ROMANCE MONOGR
Special Issue

AN ENGLISH-AROMANIAN
(Macedo-Romanian)
DICTIONARY

ROMANCE MONOGRAPHS
Special Issue

AN ENGLISH-AROMANIAN
(Macedo-Romanian)
DICTIONARY

with two introductory sketches on Aromanian

Emil Vrabie

with a Foreword by
Donald L. Dyer

UNIVERSITY, MISSISSIPPI
ROMANCE MONOGRAPHS
2000

Publication of this dictionary was made possible with grants

provided by the

Romanian Cultural and Benevolent

SOCIETY FARSAROTUL

and

Mr. Apostol Triffon - Paligora - Pomposhi - Sotiroff

from

Bitola - Moloviste

Acknowledgments

It is not possible to mention here by name the numerous native speakers of Aromanian, both in America and in Europe, who have contributed over the years, in one way or another, to the making of this book. I ask them to accept my warmest thanks. *Dumnidză s-lă agiută!* During my nine visits to Fairfield and Bridgeport, Ct., where I met so many speakers of Aromanian, Prof. Aurel **Ciufecu**, a native of Pleasa (Albania), offered me shelter and support. He introduced me to other native speakers, who subsequently became subjects of my research.

Here, in Fort Lauderdale, I have been fortunate to find a permanent and benevolent source of consultation in Mrs. Maria **Bujduveanu** (a native of Greece) and her family, active and proud preservers of Aromanian. I warmly thank them.

I also want to thank my colleagues and friends, native speakers of English, who read through various portions of the manuscript and made valuable improvements. The list includes:

Prof. James **Augerot**, Univ. of Washington; Prof. Charles **Carlton**, Univ. of Rochester; Dr. Jane **Cottrell**, Ohio State University; JD Leon **Degruchy**, Univ. of Portland; Prof. Donald L. **Dyer**, Univ. of Mississippi; Prof. Mark **Elson**, Univ. of Virginia; Prof. Ronald F. **Feldstein**, Indiana University; Prof. Grace **Fielder**, Univ. of Arizona; Prof. George **Fowler**, Indiana University; Prof. Victor **Friedman**, Univ. of Chicago; Gordon **Hogg**, bibliographer and cataloguer in the Dept. of Special Collections and Archives of the M. I. King Library in Lexington, Ky.; Prof. Michael **Impey**, Univ. of Kentucky; Prof. Brian **Joseph**, Ohio State University; Prof. Elaine **Kleiner**, Indiana State University; Dr. Richard **Laurent**, Univ. of California at Berkeley; Prof. James **Mullen**, Univ. of Birmingham, U.K.; Prof. Jan L. **Perkowski**, Univ. of Virginia; and Prof. Oscar **Swan**, Univ. of Pittsburgh.

Professor Dorin **Uriţescu** (York University, Toronto, Canada) read through the introductory part of the manuscript and made valuable observations, for which I thank him very much.

I remain particularly indebted to Mr. Charles **Ohsiek**, my extraordinary neighbor, for his invaluable assistance in various computer-related matters.

I am also thankful to Dr. Marius **Sala** and Dr. Nicolae **Saramandu** (Univ. of Bucharest), and to Prof. Gheorghe **Carageani** (Istituto Universitario Orientale, Napoli) for their advice and support.

Mr. Michael **Babu** (Fairfield, Ct.), Prof. Vasile **Barba** (Freiburg), Prof. Hristu **Cândroveanu** (Bucharest), Prof. Tiberiu **Cunia** (Boca Raton, Fl.), Dr. Sotir **Galani** (Ephrata, Pa.), Prof. Dr. Gheorghe **Mihăilă** (Bucharest), Dr. Petre **Neiescu** (Cluj-Napoca), Prof. Dr. Solomon **Vaimberg** (Bucharest), and Prof. Dr. Victor **Vascenco** (Heidelberg), helped me with documentation about Aromanians, for which I thank them very much.

FOREWORD

It is fitting that Emil Vrabie's *Aromanian-English Dictionary* is being published at the dawn of a new century. For the second half of the twentieth century, Aromanian like many others has been a language on the wane. The politics of various Balkan nation states, as well as bi- and trilingualism, has conspired to shrink the number of contemporary speakers to no more than 200,000. One arguably could make the case, however, that interest in this relatively unknown tongue has been fostered anew. The publication of this dictionary, an impressive undertaking by a storied scholar in the field of Romance and Slavic linguistics, is in fact no small testament to a revitalized cultural and indeed scholarly zeal for the Aromanian language and the Aromanian people.

As a graduate student at the University of Chicago in the 80s, I thrilled to lectures delivered by th late Balkanist, Zbigniew Gołąb, as he discussed the Aromanian people, their culture and language. Those of us who took Professor Gołąb's courses learned about the transhumant, shepherding lifestyle of the Vlachs (as the Aromanians are also known), their language's historical links to Macedo-Slavic and about the great dictionary of Aromanian compiled by Tache Papahagi (published in 1974). These were stories quite befitting courses such as "Slavic-Romance Contacts in the Balkans." The students in these courses had the sense that they were sharing a unique *learning* experience, but they were also quite aware that they might have been the only Americans learning these things.

For the Aromanian people and their language have never been extensively studied in the United States. The few book-length works on Aromanian or Aromanians have been produced abroad and, with a single exception - Gołąb's *The Aromanian Dialect of Kruševo in R.S. Macedonia SFR Yugoslavia* (1984) - primarily by Europeans: A.J. Wace and M.S. Thomson's *The Nomads of the Balkans: An Account of Life and Customs among the Vlachs of the Northern Pindus* (1974); Max Demeter Peyfuss's *Die aromunische Frage. Ihre Entwicklung von den Ursprüngen bis zum Frieden von Bukarest (1913) und die Haltung Österreich-Ungarns* (1994); and T.J. Winnfrith's *The Vlachs: The History of a Balkan People* (1987) and *Shattered Eagles. Balkan Fragments* (1995). This is not to say that studying Aromanians and Aromanian was not important.

While the ethnic origin of the Aromanian people is a matter best left to anthropologists, the history and contemporary linguistic structure of the Aromanian language are important issues for the Romance, Slavic and Balkan linguist, as well as the historical linguist, the sociolinguist and the etymologist. Emil Vrabie's dictionary provides all of the above with a wealth of information and data for study; indeed, it is a significant study for those in many fields. Given the depth and breadth of the project - its introductory grammatical sketch and remarks on lexical relationships; its multilingual entries with a focus on Latin origins; and its completness and attention to detail - scholars will find this dictionary to be extremely helpful in a number of ways.

I am proud in my own small way to be a part of it.

Donald L. Dyer
Oxford, Mississippi
January 1, 2000

TABLE OF CONTENTS

M O R P H O L O G Y   43

ABBREVIATIONS

acc.	accusative	*jur.*	juridical
adj.	adjective	*K.*	Karavlach
adv.	adverb	*Lat.*	Latin
ALB.	ALBANIA	*lit.*	literally
anat.	anatomy	*m.*	masculine
ant.	antonym	*M.*	Moscopole type
aor.	aorist	*MAC.*	The Republic of Macedonia
Arom.	Aromanian		
astr.	astronomy	*MeglR.*	Megleno-Romanian
B.	Bucharest	*mil.*	military
BG.	Bulgaria	*n.*	neuter
book.	bookish	*N.*	north(ern)
bot.	botany	*neg.*	negative
cj.	conjunction	*nom.*	nominative
coll.	collective noun	*nr.*	number; near
cond.	conditional	*num.*	numeral
CRom.	Common Romanian	*O.*	Olympus area (GR)
dat.	dative	*obs.*	obsolete
def.	definite	*ono.*	onomatopeic
dem.	demonstrative	*ord.*	ordinal numeral
derm.	dermatology	*orn.*	ornithology
derog.	derogatory	*p.*	page; past
dim.	diminutive	*part.*	participle
d/o	direct object	*PC*	personal communication
D-Rom.	Daco-Romanian		
E.	east(ern)	*pf.*	perfect
ent.	entomology	*phys.*	physiology
esp.	especially	*pl.*	plural
f.	feminine	*plupf.*	pluperfect
F.	Farsherot type	*poss.*	possessive
fig.	figuratively	*pres.*	present tense
G.	Gramoste type	*pron.*	pronoun
GBg.	G in Bulgaria	*pt*	past tense
g/d	genitive/dative	*rel.*	relative
gen.	genitive	*Rom.*	Standard Romanian
GR.	Greece	*s.*	substantive (noun)
ichth.	ichthiology	*subj.*	subjunctive
imper.	imperative	*tex.*	textile fabrics
impers.	impersonal	*TP*	Tache Papahagí
imprec.	imprecation	*Turk.*	Turkish
indef.	indefinite	*usu.*	usually
interrog.	interrogative	*vb.*	verb
invar.	invariable	*vet.*	veterinary
i/o	indirect object	*vs.*	versus
ipf.	imperfect	*voc.*	vocative
iron.	ironically	*vulg.*	vulgar
IstroR.	Istro-Romanian		

SYMBOLS

‖   separates data found in the DDA (our main source, see below) from data found in other sources.

≈   denotes approximate equivalence.

→   refers to synonyms or to entries containing additional data.

▾   preceding verbs, shows that they are accompanied by the reflexive pronoun (**mi**) in the DDA. For instance, under the English verb **ABATE** the Aromanian verb ▾*scad* is given, which means that this Aromanian verb may be used as *scad* or *mi scad*.

~   replaces the headword (e.g., under the indefinite article **A**, between **take** and **sheep**): **take ~ sheep**.

>   means becomes or became.

<   means derived or coming from.

[ ]   enclose pronunciation. Occasionally [ ] include missing words or additional explanation.

CITED WORKS

ALiA   *Aromunischer Sprachatlas. Atlasul lingvistic aromân* ('The Aromanian Linguistic Atlas'), vol. I-II (1985) Hamburg: Helmut Buske Verlag; eds. Wolfgang Dahmen, Johanes Kramer, Reiner Schlösser.

ALR   *Atlasul lingvistic român, s.n.* ('The Romanian Linguistic Atlas, new series') vol. I (1956) - VI (1969). B: Ed. Academiei (h[arta] indicates nr. of map).

B-Arch   *Balkan Archiv. Neue Folge.* I, 1976- seq. (Figures indicate number of question).

Basme   *Basme aromâne şi glosar* ('Aromanian Fairy Tales and Glossary'). 1905. Pericle Papahagi ed. B: "Carol Göbl," pp. 748. (Content: 139 tales recorded from various native speakers of Aromanian)

Bara   → Stere

Batsaria   Nicolae Batsaria (b. 1874, Kruševo, MAC; d. 1952). *Pãrãvulii* ('Anecdotes'), ECA, 1989.

Belimace   Constantin Belemace (b. 1844, Muloviște, MAC; d. 1932). *Dimãndarea pãrinteascã* ('Our parents' legacy') [Prose and Verses], ECA, 1990.

Brâncuş   Grigore Brâncuş. *Les éléments lexicaux autochtones dans le dialecte aroumain*, in Revue roumaine de linguistique 11 (1966), nr. 6: 549-565.

Brâncuş   _____ . 1983. *Vocabularul autohton al limbii române* ('The autochtonous vocablary of the Romanian language'). B: Ed. ştiinţifică şi enciclopedică, 1983.

Capidan   Theodor Capidan (b. 1879, Prilep, MAC; d. 1953). 1932. *Aromânii. Dialectul aromân. Studiu lingvistic* ('The Aromanians. The Aromanian Dialect. A Linguistic Study'). B: Imprimeria Naţională.

CapF   _____ . 1931. *Fãrşeroţii. Studiu lingvistic asupra românilor din Albania* ('The Farsherots. A Linguistic Study about the Romanians Living in Albania'). B: Cartea Românească.

CapMegl   _____ . 1925. *Meglenoromânii. Istoria şi graiul lor* ('The Megleno-Romanians. Their History and Language'). B: Cultura Naţională.

Carafoli   Tulliu Carafoli (b. 1872, Veroia, GR; d. 1937). *Pirushana shi Furlji* (two plays: 'Pirushana' and 'The Thieves'). ECA, 1995.

CarC   Matilda Caragiu Marioţeanu. 1975. *Compendiu de dialectologie română (nord şi sud-dunăreană)* ('A Compendium of North- and South-Danubian Romanian Dialectology'). B: Ed. ştiinţifică şi enciclopedică.

CarF   _____ . 1968. *Fono-morfologie aromână. Studiu de dialectologie structurală* ('Aromanian Phono-Morphology. A Study in Structural Dialectology'). B: Ed. Academiei, pp. 221.

CL   I. Mării. 1970. *Note lexicale. Cuvinte aromâne în Atlasul lingvistic român (I)* ('Aromanian Words in the Romanian Linguistic Atlas (I)', in Cercetări de lingvistică (Cluj), XV/1: 36-46 and /2: 253-64.

Cot-1957   Ion Coteanu. 1957. *Cum dispare o limbă (istroromâna)* ('How Does A Language Disappear: Istro-Romanian'). B: Societatea de ştiinţe istorice şi filologice.

Cot-1961   _____. 1961. *Elemente de dialectologie a limbii române* ('Elements of Dialectology of the Romanian Language'). B: Ed. ştiinţifică.

Cunia   Tiberius Cunia and Dumitru. S. Garofil. *Dictsiunarlu T. Papahagi turnat tu un dictsiunar rumãn-armãn* ('T. Papahagi's Dictionary Converted into a Romanian-Aromanian Dictionary'). ECA, 1995.

Cuvata   Dina Cuvata, Aromanian author (b. 1952, Dobrušána, MAC). *Sãrmãnitsa* ('The Cradle'). ECA, 1990.

Çabej-1   Eqrem Çabej. *Betrachtung über die Rumänisch-Albanischen Sprachbeziehungen*, in Revue roumaine de linguistique, 1-3 (1965): 101-115.

Çabej-2   _____. 1976. *Studime etimologjike në fushë të shqipes. II, A-B* ('Albanian Etymological Studies'). Tirana: Instituti i gjuhësisë dhe i letërsisë.

Dahmen   see ALiA

DDA   Tache Papahagi. 1974. *Dicţionarul dialectului aromân general şi etimologic* ('A General and Etymological Dictionary of the Aromanian Dialect'). B: Ed. Academiei (2nd ed.).

Décsy   Décsy Gyula. 1986. *Statistical Report on the Languages of the World as of 1985*. Bloomington, In.: Eurolingua.

DIARO   *Dicţionar Aromân (macedo-vlah). DIARO.* ('An Aromanian (Macedo-Vlach) Dictionary') by Matilda Caragiu Marioţeanu. Vol. I (A-D, 1997). B: Ed. Enciclopedică, pp. 433 + Addendum and map. Her voiced affricate *d* (with a cedilla) has been replaced by *dz* in this book. Some other minor adjustments have been made.

ECA   The Aromanian Publishing House "Editura Cartea Aromãnã," Syracuse, N.Y. (Ed. in chief Tiberiu Cunia).

FD   Fonetică şi dialectologie. B, 1958-.

Filipova   Maria Filipova-Baĭrova. 1969. *Grătski zaemki v săvremennija bălgarski ezik* ('Greek Borrowings in Contemporary Bulgarian'). Sofia: BAN.

Garofil   → Cunia

Gheţie   Ion Gheţie. *Româna primitivă* ('Proto-Romanian'), in LR (1986), nr. 6, pp. 516-527; *Diferenţieri dialectale în româna primitivă* ('Dialectal differentiations in Proto-Romanian'), in LR (1987), nr. 1, pp. 79-84; *Originea dialectelor române* ('The origin of Romanian dialects'), in LR (1987), 2: 130-146.

Gołąb   Zbigniew Gołąb → § 6

Guli   Costa Guli (b. 1916 in Livădz, GR; d. 1985). *Soneti* ('Sonnets'). ECA, 1990.

Hetzer   Armin Hetzer. *Zum Problem der Aromunishchen Entlehnungen aus dem Albanischen,* in B-Arch 7 (1982): 111-142.

Hristu   Andon Hristu (b. 1948 nr. Korçë, ALB; a native speaker of Aromanian as spoken in ALB); translator of the story *Lulja e Përgjakur* ('The Bloodstained Flower') by Dimu Tarusha (Tiranë: Shtypur në Shtypshkronjën Ushtarake, 1994) from Albanian into Aromanian. A copy of Hristu's original manuscript was sent to me by Mr. Tiberiu Cunia (→ ECA).

K-D	N. Katsanis and K. Dinas. 1990. *Grammatikí tís koinís Koutsovlachikís*. Thessaloniki: Archeio Koutsovlachikon meleton.
Ko	Vedat Kokona. 1977. *Fjalor Shqip-Frengjisht* ('Dictionnaire Albanais-Français'). Tirana: 8 Nëntori.
Kovačec	August Kovačec. 1971. *Descrierea istroromânei actuale* ('A Description of Contemporary Istro-Romanian'). B: Ed. Academiei.
Kramer	see ALiA
Kramer 88	Achille G. Lazarou. *L'aroumain et ses rapports avec le grec*. Thessaloniki, 1986. Review by Johannes Kramer, B-Arch 13 (1988), p. 324-337.
Lazarou	Achille G. Lazarou. 1986. *L'aroumain et ses rapports avec le grec*. Thessaloniki: Institute for Balkan Studies.
Liturg	*Liturghier aromânesc* ('An Aromanian Missal') published by Matilda Caragiu Marioţeanu. 1962. B: Ed. Academiei.
LB	*Linguistique balkanique*, see Sandfeld
LR	*Limba română* ('The Romanian Tongue'). Romanian periodical. B: Institutul de lingvistică, 1950-.
Mării	see CL
Merca	George M. Merca (b. 1906, Livãdz, GR). *Livãdzli - Vatrã Armãneascã* ('Livãdz - Aromanian Hearth'). ECA, 1991.
Mihăescu	Haralambie Mihăescu. 1966. *Influenţa grecească asupra limbii române până în secolul al XV-lea* ('The Greek Influence on Romanian until the 15th Century'). B: Ed. Academiei.
Mihăilă	Gheorghe Mihăilă. 1960. *Împrumuturi vechi slave în limba română* ('Old South-Slavic Borrowings in Romanian'). B: Ed. Academiei.
Murnu	George Murnu (1868-1957). *Bair di cãntic armãnesc* ('Necklace of Aromanian Songs'). ECA, 1989.

Neiescu	Petru Neiescu. 1997. *Mic atlas al dialectului aromân din Albania şi din fosta republică iugoslavă Macedonia* ('A Small Atlas of the Aromanian Dialect in Albania and in the Former Yugoslav Republic of Macedonia'). B: Ed. Academiei.
Padiotu	Gogu Pădiotu-di-Aminciu. 1988. *Cǎntiţi Armâneşti di Aminciu / Vláchika tragoúdhia tou Metsóvou /* ('Aromanian Songs from Aminciu [Metsovon]'). Athena.
Papahagi P	Pericle Papahagi (b. 1872, Avdela, GR; d. 1943) → Basme
Papahagi T	Tache Papahagi (b. 1892, Avdela, GR; d. 1977) → DDA
Petrovici	Emil Petrovici. *L'unité dialectale de la langue roumaine,* in *Revue roumaine de linguistique* IX (1964): 375-388.
Peyfuss	see § 6 below
Parallele	Pericle Papahagi. 1908. *Parallele Ausdrücke und Redensarten im Rumänischen, Albanesischen, Neugriechischen und Bulgarischen,* in: XIV. Jahresbericht des Instituts für rumänusche Sprache. Leipzig: Johann Ambrosius Barth, pp. 113-170.
Puşc-LR	Sextil Puşcariu. 1940. *Limba română.I. Privire generală* ('The Romanian Language. I. A General View'). B: Fundaţia pentru literatură şi artă "Regele Carol II" (with two exellent maps: *The Aromanians and the Megleno-Romanians,* p. 222 and 223; *The Istro-Romanians,* p. 226 and 227).
Puşc-StI	_____. 1905-1929. *Studii istroromâne* ('Istro-Romanian Studies'), 3 vols. B: Cultura Naţională.
Récatas	B. Récatas. 1935. *L'état actuel du bilinguisme chez les Macédo-Roumains du Pinde et le rôle de la femme dans le langage.* Paris: Librairie E. Droz.
REW	W. Meyer-Lübke. *Romanisches etymologisches Wörterbuch.* 5th ed. Heidelberg: Carl Winter, Universität-verlag, 1972
Rosetti	Alexandru Rosetti. 1978. *Istoria limbii române*

	('History of the Romanian Language',) 2nd ed. B: Ed. științifică și enciclopedică.
Russu	I.I. Russu. 1981. *Etnogeneza românilor. Fondul autohton traco-dacic și componenta latino-romanică* ('The Ethnogenesis of the Romanians. The Autochthonous Thracian-Dacian Stock of Words and the Latin-Romance Component'). B: Ed. științifică și enciclopedică (with an extensive French and German abstract, pp. 448-466).
Sala	Marius Sala. 1976. *Contributions à la phonétique historique du roumain.* Paris: Klincksieck.
Sandfeld	Kristian Sandfeld. 1930. *Linguistique balkanique. Problèmes and résultats.* Paris: Collection linguistique publiée par la Société linguistique de Paris.
SarA	Nicolae Saramandu. *Tratat de dialectologie românească* ('A Treatise on Romanian Dialectology'). Valeriu Rusu ed. Craiova [Romania]: Scrisul Românesc (Aromanian: 423-476).
SarD	_____. 1972. *Cercetări asupra aromânei vorbite în Dobrogea* ('Researche on the Aromanian Spoken in Dobruja' [Romania]). B: Ed. Academiei.
SarN	_____. *Neutralizarea opoziției de sonoritate în aromână* ('Neutralization of the voiced / voiceless opposition in Aromanian'). SCL, XXII/4 (1971): 377-80).
SarU	_____. *U final în graiurile Aromânei* ('Final u in Aromanian'). SCL XXIX, nr. 3 (1978): 329-340.
Sar-1988	_____. *L'aroumain and ses rapports avec le grec (à propos d'un ouvrage récent),* in Revue des Études Sud-est Européennes (B), t, XXVI/3 (1988): 251-9.
Scărlăt.	Elena Scărlătoiu. 1980. *Relații lingvistice ale aromânilor cu slavii de sud* ('Linguistic Relationships of Aromanians with Southern Slavs'). B: Litera.

Schl	Rainer Schlösser. *Historische Lautlehre des Aromunischen von Metsovon*, B-Arch., t. 3: 111-177.
SCL	*Studii şi cercetări lingvistice* ('Linguistic Studies and Researches'). B, 1950-.
Stere	Elena Stere (b. nr. Sofia, BG) and Mariana Bara. *Frãmturi di banã...* ('Bits ot life...'). ECA, 1993.
Sterghiu	Vanghea Mihañ-Sterghiu (b. 1948, Doleañ, MAC). *Trã-dzeri* ('Hardship'). ECA, 1992.
TP	Tache Papahagí, the author of the DDA (→ above)
Tulliu	Nuşi Tulliu (b. 1872, Avdela, GR; d. 1941). *Murmintsã fãrã crutsi* ('Graves without crosses'). ECA, 1993.
Tzitz.	Christos Tzitzilis. *Beiträge zur aromunishchen Wortschatzforschung*, in *Zeitschrift für Balk.* (Wiesbaden), 24/1 (1988): 173-199.
Velo	Nicolae Velo (b. 1882, Mulovište, MAC.; d. 1924). *Shana shi ardirea-a Gramostiljei* ('Shana and the Burning of Gramoste' [former Aromanian town]). ECA, 1991.
Wace	see § 6 below.
Wartburg	Walter von Wartburg. 1967. *La fragmentation linguistique de la Romania*. Paris: Klincksieck.
Winnifrith	→ § 6 below.

I. INTRODUCTION

§ 1. **The Aromanians: people and language.** The *Aromanians* (known also as *Vlachs, Koutsovlachs, Macedo-Vlachs, Macedo-Romanians,* or *Tsíntari*) are a distinct group of people in the socioeconomic, cultural and linguistic Balkan mosaic. Their ethnogenesis has been one of the many controversial topics of Balkan history. As for their origin, there is much evidence to suggest that present-day Aromanians are direct descendants of indigenous tribes of the Balkans mixed with Roman soldiers and colonists beginning with the second century B.C. and gradually assimilated by them culturally and linguistically.

§ 2a. **Aromanian as a Romance linguistic entity.** *Aromanian* - the Aromanians' native language - is a direct and uninterrupted continuation of the Latin spoken in the Balkans during the first centuries of the Christian era. Along with *Romanian (Daco-Romanian)*, it is a branch of *Common Romanian*, a member of the Romance family of languages.

During the first century AD, *Common Romance*, which developed from *Vulgar Latin*, broke into *Western Romance* (well documented by written texts) and *Eastern Romance*. Subsequently the latter gradually split into *Italo-Dalmatian* (from which Italian, Sardinian and Dalmatian emerged) and *Balkan Romance*, whence *Proto-Romanian* developed. The circumstances, duration and exact area in which *Common Romanian* formed, evolved and eventually fragmented during the first centuries of its existence has been a very controversial issue. Linguists' attempts to reconstruct Common Romanian have been made without the enormous benefit of early written records, available in French, for instance, as early as the ninth century. The earliest texts in Romanian (Daco-Romanian) date from the sixteenth century, and the earliest texts in Aromanian come from as late as the eighteenth century.[1]

In the tenth century or some time earlier *Common Romanian* split into two geographically separated groups. One was in the northern part of the Balkan peninsula (in a large area between the Black Sea and the Adriatic Sea), from which the *Daco-Romanian* branch of Common Romanian subseqently formed. The other one was in the south of

---

[1] Three brief surveys of the main existing theories concerning Common Romanian were published in 1986 and 1987 by Ion Gheţie. A systematic presentation of the main views and data on this topic can be found in Rosetti: 351 seq. and Sala: 186 seq. An insightful analysis, with illustrations, was given in Petrovici-1964.

the peninsula (Dardania, Epirus, Macedonia, Thrace), where the *Aromanian* branch of Common Romanian presumably was spoken. The eleven-century-long territorial separation of these two major branches of Common Romanian has resulted in divergent evolution to the extent that today mutual understanding between Aromanians and Romanians (Daco-Romanians) is considerably impaired. However, massive linguistic evidence shows that, in spite of their numerous differences, present-day Aromanian and present-day Romanian (Daco-Romanian) are dialects of the same theoretically reconstructed language, *Common Romanian*. By no means can one say or think, as this occasionally happens, that Aromanian is a dialect of Romanian, because today *Romanian* commonly means 'Daco-Romanian.' From a typological and sociolinguistic viewpoint, Aromanian may be considered rather a *co-language* of (contemporary) Romanian, not a dialect thereof.

> *NOTE.* When Romanian (Daco-Romanian) is viewed merely as a historical dialect of Common Romanian, its internal, centripetal dialects (*munteán or muntenésc, moldoveán or moldovenésc, bănăţeán, crişán,* and *maramureşeán*) are and should always be called *subdialects* of Romanian or *dialects* of Daco-Romanian.

Aromanian is not a homogenous linguistic entity. Its main varieties include the *Pindus* type (abbrev. **P**), the *Gramoste* type (**G**), the *Farsherot* type (**F**), the *Olympus* type (**O**), and the *Moscopole* type (**M**).[2]

§ 2b. **Megleno-Romanian and Istro-Romanian.** Two other small but intriguing external and centrifugal branches of Common Romanian need to be mentioned: *Megleno-Romanian*, spoken in a small area (*Karağova*, lit. 'the Black Plain') to the north of Salonika, near the border between Greece and the Republic of Macedonia[3] and *Istro-Romanian*, still spoken in a few communities in Croatia, on the Istrian penisula, south of Trieste.[4] Some scholars maintain that Istro-Romanian is an early branch of Daco-Romanian. As for Megleno-Roma-

---

[2] For details on these and certain other varieties of Aromanian see SarD and SarU.

[3] See CapMegl and Puşc-LR: 223-4, with map.

[4] See Puşc-SI, Coteanu-1957, and Kovačec; an excellent map is provided in Puşc-LR p. 226-7.

nian, it occupies an intermedate position between Aromanian and Daco-Romanian, being however close to the former. In spite of their
territorial discontinuity at present, these four totally independent Romance entities (*Romanian* or *Daco-Romanian, Aromanian, Megleno-Romanian* and *Istro-Romanian*) share a long series of important
phonetic, morphological, syntactic and lexico-semantic features
that lead back to Common Romanian.[5] The Aromanian linguist Achille
G. Lazarou is the author of a theory according to which Aromanian
appeared and developed as a separate entity, independently of Daco-
Romanian. This isolation theory has found little acceptance among
Romance linguists.[6]

§ 3. **Number of Aromanians today.** Since all native speakers of
Aromanian have long been citizens of the Balkan countries they inhabit (mainly Greece, Albania and the Republic of Macedonia), it is
not easy to know how many there are. In these countries they feel
at home. They are regarded and usually regard themselves as natio-
nals of Greece, Albania or the Republic of Macedonia, in spite of
the special language they know from their parents (*Aromanian* or
Vlach) and regardless of other, less important differentiating features. According to a report published in the United States in
1985, the approximate number of Aromanians is 200,000.[7] However,
this figure is to be taken with a grain of salt. One should remember that bias has always played a role in population counts.[8]

---

[5] More on this in Petrovici-1964.

[6] See Kramer-1988 and Sar-1988.

[7] See Décsy: 39.

[8] Further data on this topic may be found in Capidan: 31-32,
CarC: 218, and SarA: 423 (in Romanian); Gołąb: 16-23 and Winni-
frith-1997: 1-10 (in English.)

§ 4. **Bilingualism and trilingualism.** Aromanians, a stateless population, are bilingual: Aromanian-Greek in Greece, Aromanian-Albanian in Albania, and Aromanian-Slavic in the Republic of Macedonia). Reportedly, there are also cases of *trilingualism*. For instance, Aromanians in *Horio Gramos*, a small town in Western Greece, are fluent in Aromanian, Greek and Albanian. Some Aromanians living at present in *Struga*, a small town in the Republic of Macedonia, are also fluent in Slavic Macedonian and Albanian. When the native vocabulary required by a special topic turns out to be insufficient, Aromanians commonly shift language and continue the conversation in Modern Greek, Albanian or Macedonian. On the other hand, intermarriages between Vlachs and non-Vlachs have long been common. In such circumstances, the silent erosion of Aromanian is only natural.[9]

§ 5. **Main works on Aromanians**. Five works are particularly useful for the reader of English who needs introductory and other information about native speakers of Aromanian:

• A. J. B. Wace and M. S. Thomson. 1974 (1st ed. 1914). *The Nomads of the Balkans. An Account of Life and Customs among the Vlachs of Northern Pindus*. London: Methuen and Co. 332 pp. [Ch. XI: *The Vlach Language*, pp. 226-255; various Aromanian texts with English translation are provided, pp. 285-95];

• Zbigniew Gołąb. 1984. *The Aromanian Dialect of Kruševo in S.R. Macedonia, SFR Yugoslavia*, Skopje: Macedonian Academy of Sciences and Arts, pp. 265.

• T. J. Winnifrith. 1987. *The Vlachs: The History of a Balkan People*. London: Duckworth, pp. 180. (with 12 maps and bibliography);

• _____. 1995. *Shattered Eagles. Balkan Fragments*. London: Duckworth, pp. 26-81; *Notes*, pp. 150-153; *Maps*, p. 27, 43, 58-59 and 73;

• _____. 1997. *The Vlachs of Macedonia*, in The Newsletter of the

---

[9] See Gołąb: 14 et pass.

Society Farsarotul, vol. XI, issue 1, pp. 1-10.

There are also books on this topic in other languages. One of the best, in German, written by Max Demeter Peyfuss is *The Aromunische Frage. Ihre Entwicklung von den Ursprungen bis zum Frieden von Bukarest (1913) und die Haltung Österrich-Ungarns*, Graz [Austria]: Hermann Böhlaus, 1994.[10]

Useful data concerning Vlachs' traditional and contemporary life and language can also be found in *The Newsletter of the Society Farsarotul*, a periodical published in English (Trumbull, Ct.). Other important periodicals, mainly in Romanian and Aromanian) include *Deşteptarea. Revista aromânilor*, lit. 'The Revival. The Periodical of the Aromanians' (Bucharest, Romania), and *Zborlu a nostru*, lit. 'Our Word,' Freiburg (Germany).

§ 6. **Goal and extent of this project**. Aromanian lexicography took a large step forward in 1974 when Tache Papahagi's dictionary of Aromanian, known as the DDA, was published. The DDA is a bilingual (Aromanian-Romanian) dictionary. It also provides French glosses for each entry, a feature that makes it accessible to readers unfamiliar with Romanian. Below, an entry from Tache Papahagi's Aromanian-Romanian-French dictionary (HOÁRĂ) is reproduced and translated into English.

> **HOÁRĂ** *f.*, **horĭ** and **hoáre** *pl* = (Rom.) sat; (Fr.) village, contrée, pays. (Illustrations are given and sources mentioned); See *vlahuhoárǎ* and the synonym *sat*. - From Gr. χώρα (DDA: 663).

Thus, with the DDA at hand, the non-native reader can learn easily that Arom. *hoárǎ* is the equivalent of Rom. *sat* and of Fr. *village*. However, if what one needs to know is not the meaning of

---

[10] A Romanian version of it (*Chestiunea aromânească* 'The Aromanian Question'), with extensive bibliography, is available (Bucharest: Ed. Enciclopedică, 1994, pp. 141.)

Arom. *hoáră*, but rather the Aromanian term for 'village', the reputable DDA cannot help. The foreign scholar's frustration is increased by the sheer size of Papahagi's dictionary (1,437 pages), which makes random searching an unproductive solution. Below is the answer offered by the present work to the question raised above.

VILLAGE *s.* hoáră, *dim.* hurícă; **Aromanian** ~ vlahuhoáră; **king's** ~ vasiluhóre; **independent** ~ chifaluhoáră.

If a scholar of Aromanian happens to record the Aromanian term *uţíd* and realizes that it means 'to kill', he or she may look up the word with the DDA and find the entry:

UŢID (*mi*) *vb. III* (aor.) **uţíşŭ,** (part.) **uţís,** (inf.) **uţídire** (D-Rom.) ucide, (Fr.) tuer, CapM III, 321 (*apud Weigand*). *Syn.*: **vátăm, súrpu.** From Lat. OCCIDERE tuer, faire périr.

By contrast, this English-Aromanian dictionary lists under a single English headword (**KILL**) as many as twenty-four synonyms of Arom. *uţíd,* which are scattered here and there in the voluminous DDA.

The need for an English-Aromanian dictionary is obvious.

At first, the goal of the present work was to embrace the entire Aromanian vocabulary contained in the DDA. Along the way, additional Aromanian words and meanings from various other sources have also been included. The reader will know *at any given moment* which Aromanian data in this dictionary come from the DDA and what data come from somewhere else. Additional data, absent in the DDA, are preceded by two vertical bars: ‖ (Ex. under ABASE, ABDOMEN, etc.)

In his DDA, Tache Papahagi deliberately left out words of Romanian (Daco-Romanian) origin. The present work follows suit. Such discrimination may seem arguable, but it is stringently needed in order to offer the demanding user a clear-cut demarcation between genuine Aromanian vocabulary and neologisms imported from Romanian (Daco-Romanian).

On the other hand, the reader is cautioned that the Aromanian vocabulary presented in this work <u>is not prescriptive</u>. Aromanians have not yet decided which variety of their tongue should be taken as a standard. Native speakers seem too often inclined to believe that the version of the language they learned from their parents is the truly Aromanian one. Nobody can be a linguistic arbiter at this time. Our only major goal is to offer a research tool for scholars in the humanities and a source of general information for an educated readership.

§ 7 **Spelling and pronunciation**. These specifications refer to the characters used in the DDA and other Aromanian sources. The closest phonetic equivalent in U.S. English or other well-known languages is suggested. Letters that do not appear below (*b, d, f, h, l, m, n, p, r, s, t, v, x*) have approximately the same values as in English.

a, as *a* in Engl. *father*.

ă, as *a* in Engl. *about, sofa*.

â, identical to *î* (see *Note 5*).

ã, used by some Aromanians for both [ă] and [î].

c, as *c* in Engl. *scope*.

ce, ci [č] or [ĉ]; as *ch* in Engl. *chest, chin, each, church*.

che, chi, [ke, ki], as in Engl. *skin*; see also *k'* below.

č, see *ce, ci* above.

ĉ, as *c* in Standard Romanian *Ce faci?* [ĉé faĉ] 'How are you?' The sound [ĉ] is more palatal than [č], but the difference is not relevant phonologically. The DDA uses [č] only, but the ALR consistently differentiates [č] and [ĉ].

dh, as *th* in Engl. *this* (The DDA uses *δ*).

dz, as in Engl. *adz(e)*, a tool for shaping wood.

e, as in Engl. *elm*. See *Note 1* below.

ea, as *ya* Engl. *yacht, yak*. See *Note 2* below.

g, as *g* in Engl. *good*.

ǵ, as *ghi* in Rom. unghi 'angle'; its voiceless pair is *k'*.

ge, gi, as *g* in Engl. *ginger*.

ğ is the voiced pair of *č*, see above. The DDA uses [ğ] only, but the ALR consistently differentiates [ğ] and [ĝ]. The latter is more palatal.

ĝ is the voiced pair of [ĉ], see above.

ghe, ghi, as *g* in Engl. *get, gift*; see also *ǵ* above.

γ, see *y* below.

i, as *ea* in Engl. *each*. See *Note 3* below.

ĭ, as *y* in Engl. *boy, yacht*. See *Note 4* below.

î, high central unrounded vowel identical to D-Rom. *î*.

j [ž], as *s* in Engl. *measure*

k', as *chi* in Rom. *uréchi* 'ears'; its voiced pair is *ǵ*

ľ, (palatal *l*), as *ll* in Sp. *llave* 'key.'

lj, a digraph for [ľ] used by some Aromanians.

ñ, ń, (pallatal *n*), as *ñ* in Sp. *niño* 'boy.'

nj, a digraph for [ñ] used by some Aromanians.

o, as *a* in Engl. *fall*. See *Note 1* below.

oa In the diphthong *oa*, *o* is a labial glide. Monosyllabic clusters *oa* and *ua* (as in Engl. *wallet*) are undistinguishable in Aromanian.

ρ (rho), uvular or velar *r*, as in Arom. *bipichitós*, under ABUNDANT (in the Farsherot subtype of Aromanian). No phonological contrast with *r*.[11]

ş [š], like *sh* in Engl. *fish*.

sh, a recent digraph for *ş* [š] used by some Aromanians.

ţ, as *ts* in *zz* in Engl. *pizza*; [ţ] is the voiceless pair of [dz], see above.

ts, a digraph for [ţ] used by some Aromanians.

th, as *th* in Engl. *thin*. The DDA uses the Greek letter *θ*.

u, as *u* in D-Rom. *bun* 'good', or in It. *uno* 'one.'

ŭ, an obsolete Romanian and Aromanian letter for the bilabial

---

[11] Details in SarD 101-103.

glide [w]. In the DDA *ŭ* is used not only to designate [ŭ] in various diphthongs, but also to reflect the rounded off-glide ᵘ (after final consonants). In the dictionary section of this work such *ŭ* will not be indicated.

y In this dictionary y is used to represent the voiced velar fricative [γ], as in Mod. Greek μεγάλος 'big,' or as in Sp. *g* in *luego* 'place.' When followed by *e* or *i*, this character represents a palatal fricative reminiscent of *y* in Engl. *yet.* Ex.: Arom. *yálan* 'blue,' *ylupuéscu* 'to gulp down,' *yeácă* 'collar,' *yin* 'wine.'

ž see *j* above.

Note 1. In unstressed syllables, Arom. *e* is usually pronounced [i] and *o* is pronounced [u]. Aromanian spelling has always been inconsistent in representing unstressed **e**'s and **o**'s. (Thus, the DDA has *evlávie* alongside *ivlávie* 'devoutness'; *orolóγe* and *uru-lóγe* 'clock'). More on this in § 11.

Note 2. In the Arom. diphthong *ea*, the symbol *e* represents a glide. Monosyllabic clusters *ea* and *ia*, particularly after palatal consonants, are indistinguishable in Aromanian.

Note 3. In diphthongs *i* is a glide. In final position after a consonant *i* is either a vowel (e.g., *ári* [ári] 'he / she has'), or an off-glide (e.g., *ari* [arⁱ], 2nd sg. 'you plough'). See *ĭ*.

Note 4. In the DDA this letter is also used to represent the whispered off-glide [⁻ⁱ]. E.g., *par* 'pole,' pl. *parĭ* [parⁱ]. This traditional Romanian and Aromanian letter is outmoded. Regular *i* is used instead. Besides, one should take note that, after *l'* and *ñ* (which are palatal consonants), *ĭ* is, in fact, superfluous. The DDA *cal'ĭ* (pl. of *cal* 'horse') and *cal'* (used in this English-Aromanian dictionary) are perfect homonyms. The same is true for the DDA *poñĭ* (pl. of *pom* 'tree') and *poñ*. Redundant *ĭ*'s in various Aromanian sources have been dropped in this dictionary. However, occasionally we will use ĭ as a pronunciation guide. E.g., Arom. *oi* [oĭ] is the plural of *oáie* [oáĭe] 'sheep.' The definite pl. form is *oile* ([óĭ-li] or [ó-ĭ-li]). Spelled as *oile* (or as *oili*), this word is ambiguous phonetically. Should a non-native speaker of Aromanian pronounce it as [óĭ•li], or, maybe, as [ó•i•li]? (Cf. D-Rom. *oáie*, pl. *oi*, def. pl. *oile* [ó•i•le].) In avoidance of such doubts, now and then the obsolite but instrumental letter ĭ will be employed.

Note 5. In narrow phonetic transcription, off-glide ^î (=â) is sometimes used, as in sg. *sac*^u 'bag' vs. pl. *saţ*^î (or saţ^â). In the dictionary section of this work the off-glide ^-î (= ^-â) is not indicated, but it is implied.

§ 8. **Place names mentioned in this work**

Place names preceding an Aromanian word included in this work should not be interpreted rigidly. For example, when a given word is preceded by **Amc,** that means that it was recorded in **Aminciu** (or from a native speaker who lived there), but *it does not imply* that the word is unknown elsewhere.

On the other hand, one should take into account that in a great many localities given in this list Aromanian is not the predominant language at this time. For instance, out of 30,000 inhabitants of *Véroia* only about 5,000 are Aromanian (B-Arch 6/1981, p. 13).

ALB	= *ALBANIA*		
Am	= *Amer* (GR Miléa; SW of Turia)	**An**	= *Anílion* (N)cheáre, nr. Amc.
Amc	= *Amínciu* (GR. Métsovon, P; E. of Yanina)	Anthoússa	→ **Lep**
		Arγ	= *Arγiropoúleion* (GR; 1o km. N of Tírnavos)
AMer	= *Alli Meriá* (GR nr. Vólos)	**Arm**	= *Ármata* (GR, W of Brz)

Av	= Avdéla (GR Avdhéllo, P; N of Prv)	**Dren**	= Drenova (Korçë district, ALB)
Băi	= Băiásă (GR Vovoússa, P; S of Smr)	Elattohori	→ **Cern**
BG	= BULGARIA	**Els**	= Elassón (Arom. Lăsún, O, GR)
Bil	= Biľíşti (E of Cu, ALB)	**Fal**	= Faláni (GR, N of Larissa)
Bit	= Bitola (S-W of MAC)	**Fet**	= Fétiţa (GR, SW of Edessa)
Bl	= Beála (former village, W of Ohr, MAC)	**Flam**	= Flampourárion (GR, P; N of Grevenition)
BdD'	= Beala di D'osu nr. Ohr, MAC)	**Fu**	= Fúrca (GR, NW of Samarina)
Blţ	= Bláţa (GR Vlásti; E of Kastoria)	**Gard**	= Gardíki (GR, SE of Yanina)
Brz	= Breáza (GR Dhístraton, P; S of Samarína)	**Gop**	= Gópiş (MAC, E of Ohrid)
Cav	= Caváia (ALB; SW of Tirana)	**GR**	= GREECE
Căl	= Călárli (GR Kalarítsion; SW of Halíki)	**Gra**	= Grámostea (GR Horió Gramós; nr. the border with ALB)
Cern	= Cernéşi (GR Elattohohóri; nr. Flampourárion)	**Grăm**	= Grămatícova (Ano Γραματικόν, nr. Edessa)
Cheáre	→ **An**	**Grb**	= Grébini (GR Grévena, NE of Amc)
Cľis	= Cľisúră (GR Kleisoúra; N of Kosáni and E of Kastoria)	**Grbţ**	= Gribiníţ (GR, P; NW of Amc)
Cot	= Cótură (GR Katáfiton, P; E of Saracu)	**GSus**	= Giumaiá-di-Sus (Krúpnik, in SW BG)
Cru	= Crúşovo (MAC Kruševo)	**Hal**	= Halíki (GR, P; S of Amc)
Cu	= Curceáua (Korça, S of the Prespa Lake, ALB)	Heimádhi(on)	→ **Suf**
Cuţ	= Cutsufľeáni (GR Pana-Γía, P; E of Amc)	**Hor**	= Horopáni (GR Steními-mahos, N of Veroia)
		Horió Gramós	→ **Gra**

Kar	= *Karagióli* (GR Arɣi-ropoúleion, 10 km. N of Tirnavos)	**Mul**	= *Mulóvişte* (MAC. nr. the Preáspa lake)
Kast	= *Kastania* (GR, btw. Amc and Kalambaka)	**Muz**	= *Mizucheá* (Myzeqeja, plain in W ALB)
Kat	= *Katavóthra* (GR, W coast; btw. Igoume-nitsa and Párga)	**N**	= North of *or* north-ern area (→ **Note** below)
Kërb	= *Stan Karbunára*, ALB)	**Na**	= *Náousa* (GR, S of Edessa)
Kok	= *Kokkinopilós* (GR, O, nr. LvO)	**Nev**	= *Névisca* (GR, NE of Kastoria)
Korça	→ **Cu**	**Nic**	= *Nícea* (ALB, NW of Pls)
Krúpnk	→ **GSus**		
Lăsún	→ **Els**	**Nij**	= *Nižepole* (MAC, SW of Bitolia)
Lak	= *Lácă* (GR, S-W of Av)	**NPrv**	= *Neó Perivóli* (GR, nr. Mira)
Lep	= *Lépindza* (GR An-thoússa, S of Amc)	**Ohr**	= *Ohrid* (MAC, nr. the Ohrid Lake)
LvO	= *Livádi Olimpou* (GR, N of Kokkinopilós)	**P**	= Pindus area, GR
Lvz	= *Livădz* (GR Meɣála Livádhia, NW of Salonika)	**Pal**	= *Paľohóri* (GR, E of Yanina; nr. Saracu)
MAC	= *The Republic of MACEDONIA*	**Pals**	= *Paliuséli* (GR Pala-ioséllion; nr. Kóni-tsa)
Mal	= *Malacási* (GR Mala-kásion, P; E of Amc)	Panaɣía	→ **Cuţ**
Meɣála Livádhia	→ **Lvz**	**Pdz**	= *Pădz, Mpădz* (GR Pá-dhes, P; W of Arm.)
Métsovon	→ **Amc**	**Pe**	= *Peshta* (Vier dis-trict, ALB)
Mi	= *Míra* (GR, 7 km. SW of NPer)	**Perd**	= *Pérdhika* (GR, W coast, nr. Igoúme-nitsa)
Miléa	→ **Am**		
Mpadz	→ **Pdz**	**Peş**	= *Péştera* (former Arom. vil. in SW BG)

Për	= *Përmet* (Përmet district, ALB)	**Smr**	= *Sămărína* (GR, P; N. of Smixi)
Plat	= *Platariá* (GR, W coast, nr. Perdhi-	**Smx**	= *Smíxi* (GR, P; N of Prv)
Pls	= *Pleása di Súpra* (nr. Korçë, ALB)	**Src**	= *Săr* (GR, E of Yanina)
Po	= *Poián* (N of Vlora, ALB)	Stenímahos	→ **Hor**
Pro	= *Próti* (GR, W of Ka- válla)	**Str**	= *Strúga* (nr. Ohrid, MAC)
Pros	= *Prosotsáni* (GR, 10 km. W of Dhráma)	**Suf**	= *Suflár* (GR Heimá- dhion; NE of La- rissa)
Prv	= *Perivóle* (GR, P; SE of Brz)	**Ştep**	= *Ştépur* (nr. Berati, ALB)
Pur	= *Pournárion* (GR, 22 km. NE of Larissa)	**Tir**	= *Tirana*, ALB
Rod	= *Rodhiá* (GR, nr. La- rissa)	**Trn**	= *Trnovo* (MAC, nr. Bitolia)
S	= South of *or* south- ern area (→ **Note** below)	**Tur**	= *Túria* (GR Kranéa; W of Trikala)
Scruf	= *Scrufutína* (ALB, N of Valóna)	Vavoussa	→ **Băi**
Ses	= *Sésklon* (GR, nr. Vilistín, W of Vó- los)	Ver	= *Véroia* (GR, W of Salonika)
		Vil	= *Viliştín* (GR Ve- lestínon, SW of Vólos)
SJos	= *Sélia de Jos* (GR, NW of Veroia)	Vlaşti	→ **Blţ**
Sln	= *Selenica* (Vlora district, ALB)	**Vot**	= *Votonósion* (GR, P; 11 km. W of Amc)
		Zag	= *Zagoria* (a NW re- gion in GR)

§ 9. **SAMPLE OF NORTHERN** ("Farsherot") **AND SOUTHERN** ("Pindus") **AROMANIAN**

In his DDA (p. 84-85), T. Papahagi classifies Aromanian into *Northern Aromanian* (in Albania, Yugoslavia [now The Republic of Macedonia] and Bulgaria), and *Southern Aromanian* (in Northern Greece and on the Eastern slopes of the Olympic mountains). Below we provide fragments from a Northern Aromanian ("Farsherot") text, recorded by Th. Capidan in Albania (**Pls**) in 1928[12] and its equivalent in Southern Aromanian as spoken is the Pindus area of Greece.[13]

Northern ("Farsherot") **Aromanian:**

(1) Alăgám[14] fρráti, tu túti pắrţăli. (2) Nă băteá plóĭa ş-nu vream să ştim dip. (3) Lucrám tă nă păni. (4) Toámna, cănd z-dipuná fuméĭle to rríe, agĭundzeám păn Lárisa, Trăcól ş Lasóna. (5) Ma veñá primveára, a doáră nădzeám di le aduţeám fuméĭle la múnte. ...(6) Loam sári di Durăs ş-o aduţeám Caváĭa. (7) Stăteám căt stăteám aγcó, loam cálea ş-agĭundzeám Pikíni. (8) Oáţi nu rămăneám mult ş-nădzeám ma depárte, di-adzĭundzeám Elbasán. (9) Di Elbasán căγcám áltă părmătíĭ; făţeám dou dzắli pănă agiundzeám Curceáo. (10) Di Curceáo dipunám Flórina j-de-acó nă aflám Bítuli.

---

[12] CapF: 171-72.

[13] After the DDA: 86-8, with minor adjustments.

[14] Th. Capidan's specifications: **ă**... open e, between o and e; ρ... velar r; **rr**... apical r with several vibrations; γ... voiced guttural fricative reminiscent of New Greek γ.

Southern Aromanian (from Pindus area):

(1) Alăgám, fráte, tu túti părţâli. (2) Nă bâteá ploáĭa şi nu vream si ştim dip. (3) Lucrám trâ nă pâni. (4) Toámna, cându dipuneá fu-méľĭle tu arníŭ, agĭundzeám până Lárisa, Trâcól şi Lăsún. (5) Ma γineá prumuveára, ðéftira oáră ñirdzeám di li-aduţeám fuméľĭle la múnte. ... (6) Loam sári di Duráţu şi-u aduţeám Caváĭa. (7) Stâteám cât stâteám acló, loam cálea şi-adzĭundzeám Pikíni. (8) Aoáţe nu armăneám múltu şi nă duţeám (or nă ţeam) ma dipárti, di agĭun-dzeám Elbasán. (9) Di Elbasán ncărcám (or ngârcám) áltă prâmâtíe; fâţeám doáŭă dzâle până agĭundzeám Córiţa. (10) Di Córiţa dipuneám Flórina ş-di-acló n-aflám Bítuli.

Translation into Standard Romanian ("Daco-Romanian"):

(1) Alergám, fráte, în toate părţile. (2) Ne băteá ploáia şi nu vroiám să ştim de nimic. (3) Lucrám (or munceám) pentru o pâine. (4) Toámna, când famíliile coboráu la iernát, ajungeám până la Lárisa, Trâcól şi Elassón. (5) Când veneá prímăvara, mergeám a dóua oáră, să adúcem famíliile la múnte. ... (6) Luam (**or** cumpărám) sáre de la Durrës şi o aduceám la Kavajë. (7) Stăteám cât stăteám acólo, apoi porneám la drum şi ajungeam la Peqin. (8) Aíci (**or** acólo) nu rămâneám mult şi ne duceám mai depárte, încât ajungeám (până) la Elbasán. (9) De la Elbasán încărcám áltă márfă; făceám două zíle până ajungeám la Korçë. (10) De la Korçë coborám la Flórina şi de acólo erám curând la Bítola.

Translation into English:

(1) We used to be on the move in all directions. (2) Rain hit us, but we did not care. (3) We worked for bread. (4) In the fall, when families descended to the winter camps, we would go as far as La-risa, Trâkol and Elasson. (5) When spring came again, we had to take the families back to the mountain. ... (6) We used to buy salt in Durrës and take it to Kavajë. (7) We stayed there for a while,

then, departing again, went as far as Piqin. (8) We did not remain there very long. We then traveled until we reached Elbasan. (9) In Elbasan we loaded other goods and traveled two days until we reached Korçë. (10) From Korçë we descended to Florina and, shortly thereafter, Bitola.

II. A phono-morphological sketch of Aromanian

A. PHONOLOGY

§ 10. **Vowels.** In stressed position Aromanian has a symmetrical vowel system consisting of seven elements (in the Pindus and Gramoste subtypes):

$$i \quad â \quad u$$
$$e \quad ă \quad o$$
$$a$$

In the Farsherot and Moscopole subtypes there are six stressed vocals; *â* does not occur.

§ 11. **Unstressed vowels.** In unstressed positions /e/ and /o/ manifest a strong tendency to fuse with /i/ and /u/ respectively. The system of unstressed vowels can be roughly represented as follows:

i â u		i u
ă	or	ă
a		a

| (*mainly in the **P** and **G** subtypes*) | (*mainly in the **F** subtype*) |

An example of stressed *é* alternating with unstressed *i*: ved^u 'I see' vs. vidém^u 'we see An example of stressed *o* alternating with unstressed *u*: dórmu 'I sleep', vs. durñím^u 'we sleep

The authors of the *Aromunischer Sprachatlas* (ALIA, 1985) recorded the unstressed phoneme /e/ in the word *soáre* 'sun' as [e] in twenty-one villages and as [i] in twenty-five villages.

In subtypes of Aromanian that distinguish *ă* and *â*, the latter occurs under stress after *ţ, dz,* and *r*: *ţân* 'I hold,' *dzâc* 'I say,' *arâd* 'I laugh'; it is also heard before *m* and *n*: *câmpu* 'field,' *sân* 'breast.' In these subtypes, unstressed *ă* is pronounced [â]: *cásâ* 'house' (**P, G**) vs. *cásă* (**F** and other areas). However, an unstressed *ă* is pronounced like [ă], not [â], when it occurs in the vocative singular ending of -*ă* nouns: nom. *feátă* 'girl,' **P, G** *feátâ*, but voc. *feátă!*, not feátâ!¹⁵

---

¹⁵   See SarA: 436.

NOTE. The presence of two graphic symbols (î and â) with identical value in various Aromanian writings may be confusing. They were introduced into Aromanian spelling unnecessarily under the influence of Standard Romanian, where î and â have been spelling variants of the same sound.

§ 12. **Vowel syncope.** Syncope of unstressed vowels is frequent: *adunăm* 'we are gathering' or *annăm* (< *adnăm* < *adunăm*). Cf. also *Rămăn* 'Aromanian' vs. *Armăn* 'idem.'[16]

§ 13. **Diphthongs.** This list of diphthongs is meant to help the reader distinguish between two successive vowel letters forming a *diphthong* and two successive vowel letters representing vowels in *hiatus*. (In this English-Aromanian dictionary hiatuses are indicated in brackets. E.g., *diucľát* [i•u] 'hit by the evil eye.')

Rising diphthongs: **ea** [ea, ĭa] (*seáră* 'evening'); **ia** [ĭa] (*ma-iáuă* [ma•ĭá•ŭă] 'yeast'); cf. Engl. *yard*; **ie** [ĭe] (*iérghi* [ĭérği] 'grasses'); cf. Engl *yell*; **io** [ĭo] (*iodh* 'iodine'); cf. Engl. *yonder*; **iu** [ĭu] (*iu* 'where'); cf. Engl. *you*; **oa** [oa] or [ŭa] (*moáră* 'mill'); cf. Fr. *roi* 'king'; **ua** [ŭa] (*steáua* 'the star'); **uă** [ŭă] (*dzúuă* 'day') **uo** [ŭo] (*uóthură* 'prayer'); cf. Engl. *wall*.

Falling diphthongs: **ai** [aĭ] (*ai* '(you) have,' 2 *sg*.): cf. the Engl. pers. pron. **I**; **ăi** [ăĭ] (*măi* 'grannies,' sg. *máie*); **ei** [eĭ] (*trei* 'three'); cf. Engl. *eight, say*; **ii** [iĭ] (*cutíi* 'boxes'); cf. Fr. *ille* in *fille* 'daughter'; **oi** [oĭ] (*doi* 'two'); cf. Engl. *boy*; **ui** [uĭ] (*fuĭ* 'I was'); cf. Rom. *cui* 'nail'; **au** [aŭ] (*dau* 'to give'); cf. Engl. *now*; **ău** [ăŭ] (*arău* 'bad'); **eu** [eŭ] (*greu* 'heavy'); **iu** [iŭ] (*dilingíu* [di•lin•ğíŭ] 'tramp'); **âu** [âŭ] (*brâu* 'girdle'); **ou** [oŭ] (*bou* 'ox'); cf. Engl. *low*; **uu** [uŭ] (*véduu* [vé•duŭ] 'widower.')

The frequency of these diphthongs varies considerably. E.g., *ea* and *oa* are extemely frequent, while *uŭ* is very rare.

§ 14. **Consonants**

stops:	/p, b, t, d, k, g/
affricates:	/ţ [ts], dz, ĉ, ğ/
fricatives:	/f, v, s, z, th, ş [sh], j [zh], γ, γ', h, h'/
sonants:	/m, n, ñ, l, ľ, r/
semivowels:	/ĭ, ŭ, e (in the diphthong ea); o (in the diphthong oa)/

---

[16] See Capidan: 365-370.

In the Farsherot subtype /r/ can be apical, velar, or uvular (with no distinctive functions).

A lateral ł is common in the Farsherot subtype. Such an ł may easily become ŭ.

The *voiceless / voiced opposition* (/p/ : /b/ and so forth) is neutralized before any of its members: *nâs^u va s fug^u* 'he wants me to go' vs. *nâs va z beau* 'he wants me to drink,' where the archiphoneme /Z/ manifests itself as [s] before voiceless /f/, and as [z] before voiced /v/.

In final position, voiced consonants may become voiceless, mainly in areas of Aromanian-Slavic bilingualism.[17]

After /m/ and /n/, the voiceless / voiced opposition is neutralized and an archiphoneme appears, mainly in the areas of Aromanian-Greek bilingualism. E.g., *scúmpu* 'dear,' with an etymological *p* (< Slav. *skąpŭ*) is pronounced [skúm•pu] or rather [skúm•bu].

§ 15. **End of word.** *a*) After a single final consonant (except *ţ* and *dz*) a rounded off-glide [^u] is often noticeable. E.g., *cap* 'head' is usually pronounced [kap^u], with an lip-rounding that is rather seen than heard. After *ţ* and *dz* the off-glide is [^a]. In lexicography such off-glides may be omitted, but they are implied. *b*) After two final consonants [u] is usually heard ([zburăsku], [zburăsk^u] or simply [zburăsk] 'I speak.' However, after *muta cum liquida* final *u* is usually heard, as in *ácru* [á•kru] 'sour,' *ţércľu* [tsér•kľu] 'circle.'[18]

§ 16. BRIEF COMPARATIVE-HISTORICAL COMMENTS

§ 16.1. **Prothetic a-.** Aromanian has developed a prothetic *a-*, as in the following cases (from Latin): CLAMO 'I call,' Arom. *acľém;* COMPARO 'I compare,' Arom. *acúmpăr* 'I buy'; FUROR, Arom. *afúr* 'I steal'; LATRO, Arom. *alátru* 'I bark'; LAXO, Arom. *alás* 'I leave'; LAUDO, Arom. *alávdu* 'I praise'; LINGO, Arom. *alíngu* 'I lick'; LUCTA, Arom. *alúmtă* 'battle'; MARE, Arom. *amáre* 'sea'; MERIDIO, Arom. *amirídz* 'I rest'; RADO, Arom. *arád* 'I scrape'; RECENS (*of water*), Arom. *aráţe* 'cold'; REUS 'guilty,' Arom. *arău* 'bad'; RIDEO, Arom. *arâd* 'I laugh'; RIMOR, Arom. *arâm* 'I dig'; RIVUS, Arom. *arâu* 'river'; ROTA, Arom. *aroátă* 'wheel'; UMBRA, Arom. *aúmbră* 'shadow'; UNGO, Arom. *aúngu* 'I oil.' In light of these examples, the origin of the ethnonym *Armắn* 'Aromanian' becomes clear: from Lat. ROMANUS Roman, with loss

---

[17] More on this in SarN.

[18] More on this much debated phenomenon in CarF 65-67 and SarU.

of the unstressed *a* and with a prothetic *a-*. This peculiarity of Aromanian can also be found in words of non-Latin origin. E.g., Arom. *axén* 'stranger' (< Gr. *xénos*), Arom. *arána* 'wound' < Slav. *rána*), Arom. *ariháte* 'rest' (< Turk. *rahat*). Prothetic *a-* is very frequent in the Pindus area and rare in the Farsherot variety of Aromanian. Rare cases of prothetic *a-* have also been recorded in Daco-Romanian and in the faraway Istro-Romanian,[19] while the nearby Megleno-Romanian manifests an opposite phenomeon, i.e. the apheresis of etymological *a-*.[20] Prothetic *a-* can be also found in Greek dialects.[21]

§ 16.2. **Loss of unstressed a-.** This phenomenon sets Daco-Romanian and Aromanian apart from other Romance languages. Cf. Lat. AGNELLUS, Arom. *ñel*, D-Rom. *miel* 'lamb'; Lat. ANIMAL, *ANIMALIUM, Arom. *nămál'u* 'sheep, goat,' D-Rom. *nămáie* 'horned animal'; Lat. ANNOTINUS, Arom. and D-Rom. *noátin* 'one-year-old sheep'; Lat. AUTUMNUS, Arom. and D-Rom. *toámnă*, Istro-R. *tómna* 'fall.' In MeglR this loss of unstressed *a-* was generalized.

§ 16.3. **Diphthongization of o and e.** This CRom phenomenon, often called "conditioned" (i.e. non-spontaneous) diphthongization, distiguishes Romanian from the other Romance languages. It is common to Aromanian, Daco-Romanian, and Megleno-Romanian. Diphthongization occurs under stress, if the following syllable contains *ă* or *e*. E.g., Lat. MOLA, Arom. *moáră* 'mill'; Lat. acc. MORTEM, Arom. *moárte* 'death'; Lat. SERA *adj. f.* 'late,' Arom. *seáră* 'evening.' If these conditions are not met, *o* and *e* are preserved. E.g., Arom. *mori* [mor¹] 'mills,' *mórtu* 'dead,' *seri* [ser¹] 'evenings.'[22]

§ 16.4. **Maintenance of eá after p, b, f, v, m.** In contrast to D-Rom., Aromanian firmly keeps the diphthong *ea* (< Lat. *e*), as in: Lat. PINNA, Arom. *peánă* (D-Rom. *pánă*) 'feather'; Lat. VER, acc. VEREM 'spring,' Arom. *veáră* (D-Rom. *váră*) 'summer'; Lat. FETA, Arom. *feátă*, (D-Rom. *fátă*) 'girl'; Lat. MENSA, Arom. *meásă* (D-Rom. *másă*) 'table.'

---

[19] Pușc-StI II: 68-)

[20] More on *a-* in Sala: 44-45.

[21] Sandfeld, LB: 63.

[22] More on *ó/oá* and *é/eá* in Arom. and D-Rom. in Sala: 98-201.

§ 16.5. **Arom. *ţ* < CRom. *č* (< Lat. *ke, ki*) vs. D-Rom. *ĉ*.** E.g.,
Lat. CAELUM, Arom. *ţer* [tserᵘ] vs. D-Rom. *cer* [ĉer] 'sky'; Lat. CERA,
Arom. *ţeárǎ* vs. D-Rom. *ceárǎ* 'wax'; Lat. CERVUS, Arom. *ţérbu* vs.
D-Rom. *cerb* 'buck'; Lat. CENA, Arom. *ţínǎ* vs. D-Rom. *cínǎ* 'supper';
Lat. CINGO, Arom. *ţíngu*, cf. D-Rom. *încíng* 'to gird'; Lat. CIRCELLUS,
Arom. *ţirţél'u* vs. D-Rom. *cercél* 'earring.' It is in light of this
change that the South Slavic ethnonym *Tsíntsari* ('Aromanians') can
be understood. It derives, probably, from Arom. *ţínţi* 'five' < Lat.
*CINCE (for QUINQUE) + suffix *-ár*; the meaning then may be interpreted as 'those who say [tsíntsi'].' Some linguists believe that
the evolution of early Arom. *č* (or *ĉ*) to *ts* is due to Greek influence, but others explain this result through internal evolution.[23]

§ 16.6. **Arom. *dz* < CRom. *ǧ* or *ĝ* (< Lat. *ge, gi*) vs. D-Rom. *ĝ*.**
Examples are: Lat. GEMINUS > Arom. *dzeámin* (D-Rom. *geámǎn*) 'twin';
Lat. GEMO > Arom. *dzem* (D-Rom. *gem*) 'to groan'; Lat. GELU > Arom.
dzer (D-Rom. *ger*) 'frost.'

§ 16.7. **Lat. *kl, gl*, Arom. *kl, gl'* vs. D-Rom. *k', ǧ*.** Ex.: Lat.
CLAVO, acc. CLAVEM > Arom. *cl'eáie* (D-Rom. *chéie*) 'key'; Lat. AURI-
C(U)LA > Arom. *ureácl'e* (D-Rom. *uréche*) 'ear'; Lat. OC(U)LUS > Arom.
ócl'u (D-Rom. *ochi*) 'eye'; Lat. PEDIC(U)LUS > Arom. *pidúcl'u* (D-Rom.
pǎdúche) 'louse'; Lat. GLACIES > Arom. *gl'áţǎ* (D-Rom. *gheáţǎ*) 'ice';
Lat. acc. GLANDEM > Arom. *gl'índǎ* (D-Rom. *ghíndǎ*) 'acorn'; Lat. IN-
GLUTO > Arom. *angl'ít* (D-Rom. *înghít*) 'to swallow.' However, in the
Farsherot subtype *k'* and *ǧ* (as in D-Rom.) are common. E.g., **Plat.**
ok'u 'eye.'[24]

§ 16.8. **Maintenance of the voiced affricate *dz* (< Lat. *d+ĭ*).**
Unlike D-Rom., Aromanian keeps the affricate *dz*. E.g., Lat. RADIUS,
*radia > Arom. *arádzǎ* (D-Rom. *rázǎ*) 'beam'; Lat. DECEM > Arom. *dzáţe*
(D-Rom. *zéce*) 'ten.' (Here and there, D-Rom. subdialects still keep
the old *dz* as well.)[25]

§ 16.9. **Palatalization of labials and labiodentals.** In words of
Latin origin, labials and labiodentals underwent palatalization before *e* and *i*, as follows: p > *k'*, b > *ǧ*, f > *h'*, v > *γ'* (spelled
y in this work), and m > *ñ*. No other Romance area shows this deve-

---

[23] See Sala: 134.

[24] See B-Arch t. 9, q. nr. 183 'das Auge' ('the eye')

[25] See Cot-1961: 85 and 93).

lopment. Examples are Lat. PETRA 'stone,' Arom. *k'átră* (D-Rom. *piátră*); Lat. BENE 'good,' Arom. *ǵíne* (D-Rom. *bíne*); Lat. FERVEO, Arom. *h'érbu* (D-Rom. *fierb*) 'to boil'; Lat. VENIO, Arom. *yín* (D-Rom. *vin*) 'to come'; Lat. MEUS 'mine,' Arom. *(a) ñeu* (D-Rom. *(al) meu*). This phenomenon occurs in the Moldavian subdialect and in some other D-Rom. areas as well.[26] The same result can sometimes be noticed in Aromanian words of non-Latin origin as well, as in the vulgar word *k'ízda* 'vulva' (with *k'i-* instead of Slav. *pi-*).[27]

§ 16.10. **Maintenance of *ľ* and *ñ*.** CRom. *ľ* and *ñ* (< Lat. *l* or *n* + *e, i* in hiatus) became *ĭ* in D-Rom., but are well preserved in Aromanian. E.g., Lat. LEPUS, acc. LEPOREM, Arom. *ľépur* (D-Rom. *iépure*) 'hare'; Lat. acc. MULIEREM, Arom. *muľáre* (D-Rom. *muiére*) 'woman' and 'wife'; Lat. LIBERTO, Arom. *ľértu* (D-Rom. *iert*) 'to forgive.'

The old *ľ* and *ñ*, absent in present-day standard Romanian, are well attested in some D-Rom. subdialects.[28] A shift from *ľ* to *ĭ* and vacillation between *ľ* and *ĭ* was recorded in the Farsherot subtype of Aromanian. E.g., *F fuméĭle* 'the children' vs. *fuméľle* elsewhere (< Lat. FAMILIA); *F puĭ* 'chicks, birds,' alongside *puľ*;[29] *puĭ* or *puĭ*ᵘ, with loss of the old *ľ*, was recorded in several villages with Farsherot Aromanian: **Gra, Nij, Trn, Ses, Kok, Am, Mal, Kat,** etc.[30]

§ 16.11. **Lat. *j* + unstressed *o, u*** in words of Latin origin became *ǵ* in Arom. and D-Rom. Subsequently, D-Rom. *ǵ* evolved to *ž* (spelled *j*). In Aromanian the old *ǵ* is maintained; e.g., Lat. IUGUM, Arom. *giug* [ǵugᵘ] (D-Rom. *jug* [žug] 'yoke'); Lat. IOCUS, Arom. *gioc* [ǵokᵘ] (D-Rom. *joc* [žok]) 'dance, game'; Lat. ADIUTOR, Arom. *agiut* [a•ǵút] (D-Rom. *ajút* [a•žút] 'to help'). However, the old *ž* or *ǵ* are still heard in some D-Rom. subdialects.

§ 16.12. **Absence of rhotacism.** In contrast to D-Rom. and IstroR, neither Aromanian nor Megleno-Romanian undergoes rhotacism of

---

[26] See map nr. 13 in Cot-1961: 88 and CarC, maps 11-15, p. 163-167.

[27] See the DDA: 720.

[28] See Cot-1961: 92.

[29] See Capidan: 197-8.

[30] See B-Arch 3, 4, 5, 6, 9, q. nr. 106: 'der Vogel.'

intervocalic *n*. Cf. Lat. CANUS, Arom. *cănút* (D-Rom. *cărúnt* 'gray.' [31] However, sporadic cases of rhotacism have been recorded in the Far-sherot subtype. E,g., *păre* 'bread' (cf. D-Rom. *pâine* or *pâne*) from Lat. PANE; *skir* 'thorn' (cf. D-Rom. *spin*) from Lat. SPINU(M).[32]

§ 16.13. **Preservation of *n* in the Lat. cluster *nt*.** In contrast to D-Rom., Aromanian has preserved *n* before *t*. Cf. Lat. QUANTUS, Arom. *niscântu* 'few' (vs. D-Rom. *cât*, also spelled *cât*, 'how much'); Lat. ECCUM TANTUM, Arom. *ahântu* 'that much' (D-Rom. *atât*).

§ 16.14. **Frequent metathetical phenomena.** In varieties of Aromanian, phonemes may sometimes appear in different order, especially when /l/ or /r/ is involved. Examples of words beginning with *a-* and *b-*, selected from the DDA, are listed below: *acăchiséscu* and *achicăséscu* 'to understand'; *acroáre* and *arcoáre* 'cold'; *adávgu* and *avdág* 'to add'; *adâncá* and *andăcá* 'deeply'; *ahiursítă* and *arhiusítă* 'beginning'; *ambătruláre* and *ambăturláre* 'gallop'; *andărluséscu* and *andărluséscu* 'to become dizzy'; *arcó* (< *alcó*) and *acló* 'there'; *aróput* and *tópur* 'trot, noise'; *arujéscu* and *azuréscu* 'to neigh'; *añurzéscu* and *arñuzéscu* 'to smell'; *avigl'itór* or *avlighitór* 'guardian'; *băzácă* and *zăbácă* 'belly'; *báltă* and *blátă* 'pond'; *bârnu* and *brân* 'belt'; *brăgácică* and *buryácică* 'pail'; *búlvură* and *vúlbură* 'gunpowder'; *burdul'eác* and *dubruleác* 'bat'. Under the letter C twenty similar cases can be found (see DDA: 301-428). As long as no Standard Aromanian has come into being, none of these variants is wrong. Unusual metathetical phenomena can be heard in the Farsherot type of Aromanian: *mi dispól'u* and *mi zdăpói* 'to undress,' *dâş-t"íd* (*t"* is more palatal than *t'*) and *jdăcl'íd* 'to open' are examples.[33]

B. MORPHOLOGY

§ 17. **Morphonemic alternations**

a) **Consonant alternations** before the morpheme /$^{-i}$/, /-i/ forming the plural of nouns, the masculine plural of adjectives and the second person singular of verbs in the present tense are listed below. They may also occur in word formation.

---

[31] More on this in Rosetti: 273, 378-9, and 528-32.

[32] For details, see Saramandu, FD XI, 1992: 97-102.

[33] See Neiescu, maps 163-165).

b/ǵ. Ex. *rob* (m.) 'slave' vs. pl. *roghi* [roǵ]; *bárbă* (f.) 'beard' vs. pl. *bărghi* [băr•ǵi]; *órbu* adj. (m. sg.) 'blind' vs. m. pl. *órghi* [ór•ǵi]; *ntreb* vb. 1 sg. 'I ask' vs. 2 sg. *ntreghi* [ntreǵ].

c ([k])**/ţ.** Ex. *cuc* m. 'cuckoo' vs. pl. *cuţi* [kuţⁱ]; *núcă* f. 'nut' vs. pl. *nuţi* [nuţⁱ]; *ñic* adj. m. sg. 'small' vs. m. pl. *ñiţi*; *fac* vb. 1 sg. 'I make' vs. 2 sg. *faţi*.

d/dz. Ex. *brad* m. 'fir' vs. pl. *bradz*; *ud* adj. m. 'wet' vs. m. pl. *udz*; *ávdu* vb. 1 sg. 'I hear' vs. 2 sg. *ávdzâ* [áv•dzâ].

f/h. Ex. *sileáfe* f. 'belt' vs. pl. *siléhi*.

g/dz. Ex. *fag* m. 'beech' vs. pl. *fadzi*; *báligă* f. 'animal dung' vs. pl. *bălidzi*; *fug* vb. 1 sg. 'I run' vs. 2 sg. *fudzi*.

l/ĺ. Ex. *ñel* m. 'lamb' vs. pl. *ñeĺ*; *aţél* m. 'that' vs. pl. *aţéĺ*; *aspél* vb. 1 sg. 'I wash' vs. 2 sg. *aspéĺ*.

m/ñ. Ex. *pom* m. 'tree' vs. pl. *poñ*; *dórmu* vb. 1 sg. 'I sleep' vs. 2 sg. *dórñi*.

n/ñ. Ex. *an* m. 'year' vs. pl. *añ*; *bun* adj. m. 'good' vs. pl. *buñ*; *pun* vb. 'to put' vs. 2 sg. *puñ*.

p/k'. Ex. *pap* m. 'ancestor' vs. pl. *pachi* [pak']; *gépe* f. 'pocket' vs. pl. *gechi* [ǵek']; *nţep* vb. 1 sg. 'I start' vs. 2 sg. *nţechi* [nţek'].

s/ş. Ex. *mes* m. 'month' vs. pl. *meşi*; *căfáse* f. 'cage' vs. pl. *căfăşi* [kăfăšⁱ]; *cos* vb. 1 sg. 'I sew' vs. 2 sg. *coşi*.

sk/ ştⁱ. Ex. *péscu* m. 'fish' vs. pl. *peştⁱ* (or *péşţâ*); *fréscu* adj. 'cool, fresh' vs. pl. m. *fréşţâ*; *cunóscu* vb. 1 sg. 'I know' vs. 2 sg. *cunóştⁱ*.

t/ţ. Ex. *fráte* m. 'brother' vs. pl. *fraţ*; *murmíntu* m. 'grave' vs. pl. *murmínţâ*; *mórtu* adj. m. sg. 'dead' vs. pl. *mórţâ*; *pot* vb. 1 sg. 'I can' vs. 2 sg. *poţ*.

ţ/ĉ. Ex. *Bláţa* (a village) vs. *blâciót* [blâĉót] 'one from Blaţa.'

ŭ/ĭ. Ex. *bou* m. 'ox' vs. pl. *boi*; *dau* vb. 1 sg. 'I give' vs. 2 sg. *dai*.

v/y' (= γ'). Ex. *siv* adj. m. 'gray' vs. pl. *siγi* [siy'].

z/j (= ž). Ex. *călăúz* m. 'guide' vs. pl. *călăúji*; *caramíz* adj. m. 'dark' vs. pl. *caramíji*.

b) **Vowel alternations:**

a/ă. Ex. sg. *máie* 'grandmother' vs. pl. *măi*; sg. *cále* 'road' vs. pl. *căĺurⁱ*; sg. *páde* 'field' vs. pl. *pădz*; sg. *máre* 'big' vs. pl. *mărⁱ*; 1 sg. *cad* 'I fall' vs. 1 pl. *cădém*.

ia/ie. Ex. sg. *iárbă* 'grass' vs. pl. *iérghi*; *iárnă* 'winter' vs. pl. *iérnuri*.

e/ea. Ex. *ved* 'I see' vs. 3 sg. *veáde* (see § 16.4).
o/oá. Ex. *oárä* 'time' vs. pl. *or^i*; *pot* 'I can' vs. 3 sg. *poáte*.

This list of alternations can serve as a prerequisite for an easier understanding of Aromanian morphology.

§ 18. THE NOUN

§ 18.1. **Gender**. Nouns ending in unstressed -ă (pronounced -ă or -â) are feminine: *cásă* 'house,' *feátă* 'girl.' A few nouns in unstressed -ă are masculine because of their natural gender; e.g., *lálă* 'uncle,' *pópă* 'priest,' *tátă* 'father.' The vast majority of nouns ending in unstressed -e are also feminine: *cále* 'road,' *mínte* 'mind, opinion, idea,' *ploáie* 'rain,' *vúlpe* 'fox.' However, a few nouns ending in unstressed -e are masculine: *dínte* 'tooth,' *fráte* 'brother,' *múnte* 'mountain.' Nouns ending in a consonant, a consonant cluster, a falling diphthong, or -u are either masculine in both singular and plural, or masculine in the singular and feminine in the plural (traditionally, the latter are considered to be *neuter*). Masculines in this class are *lup* 'wolf,' *ocľiu* [ó•kľu] 'eye,' *bou* 'ox.' Examples of neuter nouns in this class are *cap* 'head,' *chiciór* 'foot'/ 'leg,' *zbor* 'word.'

All nouns ending in a stressed vowel are masculine; *pără* 'coin,' *lulé* 'smoking pipe,' *sculó* 'school' are examples.

In general, the gender of inanimate non-feminine nouns is unpredictable. There are however a few cases when meaning can be a gender indicator. For instance, all non-feminine coins and trees are masculine. Below is a list containing various non-feminine <u>monetary denominations</u> in Aromanian; all are masculine: *álbu, arslán, arúp, arúspu, áspru, bişlíc, cáţidh, căpíc, ciréc, circlíc, ducát, ducmén, frángu, γiuzlác, gălăgán, gros, icusár, mahmudé, migít, mitilíc, ngărmár, órtu, pineş, silín, statír, şiştác, zlot.* The same holds true for non-feminine <u>trees</u>: *mer* 'apple' is a neuter noun, but *mer* 'apple-tree' is masculine. However, in the vast majority of cases, m/n gender of inanimate nouns cannot be predicted. Cf. *par* 'post' (m.), *stur* 'post' (m. or n.), and *stil* 'post' (n.). To minimize gender errors in case of non-feminine nouns, the non-native student should first assume that they are neuter. Gender vacillations are frequent. For instance, 'plate' is *căţân* (n.) and *căţână* (f.), *misúr* (n.) and *misúră* (f.), *tánir* (n.) and *tániră* (f.), *tas* (n.) and *táse* (f.), *săhán* (n.) and *săháne* (f.).

§ 18.2. **Plural of feminine nouns**

a) Feminine nouns ending in -*ă* usually take -*e* in the plural: *meásă* 'table' vs. pl. *mease* [meá•si], *peánă* 'wing' vs. pl. *peáne*, *peáră* 'pear' vs. pl. *peáre*. After *ţ* and *dz* the ending -*e* shifts to -*ă*: *ţâţă* 'breast' vs. pl. *ţâţă*, *búdză* 'lip' vs. pl. *búdză*. Nouns with -*uă* in the singular take the plural ending -*le*: *căţáuă* 'bitch' vs. pl. *căţále*, *dzúuă* 'day' vs. pl. *dzâle*.

b) Many feminine nouns in -*ă* take $^{-i}$ in the plural (with vowel and consonant alternations, see § 17): *poálă* 'lap' vs. pl. *poľ*, *vácă* 'cow' vs. pl. *văţi* [văţ^{i}] (cf. D-Rom. *vácă*, pl. *vaci* [vaĉ]).

c) Feminine nouns ending in -*e* usually take $^{-i}$ or -*i* (*â* after *ţ* and *dz*), with vowel and consonant alternations in the plural: *gépe* 'pocket' vs. pl. *gechi* [ĝek'], *láfe* 'conversation' vs. pl. *lăhi* [lăh'], *hăláte* 'tool' vs. pl. *hălăţ* [hă•lăţ], *arádză* 'beam' vs. pl. *arădz* [a•rădz], *păreácľe* 'pair' vs. pl. *părécľi* [pă•ré•kľi], *noápte* 'night' vs. pl. *nópţâ*.

d) When -*e* is preceded by *ĭ*, the plural ending is -∅ (zero). Examples are: *oáie* 'sheep' vs. pl. *oi*; *nădí(i)e* 'hope' vs. pl. *nădíi* [nădíĭ]; *ploáie* 'rain' vs. pl. *ploi*.

e) Singular and plural may have the same ending: *lilíce* 'flower' vs. pl. *lilíce*.

f) -*uri* [-ur^{i}] (historically a neuter ending) often appears in the plural of feminine nouns. E.g., *cále* 'road' vs. pl. *căľuri*; *chinéfe* 'latrine' vs. pl. *chinéfuri*. This ending is always unstressed.

g) -*ate* (< Gr.): *ármă* 'weapon' vs. pl. *ármate*, *yrámă* 'letter' vs. pl. *yrámate*, *ľánumă* 'entrails' vs. pl. *ľanumáte*, *thámă* 'miracle' vs. pl. *thámate*.

h) Isolated cases: -*âñ*: *múmă* 'mother' vs. pl. *mumâñ*; *sóră* 'sister' vs. pl. *surări* [su•răr^{i}].

Plural of masculine nouns

a) The regular plural ending of masculine nouns is $^{-i}$ (or $^{-â}$) after one consonant and -*i* (or -*â*) after a consonant cluster. Alternations of consonants occur. E.g., *córbu* 'raven' vs. pl. *córghi*, *ócl'u* 'eye' vs. pl. *ócl'i* (more ex. in § 18).

b) After a vowel, the ending *-u* [-ŭ] becomes *-i* [ĭ] in the plural: *beu* 'governor' vs. pl. *bei*; *bou* m. 'ox' vs. pl. *boi* [boĭ].

c) *-âñ* (*P, G*), *-ăñ* (*F*): *tátă* 'father' vs. pl. *tătâñ* or *tătăñ*, *lálă* 'uncle' vs. pl. *lâlâñ* or *lălăñ*.

d) *-añ*, *-eañ*: *as* 'ace' vs. pl. *áseañ*, *háhă* m. 'simpleton' vs. pl. *háhañ*.

e) The plural of *om* [om^u] 'man' is *oámeñ* [ŭá-miñ].

f) *-ádz*, *-eádz* is the plural ending of all nouns whose singular ends in a stressed vowel: *dumnidză* 'god' vs. pl. *dumnidzádz*, *mehengí* 'innkeeper' vs. pl. *mehengeádz*. This ending is of Greek origin.[34]

Plural of neuter nouns. In the singular, masculine and neuter nouns look alike, but they differ in the plural. The plural endings of neuter nouns are *-e* and *-uri* [-ur^i] (always unstressed). Ex. *ac* 'needle' vs. pl. *áṭe*, *col'u* 'testicle' vs. pl. *coál'e*, *puṭ* 'well' vs. pl. *púṭuri*, *roiu* 'swarm' vs. pl. *róiuri*.

§ 19. Indefinite and definite form of nouns

In principle, this grammatical opposition is the same as the opposition we find in Engl. *a man* and *the man*. However, the definite article is enclitic and has gender and number forms:

m/n sg:	-l^u or -lu		m pl:	-l' or -l'i
f sg:	-a		f pl:	-le

Ex.: indef. sg. m. *sócru* 'father-in-law' vs. def. *sócrul^u*; indef. sg. m *lálă* 'uncle' vs. def. *lálăl^u*; indef. pl. m. *sócri*, *lălâñ^i* vs. def. pl: *sócril'*, *lălâñl'i*; indef. sg. f. *soácră* 'mother-in-law'; indef. pl f: *soácre*, vs. def. *soácrele*.

In the F subtype the definite article for m/n sg has a variant *-u*. An example is *cap* [kap^u] 'head' (n. sg. indef.) vs. *cáplu* or *cápu* [ká•pu] (sg. def.)

---

[34] Sandfeld, LB: 104.

Note. Daco-Romanian, Megleno-Romanian, Istro-Romanian, Albanian, Bulgarian and Macedonian also have enclitic articles.[35]

§ 20. **Declension of nouns**

a) Nominative and acusative singulars of all nouns are identical. So are nominative and accusative plurals for all nouns.

b) The genitive and the dative forms of all nouns are identical. The endings are: (g/d sg m/n) *-lui* (unstressed); (g/d sg f) *-ľei* (unstressed); (g/d pl m, f, n) *-lor* (unstressed).[36]

c) The g/d form is always preceded by the invariable particle *a*. Ex. nom/acc sg m: *ľépurlu* 'the hare', g/d: *a ľépurlui*; nom/acc pl m: *ľépuriľi* [lé•puri•ľi] *or* [lépurľi], g/d: *a lépurilor* [lé•puri•lor]; nom/acc sg f: *cápra* 'the goat,' g/d: *a cáprăľei*; nom/acc pl f: *cáprele or căprile*, g/d: *a cáprelor or a căprilor*.

d) A vocative singular forme in *-o* or *-e* may be heard with nouns used as terms of address for persons: *sóră* 'sister' vs. voc. *sóro! dómnu* 'sir, lord' vs. voc. *doámne!*

e) There is also a g/d form consisting of *alu* (m), *ale* or *ali* (f) used proclitically. E/g., nom/acc *préftu* 'priest' vs. g/d *alu préftu*; nom/acc *feáta* 'the girl' vs. g/d *a feátăľei* or *ali feátă*.

§ 21. **THE ADJECTIVE**

Adjectives come in *four types* depending on their gender and number forms. The vast majority of Aromanian adjectives have four nom/acc forms; e.g., m/n sg *bun* [búnᵘ] 'good,' f. sg. *búnă*, m. pl. *buni* [buñ], f/n pl. *búne*. Some adjectives have only three forms; e.g., m/n sg. *yiu* 'alive,' f. sg. *yíe*, m. and f/n pl. *yii* or m/n sg. *laiu* 'black,' f. sg. *láie*, m. and f/n pl. *lăi*. Probably the most frequent two-form adjective is m/n and f. sg *máre* 'big' m., and f/n pl. *mări* [măriᵢ]. One-form adjectives include: *cachí* 'khaki,', *scliró* 'rough.'

---

[35] Details in Sandfeld, LB: 165-170.

[36] The fusion of the genitive and dative can be found in other Balkan languages as well. Details in Sandfeld, LB 185-188.

§ 21.1. **Agreement.** Adjectives take the number and the gender of the nouns to which they refer, as in:

m. sg. om^u bun^u 'good man' vs. **m. pl.** oámiñ buñ 'good men'
n. sg. vin^u bun^u 'good wine' vs. **n. pl.** vínur^i búne 'good
f. sg. ápă búnă 'good water' vs. **f. pl.** ápe búne 'good waters'

§ 21.2. **Comparative and superlative.** Aromanian comparatives are analytical only and consist of a proclitic element (*ma* or *cáma*) followed by the adjective in the form required by the agreement rule: *Yínlu eásti ma bún di (or dicât) apa* 'Wine is better than water'; *Apa nu eásti ma búnă di (dicât) yínlu* 'Water is not better than wine.'

The *absolute superlative* is also analytical and consists of the invariable proclitic element *múltu* 'very, much' and the adjective in the form required by the agreement rule: *un câsâbă múltu muşát* (m. sg.) 'a very beautiful city' vs. *câsâbádz múltu muşáţ* (m. pl.) 'very beautiful cities' and *ună hoáră múltu muşátă* (f. sg.) 'a very beautiful village' vs. *hoáre múltu muşáte* 'very beautiful villages.'

The *relative superlative* can be formed with *cáma* + the adjective + the definite article required by the agreement rule. E.g., *Nâs^u eásti* **cáma** *muşátlu* 'He is the most handsome one' (m) vs. *Nâsă eásti* **cáma** *muşáta* (f) 'She is the most beautiful one.' In regions with Aromanian-Slavic bilingualism there is also another way of expressing a relative superlative: the proclitic *nai* (< Slav.) + *ma* or *cáma* + the adjective + the definite article required by the agreement rule. E.g., *Nâs^u eásti* **nai** *cama muşátlu* 'He is the most handsome one' (m.) vs. *Nâsă eásti nai cáma muşáta* 'She is the most beautiful one' (f.).

§ 22.1. **THE PRONOUN**

Personal pronouns

Sg. stressed forms / unstressed **Pl.** stressed / unstressed
  (**bold**)   (*italics*)   (**bold**)   (*italics*)

1st person

Nom: **io(u), eu; míni**   **noi**
Dat: **añía, añéia** *añ/âñ, ñi, ñ*   **an(o)áuă** *nă/nâ, n-*
Acc: **míni, io(u), eu** *mi*   **noi**   *nă/nâ, n-*

2nd person

Nom:	**tíni**		**voi**	
Dat:	**aţâia, aţéia**	*ăţ/âţ, ţă/ţâ, ţ*	**av(o)áu(ă)**	*vă/vâ, v-*
Acc:	**tíni**	*ti*	**voi**	*vă/vâ, v-*

3rd person m.

Nom:	**el, năs/nâs**		**eľ, năşⁱ/nâşⁱ**	
Dat:	**alúi**	*ăľ/âľ, ľi*	**alór,**	*lă/lâ*
Acc:	**el, năs/nâs)**	*ăl/âl, lu, l-*	**eľ, năşⁱ/nâşⁱ)**	*ăľ/âľ, ľi*

3rd person f.

Nom:	**ea/ia, năsă/nâsă**		**eáli, năsi/nâsi**	
Dat:	**aľéi**	*ăľ/âľ, ľi, ľ*	**alór**	*lă/lâ*
Acc:	**ea/ia, năsă/nâsă)**	*u*	**eáli, nâsi (năsi)**	*li*

Note. The accusative *io* in the 1st person singular can be explained through Albanian.[37]

§ 22.2. *Pleonastic personal pronouns*

Like the other Balkan languages, D-Rom. included,[38] Aromanian knows the pleonastic usage of the accusative or dative forms of the personal pronoun together with a direct or indirect object expressed by a noun or a pronoun. In the English translation below the pleonastic personal pronouns are given in capitals:

• *Vrea s-***lu** *veádă* **híľi-su** *dişcľís* (DDA: 488) lit. 'He wanted to see HIM his son educated.' Cf. D-Rom. *Vroia să-l vadă* **pe fiul său** *învăţat.*

• **Parádzľi** *ľi spăstrí* (DDA: 1105) lit. 'He had stolen IT the money.' Cf. D-Rom. **Paralele** le *furase.*

• *Arâulu* **ni** *u nică* **grădína** (DDA: 871) lit. 'The river had flooded IT our garden.' Cf. D-Rom. *Râul ne-a inundat* **grădina** or, in a pleonastic, but perfectly acceptable, phrasing, **Grădina** *ne-a inundat-o râul.*

• **Li** *curáşi* **pătăţle?** (DDA: 412) 'Have you peeled THEM the potatoes?' Cf. D-Rom. *Ai curăţat* **cartofii?** or **Cartofii** *i-ai curăţat?*

• **Ľi** *deáde ócľi a* **híľ-sui** *s-fúgă* (DDA: 933) 'TO HIM he gave his

---

[37] See Sandfeld, LB: 118.

[38] Sandfeld, LB: 13 and 190.

son the advice to run away.' Cf. D-Rom. *Îi dădu* **lui fecioru-său** *sfatul să fugă* or *Dădu* **lui fecioru-său** *sfatul să fugă*.

Aromanian texts contain cases of pleonastic usage of personal pronouns which would not be acceptable in D-Rom, like the following: *cu tută-ľi avuțámea* **a lui** (DDA: 246) 'in spite of his wealth,' literally 'with all **HIS** wealth of his.'

§ 23. **The reflexive pronoun**

3ʳᵈ sg/pl dat.: *ăși* or *âși*; *și, ș'-*; 3ʳᵈ sg/pl acc.: *si, să* or *sâ*; *s-, -ș*.

For the 1ˢᵗ and 2ⁿᵈ person sg/pl the unstressed dative and accusative forms of personal pronouns are used. E.g., *Mi aspel* 'I wash (myself)'; *N-aspilăm* 'We wash (ourselves).'

§ 24. **Possessive pronouns** (with variants)

a) One owner   sg: pl:

		sg	pl
1 sg.	m.	a *meu*, a *ñeu*, a *mel*	a *mei*, a *ñei*, a *meľ*
	f.	a *mea*, a *meáuă**	a *meále**
2 sg.	m.	a *tău*, a *tăl*	a *tăi*, a *tăľ*
	f.	a *ta*, a *táuă**	a *tále**
3 sg.	m.	a *lui*	a *lor*
	f.	a *ľei*	a *lor*

b) Two or more owners, *sg*:   pl:

		sg	pl
1	m.	a *nóst(r)u*	a *nóșt(r)i*, a *nóștâ*
	f.	a *noást(r)ă**	a *noást(r)e**
2	m.	a *vóst(r)u*	a *vóșt(r)i*, a *vóștâ*
	f.	a *voást(r)ă**	a *voást(r)e**
3	m/f	a *lor*	a *lor*

* REMINDER: *Unstressed /ă/ may be pronounced [ă] or [â]. Unstressed /e/ and /o/ are usually pronounced [i] and [u] respectively.* See § 11 above.

When a possessive pronoun shows "the owner" of a relative, it is used enclitically. There are twelve such forms: six for the nom./ acc. and six for the g/d:

nom./acc.: sócru-*ñu* / soácră-*mea*; sócru-*tu* / soácră-*ta*; sócru-*su* / soácră-*sa* ('my father-in-law / my mother-in-law; your father-in-law / your mother-in-law; his or her father-in-law / his or her mother-in-law');

g/d: *alu* sócru-*ñui*, *ali* soácră-*meai*; *alu* sócru-*tui*, *ali* soácră-*tai*; *alu* sócru-*sui*, *ali* soácră-*sai* ('my father's-in-law' or 'to my father-in-law' and so on).

Like in other Balkan languages,[39] the unstressed dat. sg. forms of the personal pronoun (-*ñ*, -*ţ*, -*l′*) are often used as possessive pronouns. E.g., *ínima-ñ* 'my heart' (= *ínima a mea*, cf. Engl. 'this heart of mine'). The corresponding form of the reflexive pronoun can have this function as well: *aúmbra-şi* 'his (or her) shadow.'

§ 25. **Demonstrative pronouns.** For near objects *aístu* 'this' is the only pronoun. Its forms are given below.

nom/acc **sg** m/n:	*aístu* or *aéstu*	f:	*aístă* or *aéstă*
g/d:	*aistúi* or *aiştúi*,		*aistéi*, *aiştéi*,
	aişcúi, *aliştúi*		*aişcéi*, *aliştéi*
nom/acc **pl** m:	*aíşti*, *aéşti*	f/n:	*aíste*, *aéste*
	aíşci, *aéşţâ*		
g/d m and f/n:	*aistór*[u], *aiştór*[u], *aişcór*[u], *aliştór*[u]		

For distant objects: *aţél*[u] 'that,' with the following forms:

nom/acc **sg** m/n:	*aţél*, *aţéu*, *aţăl*	f:	*aţeá*, *aţá*
g/d **sg** m/n:	*aţilúi*, *aţălúi*	f:	*aţil′éi*, *aţăl′éi*
nom/acc **pl** m:	*aţél′*, *aţéi*, *aţăl′*	f:	*aţeále*, *aţále*
g/d **pl** m:	*aţâlór*	f/n:	*aţălór*

There is also the pronoun *alántu* 'the other' with the following paradigm:

nom/acc **sg** m/n:	*alántu*, *anánt(u)*	f:	*alántă*, *anántă*
g/d m:	*alăntúi*, *anăntúi*		*alăntéi*, *anăntéi*
nom/acc **pl** m:	*alánţ(â)*, *anánţâ*	f/n:	*alánte*, *anánte*
g/d m and f/n:	*alăntór*, *anăntór*.[40]		

---

[39] See Sandfeld, LB: 188.

[40] Details in Capidan: 419-25, CarF: 170-79, and SarA: 44.

§ 26. **Relative-interrogative pronouns.** The most common relative-interrogative pronoun is *cári* (or *cai*) 'who,' 'which,' g/d:
acári, acúi, acúri. Another relative-interrogative pronoun is *țe*
pronounced *ți*, mainly in the South.[41]

§ 27. **Negative and indefinite pronouns.** These classes include
(alphabetically):

> *ahântu* or *ahându* 'that much, that many'
> *can* m/n, *cánă* f. 'nothing, nobody'
> *cániva* 'somebody, nobody'
> *cánținivá* 'nobody'
> *cánțivá* 'nothing'
> *carevá, carĭvá, cánivá*, g/d a *cuivá*
> *cárĭți, carĭțidó, cárĭțindó* 'whoever'
> *carĭchișdó ți s-híbă* 'whoever, whatever'
> *cári s-híi* or *cári s-híbâ* 'whoever, whatever'
> *erĭcari* 'whoever, whatever' (absent from the DDA)
> *íchișdó* 'whoever'
> *íțicári, íțidó, íțindó, íțipásă, íțipása s-híbâ,*
>   *íți s-híbâ, íțișĭ* 'whatever, whatever'
> *ndoĭ* m/n, *ndoáuă* or *ndáuă* f. 'a few, several'
> *niscântu* m/n, *niscântă* f., *niscânțâ* m. pl., *niscânte*
>   f. pl., var. *niscându* 'some'
> *nísti, nâști* 'some'
> *tári* 'some, certain'
> *ținivá* 'somebody'
> *țivá* 'something'
> *vâr, vârnu, vrân* m/n; *vâră, vârnă, vrână* f. 'some.'

§ 28. **THE NUMERAL**

§ 28.1. **Cardinal numerals.** *únu* m/n (absolute form, i.e. form
used by itself) and *un* (used before a noun) 'one'; *únă / únă* (or *nă
/ nă*) f.; *doi* m 'two,' *doáuă* (or *dáuă, dáo*) f/n; *trei* 'three'; *pátru* 'four'; *țínți* (2 syll.) 'five', Fărsh. *țínți* (1 syll.); *șási*
'six'; *șápti* 'seven'; *óptu* 'eight'; *noáuă* (or *náuă, náo*) 'nine';
dzáți 'ten.'
Numerals from 11 to 19 are formed with the morpheme **-spră**: *ú(n)-
spră-dzáți* (written as one word), lit. 'one (over)ten' and so on.

---

[41] Details in Capidan: 427-430.

Note. In contrast to D-Rom., these numerals are connected with the noun by the preposition *di*, as in *dósprațe* **di** *cĺei căftá* (DDA: 449) vs. D-Rom. *căutá dóuăsprezece chei* 'was searching for twelve keys'; *du-ñ... dóspradzați* **di** *curăi* (DDA: 414) vs. D-Rom. *Adú-mi... dóuăsprezece curéle* 'Bring me twelve belts (**N.B.** douăsprezece *de* chei would not be acceptable to any native speaker of D-Rom.)

'Twenty' is *yínghiț* or *yíyinț* (in the North *yínyiț*; in Gopeș and Muloviște *ghínghiț*; < Lat. **vinginti* for VIGINTI. This Latin numeral has been preserved <u>nowhere else</u> in the Balkans. Unlike D-Rom. Aromanian does not use a preposition after the numeral 'twenty.' Cf. Arom. *yínyiț cápiti* 'twenty heads' vs. D-Rom. *douăzéci* **de** *cápete*.

From **21** to **29** -*spră*- is followed by *yínyiț*, as in 21 *unsprăyínyiț* 'twenty-one,' lit. 'one (added) to twenty.' However, in Epir a form without -*spră*- is also used, as in *yíyinț únu*, lit. 'twenty-one' and so on.

Numbers representing increments of ten, from **30** to **90**, consist of the respective simple numeral and the noun 'ten' (*dzáți*) used in the plural (*dzăți̯*); e.g., *treidzăți̯* 'thirty' (lit. '*three tens*').

'One hundred' is *únă sútă* (< CSlav. **sŭtó* 'hundred'), and 'one thousand' is *únă ñíĺi* (< Lat. MILLIA).

§ 28.2 **Ordinal numerals.** 1st: *(â)ntâñu*, def. *(â)ntâñlu* m/n, *(â)ntâñi*, def. *(â)ntâña* f. This numeral (< Lat. **ANTANEUS* for **ANTEANUS*) is rare. The regular word is its synonym *prot*, def. *prótlu* m/n, *prótâ*, def. *próta* f (< Gr.) 2nd: *dóilu* m/n, *a doáua* f.; 3rd: *tréilu* or *trélu* m/n, *a tréia* f.; 4th: *páturlu* m/n, *a pátura*, *a pátra* f.; 5th: *țínțili* or *țínțirlu* m/n; a feminine form is not known; 6th: *șásili* and *șásirlu* m/n; f: ? (unknown!); 7th: *șáptili* m/n; f: ? (unknown!); 8th: *óptulu* m/n; 9th: *noáulu* m/n; 10th: *dzáțili* m/n. Another way of expressing an ordinal numeral consists of the definite form of a cardinal numeral plus -*e*. E.g., from *óptu* 'eight' the ordinal numeral is *óptuli*. Here is what Th. Capidan says about ordinal numerals in Aromanian: "*A speaker of Aromanian is very puzzled when he or she is to express numerically the order of an object or event.*"[42]

---

[42] See Capidan: 404-5.

THE VERB

§ 29. **Introductory notes.** a) **Absence of infinitive.** Unlike other Romance languages, Aromanian <u>does not have an infinitive</u> as a general label for all the verbal forms as a citation form for verbs. Convenentionally, the first person singular present indicative is used instead. Cf. Fr. *chanter*, Sp. *cantar*, It. *cantare*, Rom. *a cânta* and, on the other hand, Arom. *cântu*, which literally means only 'I sing' (or 'I am singing'). Lexicographically, Arom. *cântu* has been used as a generic word meaning 'to sing.' The Aromanian word *cântáre*, which is a direct and uninterrupted continuation of Lat. CANTARE, has ceased to funnction as an infinitive and has become a noun ('singing, song').

The DDA, the best available Aromanian dictionary thus far, provides four forms for any given verb: the first person singular of the present tense (*cântu* 'I sing'), the first person singular of the aorist, often called "simple past" (*cântái* 'I sang'), the past participle (*cântátă* 'sung'), and the deverbative noun (*cântáre* 'singing, song').

Note. The absence of infinitive is also a distinguishing trait of other Balkan languages.[43]

b) **Conjugations.** Regular Aromanian verbs fall into four conjugations which can be determined by the vowel preceding *-re* in the respective verbal noun:

1st conjugation: *cântu, cântái, cântátă, cântáre* 'to sing,' where *-á-* in the last form may be taken as a conjugation marker.

2nd conjugation: *cad, cădzúi, cădzútă, cădeáre* 'to fall,' where *-eá-* marks the conjugational class. However, *-ea-* is also found in deverbatives of verbs belonging to the 1st conjugation (after a palatal consonant): *tal^u* (in the DDA *tal'ĭŭ*) 'to cut,' with the deverbative noun *tăl'eáre*. The imperfect spelling system in the DDA is responsible for this coincidence. In reality, the latter word should have been spelled *tăl'áre*.

3rd conjugation: *dzâc, dzâş, dzâsă, dzâţeáre* or *dzâţire* 'to say,' where *-eá-* or *-i-* (unstressed) shows the conjugational class.

4th conjugation: *dórmu, durñíi, durñítă, durñíre* 'to sleep,' where *-í-* (always stressed) is the conjugational marker.

---

[43] Details in Sandfeld, LB: 173-180.

Some suffixes can also serve as indicators of conjugation. Thus, the numerous Aromanian verbs with the suffix -*édz* belong to the 1st conjugation, and the even more numerous verbs with the suffix -*éscu* belong to the 4th conjugation.

A. The indicative mood.

§ 30. **The present tense.** Endings: 1st sg: ^u (after two consonants -u); after a vowel -ŭ; 2nd sg: ⁱ (after two consonants -i or -â); after a vowel -ĭ; 3rd sg: unstressed -ă or -e; after a vowel, zero; 1st pl: -*m*^u, 2nd pl: -*ţ*; 3^d pl: as the 1st person sg (for the 1st conjugation) or as the 3rd person sg (for other verbs).

Tne distinctive contrast between various personal forms, particularly between the 1st and the 2nd person singular, is increased considerably by frequent consonantal and vowel alternations (§ 18).

Present tense paradigms for the 1st conjugation are given below (**ascáp** 'to escape'; **lucrédz** 'to work'; and **dau** 'to give').

sg:	ascáp	lucrédz	dau
	ascáchi [as•kák']	lucrédz	dai
	ascápă	lucreádză	da
pl:	ascăpăm	lucrăm	dăm
	ascăpáţ	lucráţ	daţ
	ascápă	lucreádză	da

Present tense paradigms for the 2nd conjugation (**beau** 'to drink'; **cad** 'to fall'; **pot** 'to be able'; **ved** 'to see'):

sg:	beau	cad	pot	ved
	beai	cadz	poţ	vedz
	bea	cáde	poáte	veáde
pl:	bem	cădém	putém	vidém
	beţ	cădéţ	putéţ	vidéţ
	bea	cad	pot	ved

Present tense paradigms for the 3rd conjugation (**duc** 'to carry', **dzâc** 'to say'; **fac** 'to do/to make'; and **trag** 'to pull') are given below.

sg:	duc	dzâc	fac	trag
	duţi	dzâţi	faţi	tradzi
	dúţe	dzâţe	fáţe	trádze
pl:	dúţim	dzâţim	fáţim	trádzim
	dúţiţ	dzâţiţ	fáţiţ	trádziţ
	duc	dzâc	fac	trag

Present tense paradigms for the 4th conjugation (**dórmu** 'to sleep'; **yin** 'to come'; **ávdu** 'to hear'; and **mutréscu** 'to look at'):

sg:	dórmu	yin	ávdu	mutréscu
	dórñi	yiñ	ávdzâ	mutréşţâ
	doárme	yíne	ávde	mutreáşte
pl:	durñím	yiním	avdzâm	mutrím
	durñíţ	yiníţ	avdzâţ	mutríţ
	dórmu	yin	ávdu	mutréscu

§ 31. The imperfect

Endings (for verbs of all conjugations): 1st sg: -m; 2nd sg: -i [ĭ]; 3rd sg: -∅; 1st pl: -m; 2nd pl: -ţ; 3rd pl: -∅. These endings are preceded by a suffix (-á- or -eá-, depending on phonetic environment). Sample of paradigms:

a) with the suffix -á-   **b)** with the suffux -eá-

('to escape,' 'to work,' 'to hear,' 'to fall,' 'to say,' 'to look')

sg:	ascăpám	lucrám	avdzám		cădeám	dzâţeám	mutreám
	ascăpái	lucrái	avdzái		cădeái	dzâţeái	mutreái
	ascăpá	lucrá	avdzá		cădeá	dzâţeá	mutreá
pl:	ascăpám	lucrám	avdzám		cădeám	dzâţeám	mutreám
	ascăpáţ	lucráţ	avdzáţ		cădeáţ	dzâţeáţ	mutreáţ
	ascăpá	lucrá	avdzá		cădeá	dzâţeá	mutreá

Irregular imperfects. The verbs **dau** 'to give' and **stau** 'to sit' have irregular paradigms: *dădeám, dădeái*, etc.; *stăteám, stăteái*, etc. The imperfect of **am** 'to have' is *aveám, aveái*, etc.

§ 32. The aorist (or "the simple past")

Endings: 1st sg: -i [-ĭ]; 2nd sg: -şi [-şⁱ]; 3rd sg: -∅; 1st pl: -m; 2nd pl: -t; 3rd pl: -ră. These endings are preceded by suffixes:

-á-/-ă- (for the 1st conjugation), -ú- (for the 2nd conjugation), and -í- or -â'- (for the 4th conjugation).

Samples ('to escape,' 'to fall,' 'to look at,' and 'to hear'):

sg.	ascăpái	cădzúi	mutríi	avdzâi
	ascăpáşi	cădzúşi	mutríşi	avdzâşi
	ascăpă	cădzú	mutrí	avdzâ
pl.	ascăpăm	cădzúm	mutrím	avdzâm
	ascăpát	cădzút	mutrít	avdzât
	ascăpáră	cădzúră	mutríră	avdzâră

Irregular forms of aorist: from **beau** ('to drink'): *biúi, biúşi*, etc.; from **ľau**, spelled also **ľeau** ('to take'): *loai* (1 syll.), *loaşi* (1 syll.), *lo, lom, loat, loáră*; from **stau** ('to stop, dwell, sit'): *stătúi, stătúşi*, and so on.

Verbs of the 3rd conjugation differ from the above patterns in three ways. First, the stress falls on the root (not on the suffix). Second, the suffix is -i-. Third, the 1st person singular contains no suffix; it ends in a consonant (followed by ^u) or in a consonant cluster (followed by -u). The exact form of the 1st person singular of these verbs cannot be deduced synchronically, but it is explicable historically. A list of the most frequent verbs with unpredictable 1st person singular in the aorist is given below:

adúc 'to bring': *adúş, adúsisi [a-dú-sişⁱ], adúsi, adúsim*, etc.
agiúngu 'to reach': *agiúmşu, agiúmsişⁱ, agiúmsi, agiúmsim*, etc.
alég 'to choose': *alépşu, aleápsişⁱ, aleápsi, aleápsim*, etc.
alíngu 'to lick': *alímşu, alímsişⁱ, alímsi, alímsim*, etc.
apríndu 'to catch fire': *apréşu, apreásişⁱ, apreási*, etc. or
        aprímşu, aprímsişⁱ, aprímsi, etc.
árdu 'to burn': *árşu, ársişⁱ, ársi, ársim, ársit, ársiră*
arâd 'to laugh': *arâş^u, arâsişⁱ, arâsi, arâsim, arâsit, arâsiră*
armân 'to remain': *armáş^u, armásişⁱ, armási*, etc.

arúpu 'to tear': *arúpşu, arúpsiş[i], arúpsi,* etc.

ascúndu 'to hide': *asúmşu, ascúmsiş[i], ascúmsi,* etc.

aspárgu 'to break': *aspárşu, aspársiş[i], aspársi,* etc.

aspún 'to show': *aspúş[u], aspúsiş[i], aspúsi,* etc.

astíngu 'to put out (fire)': *astímşu, astímsiş[i], astímsi,* etc.

aştérgu 'to wipe': *aştérşu, aşteásiş[i], aşteársi,* etc.

aúngu 'to oil'; *aúmşu, aúmsiş[i], aúmsi, aúmsim,* etc.

coc 'to bake': *cópşu, coápsiş[i], coápsi, coápsim,* etc.

dipún 'to go down': *dipúş[u], dipúsiş[i], dipúsi,* etc.

    or: *dipunái, dipunáş[i], dipună,* etc.

dau 'to give': *ded, deádiş[i], deádi, deádim, deádit, deádiră*

duc 'to carry': *duş[u], dúsiş[i], dúsi,* etc.

dzâc 'to say': *dzâş[u], dzâ'siş[i], dzâ'si,* etc.

fac 'to do': *feci[u], feáţiş[i], feáţi, feáţim, feáţit, feáţiră*

frígu 'to fry': *frípşu, frípsiş[i], frípsi, frípsim,* etc.

frângu 'to break': *fregi[u], freádziş[i], freádzi, freádzim,* etc.

    or: *frâmşu, frâmsiş[i], frâmsi, frâmsim,* etc.

hérbu 'to boil': *hérşu, heársiş[i], heárse, heársim,* etc.

hig 'to drive in': *hípşu, hípsiş[i], hípsi,* etc.

múlgu 'to milk': *múlşu, múlsiş[i], múlsi, múlsim,* etc.

ndrégu 'to prepare': *ndrépşu, ndreápsiş[i], ndreápsi,* etc.

ñérgu 'to go, to walk': *ñérşu, ñeársiş[i],* etc.

nvíngu 'to defeat': *nvínşu, nvínsiş[i], nvínsi,* etc.

píngu 'to push': *pímşu, pímsiş[i], pímsi,* etc.

pitrúndu 'to penetrate': *pitrúmşu, pitrúmsiş[i], pitrúmsi,* etc.

plângu 'to cry': *plâ'mşu, plâ'msiş[i], plâ'msi,* etc.

scot 'to take out': *scoş[u], scoásiş[i], scoási, scoásim,* etc.

scriu 'to write': *scriş[u], scrísiş[i], scrísi, scrísim,* etc.

    or: *scriái, scriáş[i], scrié, scriám,* etc.

stríngu 'to squeeze': *strímşu, strímsiş[i], strímsi,* etc. or:
streş[u], *streásiş[i], streási,* etc.

sug 'to suck': *súpşu, súpsiş[i], súpsi,* etc.

tíndu 'to stretch': *tímşu, tímsiş[i], tímsi,* etc.

    or: *teş[u], teásiş[i], teási,* etc.

ţíngu 'to belt': *ţímşu, ţímsiş[i], ţímsi, ţímsim,* etc.

tórcu 'to spin': *tórşu, toársiş[i], toársi,* etc.

trag 'to pull': *trápşu, trápsiş[i], trápsi, trápsim,* etc.

túndu 'to clip': *túmşu, túmsiş[i], túmsi, túmsim,* etc.

yin 'to come': *viñ[u], víñiş[i], víñi, viñím, viñít, víñiră*

    or: *viñíi [viñíĭ], viñíş[i],* etc.

§ 33. The perfect (*often called* "the compound past") consists of the present of the auxiliary verb *am* 'to have' and the feminine past participle of the given verb, regardless of the gender and number of the subject. An example paradigm would be:

    sg: *am cântátă, ai cântátă, ari cântátă*

    pl: *avém cântátă, avéţ cântátă, au cântátă*

Note. Kr. Sandfeld writes: *"Si les parlers du Sud de l'aroumain préfèrent le prétérit simple au prétérit composé c'est sans doute sous l'influence de l'aoriste grec."*[44]

§ 34. The pluperfect is also a compound tense. It consists of the imperfect (or, rarely, the aorist) of the auxiliary *am* 'to have' and the feminine past participle of a given verb, regardless of the gender and number of the subject. An example paradigm would be

    sg: *aveám cântátă, aveái cântátă, aveá cântátă*

    pl: *aveám cântátă, aveáţ cântátă, aveá cântátă*

          (or *avúi cântátă, avúşi cântátă,* etc.)

Two examples follow.

● *S-aveá aprucheátă a prândzului* (BASME 73/33) 'Lunch time had approached.'

● *Píste aţeá noápte Seávirle se-avú acăţátă di lúcru* (BASME 170/27) 'That night the north wind began (*lit.* 'had begun') its work.'

§ 35. The future. This is a compund tense consisting of the invariable particle *va* (< the 3rd person sg. of the verb *voi*

---

[44] See Sandfeld, LB: 105.

'will, want, wish'), the conjunction *s* (before a voiced consonant *z*) or *sâ*, and the present subjunctive of the given verb. The paradigms of *cântu* 'to sing,' *dau* 'to give,' and *ľau* 'to take' follow.

1-3 sg: *va s-cântu, va s-cânţâ, va s-cântă*
1-3 pl: *va s-cântăm, va s-cântáţ, va s-cântă;*
1-3 sg: *va z-dau, va z-dai, va z-da*
1-3 pl: *va z-dăm, va z-daţ, va z-da;*
1-3 sg: *va si/să/sâ ľau, va si/să/sâ ľai, va si/să/sâ ľa*
1-3 pl: *va si/să/sâ lom, va si/să/sâ loaţ, va si/să/sâ ľa.*

In the Pindus subtype, the conjunction (*si/să/sâ, s-, z-*) is not used: 1st sg: *va cântu, va dau, va ľau,* 2nd sg: *va cânţâ, va dai, va ľai,* etc.
The future particle *va* has a variant *vai.*

Note. A future auxiliary (verb or particle) derived from a verb 'will, wish, want' is found in the other Balkan languages as well.[45]

B. The subjunctive mood

§ 36. The subjunctive mood (commonly called "conjunctive") has four tenses: *present, imperfect, perfect,* and *pluperfect.* By far the most frequent of these tenses is the present subjunctive.

§ 36.1. **The present subjunctive** consists of the conjunction *sâ* (*s-, z-*) 'to' and the personal forms of the present indicative in the 1st and 2nd pers. sg. and pl.: *s-cântu, s-cânţâ, s-cântăm, s-cântáţ.* E.g., *Pot s-cântu* 'I can sing'; *Căţé nu vrei s-cânţâ?* 'Why don't you want to sing?' *Acăţărăm s-cântăm* 'We began to sing,' and so on. The 3rd pers. sg. and pl. always have a common form, the ending of which is unstressed *-ă* (or *-â*), *-e* (pronounced [i] after palatal consonants), or *-Ø* (zero). Parallel forms of the 3rd pers. sg. of the present indicative and subjunctive are given below.

---

[45] Details in Sandfield, LB: 180-185.

| 3rd pers. present indicative | vs. | 3rd pers. present subjunctive |

3rd pers. present *indicative*	vs.	3rd pers. present *subjunctive*
cântă 'sings, is singing'		vrea *s-cântă* 'wants to sing'
lucreádză 'works, is working'		poáte *s-lucreádză* 'can work'
da 'gives, is giving'		vrea *z-da* 'wants to give'
ľa 'takes, is taking'		ştie *s-ľa* 'knows how to take'
veáde 'sees'		poáte *z-veádă* 'can see'
poáte 'can, is able to'		vrea *s-poátă* 'wants to be able to'
táțe 'is silent'		vrea *s-tácă* 'wants to be silent'
trádze 'pulls, is pulling'		poáte *s-trágă* 'can pull'
arúpe 'tears, is tearing'		vrea *s-arúpă* 'wants to tear'
doárme 'sleeps, is sleping'		vrea *z-doármă* 'wants to sleep'
eáse 'comes out, is coming out'		vrea *s-eásă* 'wants to come out'

Special cases are given in the right column below:

3d sg. present **indicative**	vs.	3d sg. present **subjunctive**
eáste 'he/she/it is'	vs.	(vrea, poate) *s-híbă* or *s-híbâ*
áre 'he/she has'	vs.	(vrea, poate) *sâ áibă* or *s-áibâ*
ştie 'he/she knows'	vs.	(vrea, poate) *sâ ştíbă* or *ş-ştíbâ*

§ 36.2. The **imperfect subjunctive** consists of the imperfect indicative of the given verb preceded by *sâ (s-, z-)*: *s-lucrám, s-lucrái*, etc. Ex.: *S-aveám un gióne nu vai cripám acşíțe* (BASME: 444, from **Av**) 'Had I had a son, I wouldn't have been so distressed.'

§ 36.3. The **perfect subjunctive** consists of the perfect indicative of the given verb preceded by *sâ (s-, z-)*: *s-am lucrátă, s-ai lucrátă, s-áre lucrátă*, etc.

§ 36.4. The **pluperfect subjunctive** consists of the imperfect indicative of the auxiliary *am* 'to have' preceded by *sâ (s-)* and the
past participle of the given verb. Ex. *Se-aveái vinítă nă dzúă ma
naíntea, vreá l'-áfli tuţi púil'i* (BASME: 246) 'Had you come (just)
one day earlier, you would have found all the birds.'

C. The conditional mood

§ 37.1. The **present conditional** is a simple tense. It consists
of the stem of the imperfect indicative + the suffix *-ri-* + the
personal endings *-m^u*, *-şi* (or *-Ø*), *-Ø* in the sg., and *-m^u*, *-t^u* (or
-ţ), *-Ø* in the pl. The conditional is always preceded by the for-
mant *s-* (originally a conjunction). The paradigm of *cântu* 'to sing'
is given below.

1 sg:	*s-cântárim*	('would I sing' or 'if I were to sing')
2 sg:	*s-cântárişi* or *s-cântári*	
3 sg:	*s-cântári*	
1 pl.:	*s-cântárim*	
2 pl:	*s-cântárit* and, occasionally, *s-cântáriţ* (with *-ţ*)
3 pl:	*s-cântári*	

Examples follow.

● (1st sg. from *adúc* 'to bring') *Araplu ñ-dzáse ca* **s-nu aduţeárim**
până mâne nă avítă c-un arăpúne, va s-mi mâcă (BASME: 3) 'The Arab
said that he will eat me up if I do not bring him a branch of vine
with grapes by tomorrow.'
● (2nd sg. from *aspún* 'to tell') **Si aspuneárii** *tíne nă minciúnă
cama mári ş-cama groásă, âţi dau víptul tut* (BASME: 100) 'If you
tell me a bigger and funnier lie, I'll give you all the food';
● (3rd sg. from *áflu* 'to find') *Mă-sa l-pitricú la tátă-su, ma-l'
dimândă, că* **se-aflári** *vâră drac ân cáli, să s-toárnă năpói* 'His
mother sent him to his father, but she asked him to turn back if he
came across a devil during his journey.'

§ 37.2. The **past conditional** consists of the present conditional preceded by the invariable formant *vrea* (< 3rd sg. ipf. of *vreau*
'to want'). Examples follow.

● (from *hig* 'to drive into') *S-fúrim io tu lóclu a lui 99 di
bărţáte* **vrea s-lu hidzeárim** *tu loc* (BASME: 272) 'If I had been in
his place, I would have driven him ninety-nine feet down into the
earth.'

● (from *arúc* 'to throw') **vrea s-arcáre** *n-foc* (BASME: 179) '[The bungler] would have thrown himself into the fire.' This form of the conditional is more frequent in the Pindus area. In the North, the usual past conditional consists of the auxiliary *vrea* + the imperfect indicative: *vrea s-cântám, vrea s-cântái,* etc.

● (from *anyédz* 'to resurrect') *Şcľóplu, dúpă ţi ş-ascăpă doľi fraţi, nu o-agudí nícă nă oáră, că s-o agudeá,* **nâsă vrea s-anyiá** (BASME: 265) 'After saving his two brothers, the lame man did not hit (the monster) one more time, because, had he done so, it would have come back to life.'

There are also other types of past conditional, including ones in which the formant *s-* is absent. Ex.: *Va s-o aibă furátă di la noi, că altu cari* **vrea lu da**? (BASME: 30) 'He [the rooster] probably has stolen it from us, because, otherwise, who else would have given it to him?'

§ 38. The imperative

There are two personal forms: 2nd singular and 2nd plural. The 2nd person singular of the imperative coincides either with the 2nd or with the 3rd person singular of the present indicative, depending on conjugation. Some verbs of the 4th conjugation have the 2nd person sg. of the imperative identical with the 2nd person sg. of the present tense. Ex. (from *es* 'to come out, go out'): *tíne eşi* 'you are coming out' vs. *Eşi!* 'Come out!' or 'Get out (from *fug* 'to go, run'): *tíne fudzi* 'you are going,' vs. *Fudzi!* 'Go!' Most verbs of the 1st, 2nd and 3rd conjugation and the rest of 4th conjugation verbs have the 2nd singular imperative identical with the 3rd singular of the present indicative. Ex. (from 1st conj. *acáţ* 'to catch'): *el acáţă* 'he is catching' vs. *Acáţă!* (or *Acáţă tíne!*) 'Catch!' (from 2nd conj. *beau* 'to drink'): *el bea* 'he is drinking' vs. *Bea!* 'Drink!' (from 3rd conj. *arúp* 'to tear'): *el arúpe* 'he is tearing' vs. *Arúpe!* 'Tear!' Verbs of the 4th conjugation with *-áşte* or *-eáşte* in the 3rd person singular of the present tense lose their final *-şte* in the imperative. For example, the 3rd person sg. from *zburắscu* 'to speak' is *zburáşte* and the 2nd person sg. imperative is *Zburá!* 'Speak!' (not *Zburáşte!*).

The following imperatives are irregular:
Dắ! 'Give!' *Lắ!* 'Wash!' and *Stắi!* 'Stop!' (1st conjugation);
Du! 'Take!' or 'Carry!' *Adú!* 'Bring!' *Dzâ!* 'Say!' *Fắ!* 'Make!' or 'Do!' (3^{d} conjugation), and
Yin^{u}! Yínu! or *Yína!* 'Come!' (4th conjugation).

The 2nd person plural imperative coincides with the 2nd person plural present indicative.

§ 39. **The infinitive**. As noted earlier (§ 29a), Aromanian has no infinitive. Cf. Rom. a *cântá*, It. *cantáre*, Sp. *cantar*, Port. *cantar*, Fr. *chanter* 'to sing' and, on the other hand, Arom. *cântu*, which literally means 'I sing' (or 'I am singing') and, at the same time, is used by linguists as a citation form. After the modal verb *a puteá* 'to be able to' Daco-Romanian uses either the subjunctive mood (*Pot să cânt*) or the infinitive (*Pot cântá*). The other Romance languages use the infinitive only (It. *Posso cantáre*, Fr. *Je peux chanter*, etc.). The only possible Aromanian equivalent of this sentence is *Pot s-cântu*. However, Latin infinitives in *-re* have not been entirely eliminated from Aromanian. They have become deverbal nouns: *cântáre* 'singing, song,' *cădeáre* 'falling, fall,' *dzâţeáre* or *dzâţire* 'saying,' *durñíre* 'sleeping, sleep.' There are native speakers who feel that these deverbals have preserved some of their former verbal meaning. Cf. *Nă lipseáşte mâcáre* 'We need food,' where *mâcáre* is a noun, and *Cáşlu va mâcáre* 'The cheese should be eaten,' where *mâcáre* is felt as being a verbal form.[46]

§ 40. **The gerund**. The characteristic suffix of the gerund is *-ânda(lui)* or *-índa(lui)*. The distribution of these allomorphs depends on phonetic context: *cântândalui* or *cântânda* 'singing,' *ndzinucl̕índalui* or *ndzinucl̕índa* 'kneeling,' *durñíndalui* or *durñínda* 'sleeping.'

§ 41. **The participle**. Regular past participles end in *-át* (1st conj.), *-út* (2nd and 3rd conj.), or *-ít* (4th conj.). Examples are 1st conj. *cântát* 'sung,' *lucrát* 'worked,' *dát* 'given'; 2nd conj. *cădzút* 'fallen,' *biút* 'drunk,' *vidzút* 'seen'; 4th conj. *durñít* 'slept,' *avdzât* 'heard,' *mutrít* 'looked at.'
The past participle of 3rd conjugation verbs whose aorist is *unpredictable* (see list above, § 32) have the following past participles (listed in the same order as in the respective aorists): *adús, agiúmsu* (or *agiúmtu*), *aléptu, alímsu* (or *alímtu*), *aprímsu* or *aprímtu*), *arâs, armás, ársu, arúptu, ascúnsu* (or *ascúmtu*), *aspártu, aspús, astíngu* (or *astímtu*), *aştérsu, aúmsu* (or *aúmtu*), *cóptu, dat, dus, dzâs, fáptu, fríptu, frâmtu, hértu, híptu, múlsu, ndréptu, ñérsu, nvínsu, pímtu, pitrúmtu, plâmtu, scos, scris* (or *scriát*),

---

[46] See SarA: 460.

stres (or *strímtu*), *súptu, tes* (and *tímsu* or *tímtu*), *tórsu, tráptu, túmsu* (or *túmtu*), *țímtu, vinít* (and *viñít*).

The past participle of **hiu** ('to be') is *fut*, and of *am* ('to have') is *avút*.

When the past participle is part of a compound verb, it is its feminine singular form that is used, regardless of any agreement considerations. Examples are *Năs are dátă parádzli* 'He has given the money'; *Năsă are dátă parádzli* 'She has given the money'; *Năși au dátă parádzli* 'They (*m.*) have given the money'; and *Năse au dátă parádzli* 'They (*f.*) have given the money.'

§ 42. **The passive voice**. Personal forms of the passive voice consist of the auxiliary verb *hiu* (or *éscu*) 'to be' and the past participle of the given verb. E.g., the passive present-tense paradigm of the verb *aspél* 'to wash' is:

sg.: *hiu aspilát* ('I am washed')   **pl.**: *him aspiláț*[a]
    hii (or *ésti*) *aspilát*   *hiț aspiláț*[a]
    eáste aspilát   *sântu* (or *súntu*)
                                   aspiláț

In passive sentences, the participle agrees in gender and number with the subject that undergoes the action. E.g., 'The girl is being washed' can be expressed by *Feáta eáste aspilátă*; 'The boys are being washed' is *Ficióriľi sântu aspiláț*[a], and 'The girls are being washed' is *Feátile sântu aspiláte* (PC from **Brz**).

THE ADVERB

§ 43. Many adverbs are derived from the masculine singular form of the corresponding adjectives. E.g., *Căsăbălu eáste mușát* 'The town is beautiful,' where *mușát* is an adjective, vs. *Nâs zburáște mușát* 'He speaks beautifully,' where *mușát* is an adverb. This pattern is productive. The adjective *bun* 'good' and the corresponding adverb *ghíni* 'well' (with *ǵ < b*, see § 16.9) have preserved the situation found in Latin (BONUS ~ BENE).

There are a few suffixes specific for adverbs: *-eáște* (correlative with the adjectival suffix *-éscu*) and *-á*.

Comparatives and superlatives of adverbs are formed in the same way as those of the adjectives (see § 21.2).

THE PREPOSITION

§ 44. Daco-Romanian uses the preposition *pe* (semantically empty) to introduce direct objects in the accusative, as in *Te hrănesc ca* **pe** *o pasăre oarbă* 'I feed you like a blind bird.' A good translation into Aromanian is *Ti hrănéscu ca pul'u órbu* (DDA: 663), without the preposition *pre* or *pri* (equivalent to D-Rom. *pe*). Other examples are:

• *Amirălu... l'i streáse picurăril'i si-aspúnă alíhea* (DDA: 1124) vs. D-Rom. *Împăratul îi constrânse* **pe** *păstori să spună adevărul* 'The emperor pressured the shepherds to tell the truth.'

• *Aístă, când* **u** *vidzú feáta ahât muşátă, âl' dzâse* (BASME 254) vs. D-Rom. *Aceasta, când o văzu* **pe** *fată atât de frumoásă, îi zise,* lit. 'When she [the Gypsy] saw the girl so beautiful, she spoke to her.'

However, constructions with *pe, pi, pre, pri* are possible in Aromanian as well. E.g., **pri** *Giuvára si-l călcăm* (DDA: 307) 'so that we can rob Giuvara'; cf. D-Rom. *ca să-l jefuim* **pe** *Giuvara.*

§ 45. Constructions without preposition

Alongside prepositional constructions, Aromanians often use constructions without a preposition. Examples gathered from the DDA and BASME are given below as parallel to Daco-Romanian.

a) Spatial constructions without prepositions

• *Noi stăm Sărúnă* (DDA: 1712) vs. D-Rom. *Noi stăm* **la** *Salonic* 'We live in Salonika';

• *Iánina mi pliyuíră* (DDA: 997) vs. D-Rom. *Am fost rănit* **la** *Yanina* 'I was wounded at Yanina';

• *Aúşlu păşteá gumárlu búdza di amári* (BASME: 456) vs. D-Rom. *Bătrânul păştea măgárul pe malul mării* 'The old man was grazing his donkey on the seashore';

• *Va să cheri hăpseáne* (BASME: 17) vs. D-Rom. *Ai să mori* **la** *puşcărie* 'You will die in jail';

• *Dú-te apóea márdzinea de-amáre* (BASME: 491) vs. D-Rom. *Du-te apoi la marginea mării* 'Then go to the seashore.'

b) Temporal constructions without prepositions

• *di veáră, ahtáre oáră* (DDA: 468) vs. D-Rom. *la vară,* **la** *această oră* 'next summer at this time';

• *ună Luni di cătră seáră* (DDA: 754), vs. D-Rom. **într-o** *lune*

cǎtre searǎ 'on a Monday towards evening';
- *Iu s-duc nâşi ahtáre oárǎ?* (DDA: 933) vs. D-Rom. *Unde se duc ei pe aşa o vreme?* 'Where are they going in such (bad) weather?'
- *Na şi úrsa prândzu oárǎ!* (BASME: 48) vs. D-Rom. *Poftim (cǎ vine) şi ursoaica la ora prânzului!* 'Here comes the she-bear at lunchtime!'

c) Other constructions without preposition

- *Va-ñ ľau un duiár afrát* (DDA: 114) vs. D-Rom. *O sǎ-mi iau şoricioaicǎ de doi bani* 'I'll buy poison for two cents';
- *Añurdzeáşte prumuveárǎ* (DDA: 170) vs. D-Rom. *Miroase a primǎvarǎ* 'It smells like spring';
- *Va ti hrǎnéscu záhari* (DDA: 663) vs. D-Rom. *O sǎ te hrǎnesc cu zahǎr* 'I'll feed you with sugar';
- *Pósta i pri teľu vrea-ľ pitriţeá nǎ cárte* (DDA: 1005) vs. D-Rom. *I-ar fi trimis o scrisoare prin poştǎ sau prin telegraf* 'He/she would have sent him/her a letter by mail or by telegraph.'

THE CONJUNCTION

§ 46. An alphabetical list of conjunctions is given below.

- **a** 'and,' 'then,' 'in this case.' E.g., *driápta si dǎ,* **a** *stǎnga si nu ştíbǎ* [stress added] (Capidan: 507) 'Let the right hand give out (something) and the left one not know about it'; **a** *cǎţé ti ţǎñ pirifán,* **a** *om ţi éşti loc şi ciǎnúşǎ?* (ibid.) 'and why is it then that you keep being proud, you who are but earth and ashes?'
- **ai** or **ai cǎ** (*conjunctive or disjunctive*) 'or,' 'nor', as in **ai cǎ** *ficiór,* **ai cǎ** *feátǎ fúre* (DDA: 127) 'be it a boy or a girl'
- **áma** or **am** (*adversative*) 'but' → **ma.** Used in all Balkan languages.
- **cálai cǎ** 'though,' 'in spite of the fact that'
- **cára, cári** 'if **Cara** *s-arávdzâ hii ómlu ţe-l cáftu* (BASME 308) 'If you can stand it, you are the man I am looking for.' Also 'since,' 'in view of the fact that,' as in: *Ficiórlu..., `cara-l cântǎ şi-l discântǎ muşíca..., si nsurǎ cu védua* (BASME 362) Since the old woman had bewitched him, the young man married the widow.'
- **cǎ** 'that,' as in *Chirúta nu-şi şti* **cǎ** *tóra va-ľ taľu cáplu* (BASME 211) 'The wretched woman doesn't know that now I'll cut off her head.'

- *căţé* 'because' - *Căţé nu viñíşi?* 'Why did you not come over?'
  - *Căţé nu putúi* (DDA: 356) 'Because I couldn't.'
- *cu túte aístă* (*concessive*) 'although,' 'nevertheless,' 'in spite of the fact that'
- *di* (*comparison*) 'than,' as in *vasilcólu a ľei işí cáma uscát de a híľlui di amiră* (BASME: 202) 'Her basil came out drier than the basil of the emperor's son.'
- *dicára* 'after,' 'when,' 'subsequently'; *dicara si uscă lóclu...* (Capidan: 509) 'when the earth had dried out...'
- *dipércă, diprícă → pércă*
- *díse, disi* (*indirect question involving an alternative*) 'whether,' as in *ntribără un om disi ştíe vără háne* (BASME: 147) 'they asked a man whether he knew of an inn'; *mine aştiptám z-ved dise va-ţi yínă míntea si spuñ síngur* (BASME: 176) 'I was waiting to see whether you would change your mind and tell (it) yourself.'
- *e* 'and.' Also in Old D-Rom. Archaism replaced by *şi* (DDA: 527).
- *i* 'and,' as in *ună sútă i treidzăţi di añ* (DDA: 1148) 'one hundred and thirty years'
- *i, ícă* 'or,' as in *apóstalu Petru ícă Pavlu ľ-dişcľídi poártă ş-lu ntreábă ţe va* (BASME: 432/35-36) 'the apostle Peter or Paul opened the door to him and asked him what he wanted.'
- *i... i* 'both... and'
- *ma* (*adversative*) 'but'
- *ma calái că → ma*
- *méţe, méţi* 'though,' 'if,' as in *Apufăsíră s-u mărítă ş-meţi că nu vrea fáta* (BASME: 320) 'They decided to marry her off, though the girl did not want to.'
- *mia → ma*
- *pércă* (*comparison*) 'than,' as in *Súntu ma múlţi górţâ percă meri* (Capidan: 509) 'There are more peartrees than appletrees.'
- *s-, să → se*
- *se* (archaic) 'if' *→ díse, dísi*
- *se, să, si, s-, z-* (*connects verbs*) 'to,' 'in order to,' as in *âl băgă pi fráti-su la un prămătár si nveáţă zânáte* (BASME: 237) 'He appointed his brother to learn the trade from a merchant'; *Mítre ştea ţe s-cáftă* (BASME: 67) 'Mitre knew what (was better for him) to ask'; *Dáfnea năpói z-băgă să-l pălăcărseáscă* (BASME: 181) 'The fairy began to ask him again'; *Cât căftáţ z-vă dau...* BASME: 65) 'How much should I give you (so that...)?'
- *s-eáste că, s-éste că* 'if,' as in *Scúmpul a mel âñ dimândă... si-ľ pitréc cárte s-eáste că va s-amínţâ ficiór* (BASME: 7) 'My beloved (husband) asked me to let him know by letter if you bear a boy.' (See also LB: 124)

- *s(e)-fúre-că, fúre-că, sfúrcă* 'if,' 'whether,' as in *Huzmi-chiárlu dişcĺíse úşa şi vidzú om xen, ma nu aleápse ghíne* **fure că**-*i bărbát i fure că-i muĺáre* (BASME: 78) 'The servant opened the door and saw a stranger, but he could not tell whether it was a man or a woman.'
- *şi, ş-* (*associative, coordinating*) 'and.' This is the most frequent Aromanian conjunction.
- *tea s(ă)* 'to,' 'in order to,' as in *Eu nu vream* **ta s**-*vátăm* (DDA: 1174) 'I did not want to kill'; *Mi duc dipárte...* **tea s**-*áflu Dumnidză* 'I am going far... in order to find God.'
- *sti-că* (= *s-easte că*) 'if,' 'whether,' as in *- Avúi, ma nu ştiu* **sti-că** *bâneáză nícă* (BASME: 241) 'I did have [a brother], but I do not know if he is still alive.'

III. A Survey of Aromanian Vocabulary

§ 47. The origins of the Aromanian vocabulary

The vast majority of words in Aromanian comes down from Vulgar Latin, the language spoken by Roman common people, the language of the ignorant or uncultivated as distinguished from the educated or cultivated classes. Roman soldiers, many of them mercenaries from various regions of the Empire, and the subsequent colonists and emigrants who came into the Balkan Peninsula during and after its gradual conquest (which began with the occupation of Macedonia and culminated with the defeat and colonization of Dacia, 101-106 A.D.) did not speak Classical Latin. The vernacular of all these newcomers of various origins and, usually, modest or low socio-economic status, was *Vulgar Latin*. That is why the inherited Latin vocabulary of Aromanian, Megleno-Romanian, Daco-Romanian and Istro-Romanian (the four basic components of Common Romanian) is notable for concreteness, simplicity and rusticity. For instance, Aromanian has a word inherited from Latin to express the concrete meaning 'deep' (*adâncós, ahândós, afundós* < Lat. ADUNCUS 'concave'), but lacks an inherited word for the more abstract terms ADUNCITAS and PROFUNDITAS 'concavity, depths'). Aromanian has an inherited word *cât* 'how much, how many' (< Lat. QUANTUS), but lacks a term for the more abstract 'quantity' (cf. Lat. QUANTITAS). The adjective *nólgic* 'medium, intermediate' (< Lat. MEDIUSLOCUS, Capidan: 233) does not have a corresponding abstract noun as Classical Latin did (MEDIOCRITAS 'moderation, mediocrity'). While Daco-Romanian has coined or borrowed and fully assimilated terms able to express the most subtle and complex notions of modern thinking, Aromanian, and even more so Megleno-Romanian and Istro-Romanian, have remained in a marked state of lexical underdevelopment. One can say that there is only as much Aromanian vocabulary as needed for survival and leading traditional rustic (mainly pastoral) life with its joys and hardships. A good mirror of this traditional Aromanian life, mentality and language can be found in the invaluable anthology of Aromanian tales published in 1905 by Pericle Papahagi (1872-1943), a native of Avdela (Greece). It is apparent to anyone who reads those tales that the Aromanian vocabulary fully and adequately suffices to tell popular stories whose characters are often meant to represent real people from the Aromanian cultural background. When the topic of conversation turns to modern aspects of life (like education, politics, sports, technology and so on), terms lacking in Aromanian are spontaneously taken from a secondary language, be it Albanian, Greek, or Slavic Macedonian. Such being the situation, it appears that in fact there is no real need, at this time, for ample, deliberate and hasty development of the already existing Aromanian vocabulary.

§ 47a. Recently (in the 1980's and particularly in the 1990's) some Aromanian intellectuals abroad (mainly in the United States, Germany and Romania), enthusiastic promoters of their native tongue, have engaged in fervid activities meant to speedily introduce neologisms into the traditional Aromanian vocabulary. Their goal has been to break through the existing barrier of lexico-semantic paucity and thus to enable native speakers to use language on all occasions and for any topic (geology, psychology, philosophy and the arts are only examples.) The ostensible source for borrowing is modern Romance languages, but the real source is Standard Romanian in the vast majority of cases. It seems that the main obstacles to this cultural action of vocabulary amplification and diversification to succeed is absence of corresponding institutions genuinely interested in developing Aromanian into a modern language and, on the other hand, the rather passive response of the common native speakers themselves (See also § 60).

§ 48. **Preponderance of vocabulary inherited from Latin**

The Aromanian vocabulary inherited from Latin dominates all important lexico-semantic fields significant for the traditional Aromanian way of life and Weltanschauung. Probably the most eloquent illustration in support of this claim are the Aromanian names of the *parts of the human body*. An alphabetical list of forty-five words of Latin origin designating various parts of the body is given below (bold italics). The corresponding Daco-Romanian and Istro-Romanian terms provided after the Latin etymon offer data for comparative analysis.

anúmir 'shoulder' (< Lat. HUMERUS; cf. D-Rom. *úmăr*, IstroR *úmir*)
arnícľu 'kidney' (< Lat. RENICULUS; cf. D-Rom. *riníchi*)
braţ 'arm' (< Lat. BRACHIU; cf. D-Rom. *braţ*, IstroR *braţ*)
buríc 'navel' (< Lat. UMBILICUS; cf. D-Rom. *buríc*, IstroR *buríc*)
cap 'head' (< Lat. CAPUT; cf. D-Rom. *cap*, IstroR *cåp*)
călcâñu 'heel' (< Lat. CALCANEUM; cf. D-Rom. *călcâi*)
cheále 'skin' (< Lat. PELLIS; cf. D-Rom. *piéle*, dial. *chéle*)
chéptu 'chest' (< Lat. PECTUS; cf. D-Rom. *piept*, dial. *chept*,
        IstroR *cľept*)
chiciór 'leg, foot' (< Lat. PETIOLUS; cf. D-Rom. *piciór*, dial.
        chiciór; IstroR *piciór / piţór*)
coápsă 'hip' (< Lat. COXA; cf. D-Rom. *coápsă*)

coástă 'rib' (< Lat. COSTA; cf. D-Rom. *coástă*)

cot 'elbow' (< Lat. CUBITUS; cf. D-Rom. *cot*, IstroR *cúvât*)

críer 'brain' (< Lat. CEREBELLUM; cf. D-Rom. *créier*)

cur 'anus' (< Lat. CULUS 'buttock'; cf. D-Rom. *cur*)

dínte 'tooth' (< Lat. DENS, acc. DENTEM; cf. D-Rom., IstroR
   dínte)

dzeádzit 'finger' (< Lat. < DIGITUS; cf. D-Rom. *déget*, IstroR
   jéjet, jájet, zàzet)

dzindzíe 'gum' (< Lat. GINGIVA; cf. D-Rom. *gingíe*, IstroR
   jinjíre)

dzinúcľu 'knee' (< Lat. GENUC(U)LUM; cf, D-Rom. *genúnchi*, IstroR
   jerúncľu)

fálcă 'jaw' (< Lat. FALX, acc. FALCEM; cf. D-Rom. *fálcă*)

fáţă 'face' (< Lat. FACIES; cf. D-Rom. *fáţă*, IstroR *fáţe*)

frúmte 'forehead' (Lat. FRONS, acc. FRONTEM; cf. D-Rom. *frúnte*,
   IstroR *frúnte*)

gúră 'mouth' (< Lat. GULA 'throat'; cf. D-Rom. *gúră*, IstroR *gúre*,
   γúră; cf. Engl. *gullet* from Lat. GULA)

heáre 'bile, gall' (< Lat. FEL; cf. D-Rom. *fiére*)

hicát 'liver' (< Lat. FICATUM 'a dish made from figs and goose
   liver'; cf. D-Rom. *ficát*, IstroR *ficåt*)

ínimă 'heart' (< Lat. ANIMA 'soul'; cf. D-Rom. *ínimă*, IstroR
   ĭírime)

límbă 'tongue' (< Lat. LINGUA; cf. D-Rom. *límbă*, IstroR *límbe*)

maţ 'gut' (< Lat. MATTEA 'delicacy'; cf. D-Rom. *maţ*, IstroR *måţ*)

mână 'hand' (< Lat. MANUS; cf. D-Rom. *mână*, IstroR *mâra*)

múşcľu 'muscle' (< Lat. MUSCULUS; cf. D-Rom. *muşchi*)

náre 'nose' (< Lat. NARIS; cf. D-Rom. *nárӑ* 'nostril')

ócľu 'eye' (< Lat. OCULUS; cf. D-Rom. *ochi*, IstroR *ócľu*)

os 'bone' (< Lat. OS; cf. D-Rom. *os*, IstroR *os*)

pálmă 'palm' (< Lat. PALMA; cf. D-Rom. *pálmă*, IstroR *påma*)

pălmúnă 'lung' (< Lat. PULMO, acc. PULMONEM; cf. D-Rom. *plӑmân*)

per 'hair' (< Lat. PILUS; cf. D-Rom. *pӑr*, pl. *peri*, IstroR *per*),

pântică 'abdomen' (< Lat. PANTEX, pl. PANTICES; cf. D-Rom. *pân-
   tece*)

púlpă 'calf' (< Lat. PULPA; cf. D-Rom. *púlpă*, IstroR *púpa*)

púţă 'penis' and 'vulva' (< Lat. *PUTIUM < PRAEPUTIUM; cf. D-Rom.
   púţă, IstroR *púţă*)

schináre 'back' (< Lat. adj. SPINALIS 'spinal'; cf. D-Rom. *spi-
   náre*)

sin 'breast' (< Lat. SINUS; cf. D-Rom. *sân*, IstroR *sir*)

sândze 'blood' (< Lat. acc. SANGU(IN)EM; cf. D-Rom. *sânge*, IstroR
   sânje, sânze)

ţáţă 'nipple' (< Lat. *TITIA; cf. D-Rom. *ţâţă*, IstroR *ţíţa*)

úngľe 'nail' (< Lat. UNGULA; cf. D-Rom. **únghie**, IstroR *úngľe*)

ureácľe 'ear' (< Lat. AURICULA; cf. D-Rom. *uréche*, IstroR *urécľe*)

vínă 'vein' (< Lat. VENA; cf. D-Rom. *vână*).

Other Aromanian semantic fields also contain important words inherited from Latin. For instance, this English-Aromanian dictionary includes over forty such terms designating various animals. Like the parts of the human body presented above, almost all of them have an identical or close correspondent in Daco-Romanian, Istro-Romanian and Megleno-Romanian. But there are also cases when native terms of Latin origin have ceded their place to terms of other origin. For example, Aromanians, Daco-Romanians and Istro-Romanians have preserved their native term for 'liver' (see above), while Megleno-Romanians have forgotten *ficat* and use *drob* (< Bulg. *drob*); Aromanian, Daco-Romanian, and Istro-Romanian lost their term *corp 'body' (< Lat. CORPUS) and adopted the term *trup*, of Slavic origin, but Megleno-Romanian still preserves the old term *corp* (D-Rom. *corp* 'body' is a new word in Romanian, coined after Fr. *corps* and Lat. CORPUS); Aromanian, Megleno-Romanian, and Daco-Romanian have preserved the inherited Latin term PELLIS 'skin', while Istro-Romanian uses the term *cóje* (< Croat. *koža*).

§ 49. A classification of the Aromanian words of Latin origin

a) Inherited Latin words shared by Aromomanian and the other three dialects of Common Romanian. This is by far the the most important group of words, because it contains not only lexico-semantic items (as Lat. FILIUS 'son,' vs. Arom. *hiľiu*, MeglR *iľiu*, D-Rom. *fiu*, IstroR *fiľ*, Lat. NOMEN 'name' vs. Arom. *núme* or *númă*, MeglR *núme*, D-Rom. *núme*, IstroR *lúme*, Lat. DIES 'day' vs. Arom. *dzúŭă*, MeglR *zúŭă*, D-Rom. *zi*, IstroR *zi*, Lat. MALUM, MELUM 'apple' vs. Arom. *mer*, MeglR *méră*, D-Rom. *măr*, IstroR *mer*, Lat. DIXIT 'he/ she said' vs. Arom. *dzăsi*, MeglR *zísi*, D-Rom. *zíse*, IstroR *a zis*, etc.), but also pronouns, adverbs, prepositions, conjunctions and particles.

b) **Inherited Latin words preserved in Arom. and, locally or regionally, in D-Rom.** The standard D-Rom. term for 'snow' is *zăpádă* (< Slav.), but regionally two other terms are used: *omắt* (< Slav.) in N and N-E Romania, and *nea* (def. *neáua*) in W Romania (see map in CarC 181); cf. Arom. *neáŭă* 'snow' (< Lat. acc. NIVEM, nom. NIX). The standard D-Rom. term for 'shepherd' is *ciobán* (< Turk.), but in Transylvania, Banat, and Crişana the regular word is *păcurár* (cf. Arom. *picurár*, from Lat. PECORARIUS). The standard Romanian word for 'sand' is *nisíp* (< Slav.), but in small peripheral areas of D-Rom., as on the right bank of the Dniester river (Rom. *Nistru*), a term *anínă* is used, the same word as Arom. *arínă* 'sand' (< Lat. ARENA).

c) **Inherited Latin words common to Arom. and Old D-Rom.** In the oldest D-Rom. texts (from the 16th c.) there were some words of Latin origin that subsequently disappeared from the language. They have been preserved in Aromanian. E.g., Old D-Rom. *auo* 'grape' (in *Voroneţ Psalter*, *Schei Psalter*, *Coresi Psalter*, etc.) is a totally unknown term in Modern Romanian, while Arom. *aúă* (or *aúŭă*), from Lat. UVA, is well preserved. Other cases: Old D-Rom. *fur* 'thief' and Arom. *fur* (< Lat. FUR), Old D-Rom. *e* 'and' and the obsolete Arom. *e* (< Lat. ET). There are many similar cases.

d) **Inherited Latin words preserved in Arom. and MeglR only.** E.g., Arom. *auá*, MeglR *ŭa* 'here' (< Lat. AD HAC); Arom. and MeglR *căroári* 'heat' (< Lat. CALOR, acc. CALOREM); Arom. *hic* and MeglR *ic* 'fig' (< Lat. FICUS); Arom. *híľe*, MeglR *íľă* 'daughter' (< Lat. FILIA); Arom. and MeglR *mes* 'month' (< Lat. MENSIS).

Of particular interest for comparative Romance lexicology are those Aromanian words of Latin origin which have not ever been attested in the other three dialects of Common Romanian. Below is an alphabetical list of them.[47]

---

[47] After Roseti: 397-9, with English translation and minor modifications.

e) Latin words lost in D-Rom, IstroR, and MeglR, but preserved in Aromanian:

afreáţă 'unleavened bread' (< Lat. AFRICIA; see REW # 271)

agiún 'hungry' (< Lat. IEIUNUS; see REW # 4582)

amintáre 'gain' (< Lat. AUGMENTARE; see REW # 783)

apiríre 'dawn' (< Lat. APERIRE 'to open'; see REW # 515)

arát 'plow' (< Lat. ARATRUM; see REW # 602)

arníu 'wintering place (for shepherds and their sheep)' (< Lat. HIBERNIVUM)

arúmin 'to crunch, to munch, to crackle' (< Lat. RUMINARE)

arúp (and *rup*) 'valley, precipice' (< Lat. RUPES, see REW # 7451)

asfíngu 'to shape (dough)' (< Lat. EX + FINGO, FINGERE)

bârbútă, cf. DDA: 264: *bărbútă di praşi* 'filamentous head of a leek' (< Lat. BARBUTUS 'bearded')

bâşáre 'kiss' (< Lat. BASIARE)

blândur 'tune' (Lat. BLANDULUS)

căşáre 'cheese farm' (cf. Lat. CASEAREA)

chipuráre 'pricking' (< Lat. POPILARE)

chiuráre 'cheeping' (< Lat. PIULARE)

câstâñu 'chestnut tree' and *căstâñe*, *găstâñe* 'chestnut' (< Lat. CASTANEA, CASTANEUS)

coácă 'distinctive cut in a sheep's ear' (< Lat. COCCUM 'hole')

cúnă 'cradle' (< Lat. CUNAE)

cusurín 'cousin' (< Lat. CONSOBRINUS)

dimândáre 'behest' (< Lat. DEMANDARE; see REW # 2547)

disicáre 'split' (< Lat. DISSECARE)

dizmăláre 'ravelling' (< Lat. *DISMALLARE, cf. MALLUS)

fáuă 'lentil' (< FABA 'bean'; see REW # 3117)

fuľínă 'abdomen' (< Lat. FOLLINUS, cf. FOLLIS 'bag'; REW # 3420)

fúrnu 'furnace' (< Lat. FURNUS; see REW # 3602)

gărâre 'humming' (Lat. GARRIRE)

gruñáre 'grunt (of a hog)' (< Lat. *GRUNIARE, cf. GRUNIO)

hig, aor. *hípşu*, part. *híptu*, deverbative *hídzire* and *hidzeáre* 'to drive in' (< Lat. FIGERE)

lălătoáre 'weekday' (cf. Lat. LABORARE 'to work')

mânár 'lamb attached to people' (< Lat. MANUARIUS)

ntárdu 'late' (< Lat. IN + TARDUS)

ntricáre 'feeding' (probably from Lat. NUTRICARE)

nueárcă, neárcă 'stepmother' (< Lat. NOVERCA)

pắl'úr 'thornbush' (< Lat. PALIURUS)

pắrtăciúne 'division, sharing' (< Lat. PARTITIO, acc. -ONEM)

picúl'u 'money, hidden wealth' (< Lat. PECULIUM)

puduríţă 'treadle of a loom' (< Lat. adj. PEDULIS, from PES, gen. PEDIS 'foot')

púscă 'vinegar' (< Lat. POSCA, PUSCA)

sắrcl'áre 'weeding out' (< Lat. SARCULARE)

sfúlgu 'lightning' (< Lat. EX- + FULGUR)

sân 'healthy' (< Lat. SANUS)

săríñe 'saltlick (usu. for sheep)' (< Lat. SALINAE)

spes 'thick, dense' (< Lat. SPISSUS)

sprúnă 'ash' (< Lat. PRUNA,, see DDA: 1110)

stríngl'e 'cord' (< Lat. *STRINGULA, cf. STRINGERE 'to tighten')

suil'áre 'shearing' and *suél'u* 'wool from the caudal part of a sheep' (< Lat. *SUBILIARE 'to clip the wool from the tail')

súmă 'the best wool, wool with long fibers' (< Lat. SUMMA)

şáră 'saw' (< Lat. SERRA)

şcl'ífur 'sulphur' (< Lat. SULPHUR)

şcl'imurédz 'whimper' (< Lat. EX-CLAMORARE)

ţeáţire 'chick-pea' (< Lat. CICER)

túmbă 'grave, tomb, knob, hillock' (< Lat. TUMBA)

uín adj. 'of sheep,' *uínă* s. 'flock of sheep' (< Lat. OVINUS)

útre 'leather bottle, satchel' (< Lat. UTER)

vănát 'in vain' (< Lat. VANUS)

voámire (or *vumeáre*) 'vomiting' (< Lat. VOMERE)

yínghiţ 'twenty' (< Lat. VIGINTI; see REW # 9327)

yíte 'vine' (< Lat. VITIS).

§ 50. **Aromanian words from the Balkan substratum**. There are no written records of Thracian, Dacian, Old Macedonian, and Illyrian, the main languages of the inhabitants of the Balkan Peninsula north of Greece in antiquity. Thus, identifying and studying the words that Balkan Latin and Common Romanian took from those languages is difficult and debatable.[48] An important criterion is whether the term is identical or similar to one Albanian, the only modern descendant of Old Illyrian. If a given term has been recorded in all four dialects of Common Romanian which at this time are far apart territorially and there exists a good corresponding term in Albanian, the assumption that the word derives from the substratum can be considered well-grounded.

An illustrative list of such Aromanian words with identical or related correspondents in Megleno-Romanian, Daco-Romanian, and Istro-Romanian is given below.

Arom. *baciu* 'shepherd,' MeglR *baciu*, D-Rom. *baci*, IstroR *Baţe* (cf. Alb. *bacë, baç*, see Çabej: 454);

Arom. *bálig(ă)* 'dung,' MeglR *bálig*, D-Rom. *báligă*, IstroR *bålege* (cf. Alb. *bajgë*, see Çabej: 457);

Arom. *báltă* 'pond,' MeglR *báltă*, D-Rom. *báltă*, IstroR *båtă* (cf. Alb. *baltë*, see Çabej: 461);

Arom. *brăn, brân* 'belt,' MeglR *bron, brău*, D-Rom. *brâu*, IstroR *brâv* (cf. Alb. *brez*, see Çabej: 518);

Arom. *cătún* 'hamlet,' MeglR *cătún*, D-Rom. *cătún*, IstroR *cătún* (cf. Alb. *katund* 'village,' see Çabej: 216);

Arom. *cupáciu* 'tree,' MeglR *cupátš*, IstroR *cupáţ* 'bush', D-Rom. *copac* 'tree' (cf. Alb. *kopatsh* 'stem, trunk');

Arom. *gard* 'fence,' MeglR *gard*, D-Rom. *gard*, cf. IstroR *gård* 'gate of branches in a pen' (cf. Alb. *gardh* 'hedge', see Ko: 143);

Arom. *groápă* 'pit, hole,' MeglR *groápă*, D-Rom. *groápă*, IstroR *grópa* (cf. Alb. *gropë*);

Arom. *gúşe* 'neck, goiter,' MeglR *gúşă* 'neck,' D-Rom. *gúşă* 'goiter,' IstroR *gúşă* (cf. Alb. *gushë*, Ko: 156);

Arom. *métură* 'broom,' MeglR *miétură*, D-Rom. *mătură*, IstroR *méture* (cf. Alb. *netullë* 'mullein (from which brooms are made)';

---

[48] See Russu, *op. cit.*

Arom. **moş** 'old man,' MeglR *moş*, D-Rom. *moş*, IstroR *moş* (cf. Alb.
moshë 'age'; *burrë moshuar* 'old man').

It should be emphasized that the presence of a given Aromanian
word from the substratum in all four Romanian dialects is not con-
clusive evidence for such an interpretation. There are several cases of Aromanian words in common with Daco-Romanian but lost or
simply missing in Megleno-Romanian and/or Istro-Romanian. Such gaps
do not disqualify a term from being, potentially, from the substratum, if other conditions support the assumption. E.g., Arom. *mi*
(m)búcur 'to rejoice,' which has been almost replaced by *mi hără-*
séscu (< Gr.), has a correspondent in MeglR *búcur* and in D-Rom. *a*
(se) bucurá. A related word in Istro-R has not been recorded and,
most probably, does not exist. However, the correspondence to the
Alb. bukur[49] supports the substratum or, maybe, the Old Albanian
hypothesis of its origin. A strict etymological inquiry of the
Aromanian and Daco-Romanian vocabulary imposes a distinction between substratum and Old Albanian. Daco-Romanian scholars have had
a slight tendency to give preference to the substratum (Daco-Thra-
cian) factor, while Albanian and other scholars tend to posit Albanian as the primary source of words belonging to this category. Cf.
contrasting interpretation of D-Rom. *búză* and Arom. *búdză* 'lip' vs.
Alb. *buzë* by I. I. Russu[50] and E. Çabej.[51] A strict separation of
Daco-Romanian and Aromanian words of supposed substratum (basical-
ly Thraco-Dacian) origin from Old Albanian or from more recent dialectal Albanian words is difficult.[52]

---

[49] Çabej: 531-2.

[50] See Russu: 282.

[51] Çabej, *op. cit.* 545.

[52] See Çabej-1965, Brâncuş-1967, Hetzer-1982. An insightful
presentation of this problem, with comparative lists of autochtho-
nous words in Daco-Romanian, Aromanian, Megleno-Romanian and Istro-
Romanian, can be found in Brâncuş-1983.

§ 51. **Words of Albanian origin.** When an Aromanian word is absent from Daco-Romanian and Istro-Romanian while having an identical or comparable counterpart in Albanian, its Albanian origin is highly probable. T. Papahagi's dictionary (the DDA) contains 363 Aromanian words considered of Albanian origin. Their list includes *bésă* 'faith' (< Alb. *bésë*), *dósă* 'prostitute' (< Alb. *dósë* 'swine,' fig. 'bitch'), *dot* 'at all' (< Alb. *dot*), *duchéscu* 'to feel, to realize' (< Alb. *dúkem* 'to seem, to appear'), *étă* 'time, century, hereafter' (< Alb. *jétë* 'life'), *fátăză* ≈ 'the Fates' (< Alb. *fatë-ză*), *ghélă* 'dish, food' (< Alb. *gjéllë*), *gínde* 'rage, devil' (< Alb. *xhinde* 'witch'), *gúvă* 'pit, hole' (< Alb. *gúvë* 'cave'), *ichiş-dó* 'whoever' (< Alb. *kushdó*), *izóte* 'able' (< Alb. *i zóti*), *múndă* 'pain, suffering' (< Alb. *mund*), *po* 'yes' (< Alb. *po*), *rufé(e)* 'lightning' (< Alb. *rrufé*), *şcămbă* 'stone, rock' (< Alb. *shkëmb*). Used impersonally, the Aromanian verb *lipséscu* 'to be insufficient, to miss' means 'should' or 'must' under the influence of Alb. *lipset*.[53]

It goes without saying that the influence of Albanian on the Aromanian vocabulary is more intense in those regions of the peninsula where Albanian is spoken, primarily in Albania itself. Based on research carried out in several Aromanian communities in Albania, Gr. Brâncuş (1967) recorded cases of old Romanian (most probably Common Romanian) words from the pre-Latin substratum remodeled phonetically and semantically after recent Albanian words.

§ 52. **Words of Slavic origin.** Common Romanian formed, evolved, and eventually split apart in close contact with the Slavic tribes that crossed the northeastern borders of the Roman Empire and settled in Dacia, Pannonia, Illyricum, Moesia, Thrace, Macedonia and Greece itself (mainly in the 5th and 6th centuries A.D.). The considerable impact of South Slavic dialects on Common Romanian and its daughter languages, Aromanian included, has been studied thorough-

---

[53] Ko: 271; Sandfeld, LB: 68.

ly.[54] In his DDA, Tache Papahagi gives an alphabetical list of 585 Aromanian words of Slavic origin. Elena Scărlătoiu has arranged some of the data provided by the DDA into thematic groups (all in all, 307 words): **I.** *Terms referring to material culture* (*jar* 'ember,' *prag* 'threshold,' *sítă* 'sieve'); **II.** *Farming* (*brázdă* 'furrow,' *coásă* 'scythe,' *snop* 'sheaf'); **III.** *Plant kingdom* (*bob* 'kidney-bean,' *boz* 'elder-tree,' *jir* 'beechnut,' *mac* 'poppy'); **IV.** *Animal kingdom* (*arâs* 'bobcat,' *gúştir* 'lizard,' *rac* 'crab,' *vídră* 'otter'); **V.** *Natural evironment* (*izvór* or *ízvor* 'source,' *pádină* (or *pădínă*) 'depression, hollow,' *tínă* 'mud'); **VI.** *Human body, illnesses, folk medicine* (*aránă* 'wound,' *trup* 'body'); **VII.** *Cultural and spiritual life* (*fálă* 'pride,' *leáne* 'laziness,' *ñílă* 'pity'); and **VIII.** *Society, social life* (*năválă* 'incursion, raid,' *rob* 'slave,' *strájă* 'guardian'). Many of these words are also known in Megleno-Romanian and Daco-Romanian (occasionally also in Istro-Romanian). This indicates that they may have been borrowed by Common Romanian (i.e., during the 10th century A.D. or earlier).

G. Mihăilă has included some Aromanian words of Slavic origin in his presentation and interpretation of South Slavic words in Daco-Romanian. *Alichéscu* 'to glue,' *arăzbóiu* 'loom,' *arugóz* 'reed,' *ciudíe* 'astonishment,' *coásă* 'scythe,' *culác* 'ring-like bread,' *coş* 'basket,' *cusíţă* 'braid (of hair),' *duh* 'spirit,' *dzáre* 'horizon,' *gâscă* 'goose,' *griv* 'gray,' *hránă* 'food,' *lupátă* 'shovel,' *niveástă* 'wife,' *padínă* 'depression,' *puh* 'down (feathers),' *pulíţă* 'shelf,' *rai* 'paradise,' *scúmpu* 'expensive, dear,' *şteáie* 'sanicle,' *ştírnu* 'coxcomb,' *sútă* 'hundred,' *trup* 'body,' *tuchéscu* 'to melt, kill,' are some of the Aromanian words he mentions together with their Daco-Romanian counterparts.

Recent Slavic words in the Aromanian spoken in the Republic of Macedonia are a normal phenomenon. *Dărjávă* 'state' (< Maced. *država*) and *osmolétcă* 'eight-year primary school' (< Maced. *osmoletka*)

---

[54] See Capidan-1925, Rosetti: 310-336 and bibliography; *ibid.* 61-68; Mihăilă, *op. cit.*

are examples recorded from Kruševo in the late 1970s.[55] Such neologisms have little chance of becoming Common Aromanian words. The same observation applies to recent neologisms from Albanian in the variety of Aromanian spoken in Albania and to recent neologisms from Modern Greek in the Aromanian spoken in Greece.

§ 53. **Words of Greek origin**. This is by far the largest contingent of non-Latin words in the Aromanian vocabulary. In T. Papahagi's dictionary (DDA) there are 2,534 Aromanian words of Greek origin, more than 27% of the total of 9,236 words recorded.[56] Moreover, many of the words considered of obscure origin in the DDA (like *ayistáre* 'hoard,' *anghídhă* 'sparrow,' *căsístră* 'hennery,' *ñac* 'infant') actually come also from Greek.[57]

Here is what Kr. Sandfeld writes about the Greek words in the Balkan languages: "*Ce qui est capital, c'est que l'élément grec subsisste dans les Balkans depuis de temps immémoriaux et que malgré toutes les décadences, il n'a pas cessé d'être porteur d'une civilisation superieure à celle de ses voisins. Cette civilisation, qui avait pour centre d'irradiation Byzance, a fortement agi sur les peuples voisins.*"[58]

Daco-Romanian and Aromanian share numerous words of Greek origin. While many of the Daco-Romanian words of Greek origin entered Romanian via Old Church Slavonic or Bulgarian, Aromanian words of Greek origin have been *absorbed directly from the Greek dialects*.[59] Numerous Aromanian words of Greek origin coincide with or are very similar to Bulgarian words borrowed from Greek. Cf. Arom. *apló* and Bulg. dial. *aplós* 'simpleton' (< Gr. *haplós*), Arom. *canélă* and

---

[55] See Gołąb: 211 and 240.

[56] See Mihăescu: 171.

[57] See Tzitzilis: 173 et seq.

[58] Sandfeld, LB: 17.

[59] On this matter see Mihăescu, particularly pp. 162-174.

Bulg. *kanéla* 'cinnamon' < Gr. *kanéla* (< Ital.), Arom. *pleága* and Bulg. dial. *plĭága* 'wound' < Gr. *pligí*, and many more.[60] Greek borrowings into Albanian are also numerous. The millenium-long political preponderence of the Byzantine Empire, whose official language was Greek, Byzantine culture and civilization, the Greek Orthodox Church, and the various achievements of the modern Greek state after its independence from the Ottoman Empire (1829) have contributed to the prestige of Medieval and Modern Greek and explain the considerable influence of Greek on the other languages of the Balkans, Aromanian included. However, it should be emphasized that in terms of *word frequency*, the Aromanian vocabulary of Latin origin has remained by far the most important one. Mutatis mutandis, in this respect Aromanian words derived from Latin can be compared with the Anglo-Saxon vocabulary of English versus the vocabulary from all other sources together.

§ 54. **Words of Turkish origin.** All the regions where Aromanians had lived since their appearance in history fell under Turkish occupation in the second half of the fourteenth century A.D. Ottoman rule ended in 1912. More than five centuries of Turkish presence in the Balkans explains the relatively large number of Turkish words (some of them from Arabic) in all the languages of the peninsula. The DDA contains 1,628 words of Turkish origin, such as *acaréte* 'mansion,' *áma* 'but,' *amiră* 'emperor,' *aslán* 'lion,' *băginác* 'brother-in-law,' *băhcíşe* 'bribe,' *biľé* 'nuisance,' *buiáuă* 'color,' *budâlă* 'stupid,' *dip* 'at all,' *duşmán* 'enemy,' *geáme* 'glass,' *gépe* 'pocket,' *hăláte* 'device,' *ibríc* 'coffeepot,' *lulé* 'smoking pipe,' *muabéte* 'kaffe-clatch,' *musafír* 'guest,' *nizám* 'foot-soldier,' *sadé* 'only,' *sictír* 'Go to hell,' *sóie* 'category, kind,' *şică* 'joke,' *tăcáte* 'capacity, disposition, frame of mind,' *tuféche* 'rifle,' *urdíe* 'flock, army,' *zevzéc* 'naughty.' There are many words with the Turkish suffix *-lɪk*, such as *şiretlâche* (< Turk. *şirretlɪk*, from *şirret* 'bad'). Twenty-four such words can be found

---

[60] See Filipova: 71, 100, and 143.

in the DDA. Another large contingent of words come from Turkish nouns with the suffix *-cı*, as *hancı* 'innkeeper' (< *han* 'inn'), Arom. *hăngí* (cf. also its Arom. synonym *mehengí* (< Turk. *meyhanecı*). The other Balkan languages also have numerous words with these two suffixes. Cf. D-Rom. *şiretlíc, hangíu.*

NOTE 1. *Direct and indirect borrowings.* Sometimes a given word of non-Latin origin entered Aromanian not directly, but via another Balkan language. Thus, there are Turkish words taken from Greek or Albanian, Greek and Turkish words taken from Bulgarian or Macedonian, Italian and a few French words taken from Greek or Turkish and other linguistic pathways as well.

NOTE 2. *Absence of words of Hungarian origin.* Daco-Romanian has several suffixes and a large number of words of Hungarian origin.[61] By contrast, the DDA does not contain a single word of this origin. This suggests that Aromanians and Daco-Romanians split apart territorially some time before Hungarians occupied Transylvania in the eleventh century.

§ 55. **Aromanian word formation.** Inherited and borrowed vocabulary has been briefly dealt with above. Aromanians also have a considerable number of lexical units coined by themselves, mainly with prefixes and suffixes. Below are two lists containing the main Aromanian prefixes and suffixes from Latin, Slavic, Greek, or the Balkan substratum.

§ 56. **Main Aromanian prefixes**

apu- (< Gr.) 'again,' 'back.' E.g., *apu-víndu* 'resell' (from *víndu* 'to sale'); see LB: 43 and the DDA: 179.

ayru- (< Gr.) 'wild.' E.g., *ayru-cápră* 'wild-goat' (from *cápră* 'goat'); see LB: 43 and the DDA: 121.

---

[61] See Rosetti: 429-434.

cacu- (< Gr.) 'bad.' E.g., *cacuzburắscu* 'to slander' (from *zbu-rắscu* 'to speak'); see LB: 43 and the DDA: 302.

dis-, diz- (< Lat.) 'de-, un-.' E.g., *dizgľéț* 'to thaw, de-frost' (from *ngleț* 'to freeze'), *disfác* 'to undo' (from *fac* 'to do/make'); cf. also *diz-* in *diznóu* 'anew' (after Bulg. *iznovo*, see LB: 88).

n-, an-, am-, ân-, âm- (< Lat.) 'in-.' E.g., *mi ncred* 'to trust' (from *cred* 'to believe, to trust'), *andulțéscu* or *(â)n-dulțéscu* 'to sweeten' (from *dúlțe* 'sweet').

ni- (< Slav.) 'un-, in-, dis-, -less.' E.g., *ni-agiúmtu* 'un-ripe' (from *agiúmtu* 'ripe, baked, done'), *ni-driptáte* 'injustice' (from *driptáte* 'justice'), *ni-ascultáre* 'disobedience' (from *ascultáre* 'obedience'), *ni-aru-șinát* 'shameless' (from *rușinát* 'ashamed, shy'). This is, probably, the most productive Arom. prefix. The DDA contains as many as 345 words formed with this prefix.

paľu- (< Gr.) 'of low quality.' E.g., *paľu-óm* 'good-for-no-thing' (from *om* 'man'); see LB 44 and the DDA: 942-3.

para- (< Gr.) 1. 'beyond, too much.' E.g., *para-mâc* 'to cram oneself' (from *mâc* 'to eat'), *para-lás* 'to neglect' (from *alás* 'to leave'); 2. 'associated.' E.g., *para-báciu* 'helper of a shepherd' (from *baciu* 'master-shepherd'); 3. 'submission', as in *para-dáu* 'to surrender' (from *dau* 'to allow, to give'); see LB: 43 and the DDA: 945 seq.

pri- (< Slav.) various meanings. E.g., *pri-adár* 'to transform' (from *adár* 'to make'); *pri-avút* 'very rich' (from *avút* 'rich').

proto- (< Gr.) 'first, before.' E.g., *protozbór* 'preface' (from *zbor* 'word').

xana- (< Gr.) 'again, anew.' E.g., *xanadzâc* 'to say again' (from *dzâc* 'to say').

§ 57. **Main Aromanian suffixes.**

-**á** (< Gr.), in adverbs: *adâncá* 'deeply' (from *adâncu* 'deep')

-**ác** (< Lat., Alb., Slav.): *subțarác* 'thin' (from *subțáre* 'thin')

-**áciu** (< Slav.): *plângáciu* 'plaintive' (from *plângu* 'to cry')

-**ádhă** (< Gr.): *nustimádhă* 'savor' (from *nóstim* 'pleasant')

-**áľu** (< Lat.): *ascumtáľu* 'hideout' (from *ascúmtu* 'hidden')

-**áme** (< Lat.):[62] *alghiáme* 'many bees' (from *alghínă* 'bee')

-**án, -eán** (< Slav.): *susán* 'uplander' (from *sus* 'up')

-**ár** (< Lat.): *cudár* 'last, worst' (from *coádă* 'tail')

-**árcu** (< Gr.): *inimárcu* 'courageous' (from *ínimă* 'heart')

-**áre** (< Lat.): *gălbináre* 'jaundice' (from *gálbin* 'yellow')

-**aryó** (< Gr.): *purcaryó* 'pigpen' (from *pórcu* 'pig')

-**ăríe** → **-íe**

-**áș** (< Slav.): *cuțutáș* 'little knife' (from *cuțút* 'knife')

-**áșcu / -úșcu** (< Slav.): *lișuráșcu* 'silly' (from *lișór* 'easy');
    tinirúșcu 'very young' (from *tínir* 'young')

-**át** (< Lat.): *schinărát* 'backbone' (from *schináre* 'back' anat.)
    uricľát 'big-eared' (from *ureácľe* 'ear'); *adiľát*
    'breathing' (from *adíľu* 'to breathe')

-**átă** (< Lat.): *imnátă* 'walking' (from *ímnu* 'to walk')

-**áte** (< Lat.): *driptáte* 'justice' (from *dréptu* 'right')

-**átic** (< Lat.): *amintátic* 'birth' (from *amíntu* 'to give birth')

-**áticȧ**: *driptáticȧ* 'justice' (→ **-áte**, **-átic**)

-**át** (< Lat.): *uricľát* 'big-eared' (from *ureácľe* 'ear')

-**átă** (< Lat.): *aumbrátă* 'shade' (from *aúmbră* 'shadow')

-**ăciúne** → **-ciúne**

-**ătáte** (< Lat.): *singurătáte* 'solitude' (from *síngur* 'alone')

-**átic** (< Lat.): *avinátic* 'game animals' (from *avín* 'to hunt')

---

[62] There are fifty-two Aromanian words with this suffix in the DDA. By contrast, in D-Rom. words with *-áme* are very rare and archaic: *copiláme* 'many children,' *haiducáme* 'many outlaws,' *mișelame* 'many commoners' and a few others.

-ciúne (< Lat.): *alăvdăciúne* 'praise' (from *alávdu* 'to praise');
      uscăciúne 'dryness' (from *uscát* 'dry'); *guliciúne*
      'nudity, emptiness' (from *gol* 'naked, empty')

-cu (< Slav.): *ceacârcu* 'squint-eyed' (from *ceacâr* 'idem')

-eálă (< Slav.): *arneálă* 'sweep' (cf. *arnéscu* 'to sweep, broom')

-eán → -án

-eásă (< Lat.): *arăfteásă* 'tailoress' (from *aráftu* 'tailor')

-eáşte (cf. Alb. -*éshtĕ*): *câneáşte* 'doggishly' (from *câne* 'dog')

-eáţă (< Lat.): *multeáţă* 'multitude' (from *múltu* 'much, many')

-(e)áuă (< Lat.): *fântâneáuă* (dim. from *fântână* 'well')

-él (< Lat.): *arutél* 'pulley' (from *aroátă* 'wheel'); *grambó*
      'groom,' dim. *grămbél*

-éscu (< Lat. -*íscus* or from the Balkan substratum, see **Russu**
      57): *frăţéscu* 'brotherly' (from *fráte* 'brother')

-eş (< Slav.): *coárneş* 'with elongated horns' (from *córnu*
      'horn')

-ét (< Lat.): *frăpsinét* 'ashgrove' (from *frápsin* 'ashtree')

-gí (< Turk.): *cosagí* 'reaper' (from *coásă* 'scythe')

-íc *(m.)*, **-ícă** *(f)* (probably < Slav.): *ficiuríc* 'little boy'
      (from *ficiór* 'son'); *surícă* 'little/dear sister' (from
      sóră 'sister')

-íce (< Slav.): *fântăníce* 'little well' → **-(e)áuă**

-íciu (< Slav.): *cuţutíciu* 'little knife' (→ **-áş**)

-iciúne → -ciúne

-íe (< Lat., Gr., Slav.): *gľinduríe* 'place with many acorns'
      (from *gľíndură* 'acorn');[63]

-íľe, -âľe (< Lat.): *furíle* 'theft' (from *fur* 'to steal');
      avuţâľe 'wealth' (from *avút* 'rich')

-íme (< Lat.): *lundzíme* 'length' (from *lúngu* 'long')

-ín (< Slav.): *barbatín* 'virile' (from *bărbát* 'man, male')

-ínă (< Lat., Slav.): *sacatínă* 'deformed person' (from *săcát*
      'crippled'); *uínă* 'many sheep' (from *oáie* 'sheep')

-ínţă (< Lat.): *slăbínţă* 'weakness' (from *slab* 'weak')

---

[63] More on this in Sandfield, LB: 44.

-(i)ór *m*, **-(i)oáră** *f* (< Lat.): *gălbiñór* 'yellowish' (from *gálbin* 'yellow'); *iñoáră* 'little/dear heart' (from *ínimă* 'heart')

-(i)ót (< Gr.): *Fărşărót* (from *Fraşári*), *Sămărñót* (from *Sămărína*, a town in Greece)

-íş (< Slav.): *cărpiníş* 'hornbeam grove' (from *cárpin* 'hornbeam'); *câmpíş* (1) 'rural' (from *câmpu* 'field'); *câmpíş* (2) 'small field'

-işór (< -íş + -ór): *chinişór*, dim. from *chin* 'fir'; *bunişór*, dim. from *bun* 'pretty good'

-íşte (< Slav.): *grupíşte* 'cemetery' (from *groápă* 'grave')

-ít *n*, **-ítă** *f* (< Lat.); makes nouns from past participles: *amurţít* 'stabbing pain' (from *amurţăscu* 'to become numb'); *mutrítă* 'look, glance' (from *mutréscu* 'to look')

-itáte (< Lat.): *yiitáte* 'creature' (from *yiu* 'alive')

-ítcu (< Slav.): *nişanlítcu* 'wonderful' (from *nişanlí* 'marked')

-íthră (< Gr.): *scântălíthră* 'little spark' (from *scânteáľe* 'spark')

-íţ *m/n*, **-íţă** *f* (< Slav.) make diminutives: *buíţ* 'little ox' (from *bou* 'ox'); *gutuñíţă* 'little quince' (from *gutúñe* 'quince')

-íu₁ in adjectives ending in -ăríu, -uríu (< Lat.): *hirburíu* 'quick-cooking' (from *hérbu* 'to boil')

-íu₂ 'large amount' (< ?): *limníu* (from *lémnu* 'wood')

-iúne (< Lat.): *putigiúne* 'rot' (from *pútrid* 'rotten')

-izmă (< Gr.): *aspárizmă* 'scare' (from *aspár* 'to scare');[64]

-líche or **-láche** (< Turk.): *furlíche* 'theft' (< *fur* 'to steal')

-mén (< Gr.): *mintimén* 'wise' (from *mínte* 'mind')

-míntu (< Lat.): *acupirimíntu* 'roof' (from *acoápir* 'to cover')

-oáñe (< Lat.) *vulpoáñe* 'vixen' (from *vúlpe* 'fox')

-óce, -óciu (< Slav.): *călivóce, călvóciu* 'small hut' (from *călívă* 'hut')

-óñu (< Lat.): *vulpóñu* 'male fox' (→ **-oáñe**)

---

[64] See Sandfeld, LB: 44.

-óplu (< Gr.): *piscóplu* 'small fish' (< *péscu* 'fish')

-ós (< Lat.) *muntós* 'mountainous' (from *múnte* 'mountain'), *plu-iós* 'rainy' (from *ploáie* 'rain')

-şór m, **-şoáră** f: *bunşór* 'pretty good' (from *bun* 'good') → **-işór**

-tór (< Lat.) *arăvdătór* 'patient' (from *arávdu* 'to endure'), *ţi-ritór* 'beggar' (from *ţer* 'to ask')

-úcică (< Slav.): *călivúcică* [•úĉkă] 'small hut' → **-óce**

-úră (< Lat.): *acritúră* 'sourness' (from *acrít* 'turned sour'), *adunătúră* 'gathering' (from *adunát* 'gathered'), *căldúră* 'warmth' (from *cáldu* 'warm')

-úş (< Slav.) *picurărúş* 'little, young or dear shepherd' (from *picurár* 'shepherd')

-(u)şór: *locşór*, dim. from *loc* 'place'

-úşcu, -úşcă (< Slav.): *glărúşcu* 'simpleton' (from *glar* 'stupid'); *colivúşcă* 'small hut' → **-óce**

-út₁ (< Lat.): *curnút* 'horned' (from *córnu* 'horn')

-ut₂ (< Slav.): *plâ'ngut* 'cry' (from *plângu* 'to cry')

-utós (< Gr.): *gurguľutós* 'roundish' (from *gurgúľu* 'pebble, nipple')

-úţ (< Lat.); one case only: *ñicúţ* 'tiny' (from *ñic* 'small')

-ză, -ăz (< Alb.): *niheámăză* 'a bit' (from *niheámă* 'little'); *muşutícăz* m/n, *muşutícăză* f 'pretty' (from *muşutíc* 'pretty' < *muşát* 'beautiful').

§ 58. **Terminologies.** Since there have been no schools and no scientific research conducted in Aromanian, terminologies for various domains of activity are either rudimentary or nonexistent. There are, however, a few exceptions. For centuries, the traditional occupation of Aromanians has been sheep herding. The Aromanian vocabulary reflects this fact in various ways. Thus, as many as twelve words for 'shepherd' are known: *baciu, bagegí, birbicár, că-prár, căşeár, chihăié, cilinícu, găvărár, mătricár, muldzár, pere-gé, picurár* (main term), *stirpár,* and *uiár* (see **SHEPHERD** in this dictionary). Likewise, several terms for 'wool' are known (see **WOOL**). Not rarely, expressions from this field can be heard in situations unrelated to sheep husbandry. E.g., *Țe căşeáre áre?* (*lit.* *'What's his cheese farm like?'*) means 'How much money does he make?' or 'What property does he own?' regardless of the actual professon of the person referred to.

§ 59. **Affective (emotional) vocabulary.** Aromanian is rich in vocabulary related to affective life. Very intelligent by nature and by collective and personal experience, speakers of Aromanian value the mind and despise or mock narrow-mindedness. There can be no doubt that they enjoy the suggestive power of witty words and expressions. Under the headword **STUPID** in the dictionary presented here as many as sixty-three words can be found, some of which are very colorful and throw light on these people's character and mentality. Other affective vocabulary include: 'to steal' (twenty-two words); 'to kill' (twenty-seven words); 'devil' (forty words); 'wretched' (sixty-two words). A lazy person is called *caca-vátră* (literally, 'hearth-shitter'), and a secretive person is a *oálă acupirítă* (literally, 'covered pot').

§ 60. *Conclusion.* The future development of the Aromanian vocabulary cannot be foreseen any more than the destiny of the language itself: will it silently continue to shrink and eventually be abandoned altogether, or will it be invigorated thanks to the enthusiastic efforts of its contemporary supporters (see § 47a)? But regardless of their success or failure, Aromanian constitutes and will remain for many years to come an important field of research for students in Romance, Romanian, and Balkan linguistics.

Subject index

IV. AN ENGLISH-AROMANIAN DICTIONARY

A

A *indef. article* un *m*, únă (*or* nă) *f*; vâr *m*, vâră *f*; vârnu *m*, vârnă *f*; **should he steal ~ sheep from me** di-ñ ľa vârnă oáie; **It resounded like ~ shell** Plăscăní ca vâră tópă

A *prep.* (*for each*) tu, pri; **for 300 groshy ~ month** cu 300 [trei súti] di yroşi tu mes ‖ PC *Brz:* **twice ~ day** di doá^uâ orⁱ pri dzú^uâ; CUNIA (*in a private letter*) **I used to work two-three hours ~ day** Lucrám cãti doáuă-trei oári di chiró tu dzúã (*stress added*)

ABA *s. tex.* abă

ABACK *adv.* (*unexpectedly*) apándiha → BE TAKEN ~

ABANDON *vb.* alás, apăr(n)ăséscu, apăr(n)iséscu (*and* apărñiséscu); apăryiséscu, părăţéscu, păr(ă)tiséscu, prăhtiséscu, brăhtiséscu; bag văfía (*lit.* 'to paint, to apply paint'); **~ him!** Bágă-ľ văfía! (*to avoid*) fug; (*imprec.*) **May God's grace ~ him!** Fúgă-ľ doára a Dómnului! (*to renounce, to throw away*) ▾aleápid ‖ las; LITURG 130: **do not ~ us!** nu nă lásă

ABANDONED *adj.* alăsát; (*forgotten*) apăr(n)ăsít; (*deserted, as of a house*) aráţe (*lit.* 'cool') *m/f*; aráţĭ *pl*; **He found the house ~** U-află vátra aráţe; (*free from restraint*) azgân, *pl m* -gâñ, *f* -gâne

ABANDONMENT *s.* alăsáre, apărnăsíre, apărñisíre, apăryisíre

ABASE *vb.* ñicşurédz, cătăfroniséscu; **to ~ oneself** mi fac túrtă (*lit.* 'to make oneself a flattened cake') ‖ CUNIA 154: atimuséscu

ABASH *vb.* scol di mínte → DISCONCERT

ABATE *vb.* cúrmu, ñicşurédz, scad; (*to diminish, as of a feeling*) moľiu, slăghéscu

ABATEMENT *s.* curmáre, ñicşuráre, slăghíre

ABATTOIR *s.* → SLAUGHTER HOUSE

ABBEY *s.* → MONASTERY

ABDICATE *vb.* (*as of a monarch*) dipún di pri scámnu → GIVE UP

ABDICATION *s.* parétise

ABDOMEN *s.* pântic, pântică, *dim.* pânticúşe; plăstúre, prăstúre; tâmpiníciu; străbăşínă, străbişínă; fulínă, schimbé ‖ ALIA 179: băríc; pándică, péndică, píndică, pândică, púnducă

ABDUCT *vb.* (*to kidnap*) aráp, arăchéscu

ABED *adv.* (*in bed*) apús, băgát, culcát

ABERRATION *s.* urbáre

ABET *vb.* (*to spur to action*) píngu, anăngăséscu

ABHOR *vb.* → HATE, DETEST

ABHORRENT *adj.* ánustu, *m pl* -şţâ, *f pl* -ste → DETESTABLE

ABIDANCE *s.* ascultáre, aplicáre

ABIDE *vb.* (*to put up with*) arávdu; (*to withstand*) ţân, ţân chép-tu; (*to await*) aştéptu, apăndăxéscu

ABILITY *s.* chischineáţă, chischimeáţă; măsturí(ĭ)e, măsturlíche; muraféte, murăfitlâche

ABJECT *adj.* zgrumát; *also:* aynusós, yunusós; etepsâz, idip-, *m pl* etepsâjĭ, idip-, *f pl* -sâze ; murlái, *f* -láie; sémnu, seámnă, sémñi, seámne

ABJURE *vb.* ▾alás, ▾aleápid

ABJURATION *s.* alipidáre

ABLAZE *adj.*, *adv.* aprés

ABLE *adj.* ácşu, *pl m* ácşi; áxiu, *pl m* ácsi; **We are not ~ to steal** Noi nu him ácşi trâ furi; *also:* icanó; irbáp, *m pl* irbăchĭ; izóte *invar.*; chischín, *pl m* chischíñ; chischinéţ; sárpe *invar.* → BE ~ TO

ABLOOM *adj.* anflurít

ABLUTION *s.* láre, spiláre

ABNEGATE *vb.* (*to renounce, to give up*) alás; trag mână (*lit.* 'to draw back one's hand')

ABNEGATION *s.* alăsáre

ABNORMALITY *s.* anapudhíľe, anapudzâľe

ABODE *s.* armăneáre, şideáre

ABOLISH *vb.* ≈ bitiséscu, cúrmu, arăstórnu

ABOLITION *s.* arăsturnáre, bitisíre, curmáre

ABOMINABLE *adj.* firaón *m*, -oánă *f*, -óñ *m pl*; -oáne *f pl*; *also* firaún → ABJECT, DETESTABLE

ABORTION *s.* (*abortive person, animal, or plant; smaller than ex-pected; failure*) cacafíngu

ABORTIVE *adj.* (*imperfectly formed*) astrăchít, cácav, zvumút; ~ **child** *s.* chirchinéţ, vumutúră

ABOUND *vb.* (*to be plentiful*) artir(i)séscu; hiu di primansús

ABOUT *adv.* (*approximately*) vâră, vără; ca, ca di ~ **ten eggs** vâră dzáţe oáuă; ~ **two hours away** ca doáuă ori cále; **an elderly man ~ 70 years old** om tricút ca di şeaptidzăţi di añ; (*on all sides*) tu tú-te părţâle; (*to be ~ to, to be on the verge of*) vrea + *vb.* **The dog was ~ to tear me up** Cânile vrea mi bea (*lit.* 'The dog wants to *drink me up')* ‖ CUVATA 19: ~ **noon** aşí ca miríndi-oáră

ABOUT *prep. (indicates concern)* tă, tră; **What are you crying ~?** Tră ţe plândzi?

ABOVE *adv.* disúpră, prisúpră, pisúpră; sus, nsus di; **from ~** di sus; *(in the upper part of)* stră, disúpră (di); **~ the village** strâ hoáră

ABOVEBOARD *adj., adv.* tu fáţă, fanirá, fóra, aşchearée

ABROAD *adv. (out of doors)* nafoáră; *(out of the country)* tu a-xeáne; **from ~** dit xinitíe

ABSCESS *s. med.* cuptúră, gărnúţ *(and* gâr-*)*, găríţ, úimă, apóstimă

ABSENT *vb.* lipséscu, hiu cusúre

ABSENTMINDED *adj.* agărşít, bóşcu, hăscát, şuntít, ĺ-azboáră *(lit. '[his / her mind] is flying')*; pri múlă şeáde ş-múlă cáftă *(lit. '[he] is on the mule and is looking for [his] mule')*

ABSINTH *s. bot. (wormwood)* pilóñu, pilóñu amărós, apsíthe

ABSOLUTELY *adv. (completely)* dip

ABSOLVE *vb.* ĺértu, sălăghéscu

ABSORB *vb.* muţ, sug, beau

ABSORBED IN THOUGHTS *adj.* minduít *m sg,* -íţ *m pl*

ABSTAIN *vb.* mi ţân, mi stăpuéscu

ABSTENTION *s.* ţâneáre, stăpuíre

ABSTEMIOUS *adj. (as concerns foods and drinks)* luyursít

ABSTINENCE *s.* ţâneáre; *(diet)* piríze, perizlâche, dhiétă

ABSTRUSE *adj.* tártar, *m pl* -tarĭ

ABSURD *adj.* glăréscu, *m pl* -réşţâ; ni-minduít → STUPID

ABUNDANCE *s.* artírizmă, birichéte, bunlúche; **in ~** *adv.* cu mnáta

ABUNDANT *adj.* bólcu, *m pl* -lţi; **The crop is ~** Grâñiĺe súntu bólţe ‖ **Av:** berichitlâcu; **Pls:** birichitós, CL 38; âmbugát, BASME 14

ABUNDANTLY *adv.* di primansús; cu mnáta; *(as of sweat)* arâu *(lit. 'stream')*

ABUSE *s. (verbal ~, insult)* angiuráre, prusvusíre, prusvulíe, yu-mărsíre

ABUSE *vb.* angiúr, tăxéscu; afúm nările; rizil(ips)éscu; prus-vul(i)séscu; yumărséscu; tălăéscu tu halé; ‖ ĺ-scot óchiĺ di cutótalui, BASME 184 *(lit. 'to scoop out smb.'s eyes completely')*

ABUSIVE LANGUAGE *s.* angiuráre

ABUT *vb. (to support, hold in position)* ▾andoápăr, andoápir; *(to border upon)* sinuripséscu

ABUTTALS *s.* (*boundaries*) tráfuri *pl*, traf *sg*

ABYSS *s.* hắu → PRECIPICE

ACACIA *s. bot.* sălcắm (*and* sălcâm), bagrém, dávan, acăchíe

ACCEPT *vb.* apróchiu, a(po)dhixéscu; strắxéscu, strixéscu; u fac di căbúle; mi fac răzíă; **We ~ it the way you are putting it** Apruchém așí cum dzắţi

ACCEPTABLE *adj.* ≈ bun, *f* búnă, *m pl* buñ, *f/n pl* búne ('*good*')

ACCEPTANCE *s.* dhixíre, apodhixíre

ACCESS *s.* (*entrance*) intráre

ACCIDENT *s.* oárắ láie (*lit.* '*black time*'); páthimă → MISFORTUNE

ACCIDENTALLY *adv.* ţivá; **lest children fall ~ into the water** fi-ciórilĭi [fi•cĭórĭ•lˇi] s-nu cádă ţivá tu ápă

ACCOMMODATE *vb.* (*~ with room and board*) lu-ám / u-ám ân cunáche

ACCOMPANIMENT *s.* (*in vocal music*) ih, is

ACCOMPANY *vb.* (*to escort*) pitréc; (*in vocal music*) ţân íhlu, ţân íslu, ţân boáţea

ACCOMPLICE *s. G:* yitác

ACCOMPLISHED *adj.* adărát, axít, mburít

ACCOMPLISHMENT *s.* ad(ă)ráre, axíre ‖ BELIMACE 4: azvíndză *pl*

ACCORD *s.* (*as of musical instruments*) duzéne

ACCORDING TO *prep.* cátai; *N:* spríma ‖ CAPIDAN 510: spréma

ACCOUNT *s.* (*report*) tăcráre, tăcríre; (*record of debt*) tiftére, dhiftére; (*statement of transaction*) (h)isápe; **a man of no ~** om di ciuchi; **Short ~s make long friends** ≈ Fráte, fráte, ma cáșlu-i cu parádz; **take into ~** bag oáră (că) ‖ CUNIA: **to pay on one's own account** păltéscu cátiun (*in a private letter; stress added*)

ACCOUNT *vb.* (*to cosider, to number among*) númir; am ti

ACCOUNT-BOOK *s.* tiftére, dhiftére

ACCUMULATE *vb.* stríngu, *N:* (*rare*) strângu; adún, stivăséscu, silixéscu, lixéscu

ACCUMULATION *s.* adunáre, stríndzire, strindzeáre

ACCURATELY *adv.* giústa, sustá, tamám

ACCURSED *adj.* anăthimát, anăhi-; blăstimát, cătăryăsít, cătăryisít; nalét, nihít, ni-apucát, stímtu; (*imprec.*) **May you be ~!** Anánghea s-ţu da! **May your mother be ~!** Nathimá-ţ mắ-ta!

ACCUSATION *s.* dâvăgilâche; cătiyuríľe, cătiyuríe

ACCUSE *vb.* cătiyurséscu, arúc măhănălu pri

ACCUSER *s.* dâvăgí

ACCUSTOM *vb.* nveţ, bag tu arăstoácă, mălăxéscu

ACCUSTOMED *adj.* nviţát; (~ *to smth. harsh or unpleasant*) aryăsít (*lit. 'tanned'*); **getting ~** mălăxíre

ACE *s.* (*a playing card*) mónă, **N:** mónţă; cheţ; as (*or has*), *pl.* áseañ *and* aşi [aşĭ]

ACHE *vb.* mi doáre; âñ da dor; **The joints of their feet ~ed** Lă da dor prinódurile di la cicioáre

ACHE FOR *vb.* ĭ'-trag dórlu → LONG

ACHIEVE *vb.* adár, fac

ACHIEVEMENT *s.* ad(ă)ráre, ad(ă)rământu, (m)buríre

ACID: arsenic ~ afrát

ACIDITY *s.* **stomach ~** acríş, căúră

ACIERATE *vb.* cilicuséscu

ACKNOWLEDGE *vb.* (*to express recognition or gratitude*) cunóscu, ĭ'-u am tru cunuşteáre, ĭ'-u am tu biricheávis → ADMIT

ACKNOWLEDGMENT *s.* (*recognition, thanks*) cunuşteáre

ACOLYTE *s.* (*rare*) dupănăsătór

ACORN *s.* gĭíndă, ghíndă, ghíntă, gĭíndură; dócără, jir, văláne

ACQUAINT *vb.* dau tu şteáre ‖ CUNIA 13, 76, 300: dau hăbáre, fac hăbáre, pitréc hăbáre; dau timbíhe, fac timbíhe; dau şteáre, pitréc şteáre; dau glas

ACQUAINTANCE *s.* oáspe *m*, oáspită *f*; (*the state of being acquainted*) cunuşmáie → MAKE SMB.'S ~

ACQUAINTED → BECOME ~ WITH

ACQUIESCE *vb.* → AGREE, CONSENT

ACQUIRE *vb.* (~ *wealth*) acáţ maiáuă, ayunéscu; (~ *bad manners*) ĭ'au; (~ *a disease*) amíntu; **He ~ed heart disease** Amintă lângoáre di ínimă

ACQUISITION *s.* acăţáre, acumpăráre, acuprátă, loáre

ACQUISITIVE *adj.* → GREEDY

ACRE *s.* (*land unit*) ≈ strémă, *pl.* stémate; píndă

ACRID *adj.* ácru, -cră, -cri, -cre

ACRIMONY *s.* ústur, usturíme; ascuráme

ACRIMONIOUS *adj.* áscur

ACROBAT *s.* (*as in a circus*) pihliván

ACROSS *adv.* dhípla; **We go ~ the mountains** Lom dhípla múnţâĭ; (*face to face*) carşí; andícra, andícrita; (*from one side to the other*) disúpră di → ALONG AND ~, PUT IT ~ SMB.

ACT

ACT *s.* (*deed*) fáptă; (*a negative ~*) lăiáţă → CATCH SMB. IN THE ~

ACT *vb.* eneryiséscu; (*to pretend*) ▼prifác ‖ (*to proceed*) fac; (*to go one's own way*) faċ cúmu ñ-táľe cáplu, BASME 411 (*lit. 'to act the way one's head cuts it'*)

ACT THE PRUDE *vb.* strâmbu nárea (*lit. 'to turn one's nose away'*)

ACTION *s.* enéryie; (*lawsuit*) ayuyíe

ACTIVE *adj.* nişidzút

ACTIVITY *s.* lúcru ‖ DIARO 12: nişideári

ACTOR *s.* theatrín

ACTUAL EVENT *s.* fáptă

ACTUALLY *adv.* (n)aévea

ACUITY *s.* (*~ of perception, of judgement*) ḓhiácrise ‖ CUNIA 85, 138: iţrăľi *f*, mintimiñíľi *f*, pireáţă; DIARO 27: sârpiţâľi, sârpiţlâchi

ADAMANT *s.* yeamándă, yeamánde, yeamándu

ADAM'S APPLE *s.* *anat.* căcărdác ‖ **GSus, Pls:** núcâ, CL 257

ADAPT *vb.* ţivicuséscu, tiryiséscu, uidiséscu

ADAPTATION *s.* ţivicusíre, uidisíre

ADD *vb.* adávgu, *aor.* adápşu, adápsişi, adápsi, *etc.*, *see* § 32; *also* avdág *and* avgăţéscu

ADD WINGS *vb.* dau vímtu, inimuséscu

ADDITION *s.* adăvgáre, adăvgământu, adăvgătúră, avgăţíre

ADDLE *adj.* (*of eggs*) clúvyiu, cluvyisít, clucít, culcít

ADDLE *vb.* (*of eggs*) cluvyiséscu

ADDRESS *s.* sístase

ADDRESS *vb.* (*to turn to*) ▼ndréptu cătră

ADEPT *s.* mástur, ustă

ADEPTNESS *s.* măsturlíche, măsturíľe, măsturíe

ADEQUATE *adj.* (*sufficient*) distúr; *Mul:* distúl

ADHERE *vb.* alichéscu → STICK

ADIEU *interj.* adío

ADJACENT *adj.* ≈ viţinipsít

ADJOURN *vb.* (*to suspend*) cúrmu; (*to postpone*) amân

ADJOURNMENT *s.* curmáre; amânáre

ADJUST *vb.* ţivicuséscu, tiryiséscu

ADJUSTMENT *s.* ţivicusíre

ADMINISTER *vb.* (*to manage*) ▼chivirniséscu ‖ **to ~ justice** fac driptáti PC *Brz*

ADMINISTRATION *s.* chivernisíre

ADMINISTRATOR *s.* éfur, zăpít → MANAGER

ADMIRABLE *adj.* scóntră *invar.*

ADMIRABLY *adv.* scóntră

ADMIRAL *s.* (*Turkish officer*) amiraláiu

ADMIT *vb.* (*to give entrance*) adixéscu (*and* adhi-); (*to concede*) dau driptáte → ACCEPT; (*to make acknowledgment*) cunóscu; *I will ~ this to you* Va ţ-u cunóscu

ADMIXTURE *s.* ‖ BELIMACE 37: amisticăciúne

ADMONISH *vb.* anăcréscu, vărghéscu, trag un pirdáfe → SCOLD

ADO *s.* sălăváte; **without much ~, without further ~** níţi únă, níţi doáuă; ne únă, ne doáuă

ADOLESCENT *s.* ficiurác, ficiurángu; cândăturáş, giunóp

ADOPT *vb.* (*a child*) nhiľédz, trec prit cămeáşe, ľau di súflit

ADOPTION *s.* (*of a child*) nhiľáre

ADOPTIVE CHILD *s.* ficiór di súflit; psihupédh ‖ *Also* ficiór tră súflit (*lit.* 'son for the soul'); the same pattern in D-Rom. (**copil de suflet**), *in the Venetian dial.* (**fio d'anema**) *and in Friulian* (**fi d'anime**), PARALLELE 155

ADOPTIVE GRANDCHILD (*or* **NEPHEW**) *s.* para-nipót

ADORE *vb.* háscu n gúră

ADORN *vb.* adár, armătuséscu, muşuţéscu, nvéscu, pruvéd, stulséscu; (i)suséscu; chind(r)iséscu; viliséscu; (*to ~ with showy finery*) nsărgóciu

ADORNED *adj.* adărát; andréptu, ân-; armătusít, ânzârzălát; chind(r)isít; isusít; muşiţât, muşuţât; ncľigát; prăpsít, pripsít; prividzút, scriát ‖ HRISTU 5: stulusít

ADORNMENT *s.* muşuţâre, muşiţâre; armătusíre; privideáre; vilisíre; nsărguceáre

ADROIT *adj.* mástur → CLEVER

ADULATION *s.* culăchíe, culăchipsíre, sprelíndzire

ADULATOR *s.* tărtór

ADULATORY *adj.* tărtór; marghiól (*and* -yiól), *pl m* maryĭóľ

ADVANCE ONE'S OPINION *vb.* ‖ âñ dau mínţăli, BASME 3o2 (*lit.* 'to give one's minds')

ADVANTAGE *s.* hăíre, hăríe, scuteáre, prucuchíe → PROFIT

ADVANTAGEOUS *adj.* ≈ ári scuteáre *3 sg* (*lit.* 'it has return')

ADVENT *s.* (*coming, arrival*) vineáre, viníre

ADVENTURE

ADVENTURE *s.* (*ordeal*) páthimă

ADVENTURER *s.* azvimturát, spulbirát

ADVERSE *adj.* (*unfavorable*) laiu (*lit. 'black'*), *m/f pl* lăĭ

ADVERSITY *s.* strimturáre, stuhináre; (*bad luck*) anapudzấľe

ADVICE *s.* nveţ, nviţáre; urminíľe, -níe, -nipsíre; năsăháte, năsiháte; cále (*lit. 'path, way'*); **We do not need your ~** Noi nviţáre di voi nu vrem; **She [Eve] did that on the serpent's ~** Li feáţe cu nvéţlu a şeárpilui; **The ~ I am giving you will take you far** Cálea ţe-ţ dau io va ti scoátă náparti → ASK FOR ~; TAKE SMB.'S ~

ADVISE *vb.* nvéţ, dau un anvéţ, urnupséscu, urminipséscu, simvulipséscu, dhăscăli(p)séscu; **He ~ed him how to speak** Lu-nviţắ cum si zburáscă ‖ dau nă mínte, BASME 441 (*lit. 'to give a piece of mind'*); BATSARIA 78: dau unắ-nviţáre

ADVISER *s.* (*member of a council*)

ADVOCACY *s.* (*profession*) avucătlắche

ADZ(E) *s.* (*a cutting tool*) téslă, cópă, nócupă, nicópă, mânăcópă, schipáre, zmálă

AESTIVAL *adj.* viréscu, *m pl* -réşţâ, *f pl* -réşti

AFAR: from ~ *adv.* di lárgu

AFFABLE *adj.* evắşcu, sârbu, *m pl* -rghi, *f pl* -rbe → GENTLE

AFFABILITY *s.* uminíľe ‖ DIARO 43: adâmlắchi *f*

AFFAIR *s.* (*commercial, juridical, etc.*) artícľi *n pl*; (*activity, concern*) huzméte, lúcru

AFFECT RELUCTANCE *vb.* strâmbu nárea, fac coáde, fac năji [năjĭ]

AFFECTATION *s.* (*affected ways*) maraféte, mâ-, mu- ‖ HRISTU 26: marifet

AFFECTION *s.* vreáre; *med.* maráze → DISEASE

AFFECTIONATE *adj.* vrut; doľu, *m pl* doľ, *f pl* dóľe; **my ~ sister** dóľa a mea di sóră

AFFECTIONATELY *adv.* vrut; **She is looking at him ~** Mutreáşte vrut la el

AFFIRM *vb.* (*to assert, to maintain*) ţân, dzâc, spun

AFFLICT *vb.* lăiéscu, lipiséscu, amărăscu, părăpuñiséscu

AFFLICTED *adj.* cârtít ‖ CUVATA 4: ca bătút di gríndină (*lit. 'as if hit by hail'*) → SAD, BE ~, WRETCHED

AFFLICTION *s.* nvirín, cârtitúră, căhâre, părăpuñisíre

AFFLUENCE *s.* artírizmă; (*as of crops*) birichéte; bulắchi, bunlúche ‖ DIARO 124: bunlâchi

AFFLUENT *adj*. mbugát, -átă, -áț, -áte → RICH

AFOOT *adv*. cu cioárile

AFFORD *vb*. ñ-da di mână; **He can ~ this** Ĺ-da di mână

AFFRANCHISE *vb*. elefthiruséscu, apulséscu

AFFRONT *s*., *vb*. → INSULT

AFRAID → BE ~

AFTER *adv*. (*subsequently*) di-pri-apóia

AFTER *prep*. (*at a later time; according to, in conformity to*) dúpă, dúpu, dípu; di cára; **~ the girl's departure** dúpu plicárea a feátiľei; **~ I die?** Di cára s-mor eu? **~ a short time** tră puțăn chiró; tră puțână oáră; (*purpose*) trâ, tră, ntră; **Go ~ water** Dú-te tr-ápă; **He went ~ firewood** Nchisí ntră leámne; **~ the French fashion** a la fránga; (*succession*) cu; **year ~ year** an cu an

AFTER ALL níți că; ména; *N:* ghioa, nghioám, ghioáie; **~ Gardani** (*a masculine given name*) **is not alive** Gardáni níți că băneádză

AFTERBIRTH *s*. (*placenta and fetal membranes*) soárte

AFTERNOON *s*. **in the late ~** trâ mirínde; (*the 4:00 - 5:00 o'clock time*) cátră mirínde

AFTERWARDS *adv*. apói, apóia, apoáia, năpói, dapóia, di-apóia, di-priapóia; di-cára ‖ HRISTO 1: ma năpoi

AFTERWORLD *s*. → OTHER WORLD

AGAIN *adv*. iar, iáră, iára; diznóu, máta, xaná, *S:* pále ‖ *N:* năpói, CAPIDAN 505 → DO ~

AGAINST *prep*. tru, cóntra, cóndră cu, príste; **I was standing ~ the wind** Míni stateám cóndră cu vímtul; **He threw himself ~ him** Príste nâs si-arucă ‖ **~ one's will** di zóre, BASME 50; **The girl fell ~ a rock** Feáta si-agudí di ună k'átră, K-D 73 (*stress added*); fără ínimă (*lit. 'without heart'*), PARALLELE 140

AGAPE *adv*. cu gúra hăscátă → REMAIN ~

AGE *s*. vârstă, vrâstă, ilichíe; scáră (*lit. 'ladder'*); **He was the same ~ as the old woman** Erá tu vârsta a moáşiľei; **girls my ~** feáte tu scára a mea ‖ **of his ~** tu áñľi a lui, BASME 7

AGE *vb*. auşéscu, auşắscu → GROW OLD

AGED *adj*. (*of people*) alghít (*lit. 'whitened'*)

AGEING *s*. vicľáre, nvicľáre, vicľíre; auşíre, auşítă; muşíre; alghíre (*from álbu 'white'*)

AGENDUM *s*. (*thing to be done*) lúcru tr-avináre

AGENT

AGENT *s.* (*representative*) vichíľu *or* vichíľe, *pl.* vichíľ

AGGRAVATE *vb.* (*to vex*) guştirédz; (*to torment*) scot súflitlu, scot geánlu; (*to annoy*) sâcâldiséscu; (*a wound, etc.*) măriţéscu

AGGRIEVE *vb.* → INJURE, TROUBLE

AGHAST → ASTONISHED, STAND ~

AGILE *adj.* sárpit, sărpit (*and* sâr-), sârpid; sértu, *m pl* -rţâ, *f pl* -rte; sértic, sârbéscu; (*slender and* ~) bidiví → NIMBLE

AGILITY *s.* sârbislâche, sârpiţlâche, sârpiţâľe

AGITATE *vb.* (*as of a lake or sea*) trub, túrbu

AGITATED *adj.* ‖ (*uneasy*) sighisít, STERE 23

AGITATION *s.* → ANXIETY ‖ (*bustle*) Culóña, DIARO 277

AGO *adv.* áre (*minutes, days, etc.*) di cându; **He died a month ~** Ari un mes di cându murí; **a long time ~** dioáră, di múltu; **three years ~** auá ş-trei añ; **We sold it two days ~** U-vindúm auá ş-doáuă dzále; **a little while ~** adineávra

AGONIZE *vb.* nciómir, ncioámir, nciunirédz, ncimirédz

AGREE *vb.* (*about price, etc.*) cad tu păzáre; sinfunipséscu, căpséscu, fac razíă (*sic*); **I don't ~ with the price of this wheat** Grânlu aéstu nu-ñ cáde tu păzáre; (*to share common views*) u fac căbúle, u fac di căbúle; adhixéscu; hiu (*or* éscu) pri únă cále; ndreg; **They do not ~** Nu sunt pri únă cále; cad tu cále; **We did not ~** Nu cădzúm tu cále; (*to match, to go well together*) uidipséscu, idupséscu, ncľíd; **Will your mother ~ to give you to me?** Mâ-ta vancľídă s-ti da la míne? (*of people*) **They ~ like harp and harrow** S-mâcă ca câñľi (*lit.* 'They eat each other like dogs') ‖ HRISTU 7: fac "ghíni" ('yes') cu capu; DIARO 11: **they ~ed with each other** fúrâ dóiľi baríşu

AGREEABLE *adj.* (*pleasing*) bírcu, *m pl* -írţi, *f pl* -rţe; bírciu, *m pl* bírci; nóstim, *m pl* -tiñ, *f* -tine ‖ arisít, ară-, CUNIA 233

AGREEMENT *s.* (*harmony*) udiseáţă, udiséţă, uidisíre, úidizmă; (*understanding*) sinfuníe; (*condition*) căvúle, căúle, ligămíntu; **in ~ with** báta cu ‖ **to strike an ~** fac nă ligătúră; BATSARIA 1: **Let's strike an ~** s-făţém nă ligătúră → COME TO AN ~ WITH

AGRICULTURE *s.* zivyârlíche

AHEAD *adv.* culúi-năínte ‖ *Cru:* ăncáp, GOLAB 153

A-HUNTING ‖ *Peş:* la ávi; **He went ~** Z-dúse la ávi, CL 37 (*stress added*)

AID *s.* and *vb.* → HELP

AIGRETTE *s.* (*spray*) sărgúce, ciuciúlă, ciuciúlcă

AILING *adj.* lânţid, *m pl* -ţidz; *also* lândzit; mărăjár, nip(u)tút; zăbún, -búnă, -búñ, -búne; **to be ~** atihiséscu

AILMENT *s.* mărăze → DISEASE

AIM *s.* scupó, niéte; (*target*) nişáne → TAKE ~

AIM *vb.* (*to intend*) ñ-u bag să; (*with or as if with a weapon*) anchiléscu, dau tu sémnu, trag tu nişáne, nişinipséscu ‖ ľau la ócľu, BASME 488

AIR *s.* aéră; **Alb:** éră; (*rare word*) áir; *also* hâvă ‖ TULLIU 112: **angels were singing in the ~** ánghiľ cântá tu aéră → ASSUME ~S, GIVE ONESELF ~S, PUT ON ~S

AIRING *s.* → TAKE AN ~

AKIN (TO) *adj.* (*related, similar, identical*) únă sóie cu, nă-sóie cu (*lit.* '*the same kind as*')

ALAS *interj.* → OH

ALARM *s.* → TAKE ~

ALBANIA *s.* Arbinşíe ‖ **Cru:** Arbinişíe, GOLAB 153

ALBANIAN *s.* arbinés *m*; arbineásă *f*; ghégă *m*; *pl* gheghi (*1 syll.*) *and* ghégañ; (*sobriquet*) cápră (*lit.* '*goat*'), ghiusmăpíngă, *pl* ghiusmăpingáñ; (*~ from the mountainous regions*) malesór, *pl* malesóri *and* malesóţi; *coll.* arbinşáme

ALBANIAN *adj.* arbinşéscu; *adv.* arbinişeáşte; **the ~ language** arbinişeáşte; **Do you know ~?** Ştii arbinşeáşte?

ALBUMEN *s.* (*~ of an egg*) albúş

ALCOHOL *s.* spírtu, şpírtu; (*ethyl ~*) inóplimă

ALDER *s.* árin, arín, anín; **G:** ávar; vrăñu, *pl* vrăñ; şcľíthru, *pl* şcľíthri ‖ **GSus:** iáhlâ, CL 253

ALEMBIC *s.* lâmbíc ‖ DIARO 32: lâmbíchi; CUNIA 8: *also* căzăníţă

ALERT *adj.* (*attentive, watchful*) câştigós, -oásă, -óşĭ, -oáse

ALFALFA *s.* → LUCERN

ALIEN *adj.* (a)xén, *f* (a)xeánă, *m pl* (a)xéñ, *f/n pl* (a)xeáne

ALIENNESS *s.* ‖ CUVATA 3: xínură

ALIKE *adv.* únă; *also:* únă sóie; ómña, ómea, uigúne; **Not all the fingers are ~** ≈ Túte dzeáditile nu-s únă; **All of them were ~** Tuţ eará-ľ [ia•ráľ] únă; **All are ~** Tuţ súntu ómña ‖ MERCA 3: lis ca; DIARO 85: '*like master, like man*' ahtári tátă, ahtári híľu

ALIVE *adj.* yiu, *f* yíe, *m/f pl* yiĭ; *also* ghiu; (*still ~, of a moribund*) cu gúră; **He succeeded to catch his mother still ~** (Putú)

si-şi agiúngă mắ-sa cu gúră (*lit.* '*He managed to reach his mother with mouth*'; *i.e., she was still able to speak*)

ALL *adj. and pron.* tut; **They came back with ~ the sheep and dogs** S-turnáră cu túte oi ş-cu tuţ cáñ → AT ALL; BE NOT QUITE ALL THERE

ALL (A)ROUND *adv.* avaríg, avar(1)íga, avắríḡắ(ra), divắrlíga, divarlíga, ḏivắrlígala, deavarlíga, dinvắrlíga, varlíga ḏi varlíga; ḏi túte pắrţâle

ALL KIND OF ‖ sóie di sóie, BASME 49, 54, 83; luyíi ḏi luyíi, BASME 476

ALL OVER *adv.* toátă rádha, tu tut lóclu, prísti tot lóclu ‖ **I roamed ~ Kruševo** (*a town in MAC*) Tricúi pi Crúşuva, GOLAB 153

ALL THE SAME únă; **It's ~ to me** Únă-ñ fáţe

ALL RIGHT *adj.* bun; *adv.* ghíni; (*concessively*) as, ási → BE IT SO, LET IT BE

ALL SORTS OF sóie di sóie → ALL KINDS OF

ALL SOULS' DAY *s.* Arusále f pl

ALLAY *vb.* agăliséscu; (*as of one's hunger*) năfătéscu foámea

ALLEVIATE *vb.* (*as pain*) lişurédz (*and* ľi-), ñişurédz, agăliséscu, fac s-adíľe; (*of hunger*) năfătéscu foámea

ALLEVIATION *s.* lişuráre → RELIEF

ALLIANCE BY MARRIAGE *s.* ncuscráre

ALLOT *vb.* (*to assign, to establish*) taľu, mpártu

ALLOTMENT *s.* mpărţâre, curamánă, párte

ALLOW *vb.* alás, apróchiu, dau; dau vóľe, dau vólă; dizlég; **The law did not ~ that** Nómlu nu u dădeá; **They do not ~ them to stay in their villages** Nu ľ-aproáche s-chindrueáscă ân hórile [hórĭ•li] a lor ‖ CUNIA 226: dau izíne

ALLOWABLE *adj.* alăsát, dizligát

ALLOWANCE *s.* (*permission*) alăsáre, trat

ALLOY *s.* pacfóne

ALLUDE *vb.* (*to hint*) gréscu pri poártă s-ávdă pălthírea (*lit.* '*to speak to the gate so the window can hear*') ‖ DIARO 43: bat; PC: bat pi sumár, dau pi sumár (*lit.* '*to knock the pack-saddle*')

ALLURE *vb.* leg, amăyipséscu → ENTICE

ALLUVION *s.* lúnzimă, *pl* lunzímate

ALLY *vb.* mi leg cu; (*by marriage*) ncuscrédz

ALMOND *s.* miydhálă, badéme

ALMOND-EYED *adj.* miydalát

ALMOND-TREE *s*. míydal *m*, miydăľáuă *f*

ALMOST *adv*. aproápe, aproápea, angeác

ALMS *s*. (*usu. boiled wheat with honey offered for the souls of the dead*) (s)pumeán, pămăntu, pirpisór, eleimosíne ‖ părtăciúne, părticiúne, CAPIDAN 149; văcufi: **He looks so weak as if he lived on ~!** easti slab canda mâcâ di vâcufi! DIARO 91

ALOE *s*. (*aromatic substance*) săbúre

ALONE *adj*. síngur, singurátic, singurúş, singuríc; axólit; gol (*lit. 'empty'*), *f* goálă, *m pl* goľ, *f pl* goále; **They ~ came** (*nobody but them*) Eľ goľ viñíră; **all ~** (*and sad*) cob, *f* cóbă, *m pl* cobĭ (*sic*), *f pl* cóbe (*also invar.*); síngur cob, síngur-singuríc

ALONENESS *s*. singuráme, singureáţă, singuritáte

ALONG *adv*. ‖ CUNIA 176: dealúngului; **~ and across** crucíşalui

A LOT OF *adj*. sumăreáuă, nă crímă (di), plod (di), suríe (di), mal (di), chíhtră; **There is ~ wool at home** Lână acásă si-áflă nă crímă; **He has ~ hair** Chíhtră peri áre → LOT, MANY, MUCH

ALOUD *adv*. ‖ PC: cu sílă (*lit. 'with force'*); cu boáţe sănătoásă (*lit. 'with healthy voice'*)

ALPHA *s*. álfă

ALPINE LAKE *s*. nduhíñe

ALREADY *adv*. chióla, chiólas, véche, véce; **He ~ was on his death bed** Trădzeá véche s-moáră ‖ DIARO 363: máltu; **the sun had set ~** soárile aveá máltu scăpitátâ

ALSO *adv*. şi, ş-; **Should we ~ die, like all our ancestors?** S-murím ş-noi ca tuţ păpâñľi?

ALTAR *s*. altár *and* altáre; *also:* ayiadhímă, ayiavímă, ayiudhímă, trápeză, vímă ‖ MERCA 12: ghidímă

ALTER *vb*. → TRANSFORM

ALTERCATION *s*. strigáre → QUARREL

ALTERNATELY *adv*. cându únă, cându áltă

ALTERNATIVE: as an ~ to (*instead of*) tu loc di

ALTHOUGH *cj*. cu túte că, ţé-că, că ţe că, ţécari [ţé•carĭ], méţi, méţi că; *N:* cánai că, canúi ‖ cu-túte-că (*also in Bulg., Alb., Mod. Greek, Ital.*) PARALLELE 130; á-câ; **~ he promised, he did not do it** a-câ dzâsi, nu feáţi, DIARO 389

ALTOGETHER *adv*. deadún, dadún, dipriún, mpriúnă

ALUM *s*. cheátră álbă, stípse

ALWAYS *adv*. diúnă; tótuna, tótâna, tótna, tónna, tutdiúnă, tutú-

na, tutaúna, tutăúna, dáima, pánda; (*constantly*) tot; di únă-únă;
One of them is ~ sad Úna-i tut jilítă

  AM *vb.* *1 sg:* hiu *or* éscu → BE

  AMARANTH *s.* *bot.* ştir → COCK'S COMB

  AMASS *vb.* adún, stivăséscu

  AMASSING *s.* adunáre

  AMATEUR *s.* tiryeaclíu, tiryeaclâ, tiryeachíu ‖ DIARO 43: tiryeaclí *m*, tiryeacloáñi *f*

  AMAZE *vb.* ciud(us)éscu → MARVEL

  AMAZED *adj.* ciudisít → BE ~

  AMAZEMENT *s.* uñisíre → ASTONISHMENT, BE LOST IN ~

  AMAZING *adj.* ‖ lúcru máre (*lit.* 'great thing'), BASME 455, 487

  AMAZINGLY *adv.* → AMAZING

  AMBER *s.* chihlibáre, chihribáre

  AMBIGUOUS *adj.* ni úda, ni uscáta (*lit.* 'neither dry, nor wet'); ni álba, ni láia (*lit.* 'neither white, nor black')

  AMBLE *vb.* ímnu riváne

  AMBLING *s.* ariváne, arăvané

  AMBLING *adj.* (*of horses*) arivanlâ, -nlíu, -nlâtcu

  AMBUSH *s.* pusáte, pusíe

  AMBUSH *vb.* acáţ pusíe, limir(yi)séscu

  AMBUSHING *s.* limiryisíre

  AMEN *interj.* amín

  AMENABLE *adj.* muláşcu, *f sg* -áşcă, *m pl* -áşchi, *f pl* -áşche

  AMERICA *s.* ‖ BELIMACE 14: Americhíe

  AMIABILITY *s.* ‖ DIARO 43: adâmlâchi

  AMIABLE *adj.* eváşcu *and* iaváşcu → GENTLE

  AMID, AMIDST *adv.* → AMONG

  AMMONIAC *s.* ţapar(i)có

  AMMUNITION *s.* giuphané [ĝup•ha•né]

  AMONG *prep.* píntru, príntră, prit; nídză di (*and* ñídză di); anámisa di; nólgica di, nólgiuca di, nóljuca di, nóljua di; tu; **hidden birds singing ~ flowers** puĭ ţe cântă ascúmţâ prit flori; **They are ~ us** Sunt nólgica di noi; **~ the people** nóljua di lúme

  AMPHORA *s.* stámnă

  AMPLE *adj.* máre *m/f sg*, mărĭ *m/f pl*; múltu, *m pl* -lţâ; lărgóñu

  AMPLIFY *vb.* măréscu, adávgu, avdág, tíndu, créscu

  AMULET *s.* haimalí, haimalâ, haimaní, haimalíe, haimanlíe

AMUSE *vb*. şuitéscu

AMUSEMENT *s*. zéfcă, zéfche

AMUSING *adj*. and **-LY** *adv*. toáfe *invar*.

ANALOGY *s*. analuyíe

ANALYSIS *s*. (*as in teaching or learning grammar*) análisă

ANATHEMA *s*. afurizmó, afurizmóu, afurisíre

ANATHEMATIZE *vb*. afuriséscu, blástim, cătăryiséscu, cătăryăséscu ‖ DIARO 26: câtârâséscu

ANATHEMATIZED *adj*. afurisít, blăstimát

ANCESTOR *s*. pápu, *pl* pachi *or* păpâñ, păpáñ, păpeáñ; străpáp, ghiuş, propátor, străáuş, străuş, străpărínte, stripărínte; tot, *pl* tóteañ ‖ CARAFOLI 47: străuş

ANCESTRY *s*. (*race*) dămáră; **of noble ~** di sóie máre, di căpíe máre, di lăgámă; **of royalty ~** ciciór di scámnu → ORIGIN

ANCHOR *s*. (*as in a roof*) ‖ *SJos*: dhiplár, CL 44

ANCHOR ONE'S HOPES IN / ON SMB / SMTH. *vb*. hiu cu umútea la

ANCHORITE *s*. érmu, aschitíu

ANCIENT *adj*. străvécľu, *f* -veácľe, *m/f pl* -vécľi

AND *cj*. şi, şă, ş-, di; **Go ~ ask!** Dú-te di ntreábă! *Formerly also* e *or* i

ANECDOTE *s*. părăvulíe

ANESTHETIZED *adj*. ‖ BELIMACE 28: mbitát → DRUNK

ANEW *adv*. diznóu, iar, iára, iáră, páli, xaná; **to begin ~** pri-adár

ANGEL *s*. ánghil, *dim*. anghilúş

ANGELICAL *adj*. anghiléscu, *f* -leáscă, *m pl* -léştâ, *f pl* -léşti

ANGER *s*. amâníe (*and* amă-), năireáţă, nărleáţă, năiríre, nără-íre, yináte, ynáte, ináte, turbáre, trubáre, dzándză, gazépe, yă-zépi; (*as of a river*) bóră; thimó, uryíe, hulíe; **inflamed by ~** a-prés di hulíi; lísă, lisixíre, path, páthus, gínde, ngindáre, ză-lă, zăte, hímă; orĭ *f pl*; náxe, bóľi *f pl*; guşturáre, făsăríe

ANGER *vb*. ayrédz, furchiséscu, ngíndu

ANGINA *s. vet.* ‖ (*inflammation of the mouth, a desease of cattle and horses*) *SJos*: sufrágă, CL 261

ANGLING ROD *s*. úñiţă, vlac

ANGRY *adj*. yinătós, ynătós, furţuít, căchiusít, hulusít, cărtít (la fáţă); aprés, aprímsu, aprímtu (*lit*. 'inflamed'); năirít foc ‖ *Cru*: nirít, GOLAB 123

ANGRILY *adv.* cu hímă, cu ináte, cu nărleáţă

ANGUISH *s.* cắñisíre, cắñínă (*and* câ-), múndă, munduíre, sicliţíre, tiráñu, zahméte

ANGUISH *vb.* nciómir, ncioámir, nciumirédz, ncimirédz

ANIMAL *s.* gheáţă; právdă, *dim.* prăvdícă; nămáľu, nimáľu, numáľu; (*creature*) yiitáte [yi•i•tá•ti]; (*beast; also fig.*) zulápe

ANIMAL HUSBANDRY *s.* (*speaking of sheep*) picurăríľe, picurărátă, picurărlâche

ANIMATE *vb.* (*to enliven*) ▼ncucutédz

ANIMOSITY *s.* măcătúră, zắte

ANISE *s.* ylicánţu, ylicándzu

ANKLE BOOT *s.* gófe

ANKYLOSED *adj.* ‖ DIARO 55: acâţát (di mési, di un cicіór, *etc.*); (*immobilized*) tesu témblă

ANNEX *vb.* alichéscu, fac únă

ANNIHILATE *vb.* fac piripáchi [pi•ri•pák'], afăn(i)séscu, cătăstrăpéscu, prăpădéscu, părpădéscu; (*as an army*) astíngu, tuchéscu, stifuséscu

ANNIHILATION *s.* (*destruction*) stifusíre, prăpădíre, afănizmó

ANNOUNCE *vb.* dau glas; (*to let know*) dau / fac / pitréc hăbáre; (~ *by striking a wooden bar, as at a church or monastery*) toc; (~ *by beating a drum*) *G:* bat bărăbánca

ANNOUNCEMENT *s.* dilealâche

ANNOUNCER *s.* (*crier, messenger before the invention of radio and TV*) tilál, sihăryeát

ANNOY *vb.* scắñiséscu (*and* scâ-) → TEASE

ANNOYANCE *s.* pihtusíre; (*difficulty*) ghiúcă → GRIEF

ANNUITY *s.* airáte, airátă

ANODYNE *s.* (*any drug that allays pain*) anódhin

ANOINT *vb.* hrisuséscu, miruséscu

ANOINTING *s.* hrísmă

ANOTHER *adj.* áltu *m*, álta *f*, álţâ *m pl*, álte *f pl*; (a)lántu (*and* -ndu), anántu (*and* -ndu); **from one to ~** di la un la nántu; *g/d* alăntúi *m*, -téi *f*, -tór *m/f pl*

ANSWER *s.* apándise, apócrise, giuvápe, giuiápe [ĝu•ĭá•pi]

ANSWER *vb.* (a)păndiséscu, apocriséscu, dau apócrise, dau giuiápe, ľ-u tórnu ‖ *Cru:* apăndăséscu, GOLAB 200; fac, BASME 27

ANSWER SMB. PAT *vb.* (*promptly*) bag mănúşe (la túte cât̂e dzâc)

ANT *s. ent.* fur(n)íca, fur(n)íga; **Src:** sfârníga ‖ fârñíca, furñíga, furíya, fârmíga, *etc.* ALIA 123; *coll.* furnicáme, furnigáme

ANTEROOM *s.* haiáte

ANTHILL *s.* ‖ **GSus:** furnigárnic, CL 45; **SJos:** furmingufuľáua, CL 255

ANTIC *s.* (*ludicrous act or thing*) maimunlâche

ANTICIPATE *vb.* (*to foresee*) privéd, pruvéd

ANTIPATHETIC *adj.* (*arousing antipathy*) análut, *m pl* -luţ

ANTIPYRINE *s.* andipirína

ANTIQUE *s.* ‖ antícâ, DIARO 58

ANTIQUATED *adj.* nvicľát, *f* -cľáta, *m pl* -cľáţ, *f pl* -cľáte

ANTIQUE *s.* antíca

ANTIQUE-DEALER *s.* anticagí

ANUS *s.* cur, *pl.* curi *or* cúruri; guvaleáce, guvalíce

ANVIL *s.* amóne ‖ **GSus:** ciuc, CL 44; **PC:** stur, CL 261; **SJos, Av:** timóni *f*, CL 262

ANXIETY *s.* (*worry, concern*) (a)ngatán, gailé, **N:** gailée, gailée; frundídha, nácra, ghiúce; sicléte, sacléte; **head-splitting ~** valandúra, silu(y)íe ‖ CUNIA 205: anisihíe, niariháte [ni•a•]

ANXIOUS *adj.* **to be on the ~ side** şed ca pri schiñ → BE ~ FOR

ANY *adj.* vâr *m*, vâra *f*; (*whoever, whatever*) íţe, íţin, íţişi

ANY *pron.* vârnu *m*, vârna *f*; **You did not obey ~** Tíne vârnu nu ascultáşi; **lest she tell ~** s-nu spúna a vârnúi; barún; **Do not be afraid of ~!** Nu avéţ fríca di barún!

ANYBODY *pron.* → ANYONE

ANYMORE *adv.* iára, diznóu, xaná, póle, ma; **N:** máltu; **You do not see it ~** Nu-l xaná vedz; **They have not seen him ~** Nu-l vidzúra máltu ‖ ma, *as in:* ma ia nu ira ma aco 'but she was not there anymore,' HRISTU 21

ANYHOW *adv.* (*in any manner*) cúmţi, cúmţi s-híba

ANYONE *pron.* vârnu *m*, vârna *f*; cárevá (*sic!*), cáinivá (*sic!*), cániva; **I won't give it away to ~** Nu-l dau a vârnúi; **Don't listen to ~!** S-nu ascúlţ cáni-va; *g/d* cúniva; **Has ~ come?** Víñe cániva? **We do not do wrong to ~** Arau nu adúţim a cúniva ‖ DIARO 180: carivá; CUNIA 336: verún; **Give them to ~** Da-ľi a cúiţi s-hí-ba

ANYTHING *pron.* (*at all*) ţivá; **I did not have ~** Nu aveám ţivá; **I do not want ~** Ţivá nu voi; hir, *dim.* hirúş; **I won't give him ~** Nu-ľ dau hir; **N:** hici ţivá; **We don't want ~** Nu vrem hici ţivá;

barún; **Today I do not have ~ to do** (*I am not busy*) Nu am barún lúcru ástăz; **~ else** áltu lúcru; **They do not have ~ else to do** Altu
lúcru nu-áu țe s-fácă ‖ HRISTU 20: nițiva; **One could not hear ~** Nu
si audza nițiva

ANYTIME *adv.* ‖ TULLIU 56: cănduțidó

ANYWAY *adv.* (*at any rate*) tut ca tut

APACE *adv.* → SWIFTLY

APART *adv.* anámera (di), ahóryea, ahórea, parámira

APATHETIC *adj.* adhyeáfur [a•dhyeá•fur]; **to be ~.** (*to give no help*) stau cu mắnle n sin

APATHETICALLY *adv.* cu alăsáre

APIECE *adv.* ‖ PC: únlu *m*, únă *f*

APOLOGIZE *vb.* âñ ľau ľirtáre; cad bardón; **I ~!** Si mi ľérțâ!

APOPLEXY *s.* pícă, chícută; **hit by ~** loat di hále; **to have an apoplectic fit** nchicutédz, mi agudeáşte píca → STROKE

APOSTLE *s.* apustulă, apóstul, *pl* apóstuľ *and* apostoláñ

APOSTOLIC *adj.* apostolichíe, *pl* -chíľ (*sic*, DDA 176)

APPALLING *adj.* (*frightful*) fricós, fricuít, fuvirós

APPALLINGLY *adv.* (*dreadfully*) fuvirós

APPAREL *s.* *derog.* catrafúse *f pl*; cărăndíe

APPARENTLY *adv.* cánda

APPARITION *s.* aspúnire, aspuneáre; (*as Christ's*) alincíre

APPEAL *vb.* (*to apply for an appeal*) fac istináfe

APPEAR *vb.* aspún; alincéscu, alăncéscu; furniséscu, fărniséscu;
(*as of grass, horns, mustache*) dau, dau cap, arăsár; părăstăséscu,
părăstiséscu; (*as of the break of the day*) da dzúua; ápiră 3 *sg*;
(*of pimples*) scot; **Pimples have ~ed on my face** Scoş gărnúță; (a)n-
dzămédz; **Several drops of blood ~ed** Născânte chícute di sândze
ndzămără; (*to seem*); **in order for him to ~ handsome** ca si si-aspúnă
lărgóñu; (*as of an omen*) **A great sign ~ed to me** Ñ-si-aspúse sémnu
máre; **It ~ed in front of him** Ľ-si spúse dinínte; **Three women ~ed to
the boy** Ľ-si furnisíră a ficiórlui trei muľérĭ; **It ~ed in his dream**
Ľ-si fărnisí tu yis; (*to seem to be*) adúc → APPEARANCE

APPEARANCE *s.* videáre, vidzútă; fáță; suréte; *Tir:* asurétă; aúmbră, prep, priep; strañu; **from ~** la videáre (*or* tu vidzútă); **At the
first ~ it seemed to be silver** S-păreá la videáre di-asíme că vrea
híbă; **He has the ~ of a man** Are vidzútă di bărbát; **He had the ~ of
a prince** Aveá aúmbră di hiľu di dómnu; **From ~s and from his way of**

speaking he seemed to be from Veria (*a town in N. Greece*) Tu prep ş-tu cuvéndă aduţeá viryeán

APPEASE *vb.* apreaadún, apreadún, mbun, ambún, mbunédz; (*as one's hungar*) căléscu ‖ *Cru:* arăzbún, GOLAB 201

APPEASED *adj.* a(ră)sbunát, isihăsít, agălisít

APPEASEMENT *s.* agălisíre, isihăsíre

APPETITE *s.* órixe; **to dampen smb.'s ~** taľu tăcátea ‖ ñ-si tăľé órixea (*lit. 'my ~ has been cut [short]'*), PARALLELE 153

APPETIZER *s.* mizé

APPETIZING *adj.* nóstim, *m pl* -tiñ, *f pl* -time → TASTY

APPLAUD *vb.* plăscănéscu pălñile

APPLE *s.* mer *n*, meáre *pl*; múză; **wild ~** ayrómbul, *N:* agrómin; (*a certain variety of ~*) thiríchiu → ADAM'S ~ ‖ *Rod:* miér, B-ARCH 57

APPLE-TREE *s.* mer, *dim.* miríc, miríciu; **wild ~** ayrómbal ‖ ALIA 58: pom di meáre, améru ‖ *Rod:* miér, B-ARCH 58

APPLICATION *s.* (*request, petition*) (a)rugiuhále, argiuhále, aruzuvále; (*applying, putting, superposing*) băgáre; apuneáre, apúnire; **practical ~** píră

APPLY *vb.* apún, bag; **We are going to ~ leeches to him** Va-ľ băgăm avdhéle

APPLY ONESELF TO *vb.* cilistiséscu, cealăhtiséscu, pidhipséscu

APPOINT *vb.* (*to hire, to be hired*) ▾bag, ▾ndreg, ▾păitéscu, puitéscu, ▾zburăscu

APPROACH *vb.* apróchiu

APPORTION *vb.* mpártu

APPRAISE *vb.* → VALUE

APPREHEND *vb.* (*to grasp*) apúc, acáţ, (a)nciúp (*and* angiúp) → UNDERSTAND, PERCEIVE

APPREHENSION *s.* andírse → FEAR, SHYNESS

APPRENTICE *s.* cir(e)ác, ciuráciu, câlfă, cálfă; múcio *invar.*

APPRISE *vb.* → INFORM

APPROPRIATE *adj.* (*fit, adequate*) uidisít → MAKE ~

APPROPRIATE *vb.* (*to take possession*) ľau ‖ (*to set aside for a specific use*) → pun nanăpárti, pun parámira PC *Brz*

APPROVAL *s.* vóľe; (*consent*) căpsíre, străxíre

APRICOT *s.* caísă, hérhică, heárhiră, heárhită, cheársică, dzârdzeále *f pl*; zárzălă, *pl* zărzeále; práscă, virucneáuă, *pl* virucnéi ‖ *Gop:* căĭsíi, GOLAB 224

APRICOT-TREE

APRICOT-TREE s. cáis, cheársic, heárhic, hérhic, heárhir, heárhit, virúche f, virúchiu m, virucnéu m, virucheáuă

APPROACH vb. apróchiu; ~ **kindly** ľau cu búnlu ‖ (to come closer to) LITURG 124: 2 pl imper: apruchés-vă

APPROACHABLE adj. dóbru, m pl -bri, f pl -bre → GENTLE

APPROACHING s. aprucheáre

APPROPRIATE adj. uigúne invar; **it is** ~ acáţă, cádi 3 sg. impers. ‖ **it is not** ~ nu cádi, DIARO 193

APPROXIMATELY adv. ca; vâră, ca vâră; ~ **one month** ca vâră lúnă → ABOUT

APRIL s. apríl, apríliu, (a)prír, (a)priír

APRON s. poálă, fútă, futắ, néce, nécică [néĉ•kă], péce, mbrustélă, pistimále, bistimále, pudhyeáuă, pudeáo, puryeáuă, pureáuă; **Cru:** pişcimál

APPROVAL s. (consent) munăsípe

APT adj. ácşu → ABLE

AQUAFORTIS s. (nitric acid) ghizáp n, ghizápe f

AQUEDUCT s. ‖ **K:** apaduţitór, GOLAB 199

AQUILINE adj. (as of a nose) turnát

ARAB s. aráp, dim. arăpúş

ARABIAN HORSE s. cal arăpéscu

ARABIAN NIGHTS s. halimáuă f sg

ARBUTUS BERRY s. cumáră; **Smr:** cumăreáuă, cumureáuă

ARCH s. cubé, thol → VAULT

ARCHED adj. (vaulted, as of a forehead) ‖ DIAROM 142: gubilós (rare)

ARCHANGEL s. arhánghil

ARCHBISHOP s. arhiréu, mitrupulít, dhispóti [dhis•pótĭ] m, disputádz pl; coll. disputáme

ARCHED adj. (of smb.'s brow) gubilós

ARCHAEOLOGIST s. arhiológ

ARCHITECT s. arhitéctu

ARCHIVIST s. ‖ DIARO 72: arhiofílaxu

ARDENT adj. aprés, arăchít, azgutós, ncălurát, sértu, m pl -rţâ, f pl -rte; also sértic; sárpit, sărpit (and sâr-), sârpid

ARDOR s. cáfche, zési f

ARE vb. → BE

AREA s. loc → REGION

ARETE *s.* (*mountain*) múcľe

ARGILLACEOUS *adj.* → CLAYEY

ARGUE *vb.* mi ncaciu (cu) (*and* ngaciu); tăcânéscu, filunichiséscu

ARGUMENT *s.* strigáre → QUARREL

ARID *adj.* sec, *f* seácă, *pl m/f* seţĭ; sec gol (*sic*); (*as of a mountain*) stirnós, *f* -noáşă, *m pl* -nóşĭ, *f pl* -noáse

ARISTOCRACY *s.* dumnáme, beilíche, afindádz *pl*

ARISTOCRAT *s.* dómnu, *pl* dómñi; afindă *m*, afindoáñe *f*; arhúndu

ARISTOCRATIC *adj.* dumnéscu, -neáscă, -néşţâ, -néşti; arhundéscu

ARK *s.* cátrig, cátric

ARM[1] *s.* anat. braţ, *pl* bráţă ‖ **Cru:** anúmire, GOLAB 199

ARM[2] *s.* mil. ármă, *pl* árme *and* ármmate → TAKE ~S

ARM ONESELF *vb.* armătuséscu

ARMCHAIR *s.* cathédră ‖ **Cru:** polithróne, GOLAB 244

ARMED *adj.* armătusít

ARMED FORCES *s.* sifére

ARMFUL *s.* (*as of firewood*) braţ, brăţát, bărţát, surghíţ; (*the distance from one arm to the other*) uryíe, urghíe

ARMISTICE *s.* paidós *invar.*

ARMPIT *s.* soáră, sumsoáră, sunsoáră ‖ ALIA 164: sumsór, sumăsoáră, supsóri [sup•sórĭ], măľisát

ARMY *s.* oáste, *pl* oştĭ (*1 syll.*); aschére, urdíe (*and* urdhíe), strató, *pl* stratévmate; (*standing army*) sifére ‖ CUVATA 20: vóină

ARMY STOREKEEPER *s.* zapită

AROMA *s.* aroámă, árumă, *pl* árume *or* arómate

AROMANIAN *s.* arămăn; *N:* armăn, rămăn; *Tur:* (*self-designation*) vlah; (*Grecized* ~) gărăgún; *coll.* armănáme (*and* armâ-); armăníľe; gărăgunáme; (*nickname given by Albanians*) gog *or* gógă; (*the ~ language*) armăneáşte (*and* armă-), vlăheáşte; **He spoke ~ well** Zbură ghíne armăneáştile; **He answered back in ~** Ľ-u turnă armăneáşte

AROMANIAN *adj.* armânéscu (*and* armă-), rămănéscu, vlăhéscu

AROUND *adv.* anvarlíga, anvărlíga, nvarlíga, nvărlíga, divarlíga; dinvărlíga, văríga, vărlígalui; **all ~** di túte părţâle ‖ LITURG 124: amvrígalui

AROUND *prep.* navărlíga di, divărlíga di, vărlíga di, divarlígalui

AROUND-THE-CLOCK *adv.* dzúua ş-noáptea

AROUSAL *s.* apríndire, aprindeáre, azgănipsíre

AROUSE *vb.* aríndu, scol, azgănipséscu

ARRANGE *vb.* (a)ndrég, (â)ndrég; bag di cále; arădhăpséscu, ară-dhyi(p)séscu; **He was arranging the stones** Chéţârle li-arădhăpseá; ‖ *Cru:* iduséscu, GOLAB 221

ARRANGEMENT *s.* (*setting in order*) (a)ndreádzire, ndridzeáre, rădhyipsíre; (*order*) arádhă, nizáme; *G:* udópsu; (*secret* ~, *scheme*) dhóhă, dhóhe

ARREAR *s.* aréstu, cusúre

ARREST *s.* acăţáre

ARREST *vb.* → APPREHEND, STOP, TAKE IN CUSTODY

ARRIVAL[1] *s.* agiúmtă, agiúndzire, agiundzeáre, vinítă, yinítă, vi-níre, vineáre

ARRIVAL[2] *s.* (*one who moves to another village*) iabangíu

ARRIVE *vb.* agiúngu, acáţ; **He ~ed in the mountains** Si-acáţă di múnţâ; **to ~ at dawn** tăhinipséscu, tuhi- ‖ (*to ~ in a hurry or un-expectedly*) chic (*lit.* '*to fall*') **He ~d to Bucharest unexpectedly** Chică Bucuréştiḽi! PARALLELE 137

ARROGANCE *s.* fuduleáţă, furţuíre, fálă → PRIDE

ARROGANT *adj.* mărít, fudúl, fudulít, fălít, furduít, furţuít, făndăxít, daí *invar.*, daítcu, *m pl* daítţi; ciom, *f* ciómă, *m pl* cĭoñ, *f pl* cióme; arâñós, cămărusít, pirifán, sirbés, -béz; (*dignified*) pitrít; **to become ~** (*to give oneself airs*) li ngroş lúcrili

ARROGATE *vb.* arúc cătuhíe (pri) ‖ CUNIA 287: (a)ncálic

ARROW *s.* sădzeátă (*and* săzeá-), sudzeátă; săyítă, săítă, gilít, gilitúră; (*the* ~ *of a scale*) muciúc

ARSENIC *s.* áxif

ARSENIC ACID *s.* afrát

ARTESIAN WELL *s.* şitrăváne

ARTFUL *adj.* cumalíndru, *m pl* -índri; hítru, *m pl* -ţrâ, *f pl* -tre; píspu, *m pl* píschi, *f pl* píspe; puniripsít; (*foxy*) mástorsă *f*

ARTFULNESS *s.* (*refinement*) micáme; (*craftness*) şiretlâche

ARTHRITIS *s.* rumaticó

ARTICHOKE *s.* anghináre

ARTICULATE *adj.* (*usu. of speech*) ligát

ARTICULATION *s.* *anat.* prinód

ARTIFICE *s.* dhóhe → SCHEME

ARTILLERYMAN *s.* tupcí

ARTISTICALLY *adv.* chibăréşte ‖ cu art, HRISTU 1 *and* cu artu 4; **very ~** cu multu art, HRISTU 5

ARTISTRY *s.* micáme ‖ art, HRISTU 1

ARUM *s. bot.* călcádză

AS *cj.* (*comparison*) ca; ~ **black ~ coal** laiu ca tucínile; (*in the same manner*) ~ **they came, so they left** Cum viñíră, acşí s-dúsiră; (*while*) ~ **they were leaving** cum si duţeá; (*instead of*) trâ; ~ ... **so cáta** ... şi *or* cată şi ‖ cacúm, LITURG 125: **as in heaven, also upon earth** cacúm ţéru aşắţi şắ pi lócu; (*since*) **Av:** únă ţe, BASME 502

AS COMPARED TO spróti; ~ **the horse the mule is smaller** Spróti cálu múla eáste ma ñícă

AS FAR AS *prep.* până di

AS FAR AS ONE CAN SEE *adv.* ‖ cât veáde albul soáre (*lit.* 'as far as the white sun can see') BASME 102

AS FULL AS AN EGG *adj.* dínga, dén-, dân-; ndisát → BRIMFUL, FULL TO CAPACITY

AS FOR di; ~ **length, it is not so long** Di lúngu nu-i ahât lúngu

AS HARD AS ONE CAN LICK *adv.*: **to run** ~ (Fug) ca tórnic, ca (a)n-dórnic

AS HUCKLEBERRIES *adv.* cu mnáta

AS IF *cj.* cánda (că); ca cându, mápari [má•pari], maspár, sánchi, táha, táxi că; ~ **it were of copper** cánda că erá di hálcumă; **He behaves ~ he grew up in the woods** Si poártă ca cându criscú tu pădúre ‖ ghióia *or* ghioáia, CAPIDAN 504

AS IF ON PURPOSE ‖ CUVATA 7: ca ti ináti .

AS LIKE AS TWO PEAS ‖ DIARO 29: bitiví *m*, bitivíi [•ví•i] *f*, bitivíi [•víĭ] *pl*; *also* bitivítcu

AS LONG AS *adv.* (*temporal*) ‖ BATSARIA 70: păn-cându

AS LONG AS *cj.* (*since*) ‖ **Av:** únă ţe, BASME 502

AS SOON AS *adv.* cum; di cum; cárea, cária, cât, íţe, íţi, íţişĭ, ma; ~ **they saw her they kidnapped her** Cum u vidzúră, cum u arăchíră; ~ **love appeared** di cum andzắmă sivdắlu; cât loai să; ~ **night fell** câtu ntunicá; (*immediately after*) ~ **he comes, call me!** Ama că va s-yínă, grea-ñ! únă (+ *verbal noun*): ~ **he entered the door** únă intrátă di la úşe ‖ ~ **he saw him, he recognized him** Ma-l vidzú l-cunoscú, BASME 9

AS THOUGH *cj.* táha → AS IF

AS WELL *adv.* ómña ‖ ómia; anghióre, CAPIDAN 504-5

AS YET *adv.* tóra di tóra; di oáră; până tru hópa aístă

ASCEND

ASCEND *vb.* alín

ASCENSION *s.* al(i)náre, sculáre, análipse

ASCENT *s.* (*as of a mountain*) alináre, alnáre, anífur (*ant.* catífur); aráp; sculáre

ASH *s.* cinúşe, scrum; (*~ mixed with live coals*) sprúnă, spúză; *N:* spúră, spúrnă

ASHAMED *adj.* (a)ruş(i)nát, (a)rşunát, antirisít (*and* andirsít), antirsít; aruştít → BE ~

ASH GATHERER *s.* cinuşár

ASH-TREE *s.* frápsin, thrápsu; (*~ with red leaves*) c̦imbúciu; *coll.* frăpsinét, frăpsináme

ASHY *adj.* (*gray, as of wool*) săín, *m pl* -íñ, *f pl* -íne

ASIDE *adv.* di ună párte; parámira

ASININE *adj.* glăréscu, *f* -reáscă, *m pl* -réşțâ, *f pl* -réşti

ASK *vb.* (*to inquire*) (a)ntréb, ântréb; **If she asks about me ...** Si ntribáre ea trâ míne...; (*to consult*) **Ask even your walking stick!** (*i.e, Do not hesitate to ask*) Ş-cu cârlígu-ț s-ti-ntréghi [stin• tréǵ]; **~ a riddle** bag nă angucitoáre; (*to demand, to beg, to implore*) țer, (a)ór; **I ~ you not to anger me** Vă or nu mi cărtíț; rog (*obsolescent*); părăcălséscu, pălăcărséscu, părlăcăséscu, cáftu; **What are you ~ing from me?** Di la míne țe căftáț? (*to call, to request*) dimândédz; **~ them to surrender!** Dimândáț-lă si si nclínă; **~ a favor** (ț-) fac (a)rigeáie; fac (únă) dimândăciúne; (ț-) cad cu máre părăcălíe ‖ *P:* ndreb, SarD 82; *Cru:* mulăéscu, mulu-, GOLAB 236

ASK COUNSEL OF SMB. *vb.* ‖ ĺ-cáftu míntea, BASME 10

ASK FOR ADVICE *vb.* mi ntreb cu

ASK FOR FORGIVENESS *vb.* âñ ĺau ĺirtáre; mi simbățéscu ‖ CUNIA 133: âñ cáftu ĺirtáre

ASK FOR IT *vb.* (*to trail one's cloak*) u cáftu (ngăceárea) cu luminárea

ASK FOR PERMISSION *vb.* cáftu vóĺe, ĺau mâna a, ĺau izíne; **He went to ask for the emperor's permission** Dúse s-ĺa mâna a amirălui

ASK FOR SMB. IN MARRIAGE *vb.* ‖ **They asked for Gina in marriage** U câftárâ Gína nveástâ, DIARO 208

ASK FOR TROUBLE *vb.* ñ-bag cáplu tu tástru (*lit. 'to put one's head in a satchel'*)

ASK SMB.'S PARDON *vb.* → ASK FOR FORGIVENESS

ASKANCE *adv.* şubeilâtic

ASKEW *adv.* parámira ‖ CUNIA 221: na-năpárti

ASLANT *adv.* pládea, (a)mplátea (*and* ambládea), plainá; **The thieves ran away aslant** Fúriľi [fúrĭ•ľi] loáră ambládea

ASLEEP → FALL ~

ASPARAGUS *s.* spărángă

ASPECT *s.* vidzútă, suréte, ópse, ceahré, strañu ‖ HRISTU 1: **with the ~ of** cu fisi di → APPEARANCE, FACE

ASPHYXIATE *vb.* asfixédz

ASPHYXIATED *adj.* asfixát *and* -xít

ASPHYXIA *s.* asfixíre, asfixíe

ASPIC *s.* (*a cold dish with meat and vegetables*) pihtíe; plíhtumă, păcé (*and* pâ-)

ASS¹ *s.* yumár, tar, tăróñu, câciu, uricľát, **N:** urincľát; (*of people*) zdânglâră

ASS² *s. anat.* cur, *dim.* curéciu, şidzút, primichír, bis, ghes, fândâc, cărtéľu; (*usu. in children's talk*) cuciu

ASSASSIN *s.* catíle *invar.*

ASSASSINATE *vb.* uţíd → KILL

ASSAULT *s.* năválă, sărghíre, cităsíre, himusíre, anăpădíre, (a)urñíre; (y)irúse, (y)iurúse, (y)irúşe, (y)iurúşe

ASSEMBLAGE *s.* (*gathering*) adunătúră → ASSEMBLY, MEETING

ASSEMBLE *vb.* ▾adún; *1 pl:* adunăm *and* annăm; *2 pl:* adunáţ *and* annáţ (*of sheep*) mârşin *or* mârşinédz

ASSEMBLY *s.* adunáre, cumşóñe, diváne, giumaéte [ĝu•ma•é•ti], giumăiéte [•ié•], chinótită, sobór

ASSENT *vb.* → AGREE

ASSERT *vb.* ţân (că)

ASSERTION *s.* dzâcă

ASSESSMENT *s.* (*as of a tax*) munăsípe

ASSIGN *vb.* sémnu, simnédz, nsimnédz; (*as a salary*) taľu → ESTABLISH

ASSIGNMENT *s.* (*task*) mândátă

ASSIST *vb.* → HELP

ASSISTANT *s.* dhyeavér, dhyeaverán

ASSOCIATE *vb.* apríND aluáturile (cu), acáţ aluáturile (cu) ‖ (*to make friends with*) mi fac soţ (cu), BASME 802; **We do not ~, We do not socialize together** Nu făţém cású deadún (*lit.* 'We do not make house together'), PARALLELE 125

ASSOCIATED

ASSOCIATED *adj.* *I am ~ with* hiu únă cu; **They were ~ with the bandits** Erá únă cu aţéľ di a noáptiľei

ASSOCIATION *s.* suţátă, cumbaníe, ităríe ‖ DIARO 86: suţáľi *f*, frâţâľi *f*

ASSORT *vb.* alég, uidiséscu, iduséscu, tiryiséscu

ASSORTMENT *s.* (*as of clothes*) tăcâme; (*arrangement in groups according to established criteria*) uidisíre, tiryisíre

ASSUAGE *vb.* isihăséscu, agăliséscu

ASSUME *vb.* (*of a title*) ľau; **~ airs** li trag groáse → GIVE ONESELF AIRS

ASSURANCE *s.* siyuripsíre, siyurlíche

ASSURE *vb.* asfălséscu, săylămséscu, (a)siyuripséscu

ASSURED *adj.* asfălisít ‖ HRISTU 35: (*safe*) asfilisit

ASSUREDLY *adv.* mútlac

ASTER *s.* *bot.* flóra a Paştilui

ASTHMA *s.* ângúsă, ngústă

ASTONISH *vb.* mărmuriséscu, mărmurâséscu → AMAZE

ASTONISHED *adj.* apurisít, cihtisít, ciuduít, ciudisít, limnusít, ñirát, mărmurisít, sfuldziát, sfulguít, uiñisít, uñít ‖ BASME 25: agudít ca di sfúlgu (*lit.* 'as if hit by lightning'); BASME 325: ca agudít di chícută; BELIMACE 9: ndilisít

ASTONISHMENT *s.* apuríe, apurisíre, cĭudíe, mărmurisíre, ngurdíre, ñiráre, thăvmusíre, uñisíre; *N:* toáfe, tuáfe *invar.*; **restrain one's ~** âñ ţân apuría

ASTOUND *vb.* → ASTONISH

ASTOUNDED *adj.* ndărsít → DIZZY

ASTRAY *adv.* alăthipsít, ftisít

ASTRIDE *adj.* discăcărát

ASTRIDE OF *prep.* călár (pri); **He was ~ his chestnut horse** Sta-n călár pri ghióclu [ǵó•klu]

ASTRONOMER *s.* astronóm

ASTRONOMY *s.* astrunumíe

ASTUTE *adj.* → CLEVER, SHREWD

AT *prep.* (*on the day of*) la, ti; **~ noon** ti prândzu oáră; tu; **~ eight o'clock** tu óptule; (*when, after*) tru, tu; **~ his return from the sheep** tru turnáta di la oi; **~ his departure** tu fúgă; (*to or toward the direction of*) câtră la; **He is looking ~ my in-law** mutreáşte câtrâ la cúscra; (*against*) prísti; pi; **He rushed blindly ~**

him Prísti nâs si-arúcă zúrlu; **Because of that he was angry ~ the girl** Di aéstă hirbeá pi feátă

AT ALL adv. can, dip, di-a dip, dot; *N:* hici; cât ghitríşca, cât trâ yitríe, iuvá ş-iuvá, şcrau; (*of money*) tiniché; **I am not going to be quiet** ~ Nu tac ş-dip (PC: [jdip]); **He is not choosing anything** ~ țevá di dip nu aleádze; **We do not understand** ~ Cât ghitríşca nu achicăsím; **He did not speak Latin** ~ Nu şcrăpuiá can latineásca; (*of a foreign language*) níți élif be; di-a-cutótalui, dicutót; **The wool has not been carded** ~ Lâna nu-i dot scărminátă ‖ hir, iciu, sărmă, CAPIDAN 504; *F:* dot, DIARO 77; VELO 106: di dibidús

AT ANY PRICE ‖ DIARO 241: cum-di-cum

AT LEAST báre, bári, bárim, mácar, macárim, măcár, mácă, cánim; *N:* canáe, canái, cánai-că; *S:* can; **~ I married a woman who is the way I wished her to be** Loai feátă, canáe, aşí cum vream; **If you break your fast, ~ eat lamb!** Máca ti purínțâ, mâcă cánim ñeì! ‖ BELIMACE 86: bar

AT ONCE adv. dinăcále. di nă oáră, tu oáră; **It used to be done ~, that very second** S-fățeá tu oáră, tu ațeá minútă

AT ONE'S OWN SWEET WILL ‖ STERGHIU 11: cum ță tálí míntea

ATHEISTIC adj. athéu *m*, athéă *f*; *m pl* athéi, *f pl* athée

ATHWART adv. amplátea, dhiplá

ATHWART prep. cóntră (*and* cóndră) cu

ATMOSPHERE s. aéră, atmusféră

ATOM: not an ~ cât trâ hitríe, cât ghitrúşca → AT ALL

ATOP adv. and prep. (*on top of*) di súpră, pri súpră

ATROCIOUS adj. crud, -dă, -dz, -de; arău, *f* aráuă, *m pl* arăi, *f pl* arále; ni-ñilós, -oásă, -óşi, -oáse

ATROCITY s. ni-ñílă

ATTACH vb. (*to put, to hang*) chic; **He ~ed the sword to her neck** âl̦ chică apála di gúşe ‖ (*to pay attention*) bag oáră (*with dat.*), HRISTU 30

ATTACK s. (a)urñíre

ATTACK vb. (*with stones*) ambuliséscu → FIGHT

ATTAIN vb. aséscu, agiúngu; **to ~ one's end** (a)pugudéscu

ATTAINMENT s. → ACHIEVEMENT

ATTEMPT s. cătăpățíre, dhuchimăsíre

ATTEMPT vb. cătăpățéscu, dhuchimăséscu

ATTEND vb. (*to accompany*) fac suțátă; (*to escort, to see*) pitréc;

ATTENDANCE

(*to look after*) mutréscu, câştighédz ‖ CUVATA 7: **to ~ to one's business** ñ-mutréscu lúcurlu

ATTENDANCE *s.* câştigáre → DANCE ATTENDANCE TO SMB/SMTH.

ATTENTION *s.* (*applying the mind to an object*) méngă; (*care*) (a)ngătán, ângătán, mutrítă; (*consideration, mindfulness*) usúle ‖ **Cru:** dicáte, GOLAB 211 → SHOW SMB. MUCH ~

ATTENUATE *vb.* minutédz, minuţăscu; scad; slăghéscu, sclăghéscu

ATTESTATION *s.* (*proof*) imzáe, *pl.* imzăi

ATTIC *s.* hátule ‖ **Peş:** dăváne, CL 44

ATTIRE *s.* stólidhă, stulídhă

ATTITUDE *s.* (*posture*) purtátic

ATTITUDINIZE *vb.* fac gilfédz

ATTORNEY *s.* avucát, dhichiyór

ATTRACT *vb.* (*to beguile*) plănăséscu; (*impers., usu. in negative phrases*) (nu) mi ncăldzáşte ‖ BASME 426: ñ-fáţe cu ócĭul; ALR 1348: (*as a dog, by showing it a piece of bread*) Angán cânli c-ună cumátă di páni

ATTRACTIVE *adj.* arâsít; nóstim, *m pl* -tiñ, *f pl* -time; pălít

AUBERGINE *s.* pitligeánă, pâtlâgeánă

AUCTION *s.* vindeáre, víndire

AUDACIOUS *adj.* curajlí → BOLD, BRAVE

AUDACITY *s.* fidănlâche, cutidzáre

AUGMENT *vb.* măréscu, adávgu → ADD

AUGURY: of good ~ ugúre *invar.* **Meeting him was of good ~** âñ işí ugúre n cále

AUGUST *s.* águstu, ávyustu

AUNT *s.* ţáţă, tétă, dódă

AURORA *s.* hărghíe, hăryíe → DAWN

AUSTER *s.* (*a wind blowing from the south*) iug, not

AUTHENTIC *adj.* alithhiós (*sic*); di tamamá; (*perfect*) tamamaná, ynisíu; (*genuine*) sayláme *invar.*

AUTHORITY *s.* (*police*) zabitlăcă; (**power**) exusíe; **on good ~** (am) ápă di la múmă ‖ iuchiuméte [iu•k'u•mé•ti], BASME 277

AUTHORIZATION *s.* (*permission*) tischiré(e), trat; (*formerly*) rusatnaméi → PERMISSION

AUTUMN *s.* toámnă → FALL

AUTUMNAL *adj.* di toámnă, tumnátic, tumnăréscu, tunăréscu, tumníş

AUTUMNAL SEASON *s.* (*from a shepherd's viewpoint*) tumnátic

AVAIL: chirútă; **All he did was to no ~** Íți feáțe fu chirútă ‖ CUVATA 3: **tears were of no ~** lăcărñili nu fățeá țivá

AVALANCHE s. (of snow) **Băi:** rungă

AVARICE s. sclinceáme → STINGINESS

AVENGE vb. ▼arăzgán; âñ ľau áhtea, ñ-scot áhtea, ñ-scot arăzgánlu, ñ-ľau sândzile, ľ-u scot prit nări, ľ-u scot análma prit gúră; **N:** mi ascúmpăr; **You should ~ me!** S-mi ascúmpări! **We are ~d!** Nă scoásim áhtea!

AVERAGE adj. nólgic; (common) paráspur

AVERSION s. límă

AVID adj. **be ~** nu am sat di, nu am sátru di → GREEDY

AVOID vb. amfiréscu, afiréscu; **~ like a pest house** fug ca u-vréulu di cărăvídhă; fug ca di per di lup; fac ilealá (di); âñĭ dau limăreáua (di); dau dabóga (di); impers. s-țâ dai cămeáşa (i.e., it is better to renounce even your shirt in order to ~ danger)

AVOW vb. dzâc fanirá

AWAIT vb. aştéptu, apăndăxéscu

AWAKE adj. (not sleeping any longer) sculát, diştéptu, diştiptát

AWAKE vb. diştéptu ‖ **Cru:** mi discéptu, GOLAB 212

AWAKING s. diştiptáre, diştiptátă

AWARD vb. dau nişáne; **to be awarded** ľau nişáne

AWARE adj. ‖ **I am ~** ñ-u am míntea; **I am fully ~** éscu cu tútâ míntea, DIARO 289

AWAY adj., adv. dipárte, náparti, lárgu

AWAY interj. **~ with you!** Adúnă-u di auá! → GET LOST!

AWFUL adj. lăhtărós, f -roásă, m pl -róşĭ, f pl -roáse

AWKWARD adj. astângu, m pl -ndzi; stângáciu (ant. driptáciu); zérvu, m pl -ryi, f sg -rvă, f pl -rve

AWL s. súlă, țângârsúlă, țungursúlă, țungrusúlă

AXE s. tupór, tăpór, tupoáră, tupoáre, tăpoáre, țupátă; dim. tupuráț, tâpuríc, țupătíce; **Băi:** ľátă

AZURE s., adj. (as of the sky) albástru, -stră, -ştri, -stre

B

BAA *interj.* (*of goats*) mea; (*of sheep*) bea

BABBLE *vb.* (*to talk idly*) băbăléscu, dărdăréscu (*and* dârdă-), discântu, máţin (pi virisíe); *3 sg* dâr-dâr gúra ľ-si dúţe

BABBLER *s.* băbăľár, dârdâră, dârdârós, fafaľán, farafúră, fărfár, farfará, fărfără

BABBLING *s.* (*of people*) dârdâr(s)íre, poliloyíe; (*chatting*) láfe, lăcărdíe (*and* lăcâr-), lăpărdíe; (*of birds*) pilidáre; (*of infants*) guguráre

BABEL *s.* → HUBBUB, UPROAR

BABUSHKA *s.* bálţu, dărmă, dártumă

BABY *s.* beb, *pl* bebi (*The DDA cautions: not* beghĭ!) *m*, bébă *f*; ciuciu, cópan, *N:* gad, gat; fet, ficiuríc, luţ, nat, ñic, níphiu [níp•hiu], ñac, ñat, ñiţicó; (*before baptism*) pij *m*, píjă *f*; sărmăníţă, ţup, *pl* ţuchi [tuk']; *Nic:* (*baby girl*) púpă ‖ pup, CAPIDAN 149; STERE 14: técnu

BACHELOR *s.* bicheár; *derog.* mărtătór → SINGLE ‖ DIARO 198: câlúgâr, calóyir

BACHELOR'S BUTTON *s. bot.* zărzăríche

BACK *s. anat.* schináre, schinărát; plătáre, păltáre, pultáre; spálă; (*in a children's game*) lásă-spátă; (*middle of the ~*) crúţe; *on the ~* ncrâşca (*and* ngrâşca); **at the ~ of beyond** dúpă soáre; tu ascápitlu a lóclui; iu bea púľi ápă → BREAK ONE'S ~

BACK *vb.* andrupăscu, ţân, agiút, dau mână di agiutór

BACK DOWN *vb.* frângu năpói

BACK UP *vb.* ‖ (*to retreat*) mi strag; *2 pl imper.* Strădzeţ-vă! HRISTU 34

BACK *adv.* năpói; **~ and forth** năpói ş-năínte; *F:* pi-aroá, pi-arcó → FALL ~

BACKBITE *vb.* cacuzburăscu

BACKBONE *s. anat.* schinărát

BACKGAMMON-BOARD *s.* táblă

BACKWARD(S) *adv.* napudhíşalui, năpu-; **go backward(s)** cătră năpói; ca cávurlu; anáschila

BACON *s.* (*fat bits of pork*) ţiyărídhă (*and* tiyărídă); *Cľis:* pisurídă

BAD adj. (wrong, vicious, lousy, ugly) (a)rău, f (a)ráŭă, m pl (a)răĭ, f pl arále; also: ca vai di míni, ca vai di tíni, etc; chiutandál; nibún, pabés, s(c)lab, m pl s(c)laghi, f pl slábe; sab, f sábă, pl m saghi, f pl sábe;; uchinát; ~ **people** bicimsâj [•sâž] oámiñ ‖ **I feel** ~ Ñ-u arău, BA 6; ~ **person** ínimă láie, BASME 346

BAD HABIT s. tăbiéte → HABIT

BAD LUCK s. anapudhíľe, tirsilâche

BAD TEMPER s. sisimlâche

BADGER s. zool. ázvu, baľadós; **Cru:** dzóyiur; yédzăre, yédzură ‖ **Lvz:** dzóyiură; **GSus:** brâsúc, CL 39; **G:** zóyiar, zóyir, SarD 34; **Kёrb:** dozbáľt; **Bil:** baľdósâ, cunávă; **Pls:** palidósâ, NEIESCU 142

BADGER vb. nu dau bánă, scăñiséscu, acáţ limăreáua

BADINAGE s. şuguíre

BADLY adv. (a)rău; also: ahamná; ca vai di míne; ghíne (lit. 'well'; **The rain soaked us** ~ Nă udă ghíne ploáia

BAFFLE vb. cărşilătiséscu

BAG s. sac m; also: búrdhă, hărár, săcúľu, tástru; (as for carrying food) **G:** târváciu, tărváş; vúryă; **with** ~ **and baggage** cu síndu cu pándu ‖ **Cru:** púngă, GOLAB 246

BAGATELLE s. → TRIFLE

BAGEL s. clúră; ghivréc, ghiuvréc

BAGGAGE s. călăbălâche, cătăndíe → BAG

BAGPIPE s. gáidă

BAIL[1] s. (security) bifă, chifíle, chifiliméi [ki•fi•li•mé•i]

BAIL[2] s. (handle) mănúşe, turtoáre

BAIT s. căpáne → TRAP

BAKE vb. coc, aor. cópşu, part. cóptu; **The bread is not ~ed; it is not done** Pânea nu s-coápse, eásti yíi; (~ in hot ashes) sprunédz

BACKBONE s. anat. cătínă, schinărát

BAKER s. cilipár, ciripár; furnagí, furnăgí, furnucíu, furnár; psumă; (~ of pretzels, etc.) covrigár ‖ pânár, CAPIDAN 149; **Cru:** cilipár, GOLAB 210

BAKER'S PROFESSION s. cilipârlâche

BAKERY GOODS s. cilipârlâche

BAKING s. (of bread, etc.) coáţire, cuţeáre

BAKING OVEN s. → FURNACE ‖ **K:** ciriáp, GOLAB 210

BAKING PLATE s. siníe, tăpsíe, tipsíe, tâvă (and tăvă)

BALANCE *s.* cântáre (*and* căntáre, căndáre); palándză, pălándză; statéră, statíre; tirizíe, zíyă ‖ (*large ~*) **Prv, SJos:** plastíngă, CL 259 **to lose one's ~** *vb.* păléscu

BALANCE *vb.* → WEIGH

BALCONY *s.* balcóne, cirdáche → TERRACE

BALD *adj.* chiléş; *also:* cálvu, *pl m* -lyi; chel, *f* chélă (*sic*), *m pl* cheľ, *f pl* chéle; chirós; şúplid, -pliv, *f* -vă, *m pl* -pliyĭ, *f pl* -plive; *3 sg:* áre lúnă n cap ‖ **Amc:** fără peri, SCHL 114; ALIA 146: bel, bilít; falacró, falácru, falávcu; gol, şut, urdát, zarcuchéfalu

BALD SUMMIT *s.* gól(i)nă; (*~ of a hill*) acâre

BALDACHIN *s.* (*a rich embroidered fabric*) cuvúcľu

BALDERDASH *s.* → NONSENSE

BALE *s.* bal, hărár, hăráie

BALEFUL *adj.* lăhtărós, *f* -oásă, *m pl* -óşĭ, *f pl* -oáse

BALLYHOO *s.* giufă

BALK *s.* (*as a support in a wall*) dhémă

BALK *vb.* cărşilătiséscu

BALL *s.* (*spherical body*) bel, *pl.* beále; (*~ of food, paper, cotton, etc.*) arómbu; gumóľi, gumúľu; toc, top; (*of thread*) gľem, gľom; (*of snow, of gold, etc.*) zbúldzu; (*toy*) ansăritoáre, şúcă, **S:** tópă, **N:** tópcă → CLEW

BALL OF FIRE *s.* şpírtu

BALLYHOO *vb.* alávdu

BALONEY *s.* bişíñ di cuc, *pl* (*lit. 'cuckoo's farts'*) → NONSENSE

BALSAM *s.* bálsam, bálsan

BAMBOOZLE *vb.* ncálţu, fac tirtípe → DECEIVE

BAN *vb.* nu alás, nu dau voľe, nu dau vólă; zăptăséscu

BAND *s.* (*strap*) ghíncală, yínglă; (*strip of fabric or leather*) lurídhă; (*group*) plătúră, tăbúre; (*~ of musicians*) bándă, múzică ‖ HRISTU 38: cetă ('group')

BANDAGE *s.* peática, fáşe

BANDAGE *vb.* leg; **~ed his wound** (C-únă peática) ľ-ligă arána

BANDIT *s.* caceác → BRIGAND

BANDY-LEGGED *adj.* discăcărát

BANE *s.* (*poison*) fărmác, virín; (*misfortune*) pácus, uryíe

BANG *s.* agudíre, plăscăníre

BANG *vb.* (*a door, an adversary, etc.*) agudéscu, luvéscu; plăscănéscu, zdupănéscu → HIT, STRIKE

BANG! tâc!

BANGLE s. mănóchir (and mâ-), haimalí, haimalâ, haimaní, haima(n)líe

BANG-UP adj. → EXCELLENT

BANISH vb. agunéscu, ayunéscu, azgunéscu; xinumséscu

BANISHED adj. a(z)yunít, xinumsít

BANISHMENT s. aurláre; ayuníre, azguníre; xinumsíre

BANK[1] s. (as along a river) mal ‖ MERCA 7: ameál; **G, M:** meal, SarD 27; Brâncus could not obtain mal 'bank' in ALB (**Dren, Kёrb, Pe, Pёr, Sln**)

BANK[2] (financial institution) báncă

BANK[3] s. (mass) cup → PILE

BANKRUPT adj. muflúz, m pl -lújĭ; mufluzít, mufluzipsít

BANKRUPT vb. făľurséscu

BANKRUPTCY s. faliméntu, făľursíre, mufluz(ips)íre, mufluzlắche

BANNER s. bandéră, flam(b)úră; **church** ~ sígne → FLAG

BANQUET s. cimbúze, giumbúse, uspéţ; (~ given by the parents of the bride eight days after the wedding party) mbăryíce, băryíc, păryíce, păryíţă; (~ given three days after the birth of a child) puguníc

BANQUETTE s. báncă

BANTER s. arâdeáre, arâdire; mbizuíre, mbizuitúră; şuguíre, şúpur, şupuráre

BANTER vb. şupurédz, şuguéscu → RIDICULE

BANTERING s. arâdeáre, măitápe, mbizuíre, péză

BANTLING s. → CHILD

BAPTISM s. pătidzáre, bătigiúne

BAPTIZE s. pătédz

BAPTIZED adj. pătidzát (ant. ni-pătidzát); (as of a Turk) niñiruít

BAPTIZER s. pătidzătór

BAR vb. (to forbid) nu alás → BAN

BAR SMB.'S WAY vb. ľ-taľu cálea

BARBARIAN s. várvar

BARBARIC adj. várvar

BARBARITY s. vărvăríľe

BARBEL s. ichth. bărbúne m, mreánă, breánă

BARBER *s.* barbér, birbér, bilbér

BARE *adj.* bilít, goáliş ‖ DIARO 388: (*empty*) dişértu

BARE *vb.* dizguléscu, biléscu

BAREFACED *adj.* fanirá *invar.*

BAREFACEDLY *adv.* fanirá, fára; ᴛᴜ fáţă

BAREFOOT *adj.* discălţát, discálţát, discúlţu, nincălţát, xipóltu

BAREHEADED *adj.* cu cáplu gol; discufusít; (cu cáplu) discufút

BARELY *adv.* ayeá, cu di-ayeá, cu di-ayía, (cu) adiyíe, ayía, cât-cât (*and* căt-cắt), mizíe; **They ~ remember** şi-adúc cu adiyíe amínte

BARENESS *s.* gulăciúne

BARGAIN *s.* (*negotiation*) păzáre, păzăripsíre; (*smth. acquired at a price advantageous to the buyer*) pleácică (*and* pľácică) [pleáĉ•kă] *or* [pľáĉ•kă] ‖ CARAFOLI 81: chilipúri → MAKE A GOOD ~

BARGAIN *vb.* păzăripséscu; **Better ~ing before than complaints after** Dicât zboáre năpói, ma ghíne păzáre năínte; (*to dicker, to haggle*) yiftuséscu

BARK[1] *s.* (*of dogs*) (a)lătráre (*and* alâ-)

BARK[2] *s.* (*of trees*) coáje; *Băi:* şcoárce

BARK[1] *vb.* (*of dogs*) (a)látru, bat; **The dog began to ~** Cânile acáţă s-bátă

BARK[2] *vb.* (*to peel off, as trees*) dizgóľu, disbiléscu

BARK UP THE WRONG TREE *vb.* ≈ u-adár taratóre

BARKEEPER *s.* ambirigí

BARKING *s.* (*as of trees*) disbilíre

BARLEY *s.* órdzu, hăsíľu ‖ ALIA 72: órzu; *Els:* orţ, ʙ-ᴀʀᴄʜ 72

BARN *s.* (*for animals, straw, etc.*) ahiroánă, pleánţă, tream ‖ *Av:* ahirónâ, ᴄʟ 36; *SJos:* cópă, ᴄʟ 42

BARRACKS *s.* câşlă

BARREL *s.* (*of a gun*) glup, ylup, nămlíe; (*cask*) varélă; (*small ~ for water and wine*) búclă, *dim.* buclíţă; búte, vóză

BARREN *adj.* stérpu, *m pl* stérchi, *f* steárpă, *pl f* steárpe; stirpuít; (*of sheep*) marmáră; *coll.* **~ sheep** *s.* stirpurét, stirpuríu; (*of soil*) hărhálă

BARRENS *s. pl* gulínă, gól(i)nă, acâre

BARTENDER *s.* ambirigí

BARTER *s.* trámpă (*and* trámbă)

BARTER *vb.* fac trámbă, fac tigiaréte [•ĝa•]

BASE *s.* (*main component*) múmă; **be off one's ~** zurluséscu

BASE *adj.* ápcu, *m pl* ápţi, *f pl* ápţe; átim, *m pl* átiñ, *f pl* átime; babés *or* pabés, *m pl* -béşĭ; próstih, *m pl* -hĭ; zgrumát

BASE *vb.* thimiľuséscu

BASEBORN *adj.* próstih

BASENESS *s.* şăneáţă → INFAMY

BASH *s.* (*blow*) goádă, agudtúră

BASH *vb.* → BEAT, STRIKE

BASHFUL *adj.* ar(u)şinós → BE ~

BASHFULNESS *s.* andírise → SHYNESS

BASIL *s. bot.* busiľóc, busuľóc, văsileác, văsilác, bizealóc

BASIN *s.* cuvátă, *dim.* cuvátícă, cuvátíce; *also:* cărnéciu (*and* câr-), cârníciu, chipinác

BASIS *s.* thiméľu

BASK IN THE SUN *vb.* nsurín, nsurinédz, nsurnédz

BASKET *s.* coş; căláthă, *dim.* călăthícă, -thíce; (*for shaping cheese*) căláthă di căşcavál; cănéstră, cănístră, cănistreálă, cărínă, căşúg; cufínă, -fíţă; cuşéľu, cuşór, cuşóre, cuşórā; yâlícă; (*made of rush*) zămbílă, zimbíle; **left in the** ~ (*i.e., a loser*) (Armân) ca găľína údă *or* (Armân) ca Sultána cu ucălu

BASKING IN THE SUN *s.* nsur(i)náre

BASSWOOD *s.* tiľu, lípă

BASTARD *s.* báştu, cópil, cupílciu, **N:** cochiu, *pl.* cochi; *also* cóchiul; copélă *f*; **F:** dociu; lud *m*, lúdă *f*; luţ; suisâz; (*a disagreeable person*) análut ‖ **Av:** băştárcu, CL 38

BASTE[1] *vb.* → BEAT

BASTE[2] *vb.* (*to sew provisionally*) căţéscu ‖ **SJos:** căséscu, CL 41

BASTING *s.* căţíre, şuláre

BAT[1] *s. zool.* bubureác, burduľác, dubărác; **Gop:** dubruľác; nihtiré, nihtirídhă, puľu di noápte, puľu di-a noáptiľei → HAVE ~S IN THE BELFRY ‖ ALIA 105: órbu-şoáricu, puiu a nóptiľei, puľu órbu; **GSus:** puľu órbu, CL 259

BAT[2] *s.* (*as for crushing grapes in a vineyard*) mútcă

BATCH *s.* → OUT OF THE SAME ■

BATHE *vb.* (a)scáldu, culimbiséscu; (*children talk*) luşi

BATHED IN SUNSHINE: a place ~ surín, surinél (*ant.* cheáre)

BATHED IN TEARS *adj.* (*of eyes*) aruv(r)inát

BATHING *s.* (a)scăldáre; ~ **place** scăldătoáre

BATHS *s. med.* láge *pl f*

BATHTUB

BATHTUB *s.* báñe, hămáme

BATTALION *s. mil.* tabór, tabóre, tăbúre

BATTER *s.* tiyáñe, lănghídhă; **We make our ~ in a pan** Tiyắñle li-adrăm tu tiyáne

BATTERY *s.* → BEATING

BATTLE *s.* bátire, băteáre ‖ DIARO 118: (*rare*) bâtíe

BATTLE *vb.* bat, (a)lúptu, lúmtu → FIGHT

BATTY *adj.* şcret, *f* şcrétă (*sic*) → CRAZY

BAUBLE *s.* minuţáľe → BANGLE

BAWD *s.* → PROSTITUTE

BAWL *s.* aurláre, (i)strigáre, zghíc

BAWL *vb.* zghiléscu, aúrlu, bag boáţe; (*to scold*) nţértu

BAWLING *s.* → BAWL

BAY *vb.* (*of dogs*) nciuñédz

BAYADERE *s.* (*usu. a Gypsy*) cinghíe

BAYING *s.* (*a dog's ~*) ceáună

BAYONET *s.* băĭnétă, lóhe, sunhíe, şpángă; **at the point of the ~** sunghiutác, *adv.*

BAY-TREE LEAF *s.* dáf(i)nă

BAZAAR *s.* bizusténe, cirşíe, păzáre

BE *vb.* hiu [hiŭ] *or* him; *N:* éscu; *2 sg* hii [hiĭ], *3 sg* eáste *or* e, i, -i [-ĭ], i- [ĭ-]; *1 pl* him, *2 pl* hiţ, *3 pl* sântu, súntu, sun, s- *or* -s; **Only two people are such in the whole village** Maşi doi s-ahtări tu hoáră; **They are not like me** Ca míne nu-s; *aor.* fuĭ, fuşi, fu, fum, fuţ, fúră; *ipf:* earám, iram, *or* ireám, *etc*; *imper:* *2 sg* Sâ hii! [hiĭ] *3 sg:* Sâ híbă! *2 pl:* Sâ hiţ! *part.* fútă; *gerund* hínda(lui) *or* fúnda(lui); **Who is the man at the water pipe?** Ţi om áre la şóput? **He was nowhere** Nu lu-aveá iuvá; **Where is he?** Iu lu-áre? **This girl was stupid second to none** Feáta ístă şi-irá gláră cum soţ nu-aveá ‖ estu 'I am,' HRISTU 20; eşt 'you are,' *2 sg*, HRISTU 9; **You will ~ my wife** Tini u-s eşti muiera a mia, HRISTU 21

BE ABLE TO *vb.* hiu di căíle; **Are you able to bring the forest here?** Hiţ di căíle si-u aduţéţ pădúrea auá? → ABLE

BE ABOUT TO *vb.* (*be on the point of*) **He was about to die** Vrea s-moáră; **I was about to burst with anger** Ñ-yineá tâc s-fac; **Once the dog was about to tear me to pieces** Câñľi va s-mi dizvucá tr-únă dzúuă; **The dogs were about to tear me to pieces** Vrea mi bea (câñľi); **(He) was about to send the ring** Erá s-pitreácă nélu; mi angréc si (+ *vb*), as in: **The house was about to crumble** Cása an-gricá s-cádă

BE ABSENT *vb.* hiu cusúre, lipséscu

BE A BUTTON SHORT *vb.* hiu loat di mínte; ñ-lipséscu drãñ

BE A CURSE TO *vb.* hiu púşcĺe trâ

BE AFFLICTED *vb.* părăpuñiséscu

BE AFRAID *vb.* aspár, ñ-u frícă, am stricătoárea arúptă, şápte-óptu ñi si dúţe; **If the wolf were afraid of rain, it would wear a cloak** Si s-aspăreá lúplu di ploáie, vrea poártă tămbáre; (*to dance the back steps*) **He began to ~** Ĺ-arăţí bişína; (*to panic*) târ-târ ñi si dúţe; (*~ a little*) ñi ca si-aspáre ócĺul

BE AGOG SMB. *vb.* ‖ ñ-fac ântr-ócĺi, BASME 303

BE A GOOD HAND AT DOING THINGS *vb.* ñ-gioácă ócĺul; ñ-ĺa ócĺul la túte

BE ALL AT SEA *vb.* u chér pusúla

BE ALL OVER ONESELF *vb.* nu mi ţâne lóclu di haráuă; nu mi ncap strãñile

BE ALL THE SAME TO SMB. *vb.* únă ñ-fáţe; adheafuriséscu

BE AMAZED *vb.* ciudiséscu → WONDER

BE AN ARTFUL DODGER *vb.* âñ tricú rúglu prit náre

BE ANGRY *vb.* (*with frustration*) ñ-u sémnu

BE AN OLD HAND AT SMTH. *vb.* ñ-ĺa ócĺul (la)

BE ANXIOUS ABOUT SMTH. *vb.* trag căştíga a; **You are anxious about other people's problems** Tradz căştíga a lúmiĺei

BE ASHAMED *vb.* (a)ntiriséscu (*and* andir-), aruşdiséscu, (a)ruş-téscu, ar(u)şinédz, aruşunédz ‖ BATSARIA 35: **I am ashamed to show up in the village** Nu-ám fáţă s-es ãn hoáră

BE ASTONISHED *vb.* ncruţéscu → WONDER

BE ATHIRST FOR *vb.* nu am sat di, nu am sátru di

BE AT ONE'S LAST GASP *vb.* hărchéscu

BE BASHFUL *vb.* (a)ndiriséscu, ândiriséscu, ntiriséscu, aruşdi-séscu, (a)ruştéscu, aruş(i)nédz, arşinédz, aruşunédz

BE BESIDE ONESELF WITH JOY *vb.* nu mi ţâne lóclu (di haráuă); nu mi ncap strãñile (di haráuă) ‖ **I was beside myself with joy** Míni earám agno haráuă, CUVATA 9

BE BITTEN *vb.* (*by or as by a snake*) şirpichédz; S-nu vă şirpicáţ! (*lit. 'Don't get bitten by snakes!'*)

BE BORED *vb.* ñi si aurắşte (di), biziréscu, buhtiséscu, plicti-

BE BORN

séscu, sâcâldiséscu

BE BORN *vb.* áflu, amíntu, fac, fet, náscu, príndu; **I was born in 1892** Mi-amintái tu únă ñíľe óptu súte noáuadzăţi doi; **You were born in winter** Tíne ti-aflăşi iárna; **He was born like that** Nâs ahtáre s-preáse; **where our ancestors were born** iu áuşiľi a noştĭ s-fitár̆ă; **I was born only once!** Nă oár̆ă mi feáţe mú-mea! ‖ **That's the way I was born, that's the way I am!** Aşí mi plâsái, ahtári éscu, DIARO 306; ZbN: **She was born in 1906** S-aveá fáptă la 1906; STERGHIU 4: **Cata was born in 1976** Tu anlu 1976 s-feaţi Cata

BE CAREFUL *vb.* (*to look out*) am ócľilu, am peána

BE CAUGHT BY THE EVENING *vb.* nsirédz; **He had been caught by the evening in the valley** Aveá nsirátă tu vále

BE CAUGHT BY THE NIGHT *vb.* murdzéscu, nuptédz

BE CAUGHT IN THE NET (IN THE SNARE, IN THE TRAP) *vb.* cad tu bátă, cad tu yrip → FALL INTO THE TRAP

BE COLD *vb.* afiriséscu, sec; **Put on your cloak or you will ~** Ľa-ţ tâmbárea că va seţi

BE CONCERNED *vb.* sicliţéscu, ñ-u zórea di → CARE

BE CONSPICUOUS *vb.* aleg

BE DISGRACED *vb.* (*to get low, to sink, to decay*) cătăndiséscu pri hála éstă

BE DISGUSTED *vb.* aynuséscu, aynusédz; dizvăléscu; **We were ~ed with what we saw** Nă dizvălím di ţe vidzúm; ñ-i greáţă (di); ñ-u ynos (di); him disvălít (di); ñ-vérsu máţăle

BE DISPLACED *vb.* mi strămút

BE DISPOSED TO *vb.* hiu di căbíle s; **He is disposed rather to die** I di căbíle ma ghíne s-moár̆ă

BE DISTRESSED *vb.* sicliţéscu

BE DOING WELL *vb.* (*as of a sick person*) ľau trâ năínte; (*as of a student*) nveţ ápă

BE DUMBFOUNDED *vb.* armân ca tul, cicărdiséscu, cictiséscu, cihtiséscu, ciăhtiséscu, ñ-fac crúţe, nmărmuriséscu ‖ armân ca mármura, BA 439; CUVATA 12: mi sturuséscu

BE ELSEWHERE *vb.* (*of one's thoughts*) **His thoughts are elsewhere** Ľ-asboár̆ă

BE ENCHANTED *vb.* **He has been enchanted** Lu călcă aúmbra

BE ENGLUTTED *vb.* vărcuséscu, vultuséscu; **He was englutted in tar up to the neck** Pân di gúşe vultusí tu cătráne

BE ENTICED vb. (*to be about to yield to temptation*) dau coáda

BE EQUAL TO vb. ahârdzéscu; **Those sixty days were equal to sixty years** Aţeále şaidzăţi di dzâle ahârdzíră cât şaidzăţi di añ

BE FAR WRONG vb. ‖ HRISTU 37: fac lath mari

BE FOND OF vb. lu háscu n gúră; lu am ca núca n sănătór

BE IN FOR IT vb. ñ-cáde chicútă máre → TO GET IT HOT

BE IN LOVE WITH vb. alughéscu, amíntu; *Clís*: **With whom were you in love?** Cu ţe gióne ñ-amintái?

BE IN LOW WATER vb. ñi si dúţe tersiné ‖ ñi si dúţe strâmbu, BASME 280

BE IN NEED vb. ñ-eáste lipsítă (di) → NEED

BE IN READINESS FOR ACTION vb. mi áflu sti cior

BE GOING ON vb. trăxéscu; *3 sg*: **in order to see what is going on** s veádă ţe trăxeáşte → HAPPEN

BE GONE vb. (*to depart as fast as possible*) li tíndu; **Be gone!** Tíndi-le! (*to come to an end*) duc; **Summer is gone** S-dúse veára

BE HAND AND GLOVE WITH SMB. vb. ‖ (*to be very good friends with smb.*) **The too women are hand and glove with each other** doáuli bes tu ună curcubétâ (*lit. 'both fart into the same pumpkin shell'*), DIARO 333

BE LEFT IN THE BASKET vb. armân ca găĺína údă; armân ca Súlta cu ucălu

BE LEFT WITH SMTH. vb. (*to gain a profit*) mi alég cu

BE LIKE A THORN IN ONE'S SIDE vb. *3 sg*: ñ-şeáde ntr-ócĺi

BE LOOKING FOR IT vb. u-cáftu (ngăceárea) cu luminárea

BE LOOSE IN THE SADDLE vb. (*to be insecure*) şuvăéscu

BE LOST IN AMAZEMENT vb. armân mărmurisít, şed ca mărmurisít ‖ BELIMACE 9: **they were lost in amazement** armásiră ca ndilisíţ

BE LUCKY vb. ‖ ñ-ímnă tíhea, BASME 66

BE MISSING vb. lipséscu; **Three thousand are missing** Lipséscu tréi ñíĺe

BE NOT QUITE ALL THERE vb. *3 sg*: ĺ-lipseáşte únă scândură

BE NUTS ABOUT/ON SMB. vb. (*to take a fancy to smb.*) ñ-cáde tu vreáre máre ‖ **He is nuta about her** Âl mâşcâ buríclu ti nâsâ, DIARO 160

BE OFF vb. (*to leave*) li scármin; u adún ‖ ñ-ĺau zvérca, BASME 458

BE ON A SPREE vb. (*to give free rein to fun*) u fac uzungióva

BE ON BAD TERMS WITH

BE ON BAD TERMS WITH SMB. *vb.* ‖ hiu cârtít cu, DIARO 94; *aor:* mi astăleái cu, DIARO 148

BE ON ONE'S BEAM-ENDS *vb.* am anánghia, mi áflu tu strâmtúră

BE ON ONE'S DEATH BED *vb.* trag s-mor → BE ON ONE'S LAST LEGS

BE ON ONE'S LAST LEGS *vb.* hiu cătră soáre, ľau cálea máre, trag s-mor, trag trâ moárte ‖ ▼ncárcu dit lúmea aéstă, BASME 488

BE ON ONE'S GUARD *vb.* ▼amfiréscu, afiréscu; **All** (*f*) **were on their guard, as if from a great danger** Túte s-afireá ca di per di lup; ▼avégľu, ▼apreavégľu; *imper.* (*Beware!*) Lárgu!

BE ON THE GROWING HAND *vb.* *3 sg impers:* ñ-cústă → THRIVE

BE ON THE LOOK-OUT FOR *vb.* păndixéscu

BE ON THE POINT OF *vb.* vrea (si), ▼angréc (si) → BE ABOUT TO

BE ON WATCH *vb.* privégľu, ▼avégľu → WATCH

BE OPPOSED TO *vb.* ▼duc contră → DISAGREE

BE OUT *vb.* (*to come to light*) es to páde

BE OUT FOR SCALPS *vb.* (*to be ready to fight*) dau tâmbárea di páde; u cáftu ngăceárea cu luminárea

BE OUT OF HUMOR WITH SMB. *vb.* lu-ám şíľe ntr-ócľi

BE OUT OF ONE'S DEPTH *vb.* nu-ñ táľe (cáplu), nu-ñ táľe puscárlu (*or* cărăfétea), nu ñ-si úmple ftína

BE OUT OF ONE'S MIND *vb.* ñ-asbură gáia

BE OUT OF POCKET *vb.* (*at a loss*) ≈ lu adár yróslu zloátă

BE OVERCOME BY HUNGER *vb.* ‖ ñ-intră lúplu tu máţă, BASME 25

BE OVERCOME BY SLEEP *vb.* mi ľa sómnul

BE OVERJOYED *vb.* nu mi ncap stráñile, nu mi ţâne lóclu di haráuă

BE OVERTAKEN BY THE NIGHT *vb.* ntúnic, ntuneáric

BE OVERWHELMED BY LONGING *vb.* ▼sicliţéscu

BE PARALYZED WITH FEAR *vb.* mi fac (tu fáţă) ca mórtu (di frícă); ñ-beau tut sândzile (di frícă)

BE PARCHED WITH THIRST *vb.* crep di seáte

BE PATIENT *vb.* *imper.* ≈ Ndreádzi-ţ mustăţle!

BE PERMITTED *vb.* am izíne di (*lit.* 'to have permission from')

BE PERPLEXED *vb.* u am cumbúră

BE PLEASED *vb.* ▼ifharistiséscu

BE POSSIBLE *vb.* **if it were possible** s-híbă di cáíle

BE POURING (WITH RAIN) *vb.* *3 sg impers:* veársă cu găleáta

BE PRACTICABLE *vb.* (*of roads*) ▼urdín; **The roads were not practicable** Căľuríle nu urdiná

BE PRESSED *vb.* (*by bodily necessities*) **I am pressed** mi loárǎ pri cioáre

BE PROUD OF *vb.* arhundipséscu

BE PUFFED UP *vb.* arhundipséscu

BE QUICK ON THE UPTAKE *vb.* ñ-gioácǎ ócľul

BE QUIET *vb.* (*to stop talking or making noise*) amút, ▾tac; **Be quiet!** Amúte! ~, **brother!** Tás-ţâ, fráte!

BE QUITS WITH SMB. *vb.* hiu ísea

BE RATHER UNWELL *vb.* (*to be ailing*) atihiséscu

BE READY *vb.* hiu pri cior (*or* pri ciciór); **He was ready to throw himself into the fire** Vrea s-arcáre n foc → READY

BE RECONCILED *vb.* ▾disvér

BE RIGHT *vb.* am ndréptu ‖ BELIMACE 39: am ndriptáte

BE RUINED FINNACIALLY *vb.* cad nafoárǎ

BE SAD *vb.* ▾nver, ▾nvirín, ▾(a)nvirinédz

BE SATISFIED *vb.* ▾ifharistiséscu

BE SCARED *vb.* ▾(a)spár → BE FRIGHTENED, GET SCARED

BE SEIZED *vb.* strǎbát, stribát; **I was seized with cold** Mi strǎbǎtú arcoárea; (~ *with fright*) mi ľa lǎhtárlu, mi acáţǎ fríca, mi ľa ceáşlu (di fríca)

BE SICK *vb.* (*to be ill*) nu pot, nu-ñ pot; trag di; trag niputeáre; (*to be disgusted*) ▾(a)ngusédz, ▾nguséscu

BE SILENT *vb.* ▾tac (ca peáştile)

BE SIMILAR TO *vb.* ñ-u adúc cu → AS LIKE AS TWO PEAS

BE SITTING *vb.* şed n cur; **He was seated by the stove** şideá n cur-şu níngǎ sóbǎ → SIT

BE SLOW ON THE UPTAKE *vb.* nu ñ-si umplú ftína

BE SORRY *vb.* (*to have sympathy*) ñiluéscu; (*to regret*) ñ-u am caimó, ñľ-u am dor; **I will be sorry to die** Va ñ-u am dor cǎ mor; ñ-páre arǎu; ▾tuniséscu (*and* tuñi-), ▾tunuséscu; **He was sorry that he was born** S-tunisí cǎ s-feáţe; **Now the thief was sorry** Tóra fúrlu s-tunusí; (*to repent*) ñ-múşcu búdzǎli (*or* mâñle); âñ yíne chiaméte [k'i•a•mé•ti]; ▾pişmǎniséscu ‖ ▾mituñiséscu, BASME 85; âñ chícǎ tu ínimǎ, BASM 203; âñ páre arǎu, PARALLELE 152

BE SPOILING FOR FIGHT *vb.* u cáftu (ngǎceárea) cu luminárea → TRAIL ONE'S CLOAK

BE SPOONY ON SMB. *vb.* *3 sg pt*: ñ-cǎdzú tu ínimǎ

BE SOARING *vb.* ľau sǎlǎghíre

BE SQUARE WITH SMB. *vb.* hiu ísea

BE STARTLED *vb.* ▼aspár

BE STRUCK DUMB *vb.* arămân ca hut, armân cihisít, ñ-si ľa ócľiľ

BE STRUCK WITH *vb.* **I was struck with cold** Mi strãbãtú arcoárea;
(~ *with amazement*) armân ca cihãsít; (~ *with apoplexy*) nchicutédz
→ HAVE A STROKE

BE SUITABLE *vb.* ▼uidiséscu, ▼idusēscu; fac (trâ) → FIT ‖ ñ-da
mâna, BASME 432

BE SURE *vb.* ñ-si úmple ócľul (cã); **As for you, I am sure that you
will kill her** Di tíne ñ-si úmple ócľul cã va s-u vãţãñ

BE TAKEN ABACK *vb.* mi (a)ñír

BE TAKEN IN THE TOILS *vb.* cad tu yrip → FALL INTO THE TRAP

BE TEMPTED *vb.* (*be about to give up*) dau coáda

BE THANKFUL *vb.* cunóscu; ľ-u am tu biricheávis

BE THAT AS IT MAY ţi s va, las s híbã

BE THE FABLE OF THE TOWN *vb.* agiúngu pãrãmíth

BE THE SAME *vb.* ‖ (*it makes no difference*) únã fáţe, BASME 247

BE THREATENED *vb.* mi pášte perícľul

BE THRIVING *vb.* ñ-si dúţe príma; ñ-ñárdze ghíne → PROSPER

BE THROWN HERE AND THERE *vb.* (*as of a bird caught by a cat*) mi
zbat

BE TICKLED TO DEATH *vb.* ▼arâd cã mi zmúrtic; ▼cãpãéscu (*or* ▼li-
şín, ▼lişinédz) di-arâdeáre

BE TIRED *vb.* (*to be reluctant to repeat*) *impers.* ñ-angreácã; (*of
smth. perceived with the eyes*) ñ-si úmple ócľul (di)

BE TOO LATE IN THE FIELD *vb.* armân ca gãľína údã

BE UNDER A SPELL *vb.* hiu diucľát

BE UNLIKE *vb.* (*to differ*) am fárche

BE UP TO ALL THE DODGES OF SMTH. *vb.* ştiu hunérea

BE UP TO A THING OR TWO *vb.* (*to be an old hand; to be up to
snuff*) âñ tricú rúglu prit náre

BE UP TO SMTH. *vb.* (*to roll up one's sleeves as to begin work*)
▼scumbuséscu ‖ ñ-bag poálile m-brâu, BASME 682

BE VEXED WITH SMB. *vb.* ▼cãrtéscu (*and* câr-); **We have been vexed
with you because of what you said** Nã cãrtím di zboárile ţe dzâsişi

BE WARY OF *vb.* (*to be very cautious*) ▼(a)firéscu, ▼amfiréscu,
▼avégľu

BE WELL-OFF *vb.* (*to be prosperous*) am cheag, huzuripséscu

BE WHAT MAY ţi s va, las s híbă

BE WILD WITH DELIGHT *vb.* nu mi ţâne lóclu di haráuă; ñ-si fătă Hristólu n cásă

BE WORTH *vb.* (a)hărdzéscu (*and* ahâr-), axizéscu; *3 sg impers.* fáţe ‖ *it is not worth it* nu fáţe paráţ, PARALLELE 146

BE WORTHLESS *vb.* (*or inferior*) nu fáţe parádz

BE WRONG IN THE UPPER STORY *vb. 3 sg:* ľ-lipseáşte únă scândură

BEAD *s.* mărdzeáuă (*and* mâr-), *dim.* mârdzilúşe; mânúşe; (*made of colored marble*) mirmér; *N:* culubác ‖ mârgheáľi *pl f,* DIARO 307

BEADLE *s.* (*in a church*) candilanáftu ‖ *Pls:* candilináf, CL 40

BEAD-LIKE *adj.* (*as of smb.'s eyes*) mărdzilát (*and* mâr-)

BEADS *s.* (*rosary*) ori *f pl*

BEAK *s.* (*as of a rooster*) cărăntáne (*and* cărân-); *also:* chípită, cioc, dintánă, ghintánă, dhinténă → BILL ‖ *Peş:* ciófcă, CL 43

BEAKER *s.* birbíľu → PITCHER

BEAM *s.* (*a ~ of light*) (a)rádză; arpăyi [•păy^i] *f pl*; cilístră, ţilístră, diligitúră, gilít, *pl* gilíte, gilíturi *or* gilídz; măndă, múndă, şíţă; (*a long piece of timber, as in a wall*) gréndă, pótan, pótană, pótane, tăbáne

BEAM *vb.* (a)nyil(i)séscu, lumbrăséscu, lumbriséscu, lumbruséscu

BEAM-ENDS: be on one's ~ am anánga; mi áflu tu strimtúră

BEAMING *adj.* lumbărsít → BRILLIANT

BEAN *s. N:* făsúľu, fisúľu, *S:* făsúľe; păscúľu; cucheáuă; **boiled ~s** şúşcă; **stewed ~s** făsúľe yeayné; **broad ~** fávă

BEAR *s. zool.* (a)úrsă; **~ cub** ursóplu; (*rare*) úrsu; **~ tamer** ursár

BEAR *vb.* (*to carry*) ▾duc, mut; (*to give birth*) nfăşédz; **His wife bore two children** Nveásta nfăşé doi ficióri; (*to endure, to stand*) arávdu, apufirséscu, (a)stráxéscu, hunipséscu; **The water should be as hot as the hand can ~** Apa s-híbă cáldă cât astrăxeáşte mâna; **He cannot ~ the burden** Nu poáte s-hunipseáscă várlu

BEAR MALICE AGAINST SMB. *vb.* (*to bear smb. a grudge*) ľ-ţân cáche; ľ-duc zăte → ROD

BEARD *s.* bárbă, métură ‖ **to grow a ~** ñ-alás bárbă PARALLELE 144

BEARD *vb.* ncucutédz, stau cucót

BEARDED *adj.* bărbós, săcălă

BEARDLESS *adj.* chióse *invar.*; spân, spânác; **a ~ face** fáţă spânácă ‖ *Peş:* chiusé, CL 254

BEARING *s.* (*comportment*) aréu, cúmpite *f pl*; purtátic

BEAST

BEAST s. ayríme, agríme; beau *m*, bei *pl*; (*and fig.*) z(u)lápe, *pl.* zulắchi

BEASTINGS s. culástră, curástră

BEAT vb. (*to strike repeatedly*) bat; **Bells were ~ing** Clópute bắteá; asún; (*as a tree for its fruit*) alúmtu; **I began to ~ the tree with stones** Acáţ s-lu alúmtu cu chétrili; (*to get lost*) **Beat it!** Adúnă-u di auá! (*to trash*) adár pipiríă, ansár, bat dála, bat pistíle, cos, dau fúşte, fac pistíle diq chiutécă, adár pipiríţă, ľ-u íntru, âmpărjinédz, ndărséscu di chiutécă, ľi-ndreg chiúrcu, para-bát, păpuriséscu, tălăéscu, tuchéscu di băteáre, lu tuléscu di fúşte, trag ţurţúfe, úmflu, ľi úmflu cheálea, ľi úmflu sămárlu; (*to beat with one's foot or feet*) cluţéscu; (*to beat smb. black and blue*) astíngu di băteáre, l-bag tu cheále, chisédz oásili, frângu arídzle, frângu călámea di cior, frângu chilúnghea, lu frângu di şcop, stulcinédz di chiutécă, lu vátăm di şcop, lu vátăm di părjínă, lu fac pândză bilítă, lu fac víñită, cruéscu rásă, psuséscu di şcop ‖ cruéscu un sumár, BASME 431; cruéscu un şcop, BASME 43; ľi am únă, BASME 135 → BEAT THE BUSH

BEAT ABOUT THE BUSH vb. bat n-aľúrea; xínu-zburắscu

BEAT DOWN vb. cúlcu, afiriséscu

BEAT FLAT vb. nturtédz, ciupléscu

BEAT HELL vb. (*to play a shaby trick*) ľi scot ócľiľ; para-fác

BEAT ONE'S BRAINS WITH / ABOUT vb. ñ-disíc cáplu; ñ-vátăm míntea

BEAT ONE'S BREAST vb. ñ-u dau ăn chéptu (*or* pri chéptu) cu búşlu

BEAT SMB. BLACK AND BLUE vb. ‖ BATSARIA 61: lu-astíngu di părjínă

BEAT THE BUSH vb. ‖ **one beets the bush and another catches the bird** ≈ áltu háscâ şi-áltu s-cumânicâ, DIARO 205 (*lit.* 'one opens the mouth and another one gets the communion')

BEAT THE TAR OUT OF SMB. vb. ľi-scútur yicắlu

BEATER s. (*cynegetics*) aurlătór

BEATING s. şcop; *also:* ansăráre, avráre, băteáre, bătíche, calcavúr, chisáre, csáre, chiúrcu, chiutécă, cláră; (*with kicks*) cluţuíre; cruíre, fúşte *f pl*; papáră, păpáră, pupáră; pipiríţă, pistíle, pârjínă, plíhtumă, ţurţúfe, umpleáre; **He deserves a ~** Sumárlu-ľ va umpleáre; **They were put to a ~** Fúră arcáţ tu şcop; **He needs a ~** Va ansăráre; **He escaped from a ~** Ascắpă di chiutécă → DRUBBING

BEAUTIFUL adj. m(u)şeát, mşat, muşutíc, muşitíc, muşitícăz; chicát dit steále (*lit. 'fallen from the stars'*); dulbér; mǎ-sa a steáuľei; scriát (*lit. 'written'*); (*of a woman*) alímtǎ (*'licked'*); **A ~ woman passed by** Tricú únǎ alímtǎ ‖ (*very ~*) chicát din soáre (*lit. 'fallen from the sun'*), PARALLELE 157; s-lu sórghi tu cúpǎ, BASME 36 (*i.e. you are tempted to sip him down with your coffee*); **a ~ girl** únâ cadânâ di feátâ, DIARO 165

BEAUTIFULLY *adv.* muşeát

BEAUTIFY *vb.* muşiţéscu

BEAUTY *s.* muşiteáţǎ, muşuteáţǎ; (*a beautiful woman*) alímtǎ, béce, dulbérǎ

BEAVER *s. zool.* castóre *m*

BECAUSE *cj.* cari, cǎ, cǎ ţe, ciúnche, déca; **- Why don't you buy it? - Because it is too expensive** - Cǎ ţé nu lu-acúmpǎri? - Cǎ ţe-i scúmpu; **~ it was in the fall, with many fogs** cari eará toámnǎ, cu néguri; **Help, 'cause I am drowning!** Agiutór, cǎ mi nec! ‖ **An:** catacúm, Réc. 47

BECAUSE OF *prep.* di, di itía a, di sibépea a, di trǎ simbétea a, di trǎ, tru; **People are dying of thirst** Moáre plásea di ápǎ; **The head gets beaten ~ the mouth** Di gúrǎ s-báte cáplu; **~ too much rain the rivers flooded** Di ploi múlte arâurile inşírǎ; **~ her they won** Di nâsa sibépe azvímsirǎ; **~ you we will suffer as well** Di trǎ tíne vai trǎdzém ş-noi; **~ a horse** tru un cal; **Has he not suffered enough ~ his shortness?** Câte nu áre tráptǎ di itía a şcurtámiľei! ‖ **~ him** di nâs itíe, BASME 13; **~ his wife** di muľáre-sa itíe, BASME 474; dítrǎ, dírtǎ; **~ him we ran away from the village** Dítrǎ nâs fudzím din hoárǎ, BASME 37

BECLOUD *vb.* ntúnic

BECOME *vb.* → GROW

BECOME *vb.* fac, adár, agiúngu; **as soon as he became an emperor** agiúmtu amirǎ; **He wants to ~ a doctor** Va si-agiúngǎ yeátru; **Have you ~ a beggar?** Ţiritór ti-ai fáptǎ? (*to reduce to, to be reduced to*) cǎtǎndiséscu

BECOME A BYWORD *vb.* agiúngu pǎrǎmít

BECOME ACQUAINTED WITH *vb.* fac cunuşmáe cu

BECOME ANXIOUS *vb.* pǎleáşte peána → WORRY

BECOME BLIND *vb.* urghéscu

BECOME CLEAR *vb.* limbiséscu, limbidzǎscu

BECOME CLOUDY *vb. 3 sg* niureádzǎ, nǎureádzǎ, nuoreádzǎ; **The sky**

BECOME CONSUMPTIVE

is becoming cloudy Acáţă s-niureádză

BECOME CONSUMPTIVE *vb.* mi stric di chéptu; *also*: mi cârtéscu di chéptu, mi tihtuséscu, mi uftichédz, uhtichédz

BECOME CORRUPTED *vb.* aspárgu, distórcu; **Today children become easily corrupted** Ásândz ficĭórľi si-aspárgu lişór

BECOME DELIRIOUS *vb.* aľurédz

BECOME DEPRAVED *vb.* → BECOME CORRUPTED

BECOME DETESTABLE *vb.* (*to worsen*) cacurizipséscu

BECOME DIM *vb.* (*of one's eyes*) pãniséscu (*and* pâ-) → BECLOUD

BECOME DIZZY *vb.* andrălăséscu, andrăliséscu, andrăluséscu, ñ-yíne andrálă

BECOME DUSTY *vb.* (*as of clothes*) mi ncarc (di púlbire)

BECOME ENLIGHTENED *vb.* (*to grow wiser*) diştéptu ‖ dişcľíd, BASME 34

BECOME FACT *vb.* (*to come true*) 3 *sg aor.* s-feáţe; **What you dreamed of has become fact** Ţe nghisáşi s-feáţe

BECOME FRENZIED *vb.* (*to frenzy*) aľurédz

BECOME FROSTY *vb.* (*to cover with frost*) 3 *sg impers.* mbrumeádză, brumeádză

BECOME HELPLESS *vb.* cad stog

BECOME ILL-NATURED *vb.* nşárpic, nşárpit, nşirpichédz, nşirpitédz nyispinédz, yispinédz

BECOMING *adj.* (*fit*) uidisít, idusít

BECOME INTIMATE WITH SMB. *vb.* 3 *pl*: şi-ľa dúhurile

BECOME LEAN *vb.* (*to lose weight*) slăghéscu; s-tucheáşte cárnea di pri míne

BECOME OLD *vb.* mbitărnéscu, auşéscu, auşắscu

BECOME OVERABUNDANT *vb.* para-agiúngu

BECOME OVERRIPE *vb.* (*as of fruit*) para-agiúngu

BECOME RICH *vb.* arhundipséscu; avuţắscu, mbugăţắscu

BECOME SICK *vb.* (*disgusted*) anusţắscu, aynuséscu

BECOME SORROWFUL *vb.* nvirín, (a)nvirinédz, **N:** nver; *impers.* ñ-chícă

BECOME STERILE *vb.* (*as of sheep*) stirpuéscu, stirpéscu

BECOME THINNER *vb.* (*as of thread*) minutédz, minuţắscu, supţirédz

BECOME TUFTED *vb.* (*as of the tail of an animal*) tufuséscu; (*as of forests in spring*) funduséscu, nvirdzắscu

BECOME WORSE *vb.* cacurizipséscu

BECOMING *s.* agiundzeáre, agiúndzire

BECOMINGLY *adv.* cum prínde

BED *s.* pat, criváte; (*with bedclothes*) aşcirnút, yitáche; (*as of flowers or vegetables*) strat *n*; úrdin *m*, úrdiñ *pl*; (*of people*) culcát; **be on one's death ~** trag *s* mor; (*to say, to utter*) **from one's death ~** cu límbă di moárte; **in ~** culcát, apús, băgát (*ant. out of ~*) → MAKE THE ~, PUT TO ~

BED *vb.* pun, cúlcu

BED IN *vb.* (*as seedlings*) plântu; fitipséscu, seámin

BEDAUB *vb.* ▾ncárcu, ▾mârghéscu

BEDBUG *s. ent.* córţă, tartabíc, tahtabíc

BEDCLOTHES *s.* aştirnút, aşcirnút, circiáfe, strózmă

BEDDING *s.* strózmă; (*mattress*) duşéc

BEDEVIL *vb.* scăñiséscu → HARASS

BEDFAST *adj.* dzăcút (*and* ză-) → BEDRIDDEN

BEDIZEN *vb.* ▾fac, ▾ndreg, ▾muşuţăscu ‖ CUNIA 88: ▾pruvéd

BEDEW *vb.* ud

BEDRIDDEN *adj.* culcát, dzăcút (*and* ză-); **to be ~** hivréscu, hiuvréscu, lândzidzăscu

BEDROOM *s.* (*with no floor*) yuneáuă

BEDSIDE *s.* (*esp. the pillow*) căpitíñu, căpitâñu; pruschéfal

BEDSPREAD *s.* cérgă, ciórgă, cuvérte, cuvértă, doágă, yeámbulă, iámbulă, hreáme, *pl* hreñ; măcáte, mândzále, mutáfe, téndă; (*old, worn out ~*) tóblă; viléndză, *dim.* vilindzícă

BEDTIME *s.* culcáre, oára trâ culcáre ‖ DIARO 321: bâgári

BED-WETTER *s.* (*as children who urinate when sleeping*) ciúşe *m/f*; *pl* ciúşeañ *m*, ciúşane *f*

BEE[1] *s. ent.* alghínă; *coll.* alghináme; múşti di alghíñ; *coll.* stup; **The smoke drives away the ~s** Fúmlu aznắşte stúplu ‖ **An:** aghínă, **Pals:** alăghínă; **Kok:** milísă, **Pdz:** mélisă; **Na:** iáspă, **LvO:** iáspe, **Hor, Rod:** iáspi, **Smx:** geáspe, B-ARCH 342

BEE[2] *s.* (*gathering*) bărţát, ţícna-préfte

BEECH *s.* fag *m*; **Gop:** fau

BEECH-GROVE *s.* fădzét, fădzíme

BEECHNUT *s.* fágă, *no pl*

BEEF *s.* → MEAT

BEEF-WITTED *adj.* ‖ cap di strúmciu, DIARO 150 → STUPID

BEEFY *adj.* cărnós, muşcľós

BEEHIVE

BEEHIVE *s.* stup di alghíne, crin di alghíñ, cuşór, cuşóre

BEEKEEPER *s.* alghinár

BEELINE *s.* (a)ndréptu *adv.*

BEER *s.* bérǎ

BEESWAX *s.* țeárǎ ‖ *Av:* chilíthrǎ, CL 254

BEETLE-BROWED *adj.* dzinós

BEETROOT *s. bot.* (a)ripáne, râpáne, pangiáre ‖ (*red beetroot*)
Prv: cuchinoyúli, CL 42

BEFORE *adv.* **shortly ~** (a)piríndu, (a)príndu ‖ *Cru:* (a)nínte, GOLAB
199

BEFORE LONG *adv.* ayóña, curúndu, crúndu

BEFORE YOU SAY KNIFE / JACK ROBINSON ≈ ‖ pânǎ s-țǎ frețĭ ó-cľiľi,
BASME 494; pânǎ z-dzǎți țínți, BASME 427, BATSARIA 12

BEFORE *prep.* ntrâ, ntrǎ ; **They took him ~ the emperor** Lu scoásirǎ
ntrǎ amirǎlu; (*in front of*) **All the birds paralyzed with fear ~ the
dreadful vulture** Tuț púľi ngľițárǎ di frícǎ ntrǎ fuviróslu vúltur;
nǎínte di, nínte di, dinǎíntea a; **~ his eyes** dinǎíntea a ócľilor a
lui; **~ leaving** piríndu fúgǎ; **~ dawn** pânǎ din dzáre; nínte di
hǎrghíe; **Why don't you make your promise ~ crossing the river?** Țe
nu tǎxéşti pânǎ s-treți arâulu [a•râu•lu]? ‖ CUVATA 9 agnánghea di
(*spatially*)

BEFOREHAND *adv.* nǎínte, nǎínde

BEFOUL *vb.* liruséscu → DIRTY, SOIL

BEFUDDLE *vb.* cutúlbur → MUDDLE

BEG *vb.* aór; (*to ask earnestly*) pǎrǎcǎlséscu, pǎrlǎcǎrséescu,
țer; **He who begs does not die, but neither is he esteemed** Cari
țeáre nu cheáre, ma néca-i tr-alǎvdáre; rog (*anemic word*); (*to ask
for alms*) cirşéscu, parastáu la úşile a lúmilor; (*to go a-begging*)
yiftuséscu; **~ smb.'s pardon** ñ-ľau ľirtáre; **I ~ your pardon** bardhón

BEGET *vb.* (*to ~ offsprings*) nfumiľédz

BEGGAR *s.* dhicuñár, pitáciu, proseác, țǎrǎpín, țârpân, țiritóñu,
zicľár; (*Gypsy woman ~*) mástorsǎ ‖ *Smr:* ştoh; *Prv, SJos:* ftoh, CL
261; *adj.* țǎrǎpânéscu, di țiritór

BEGGARLY *adj.* fucǎr(ǎs)éscu, țǎrǎpânéscu

BEGGARY *s.* ftuhipsíre greáuǎ ‖ DIARO 230: dhicuñirláchi

BEGGING *s.* dicúñe, yiftusíre

BEGIN *vb.* (a)cáț (sǎ), nțep (sǎ), arhinséscu (sǎ), *S:* ayiurhéscu,
N: ahiurhéscu, arhiuséscu; bag sǎ, bag di; dau sǎ, dau di; apǎr-

ñéscu (să), apúc (să), ľau să, purñéscu (să), pârñéscu (să); *Src:*
purnéscu (să); stau să, yin (di) **They began to show up** Acățără s-da
cap; **The trumpets began to blow** Cățără buríile s-bátă; **They began
to leave** Ahiurhíră s-fúgă; **She ~s to work like a slave** Ca scláva s-
lucreádză-apărñáște; **They began to eat** Arhiusíră să mângă; **The girl
began to scream** Feáta bágă zghíclu; **The wife came out and began to
shout** Eáse nveásta, bágă boáțea; **when the slope ~s to turn green** ma
s-da si-nveárdă pláilu; **Snow began to fall abundantly** Neáua loa
s-cádă pále, pále; **Then she began to sing** Nțipú di priapóia s-cântă; **Let's ~ harvesting** S-purním la sițiráre; **~ a war** mut pólim; **~
to hate each other** cad tu dușmăníľe; **He began to get angry** Víñe di
ariciuí; **~ anew** pri-adár ‖ ľau; **no sooner had they begun to sing
the song** níca no-aveá loátă ghíne cânticlu, BASME 439; **He began to
laugh** Aéstu bágă s-arâdă, BASME 501; ânchiséscu, CUNIA 145

BEGINNER *s.* ageamít

BEGINNING *s.* ahiurhíre, ahiurhítă, ahiursítă, ahiursitúră, ar-
hinsíre, arhiusítă; **from the ~ of the spring** ditu ahiurhíta a
primăveáriľei; *also:* arhíe, árhizmă, apărñítă, apărñíre, apăr-
ñitúră; (*as of the fire in a stove*) anguñáre; cap, intrátă; **at the
~ of the year** tu intráta a ánlui; **from the (very) ~** di prótă; **from
the ~ till the end** din cap până tu coádă; dit apărñítă pân tu bitisítă; (*handsel*) xifté, sifté → MAKE A BAD ~ ‖ **A good ~ is half
the battle** ≈ dzúua búnă s-cănoáște di tahiná, ALR 1470

BEGOTTEN *adj.* acățát; **children ~ on Saturday** ficióri acățáț Sâm-
băta

BEGRIME *vb.* murdăripséscu → DIRTY, SOIL

BEGROUDGE *vb.* zilipséscu, zuli-

BEGUILE *vb.* arâd, plănăséscu; **The snake ~ed her** șárpile o plă-
năsí; **~ the time** mi șintéscu ‖ BASME 234: bag pi plan → DECEIVE

BEHAVE *vb.* (a)pórtu; **~ properly!** Poártă-ti cum prínde! fac; **He ~s
like a janissary** ca yeaníțar fáțe; (*as of a child*) șed ghíne;
(*iron. of smb. who is anything but young*) mi túndu cu noátiñľi
→ MAKE SMB. ~

BEHAVE! (*a shout to the mules*) moț!

BEHAVIOR *s.* purtátic, pórtu, práxe, aducătúră **His ~ shows that he
has lived in a city** Purtáticlu u spúne că áre bănátă tu căsăbă;
(*good ~*) frumineáță, frunimeáță, frunimádhă

BEHEAD *vb.* gușuéscu, hrăștuéscu, ľau cáplu, șcurtédz, șcurti-

BEHEST

chédz

BEHEST *s.* dimândátă, dimândáre

BEHIND *adv.* năpói, dănăpói, dinâpói, dânâpói; ~ **the back** pri dĭnăpói; (*late*) amănát, şintít ‖ **Cru: from ~** di apóia, GOLAB 200

BEHIND *prep.* dúpu, dúpă (DDA: 1118), dípu

BEHINDHAND *adj.* (*lagging ~*) amănătór

BEHOLD *interj.* na; na că; na iu; ~, **a shepherd passed by** Na că treáţe pri-acló un picurár; ~, **he encounters a wolf** Na iu da chéptu cu un lup

BEHOLDEN *adj.* burgilâ, burgilipsít

BEHOOF *s.* prucuchíe

BEING *s.* (*from* BE) fúndalui; ~ **next to him** fúndalui aláturea di nâs; híndalui

BELABOR *vb.* (*to thrash soundly*) → BEAT

BELATED *adj.* amânát

BELCH *s. phys.* aruguíre, răgăíre, arăguráre

BELCH *vb.* arăgăéscu, arăgurédz, arăguédz ‖ ~ **out Amc:** sărghéscu; **The rooster belched the fox out of his belly** Cucótlu sărghiáşte vúlpea di tu pántică, RÉCATAS 37

BELCH OUT SMOKE *vb.* (*as of a stove*) afúm

BELDAM *s.* muşurécă

BELFRY *s.* cambanaryió, símandru

BELGRADE *s.* (*city*) ‖ **Cru:** Biligrád, GOLAB 208

BELIEF *s.* crideáre, creádire → FAITH, TRUST

BELIEVE *vb.* cred, ncréd; ñ-u am că; **An intoxicated man ~s that he is the emperor** Mbitátlu şi-u áre că nâs i amiră; (*to trust*) pistipséscu, pistup-; **If you don't ~, measure you again!** S-nu pistipsíre, misúră tíne diznóu! ‖ TULLIU 121: acred; (*to take it seriously*) ľau tră búne, BASME 399; ñ-si úmple óclul, BASME 264; **I can scarcely ~ it** nu ñ-u va míntea, BASME 68; nu ñ-u ncápe míntea BASME 236; **Believe me!** (*I promise!*) Pistusiţ-mi mini! HRISTU 39; **they could scarcely ~ it** nu lă pistusia a ochĭlu, HRISTU 62

BELIEVER *s.* pistipsít

BELITTLE *vb.* ñicşurédz, cătăfroniséscu ‖ CUNIA 90: atimuséscu

BELL *s.* cămbánă; *F:* clóput; (*for animals*) ciocán di oi, trácă; (*small ~*) gărgăríciu, yăryălíciu

BELL TOWER *s.* cămbănăríe, cambanaryió, símandru

BELLADONNA *s. bot.* măseáuă

BELLFLOWER *s. bot.* minghiúşe

BELLICOSE *adj.* căvyă(n)gí, ghiurultagí

BELLMAN *s.* ‖ *Peş:* câmbănargí, CL 41

BELLOW *vb.* mug, mudzéscu, mung(ă)ri(p)séscu

BELLOW(ING) *s.* mudzíre, mugrisíre

BELLOWS *s.* (*as in a blacksmith's shop*) miháne ‖ *Prv:* buháne, CL 39; *GSus:* fuĺínă, CL 45

BELLY *s.* bícă, bică, pântică; **You cannot fill up a ~ with words** Cu zboáre pântica nu s-úmple; (*the lower part of the ~*) stripóchiu

BELLY BUTTON *s.* → NAVEL

BELLY-BAND *s.* ghíncală, yínglă

BELONG *vb.* l-am *or* lu-ám *m*, u-ám *f*, ĺi ám *m pl*, li ám *f pl*; **Albanians who ~ed to the sultan** Arbinéşi ţe ĺ-aveá sultánlu

BELONGINGS *s.* lúcru, *pl* lúcre *and* lúcrurĭ; cărcăndíe, cărcăndă, cătăndíe, cătândíe, nicuchirátă

BELOVED *adj.* vrut; *also:* alughít, daş, dáşur, durút, zdrod ‖ LITURG 126: **of your ~ son** a dorrútlu híĭlu atău

BELOW *adv.* dinghiós, dighiós; **from ~** di pri nghios; **They encircled us from ~** Ni-anvărtíră di pri nghios

BELOW *prep.* **~ the forest** di-ghiós di pădúre

BELT *s.* curáuă, *N:* curáo; *also:* băr *or* bărnu, zónă, zúnă, *dim.* zuníţă; (*leather ~ with cartrige loops*) cileáhe, şileáhe, sileáf, sileáfe → CARTRIDGE ~

BELT *vb.* (*to encircle with a belt*) ţíngu (→ § 32)

BEMIRE *vb.* bârbâtéscu, mâryéscu → DIRTY

BEMIRED *adj.* (*as of horses*) lăspusít

BEMOAN *vb.* plângu, buiséscu

BENCH *s.* (*at school; also a tailor's ~, a joiner's ~, etc.*) báncu (*and* bángu), trápeză; (*along or around a house*) pizúĺu ‖ STERGHIU 3: scámie

BEND *s.* anduplicătúră; bástă; (*knot*) nod, *pl* noáde → FOLD

BEND *vb.* andúplic; (*to lean over or out*) apléc; **He bent over to drink some water** S-aplícă s-bea ápă (PC *Brz* [zbea]); (*of a road*) frângu amplátea; ncârlighédz; (*as a metalic bar*) strâmbu ‖ (*in token of submission*) apún, LITURG 124 (*the d/o is* caplu 'the head')

BEND ONE'S STEPS TOWARDS *vb.* (*to turn to*) ĺau cătră

BENDING *s.* (*as of an old man*) gribuíre

BENEATH *adv.* dinghiós, di-ghiós, prighiós di prighiós → UNDER

BENEDICTION

BENEDICTION s. (*agreement, consent*) evluyíe, vluyíe, evluyisíre; vluitó; urăciúne (*and* urâ-), răciúne, urucíne, urăcínă, urcíne, rucíne; (*prayer*) ifchíe, ifcheáuă, ifhíe; **to give ~** bag vluitó

BENEFACTION s. bunăteáţă, filanthropíĺe, filanthropíe, sivápe

BENEFIT s. prucuchíe; ufélie; (*undeserved ~*) yeayláră; **Forget about your ~s!** ≈ S-mută yeaylára!

BENEFIT vb. aduchésc ţivá di; **Do you think he ~ed life at least a bit?** Ţ-u ai că aducheá ţivá di bánă? **~ from** hăiruséscu

BENEVOLENCE s. bunătáte, bunáţă, bunăteáţă; (*grace*) cherémi, cheremlâche

BENIGHTED adj. (*overtaken by darkness or night*) ntunicát

BENIGN adj. eváşcu *and* iaváşcu; *med.* aţél búnlu

BENT s. (*inclination, talent*) doáră

BENT adj. (*as under a burden*) gribuít; fáptu andáulea [•dáŭ•lᵉa] → CROOKED

BENUMB vb. (a)múrtu, amurţăscu; **His body had become ~ed** Trúplu ĺ-aveá amurţâtă; ▼ncărfuséscu; **Cold weather had ~ed us** Arcoárea nă aveá ncărfusítă; (*to ~ with or as if with cold*) ncucinédz, ngu-; ncucinéscu, ngu-

BENUMBED adj. (*as of one's voice*) pirít; (*of a limb*) amurţât; nstugát

BEQUEATH vb. alás; ĺ-alás dhyeátă

BEQUEST s. lásă, miráze

BERATE vb. trag un pirdáfe → SCOLD

BEREAVEMENT s. amăreáţă, cripáre, dureáre

BERET s. (*worn by the Albanians*) chéce, cuc, cúcă, fésti → CAP

BERGAMOT PEAR s. górţă apídhye

BERRY s. *bot.* báclă

BESEECH vb. ▼(a)ngréc, ▼cáftu, ţer → BEG, IMPLORE

BESET vb. anăpădéscu, ▼mintéscu, ▼stinuhurséscu

BESIDE prep. (*next to*) níngă; (*in addition to*) pri níngă

BESIEGE vb. anvăríg, anvărlíg, nţercĺu, ţircĺédz, nţircĺédz

BESMEAR vb. → SMEAR, SOIL

BESMIRCH vb. → BESMEAR

BESMIRCHMENT s. lăvăşíre, lavuşíre, lăvuşíre, lichisíre, lirusíre, mâryíre, murdăripsíre, ngăláre, pângân(ips)íre, putusíre; (*with mud*) lăspusíre

BESOM s. métură

BESPRINKLE *vb.* nţilistrédz

BEST *adj.* nai bun; **brandy of the ~ quality** arăchíe di nai búna; **The large chimney is the ~** Nai bun eáste ugeáclu máre; **the ~** nai ma búna; cáma búna; dip ma búna ‖ (*the ~ part of smth.*) frúntea (*lit. 'the forehead'*), PARALLELE 157 → DO ONE'S (DAMNED) ~

BEST MAN *s.* (*sponsor of a marriage*) nun

BEST MAN'S FATHER *s.* muş, mămúş

BEST MAN'S MOTHER *s.* múşe, mămúşe

BESTIR *vb.* (*to rouse to action*) ▾scol

BESTOW *vb.* (a)hărzéscu; **~ a benefit upon smb.** ĺ-fac bun → PRESENT

BESTRIDE *vb.* ncálic, ngálic

BET *s.* stíhimă → WAGER

BET *vb.* mi acáţ, mi acáţ cu báste ‖ bag báste, PARALLELE 155

BETOKEN *vb.* adúc sémnu, dau sémnu, fac ispáte, apudixéscu

BETRAY *vb.* ▾pridáu, ▾prudáu; **You have ~ed us** Tíne nă prudédişi; ▾prudhuséscu, scot mpáde; (*to mislead*) ▾plănéscu, plănăséscu ‖ (~ *oneself*) mi dau di páde, BASME 448

BETRAYAL *s.* pridáre, prudare

BETROTH *vb.* ▾isuséscu, u-adár di fărínă ‖ alăxéscu neálile, BASME 438

BETROTHAL *s.* arăvuñisíre, isusíre, isósmă, isósmată

BETROTHED *adj.* isusít

BETTER *adj.* ma bun; anótir

BETTER *vb.* antréc

BETTER *adv.* cála, ma ghíne, ma mbar

BETWEEN *prep.* (a)námisa di; ntră; **~ the two of us** ntră noi dóĺi m; díntră; **the road ~ these two villages** cálea díntră aéstă doáuă hoáre; nóĺjica di, nólgica, nólgiuca, nóĺjuca

BETWEEN WIND AND WATER (*i.e., in a very bad state*) ≈ cătră soáre (*lit. 'towards the sun'*)

BETWIXT AND BETWEEN *adj., adv.* ceat-pat; ne úda, ne uscáta (*lit. 'neither wet, nor dry'*)

BEVERAGE *s.* phitó

BEVY *s.* (*girls*) fitáme; (*women*) muĺiráme

BEWAIL *vb.* arăvdăséscu, arăbdăséscu → LAMENT

BEWARE *vb.* ▾(a)firéscu, ▾amfiréscu → BE ON ONE'S GUARD

BEWARE! *interj.* Ai-ţâ ócĺlu! Ai-ţâ peána! Lárgu! Mutreá! Sacân!

BEWILDER

Várda! ‖ Dişcľíde-ţ ócľiľ! BASME 131

BEWILDER *vb.* ▾cicărdiséscu, ▾cictiséscu, ▾cihtiséscu, ▾şişirdi-séscu, ▾şiştiséscu

BEWILDERED *adj.* aumbrát, nămătisít, schirdút, şişirdisít, şiştisít; şarfúra *invar.*; t.ul; (*fascinated*) măndipsít → GIDDY

BEWILDERMENT *s.* şişirdisíre, şiştisíre; (*as after a beating*) tulíre

BEWITCH *vb.* (a)măyipséscu, (a)măghipséscu, căidiséscu, ▾leg; măndipséscu, nămătiséscu **Romanian women have bewitched Goga** Vlă-hútile lu-áu ligátă pi Góga

BEWITCHED *adj.* loat di vále, ligát, măghipsít, măyipsít

BEWITCHMENT *s.* căidăsíre, măyipsíre, măndipsíre, nămătisíre

BEY *s.* beiu, beu

BEYOND *prep.* nclo di; **went ~ the sea** trápse nclo di-amáre; **at the back of ~** dúpă soáre; tu ascăpitátlu a lóclui; iu bea púľi ápă; **~ measure** prísti misúră; **They are ~ my strength** Nu-s trâ ándzăle a meále

BEYOND ALL DOUBT *adv.* fără di áltă

BEYOND ALL MEASURE *adv.* (*very much, immeasurably*) a mórtului; **She loves him ~** L-va a mórtului; fâr isáfe

BEYOND SMB.'S STRENGTH *adv.* → BEYOND

BICKER *s.* căvyă, ncăceáre

BICKER *vb.* → SQUABBLE

BID FAREWELL *vb.* or cale-ambár; mi ľértu (di)

BID GOOD-BYE *vb.* (a)lás sănătáte; ñ-ľau sânătáte (di la); urédz cale-ambár ‖ ñ-ľau oáră búnă, BASME 439, 440, 442; ñ-ľau dzúuă búnă (di la), BASME 423

BIDDY *s.* púľe, puľíţă, găľínă, găľinúşe

BIG *adj.* máre *m/f*; *pl* mări; (*as of a blanket*) bólic; (*corpulent*) căbátcu, *m. pl* căbátţi, *f pl* -tţe; (*spacious*) lărguríu, ncăpătór, vlíhur; (*used emphatically*) cugeá, gugeá, cugeámite; **You are ~ guys and you don't have any sense** Hiţ gugeá ficióri ş mínte nu-avéţ; **such a ~ ...** gugeámite; **such a ~ girl** gugeámite feátă

BIG DIPPER *s. astr.* trăpód (*and* trăpódh), lătrăpód (*and* -pódh)

BIG-BELLIED *adj.* pânticós, buricós, fuľinós, băzăcós, jibăcós, jibicós; *s.* băzácă, zăbácă

BIG-EARED *adj.* uricľát

BIG-HEADED *adj.* căpós, *f* -oásă, *m pl* -óşĭ, *f pl* -oáse

BIG-MOUTHED *adj.* gurahán, *m pl* -háñ

BIG-NOSED *adj.* nărós, *f* -oásă, *m pl* -óşĭ, *f pl* -oáse

BIGOTRY *s.* → FANATICISM

BIGWIG *s.* (*an important person*) greu

BILBERRY *s. bot.* afíngă, afínghe ‖ *Av:* ţápurnă, CL 262

BILE *s. anat;* also *fig.* (*irascibility*) heáre, hulíe

BILGE *vb.* (*as a cask*) disfúndu

BILIOUS *adj.* (*irritable*) căchiós, *f* -oásă, *m pl* -óşĭ; inagí

BILK *vb.* aplăniséscu → CHEAT

BILL *s.* cioc; *also:* cărăntáne, chipítă, ciuplitúne, dintánă, ghintánă → BEAK ‖ ALIA 107: chirintánă, cimbél, clun, dáltu al púilu, mitícă *or* mítcă, náre di puľu; *M:* dănténă, SarD 27; *G:* dâltánă, *ibid.;* *Cru:* tindánă, GOLAB 254

BILL *vb.* (*to caress*) gugiléscu

BILL CASE *s.* purtufóle, pirtufóle, portafél

BILLFOLD *s.* → BILL CASE; (*small ~*) priftáciu

BILLINGSGATE *s.* ngiurătúri *f pl* → ABUSE

BILLION *s.* biliúnă

BILLOW *s.* úndă → WAVE

BILLOW *vb.* ▾turculéscu, ▾arucutéscu

BILLY GOAT *s.* → HE-GOAT

BIN *s.* săndúche, sindúche, sfindúche

BIND *vb.* ▾leg; ~ **hand and foot** ľ-taľu mâñle

BINOCULARS *s.* → FIELD-GLASS

BIRCH-PLANTATION *s.* *G:* pilpét, *Lvz:* pulpét

BIRCH-TREE *s.* ‖ *Av:* léfcâ, CL 258; *GSus:* pelipét, pilpét CL 258

BIRD *s.* puľu; (*small ~*) iavríu; ~ **of prey** orñu ‖ ALIA 106: *also* pui, *Am, Gra, Grbţ, Mul, Nij, Ses, Trn;* puiu, *GSus, Kok*

BIRTH *s.* amintáre (*and* amindáre) amintátic, soárte; **from ~ to death** di tu soárte pân-tu moárte; **person of low ~** cătrănár, suisâz, xisóiastu ‖ *Cru:* făţeáre, GOLAB 215

BIRTH CERTIFICATE *s.* năfúze, nufúze

BISHOP *s.* epíscop, dhispótĭ (*and* dis-)

BISHOPRIC *s.* eparhíe. episcopát, episcupíe, dhispuţâľe

BIT[1] *s.* (*the steel part of a bridle*) ‖ *Prv:* halinó, CL 253

BIT[2] *s.* (*small amount or fragment*) anghídhă, ghídhă; **Give them a ~ of cheese** Dáţ-lă nă anghídhă di caş; hir, *dim.* hirúş; heámă, theámă; **It is a ~ too late** Eáste theámă amânát; **not a ~** cât trâ

BITCH

yitríe; cât ghitrúşca; dhráme (*and* dráme), ténghiu, ténghe; **When he returned he did not find a single ~ of it** Când s-turnă nu-află un ténghiu; sálmă, sâlmă, şilé; **~ by ~** câte puţân; (*as of money*) părălâche; **a ~ ago** adineávra, adeaneávra, daneávra ‖ **not a ~** (*as in a blunt refusal*) fărmác; **I won't give you a ~!** Fărmác nu-ţi dau! BASME 226 ‖ **not a ~** níţi tră ileáce (*lit.* 'not even for a cure'; details in PARALLELE 120)

BITCH *s.* căţáuă ‖ *AMer, Nij:* căţá; *Gra, Grăm, Mi, Pals, Trn:* căţáu [•ţáᵘ]; *Cľis, Prv:* căţeáu [•ţ°áᵘ]; *Suf:* căţeáuă, B-ARCH 91 ‖ cúcicâ [kúĉ•kâ], DIARO 208

BITE *s.* (*an instance of biting*) muşcáre; (*as by a snake*) şirpicáre, chipináre, chipinătúră

BITE *vb.* ▼mâşcu, múşcu; (*as of a harsh wind*) seáţir, ▼ciuléscu; **The cold wind was ~ing our ears** Vímtu aráţe nă ciuleá urécľile; (*by or as if by a snake*) ▼şirpichédz ‖ (*as by fleas or flies*) **The flea has bitten me** Mi mâcă púriclu (*lit.* 'The flea has eaten me'), PARALLELE 120

BITE ONE'S LIPS *vb.* (*with worry, regret, etc.*) ñ-múşcu búdza (di cripáre)

BITING *adj.* (*as of a thorn*) nţăpătós, *f* -oásă, *m pl* -óşĭ; (*as of a knife*) tăľós, *f* -oásă, *m pl* -óşĭ; struxít, *m pl* -xíţ

BITTEN *adj.* (*by or as if by a snake*) chipinát, (n)şirpicát

BITTER *adj.* amár, amărós, fârmăcós, zămărát, *G:* merahún

BITTERLY *adv.* amár

BITTERNESS *s.* amăráme, amăreáţă; *N:* amăráre; cémir, fărmác *and* fármac, farmúc, nvirináre, nvirnáre, pilóñu, virín

BITUMEN *s.* pécură → PITCH

BIZARRE *adj.* alócut, anápudh, *f* -dhă, *m pl* -dz, *f pl* -dhe; ciudós, *f* -oásă, *m pl* -óşĭ; paráxin; toáfe *invar.*; trónciu, *f sg/pl* trónce, *m pl* trónci

BLAB *vb.* (*to talk idly*) discântu, máţin, máţin pi virisíe

BLACK *s.* (*a black person*) Aráp, *pl* aráchi, *f* Arápsă, *pl* -pse

BLACK *adj.* laiu, *f* láĭe, *m/f pl* lăĭ; córbu, *f* córbă *or* coárbă, *m pl* córghi, *f pl* córbe *or* coárbe; (*as of eyes*) gâilé, gălăíţ *or* lăíţ; négru *and* négur, *f* neágră, *m pl* négri, *f pl* neágre; sumulă-íţ; (*of wine*) carás *or* crasát; (*of dogs, etc.*) aráp, *f* -pă, *m pl* aráchi, *f pl* arápe ‖ *Amc:* (*of eyes*) castáncu, SCHL 114

BLACK ALDER *s. bot.* soárbă

BLACK AND BLUE *adj.* siñicát

BLACK ART *s.* amáie, măndíe, (a)măyipsíre, aumbráre

BLACK WOMAN *s.* Arápsă

BLACK SEA *s.* Amárea-láie, Láia-amáre

BLACKBERRY *s. bot.* (a)múră; căpíncă, dúdă, mănáze

BLACKBERRY BUSH *s.* (a)rúg, pilivúre ‖ *Cru:* amúr, GOLAB 198

BLACKBIRD *s.* (a)nírlă, ñérlă (*and* nérlă); *also:* cóciuv, cójvu, coşáv, cóşuv, cóciuvă, cóşavă, málin, mălắñe, mălíñu ‖ *Prv:* cóşurvă, CL 42; *SJos:* gógiuvă, CL 45

BLACKBOARD *s.* pínac, pinácă

BLACKEN *vb.* (*to make black*) lăiéscu, sumulăéscu, ▾ncărñidzédz; (*to denigrate*) zburăscu

BLACKENED *adj.* lăít

BLACKENING *s.* lăíre, ncărñidzáre

BLACK-EYED *adj.* mavrumát

BLACKGUARD *s.* púşcľu, *G:* dărmálă → RASCAL

BLACKISH *adj.* caramúz; (*of a horse*) cârắ, gal; (*tanned by the sun*) lăít di soáre; sumulăít, sumulăíţ

BLACKNESS *s.* lăitúră

BLACKSMITH *s.* hirár, hălché, yíftu ‖ *Amc, An, Els:* sidhiró, *Src:* sidhărár, *Na:* sidhirău; *Plat:* hiró; *Mul:* cóvaci [kó•vaĉ], B-ARCH 380

BLACKTHORN *s.* ţápurnu, iapurnéu, iapurneáuă

BLADDER *s. anat.* bişícă

BLADE *s.* lámă; (~ *of grass*) hir; (*as of a knife*) lipídhă

BLAIN *s. med.* → ABSCESS

BLAME *s.* cătiyuríe, cătiyuríľe, furñíe, măhănă → CAST THE ~

BLAME *vb.* arúc măhănălu (*or* fáia, furñía);, ▾cătiyurséscu, giúdic

BLAMELESS *adj.* fâră (níţi un) stépsu; făr di catmére; (*of people*) ápă di lituryíe (*lit. 'holy water'*) → INNOCENT

BLAMING *s.* cătiyursíre

BLANCH OVER *vb.* (*to prove innocent*) ‖ scot cu fáţa álbă, BASME 177

BLAND *adj.* (*mild*) eváşcu *or* iaváşcu; *m/f* moále, *m/f pl* moľ

BLANDISHMENT *s.* culăchipsíre, cănăchipsíre, hăidhipsíre

BLANKET *s.* cérgă, ciórgă; viléndză → COVERING

BLASPHEME *vb.* ▾blástim, blástin, ▾uryiséscu

BLASPHEMER *s.* blăstimătór

BLASPHEMY *s.* uryisíre

BLATHER *s.* → BABBLER

BLATHER *vb.* *(to talk foolishly)* xenu-zburắscu

BLAZE *s.* lumbrăsíre, lumbrusíre, luñínă, luñináre

BLAZE *vb.* árdu dumáne, árdu bărbărútă; *(of a fire, 3 sg)* bur-bureádză, bubureádză

BLEACH *vb.* alghéscu, biléscu, clucutéscu

BLEAK *adj.* astrăchít; sec, *f* seácă, *m/f pl* seţĭ; stérpu, *f* steárpă, *m pl* stérchi, *f pl* steárpe

BLEARY-EYED *adj.* ţălpós, -oásă, -óşĭ, oáse

BLEAT *s.* azghiráre, azghirát ‖ zghirară, HRISTU 21

BLEAT *vb.* *(of sheep and goats only)* (a)zghér, ber

BLEATING *s.* azghiráre, azghirárrát, azghirátic

BLEED *vb.* ▼ancrúntu, ▼sândzinédz; *(as of one's nose)* ñ-cúră nárea

BLEED SMB. WHITE *vb.* (a)fuléscu (di parádz)

BLEEDING *adj.* sândzinát; *(stained, soiled)* mârşusít

BLEMISH *s.* cusúre, scárţu

BLEMISH *vb.* ▼stric, tălăéscu

BLENCH *vb.* *(to renounce, to retreat)* trag mână → ABNEGATE

BLEND *vb.* ▼ameástic, ▼mintéscu ‖ PC: ▼fac únă

BLESS *vb.* dau urăciúnea; **I give you my blessing!** Sâ ñ-ai urăciúnea! evluyiséscu, vluiséscu; *(of a priest)* bag vluitólu

BLESSED *adj.* evluyimén, vluyimén; *(interjectionally)* **~ is / be / are ...** Hará di ...; **~ed be the mother who brought him into the world!** Hará di mă-sa ţi şi-lu-áre! ‖ CARAFOLI 63: vlu(gh)isít

BLESSED VIRGIN, THE *s.* Dumnidză-Făcătoáră *(calque from Greek, unusual)*

BLESSING *s.* urăciúne *(and* urâ-*)* → BENEDICTION; **it is a ~ that** cálai-că, calái-ţe

BLIGHTED *adj.* *(affected with blight, of plants and fig.)* pălít

BLIND *adj.* órbu, *f* oárbă, *m pl* órghi, *f pl* oárbe; chior; gav, *m pl* gayĭ; **Áre you ~?** Ai gavumáră? ‖ *Els, Fal, Fu, Hor, LvO, Na, Pdz, Pur, Smr, Vil:* gav, B-ARCH 190; *Amc:* strâmbu, SCHL

BLIND *vb.* urghéscu

BLINDER *s.* *(on a horse's bridle)* ‖ *Peş:* căpáche, CL 41

BLINDFOLD *vb.* ñ-u toárnă míntea

BLINDLY *adv.* urghíşalui, di-aurghíşalui; zúrlu

BLINDMAN'S BUFF *s.* ‖ agiucárea cu óclĭĭ ligárea; agiucárea aurghíşului; Orbu-Yeáni *is the blindman*, DIARO 101

BLINDNESS *s.* urghíre, urgheáre, urbáre, urbeáţă, gavumáră; (*passing dimness of sight*) túrbu; urbárea a găľíñlor; *fig.* primoáră

BLINK *vb.* (*of light*) licurédz, licuricéscu, licrăséscu; ‖ PC: (*as because of smoke*) scápir ócľiľ

BLISTER *s. derm.* bişícă, fultácă, arópun, rópan ‖ DIARO 172: cândílâ

BLISTER *vb.* ▾bişichédz, ▾fultăchédz

BLISTERING *s.* bişicáre, fultăcáre

BLISTERY *adj.* bişicát, fultăcát

BLITHE *adj.* → HAPPY, MERRY

BLIZZARD *s.* nturín, nturináre, azvimturáre, zvinturáre; **the ~ is raging** nturínă, nturineádză

BLOATING *s.* umfláre; (*as of boiling milk*) căbărdisíre

BLOB *s.* chicătúră, chícută, lánguţă, lóscut

BLOCK[1] *s.* (*for cleaving firewood*) discătór

BLOCK[2] *s.* (*large piece*): **~ of cheese** dánă

BLOCK *vb.* (*to trap*) ▾(a)pitruséscu, *N:* (a)putruséscu; **It's just here that we ~ed the snake** Auá apitrusím nipârtica; **They will ~ me in the house** Va mi-apitruseáscă n cásă

BLOCKADE *s.* (*siege*) anvărligáre

BLOCKAGE *s.* apitrusíre

BLOCKHEAD *s.* glar → STUPID

BLOND *adj.* (a)rús; beal, *m pl* beľ, *f pl* beále; (*of lambs*) beálbiş, beáliş

BLOOD *s.* sândze *n;* **a drop of ~** nă chícută di sândze → MAKE BAD ~ BETWEEN ‖ ALR 1119: *art sg:* sândza (*sic*)

BLOOD PRESSURE *s. med.* ‖ STERE 42: piási

BLOOD VESSEL *s.* vínă, flévă

BLOODHOUND *s.* (câne) zăyár (*and* ză-)

BLOOD-LETTING *s.* lăsáre

BLOODSHED *s.* cârléşi di sândze; sîndzináre

BLOODY *adj.* sândzinós, *f* -oásă, *m pl* -óşĭ, *f pl* -oáse

BLOOM *s.* floáre, *N:* floárắ; **in ~** *adj.* anflurít → FLOWER

BLOOM *vb.* (a)nfluréscu, dau floárắ, ▾dişcľíd; **I was growing and ~ing like a rose** Eu crişteám ş dişcľideám cum dişcľíde trandáfi-la; flituriséscu, luludhyiséscu ‖ ALIA 38: *3 sg:* anthiseáşti, anthălúcheşte, bubuchiséşti, da bumbúchi [•búk'], da flori, da lilíţi

BLOOMER

[•líţi], scoáte flori, scote lílă, scoáte lulúdhă, dischíde

BLOOMER: **make a ~** u adár bóză → PUT ONE'S FOOT INTO IT

BLOOMING *s.* nfluríre, luludhyisíre

BLOOPER (*blunder*) *s.* ‖ CUNIA 118: **make a ~** cálcu tu pítă

BLOSSOM *s.* and *vb.* → BLOOM, FLOWER

BLOT *s.* dámcă → STAIN

BLOT *vb.* ▼lichiséscu

BLOTCH *s.* (*as of ink*) dámcă; *derm.* (*on an infant's face*) blândă, hrúpă

BLOW *s.* únă; **a ~ with a club** únă cu buzdugánea; bătíche, goádă; (*with the fist*) súplu, şúplu, şub; (*with an axe*) tâpureáuă; (*a ~ with the thick end of a rifle*) cundăcheáuă; (*a ~ with the foot or hoof*) (s)clóţă, cloáţă, culţátă, scluţátă; (*unexpected calamity*) pusoágă → COME TO ~S ‖ **The first ~ is half the battle** ≈ dzúua búnă s-cănoáşte di tahiná, ALR 1470

BLOW *vb.* (*of the wind*) súflu; trag; **~ your nose!** Súflă-ţ nările! **~ up the lamp!** Súflă lámpa! **~ up the fire!** Súflă tu foc! **when the wind ~s** víntul când vai trágă; (*of a light wind*) adíĺu; **The breeze is ~ing softly** Lişór adíĺe ávra; (*as of a trumpet*) bat; **The trumpet blew** Bătú buría; (*to rage, as of a blizzard*) năvăéscu ‖ ALIA 12: **(The wind) is ~ing** (a)súflă, báte, trádze

BLOW ONE'S TRUMPET (*to boast*) ≈ Murí yífta ţe ti-alăvdá (*said to a boaster; lit. 'The Gipsy woman who used to praise you has died!'*)

BLOWING HOT AND COLD *adj.* (*to be ambiguous*) ni úda, ni uscáta

BLOWSY *adj.* buzgúni *invar.*

BLUBBER *vb.* ▼plângu, ▼deápir

BLUBBERER *s.* (*as of a child*) lătiníciu

BLUDGEON *s.* şcop → CUDGEL

BLUDGEON *vb.* dau cu ciumága

BLUE *adj.* albástru, *m pl* -ştri *or* -ştrâ, *f* -stră, *pl* -stre; *also:* yálan; (*as of eyes*) yălănós, *G:* muşinghínă; niruyálaz, niúr, năúr, ñírlu, uraníu; **make** *or* **become ~** *vb.* albăstréscu, (n)viñiţăscu; **turning ~** *s.* nviñiţâre ‖ *Cru:* acíc, GOLAB 195; *Gop:* vinít, GOLAB 259 → OUT OF THE BLUE

BLUE FUNK *s.* lăhtár → FRIGHT

BLUEBELL *s.* *bot.* minghiúşe [•ģú•]

BLUDGEON *s.* (*club*) şcop

BLUEBERRY *s.* *bot.* afíngă, afínghe

BLUEBOTTLE *s. bot.* zărzăríche

BLUES *s.* (*state of depression*) milancolíe; **He has the ~** ≈ cánda ĺ-si nicáră cărắyĭle (*or* ghimíĭle)

BLUFF *s.* cacearmáie

BLUISH *adj.* vínit (*and* víñit); yioáră [yi•oá•]

BLUISH-GREEN *adj.* ghérdu, *f* -rdă, *m pl* -rzâ *f pl* -rde

BLUNDER *s.* glăreáţă → MAKE A ~

BLUNDER *vb.* → MAKE A BLUNDER

BLUNT *adj.* (*worn-out*) mâcát; (*rough, rude*) jupânéscu, păduríş ‖ HRISTU 46: dudum

BLUNT *vb.* (*to wear out*) mâc; (*to deaden, to lessen, as of pain*) amúrtu, amurţắscu

BLUNTLY *adv.* cu ţupáta → PUT IT ~

BLURRED *adj.* alăcít

BLUSH *s.* aruşeáţă

BLUSH *vb.* (*as of shame or embarrassment*) aruşắscu, ▾păléscu, mi-adár pipér tu fáţă; (*to ~ up to one's ears*) ▾păléscu pân di urécĭi

BLUSHING *s.* aruşíre

BLUSTER *vb.* (*as of a storm*) huhutéscu, văzéscu; (*to talk or act boisterously*) ñ-u fac sílă (cu)

BLUSTERER *s.* fanfarón, scandaĺár

BOAR *s. zool.* ‖ **GSus:** néris; **Cru:** pórcu nipăstrít, GOLAB 244 → WILD BOAR

BOARD *s.* scândură, *dim.* scânduríce (*and* scăn-); blánă; (*in a fence*) plătíţă → CHOPPING ~

BOARD OF DIRECTORS *s.* efuríe, efurlíche

BOAST *s.* **Great ~, small roast** ≈ Zboáre múlte, ftóhe máre

BOAST *vb.* ▾alávdu, ▾căbărdiséscu, ▾cămăruséscu, cămărséscu, ▾curduséscu, ▾făléscu, ▾frângu; ▾fuduléscu; **They ~ with their golden necklaces on their chests** Eále si frângu cu fluríile pi chéptu; ĺ-trag cămára *or* trag cămări; ▾ţân pi cămări; víndu línte, víndu curcubéte di Chirásova ‖ ▾măréscu, PARALLELE 133 → BLOW ONE'S TROMPET

BOASTER *s.* tartabés → BOASTFUL

BOASTFUL *adj.* fălós, -lít; *also:* (a)lăvdát, -dătór, -dós; **N:** cămăr(u)sít; cu fúmuri; fu(r)dulít; pălăvrăgí; piñisít; tartabés *or* tartarés; **~ in words and timid in deeds** ≈ căcát di guştiríţă (*lit.* 'lizard shit') ‖ MERCA 19: béngastu

BOASTING *n.* fălíre → BRAGGING

BOASTING *adj.* → BOASTFUL

BOAT *s.* căíche, căiác, căiácă, căráve; *G:* cărádhi; ghimíe, lăn-dură (*and* lân-), lúntre, náie, şáică, várcă ‖ *Peş:* sále, CL 260

BOATMAN *s.* căiccí, cărăvyeár, cărăvyiót, varcagí ‖ *GSus, Peş:* sălgí, CL 260

BOBBIN *s.* cărúľu

BOBCAT *s. zool.* arâs

BOBWHITE *s. orn.* → QUAIL

BODE *vb.* ▾pruvéd, prufitipséscu; **This ~s ill** Nu va s-cúră lúcru bun; Nu undzeáşte s-híbă lúcru bun

BODKIN *s.* súlă

BODY *s. anat.* trup, *dim.* trupulíciu; (*rare*) córpu; (*group*) ur-táuă → COME IN A ~

BODY LOUSE *s.* → LOUSE

BOG *s.* (*poorly drained area*) váltu, varcó

BOGEYMAN *s.* bóşea → BUGBEAR

BOGGLE *vb.* ▾aspár

BOGGY *adj.* băltós, -oásă, -óşĭ, -oáse; *also* văltós

BOGUS *adj.* cálpu, *m pl* -lchi, *f* -lpă, *pl* -lpe; *also* cálpic *or* -cálbic, *pl m* -lpiţĭ, -lbiţĭ

BOIL[1] *s. derm.* cuptúră, gărnúţ (*and* gâr-), gărâţ, grănúţ, grănţu, frinţél, frân-, furni-, furnu-, sfrânu-, sufrân-; sufrândzéľu; (*big* ~) ócľu buín

BOIL[2] *s.* (*boiling*) clócut, *N:* cólcut

BOIL *vb.* hérbu (→ § 32); *fig.* hérbu (pi); clucutéscu, undzéscu; **He was ~ing over with rage at the girl** Hirbeá pi feátă; **~ing water** ápă undátă ‖ *Cru: 3 sg:* (*of a meal*) s-hunipseáşce, GOLAB 220

BOILER *s.* căzáne; *dim.* căzănúľe

BOILING *s.* heárbire, hirbeáre; undáre

BOILING WATER *s.* crop, ápă undátă

BOISTEROUS *adj.* (*blusterer*) asiyúriftu, *m pl* -fţâ; năpudheárnic, scandaľár, dzarzára (*and* zar-); (*as of a child*) sirsén, -sém

BOLD *adj.* ncucutát (*and* ngu-) ‖ om cu doáuă cápiti, BASME 43

BOLDNESS *s.* cutidzáre

BOLE *s.* brándu → STUMP

BOLERO *s.* (*jacket*) ghiurdíe

BOLETUS *s. bot.* arţivúrţe *f pl*

BOLSTER *vb.* ▾nvârtuşédz, ▾stiriuséscu

BOLT s. (*as in a door*) cătălăhtu, căpălăhtu, dzángră, lóstru, lóstur, lóthru, mándal, sírtu

BOLT[1] vb. ▼ţérnu, nţérnu (*and* ndzérnu) → SIFT

BOLT[2] vb. (*to run away*) u-adún, u-afúm (di-acló), (ñi-) u angán, u-arúp, li (a)spél, aspún păltările, li-aştérgu, bisguléscu, li că-léscu, li (*or* mi) căpsălséscu, li ciuléscu; (*interjectionally*) ciú-lea! *or* ľa-ľ fúmlu! *Also:* li deápin, fac, fac náparte, ▼frângu (di-acló), u frângu zvérca, ▼fug, fug di mi frângu, fug di nu mi ved, u ľau bisgúľa, ñ-ľau cáplu, ñ-ľau cărăndíile, ñ-ľau păltările [•tărĭ•], ñ-ľau pľácichile [pľáĉ•k'i•li], ▼măşcăturédz (di-acló); li scármin, li şpirtuéscu, li tíndu; **Seize the bag and ~ out thru the gate!** Úmflă sáclu şi ľa-ľ fúmlu prit poártă afáră! ‖ o-adún, BASME 35; o-angân cáţáua (di auáţe), BASME 404; ñ-ľau ócľiľ (de-auáţe), BASME 4; ñ-ľau zvérca, BASME 458; *imper.* fă-ţ paspórtea! BASME 431; DIARO 197: u câléscu; BATSARIA 8: ñ-ľau pérľi

BOLTING s. (*of flour, etc.*) nţirneáre (*and* ndirneáre), ţirneáre

BOLUS s. (*the soft mass of chewed food, speaking of cattle and sheep*) păstúră

BOMB s. top, tópă, bómbă ‖ CUNIA 32: búmbă

BON VOYAGE! cále-ambár!

BONBON s. → CANDY

BOND s. ligătúră

BONDAGE s. sclăvíľe, sclăvíe

BONDMAN s. rob, sclav; (*farmer-serf*) cifcí

BONDSMAN s. → BONDMAN

BONE s. os, *dim.* usíc, cioľu, *pl* cioáľe → BREAK SMB.'S ~S, CAST A ~ BETWEEN

BONELESS MEAT s. ‖ *N:* cárne mácră, CAPIDAN 152

BONER s. glăreáţă

BONHOMIE s. imireáţă, imiráme

BONNET s. cuc, cúcă, chilipóşe

BONNY adj. bírbu, *m pl* -rghi, *f pl* -rbe → HANDSOME

BOO interj. (*contempt or disapproval*) u! **~, shame on you!** U! Arşíne!

BOO vb. ľau hududú; aruşinédz, arşinédz

BOOBY s. léfcă, témblă

BOOBY adj. hascanífur; *G:* başinghél → STUPID

BOODLE s. (*bribe*) mítă, arusféte; (*big money*) sirmaié, sirmaé, picúľu

BOOK *s.* cárte, chiutúc, chitápe, vivlíe

BOOKLET *s.* afládhă

BOOKSELLER *s.* chitapcí

BOOM *vb.* (*to resound*) plăscănéscu

BOOR *s.* jupân

BOORISH *adj.* jupânéscu, *f* -neáscă, *m pl* -néşţâ, *f pl* -néşti

BOORISHLY *adv.* huryiteáşte

BOOST *vb.* mut nsus, ▾análţu, ▾alín, créscu, ▾agiút

BOOT *s.* cízmă, cíjmă; **a pair of ~s** nă păreácľe di cíjme; (*ankle ~*) călăpódă; gófă, scórnă, pudhúmată, pudhímată; (*half ~*) stiváľe, stivalétă, stifalétă, ştíflă; (*chidren talk*) pópă

BOOTBLACK *s.* lustragí

BOOTH *s.* chiósche, chióşcu

BOOT-LAST *s.* călăpe, călúpe, călupódhe, călăpódhe

BOOTLESSLY *adv.* ncot → VAINLY

BOOT-POLISH *s.* gileáe, lústru

BOOTSTRAP *s.* leápă, ureácľe

BOOTY *s.* alimúră → PREY

BOOZE *vb.* → TIPPLE

BORAX *s.* vórax

BORDELLO *s.* putanaryió

BORDER *s.* márdzină; *Grbţ:* márne; *also:* dhyeárgu, grániţă; *G:* gârníţă; sémte, sínur, *pl* sinurómate ‖ *Av, GSus, Prv:* (*between fields or plots*) sínur, CL 260 ‖ STERE 27: gărniţă

BORDER *vb.* (*to lie on the ~*) ▾viţinipséscu, ▾sinuripséscu

BORE[1] *vb.* (*to perforate*) ▾pitrúndu, ▾spitrúndu; *also:* **N:** ▾ampíhiur; azvundéscu, azundéscu, cărtilédz, sfreádin, străpúngu

BORE[2] *vb.* (*with ennui or tedium*) âľ şed şindáme → BE BORED ‖ *Cru:* aurăscu, GOLAB 203

BORED *adj.* (*weary*) bizirsít, plictisít → BE ~

BOREDOM *s.* aurâre, bizéryiu, bizirsíre, plictisíre, plixe, sâcâldisíre

BORER *s.* ent. ‖ DIARO 177: sâráchi

BORING *s.* (*piercing*) ampihiuráre, azvúndzire; (*tedious*) ánustu

BORN *adj.* amintát, fáptu, *m pl.* -pţâ, *f pl* -pte; fitát → BE BORN

BORROW *vb.* ▾mprumút → LEND

BOSKY *adj.* pădurós, *f* -oásă, *m pl* -óşĭ, *f pl* -oáse; *G:* sănluós

BOSOM *s.* sin

BOSS *s.* afindicó, cap

BOSS *vb.* cumăndărséscu

BOTCH *vb.* ▾mpeátic

BOTH *adj.* and *pron.* dóili *m*, dáule [dáŭ•li] *f*; andóľ [•dóľ] *m*, andoále *f*; amindóiľĭ [•dói•ľi], amindóľi [•dó•ľi] *m*, amindoále, amindále *f*; şamindói *m*, şamindoáuă(le) *f*; şándoi *m*, şandoáuă, şandoále, şandáule [•daŭ•] *f*; **She will be wife to ~ of them** Are să lă híbă niveástă a şandulór ‖ BASME 706: şamijdóiľi *m*, şamijdoále *f*; CARAFOLI 56: şamizdoľ *m*

BOTH OF A HAIR → LIKE

BOTH... AND *cj.* i...i; em... em ‖ TULLIU 108: **his black and bushy beard made him seem both dreadful and attractive** bárba lai şi stufoásă făţeá ca s-pără em fuvirós, em arăsít

BOTHER *vb.* (*to annoy, to trouble*) *N:* ▾angulcéscu → DISTURB ‖ **It does not ~ me!** Nu-ári zñíe, DIARO 350; **Leave it there, it doesn't ~ me** Nu mi cârteáşti, alásâ-lu acló, DIARO 94

BOTHER THE LIFE OUT OF SMB. *vb.* aród dit hiáte; mâc hicátlu; **You have ~ed the life out of me!** Mi-aroásişi dit hicáte! *3 sg aor:* Ñ-mâcă hicátlu!

BOTTLE *s.* şiş *and* (a)şíşe; *also:* bóţă, butíľe, chélche; (*of leather*) chilíţ *or* chilíţă; clondír, dulíe, fiálă, vóză; (*~ of 1,000 units*) hiľárcă; **Give me a ~ of wine!** Dă-ñ nă hiľárcă di yin! ‖ *Peş:* hunétă, CL 253; *Cru:* (*wooden ~*) plóscă, GOLAB 244; *F:* şuş; *M and Pls:* şíşă; *P:* şuş, SarD 34

BOTTOM *s. anat.* cur; (*as of a river*) fúndu; **from the ~ of the heart** di tru hicáte → DEPTH

BOTTOMLESS *adj.* fâră fúndu; afóndut

BOUGH *s.* cráncă, crángă

BOUGHT *adj.* acumpărát, *N:* ancumpărát

BOULDER *s.* bărţíre, cheátră; şcămbă; şómbur *and* şómbură

BOUNCE *s.* sáltă, (a)săltáre

BOUNCING BET *s. bot.* (*soap-worth*) sărpúñe, *G:* şărpúñe

BOUNDARY *s.* sémte; (*between two plots*) dhyeáryu → BORDER

BOUNTEOUS *adj.* cuvurdhă; giumértu, *m pl.* -rţâ, *f sg* -rtă; sălghít

BOUNTIFUL *adj.* giumértu, -rtă, -rţâ, -rte → GENEROUS

BOUNTIFULLY *adv.* (*abundantly*) di-primansús

BOUQUET *s.* (*as of flowers*) mănúcľu, túfă, dhimáte, buchét ‖ DIARO

BOURGEOISIE

153: stog di lilíci

BOURGEOISIE *s.* arhundilắche, ciorbagilắche

BOW *s.* árcu, dhuxár; (*reverence*) ncľináre → DRAW THE ~, DRAW THE LONG ~

BOW *vb.* ▾ncľin ‖ **Cru:** apléc, GOLAB 200; (*to ~ in greeting, courtesy or submission*) ľ-fac taéte, ľ-fac timínă

BOW OF RIBBON *s.* fľóngu, fióngu, fúndă

BOWL OVER *vb.* ▾súrpu

BOW WOW *interj.* ham-ham; gap-gap

BOWEL *s.* anat. maţ, *pl* máţă

BOWL *s.* (*vessel, usu. made of wood*) cărnéciu (*and* câr-); căţân, căţănă, câţón; (*made of clay*) ceam, cinác, cinácă, cináche, clidhupirác (*and* clidu-), cupác; (*madewooden*) cuvátă, guvátă, *dim.* cuvatícă; yăváthă, găvănă, misúră; piripinác, pirpinác; (*usu. for cheese*) rácică [rác•kă], *pl* ráciche [rác•k'i]; săcă, scuteále ‖ **GSus:** misúr, CL 256

BOWLDER *s.* → BOULDER

BOX[1] *s.* cásă, cutíe, *dim.* cutúcă, cutíce ‖ DIARO 339: *also* cutícâ

BOX[2] *s.* (*slap*) báţă, flíscută, flâscută, flúscută, fláscută, şúbă, şupleácă; (*on the nape*) ghiúştă, ghiuştăreáuă, zvârcăreáuă

BOX THE EARS OF SMB. *vb.* ľ-trag únă báţă; ľ-am nă şupleácă

BOX-TREE *s.* băngiu, yăreáuă, píscu, píxu, plíscu, şimşír

BOX WOOD *s.* pixáre; (*made of ~*) *adj.* pixăríş

BOY *s.* alabáciu, talabáciu, ciuliméan, cupiláciu

BRACE *s.* (*stay, support*) **Gop:** potpár *m*

BRACE *vb.* ‖ BATSARIA 61: *to ~ for a beating* mi-ndreg ti băteáre → PREPARE

BRACELET *s.* biligéche, bilgéche, biligíc, biligícă, bilingícă, bilingiúcă, bişlíc, bizilícă, biliczíe

BRACES *s. pl* (*pair of ~*) tarăndzâ *f pl*

BRAG *vb.* ▾măréscu → BOAST

BRAGGART *s.* tartabés → BOASTFUL

BRAGGING *s.* (a)lăvdáre, (a)lăvdătúră, fălíre, palávră, pălávră, piñisíre

BRAID *s.* cusíţă, cuseáuă → BRAID); (*cord or ribbon*) **S:** ciupáre

BRAID *vb.* (a)mplătéscu (*and* amblă-)

BRAIDED *adj.* (*of hair*) mblătít

BRAIN *s.* críer, mădúuă, midúuă, midúľu; (*rare*) mindúuă → BEAT

(BREAK, CUDGEL) ONE'S BRAINS, MAKE SMB.'S ~ REEL

BRAINLESS *adj.* fâră mădúuă → STUPID

BRAISE *vb.* hérbu

BRAKE s. (*for hemp*) limădhúră (*and* -dúră)

BRAMBLE s. *bot.* chíngher, ciun, yumarángath, mărăţíne, schínu a tárlui

BRAN s. grúndză, târţă

BRANCH s. (a) lumáche, alămáche, *dim.* lumăchíţă; *also*: aluneáuă, alneáuă, angheáuă, (a) rắzgă, cârcóciu, câtáľe, creángă, cráncă (*and* crángă), grángă, dărmă, drămă, dărmăţeáuă, dégă, deágă, dúşcu; (*small ~s of fir*) şíţă; (*dead ~s used as firewood*) uscătúră; *coll.* vreáşturi, vréşturi; (*trimmed off, coll.*) clăstúră; (~ *of a stream*) mânicǎ

BRANCHY *adj.* alumăchiós, -oásă, -óşĭ, -oáse

BRAND s. (*a piece of burning wood*) tăciúne [•ĉú•] ‖ VELO 106: tuciún; (*mark*) sémnu, dámcă

BRAND *vb.* sémnu, nsimnédz, simiuséscu; (*to attest ownership of sheep*) noáţin; ~ **on one's memory** ▼stămbuséscu tru mădúuă

BRANDING s. (*of sheep*) nuţináre, **G:** nutáre

BRAND-NEW *adj.* (*of clothes*) nou dit ac; (stráñe) dit foártică ‖ ca scos dit ou (*lit.* 'as if taken out from an egg'), BASME 473; ca óulu aróş, BASME 458; ca óulu aţél aróşlu, BASME 473

BRANDY s. (a) răchíe di prúştină; (arăchíe) ţipuríşe; măstíhă (*and* măsthícă) ; **French** ~ cuñác

BRASH *adj.* furtunós, -oásă, -óşĭ, -oáse

BRASS s. bácră, băcáre, hálcumă, *pl* halcómate

BRASS FARTHING s. (*coin of low value*) cărădánă; mângâr *or* mấngâr, mângâră, mángară

BRAT s. (*usu. of a child*) disgrădít → IMPERTINENT

BRAVE *adj.* **1.** gióne *or* jóne *m*, gioánă *f*; giunél, junél; *also*: alipidát; aslán, arslán, babageán, bărbát *m*, bărbátă *f*; **their ~ women** muľérile a lor bărbáte; babáşcu, babáşcan, bir *or* bírciu; (*of a woman or girl*) birbeácă, biroáñe; cădigí; **Cľis:** ciupérnic; ghirăchín, palicár, putút, şaín, vârtós; **a ~ young man** vârtós gióne; xiftér, zot; **2.** *adj.* (*pertaining to a ~ person*) giunéscu; **3.** s. giunác, giunár

BRAVELY *adv.* bărbăteáşte; cu giunátic

BRAVERY s. giuneáţă, giunátic, junátic, giunáme, junáme; *also*:

BRAVO

bărbăteáţă, bărbăţắľe, livindeáţă, livindlâche, pihlivănlâche, sărpiţắľe; **unsurpassed in ~** tru junátic nintricút

BRAVO *interj.* áferim, áşcolsun, brávo, brávu

BRAWL *s.* dăndắnă, ncârligáre → SCUFFLE

BRAWLER *s.* ‖ DIARO 154: buclucgí

BRAWN . vâruşáme, vârtúte

BRAWNY *adj.* muşcľós, cărnós, putút, vârtós

BRAY *s.* (*of donkeys*) angărsíre, (a)zghiráre, azghirát

BRAY *vb.* (*of donkeys only*) angărséscu; (*also of sheep*) azghér

BRAZEN *adj.* ni-aruş(i)nós

BREACH *s.* (*of a law, etc.*) călcáre; **~ of habit** dizvéţ

BREACH *vb.* (*to infringe*) ▾cálcu

BREAD *s.* păne (*and* pâ-); (*white ~*) asicmécă, frangiólă, somúnă *or* sămúne; (*unleavened ~*) ftazmítcă, stazmítcă; **ring-like plaited ~** culác, *dim.* culăcúş; **a crusty end of ~** călcâñu; **~ crumbled in hot milk** tripsánă → CONSECRATED ~ ‖ **to make ~** *vb.* **N:** firmít, CAPIDAN 152

BREADTH *s.* lărdzíme

BREAK *s.* (*respite from work or duty*) páfse, pápse; (*result of breaking; fragment, debris*) aspărgătúră; (*an instance of breaking*) arupeáre, arúpire, (a)spărdzeáre, (a)spárdzire, cripáre, frândzire, frândzeáre; (*infringement*) călcáre → MAKE A BAD ~

BREAK *vb.* ▾aspárgu (→ § 32); (*to damage*) **You've broken my watch!** Ñ-aspársişi oára! (*of a new day*) ápir; **Call Níca because the day has broken!** Gríţ-ľi al Níca c-apirí; **The day was beginning to ~** Loa s-ápiră; *impers.* hărăxeáşte; **~ the heart** árdu iñoára; **How many hearts he has broken!** Câte iñóri nu-áre ársă! ▾frângu (*and* frăngu), *aor.* fregiu *or* frâmşu; ▾stric, ▾zdrúmin, zdroámin; (*as of one's back*) ▾dişilédz, ▾misucupséscu; (*as of a branch of a tree*) ▾dijgľín, dizgľín, dizghín

BREAK AN ENGAGEMENT *vb.* ▾disuséscu

BREAK AWAY FROM *vb.* (a)scáp

BREAK DOWN *vb.* (*to collapse*) vérsu mpáde; çad stog (ân páde)

BREAK EVEN *vb.* ‖ u scot ân cap (cu), BASME 461

BREAK FAITH WITH SMB. *vb.* ‖ ies di zbor, BASME 502

BREAK FAST *vb.* (*to eat meat*) mi puríntu (*and* puríndu)

BREAK IN *vb.* aspárgu, íntru, ▾pitrúndu, ▾spitrúndu

BREAK INTO A CONVERSATION *vb.* ▾ameástic

BREAK INTO A RUN *vb.* fac náparte → BOLT

BREAK INTO FLINDERS *vb.* ▾zdrúmin, zdroámin; (*as of a plate*) ▾adár țívale

BREAK INTO PERSPIRATION *vb.* mi-arúp sudóri ‖ BATSARIA 61: (*from fear*) ñ-treáțe n-asudoáre

BREAK INTO PIECES *vb.* (*as of a cloud*) ▾diñíc

BREAK OF DAY → BY THE BREAK OF DAY

BREAK OFF *vb.* ▾bitiséscu, pricúrmu; (~ *a conversation*) u mor láfea; (*to ~ relations with smb.*) u-arúp cioára (cu) ‖ *3 pl:* nu-și gréscu cu gúra, BASME 605

BREAK ONE'S BACK *vb.* ▾dișilédz, ▾misucupséscu; (*as of a horse*) dăulédz

BREAK ONE'S BRAINS ABOUT / WITH *vb.* ñ-disíc cáplu

BREAK ONE'S WORD / OATH *vb.* ▾strâmbu, ▾cálcu giurátlu, ▾tórnu di graiu, ies di(n) zbor, ñ-cálcu zbórlu dat, ñ-cálcu giurátlu

BREAK OPEN *vb.* plăscănéscu (*and* plâscă-)

BREAK OUT *vb.* (*of the break of day*) *3 sg:* dă; **The day broke out** Deáde dzúua; (*of a rash*) ▾fultăchédz, ▾bișichédz, ▾bișchédz; **to ~ in pimples** gărnuțădz

BREAK SMB.'S BONES *vb.* chisédz oásile, stulcinédz di chiutécă → BEAT

BREAK THE DEADLOCK *vb.* ĺ-áflu căpáchea

BREAK THE SEAL *vb.* (*to unseal*) dizvuluséscu, dizvuliséscu

BREAK THROUGH THE ENEMY'S RANKS *vb.* ▾arúp; **They were thinking to break the ranks uphill** Nâși minduiá si-arúpă dzeána nsus

BREAK TO SMITHEREENS *vb.* ▾adár țivále, ▾fac sârme, ▾zdrúmin sârme-sârme

BREAK UP *vb.* (*as of a gathering*) ▾aspárgu; (*as of a cloud*) ▾diñíc

BREAK WIND *vb.* (*to expel intestinal gas*) zdângânéscu únă

BREAK WITH SMB. *vb.* (*to fall out with smb.*) arúp cioára (cu)

BREAKDOWN *s.* cădeáre, arăvuíre

BREAKFAST *s.* (a)ngustáre (di tahiná); **~ is waiting!** La meásă! *or* La meásă s cupuséști! ‖ *Peș:* gústu, CL 46; *Cru:* gustáre, GOLAB 218

BREAKFAST *vb.* (a)ngústu ‖ ĺau ngustárea, BASME 86

BREAKING *s.* arupeáre, arúpire → BREAK

BREAKING IN *s.* (*as of a ship*) fundusíre; (*forcible entry*); aspărgăciúne, spărgămíntu

BREAKING OUT *s. derm.* fulticáre, bișicáre

BREAKNECK: ‖ **run at a ~ speed** fug di mâc lóclu, BASME 500

BREAM

BREAM s. *ichth.* plătícă

BREAST s. *anat.* chéptu, sin, țâță → BEAT ONE'S ~

BREAST-BONE s. (*wishbone*) iádeș, trágă

BREAST-FEED vb. dau si súgă, alăptédz, țâțuéscu

BREATH s. suflắre, suflát; *also:* adiľátic, adiľáre, (a)hnoátă *or* honoátă, anásă, duh, sulúche; **all in a ~** t-un adiľátic, t-únă anásă, t(r)-un súflet; **to recover one's ~** ñ-víñe sulúchea; **take smb.'s ~ away** ñ-si cúrmă adiľárea → TAKE ~, TO ONE'S LAST ~

BREATHE vb. súflu, adíľu, ľau anásă

BREATHING s. adiľát → BREATH

BREATHING ONE'S LAST adj. *and* adv. ‖ pi hírlu di moárte, BASME 144

BREATHLESS: stand ~ vb. ñ-si cúrmă adiľárea

BREECHES s. púturi f pl; *also* pắturi

BREECHING s. (*wool from the codal part of a sheep*) suéľu; (*a part of a harness; a wide strip protecting the back of a horse*) bâldúme, buldúme, pắldắmă, pisteáuă, pișteáuă

BREED vb. (*to give offsprings*) mpuľédz, mulțắscu

BREED DISCORD vb. arúc chétri, arúc múști, bag anghídz, bag fití-ľe, bag munắfícuri, bag schiñ, bag súle, bag zizáñe, ▼nțap, sâr-gľéscu múște

BREEDING s. mpuľáre, mulțâre

BREEZE s. adiľátic, (a)éră, ávră

BREEZE vb. (*of winds*) adíľu

BREVIARY s. (*a Greek-Orthodox prayer for the saints of the month*) minéu

BRIBE s. (a)rușféte, băhcíșe ‖ *GSus, Prv:* băccíșe, CL 38

BRIBE vb. aúngu; **We've ~ed the watchman** Pândárlu lu-avém aúmtă

BRIBETAKER s. rusfitcí

BRICK s. chirắmídhă, chiriñídhă, ciuruñídă, túvlă, túlă; **a ~ house** cásă cu túvle; **row ~** plitháre; **a ~ of a boy** un sémnu di fi-ciór; un gióne nă nișáne → DROP A ~

BRICK-FIELD s. chiramaryió

BRICKLAYER s. (*mason*) mástur

BRICKMAKER s. chirắmidhár, tuvlár

BRIDAL adj. nuntár; **a ~ song** cântic nuntár

BRIDE s. niveástă, nveástă, *dim.* nivistícă; *N:* mắireásă, *S:* niveástă noáuă; crúnă, dudíe, dudușeánă; (*adj: pertaining to a ~*) nivistéscu, nvistéscu, niviștéscu

BRIEF *adj.* scúrtu → SHORT

BRIDEGROOM *s.* yambró, yrambéu

BRIDESMAID *s.* (*maid involved in the wedding ritual*) surátă; (*female sponsor of a marriage*) núnă

BRIDGE *s.* ‖ púnte; *with reference to the ~ over the Danube river at Cernavoda, Romania:* puntea di la Cerna Voda, BELIMACE 52

BRIDLE *s.* fărnu (*and* fâr-); *N:* afăr; frân; *also:* (a)ghéme, căpéstru, cătărmă, cătărmău, *G:* tricătoáre

BRIDLE *vb.* ▼căpistruséscu, ▼căpistruéscu, ncătrămédz, ▼stăpuéscu

BRIDLE ONE'S TONGUE *vb.* (*ant.* to divulge, to reveal) nu dau pri toácă

BRIDLED *adj.* (*curbed, subdued*) căpistrusít

BRIDLING *s.* căpăstrusíre

BRIEFCASE *s.* geántă

BRIER *s.* măcéş → EGLANTINE

BRIGAND *s.* caceác; *G:* furcudár; haramíu; (*Turkish brigand*) cărjilí, cărjalíu, cărgialíu

BRIGANDAGE *s.* furlíche, furlíľe

BRIGHT *adj.* lumbărsít; **as ~ as a new button** ca scos dit ou → BRILLIANT; (*intelligent*) disfáptu

BRIGHTNESS *s.* (*gleam*) lámpse

BRILLIANT *s.* brilántu → JEWEL, DIAMOND

BRILLIANT *adj.* scântiľós; *also:* **Smr:** cărtătirát, grindinát, grân-; limbisít, lumbărsít, lubrisít, luñinós, luţít; (*as of a face*) şcălichiceát

BRIM *s.* (*as of a well*) búdză, márdină *and* márdine; (*as of a glass*) zvíţă

BRIMFUL *adj. and adv.* (*as of a glass*) plin, umplút víţă; písti zvíţă; (*as of a bag: full to capacity*) ndisát

BRIMSTONE *s.* schífură, teáfe

BRINE *s.* (*of cabbage*) moáre, salamúră, sălămúră; *also:* ármă, armíră, armázmu, yar

BRING *vb.* adúc (→ § 32); (*to be brought*) cătundiséscu; **You, sons of an emperor, to be brought so low!** Hiľ di amiră ş cătăndisíţ pri hála aéstă!

BRING A HORNET'S NEST ABOUT ONE'S EARS *vb.* ≈ ñ-si áre urâtă bána

BRING AN ACTION / A SUIT AGAINST SMB. *vb.* → SUE

BRING DISCREDIT ON ONESELF *vb.* mi fac părăvulíe; **The cute miss**

BRING DOWN

went to the woods and brought discredit on herself Dúse ñíca tu curíe di s-feáțe părăvulíe; ▼fac birbáte

BRING DOWN vb. (as the price, an enemy, etc.) (a)firiséscu

BRING DOWN A PEG OR TWO vb. ľ-u apléc nárea

BRING FORTH vb. ▼(a)fét, fac, ▼dizvóc, nfaș or nfășédz → GIVE
BIRTH

BRING GRIST TO ONE'S MILL vb. ñ-u bag ápa tu avláche

BRING IN vb. ▼bag

BRING INTO A POUND vb. (to put pressure upon smb.) bag súla n
coáste

BRING INTO SERVITUDE vb. ▼sclăvuséscu, ▼sclăvuéscu, (a)rubuéscu

BRING OFF vb. u scot náparti → SUCCEED

BRING OVER vb. adúc

BRING TO AN END vb. scot lúcrulu n cap; u scot n cap → END,
FINISH

BRING TOGETHER vb. (of sheep on a pasture) ▼mârșin

BRING TO HIS / HER WIT'S END vb. disíc cáplu

BRING TO LAW vb. → SUE

BRING TO LIGHT vb. (as a forgotten debt) dizgróp

BRING TO TRIAL vb. scol → TRIAL

BRING UNDER CONTROL vb. ▼căpistruséscu → BRIDLE

BRING UP vb. (to educate) créscu, prăxéscu

BRINGING FORTH s. (a)fitáre; (the process, place or time of ~,
usu. of sheep) fitáľu

BRINGING UP s. creáștire

BRINK s. márdzine

BRISK adj. sárpit → AGILE

BRISTLE vb. ▼ariciuéscu, ▼ariciuséscu ▼zbârléscu, zburléscu; **His
hair ~ed up** Pérlu ľ-si ariciusí or ľ-si zbârlí

BRISTLE UP vb. (to startle) ▼mpirușédz (and mbi-), mpirșédz

BRISTLING UP adj. (of hair) (cu pérlu) arăciusít, ariciuít, mbirșát, zbârlít

BROAD adj. lárgu, f -rgă, m/f pl lárdzi → WIDE

BROAD BEAN s. cucheáuă; fávă ‖ fáo, CAPIDAN 148

BROAD-CHESTED adj. (as of a horse) chiptós, -oásă, -óșǐ, -oáse

BROADEN vb. ▼lărdzéscu, lărguéscu

BROAD-SHOULDERED adj. lárgu tu plătări; dhiplárcu, m pl -rțâ

BROCADE s. ‖ DIARO 150: curazé

BROCHURE *s.* (*booklet*) aflá dhă

BROIL *vb.* ▼frig, ▼pârjiléscu

BROKE *adj.* oárfăn di părádz; fără pră → PENNILESS

BROKEN *adj.* frâmtu; (*dissolved, as of an association*) disfáptu

BROKEN DOWN *adj.* (*by age or heavy work*) sarával, miscupsít

BROKEN-HEARTED *adj.* văpsít → SAD

BROKER *s.* misít, sămsár; *adj.* sămsăréscu, *m pl* -réşţâ, *f pl* -şti

BROKERAGE *s.* misitíe, sămsărlâche

BRONZE *s.* brúndzu, tuciu, túnge ‖ DIARO 150: strúmciu; HRISTU 1, 5: bruz

BROOCH *s.* cărfíţă

BROOD *s.* (*people*) zintúne

BROODY HEN *s.* clóţă, clóce, cloáce, clóşcă

BROOK *s.* avláche, avláchiu, pivóñu, puvóñu; *Muz:* răcheá, răchée; víe

BROOM *s.* métură, *dim.* miturícă, mituríce

BROOM MONGER *s.* métur, miturár

BROTH *s.* hirtúră, ciurbă, ciórbă, súpă

BROTHEL *s.* putanaryió

BROTHER *s.* fráte, *dim.* frătíc, fărtíc; *F:* fărtát, frătát, furtát ‖ CUVATA 4: (*term of respect for an elerly ~*) baci; BATSARIA 6: **his** ~ fărtá-su

BROTHERHOOD *s.* frăţâľe, frătătlâche; (*bond preceeded by a special ritual*) fărtăţâľe

BROTHER-IN-LAW *s.* cumnát, băginác ‖ *F:* bigianác, SarD 29; (*wife's brother*) dzíniri di sórâ, DIARO 325

BROTHERLINESS *s.* cărdăşlâche

BROTHERLY *adj.* frăţéscu, *f* -ţeáscă, *m pl* -ţéşţâ, *f pl* -ţéşti

BROTHERLY *adv.* frăţeáşte, frăţáşte

BROUGHT UP *adj.* criscút, *f* -tă, *m pl* -ţ, *f pl* -te

BROW *s.* anat. dzeánă, (s)frânţeáuă, sufrânţeáuă (*and* -ndzeáuă), sprândzeánă → CLEAR UP ONE'S BROWS

BROWBEAT *vb.* (*to intimidate*) cănuséscu

BROWN *s.* murneáţă

BROWN *adj.* múrnu, *m pl* -rñi, *f pl* -rne ; caferengíu; (*of hair*) căstănát, ismér, scur; (*of goats*) cul ‖ *Cru:* cafeiáv, GOLAB 223; STERE 69: mórcu

BROWN *vb.* (*by frying or cooking*) ţiyăr(ip)séscu

BRUISE

BRUISE *s.* (*contusion*) ciuplíre, murníre, vătămătúră, viñiteáţă, viñiţâre ‖ *Prv:* cucuşúrâ, CL 42

BRUISE *vb.* ▾ciupléscu, ▾zdrúmin, zdroámin, zmoátic

BRUNET *adj.* múrnu, *m pl* -rñi; smead, -ă, -dz, -de (*sic*); sumuláiu

BRUSH *s.* vúrţă; cétcă, fârce

BRUSH *vb.* ▾vurţéscu

BRUSHING *s.* vurţusíre

BRUTAL *adj.* → BRUTE

BRUTE *s.* ni-ñilós. ni-ñiruít; túrcu (*lit.* 'Turk')

BUBBLE *s.* fúscă, plúscută; (*also* anat., derm.) bişícă, căndílă, făltácă, fultácă; (~ *of soap*) hăboátă di săpúne

BUBBLE *vb.* (*as of boiling water*) clucutéscu, clucutédz, gruhutéscu, gruhtéscu, hurhuréscu, şuñédz; adár căndíle

BUBBLING *s.* (*of boiling water*) clucutáre, clucutúră, gróhut, heárbire, hirbeáre, şuñáre, undáre; (*effervescent talk*) láfe

BUCHAREST *s.* ‖ MERCA 7: *def.* Bucuréştea

BUCKET *s.* 1. căldáre, cărdháre; *G:* căldúş; *dim.* căldărúşe; *also:* (*wooden*) ciótră, cófă, cóvă, cuvă, cufínă; *Cl'is:* (*one decaliter*) curóiu; măldzărúşe; (*small*) tăryăcícă, úrnă, viţélă, viţeálă; (*of copper*) bărcáce, băryáce, brăyáce, bruyáce; 2. (*the ~ of a water mill*) cărútă

BUCKETFUL *s.* cufínă

BUCKLE *s.* (*as in a belt*) cătrămă; (*ornamental ~*) gubé, páftă, ploáce; (*head ornament*) culáre ‖ *Pls:* (~ *in a belt*) piástă, CL 258; *GSus:* phiástor, *ibid.*

BUCKLE DOWN TO WORK *vb.* mi astérnu tu lúcru (*or* pri lúcru)

BUD *s.* bot. bubúche, cl'eciu, ţípur; (~ *of a flower*) buzbucheáuă ‖ MERCA 9: *pl:* băbúchi [bă•búk']

BUD *vb.* bubuchiséscu, mbubuchiséscu, dişcl'íd, ţipurédz

BUDDING *s.* bubuchisíre, ţipuráre

BUDGE *vb.* ▾ñíşcu, ▾bat; litéscu; ▾min; **They did not ~ from him** Nu s-băteá di nângă nâs

BUFF (*the bare skin*): **in ~** *adj.* gol-gulişán ‖ gol ca tuféchea, BASME 419 (*lit.* 'as naked as a rifle')

BUFFALO *s.* bívul, búval, búvul; (*cow ~*) bivulíţă, buvălíţă, buvulíţă, búvală; (*young ~*) bic, buvălíciu *m*, buvălíce *f*

BUFFET *s.* şúplu, cluţátă → KICK, BLOW

BUFFOON *s.* bal'áciu → CLOWN

BUG *s. ent.* bumbărác, rímă

BUG *vb.* → ANNOY, BOTHER

BUGBEAR *s.* Gióia; *also:* Bóşea, Góşea, Tărăbóş; búbă, fántase, fántasmă (*and* fandásmă), fándaymă ‖ ALB, **Kërb:** gangólu, gogólu; **Dren:** găgól', Brâncuş 557; (*scarecrow*) **Amc, Mal, Perd:** păpúş; **An:** schiásmă; **Am, Pal:** schiázmă; **Gard, Kast, NPrv, Pur, Smr, Ver, Vil, Vot:** schiáhtru; **Arγ, Arm, Cern, Grăm:** aúmbră, B-ARCH 339; STERE 19: buşurácă

BUILD *vb.* ▾adár, ▾álţu, ▾análţu, (a)stăséscu; (*to set up, to install*) bag; **Where did you ~ your sheepfold?** Iu băgáşi căşáre? ‖ (*to make, to construct*) scol, HRISTU 22

BUILD IN *vb.* stizmuséscu; **in order to build her (in the wall) alive** yíe s-u stizmuseáscă

BUILDING *s.* (*as a process*) astăsíre; (*a roofed and walled structure*) adărămíntu, bináe, bină; ghevghíre

BUILDING IN *s.* stizmusíre

BUILT *adj.* ncl'igát → MADE

BULB OF GARLIC *s.* cap di al'u

BULGARIA *s.* ‖ **Cru:** Vurgăríe, GOLAB 259

BULGARIAN *s.* vârgăr, vâryăr, vúlgur, vúrgar, vúrgăr, vúryar, vúryur; ócan; şop, *pl* şópeañ; zdángan; *coll.* vurgăráme; *adj.* vulgăréscu, vur-, *m pl* vulgăréştâ, vur-; *f/n pl* vulgăréşti, vur-

BULGARIZE *vb.* **G:** ▾vârgârédz

BULGE *s.* umflătúră

BULGE *vb.* ▾úmflu, ▾căbărdiséscu

BULK OF FOOD *s.* (*loaf*) dérlic

BULKY *adj.* mplin; ncărcát; dínga, dânga, dénga; căbătcu; ~ **cargoes** furtíi căbátţe *f pl*

BULL[1] *s.* bic, bică, buyă, dhămál, távru ‖ **Cru:** giúngu, GOLAB 261

BULL[2] *s.* (*idle talk*) bişiñ di cúc (*lit.* 'cuckoo's farts') → NONSENSE

BULLET *s.* curşúm, curşúme, gugóş, făndéc, fândâc, mulíve, mulídhe (*and* mulíde); plúmbă, pl'úmbă, pl'úmbu (di gră); top; (*of tow*) ciuciumág (di stúpă) *m*

BULLOCK *s.* giúncu ‖ **Av:** dhămulóplu, CL 44

BULLY *adj.* → EXCELLENT

BULLY *vb.* ñ-u fac sílă (cu)

BUM *s.* haihúi → LOAFER

BUM AROUND

BUM AROUND *vb.* alág loc di loc; hălăndăréscu; misúr steálile (*lit. 'to measure the stars'*)

BUMBLE *vb.* zăzăéscu → BUZZ

BUMBLEBEE *s. ent.* heávră, zăngănár, zăngrănă

BUMP *s.* (*swelling of tissue*) ‖ **Amc:** buşuĺé n cap, SCHL 113

BUNCH *s.* (*of grapes*) reápin *m*; *also:* arápun (di aúuă) *m*; arápune *m*, areápune, areápine; *dim.* aripinúş, bărbărúş, căirúş, cruş, călă-rúş (di aúuă); **Pdz:** cărmăstár, ripinídhă; (~ *of flowers*) buchét (di flori); **G:** chítcă; făndáche, văndáche, mâldár → BOUQUET; (~ *of flowers or fruits*) bărbătúş, bubúche; (*of wild strawberry*) bărburíş di frándzĭ

BUNDLE *s.* (*of garlic or onion*) arămătheáuă, chíscă; **a ~ of gar-lic** únă chíscă di aĺu

BUNDLE OFF *vb. imper. 2 sg:* Adúnă-u di auá! → BOLT, GET LOST!

BUNG *s.* (*in a barrel or cask*) cep, til

BUNG-HOLE *s.* vránă

BUNGLE → MAKE A ~ OF SMTH.

BUNGLE *vb.* ▼mpeátic

BUNGLER *s.* măsturíciu, mbalumatí, mpiticătór

BUNK *s.* chiritúră → NONSENSE

BUNNY *s.* ĺepur, ĺépure → HARE

BURDEN *s.* bróstu, furtíe, greáţă, ncărcătúră, sárţină, sálţină, var; **They got relieved of the ~ they were carrying** S-ĺişuráră di greáţa ţe purtá

BURDEN *vb.* ▼nşiédz, ▼nşiuédz [nşi•u•édz]; ncárcu

BURDOCK *s. bot.* bróstu, bróştu, bróştur, brúşir, brúştură

BURGLARY *s.* furíĺe, furlíche

BURIAL *s.* ngrupáre, ngrupăciúne, ngrupiĺáre

BURLY *adj.* căbátcu, *m pl* -tţi, *f pl* -tţe → THICK-SET

BURN *s.* árdire, ardeáre, căpsálă; (*with a hot liquid*) upăritúră ‖ (*injury from fire*) arsurâ, DIARO 78

BURN *vb.* ▼árdu (→ § 32); ▼frig; **The sun is ~ing** Soárĭle frídze; (*of food*) ▼pârjéscu, pârjiléscu; ▼scrumédz, ▼nscrumédz; **The food had ~ed on the fire** Mâcárea si-aveá scrumátă; ▼ţicnuséscu; (*usu. of skin*) ▼ústur; (*to harm with hot water, milk, etc.*) ▼upăréscu, **N:** upuréscu; (*of hair or brows*) ▼căpsălséscu (pérlu); ▼ghimtuéscu; (*to ~ down, to melt away in fire*) hunipséscu; **The firewood burnt down** Leámnile hunipsíră tu foc

BURN ONESELF *vb.* (*with a hot liquid*) ▼upăréscu, upuréscu
BURN WITH SHAME *vb.* mi ngroápă lóclu di-arşíne
BURNED *adj.* ársu, *f* -ă, *m pl* árşi, *f pl* árse
BURNING *s.* (*also:* ~ **down**) árdire, ardeáre
BURNING *adj.* (*and fig., as with thirst*) şcrumát
BURNT *adj.* (*of food*) ţicnusít
BURNT SMELL *s.* (*of food*) ţícnă
BURNT OFFERING *s.* afiérumă, curbáne
BURP *s. and vb.* → BELCH
BURROW *s.* culcúş → LAIR, DEN
BURST *s.* (*of laughter*) cachín, căchín, căhtíre, hărhăríre
BURST: with ~ eyes cu ócľi cripáţ
BURST *vb.* (*as with anger*) crep, plăscănéscu, zdângânéscu, dân-gânéscu; (*to ~ with sadness or sorrow*) âñ yíne tâc s-fac; (*to ~ with envy*) crep di éryu ‖ (*to ~ with anger or envy*) ñ-víne z-dân-gânéscu tu cheáli, BASME 115; crep tu cheále, BASME 399; ñ-yíne cripárea, BASME 406; nu-ñ áflu lóclu di érgu, *ibid.*
BURST INTO TEARS *vb.* mi ľa lăcriñle; lăcrămédz, lăcrimédz, lă-cărmédz
BURST ONE'S BUTTONS *vb.* (*to be or grow too fat*) mi-adár şut
BURST OUT *vb.* ▼zvom
BURY *vb.* ▼(a)ngróp, ▼ngrupiľédz; *Smr:* grop; ▼acoápir; **They buried them under a pine** Ľ-acupiríră sun chin; (*to be buried*) ▼úmplu groápa (*lit. 'to fill out one's own grave'*) ‖ (*as a threat*) Ti bag tu loc (*lit. 'I will put you in the ground'*), PARALLELE 124
BURY IN OBLIVION *vb.* ▼agărşéscu, trec tu cártea a mórţâlor, trec tu psihuhárte → FORGET
BUSH *s.* túfă, *dim.* tufícă → BEAT ABOUT THE ~
BUSHED *adj.* curmát → TIRED
BUSHEL *s.* (*unit of dry capacity*) ≈ alcéchi *f*; (*about 45 kg.*); chiló, crínă, cútlă, cuveále, cuvéle (*and* cuvéľe), munzúră, mân-zúră, stambóle, şiníc, tăyáre, tăgáre, usmác
BUSHY *adj.* tufós, -oásă, -óşľ, -oáse → TUFTED
BUSINESS *s.* lúcru, ipóthise; (*a piece of ~*) daravéră, dáre-loáre ‖ BATSARIA 59: **What's your ~?** (*why should you care?*) Ţi ţi-u zóre? → DO A GOOD ~, MAKE A SWEET ~ OF IT; (*killing*) DO THE ~ FOR SMB.
BUSTARD *s. orn.* ceámñe
BUSTLE *s.* (*run*) alăgáre; *G:* (*fuss, stir, uproar*) lávă, vreávă,

BUSY

giufă ‖ BG: Culóña, DIARO 277; *also* treáţiri, *ibid.*

BUSY *adj.* acăţát

BUT *adv.* (*only, merely*) mânghi, sai, maşi; **Cola regreted ~ one thing** Mânghi di únă ĺ-păreá arău al Cóla; (*other than*) **The shemer was nothing ~ joy** Curcusúra sai haráuă erá; **This man is ~ rancor** Ómlu aéstu eáste maşi heáre → ONLY

BUT *prep.* (*except*) hórghea di

BUT *cj.* áma, ma, maşi, ámea, mea, amí, brem, dea, eleachím, ghioa, *N:* ghioám; măni (*and* mâni), ména, mu; **The bride is good, ~ she is not Aromanian** Niveásta eáste búnă ma nu eáste Armână; **another devil, ~ this time more skillful** áltu drac, gioam cáma mástur

BUTCHER *s.* cărnár, căsáp, hăsáp; (*Turkish tyrant*) cărgialíu, cărjilí, cărjilíu; *adj.* (*as of a knife*) hăsăpéscu

BUTCHER *vb.* ▾gilitipséscu, ▾măchilipséscu

BUTCHER'S SHOP *s.* căsăpníţă, hăsáp-, *Cĺis:* hăsămníţă; hasapĺó

BUTCHERY *s.* (*trade*) hăsăplâche

BUTT[1] *s.* varélă → CASK

BUTT[2] *s.* (*with the head or horns*) (a)mbuiráre

BUTT *vb.* ▾(a)mbúir

BUTT IN *vb.* (*to break into a conversation*) ▾ameástic

BUTT-END *s.* (*of a rifle*) cundác, strat → FAG END

BUTTER *s.* úmtu

BUTTERFLY *s.* flítur, fliútur, fliútură, flútur, flítură, fítur, pirpirúnă, pitălúdhă; (*metal trinket on shirts etc.*) (a)sprí(n)ciu

BUTTER-FRITTER *s.* lăhídhă, nălăhítă

BUTTERMILK *s.* dhálă (*and* dálă)

BUTTERY *adj.* umtós, -oásă, -óşĭ, -oáse

BUTTOCK *s.* anat. şidzút; (*runk of a horse, etc.*) căpúĺe, căpúĺu

BUTTON *s.* (a)nástur *m*; fólă; **be a ~ short** ≈ nu lu ári súbaşi la loc; eásti loat di mínti; i-lipséscu drăñ; **as bright as a new ~** ≈ ca scos dit ou (*lit.* 'as if taken out from an egg') → BURST ONE'S ~S ‖ *GSus:* cópci, *Prv:* cumbí, *Pls:* cumbíe, CL 42

BUY *s.* (a)cumpăráre

BUY *vb.* ▾(a)cúmpăr (*and* acúmbăr); *N:* (a)cúmpru, *G:* cúpăr; ĺau (*lit.* 'to take'); (*to bargain, to shop*) păzăripséscu

BUYER *s.* muştirí, muştiră; *coll.* muştiráme

BUZZ *s.* zângâníre

BUZZ *vb.* zăzăéscu, zângânéscu, zvângânéscu, vângânéscu; (*as bees*

in a hive) hérbu (lit. 'to boil'); (of crickets) jujuéscu

BY prep. 1. (near) níngă; 2. (pledge) pri; **I swear ~ my eyes** Mi giur pri ócľiľ a mei; 3. (distribution) câte un m, câte únă f; **One ~ one all passed** Câte un, un tuţ tricúră; **The leaves are fall-ing down one ~ one** Fründzăle cad câte únă; **~ how many?** câte câţ? m, câte câte? f; 4. i/o di; **They seized him ~ the collar** L-loáră di limăreáuă; 5. (conformity) dúpă, di pri, di písti; **~ the barking of the dogs one could tell that there were some strangers** Dúpă ală-tráre aducheái că săntu oámiñ xeñ; **He could recognize sheep by wool and lambs ~ eyes** Li cunoşteá óile di pri lână, ñéli di písti ócľi

BY ALL MEANS adv. cum di cum; **They were trying to kill him ~** Mu-treá cum di cum s-lu vátămă ‖ BELIMACE 49: cu iţidó di trop

BY ANY MEANS adv. → BY ALL MEANS

BY CHANCE adv. (perhaps) nápa, nápă, ţivá

BYE-BYE (go to sleep) lu-ľu-ľú, lu-lu-lú; náni-náni

BY DINT OF TALKING adv. di zbor zbor; di cuvéndă cuvéndă

BY EVERY MEANS → BY ALL MEANS

BY FITS AND STARTS adv. (with difficulty) rúfu-n-búfu [rú•fum•-bú•fu]

BY HEART adv. di nafoáră

BY HOOK OR BY CROOK adv. → BY ALL MEANS

BY JOVE! dzău!

BY NO MEANS pa-pa-pá! ba-ba-bá! iuvá ş-iuvá ‖ dip-di-dip, DIARO 241

BY ONESELF adv. di síngur; **The doors began to open by themselves** Pórţăle acăţáră să s-dişcľídă di síngure

BY STEALTH adv. pri niaduchíte → STEALTHILY

BY THE BREAK OF DAY adv. di andzáre, di tahínimă, di tiheánă, tu işíta a soárĭlui

BY THE DAY adv. (as to work ~) ‖ ALR 1828: cu ghiunlúche

BY THE LUMP adv. cu cárlu

BY THE SKIN OF ONE'S TEETH adv. rúfu-n-búfu [•fum•bú•]

BYGONE adj. di zămáne; **bygone invaluable people** lai oámiñ di ză-máne

BYPASS vb. nvărlíg, nvărlighédz, ▾şuţ

BYWORD s. susúme → NICKNAME; **become a ~** agiúngu părămíth

C

CAB *s.* (*with horses*) cucíe → CARRIAGE

CABAL *s.* mâcătúră

CABBAGE *s.* veárdzu, vérdzu, cuceán, geáhtu ‖ ALIA 75: veárdză *and* veárză

CABBAGE BRINE *s.* ármă

CABBAGE HEAD *s.* ‖ *GSus:* túmbâ di veárdzâ, CL 262

CABLE *s.* pălimár, spărtínă → ROPE

CACHE *s.* ascumtíş, ascumtáĭu

CACHET *s.* (*with powder of quinine*) scónă → PILL; (*seal*) dámcă

CACKLE *s.* (*of hens*) cărcărăre, cărcărizáre

CACKLE *vb.* (*of hens and fig.*) cărcărédz; *of chickens*) cârcârédz (*to blab*) máţin, máţin pi virisíe, discântu

CAD *s.* (*an ungentlemanly person*) păstúră, plăstúră

CADAVER *s.* cúfumă, mârşe

CADDISHNESS *s.* nĭ-aruşináre, yumărlâche

CADDY *s.* cásă, cutíe → CHEST

CADRE *s.* (*frame*) curnídhă

CAGE *s.* culuvíe, cluvíe; (*as for a lion*) căfáse, căfắşe, căfése ‖ *M:* caféză, SarD 26

CAITIFF *s., adj.* cătăryár; idipsâz, *m pl* -âjĭ, *f pl* -âze; zgrumát

CAJOLE *vb.* ▾gúdur, ▾guduréscu → WHEEDLE

CAJOLERY *s.* guduráre, gudance → BLANDISHMENT

CAJOLING *adj.* disñirdătór, *f* -oáre; disñirdós, *f* -oásă

CAKE *s.* (*thin flat ~*) túrtă; (*~ made of wheat flour*) grânáţă; (*~ made with vegetables*) virdzáre, vărdzáre; (*on Saint Basil's Day, Jan. 1*) vasiloáñe; (*cheese ~*) pítă; (*meat or vegetable ~*) colburécă; (*apple and almond ~*) ghiulvarácă; *N:* cólpide; (*milk ~*) lăptáre, lăptúcă

CALAMITY *s.* pácus → MISFORTUNE

CALCULATE *vb.* ▾luyuryiséscu, luyurséscu, lugărséscu, ▾minduéscu

CALCULATED *adj.* (*of people*) adunát

CALCULATION *s.* cicuteálă; (*rumination*) hisápe, isápe, ricáme, luyaryeazmó, luyareazmó, luyureazmó, minduíre

CALENDAR *s.* calindár

CALF[1] *s.* yiţắl *m*, yiţáuă *f*; muscár *m*, muschídhă *f*; (*one-year old*

~) demúş; (*young bullock*) giúncu (*and* giúngu), júncu; mânzát

CALF² *s*. anat. púlpǎ, ándzǎ; *adj.* (*with large calves*) pulpós

CALICO *s*. (*cotton cloth*) amiricáncǎ; (*printed ~*) stámpǎ (*and* stámbǎ); ghiuralántǎ

CALL *s*. (a)clʼimáre; (*as of a horse*) angǎnáre; **at ~** (*i.e.,* *cut and dried*) țâțǎ n gúrǎ

CALL *vb.* ▼(a)clʼém, *F:* chem; **Why should it matter what they ~ it?** țe-áre s-fácǎ cum si-aclʼámǎ? (*to invite*) ▼acǎliséscu (*and* -lʼi-); **He is calling guests in** Cǎliseáște oáspiț; (*to ~ a dog*) angán; (*to shout, urging someone to come or show up*) (a)strig, ▼aúrlu; **Have you ~ed him?** Lu-aurláși? [lʼa•ur•láși]; (*to make a request or demand*) dimându ‖ *Amc:* **to ~ again** matangán, RÉCATAS 36

CALL AT *vb.* (*to drop by*) *N:* trec pir la cása a, trec pir la poárta-ț, poárta-i, *etc.*

CALL DOWN *vb.* → SCOLD

CALLIGRAPHY *s*. caliyrafíe

CALL IN *vb.* (*to invite*) ▼(a)clʼém, ▼(a)cǎliséscu (*and* -lʼi-)

CALLING *s*. (*verbal ~*) gríre, grítǎ

CALL NAMES *vb.* ▼(a)ngiúr, ▼tǎxéscu

CALL OFF AN ENGAGEMENT *vb.* ▼disuséscu

CALLOSITY *s*. derm. bǎtǎtúrǎ

CALLOUS *adj.* cu bǎtǎtúri; *fig.* ni-durút

CALLOUS *vb.* ñ-si báte (mâna, *etc.*)

CALL TO THE COLORS *vb.* clʼem tu sifére

CALL UP *vb.* (*to summon for military duty*) → CALL TO THE COLORS

CALLUS *s*. derm. bǎtǎtúrǎ

CALLUS *vb.* ñ-si báte (mâna, *etc.*)

CALM *s*. (a)rǎpás, (a)ripás, (a)rupás, (a)riháte, arǎháte, isihíe, stámǎ, arihǎtlâche ‖ HRISTU 37: sihii → SILENCE

CALM *adj.* ísih, *f* -hǎ, *m pl* -hǐ, *f pl* -he; (*tranquil*) arihǎtipsít; (*untroubled*) sirín; (*slow*) minghét

CALM *vb.* ▼urséscu; **to ~ down** agǎliséscu; (*to ~ after anger*) ▼diznǎiréscu, ▼irini(p)séscu, ariñiséscu; ▼arihǎtipséscu, ▼isihǎséscu, ▼acúmtin; **Calm down!** Şedz pri cúr-țâ! (*lit.* '*sit down on your ass*'); Bea púscǎ s-țâ treácǎ! (*lit.* '*Drink vinaigre and it will pass*')

CALM DOWN *vb.* (*intrans.*) îñ vin cǎprili; (*trans.*) **Calm him down!** (*i.e., Slap him!*) Avreádzǎ-l!

CALMING

CALMING *adj.* rupusós, -oásă, -óşĭ, -oáse

CALMNESS *s.* imiráme, imireáţă

CALUMNIATE *vb.* arúc efteríe (pri); ▾catiyurséscu → SLANDER

CALUMNY *s.* efteríe → SLANDER

CAMBRIC *s. tex.* pricál, pircálă

CAMEL *s.* cămílă, gămílă, gámilă

CAMEL-DRIVER *s.* cămilár, gămilár

CAMELLIA *s.* balíciu

CAMOMILE *s. bot.* arménă, hamómilă ‖ *SJos:* iarméñ, CL 253

CAMP *s.* ‖ (*body of persons*) BELIMACE 7: taráfe, *pl* -furi

CAMPANULA *s. bot.* minghiúşe

CAMPECHE WOOD *s.* (*used to redden Easter eggs*) băcáme

CAMPHOR *s.* cámfură

CAN *s.* (*cóntainer*) chisále, cíne, cófă, păyúr, tiniché(e)

CAN *vb.* pot, *part.* putút, ptut

CAN AFFORD IT *vb.* ñ-da di mână

CAN SCARCELY BELIEVE *vb.* nu ñ-u ncápe míntea ‖ **They could** *scarcely believe their eyes* Nu lă pistusia a ochĭlu, HRISTU 62

CAN TELL *vb.* pricunóscu; **At that time one could tell if a wife was getting along well with her husband** Atúmţea s-pricunuşteá că únă muĺáre băná ghíne cu sóţlu a ĺei

CANAL *s.* avláchiu, canále, cănále, cărútă, chiúncu (*and* chiúngu), chiúnce (*and* chiúnge), luyúme, lăyúme, gălúme, sulinár, víe ‖ *Cru:* ghiríz, GOLAB 218

CANARY *s. orn.* canár, canarín

CANCEL *vb.* ▾aştérgu, fac aríste

CANCELLATION *s.* risíte *invar.*

CANCER *s. med.* carchín, cărchín, hărchín, per ‖ *GSus, SJos, Prv, Av:* bun, CL 39

CANDESCENT *adj.* aprés, -eásă, -éşĭ, -eáse; aprínsu, *or* -ímsu; *also* -ímtu; aryuñát

CANDLE *s.* ţeáră, căndílă (*and* cân-); *Prv:* ayiuchére; **the game is not worth the ~** ≈ yumár aspéĺ, săpúnea-ţ cherĭ (*lit.* 'if you wash a donkey you waste your soap'); (*small bowl with oil or kerosine and a snuff*) lihnár; finghít, gaz, căzinár

CANDLE MANUFACTURER *s.* căndilár

CANDLESTICK *s.* şandán, şă-, şi-; şindáne; (~ *for many candle-lights, as in a church*) mănále, mănáre

CANDY *s.* cócă, cufétă, toápă, zăhărátă, zăhărtáre ‖ *SJos, Prv:* bilbíci, CL 39; *Pls: pl* zahapéti, CL 263

CANDY MAKER *s.* şichirgí

CANE *s.* (*walking stick*) băstún, băstúne

CANINE TOOTH *s.* cârínti (*and* câríndi); *Gop:* cl̆ínti → TOOTH

CANNED MEAT *s.* căvrămă

CANNY *adj.* aştirnút, cu cáli, cu cap ligát, siluyisít

CANON *s.* (*law*) canónă, canóne, nom

CANON *s. mil.* tópă, canóne

CANOPY OF HEAVEN *s.* cubélu a ţérlui; gubé

CANOPY OF LEAVES *s.* frundzár

CANT *s.* făţ-făţ *f pl* → HYPOCRIT

CANT *vb.* (*to talk hypocritically*) hiu cătúşe

CAN'T *vb. 1 sg* nu pot

CANTICLE *s.* (*song to praise a saint*) cundác, hirovicó

CANVAS *s. tex.* cănăvă

CANYON *s.* ‖ *Cru:* clisúră, GOLAB 226

CAP *s.* şápcă, *pl* şépchi; (*winter* ~) căciúlă, căciúuă; *dim.* căciulícă; (*for women*) táblă; (*small, light* ~) tichíe, tăchíe; chilipóş *or* chilipóşe; (~ *of low quality*) sămúră, sămúre; sărpoáşe, scufíe, chifălúcă; (*a Greek priest's* ~) cămăláfche, cămiláfe, *S:* cămbláfche; (*conical* ~) chiuleáfe, chileáfe; (*cylindrical* ~) ciuváñu; (*Turkish* ~) fése ‖ *Cru:* capélă, GOLAB 224; (*fur* ~) *Cru:* şubáră, GOLAB 253 → FUR CAP

CAP DEALER *s.* şepcár

CAP MAKER *s.* şepcár

CAPABLE *adj.* ácşu → ABLE

CAPACITY *s.* tăcáte; **It's beyond my** ~ Nu-i (*or* nu-s) trâ ándzăle a meále

CAPARISON *s.* (*ornamental covering for a horse*) óplă → COVERING

CAPITAL *s.* cap, cap di parádz, capitál, căpitál, capitál̆u; sirmaé; *G:* (*joint* ~) chiúne

CAPITAL *adj.* (*first-rate*) → EXCELLENT

CAPITATION *s.* (*taxation on non-Moslem inhabitants*) haráce, hăráce

CAPITULATE *vb.* ▾ncl̆in, părădhuséscu → GIVE UP, SURRENDER

CAPITULATION *s.* pridáre

CAPON *s.* căpón, căpóñu

CAPRICE *s.* chéfe, chéifă, gústu, yústu, căpríciu, camómate *f pl*;

fărfúdă

CAPRICIOUS *adj.* cu oára, cu órile [óri•]; nizeárcu, *f* -ă, *m pl* -rţi, *f pl* -rţe; căpriţusít; căpriceár, -ă, -rĭ, -re; căpriceárcu, -árcă, -árţi, -árţe

CAPSIZE *vb.* ▾arăstórnu → OVERTURN

CAPSULE *s.* *bot.* ‖ (~ *of poppy*) **Av:** căciúli *f pl*, CL 40

CAPTAIN *s.* căpidán, bulubáş, yiuzbáş, yiuzbăşé

CAPTIOUS *adj.* scandzóhir

CAPTIVATING *adj.* ≈ nóstim, *m pl* -tiñ, *f pl* -time

CAPTIVE *s.* sclav, rob; **to take away** ~ ľau sclav, acáţ sclav

CAPTURE *s.* acăţáre, ľoáre

CAPTURE *vb.* ▾acáţ, príndu, bag tu mână

CAR *s.* (*automobile*) máchină ‖ DIARO 98: aftuchinát

CARAFE *s.* bucál, bucále, gắră

CARAPACE *s.* (*a turtle's* ~) samár di broáscă

CARAVAN *s.* (*shepherds and their belongings on the move*) cărăváne, carváne; *adv.* n cărváni

CARBINE *s.* tuféche → RIFLE

CARBONIZATION *s.* scrumáre

CARBONIZE *vb.* ▾scrumédz, şcrumédz, ▾nscrum, ▾nscrumédz

CARBONIZED *adj.* (*as of a tree*) scrumát

CARBOY *s.* trimindzáně

CARBUNCLE *s.* *med.* dalácă, dălácă, duloáge

CARD *s.* → PLAYING CARD, SHUFFLE THE CARDS

CARD *s.* (*as of wool*) cheáptine *m*

CARD *vb.* (*by hand*) scármin; fac clậndu; (*by a special comb*) trag tu cheápţâñ

CARDER *s.* chiptinár, hăláciu

CARDINAL POINT *s.* párte a lúmiľei

CARDING *s.* (*by hand*) scărmânáre, scărmânătúră

CARDING BOARD *s.* cheápţâñ *m pl*; scámnu, zórnă

CARDPLAYER *s.* agiucătór, hartupéxi [•péksĭ], *pl.* hartupéxeañ

CARE *s.* mutríre; **A sick person needs** ~ Niptútlu va mutríre; mutrítă, (a)ngătán, bruítă; (*suffering of mind*) săráche; (*safe-keeping*) (a)firítă; căştíg (*and* câş-); cumándă

CARE *vb.* ñ-u zórea (di / că); ñ-si báte urécľa (di *or* că); ñ-u mâc ínima; (*to be anxious for*) trag căştíga a; mi sinfiriseáşte; mi ntiriseádză; **I don't ~ a rap** Nu mi meálă; Nu mi doáre cúrlu; Hăbáre nu am; Nu ñ-u zórea (di *or* că), Nu ñ-u zóre (că); **Úna-ñ fáţe**; **I ~ much about this** Ñ-u am ca núca n sănătór → TAKE ~ ‖ **It was not wealth that he cared about** Nu-ľ erá a lui di aveáre, BASME 420; ALR 1846: **I don't care (It makes no difference to me)** Añía ñ-u únă; DIARO 116: **I don't care!** Nu-ñ si beási! DIARO 153; nu-ñ creápâ dip, DIARO 371 *and* 431; STERGHIU 4: nu mi doári buriclu (ti)

CAREFREE *adj.* fârã gailéi, cu căciúla scoásă ‖ STERE 4: tărăsít

CAREFUL *adj.* angătán, câştigós, cu câştígă → BE ~

CAREFULLY *adv.* angătán, ângătán, cu angătán, cu tahmíne, cu usúle, cu câştígă, câştigós; **Walk ~!** *(2 pl)* Imnáţ câştigós! ‖ MURNU 33: cu ocľi pátru

CAREFULNESS *s.* mucaitlâche

CARELESS *adj.* (*free from care*) fârã ghidérĭ; (*negligent*) *G:* pálaz

CARELESSLY *adv.* fârã ghidérĭ

CARELESSNESS *s.* (*neglect*) ni-mutríre

CARESS *s.* dizñirdáre, adiľáre, cănăchipsíre, gălinisíre; hăidhipsíre, hádhye, puşputíre; (*comfort*) sămănáre ‖ *Amc:* zdrudíre, PADIOTU 152; haidhâ, *pl.* hăidhi, DIARO 396

CARESS *vb.* ▾dizñérdu, adíľu, ▾cănăchipséscu, ▾găliniséscu, ▾puşputéscu, ▾hăidhipséscu

CARESSING *adj.* disñirdós, -oásă, -óşĭ, -oáse; dizñirdătór, -oáre

CARESSIVE *adj.* sămănătór, -oáre

CARETAKER *s.* cumandărgí

CAREWORN *adj.* sicliţít

CARGO *s.* furtíe → LOAD

CARIOUS *adj.* gof, *f* -fă, *m pl* gohĭ, *f pl* gófe; cúfchiu

CARNAGE *s.* → MASSACRE

CARNIVAL *s.* carnavál

CAROB *s.* róşcuvă, curnuţél, xiluchérată ‖ *Peş:* xarachérate *f pl*, CL 42

CAROL *s.* culíndă, culíndu, cólindă

CAROL *vb.* mi duc cólinda; culindédz

CAROLER *s.* culindár

CARP *s.* *ichth.* crap ‖ *Prv:* yrivádh; *SJos:* yrivă, CL 46

CARP *vb.* áflu acăţătúră → CAVIL

CARPENTER *s.* dulghér, dugramagí, duyramgí, maréngu, marangó ‖ *Pls:* dăvăngér, CL 44; *Mul:* lemnár; (*almost everywhere in GR*) marangó, B-ARCH 369

CARPET

CARPET *s.* cérgă, cíftă, mutáfe, pocroává, téndă → BEDSPREAD, COVERING

CARRIAGE *s.* (*vehicle*) talíngă, dalíngă, caleáscă, căleáscă, caráţă, carétă, landón, landóne, landóne, cucíe, paitóne; (*transportation of goods*) chiragilâche; (*manner of holding or carrying oneself*) purtátic

CARRIER *s.* (*mainly on mules*) chiragí, cărvănár, *G:* cârvuchír

CARRION *s.* leş, mârşe, murţínă, murtuţínă, cúhmă, cúfumă, cúfmă, psuthíme

CARROT *s.* mer dit loc ‖ *Av:* hâvúci, CL 253; *Prv:* carótâ; cuchino-yúli, CL 40, 42

CARRY *vb.* duc (→ § 32); (*to take, to transport*) ▾pórtu (*to wear, as a medal*) *Smr:* (a)pórtu; (*to ~ on one's back*) duc ncrâşca (*and* ngrâşca); (*to make the rounds or go on a business errand*) fac uná cále, arúc únă cále

CARRYING *s.* (*transportation*) purtáre; **is fit for ~ing water** tră purtáre ápă fáţe

CARRY OFF *vb.* (*by or as by force*) ▾aráp, ▾aráchiu

CARRY ON / OUT *vb.* (*to manage*) trag; **to ~ trade** fac tigiaréte

CARRY OUT *vb.* ▾fac, buréscu, mburéscu

CARRY THROUGH *vb.* u scot n cap, scot lúcrulu n cap

CART *s.* cărúţă ‖ *Cru:* amáxe, GOLAB 198; *GSus:* máxi; *Peş:* máxe, *Prv:* amáxe, CL 255

CARTER *s.* cărvănár, căruţár, căruţér, amăxă, ayuyeát, arăbăgí → CARRIER, COACHMAN

CARTILAGE *s.* scârcic, scârciu

CARTRIDGE *s.* fuşéche, fişéche, fşéche, mulíde, patrónă

CARTRIDGE BELT *s.* fuşiclíche

CARTRIDGE BOX *s.* paláscă, păláscă, *G:* pălăpáscă; pudyeáuă, tócăză

CARVE *vb.* (*as with a spade*) sap, scălséscu; (*as with an ax or knife*) pilichiséscu

CARVED *adj.* (*as of a piece of furniture*) scălsít

CARVE ONE'S WAY *vb.* ▾alúmtu; **He ~ed his way through towns** Alumtá hăspádzľi

CASCADE *s.* (*waterfall*) ghirdápe

CASE *s.* (*box*) sfindúche, *dim.* sfinduchíţă → TRUNK

CASE *s.* (*actual event*) fáptă → MAKE OUT ONE'S ~ ‖ *PC:* únă; CUNIA: **in any ~** íţicum (*private letter*)

CASH *s.* (*coins*) uscát, fluríi uscáte, náhte; **be in ~** li súflu

CASH-BOX *s.* cugiré

CASH DOWN *adv.* dismână

CASHIER *vb.* fac argó; dau poárca, dau tástrul, dau ţărúhile [ţă•rúhĭ•li]

CASHIER'S DESK *s.* tisgheáfe → COUNTER

CASHMERE *s. tex.* caşmíre, cazmíre, căsmíre; **Băi:** *adj.* ľáhură; **She put on a ~ dress** Si nviscú cu ľáhură fustáne

CASK *s.* săsăngă, tálar, *dim.* tălăríc, tălărícĭu, varélă, vurélă, vuléră, vuryélă, vărţeálă, vurţeálă, vóză, cádză, bútin, *dim.* butinél, butiñór ‖ VELO 57: buclíţă

CASSOCK *s.* (a)rásă, ráze

CAST *s.* arucătúră

CAST *adj.* (*taken in a mold, as of a bell*) virsát

CAST *vb.* ▾arúc → THROW

CAST A LOOK *vb.* ▾arúc mutríta pi, *N:* arúc ócľi

CAST A SPELL UPON *vb.* ▾leg → BEWITCH

CAST DIRT AT SMB. *vb.* rizil(ips)éscu, tălăéscu tu halé

CAST EYES ON *vb.* dau cu ócľiľ di → CATCH SIGHT OF

CAST LOTS *vb.* arúc şcurtíţa, arúc clir, trag ciop; *G:* arúc lâhmălu

CAST SHADOW *vb.* ▾(a)umbrédz, (a)umbréscu, (a)umbrăscu

CAST THE BLAME (ON) *vb.* → BLAME

CAST THE EVIL EYE *vb.* ľau di ócľu, ▾diucľédz; (*ant.* ▾disucľédz (*i.e., to annihilate the effect of the evil eye*)

CASTAWAY *adj.* ar(u)cát

CASTIGATE *vb.* → PUNISH

CAST IT IN SMB.'S TEETH *vb.* (*to say smth. bluntly*) ľ-u dzâc tu fáţă

CASTLE *s.* (a)cúlă, (a)gúlă ‖ HRISTU 104: castelă

CAST-OFF *adj.* ar(u)cát

CASTRATE *vb.* (*a horse*) ascúchiu, scuchéscu, şuţ, şuţăscu; (*a he-goat, a ram*) ciucuţéscu, *F:* dzigăréscu

CASTRATED *adj.* scupát, strif; (*of a horse*) şuţât; (*of a he-goat*) ciucutít, gágur, gí-, gâgúr; (*of a ram*) munúh, monóh; (*incompletely ~ed horse*) arungáciu ‖ **Cru:** (*of a ram*) hudúm birbéc, GOLAB 220

CASTRATION *s.* şuţâre

CASUALTY *s.* chidére, ghidére, arăníre, chiríre, chireáre; moárte; (*of a person*) arănít, pliguít, chirít

CAT *s.* cătúşe (*and* câ-), máţă, păsă, pésă ‖ mắţă, măciócă, ALIA 96; **LvO:** cătúse (*sic*), **Cot:** písă, B-ARCH 96

CATACLYSM *s.* sindilíe, şindíľu, cataclizmó, halazmó

CATAPLASM *s.* lâpắ

CATARACT *s. med.* teáră; (*of a river*) ghirdápe

CATARRH *s.* arémă

CATASTROPHE *s.* lăiáţă, dhistihíe, taxiráte ‖ DIARO 187: catástrufi, catastrufíe

CATCALL *s.* ñiuráre [ñi•u•]

CATCH *vb.* ľau, ▾apúc, ▾acáţ, pruftuséscu; (*acquire, as a disease*) amíntu; (*to capture*) **We caught him in the forest** Lu-acăţăm tu pădúre; (*to be effective*) **Your words have caught on** Zboárile a tále acăţáră; **The morning will ~ us still sleeping** Va nă ľa dzúua

CATCH A CHILL *vb.* ľau arăţíme, ľau arcoáre, (ñ-) arăţéscu, arcurédz

CATCH A COLD → CATCH A CHILL

CATCH A WEASEL ASLEEP *vb.* (*to steal*) ñ-seácă mâna

CATCH FIRE *vb.* ľau foc; mi apríndu (→ § 32)

CATCH ONE'S BREATH *vb.* ñ-ľau adiľáticlu, ñ-víñe sulúchea; (*as of a horse*) ľau anásă

CATCH PLEURISY *vb.* arcurédz, plirutuséscu, plivrituséscu, plivricéscu

CATCH SIGHT OF *vb.* ▾(a)ndzăréscu, dau cu ócľiľ di

CATCH SMB. BY THE THROAT *vb.* ascálin (*or* ascálnu) di gúşe

CATCH SMB. IN THE ACT *vb.* (*red-handed*) acáţ tu ayíñe ‖ lo-acáţ tu praşi, BASME 305

CATCH TUBERCULOSIS *vb.* ▾uftichédz, uhtichédz, tihtuséscu; ▾vlăpséscu, ▾umbărnédz

CATCH UP WITH *vb.* ▾apróchiu, agiúngu

CATEGORIC(AL) *adj.* stres, *f* -reásă, *m pl* -reşĭ, *f pl* -reáse

CATEGORICALLY *adv.* stres

CATEGORY *s.* (*kind*) sóie, luyíe, turlíe

CATERPILLAR *s.* uñídă (*and* uñídhă), luñídă, gâşníţă

CATERWAUL *vb.* ñiurédz [ñi•u•]

CAT-FISH *s. ichth.* soámă, guľanó

CATHARTIC *s.* chinitcó → PURGATIVE

CATHOLIC *adj.* látin, lătín, papistán

CATTAIL *s. bot.* vuľár

CATTLE *s.* văcăríu; văţi *f pl*; právdă

CATTLE-BELL *s.* chípur, chípru, *dim.* chipuríciu, chipuríş

CAUGHT *adj.* apucát

CAUL *s.* soárte; (*a lamb's omentum*) schépe

CAULIFLOWER *s.* cunupídhă, cărnăbétă

CAUSE *s.* (*motive, reason*) cicuteálă, furñíe, isápe, itíe; luyar-yeazmó, madé, madée

CAUTION *s.* (a)firítă, pruvideáre, mintiminíľe (*and* mindi-)

CAUTION *vb.* ▾anvéţ

CAUTIOUS *adj.* lughearic, luyeáric → PRUDENT

CAUTIOUSLY *adv.* (a)ngătán, câştigós

CAVALRY *s.* căvălăríe, călăríu

CAVALRYMEN *s. coll.* căvălăríe

CAVE *s.* spílă, spilée, spiľáuă, spiľu, piştireáuă, pişcireáuă, gúvă, pudrúme, bădrúme, budrúme

CAVE-IN *s.* surpătúră

CAVE IN *vb.* ▾súrpu, ▾surúp, sărúp, ▾arăvulséscu

CAVERN *s.* → CAVE

CAVIAR *s.* ícre *f pl*; hăvyeár; (*red caviar*) vutarác; límbi *f pl*

CAVIL *vb.* ľ-áflu nă acăţătúră; ľau părătúră; ~ **at smb.** trag tămbárea azvărna → SPOIL

CAVILING *s.* părătúră

CAVITY *s.* cúfumă → HOLLOW

CAW *s.* strigáre, cârlédz

CAW *s.* (*the call of a caw*) mudzíre

CAW *vb.* mug, mudzéscu

CEASE *vb.* ▾curmu, ▾acúmtin, ▾taľu; **Friends ~ed visiting him** Oáspiţľi ľ-si tăľără; (*as of milking sheep*) ▾stărchéscu; ▾ľau; astămăţéscu, păxéscu (*and* pâ-), păfséscu, păpséscu, pupséscu

CEASELESS *adj.* ni-cumtinát, ni-curmát

CEASELESSNESS *s.* ni-curmáre, ni-păpsíre

CEASELESSLY *adv.* índa → CONTINUOUSLY

CEDE *vb.* trag mână (di) → ABNEGATE

CEIL *vb.* (*to furnish with a ceiling*) tăvăñuséscu, dăvăñuséscu

CEILING *s.* tăváne, dăváne; (*process*) tăvăñusíre, dăvăñusíre ‖ DIARO 102: bâgdâtíe (*rare*) = tâváne

CELANDINE *s. bot.* alânduríşe, hilidhuñáuă, hilidhruneáuă

CELEBRATE *vb.* yiurtiséscu, yiurtuséscu

CELEBRATED *adj.* cu númă → FAMOUS

CELEBRATION *s.* yiurtisíre

CELEBRITY *s.* númă → RENOWN

CELERY *s.* sélin, şéleană

CELIBACY *s.* bichireáţă, bichirlâche, ayamíe

CELIBATE *adj.* (*single, speaking of men*) bicheár, *pl* -cheárĭ

CELL *s.* (*small room in a convent*) chilíe, ţilíe

CELLAR *s.* chilár, ţilár, ţâlár, ţăláre, pleámniţă, plávniţă, pímniţă, bímţă, catóye, ízbă, **G:** zímnic

CELLARER *s.* chilargí

CEMENT *s.* ciméntu

CEMENT *vb.* ‖ CUNIA 51: bag ciméntu

CEMETERY *s.* mărmínţâ, murmínţâ (*and* -ndzâ) *n pl;* chimitír, chimitír(y)iu; grochi *f pl;* grupíşte ‖ **Cru:** ăn-geánă, GOLAB 206; ALiA II q. 216 *also:* nekrotafíu (*in GR, frequently*)

CENSER *s.* thimñató ‖ **Peş:** thimñitór, CL 262

CENSUS *s.* cătăyrăfíe

CENTAUR *s.* sâtâr

CENTER, CENTRE *s.* mése, buríc, chéntru, chéndră, ínimă; (*central area*) múmă; **to the very ~ of Europe** pân-tu múma a li Evrópe

CENTURY *s.* étă

CEREALS *s.* yípturi *n pl;* yinimáte *n pl*

CEREBELLUM *s.* ‖ **N:** (*nr.* Bit.) mădulár, CAPIDAN 152

CEREMONIAL *s.* ţirimóñe

CEREMONY: without further ~ fâră múlte pricădéri; **stand upon ~** ▼antiriséscu (*and* andi-), ▼aruşdiséscu (PC: [a•ruž•di-], ▼aruş-téscu; ▼aruşinédz, ▼aruşnédz, ▼aruşunédz, ▼arşinédz

CERTAIN *adj.* (*sure*) sígur, síyir; saylám, saylámcu, -mcă, -mţi

CERTAINLY *adv.* bezbilé, curmátă → OF COURSE

CERTIFICATE: birth ~ năfúze, nu- ‖ **~ of title** tâpíe *obs.*, DIARO 12

CESSATION *s.* acúmtin, acúmtil, acumtináre, curmáre, astămăţíre, pápse, páfse, păpsíre, păfsíre

CHAFE *s.* ‖ **in a ~** năirít foc *adj.*

CHAFE *vb.* ▼guştirédz → IRRITATE

CHAFF *s.* (*teasing*) şúpur, şupuráre

CHAFF *s.* (*husks*) cóţală, cóţule *f pl;* (*remainder of impurities in grains*) gúşte; (*smth. light and worthless*) scámă ‖ curâtúrâ, DIARO

331

CHAFF *vb.* → TEASE

CHAFFER *vb.* ▼păzăripséscu, yiftuséscu

CHAIN *s.* alisídă, alsídă, *N:* ális; álţu, cadhénă (*and* cadénă), cartéľu, chiustécă, chiustéche, cinghéľu, silivár, sulivár, singír, zingír, şingír, şingíre

CHAIN *vb.* leg tu singír → PUT IN CHAINS

CHAIR *s.* scămnu, *dim.* scămníciu; căpitâñu, căpitúñu, caréclă, cathédră, amvóne, ámvun, amvúnă ‖ *F:* scammu, SarD 98; *SJos:* calécră, CL 40; *Peş:* stol, CL 261 ‖ *Rod:* scámu (*sic*); *GSus:* stol, B-ARCH 416

CHAISE *s.* caleáşcă → CARRIAGE

CHALK *s.* tibişíre

CHALLENGE *vb.* mi acáţ (cu); arniséscu; (*to issue a* ~) ≈ u-cáftu (ngăceárea) cu luminárea ‖ Ľi stau cucót *or* ľi stau cócut (*lit.* 'to oppose smb. [like a] rooster'), PARALLELE 135

CHAMBER POT *s.* ciuváñu, ţucál

CHAMOMILE *s.* lilíce álbă

CHANCE *s.* (a)mbăreáţă, ugoádă, ugúre; **by** ~ cu tahmíne; tu tíhe; ţiva; **Have you seen my goats by** ~? Nu-ñ vidzúşi ţivá căpârli? ‖ *Cru:* tíhe, GOLAB 254; PC: **I came on the off** ~ **that I would find you** Viñiu cu míntea că va s-ti áflu acásă

CHANCELLOR *s.* logothét

CHANCY *adj.* (*risky*) ‖ PC: ndáo

CHANDELIER *s.* poliéleu, puliléu

CHANGE *s.* minúţ *m pl*; minuţáľe, minţále *f pl*; parádz frâmţâ *m pl* (*lit.* 'broken money'); (a)ngărmári, gărmári *m pl* ‖ minúţi paráţi (*lit.* 'small money'), PARALLELE 125

CHANGE *s.* (*as of place*) mutáre, mtáre

CHANGE *vb.* ▼mut; (*to* ~ *one's place, one's mind*) ▼strămút; (*of money*) ▼aspárgu, ▼alăxéscu (*and* alâ-); (*to put on other clothes, linens*) **Change your linen!** Alăxeá-te! (*to* ~ *policy, tactics*) u şuţăscu frândza; **to** ~ **color** (*as of embarassment*) scot făţ-făţ; únă fáţă ñ-fúdze, álta ñ-yíne

CHANGEABLE *adj.* nu sta pri únă; ni-síyur

CHANGE COLOR *vb.* → CHANGE

CHANGE ONE'S MIND *vb.* u mut míntea, ñ-tórnu míntea

CHANGE ONE'S TUNE *vb.* (*to step back, to yield*) li apľéc urécľile

CHAOS

CHAOS *s.* pálaz → DISORDER, CONFUSION

CHAOTIC *adj.* ahundós, -oásă, -óşĭ, -oáse

CHAP *s. anat.* fálcă

CHAP *s.* giunóp, junóp → FELLOW

CHAP *vb.* (*to crack open, to split*) crep

CHAPEL *s.* (*small monastery*) schit, paraclís

CHAPFALLEN *adj.* (*dejected*) mbudzinát, mbufnát

CHAR *vb.* cămiñuséscu, nscrumédz, nscrum

CHARACTER *s.* híre, haractír, húche, idhíumă, físe, sáre, véte, vóvlă; **Such is his ~** Acşí ľ-u vétea; Ahtáre ľi-eáste físea (*or* sárea, vóvla)

CHARCOAL *s.* măngál (*and* mân-), mângáne; (*live coal*) tucíne *m*, tăciúne *m*; **Src:** stăčăn *m*

CHARCOAL SELLER *s.* cărbunár, cârvânár

CHARGE *s.* (*load*) ncărcătúră; (*task or duty imposed*) sárţină, sálţină

CHARGE *vb.* (*to load*) ▼ncárcu; (*to blame, to impute*) cătigurséscu, cătiyurséscu; (*to charge for borrowed money*) tuchiséscu ‖ dau / ľau parádz cu toc, DIARO 410

CHARITABLE *adj.* giumértu, -rtă, -rţi, -rte; sălghít

CHARITY *s.* bunăteáţă, sivápe; (*clemency*) ñílă

CHARISMATIC *adj.* arâsít, yustós, gus-; nóstim, nustimác, lugheáric, pălít

CHARLATAN *s.* şarlatán

CHARLEY HORSE *s. med.* ‖ CUNIA 55: cărcĭór

CHARM *s.* măndíe, gilfé, gilvée, háre, hárismă

CHARM *vb.* ▼leg → BEWITCH

CHARMING *adj.* dulbér, ghiurghiulíu; sârbu, -rbă, -rghi, -rbe; zâmbác; (*of a woman*) ghirghínă

CHARY *adj.* → CAUTIOUS

CHASE *s.* (*banishment*) aurláre, ayuníre, azguníre, avináre

CHASE *vb.* azgunéscu, agunéscu, asñéscu, *N:* azuñéscu, azñéscu; amín, ▼xinumséscu, fúg, *N:* afúg; **Chase them away from the village!** Fugíţ-ľi din hoáră! (*as with a whip*) ▼avín, anăngăséscu; (*to ~ away*) ▼aúrlu, dau poárca; **I will ~ you away from the house!** Poárca va-ţ dau din cása; ▼surgunipsescu, ▼surghiunipséscu, ▼xipundiséscu

CHASSIS *s.* curnídhă, curníză, curníţă

CHASTE *adj.* curát, ni-amurtipsít, ni-stipsít; ápă di lituryíe;

(*innocent of unlawful sexual intercorse*) CARAFOLI 121: vérgur

CHASTISE *vb.* → PUNISH

CHASTITY *s.* viryireáţă, născăríe, şpástră

CHASUBLE *s.* filóne

CHAT *s.* láfe, lăcărdíe (*and* lăcâr-) ‖ *GSus:* moaéti, CL 256 → TALK

CHAT *vb.* lăfuséscu, discântu, máţin, máţin pi virisíe ‖ *GSus:* fac moabéti, CL 256; TULLIU 66: lăfuéscu

CHATTER *s.* láfe

CHATTER *vb.* (*to talk idly*) discântu; máţin pi virisíe; am múlte măslăţ; (*to cause the teeth to click with cold*) dau dínţâľ; cicăléscu → THIRTEEN

CHATTERBOX *s.* farfúră, *pl* farfuráñ; farfará; moáră aspártă ‖ CUNIA 111: băndur

CHATTERING *s.* (*of the teeth*) trimurárea a dínţălor, trămuráre

CHATTY *adj.* fărfár, fărfără → TALKATIVE

CHEAP *adj.* (*inexpensive*) éftin, *m pl* -tiñ; (*dejected*) **He feels ~** cánda ľ-si nicáră cărăyile [•răyĭ•li] → DO IT ON THE CHEAP

CHEAPEN *vb.* eftinipséscu

CHEAPNESS *s.* iftinătáte

CHEAT *vb.* ▾arâd, ▾(a)plănăséscu, plăn(ips)éscu → DECEIVE

CHEATER *s.* pişichér; *G:* ehlé

CHEATING *s.* aplán, arâdeáre, aplănăsíre, ilée *and G:* ehlé; zăryíe

CHEAT TIME *vb.* (*to put off, to be late; to do nothing*) ▾şintéscu

CHECK *vb.* (*to verify, to test*) cătăpăţéscu; (*as of a scale*) ľau aiárea; (*to monitor*) privégľu; (*to control, to curb*) adún curăile

CHECKING *s.* cătăpăţíre

CHEEK *s.* búcă, búdză, fáţă ‖ ALIA 155: bulcíe, bucíe, soráţă

CHEEKY *adj.* (*as of a healthy child*) bucicós [buĉ•kós], -oásă, -óşĭ, -oáse; (*impudent*) abráşcu, *f* -şcă, *m pl* -şţi, *f pl* -şte

CHEEK-BONE *s.* anat. meárile di fáţă *n pl*

CHEEP *vb.* (*of birds, fig. of children*) ▾ngârnéscu; chíur, chiurédz

CHEEPING *s.* chíur, chiuráre

CHEER UP *vb.* dau ínimă, ľ-fac găiréte [gă•i•], ▾arăzbún, inimuséscu ‖ ľ-fac ínimă, BASME 226

CHEERFUL *adj.* hărăcóp, -cóchi, -coápă, -coápe; hărós, yiós

CHEERFULNESS *s.* hilăríe

CHEERS *interj.* (*when clinking glasses, toasting someone*) cióca!

CHEESE

tóca! víva! hair-lítca, hairlâtca, haírula ‖ BATSARIA 2: tră ghíni!

CHEESE s. caş, brândză; (*fresh oval loaf of ~*) combóli; **fat ~** mănúre; (*~ from secondary buttermilk*) ghíză; *G:* (*sheep's milk ~*) zbúldzu; *other kinds of ~:* úrdhă (*and* úrdă), telemé, căşcăvál (*derog.* căşcăvrác); mizítră, mindzíthră, bagiu, gavruyeáni [ga•vru•yeáñ]; **block of ~** dánă → GREEN ~

CHEESE *adj.* (*made with ~*) căşeát; ~ **cake** pítă căşeátă

CHEESE CAKE s. pruscutátă, câmbăcúche, pítă căşeátă

CHEESECLOTH s. stricătoáre

CHEESE LOAF s. dánă

CHEESE-MAKER s. căşár, căşeár, ghizár, baciu, bagiu, căşcăvălár, şâgăr (*sic*)

CHEESE-MAKING s. (*viewed as a profession*) căşirlâche

CHEESE-MITE s. streápit

CHEESE MOLD s. (*for molding căşcăvál*) stifáne

CHEESEPARING s. sclingiureáţă, sclinceáme

CHEESEPARING *adj.* → STINGY

CHEMIST s. (*pharmacist*) spiţér

CHERRY s. cireáşe

CHERRY-LAUREL s. lívan

CHERRY-TREE s. círéş

CHERRY-VENDOR s. cirişár

CHERVIL s. *bot.* smeáră

CHEST s. *anat.* chéptu

CHEST s. (*coffer*) cásă, casélcă, căsélă, hasélă, casénă, săndúche, sindúche, sfindúche, sundúche; *dim.* sfinduchíţă

CHEST MAKER s. cufciugár

CHEST OF DRAWERS s. scrínă

CHESTNUT s. căstâñe, gâstâñe

CHESTNUT *adj.* (*color of eyes*) ‖ *Av, Băi, Smr:* câstâñós, CL 42; *Amc:* rúşâ ócľi, SCHL 45

CHESTNUT COLORED HORSE s. aróibu, durí, durín, cu pérlu durí, cúlcu; ghioc

CHESTNUT GROVE s. castanaryió

CHESTNUT TREE s. căstâñu, câstâñu, câstíñu, găstíñu

CHEW *vb.* (*a*)meástic, mástic; (*to nibble*) măcilséscu; (*to ruminate*) ▾aroámig, arúmig, zdroámig ‖ (*to ruminate, as of cattle, 3 sg*) *Amc:* rúmică, *LvO:* rămică, *Mal, Rod:* arómică, *Mul:* arómegă, *Smx:*

xanaroámică, **An:** mástică, **Vil:** giumuleáşte, B-ARCH 317

CHEWING s. măcilsíre

CHIC s. hu *invar.*

CHIC *adj.* → STYLISH

CHICK s. gălinúş, puľu, *dim.* puľişór

CHICKENHEARTED *adj.* fricós, -oásă → COWARD, FEARFUL

CHICKEN OUT *vb.* ▾aspár

CHICKEN POX s. luţítă, mălţeádză, multeádză

CHICK-PEA s. aróv, chéchiră, ţeáţire, niblibíe, nibilbíe, nibir-bíľu; (*roasted ~*) bilbíce *f pl*

CHICORY s. *bot.* ţicoáră

CHIDE *vb.* ▾anăcréscu → SCOLD

CHIDING s. văryíre, zăvráche, zbárdhu

CHIEF s. căpíe (*and* câ-) → LEADER

CHIEFSHIP s. căpitănátă, căpităníľe, căpitănláche

CHIEFTAIN s. arhilistín ‖ **Cru:** căpidán, GOLAB 235

CHIFFONIER s. scrínă

CHILBLAIN s. lúngă

CHILD s. ficiór; *dim.* ficiuríc, ficiurúş; *coll.* ficiuráme; ñic, míncu, hurhutaláş, cóchil, *dim.* cochilúş, *coll.* cuchiláme; cóchil *or* técnon *invar*; **F:** fet; *adj.* (*of a parent with children*) familít, fumiľít, nfumiľát; **children** fumeáľe, **N:** fuméľu → ABORTIVE ~ ‖ **He is my ~** Este fuméľu añéu, CAPIDAN 152; STERE 14: técnu

CHILDBED s. (*condition of woman in process of giving birth*) li-huníľe *f pl*; **in ~** (muľáre) mitrícă

CHILDBIRTH s. → PARTURITION

CHILDHOOD s. ficiuríľe, ficiuráme, ficiureáţă

CHILDLESS *adj.* ni-fumiľát

CHILDISH *adj.* ficiuréscu, *f* -eáscă, *m pl* -éşţâ, *f pl* -éşti

CHILDISHLY *adv.* ficiureáşte

CHILL s. arăţíme, arcuráme → CATCH A ~, TAKE THE ~ OFF

CHILL *vb.* (*to be seized with cold*) ľau arăţíme

CHILLED *adj.* arăţít; (*to the marrow*) corcán *invar*; cóţâ *invar.*

CHILLY *adj.* arcurós, -oásă, -óşǐ, -oáse

CHIME IN *vb.* ▾ameástic

CHIMERA s. stihíe, stihió

CHIMNEY s. coş, băgé, bugé, buhár, buharé, fungár, ugeác, ugeáche, ugeáţe, ujác

CHIN *s. anat.* gruñiu; *Smr:* grúnghiu; **double ~** bărghéľ → TAKE IT ON THE ~

CHINA *s.* fărfuríu, fărfăríu

CHINK *s.* cripătúră, cripitúră

CHIP *s.* áşcľe; găgi [găĝ] *f pl*; minuţáľe, minţále, pilucúdhă, scárpă, spíţă; (*used as fuel*) surţél, surţeáuă, *dim.* surţilúş ‖ *SJos:* pelecúdhă, CL 258

CHIPPER *adj.* hărăcóp, -oápă, -óchi, -oápe

CHIRP *s.* pilidáre, piridáre, băteáre, ţíur, ţiuráre

CHIRP *vb.* ţíur ‖ găréscu, CAPIDAN 149; STERE 31: chirchirédz

CHIRR *vb.* (*as of crickets*) jujuéscu

CHIRP *ono.* (*of birds*) ‖ ţíţir-víţir, DIARO 253

CHISEL *s.* zmiláră

CHITCHAT *s.* láfe

CHOKE *vb.* ▾zgrum, zdrúmin di gúşe, ▾(a)pitruséscu, *N:* (a)putruséscu; (*on food, water, etc.*) ▾mbeciu

CHOCK-FULL *adj.* plin, mplin, umplút, para-umplút; durdusít; dângusít, surusít

CHOCKING HEAT *s.* (*as in July*) zădúh

CHOCOLATE *s.* ciuculátă

CHOICE *s.* aleádzire, alidzeáre; (*the best part*) danélă; ‖ *adv.* **at one's ~** pri aleádzire, BASME 286

CHOICE *adj.* alépsu, *f* aleápsă, *m pl* alépşi, *f pl* aleápse; aléptu, *f* aleáptă, *m pl* alépţâ, *f pl* aleápte; biringí, has, *f* -ă, *m pl* haşǐ, *f pl* háse; háscu, *f* -scă (*no pl*); prot; un şi un (*lit.* 'one and one'; *the same construction in Albanian*, PARALLELE 125)

CHOKE *vb.* ▾ascálnu, ▾ascálin di gúşe

CHOLERA *s.* huléră

CHOLERAIC *adj.* hulirós

CHOLERIC *adj.* inacíu, inací, inagí, căchiós → ILL-NATURED

CHOOSE *vb.* ▾alég (→ § 32); (*too much and/or too long*) pri-alég

CHOOSEY, CHOOSY *adj.* căpriceár, căpriceárcu, nizeárcu

CHOP *s.* (*seal, stamp*) túră, vúlă, miúre; (*kind, brand*) turlíe → CHOPS

CHOP *vb.* (*to hack*) toc; (*to tear into pieces*) diñíc; **to ~ smb.'s head off** ľau cáplu → BEHEAD

CHOPPING BOARD *s.* mbrustár; *Bit:* dácă

CHOPPY *adj.* (*changeable, variable*) nu sta pri únă

CHOPS s. pl. fălţi f pl, fálcă sg

CHORD s. → STRING; (in tune, accord, in music) duzéne

CHORE s. lúcru, huzméte

CHORTLE vb. ▾arâd

CHOSEN adj. aléptu, f -eáptă, m pl -épţâ, f pl -eápte

CHRISM s. mir, ñir

CHRIST Hristó(u), Hriştó; **They died for ~** Tră Hristólu năşĭ cădzúră

CHRISTENDOM s. criştinătáte, crăştinătáte, criştinitática

CHRISTIAN s. crâştín, criştín; coll. criştináme; **We are ~** Ţâném păreásiñ (lit. 'We observe fasts')

CHRISTIAN adj. criştinéscu, -eáscă, -éşţâ, -éşti

CHRISTIANIZATION s. criştináre, criştinipsíre, pătidzáre

CHRISTIANIZE vb. ▾criştinédz, criştinipséscu, ▾pătédz

CHRISTIANIZED adj. criştinát, criştinipsít, pătidzát

CHRISTIANLY adv. crăştineáşte (and crâş-)

CHRISTMAS s. Crăciún, Cărciún (and Câr-); **on ~ day** tră Crăciún

CHRISTMAS EVE s. Cólinda invar.

CHRISTMAS TREE s. ‖ BELIMACE 50: pómlu veárde

CHROME s. hrom

CHRONIC DISEASE s. măráze veácľe

CHUB s. ichth. clen m

CHUBBY adj. grăsíc, -că, -íţĭ, -íţe; şíşcu, -că, şíştâ, şíşte ‖ DIARO 143: şúşcu

CHUCK IT vb. (to give up) trag mână (di) → ABNEGATE

CHUM s. (mate) soţ, oáspe

CHUMP s. zúrlu

CHUNK s. bucátă, cumátă, ţópă

CHURCH s. băseárică, băseárcă; N: also biseárică

CHURCH BANNER s. sígne

CHURCH STALL s. stálă, stisídhă

CHURCHWARDEN s. pítrup

CHURL s. (rude, ill-bred person) jupân, păduríş

CHURLISH adj. (rude) păduríş ‖ **Peş:** distórsu, CL 44

CHURLISHNESS s. huryeátă

CHURN s. (container to make butter) butín, bătín; tálar

CHURN-STAFF s. (s)fârlíciu

CICADA s. ent. carcaléc, cicalédz, scarlédz, curcaléc, caculéţ,

CIDER

Gop: scucalét; scarcalít, scărcălít, acrídhă, lăcústă → CRICKET

CIDER *s.* bóză, buzắ

CIDER DEALER *s.* buzagí

CIGAR-CASE *s.* ţiyarét, ţiyăréte

CIGARETTE *s.* ţiyárắ, fum

CILIUM *s.* peánă → EYELASH

CINCTURE *s.* páhtă → GIRDLE

CINDER *s.* zgúră, zgureáuă

CINDERY *adj.* zgurós, -oásă; zgúrav, -avă, -ayĭ, -ave

CINNAMON *s.* canélă

CIRCA *adv.* ‖ PC: cam

CIRCASSIA *s.* Circhizáme

CIRCASSIAN *s.* and *adj.* circhéz; *coll.* circhizáme

CIRCLE *s.* arucót, arócut, rucóciu, *G:* arcoátă; yiur, yiúră, yir, ghírgal, stipáre, suzé, târcól; ţércĭu, ţérchiu; (~ *marked on the ground in children's games*) sóir; (~ *under the eyes*) arúptu

CIRCLE *vb.* ▾anvărlighédz, anvăríg, anvărlíg, nţércĭu, nţir-cĭédz, ţirclédz, ▾ţíngu; (*to drive smb. into a corner*) anăpădéscu

CIRCULAR *adj.* arucutós, -oásă; strónghil, *m pl* -nghiĭ

CIRCULATE *vb.* (*to move or pass to and fro*) ▾úrdin, cur, trec

CIRCULATION *s.* treáţire, triţeáre; **to be in ~** (*as of money*) trec, ▾úrdin

CIRCUMCISED *adj.* (*of Muslim Turks*) tăĭát, *m pl* -ĭáţ

CIRCUMCISION *s.* siréte, sâréte, suréte

CIRCUMSPECT *adj.* câştigós, -oásă, -óşĭ, -oáse

CIRCUMSTANCE *s.* pirístase, oáră; **narrow ~s** cacurizipsíre → UNDER NO ~S

CIRCUMVOLUTION *s.* (a)nvârtitúră, (a)nvârtíre (*and* nvăr-); (*as around an axis*) şuţâre

CISTERN *s.* (*water wagon*) buduváie, stérnă

CITADEL *s.* cástru, ţitáte, grădítă, calé

CITATION *s.* (*summons*) iczáre, clíse

CITRIC ACID *s.* limóntus

CITRON *s.* chítră

CITY *s.* căsắbă, câsâbắ, câsâbắu, hâsâbắ, hăsăpắ, (a)pulitíe, póli, misíre, păzáre

CITY LIMIT *s.* ‖ *Cru:* sinúr, GOLAB 248

CIVIL STATUS *s.* óhe

CIVILITY *s.* uminíľe → ELABORATE CIVILITIES

CIVILIZATION *s.* (*the act of civilizing*) pulitipsíre

CIVILIZE *vb.* ▼pulitipséscu. ▼fruminéscu

CIVILIZED *adj.* (*polite, urbane, refined*) pulitipsít

CLACK *s.* (*rapid talk*): **His ~ goes thirteen to the dozen** Ápă-ľ ñárdze gúra → CHATTER

CLAD *adj.* viscút, (a)nviscút

CLAIM *s.* ţeárire, ţireáre; (*as in court*) nadé, nadée → CAUSE, PUT UP A ~

CLAIM *vb.* ţer, cáftu

CLAMBER UP *vb* ▼(a)ngărlím (*and* angâr-) → CREEP UP

CLAMMY *adj.* mâzgós, -oásă, -óşĭ, -oáse

CLAMOR *s.* strigáre → HUBBUB

CLAMOR *vb.* strig, fac ghiurultíe → SHOUT

CLAM UP *vb.* amuţắscu, tac

CLAN *s.* ‖ MERCA 3: ghireáuă

CLANK *interj., ono.* glungurú

CLAP *vb.* (*to applaud*) plăscănéscu; (*while dancing*) dau mâñle n pláscu, ñ-gioc mâñle n pláscu ‖ BASME 249: plăscănéscu pălñile

CLARET *adj.* (*red to purplish pink*) vişinát; víş(i)nă *invar.*

CLARIFICATION *s.* (*as of water*) limpidzâre, limbisíre, dizlăcíre, lăyărsíre

CLARIFY *vb.* limpidzắscu (*and* limbi-), ▼dizlăcéscu, ▼lăyărséscu

CLARINET *s.* gârnétă, súrlă, clărinétă

CLARINETIST *s.* gârmetăgí

CLASH *s.* ciucutíre, acăţáre, ncârligáre, fricáre

CLASH *vb.* ▼ciucutéscu → COLLIDE

CLASP *s.* (*fastener*) ceapráche, cipráche, ciupráche, cârlíg, cârligár

CLASP *vb.* ▼stríngu, *N:* (*rarely*) strângu; **to ~ one's hands** (*as in astonishment*) ▼ncľidz mâñle; **to ~ to one's heart** stríngu la sin

CLASS *s.* (*body of students*) táxe ‖ **Cru:** rázred GOLAB 246

CLAW *s.* úngľe; **Cľis:** zgrâñe

CLAY *s.* lut, ţáră, cľísă, nigľánă; (*the human body in distinction from the spirit*) → DUST ‖ ALIA 31: lắschi, múzgă

CLAY *vb.* (*to apply a coat of ~*) ▼aúngu

CLAYEY *adj.* lutós; **~ soil** plăvúc *n* ‖ CUNIA 177: alutós, nigľinós

CLEAN *adj.* curát, spástru, *m pl* -ştri, *f pl* -stre; ascuţât, aspi-

CLEAN

lát; lat, *f* -ă, *m pl* laţ, *f pl* láte; lăyárǎ *invar.*; cârţǎnós, chischín; yilíe (*lit.* 'mirror'); cǎthǎrusít; (*rare*) nyiurát [nyi•u•]; **as ~ as a whistle** ca scos dit ou ‖ **Cru:** (*pedantically ~*) chibár, GOLAB 230

CLEAN *vb.* ▾spǎstréscu, pǎstrǎséscu, pǎstréscu; (*to extirpate, to weed*) cur, cur di érghĭ; adár lǎyárǎ; cǎthǎrǎséscu; **to ~ smb. out** (*as at cards*) (a)fuléscu (di parádz); fufuléscu; **~ed him out** l-fufulí; **to ~ off** (*as of a blackboard*) ▾aştérgu, ▾astíngu; **to ~ up** (*as a room*) nǎscǎréscu

CLEANING *s.* spǎstríre, pǎstrire, curáre, cǎthǎrsíre, (a)nǎscǎrsíre, nǎscáríe

CLEANLINESS *s.* pástru, spástrǎ, pástrǎ, chischimeáţǎ, -neáţǎ

CLEANSE *vb.* trec tu ápǎ ‖ CUNIA 56: trec prit ápǎ

CLEANSING *s.* (*as raw cotton*) scǎlsíre

CLEAR *adj.* (*cloudless*) curát; lǎyárǎ *invar.*; (*as of a lake*) límpid

CLEAR *vb.* (*to make or to become clear*) limbidzǎscu, limbiséscu; **to ~ the table** ▾scol meása, créscu meása, mut meása; (*to ~ smb. out of money, etc.*) (a)fuléscu (di parádz) ‖ (*to ~ from accusation or blame*) scot cu fáţa álbǎ, BASME 177

CLEARLY *adv.* ‖ ca tu cutii (*lit.* 'like in a mirror'), HRISTU 23

CLEAR OUT: Clear out! Adúnǎ-u di auá! → GET LOST

CLEAR UP *vb.* (*of the sky*) ▾dişcľíd; *3 sg impers.* ▾disvirneádzǎ, ▾nsirineádzǎ, ▾nsirínǎ, ▾gǎľáşte; (*as of a puzzle*) ľ-dau di fún-du; **to ~ one's brow** (*i.e., to calm down*) ñ-yin cǎprâle (*lit.* 'my goats are coming [home]!')

CLEARANCE *s.* (*of merchandise*) mǎrdáie

CLEAT *s.* (*as on the bottom of a shoe to protect it from being worn down*) nálce

CLEAVAGE *s.* (*break*) disicáre, discáre

CLEAVE *vb.* ▾disíc

CLEFT *s.* cripǎtúrǎ, ţânţânǎ → SLIT

CLEMENCY *s.* ñílǎ, imiráme, isáfe, merhaméti ‖ limusíni, CUNIA 56

CLEMENT *adj.* ímir; ñilós, -oásǎ, -óşĭ, -oáse

CLENCH *vb.* stríngu

CLERGY *s.* clir

CLERK *s.* mimú

CLEVER *adj.* drǎcós, drǎcurós, chischín, chischinéţ, epitídhiu, ítru, mástur, pir, pirgác, theámin, ustă ‖ *Cru:* prucupsít, GOLAB 245

CLEVERNESS *s.* pireáţă ‖ CUNIA 138: iţrăľi

CLEW *s.* gľem, gľom; cuváre, cuvalístra

CLICK *vb.* (*to fit or work together smoothly*) ▾uidiséscu

CLIENT *s.* muştirí, muştiră

CLIFF *s.* şcárpă, şcăbă, piştireáuă, *N:* pişcireáuă

CLIMATE *s.* aváie, aváe; hâvă, *N:* hăváie; **Here is a harsh** ~ Auá eáste hâvă greu

CLIMB *vb.* (*as a mountain, a ladder*) ▾alín; (*as of a goat on a steep hill*) ▾aspíndzur; (*as up a tree*) ▾ascálin, ascálnu, ▾an-gărlím

CLIMBING *s.* (*as a mountain*) anifuráre, anífur

CLIMBING *adj. bot.* ascălnătór, *m pl* -tórĭ, *f sg/pl* -toáre

CLINCH *s.* ncărfusíre

CLINCH *vb.* (*to fasten*) ▾ncărfuséscu

CLING *vb.* ▾ascálin, ascálnu, mi ţân scaľu, ľ-acáţ yeáca; ~ **to him!** Ascálnă-te di el!

CLING TO ONE'S OPINION *vb.* u leg tu greáuă, u leg greáua

CLINK *vb.* asún; **to** ~ **glasses** fac cíóca, ▾cingărşéscu; (*to* ~ *and drink*) ▾ciucutéscu ‖ ALR 1270: fac tóca

CLINK-CLANK *interj., ono.* (*as of a bell*) glungurú

CLIP *s.* foártică

CLIP *vb.* (*usu. of hair or wool*) túndu (→ § 32); foártic, fur-tichédz; (*of the wool on the head of a sheep*) cápit, căpitédz; (*of the wool on the belly and under the tail*) suilédz; (*to trim with scissors*) aruféc; (*to clasp*) ▾acáţ, ▾stríngu

CLIQUE *s.* táymă, suţátă; **a** ~ **of liars and rascals** ună suţátă di psívţâ (*or* di spindzuráţ)

CLITORIS *s.* caţaflác ‖ múscâ, závâ, DIARO 264

CLOAK *s.* tămbáre (*and* tâm-); *dim.* tămbărúşe; tălăgán, tăligáne; (~ *with a hood*) cápă, pănucáplă, pănucápă giúbă, giubé; măľót; (*with the hair outwards*) sárică, sárcă; gioc, giócă; (~ *for rainy days*) brúţă; (*Turkish* ~) căplămă; (*for children*) sărcótă; cacúţă; *Bl:* (*made* ~ *of goat hair*) ľáră; *Blţ:* (~ *made of black wool*) dzaţ; *N:* (*sleeveless* ~) şigúnă, şigúne; *N:* (*for women*) căndúşe, cundúşe; şcúrtă; *S:* ţipúne; (*sleeveless*) capótă

CLOAKROOM *s.* sărceáne

CLOBBER *vb.* ▾agudéscu, ▾păléscu, dau

CLOCK

CLOCK s. săhát(e), s(ă)áte; oárӑ, órnic, urulóye; **The ~ struck five** Sӑhátea deáde țínți ‖ *Peş:* (~ *on the wall*) sihӑte, CL 260

CLOD s. (*lump of earth with grass*) zvol, zvoĭu, zvólar, zvulár

CLOG s. (*sabot*) nalóne, nӑlúne, **N:** nalínӑ; (*a weight attached to an animal's leg to hinder motion*) chédicӑ, cheádicӑ

CLOG vb. ▾ancheádic → SHACKLE

CLOISTER-WALL s. bӑgdӑtíe, citmӑ → WALL

CLOP s. aróput, tópur, tróput

CLOP vb. arupӑțéscu, ruputéscu

CLOSE s. (*end*) bitisítӑ: **at the ~** nai ân coádӑ

CLOSE adj. ncĭis; (*intimate, as of a friend*) bun; (*tight, stingy*) stres; (*crowded*) ndisát, strímtu; (*near*) di-anvӑrlíga: **a ~ village** unӑ hoárӑ di-anvӑrlíga; **~ at hand** próhir

CLOSE vb. ▾ncĭid, **F:** nchid; (*as one's fists*) ▾stríngu

CLOSE adv. (*intimately*) aproápe, alӑturi, alӑturea

CLOSED adj. (*very tightly ~, as of one's lips*) ncliştát

CLOSE-FISTED adj. stres, *f* -reásӑ, *m pl* -reşĭ, *f pl* -reáse

CLOSEMOUTHED adj. câştigós, -oásӑ, -óşĭ, -oáse

CLOSET s. dulápe; (*in a wall*) dulape dit stízmӑ; firídhӑ (*and* firídӑ), frídhӑ; cӑrghíe, cӑryíe, cumárӑ, misándrӑ, cuşúg ‖ *Cru:* camárӑ, GOLAB 224

CLOSE TO prep. ntrӑ, ntrâ, ndrӑ, trӑ; príngӑ, priníngӑ, níncӑ (*and* níngӑ), nângӑ, língӑ, alӑturea di, pri níntrӑ; **Go ~ him** S-vӑ prucheáț príngӑ nӑs; **He kept him ~ the sheep** L-țӑnú pri níntrӑ steárpe; **They are sitting ~ him and are smoking** Sta trâ nâs di trag țiyárӑ

CLOT s. (*of blood*) cĭag di sândze ‖ *Peş:* (*as a ~ of butter in sour cream*) grundíce

CLOTH s. (*linen*) pândzӑ; (*coarse woolen ~*) şiác, şaiác, véştu; (*piece of ~*) peáticӑ; (*silk ~*) silinícӑ, sӑlinícӑ (*and* sâ-); (*thick ~*) pustáve, pultúrӑ ‖ (~ *used by women undegoing menstruation*) spástrâ, zóstrâ, DIARO 105

CLOTHES s. stráñe *pl*, strañiu *sg*; stóle *no pl*; **European ~** (*coat and pants*) strímte *f pl*, frânțéşti *f pl*; **He put on E. ~** Intrӑ tu strímte; **I see him in E. ~** L-ved tu frânțéşti; (*girlish ~*) fitéştile *f pl def.*

CLOTHES-BRUSH s. → BRUSH ‖ *Peş:* fӑrce, CL 45

CLOTHESLINE s. ‖ fúni, DIARO 215

CLOTHESPIN *s.* ‖ cľáe, DIARO 215

CLOTHING *s.* vistămínte *n pl*, vistămíntu, viscămíndu *sg*; stráñie *n pl*, strañiu *sg*

CLOUD *s.* niór *m/n*; nor, nuór, năór ‖ *Cľis:* năúr, BASME 651; ALIA 9: ñĭór, neór, neóre

CLOUD OVER *vb.* niureádză *3 sg*, nigureádză *3 sg*; *fig.* mi nigurédz *or* mi nigurédz la fáţă ‖ **The sky has clouded over, it's going to rain** Ţérlu niură, s-feáţi ciórgâ, va s-da ploáe, DIARO 229

CLOUDBURST *s.* zof, zdârce

CLOUDED *adj.* vurcusít; ~ **over** (*of the sky*) astupát, alăcít

CLOUDLESS *adj.* sirín, curát, gălít, límpid, lăyáră *invar.* ‖ *SJos:* strufingíe, CL 261; *Prv:* xistiriyeáuâ, CL 42

CLOUDY *adj.* astupát, niurós, nigurós, niurát → BECOME ~ ‖ *SJos:* muntós, CL 256

CLOUT *vb.* ▾agudéscu → HIT

CLOVE OF GARLIC *s.* căţăl di aľu ‖ *Av:* cior di aľu, CL 43

CLOVER *s.* trifóľu → TREFOIL

CLOWN *s.* baľáciu, soitár, casoitár

CLOWN AROUND *vb.* ‖ **Why are you clowning around?** ţi faţi ca vârnu caraghióz? DIARO 179

CLOY *vb.* ▾(a)năfătéscu, ▾fănătéscu, fănitéscu; ▾pristăniséscu, pristănéscu, prâstânéscu, ▾cos di mâcáre, ▾adár ciufulícă (*or* ciu-fľácă, cĭuflécă, ciuflícă); (*to disgust with excess*) ñ-i greáţă → NAUSEATE

CLOYED *adj.* (*stuffed, full*) sătúl, *m pl* -túľ; săturát

CLOYING *adj.* (*excessively sweet*) liyusít

CLUB *s.* (*staff*) gărbáce, gărbáciu; (*weapon*) buzdugán, buzdugáne, buzdugánă → CUDGEL

CLUB *vb.* agudéscu cu ciumága

CLUBS *s.* (♣ *on playing cards*) ‖ DIARO 204: lăi (*pl of* laiu 'black')

CLUCK(ING) *s.* (*of hens*) cărcăridzáre

CLUCK *vb.* ▾cărcărédz, cacărédz

CLUMSY *adj.* astângu, *m pl* -ndzi, *f pl* -ndze; angricós, -oásă

CLUSTER *s.* (a)pálă; *in* ~s păľi-păľi ‖ *Pls:* (*tuft of hair*) tumb, CL 262

CLUTTER *s.* mintitúră, mintireáje, mintireáţă

CLYSTER *s.* (*enema*) ylistír

COACH *s.* cucíe → CARRIAGE

COACH-HOUSE *s.* pľánţă (*and* pľándză)

COACHMAN *s.* cucigí, chiragí, sindúş; (*in children's games: the player who has the whip*) tombulár → CARTER ‖ ALR 281: cărvănár; BELIMACE 48: cociáş

COAGULATE *vb.* (*usu. of milk or blood*) ▾cľeq, (a)ncľég; (*of a dish*) pihtuséscu ‖ ALR 1121 (*as of fat, 3 sg*) ngľáţă

COAGULATED *adj.* (*of a dish*) căpăít

COAGULATION *s.* ncľigáre

COAL *s.* cărbúne *m*; chiumúre *f*; *coll.* cărbunáme

COALESCE INTO ONE *vb.* ▾fac únă

COALIFICATION STATION *s.* cărbunărlíche

COALITION *s.* tăráfe

COARSE *adj.* (*as of wool*) áscur, áyru; scliró

COARSEN *vb.* (*as of the skin*) ▾ascurédz

COARSENESS *s.* (*of behavior*) ascuráme, huryeátă

COAT *s.* (*for men*) surtúc, sultúc, siurtúc; (*velvety ~*) mindán; **Blţ:** (*black woolen ~*) dzaţ; (*sleeveless furred ~*) cheptár; (*for women*) bértă, bidéne, búndă; yúnă, sac ‖ **Cru:** (*~ worn by shepherds*) giumădáne, GOLAB 261

COAT *vb.* → PLASTER

COAX *vb.* culăchipséscu → WHEEDLE ‖ PC: cândiséscu

COBBLER *s.* păpugí, cârpáciu → SHOEMAKER

COBBLER'S SHOP *s.* cunduragilắche

COBWEB *s.* pândză di păiángu; pândzină di păiángu; cánă

COCK *s.* (*of a gun*) ceárcu ‖ **Peş:** mânár; **GSus:** mânáră, CL 255

COCK *s.* (*a small pile, as of hay*) căpíţă, cupíţă

COCK-A-DOODLE-DOO *ono.* cucurígu, cucurícu, câ-câ-câ; cắcă, chichi-chí

COCK A SNOOT AT SMB. *vb.* ▾mundzuéscu; ľ-dau mắndzăle (*or* mún-dzăle) → THUMB ONE'S NOSEB. *vb.*

COCKCHAFER *s. ent.* cľeg, zăngănár (*and* zângâ-); **green ~** júnă

COCKCROW: (*dawn*) nícă nicântátă cucóţľi

COCKEREL *s.* (*young rooster*) cucutíciu

COCK-EYED *adj.* ‖ (*squint-eyed*) **Av:** zăvumát CL 263 → SQUINT-EYED

COCK'S COMB *s. bot.* ştíră, ştírnu; (*yellow flowers:* máranthu, marándu, *vague meaning in the DDA*)

COCKSURE *adj.* saylám(cu)

COCKY *adj.* saylám, saylám(cu), thirisít

COCOON *s.* gâgoáşe di sírmă, gugóş di sârmă; búbă, cucúľu

CODDLE *vb.* (*to baby, to spoil*) ▾dizñérdu, ▾cănăchipséscu, ▾hăidhipséscu, puşputéscu, ▾zdrudéscu

CODFISH *s.* (*salted and dried*) bacaľár *m*

CODGER *s.* om şuţât, om aruşuţât

COEQUAL *adj.* ísea → EQUAL

COERCE *vb.* ▾stríngu, bag súla n coáste → COMPEL

COERCION *s.* cilihtisíre → CONSTRAINT

COFFEE *s.* café, *N:* cafée → TURKISH ~

COFFEE CUP *s.* ceáşcă, filigeánă, filgeánă, fligeánă

COFFEE HOUSE *s.* cafiné, cazín

COFFEE-HOUSE KEEPER *s.* cafigí *m*, cafigioáñe *f*

COFFEE-MILL *s.* moáră di café

COFFEE POT *s.* (*with a long handle*) ibríc, **Gop:** iubríc; yiumác, iamácă, ghiumác, ghiumáciu, cafébric, gigivé, giugivé, gijivé, gijvée, gisvé, gisvée

COFFEE ROASTER *s.* dulápe

COFFER *s.* căsélă, casélă, hasélă, măláthă, săndúche, sindúche, sfindúche

COFFIN *s.* svindúche, sindúche; căvúre, chivúre; xilucrevát; *N:* cufciúg; scámnu, cutíe di mórtu ‖ ALiA II q.214: cutíe, cásă

COFFIN MAKER *s.* cufciugár

COGITATE *vb.* ▾minduéscu

COHERENT *adj.* ligát

COIL ONESELF UP *vb.* ▾fac culác ‖ (*as under a warm blanket*) mi cutuléscu, DIARO 271

COIN *s.* pără, *N:* pră; *F:* căţíth *n*; *G:* gălăgán *m*; mitilíc *m*; pénge; sfânţíc *m*; spéndză; şitác *m*; statíră, munédhă, găzétă; pineş (*gold* ~) gálbină

COITUS *s.* → COPULATION

COL *s.* (*saddle-shaped depression in the crest of a ridge*) şilătúră, şulătureáuă; coácă

COLD *s.* (*low temperature*) (a)răcoáre, arcoáre, arcuráme; arăţíme; frig; (*severe* ~) virvér, dzer; **It was extremely** ~ Cripá chétrile di dzer ş di virvér; (*bodily disorder, malady in the head or chest*) arémă, aréme; bútur, ceáră, guhtíc, rufă, sirmíe → CATCH A ~ ‖ **Cru:** **I caught** ~ Arémă mi acáţă; Am arémă, GOLAB 201

COLD *adj.* (a)ráţe, *m/f*; (a)răţĭ, *m/f pl*; (*susceptible of being* ~)

COLD

frigurós, arcurós; **The weather was ~** Chirólul erá arcurós; **as ~ as ice** córcan *invar.*; (*harmed by frost*) cóţâ *invar.* → BE ~

COLD *adv.* (*with utter finality*) dip → TOTALLY

COLD FEET *s.* trimuráre, trimurárea a dínţălor; cărcicáre

COLDLY *adv.* aráţe; **He spoke to me ~** Ñ-zburá aráţe

COLDPROOF *adj.* **G:** sărcás, sărchicós

COLIC *s.* **I suffer from ~** Mi múşcă buríclu; (**a sheep disease**) strof; **sick with ~** strufchisít; **to be diseased with ~** strufchiséscu

COLLAPSE *s.* arăvuíre → FALLING IN

COLLAPSE *vb.* cad, ▾aruvuéscu, ▾hărdăcuséscu, tălcéscu; (*to shrink, to deflate*) ▾disúmflu, disúflu; (*financially*) cad nafoáră ‖ (*to break down in vital energy, stamina or self-control through exhaustion or desease*) cad di cicioáre (*lit.* 'to fall from one's legs'), PARALLELE 127

COLLAR *s.* yică, **N:** iácă, yeácă; limăreáuă; (*detachable ~*) culár; (*of a blouse for women*) părtíţă; (*of fox fur*) ilmă, ilmáe

COLLEAGUE *s.* simathití

COLLECT *vb.* ▾adún, lixéscu, silixéscu

COLLECTED *adj.* (*cool*) stăpuít; cap ligát (*lit.* 'tied head')

COLLECTION *s.* adunătúră

COLLECTIVE FARM *s.* ‖ **Cru:** stopánstvo, GOLAB 250

COLLECT ONE'S FACULTIES *vb.* ñ-yin tu orĭ; ñ-yíne sulúchea; *3 sg m, pt:* víne ântr-ésu ‖ **Alb:** âñ ľau vétea, CAPIDAN 177

COLLIDE *vb.* ▾cingărşéscu, ▾ciucutéscu; mi dau; **they ~ed with such force that** s-deádira cu ahântă fórţă că ‖ **Cru:** mi gudéscu, GOLAB 218

COLLISION *s.* cingărşíre

COLLUSION *s.* ţeásire, ţăseáre, cuţeáre

COLONEL *s.* culási [•lási], *sg. and pl.* (*rare*) cólasă; alái-bei

COLONNADE *s.* témplu

COLOPHON *s.* săcâze, ceamceacâză, samsacâze; măstíhe

COLOR *s.* bóie, buiáuă, réngă, rénghe, hrómă; (*of the face*) máste

COLOR *vb.* chindriséscu, ncărdzéľu, dau réngă

COLORATION *s.* văpsíre, văpsitúră

COLORFUL *adj.* cu buiéi [bu•iéi] (*lit.* 'with colors')

COLOSSAL *adj.* balaváncu, *m pl* -ánţi, *f pl* -ănţi; évil

COLOSSUS *s.* (*of a very large person*) ľúftă

COLT *s.* măndzu (*and* mân-), mândzác; **G:** dintác; (*two-year old ~*) dhiót *m*, dhioátă *f*; (**as**) **sound as a ~** sănătós ca grij di dzádă →

ROACH

COLUMN *s.* (*pillar*) culoánă

COLZA *s. bot.* **wild ~.** ‖ *Pls:* sinápĭ, *SJos:* snápi, CL 261

COMB *s.* cheáptine *m*; *dim.* chiptiníciu; (*with large sparse teeth*) zuyránă, zug-; discăciór, -citór; gríbă, glí-, ylí-, gríblă, zórnă; (*a rooster's ~*) creástă, giúfcă ‖ *Trn:* zuyrámă, NEIESCU 111

COMB *vb.* ▾cheáptin, chéptin; (*to curry a horse*) xistriséscu; *N:* histriséscu

COMBAT *s.* alúmtă, băteáre, bátire, bătíc, bătíe, ncârligáre

COMBAT *vb.* → FIGHT

COMBATANT *s.* and *adj.* alumtătór, -toáre; lumtáş

COMB DOWN *vb.* (*to scold severely*) ľ-afúm nărĭle (*lit.* 'to smoke smb.'s nose')

COMBINE *vb.* ▾alăchéscu, ▾ameástic

COMBUSTION *s.* ardeáre, árdire

COME *vb.* yin (→ § 32); agiúngu, cupăséscu; **Why have you come?** Ţe ţ-u viníta? **There they ~!** Ia-ľ, agiúngu! (*of the ~ing of the night*) ntúnică *3 sg impers.*; **to ~ over** urséscu; **Come over tonight, if you wish** Urseá, ma s-vrei, astáră; **Come closer!** Éla! *or* Fă-ñ-te ncoáţe! *2 sg*; Iláţ! *2 pl*; **Where have you come from?** D-ĭu nă cupă-síşi?

COME ACROSS *vb.* dau di, ▾mpichiu, mi áflu pri cále; **There you will ~ a dog** Acló va s-dai di un câne; **I came across a rich man** Ded di om cáldu; (*by chance*) tihiséscu, ▾astáľu; **If you ~ a snake, smash its head in !** Astáľ şárpe, chiseádză-ľ cáplu ! ▾(a)ndămuséscu; (*~ smth. bad, unpleasant*) (a)ndiséscu; **I came across trouble** ñi-ndisíi lăiáţă; ▾ndizmuséscu, andămiséscu, dau chéptu (cu)

COME BACK *vb.* ▾tórnu, *F:* tórru

COME BETWEEN *vb.* ▾bag

COME DIFFICULT TO SMB. *vb.* mi (a)ngréc; *impers.* ñi-ngreácă; **Work comes difficult to you, doesn't it?** Lúcrulu ţă-ngreácă

COME DOWN *vb.* ▾dipún, ▾scad, năvăléscu; **came down from the tree** năvălí di pi oárbări → DESCEND

COME DOWN HEAVILY ON *vb.* (*as a threat*) lu-nvéţ eu panachída! *I'll come down heavily on you!* Va-ţ arát!

COME DOWN A PEG OR TWO *vb.* li dipún urécľile; l-dipún tâmbárălu

COME FORTH *vb.* ies, es; *aor.* inşíi, işíi, i(n)şái

COME IN! Triţéţ năúntru! (*2 pl*)

COME IN THE NICK OF TIME *vb.* (a)pugudéscu

COME IN STAGE

COME IN STAGE *vb*. dişcľíd tu lúme

COME NEAR TO *vb*. ▼apróchiu

COME NOW! ştu-cará!

COME OFF *vb*. u scot náparti, căturthuséscu, mi alég (cu) ‖ CUNIA 259: u scot n cáli, u scot n cap, scot lúcurlu n cap; acáţ péşti

COME ON! ‖ *Cru:* ai! áide! GOLAB 196; DIARO 89: (*used challengingly*) ba! ~, **who told you that?** ba, di iu u scoásişi şi aéstâ?

COME OUT *vb*. ies, es; ~ **with clean hands** es cu fáţa álbă; ~ **in procession** scot sígnile

COME OVER *vb*. cupăséscu, urséscu; **Turks came over to his house** Túrţi ľ-cupăsíră n cásă; **Come on over!** Cupăseá ñăúntru n cása! → INVITE; (*to ~ unexpectedly, as of thieves, guests, etc.*) ▼cálcu; **We will ~ to your place unexpectedly** Va vă călcăm când nu va ştiţ

COME ROUND *vb*. *med*. ñ-yin pri mínte; ñ-yin tu orĭ ‖ VELO 98: âñ vin pi veti

COME TO A HEAD *vb*. (*of a boil*) adún; **My boil is coming to a head** Gârnúţlu ñ-adúnă; cluvyiséscu

COME TO AN AGREEMENT WITH *vb*. mi (a)ndrég (cu)

COME TO AN END *vb*. (a)scáp; **The day is coming to an end** Dzúua ascápă ‖ *Amc:* **The story has come to an end** Si scăpă părămíthlu, RÉCATAS 37; **The day has come to an end** Frâmse dzua (*lit. 'the day has broken'*), PARALLELE 124; si-ncľié 3 *sg*. aor., TULLIU 124

COME TO BLOWS *vb*. ▼(a)nciúp (cu), ▼(a)ngiúp; ▼acáţ (cu); ▼acáţ di per (cu); ▼agiúngu la par (cu); ▼(â)ncârlighédz (cu)

COME TO CUFFS *vb*. mi-acáţ di per (cu), ▼agiúngu la par (cu)

COME TOGETHER *vb*. (*to congregate*) ▼adún; (*of sheep*) ▼mârşin, ▼mârşinédz

COME TO KNOW *vb*. mi cunóscu cu, fac cunuşmáie cu; (*to learn*) ľau di hăbáre

COME TO LIFE *vb*. ñ-yin tu orĭ → COME ROUND

COME TO LIGHT *vb*. ies tu páde; (*as of a theft*) ies to miydáne

COME TO LOGGERHEADS *vb*. ▼agiúngu la par → COME TO BLOWS

COME TO NOTHING: **It came to nothing** Ţívale si aleápse; (*in vain*) ti éră ş-ti séră ‖ Cinúşe s-feáţe (*lit. 'It became ashes'*; details in PARALLELE 120)

COME TO ONE'S MIND *vb*. ‖ *Cru:* ñ-tăcăiáşte, âñ tihneáşce, GOLAB 253

COME TO ONE'S SENSES *vb*. (*to come to reason*) dipún mínte

COME TO REASON *vb*. dipún mínte, bag mínte, ▼fruminéscu, ▼aştérnu

COME TO TERMS WITH SMB. *vb.* → AGREE ‖ u scot náparte cu, BASME 494

COME TRUE *vb.* (*to become fact*) *3 sg aor.* s-feáţe; *pf.* s-áre fáptă; acáţă loc; **dreams ~** yísile s-fac; **Your words have come true** Zboárile a tále acáţără loc

COME UP *vb.* ies; (*to ferment, to rise, of dough*) *3 sg pf* **The bread has not come up** Pânea nu eáste viñítă; (*of plants*) dau ‖ **I want to see how the grass comes up** Vroi s-vedu că cum u-s da iarba, HRISTU 45

COME UP TO THE BIT *vb.* (*to sit, of a dog*) stau sústa

COME UP WITH SMB. *vb.* (*to reach*) ▼apróchiu, agiúngu, ▼axéscu, aséscu

COME WHAT MAY! ţi va, las s-híbă! ‖ Ţe s-eásă, z-beásă, BASME 489; iu s-eásă, z-beásă, BASME 405; tângăr-mângăr, BASME 405

COMEBACK *s.* năpuíre, túrnáre, turnátă

COMELY *adj.* aléptu, -eáptă, -épţâ, -eápte → HANDSOME

COME-ON *s.* culăchíe, culăchipsíre, băgáre pri sómnu

COMESTIBLES *s. pl* mâncătúră → FOOD

COMEUPPANCE *s.* pirdáfe

COMFORT *s.* (*solace*) sămănáre, păriyuríe

COMFORT *vb.* azbún, asbún; ▼păriyuriséscu, ▼păryuriséscu → CONSOLE, RECONCILE

COMFORTS *s. pl.* zéfche, zéfcă

COMING *s.* vinítă (*and* viñítă), vineáre, viñáre, viñíre; **What is the purpose of your ~?** Ţe ţ-u viníta? **~ of summer** nviráre

COMING BACK *s.* turnátă, turnătúră

COMING DUE *s.* (*deadline, as of a payment*) murmín

COMING IN *s.* intráre (*and* indráre)

COMING OUT *s.* inşíre, işíre

COMMAND *s.* endolíe, ordhiníe, părănghilíe, cumándă

COMMAND *vb.* dau dimândáre → ORDER

COMMANDER *s.* silihtár, tăpár, cumandár

COMMANDER-IN-CHIEF *s.* arhistratiyó, seraschér

COMMANDMENT *s.* dimăndáre ·(*and* dimân-), părănghilíe

COMMEMORATION *s.* (*a Christian ritual and banquet*) pumeán, pumíníe, trisáyiu

COMMENCE *vb.* → BEGIN, START

COMMERCE *s.* embóriu, emburlíche, tigearéte, tugearlíche ‖ *Peş:* prămăteftălâche, CL 517

COMMERCIAL

COMMERCIAL *adj.* tugiréscu, -eáscă, -éşţâ, -éşti

COMMISSION *s.* pitrupíľe

COMMIT *vb.* (*to carry into action*) fac, adár; u adár muşiteás-
că; **What sacrilege have they ~ed?** Ţe lăĭéţ au fáptă? ‖ **~ oneself**
(*to pledge*) leg zbor, CAPIDAN 176

COMMIT AN ERROR *vb.* (a)lăthipséscu → MAKE A MISTAKE

COMMIT A SIN *vb.* → SIN

COMMITTEE *s.* efuríe, efurlíche, pitrupíľe

COMMODITY *s.* (*merchandise*) prămătíe, părmătíe; săváte, *pl.* su-
văţ

COMMON *adj.* (*ordinary, usual*) paráspur

COMMON PEOPLE *s.* ciuplicheáuă

COMMON SENSE *s.* aduchíre, aduchitúră

COMMONER *s.* (om) di arádă (*and* arádhă); paráspur

COMMOTION *s.* trunduíre, mintíre (*and* mindíre), mintitúră

COMMUNICATE *vb.* (*to inform, to let know*) dau di şteáre; dau di
hăbáre

COMMUNION *s.* cumnicătúră; (*before Easter*) păştíc; **to administer
or receive ~** ▾cumânic

COMMUNIQUÉ *s.* şteáre, timbí(h)e

COMMUNITY *s.* giumaéte, giumăéte, chinótită

COMPANION *s.* soţ *m*, soáţă *f*; curcóñu *m*, curcoáñe *f*

COMPANY *s.* sinastrufíe; **in ~** carşí *adv.* → ASSOCIATION, SOCIETY

COMPARATIVE *s.* (*the ~ degree*) singriticá

COMPARATIVELY *adv.* singriticá

COMPARE *vb.* ▾fac biáne [bi•á•ne] → AS COMPARED TO

COMPARED TO *prep.* spróti

COMPARISON *s.* biáne [bi•á•ne] *invar.*

COMPASS *s.* pusúlă

COMPASSION *s.* ñílă

COMPASSIONATE *adj.* ñil(ă)ós, -oásă; adiľós, -oásă

COMPEL *vb.* bag súla tu coáste → CONSTRAIN

COMPELLED *adj.* stres, *f* -eásă, *m pl* streşĭ, *f pl* -eáse

COMPENSATE *vb.* ▾plătéscu

COMPENSATION *s.* plátă, muştinare

COMPETE *vb.* ▾sinirséscu; mi ľau la ntriţeáre

COMPETENT *adj.* ácşu → ABLE

COMPETITION *s.* ntreáţire, astreáţire, astriţeáre

COMPLAIN *vb.* ▾rucuiéscu, ▾buiséscu, cắñiséscu (*and* câ-)

COMPLAINING *adj.* parapuñárcu, *pl m* -rţi, *pl f* -rţe → PLAINTIVE

COMPLAINT *s.* plâgu, (a)rugiuhále, (a)rgiuhále, aruzuvále, parápun; (*reproach*) zboáră năpói *n pl*; **to lodge a ~** → PUT IN A CLAIM

COMPLECTED *adj.* (*entangled*) cărşiľát

COMPLETE *adj.* (*finished, done*) susít, mplin

COMPLETE *vb.* (*to bring to an end*) ▾mburéscu, bitiséscu

COMPLETELY *adv.* dot, dip, dibínă, dicutót, dicutótalui, acutótalui, fáre; *G:* pandilós; xintopándo; cu síndu, cu pándu ‖ BASME 95: de-a ghínealui

COMPLETION *s.* buríre, susíre, sculusíre, scărchíre (*and* scâr-), scărchitúră

COMPLEXION *s.* fáţă

COMPLIANCE *s.* ascultáre; **full ~** pára-ascultáre

COMPLIANT *adj.* ascultătór, -oáre; tibié *invar.*

COMPLICATED *adj.* cărşileát

COMPLICATION *s.* (*embroilment, perplexity*) birdhipsíre; mintitúră, síyise → CONFUSION

COMPLICE *s. G:* yitác

COMPLY *vb.* ▾ascúltu (di); **They do not want to ~ with anything** Di ţivá nu vor si-ascúltă

COMPORT *vb.* mi (a)pórtu → BEHAVE, CONDUCT

COMPORTMENT *s.* (*behavior*) aréu; cúmpite *f pl*

COMPOSE *vb.* ▾fac, ▾adár

COMPOSITION *s.* (*putting together*) adăráre, adráre

COMPOSITOR *s.* tipuyráf

COMPOSURE: *to recover one's ~* vin pi ópse → RECOVER

COMPOTE *s.* ‖ cuşáfi, huşáfi, uşáfi, DIARO 281

COMPREHEND *vb.* → UNDERSTAND; (*to include*) ncurpíľu, ncurpi-ľédz (*and* ngur-), ngrupiľédz

COMPREHENSION *s.* achicăsíre, chicazmó, ayrăxíre; (*grasp*) ncurpiľáre

COMPRESS *vb.* ▾(a)ndés, andiséscu, ▾apitruséscu, putruséscu; ▾strimuxéscu

COMPRESSION *s.* (a)ndisáre, apitrusíre, strimuxíre, strândzire, strândzeáre

COMPRISE *vb.* (*to contain*) ncurpíľu, -piľédz, -puľédz

COMPROMISE *vb.* (*to endanger the reputation of smb.*) ▾nvăpséscu, ▾buiséscu

COMPULSION *s.* stañó → CONSTRAINT

COMPULSORY *adj.* ipuhriuticó [•hri•u•]

COMPUNCTION *s.* săráche → REMORSE

COMPUTATION *s.* hisápe, isápe, ricáme, luyaryeazmó, luyareazmó, cicuteálă

COMRADE *s.* soţ, fărtát, urtác; (*after or as after a ritualistic alliance*) (a)vlámi [a•vlámi] *m sg*, (a)vlámeañ *m pl* ‖ (*form of address among comunists*) soţ; soţu Enver (Hoxha), HRISTU 32

COMRADESHIP *s.* fărtătlíche, fărtăţâľe; cărdăşláche

CONCAVE *adj.* cuvutós, -oásă, -óşĭ, -oáse

CONCEAL *vb.* ▾ascúndu, căpăchiséscu, ▾mistiryipséscu

CONCEALMENT *s.* păpărusíre, zurusíre, mistiryipsíre

CONCEDE *vb.* (*to admit*) dau driptáte; (*to concede*) alás

CONCEIT *s.* căbărdisíre, pirifáñe → PRIDE

CONCEITED *adj.* fudúl, *m pl* -úľ; făndăxít, cu nările mutáte; *to be* ~ am nările mutáte ‖ DIARO 275: cuľós

CONCEIVE *vb.* (*to become pregnant*) ▾acáţ, armân sárţină; **to be ~ed** mi príndu; (*to invent*) ▾curduséscu; **He had ~ed the lies well** Li-aveá curdusítă ghíne minciúñle

CONCERN *s.* (*anxiety, worry*) căsăvéte, casavéte, căştígă, dérte, dértă, fină, frundídhă, frundixíre, gailé, găilé, găiléie, nácră, (a)ngătán, pihtíe, săráche, siluyíe, siluíe, strimturáre, vălăndúră, *G:* găiréze ‖ ALR 1392: **She told me all her ~s** âñ le-aspúse túte pricíñli → WORRY

CONCERNED *adj.* (*worried*) sicliţít → BE CONCERNED

CONCESSION *s.* (*favor, privilege*) hătâre

CONCILIATE *vb.* ▾(a)mbunédz, ▾(a)mbún, apreaadún → APPEASE

CONCILIATION *s.* ambunáre, arăzbunáre, arăzbâ-, asbunáre, bărşíe, disvér, puitíre

CONCISE *adj.* şcúrtu, *m pl* -rţâ, *f pl* -rte

CONCLUDE *vb.* ▾bitiséscu

CONCLUSION *s.* bitisíre, bitisítă

CONCOCT *vb.* ▾ameástic, ▾anăcătuséscu

CONCORD *s.* (*agreement*) uidisíre, udiseáţă, udiséţă, úidizmă

CONCRETE *s.* ciméntu

CONCRETION *s.* (*coagulating*) ncľigáre

CONCUBINE *s.* muróză → MISTRESS

CONCUSSION *s.* trunduíre

CONDEMN *vb.* cătădhicăţéscu, giúdic

CONDENSE *vb.* ▼strimuxéscu → COMPRESS

CONDESCEND *s.* cătădhixéscu, trag boză máre, li ngroş hăbările [•bărĭ•]

CONDESCENSION *s.* cătădhixíre

CONDITION *s.* (*premise of agreement*) ligătúră, ligămíntu; **on ~ that** cu ligătúra si, cu căvúlea că, cu simfunía si, cu dimândárea să ‖ cu zbórlu că (*lit. 'with the word that'*), PARALLELE 151 → PROVIDING

CONDUCT *s.* purtátic

CONDUCT ONESELF *vb.* ▼(a)pórtu

CONDUIT *s.* (*in a well or spring*) şóput; *dim.* şuputíc, sulináre, şulinár, şúrcă; (*for water or smoke*) chilúnghe

CONE *s. bot. G:* cucúciu; cuculíciu, gugulíciu

CONFECTIONER *s.* (*of candies, pastries, etc.*) şichirgí

CONFECTIONER'S SHOP *s.* şichirgeríe

CONFER *vb.* (*to consult*) ñ-dau mínţâle

CONFERENCE *s.* (*deliberation*) cunsóltu, consúltu

CONFERVA *s.* (*frog spit*) jághină

CONFESS *vb.* (*as under pressure, derog.*) vom; **You'll confess everything** Va li voñ túte; (*to ~ one's sins, as to a priest*) ▼dizlég, ▼ximistiripséscu, ▼ximuluyiséscu, exumuluyipséscu; **Women ~ to the confessor** Si ximuluyiséscu mľérile la plimatcó

CONFESSION *s.* exumuluyíe, xumuluyíe; (*~ of sins*) ximuluyisíre, exumuluyisíre; **to administer a ~** xumuluyiséscu, sulmuxéscu; **to take a ~** ▼ximuluyiséscu

CONFESSOR *s.* pramaticó, prămaticó, plimatcó

CONFIDE *s.* ▼ximistir(ghip)séscu

CONFIDANT *s.* embistimén, mbistimén

CONFIDENCE *s.* mbithár; (*self-assurance*) embistosíne → TAKE INTO ONE'S ~

CONFIDENT *adj.* umplút

CONFINE *vb.* ▼sinuripséscu, âncľíd (tu); **I am ~ed to my bed** hiu di-amplátea

CONFIRM *vb.* apuchiruséscu ‖ (*to ratify a document*) CARAFOLI 31: vuluséscu

CONFIRMATION

CONFIRMATION *s.* apuchirusíre, tăcráre, tacríre

CONFLICT *s.* acăţáre, ceamăúnă *no pl*; ncârligáre → DISCORD

CONFORM *vb.* (*to be fitted*) pripséscu; *3 sg impers.* prínde

CONFOUND *vb.* ▾trub, ▾alăcéscu, ▾mintéscu → CONFUSE

CONFRONT *vb.* dăldăséscu, ▾ncucutédz, ľi stau cucót

CONFUSE *vb.* ▾mintéscu, ▾(a)lăcéscu (*and* alâ-), ▾birdhipséscu, ▾mbirdhuéscu, ambărtuéscu

CONFUSED *adj.* cutruburát, cutulburát, cihisít; şarafúra *invar.*; **to be ~** mi scol di mínte; *to get ~* ▾cirtuéscu

CONFUSEDLY *adv.* alandála, darmadán → HIGGLEDY-PIGGLEDY

CONFUSION *s.* alăcíre, (a)misticătúră, buzgúne *invar*; cărşéľu (*and* câr-), cildisíre, cihtisíre, cistisíre, mintitúră, şişirmáe, şişirdisíre, şiştamáră, şiştimáră → HUBBUB, PERPLEXITY; **in ~** *adv.* cióra-bóra *or* cioáră-boáră

CONGENIAL *adj.* arâsít

CONGRATULATE *vb.* (a)ór; **Let the friends come and ~ me** S-yínă soáţăle si-ñ oáră

CONGREGATE *vb.* ▾adún

CONJECTURE *s.* angucíre, pripuneáre

CONJECTURE *vb.* pripún, ▾făndăxéscu

CONJURATION *s.* (*solemn appeal*) sprigiurát, sprigiuráre

CONJURE *vb.* (*to entreat solemnly*) ▾sprigiúr, ▾spigiúr

CONJURER *s.* ghioz-boiagí

CONNECTED *adj.* amisticát; **a well ~ man** om amisticát

CONNECTION *s.* (*relationship*) shési *f*; cioáră

CONNIVANCE *s.* munăsípe

CONQUER *vb.* (*as a town*) ľau → WIN OVER

CONQUEST *s.* loáre

CONSCIENCE *s.* súflit; **I have her on my ~** U-ám pri súflit; siníthise, suméñe; **to have smb. /smth. on one's ~** am pri súflit, am pri gúşe, ľau pri gúşe, trag pri gúşe

CONSCIOUSNESS *s.* (*the upper level of mental life; mind*) ‖ LITURG 128: fichíri

CONSCRIPT *s.* ridíf *m*

CONSCRIPT *vb.* (*lasso*) ľau pidichíe; scriu

CONSECRATE *vb.* ayiséscu, ayiuséscu; (*of bread and wine*) lituryiséscu

CONSECRATED BREAD *s.* anáfură; ártu *m*, pindeártu *m*; lituryíe, píscur, piscúre, piscúră, *dim.* piscuríciu; pănăyíe; (~ *having the form of a ring, at Easter*) şirpişór

CONSECRATION *s.* ayisíre

CONSENSUS *s.* sinfuníe → AGREEMENT

CONSENT *s.* străxíre, strixíre, munăsípe

CONSENT *vb.* străxéscu, strixéscu → AGREE

CONSERVATION *s.* păstráre

CONSIDER *vb.* (*to meditate*) ▾săluşéscu, ▾siluyiséscu; (*to regard*) ▾(a)númir, am ca, ľau ti; **I ~ myself a gentleman** Mi númir om; **He ~ed him as one of theirs** Lu-aveá pri únlu di-a lor-lă ‖ mi dau; **I ~ myself a gentleman** Mi dau om, DIARO 286 ; (*to have regard for*) ‖ TULLIU 104: lu-ám (u-ám) tu (mári) angătán; STERE 66: hăbărséscu

CONSIDERATION *s.* ipólipse, ihtibáre, cumşóñe, *G:* mále; (*pondering*) arumigáre, minduíre, siluyisíre; **on no ~** iuvá ş iuvá → TAKE INTO ~

CONSOLATION *s.* meyléme, miyléme, mihléme, păriyuríe, sămănáre

CONSOLATORY *adj.* sămănătór, -oáre

CONSOLE *vb.* ▾asbún, ▾păriyuriséscu, părăyuriséscu; (~ *oneself*) ñ-fac păriyuríe

CONSOLIDATE *vb.* ▾stiriuséscu → FASTEN

CONSOLIDATION *s.* stiriusíre

CONSONANT *s.* símfonă

CONSPICUOUS *adj.* → BE ~

CONSPIRE *vb.* plitéscu, mplitéscu

CONSTANT *adj.* (*immobile*) ni-minát; (*as of a noise*) ni-tăcút; (*faithful and trustful*) di bésă

CONSTANTLY *adv.* índa → CONTINUOUSLY

CONSTANTINOPLE (*Istanbul*) Póle

CONSTELLATIONS (*some names of ~ are:*) Iriríţă, Látură, Lătră-pódh (*or* Trăpódh) ·

CONSTERNATION *s.* mbudzináre

CONSTIPATED *adj. phys.* astupát, cu cápse

CONSTIPATION *s.* cápse, astupáre

CONSTRAIN *vb.* (a)năngăséscu, ▾leg, sălnăéscu, stríngu, bag súla tu coáste; **when hunger ~ed him** cari lu strímse foámea

CONSTRAINT *s.* cilihtisíre, sălnăíre, stañó

CONSTRICT *vb.* ▾stríngu

CONSTRICTION

CONSTRICTION *s.* stríndzire, strindzeáre

CONSTRUCT *vb.* ▼fac, ▼adár; (*as a building*) stizmuséscu

CONSTRUCTION *s.* făţeáre, adăráre, adráre; (*as of walls*) stizmu-síre

CONSUL *s.* (*official who issues visas*) caidigí, cónsul

CONSULATE *s.* cunsulátă

CONSULT *vb.* (*to ask advice*) mi (a)ntreb (cu); ñ-dau mínţâle

CONSULTATION *s.* consúltu

CONSUME *vb.* (*to destroy, to spend, to waste*) aspárgu; (*to do away with smth.*) fac ghíne; (*as of firewood*) ▼hunipséscu; (*to be ~ed by fire*) ▼árdu; (*to eat*) măc; (*to cause to deteriorate, as of clothing*) ▼aród ‖ BASME 607: adár ghíne

CONSUMPTION *s.* hunipsíre; *med.* ftíse, óftică, óhtică, tíhtă, zúră

CONSUMPTIVE *adj.* ftisicó; ofticós, uhti-; tihtós, cărăúş, cărtít (*and* câr-) → BECOME ~

CONTACT *s.* (*relationship with people*) (a)misticáre

CONTACT *vb.* ▼cârtéscu (*and* cár-) → TOUCH

CONTAGION *s. med.* mulipsíre

CONTAIN *vb.* ncurpiľédz → COMPREHEND, INCLUDE

CONTAINER *s.* vas, búclă, *dim.* buclíţă; văţélă; (*wooden* ~) búrlu

CONTAMINATE *vb. med.* ▼mulipséscu

CONTAMINATION *s.* mulipsíre

CONTEMPLATE *vb.* bruéscu, ▼mutréscu; (*mentally*) ▼minduéscu; (*from a distance*) aynăndipséscu, aynănghioséscu; (~ *for pleasure or out of curiosity*) fac síre

CONTEMPORARY *adj.* di az, di ádză

CONTEMPT *s.* catafrónise → SCORN

CONTEMPTIBLE *adj.* etepsâz, idip-; zgrumát; plăstúră, păstúră; om fâră cătúnă (*lit.* 'man without cottage'); ~ **person** *s.* chirătă, *pl.* chiratádz ‖ DIARO 191: únu di aţéľ di tahiná (*i.e., an excrement*)

CONTEMPTUOUS *adj.* pirifán, *m pl* -áñ → ARROGANT

CONTEND *vb.* (*to assert, to maintain*) fac incheáre; (*to argue over the price, to negotiate*) ▼păzăripséscu; (*to compete*) mi ľau la ntriţeáre (cu), mi sinirséscu (cu); (*to fight*) mi bat

CONTENT *s.* → TO ONE'S HEART'S ~

CONTENT *adj.* arăsbunát, asbunát

CONTENT *vb.* ▾arăzbún, ▾arăzbunédz, apudiséscu, efharistéscu, ifhăristéscu

CONTENTMENT *s.* ambăreáţă, efharistíre, efharistíse, uşnurlắcă

CONTEST *s.* ntreáţire, ntriţeáre

CONTEST *vb.* (*to deny*) fac incheáre

CONTIGUOUS *adj.* viţinipsít cu; **to be ~ to** ▾viţinipséscu (cu)

CONTINENCE *s.* ţâneáre

CONTINUAL *adj.* ni-curmát → CONTINUOUS

CONTINUALLY *adv.* índa → CONTINUOUSLY

CONTINUOUS *adj.* (*as of a sound*) ni-acumtinát, ni-curmát, ni-tăcút

CONTINUOUSLY *adv.* ápă, di-priúnă, dáima, di únă únă, dzúuă ş noápte, índa, nĭ-acumtinát; ni-curmát, pánda, picná, tot, tótuna, tótna, totúna, únă-únă, víra, víra-víra ‖ tot; **He / she cries ~** Tot plândze (*lit. '[He /she] cries all [i.e., all the time]'*), PARALLELE 130

CONTORT *vb.* ▾şuţ

CONTORTION *s.* şuţâre

CONTRABAND *s.* cacearmáie

CONTRACT *s.* cundráche, cundrátă, hundrátă; (*~ between the council of a village and a doctor*) cundátă

CONTRACT *vb. med.* ▾fac, ľau, ▾mulipséscu; **to ~ tuberculosis** ▾umbărnédz

CONTRACTING *s.* (*tightening*) stringătúră

CONTRACTOR *s.* ‖ DIARO 291: cuntraccí

CONTRARIETY *s.* (*quarrel, disagreement*) guşturáre

CONTRARY *adj.* (*tending to find fault*) dzăndzăvós (*and* dzân-), dzăndzós; (*of a woman*) geálă

CONTRAVENE *vb.* ▾cálcu

CONTRIBUTE *vb.* (*to play a part in bringing about an end or result*) bag mâna; bag mâna pi lúcru

CONTRITE *adj.* pişmán, *m pl* -áñ → PENITENT

CONTRITION *s.* pişmănipsíre → REPENTANCE

CONTRIVANCE *s.* frâmtúră, dhóhe → SCHEME

CONTRIVE *vb.* (*to plot*) ▾ţas

CONTRIVED *adj.* gurguľitós, -oásă, -óşĭ, -oáse; **a well ~ lie** nă minciúnă gurguľitoásă

CONTROL

CONTROL → BRING UNDER ~

CONTROL *vb.* (*to curb, to check*) adún curăile; (*to dominate*)
▼zăptăséscu, ▼zăptiséscu

CONTROLLER *s.* (*inspector*) meimúr, *pl* meimureáñ

CONTROL ONESELF *vb.* ▼stăpuéscu

CONTROVERSY *s.* ncăceáre → DISPUTE

CONTUSE *vb.* ▼ciupléscu → BRUISE

CONTUSION *s.* (*bruise*) vătămătúră, ciuplitúră, viñiteáţă

CONUNDRUM *s.* scutúră

CONVENT *s.* → MONASTERY

CONVENTION *s.* → AGREEMENT

CONVERSATION *s.* cuvéndă, láfe, măsláte, umilíe; **in the flow of**
~ di zbor zbor → BREAK INTO A ~

CONVERSE *vb.* lăfuséscu

CONVERSELY *adv.* anáschila

CONVERSER *s.* ‖ muabetcí, DIARO 292

CONVERT *vb.* tórnu míntea; **They ~ed to Mohammedanism** S-turnáră
túrţi; (*to ~ almost completely*) apu-adúc

CONVEY *vb.* (*to hand over*) pitréc, fac tislíme

CONVEYANCE *s.* pitriţeáre

CONVICT *s.* hăpsânít, âncľís

CONVINCE *vb.* adúc n cále, ▼(a)ndúplic, apu-adúc, bag di cále,
bag tu bóndu, cândă(r)séscu, cândi(r)séscu, úmplu cáplu; **You
cannot ~ him easily** Nu si-andúplică lişór ‖ (*to come to realize*)
Have you convinced yourself that... Ţi si umplú cáplu că... (*lit.
'Has your head become full that...'*), PARALLELE 126; **You cannot ~
him** nu poţ si-ľ badzi mânâ, DIARO 113; **We have to ~ him** Cáplu-ľ va
umpleáre; **I cannot ~ my husband** Nu pot s-bag di cále bărbát-ñu (*3
syll.*) ‖ **Cru:** bag pri mínte, GOLAB 207

CONVINCED *adj.* căndisít

CONVIVIAL *adj.* hăriós, -oásă; hărăcóp, -coápă, -cóchi, -coápe

CONVOKE *vb.* acľém

CONVOCATION *s.* acľimáre

CONVULSE *s.* mi zbat

CONVULSION *s.* târculíre, zbátire, spazmó

COO *s.* guguráre

COO *vb.* gugurédz, guguréscu

COOK *s.* máyir, mayirgí, măyirgí; băcătár (DIARO 153: *rare*);

ahcí, ahcíu (DIARO 153: *obs.*); **Too many ~s spoil the broth** ≈ Iu-s mămíi múlti lu scot ficiórlu órbu

COOK *vb.* măyiripséscu ‖ *3 sg:* **Amc:** măghiripseáşte, **An:** măiripseáşte; **AMer, Gra, Vil:** adáră ghélă; **Fu, Rod:** fáţi ghélă; **Els:** adáră mâcáre, **Kast:** adáră mângáre; **Kok:** adáră mándză, B-ARCH 221

COOKERY *s.* ahcilâche ‖ CUNIA 70: măyiryilâche

COOKIE *s.* zăhărátă, zăhărtáre; **N:** toápă; (*in children's talk*) cócă ‖ **Cru:** dulţeáme, GOLAB 213; BASME 416, 426: dulţéñ *f pl*

COOKING-POT *s.* (*clayey ~*) ghiftă; (*with missing handles*) sut; ciuváñu

COOK SMB.'S GOOSE *vb.* ĺ-u coc, ĺ-u hérbu

COOL *s.* ávră

COOL *adj.* (a)ráţe *m/f*; (a)răţĭ *m/f pl*; (*collected*) stăpuít

COOL DOWN *vb.* (*from anger*) ▾diznăiréscu → CALM DOWN

COOLED OFF *adj.* arăţít, avrát

COOLING *s.* arăţíre, arcuráre, avráre

COOLNESS *s.* ávră

COOP *s.* cumás

COOT *s.* ayru-bíbă

COOPER *s.* buclár, butár, dugár ‖ **Av, Pls:** tălărgí, CL 262; **Prv:** varilă, varilár, CL 263

COOTIE *s.* pidúcĭu

COPE *s.* (a)rásă

COPE *vb.* ĺ-agiúngu, trec, ▾ţân chept; **I cannot ~ with everything** Nu pot s-ĺi agiúngu túte → WITHSTAND

COPIOUS *adj.* bólcu, *m pl* -lţi, *f pl* -lţe; bugát

COPIOUSLY *adv.* chíhtră, bólcu, di primansús

COPPER *s.* bácră, băcâre, hálcumă; (*copper coin*) cărăndánă ‖ ALIA 32: băcâr, bucáră, băkéri, băkéră

COPPERAS *s.* ‖ **GSus:** călcáni, CL 40

COPPERSMITH *s.* căzăngí ‖ **Peş:** băcărgí, CL 38

COPPER SULPHATE *s.* yeáre, yealopítră

COPULATE *vb.* ▾fut, ▾ambáir, ▾ampíhiur, ▾ciumuléscu, ▾âmprăéscu; (*of sheep and goats*) ▾mârléscu; (*of goats*) ▾pârcéscu

COPULATED *adj.* (*of a sow*) vurţítă; (*of a ewe*) mârlítă; (*of a goat*) pârcítă

COPULATION *s.* futeáre, ambăiráre, ampihiuráre, ciumulíre; (*of goats*) pârcíre; (*of sheep and goats*) mârlíre

COPY-BOOK *s.* filádhă, tetrádhiu

CORAL *s.* mirgeáne, milgeáne

CORAL-LIKE *adj.* mirginós, -oásă

CORD *s.* fúne, fórtumă, sigíme, şigíme; (*made of goat hair*) tru-şínă ‖ (*as to hold stockings up*) stríngľe, CAPIDAN 147

CORD *vb.* ▼leg

CORDIAL *adj.* dóbru, ímir

CORDON *s.* (*ornamental belt*) curdhóne

CORDOVAN *s.* (*Morocco leather*) curdhuváne

CORK *s.* astupătoáre → STOPPER

CORK *vb.* ▼astúp

CORN *s. bot.* arapósite, arăpusít, arpusít, călămbúchiu, gărni-şór (*and* gâr-), grânişór; (*baked on corncob*) cucuţăl → EAR OF ~

CORN *s.* (*hardening of the skin*) (a)róz

CORN BREAD *s.* babanáţă, bubótă

CORN CRIB *s.* cuciuró

CORN LOFT *s.* ambáre, hămbáre

CORNCAKE *s.* (*sprinkled with cheese*) pispilítă, pítă di bubótă, câmbăcúche

CORNCOB *s.* tópă di gărnişór, gugúciu; *F:* (*cob*) cărbúş ‖ PC: (~ *with grains on it*) cuceán; (*after the removal of grains*) cu-cúciu; STERE 100: cuculíci

CORNEL BERRY *s.* coárnă, *F:* coáră

CORNEL-TREE *s.* córnu

CORNER *s.* cohe, *N:* ohiu; ángun, ángună; (*as of a street*) chiu-sé, chiuşé; **at the ~ of a street** tu un chiuşé di sucáche; (*re-mote, hidden place*) cicmácă → DRIVE INTO A ~

CORNER-BOY *s.* gulimán → LOAFER

CORNER-STONE *s.* angunáre

CORNFIELD *s.* călămbucheáuă

CORNFLOWER *s. bot.* zărzăríche

CORNMEAL *s.* bubótă, băbótă, fărínă di bubótă; (*milldust of ~*) păspálă (*and* pâs-)

CORNMEAL MUSH *s.* mămulíg → POLENTA

CORN-POPPY *s.* cucuţăl, mălăcúche

CORNSTALK *s.* ‖ CUVATA 14: şaşan *n*

CORNY *adj.* (*tiresomely simply*) paľu ntr-ócľi

CORNSTALK *s.* cuceán

CORPORATE ARTISAN *s.* isnafcí

CORPORATION *s.* (*guild*) isnáfe, táymă

CORPSE *s.* mârşe → CARRION

CORPULENT *adj.* (*of people*) dúrdu; (*as of a cow*) binalític

CORRECT *adj.* ndréptu, *f* -eáptă, *m pl* -épţâ, *f pl* -eápte

CORRECT *vb.* ▼ndriptédz, ▼ndréptu

CORRECTION *s.* ndriptáre

CORRESPONDENCE *s.* (*agreement*) uidízmă, uidisíre, udiséţă; (*letters*) cărţâ, pistulíi *f pl*; scriitoáre [scri•i•] *f pl*

CORRIDOR *s.* ‖ CUVATA 2: hódnic

CORRODE *vb.* ▼aród; (*of rust*) arudzinédz, ▼zgurghiséscu, mâc

CORROSION *s.* aroádire, arudziníre, zgurghisíre

CORRUGATE *vb.* ▼zbârcéscu

CORRUGATION *s.* zgáibă

CORRUPT *adj.* aspártu, *m pl* -rţâ, *f pl* -rte → VICIOUS

CORRUPT *vb.* ▼aspárgu, cacurizipséscu, ▼distórcu, ▼disţíngu, ▼dişúţ, ▼dizlég, ▼dizmál, ▼fac cioáră, ciurutipséscu → DISSOLUTE

CORRUPTED *adj.* distórsu, geadíu → BECOME ~, CORRUPT

CORRUPTOR *s.* aspărgătór

CORRUPTION *s.* pănghíe (*and* pân-), chirdăciúne, *N:* asperdiciúne

CORYZA *s.* vet. şap, zurlumă

COS LETTUCE *s.* mărúľu, mărúľe

COSMETIC BLEACH *s.* ‖ *Cru:* albeáţă, GOLAB 197

COST *s.* cústu; ~ **of milling** (*paid in flour*) axáyiu

COST *vb.* fac, custiséscu, custuséscu, ▼acáţ; (**In the long run**) **an expensive thing costs you less** Scúmpa luyuríe ti-acáţă ma éftin ‖ **How much does it cost?** Cât áre? (*lit. 'How much does it have?'* PARALLELE 134

COSTIVE *adj.* (*afflicted with constipation*) astupát; cu cápse

COSTLY *adj.* scúmpu, -mbu, *pl m* scúnchi, -nghi; arúspu, *m pl* arúschi

COSTUME *s.* (*clothes*) armátă, ármă, tăcâme, custúme, fórimă, furişeáuă; pérpiră; (~ *specific to a certain village or area*) pórtu

COTE *s.* parángă, barángă

COTERIE *s.* fărtătlíche, fărtăţâľe, cărdăşlăche, isnáfe, táymă

COTTAGE *s.* călívă, colíbă, culíbă, cólibă; *dim.* călivúce, călivúşcă, călivúcică [•vúc•kă], caleáo, cătrínă, arăbătíe; (*as for the guardian of a vineyard*) drăyăsíe, parángă, barángă

COTTON *s.* bumbác

COTTONCLOTH *s.* stámpă (*and* stámbă), bâsmă, buyuzíe, buhasíe, buhăsíe, ghiuralántă

COTTON FIELD *s.* bumbăchíe

COTTON-WOOL *s.* scămángu, scămánghe, cămángu, cămânchĭ → WADDING

COUCH *s.* canapé *and N:* canapéi; sufă, sufáte, sufătlắche

COUCH GRASS *s.* ayreádhă

COUGH *s.* túse

COUGH *vb.* tuşéscu, tuşédz, guhtusădz

COUNCIL *s.* (*town council*) miglíse, mingilíze, mizilíse, mizilíşte, dhimuyerundíe

COUNCILLOR *s.* ază

COUNSEL *s.* (*deliberation*) simvulíe, sinvvulíe, muşafére, muşăfére, muşaviréi, urminíe, urminíľe → ASK ~

COUNSEL *vb.* ▼urminipséscu, ▼simvulipséscu

COUNT *vb.* (a)númir, misúr; **I cannot ~ all those I saw** Nu pot si-ľ númir cât tricúi; (*to count*) → RELY

COUNTED *adj.* numirát, misurát, aruminát

COUNTENANCE *s.* (*face, visage*) iapíi

COUNTENANCE *vb.* (*to approve, to encourage*) dau ínimă

COUNTER *s.* tisghireáuă, tisgheáfe, tizáhe, báncu

COUNTERFEIT *adj.* cálpu, *m pl* -lchi, *f pl* -lpe; calpuzán

COUNTING *s.* numiráre (*word unknown to TP*); arumin– áre

COUNTLESS *adj.* ni-numirát, ni-misurát, ni-ruminát; fără númir; cu sácul (*lit. 'by the bag'*)

COUNTRY *s.* loc, vilaéti; **people from his ~** oámiñ dit lóclu a lui; **other countries, other ways** ≈ áltu loc, áltu port

COUNTRY *adj.* (*unsophisticated*) apló ‖ CUNIA 317: huryitéscu

COUNTRYMAN *s.* huryeát

COUNTY *s.* ‖ *Av:* numó, *Prv:* nomón

COUPLE *s.* păreácľe, preácľe, căftíe; **a ~ of** ândói, ndoi ‖ **a ~ of years** cătiva părecľi di añ, BELIMACE 45 → PAIR

COUPLE *vb.* (*to marry*) ▼ngiug

COURAGE *s.* anácră, basaréte, curáiu, cutidzáre, físe, thar, iárbă di ţâneáre; **to have the ~** ñ-ţâne; **Do you have the ~?** Ţ-ţâne? → TAKE ~, PLUCK UP ONE'S ~, LOSE ~

COURAGEOUS *adj.* dăldăsít, dâld-; inimárcu, *m pl* -rţi, *f pl* -rţe; curagiós, -oásă, -óşĭ, -oáse → BRAVE ‖ CUNIA 72: curajlí

COURIER *s.* pisudhróm

COURSE *s.* (**series of instruction**) parádhuse

COURT *s.* giudéţ, huchimáte, huchiumáte, mekhemé [mek•he•mé]; críse, curnáche; (~ *for transfers from a lower court*) istináfe; (*court-martial*) urfíe, rufíe

COURTEOUS *s.* supţâre

COURTESY *s.* (*affability*) uminíľe ‖ (*elegant and kind behavior*) adâmlâchi, DIARO 336

COURTHOUSE *s.* bilidé → COURT

COUSCOUS *s.* cuscúsă

COUSIN *s.* ver *m*, veáră *f*; cusurín *m*, cusurínă *f*; cuşurí, cu-şiurí, cuşearí *m*; cuşearoáñe *f*; **first** ~ cusurín bun *m*; prótă cusurínă *f*; cusurínă veáră *f* ‖ **Cru:** (*second degree* ~) cusurín andáulea [-dáᵘ•lᵉa]; (*third degree* ~) cusurín antréilea; (*fourth degree* ~) cusurín apátrulea, GOLAB 199

COVENANTOR *s.* contraccí

COVER *s.* (*as on a pot*) căpáche; (*of a book*) pinichídhă, pină-chídhă, pilichídhă; (*shelter*) apărătúră

COVER *vb.* (*to put on, to hide*) ▾acoápir, ▾astúp; **We ~ed the whole thing** U-acupirím luyuría; (*to wrap*) ▾(a)nvăléscu, (a)n-viléscu, amvăléscu, amviléscu; (*to ~ with a shroud*) săvănuséscu, săvăniuséscu; (*to ~ the face, as Muslim women do*) ▾mbuliséscu, mbulitédz; (*to ~ the chin with a veil as a sign of mourning*) ▾bărbuľiséscu; (*of sheep, to copulate*) ▾mârléscu; (*to ~ with flour*) ▾nfărinédz; (*to ~ with a lid*) căpăchiséscu; (*speaking of the sky, 3 sg*) si vărcuseáşte, niureádză; (*to ~ with dust*) (a)spúlbir ‖ **The girl ~ed her face with her hands** Fiata anvili faţa cu măñli, HRISTU 70

COVERAGE *s.* acupríre

COVERING *s.* (*process*) acupiríre; (*rug, mat, fabric*) acupiri-míntu (*and* -míndu), acupiritúră, amvilimíntu, avilimíntu, (a)ş-tirnămíntu, aştirnu-; *G:* bătăníe; bilíţă, căpérdhă, cérgă, ciór-gă, cidáre, câftă, cuvértă, doágă, (*of cloth*) ftă; hreáme, yeám-bulă, iámbulă; (*for mules and horses*) óplă; sázmă, sărpoáşte, vi-lénză, zilíe; (*copulation of pigs*) vurţíre → COVERLET, BEDSPREAD

COVERLET *s.* hreáme → COVERING

COVERT *s.* (*hiding place*) ascumtíş, ascumtáľu, ascumtátic

COVERT *adj.* ascúmtu, -mtă, -mţâ, -mte

COVER-UP *s.* căpăchisíre

COVER-UP *vb.* căpăchiséscu

COVET *vb.* zilipséscu, zulipséscu → ENVY

COVETER *s.* limăryisít

COVETOUS *adj.* ânchismatáric, *m pl* -riţĭ, *f pl* -riţe → ENVIOUS

COVETOUSNESS *s.* pízmă → ENVY

COW *s.* vácă, *pl* văţĭ; *dim.* văchícă

COWARD *s. and adj.* fricós; *also:* bişinós, căcăcĭós, căcătós, chĭutí, cufurós, cufuryeár, pantalunár (*and* panda-)

COWARDICE *s.* chiutilíche

COWER *vb.* (*as of fear*) mi fac gľem, mi fac guzmóľu, ▾nguzmulédz → CRINGE

COWHERD *s.* văcár, buyeár

COY *adj.* aruşdisít → SHY

COZEN *vb.* → CHEAT, DECEIVE

CRAB APPLE *s.* mer ágru; ayrómin, ayrómbal

CRABBED *adj.* yispinát → ILL-NATURED, SULKY

CRABBY *adj.* guşturát → CRABBED

CRACK *s.* cripitúră, cripătúră, cărpătúră, călpătúră, firádhă; *dermat.* dzidzirătúră; (*a short resounding sound*) plăscăníre; instant → IN A CRACK

CRACK *vb.* crep, cărţănéscu; (*as with shame*) dângănéscu (tu cheále); (*to explode*) plăscănéscu

CRACK ON ALL HANDS *vb.* (*to put oneself out*) ‖ mi fac cumắţ (ti), DIARO 152

CRACKBRAINED *adj.* şcret, -étă (*sic*) → CRAZY

CRACKED *adj.* cicnít → CRAZY

CRACKERJACK *adj.* spániu, *f* spánie, *pl m/f* spáníĭ → EXCELLENT

CRACKER *s.* ghivréc, ghiuvréc; (*dried piece of bread*) păximádhe, piximádhe, puximádhe; (*a toy*) pliófcă

CRACKING *s.* cripáre

CRACKLE *s.* (*as of a fire, of a candle*) buburáre

CRACKLE *vb.* scárţăn; cârţănéscu (*and* cărţă-), crăţănéscu; (*to make the sound of onions frying*) ţărţăréscu; (*of a fire or a candle*) buburédz → CRACK

CRACKLING *s.* cârţăníre, ţărţăríre, buburáre

CRACKPOT *s.* trónciu, toáfe

CRACKPOT *adj.* şcret, *f* -étă (*sic*) → CRAZY

CRADLE *s.* sărmăníţă, níţă, cúnă, cúñe, leágăn, mănúşe, nánă, trócnă

CRAFT *s.* (*trade*) téhne, măsturíe, măsturíľe, măsturlíche, mu raféte; (*guile*) dhol, punirlíche

CRAFTINESS *s.* (a)plán → CRAFT, SLYNESS

CRAFTSMAN *s.* zanahcí, zănatcíu

CRAFTSMANSHIP *s.* (*refinement*) micáme

CRAFTY *adj.* hítru, *pl m* híţrâ, *pl f* hítre; şirét, *f* -eátă, *m pl* -éţ, *f pl* -eáte; cătăryár, cumalíndru, -ndră, -ndri, -ndre

CRAGGY *adj.* arâpós, -oásă; scârpós, -oásă

CRAM *vb.* ▾adár fuşéche, ▾(a)ndés, ▾andiséscu, ▾andóp, angľít; ▾arucutéscu, ▾arufeáric, aruféc, ▾astúp, ▾cos (di mâcáre), ▾disvóc (di mâcáre), ncurpiľédz, ncurpulédz, paramâc, primâc, ▾pristănéscu, prâstânéscu, ▾stivăséscu; **Cram yourself and shut up!** (= *Shut up and eat!*) Ncurpíľe ş-taţi!

CRAMP: **I have ~s in my stomach** Mi múşcă buríclu; (*of a horse*) cârciór

CRANE *s.* orn. ‖ **SJos:** yirănă, **Prv:** yiracnó, CL 263

CRANIUM *s.* anat. cărápă → SKULL

CRANKY *adj.* şcret, -étă (*sic*); căchiós, -oásă; inagí; **He is a bit ~** Eáste heam ca şcret → ILL-NATURED

CRASH *vb.* ▾zmoátic, zdrúmin, zdroámin

CRASS *adj.* (*crude, unrefined, of people*) budălác

CRAVE *vb.* (*smth.*) zilipséscu; (*to ask for earnestly*) âţ pricád, ▾angréc; (*to beg, to desire*) ţer

CRAVEN *adj.* ≈ şápte-óptu ñ-si dúţe → COWARD

CRAVING *s.* caimó

CRAWL ALONG *vb.* zvărñéscu, ▾azvărnăéscu, ▾azvărnuéscu, ▾trag azvárna, adúc azvárna ‖ ímnu abúşalui, DIARO 161

CRAWLINGLY *adv.* azvárna, azvárnalui, pri pântică ‖

CRYBABY *s.* lătiníciu

CRAYFISH *s.* cărăvídhă, cávur, cávru, căvúr, (a)rác, hărhídhă ‖ *Pls:* cănăvúr, CL 41

CRAZE *vb.* glăréscu, hăzăséscu (di mínte)

CRAZILY *adv.* zurleáşte

CRAZINESS *s.* zurleáţă, zureáţă, zurláme, zuráme, zurlíľe, zurlamără, zúrlu; **Wisdom and ~ are sisters** Míntea cu zurleáţa surări súntu

CRAZY

CRAZY *adj.* acăţát di hále, agudít, alăcít di mínte, astráptu, bărliv, cărtít di mínte, chirít, chirút, cicănít, cicnít, cicărdisít di mínte; cşúra, *f* cşúră, *m pl* cşúrañ, *f pl* cşúre; cu treĭ scânduri, cu zíya ma nafoáră, dat n cap, loát, loat di hále, loat di mínte, loat di vímtu, parmén, préşcav, şarafúra, şcret, tul, zăpălít, zúrlu, zurlít, zurlusít; **They are a bit ~** Ĺ-agudí ună apumoáră; **Don't you think I am ~** Ţe, ñ-lo gáia míntea? **He must be ~** U-ári asbuirátă *or* Ĺ-asbuiră gáia; **As far as I can tell, you are ~** Văd că-ţ asboáră ‖ **He she is ~** Nu-i tu mínţăle túte (*lit.* 'He /she is not in all his / her minds'), PARALLELE 157; *F:* zur, HRISTU 20; **Are you ~?** Ţ-fudzí mín-tea? BATSARIA 23; **You're ~** hiţ tu ligáre, BATSARIA 57 → BE ~ WITH DELIGHT, DRIVE ~

CREAM *s.* áică, teáră; (*coat on boiled milk; also, the choicest part of smth.*) peáţă, peáză; *N:* căimác, *S:* căimáche; danélă ‖ *K:* álcă, GOLAB 197

CREASE *s.* (*in a garment*) bástă, fúrtă

CREASE *vb.* ▾stăfidhuséscu

CREATE *vb.* (*to bring into being*) ▾plăsédz; **God has ~ed you thus** Ahtári vi áre plăsátă Dumnidzắu

CREATION *s.* făţeáre, fáţire

CREATOR *s.* făcătór

CREATURE *s.* yiitáte, făptúră, pláse, plázmă ‖ BASME 87: príce

CREDENTIAL *s.* sémnu, ispáte

CREDIT *s.* (*good name, esteem*) treácă, ihtibáre; (*financial*) crédit, virisé, virisíe; **on ~** pi virisíe

CREDITABLE *adj.* besalâ

CREED *s.* (*religion, rite*) thrischíe

CREEK *s.* arâu, avláchiu, răcheá, răchée ‖ ALIA 72: (a)răcheá, avéşe, avlác, cândalícă, csândácu, val, vulăceáuă, rău → RIVER

CREEP *vb.* (*~ in, out, away*) ▾ciun, ▾ciuléscu, ▾fur; **I crept away from them** Mi ciunái di níngă nâşi; **He crept out from home** S-fură di-acásă; (*to have a tingling sensation*) ▾azvărnuéscu, azvărnăéscu, zvărñéscu, archíşur, archiuşurédz, ▾virvirédz, ▾viţăréscu; **It makes my flesh ~** Ñ-si viţăreáşte trúplu

CREEP UP *vb.* (*as of ivy*) ▾(a)ngârlím (*and* angâr-)

CRENATE *adj.* (*as of a leaf*) chipurát ‖ DIARO 405: dinţălós

CRESCENT *s.* (*new moon*) lúnă noáuă

CRESS *s. bot.* cardhám

CREST s. (*the top line of a mountain or hill*) aráhe, creástă, crésă; schinărát; (*on a bird's head*) hărháľu, hărháľe, giúfcă ‖ (*on a rooster's head*): (a)reáhă *and* aréhi, DIARO 307

CRESTFALLEN adj. cripát → SAD

CREVICE s. (*fissure*) cripitúră, firídhă

CRIB s. (*manger for feeding animals*) păhníe; (*building for storage, as of grain*) ambáre, hămbáre

CRICKET s. carcaléc, carcaléţ, carcalédz, cărcăléţ, chirchinéc, chirchinéz, dzéndzer, dzíndzir, dzindzinár, ghincálă, yincálă, jujunár, giungiunár, ţínţir, ţíndzir

CRIER s. tileál, tiľál, tilál, leán; cărătór

CRIME s. lăiáţă, ur(â)teáţă, aspărgăciúne

CRIMINAL s., adj. catíle

CRIMP vb. ▼şuţ, ▼strâmbu

CRIMSON s. (*stuff*) gariváli, gariváldu

CRINGE vb. (*to cower*) culchipséscu, ľ-fac taéte, ľ-fac ti-mină; (*as in fear*) ▼mihriséscu, păpăruséscu, ▼şuţ, ▼zuruséscu

CRINGING s. mihrisíre, păpărusíre, zurusíre, ñicşuráre

CRINKLE vb. → CRIMP

CRINOLINE s. (*full stiff underskirt*) malacó, malacóv

CRIPPLE vb. (*of legs or feet*) uludzéscu, ▼săcătipséscu, **N:** cărág

CRIPPLED adj. ulóg, -oágă, -ódzĭ, -oádze; ólug; *also*: cărăyát, ciulác, m pl ciuláţĭ, f pl -ţe; ciúngu, m pl ciúndzi, f pl -ndze; cúciub, m pl cúciughĭ; săcát, sicát di cicioáre, săcătipsít, şbut ‖ **Peş:** oláh, CL 257

CRIPPLING s. cărăgáre

CRISIS s. (*economic ~*) chisáte

CRITICAL POINT s. oára a oárăľei ˆ

CRITICIZE vb ▼cătiyurséscu, giúdic

CROAK vb. (*as of a raven*) aúrlu; (*of frogs*) brutichédz

CROAKING s. bruticáre

CROCHET vb. (*as socks*) ncărdzéľu

CROCHET-HOOK s. cârlíg

CROCK s. stámnă, pótă

CROCODILE s. crucudhíl

CRONE s. (*withered old woman*) moáşe

CRONY s. oáspe → FRIEND

CROOK¹ *s.* (*swindler*) pľaşcagí, zulumgí

CROOK² *s.* (*hook*) cánge, *dim.* căngíche; cârlíg

CROOK *vb.* (*to curve, to wind*) cămburyi(p)séscu; ▾ncucuşédz (*and* ngu-), gribuéscu, ▾mihrisescu, ▾ncusór, ncusurédz

CROOKED *adj.* adunát găzămóľu; adús, adús di plătări, anduplicát; bubót, cambúr, cucuşeát, cusurát, gusurát, găzămóiu, gârbuv, *m pl* -buyĭ, *f pl* -buve; gribuít, guvór, gubés; (~ *old man*) âmbógru, ncusurát; (*as of claws*) ânvârligós, -oásă; strâmbu, *m pl* strânghi, *f pl* strâmbe; zgólub, zgrob ‖ **Peş:** ncusurós, CL 257

CROOKEDNESS *s.* strâmbătúră

CROOKING *s.* ncucuşáre

CROP¹ *s.* (*harvest*) grâu, grânár

CROP² *s.* (*sacklike part of a bird's gullet*) mámă, mámcă

CROP UP *vb.* (*to come to light*) es tu páde

CROSS *s.* crúţe, *dim.* cruţícă; **N:** cărúţe

CROSS *adj.* (*sulky*) mutrusít; (*ill-tempered*) căchiós; **What makes you so ~?** Ţe jále ñ-ti străbáte?

CROSS *vb.* (*to intersect*) ncruţilédz; (*to meet and ~*) ▾astáľu, ▾stăvruséscu; (*as a bridge*) trec; (*to pass through, to traverse, as a forest*) ▾spitrúndu, ▾pitrúndu, străbát, stribát; (*to go over a hill, etc.*) píngu; **~es hillocks** píndze oáhte

CROSS OFF *vb.* (*as a name from a list*) fac arisíte

CROSS ONE'S MIND *vb.* 3 *sg impers.* ñ-tâc(â)neáşte, ñ-treáţe prit mínte, ñ-cântă tu núcă; hupéscu → FLASH ACROSS ONE'S MIND

CROSS OUT *vb.* fac arisíte

CROSS THE THRESHOLD *vb.* (*to drop by*) andrisár práglu

CROSS-EXAMINATION *s.* discoásire

CROSS-EYED *adj.* ‖ **Av:** zăvumát, CL 263 → SQUINT-EYED

CROSS-GRAINED *adj.* mutrusíť, zăpăľít → ILL-TEMPERED

CROSSING *s.* (*intersection*) astălitúră, treáţire, triţeáre

CROSSING OUT *s.* (*cancellation*) (a)risíte *invar.*

CROSS-LEGGED *adj.* and *adv.* cior pri cior; cu ciórlu un prísti alántu; stavrutá, ncruţíşalui, ncruţíş

CROSSROADS *s.* cruţícăľuri *f pl*

CROSSWISE *adv.* crucíşalui ‖ DIARO 316: âncruţíşalui

CROUCHED *adj.* adunát gădzămóľu (*or* găzmóľu); cuculít; nstrugát

CROUP *s. vet.* (*a disease of pigs*) gurlíţă; (*a sheep disease*)

dzâpe

CROW *s.* gáie, háşcă, hâşcă; *Cuţ:* cioáră ‖ Brâncuş 555 did not find *cioáră* in Albania, but he did record: *Pe, Për:* gáie, *Kërb:* córbu, *Sln:* sórră

CROW *vb.* (*of a rooster*) cântu

CROWD *s.* lúme, multíme, multeáţă; *also:* călăbălăche; ca tră Stâmăríe, chídră, ciuplicheáuă, crímă; *Smr:* fúlmin (di), fúmin (di), ghíntă (*and* ghíndă), ghímptă, gloátă, jurdúnă, *G:* năfámă di oámiñ; plithizmó, sumăreáuă

CROWD *vb.* ▾(a)ndés, (a)ndiséscu, ▾ambărtuéscu, ▾strimuxéscu

CROWDED *adj.* ndisát, strímtu, *m pl* -mţâ; strimuxít, strâmuxít; apitrusít; ca alghíñle tu cufínă (*lit.* 'like bees in a hive')

CROWDEDNESS *s.* (*as at a ball*) strimtúră

CROWN *s.* curúnă, cărúnă, crúnă, stifáne

CRUCIAL *adj.* **The ~ moment has come** Víne oára-a oárăľei

CRUCIFIED *adj.* ncruţiľát, ncărfusít ‖ stăvrusít, DIARO 316

CRUCIFIXION *s.* ncărfusíre

CRUCIFY *vb.* ▾ncârfuséscu, ncrăfuséscu

CRUEL *adj.* crud, *pl m* -dz, *f pl* crúde; pabés, scliró; **~ fate** tíhe neárcă *or* scriátă nfărmăcoásă; **my ~ destiny** míra mea căţáuă (*lit.* 'my bitchy destiny') ‖ HRISTU 6: ayur

CRUELTY *s.* ni-ñílă

CRUET *s.* păyúr, *N:* cutróv → CAN

CRUISE *vb.* **He is ~ing for a bruising** U-cáftă cu luminárea; va ansăráre *3 sg*; sumárlu-ľ va umpleáre

CRUMB *s.* cărşéľu, fărămitúră, sârmă, *dim.* sârmótă ‖ ALB, **Dren, Kërb, Pe, Për, Sln:** sărrămă, BRÂNCUŞ 556

CRUMBLE *vb.* dărâm, ▾diñíc, fármu, ▾zminút; (*to fall apart*) cad; **The house was on the point of ~ing** Cása angrícá s-cádă ‖ ALR 1319: (*spealing of bread*) sărmu

CRUMBLING *s.* dărâmáre; diñicáre, dingáre, diñicát, diñicătúră, fărmáre, zminutáre

CRUMPLE *vb.* sufruséscu, ciumuléscu

CRUMPLED *adj.* (*as of clothes*) sufrusít; guzmóľu *invar.*

CRUMPLE IN A BALL *vb.* ▾cuculéscu

CRUMPLING IN A BALL *s.* cuculíre

CRUNCH *vb.* arúmin

CRUNCHY *adj.* (*as of a pie crust*) cârţacóñu, *f* -oáñe

CRUPPER-LOOP *s.* sumcoádă, bâldúme, cuscúne

CRUSH *s.* stulţináre, apitrusíre

CRUSH *vb.* ▼(a)pitruséscu, aputrupéscu, chisédz, stúlţin, stulcin, stulcinédz, stúrcin, strúcin, strucinédz, zdroámin, zdrúmin, ▼zmoátic ‖ zmútic, CAPIDAN 150

CRUSHED *adj.* apitrusít, chisát, stulcinát, zdruminát, zdru(n)cinát, zmu(r)ticát; ~ **grains** (*used as food for cattle and sheep*) ruiálă, uróv

CRUSHING *s.* stulcináre; zdrumicáre; zdruncináre, zdrucináre

CRUST *s.* coáje, cúuă, coáră → EARN ONE'S ~

CRUSTY END OF BREAD *s.* cultúc, márdzine di pâne

CRUTCH *s.* pătăríce, pătăríţă ‖ **Peş:** năgáltă, CL 257

CRY *s.* plângu, plândzire, plândzeáre, strigáre, zghic, zghícut; **much ~ and little wool** (≈ *many words will not fill a bushel* ≈ *all talk and no cinder*) → WOOL

CRY *vb.* plăngu (*and* plâmgu), *aor.* plâmşu *or* plâmtu; lăcrimédz, lăcrămédz; şcľimurédz, şcľumurédz; **to ~ one's eyes out** plângu ca şurpicát; plângu di crep ca núca; scârlédz

CRY FOR VENGEANCE *vb.* âľ pórtu múltă seáte

CRY UP *vb.* ▼făléscu → BOAST

CRYING *s.* asplândzire → CRY

CRYSTAL *s.* crústal; biľúre

CUBBYHOLE *s.* ascumtíş → RECESS

CUBIC METER *s.* (*measurement for wood*) ‖ **Cru:** cármă, GOLAB 224

CUBIT *s.* (*unit of length*) cot *m,* cod

CUCKOLD *vb.* (*to deceive, to make a cuckold of*) ▼ampíhiur

CUCKOO *s. orn.* cuc

CUCKOOPINT *s. bot.* călcádză

CUCUMBER *s.* căstrăvéţ, castravéţ, angúr ‖ ALIA 77: crăstavéţ, peápin, peápine; **Suf:** căstăvécu, B-ARCH 77; DIARO 184: *also* câstrăveáţă; *dim.* câstrăviţúş; ángur (*rare*)

CUDGEL *s.* puleán (*and* puľán); *also:* biştóc, cut; (*carol singers'* ~) cólindu, cólindă; ciumág, giumág, ciumágă; (*bifurcated*) ciutáľu; dhicániche; sfálangu, fálangu, fultutíre, furtutíre, sópcă; stupagánă, şcop; **Gop:** tuiág *or* tuiágă, teag, teg; (*war cudgel*) tupúz *or* tupúză; tupuzgánă, ţoápit, ţópit

CUFF *s., vb.* → BOX

CUISINE *s.* ahcilâche

CUKE *s.* angúr → CUCUMBER

CULMINATION POINT *s.* oára a oárăľei

CULPABLE s. (*offender*) ánom, *pl* anómiñ

CULTIVATE *vb.* (*to till*) ‖ fac ágru, BASME 512; (*to ~ a vegetable garden*) adár grădínă, BASME 9

CULTIVATED FIELD *s.* ágru

CUMIN *s.* chímin

CUNNING *s.* (*guile*) punirlíche

CUNNING *adj.* şirét, -eátă, -éţ, -eáte → SLY

CUP *s.* ceáşcă, filigeánă, géjve, tas *or* tásă; (*goblet*) măstră-pă (*and* mâstrâpă); **to be in one's ~s** éscu cu chéfe ‖ DIARO 223: fligeánâ

CUPIDITY *s.* sclingiureáţă → STINGINESS

CUPOLA *s.* cubé, gubé, cubée, thol

CUPPING GLASS *s.* fântânélă; vintúză (*and* vindúză)

CUPPING VESSEL *s. vet.* cuvátă, guvátă

CUPULE *s. bot.* (*shell, as of an acorn*) cufcúlă

CURABLE *adj.* áre ileáce (*lit. '[it] has a cure'*)

CURB *s.* (a)ghéme; fărnu (*and* fârnu)

CURB *vb.* (*to check, to control*) adún curăile [ku•răi•li]

CURB ONE'S TONGUE *vb.* (*ant. to divulge, to reveal*) nu dau pri toácă

CURBED *adj.* (*subdued, bridled*) căpistrusít

CURD *s.* (*a kind of fresh soft sheep cheese*) străgľátă, ármă, F: áică; **The milk has turned into ~** Láptili ngľigă

CURD *vb.* ▼(a)ncľég , (a)ngľég

CURDLE *vb.* → CURD

CURDLED *adj.* (*usu. of milk*) ncľigát (*and* ngľigát), strivuít, vinít

CURDLING *s.* ncľigáre

CURE *s.* ileáce; **There is a ~ for this!** Are ileáce! → REMEDY

CURE *vb.* ▼víndic; (*speaking of sight*) dau ócľi; **the well that cures one's eyes** (*in tales*) fântâna ţi da ócľi

CURIOSITY *s.* perieryíe

CURIOUS *adj.* (*nosey*) períeryu, *m pl* -yi, *f pl* -ye; curyiós, -oásă, -óşĭ, -oáse; (*strange*) ciudós; paráxin, *m pl* -xiñ

CURL *s.* ţalúfră, ţâlúfră, ţulúfră, zulúfe

CURL ONE'S LIPS *vb.* ▼strâmbu búdzăle

CURL UP *vb.* (*of one's body*) mi adún, mi adún gľem (*or* guzmóľu)

CURLED *adj.* (*of smb.'s hair*) (cu pérlu) cârciľós; ncărciľát; cu pérlu neále; cu perlu avoále; cățărós, zgur ‖ **Amc:** cațaramán, SCHL 113

CURLED UP *adj.* (*as with cold*) adunát gľem, adunát guzmóľ, nstrugát, âncucinát, apreaadunát [•prea•a•]

CURLY *adj.* cățărós, -oásă → CURLED

CURRANT *s.* coácăză, aúuă frânțeáscă, brágană, cúmară

CURRANT BUSH *s.* coácăz, braganéu, cúmar

CURRY *vb.* striséscu, xistriséscu, sistriséscu, *N:* histriséscu

CURRY-COMB *s.* xístră, sístră, xistríe

CURRYING *s.* xistrisíre, sistríre, histríre, timáre, dimáre

CURSE *s.* blăstém → MALEDICTION

CURSE *vb.* ▼(a)ngiúr; *also:* ▼afuriséscu, ▼(a)náthim, ▼(a)năthi-médz, *N:* ▼anăhimédz; ▼blástim, ▼blástin, ▼cătărnăséscu, ▼cătără-séscu, ▼cătăryiséscu, ▼culédz, ▼hulédz; **She is cursing him** Lu cu-leádză di blăstáme; dzâc sărindár, tăxéscu

CURSED *adj.* cătăryisít, cătăryăsít → ACCURSED

CURSORY *adj.* cu avrápă

CURSORILY *adv.* cu avrápă

CURT *adj.* arăchít

CURTAIL *vb.* ▼scurtédz, ▼șcurtédz → SHORTEN

CURTAILMENT *s.* șcurticáre, șcurtáre

CURTAIN *s.* pirdé, pirdée, birdé ‖ STERGHIU 3: pirdă

CURVATURE *s.* anduplicătúră

CURVE *vb.* ▼andúplic

CURVED *adj.* (*as of a nose*) turnát

CUSHION *s.* (*for carrying loads on top of the head*) pidilóc, pi-tălóc; (*a ~ to rest or sleep on*) pruschéfal; *N:* căpitíñu, *S:* că-pătâñu, căpătúñu

CUSTODY *s.* căștígă (*and* câs-) → SAFE-KEEPING, TAKE IN CUSTODY

CUSTOM *s.* dat, dátă; *also:* adéte, aréu, mor, táxe, zăcóne; **our language and our ~s** límba ș-mórlu a nóstru; **Aromanian ~s** aréurile armănéști; **Such is the Aromanian ~** Așá-i dátlu armănéscu

CUSTOMER *s.* muștirí, muștiră; *coll.* muștiráme

CUSTOMHOUSE *s.* cumérche, dărvéne, dirvéne, ghiumbrúcă, yimbrú-che, yiumbrúche

CUSTOMHOUSE OFFICER *s.* băjdár, imbruccí, yimbruccí, yiumbruccí, dirvingí

CUSTOMS *s.* ‖ BELIMACE 3: dirvinlắche

CUT *s.* (*reduction*) ñicşuráre; (*shape and style of clothes*) cruitúră; (*gash*) tăĺitúră; (*distinctive mark in the ear of a sheep*) coácă → NOTCH; (*blow*) únă

CUT *adj.* tăĺát

CUT *vb.* ▾taĺu; (*to diminish*) ñicşurédz; **Cut their pay!** Ñicşureádză-lă arúga! (*of hair*) ▾túndu, ▾cutruséscu; (*to trim*) schizédz; (*with or as with scissors*) foártic, furtichédz

CUT A DASH (A FIGURE, A FLASH, A SHOW) *vb.* ▾căbărdéscu → GIVE ONESELF AIRS

CUT AND DRIED *adv.* n gúră; ţâţă n gúră; mboálă; cadz hícă s ti mâc!

CUT BY HALF *vb.* ▾ngiumitichédz

CUT DOWN *vb.* afiriséscu

CUT IN TWO *vb.* ▾ngiumitichédz

CUT INTO PIECES *vb.* diñíc, ▾cumithiséscu

CUT IT FAT *vb.* (*to lie*) ‖ BATSARIA 60: taĺu crúde; CUNIA 187: mâc chéţrâ (*lit. to eat pebbles / stones'*)

CUT OFF *vb.* (*to discontinue, to end*) scărchéscu, ▾cúrmu, ▾scol, *N:* ascól; (*to trim*) ▾ciuléscu, schizédz; (*speaking of benefits*) usúc língra; **He has ~ your benefits** Ţ-uscă língra; **They cut us off from school** Nă curmáră di la scuĺó; **They ~ his income** Ĺ-u scărchí dhyeárea; **To begin with, cut off his (portion of) wine!** Próta yínlu si-ĺ si scoálă!

CUT ONE'S FINGERS *vb. fig.* mi-acáţă di ócĺi → GET IT IN THE NECK

CUT OPEN *vb.* ▾disíc, ▾spântic, ▾dispântic

CUT OUT *vb.* (*a coat, etc.*) cruéscu, *N:* cuiréscu, curéscu

CUT SHORT *vb.* ▾bitiséscu, cúrmu → FINISH

CUT SMB. SHORT *vb.* ĺ-cúrmu (*or* ĺ-taĺu) zbórlu; ĺ-u taĺu cu tăpórlu

CUT THE GROUND OUT FROM UNDER SMB. *vb.* ncheádic; ĺ-taĺu mâñle

CUTLER *s.* cuţâtár, cuţutár

CUTTING *s.* (*process*) tăĺáre; (*result*) tăĺitúră; (*recording on wood or stone*) arăbúş, arbúş, răbój, cârníciu

CUTTING *adj.* (*sharp*) tăĺitós, -oásă *and* tăĺós, -oásă

CUTTING OUT *s.* cruíre, curíre

CYCLOPS

CYCLOPS *s.* ‖ chiclúp, DIARO 244
CYLINDER *s.* (*in a loom*) sul, vǎltór (*and* vâl-), vultór, vâltúr, vólbu, vólvu, bǎlbǎtór, bǎrbǎtór, chélindru, ghélindru, chélindu; *G:* nǎvóiu
CYMBAL *s.* chimvál
CYPRESS *s.* chiparíş, chiparóş, chiparíciu *m*, silvíu *m*, silvíe *f*

D

DAB *adj.* (*skillful*): **to be ~ at doing smth.** ñ-gioácǎ óclˇul
DAD *s.* tǎtíc → FATHER
DADDY *s.* néni
DAFFODIL *s.* *bot.* **Amc:** gugúţǎ; guláce
DAFFY *adj.* cicnít, cicǎnít → CRAZY
DAFT *adj.* zúrlu
DAGGER *s.* acámǎ, şiş, (a)láz; (*curved* ~) hǎngeár, hangeárǎ, hǎnjár
DAILY *adv.* (*every day*) tútǎ dzúua ‖ PC: (*computed in terms of one day*) tu dzúuǎ; ~ **wage** udâlâchi, udulúchi, DIARO 409
DAINTY *adj.* nóstim, *m pl* -tiñ, *f pl* -time; gustós, yu-; ndálic; (*charming, as of a flower*) zâmbác → DELICATE
DAIRY FARM *s.* (*of sheep*) cǎşeáre (*and* câ-), cǎşǎríe; (*the place of a former dairy farm*) cǎşiríşte
DAIRY MAN *s.* iargí
DAIRY PRODUCTS *s.* ‖ *K:* mǎcúli *f*, GOLAB 234
DALE *s.* (*hollow*) trǎpíc → VALLEY
DALLY *vb.* (*to act heedlessly, to trifle*) ▾avín guşturíţǎle (*lit. 'to chase lizards'*)
DAM *s.* dhési *f*; próhumǎ
DAMAGE *s.* aspǎrgǎciúne, cheárdire, chirdeáre, gazépe, pácus, pácuz, sǎcǎtlâche, vlǎpsíre, vlǎpsitúrǎ, zǎráre, zimñusíre, zmurticáre, zñíe, zñisíre
DAMAGE *vb.* ▾stric, ▾aspárgu, ▾zǎrǎriséscu, ▾zimñiséscu, ▾zñi-(i)séscu; u-adár bózǎ

DAMAGED *adj.* (*out of order*) săcát (*and* sâ-)

DAMASK *s. tex.* şem, (a)şáme

DAME *s.* doámnă; *also:* arhóndisă, arhundoáñe, biíñă, bioáñe, bó-je, păşoáñe

DAMN *vb.* âl̃ bag láia → CURSE

DAMNABLE *adj.* → ACCURSED

DAMNATION *s.* usândă ‖ **May ~ take you!** BATSARIA 1: Dumnudză s-ti bátă! PARALLELE 128: S-ţi-o-áfli dila Dumnidzău! (*lit.* 'May you find it from God!')

DAMNED *adj.* → DO ONE'S ~ BEST

DAMP *adj.* nuţít; **~ stains** (*on walls*) iyrasíe; nóti *f*, nutíe

DAMP *vb.* ▼nuţéscu; **to ~ smb.'s appetite** l̃-tal̃u tăcátea

DAMP SMB.'S APPETITE *vb.* l̃-tal̃u tăcátea

DAMP SMB.'S SPIRITS *vb.* l̃-tal̃u basarétea

DAMPEN *vb.* → DAMP

DAMPNESS *s.* (*of weather*) mul̃itúră, nóti *f*, nutíe, udál̃, udă-túră, vlágă, vlắngă; (**~** *coming from a close river*) búndă → HUMI-DITY

DANCE *s.* (a)gióc; (*some dances are:* ceámcea, ceámcu, singastró, singaţcó, sirtó)

DANCE *vb.* ▼(a)gióc, arăsár; (*of the dance called singaţcó*) sin-găţéscu; **~ after smb.'s pipe** gioc cúmu ñ-cântă

DANCE ATTENDANCE ON SMB./ SMTH. *vb.* dau tărcoále (*and* târ-), dau trâcoále, dau dulắi di-avarlígalui, adúc vârlíga

DANDER *s.* năireáţă → ANGER

DANDLE *vb.* (*a baby*) ▼leágăn

DANDRUFF *s.* mătreáţă, mătráţă, piturídhă ‖ *Pls:* mutuⲣeáţă, mu-tuⲣeáñţâ, CL 256; *Prv:* piturlídhă, CL 259; *F:* mutreáţă, SarD 48

DANGER *s.* pirícl̃u; *also* perícul, pirícul, chíndhin; **to be in ~** hiu pi chíndhin; mi páşte pirícl̃ul (*lit.* 'a danger is grazing on me') ‖ BASME 49: chíndin

DANGEROUS *adj.* laiu, *f* láie, *m/f pl* lăi; s(c)lab, *m pl* s(c)laghi, *f pl* s(c)lábe

DANGLE ABOUT / ON / AFTER SMB./ SMTH. *vb.* lu adúc vârlíga → DANCE ATTENDANCE

DANK *adj.* vlắngu, -ngă, -ndzâ, -ndze → HUMID

DANUBE *s.* Dúna, Dúnav, Túna

DARE *s.* (*an act or instance of daring*) cutidzáre, căidăsíre,

DARE

dăldăsíre (and dâldâ-)
  DARE *vb.* c(u)tédz, căindiséscu [kă•in•], căidiséscu, dăldăséscu (and dâldâ-), dăvrănséscu, am iárbă di ţâneáre (*lit. 'to
possess the strengthgiving herb'*), ñ-ţâne
  DARING *s.* cutidzáre
  DARING *adj.* ncucutát (and ngu-), inimárcu, inimós, căidigí
  DARK *adj.* lăít, cérnu, ntunicát, ntunicós, scutinós, scutidhós;
písă; **It is ~ outdoors** Afără eáste písă; **It had grown** ■ Aveá ntu-
nicátă ‖ (*of the hair of animals*) muĺu, CAPIDAN 147; **It is get-
ting ~** Nduniarícă *3 sg impers.*, K-D 114
  DARK-COMPLEXIONED *adj.* scur, muĺu, múrnu, oácĺiş, sumuláiu,
ismér; *s.* (*usu. derog.*) gáie, gărăvéĺu
  DARK-EYED *adj.* ‖ *Cru:* mavrumát, GOLAB 233
  DARKEN *vb.* ntúnic, ▼nciórnic (and ngiór-), nciornichédz; *im-
pers.* **It is ~ing** Ntúnică
  DARK-HUED *adj.* (*sad*) jilós, -oásă, -óşĭ, -oáse
  DARKLE *vb.* ▼(a)umbréscu, (a)umbrăscu → DARKEN
  DARKLY *adv.* aráulea, n-aráulea; **They looked at him ~** L-mutríră
n-aráulea
  DARKNESS *s.* lăiáţă, ntuneáric, ntunéric, (a)scutídhe, písă, fu-
măríe; **the ~ of the night** fumăría a noáptiĺei ‖ HRISTU 35: scu-
tidhi; **pitch ~** chísă zăndáne, BELIMACE 46
  DARK-RED *adj.* ‖ *Cru:* aspríce, GOLAB 203
  DARK-REDDISH *adj.* (*of animals' hair or wool*) ghesuláiu
  DARK-SKINNED *adj. usu. derog.* gáie *invar.*
  DARKSOME *adj.* niurós, niurát
  DARLING *s.* ñícă *f*, şcrétă *f* ‖ DIARO 420: nástur *m*, násturâ *f*
  DARN *vb.* (*to mend, usu. of clothes*) măsturipséscu
  DARNEL *s. bot.* góngulă, cheánţă (and cheándză), cheániţă
  DART *vb.* ▼sărgĺéscu (and sâr-), sărghéscu; **to ~ away** li tíndu →
BOLT, DECAMP
  DASH *vb.* (*to collide*) ▼cingărşéscu, ▼ciucutéscu; (*to throw*)
▼aúrlu; (*to knock down*) ▼agudéscu, dau di pádi, ▼súrpu; (*to ~
into pieces*) fac bucatíce; (*to pound, to crash*) chisédz
  DASTARD *s.* mangúfă *m*, mangúfeañ *pl* → GOOD-FOR-NOTHING
  DATE *s.* (*time of an event*) imerominíe; **to ~** *adv.* (*thus far*) pân
tru hópa aístă
  DATE *s.* (*fruit*) curmă, hurmă, hurmáe

DAUB *vb.* ▼aúngu

DAUGHTER *s.* híl̃e, cóchilă, ciúpră

DAUGHTER-IN-LAW *s.* nóră, nor, *pl* nurări ‖ *Alb*: noáuă, CAPIDAN 177; *Cot, Mal, Mi*: mveástă; *Palius*: niveástă, *Pdz*: nă-, B-ARCH 470

DAUNT *vb.* piculéscu, ▼imirédz, ▼fruminéscu, ▼dipún

DAUNTLESS *adj.* ni-aspăreát → BRAVE

DAWDLE *vb.* misúr steálile (*lit.* 'to measure the stars')

DAWDLER *s.* adúnă-vímtu (*lit.* 'wind-gatherer'), hásca, hascanífur; *G*: başinghél

DAWN *s.* apirítă, apiríre; háragmă, hárasmă, -zmă, hărăxíe, hăryíe, -ghíe; cripátă, cripátă a hăryíil̃ei; **before ~** d(e)adoára, di c-noápte, níntea a li háragmă, nínte di hărghíe, nĭ-apirít, până s-creápă dzúuă, tu cripáta a dzâul̃ei; **at ~** di ndzáre, ni-dátă soárĭle *or* ni-dátă soáre; nícă ni-cântátă cucóţl̃i, nícă nĭ-apirítă ghíne, până di ndzáre, tu hăryíe, haraiméra; **He arrived before ~** Agiúmse ni-apirít; **I departed before ~** Fudzíi hăryíe

DAWN *vb. 3 sg impers.* (s-) creápă dzúua, algheáşte (di nghiós), ápiră; **It is ~ing** Da dzúua

DAWN UPON SMB. *vb.* (*to guide, to inspire*) ñ-şuiră; **as God will ~ upon him** cum va-l̃ şuiră Dumnidzău

DAY *s.*carry *vb.* dzúuă (*and* zúuă), *pl* dzâle; *N*: dzăuă; **good day** (*greeting one person*) Búnă-ţ oára! (*more than one person*) Búnă-vă dzúua! *or* Búnă-vă oára! **during the ~** dzúua; **next ~** dzúua alántă *or* a dáuaz; **the ~ after tomorow** păimâne (*and* pâi-), paimâne; **~ and night** (*all the time*) dzúua ş-noáptea ‖ BASME 439: dzúuă-noápte

DAY LABORER *s.* aryát; prichindé, pirchindé

DAYBREAK *s.* hăryíe → DAWN

DAYLIGHT *s.* **in open ~** *adv.* ñádză-dzúuă

DAZE *vb.* zăléscu → STUN

DAZZLE *vb.* (*with or as with light*) ñ-l̃a ócl̃il̃, ñ-si l̃au ócl̃il̃ ‖ BASME 499: ñ-si l̃a videála

DEACON *s.* dhyeac, *pl* dhyeáţĭ

DEAD *s.* (*innermost part*) ñedz, ínimă, dísă, váhte; **the ~ of the winter** ñádză-iárnă; **in the ~ of the night** tru dísa di noápte; **in the ~ of the heat** tu váhtea a li căloáre

DEAD *adj.* mórtu, -rţâ *m sg/pl*; moártă, -rte *f sg/pl*; murít, astés, dus, dus tu-alántă étă, siţirát, cătră soáre; (*of animals*) psohiu, *pl* psohĭ, *f sg/pl* psoáhe; *m* hiópsu, -pşi, *f* hioápsă,

-pse; psusít; **You will be ~ by then** Va-ţ bea curcubéta ápă; **The fox pretended to be ~** Vúlpea s-feáţe psoáhe; **~ beaten** (*very tired*) curmát, vătămát; **You will be ~ by then** Va-ţ bea curcubéta ápă (*lit. 'Your gourd will drink water'*)

DEAD-DRUNK: to get ~ mi fac trácă → DRUNK

DEADEN *vb.* (*to blunt, to lessen*) amúrtu, amurţắscu

DEADLINE *s.* dhiuríe [dhi•u•], murmír, muvléte, trat, prothesmíe, vadé, vadéie, vadimíe

DEADLOCK: to break the ~ ľ-áflu căpáchea

DEAF *adj.* súrdu, *m pl* -rdzâ, *f pl* -rde; cuf, *m pl* cúhľ; fudúl di urécľi ‖ **Cru:** sud, GOLAB 251

DEAFEN *vb.* (a)surdzắscu, şurduéscu, cufédz, cufuséscu (di uré-cľi); **to ~ smb.** ľ-ľau urécľile

DEAFENING *s.* (a)surdzâre, surduíre, şurduíre

DEAL *s.* (*arrangement, transaction*) lúcru, dáre-loáre; (*a lot of*) múltu, nă crímă di

DEAL *vb.* (*to have to do with*) am dáre-loáre cu; (*to distribute*) ▼(a)mpártu

DEAR *adj.* durút; scúmpu, *f* -mpă, *m pl* scúnchi, *f pl* -mpe (*and* scúmbu, -mbă, -nghi, -mbe); ghiurghiuván; **my ~** (*to a male*) ghiurghiuvánlu a ñeu; (*to a female*) geánă, geána-a mea; (**my ~,** *of a male or female*) geánăm (*and* -nân); iarán, yea-, a-; soáre; **Get up, my ~!** Scoálă, soáre! ahár, ahâr, ahári, daş, marát, mă-; (*voc., to a male*) corbáne; (*to a female*) sărmáie; (*~ and/or unfortunate*) gále, lai

DEARTH *s.* foámită, foámite, lipsítă → NEED

DEATH *s.* moárte; (*destruction, ruin*) chiríre, -răciúne, chiri-, chir(d)eáre, ciupălíc, ciupu-; **to be smb.'s ~** mâc yiu; **at ~'s door** pi hírlu di moárte; **to be on one's ~ bed** trag s-mor

DEATHLESS *adj.* athánat; (*rare*) ni-mórtu

DEATHWATCH *s.* nihtéryiu

DEATHWATCH BEETLE *s.* săráche *f*; saracufái *m*, -fáiañ *pl*

DEBACLE *s.* survóľu, arăvuíre

DEBAR *vb.* nu dau vóľe, nu dau izíne

DEBASE *vb.* (*because of long use*) ▼(a)nvicľédz, nvicľéscu; (*to demean*) ▼ñicşurédz, ▼scad; (*to make worse*) cacurizipséscu

DEBASED *adj.* aspártu, -rtă, -rţâ, -rte → CORRUPTED

DEBATE *s.* (*formal discussion*) zítise, sítise; filunichisíre

DEBAUCHEE *s.* púştean, puştán → RAKE

DEBAUCHERY *s.* ceapcânlâche, curvăríľe, dişuţâre, iaranlâche

DEBILITATE *vb.* adhinăţéscu

DEBILITY *s.* slăbeáţă, slăbíľe, slăbínţă

DEBRIS *s.* (*fragment, chip*) aspărgătúră; (*ruin*) surpătúră, súr-puri *pl*; murísce *f pl*

DEBT *s.* bórge, hreu, hréus, hursíre; **I am heavily in ~** Am bórge pân di gúşe → RUN INTO ~ ‖ *GSus:* luyuríe, *Prv:* lâyuríe, CL 255

DEBTOR *s.* burgilâ, burgilău, burgilipsít ‖ ALR 1006: burgilí

DEBUNK *vb.* ▾scad

DECAMP *vb.* (*to run away*) li tíndu (*lit. 'to stretch them'* [*one's legs*]) → BOLT

DECANTER *s.* cunétă; (*carafe*) gără

DECAPITATE *vb.* ▾şcurtédz → BEHEAD

DECAPITATION *s.* şcurticáre, şcurtáre, hrăştuíre

DECAY *s.* hărápă, ruzuíre; **houses in ~** cáse ruzuíte → RUIN

DECAY *vb.* (*of or as of tuberculosis*) lăvrăséscu

DECEASE *s.* moárte

DECEASE *vb.* mor

DECEASED *adj.* astés, -eásă, -éşĭ, -eáse (*lit. 'extinct'*) → DEAD

DECEIT *s.* aplănăsíre, ardeáre, árdire, bătăhcilâche, căláie, furlíche, ilée

DECEITFUL *adj.* plan, -ă, -añ, -ne → TRICKY

DECEITFULNESS *s.* (*disloyalty*) băbislíche

DECEIVE *vb.* (a)ncálţu, (a)plănăséscu, (a)plănéscu, plăni(p)-séscu, ▾ard, lu-árdu, ▾(a)mpíhiur, ľ-bag cuváta, ľ-bag yi-líile, ľ-bag yilíile pánă la ócľi, ľ-bag şáua, ľ-bag samárlu, ▾ciumur-léscu, cos, ľ-fac rénghea, nşiuédz [nši•u•édz], nşiédz, ľ-trag únă căláie, ľ-trec tástrulu; **to ~ smb. easily** (a)ncálţu şi dis-cálţu; **Do not ~ me!** Nu mi ncálţă! ‖ BASME 80: fac minciúñ; BASME 467: ľau ócľiľ; **How badly she deceived him!** Ţi yánumâ-ľ trápsi! DIARO 299

DECEIVED *adj.* ars, ársă, árşi, árse; ncălţát

DECEIVER *s.* arditór; calpuzán, căl-; farmazón; *G:* (om) ehlé

DECEMBER *s.* Andréu, Andrelúş, Ndreu, Ndriu

DECEPTION *s.* ardeáre → CHEATING

DECEPTIVE *adj.* bírbu, -rghi, -rbă, -rbe; plan → TRICKY

DECIDE *vb.* ñ-u bag si, taľu, ▾apufăséscu, căndăséscu, mi fac di

DECIDED

căíle, ▾vulipséscu; **I have ~ed to sell the sheep** Mi băgái s-li víndu óile; **You decide!** Táľ-u tíne! **She ~ed to go to find him** S-vulipsí si s-dúcă s-lu áflă ‖ (*to make a choice or judgment*) PC: mi nămăşéscu

DECIDED *adj.* (*determined*) apufăsít, dâlâdsít

DECIMATE *vb.* (*to destroy*) tuchéscu → PULL TO PIECES

DECISION *n.* (*determination arrived at after consideration*) apufăsíre, apufăseáre, apófase, vulíe; **to take a ~** taľu → MAKE A DECISION

DECK *s.* (*of a ship*) cuvértă

DECK *vb.* (*to clothe elegantly; to ~ oneself out*) ▾viliséscu, ▾adár → ADORN

DECKED OUT *adj.* (*rigged out*) tăcmâlát

DECISION *s.* → MAKE A ~

DECLENSION *s.* (*deterioration*) cacurizipsíre

DECLINE *s.* (*of life*) ascápit

DECLINE *vb.* (*to slope downward, as of a celestial body; fig. of life*) hiu tu ascápit, apún ‖ (*to refuse smb. bluntly, unceremoniously, or provocatively*) ľ-aspún cótlu (*lit. 'to show smb. one's elbow'*), PARALLELE 126

DECLIVITY *s.* (*slope*) tăľitúră

DECOMPOSE *vb.* ▾aspárgu, ▾disfác, ▾diñíc

DECOMPOSED *adj.* anăl(i)sít

DECORATE *vb.* (*to adorn*) muşiţăscu (*to award a decoration*) dau nişáne

DECORATED *adj.* ncligát; **those rooms ~ed with carpets** udádzľi-aţéľ cu ciórgi ncľigáţ → ADORNED

DECORATION *s.* (*embellishment*) muşiţâre; (*badge of honor*) nişáne; **to receive a ~** ľau nişáne

DECORUM *s.* (*aspect, fitness*) prep

DECOY *s.* → TRAP

DECOY *vb.* plănéscu, plănăséscu, bag pri sómnu

DECREASE *s.* discreáştire, scădeáre; (*of the moon*) mângátă → LESSENING

DECREASE *vb.* discréscu, ▾arăiéscu (*and* arâ-) → DIMINISH

DECREMENT *s.* scădeáre

DECREPIT *adj.* trecút; (*mentally ~*) lişurát; (*broken down, as of a horse*) sarával

DECRY *vb.* săhunéscu

DEDICATE *vb.* (*to commit*) tăxéscu; (*to offer*) dăruéscu

DEDUCT *vb.* (*to reduce, to lessen*) afiriséscu

DEED *s.* fáptă; (*a blamable ~*) lăiáţă

DEEM IT RIGHT TO *vb.* u áflu cu cále să ‖ BASMEA 302: u-áflu ghíne

DEEP *adj.* adânc, adâncós, ahândós; (*of sleep*) greu ‖ ALIA 27: (a)hăndós, (a)hundós, acundós, afunducós; hăndó, hăndá, handá, handacá, andicó, dangá, andacós

DEEPEN *vb.* ▼afúndu, ▼afunduséscu, ahânduséscu

DEEPLY *adv.* adâncá, (a)handá, (a)hândá, afundá, afúndu; **Study this problem ~** Tíni sápă-l lúcrul afúndu; **He sighed ~** Suschiră adâncá

DEEP-ROOTED *adj.* aruzusít

DEEP-SET *adj.* (*of eyes*) *m pl*: ahândusíţ (n cap), hăusíţ

DEER *s.* ţérbu, *pl* ţérghi; ndrel, elén

DE-ESCALATE *vb.* ▼acúmtin, ▼scad, ñicşurédz, agăléscu, agălisés-cu

DEFACE *vb.* tălăéscu

DEFAMATION *s.* săhuníre

DEFAMATORY *adj.* laiu, *f* láie, *m/f pl* lăĭ

DEFAME *vb.* săhunéscu, zburăscu, cacuzburăscu

DEFAULT *s.* mărdáie, smârdhă

DEFEAT *s.* azvíndzire, azvindzeáre, anixíre, hăndăcusíre ‖ CUNIA 152: zăbunusíre, zăbunuseáre

DEFEAT *vb.* ▼(â)nvíngu (→ § 32); *also:* ▼alúptu, ĭ́-u (a)mpót, (a)nichiséscu, anixéscu, ▼azvíngu, ĭ́-bag mână, bag n páde, ▼bat, ▼ciucutéscu, ▼frângu, ▼súrpu; **Pisuderea** (*an Aromanian village*) **cannot be ~ed!** Pisudérea nu s-báte! **and you ~ed your enemies** şă ĭ́-aluptáşi éhsriĭi a tăi; **He ~s all the evils of the body** Ĺ-u mpoáte a tutulór rálile a trúpului; **He ~ed me, I did not ~ him** Ñ-u putú, nu ĭ́-u putúi; **He had ~ed him** Lu aveá azvím-tă; **those whom he could not ~** a curór nu putú s-lă bágă mâ-na; **He ~ed Bură three times** Trei ori l-freádze Búră; **In a fight he ~ed ten young fellows** Surpă tr-un alumtátic dzáţe gioñ; **Illness ~ed him** Ĺ-u băgă mână lângoárea ‖ **I ~ him** ĭ́u pot, PARALLELE 142

DEFEATED *adj.* azvímtu, azvínsu, anixít, frâmtu, nichisít

DEFECATE *vb.* ▼cac, ñ-fac ápa aţeá groásă, ñ-scot ócĭiĭ; (*to*

DEFECT

mess) ▾fac; **The baby has ~ed in his diapers** Ñíclu eásti-l fáptu tu culpáne *or* Ñíclu s-feáţe ‖ es, CAPIDAN 176

DEFECT *s.* cusúre, mărdáie, smrâdhă

DEFECT *vb.* (*to desert*) ▾alás → ABANDON

DEFECTIVE *adj.* (*as of a newborn*) ‖ BELIMACE 36: cu sémnu

DEFEND *vb.* (*to protect*) ▾ápăr; **May God ~ us!** Si-ápără Dumnidzău! ▾avégľu, (*rare, obs*) ▾vleghiu; (*rare*) ▾pădzéscu (*and* păzéscu), pidzéscu ‖ CUVATA 14: mi ápur

DEFENDANT *s.* giudicát

DEFENSE *s.* apăráre

DEFER *vb.* (*to put off*) ▾amân

DEFIANCE: in ~ of pri inátea a, trâ píca a

DEFICIENCY *s.* scárţu → FAILURE

DEFICIENT: to be mentally ~ *3 sg*: ľ-lipseáşte únă scândură

DEFICIT *s.* scárţu

DEFILE *s.* angusteáţă, arăstoácă, buyáze, coácă, dirvéne, strimtúră, şilătúră

DEFINE *vb.* nsimnédz

DEFLATE *vb.* ▾disúflu

DEFLATION *s.* disufláre

DEFLOWER *vb.* (*of a virgin*) ľ-áflu cuibárlu ‖ aspárgu, arúp, disíc, DIARO 361, 383

DEFORM *vb.* (*to distort*) ▾şuţ ‖ CUNIA 88: (*to make ugly*) sluţăscu

DEFORMATION *s.* şuţâre

DEFORMED *adj.* urât; (*of a person or animal*) săcătúră

DEFORMITY *s.* slutíche

DEFRAUD *vb.* plănéscu, aplăniséscu → CHEAT

DEFT *adj.* epitídhiu, *f* -dhie, *m/f pl* -dhiĭ; chischín, izóte *invar.*

DEFY GOD *vb.* nu ncľin Dumnidzău

DEGENERATE *vb.* (*morally*) cătăndiséscu, ciurutipséscu; **People have ~ed morally** Ciurutipsí lúmea

DEGENERATION *s.* cătăndisíre, ciurutipsíre

DEGRADATION *s.* scădeáre; (*of smb.'s mental condition*) glăríre, hăzusíre, huţâre

DEGRADE *vb.* ▾ñicşurédz, ▾scad, ▾şcurtédz, ▾şcurtichédz, ▾dipún, cacurizipséscu; **to ~ oneself** mi fac túrtă

DEIGN *vb.* cătădhixéscu ‖ *Cru:* dăxéscu, GOLAB 211

DEITY *s.* (*male*) dzân; (*female*) dzână ‖ ~ **of the sea** dzânlu a mărilʲei, BASME 250

DEJECTED *adj.* jilós; búză cripátă (*lit.* 'cracked lip') → SAD

DEJECTION *s.* milancolíe

DELAY *s.* amnáre, muvléte; **Give me a three-day ~** Să-ñ alăşi trei dzâle muvléte; şintíre; (*waiting, inactivity*) stáre; **There was no time for ~** Nu erá trâ stáre; armăneáre; **without much ~** ni únă, ni áltă

DELAY *vb.* şintéscu → POSTPONE

DELAYED *adj.* amânát

DELETE *vb.* ▾aştérgu

DELIBERATE *vb.* 3 *pl:* şi-da mínţâle (PC: [žda]); fac muşaviréi; u fac cunsóltu; ▾vulipséscu, ▾luyurséscu

DELIBERATELY *adv.* priagálea [pri•a•], castílea, máxus, maxús, xaryú **DELIBERATION** *s.* muşaviréi [•ré•i], cunsóltu, consúltu, luyursíre

DELICATE *adj.* N: créfcu, -fcă, -fţi, -fţe; créftu; S: créhtu; (n)dilicát, ndálic, pirpişór; (*of a face*) ~ **like a rose** créhtă ca nă trandafílă

DELICIOUS *adj.* scóntră *invar.*

DELIGHT *s.* (*good things of life*) zéfcă, zéfche, glingé → BE WILD WITH ~

DELIGHTED *adj.* **to be ~ (very happy)** nu mi ţâne lóclu di haráuă

DELIGHTFUL *adj.* ghiurghiulíu; (*of a pretty woman*) ghirghínă, ghirgheánă

DELIMIT *vb.* (*of borders, limits*) ▾sinuripséscu

DELINQUENT *adj.* batác, bătác

DELIRIOUS: to become ~ alʲurédz

DELIVER *vb.* (*to rid from, to set free*) (a)scáp, cuturséscu; (*to hand over, to send to a destination*) fac tislíme; **We have ~ed them the man** Ómlu lă lu feáţim tăslíme; (*to give birth*) dizvóc, lihunipséscu; (*to ~ a speech*) bag zbor

DELIVERANCE *s.* (a)scápáre, cutursíre, cutrusíre, elefthirusíre; (*salvation*) nchiuluíre

DELIVERED *adj.* (*rescued, saved*) (a)scăpát, cutursít, elefthirusít

DELIVERY *s.* (*giving birth*) fáţire, făţeáre, amintáre, amintá-

DELOUSE

tic, lihuneáţă, lihuníľe, lihunlíche, nfăşáre, părădhusíre

DELOUSE *vb.* ▾dispiducľédz, ▾caftu n cap

DELUDE *vb.* ▾ard → DECEIVE

DELUGE *s.* cataclizmó → FLOOD

DELUSION *s.* ardeáre

DEMAGOGUE *s.* ≈ alávdă făsúľĭle ş mâcă cárne *(lit. 'praises beens but eats meat')*

DEMAND *s.* treácă, treáţire, triţeáre; **to be in ~** trec, am treácă, am triţeáre; **Wax is in greater ~** Ma múltă triţeáre áre ţeára; **upon ~** pi dimândát, pi dimândáte; *adj.* **made upon ~** maxutárcu, -rcă, -rţi, -rţe; **in ~** căftát

DEMAND *vb.* ▾cáftu; **What are you ~ing from me?** De la míne ţe căftáţ? → REQUIRE

DEMARCATE *vb.* ▾dispártu, ▾sinuripséscu → SEPARATE

DEMARCATION *s.* dispărţâre, dispărţătúră; (~ *between plots of land*) traf

DEMEAN *vb.* (*to behave*) ▾pórtu; (*to degrade*) ▾ñicşurédz

DEMEANOR *s.* purtátic

DEMENTED *adj.* zúrlu (*or* zur) → CRAZY

DEMENTIA *s.* zurleáţă, zurláme, zurlíľe

DEMIJOHN *s.* buján, căráfă, damageánă, trimindzánă

DEMOLISH *vb.* dărâm, ▾răzuéscu, ruzuéscu

DEMOLITION *s.* dărâmáre

DEMON *s.* → DEVIL

DEMONIAC *adj.* drăcusít, dhimunsít

DEMONIC *adj.* → DEMONIAC

DEMONSTRATE *vb.* (*to evince*) ▾aspún, ▾apudhixéscu, adúc sémnu, ▾limbidzăscu

DEMORALIZE *vb.* ▾aspár, ▾aspárgu

DEMOTE *vb.* → DEGRADE

DEN *s.* (*lair*) culcúş, loje, loj, lujár, scrob

DENIAL *s.* cheáre *invar.*

DENIGRATE *vb.* zburắscu, cacuzburắscu

DENIGRATION *s.* cacuzburáre → SLANDER

DENOMINATION *s.* númă

DENOTE *vb.* ▾aspún, ▾făniruséscu

DENOUNCE *vb.* ▾discoápir, scot n páde, scot tu páde, cătărăséscu, cătăryiséscu, cătăryăséscu, ▾afuriséscu

DENOUNCEMENT s. (*blame*) cătăryisíre; (*accusation, information against*) părătúră

DENSE adj. des, deásă, deşi, deáse; spes, speásă, speşĭ, speáse; picnós, -oásă; (*as of fog*) ndisát → THICK

DENTICULATE adj. (*as of a leaf*) chipurát

DENUDATION s. disgulíre, disbilíre

DENUDE vb. ▼guléscu, ▼dizgól̆u, disguléscu, disbiléscu → STRIP

DENUDED adj. (*as of a tree in winter*) goáliş, disgulít

DENUNCIATION s. angăl(i)síre

DENY vb. arniséscu, fac incheáre, ▼agắţ di steále, fac háşa; **a thousand times no** ≈ háşa ş-háşa; **He has ~ed all his kinsmen** şĭ-a-risí tútă sóia

DEODORIZE vb. ‖ DIARO 385: ▼dispút

DEPART vb. nchiséscu, (a)fúg, purnéscu, ▼trag cále, u-adún, u afúm, u-litéscu → BOLT, DECAMP

DEPART FROM ONE'S WORD vb. ies di zbor

DEPARTMENT s. (*of a government*) ipuryíu, chivérnise

DEPARTURE s. dúcă and túcă; *also*: angănáre, (a)plicáre, chinímă, duţeáre, dúţire, fúgă, litíre, nchisíre, purñíre, sărmáre ‖ DIARO 432: dúsâ (*ant.* turnátâ)

DEPEND vb. discálnu, dispíndzur, ▼ţân (di) ‖ HRISTU 42: **Aromanians' life depended on milk from these sheep** Cu laptili a lor ira ligată bana a rămăñlor

DEPENDABLE adj. saylám, saylámcu, sayláme, síyur, siyuripsít

DEPENDENT s. (*one relying on another for support*) pl coáde pri dinăpói; **I have ~s to feed** Am coáde pri dinăpói

DEPICT vb. (*to describe, to portray*) ▼zugrăpséscu, zugrăvséscu

DEPILATION s. dipiráre

DEPLETE vb. sec, astărchéscu, scot pétalile

DEPLETION s. sicáre, astărchíre

DEPLORE vb. ▼plângu

DEPLORED adj. (*regretted, lamented*) arăbdisít

DEPLORINGLY adv. ca vai di míne (ca vai di tíne, *etc.*)

DEPORT vb. ▼xipundiséscu

DEPORTATION s. xipundisíre

DEPORTEE s. xipundisít

DEPOSIT s. (*pledge*) nişáne, péie, arăvoánă, aruvúnă, arvúnă, căpáră, căpărusíre, alíl-hisáp → MAKE A ~

DEPRIVATION

DEPRAVATION *s.* pănghíe (*and* pân-)

DEPRAVE *vb.* ▼aspárgu

DEPRAVED *adj.* aspártu, -rtă, -rţâ, -rte → DISSOLUTE, BECOME ~ ‖ ~ **woman** dis(i)cătúrâ, DIARO 383

DEPRAVITY *s.* edepsâzlâche

DEPRESS *vb.* (*to press*) ▼(a)ndés; (*to lower*) ▼scad; (*to diminish*) ▼ñicşurédz; (*to sadden*) lăéscu tu hicáte, ▼amărăscu

DEPRESSED *adj.* cripát, dipús → SAD

DEPRESSION *s.* (*sadness*) amárăme, amărăre, căñínă; (*hollow*) hambílumă, súdhă; (*funnel-shaped* ~) húne; (*depressed area*) cócă; surpătúră, grem, grémur, grimúră; (*low economic activity*) chisáte

DEPRIVE *vb.* ľau, urfănéscu

DEPRIVED *adj.* istirisít, lipsít, urfănít; (*poor*) gol, gulişán

DEPTH *s.* ahândusíme, ahăndáme; (*as of one's being*) frúndză; **from the ~ of one's heart** di tru hicáte *or* dit frúndza di hicáte; dit frândzle di ínimă; dit báirĭle di ínimă; (*dreadful* ~*s, as of the earth*) tartáră → BE OUT OF ONE'S ~

DEPURATION *s.* (*as of raw cotton*) scălsíre

DERACINATE *vb.* scot dit rădăţínă

DERANGE *vb.* fac acătăstăsíe; **to make insane** zurléscu, zurluséscu, glăréscu, lişurédz

DERANGEMENT *s.* zurleáţă → INSANITY

DERELICT *s.* azvărnătúră → GOOD-FOR-NOTHING

DERELICT *adj.* alăsát; alăsătóñu, -tóñ, *f sg/pl* -toáñe

DERIDE *vb.* şúpăr → RIDICULE

DERISION *s.* ardeáre, măitápe, măscără (*and* mâscâ-), măscărlíche, măscărlíľe, mâscâripsíre, mbizuíre, péză, rizíle; *in* ~ tră şúpir

DERISIVE *adj.* pizuiáric, -rică, -riţi, -riţe → SCOFFING

DEROGATE *vb.* cătăfroniséscu → BELITTLE, DISPARAGE ‖ CUNIA 90: atimuséscu

DERVISH *s.* dirvíş

DESCEND *vb.* ▼dipún, dipún híma, ľau híma, ▼apléc, ▼vérsu, ▼aripidinédz; **The sheep ~ed towards the fir forest** Óile virsáră cătră tu chinét

DESCENT *s.* dipuneáre, dipneáre, dipúnire, dipunát; aripidináre, catífur; (*origin*) **of aristocratic** ~ ciciór di scámnu → ANCESTRY

DESCRIBE *vb.* (*to portray, to depict*) zugrăpséscu, zugrăvséscu, zugrăfséscu

DESCRIPTION *s.* zugrăfsíre

DESERT *s.* (*reward or punishment deserved*) axítă; (*scolding, punishment*) pirdáfe

DESERT *s.* pustilíu, pustilíe, irñíe, erimíe, urñíe, pundíe, chirítă

DESERT *vb.* (*to forsake, to abandon*) alás, fug caceác ‖ (*to absent oneself from military duty*) MERCA 31: li spingéscu

DESERTED *adj.* (*desolate and unoccupied*) irmuxít, pondít, pundixít → DEVASTATED

DESERTER *s.* caceác

DESERVE *vb.* ñ-eáste bun; **You ~ a beating** ţi-i búnă păpáră; ▾axiuséscu, ▾axéscu → MAKE SMB. ~ SMTH.

DESERVEDLY *adv.* driptátic, driptáticǎ

DESERVING *adj.* ácşu, ácşă, ácşi, ácşe (*or* ácse); áxiu

DESIDERATUM *s.* dor

DESIGN *s.* (*planning, calculation*) isápe, cicuteálă

DESIGNATE *vb.* (*to destine*) număţéscu

DESIRE *s.* (*longing*) dor; (*whim*) chéfe, chéifă; (*passionate ~*) miráche, geáhte

DESIRE *vb.* ▾urséscu, ñ-si dişclíde ínima (tră); (*covetingly*) zilipséscu

DESIROUS *adj.* arslíu, *f* -líe, *m/f pl* -líĭ; durút → EAGER

DESK *s.* (*counter*) tisghireáuă, tisgheáfe

DESOLATE *adj.* érmu, érim; **in this ~ place** tu-aéstu érim loc

DESOLATE *vb.* pustiéscu → DEVASTATE

DESOLATION *s.* ñílă

DESPAIR *s.* deáspir, apilpisíe, apilpisíre

DESPAIR *vb.* ▾apilpiséscu

DESPERATE *adj.* apilpisít

DESPERATION *s.* deáspir, apilpisíe

DESPICABLE *adj.* idipsâz, zgrumát → CONTEMPTIBLE

DESPISE *vb.* cătăfroniséscu ‖ CUNIA 90: atimuséscu; DIARO 376: bag la cur → DISREGARD

DESPITE *prep.* cu túte că, cánai-că

DESPOIL *vb.* ayízmu, biléscu, ▾dispól̦u, ▾gulişinédz, guluşnédz

DESPOLIATION *s.* arăchíre, arăchitúră, bilíre, dispul̦áre, guli-

DESPOND

şináre, gulişnáre

DESPOND *vb.* ▾apilpiséscu

DESPONDENCY *s.* apilipsíre

DESPONDENT *adj.* dipús

DESTINE *vb.* urséscu

DESTINED *adj.* (*meant*) simnát

DESTINY *s.* soárte; *also:* fátăză; (*Fates*) míră, ñíră, scriátă, scriitúră, tíhe, ursítă, ursíre; (*ill fate*) aráua; **You cannot change ~** Ţe-i scriátă, scriátă armâne; **Such has been your ~!** Ahtáre-ţ fu ursírea (*or* scriitúra); **We are the Fates** Noi him mírile; **They are deploring their own ~** şi-plângu míra ‖ BELIMACE 14: nependéche; HRISTU 22, *F:* fati

DESTITUTE *adj.* partál, spătăĺusít

DESTROY *vb.* aspárgu; *also:* afăn(i)séscu, buréscu, cătăstrupséscu, dărâm, ĺau pri gúşe, mâc yiu, prăpădéscu, stifuséscu, sutrupséscu, tuchéscu

DESTROYER *s.* aspărgătór

DESTRUCT *vb.* → DESTROY, RUIN

DESTRUCTION *s.* afănisíre, afănsíre, arăvuíre, aspárdzire, aspărgăciúne, chiríre, chirdeáre, chireáre, chirdăciúne, halazmó sutrupsíre, *G:* colóña

DETACHMENT *s.* dislăchíre, dislăchitúră ‖ *mil.* apóspazmă, MERCA 9

DETAIL: **in ~** *adv.* pân tu per, pân la şíle, di hir hir

DETAILEDLY *adv.* → DETAIL, HAIR

DETAIN *vb.* am, ▾ţân, ▾stăpuéscu

DETAINED *adj.* ncĺis

DETECT *vb.* ▾áflu, ▾discoápir

DETER *vb.* (*to inhibit*) dau ibréte (la), bag ceáşlu (tu), ▾aspár

DETERIORATE *vb.* ▾(a)nvicĺédz, (a)nvicĺéscu, ▾aspárgu, cacurizipséscu, ▾tălăéscu

DETERIORATED *adj.* (*as of a fence*) aspártu; (*by scratches, as of a wall*) armát

DETERIORATION *s.* cacurizipsíre, aspărdzeáre; (*as of a coat*) tălăíre

DETERMINATION *s.* (*firmness, resolution*) apufăsíre; (*prices imposed by sellers' consensus*) curmătúră

DETERMINE *vb.* (*to decide*) ▾apufăséscu; (*to convince, to influence by argument*) aduc n cále; **He could not ~ her** Nu putú s u-adúc n cále → PERSUADE

DETERMINED *adj.* (*decided*) apufăsít, dâlâdsít

DETEST *vb.* nu lu-am tu stumáhe, nu pot s-lu ved, ñ-víni aynós di năs ‖ lo-ám şíľe ntr-ócľi, BASME 115

DETESTABLE *adj.* afurisít, aumbrós, blăstimát, cacurízic, sal-chíu, şulúndu; **a ~ person** ca-di-câne, ca-di-câneán, schínu ntr-ó-cľi ‖ CARAFOLI 11: agíúmtu; *imprec.* (*to a female*) Mor, lea agiúm-tă! ≈ Go to hell!

DETOUR *vb.* ▼(a)nvărtéscu, ▼şuţăscu

DETRACT *vb.* ñ-tórnu míntea

DETRIMENTAL *adj.* zñiseáric; **to be ~ to smb.** ▼zărăriséscu

DEUCE: *imprec.* **The ~ take her!** ≈ S nu şi-apúcă! **What the ~?** ≈ Ţe zále?

DEVASTATE *vb.* pustuxéscu, pustuéscu; *also:* bag stróflu tu, băs-tiséscu, ermuxéscu, irmu-, pundixéscu, punduxéscu, pundéscu, rimuéscu, şcrituéscu

DEVASTATED *adj.* pustuít; *also:* băstisít, ermuxít, pundixít, şcrituít

DEVASTATION *s.* pustuíre, băstisíre, irmuxíre, pundíre, şcritu-íre, văpsitúră

DEVELOP *vb.* (*to acquire wealth gradually*) acáţ maiáuă

DEVIATE *vb.* ▼abát, ▼strâmbu; **Don't ~ at all!** (*Go straight ahead!*) S-nu strânghi dip! → DIVERT, SWERVE

DEVIATION *s.* abátire, abăteáre, părmărăsíre, părmăsíre; (*turn in a road*) şuţitúră, turnătúră

DEVICE *s.* hăláte

DEVIL *s.* drac, darác, *dim.* drăcúş; *also:* acló s-ľi híbă, antí-hrist (*and* andí-); (*little ~*) anghiúdhă; aţél c-un ciciór, aţél cu coádă, aţél cu-un córnu, aţél din vále, aţél di sum púnte, ca-lacándzu, caracándzu, carcalándzu, curnút, dheávul, dheául, yeá-vul, yeául, dhémun, dzardzavúľ (*and* zarzavúľ), dzardzacúchi [•kúk'], gáţal, iándza, lup s-lu mâcă, nihítlu, parparíe, pi-razmó, saïtán, si-ľ creápă núma, s-lu ngľítă lóclu, stimpinát, sătănă (*and* sâtână), sirsém, sirsén, sirsénlu a sirséñlor, şutlu, tártar, tartacútĭ [•kútĭ], triscatárat; **The ~ take him!** Bágă-ľ cuváta! **What a dévil!** Ţe drac ş-ţe darác! ‖ Eusfór, BASME 499; Chirătă, BASME 23; duşmán, BASME 460; DIARO 151: **Go to the devil!** Dú-ti Brúsa! **little ~** (*as of a child*) drâclíc, DIARO 421

DEVIL

DEVIL *vb.* ▾schin → TEASE

DEVILFISH *s.* (*octopus*) uhtapódhe, htapódhe

DEVILISH *adj.* (*passionate, hot*) sárpit, sărpit (*and* sâr-), sâr-pid, sértu, sértic; (*unpredictible, evil*) drăcós, drăxít, drăcu-ít, drățéscu, drăcuréscu, drăcurós; zarzavúl; **a ~ girl** un darác di feátă; **the ~ mother-in-law** drățeásca di soácră

DEVILRY *s.* drăcuríe, drăcuríľe, dhyeavulíe, dhimuneáță, dhimu-níľe; **through witchcraft and ~** cu amăi, cu daráți

DEVIOUS *adj.* șuțât, cănghéľu

DEVISE A SNARE *vb.* croiéscu únă căpáne → SET A TRAP

DEVOTION *s.* evlávie, ivlávie (DDA 535, 686)

DEVOUR *vb.* ▾mâc ca nă lámñe → GULP DOWN

DEVOUT *adj.* evlaviós, iv-; thríscu, -scă, -schi, -sche

DEW *s.* (a)ráuă, aroáuă

DEW *vb.* *3 sg impers.* (a)rureádză

DEWFALL *s.* ruráre

DEWLAP *s.* ‖ *GSus:* burgheáli, CL 40

DEXTERITY *s.* (*adroitness*) hunéră, hunére, murafitlâche

DEXTEROUS: to be ~ ñ-acáță mâna; **a woman ~ in every respect** muľáre țe ľ-acáță mâna di túte

DIABOLIC *adj.* drăcuréscu, -eáscă, -éșţâ, -éști → FIENDISH

DIALECT *s.* dhiálect

DIALOGUE *s.* dhiáloy

DIAMOND *s.* brilántu, dhyeamándi, yeamándă, yeamánde, yeamándu, ghinére ‖ *Str:* geváíre, GOLAB 261

DIAMOND *adj.* (*in cards*) ghinére; **ten of ~** dzáțea ațeá búnă (*lit.* '*the good ten*') ‖ chiușilitíc, chiușulitíc, DIARO 181, 204 *and* 278

DIANTHUS *s.* (*pink*) garáfilă, garoáflă, garofíl, garufír, garu-fľáuă ‖ *SJos:* lúdhă, CL 254

DIAPER *s.* culupán, culpán, spárgan → SWADDLING CLOTHES

DIARRHEA *s.* cufoáre; *also:* chínise, dhiárie, inșíre, ișíre, sprimáre, străbátire, stribátire, străbăteáre, surdisíre, urdi-nát, urdináre; *vb.* **to have ~** surdiséscu, mi úrdină, mi scoáte na-foáră ‖ DIARO 319: cufureálâ, tartacúti

DICE *s.* (*as in gambling*) → DIE

DICKER *vb.* (*to bargain*) yiftuséscu

DICTATORSHIP *s.* síndaymă ‖ dictatúră, HRISTU 1

DIDDLE *vb* ▾ciumuléscu → DECEIVE

DIDO *s.* chirtúră, glăreáţă

DIE *s.* (*for playing*) záre, *pl* zárări

DIE *vb.* mor; *also:* adár pádea óhtu (*lit.* '*to change the plain into a hillock*'; *i.e., to make a grave*), angán căţáua (*lit.* '*to recall the bitch,*' *as before a leavee*), arúc pétalile (*lit.* '*to throw away one's horseshoes*'), ▾arúc tópa (*lit.* '*to throw the shell*'), ñ-si-astíndze fitíľlu (*lit.* '*my wick is burning out*'), ▾cher ('*to perish*'), dau arñacólu (*lit.* '*to return [one's] lamb-skin*'), dau cheálea a préftului (*lit.* '*to give one's skin to the priest*'), dau dóľi a préftului (*lit.* '*to give two [coins] to the prist*'), li dau cľéile (*lit.* '*to hand over the keys*'), dau şi ľau dit lúmea aéstă (*lit.* '*to give and gete from this world*'), mi duc s-adár chirămídz / oále) (*lit.* '*to go to make bricks / earthen-ware*'), ▾fac tâmpână (*lit.* '*to become a drum*'), mi fac bărsíe (*lit.* '*to become grounds*'), ies cu pátile (*lit.* '*to go out with the ducks*'), mi ľártă Dumnidzău (*lit.* '*to be forgiven by God*'), mi ľa gáia (*lit.* '*to be taken away by the crow*'), mi ľa úta (*lit.* '*to be taken away by the eagle*'), ▾mâşcu lóclu (*lit.* '*to bite the earth*'), ľi-ncľíd, ncľid ócľiľ (*lit.* '*to close one's eyes*'), ncárcu (*lit.* '*to load [one's belongings, as for a departure]*'), ñ-arăţeáşte bişína (*lit.* '*my fart is cooling down*'), ñ-ľau dhípla (*lit.* '*to take one's fold*'), ñ-ľau lélea (*lit.* '*to take one's terminal [leave]*'), ñ-ľau zvérca (*lit.* '*to take one's nape*' *i.e., to show one's nape, to depart*), scap (*lit.* '*to es-cape*'), li tín-du (*lit.* '*to stretch them out [one's legs]*'), trag tu lúmea alán-tă (*lit.* '*to pull out to the other world*'), ▾úmplu groápa (*lit.* '*to fill up the [= one's] pit*'); (*mainly of animals*) p(u)suséscu, supséscu, *N:* hiupséscu; **You will be dead by then** Va-ţ bea curcu-béta ápă; **Do you want me to ~?** Vrei si-ñ mâţi grân-lu? **You will ~** Va ţ-apríndu ţeára (*lit.* '*I will light up your candlelight*') ‖ BASME 370: ncárcu dit lúmea aéstă (*lit.* '*to pack off from this world*'); BASME 488: trag tră tótna; *Cru:* mi astíngu, GOLAB 203; locu s-feáţe (*lit.* '*became earth*'), PARALLELE 124; BATSARIA 46: mi duc

DIE FROM SHAME *vb.* lu ngrop lóclu

DIE IN THE PRIME OF YOUTH *vb.* mor tu lilícea a áñlor (*lit.* '*to die in the flower of one's years*')

DIE OF LAUGHTER *vb.* arâd di mi lişín

DIE OUT *vb.* (*as of a fire*) agăliséscu

DIET *s.* → REGIMEN

DIFFER *vb.* ▾alég; **He ordered a silversmith to make him a plate which did not ~ from the old man's** Adáră un san la un fávru di nu alidzeá di sánlu a aúşlui; *also:* alăxéscu; **He did not ~ from him at all** Tu ţivá nu-ĺ alăxeá; am fárche; **Thieves ~ from each other** Fur di fur are fárche; fug, *N:* afúg; **They ~ a lot from each other** Fúdze múltu únă di alántă ‖ CUNIA 81: nu ñ-u adúc cu; hiu áltă sóie

DIFFERENCE *s.* fárca, fárche, dhyeafuráuă ‖ BASME 247: **It makes no ~** Únă fáţe (*lit.* 'it makes one'), ñ-u tut únă (*lit.* 'it is all the same to me'), PARALLELE 126

DIFFERENT *adj.* áltă sóie ‖ *Cru:* áltă turlíe, GOLAB 197

DIFFERENTIATE *vb.* ▾alég

DIFFERENTIATION *s.* aleádzire, alidzeáre

DIFFERENTLY *adv.* aĺúmtre → OTHERWISE

DIFFICULT *adj.* greu, greáuă, grei, greále; zóre, dhíscul; **Communion, what a ~ thing to take!** Zóre lúcru cumnicárea! (*of a person hard to deal with*) biĺagí

DIFFICULTY *s.* angusteáţă; (*financial ~*) cacurizipsíre; dhisculíe, gărămínă, greáţă, ghiúcă, strimtúră, strimturáre, zóre; greálile *f pl def*; mărăţíñ *f pl*; **with ~** (*barely*) cu mizía, cu zóre; *N:* cu zórte; **with no ~** fără zóre; **Difficulties appear in the end** Năpóĭ sun greálile; **to overcome a ~** lu arsár tráplu (*or* gárdul)

DIFFIDENT *adj.* fricós, -oásă, -óşi, -oáse → FEARFUL, SHY

DIFFUSE *vb.* (*as of a smell*) ▾arăspândzu, -pândéscu, -pândzăscu

DIG *vb.* sap, *G:* ţap; **He is ~ing a pit for him** (*fig.*) L-sapă; (*fig.*) adár groápa; *Brz:* târchéscu; (*of chicken when feeding outdoors*) scălcéscu; (*to excavate, to bring out, also fig.*) dizgróp ‖ CUNIA 87: scot tu miydáne

DIGEST *s.* (*as a ~ of legal rules*) chiutúc, chiúche, chitápe

DIGEST *vb. phys.* hunipséscu; **This pie ~s badly** Píta aéstă hunipseáşte greu ‖ (*of food*) máţin, CAPIDAN 176

DIGESTION: My ~ is upset ▾spriímnu; *impers.* (*to have frequent stools*) mi úrdină

DIGGER *s.* (*person*) săpătór

DIGGING s. săpáre, săpătură; **The vineyard needs a** ~ Ayíña va săpáre; (*rooting, searching, usu. with one's hands, or an animal's claws, legs, snout*) (a)rmáre, armătúră

DIGNIFIED adj. (*proud*) pitrít; (*proper and* ~) prímtu, m pl -mţâ; chibár, chibárcu, m pl -rţi, f pl -rţe ‖ aumbrós, DIARO 408

DIGNITARY s. (*in a pastoral Vlach society*) célnic → SHEEP-OWNER

DIGNITY s. (*self-respect*) cheaféte, érye, (i)htibáre; (*honor*) (a)nămúze

DIG OUT / UP vb. dizgróp

DIKE s. dhési, próhumă

DILAPIDATED adj. căhtít, halazmó, hárval

DILATORY adj. (*of people*) alăsătúră s.

DILEMMA s. → QUANDARY

DILIGENT adj. ni-şidzút; lucrătór, -oáre; cilistisít

DILL s. măráľu, málathru ‖ **Av:** máranthu, CL 255; ALB, **Kërb**, **Për:** măráiu, **Sln:** murái, Brâncuş 558

DILLY-DALLY vb. hălăndăréscu

DILUTE vb. apătuséscu

DILUTION s. apătusíre

DIM adj. (*of eyes*) alăcít, păngusít, pañisít

DIM vb. (*to make* ~, *to become* ~, *as of eyes*) pañiséscu; **My eyes became** ~ Ñ-si pañisíră ócľiľ; (*as a lake*) ▾mintéscu ‖ (*to* ~ *smb.'s mind, to disturb, to confuse*) niguredz, HRISTU 24

DIMINISH vb. discréscu, ▾frângu, ▾mpuţânédz, ▾psânédz, ▾ñicşurédz, ▾ñicurédz, ▾şcurtichédz, ▾şcurtédz, ▾mihriséscu; (*of sadness, etc.*) ▾moľu, ▾(a)firiséscu, hiriséscu, hirăséscu; (*as of a fire*) apún; (*as of a river*) ▾scad, ▾trag; (*to become less frequent, as of visitors*) ▾arăéscu; (*of prices*) eftinipséscu; **The day began to** ~ Dzúua lo ca s frângă; **His love did not** ~ Nu u ñicură vreárea

DIMINISHED adj. discriscút, mpuţânát, ñic(ş)urát, scădzút, şcurt(ic)át

DIMINUTION s. discreáştire → LESSENING

DIMMING s. pañisíre; (*passing dimness of sight*) urbárea a găľíñlor (*lit. 'chickens' blindness'*)

DIMNESS OF SIGHT s. → DIMMING

DIN s. lávă

DINE vb. miríndu, mirindédz

DINGY

DINGY *adj.* ntunicát → DARK

DINKY *adj.* ñícăz, *m pl* -căjĭ

DINNER *s.* *(at 4:00 - 5:00 PM or so)* mirínde; ~ **(breakfast, sup-per) is ready!** La másă s cumpăséşti! *sg,* s-cumpăsíţ! *pl*

DINT: **by ~ of talking** di zbor zbor

DIOCESE *s.* eparhíe, iparhíe

DIP *vb.* ▾afúndu, ▾moĭu; *(to decrease, as of prices)* scad

DIPLOMA *s.* dhíplumă; *(appointive ~ in the former Ottoman Empire)* biráte, firmáne

DIPLOMACY *s.* dhiplumătíe

DIPLOMAT *s.* dhiplumát

DIPPER *s.* → BIG ~

DIRE *adj.* urât → FRIGHTFUL

DIRECT *vb.* *(to address or show the way to a destination)* ▾ndréptu, ndriptédz, ▾mbróstu, mbrustédz; *(to manage, to handle)* trag; *(to supervise)* cumăndărséscu

DIRECT ONE'S STEPS TO *vb.* ▾mbróstu, mbrustédz; ĭ-u dau cătră

DIRECTION *s.* párte; **He left in that ~** Lití cătră aţeá párte; **in all ~s** tu túte părţále ‖ **in that ~** cât aco, HRISTU 54; **in all ~s** tu paturli, HRISTU 55

DIREFUL *adj.* fricós, fuvirós

DIRGE *s.* boáţit, miryiulóy, miyiulóiu

DIRK *s.* şiş → DAGGER

DIRT *s.* *(filth)* murdăríĭe → CAST ~; *(earth, soil)* ţáră ‖ *Pls:* mutureáţă, mutureánţă, CL 256

DIRTILY *adv.* *(~ and untidily)* troc; cărñídă; áţala-máţala

DIRTINESS *s.* murdăríĭe → FILTH

DIRTY *adj.* murdár; *also:* áţal, başúr, başúrcu, birbáte *invar.*; cărñídă *invar.*; (á)ngălát, lăturós, lăvós, lăvăşít, lirós, lirusít, pişlirós; *(disgusting, treacherous)* (a)zvărñár; *(in superstitions)* pângân(ips)ít; lu alímsiră cătúşile *(lit. 'Cats licked him')*; **Your face is ~** Hii başúr tu fáţă ‖ *Cru:* ăncărcát, GOLAB 205; nispăstrít, *ibid.* 238

DIRTY *vb.* ▾murdăr(ips)éscu; *also:* ▾fac birbáte, ▾fac ntroc, ▾lăspusescu, ▾lăvăşéscu, lăvuşéscu, ▾liruséscu, ▾ncárcu (di lăchi), ▾ngălédz, ▾ntinédz, ▾putuséscu, ▾smâryéscu, mâryescu, ▾úmplu di; *(to stain, to spot)* ▾lichiséscu

DIRTYING *s.* lăvuşíre, lirusíre, murdăripsíre, putusíre, → BES-

MIRCHMENT

DISABLE *vb.* ▼săcătipséscu

DISABLED *adj.* ulóg, -oágă, -odzĭ, -oádze → CRIPPLED

DISACCUSTOM *vb.* ▼dizvéţ (di)

DISACCUSTOMED *adj.* dizviţát

DISAGREE *vb.* mi duc cóntră; nu mi fac căbúle; nu hiu pri ună cále (cu); *ant.* → AGREE

DISAGREEABLE *adj.* salchíu, -chíe, -chíĭ

DISAGREEMENT *s.* (*quarrel*) cârtitúră, făsăríe, guşturáre

DISAPPEAR *vb.* ▼(a)spúlbir, ▼astúp, căipuséscu, cher; (*to lose track of*) mi fac căípe, mi fac lóclu, mi fac stifă, mi stifuséscu; **They ~ed from sight** S-feáţiră stifă dintr-ócĭi; ▼zăgădéscu (*and* zâgâ-); (*to ~ below the western horizon, speaking of the sun*) ascápit; (*to ~ by theft*) fac cicioáre; **The tobacco may disappear** Tutúnea poáti s-fácă cicioáre; (*to ~ by hasty departure*) angán căţáua ‖ BASME 438: cher din vidzútă; BELIMACE 37: mi fac afándu; MERCA 7, 8: mi fac áfana; TULLIU 122: mi afăniséscu

DISAPPEARANCE *s.* căipusíre

DISAPPOINT *vb.* bizdiséscu

DISAPPOINTED *adj.* cu nările spindzuráte (*lit.* 'with a hanging nose')

DISAPPOINTMENT *s.* (*bitterness*) fărmác

DISARRANGE *vb.* alúmtu

DISARRAY *s.* şişirmáe → CONFUSION

DISASSEMBLING *s.* disfáţire, disfăţeáre

DISASTER *s.* chiaméte [k'i•a•mé•ti] → MISFORTUNE

DISAVOW *vb.* arniséscu; **He ~ed his faith** şĭ-arnisí thrischía; (*to give up an opinion*) es di míntea a mea

DISBAND *vb.* ▼aspárgu → DISPERSE

DISBURDEN *vb.* lişurédz

DISCARD *vb.* arúc, ascáp (di)

DISCERNMENT *s.* aleádzire, dhiácrise

DISCHARGE *s.* discărcáre, sălăghíre, lişuráre; (*firing off*) amináre, tufichisíre, tifixíre; (*lay-off*) sărchíre

DISCHARGE *vb.* (*to relieve*) lişurédz; (*to unload*) ▼discárcu; (*to set free*) dau díra; (*of a rifle, etc.*) *N:* amín; ▼vérsu; **The cannons ~ed** Martíñle s-virsáră; trag (tuféchea), ▼arúc tuféchea; (*of a debt*) mi lau di bórge

DISCHARGED *adj.* (*of a gun*) aminát

DISCLOSE *vb.* ▼discoápir, scot tu páde, ies tu miydáne ‖ CUNIA 124: dau mpáde; (*to give oneself away*) mi dau di páde

DISCONCERT *vb.* tuléscu, ▼ciurtuéscu, ▼scol di mínte

DISCONTENT *s.* (*uneasiness*) sicléte, sácléte

DISCONTINUE *vb.* (*of salaries, benefits, etc.*) scărchéscu; **He ~ed his wage** Ľi scărchí lufélu → CUT OFF

DISCORD *s.* anghídhă; *also:* ceamúnă; *G:* dălgáne; ângrắñe (*and* -grâ-), ngrắñe, gríñe, mâcătúră, munăfíe, ncáce, ncăceáre (*and* ngă-) ncăcitúră, ndăríe, *N:* ndiríe; zizáñi → BREED ~

DISCOUNT *s.* scóntu

DISCOURAGE *vb.* dau ibréte (la), bag ceáşlu (tu), taľu nărĭle, frângu nárea; (*to damp smb.'s appetite*) taľu tăcátea; (*to be or to become discouraged*) ▼apilipséscu ‖ MERCA 13: ľ-ľau bastrétea

DISCOURTEOUS *adj.* → RUDE

DISCOVERY *s.* afláre

DISCREDIT → BRING ~ ON ONESELF

DISCREDIT *vb.* buiséscu, cacuzburắscu, fac părăvulíe → SLANDER

DISCREDITABLE *adj.* pârghiós, tr-ascucheáre

DISCREET *adj.* oálă acupirítă (*lit. 'covered pot'*)

DISCRETION *s.* (*good behavior*) frunimádhă; **at smb.'s ~** dúpă vóla a

DISCRIMINATION *s.* (*discernment*) aleádzire, dhiácrise

DISCUSS *vb.* (*to examine*) ved; ▼siluyiséscu, ▼minduéscu

DISCUSSION *s.* (*debate*) cuvéndă, zítise ‖ CUNIA: muabéţ *f pl* (*from a private letter*)

DISDAIN *s.* péză → SCORN

DISDAIN *vb.* cătăfroniséscu

DISDAINFUL *adj.* daítcu, *m pl* -tţi, *f pl* -tţe → ARROGANT

DISEASE *s.* lângoáre, ni-puteáre, nipteáre, niputeáţă; **chronic ~** măráze veácľe

DISEMBOWEL *vb.* (*to wound or kill smb.*) vérsu máţăle, ▼dis-pântic, spântic

DISEMBOWELMENT *s.* dispânticáre, spânticáre

DISENCHANT *vb.* bizdiséscu

DISENCUMBER *vb.* ▼discárcu → DISCHARGE

DISENTANGLE *vb.* ▼discáciu, ▼dizmeástic, ľ-u dau di fúndu

DISENTANGLEMENT *s.* discăceáre

DISGRACE *s.* arşíne, aruşináre → SHAME

DISGRACE *vb.* aruşinédz, arşinédz, ▾fac birbáte, ▾fac páde tu lúme, fac ti-arşíne; **You have ~ed me** Ti-arşíne mi fắţéşi; (*to ~ oneself*) ▾scad ‖ BASME 344: ĺi scot ócĺiĺ; BATSARIA 4: mi fac di péză; 85: *1 pl aor* nă feáţim fără fáţă

DISGRACED → BE ~

DISGRACEFUL *adj.* tr-ascucheáre (*lit.* 'such as to spit on')

DISGRUNTLE *vb.* ĺ-u aspárgu (chéfea)

DISGUISE *s.* tiptíle *invar.*

DISGUISE *vb.* mi adár ca, mi fac tiptíle

DISGUST *s.* aguñós, ayunós, (a)ngustáre, anusteáţă, buhtisíre, lăíle; **to have ~ for** ▾anusţắscu

DISGUST *vb.* ▾aynuséscu, ▾aynusédz, ▾anusţắscu; mi dizvăléscu (di) ‖ **Amc:** ñĭ-eáste yunósu, PADIOTU 119

DISGUSTED *adj.* anusţât, buhtisít, dizvălít (di), ngusát (di); **to be ~ with** ñ-u ynos di

DISGUSTING *adj.* aynusós, gunusós, griţós

DISH *s.* (*food*) mâcáre; *also:* ghélă, ghivár, măyiríe, miyiríe; (*shallow container*) vas → PLATE

DISH-CLOTH *s.* păcivúră, păciúră

DISHEARTEN *vb.* dau ibréte (la) → DISCOURAGE

DISHEVEL *vb.* (*of hair or clothing*) ▾distrám, distrămédz; (*rare*) dizmóĺu → TOUSLE

DISHEVELLED *adj.* (*of hair*) displătít ‖ cealpér, DIARO 256

DISHEVELLING *s.* dismăiráre, dizmăĺáre

DISHONEST *adj.* plan, *m pl* plañ; da pâne a fúrĭlor [fúrĭ•] ‖ **Cru:** nitiñisít GOLAB 238; BASME 313: fáţă láie

DISHONOR *s.* arşíne → SHAME

DISHONORABLE *adj.* pânghiós [•ǵós], tr-ascucheáre (*lit.* 'such as to spit on')

DISHWARE *s.* váse *n pl*, vas *sg*

DISHWATER *s.* lătúră

DISINTER *vb.* (*to exhume*) dizgróp

DISINTERMENT *s.* dizgrupáre

DISJOIN *vb.* ▾disfác; (*as of a cloud*) ▾diñíc

DISLIKE *vb.* nu-ñ pláţe

DISLOCATE *vb.* (*as of a finger*) ▾scot, ▾mut, ▾cluzunéscu, ▾strănguléscu → SPRAIN

DISLOCATED *adj.* (*as of a joint*) cluzunít

DISLOCATION *s.* (*luxation*) cluzuníre, străngulsíre

DISLODGE *vb.* scot

DISLOYAL *adj.* pabés, -ésă, -éşĭ, -ése → UNFAITHFUL

DISLOYALTY *s.* băbislíche

DISMAL *adj.* laiu, *f* láie, *m/f pl* lăi; ntunicós → EVIL

DISMAY *vb.* bag ceáşlu (tu) → DISCOURAGE

DISMISS *vb.* scărchéscu, ĺ-dau ţărúhile [•rúhĭ•li], ĺ-dau poárca; **to be dismissed** hiu scărchít

DISMOUNT *vb.* ▾dipún di pri cal, discálic ‖ HRISTU 62: dipun di ncalar

DISMOUNTING *s.* discălicáre, discălicátă, discălicătúră

DISMOUNTING AREA *s.* discălicătoáre

DISOBEY *vb.* nu ascúltu

DISOBEDIENCE *s.* nĭ-ascultáre

DISOBEDIENT *adj.* naprán, *m pl* -áñ

DISORDER *s.* alăcíre; *also:* acatástase, acătăstăsíe, arăiátă, atăxíe; ghilítĭ *f pl*; ni-arádhă; (*pell-mell*) darmadán *invar.* ‖ (*mess*) círtâ, DIARO 253

DISORDERED *adj.* (*physical or mental* ~) cearpér; (*of hair*) mbirşát

DISORDEREDLY *adv.* ‖ ca pérĺi ali zúrle, ca pérĺi a zúrlăĺei (*lit.* 'like the hair of an insane woman'), PARALLELE 134

DISORDERLY *adj.* alócut, anápudh (*and* anápud), năpudheáric, cearpér, áţala-máţala, sirsém, sirsén, minditór, *G:* pálaz ‖ DIARO 397: áţal, dizbârnát

DISORDERLY *adv.* átacta, áţala-máţala

DISORGANIZE *vb.* ▾aspárgu

DISORIENT *vb.* ▾chérdu, ▾schérdu, cher cálea

DISPARAGE *vb.* săhunéscu, cătăfroniséscu

DISPARAGEMENT *s.* cacuzburáre → SLANDER

DISPARATE *adj.* ni-uidisít; áltă sóie (*lit.* 'another kind')

DISPASSIONATE *adj.* ísih

DISPATCH *vb.* → SEND

DISPEL *vb.* ▾aruvérsu, arăéscu; (*as of fog*) ▾tuchéscu

DISPENSE *vb.* mpártu

DISPERSE *vb.* ▾aspárgu, ▾arăspândéscu; (*as of thoughts*) ▾arăés-cu; (*as coins*) ▾aruvérsu, aruvirsédz, ▾scrupuséscu; (*to spend, to*

waste) ngărmiséscu; (*as of fog*) ▼tuchéscu

DISPERSED *adj.* arăít, (*disheveled*) arăshirát

DISPERSION *s.* arăíre, arăspândíre, arăspândzâre, scrupsíre, scurpisíre → SCATTERING

DISPIRIT *vb.* → DISCOURAGE

DISPIRITED *adj.* cripát → SAD

DISPLACE *vb.* ▼mut; (*as things in a room*) alúmtu, ▼strămút; ~ a *bone* cluzunéscu, ▼strănguléscu; âñ mut (mâna, *etc.*)

DISPLACED *adj.* strămutát; ~ **person** muageár, muagír; prósfingu, *m pl* -nghi → BE ~

DISPLACEMENT *s.* mutáre, mtáre

DISPLAY *vb.* scot, ▼aspún; **They ~ed great courage** Si-aspúsiră asláñ; **to ~ one's true colors** (*to become shameless*) ñ-arúc făţle n páde

DISPLEASE *vb.* pihtuéscu

DISPOSAL *s.* (*polite reply*) **I am at your ~** (*please! I am listening, I am wating for your orders, etc.*) Ursea!

DISPOSED → BE DISPOSED TO

DISPOSITION *s.* (*frame of mind*) tăcáte; (*formal expression of opinion*) timbíhe, timbíe → ORDER

DISPUTATEOUS PERSON *s.* căvgăgí, căvyăngí → GOOD-FOR-NOTHING

DISPUTE *s.* daravéra, filunichisíre, strigáre → QUARREL

DISPUTATION *s.* filunichisíre

DISPUTE *vb.* (*to deny*) fac háşa, filunichiséscu

DISQUIET *s.* angúsă, ar1háte, sicléte, săcléte, stinuhuríe

DISQUIET *vb.* ▼stinuhurséscu → DISTURB, FLURRY

DISREGARD *vb.* (*to disrespect*) fac mânică di tămbáre, nu-l dau di curáuă; (*to forget, as a concern*) u bag strâmbă; ~ **it!** Băgă-u strâmbă! (*to deny*) fac incheáre, filunichiséscu; (*to neglect*) paralás ‖ lu trecu ti puţâ di ľépuru, DIARO 286; lu am ti púţâ di ľépur. 422; **I ~ this man** Nu lu am ti ţivá aést om, DIARO 99

DISREPUTABLE *adj.* tr-ascucheáre (*lit.* 'such as to spit on')

DISREPUTE *vb.* → DISGRACE

DISRESPECT *vb.* fac mânică di tămbáre, nu-l dau di curáuă

DISROBE *vb.* → UNDRESS

DISRUPT *vb.* ▼aspárgu, ▼cúrmu

DISSEMINATE *vb.* → STREW

DISSENSION *s.* mâcătúră, ceamăúnă → WRANGLE

DISSIMILAR

DISSIMILAR *adj.* áltă sóie (*lit. 'a different kind'*)

DISSIPATE *vb.* (*as of fog*) ▾tuchéscu, ▾diñíc; (*as of wealth*) spătăľuséscu → DISPEL, SCATTER

DISSIMULATE *vb.* ▾acoápir, ▾ascúndu, mi fac

DISSIPATION *s.* tuchíre, tucheáre; (*as of money*) spătăľusíre

DISSOLUTE *adj.* aspártu, -rtă, -rţâ, -rte; distórsu, -toársă, -tórşi, -toárse; púrnu, -rñi, -rnă, -rne; *s.* om distórsu; curvár

DISSOLUTENESS *s.* anăpudzâľe, curvăríľe, curvăríe, dişuţâre, iaranlâche, pănghíe, purníľe, putănlâche

DISSOLUTION *s.* anălsíre; (*also fig.*) aspărdzeáre

DISSOLVE *vb.* anăliséscu, anălséscu, ▾tuchéscu, ▾aspárgu

DISTAFF *s.* fúrcă; *also:* culístră, drúgă; *F:* cărbúş; (*the female side of a family*) muľiráme

DISTAFF *adj.* muľiréscu

DISTANCE *s.* dipărtáre; (*~ between two given points*) dhiástimă; (*~ between two stops*) cunáche; (*spacial remoteness*) záre (*and* dzáre); **in the ~** tu ndzáre; **far in the ~** dipárte n záre ‖ **from a ~** *adv.* (*from far*) di lárgu, CUVATA 29

DISTANCE *vb.* (*to leave behind*) ľau cior, ľau loc, trag cior; ▾dipărtédz (*and* -pâr-); **They had ~ed themselves greatly** Aveá loátă loc múltu

DISTANT *adj.* dipărtát, dipărtós (*and* -pâr-)

DISTASTE *vb.* (*to feel aversion to*) ▾aynuséscu, aynusédz, ▾anusţăscu

DISTEND *vb.* (*to swell*) ▾úmflu

DISTILL *vb.* limbiséscu

DISTILLATION *s.* limbisíre

DISTINCT *adj.* (*plain, clearily seen*) límpid (*and* límbid)

DISTINCTION *s.* (*as a decoration*) nişáne ‖ (*as a personal quality*) aumbrâ; **She is not beautiful, but she has ~** Nu-i muşátâ, ma ári aúmbrâ, DIARO 408

DISTINGUISH *vb.* (*to single out from, to ~ oneself, to be better*) ▾alég (di); (*to discern, to detect, to recognize*) ▾ved, ▾ávdu ‖ **~ed from the others** si alidzea di alanţ, HRISTU 49

DISTINGUISHED *adj.* chibárcu, -rţi, -rcă, -rţe; aléptu, *f* aleáptă, *m pl* alépţâ, *f pl* aleápte → ELEGANT, FAMOUS ‖ BATSARIA 1: cu sémnu; (*having distinction*) aumbrós [a•um•], DIARO 408

DISTORT *vb.* ▾şuţ

DISTORTED *adj.* anvârligát → TWISTED

DISTRACTION *s.* (*amusement, gaping about*) siryeáne; (*mental disturbance*) pumoáră, şuşăre

DISTRAIN *vb.* (*to sequester*) fac sucréstu

DISTRAIT *adj.* agărşít, hăscát, hascanífur, adúnă-vímtu

DISTRESS *s.* (*seizing*) sucréstu, catáshise; (*pain, sorrow*) căhâre, ghiúce, nvirín, parápun, părăpuñisíre

DISTRESS *vb.* (*to afflict*) ▼părăpuñiséscu

DISTRESSED *adj.* părăpuñisít, părpuñisít, ncimirát, nciumirát; (~ *because of longing*) siclitít ‖ CUVATA 4: ca bătút di gríndină → BE ~

DISTRESSFUL *adj.* niurát, niurós, vurcusít

DISTRIBUTE *vb.* ▼âmpártu, mpártu

DISTRIBUTION *s.* (*as ~ of goods to the needy*) mpărtâre

DISTRICT *s.* (*in former Turkey*) singeáche; vilaéte, viléte, câză ‖ *G, P:* vilaét, SarD 30

DISTRUST *s.* şubé, şubée; apistíe ipupsíe

DISTRUSTFUL(LY) *adj., adv.* ípaptu, ípuptu, şubeilâtic

DISTURB *vb.* (*of a river, of mind*) ▼alăcéscu, ▼túrbur, túlbur, ▼cutúlbur, cutúrbur, *N:* cutrúbur; căscăndiséscu, ▼mintéscu, *N:* ▼angulcéscu; **Frightful dreams ~ his sleep** yíse lăhtăroáse ĺ-cutúlbură sómnul; (*to tease*) pirăxéscu; (*to ~ from work*) gréscu tu mână ‖ (*to interrupt smb.'s thoughts*): **Shut up, you've ~ed my thoughts!** Taţi câ-ñ loaşi sistasea! DIARO 371

DISTURBANCE *s.* alăcíre, mintíre (*and* mindíre), mintitúră, mintireáţă, turburáre; (*fatigue*) bréngă; (*interruption*) biuzúre; (*mental ~*) pumoáră, şuşăre; (*teasing*) pirăxíre; (*hubbub*) tăvătúră

DISTURBED *adj.* (*as of a body of water*) mintít; (*emotionally sick*) aprés, *f* apreásă, *m pl* apréşĭ, *f pl* apreáse; glărít, hăzusít, şuşăt

DISUNITE *vb.* ▼dispártu; (*to make bad blood between*) hăzmuséscu ‖ HRISTU 37: fac azmălichi (cu)

DISUNITY *s.* → DISAGREEMENT

DITCH *s.* endéc, hăndác, hăndáche

DITHER *s.* hir arăţe, hiór, mpiruşáre; hórhut; hirbeáre, heárbire

DIVAN *s.* canapé

DIVE *vb.* ▼afunduséscu → PLUNGE

DIVERS

DIVERS *adj.* alǘmtrea *invar.*; áltă turlíe, áltă sóie, áltă lă-ghíe

DIVERSION *s.* (*pastime*) dhiaschédhese

DIVERT *vb.* ▾abát, părmărăséscu, părămăséscu

DIVERTISSEMENT *s.* ylinghé, ñirătúră

DIVEST *vb.* ▾dispóľu

DIVIDE *vb.* ▾mpártu, ▾cúrmu; ~ it into two parts! Cúrmă-l tu doáuă! ‖ (*to disunite as by intrigue*) bag pi azmălichi, HRISTU 38

DIVINE *adj.* dumnidzăscu, -dzáscă, -dzắşţâ, -dzắşti; sâmtu, -mtă, -mţâ, -mte; ayiu, *m pl* ayĭ, *f s/pl* áye

DIVINATION *s.* angucíre, măndíe ‖ PC: arcáre tu steále

DIVINITY *s.* dumnidzắľe, theoloyíe

DIVISION *s.* (*sharing*, *partition*) mpărţâre, mpărtăciúne, păr-tăciúne; (*quarrel*) cârtitúră

DIVISIVE *adj.* muzavír → INTRIGUER, SCHEMER

DIVORCE *s.* dispărţâre

DIVORCE *vb.* ▾dispártu (di), ▾dismărít

DIVULGE *vb.* dau pri toácă, scot n páde, scot tu páde; I won't ~ you Nu va ti scot tu páde

DIZZINESS *s.* andrálă, cildisíre, cistăsíre, cistisíre, scútură, uténţă ‖ **F:** urteániţă, uteániţă SarD 105; DIARO 49: ânvârleári

DIZZY *adj.* andrălăsít, andăr-, cicărdisít, cirtăsít → BECOME ~

DIZZY *vb.* ▾cirtăséscu, mindéscu di cap

DO *vb.* ▾fac, ▾adár, apu-adár; God's will be done Al Dumnidzắu sĭ s-fácă; What's to be done? ţi-i ti-a fácă? Who knows what he is going to ~? Cári-şti ţe va apuadáră? (*to accomplish*) What have you done? Ţe péşţ acăţáşi? (*lit.* 'What fish have you caught?'); what he should ~ cum s-adáră; (*to travel*) alág; You did the whole world Alăgát tut lóclu; (*to clean*, *to arrange*) ndreg; (a)născăr-séscu, anischirséscu

DO A BAD TURN *vb.* l-gioc, l-gioc pri tăpsíe

DO A FAVOR *vb.* fac háre; Do me this favor Fă-ñ aéstă háre

DO AGAIN *vb.* pri-adár

DO A GOOD BUSINESS *vb.* adár căşáre

DO ALL IN ONE'S POWER *vb.* mi fac páde

DO AWAY WITH *vb.* (*to deny*) arniséscu; (*to use up, as money or food*) fac ghíne; (*to kill*) ľ-astíngu ţeára ‖ BASME 607: adár ghíne

DO EVIL *vb.* adár slăbínţă, adúc slab

DO FOR SMB. *vb.* ĺ-u pot; ĺ-vin di indihàche (*or* di induhàche)

DO GOOD *vb.* (*speaking of food, climate, etc.*) mi acáţă; **The water had not done him any good** Apa nu lu-aveá acăţátă; (*as of a good deed*) fac bun, mi bunuéscu

DO IN *vb.* ▼aspárgu → KILL; (*to ruin*) dărâm; (*to exhaust*) căpăéscu; (*to cheat*) (a)ncálţu

DO IT FAT *vb.* (*to do it fine*) u trag chióşea dumneáşte, âñ gioácă cálu, huzuripséscu

DO IT ON THE CHEAP *vb.* (*to live in poverty*) bat tămbărălu

DON'T ‖ BATSARIA 92: ~ **eat too much grapes!** s-núpu măţ aúuă múltă!

DO OF / WITH THIRST *vb.* crep di seáte, (a)năschirséscu, născărséscu

DO ONE'S (DAMNED) BEST *vb.* mi fac páde; ▼apufác; **Do your best for her!** Apufă-ti trâ nâsă!

DO ONE'S DUTY *vb.* (*to get married*) ‖ BASME 256: ñ-fac aráda

DO OUT *vb.* (*to clear smb. out, to defeat at cards*) (a)fuléscu

DO SMB. IN *vb.* (*to hurt or kill*) ĺ-vin di indiháche (*or* induháche)

DO SMB. AN ILL TURN *vb.* ĺ-gioc únă hunére

DO THE BUSINESS FOR SMB. *vb.* astíngu bána → KILL

DO THE GRAND *vb.* mi ngroş → GIVE ONESELF AIRS

DO UP *vb.* (*to launder*) ▼aspél; (*to clean, as a room*) (a)născărséscu

DO WELL *vb.* (*to afford, to suit*) ñ-da di mână

DO WRONG *vb.* ĺ-adúc slab; **He did not do any wrong to her** Nu ĺ-adúse vârnu slab

DOCILE *adj.* ascultătór; ñilúş (*lit. 'little lamb'*)

DOCK *s. bot.* nánă, nénă

DOCKHAND *s.* hămál

DOCTOR *s.* gheátru, yeátru; yeatrísă *f*; iichím (*sic*) ‖ ALiA II q. 207: iátru, iáturu; (*rare*) dóktoru

DOCUMENT *s.* cárte

DODDER *vb.* auşéscu, slăghéscu, sclăghéscu

DODDERED *adj.* auşít, tricút, s(c)lab, slăghít

DODDERY *adj.* → DODDERED

DODGE *s.* (a)firíre, amfiríre, féstă, frâmtúră, tirtípe → TRICK

DODGE *vb.* ▼(a)firéscu, amfiréscu

DODGER: be an artful ~ ≈ ñ-tricú rúglu prit náre
DODO *adj.* (*hopelessly behind the time*) cudár, códus; (*unin-telligent*) şulúndu → STUPID
DOE *s.* şútă; (*hornless ~*) cărşútă, corciútă; (*rare*) căprioáră *f*, căpriór *m*; zărcádhă *f*, zărcângé *m* ‖ BASME 340: ágru-cápră
DOFF *vb.* ▾alás, scot; ▾dispóĺu, ascáp di, mi cuturséscu di
DOE-HARE *s.* ĺipuroáñe
DOG *s.* câne (*and* căne); *coll.* câníu; (*children's talk*) cútă ‖ (*old ~*) **SJos:** paĺuşchiul, CL 257; **Gra, Perd:** kéni, **Pdz:** kéne, **Kat:** keáni, B-ARCH 89 → LUCKY DOG
DOG HOLE *s.* cumás di câne
DOGGED *adj.* apufăsít
DOGGISH *adj.* cânéscu, -eáscă, -éşţâ, -éşti
DOGGISHLY *adv.* câneáşte
DOGGY *adj.* → DOGGISH
DOGLEG *s.* şuţâtúră (a cáliĺei); turnătúră
DOGMA *s.* dhóymă, *pl.* dhóbmate
DOG-ROSE *s. bot.* coárne bífe *f pl* → EGLANTINE
DOG-ROSE BUSH *s. bot.* măcéş
DOING *s.* făţeáre, fáţire
DOLE *s.* (*alms, donation*) pirpişór, pămăntu, eleimosíne
DOLEFUL *adj.* (*as of a voice*) suschirát, flivirós → PLAINTIVE
DOLL *s.* păpúşe, pupúşe, cúclă, geamálă
DOLL UP *vb.* (*to deck out*) muşuţăscu
DOLLOP *s.* bărţíre, bizbíle, cumátă
DOLT *s.* (*dullard*) budălă; măscălídhă → STUPID
DOLTISH *adj.* budâlă, budâládz, *f sg/pl* budâloáñe
DOMAIN *s.* numíe, sireáuă; mulălíche
DOMESTIC *s.* huzmicheár → SERVANT
DOMESTIC *adj.* dumuşár, dumuşárcu); (*for ~ use*) **Smr:** di-a víşti
DOMESTICATE *vb.* ▾imirédz → TAME
DOMINANCE *s.* (*reign*) dumníĺe
DOMINATE *vb.* ▾zăptăséscu, zăptiséscu, (a)ncálic
DOMINATION *s.* exusíe; (*subdueing*) (a)zápe
DOMINEER *vb.* → DOMINATE
DOMINOES *s.* dómină
DOMICILE *s.* (*residence*) cásă
DON *vb.* ▾(a)nvéscu; ñ-trec (cămeáşea, *etc.*)

DONATE *vb.* (a)hărzéscu, dăruéscu, duruséscu

DONATION *s.* dar, dhoárǎ, durusíre, dursíre; (*alms*) eleimosíne

DONE *adj.* adrát; fáptu, -ptǎ, -pţâ, -pte

DONKEY *s.* yumár; *dim.* yumăríc, yumăríţ; *also:* câciu, *pl* câci [kâc] *and* câceáñ; dângǎ, dânglârǎ *m*, dânglâroáñe *f*; şoñiu; tar *m*, tárǎ *f*; tăróñu *m*, tăroáñe *f*; uciu, uricľát

DONKEY-WISE *adv.* yumăreáşte

DON'T *particle* nu, mi; ~ **sadden her!** Nu u-nvirínǎ ş-tíne! ~ **you ever dare!** S-nu ti píngǎ dráclu! ~ **come here!** Mi yiñ nculeá!

DOOMED *adj.* hiu scris; *N:* éscu scris; **as it was** ~ cum fu scris

DOOR *s.* úşe; (*entrance*) intráre; (*in a sheepfold*) leásǎ, liseáuǎ ‖ *LvO:* úsǎ (*sic*), B-ARCH 402; **He had left the door open carelessly** úşa u-aveá alâsátâ háni, DIARO 375

DOOR-CATCH *s.* cărcheáuǎ

DOOR-FRAME *s.* márgurǎ

DOOR-KEEPER *s.* purtár, cafás, caváz, calafáz, calaváz

DOOR-SHUTTER *s.* poálǎ di poártǎ

DOORSTEP *s.* prag, preag

DOPE *adj.* hascanífur → STUPID

DOTTY *adj.* (*mentally unbalanced*) şcret, cu zíya ma nafoárǎ

DOUBLE *adj.* dúblu, *m pl* -bľi *and* dúplu, *m pl* -pľi

DOUBLE *vb.* (*to make of two thicknesses*) dhipluséscu

DOUBLE *adv* dhipló, dúblu, cu dúblu

DOUBLE-CROSS *vb.* → DECEIVE

DOUBLE GAIN *s.* (*at backgammon*) márţu

DOUBLE-BARRELLED GUN *s.* (*for hunters*) cifté

DOUBT *s.* induíre, nisiyurlíche; **without** ~ (*beyond all* ~) fărǎ di áltǎ; aiá; **There is no** ~ **that God does not like you** Aiá, nu ti va Dumnidzǎ → BEYOND ALL ~

DOUBT *vb.* ▼induéscu, stau pri doáuǎ

DOUBTFUL *adj.* (*undecided*) induít, ni-umplút, ni-síyur, andáulea [•daŭ•]; (*suspect*) ípuptu, şubiilâ [su•biľ•lâ]

DOUBTFULLY *adv.* andáulea [•daᵘ•]

DOUBTLESS *adj.,* ~LY *adv.* besbelé, bezbilé

DOUGH *s.* aluát, aloát

DOUGH LEAF *s.* pétur

DOUGHTY *adj.* gióne, *f* -oánǎ, *m pl* gǐoñ, *f pl* -oáne

DOVE *s.* părúmbu *m*, părúmbǎ *f*; purúmbu, purúngu, culúmbu, pilisţér, piristér

DOWN s. (*from birds*) puh; (*first human beard*) múhlu; (*as from a rug*) frúmă ‖ **Prv:** (*from a bird*) púpulu m, CL 260

DOWN adv. ghios, nghios (*ant.* nsus); npáde, mpáde; **fall ~** cad n páde → BRING ~, PUT ~

DOWN IN THE MOUTH adj. cu cúrlu n sus

DOWN PAYMENT s. aruvoánă, arăvoánă; căpáră

DOWN SMB. vb. arúc mpáde

DOWNCAST adj. dipús, jilós → SAD

DOWNFALL s. hăndicusíre

DOWNGRADE s. dipuneáre, dipúnire

DOWNGRADE vb. ▾apléc, ▾dipún, cad

DOWNHEARTED adj. dipús → SAD

DOWNHILL adv. (*on a road*) sum cále (*ant.* tră cále) ‖ **Cru:** catífurlu; **I am descending ~** Mi dipún catífurlu, GOLAB 224

DOWNPOUR s. zof → RAIN

DOWNSTREAM adv. păgór, n vále

DOWNTRODDEN adj. ncălicát, stulcinát

DOWNWARD adj. di ahímura; **the ~ road** cálea di ahímura

DOWNWARDS adv. n vále, păgór, pugór, híma, cătră híma, trâ híma, ahímura, n páde, mbáde, ânghios, nghios, nghiósura ‖ **Cru:** ănghiós, GOLAB 205

DOWRY s. pái, páie, pirţíe, priţíe, prícă, zéstră ‖ **Amc:** părţíe, prăţíe, PADIOTU 141

DOZE: take a ~ vb. ľ-coc un sómnu

DOZE vb. cad di sómnu; **to ~ off** mi fúră sómnul ‖ BASME 309: mi ncľin

DOZEN s. duzínă

DRAB adj. bágav, m pl -gaYĭ, f pl -gave

DRAFT s. (*drink made by a sorceress*) tatulát

DRAFT vb. ▾trag

DRAG s. (*smth. boring*) bizéryiu, plixe

DRAG vb. ▾trag; ▾azvărnuéscu

DRAG ONE'S BRAIN ABOUT/WITH vb. ñ-disíc cáplu

DRAG ONESELF ALONG vb. ▾azvărnăéscu, azvărnuéscu, zvărñéscu

DRAG OUT vb. scot (nafoáră), trag (nafoáră)

DRAGGING s. azvărnuíre

DRAGGINGLY adv. azvárna, azvárnalui; **F:** azvárra

DRAGON *s.* lámñe, láme; zmeu; (*the mooneating* ~) vurculác; (*winged serpent*) stihió, stihíu → MONSTER

DRAIN *s.* (*as in a kitchen*) niruhíte, **N:** nuruhídhă; uz; Lac: gólniţă ‖ (*trough*) **GSus:** misúr, CL 256

DRAIN *vb.* dişértu, ▾stricór, ▾vérsu

DRAINER *s.* (*a stake with trimmed branches at the upper end*) ţirutór

DRAINING *s.* stricuráre, virsáre

DRAKE *s.* bib, pataróc, patóclu, ros, rusác ‖ **SJos:** nis, **Av, Prv:** pap, CL 257 → MAKE DUCKS AND ~S WITH MONEY

DRASTIC *adj.* áscur, ágru

DRAW *vb.* ▾trag, scot, cundiľédz, cundiľiséscu; **to ~ aside** ▾trag di nă párte; **to ~ closer to** ▾apróchiu; **to ~ smb. into a scrape** (*to trick*) ľ-gioc únă hunére ‖ **to ~ aside** ALR 1376: mi dau na nă párte

DRAW IN ONE'S HORNS *vb.* li dipún urécľile

DRAW LOTS *vb.* arúc şcurtíţa → CAST LOTS

DRAW OUT *vb.* scot

DRAW THE BOW *vb.* surrender sădzitédz

DRAW THE LONG BOW *vb.* ▾arădhăpséscu → TITTLE-TATTLE; (*to exaggerate*) spun únă căpáche; u fac di per fúne

DRAW THE WOOL OVER SMB.'S EYES *vb.* ľ-bag pirdé tu ócľi → DECEIVE

DRAW WATER TO ONE'S MILL *vb.* ñ-u bag ápa tu avláche

DRAWER *s.* (*as in a table*) sirtár, cicmigé, cicmigée

DRAWERS *s.* (*for men*) cihşíre, sindrófe; **Cľis:** dónuri *f pl*; (*for small children*) dónce ‖ **Peş:** zmeáne, CL 258; **K:** păndzătúri *pl.* GOLAB 241

DRAWERS LACE *s.* prăcăzón (*and* prâ-), părcăzón, prucuzúnă

DRAW-KNIFE *s.* sgáibă, zgoábă

DRAWLING(LY) *adj., adv.* (*as of a speech*) trăgănós

DRAWSHAVE *s.* → DRAW-KNIFE

DREAD *s.* lăhtár → FEAR

DREAD *adj.* → DREADFUL

DREAD *vb.* ▾nfrichédz

DREADFUL *adj.* fricós, -oásă, -óşĭ, -oáse; fuvirós, lihtărós

DREADFULLY *adv.* fuvirós, -oásă, -oşĭ, -oáse; lihtărós

DREAM *s.* yis; **It appears in their dreams** Tu yis lă si-alin-

DREAM

ceáşte; **They see their village in their ~** Hoára-şi ved tu yis

DREAM *vb.* ved tu yis; ved yíslu (că); ▼(a)nyisédz

DREAMING *s.* (a)nyisáre

DREARY *adj.* cérnu, ngérnu → GLOOMY

DREDGE *vb.* (*to coat food by sprinkling*) pispiléscu

DREDGED *adj.* (*covered*) pispilít; **a field ~ with snow** câmpu pispilít cu neáuă

DREDGING *s.* pispilíre; acupiríre

DREGS *s. pl.* bărsíe, blúzgă, brúzgă; *N:* cómină, cuméñe; príştină (di aúuă), prâştină, prúştină, pruştínă, priştínă, prâştínă,
piştínă, purúştină, ţípur, ţípură; (*from apples, pears or plums*)
stipsunére

DRENCH *vb.* ▼adár chícută, ▼ud chícută

DRESS *s.* fustáne, *N:* fâstáne; júpă, giúpă, aróbă; (*of silk*)
cumáşe → CLOTHES, COSTUME

DRESS *vb.* ▼véscu, nvéscu, amvéscu, anvéscu; (*to deck, to adorn*)
▼adár, schez; **to ~ in colors** mi adár tu lăile [lăi•]

DRESSED *adj.* viscút, (a)nviscút, nviscúlt, alăxít, angl'igát,
armătusít, isusít; (~ *smartly*) galántu, -ntă, -nţâ, -nte

DRESSY *adj.* prăpsít

DRIBBLE *s.* chicuráre, pruscutíre

DRIBBLE *vb.* ▼pic, chic, chícur, chicurédz, chicutédz; (*sprinkle*) ▼pruscutéscu

DRIBLET *s.* chicătúră; (*a trifling amount*) dhráme → DROP

DRIED → CUT AND ~

DRIED TREE *s.* xérac

DRIED UP *adj.* uscát; *also:* astrăchít, sec, sicát, şcrumát

DRIFT *s.* (*of snow*) năvál'u, nivál'u; (*alluvion*) lúnizmă

DRIFTER *s.* alăsát, alăsătóñu

DRIFT UNDER BARE POLES *vb.* (*to live in poverty*) bat tămbărălu

DRILL[1] *s.* (*as of vegetables or flowers*) úrdin, úrdine; *mil.*
tilíme, tălíme ‖ *Mac. mil.* véjba, CUVATA 1

DRILL[2] *s.* (*tool*) burghíu, burghíe; *also:* biză, sfreádin, sfreá-
dine, sfrédin, sfrédine

DRILL *vb.* sfreádin, *N:* ▼ampíhiur

DRILLING *s.* (*piercing with or as with a drill*) sfridináre, ampihiuráre

DRINK *s.* biutúrǎ, pihtó; (*~ offered by the seller to the buyer*) crâşmǎ; **I've made a good sale, so I'll buy you a ~** ≈ Dau crâşmǎ

DRINK *vb.* beau, *aor.* biúi *and* bii (→ § 32), *part.* biút; **to ~ too much** pára-beau; (*to have a booze*) u árdu; (*to ~ almost completely*) apu-beáu; (*to booze, 3 sg*) ľ-arúcǎ múltu tu cǎrcheáuǎ; (*to drink up, to dry up*) astráchiu ‖ LITURG 125: *2 pl imper:* béţǎ

DRINK ONESELF POOR *vb.* u árdu tâmbárea (*lit. 'to burn out one's cloak'*)

DRINK ONE'S MONEY AWAY *vb.* ▼ciucutéscu prádzľi

DRINKING *s.* beáre

DRIP *s.* (*flow, stream*) ‖ **Cru:** şóput, GOLAB 252

DRIP *vb.* ▼pic, chic, chícur, chicurédz, chicutédz

DRIPPING *s.* chicáre, chicutáre; ţurţuríre

DRIVE *vb.* (*animals*) avín, dau dúpǎ; (*sheep*) ciuiéscu; **He was appointed to ~ the sheep** L-bǎgárǎ s-da dúpǎ oi; (*to exert pressure on*) ▼astrág; **Mother is driven by longing** Pi máma u-astrádzi dórlu

DRIVE A NAIL IN SMB.'S COFFIN *vb.* (*to take smb.'s heart out*) scot súflitlu

DRIVE AWAY/OUT *vb.* agunéscu; ▼cicutéscu; **Let's drive him away from here!** Si-ľ dǎm pálmili di-auá!

DRIVE CRAZY *vb.* cihtiséscu, glǎréscu, hǎzuéscu (di mínte), ▼şi-şirdiséscu

DRIVE IN(TO) *vb.* ▼bag, ▼nhig (→ § 32), plântu, ▼ciucutéscu; **~ the knife into his chest!** Hídzi-ľ cuţútlu tu chéptu! **Has he driven in the nails?** Li plântǎ pénurile?

DRIVE INTO A CORNER *vb.* ▼aplucuséscu, anǎpǎdéscu; **The dogs had driven him into a corner** Câñľi lu-aveá anǎpǎdítǎ

DRIVE MAD *vb.* nzurluséscu, zurluséscu

DRIVE OUT *vb.* scot

DRIVE SMB. OUT OF HIS SENSES *vb.* ▼cihtiséscu; ľ-mâc urécľile

DRIVE SMB. TO HIS WIT'S END *vb.* disíc cáplu

DRIVEL *s.* → NONSENSE, TWADDLE

DRIVEL ON / AWAY *vb.* (*to talk idly*) discntu, máţin (pi virisíe)

DRIVEL *vb.* bǎbǎléscu

DRIVEN IN *adj.* (*as of a pole*) (n)híptu, -ptǎ, -pţâ, -pte

DRIVING IN *s.* (*a knife, a peg, etc.*) plântáre, nhidzeáre, hidzeáre, nhídzire, hídzire; (*in water*) fundusíre

DRIZZLE

DRIZZLE *s.* pluínă ‖ ploáe minútă, PARALLELE 125

DRIZZLE *vb. 3 sg impers.* ndzeárnă ‖ **Peş:** *impers.* asprucucheáş-
te, CL 37

DROLL *adj.* caraghiós, -oásă, -óşĭ, -oáse

DROLLERY *s.* caraghiuzlâche

DRONE *s. ent. (and fig.)* ayru-cúmban ‖ **SJos:** bámbăr, CL 38

DRONE *vb.* zăzăéscu; *(of a spinning top)* zvângânéscu → BUZZ

DROOL *vb.* ñ-cúrgu bálile

DROOP *vb.* ▾apléc, ▾dipún

DROP *s.* chícă, pícă, chicută, chicătúră, lánguţă, staxeáuă; *(a
squeezed drop)* străchitúră; *(a small quantity)* dhráme *(and dráme)*, lóscut, próscut → FALL IN ~S

DROP *vb. (to let fall)* ascáp; **to ~ a stitch** *(as in a sock)*
ñ-ascápă un ócĭu (di lăpúdă)

DROP A BRICK *vb.* u-adár dhálă, u-adár taratóre ‖ CUNIA 118:
cálcu tu pítă → PUT ONE'S FOOT IN IT

DROP A HINT *vb.* gréscu pri poártă s-ávdă pălthírea

DROP BY/IN *vb.* urséscu, trec pir la, dau pân di, am turnătúra
la; **He dropped by your gate** Tricú pir la poárta-ţ; **Go and ~ my
beauty** Dú-ti, dă pân-di muşeáta; **Everybody dropped in on him** Nu
erá om ţe s-nu áibă turnătúră la nâs; *(~ hastily)* ▾sărgĭéscu *(and
sâr-)*, sărghéscu ‖ dau pi la, BASME 420; trec pr-acló, BASME 437

DROP INTO A SNOOZE *vb.* mi fúră sómnul, mi fúră un ócĭu di som-
nu, ĭau un ócĭu di sómnu, mi-ncĭín, mi ĭa ncĭinárea

DROP OFF *vb.* mi ĭa sómnul, mi fúră sómnul → DROP INTO A SNOOZE
‖ CUNIA 6: âñ víni gavuiáni

DROP OUT OF SCHOOL *vb.* u-leg cártea di cârnicócilu di par

DROP-EARED *adj.* plahúrcu, pĭa-; *m pl* -rţi, *f* -rcă, *f pl* -rţe

DROP-OFF *s.* súrpu, surpătúră, hímă, háu, háuă; *fig. (decline)*
cădeáre

DROPPING(S) *s.* báligă; *(of chicken)* găĭinát, gĭinát *m*; *(of
birds)* gĭináţ di puĭ *m pl*

DROPSICAL *adj.* idhrópic

DROPSY *s. (edema)* andrópică

DROSS *s.* zgúră, zgureáuă

DROSSY *adj.* zgurós, -oásă; zgúrav, *m pl* -rayĭ, *f pl* -rave

DROUGHT *s.* seáţită, *also:* sicătúră, uscăciúne, uscătíciu, us-
cătíş, xéră, xére

DROVE *s.* (*group*) gârdéľu, văcăríe, văcăríu

DROWN *vb.* ▼nec

DROWNING *s.* nicáre, nicătúră

DROWSE *vb.* cad di sómnu

DROWSINESS *s.* agărşíre

DROWSY *adj.* sumnós, -oásă, -óşĭ, -oáse

DRUB *vb.* ansár, ▼úmflu

DRUBBING *s.* şcop; **to be itching for a ~** ti mâcă sândzile? (*lit. 'is your blood itching?'*) ‖ ti mâcă schinárea? (*lit. 'is your back itching?'*) PARALLELE 120 → BEATING

DRUDGE *vb.* cilistiséscu

DRUDGERY *s.* havalé, cilistisíre

DRUGGET *s.* abă, bulubóţă, garvanó, gravanó, grăvăníciu, nvéscu

DRUGGIST *s.* spiţér, spiţár

DRUGSTORE *s.* spiţăríe

DRUM *s.* G: bărăbáncă; dăúľe, ghium, tâmpână (*and* tâmbână), *dim.* tâmpâníciu; **to beat the ~** bat bărăbánca

DRUMMER *s.* dăulgí [dă•ul•], tâmpânár

DRUNK *s.* (*excessive drinking*) parabeáre

DRUNK *adj.* (a)mbitát; *also:* afumát (*lit. 'smoked'*), arucutít, bicríu, biút; ciucutít (*lit. 'knocked'*) → MAKE ~ ‖ BASME 510: adrát (*lit. 'done'*)

DRUNKARD *s.* (a)mbitătór, bicríu, ciucutóniu; şóşe *m*, şóşañ *pl* ‖ *Cru:* ămbitătór, GOLAB 204; *Prv:* bicroáñe *f*, CL 39

DRUNKEN *vb.* (*to make drunk*) ▼(a)mbét

DRY *adj.* uscát; (*as of firewood*) frigănát; sufín; (*as of laundry*) zvinturát, azvimturát; (*as of bread served and eaten without butter*) gol, goálă, goľ, goále

DRY *vb.* (*to make or to become dry*) ▼usâc, usúc, ▼azvímtur, ▼frigănédz, ▼sufinédz; (*as of a well, a tree, a flower*) sec; **The well has dried up** Sică púţlu; (*of grapes*) ▼stăfidhuséscu; (*of rivers*) (a)stărchéscu, (a)străchéscu

DRY LAND *s.* (*as opposed to the sea*) uscát

DRYER *s.* (*basket of tangled branches for laundry*) câsnác ti uscáre stráñĭle

DRYING BARN *s.* (*for corn*) cuşáre

DRYING UP *s.* uscáre, (a)străchíre, stăfidhusíre → DRY UP

DUB *s.* astângu, zérvu

DUBIETY *s.* ni-siyurlíche

DUBIOUS *adj.* ni-síyur; andáulea [•daŭ•] *invar.*

DUCAT *s.* (*golden coin*) fluríe

DUCK *s.* bíbă, pápă, pápcă, páphe, pátă, pátcă, rósă → PLAY ~S AND DRAKES WITH MONEY ‖ ALIA 118: pápe, páte, pápher

DUCK *s. tex.* arițína

DUCKLING *s.* patóclu ‖ *SJos:* bibóplu, CL 39; *GSus:* pap, *Prv:* pă-póplu, CL 258

DUCT *s.* (*canal*) chilúnge, sulinár

DUDE! *interj.* ‖ STERE 24: olangim

DUDGEON *s.* năireáță, nărleáță, cărtíre

DUDS *s. pl* (*belongings*) catrafúse *f pl*

DUE *adj.* (*expected to happen*) ‖ PC: lipseáște să; **He is ~ to arrive** Lipseáște z-yínă

DUE TO *prep.* dítră, șúchiur al → BECAUSE OF

DUFFER *s.* agemí, agemíu, agemít; astângu → GOOD-FOR-NOTHING

DULL *adj.* (*vapid, tedious*) análut; **~ of hearing** fudúl di uré-cl̦i

DULL-WITTED *adj.* divană, *pl m* divanádz → STUPID; (*slow in action*) → SLUGGISH; (*blunt*) nituryisít; (*not resonant*) cuf; (*boring*) plictisít; (*of a color*) sálbit

DUMB *adj.* (a)mút; *s.* muteái, *m pl* muteáiañ; mutule(n)ágă → BE STRUCK ~, BE ~ WITH

DUMBFOUND *vb.* ▾cildiséscu → AMAZE

DUMBFOUNDED *adj.* mărmurisít → BE ~, ASTONISHED

DUMMY *s.* glar → STUPID

DUMP DOWN *vb.* arúc mpáde

DUMPS: **in the ~** cu cúrlu n sus; **to be in the ~** nu éscu tu ori

DUMPY *adj.* scurtác, scurtabác, scurtabéc, șcurtabéc; *also:* ciu-púngu, giúgea *m*, giúgeañ *pl*; jabéc, mușmoálă, mușmúlă *invar*; nă-réce *invar*; scúndu, -ndzâ, -nde; șíșcu, -șcă, -șțâ, -ște

DUN *adj.* bágav, *m pl* -gayĭ, *f pl* -gave → GRAY

DUN *vb.* (*to pester, to ask repeatedly*) ĺ-cad furtíe

DUNCE *s.* → STUPID

DUNDERHEAD *s.* cap di grij

DUNG *s.* báligă; (*from sheep and goats*) căcăreádză, căcărádză, găgăreáță, gărgăráță; (*from a mouse*) căcăstór *m* ‖ ALB: **Kërb,** *Pe:* báĺgă; *Për:* bálike; *Dren:* báligă; *Sln:* báigă, BRÂNCUS 551

DUNG *vb.* ▼bálig, trag bắlidzi

DUNG-HILL *s.* cupríe, coprăe

DUNK *vb.* (*usu. of bread*) ▼diñíc → CRUMBLE; ▼afunduséscu → SUB-MERGE

DUPE *s.* apló, tivichél

DUPE *vb.* ▼ardu, (a)ncálţu → DECEIVE

DUPLICITY *s.* tácmă, ipucrisíe

DURABLE *adj.* arăvdós; nu ári moárte (*lit. 'it does not have death'*)

DURANCE *s.* hăpsâníre → IMPRISONMENT

DURESS *s.* → CONSTRAINT

DURING *prep.* pi; **~ the days when** pri; pi dzắlile cându; **death ~ the wedding** hárlu pri curúnă; (*over*) písti; **~ the night** pisti noápte

DUSK *s.* amúrgu ‖ **Cru:** murgíş, GOLAB 236

DUSK *vb.* (*to become dusk*) 3 *sg:* ntúnică, *aor.* ntunică

DUSKY *adj.* ntunicát; (*shadowy*) umbrós

DUST *s.* púlbire, pulvire, curñahtó, puh; (*cloud of ~*) pulbiráme, puhó; (*the human body in distinction to the spirit*) loc; **We are but dust** Him loc ‖ HRISTU 52: plubări

DUST *vb.* ▼ascútur ‖ (*as a room*) BASME 125: spúlbir

DUST OFF / OUT *vb.* (*a rug, a covering, etc.*) ▼(a)scútur, ▼spúlbir

DUST SMB.'S COAT / JACKET *vb.* (*fig. to brush off smb.'s coat*) ľi scútur yicắlu → BEAT

DUSTER *s.* (*house-cloth*) păciúră, păcivúră

DUSTING *s.* ascuturáre, spulbiráre

DUSTPAN *s.* fărắşe, făráse

DUSTY → BECOME ~

DUTEOUS *adj.* → DUTIFUL

DUTIFUL *adj.* ascultătór, -oáre; tibié *invar.*

DUTY *s.* (*moral obligation; tax*) dat; bórge; **my ~ as a teacher** dátlu a ñeu di nviţătór; (*taxation on sheep*) gilép; (*custom ~*) cumérche, yimbrúche, ghiumbrúcă; (*assigned service*) sárţină, sálţină

DWARF *s.* giugía *m, m pl* giugíañ; căcărdác (*and* -rdhác), pívul

DWARFED *adj.* pívul; *also:* astrăchít, chirchinéc, piliciós, zvumút, p(r)uzúme, *pl* p(r)uzúñ; străchitúră, vumutúră

DWARF-ELDER *s. bot.* fiĺu, ibóz, săúc, vúje *f or* vuj *m*

DWARFISH *adj.* giugía, şcurtabác → DUMPY, DWARF

DWELL *vb. (to reside)* şed; stau (→ § 32); cătichéscu; *(as of a fox)* lujéscu

DWELL UPON *vb.* para ngréc

DWELLING *s.* cásă

DWINDLE *vb.* discréscu

DYE *s.* buiáuă, hrómă, réngă, rénghe, văfíe; *(black ~ for the hair)* cână ‖ BELIMACE 29: băiáuă

DYE *vb.* ▼buiéscu, ▼văpséscu, dau réngă; *(to ~ with a dye made from dregs)* stipsuséscu; *(to ~ dark yellow)* gănguripséscu

DYEING *s.* buisíre [bui•]

DYER *s.* buiangí, buiagí, bugeáiu

DYE-WORKS *s.* buiagilấche

DYSENTERY *s.* ‖ DIARO 409: sindiríe, cufoári cu sândzi

E

EACH *pron. (every one of a group)* cariţi(n)dó [karĭ•], íchişdó (PC: [i•k'iž•dó]); *(shows the share)* câte (+ *numeral*); **You will have to pay one lira ~** Va plătíţ câte únă líră di căcĭúlă; **~ and all** cu mărĭ cu ñiţĭ; şi ñic şi máre; *adv.* → APIECE

EAGER *adj.* lingársu (dúpă); *also:* arslíu, ársu, ársu tu hicáte, iraclâ, lémaryu, *m pl* -ryi; ni-săturát

EAGERNESS *s.* cáfche, sirtlấche

EAGLE *s.* iacamgeáie → FALCON

EAR *s. anat.* ureácĺe, *dim.* uricĺúşe; *(usu. derog.)* zíĺe; *with small ~s (adj., usu. of sheep and horses)* ciul; *(of smb. with protruding ~s)* plahúrcu, pĺahúrcu, maltécicu ‖ **SJos:** stáhi, *pl* stăhi, CL 261; **Kat, Perd, Plat:** uréchi, B-ARCH 192

EAR OF CORN *s. bot. (the fruiting spike of a cereal)* schic, schícă, schícură; cuculíciu di misúr; tópă ‖ **GSus:** căcúş, *pl* căcúci (*sic*), CL 40; ALR 1o8: cucúciu 'ear of corn'

EAR OF WHEAT *s.* schic di gârnu

EARLOBE *s. anat.* ureácľe, lăpúşe

EARLY *adj.* (*usu. of vegetables or fruit*) turfandá *invar.*

EARLY *adv.* (*earlier than expected*) timpuríu, cáma tr-oáră; **earlier** ma năínte; **very ~ in the morning** di cu ndzáre; n-dzáre, andzáre; di cu noápte; tu cântáta a cucóţlor (*lit.* '*at the roosters' crowing*')

EARMARK *s.* coácă, *pl* coţi

EARN *vb.* (*to obtain*) scot, ▾amíntu, nchirdhăséscu, ▾agudéscu; **Try to ~ your bread!** Mutreá-ţ s-ţâ scoţ pânea! **He could not ~ a single nickel** Nu puteá s-agudeáscă vâră pindáră; **to ~ a living** ñ-scot pânea

EARN ONE'S CRUST *vb.* ñ-scot pânea

EARNEST MONEY *s.* căpărusíre → DEPOSIT

EARNINGS *s. pl.* scoátire, scuteáre, amintátic (*and* amindátic), amintáre, cheáre, nchirdăsíre; **There are no ~ from staying at home** Acásă nu áre scuteáre; (*illicit ~*) ghilír; (*the first year ~ of a priest paid to his bishop*) embatíche

EARRING *s.* ver *n or m*; veáre *f*, veri *pl*; ţirţél, ţirţéľu, dzirdzéľu, mănghiúş, măngiúş, minghiúş, minghiúşe; (*coin used as an ~*) péngiu [•ĝu] *m*, pénge *f*

EARTH *s.* (*world*) loc; (*soil*) ţáră, ţărnă; (*rare word*) pimíntu; **in the ~** ntroc, nturóc → ON EARTH

EARTHEN POT *s.* pótă; **earthen ware** puceáme

EARTHQUAKE *s.* cutrém, cutrémur, cutreámur, cutrimburáre a lóclui, trunduíre

EARWIG *s. ent.* gugiufoártică ‖ *Prv:* burdufoártică, CL 45

EASE *s.* efcolíe, ifcolíe, lişureáţă, zéfcă; **at ~** (*leisurely*) pri tiniháe, *N:* pi tihnáe

EASILY *adv.* lişór, éfcula, culái (*ant.* cu zórte *or* nu cu únă cu doáuă) ‖ culáina, CAPIDAN 504

EASINESS *s.* lişureáţă → FACILITY

EASING *s.* (*as of a belt*) disţíndzire; (*a bolt, a muscle*) distríndzire

EAST *s.* apreásă, dáta a soárïlui; **from the ~** di tu apreásă ‖ *Cru:* dátă, GOLAB 211 ‖ TULLIU 132: apirítă

EASTER *s.* Páşti, Gráilu-máre, *N:* Ngrei-mari ‖ *Căl:* lambrâdză,

B-ARCH 501

EASTER VESPERS *s.* ‖ ayripníe, DIARO 366

EASTER-EVE *s.* Sâmbăta-máre

EASTWARD *adv.* cătră tu apreásă, cătră soári, câtră tu dáta a soárĭlui → WESTWARD

EASY *adj.* lișór, éfcul, culái; **It doesn't come ~ to us** Nu nă yíne culái → MAKE ~

EASY COME, EASY GO (*unfairly*) ≈ haráme víñe, haráme s dúse

EAT *vb.* ▾măc, mâc, măncu (*and* mâncu, mângu), *part.* mâcát, mcat, ngat; (a)mbúc; ▾ciupléscu; **Fry this kid and ~ it!** Édlu aéstu frídzeţ-lu și ciuplíţ-lu! (*to ~ much and/or greedily*) ľau pântică, ľau búrtă, ľ-u astúp; ▾ndes, ▾deápin; **You are not going to ~ the whole cake, are you**? Va si-u deápiñ píta ntreágă? **He ~s a lot** Ľ-arúcă múltu tu cărcheáuă ‖ BATSARIA 6 *and* 93: bag sum náre; CAPIDAN 151: (a)ngán

EAT HUMBLE PIE *vb.* ≈ lu aspândzur cáplu

EAT MEAT *vb.* ▾puríndu; **If you ate meat you should not take the sacrement** Máca ti purindáși, s-nu ti cumâniţi

EAT THE FAT OF THE LAND *vb.* bănédz ca dzúua ţea álba

EAT TO A SURFEIT *vb.* ▾sátur, ▾(a)năfătéscu; adár pântica ciuflĭícă → SURFEIT

EATER *s.* mâcătór; **great ~** ľúftă *m*, ľúfteañ *pl*

EATERY *s.* mihănă, mihéne, miéne, lucántă, háne

EATING *s.* (*much and/or fast*) arucutíre

EAVES *s. pl.* (a)streáhă, (a)stráhă, chícută, hátule, hutúle, puiátă

EAVESDROP *vb.* ascúltu, bag ureácľa, ▾ciuléscu cu ureácľa ‖ *Prv:* crifascúltu, *cf.* B-ARCH 194

EBONY *s.* abanózi *f*

ECCENTRIC *adj.* (*curious, strange*) paráxin; tuţ cálea - nâs válea (≈ [*when*] *all are going up - he is going down*)

ECCLESIASTICAL *adj.* văc(u)féscu

ECHO *s.* arăsunáre, aru-

ECONOMICAL *adj.* (*thrifty*) icunumiseáric

ECONOMIZE *vb.* (*to ~ stingily*) șcľinciuéscu [•ĉu•és•]

ECONOMY *s.* icunumíe, cumándă

ECZEMA *s. med.* aruvirsáre, arăbudzináre

EDDY *s.* vâltoáre

EDEMA *s.* (*dropsy*) andrópică

EDGE *s.* márdzine, márdzină, múhľe; (*the cutting side of a knife*) tăľitúră, lipídhă; (*a steep edge of a brook*) arâpă, rípă; **to be on the ~** şed ca pri schiñ ‖ **Peş:** (*the cutting ~ of a scythe*) mirahúni, CL 255

EDUCATE *vb.* créscu, prăxéscu; (*to study*) ▼yrămătipséscu; ▼nvéţ cárti

EDUCATED *adj.* cu cárte, cu pátru ócľi, dişcľís, yiuvăsít, nviţát, ócľi discľíşi, ştiút, prucupsít, purcupsít; (*refined, well-mannered*) pilichisít

EDUCATION *s.* creáştire, prucuchíe

EEL *s. ichth.* uhéľe, hióle [hǐó•]

EERIE *adj.* lăhtărós, ciudós, fricós

EFFACEMENT *s.* (a)şteárdzire

EFFECT: → TAKE ~

EFFEMINATE *adj.* fiteái [fi•teáǐ] *m*, fiteáiañ *pl*

EFFLORESCENCE *s.* luludhyisíre

EFFORT *s.* spreámiţă, eneryisíre → MAKE AN ~, MAKE ~S; (*trouble*) cópus ‖ CUNIA 98: alămăseári

EFFRONTERY *s.* nĭ-aruşináre, yumărlâche, cutidzáre

EGG *s.* ou, *pl* oáuă; (*painted or decorated ~ at Easter*) pirdhíc; (*premature ~ with no shell*) prólog, *pl* proloádze; **fried ~s** oáuă ócľi, oáuă mproáste; **Gop, Mul:** ghélă din cur; **nest ~** (*used to make hens lay ~s*) foľu

EGGHEAD *s.* prucupsít → EDUCATED

EGGPLANT *s.* pitligeánă

EGGSHELL *s.* coáje di ou ‖ **Cern, Pdz:** coájă, **Trn:** coáze di uou; **Grăm:** cíflă, **Mul:** cíflă di ou, **Smx:** ceáflă, **Grbţ:** céflă di ou, **Prv:** cióflă di ou *and* flúdhă di ou, **Hor:** peájă di ou, **Pals:** şcoárchi di ou; **Kast:** ţâflă, **Am:** ţúflă, **Hal:** ţôflă, B-ARCH 295

EGLANTINE *s. bot.* măcéş (*and* mâ-); *also:* arúg; **Smr:** bubzél; culumbrí; curubíţ, şípcă, zíyră, ayru-trandafiľáuă; (*the fruit*) măceáşe, muceáşe *sg*

EGYPT *s.* Misiríe

EIGHT *num.* óptu; **~ of them were wise and the ninth was dumb** Óptuľ eará mintióşi şi noáulu eará chirút; **the room where the ~ girls were sleeping** udălu iu durñá óptule feáte; **during the ~ days that I remained there** óptuli dzále ţe şidzúi acló

EIGHTEEN *num.* óptusprădzaţe, óptuspraţi, óptusprǎ

EIGHTY *num.* opdzăţi, ubdzăţi ‖ optudzătsi, opdzătsi, ᴋ-ᴅ 70

EITHER ... OR (*and* **NEITHER ... NOR**) ba ..., ba ...; i ...,
i ...; ia ..., ia ...; ne ..., ne ...; ori ..., i ...; va ..., va
...; ~ **a man, or an animal** ba om, ba právdǎ; ~ **you, or we**; i voĭ,
i noĭ; ~ **you, or he** ia tíne, ia el; **neither white, nor black** ne
álbu, ne laiu; **either dead, or alive** va moártǎ, va yíe (*f sg*)

EKE OUT ONE'S EXISTENCE *vb.* puripséscu, prăpséscu, am yitríe

ELABORATE POLITENESS *s. pl.* náze *f*, năji *pl*; camómate *f pl*; cod
n, coáde *pl*

ELAPSE *vb.* (*of days, weeks, etc.*) trec; ▾deápin

ELASTIC *adj.* **Cĺis:** jílav

ELATE *vb.* ▾hăriséscu → REJOICE

ELBOW *s.* cot *or* cod, *pl* coáte *or* coáde, cóturi, coţ

ELDER *adj. m/f sg* máre, *pl m/f* mărĭ; ma máre

ELDERBERRY FLOWERS *s.* lilíce de usâc; lălíţĭ

ELDERBERRY JUICE / WINE *s.* lilícǎ; **Amc:** lalíţǎ

ELDERLY *adj.* tu añ

ELDER-TREE *s. bot.* soc; *also:* (i)bóz, prófe, sâmbúc (*and*
zâmbúc), sǎúc, suúg, sug, usúc; ştog; vuj *m, and* vúje *f*

ELECTIONS *s. pl.* ‖ **Cru:** icluyíi, ɢᴏʟᴀʙ 221

ELEGANT *adj.* chibárcu, prăpsít, pripsít

ELEPHANT *s.* eléfandu, fildişín, fiĺu, fil, sfildíciu

ELEVATE *vb.* ▾álţu → RAISE

ELEVATION *s.* nălţíme, (a)nălţáre, m(u)táre; (*elevated place*)
óhtu, *pl.* oáhte → HILL

ELEVEN *num.* únăsprădzaţe, únspraţi, únsprǎ, úsprǎs

ELIMINATE *vb.* scot; (*as a name from a list*) fac arisíte

ELITE *s.* athérǎ, danélǎ; **the ~ of his army** danéla a oástiĺei a
lui; **N:** căimác *n*, **S:** căimáche *f*

ELL *s.* (*unity of length*) píhe

ELM *s.* úlmu, cărăyáciu, meĺu ‖ **SJos:** miringéu, ᴄʟ 255

ELONGATE *vb.* ▾lundzéscu, spirlundzéscu

ELONGATED *adj.* spirlúngu, spri-; spirlungós

ELONGATION *s.* lundzíre, sprilundzíre

ELOPE *vb.* fug

ELOPEMENT *s.* fúgǎ, fudzíre

ELSE *adj.* alt *or* áltu *m*, álta *f*

ELSEWHERE *adv.* naľúrea; **to be ~** ñ-azboárǎ (→ ABSENTMINDED); **His thoughts were ~** şi-imná cu míntea cǎtrǎ naľúrea

ELUCIDATE *vb.* ľ-dau di fúndu (*lit. 'to get to the bottom of it'*)

EMACIATE *vb. med.* ▼usâc, usúc; **~d** *adj.* súptu (*lit. 'sucked'*)

EMACIATION *s. med.* zúrǎ; (*process*) supţâráre, slǎghíre

EMANCIPATE *vb.* → SET FREE

EMBALM *vb.* mbǎlsǎmédz; **~MENT** *s.* bǎlsǎmusíre

EMBANK *vb.* ▼apitruséscu ‖ PC: fac óhtu, adár oáhte

EMBARK *vb.* (*on a boat*) ▼vǎrcǎrséscu

EMBARKATION *s.* vǎrcǎrsíre

EMBARRASS *vb.* (*to place in difficulty*) ▼stinuhurséscu, buiséscu

EMBARRASSING *adj.* béte *invar.;* **a quite ~ situation** ca béte luyu-ríe

EMBARRASSMENT *s.* biľé, biľáuǎ, cánge, scánce (*and* scánge)

EMBELLISH *vb.* muşiţǎscu, muşuţǎscu

EMBELLISHMENT *s.* (*decorations, as in a rich house*) stóluzmǎ, stólizmǎ

EMBER *s.* jar, tǎciúne *m,* citúne *m;* cirlác *m;* (*small ~*) **Bit:** clécicǎ [kléĉ•kǎ]; **to make** *or* **to become ~** (*of firewood*) njirédz ‖ HRISTU 7, 42: juráti

EMBITTER *vb.* ▼amǎrǎscu, ñ-si nfǎrmácǎ ínima, mi nfármǎc

EMBITTERMENT *s.* amǎrâre, nfǎrmǎcáre → BITTERNESS

EMBODY *vb.* ▼(ân)trupuéscu, ▼ntrupuşédz

EMBOLDEN *vb.* âñ bag ciulíche la iñoárǎ → ENCOURAGE

EMBRACE *s.* ambrǎţáre

EMBRACE *vb.* ▼ambráţ, ▼mbrǎţişédz, mbrǎţuşédz, ▼stríngu ân brá-ţǎ, N (*rare*) strângu; angǎliséscu, puştuéscu, ncurpíľu, ncurpi-lédz (*and* ngur-), ncrupilédz, ngrupilédz, ncrupulédz

EMBRACING *s.* mbrǎţişeáre, ngurpiľáre, angǎľisíre, puştuíre

EMBROIDER *vb.* chindiséscu, trimédz, trǎmédz, vizuéscu

EMBROIDERY *s.* chéndimǎ, chíndimǎ (*and* chíndhimǎ), chindínǎ, şabác, şubác; (*on the sleeves of a woman's blouse*) óimǎ

EMBROIL *vb.* (*to entangle*) ▼(n)cǎrşilédz, ▼birdhipséscu, ▼mbir-dhuéscu, ▼ambǎrtuéscu, hurhuléscu

EMBROILING *s.* cǎrşire

EMBROILMENT *s.* (*complication, misunderstanding*) birdhipsíre, mintitúrǎ, síyise → CONFUSION

EMBRYO *s.* (*of a child*) fitáľu, CAPIDAN 146

EMERGE *vb.* ies, *aor.* i(n)şíi *or* i(n)şái

EMINENT *adj.* aléptu, *f* -eáptă, *m pl* -épţâ, *f pl* -eápte

EMIT SMOKE *vb.* afúm

EMOTION *s.* sínhise

EMPEROR *s.* amiră(u), văsiľé; **EMPRESS** *s.* ami(ră)roáñe, văsiloáñe

EMPEROR MOTH *s.* *enthom.* câne di la oi

EMPIRE *s.* amiráľe, amirăríľe, amirălíche

EMPLOY *vb.* (*to hire, to be hired*) ▼arughéscu, ▼bag tu pâne

EMPLOY ALL ONE'S WITS *vb.* ▼frimíntu

EMPLOYED *adj.* (*hired*) arugát, păitít, puitít

EMPLOYMENT *s.* lúcru, pâne

EMPTY *adj.* dişértu, -eártă, -érţâ, -eárte; gol, goálă, goľ, goále; pústu, *m pl* púşti *and* púşţâ, *f pl* púşte; (*vain*) şcret; (*unloaded, emptied*) dişirtát; (*of empty eggshells and fig. as of smb.'s head*) clúvyiu ‖ BATSARIA 60: **to feed smb. on ~ words** ľ-víndu goále

EMPTY *vb.* dişértu, guléscu, pustuxéscu, pustixéscu; (*of a liquid*) ▼vérsu, ▼stricór ‖ STERE 101: durduséscu

EMPTY TALK *s.* vrúte şi ni-vrúte

EMPTY-HEADED *adj.* cap-di-gáie (*lit. 'crow's head'*) → STUPID

EMPTYING *s.* dişertáre, gulíre, virsáre

EMPTINESS *s.* gulăciúne, vânătáte

ENAMEL *s.* smáltu

ENAMOURED *adj.* erotipsít; sivdălâ, sivdaľíu, -dălíu, sivdălós

ENCAMPMENT *s.* câşlă, ştirnumíntu

ENCHAIN *vb.* leg tu singír

ENCHANT *vb.* ▼alín, ▼aumbrédz, amăyipséscu, bizdiséscu; căidiséscu, cântu, ▼leg; **They will ~ them with nice words** Va li alínă cu zboárile; **The boy is not doing well; someone might have ~ him** Ficĭórlu da năpói; va lu-aumbráră

ENCHANTED *adj.* amăyipsít, aumbrós, căntát (*and* cân-), discântát, loát di vále; di fáptu; **Some were saying that he was ~** Nâscânţâ dzâţeá că-i di fáptu; **~ bird** puľu cântát; **~ water** ápă discântátă

ENCHANTMENT *s.* cântáre, discântáre, fáptu, cântáre ş discântáre

ENCHANTER *s.* măyístru, palongheár

ENCHANTRESS s. mándisă, măyístră, palongheáră

ENCIRCLE vb. țírcľu, nțírcľu, țircľédz, nțircľédz; anvărlighédz
→ SURROUND

ENCIRCLE WITH WALLS vb. stizmuséscu

ENCIRCLEMENT s. (with walls) stizmusíre

ENCIRCLING s. (as on the battlefield) anvălíre, anvărligáre,
ngurpíre, nțircľáre

ENCLOSE vb. ▾ncľid, **F:** nchid; (~ with walls) stizmuséscu; (with
a fence) ngărdédz, ngărdéscu; nțércľu

ENCLOSURE s. (with a fence) ngărdíre, nțărăcáre; (with walls)
stizmusíre

ENCOMPASS vb. ▾anvăr(l)íg, anvărlighédz, nțércľu; țircľédz,
nțircľédz

ENCOUNTER m. adunáre, astăleáre, astălitúră, andámuse, andă-
musíre, stăvrusíre, afláre; (combat) băteáre, ncârligáre

ENCOUNTER vb. ▾adún, ▾astáľu, dau chéptu cu

ENCOURAGE vb. ▾mbărbătédz, ľ-fac găiréte [gă•i•ré•ti], inimuséscu ‖ HRISTU 29: dau giunami

ENCOURAGEMENT s. inimusíre, mbărbătáre, găiréte; **N:** găirée

ENCROACH vb. arúc cătuhíe (pri), ▾zăptiséscu

ENCROACHMENT s. zăptisíre

ENCUMBER vb. ▾ambudhiséscu, mbudhuéscu

END s. (as of a meeting, of a market day) aspártă, bitisíre,
bițíre, bitisítă, burítă, buríre, cap, cápit, coádă, ișítă, măr-
dzínă, scólzumă, sculáre, sóne; **at the ~** năpói; **at the world's ~**
(very far away) dúpă soáre; iu bea púľi ápă; tu ascápitlu a ló-
cului; **in the ~** tu bitisítă, tu coádă; **the ~ of the world** biti-
síta a lúmiľei; **The ~ crowns the work** Sónea aleádze; **until the ~
of your life** pân-tu buríta a bánăľei a tăei; **It won't have an ~**
Nu va s-áibă scólzumă; **All will have such an ~** Toț va s-áibă sónea țea; **at the ~ of the month** tu ișíta a méslui; **no ~ of** (innumerable) ca sprúna ș-ca arína; **right to the bitter ~** pân tu amín;
pánă tu chiaméte; pánă la ploáce; (as of a burning house) pân di
furígă ‖ HRISTU 101: son → BRING TO AN ~, COME TO AN ~, MAKE BOTH
~S MEET, MAKE AN ~ OF SMTH.

END vb. (to break up) ▾aspárgu; (of a month, year) es, ies; (of
summer, of youth, etc.) ▾duc; (to ~ almost completely) ▾apu-fac;
(last stage of a series of changes) cătăndiséscu; **They ~ed up by**

END IN SMOKE

becoming brigands Cătăndisíră cu furlíchea ‖ TULLIU 124: *3 sg.*
aor. si-ncľié → FINISH, CUT OFF

END IN SMOKE *vb.* fac piripáchĭ; **It ~ed in smoke** Ţívale si-a-
leápse; fac jir; **His money ~ed in smoke** Parádzľi jir ľi feáţi; ≈
ti éră ş-ti séră ‖ BASME 364: li mâcă lúplu (*lit. 'The wolf ate*
them')

ENDANGER *vb.* ▾chindinipséscu

ENDEAR *vb.* âñ cáde tu vreáre

ENDEARMENT *s.* miyléme, cănáche, hăidhipsíre

ENDEAVOR *vb.* ▾dhuchimiséscu, cătăpăţéscu

ENDLESSLY *adv.* păn tru éta a étiľi

ENDMOST *adj.* din coádă, cudár, códus, coáda

ENDORSMENT *s.* izíne, vóľe, astrăxíre, sinfonipsíre

ENDOW *vb.* dhuruséscu (*and* duruséscu), dhurséscu → PRESENT

ENDOWMENT *s.* dhurusíre (*and* durusíre)

ENDURANCE *s.* arăvdáre, arăvdăciúne, văstăxíre → PATIENCE

ENDURE *vb.* ▾arávdu; *also:* (*to tolerate*) apufiréscu, astăxéscu,
hunipséscu; (*to suffer*) trag

ENEMA PUMP *s.* *med.* clistír, ylistír

ENEMY *s.* duşmán, éhtru, éhtur, házmu, ni-oáspe ‖ HRISTU 19, 25:
azmu, *pl* azñĭă; DIARO 433: **I do not have enemies, I have only**
friends Nu-ámu éhţri, am maşi oáspiţ

ENERGETIC *adj.* bărbătín, sárpe; **an ~ woman** mure bărbătínă

ENERGETICALLY *adv.* bărbăteáşte

ENERGY *s.* p(u)teáre, véte, enéryie

ENFEEBLE *vb.* (*to weaken*) adhinăţéscu

ENFEEBLED *adj.* loat la fáţă

ENFOLD *vb.* (*to cover*) ▾anvăléscu; (*to embrace*) ▾mbrăţişédz

ENFRANCHISE *vb.* → SET FREE

ENGAGE *vb.* (*to pledge to marry*) ▾arăvuñiséscu, ▾isuséscu, ▾a-
rúc tuféchea

ENGAGED *adj.* arăvuñisít, isusít

ENGAGEMENT *s.* arăvoánă, arăvuñisíre, isósmă, isósmată; **to break**
an ~ ▾disuséscu

ENGAGING *adj.* arâsít; nóstim, *m pl* -tiñ, *f pl* -time

ENGENDER *vb.* fac, dau

ENGINEER *s.* mindíz

ENGINEERING *s.* mindizlâche

ENGLISH *adj.* ingléz, -ză, *m pl* -éjĭ, *f pl* -éze; inglizéscu, -zeáscă, -zéşţâ, -zéşti

ENGRAVE *vb.* sap; **ENGRAVING** *s.* săpătúră

ENGROSSED *adj.* (*absorbed in thought*) minduít

ENHANCE *vb.* ▾ndreg

ENJOY *vb.* ▾hăriséscu, hărăséscu, hărséscu, ▾fac cu haráuă, mi ľa haráua; **I don't ~ looking at him** Eu nu-l fac háze

ENJOYMENT *s.* → FUN

ENLARGE *vb.* ▾măréscu, ▾adávgu, ▾ngróş

ENLARGEMENT *s.* măríre, ngruşeáre → INCREMENT

ENLIGHTEN *vb.* fac tirbié, ▾nvéţ

ENLIGHTENED *adj.* (*educated*) dişcľís → BECOME ~

ENLIST *vb.* (*to enroll*) mi scriu

ENLIVEN *vb.* (*to animate*) ▾ncucutédz

ENMITY *s.* arăiáţă, duşmăníľe, éhtră, ihtríľe, ni-uspiţâľe, zăte ‖ TULLIU 59: hăzmălăchi

ENORMITY *s.* (*monstrousness*) urâteáţă, lăiáţă

ENORMOUSLY *adv.* ‖ fără márdzine, CAPIDAN 175

ENOUGH *adj.* and *adv.* distúr, *Mul:* distúl; *adv.* distúre; dúre, i(n)sáfe, nisáfe, máltu, nimál, nimálo, nămálo, di nimál; **There was ~ heat in the house** N cásă erá căldúră distúra; **These words are ~** Máltu aíste zboáră; **(Stop it,) you have had enough!** Dúri-ţ-u! **God gave me ~ wealth** Ñ-deáde Dumnidză aveáre di nimál; **to have ~** (*plenty*) ñ-aséscu; **I have more than ~** Am ş pri am; **It is ~** Agiúndze ('It suffices') ‖ (*interjectionally or as a command*) báea, DIARO 387

ENRAGE *vb.* ▾ngíndu, inătuséscu, túrbu, trub, lisixéscu ‖ PC: mi-acáţă inátea; **Don't enrage me!** Nu mi adáră s-mi acáţă ináteá! *or* Nu mi crápă! → MAKE SMB. BESIDE HIMSELF

ENRAGED *adj.* inătusít; (*of a woman*) arápsă (*lit.* 'Arab woman')

ENRAPTURE *vb.* (a)măyipséscu, ▾leg → BEWITCH

ENRICH *vb.* avuţéscu, bag zvércă, ▾mbugăţăscu → BECOME RICH, MAKE RICH

ENROLL *vb.* scriu; **We were ~ing the young men into the army** Scriám gióñľi tru nizáme

ENSLAVE *vb.* (a)rubuéscu, ▾sclăvu(s)éscu

ENSLAVEMENT *s.* (a)rubuíre, sclăvu(s)íre

ENSNARE *vb.* ▾acáţ

ENTANGLE

ENTANGLE *vb.* (*to embroil, to confuse*) ▾ncărşiľédz, ▾cărşiléz

ENTANGLED *adj.* ciuf, *m pl* cĭuhĭ, *f pl* ciúfe; ncărşít, cărşiľát

ENTANGLEMENT *s.* (*intricacy, perplexity*) birdhipsíre, mbirdhu-íre, cărşéľ, cârşíľ, mintitúră, síyise → CONFUSION

ENTER *vb.* ▾bag, mi arúc tu, dau tu, íntru; ([**He**] ~s the vine-yard si-arúcă tu ayíñe; **I ~ed the house** Intrái n cásă

ENTERING *s.* intráre (*and* indráre): intrátă

ENTERTAIN *vb.* (*to amuse*) ▾şuitéscu

ENTHUSIASM *s.* ‖ PC: haráuă mári

ENTHUSIASTIC *adj.* miraclí; ľ-si fătă Hristólu n cásă → HAPPY

ENTICE *vb.* bag pri sómnu, plăn(ăs)éscu

ENTICED → BE ~

ENTICEMENT *s.* băgáre pri sómnu, plăníre, plănăsíre

ENTIRE *adj.* tut *m*, tútă *f*

ENTIRELY *adv.* dicutót → COMPLETELY

ENTRAILS *s.* minuţále *f pl*; ľánumă, *pl* ľanómate; *G:* yinómate *pl* ‖ *Prv:* ľácăti, *SJos:* leácati, CL 254

ENTRANCE *s.* intráre (*and* indráre)

ENTRAP *vb.* ▾acáţ

ENTREAT *vb.* ţer, ▾(a)ngréc, cilistiséscu, pălăcărséscu, părlă-căséscu; (*rare word*) ▾rog

ENTREATING *adj.* rigeagí, *m pl* rigeageádz

ENTREATY *s.* arigé, cilistisíre → REQUEST

ENTRENCHMENT *s.* fusáte, fsat, tábye, tăbyíe

ENTRUST *vb.* fac tislíme, para-dáu; **I've ~ed the sheep to him** Óile ľi li feciu tislíme

ENTRY *s.* intráre (*and* indráre)

ENUMERATE *vb.* (a)númir

ENVELOP *vb.* ▾(a)nvăléscu, (a)nvilscu, amviléscu → COVER, WRAP UP

ENVELOPE *s.* plic, fáchil

ENVELOPMENT *s.* anvălíre

ENVIABLE *adj.* trâ ziľu

ENVIOUS *adj.* eryatáric, ftuñárcu, ftuñirós, nchismatáric ‖ ALR 1250: zilipsít

ENVISION *vb.* ▾privéd, pruvéd

ENVY *s.* písmă, pízmă, nchísmă, chísmă, chízmă, nchizmuíre, limăryisíre, ziľ, zilíe, zilipsíre; **out of ~** di zilíe

ENVY *vb*. nchizmăséscu, nchizmuséscu, zilipséscu, zulipséscu, am ziľu (pri); ▼fingărséscu, ▼ftuniséscu, ftunséscu, limăryiséscu, limăxéscu, limuxéscu ‖ fac ntr-óčľi, BASME 308

EPIDEMIC *s*. epidhimíe, mólimă, ni-puţáme

EPIGASTRIUM *s*. *anat*. linguríce

EPILEPTIC *s*. *3 sg*: cáde nafoáră

EPIPHANY *s*. Buboáte, Boboátim, Bubuteáză, Pătigiúne, Fóta *f sg*, *or* Fótile *f pl def*

EPISCOPATE *s*. eparhíe, episcopíe, episcopát

EPISODE *s*. (*occurrence*) tihisíre

EPITAPH *s*. (*funeral oration on Easter's eve*) pitáfil, epitáfiu

EPSOM SALT *s*. sáre

EQUAL *adj*. is *m*, ísă *f*, işĭ *m pl*, íse *f pl*; ísea, íşea, únă cu, uigúne; **Not all are equal** Nu súntu tuţ uigúne → BE ~ TO

EQUAL *vb*. ▼agiúngu, ahârdzéscu; **You have ~ed him in bravery** Lu-agiúmsişi tu giuneáţă

EQUALLY *adv*. ísa, ísea, íşea, únă; **The sun rises ~ for every-body** Tră toţ soárĭle da únă

EQUILIBRIUM *s*. tirizí

EQUIPAGE *s*. (*outfit*) tăcâme

EQUIPMENT *s*. tăcâme

EQUIPPED *adj*. (*rigged out*) armătusít; *G*: (*as of horses*) tăc-mâlát

EQUITABLE *adj*. ímnă cu zíya n brân (*is always with a balance at his/her belt, i.e. is ready to impart justice*)

EQUIVOCAL *adj*. anvărligós; ~ **words** zboáre anvărligoáse; ne úda, ne uscáta (*lit. 'neither dry, nor wet'*)

EQUIVOCALLY *adv*. ne úda, ne uscáta

-ER *suffix of the comparative* **1.** ma + *adj. or adv*. (**smarter than him** ma diştéptu di nâs); **2.** cáma + *adj. or adv*. (**The older caravanner said** Dzíse cama aúşlu chiragí)

ERADICATE *vb*. ▼zmúlgu; (*exterminate*) ▼(m)buréscu

ERADICATION *s*. zmúldzire, zmuldzeáre

ERASE *vb*. ▼aştérgu

ERASED *adj*. aştérsu, -eársă, -érşi, -eárse

ERECT *vb*. (*to build*) ▼álţu, (a)nálţu; (*as a hut, a swing*) (a)stăséscu, (a)stiséscu, bag, ▼mbróstu

ERELONG *adv*. ayónea, curúndu, crúndu

ERODE *vb.* ▼aród

ERR *vb.* (a)lăthipséscu, lăthăséscu, fti(p)séscu, stipséscu

ERRATIC *adj.* cu órile

ERRONEOUS *adj.* (a)lăthipsít, lăthăsít, ftixít, ftisít, stipsít

ERROR *s.* sfálmă → COMMIT AN ~; MISTAKE

ERUDITE *s.* iľumáie *f*, iľumăi *pl*

ERYSIPELAS *s. derm.* fócă, nimupírimă

ESCALATE *vb.* créscu

ESCALATION *s.* creáştire, crişteáre

ESCAPE *s.* (a)scăpáre, discăpáre; (*safety, salvation*) sileaméte; **I had a narrow ~** Pi hir víñe s-chérdu cáplu; (*getting rid of*) cutursíre → MAKE ONE'S ~

ESCAPE *vb.* (a)scáp (→ § 32), discáp, asuséscu, ▼curturiséscu, curturséscu; (*to get away, usu. by flight*) ľ-ľau fúmlu; **He ~ed** Ľ-loai fúmlu (*lit.* 'I got his smoke,' i.e. his fart)

ESCAPE BY A HAIR'S BREATH *vb.* ‖ ascáp ca di pri per, BASME 295

ESCAPE WITH LIFE AND LIMB *vb.* (*to escape with one's life*) ▼(a)scăp cu yeáţă, (a)scáp di moárti

ESCARPMENT *s.* (a)râpă, rípă

ESCORT *vb.* pitréc, duc

ESCORTING *s.* pitreácă

ESOPHAGUS *s. anat.* glâcă

ESPECIALLY *adv.* maxutárcu ‖ LITURG 123: ahóryea

ESPIONAGE *s.* spiunlâche

ESSENCE *s.* usíe

ESSENTIAL *adj.* (*necessary, indispensable, inherent, unavoidable*) ≈ cáşlu nu s-adáră fâră cľag (*lit.* 'Cheese cannot be made without rennet')

ESTABLISH *vb.* ▼(a)stăséscu, ▼taľu; **A salary will be ~ed for him** Va să-ľ si táľe únă arúgă; (*a church, etc.*) ▼stiriuséscu

ESTABLISHMENT *s.* (*religious ~*) văcúfe

ESTATE *s.* (*property in land*) ciflíche, ciuflíche, fármă, múlche, numíe; **small ~** báştină, báşnă

ESTEEM *s.* (i)htibáre, măríľe, treácă; *G:* mále; **He does not esteem you at all** Ici nu ti fáţe mále

ESTEEM *vb.* am ihtibáre (ti), ľi fac ihtibáre; lu fac mále

ESTEEMED *adj.* anguñát, tiñisít; cu anamúze

ESTIMABLE *adj.* (*worthy of esteem*) tiñisít → ESTEEMED

ESTIVAL *adj.* → AESTIVAL

ESTRANGED *adj.* (a)xinitór, -oáre; axenít; xinitimén, *m pl* -méñ

ETERNALLY *adv.* (*forever*) tră tótna, di dáima

ETERNITY *s.* zămáne, étă

ETHER *s.* anódhim

ETIQUETTE *s.* țirimóñe

EULOGIZE *vb.* ▼álțu

EULOGY *s.* alăvdăciúne

EUNUCH *s.* hadúm, *pl* hadúmeani, *G:* hudúm

EUPHORIA *s.* ghineáță

EUROPE *s.* Evrópe

EUROPEAN *adj.* (*civilized, ant. of Levantine, Balkan*) frâncu (*and* frângu), fréncu, frânțéscu (*and* frănțéscu, frăndzéscu); *adv.* a-la-fránga (*ant.* a-la-túrca)

EVACUATE *vb.* (*to empty*) dișértu, guléscu

EVADE *vb.* (*to elude*) ascáp, ▼a(m)firéscu, fug

EVALUATE *vb.* → VALUE

EVAPORATE *vb.* (*to pass off in vapor*) hiriséscu, ▼azvímtur

EVASION *s.* (*expedient, dodge*) frâmtúră; (*escape*) fúgă

EVE: **on the ~ of** (a)piríndu, apríndu ‖ BASME 679: príndu

EVEN *adj.* ísea; **Even reckoning makes long friends** ≈ Fráte, fráte, ma cáșlu-i cu parádz → EQUAL; BREAK ~

EVEN *vb.* hiu ísea ‖ PB: fac ísea; (*to level*) ▼ischédz

EVEN (*used as an intensive word*) și, ș; **~ if I tell you, you cannot help me** și s-țâ spun, s mi-ajúț nu poț; mácar, macárim; **He would not commit perjury ~ if you tortured him** Nu giurá strâmbu, macárim si-l vătămái; **Not ~ a crumb has remained** Uná sârmă nu-și armáse

EVENHANDED *adj.* driptátic

EVENING *s.* seáră; **this ~** astáră, ástă-seáră; **It was late in the ~** Erá seáră oáră; **towards ~** tu nsirátă, pi nsirátă, ñádză-oáră, di cátră seáră; **Good ~!** (*when coming in*) Búnă seáră! (*when leaving*) Seáră búnă! ‖ CUVATA 8: **toward the ~** piningă seáră → BE CAUGHT BY THE ~

EVENING *adj.* di seáră

EVENING PARTY *s.* suțâľe

EVENING STAR *s.* luțeáfir *or* luțeáfire *m*; luțeáfirlu di seáră

EVENT *s.* (**actual ~**) fáptă

EVENTUALLY *adv.* (**in the end**) tu burítă, tu sónă; tu márdzine, cáma tu márdzine, până ma dinăpói; *N:* daporpóia ‖ n-coádă PC

EVER *adv.* vârnăoáră, nițidânâoáră; **Have you ~ seen him? Never!** L-vidzúşi vârnăoáră? Várnăoáră → NEVER

EVERMORE *adv.* → FOREVER

EVERY *adj.* íțe, íțişi, cáthi, *N:* cáfe; *Gop:* cáse-un *m*, cáse-únă *f*; cátheşi-un; pása, pásă; şi ñic şi máre; sfáca *invar*; **in ~ place, in ~ house** tu íți loc, tu íți cásă; **~ one of you** cáfi un di voi; **He goes there ~ other year** S-dúțe cáthi doi añ; **~ evening** pása seáră; **~ now and then** di oáră oáră

EVERY NOW AND THEN *adv.* ori, ori → FROM TIME TO TIME

EVERY ONCE IN A WHILE *adv.* ori, ori

EVERYBODY *pron.* tut ínslu, íți om, duñáe, *N:* duñáuă, *pl* duñéi; **~ cried** plâmse nă duñáe ntreágă; **You should also listen to what ~ is saying** Ascúltă şi zboárile a duñáuăľei

EVERYONE → EVERYBODY

EVERYTHING *pron.* tut, íțe; **She had a son and he was ~** şĭ-aveá un ficiór ş-tut

EVERYWHERE *adv.* tu tot lóclu, n toáte părțâle, toátă rádha ‖ BASME 25: din sus ân ghios

EVICT *vb.* (*to force out*) scot (din)

EVIDENCE *s.* (*attestation*) imzáe

EVIDENT *adj.* límbid, límpide, ayimlíu → CLEAR

EVIL *s.* (a)rău, *pl* arále; s(c)lab; slăbínță, aspărgăciúne

EVIL *adj.* s(c)lab, *pl m* s(c)laghi, *f pl* s(c)lábe; laiu, *f* láie, *m/f pl* lăi; puşcľós, niñiruít, uchinát, murtăráuă *f*; **I came across an ~ man** Ded di om laiu; **to have ~ designs on/against smb.** lu mutréscu n-aráulea

EVIL EYE *s.* **to fall under the spell of an ~** ľau di ócľu; **You may have fallen under the spell of an ~** Nápa ñ-loaşĭ di ócľu → CAST THE ~ ‖ ócľu aráu (*Also in Mod. Greek*, see PARALLELE 121); BASME 136: **God protect you from the ~** S nu-ț híbă di ócľu!

EVIL SPELL *s.* văscăníe

EVIL SPIRIT *s.* har, DIARO 426

EVIL-DOER *s.* cacurízic, batác, bătác; cătíle *invar.*

EVIL-DOING *s.* strămbeáță, urâteáță

EVIL-MINDED *adj.* andíhristu, -stă, -şțâ, -ste; antártu

EVINCE *vb.* ▾apudhixéscu

EVISCERATE *vb.* ▾(di)spântic , vérsu máṭăle

EVISCERATION *s.* (di)spânticáre, dizmăṭáre

EWE *s.* oáie; (*milking ~ without lamb*) mătrícă, mitrícă, muldzá-ră, muldzárcă; *Src:* ṭangádhe; *coll.* mătricáme ‖ *GSus:* mutrícâ, CL 256; **sterile ~** biroáñe, GOLAB 208; **~-lamb** ñálă, m(b)ľoáră

EWER *s.* liyén, liyéne, lién, liéne, iléne

EXACTION *s.* (*extortion, excessive taxation*) haráṭumă

EXACT *adj.* saí *invar.*

EXACTITUDE *s.* (*of a scale, of a clock, of smb.'s mind*) aiáre

EXACTLY *adv.* giústa, giústu, n cap, pắnă tu per, saí, tam *or* tamám; **~ at six o'clock** la şeáse oára giústa; **~ at this time** giústu tu aístă oáră; **It is ~ the middle of the summer** I tamám ñádză-veáră; **~ when she was combing her hair** tamám tu oára cându-şi chiptiná pérlu; **Since then ~ two years have passed** Di-atúmṭea tricúră doi añ ân cap; **~ one year** un an cu ánlu; (*of time*) cu oára ‖ (*to a hair*) BASME 438: pắnă tu per; HRISTU 47: **~** tamam aşă

EXAGGERATE *vb.* li ngruşédz, li adávgu, li adávgu lúcrile, adár hírlu fúne, u fác di per fúne ‖ (*to misinterpret, as smb.'s words*) li créscu (zboárâli), DIARO 311

EXAGGERATION *s.* adăvgáre

EXAGGERATED *adj.* (*of statements, news, etc.*) ncoárniş

EXALT *vb.* eftihipséscu, eftihiséscu

EXAMINATION *s.* exétase, dhuchimăsíre, *G:* íspit

EXAMINE *vb.* (*inspect closely*) xităxéscu, xităséscu, sătăxéscu, sităséscu; (*of a doctor*) ved; **The doctor ~ed me thoroughly** Yeátrul mi vidzú ghíne ‖ (*to interrogate, to question*) TULLIU 115: căftărescu

EXAMPLE *s.* parádhiymă, urnéche, iurnécă; (*harsh reprimand, lesson*) ibréte; **give ~s** (*by terror*) dau ibréte

EXARCH *s.* (*head of an independent church; governor*) exárhu

EXARCHATE *s.* exarhát, exarhíe

EXASPERATE *vb.* scot geánlu, scot súflitlu

EXCAVATE *vb.* sap; târchéscu; (*with one's feet, hands, cláws*) răcăéscu

EXCAVATION *s.* săpáre, târchíre, râcăíre

EXCAVATOR *s.* (*onc who investigates*) guzgún

EXCEED *vb.* ▾(a)ntrec, ▾astréc; **~ the limits** (*in doing smth.*) para-fác → SURPASS

EXCEEDINGLY *adv.* múltu, cum soţ nu áre, turbát ‖ BASME 455, 487 lúcru máre

EXCEL *vb.* (*to surpass*) ▼(a)ntréc; **He ~ed him in telling lies** Lu-antreápsi cu minciúna

EXCELLENT *adj.* aléptu, -eáptă, -épţâ, -eápte; háscu, *f* -că (*no pl forms*); di prótă (≈ *first class*); spañu, scóntră; **an ~ boy** un sémnu di ficiór

EXCEPT *prep.* (*other than*) afoáră di, (a)hórea di, (a)hóryea di; **She did not have anyone ~ him** Nu aveá áltu afoáră di nâs ‖ CUVATA 23: madan; **who else would send me a letter ~ for my brothers from Romania?** Cari áltu vrea-ñ pitrácă a ñíia cárti, madan fráţľi di tu-Armăníi? DIARO 359: **Nobody should know that ~ you** S-nu u ştiţ aéstâ dicât voi *or* aéstâ si-u ştiţ maş voi, DIARO 359

EXCEPT THAT *cj.* maşi că

EXCEPTIONAL *adj.* (*superior*) spáñu, *f* -áñe, *m/f pl* -ñiĭ

EXCESS *s.* **to do to ~** *vb.* para-fác

EXCESSIVELY *adv.* până di urécľi; turbát

EXCHANGE *s.* (*commercial transaction*) alăxíre, dáre-loáre, trámbă, *pl.* trănghi; *also* trámpă, *pl* trănchi; (*sale*) alişveríşe

EXCHANGE *vb.* (*to trade*) ▼alăxéscu (*and* alâ-), fac dáre-loáre

EXCITATION *s.* asplindíre, asplinsíre, azmuţáre, azmuţâre

EXCITE *vb.* (*call to activity, set smb. at*) azmúţ; (*to sensualize*) azdiséscu, azgânipséscu

EXCITED *adj.* aprés, -eásă, -éşĭ, -eáse; asplinsít, azmuţât *or* -ţát; azdisít

EXCOMMUNICATE *vb.* ▼afuriséscu, cătărăséscu

EXCOMMUNICATED *adj.* cătărăsít

EXCORIATION *s.* zgrâmătúră, sgârietúră, zgáibă

EXCREMENT *s.* căcát; *also:* găvún *m*, guvún; guluméu *m*, guluván *m*; mérdu *m*; spreámit *m*; (*in children's talk*) cácă *f*

EXCRESCENCE *s.* júmbă

EXCUSE *s.* simbăţíre

EXCUSE *vb.* (*to forgive*) ▼ľértu, ▼simbăţéscu, *N:* ▼ascúmpăr; **Excuse mi!** Bardhón! *or* Cu ľirtáre!

EXECRABLE *adj.* → ACCURSED

EXECRATION *s.* blăstém → MALEDICTION

EXECUTION *s.* (*puting to death with a firearm*) tufixíre

EXECUTIONER *s.* gilát

EXEMPT *adj.* ni-sudít, ľirtát

EXEMPTION *s.* (*as of a tax*) ľirtáre

EXERCISE-BOOK *s.* tetrádhiu *n*, tetrádhii [•dhiĭ] *pl*

EXERT ONESELF *vb.* pidhipséscu ‖ *Cru:* pidipséscu, GOLAB 242

EXERTION *s.* eneryisíre

EXHALATION *s.* (*of steam*) aburáre

EXHAUST *vb.* (*as of walking or hunger*) ▾băildiséscu, ▾căpăéscu, ▾nicuséscu, ▾zmurtic; (*as of crying*) ▾agăľiséscu (di plângu), ▾ayăliséscu, mi dirín (di plângu), ▾miucăéscu, ▾măcăéscu (di plângu); (*to overwork, to weary smb.*) ľ-scot pétalile

EXHAUSTED *adj.* curmát; *also:* ayăľisít, băldăsít, căpăít, dirinát, dirnát, liyusít, lişinát, lişnát, stuhinát, tălăít, vătămát

EXHAUSTION *s.* ayăľisíre, căpăíre, curmáre, dirináre, dirnáre

EXHIBIT *vb.* (*to display*) ▾aspún, scot, ▾alávdu

EXHORT *vb.* (*to urge on, as horses*) văryéscu (*and* vâr-), parachiniséscu (*and* pără-)

EXHORTATION *s.* anăngăsíre, anángasi *f*; părăchinisíre, părăchinsíre, parachínise, ştĭúri *f*, văryíre

EXHUMATION *s.* dizgrupáre, dizgropăciúne

EXHUME *vb.* dizgróp

EXILE *s.* exuríe, ixuríe, surgúne, suryiúne, suryiunipsíre, xipundisíre

EXILE *vb.* ▾surgunipséscu, ▾xipundiséscu

EXISTENCE *s.* (*life*) bánă, bănáre → EKE OUT ONE'S ~

EXIT *s.* işíre, inşíre; (*escape, way out*) cărăre ‖ HRISTU 5: işari → MAKE ONE'S ~

EXONERATE *vb.* ‖ scot cu fáţa álbă, BASME 177

EXORCISM *s.* (a)măyipsíre, măndipsíre, nămătisíre → BEWITCHMENT

EXORCIZE *vb.* (a)măyipséscu, cărmuéscu

EXPAND *vb.* ▾tíndu ‖ (*of dough*) asfíngu, CAPIDAN 148

EXPANSION *s.* tíndire, tindeáre, creáştire, crişteáre

EXPATIATE *vb.* para-ngréc

EXPATRIATED *adj.* xinít; xinitimén, -énă, -éñ, -éne

EXPECT *vb.* ▾aştéptu, ▾(a)păndixéscu, ▾apăndăxéscu

EXPECTANT *adj.* (*pregnant*) greáuă *f* ‖ ALR 328 (*of cows*) afeátă

EXPECTATION *s.* apăndixíre, apăndăxíre

EXPECTORATE *vb.* hârpuéscu

EXPECTORATION *s.* hârpuíre

EXPEL

EXPEL *vb.* agunéscu, *N:* azgunésu; scot ‖ *Cru:* ayunéscu, GOLAB 196; → FORCE OUT

EXPEND *vb.* (a)spárgu, hărgéscu, hărgiuéscu, ▾hiriséscu, hunipséscu, bitiséscu

EXPENSE *s.* éxudh, hárge, hărgilâche; **He needed that for travel expenses** Ľ-lipseá tri hárge pri cále; (*act of spending*) hărgíre, hărgiuíre ‖ CAPIDAN 155: exúdă; BATSARIA 6: **at the ~ of another** pi cheále xeánă

EXPENSIVE *adj.* scúmpu, -mbu *m pl* scúnchi, -nghi; custisít; (*excessive, of price*) (a)nsărát ‖ **very ~** scúmpu foc (*lit.* 'expensive fire' = *you cannot approach it as you cannot approach fire, because it burns you*), PARALLELE 128

EXPERIENCE *s.* (*practice*) practichíe

EXPERIENCE *vb.* (*to undergo*) trec prit

EXPERIENCED *adj.* (*hard-boiled*) păţât, fricát; tricút prit ţir ş-prit sítă; (*of a thief*) cu cízme (*lit.* 'with high boots') → SMART, VERSED

EXPERT *s.* → ADEPT

EXPIRATION *s.* suflăre

EXPLAIN *vb.* ▾limbidzăscu, limbiséscu; ▾exiyiséscu, ▾xiyiséscu

EXPLANATION *s.* limbidzăre, exíyise, xíyise, xiyisíre

EXPLICATE *vb.* → EXPLAIN

EXPLODE *vb.* crep, plăscănéscu (*and* plâscâ-)

EXPLOITED *adj.* (*used unfairly*) múlsu, -lsă, -lşi, -lse; dipirát

EXPLORED *adj.* zgruñít

EXPLOSION *s.* cripáre, plăscăníre

EXPOSE *vb.* (*to fall, to lay open*) cad; **Today we will ~ ourselves to rifles** Vai cădém az pri tuféchi [●fék']

EXPOSED *adj.* (*unprotected*) ni-afirít; (*~ to winds, rain*) bătút (di); (*~ to the sun*) nţilistrát di soáre

EXPOSURE *s.* (*~ to danger*) dăldăsíre

EXPRESSLY *adv.* (*for the express purpose*) castíli; **It has been done ~ for such occasions** Eásti fáptu castíli ti aşă → INTENTIONALLY

EXTEND *vb.* ▾tíndu, ▾ntíndu, ▾lărdzéscu, créscu, ▾lundzéscu, ▾spirlundzéscu

EXTENSION *s.* tíndire, tindeáre, măríre, lărdzíre, creáştire, crişteáre

EXTENT: → TO THE UTMOST ~

EXTENUATION *s*. căpăíre → EXHAUSTION

EXTERMINATE *vb*. buréscu; (*to ~ lice*) ▼dispiducľédz

EXTERMINATION *s*. (*of lice*) piducre, biducre, mbiducre

EXTINGUISH *vb*. (*of a fire and fig*.) ▼(a)stíngu

EXTINGUISHED *adj*. (a)stímtu, *m pl* -mţâ, *f pl* -mte

EXTIRPATE *vb*. (*as of weeds*) zmúlgu; (*as of mice*) ascáp (di)

EXTOL *vb*. (*to glorify*) cântu, ▼álţu, lávdu, dhuxăséscu, dhuxuséscu

EXTOLLING *s*. lăvdáre, dhuxăsíre, dhuxusíre

EXTORT *vb*. (a)ghizmédz

EXTRA *adj*. (*additional, more than needed*) nsus, ma nsus, pri ma nsus; **I have a few** ~ Am născânte pri ma nsús

EXTRACT *vb*. scot; (*forcibly*) ▼zmúlgu

EXTRACTION *s*. scoátire, scuteáre; **of high** ~ (*origin, lineage*) di sóie máre → ANCESTRY

EXTRANEOUS BODY *s*. (*as in wheat*) plătíţă

EXTRAORDINARY *adj*. (*remarkable*) nţirnút cu sită di mătáse (*lit.* 'sifted with silken sieve') ‖ (*luxurious*) ţivá éxtra di tut, BE-LIMACE 57

EXTRAVAGANT *adj*. (*wasteful, spendthrift*) hărgiuitór, spátal

EXTRAVAGANTLY *adv*. **to spend money** ~ fac părádzľi jir

EXTREMELY *adv*. (*very*) múltu; câtu s-dzâţi ‖ ALR 1367: di cále nafoáră

EXTREMITY *s*. (*end*) cápit

EXUBERANT *adj*. yiós; hărós, -oásă; ľ-si fătă Hristólu n cásă

EXULTANCE *s*. azdisíre

EYE *s*. anat. ócľu; *derog*. dzíf *m*, burlídhă, pălăthíre (*lit.* 'window'); *imprec*. **Damn your eyes!** S-ţ-arsáră pălăthírĭle! (*orifice of a needle*) coáca (*or* gúva) a áclui; măgheáuă; ureácľe; (~ *of a clasp*) záva theámină; **with burst** ~s cu ócľi cripáţ → EVIL ~, PUT OUT SMB.'S EYES, SET ~S ON, UNDER SMB.'S EYES ‖ *Arm, Kok, LvO, Mal*: óclu; *Mul, Plat*: ochiu, B-ARCH 183; **with the tail of one's** ~ cu coáda ócľului *or* cu coáda di ócľu, see PARALLELE 154

EYE *vb*. mutréscu; ~ **carefully** mutréscu di la úngľi pân la cap

EYE SOCKET *s*. anat. cáfcală

EYEBALL *s*. ‖ *Peş*: om, CL 257 (*lit.* 'man')

EYE-BOLT *s*. (*of a steel-yard*) bilcíc, muştúc, sérghe

EYELASH

EYELASH *s.* peánă ‖ ALIA 187: mătuţináră, peánă di ócľi, pénă

EYELID *s.* dzeánă ‖ *GSus, SJos, Peş, Pls:* căpáche, CL 41; *Amc:* frândză di ócľu, SCHL 116

EYESORE *s.* vazmó

EYEWITNESS *s.* mártur, şaít

F

FABLE *s.* părăvulíe, părămíth; **to become the ~ of the town** agiúngu părămíth

FABRIC *s.* (*rather thick, as for coats*) stófă, pulúră; (*of cotton or wool*) fótă; (*of silk*) díbă, geamfése; (*printed cotton*) chităbí, chităbíe; (*satin mixed with cotton*) cutníe; (*for tents*) cidâre, téndă

FABRICATE *vb.* ndreg, ţas

FABULOUS *adj.* ‖ BELIMACE 57: ca ţivá di spúnirli a părmítilor

FACE *s.* fáţă, prósupă, surétă, máste; **He saw her pretty ~** Vidzú muşeáta-ľ máste; (*aspect, face*) ceahré; **~ to ~** andícra, andícrita, carsí ‖ LITURG 128: fiutiúră; CUVATA 3: prósup

FACE *vb.* (*to meet, to encounter*) dau chéptu cu

FACILITATE *vb.* lişurédz, ▾ifculipséscu

FACILITY *s.* (*ease*) lişureáţă, nişureáţă, ifculíľe, ifculíe

FACT *s.* fáptă, lúcru → BECOME ~ ‖ PC: (*case, instance*) únă

FACTORY *s.* fábrică, fámbrică, fávrică

FACULTY → COLLECT ONE'S FACULTIES

FADE *vb.* (*as of flowers*) ▾aludzăscu, ▾arăhñiséscu, ▾aspárgu; (*of a person's face*) ñ-si bubuchiseáşte fáţa, ▾bubuchiséscu, ▾mărăndédz, mărănghipséscu, mărănghiséscu, ▾paléscu, ▾víntin, ▾viştidzăscu, ▾nviştidzăscu

FADE AWAY *vb.* (*as of beauty*) ▾apún; ▾paléscu

FADED *adj.* arăhñisít, bubuchisít, mărănghisít, pălít, veáştid, víştiz, viştijít, vintinát; (*of meat*) aludzât

FADING *s.* viştijíre; *also:* arăhñisíre, mărănghisíre, pălíre, vintináre

FAECES *s.* → FECES

FAG *vb.* ▼zgrum tu lúcru, agăliséscu, ▼nicuséscu → EXHAUST

FAG END *s.* ‖ (*unburned end of a cigarette*) PC: armăsitúră di la ţiyáră

FAGGED OUT *adj.* curmát → TIRED

FAG(G)OT *s.* (*sticks or twigs of pine-tree used for fuel*) dzádă

FAIL *vb.* cad, cad niptút; nu ñ-si văpseáşte óulu [oᵘ●] ‖ **The two men failed to do business together** nu feáţirâ vârnâ câşári dóiľi, DIARO 206

FAILING *s. med.* slăbeáţă, slăbínţă, slăbíľe

FAILURE *s.* (*of a person*) ni-prucupsít, om fâră prucuchíe → GOOD-FOR-NOTHING; (*fiasco*) ni-prucupsíre, căcătúră; (*used as an interj.*) căcátă luyuríe!

FAINT *s.* (*fainting fit*) lişín, lişináre, lişinătúră; *also:* milíe, căhtíre, căpăíre, liyursíre

FAINT *adj.* lişinát, lişnát; **to feel ~** atihiséscu ‖ **~ with hunger** lişinát di nimâcáre, BASME 57

FAINT *vb.* ▼lişín, ▼lişinédz; *also:* ayăliséscu, agă-, ayă-, liyuséscu, mi-arúc n-a-răului, ñ-cáde milíe, ñ-víne milíe

FAINT-HEARTED *adj.* pabés, ba-; *f* -ésă *m pl* -éşĭ, *f pl* -ése

FAIR *s.* păzáre, pănăyír, păniyír

FAIR *adj.* (*not dark*) (a)rús, *m pl* (a)rúşĭ; (*pleasing*) arisít; (*beautiful*) muşát; (*clear*) curát; (*favorable*) fursatlí; (*light in coloring*) albér, -éră; albúş, arús; **by ~ means** → ABOVEBOARD ‖ DIARO 135: arúscâ **f** ('blond')

FAIRNESS *s.* driptáte, driptáticã, dhíche

FAIRY *s.* dzână (*and* zână), argheándă; álbile *pl f def*; muşeátile *pl f def* (*lit.* 'the pretty ones') ‖ **I am not a ~, I am only your fiancée** Nu estu ghindă, estu goală susita a ta, HRISTU 64

FAIRY *adj.* cântát; **~ horse** cal cântát; **~ bird** puľu cântát

FAIRY TALE *s.* părămíth, *N:* părămís

FAITH *s.* bésă, dínă, féde, imáne, píste, vereáuă; (*religion*) thrischíe, nom → BREAK ~ WITH SMB.

FAITHFUL *adj.* di bésă, besalâ, pistó, pistimén, -énă, -éñ, -éne; *also* mbistimén

FAITHLESS *adj.* dinsâz, -âză, -âjĭ, -âze → INFIDEL

FAITHLESSNESS *s.* apistíe, băbislíche

FAKE *adj.* cálpu, -lpă, -lchi, -lpe; *also:* cálpic, cálbic; **A ~**

FAKE

coin never gets lost Părălu cálbic puté nu cheáre → FALSE

FAKE *vb.* plăn(ăs)éscu → DECEIVE

FALCON *s.* (*various species of birds of prey*:) aitó, áţiră, caracáxă, ciuligán, fiturísçhe, gărăchínă, ghirăchínă, yirăchínă, yearăchínă, yirác, hútă *or* útă, iacmageáie *or* acmageáie, ľipurár, órñu *m*, órñe *f*, pirít, săcól, stavraít, schipóñiu, şchi-póñu *m*, schipoáñe *f*, sfrindzél, şaín, vúltur, schifţér, xiftér

FALL *s.* (*an instance of falling*) cădeáre; (*autumn*) toámnă; (*long mild ~*) tumnăríu; **~ is coming** Ntumneádză; **~ has come** (Chi-rólu) ntumnă; **last ~** ástă-toámnă; **~ of night** ntunicátă; **at the ~ of night** tru ntunicátă ‖ **~ is coming** Ndumniádză, K-D 114

FALL *vb.* cad (→ § 32); (*to ~ heavily, of snow or rain*) ľ-u ndeásă; **Snow began to ~ heavily** Neáua acáţă s-ľ-u ndeásă; (*of night*) murdzeáşte, ntúnică; (*of frost*) brumeádză, mbrumeádză

FALL ASLEEP *vb.* dórmu, ▾agărşéscu; **The woman fell asleep and slept** Niveásta s-agărşí ş-durñí ‖ TULLIU 80: agărşéscu

FALL BACK *vb.* ▾scad, ▾trag năpói

FALL DOWN *vb.* sărúp, surúp

FALL GUY *s.* apló, ageamít

FALL HEAVY UPON SMB. *vb.* (*as a threat*) Lu-nvéţ eu panachída! ľ-arăt; **He'll fall heavy upon him!** Ľ-arátă năs!

FALL HELPLESS *vb.* (*to collapse*) cad stog (n páde)

FALL ILL *vb.* cad niptút, hivréscu, hiuvréscu, lăndzidzăscu; *impers.* mi hiuvrueáşte ‖ (*to fall terminally ill*) ñ-ľau lélea, BASME 627; cad greu lăndzit

FALL IN *vb.* (*of land, etc.*) cad, ▾ahânduséscu, afunduséscu, ahunduséscu, ▾hăndăcuséscu, sărúp, surúp; (*as of an old house*) ▾ruvuéscu, ruvuléscu, arăvulséscu, ruvulséscu, ▾arăsvuéscu, cad n páde, cad stog, ▾gărmiséscu, ▾ruzuéscu, ▾survuľiséscu, tălcéscu, ▾vérsu mpáde ‖ *Peş:* zvurnuéscu, CL 269

FALL IN DROPS *vb.* (*to let fall in drops, to drip*) chicutédz

FALL IN LOVE *vb.* ñ-cáde tu ínimă, ñ-arúc vreárea pri, ▾alu-ghéscu, ñ-si alăcheáşte buríclu; **She had fallen in love with an Arab** şi-aveá arcátă vreárea pri un aráp ‖ *Cru:* mi erotipséscu pri várnu, GOLAB 214; ñ-íntră tu ínimă, BASME 60

FALL INTO ABEYANCE *s.* bătăľusíre

FALL INTO A PASSION *vb.* ľau vímtu → FLY INTO A TEMPER

FALL INTO DISUSE *vb.* ▾nvicľédz, ▾nvicľéscu

FALL INTO RUIN *vb.* tălcéscu

FALL INTO SIN *vb.* íntru tu amărtíe

FALL INTO THE TRAP *vb.* cad tu bátă (*or* tu yrip, tu tăpíţă); ñ-cad ăn príncă, mi acáţ di páturli cicioáre

FALL OF NIGHT *s.* nsiráre

FALL OUT WITH SMB. *vb.* u-arúp (*or* u-táľu) cioára (cu); u-aspárgu uspiţâľa (cu); ▼ancáciu (*and* angáciu) ‖ aspárgu aloáturle, BASME 351

FALL PROSTRATE *vb.* ľ-fac taéte, ľ-fac timină

FALL SICK *vb.* ▼lândzidzăscu

FALL SILENT *vb.* (*to get dumbfounded*) ‖ *Cru:* amút, GOLAB 198

FALL TO PIECES *vb.* ndăcănéscu

FALL UPON SMB. *vb.* urñéscu → RUSH ON

FALLACIOUS *adj.* → TRICKY

FALLACY *s.* ≈ dzăgădíre

FALLEN *adj.* (*injured or dead*) cădzút; (*as of a cellar; fig. as of a sinner*) sur(u)pát; (*as of smb.'s looks or hair*) sălăghít

FALLEN OUT WITH SMB. *adj.* ncăceát (cu)

FALLING ASLEEP *s.* adurñíre

FALLING DUE *s.* (*deadline, as of a payment*) murmín

FALLING IN *s.* arăvuíre, aruvuíre, ruvursíre, ruvulsíre, ruzuíre, survóiu

FALLING IN *adj.* cădzút, aruvulsít, arăvăít, aruvuít

FALLING-OUT *s.* → QUARREL

FALLOW *adj.* (*of land*) apăryisít

FALSE *adj.* bírbu, *m pl* -rghi; plan, *m pl* plañ; (*as of money*) cálpu, *m pl* -lchi; cálpic; călpăzán; (*as of a witness*) strâmbu, *m pl* -ânghi, *f pl* -âmbe; **to take a ~ step** cálcu strâmbu

FALSE OATH *s.* yealán-giurátic

FALSE STEP → TO TAKE A FALSE STEP

FALSEHOOD *s.* tácmă → LIE

FALTER *vb.* ▼clátin, ▼clătín

FALTERING *s.* (*broken or weak speech*) băbălíre, bărbăríre, dârdáră

FAME *s.* anáme → RENOWN

FAMILIARIZE *vb.* → ACCUSTOM

FAMILY *s.* fămeáľe, fumeálă, *N:* fuméľu; **of good ~** di cásă máre, di ugeáche, di poártă máre; **old ~** ugeác vécľu ‖ *Cru:* fămilíe,

FAMILY MAN

GOLAB 215; MERCA 3: (*clan*) ghireáuă

FAMILY MAN *s.* (*usu. with many children*) familít

FAMINE *s.* zíe, foámită, foámite

FAMISH *vb.* (*to starve continuously*) agiún, agiunédz

FAMISHED *adj.* líhud, *m pl* -hudz

FAMOUS *adj.* lăvdát, avdzât, cu númă, cu sémnu, mărít

FAN *s.* (*device*) avríţă

FAN *vb.* (*of seeds*) ndzirnédz ‖ PC: dau la vímtu

FANATICAL *adj.* fanátic

FANATICISM *s.* fanatizmó

FANCIFUL *adj.* căpriceárcu, -rcă, -rţi, -rţe → CAPRICIOUS

FANCY *s.* gústu; **to take a ~ to smb.** ñ-cáde tu vreáre máre →
CAPRICE ‖ **Alb:** chéfe; **His ~ is gone** Ĺ-armási chéfea, CAPIDAN 177

FANCY *adj.* căpriceárcu, -rcă, -rţi, -rţe; (*ornamental*) stulsít

FANCY *vb.* ▼făndăxéscu; **Just ~!** Ba!

FANG *s.* cărínte (*and* cărínde)

FANTASY *s.* făndăsíe, făndăzíe, făndăxíre

FAR *adj.* dipărtát, dipărtós; lúngu, -ngă, -ndzi, -ndze

FAR *adv.* dipárte, nclo dipárte, náparte; **~ from me** náparte di
míne; lárgu; **from ~** di lárgu; **thus ~** pân tru aístă hópă → AS ~
AS, AS ~ AS ONE CAN SEE ‖ **~ away, very ~, as ~ as:** **He went very ~**
S-dúsi Brúsa (*Brusa is a city in Turkey*), DIARO 368

FARAWAY *adj.* → FAR

FAREWELL *s.* dispărţáre; *s. and interj.* cále-ambár, oáră búnă;
Dú-te ambár! **to bid ~** or cale-ambár; mi ĺértu (di) → BID ~

FARRIER *s.* albán, nalbán, pitălár

FARINACEOUS *adj.* fărinós, -oásă, -óşĭ, -oáse

FARM *s.* fármă; (*~ of a monastery*) mitóh, mitóhe

FARM HUSBANDRY *s.* zivyărlíche

FARMER *s.* (*prosperous ~*) chibúr ‖ **Cru:** huniát, GOLAB 220

FARMING *s.* zivyărlíche; **sheep ~** cilnicátă; **Sheep farming is no
easy job** Cilnicáta nu si scoálă ĺişór

FARMSTEAD *s.* catándă, nicuchirátă

FARMYARD *s.* cúrti → YARD

FAR-OFF *adj.* dipărtát; dipărtós, -oásă, -óşĭ, -oáse

FARRIER *s.* nalbán, pitălár

FARSIGHTED *adj.* (*wise*) aduchít

FART *s.* bişínă; (*as ono.*) pârţ ‖ DIARO 111: fum (*lit. 'smoke'*)

FART *vb.* ▾bes, ▾bişinédz, arúc bişíñ; **to ~ noiselessly** li-arúcă cúfe *3 sg.* ‖ DIARO 117: trag fúmuri

FARTHER ON *adv.* cáma nclo *or* cama nclóţec ‖ HRISTU 18: ma nclo

FARTHING: ≈ cărăndánă (*and* cărântánă, cărândánă); **I don't care a brass ~!** (= *I don't give two cents*) Hăbáre nu am! **It is not worth a ~!** Nu fáţe níţi únă cărăndánă! **to the last ~** (*everything*) pân tu ac (*lit. 'up to a needle'*)

FASCIA *s.* (*as for swaddling infants*) fáşe

FASCINATE *vb.* măndipséscu

FASCINATED *adj.* măndipsít

FASHION *s.* (*vogue*) módhă; **after the French ~** a-la-fránga

FASHION *vb.* (*to form, to shape, to mold*) turnipséscu

FASHIONABLE *adj.* galántu, -ntă, -nţâ, -nte → MODISH

FASHIONING *s.* turnipsíre

FAST *s.* (*a time of fasting*) păreásiñ *f pl*

FAST *adj.* (*firmly fixed*) ni-minát; (*deep, as of a sleep*) ahân-dós; (*tight*) stres, *f* -eásă, *m pl* streşĭ, *f pl* -eáse

FAST *vb.* ţân păreásiñ, mărsinédz; **~ing woman** trimiroáñe

FAST *adv.* ayiú, ayíu, anyíu, nyíe, yíe-yíe; cu ayiuseálă, cu avrápă; alága (*or* alága-fúga), dălága, gudalágă, *N:* curúndu *or* crúndu; agúña, *Gop, Mul:* agóña; máni-móni, prápa, ân prápă; cáma troáră (DDA: 955); **very ~** apálă, ca curşúmlu; (*of smth. that sells well*) ca pânea cáldă; **Come ~er, because they have been waiting for you!** Cáma crúndu, că ti-aşteáptă! **Climb up the poplar fast!** Ayiú alínă-te sti plup! **as ~ as possible** t-un aditic, pi arăchí-tă; **~ and much** cu língura; **The boy learned to read and write very ~** Ficiórlu li nviţă cu língura ‖ STERE 21: cuşíi; CUVATA 9: **as ~ as possible** ţi ma-agóña

FAST BREAKER *s.* puríntu (*and* puríndu)

FAST BREAKING *s.* purintáre

FAST DAY *adj.* (*of food*) mársin; **~ pie** pítă mărsinátă

FAST DAY FOOD *s.* puríndă, mărşineáţă

FASTEN *vb.* ▾stríngu, ▾stiriuséscu; (*as a dog*) ▾leg; (*to ~ nails*) ▾sfinuséscu; **to ~ one's eyes on smb./smth.** mi si alăchés-cu óclĭĭ (nínga)

FASTENER *s.* cipráche, ciupráche, ceapréche, clʼişúţă; *N:* ciu-précă, cupceáuă, cupíţă ‖ *Peş:* filíche, CL 45

FASTIDIOUS *adj.* garamitlíu, *f* -líe, *m/f pl* -líĭ

FASTING s. mărsináre, păreásiñ f pl; trímir

FASTNESS s. ni-mináre

FAT s. grăsíme, umtúră, líydhă, lărdhíe (and lărdíe); the best part of smth. ‖ CUVATA 28: păstó → EAT THE ~ OF THE LAND

FAT adj. gras, **N:** greas; dim. grăsíc → CUT IT ~, CUT IT TOO ~

FATE s. míră, **N:** fátăză → DESTINY

FATED adj. ursít

FATHER s. tátă, pl tătáñ; tátu, táte, táti, aféndi, aféndu, bába, pl bábañ; **Zag:** andíc; (in swearing) yuñó; **To the devil with your ~!** Lo-ţ dráclu yuñólu! (rare) patéra; (priest) aféndi; préftu; (addressing a priest, voc.) yisíte!

FATHER vb. nfumiľédz

FATHER-IN-LAW s. sócru, sócur; **his/her ~** sócur-su

FATHERLAND s. pătrídhă (and pătrídă); (the place where one lives) vădáne

FATIGUE s. curmáre; also: apustusíre, buhtíre, bréngă

FATIGUE vb. apustuséscu → TIRE OUT

FATTEN vb. ▼ngraş, ▼ngrăşédz, sărcuséscu; iron. bag sândze

FATTENING s. ngrăşeáre

FATTISH adj. grăsíc

FATTY adj. gras

FATUITY s. huţáme

FATUOUS adj. dabóľa invar. → STUPID

FAUCET s. (of a barrel) canélă, sóche → BUNG

FAULT s. căbáte, stépsu, stipsíre ‖ **Cru:** măhănă, GOLAB 234 ‖ CARA-FOLI 67 and 85; căbăháti; ibid. 33: căbăhsíti; 85: ftéxim; **it's not their ~** ftéximlu nu-i a lor

FAULTLESS adj. ni-stipsít → INNOCENT

FAULTY adj. stipsít

FAVOR s. (service) huzméte, usméte, arigé, rigeáie; **Gop, Mul:** arâjéie; **Do me a ~** Fă-ñ únă huzméte (or: Ţ-fac únă rigeáie); **to be in ~ with** am plătări → REQUEST, DO A ~

FAVOR vb. (to support, to prefer) fac háre; (to resemble) °aun-dzéscu (with dat.); ñ-u adúc (pri or cu)

FAVORABLE adj. cu hăíre, tihiró, fursatlí, -sătlí

FAWN vb. ▼gúdur, ▼guduréscu, culăchipséscu

FAY s. → FAIRY

FAZE vb. (to disturb) alăcéscu míntea; (to dishearten) ▼apilpiséscu

FEALTY *s.* bésă

FEAR *s.* frícă; **out of ~** di frícă, di aspárizmă, di aspáryiu →
BE PARALYSED WITH ~, PUT ~ IN SMB.'S HEART

FEAR *vb.* ñ-u frícă

FEARFUL *adj.* fricós, aspărós, chiutí, dzadílă; áre ínimă di ľépure (*lit.* 'has a hare's heart'); ľépur eáste (*lit.* 'is a hare');
nu-áre arândză ‖ HRISTU 34: fricăros *and* 37: friăros

FEARLESS *adj.* ni-aspăreát, inimárcu, inimós, caidigí

FEARLESSNESS *s.* cutidzáre

FEARSOME *adj.* → FEARFUL

FEAST *s.* uspéţ; **to give a ~ for** ľ-aştérnu tavérnă → BANQUET

FEAST *vb.* (*to celebrate*) yiurtiséscu, yiurtuséscu; **to ~ one's
eyes on smb./smth.** ylindipséscu, l-fac síre, siryinséscu

FEASTING *s.* băiráme

FEATHER *s.* peánă

FEATHER ONE'S NEST *vb.* acáţ maiáuă → PROSPER

FEATHERED *adj.* (*as of a dragon*) cu peáne

FEATURE *s.* (*as of smb.'s face*) físe, măsídhă, misídhă, ñisídhă

FEBRUARY *s.* Scúrtu, şcúrtu, Flivár; **~ the nasty** şcúrtu aţél rău

FECES *s.* → EXCREMENT

FECKLESS *adj.* ni-ácşu; náxu, *f* -xă, *m pl* -cşi, *f pl* -xe

FED *adj.* (*well ~, of a horse*) urdzát; (*milk fed, speaking of a
suckling*) aplicát

FEE *s.* plátă, dat → TAX

FEEBLE *adj.* s(c)lab, *m pl* s(c)laghi; *also:* azmét, chirchinéc,
hárval, piliciós, -oásă, -óşĭ, -oáse; *m/f* pruzúme, *pl* -zúñ;
ţărós, -oásă, -óşĭ, -oáse; zaíf, *m pl* -ífĭ, *f pl* -fe; zaífcu

FEEBLEMINDED *adj.* ľócă *invar.* → STUPID

FEED *s.* ‖ **to be off one's ~** nu ñ-si mácă, BASME 132; nu ñ-si
bágă ţivá n gúră, BASME 39

FEED *vb.* ▾hrănéscu, ▾hărnéscu, ▾hăréscu, tăiséscu; (*to support*)
▾ţân; (*to cram*) ▾astúp; (*to ~ from the mother's mouth*) mătríc,
mitríc, nitríc, nutríc, ntric

FEEDING *s.* hrăníre, hărníre, mătricáre, ntricáre

FEEDING BOTTLE *s.* lástic

FEEDING TROUGH *s.* (*for animals*) păhníe

FEEDLOT *s.* păşúne

FEEL

FEEL *vb.* (*to perceive, to be aware*) símtu, síntu, sâmtu, ▾simţéscu, duchéscu; (*to touch*) ahuléscu; (*to examine by the feel*) păspătéscu, pusputéscu, pusputipséscu; (*to have a presentiment*) ▾privéd, ▾pruvéd; **I ~ a cold shiver go down my back** Mi treáţe un hir aráţe pi tu păltări; Mi treáţe gĺáţă di frícă; **to ~ a longing** mi ĺa dórlu (di); **to ~ a thrill** tríhir, trihirédz; ▾nhiu-rédz [nhi•u•]; **to ~ bad about smth.** ñ-víne cripáre; **to ~ dithery** ñ-fug bişíñ; şeápti-óptu ñ-si dúţe; **to ~ enmity** ▾pizmuséscu; **to ~ faint** atihiséscu, mi-arúc n arăului; **to ~ hungry** (*intensively*) ñ-si dúţe gúra la ureácĺe; **to ~ ill** atihiséscu; **to ~ peckish** (*to starve*) crep di foáme; **to ~ sick** ñ-yíne greáţă; ñ-eáste greáţă (di); **to ~ the pinch** (*to rough it*) bat tămbărălu; **I don't ~ up to it** (*I do not have the courage*) nu-ñ ţâne stricătoárea ‖ **~ vexed**; *imper. 2 sg*: Nu ţ-u mâcă ínima! BASME 52; **to ~ relieved** ñ-yíne ínima la loc, BASME 289; ALR 1367: **I ~ very ill** Mi duchéscu arău di cále nafoáră

FEEL A LUMP IN ONE'S THROAT *vb.* ‖ STERGHIU 3: noádi ñi s-acáţă tu gurmáz

FEELING *s.* sâmţâre

FEELING *adj.* adiĺós

FEIGN *vb.* mi fac; **Father Coma ~ed ninny** Pópa Cóma s-féţe glar

FELL *adj.* ni-ñilós; fuvirós, -oásă, -óşĭ, -oáse

FELL *vb.* (*to ~ smb. to the ground*) cúlcu n páde [mpádi]

FELLOW *s.* soţ; (*chap, lad*) junóp, giunóp, firfirúş

FELLOW-TOWNSMAN *s.* huryeanít

FELLOW-COUNTRYMAN *s.* patriót

FELLY *s.* (*of a wheel*) ‖ *SJos*: cóthor, cóthar, CL 42; PC: rahótă; culiló

FELT *s.* mătáfe

FEMALE *adj.* theámin, heá-, seá- (*ant.* máscur); **a ~ mule** múlă seámină; muĺiréscu, -reáscă, -réşţi, -réşti; *the part of a church reserved for women* muĺireásca

FEMININE *adj.* → FEMALE

FEN *s.* váltu, varcó

FENCE *s.* gárdu, ploc; (*~ made of boards*) tarácă ‖ ALB: *Kërb*, *Pe*: gardhu, BRÂNCUŞ 557

FENCE *vb.* ngărdédz, ngărdéscu, ntărác

FEND *vb.* ▾ápăr

FENDER *s.* (*fireguard of stone, as in a stove*) pirumáh

FENNY *adj.* băltós, -oásă, -óşĭ, -oáse; *also* văltós

FERAL *adj.* ágru, áyru

FERMENT *s.* (*for dough*) maiáuă, piteáuă, *G:* zaciu

FERMENTATION *s.* (*of dough*) yineáre

FERN *s. bot.* feárică

FERRYMAN *s.* varcagí, căiccí

FERTILE *adj.* ‖ âmbugát, BASME 18

FERVENT *adj.* aprés, -eásă, -éşĭ, -eáse

FERVID *adj.* aprés, -eásă, -éşĭ, -eáse

FESTER *s. med.* cuptúră, proñ

FESTER *vb. med.* adún puróñ

FESTIVE *adj.* písim, -mă, -siñ, -sime

FETCH *vb.* adúc

FETCH ONE'S BREATH *vb.* ñ-ľau adiľáticlu

FETCHING *adj.* nóstim, -timă, -tiñ, -time

FETID *adj.* ambuţós, -oásă; dâh(â)nít; (*as of meat*) añurzít

FETLOCK JOINT *s.* puľu

FETTER *vb.* leg tu singír, ▾ncheádic → SHACKLE

FETTERS *s.* heáre *n pl* → MANACLES

FETTLE: (*as of a horse*) **in good ~** pri trup

FEVER *s. med.* căldúră; *fig.* **throw smb. into a ~** ľ-frig máţăle → TEMPERATURE

FEVER *vb.* hivréscu, hiuvrescu

FEW *adj.* niscântu (*and* nscându); **a ~ hares** niscânţâ ľepuri; **a ~ sheep** niscânte oi; puţân, pţân, psân; ndoi *m*, ndoáuă *f*; vârnă ndoi *m*, vârnă ndoáuă *f*

FEWER (*as of smth. missing*) ‖ un cama nghios (*lit. 'one lower'*) BASME 312

FEZ *s.* (*white cotton ~*) tirlíche, barbarúsă (*and* bărbă-)

FIANCÉ *s.* duduşeán, isusít

FIANCÉE *s.* duduşeánă, isusítă ‖ MURNU 12: pruxinítă; *F:* susită, HRISTU 64

FIASCO *s.* ni-prucupsíre

FIB *s.* minciúnă → LIE

FIB *vb.* uidiséscu nă minciúnă; másin curnuţeále → LIE

FIBER, FIBRE *s.* íne *f pl*

FICKLE *adj.* (*flighty*) 3 *sg:* nu-áre fuľór ân cap; nu-i angreácă

FIDDLE

míntea; nu sta pri únă

FIDDLE *s.* avyiulíe, chimané, chimanée, zancacrútă, zăngănă ‖
Peş: zăngălăcútă, CL 263

FIDDLER *s.* avyiulgí; **N:** cealyagí; chimanigí; dumdúm *invar;* sa-
segí, yíftu; (Tirana) sazagí; zăngănár; *coll.* ghiúmuri; **The ~s
have arrived** Viñíră dum-dúm ‖ *Peş:* zăngălăcutár, CL 263

FIDDLESTICKS! *interj.* ≈ Hăbáre nu ám!

FIDELITY *s.* bésă

FIDGET *vb.* am furnídzi la cicioáre; am yérmu la ínimă; nu mi-
acáţă (*or* nu mi áre / nu mi áflă) lóclu; nu-ñ si aşteárne

FIDGETY *adv.* asiyúriftu

FIELD *s.* cămpu (*and* câmpu); *dim.* câmpíş, câmpíc; (*land for
tillage*) ágru, águr; **sown ~** simănătúră ‖ *Cru:* áyru, GOLAB 196

FIELD-GLASS *s.* (*binoculars*) chéle, dulbíe

FIEND *s.* drac → DEVIL

FIENDISH *adj.* drăcuréscu, -reáscă, -réşţâ, -réşti → DEVILISH

FIERCE *adj.* (*as of a look*) gúvru ‖ arnăút *m,* -ă *f,* DIARO 75

FIERY *adj.* sértu, -rtă, -rţâ, -rte; sértic → ARDENT, IRRITABLE

FIFTEEN *num.* ţísprădzaţe, ţíspră ‖ CUVATA 1: ţísprădz

FIFTH *ord.* ţínţirlu ‖ *Cru:* pémtu, GOLAB 242 → § 28.2 *above*

FIFTY *num.* ţindzăţi

FIG *s. bot.* hícă; **I don't give a ~** Hăbáre nu ám

FIGHT *s.* alúmtă, alumtáre, aluptáre, alumtátic; lúptă, lúftă,
ľúftă, ľuftuíre, ľuftíre, bătíe, géngă ‖ HRISTU 6: polim

FIGHT *vb.* ▾bat, ▾lúptu, lúmtu, ľúftu, ľuftuéscu, ľuftéscu, ▾am-
pulimséscu, ▾ampuliséscu, ▾deápir, ▾azvíngu; *3 pl:* şi-arúp su-
márili *or* şi-mâcă sămárili ‖ (~ *like bitter enemies*) s-mâcă ca
câñľi *3 pl* (*lit. 'they eat one other like dogs'*), PARALLELE 120

FIGHTER *s.* ľúftă, *pl* ľúfteañ

FIGMENT *s.* sufíe

FIG-TREE *s.* hic

FIGURE *s.* (*of people*) figúră, fighiúră, fiutiúră [fĭu•tĭú•ră]
→ CUT A ~

FIGURE *vb.* (*to represent, to be*) ▾părăstăséscu, ▾părăstiséscu

FIGURE OUT *vb.* ‖ **I can't figure it out** Nu ñ-u-ncápe míntea
(*lit. 'my mind cannot comprehend it'*), PARALLELE 126; (*to imagine,
to invent*) chiuluéscu, CUVATA 3

FILAMENT *s.* (*as the ~ of a lamp*) fitíle *or* fitíľ

FILCH *vb.* ciun, ▾ahuléscu, ▾anvăléscu, ▾anvărtéscu, sufruséscu ‖ DIARO 197: câléscu

FILE[1] *s.* (*for rubbing down a hard substance*) límă, ariníe, arníe, arneálă

FILE[2] *s.* (*row*) arádhă; (*record*): **to be old** ~ (*i.e., to be experienced, to be an old hand at smth.*) âñ tricú rúglu prit náre

FILE *vb.* (*to smooth, to rub down*) arinsécu

FILIGREE *s.* sermáe, sirmatiró

FILL *vb.* ▾úmplu; (*to satisfy, to sate*) ▾tâpuréscu; (*to* ~ *to capacity*) dânguséscu, suruséscu; (*to put close together*) ▾stimuxéscu; **to** ~ **up** para-úmplu; (*as a pipe*) ▾úmflu ‖ ~**ed with mud** fapt di muzgă, HRISTU 60

FILLET *s.* pánglică, pántlică

FILLING *s.* umpleáre, úmplire; (~ *to capacity*) dângusíre, surusíre

FILLY *s.* iápă

FILM *s.* (*thin skin*) peáje, pijilínă

FILTER *vb.* ▾stricór

FILTH *s.* murdăríľe, murdărlâche, smágă, cóthră; lăvăşitúră, lăvuşitúră, lăşitúră, lăvíľe, léră

FILTHY *adj.* murdár → DIRTY

FILTRATE *vb.* → FILTER

FILTRATION *s.* stricuráre

FIN *s.* (*of fish*) leástră

FINAGLE *vb.* ncálţu → SWINDLE

FINAGLER *s.* (*swindler*) zulumgí

FINCH *s. orn.* angícă

FIND *s.* → MAKE A LUCKY ~

FIND *vb.* ▾áflu, ▾apúc, ugrădiséscu; **We found him exactly as he was having dinner** Lu-apucăm análtu pri meásă; ~ **a job** ▾zburăscu (la); **He found a job in a bakery** Si zbură la únă fúrnă; **to** ~ **fault with** (*to criticize*) ľau părătúră; **to** ~ **fault with a fat goose** ľ-áflu coáde, ľ-bag coáde; **to** ~ **it hard to** ñ-yíne béte; **to** ~ **one's way in** (*as of a wolf trying to get to the sheep*) ▾aúrlu; *to* ~ **shelter** ľau pâne; **They learned out where the emperor had found shelter** Loáră di hăbáre iu ľa pâne amirălu; **to** ~ **smb. out in a lie** lu acáţ tu praşi; **to** ~ **use for** ufiliséscu

FIND OUT *vb.* ▾áflu. ▾(a)nveţ, veţ, ľau di hăbáre; **Let's run**

FINDER

before they ~ S-fudzím pânǎ nu nǎ loárǎ di hǎbáre; **He finds out what is going on** Nveáțǎ țe cúrǎ

FINDER *s.* (*one that finds*) aflǎtór

FINDING *s.* afláre

FINE *s.* (*penalty*) ghiz, giz, ghizáe, girimé, girimée ‖ BELIMACE 79: geazáe

FINE *adj.* fin, *m pl* fiñ; háscu, -scǎ (*no pl*); (*thin*) minút; (*conventional answer to the greeting* Ți hǎbǎrǐ? 'How are you?' (*lit.* 'What news?'*) Ghinǎtéț! (*lit.* 'Good things!')

FINE *vb.* girimit(is)éscu, glub(u)éscu ‖ CUNIA 11: arúc ghizáe

FINE *adv.* ghíne, **F:** ghéni

FINERY *s.* stóle, *no pl*; stólídhǎ, stulídhǎ, stulíe

FINESSE *vb.* puniripséscu

FINGER *s.* dzeádzit, deádzit; *dim.* dziditíc; **Gop, Mul:** dézet ‖ **Mul:** get; **Cot, Hal:** geádit, **Els:** geágit, B-ARCH 169

FINGERLING *s.* piscóplu ‖ CUNIA 227: *also* pischíț

FINGERNAIL *s.* úngľe

FINGERNAIL SPOT *s.* ñel (*lit.* 'lamb')

FINICKY *adj.* garamitlíu, -líe, *m/f pl* -líǐ

FINIS *s.* bitisítǎ

FINISH *vb.* ▾apulséscu, ▾bitiséscu, ▾buréscu, mburséscu, scap, scǎrchéscu, sculuséscu, suséscu, ▾tiléscu ‖ STERE 101: dǎnǎséscu → END

FINISHED *adj.* bitisít, bițít, mburít; (*done, accomplished, as of a chore*) huzmitipsít

FIR *s.* brad *m*, *dim.* brǎdíc; **G:** iéhlǎ; **needles from a ~** șíțǎ

FIRE *s.* foc; (*destructive ~*) yeangâne; **to catch ~** ľau foc; ▾apríndu ‖ **fire and fury** fríte; BELIMACE 20: **Poor Maria became fire and fury** Fríte s-feáțe mǎrata di Mǎrie → PUT SMB. TO ~ AND SWORD

FIRE[1] *vb.* (*of a gun*) amín (cu tuféchea); trag (tuféchea); **to ~ a shot** foc ľ-u am; **He ~ed and killed him** Foc ľi áre și-l vǎtǎ-mǎ; **to ~ a cartridge** amín únǎ patrónǎ; **to ~ at a target** dau tu sémnu, trag tu nișáne; **to ~ into the wrong flock** ≈ u-adár taratÓ-re

FIRE[2] *vb.* → DISMISS

FIRE FIGHT *s.* tuficheáuǎ

FIRE FIGHTER *s.* tulumbagí

FIREARM *s.* tuféche

FIREFLY *s. entom.* licuríciu, ľúleac ‖ *SJos:* culufécsâ, *Prv:* culufuth-h'éi (*sic*) CL 43

FIREGUARD *s.* (*in a stove*) pirumáh

FIREMAN *s.* tulumbagí

FIRE-PAN *s.* (*the ~ of an ancient fire-arm*) fáľe

FIREPLACE *s.* vátră

FIRERAKE *s.* căţíe, (*rare*) giugár; jáglu *m*, lupátă, máşe

FIREWOOD *s. CľIs:* cărmucăñ *f pl*

FIRING OFF *s.* tufixíre

FIRM *adj.* (*solid, as of a new bridge*) sănătós, -oásă, -óşĭ, -oáse; (*resolute*) ligát; (*fixed, steady*) ni-minát; **with a ~ voice** cu un graiu ligát → MAKE ~

FIRMAN *s.* firmáne, thirmáne

FIRST *ord., adv.* ntâñu, biringí, prot; **a ~-hand inn** hánea ţea cáma próta; **the ~ time** ntâña oáră; **He did to him what he had done to the ~ one** Ľ-feáţe ca a prótlui; **The ~ went out** Işíră antâñľi; **at ~ glance** la videáre; **at ~** próta → § 28.2

FIRST CLASS *adj.* (*excellent*) aţél ma búnlu; di prótă mână; mă-sa-ľ fu!

FIRST COUSIN *s.* cusurín bun *m*, -ínă búnă *f*

FIRST-BORN *s.* prutárcu, purtárcu, purtáric

FIRST RATE *adj.* → FIRST CLASS

FIRST-HAND *adj.* ţel cáma di próta (*resp.* ţeá, ţéľ, ţeále)

FIRSTLING OF SPRING *s. bot.* (*primula*) (flori di) ligoáce

FIRSTLY *adv.* próta; di próta, năínte, ânínte; (*first of all*) únă; **I am not going. First of all, I am sick.** Nu mi duc; únă, că nu pot

FISH *s.* péscu, *dim.* piscóplu; peáşte; **neither ~ nor fawl** ne álbu, ne laiu; ni úda, ni uscáta

FISHERMAN *s.* piscár; **a ~'s wife** piscăroáñe ‖ *Amc, An, Gard, Na:* psărár, *Fal:* psărél, B-ARCH 360

FISHERY *s.* piscăríľe

FISHHOOK *s.* úñiţă → LINE

FISHING *s.* piscăríľe

FISHING ROD *s.* úñiţă, vlac

FISHING-LINE *s.* vlac, grep, grip

FISHY *adj.* (*questionable*) ni-síyur, ípaptu; şubiilâ, *f sg/pl* -loáñe, *m pl* -ládz; şubeilâtic

FISSURE

FISSURE *s.* cripitúră, firádhă

FIST *s.* buş, búştu, búşur *m;* púlmu ‖ ALIA 161: bus, pum, stúmbu

FISTFUL *s.* púlmu, *pl* púlñi

FISTICUFFS *s.* ncârligáre, fuľór

FISTULA *s. med.* fístulă, fíştură

FIT[1] *s.* (*the quality, manner or state of being fitted or adapted*) uidisíre, undzíre

FIT[2] *s. med.* loáre di lúnă; ~ **of malaria** hivríre; ~ **of anger** inătusíre; **to beat smb. into ~s** l-fac léşi → BY ~S AND STARTS

FIT *adj.* bun, undzít; (*flat, even, adequate*) dúze *invar;* duziñárcu; 3 *sg.* fáţe tră; **as ~ as a fiddle** sănătós ca grij di dzádă

FIT *vb.* **It ~s me** Ñ-undzeáşte; (*to suit each other, to be well suited with*) ▾uidiséscu, iduséscu; **We ~ each other** Dóľi nă uidisím ‖ (*as of a pair of shoes*) âñ vin 3 *pl,* see PARALLELE 142

FITTING *s.* tiryisíre

FITTING *adj.* uidisít, idusít; uigúne *invar.*

FITTINGNESS *s.* undzíre

FIVE *num.* ţínţi; **the ~ brothers** ţínţiľ fraţ ‖ **the ~ of us, of you, of them**) amintsintsiľ, K-D 72

FIVER *s. med.* foc, căldúră, heávră

FIX *s.* (*a position of difficulty or embarrassment*) stinuhuríe; angúsă; **in a bad ~** tu angúsă máre; **to be in a bad ~** ≈ şed cu cúrlu tu neáuă

FIX *vb.* (*to fasten with nails*) pirunséscu, ▾ncărfuséscu; (*repair*) ▾ndirég, ndreg, ▾ndréptu; (*to assign, to establish, as smb.'s salary*) ▾taľu; **to ~ one's eyes on smb.** bag tu ócľu, ñi si alăchéscu ócľiľ di; **A muleteer had ~ed his eyes on him** Un cărvănár l-băgă tu ócľu

FIXING OF PRICES *s.* nárche

FIXED *adj.* (*immobile, stationary*) ni-minát

FLABBERGASTED *adj.* aumbrát, chirút, cildisít, cildăsít

FLABBINESS *s.* slăbeáţă → WEAKNESS

FLABBY *adj.* mólav, *m pl* mólavi (*sic* DDA 819); prăhár

FLAG *s.* bandéră, pandéră, băiráche, băryeáche, flámură, flámbură; **to raise the ~** u scol pandéra

FLAGELLATED *adj.* frăştuít

FLAGITIOUS *adj.* zgrumát

FLAGSTONE s. ploáce

FLAKE s. (*of snow*) fúlgu (di neáuă), spíthă (di neáuă), ciómbu-ră (di neáuă) ‖ GULI 31: peánă di neauă

FLAME s. píră, băbărútă (*and* bâbâ-), bărbărútă, bubúnă, bubu-ránă, bubútă, curmicáme, flámă, fleámă, fleácă (*and* fľácă), *pl* fléțe; **Gop:** gâlmădz *f pl*; **Clis:** gârgáľu; lămbíe, lumbárdhă (*and* lumbárdă), plámină ‖ (*big* ~) GULI 25, 47: cărmăgáne, *pl* -găñ

FLANNEL s. fanélă, flanélă; *also:* catasárcă, catasárcu; cămi-geálă, camigeánă, **GSus:** cămăgeálă; sălnícă, silnícă; **G, Lvz:** gă-dzoáfe, **N:** coáce

FLANK s. árpă; ~ **of a mountain** plaiu, *pl* -iuri ‖ MURNU 2: *pl* pláie

FLAP s. (*of a garment*) yeácă; (*the motion or sound of smth. broad*) flítur, flituráre

FLAP vb. flítur; (*as of a rooster*) ascútur (árichile)

FLAPPING OF WINGS s. flítur

FLASH ACROSS / THROUGH ONE'S MIND vb. ñ-şúiră (*or* ñ-şíură) prin cap, ñ-cântă tu núcă, ñ-ticneáşte; hupuéscu → CROSS ONE'S MIND

FLASH-FLOOD s. nicătúră, plimíră

FLASHY adj. jupânéscu, -neáscă, -néşţâ, -néşti

FLAT adj. buimátcu, -tcă, -tţi, -tţe; nturtát; paciŭ, *m pl* pacĭ [pač], *f sg/pl* páce; placeán, plăsát, plisát, pliciós, plicitós, plâciutós; (*even*) dúze *invar.* → BEAT ~

FLATLAND s. câmpu, páde; *obs.* şes

FLATTEN vb. plăsédz, plăciutédz, pli-, plăciuséscu, nturtédz (*and* ndur-); **to** ~ **out** ischédz; **to** ~ **out smb.** ľ-pliciutédz nările

FLATTENED adj. nturtát → FLAT

FLATTENING s. plăsáre, plăciutáre, plăciusíre, plăcitúră, ntur-táre (*and* ndur-), ciuplitúră

FLATTER vb. ▼alín cu zboárile, culăchipséscu, ▼sprilíngu

FLATTERER s. cólac, tărtór

FLATTERING adj. gudiľár, -lárcu; marghiól, *f* -ghioálă; tărtór

FLATTERY s. culăchíe, culăchipsíre, sprilíndzire

FLAUNT s. căbărdisíre

FLAUNT vb. ▼fuduléscu, ▼căbărdéscu, ▼căbărdiséscu

FLAVOR s. (*smell*) ñurdíc

FLAW s. mărdáie, smârdhă → SHORTCOMING

FLAX s. *bot.* ľin

FLAX OIL *s.* bizíre

FLAX-COMB *s.* tépcă

FLAXEN *adj.* di ľin

FLAY *vb.* (*to strip off the skin or crust*) disbiléscu; ▼disgu-léscu, ▼dizgóľu

FLEA *s.* púric; *coll.* puricáme ‖ *Gop:* pric^u (*sic*), GOLAB 246

FLEE *vb.* ▼fug, li tíndu; **to ~ for one's life** fug di mi frângu, fug di nu mi ved → BOLT

FLEECE *s.* báscă ‖ *Cru:* báscă di lănă, GOLAB 207

FLEECE *vb.* (*to strip of money, as at cards*) afuléscu

FLESH: neither fish nor ~ ni úda, ni uscáta; ne álbu, ne laiu → PUT ON ~

FLESH AND BLOOD *adj.* yiu, *f* yíe, *m/f pl* yiĭ ; **He was the devil in ~** Aéstu erá şútlu yiu ‖ cárne ş-oáse, BASME 28

FLESHY *adj.* (*as of cheeks*) cărnós, buciós, bucicós [buč●kós]; **~ cheeks** fáţă bucicoásă [buč●koá●să]

FLEXIBLE *adj.* (*pliant*) *Clis:* jílav

FLICK OUT OF SIGHT *vb.* ▼fac cáípe → DISAPPEAR

FLIBBERTIGIBBET *s.* sirsém, asiyúriftu, pirídhrum, zevzéc

FLIGHT *s.* zbor, azburáre, azbuiráre, azburát, azbuirát; (*running away*) alágă, fúgă, fudzítă, fudzíre, fudzeáre, angănáre, căpsălsíre, şpirtuíre; (*caprice*) fărfúdă; (*group of birds or insects*) gârdéľ, grúmur, suríe, urdíe

FLIGHTY *adj.* căpriceárcu, nizeárcu; **He is ~** Nu-ľ angreácă míntea

FLIMFLAM *s.* ilée

FLIMSY *adj.* slab, *m pl* slaghi; lişurác, -ráşcu, -rátic; sersém

FLINDERS *s. pl.* (*bits, splinters*) ţívale *invar*; **to break into ~** mi adár ţívale; ▼zdrúmin sârme-sârme → SPLINTER

FLING *s.* arucătúră: **at one ~** tu úna → SUDDENLY

FLING *vb.* (*to throw*) arúc; (*to hit, to blow*) plăscănéscu; **I'll ~ you into the hollow!** Am s-ti plăscănésc tu trap! *to* **be flung to and fro** (*as of a bird*) mi zbat, mi dirín; **to ~ dirt at smb.** riziléscu, rizilipséscu; **to ~ the hatchet** (*to beat hell*) para-fác, li ngruşédz lúcrile

FLINT *s.* crémine, sturnáre

FLINT-LOCK GUN *s.* flíntă, sturnáre

FLINTY *adj.* (*of an area*) sturnărós, -nurós

FLIPPANCY *s.* lişuráme, xinăstrăpsíre

FLIPPANT *adj.* dúrdur, giadíu, ni-aştirnút; **to be ~** xinăstrăp-séscu

FLOAT *vb.* anót, (m)plătéscu (*and* mblă-), mplitéscu, avuzéscu; **~ed like a feather** ca nă peánă amplăteá; **Boards from broken ships ~ed here and there** Scânduri di căíchi aspárte anutá pri-auá ş-pri-acló

FLOCK[1] *s.* (*of sheep, etc.*) cupíe, túrmă, uínă; (*cattle or birds*) suríe; *also:* árpă (di oi, di ñále); bándă, bulúche; (*small ~ of milking sheep kept in the village*) cănără; grúmur, tăbăbíe; uiríu; (*of birds*) trâmbă (di puľ), urdíe (di puľ) ‖ SarD 63: bi-liúc; BASME 701: stog

FLOCK[2] *s.* (*of wool, etc.*) floc, *pl* floáţe; (*tuft*) ciúmă; *adj.* flucát, flucós

FLOCK *vb.* (*to congregate*) ▾adún

FLOE *s.* (*floating ice*) ‖ PC: gľeţ

FLOG *vb.* frâştuéscu

FLOGGING *s.* frâştuíre

FLOOD *s.* nec; *also:* cataclizmó, chiaméte, plimíră

FLOOD *vb.* (*of a river*) ies, es; ▾dipún; **The river has ~ed** Di-púse) arâulu [a•râᵘ•lu]; (*to overwhelm with water*) ▾pudidéscu, ▾nec

FLOODED *adj.* (*overflown*) dipús túna

FLOOR *s.* (*story*) pat, pátumă; **a palace with four ~s** únă păláte cu pátru páturi ‖ HRISTU 1: cat

FLOOR *vb.* pătuséscu, pătuñiséscu; (*to flatten*) nturdédz; (*to put smb. down*) dărâm

FLOTSAM *s.* nicătúră

FLOUNCE *s.* (*as of a scurt or curtain*) fărbálă; frúte *f pl*

FLOUNDER *vb.* (*to play in water, of children or animals*) ▾nciu-muléscu, ciumuléscu

FLOUNDERING *s.* nciumulíre

FLOUR *s.* fărínă; **wheat ~** gărneáţă, grăneáţă (*and* grâ-), găreá-ţă; (*best quality ~*) fluríţă ‖ *Kok, Rod:* firínă; *Kar, Plat, Perd:* frínă, B-ARCH 353

FLOUR DEALER *s.* fărinár

FLOUR PAN *s.* căpisteáre

FLOURISHING *adj.* tihiró, -rádz, *f sg/pl* -roáñe; cu hăíre

FLOUT

FLOUT *vb.* ñ-arâd → MOCK

FLOW *vb.* cur, fug

FLOWER *s.* lilíce; lălúdă, lulúdhă; floáre (*DDA: anemic word*); *N:* floárä ‖ ALIA 35: chítcă, lílă

FLOWERPOT *s.* ciuváñu, găvanós, ghi(u)véciu

FLOWING *s.* curáre

FLUE *s.* ugeác → CHIMNEY

FLUENTLY *adv.* ápă; **talks ~** ápă-ľ ñárdze gúra

FLUKE *s.* (*luck*) ambăreáţă, báftă, căsméte, hăíre, tíhe

FLUMMOXED *adj.* limnusít → DUMBFOUNDED

FLURRY *s.* (*stir*) lávă, vreávă

FLURRIED *adj.* aumbrát → GIDDY

FLURRY *vb.* (*to discompose, to fluster*) ▼mintéscu, armân ca tul, ▼cirtuéscu, ▼cicărdiséscu, ▼cihtiséscu, ▼şişirdiséscu ‖ (*of snow*) CUNIA 115: da spíti di neáuă *3 sg impers*

FLUSH *s.* (*tinge of red*) aruşeáţă

FLUSH *adj.* (*having an unbroken or even surface*) buimátcu; dúze *invar.*; (*abundant*) bólcu, -lcă, -lţi, -lţe

FLUSTER *vb.* (*to put into a state of agitated confusion*) mi cirtuéscu, ciurtuéscu, cirtăséscu; **They ~ed the state** Duvlétea u ciurtuíră → FLURRY

FLUTE *s.* fluiáră, fiľoáră, flúir, cavál, căvál, dzamáră, dză-máră ‖ ALB: *Kёrb, Pe:* fuléru; *Sln:* făléru; *Dren:* fleru, Brâncuş 556; HRISTU 52: dzumar

FLUTTER *vb.* flítur, fliturédz

FLUTTERING *s.* (*as of a light fabric in the wind*) flituráre, arăschiráre

FLY *s. ent.* múscă; *coll.* muscáme ‖ CUVATA 14 mújdzăli *pl def*

FLY *vb.* zbor, asboáir, arăsbór; **to ~ about** (a)ruéscu, arăéscu; ‖ (*in folk poetry*) bor, CAPIDAN 148

FLY INTO A PASSION (or TEMPER, TANTRUM) *vb.* mi acáţă báľile, mi acáţă cľínlu, mi acáţă daráţľi (di urécľi), mi acáţă órĭle, mi acáţă zála; ▼ayrédz, mi apríndu, ▼aráchiu, ñ-arsáre dzâfna, ñ-ar-sáre scârpa, lu arúc samárlu, ▼dhimunséscu, ▼drăcuséscu, drăcul-séscu, mi fac Frâncu (*and* Frângu); ñ-yíne zurleáţa, ñ-yin órĭle, ▼inătuşéscu, ľau vímtu, ▼năiréscu, nărăéscu, inrăéscu, mi ncálică daráţiľ, ▼thimuséscu, ñ-víne únda

FLY IN(TO) PIECES *vb.* (*as of a vase*) ▼adár ţívale; (*to spend*

irresponsibly, usu. of money) fac jir, asbór pi víntu

FLY OFF THE HANDLE *vb. (of joy or anger)* ▾chérdu míntea, mi schérdu (di haráuă, di yináte)

FLY OVER *vb.* trec

FLY ROUND *vb.* lu adúc varlíga; *to ~* **and round** *(as of a vulture)* adúc roátă, ▾nvârtéscu

FLY TO THE WINDS *vb.* → FLY IN(TO) FLINDERS

FLYING START *s.* fúzmă, paramázmă, vánţu, vímtu; vrápă

FLYSPECK *s. (trifle)* chiritúră

FOAL *s.* măndzu *(and* mândzu) → COLT

FOAM *s.* spúmă, spumătúră, scámată ‖ *Peş:* scámă, CL 260

FOAM *vb.* spumédz

FOAMING *s.* spumáre

FOAMING *adj.* spumós, -oásă, -óşĭ, -oáse

FOE *s.* → ENEMY

FOG *s.* négură; *also:* andáră, brúmă, cătăháie, cătăcníe, dumáne, iámă, sineácu ‖ *Els:* ñégură, B-ARCH 8

FOGHORN *s. (of a steamer)* pízgă

FOIBLE *s.* slăbínţă

FOLD *s. (pleat)* clin, anduplicătúră, bástă, dhíplă, pultéţă; *(pocket-like ~)* budzănáră; *adj. (with folds)* fustănát

FOLD *vb.* dhipluséscu, dipluséscu; ▾andúplic ‖ *Peş:* andăplăséscu, CL 37

FOLDED: **with ~ arms** *adv.* cu mâñle ncurţite *(or* ncruţíte); **to stand with ~ arms** stau cu mâñle n sin

FOLDEROL *s. (conceit)* căbărdisíre; *(nonsense)* bişíñ di cuc

FOLIAGE *s.* frundzáme, şúmă, şúmcă; *(~ and wood chips)* şúştali *f pl*

FOLK *s.* fáră → PEOPLE, TRIBE; *(relative)* cărdu

FOLLOW *vb.* ▾avín, lʼau n cicioáre; **He will ~ me until my death** Va s-mi avínă până tru mărmíntu; **Thieves are ~ing him** Lu-avínă fúrilʼi; *to ~* **on the track of smb.** (mi lʼau dípu díra a; *(to ~ by smell)* úlmic; **to ~ in smb.'s footsteps** ▾cálcu pi úrma a; **to ~ smb. like a sheep (like St. Antony's pig)** mi ţân scalʼu, mi ţân ca mânár ‖ mi lʼau dúpă, BASME 22; CUVATA 13: **I ~ed him** Mini u loai dupu el

FOLLY *s.* cicăníre, cicníre, cicărdisíre, zurleáţă

FOMENT *vb. (to instigate)* ▾schin

FOND

FOND *adj.* ~ **of smb.** l-háscu n gúră → BE ~ OF

FONDLE *vb.* ▾cănăchipséscu, ▾dizñérdu, ▾gălinăséscu, gălini-
séscu, ▾gugiléscu, ▾hăidhipséscu, ▾puşputéscu, ▾zdrudéscu

FONT *s.* (*receptacle for baptismal water*) culimbíthră ‖ **Peş:** cu-
limvíthrâ, CL 43

FOOD *s.* măcáre, mcáre, mângáre, mâncătúră (*and* mângă-), ciumeá-
lă, fáie, ghélă, mánge, hránă; (*free ~*) bugiórnă; (*from a mother's mouth*) mámă; (*children talk*) pápă; (*liquid food*) muḷitúră

FOOD SUPPLIES *s.* mánge, psúne; zaíre, zăiré, zairée

FOODSTUFF *s.* ‖ (*for cattle*) PC: hránă di oi, hránă di văţ

FOOL *s., adj.* zúrlu, dátu-n-cáp, cicănít; (*dupe*) apló; tivichél, *f* -chélă → MAKE A ~ OF ONESELF, MAKE A ~ OF SMB.

FOOL *vb.* (*to deceive*) ancálţu

FOOL AROUND *vb.* ▾agióc; **The man kept working; he was not ~ing
around** Lucrá ómlu, nu si-agiucá

FOOLERY *s.* glăríle, chiritúră, cicăníre, cicníre, cicărdisíre

FOOLHARDY *adj.* azvimturát, cuturgí, distórsu; ≈ nu áre meḷu tu
ciútură (*lit. 'does not have millet in his/her bucket,' i.e. mind
in his/her head*) → RECKLESS

FOOLISH *adj.* cap-di-gáie (*lit. 'a crow's head'*) → STUPID, PENNY

FOOLISHNESS *s.* chiritúri *f pl*; curcubéte (di Chirásova) *f pl*;
glarumáră, glăreáţă → STUPIDITY

FOOT *s.* ciciór (*mainly* **N**); cior (*mainly* **S**); **S Pind:** chiciór;
pătúnă, pâlmúţă; (*jokingly or derog.*) cloáţă → ON ~, PUT ONE'S ~
INTO IT ‖ ALIA 171: chiţór, dixáḷă; **LvO:** ţor

FOOTBRIDGE *s.* púnte (*and* púnde), púnghe, púmhe (*sic*) ‖ (*small
~*) **Av, SJos:** purdícâ, **Prv:** puntícâ, CL 259

FOOTLE (ABOUT) *vb.* mi avín guşturíţăle

FOOTPATH *s.* căráre, *dim.* cărărícă, cărăríce, călíţă, călíce,
călişoáră, munupáte; (*in the snow*) părtícă

FOOTPRINT *s.* úrmă, tor; **G:** toáră

FOOT-SOLDIER *s.* nizám → INFANTRY MAN

FOOTSORENESS *s.* med. (*chronic ~*) dátură

FOOTSTEP *s.* călcătúră → FOOTPRINT

FOOTWEAR *s.* cálţă, pódhimă

FOR *prep.* (*to be used ~, to benefit from*) dit, sti, tră (*and*
trâ), tri, ti, ti la; **Winter is good ~ the rich** Iárna-i búnă, ma
trâ domñi; **clippers ~ clipping sheep** foártiţi tră tundeáre óḷli;

in order to make money ~ (purchase of) salt s-fắţém sirmaié trâ
la sáre; **What are you getting ready ~?** Trâ iu ti ndredzi? **a pawn
~ the payment of the tax** amanéte tri plătíre a dátlui; **medicine ~
cough** yitríe trâ túse; **small houses ~ small people** căsi trâ oámiñ ñiţĭ; **~ a pair of brows** (*i.e., for a woman with beautiful
brows*) ti dáule sufrâmţeále; (*because of*) tră, sti; **The poor boys
were burning ~ a girl** Ardeáu măráţľi tră nă feátă; **to die ~ a
drop of water** (*3 sg*) s-moáră sti nă chícă di ápă; (*~ the benefit
of*) **Such a man was needed ~ the flock** Ahtáre om erá lipsít ti la
túrmă; pri, dípu, sti, stră, trăt, di; **He searched them ~ salt**
(*salt was an expensive commodity*) Ľ-mutrí di sáre; (*purpose: in
order to*) tră; **The enemies are coming ~ plunder** yin duşmáñľi tră
călcáre; **He carried more ~ his fishing** Ma múltu ţâneá pri piscă-
ríľi; **She died ~ flowers** Mureá dípu lălúdz; **poison ~ two pence** un
duiár afrát (NB: *no preposition before the noun* afrát); *other
uses*: **~ months** cu méşľi; **~ sale** di-a vínde; **~ a long time** di múltu; **~ ever** tră tótna; di únă

FOR A WHILE: After she had mourned him ~ Cára l-plâmse ţe
l-plâmse; **After they had walked ~ ...** Ñársiră ţi ñársiră ...

FOR BETTER OR FOR WORSE (*haphazardly, regardless of consequences*) tu tíhe

FOR GOOD → FOREVER

FOR NOTHING *adv.* (*having no purpose; in vain*) ‖ tră oáuă aróşă,
BASME 165

FOR ONE THING únă (că) → FIRST OF ALL

FOR SO LITTLE (*for such a trifle*) ‖ tr-ahât lúcru, BASME 10

FOR SOME TIME NOW *adv.* *N:* di la un chiróu şi coa

FOR THE TIME BEING *adv.* tóra di tóra, di oáră, ti oáră, tră oáră

FOR THE SECOND TIME *adv.* dea-doára, da-doára

FORAY *vb.* fac iurúşe, dau iurúşe → PLUNDER

FORBEAR *vb.* (*to abstain*) ▾ţân, ▾stăpuéscu; (*to be patient*)
▾arávdu

FORBEARING: He is as ~ as a dog Arávdă ca un câne

FORBID *vb.* (*to bar*) nu alás; **God ~!** Ilealá; **The whole village
keeps saying God forbid of this man** Tútă hoára fáţe ilealá di
aístu om → GOD ~!

FORBIDDEN *adj.* yeasáche *invar.*

FORCE

FORCE *s.* puteáre, pteáre; *also:* azgáte, azváte, cuvét(e), dhí-name, fórţă, fuchíi, părădhúnă, seu, sílă; (*compulsion*) stañó; (*resources, capability*) tăcáte; (*moral ~*) véte, vârtúte, vir-túte, vurtúte, vârtuşáme; **It is lacking ~** Nu áre tăcáte; **He took her by ~** U-ló cu stañólu; **by ~** cu părdhúmă, cu zórba, cu zórea, zórca ‖ **GSus:** séftu, CL 260; **God's ~ is great** Dhínamea a Duⁿnu-dzắuli eáste máre, RÉCATAS 51; **with all one's ~** cu tută forţa ţi avia, HRISTU 34

    FORCE *vb.* sălnăéscu, ▾stríngu, bag súla n coáste → COMPEL

    FORCE OUT *vb.* scot; (*to expel, to drive away / out*) ľ-dau pál-mili di-auá (*or* di-acló) → EXPEL

    FORCED *adj.* (*compelled*) stres, -eásă, -eşĭ, -eáse

    FORCEDLY *adv.* cu síla

    FORCEFULLY *adv.* cu zórca

    FORCEPS *s.* ţimbídhă, ţimbístră

    FORCIBLE *adj.* (*robust, strong*) zdúmban

    FORCIBLY *adv.* cu síla, cu zórba, zórca ‖ cu arắulu, BASME 94; cu angăríe greáuă, BASME 89; HRISTU 26: cu forţă; STERE 81: zórlea

    FORD *s.* por, puréauă ‖ **SJos:** báră, CL 38

    FORDABLE *adj.* plítcu, -tcă, -tţi, -tţe

    FOREARM *s.* ‖ **Peş:** biľigícă, CL 39

    FOREBODING *s.* érgu, nóimă; (*of smth. bad*) nóimă slábă → HAVE A HUNCH

    FORECAST *vb.* ▾privéd, pruvéd, prufitipséscu ‖ (*by reading the stars*) arúc tu steále; (*by reading the [playing] cards*) arúc tu cărţâ PARALLELE 157-158

    FOREFATHER *s.* stripărínte → ANCESTOR

    FOREFINGER *s. anat.* ‖ ALR 1604: pilicár

    FOREHANDED *adj.* (*cautious*) câştigós (*and* că-), -oásă

    FOREHEAD *s.* frúnte, **S:** frúndi; frâmte, frúnghe

    FOREIGN *adj.* xen, xeñ, xeánă, -eáne **N:** căsén; strin; **completely ~** pataxén, xen-pataxén; **~ language** límbă axeánă

    FOREIGN COUNTRIES curbéte, xeánă, xinitíe, xinitíľe, xinătá-te; **the cursed ~** pónda xinitíe

    FOREIGN-BORN RESIDENT *s.* sudít

    FOREIGNER *s.* (a)xén, om (a)xén, om dit axeáne ‖ CARAFOLI 49: xintimén

    FOREMAN *s.* căpíe (*and* câ-), máru, maimár, măimár; **G:** căliúş

[•lĭúş]

FORERUNNER *s.* pródhrom

FORESEE *vb.* ▼privéd, pruvéd ‖ (*as of a magician*) arúc tu steá-li, DIARO 255

FORESEEING *s.* pruvideáre

FORESIGHT *s.* pruvideáre

FOREST *s.* pădúre, *dim.* păduríce, pădurícă; **large** ~ păduráme; pădurlíche; *also*: códru, códur *or* códure; *N*: curíe; dhas, dubrác, urmáne ‖ ALIA 47: múnte; *Po*: bâdúri, NEIESCU 283

FOR(E)FEND *vb.* ▼ápăr → PROTECT

FOR(E)GATHER *vb.* ▼astálʼu → MEET

FORENOON *s.* dimineáţă → MORNING

FORETASTE *vb.* dhuchimăséscu

FORETELL *vb.* prufitipséscu → FORECAST

FORETHOUGHTFULLY *adv.* cu usúle

FORETHOUGHTFULNESS *s.* usúle

FOREVER *adv.* tră tótna, tră tótăna, ti tótnă; păn tu éta a étilʼi; (*rare*) salím ‖ HRISTU 21: ti etă

FORGE ABOUT *vb.* (*of scavengers and fig.*) ▼mârşuéscu

FORGE AHEAD *vb.* ▼disíc năínte

FORGED *adj.* (*as of a lie*) gurgulʼitós, -oásă; (*counterfeit*) cálpu → CONTRIVED

FORGER *s.* plastoyráf

FORGERY *s.* plastoyrafíe

FORGET *vb.* ▼agărşéscu, agrăşéscu, ▼xihăséscu; *obs.* ▼últu; **Forget it!** Bágă-lʼ crúţea! Lʼa-ţ curátile! Mútă-u míntea! *or* Mútă-ţ míntea! Sănătáte! **Let's now ~ everything that has been said!** Hai tóra ápă şi sáre túte câte dzâsim! ‖ Mutreá-ţ lúcrulu! BASME 465

FORGET ONE'S PLACE *vb.* ▼disgărdéscu

FORGETFUL *adj.* agărşít, agărşitór

FORGETFULNESS *s.* agărşáre, agărşíre, xihăsíre

FORGETTING *s.* agărşáre, agărşíre, xihăsíre

FORGIVE *vb.* ▼lʼértu; (*to have the final conversation with a Christian moribund*) dau lʼirtăciúne (*lit.* 'to give him/her one's forgivness')

FORGIVENESS *s.* lʼirtáre, lʼirtăciúne → ASK FOR ~

FORGIVING *s.* → FORGIVENESS

FORGO *vb.* trag mâna di → ABNEGATE

FORGOTTEN

FORGOTTEN *adj.* agărşít, xihăsít

FORK *s.* **1.** (*at the table*) bunélă, furculíţă, pirínghe, piróñe, pirúnă, pirúye, pirúľe, puñáuă, păneáuă, pingheáuă ‖ *Prv:* proácă, CL 259; **2.** (*implement for hay, etc.*) fúrcă; *also:* carpulóy, cârpâlóg, dihálă, fultutíne, furcáce; (*Y-shaped wooden spool ~*) ftíuă

FORLORN *adj.* (*as of a grave*) (a)lăsát, (a)părnăsít; (*desolate*) érmu

FORM¹ *s.* (*shape*) bicíme; **will assume such a ~** ahtáre bicíme va s-ľa; (*condition*) **in good ~** (*as of a horse*) pri trup

FORM² *s.* (*resting place of a hare*) pitúľ

FORM *vb.* phys. ▾fac; **A wart has ~ed just on the top of my nose** Ñ-si feáţe nă lúznă trâşĭ pi chípita a nárĭľei; *bot.* (*to set, of a fruit*) leg; (*to fashion*) turnipséscu

FORMALITY *s.* (*etiquette*) ţirimóñe

FORMER *adj.* vécľu; **at their ~ innkeeper's** la vécľul a lor hăngí

FORMERLY *adv.* năoáră, unăoáră, unoáră; (*previously*) năínte (*and* năínde), nínte (*and* nínde)

FORMIDABLE *adj.* (*arousing fear*) fuvirós, lăhtărós

FORMLESS *adj.* bicimsâz, -âjĭ, -âză, -âze

FORSAKE *vb.* (*to abandon, to desert*) ▾alás, fug caceác

FORTH *adv.* năínte (*and* năínde) nínte (*and* nínde) → BRING ~

FORTHRIGHT *adj.* (*direct, straightforward*) fóra, tu fáţă

FORTHRIGHTLY *adv.* → FORTHRIGHT

FORTHWITH *adv.* diunăoáră, dinăoáră → SUDDENLY

FORTIFY *vb.* ▾nvârtuşédz → STRENGTHEN

FORTITUDE *s.* virtúte, vârtuşáme

FORTRESS *s.* cástru, căstríe, calé, víglă

FORTUITOUS *adj.* tihiró

FORTUNATE *adj.* calótih; **I wish you to be pretty and ~** S-ti faţi muşátă ş-calótihă! (*predicative*) **It is ~ for you/him/ her, etc.** calíheal di, calótih di, calóit di tíni/năs/năsă, etc.

FORTUNATELY *adv.* spuláite; cálai-că, caláí-ţe

FORTUNE *s.* (*property, wealth*) căşeáre; (*livestock*) tutípută; cătúnă, catándă, cătăndíe → MAKE A ~

FORTUNE-TELLER *s.* mándu *m*, mándisă *f*

FORTY *num.* patrudzăţi

FORTY WINGS *s.* sómnu, *dim.* sumnúş

FORWARD *adj.* di frắmti; prot, -ótă (*sic*), proţ, -óte; biringí, *m pl* -geádz, *f sg/pl* -gioáñe

FORWARD *adv.* năínte (*and* năínde), nínte (*and* nínde)

FORWARD *vb.* dau năínti

FOSTER *vb.* ▾bréscu, créscu, ▾mutréscu; (*to nurture*) ▾hrănéscu, hărnéscu

FOSTERLING *s.* ţup, ciup → BABY

FOUL *adj.* blắstimát, murdár; sălchíu, *f* -íe → DETESTABLE

FOUL PLAY *s.* aplá, ilée ‖ CUNIA 113 *also:* dubáră, duculeáchi

FOUL *vb.* cacurizipséscu, ▾lăvăşéscu → DIRTY, DISGRACE

FOUL UP *vb.* ▾aspárgu, ▾stric, u-adár bóză

FOUL-UP *s.* (*confusion*) cârşéľ, mintitúră

FOUND *s.* (*ground*) usíe

FOUND *vb.* thimiľuséscu, bag par

FOUNDATION *s.* thiméľ; (*process*) thimiľusíre

FOUNDER *s.* ctítor

FOUR *num.* pátru; **the ~ of them** şaminpáturľi; **from the ~ corners of the earth** dit páturile chioşi a lúmiľei

FOURTEEN *num.* pásprădzaţe, páspraţi, pásprăţi, pátrusprădzaţe; **~ people** pásprăţi di (*sic*) oámiñ

FOURTH *ord.* páturlu *m*, a pátura *f*; **on the ~ day** a pátura dzúuă ‖ **Cru:** tetártu, GOLAB 254; tetartlu, tetarta, K-D 71; **the ~ time** a patruuară, K-D 72 → § 28.2

FOWL *s.* pitúmin; **neither fish nor ~** → FISH

FOX *s.* vúlpe *f*, schílă; vulpóñu *m* ‖ (*in fairy tales*) Chíra Mára, BASME 271

FOX *vb.* ncálţu → TRICK, OUTWIT

FOXGLOVE *s. bot.* culeáţă

FOXINESS *s.* vulpíľe → SLYNESS

FOXY *adj.* drăcurós, -oásă, -óşľ, -oáse; pónir → CLEVER, SLY

FRACAS *s.* → BRAWL, ROW

FRACTION: to a ~ pân tu ac

FRACTIOUS *adj.* ghiurultagí, căvyăgí

FRACTURE *s.* frâmtúră

FRAGILE *adj.* pirpişór, -oáră; vlângu, *m pl* -ndzi → FRAIL

FRAGMENT *s.* (*debris*) aspărgătúră ‖ **~s of speach** bucăţ di zburari, HRISTU 51

FRAGMENT *vb.* (*as of a cloud driven by the wind*) ▾diñíc

FRAGRANT

FRAGRANT *adj.* mirudhát, ñurdzitór, ñurizmós

FRAIL *adj.* → FRAGILE; *derog.* Cánda l-uuắ mâ-sa (*lit. 'As if his mother laid him'; i.e., he is or seems to be as frail as an egg*)

FRAME *s.* (*outline*) chináre, curníṭă, curníză, curnídhă, márgură

FRAME OF PLOUGH *s.* plaz

FRAME UP *vb.* arúc mắhănăulu pri

FRAME-UP *s.* dâvăgilâche

FRANC *s.* (*a French monetary unit*) frángu

FRANK *adj.* curát, cu priéplu diṣcľís, cu ínima diṣcľísă; li-ám curáte (zmeánile) (*lit. 'I have them clean,' i.e. my underwear is clean'*)

FRANKLY *adv.* → FRANK

FRANTIC *adj.* ≈ li si fită Hristólu n cásă

FRATERNAL *adj.* frăṭéscu, -ṭeáscă, -ṭéṣṭâ, -ṭéṣti

FRATERNITY *s.* cărdăṣlâche

FRAUD *s.* bătăhcilâche, ilée → DECEIT

FRAUGHT *adj.* mplin (cu)

FRAZZLE *vb.* (*as of clothes*) mâc, ▾tuchéscu

FRAZZLED *adj.* (*tired*) curmát, arúptu; (*of clothes*) măcát di purtáre

FREAK *s.* fărfúdă

FREAKISH *adj.* anápudh, *m pl* -nápudz, *f pl* -nápudhe; *m* térsu, *f* térsă (*sic*), *m pl* térṣi, *f pl* térse

FRECKLE *s.* pécnă, pícnă, précnă ‖ M: píclă, SarD 32 and 95

FRECKLED *adj.* picn(ăv)ós, -oásă, -óṣĭ, -oáse

FREE *adj.* léfter, eléfthir; (*unemployed, independent*) vlíhur; G: fílcu; (*~ of charge*) batiavá, bathavá [bat•ha•vá]; pi virisíe; **to set ~** dau cále

FREE *vb.* ▾elefthiruséscu, dau cále

FREED *adj.* elefthirusít

FREEDOM *s.* iliftiríi → LIBERTY; (*exemption*) ľirtáre

FREELY *adv.* G: dilíe

FREEMASON *s.* masón, farmazón

FREEZE *s.* ngľeṭ

FREEZE *vb.* ▾ngľeṭ (*to be affected by cold*) arcurédz, dzeádzir (di arcoári), (n)frigurédz, sec; (*as a command*) Dur! ‖ xipâyiséscu (di-arcoári), DIARO 362; (*as a command*) Stăi! PARALLELE 157

FREEZING *s.* arcoáre, dzeádzir, ngľiṭáre ‖ xipâyiseári, DIARO 362

FREIGHT *s.* návlu

FREIGHT *vb.* arúc nă cále

FREIGHT CART *s.* arâbă

FRENCH *s.* ‖ BELIMACE 50: **until the arrival of the French** pănă la vineárea a frânţălor

FRENCH *adj.* frânţéscu (*and* frânţéscu, frândzéscu)

FRENCH BEAN *s.* spătáľe, păstáľe

FRENCHMAN *s.* Fréngu ‖ **Cru:** yal, GOLAB 220

FRENZIED *adj.* plin di bubulíţi

FRENZY *s.* farfúdă

FRENZY *vb.* (*to be, to become delirious*) aľurédz

FREQUENT *vb.* (*derog. as to ~ taverns*) alág

FREQUENTLY *adv.* des, dipriúnă, índa, picná

FRESH *adj.* proáspit; *also:* (*as of bread, of flowers*) afrát, fréşcu; (*of meat*) tazé *or* tazétcu; (*of cheese*) tínir

FRESHET *s.* ‖ CUNIA 139: (*as of a river*) (a)zvumeáre, azvoámire

FRET *vb.* ▾uftichédz, uhtichédz, ▾nvirín, nvirinédz; *N:* ▾nver; ▾munduéscu; **Don't ~ about that!** Bag-u strâmbă cămăláfchea! **to ~ and fume** ▾cârtéscu ‖ ▾nfármăc, BASME 656

FRETFUL *adj.* şcľimurós, -oásă, -óşĭ, -oáse; mutrusít

FRIABLE *adj.* (*usu. of pears*) *m sg/pl* muluéţ, *f pl* mulueáţă

FRICTION *s.* fricáre

FRIDAY *s.* víñirĭ ‖ **Vil:** vínir, **Na:** víñir, **Pal:** vínira, B-ARCH 537

FRIED *adj.* tiyănsít, ţăyărsít, ţiyărsít

FRIED EGGS *s.* oáuă ócľi, oáuă mproáste

FRIED LAMB *s.* (*or any other animal*) curbáne

FRIEND *s.* oáspe *m*, oáspită *or* uspitoáñe *f*; *also:* fărtát, furtát, frătát, fărtíc, frătíc, patriót, soţ *m*, soáţă *and* surátă *f*; urtác; (*a friend's ~*) pára-oáspe ‖ VELO 96: fărtătíciu; **We are very good ~s** Sáre ş-pâne mâcăm deadún (*lit. 'We eat together salt and bread'*) → BE HAND AND GLOVE WITH SMB., MAKE A ~, MAKE ~S WITH, MAKE ~S AGAIN

FRIENDSHIP *s.* uspiţáľe, uspitláche, filíe; **to strike up a ~ with** li apríndu aluáturile [a•luă•turĭ•li] cu → PAL IN WITH SMB.

FRIENDLY *adv.* baríş

FRIGHT *s.* frícă; *also:* aspáryiu, aspárimă, aspárizmă, bubuíre, ceáş, chiutilíche, cişíre, cutrém, cutróm, cutrémur, cutreámur,

FRIGHTEN

cutreámbur, dátă, fricuíre, fricuşári, nfricuşári, lăhtár, păvríe, pirdéşe, tartacútă, târtile, trom, trumáră → TAKE ~

FRIGHTEN *vb.* ▾fric, fricuéscu, fricuşédz, ▾nfrichédz, ▾spár, u
aspár huzmétea, ▾bubuéscu, ▾căşéscu, ñ-fúdze buríclu (di frícă),
ñ-beau sândzile di frícă, ñi-ngľáţă sândzile di máre lăhtáră, li
úmplu (di frícă), mi ľa dáta, mi ľa lăhtárlu, mĭ-acáţă hérile (*or*
limăreáua) di frícă, mĭ-acáţă lăhtárea, ▾lăhtărséscu, li cac (*or*
li cufuréscu) zmeánile (*or* cicioárĭle), ľau păvríe, ▾şirpitédz,
trag frícă, trâmuxéscu, trumuxéscu, trumăxéscu, mi úmplu di cutrémur, ñ-yíne cutrémur, mĭ-acáţă cutrémurlu ‖ mi ľa ceáşlu di
frícă, BASME 35

FRIGHTENED *adj.* lihtărsít, şirpitát

FRIGHTFUL *adj.* urút; *also:* ceáşav, *m pl* -şayĭ, *f pl* -şave; fricós, fricuít, lihtărós, fricuşát, fricuşeát, nfricuşát

FRIGHTFULLY *adv.* ceáşav, fricós, fuvirós, cu lăhtár, lăhtărós

FRIGID *adj.* dzidzirós, virvirós; (*as of a wind*) turinós

FRINGE *s.* arâsă, fúndă, pischiúle

FRISK (ABOUT) *vb.* trub, ▾zburdălipséscu; **The boy began to ~
about** Ficiórlu băgă s trúbă

FRISKY *adj.* astráptu, *m pl* -pţâ, *f pl* -pte → FROLICSOME

FRITTER *s.* (*small cake*) lănghídhă, nălănghítă

FRITTER *vb.* toc; **to ~ away** (*to spend wastefully*) dau di zvércă, tuchéscu; **to ~ one's time to no avail** ñ-cher săpúnea

FRIVOLITY *s.* lişuráme

FRIVOLOUS *adj.* chirút; lişór (*and* ľi-), ñişór, lişór di mínte;
gláru-lişór; lişurác, lişuráşcu; **He is ~** U băgă tu lişoára

FRIZZLE *s.* zulúfe → CURL

FRIZZY *adj.* căţărós, -oásă; zgur

FRO: to and ~ ≈ **F:** pĭ-aroá pĭ-arcó (DDA: 207)

FROG *s.* broáscă; (*male*) bruscóñu, (*female*) broscoáñe; *coll.*
broscáme ‖ ALIA 132: broátic, bróscu, brótic; farfaľópă; **Pls:**
fiρfiľópâ, CL 45

FROGS AND LOOPS *s.* (*on a uniform*) găitáne, yăitáne

FROG SPIT *s.* jághină, jeghiu, jéynă; *G:* jighinitúră

FROLIC *s.* (*an infant's ~s*) gáduri *n pl*

FROLIC *vb.* xinăstrăpséscu ‖ CUNIA 319: ▾gioc, ansár di pi un
chiciór pi-alántu; CUVATA 22: (*of lambs*) hamuansár nsúsu-nghiós

FROLICSOME *adj.* (*as of a child*) astráptu; *G:* ciórnic; (*as of a*

horse) dúrdur, fliturác, geadíu, ni-aştirnát, xinăstrăpsít

FROM *prep.* **1.** di; ~ **good the apples grew even better** S-feáţiră meárile di búni ma búni; ~ **village to village** di hoáră-hoáră; ~ **year to year** an di an; (*as a piece of advice*) **You can take it ~ me!** Si ştiţ di míne! **Get away ~ me!** Fudzi di míne! ~ **here** di auá; ~ **here to there** di-auá pănă acló; ~ **here** di auáţi; **2.** di di; **the necklace ~ her neck** fluríile di di gúşe (*sic*); **3.** di la; di la pănă la; ~ **the smaller gate to the larger one** di la poárta ţea ma ñícă pân-la poárta ţea ma máre; **4.** di nângă; **They did not budge ~ his side him** Nu s-băteá di nângă nâs; **5.** di ntre; **I've come back ~ water** Mi turnái di ntr-ápă; **6.** di pi; **He broke all the plates ~ the table** Aspárse túte căţănile di pi meásă; **7.** di pin; ~ (**various**) **Aromanian villages** di pin hórile armănéşti; **8.** di sti; **all the animals ~ the earth** prăvdzâle túte di sti loc; ~ **a thorn a rose arises** Di schin trandafír arsáre; **She learned that either ~ you or ~ me** Di tíne, di míne nviţă; **Blood was flowing ~ me in streams** Sândzile curá di míne şurúñ; **9.** dit; **They came back ~ Bucharest** Viñíră di trâşi Bucuréşti; **10.** di tu; **We are taking the kids ~ the pen** Scotém édzĺi di tu ţárcu; **11.** pri; **He suddenly awoke ~ the dream he was seeing** S-dişțiptă dinăoáră pri yíslu ţe vidzú; ~ **all parts** ti túte părţâle

FROM ABOVE *adv.* di-pri-súpră

FROM A DISTANCE *adv.* pri lárgu, di dipárte

FROM AFAR *adv.* di nculó, di dipárte

FROM A RELIABLE QUARTER ≈ (*am, are, avem, etc.*) ápă di la múmă

FROM A TO Z ≈ din cap pănă tu coádă

FROM BEHIND *adv.* dinăpói, dănăpói

FROM BEHIND *prep.* di dúpă; **They suddenly jumped out ~ the beeches** Diunăoáră ansăríră di dúpă fadzi

FROM GENERATION TO GENERATION bârnu di bârnu

FROM HAND TO HAND *adv.* ‖ CUVATA 27: di mănă tu mănă

FROM HEAD TO FOOT *adv.* di la cap pănă la cioáre

FROM HEARSAY *adv.* di pri avdzâte ‖ ALR 1399: **I know it ~** U ştiu pi avdzât

FROM INSIDE *adv.* dinăúntru ‖ di didínde, BASME 500; HRISTU 4: pi tu nuntru

FROM MORN(ING) TILL NIGHT di andzáre pănă seára, di cându creápă dzúua ş-pân tu-ascăpătátă

FROM NOW ON *adv.* di-auá ş-năínte (*or* ş-nínte), di-auá nculeá, di ástândzâ nâínte ‖ **Av:** di tóra şi nclo, BASME 503

FROM OLD *adv.* di pap-străpáp

FROM ONE PERSON TO THE OTHER om di om

FROM THE BEGINNING *adv.* di prótă

FROM THE DEPTH OF THE HEART dit fründza di hicáte

FROM THE DIRECTION OF *prep.* di cătră

FROM THE FOUR CORNERS OF THE EARTH *adv.* dit páturile chioşi [k'oş'] a lúmiľei

FROM THE MOMENT WHEN di tu oára cându

FROM THE VERY BEGINNING *adv.* di prótă

FROM TIME IMMEMORIAL *adv.* di la aúşi-străaúşi, di pap-străpáp

FROM TIME TO TIME *adv.* câti únă oáră; ndáse, ndáse; di oáră oáră; ori, ori; ~ **he faints** Ori, ori lişínă ‖ di cându cându, DIARO 211

FROM TIP TO TOE *adv.* di la cap până la cioáre

FROM ... TO: ~ **elm to elm** di úlmu úlmu; **from tree to tree** di pom pom

FRONTIER *s.* grániţă, sínur

FROST *s.* (*freezing temperature*) dzer, ţícnă, ţeáfem ţingríme, cingríme, virvér; (*dry frost*) dzidzér, dzeádzir, xirupăyíe; (*minute ice crystals on grass, trees, etc.*) brúmă

FROSTBITE *s.* dzidzirătúră

FROSTBITTEN *adj.* dzidzirát, (m)brumát

FROSTY *adj.* (*covered with frost*) (m)brumát, brumós → BECOME ~

FROTH *s.* spúmă; (*of soap*) scámată, fuscălíthră; (*on coffee*) **N:** căimác, **S:** căimáche

FROTHY *adj.* spumós, -oásă, -óşĭ, -oáse

FROWARD *adj.* (*disobedient*) naprán → INTRACTABLE

FROWN *vb.* niurédz [ni•u•], dipún dzeánile; ▾ancrúntu ‖ HRISTU 18: scol sufurţelili

FROWSY *or* **FROWZY** *adj.* átacta *invar.*

FROZEN *adj.* dzidzirát, sicát, ngľiţát, ngucinát, ngordu

FROZEN TO THE BONE/MARROW *vb.* ngľeţ córcan

FRUGAL *adj.* icunóm, -noámă, -nómĭ (*sic*), -noáme; icunumiseáric

FRUGALITY *s.* → THRIFT

FRUIT *s.* pom, *pl* poáme; carpó *invar.*; frut *or* frútă; frúctu; yimíş; (*children's talk*) bóbă ‖ **Gop:** emíş 'fruits', GOLAB 214

FRUIT JELLY *s.* pelté

FRUITFUL *adj.* ‖ (*as of a good year*) **Av:** berichitlâcu, birichitós, CL 38-9; (*ant.* aclirát)

FRUIT-TREE *s.* pom

FRUITERER *s.* *sg* manáfi [•náfi], *pl* manáfeañ

FRY *vb.* ▾frig (→ § 32); ▾ţiyăr(ip)séscu, ţăyăripséscu, tiyănséscu, tiyniséscu; ~ **your eggs!** ('Mind your business!', 'What are you talking about?') ≈ Nu-ţ lipséscu căstrăvéţ truşíe?

FRYING PAN *s.* tiyáne

FUCK *vb.* ▾ambáir → COPULATE

FUCKING *s.* futeáre, ambăiráre, ampihiuráre, ciumulíre

FUDDLE *vb.* mi afúm, mi adár cáplu

FUDDLED *adj.* călít

FUDGE *s.* → NONSENSE; **All ~!** Bişíñ di cuc! (*lit.* 'cuckoo farts')

FULFILMENT *s.* buríre

FULFIL ONE'S WISH *vb.* ñ-u fac ursírea

FULL *adj.* plin, mplin, nglígát; (*of food and fig.*) sătúl; ~ **moon** lúnă mplínă; **a garden ~ of flowers** grădínă mplínă (*or* nglígátă) di lilíce; ~ **to capacity** (*as of a glass of water*) plin (*or* umplút) víţă; (~ *to overflowing*) písti zvíţă, dénga, dínga, dânga ‖ **Prv:** *adv.* bóldu, CL 39 → AS ~ AS AN EGG

FULL-BREASTED *adj.* ţâţoásă *f*

FULLING-MILL *s.* drăşteálă, **G:** grăşteálă; *also*: bătáľe, bătáñe; **Tur:** mândáñe

FULLING-MILL WORKER *s.* bătăr ‖ **GSus:** bătâñár, CL 38; **Av, SJos:** drăştir, **Prv:** dârştileár, CL 44

FULL-UDDERED *adj.* (*as of cows*) udzárcă, udzirátă

FULSOME *adj.* aynusós, -oásă, -óşĭ, -oáse → DISGUSTING

FUME *vb.* (*to be angry*) hérbu (pi); (*to ~ over smth with frustration*) ñ-u sémnu

FUMITORY *s. bot.* brubuştínă

FUN *s.* (*enjoyment*) siryinsíre, ylindipsíre, ylindisíre; **for ~** trâ arâdeáre → MAKE ~ OF

FUN *adj.* nóstim, -mă, -tiñ, -time

FUNCTION *s.* (*rank, post*) thése

FUNK *s.* (*fright*) lăhtár; (*coward*) pantalunár

FUNK *vb.* li yănuséscu vásile

FUNKY

FUNKY *adj.* (*fearful, scared, terrified*) fricós, -oásă; căcăciós, -oásă; cu ínima strímtă (*lit. 'with narrow heart'*); He/she
is very ~) u ári aspăreátă huzmétea

FUNNEL *s.* huníe, ghíncă, híncă, *G:* plăríe ‖ *An, Arγ, Els, GSus,
Mul, Na, Pal, Pur, Ses, Vil, Vot:* huní, B-ARCH 420

FUNNY *adj.* caraghiós, -ghioásă

FUR *s.* (*dressed animal pelt*) chiúrcu, nafée

FUR CAP *s.* căciúuă [•ĉú•ŭă] ‖ ALB: *Kërb, Pe, Sln:* căciúuă;
Dren: căciúlă; *Për:* kiciúlă, *Pe:* căsúuă, BRÂNCUŞ 554 → CAP

FURIOUS *adj.* vârlu → INFURIATED, MAD

FUR-LINED COAT *s.* gúnă, yúnă, sac

FURLOUGH *s.* pápse, páfse

FURNACE *s.* cuptór, căftór, cuftór; *also:* cireáp, cileáp, *G:* ciriché, cirichíe, *dim.* ciripíc, cirichél, circhén; fúrnu, furn,
fúrre; *G:* pişníc; (*lid of clay under which one can bake bread,
etc.*) cirichéĺu; yástru, yástră, pónţă (*and* póndză), póñiţă, *Gop:*
póinţă; (*for coal*) camíñe

FURNITURE *s.* mómilă (*sic!*), stólizmă, stóluzmă

FUROR *s.* mâníe, amăníe → ANGER

FURRIER *s.* cojocár, *Gop:* cujuhár; chiurcíu, chiuruccíu ‖ *Cru:*
chiurcí, GOLAB 231

FURRIERY *s.* ‖ BELIMACE 21: chiurcilắche

FURROW *s.* brázdă, avláchiu, vrag

FURROW *vb.* ar, vruguéscu, nvrag

FURTIVELY *adv.* tiptíle → STEALTHILY

FURUNCLE *s. med.* frânţél → BOIL

FURY *s.* (a)măníe (*and* amâ-) → ANGER

FUSE *vb.* (*to merge*) ▾fac únă

FUSILIER *s.* (*fusileer*) tuficcí

FUSILLADE *s.* tuficheáuă

FUSS *s.* camómate *f pl;* maraféte, mârâféte, muraféte; (*stir,
uproar*) *G:* giufă

FUSS *vb.* ‖ STERE 3: mi sighiséscu

FUSSY *adj.* căpriceárcu, nizeárcu

FUSTIGATION *s.* frâştuíre

FUSTY *adj.* (*impaired by dampness*) múhlid, *m pl* -lidz → MOLDY

FUTILE *adj. and adv.* (*vain, vainly*) áhristu, *m pl* áhrişţâ; n
vímtu; (*useless*) di-pristanéu; di-pri-súpră, parapaníş

FUTURE *s.* ‖ HRISTU 42: vinită

FUZZ *s.* (*as from birds*) puh, frúmă; (*as from wool or cotton*) scámă, cánă

G

GAB *vb.* discântu → CHATTER

GABBLE *vb.* (*of geese*) găgărédz → BABBLE, GAB

GABBY *adj.* zburyeárcu → TALKATIVE

GABFEST *s.* láfe

GAD ABOUT *vb.* (*to roam*) hălăndăréscu; alág sucăchile [●căk'●li]

GADFLY *s. ent.* tăún

GAFF *vb.* (*to abuse*) tălăéscu tu halé

GAFFER *s.* béhlu → OLD MAN

GAG *s.* (*smth. thrust into the mouth to prevent speech or outcry*) călúş; (*hoax*) ncălţáre

GAG *vb.* bag călúşlu n gúră, bag liyăreáua; (*to hoax, to trick, to make quips*) gioc hunérea, gioc únă hunére

GAGGLE *s.* túrmă di găşte

GAIETY *s.* hărăcupíľe, hilăríe

GAILY *adv.* hăriós, hărós

GAIN *s.* amintáre; (*win*) amintátic; *scoátire* → EARNING

GAIN *vb.* amíntu (*and* amíndu); *also:* (a)căzănséscu, ▾agudéscu, mi alég cu; chindiséscu, ▾chirdhăséscu, nchirdhăséscu; (*to earn*) scot

GAIN WEIGHT *vb.* ▾astúp cárne

GAINFUL *adj.* cu hăíre; *3 sg:* Ari scuteáre (*lit. 'It has return'*)

GAINSAY *vb.* fac incheáre, fac háşa

GAIT *s.* imnát

GAL *s.* feátă

GALE *s.* (*emotional outburst*) arúpire, arupeáre

GALL *s.* heáre, hulíe; (*bitterness*) nvirináre

GALLANT *adj.* căĭdigí → BRAVE

GALLANTRY *s.* sărpiţâľe

GALLIMAUFRY

GALLIMAUFRY *s.* mintitúră → JUMBLE

GALLIVANT *vb.* alág sucăchile [•căk'•li]

GALLNUT *s.* (*black fard*) măzíe, măzeáuă

GALLON *s.* (*bottle*) yalóne

GALLOP *s.* ambătruláre, ambăturláre; **at a gallop** anpátrulea, am-bátrulea ‖ *Cru:* ampăturáre, GOLAB 198; *Peş:* clíncă, CL 42; (*run*) **at full ~** (fug) di mâc lóclu, BASME 500

GALLOP *vb.* (a)mpátur, ampăturlédz (*and* ambă-), ampăturédz, ▾am-báturlu; **Do not ~ your horse with your boss!** Cu mamárĭle s-nu am-báturlĭi cálu!

GALLOPING *s.* ampăturláre (*and* ambă-), ampătruláre

GALLOWS *s.* aspindzurătoáre

GALORE *adj.* artisít, bólcu, giumértu; **no end ~** (*esp. of food*) de-a sătúlui

GAMBLE *s.* cumáră, lahnó

GAMBLE *vb.* gioc cumáră

GAMBLER *s.* (a)giucătór, cumargí, hartupéxi *m sg*, hartupéxeañ *pl* ‖ DIARO 182: hartufór

GAMBOL *vb.* trub, ▾zburdălipséscu

GAME *s.* (*amusement*) (a)gióc, joc; (*as of cards or knucklebones*) zdârtă; **~ of cards** óină

GAME *s.* (*hunting*) avináre; (*catch*) avinátic

GAME *adj.* (*lame*) şcľop, *m pl* şcľochi, *f sg* şcľoápă, *f pl* -oápe

GAME BAG *s.* ceántă, *pl* cénţâ; táşcă, *pl* tăşti

GAMESTER *s.* cumargí → GAMBLER

GAMMON *s.* (*double win at backgammon*) márţ

GANDER *s.* gâscu, *N:* gusác; (*simpleton*) apló

GANG *s.* sinastrufíe, suţáte, tăbúre; túbă; **~ of thieves** furáme ‖ MURNU 63: suţátă di furi

GANGLION *s. med.* broáscâ, DIARO 149

GANGRENE *s. med.* cángrenă, yangrénă

GANGWAY *s.* cicmácă

GAOL-FEVER *s. med.* tif

GAPE *s.* (*an act of gaping*) zgârlíre, zgârleáre

GAPE ABOUT *vb.* háscu, ylindipséscu, ylindiséscu, siryinséscu

GAPING ABOUT *s.* síre, siryeáne, zgârlíre

GAP-TOOTHED *adj.* jímbu, *pl m* jínghi, *f pl* jímbe; *also* júmbu; strábal; ştírbu, -rbă, -rghi, -rbe

GARBAGE *s.* (*waste*) armăsătúră

GARBANZO *s.* (*chick-pea*) nibirbíľu *or* nibirbíi [•bíĭ]

GARBLE *vb.* (*to alter, to distort*) ▼adávgu

GARDEN *s.* grădínă, gărdínă (*and* gâr-), perivóle; *dim.* gârdiníce, gârdinúşe

GARDENER *s.* grădinár, gărdinár

GARDEN-VARIETY *adj.* paráspur → ORDINARY

GARGLE *s.* yăryáră

GARGLING *s.* yăryáră

GARISH *adj.* jupânéscu, -neáscă, -néşţâ, -néşti

GARLIC *s.* aľ; **bulb of ~** cap di aľ, căpiţână di aľ → CLOVE OF ~
‖ *Suf, Paleoh, Flam:* ai; *Am, Hal, passim* aiu, B-ARCH 80

GARLIC SAUCE *s.* aľ chisát; scurdháme

GARMENT *s.* strañiu, *dim.* strănúş; veştimíntu, nviscămíntu (*and* -índu), vistămíntu; ânvescamínte *f sg*; strânót, *pl.* -nóte; *coll.* strañiríu, strañíu; (*winter coat*) găbún; (*sleeveless, rimmed with fur*) firméne; (*black woolen coat*) *Blţ:* firigé(e) → SET OF ~S

GARNER *vb.* ambăruséscu, silixéscu *or* lixéscu; ▼adún

GARNISH *vb.* ▼muşăţăscu, ▼armătuséscu, ▼stulséscu, ▼susuéscu

GARRET *s.* anóye, hátule; **to be a bit wrong in the ~** *3 sg:* nu lu ári súbaşi la loc

GARRISON *s.* mirchéze

GARRISON TOWN *s.* mirchéze

GARROTE *s.* sgrumătúră

GARRULITY *s.* láfe, poliloyíe

GARRULOUS *adj.* zburyeárcu → TALKATIVE

GARTER *s.* buveátă, buvétă, vuvétă, călţăvétă, stríngľe

GAS *s.* (*idle talk*) vrúte şi nevrúte

GASH *s.* tăľitúră; (*sign in the ear of a sheep to be recognized*) coácă

GASH *vb.* ▼taľu

GASP: **to be at one's last ~** hărchéscu; *adv.* **to the last ~** pânla ploáce

GASP *vb.* hărbulédz, hărbuléscu, hărchéscu

GATE *s.* poártă, *dim.* purtíţă; déră; *Mul:* părníşcă; (*opening through which sheep pass one by one to be milked at a sheepfold*) (a)rúgă, arăstoácă, arustoácă, strúngă, străgă; (*~ of a fortified building or town*) dirvéne

GATEWAY *s.* dişcĺidzătúră

GATHER *vb.* (*to assemble, to pick up*) ▼adún; **I don't know why they** ~ Nu ştiu ţe si-adúnă; **He ~ed flowers for her** Ĺ-ană lălúdz; **He began to ~ grapes** Ahiursí s-adúnă aúuă; ▼mârşin, mârşinédz; (*to reep*) silixéscu, lixéscu; (*to buy, to collect*) ▼bag; **I have learned that you ~ he-goats** Anviţái că badzi ţachi

GATHERED *adj.* (*as of a vineyard*) ayizmát

GATHER GROUND / WAY UPON SMB. *vb.* ĺau vrápă

GATHER MOMENTUM *vb.* ĺau fúzmă, ĺau vánţ, ĺau zvórimă

GATHERING *s.* adunáre, adunătúră → MEETING

GATHER SPEED *vb.* → GATHER MOMENTUM

GATHER UP ONE'S SPIRITS *vb.* ĺau ínimă, ▼ncucutédz → COLLECT ONE'S FACULTIES

GAUCHE *adj.* stângáciu, *f sg/pl* -gáce; stângár; zérvu, -ryi

GAUD *s.* → BANGLE

GAUGE *s.* misúră, métru; (*template, pattern*) călăpódhe

GAUGE *vb.* ▼misúr

GAUNT *adj.* (*excessively thin*) gúndu; (*haggard*) s(c)lab; (*grim*) fuvirós; (*desolate*) érmu, *m pl* érñi, *f pl* érmă; *also* érim

GAWK *s.* durñít

GAWK *vb.* azgârléscu ócĺiĺ

GAWKY *adj.* durñít; angricós, -oásă → AKWARD

GAY *adj.* (*merry*) hărăcóp, -coápă, -cóchi, -coápe; hăriós

GAZE *s.* síre, siryeáne

GAZE *vb.* 1-fac síre; (*to ~ with rupture at smb.*) 1-sórbu

GAZER *s.* zgârleáiu *m sg*, -leáiañ *pl*

GAZETTE *s.* gazétă → NEWSPAPER

GEE *interj.* **1.** i! iĭ! ih! **Gee, how late he is!** I, cum amână! **2.** (*command to a donkey or mule to go*) uş! pâr! ai prââ prââ úş! (*to a horse*) i! Gee, Murgu! *or:* Múrgu, i!

GEEZER *s.* tronciu

GHEG *adj.* (*pertaining to a native of northern Albania*) ghigă-néscu

GHEGS *s. coll.* Ghigăríe; *the Albanians from the Gheg region* ghégañĺi dit Ghigăríe

GELD *vb.* → CASTRATE

GELDED HORSE *s.* cal şuţât

GELDING *s.* scuchít

GEM *s.* giuvaír, giuvaíre

GENDARME *s.* (*in the old Turkish army*) seimén, semén, biráciu, zaptié, zăptié; jandár, geandár, gindár ‖ ALR 982: şcherládzľi *m pl def*

GENERAL *s. mil.* stratiyó

GENERALISSIMO *s.* arhistratiyó

GENERAL STORE *s.* dugáne, măgăză, măgăzíe

GENERATION *s.* ţárcu, scáră; **of my ~** (*age*) tu scára a mea; brânu, *N:* bârnu; **from ~ to ~** bârnu di bârnu; **until the ninth ~** pân tu noáuăle brâne

GENEROSITY *s.* cuvurdhălâche

GENEROUS *adj.* (*liberal in giving*) cuvurdhă, giumértu, sălghít; (*large, liberal*) filótim

GENEROUSLY *adv.* ‖ cu mânǎ dişcľísă (*lit.* 'openhandedly'), *see* PARALLELE 136

GENTIAN *s. bot.* lulúdhă gálbină

GENTLE *adj.* bunác, dóbru, eváşcu, sârbu ‖ DIARO 159: bunáşcu

GENTLY: to approach smb. ~ ‖ ľau cu búnlu PARALLELE 134

GENTLEMAN *s.* (*man of correct behavior*) om, *pl.* oámiñ ‖ (*of high rank*) *Av:* chiríu, CL 254

GENTLENESS *s.* (*mildness*) adire, imiráme, imireáţă

GENTLY *adv.* dúlţe; *F:* câteañór, câtelín ‖ HRISTU 9: cu zdruderi

GENUFLECTION *s.* (*in worship*) mitáñe

GENUINE *adj.* alithinós, -oásă; aslâ *invar.*; ynisíu, -íe, *pl* -íǐ ‖ CUNIA 5: alihiós

GERMAN *s. N:* neámţu ‖ *Cru:* ghermán, GOLAB 221

GERMAN *adj.* nemţéscu, -eáscă, -éşţâ, -éşti

GERMANY *s.* ‖ BATSARIA 48: Nemţía; *Cru:* Yermaníe, GOLAB 221

GERMINATE *vb.* (*to appear, as of wheat*) fitruséscu

GERMINATED adj. fitrusít; (*as of wheat*) biscuít

GERMINATION *s.* fitrusíre

GESUNDHEIT! ‖ (*words used to wish good health to one who has just sneezed*) PC: S-ţâ híbă di ghíni! *In fact, Aromanians do like other people's sneezing and say reproachfully:* cárnax! *or* cárnas! ≈ Go to hell! DDA 317, DIARO 181

GET *vb.* (*to ~ possession of*) adár, ▾agudéscu, ▾bag; **I got a couple of sheep** Adrái niscânte coáde; **Where did you ~ such a horse?** Di iu lu-agudíşi ahtáre cal? **He got a load of dung** Băgă nă

GET ACCUSTOMED

furtíe di bălidzi; (*to succeed in coming or going*) agiúngu; (*to receive, as a name, a letter*) ľau, ▾(a)próchiu; **He got a sad letter** Lo nă cárte láie; (*to understand*) achicăséscu; (*to possess*) am

GET ACCUSTOMED *vb.* ▾(a)nvéţ, ▾veţ, ▾mălăxéscu

GET ACQUAINTED *vb.* ▾cunóscu

GET ACROSS *vb.* scăpit; **I got across the snowy mountains** Scăpitái múnţâľ cu neáuă

GET A HAIRCUT *vb.* mi túndu; mi bărbiriséscu, mi bărbirséscu

GET A HALF NELSON ON SMB. *vb.* bag tu tástru ‖ lu-ám tu mână, BASME 307

GET A JOB *vb.* ‖ íntru tu pâne, BASME 187

GET ANGRY *vb.* mi-acáţă zála, ▾ayrédz, ▾(a)hulséscu, lu arúc sămárlu, ▾astáľu, căchiuséscu, chicuséscu, mi fac foc, ▾furţués-cu, ▾yinătuséscu, ynătuséscu, inătuséscu, ▾huluséscu, huľiséscu, mi inrăéscu, năraéscu, năiréscu, năréscu, ▾nguvujdédz, ▾ni-pârtic, ▾nşárpic, nşarpit, ▾nvipirédz, ▾thimuséscu → FLY INTO A TEMPER ‖ úmflu nărle, BASME 321; mi acáţă inátea, RÉCATAS 47

GET A SCENT OF *vb.* dau di úrmă a

GET A SOAKING *vb.* (*to be punished severily*) ▾mâc păpáră, mâc şcop (*lit. 'to eat club'*)

GET A VISA *vb.* (*on a passport*) ñ-fac cáide pasapórtea

GETAWAY *s.* (a)scăpáre

GET AWAY *vb.* fug di; ~ **from me!** Fudzĭ di míne! (*to escape, as by flight*) ľ-áflu fúmlu, ľ-ľau fúmlu

GET BACK ONE'S WIND *vb.* (*to recover*) ‖ CUNIA 329: mi apuituéscu, ăñ vin tu aéri

GET BEANS *vb.* (*to catch hell*) li-adún; Si ncáce cáľi, li-adúnă yumárľi (= *injustice*; *lit. 'Horses make a rumpus and donkies get beans'*)

GET BENUMED *vb.* amurţăscu → BENUMB

GET BITTEN BY A SNAKE *vb.* ▾nipârtichédz

GET BY *vb.* (*to proceed without being discovered or punished*) (a)scáp

GET CLARIFIED *vb.* (*to understand*) ▾lăyărséscu

GET COLD *vb.* arcurédz, arăţéscu **The weather got cold** Arcurí (*or* arăţí) chirólu

GET COLD FEET *vb.* (*to go down one's boots*) u aspárg huzmétea

GET CONFUSED *vb.* ▾cirtăséscu, ▾ciurtăséscu, ▾cirtuéscu, ▾cistiséscu, ▾scol di mínte

GET COOL *vb.* (*of weather*) *3 sg impers.* arăţeáşte, arcureádză

GET DARK *vb.* *3 sg:* ntúnică ‖ CUVATA 2: **it had become quite dark** s-aveá scutidisítă ghíni; BELIMACE 92: **until it got dark** pănă deáde múrgul

GET DIRTY *vb.* ▾mâzgăléscu; (~ *with ashes*) ▾ncinuşédz, cinuşédz ‖ *Cru:* mi fac óndus, GOLAB 240

GET DOWN *vb.* ▾dipún (→ § 32); **Get down from the appletree!** Dipúni-ti di pri mer! (*to* ~ *from a horse, etc.*) discálic

GET DOWN TO WORK *vb.* mi-aştérnu tu lúcru

GET DRESSED *vb.* ▾nvéscu, véscu ‖ *Cru:* mi andrég, GOLAB 205

GET DRUNK *vb.* mi (a)mbét, âmbét; mi adár cúrpit, mi adár cândílă, mi adár órbu, mi adár stíngale, lu adár cáplu, mi fac cucútă, mi fac hrup, mi fac ciúrla, mi fac ciúrla ş-cazáca, mi căléscu; (*a little*) ▾cămiñuséscu ‖ BASME 307: mi fac dzádză; STERE 50: ñ-adár cârţúna

GET DUMBFOUNDED *vb.* (*to fall silent*) ‖ *Cru:* ▾amút, GOLAB 198

GET FAR *vb.* (*of smb. who is walking*) ľau chiciór; **He has got far** Lo chiciór

GET FOUL *vb.* (*with grease, dust, etc.*) mbăxéscu

GET HELL *vb.* dau di arále → CATCH HELL

GET HOLD OF *vb.* arúc cătuhíe (pri); **They got hold of the house** Arucáră (*or* arcáră) cătuhíe pri cásă

GET HUNGRY *vb.* (*severily*) ñ-si dúţe gúra la ureácľe

GET IN *vb.* ▾bag

GET IN A HUFF *vb.* spíndzur nările → HUFF

GET INFECTED WITH SHEEP-POX *vb.* *vet.* (*of sheep*) gălbidzăscu

GET INTO *vb.* ▾(a)ndés; **He got into the river** Si andisă tu arâu

GET INTO A HEAT *vb.* (*as of thirst*) ▾apríndu (→ § 32)

GET INTO A TANTRUM *vb.* mi acáţă dráţiľi di urécľĭ, mi acáţă dzándza, mi acáţă zála, mi acáţă órile, âñ víñe zurleáţa, âñ víne inátea, âñ yin órile → GET ANGRY ‖ *Cru:* glăréscu, anglăréscu, GOLAB 205; CARAFOLI 30: mi furchiséscu

GET INTO HOT WATER *vb.* şed cu cúrlu tu neáuă → BE IN A BAD FIX

GET INTO A WAX *vb.* → GET INTO A TANTRUM

GET INTO THE FAMILY WAY *vb.* ▾acáţ ‖ armân sárţină, BASME 438

GET INTO TROUBLE *vb.* dau di arále; ved scânteáľe, ñ-ascápiră

GET INTOXICATED

ócĭiǐ, ñ-cáde chicútă máre, ñ-undiséscu, u-pát hunérea, dau di
bilé; ▾mâc păpárǎ; (as a threat) Gúştur veárde va ti mâcǎ! Nu
va-ñ dai giuvápe! (lit. 'You will not give me an answer,' i.e.
You will be dead) dau di arále ∥ pǎţéscu; He got into trouble U
pǎţâ, PARALLELE 127

GET INTOXICATED vb. → GET DRUNK

GET IRRITATED vb. ∥ *Cru:* mi nivruséscu, GOLAB 238

GET IT IN THE NECK vb. ▾mâc pri zvércǎ, ñ-iáse fum prit nǎri,
mi ĭa arâulu, ▾mâc păpárǎ; **He got it in the neck** U mâcǎ pâpára;
mi-acáţǎ di ócĭi; **You'll ~!** Va ti-acáţǎ di ócĭi! ∥ mâc şcop (lit.
'to eat a club'), PARALLELE 127

GET IT INTO ONE'S HEAD (TO) vb. ñ-íntrǎ (sǎ)

GET LOST! (interjectionally) Adúnǎ-u di auá! Angánǎ-u di aua!
Arúpi-ţ-u di aţía! Arúpi-ţ gúşea (or zvérca)! Aspeálǎ-li di auá!
Cǎpsǎlseá-li di auá! Dé-vǎ (di auá)! Fǎ-te cusúre! Fǎ-te stifǎ!
Frândzi-ţ gúşea! Ĭa-ţ zvérca di auáţe! Mânǎ-te di auá! Risíte
s-ti faţi! Scoáti-ţ mǎdulárlu! Scǎrminá̧t-li di auáţe! Stifuíţ-vǎ!
Súrpǎ-te di aţía! Tíndi-le! (to a dog) at! oşti! titi! ∥ BASME 47:
Hǎndǎcuseá-te! BASME 122: Ĭa-ţ pérlu de-auá! DIARO 152: fǎ-ti cu-
mǎţ, dú-ti di-auá; DIARO 180: fǎ-ti défi! DIARO 238: şpirtuiá-u di
auá!

GET LOW vb. (to sink to a much lower state) cǎtǎndiséscu pri
hála éstǎ

GET MARRIED vb. → MARRY

GET MISTY vb. 3 sg nigureádzǎ, ngureádzǎ

GET NERVOUS vb. (to get irritated) ∥ *Cru:* mi nivruséscu, GOLAB
238

GET OFF CLEAR vb. (to save face) es cu fáţa álbǎ

GET OFF ON THE WRONG FOOT vb. calc cu zévul

GET OFF SCOT-FREE vb. (a)scáp ∥ ALR 1439: **to get off safely** 1
sg pt: ascǎpái sǎnǎtós

GET ON BADLY/WELL WITH SMB./SMTH. vb. trec ghíne (cu) / nu trec
ghíne (cu); **She was not getting on well with her mother-in-law**
Nâsǎ nu triţeá ghíne cu soácrǎ-sa; (to cope with life's problems)
ĭ-u trec; **How are you getting on?** Cum ĭ-u treţi?

GET ON WELL vb. (to be thriving) ∥ BATSARIA 57: ñ-ñárdze ti am-
bǎreáţǎ

GET ONE'S BREATH vb. ñ-víñe sulúchea

GET ONE'S HANDS (UP)ON *vb.* (*to catch, to capture*) bag mână pi

GET ONE'S RAG OUT *vb.* (*to fly into a tantrum*) ñ-arsáre scârpa

GET ONE'S SECOND WIND *vb.* ñ-ľau adiľátlu

GET ONE'S TOES UP *vb.* li tíndu → DIE

GET ONE'S WIND *vb.* ñ-ľau adiľátlu

GET ON SMB.'S NERVES *vb.* ľ-mâc urécľile

GET OUT *vb.* ies *aor.* i(n)şíi *or* i(n)şái

GET OUT OF AN ENCUMBRANCE *vb.* ascáp di nă sfínă

GET OUT OF ORDER *vb.* ndăcănéscu

GET OUT OF TROUBLE *vb.* purbuléscu

GET OUT OF ONE'S ELEMENT, COUNTRY, *etc. vb.* ▼xinitipséscu

GET PREGNANT *vb.* ‖ BASME 438: armân sárţină

GET READY *vb.* ▼(a)ndrég, ▼etimăséscu; **Get ready so that we can leave tonight!** Ndreádzi-te s-fudzím astárá!

GET RID OF *vb.* (a)scáp (di), ▼cuturséscu (di), cutruséscu

GET SCARED *vb.* ▼lăhtărséscu; u-ám aspăreátă huzmétea; li yănuséscu vásile; ▼cişéscu ‖ CARAFOLI 41: ciuşiéscu; 43: ▼cişiéscu; BASME 213: ngălbinéscu ca ţeára; *Pls:* ▼lictârséscu, CL 254; ▼nfricuşédz, BASME 656; şápte-óptu ľĭ si dúţe pi dinăpói, BASME 706; *Pls:* li úmplu zmeánile di frícă, BASME 477; ñ-aspargu săndzăli, HRISTU 37

GET SICK *vb.* ñ-ľau lélea; **He got sick** L-chişárá moáşile

GET SICK OF *vb.* (*to get saturated of things seen*) ñi s-úmple ócľul (di)

GET SIGHT OF *vb.* (*intentionally*) ▼arúc mutríta (pi); (*unintentionally*) dau cu ócľiiľ di

GET SMB. INTO A SCRAPE *vb.* (*to put smb. to trouble*) ľ-gioc únă hunére

GET SMB. INTO DEBT *vb.* ▼hriuséscu → RUN INTO DEBT

GET SMB.'S NUMBER: I got your number, you harlot! ştiu tu ţe ápe ti-adắchi, lea dósă!

GET SMTH. ON THE BRAIN *vb.* nu-ñ iáse dit mínte

GET SOBER AGAIN *vb.* ▼disbét

GET SPOONY ON *vb.* ñ-cáde tu ínimă

GET SQUARE WITH SMB. *vb.* hiu ísea cu

GET TERMINALLY ILL *vb.* ñ-ľau lélea

GET THE BEST OF IT *vb.* (*to get off scot-free*) (a)scáp; es cu fáţa álbă

GET THE BETTER OF SMTH.

GET THE BETTER OF SMB. *vb.* ĺ-u pot, âĺ yin di háche (**or di in-dih
áche, di ânduháche**); **A woman can get the better of the devil himself** Muĺárea şi-a dráclui âĺ yíne di háche; (*to defeat, to put an end to*) bag mână

GET THE BOOT ON THE WRONG FOOT *vb.* u-adár taratóre

GET THE CHEESE *vb.* (*to come off a loser*) nu ñ-si văpseáşte óulu; armân ca Súlta cu ucnălu

GET THE TRICK OF IT *vb.* ĺ-áflu căpáchea, ĺ-dau cále; **The problem is so complex that nobody can ~** Lúcrul eáste ahântu mindít că vâr nu poáte si-ĺ da cále

GET THE WIND UP *vb.* li yănuséscu vásile → GO DOWN IN ONE'S BOOTS

GETTING *s.* (*a trip to a place; the first half of a round trip*) imnătúră (*ant.* turnătúră); **~ there takes two months and coming back another two** Doi meş ţâne imnătúra şi-álţ ahânţâ turnătúra

GETTING A COLD *s.* arcuráre

GETTING ALONG *s.* treácă

GETTING DRESSED *s.* (a)nvişteáre, nveáştire

GETTING UP *s.* (*on one's feet*) mbrustáre; (*as from bed in the morning*) sculáre, sculátă

GET TIPSY *vb.* ▼afúm → GET DRUNK

GET TIRED *vb.* ▼cúrmu, ▼avurséscu, avruséscu, apustuséscu, lăvruséscu; (*to get saturated of things seen*) ñ-si úmple ócĺul di

GET-TOGETHER *s.* adunáre, suţâĺe

GET TOGETHER *vb.* ▼adún (cu)

GET TO LOGGERHEADS *vb.* ▼agiúngu la par, mi acáţ di per (cu)

GET THE SCENT (THE WIND) OF *vb.* (*to learn*) u ĺau di viş (*or di* vij)

GET THROUGH *vb.* (*to be successful*) u scot náparti; **You will not get through with lies** Cu minciúna nu u scoţ náparti

GETTING SOBER AGAIN *s.* disbitáre, disbitătúră

GET TO KNOW *vb.* ĺau di hăbáre

GET UNDER WAY *vb.* trag; **Well, ~, go!** Hai trádze, fudzi!

GET UP *vb.* (*as from sleep*) ▼(a)scol; **~ at daybreak** ▼scol cu noáptea n cap

GET UP SPEED *vb.* (*and fig.*) ĺau vímtu, ĺau fúzmă, ĺau paramázmă, ĺau vánţu, ĺau zvórimă

GET UPPITY *vb.* (*to put on airs of superiority, to forget one's*

place) ▾disgărdéscu

GET WIND OF *vb.* ľau di hăbáre

GET WORK *vb.* (*to be hired*) ▾arughédz, ▾ndreg, ▾păitéscu, ▾puitéscu, ▾puituéscu

GET YOU GONE → GET LOST

GHOST *s.* súflit, duh, stihíe ‖ aúmbră (*lit. 'shadow'*), PARALLELE 152 → HOLY ~

GHOUL *s.* strígă

GIANT *s.* thiríu, gaľamán, évil, ľúftă, ghigántu; **They came across a ~** Deádiră di un gaľimeán di om; *adj:* div ‖ HRISTU 1: yigan

GIBBER *vb.* dârdăréscu; *3 sg:* gúra ľ-si dúţe dâr-dâr → PRATTLE

GIBBERISH *s.* dârdârsíre

GIBBET *s.* aspindzurătoáre

GIBBET *vb.* (*to hang*) ▾aspíndzur

GIBBOSITY *s. med.* (*protuberance, swelling*) cambúră

GIBE *vb.* tălăéscu tu halé → ABUSE, RIDICULE

GIDDAP! (to a horse) ‖ ALR 279: dée! or díi!

GIDDINESS *s.* (*swimming in the head*) andrălăsíre, ndărsíre, scútură; (*playfulness*) zburdălipsíre

GIDDY *adj.* aumbrát, avdálcu, burdál, zdurdít; **to be ~** vârléscu

GIFT *s.* dar, dhoáră (*and* doáră), durusíre, háre; **Never look a ~ horse in the mouth** Cálu di dhoáră nu s-cáftă la dínţâ; (*a ~ to the bride*) pălăríe; (*for as for one who brings a good piece of news*) mujdé, sihăríeľe, sihăríche ‖ VELO 53: săcăríchi

GIFTED *adj.* durusít

GIGANTIC *adj.* balaváncu, *m pl* -nţi, *f pl* -nţe; évil → HUGE

GIGGLE *s.* căhtíre

GIGGLE *vb.* ▾căchín, ▾căhtéscu, ▾păhăéscu

GILD *vb.* afúm, hrisuséscu, ▾mălămuséscu, nglubudédz; **We gild our earrings at the silversmith's** Afumăm vérile la hrísic ‖ alâmâséscu, DIARO 97

GILDED *adj.* afumát, glubudán, hrisusít, malamatérñiu, mălămusít

GILDING *s.* (*stuff*) văráche, văráchiu; (*process*) afumáre, afumătúră, hrisusíre; mălămusíre, nglubudáre

GILLYFLOWER *s.* canacíche, caranfíl, caranfir, caranfílă, şibóie

GILT *s.* (*a young female swine*) purţeáuă

GIMLET *s.* (*a tool for boring*) arídhă, biză, sfreádin

GIMPY *adj.* săcát → CRIPPLED

GINGER *s. bot.* chitribóbule, chitribóbală

GINGERBREAD *s.* ≈ spinşoáră, pandişpáñe

GINGERLY *adj.* câştigós, -oásă, -óşĭ, -oáse → CAUTIOUS

GIRD *vb.* ▾ţíngu

GIRDED *adj.* ţímtu, *f* -mtă, *m pl* -mţâ, *f pl* -mte

GIRDER *s.* (*in a wall*) dhémă

GIRDLE *s.* bărnu; *F:* băr, *pl.* bără; páftă, páhtă, paptă, pahtá-uă, ploáce, zónă, zúnă, *dim.* zuníţă; (*woolen or cloth* ~) tízgă, dízgă

GIRL *s.* feátă, *dim.* fitícă, fitíţă, copélă, cupélă, cóchilă, heárhiră, heárhită; (*baby girl*) púpă; (*caressingly*) tănúşe; *coll.* fitáme, fitiryĭó, fituríu; **A boy, or a girl?** Ficiór, i feátă? **He did not marry the ~, but her money!** Nu lo feátă, lo parádz!

GIRLHOOD *s.* fitíľe

GIRLISH *s.* fitéscu

GIRTH *vb.* (*as a saddle on a horse*) yingluséscu

GIVE *vb.* (*pres.* dau, dai, da, dăm, daţ, da; *ipf.* dădeám; *s. p.* ded, deádiş, deáde, deádim, deádit, deádira; *imper. 2 sg* dă! *3 sg* s-da (PC: [zda]); *2 pl* daţ! *and* didéţ! *3 pl.* s-da [zda]); **~ me a little water!** Dă-ñ nă chícă di ápă! **~ me my pay!** Să-ñ dai rúga! (*to present*) ahărzéscu; (*to offer for sale*) apún; **He is trying to ~ you an ordinary fur instead of a (genuine) beaver** Mutreáşte tra s ţ apúnă trâ castóre nă mişíne

GIVE A BATH *vb.* (a)scáldu ‖ DIARO 102: **~ to an infant or a child** (*hypoco-ristically*) fac lusi a ñíclui

GIVE A BEATING *vb.* ▾bat → BEAT, THRASH

GIVE A CUE TO *vb.* nveţ, veţ, dau un anvéţ, ▾dhăscălipséscu, dhăscăliséscu

GIVE ADVICE *vb.* dau un anvéţ

GIVE A HAND *vb.* (*to help*) agiút, dau mână di agiutór

GIVE A JOB *vb.* bag pri pâne

GIVE ALMS *vb.* ‖ dau tră súflit, BASME 165

GIVE A MASS FOR SMB. *vb.* dau dáre; **He was giving the mass for the old man** Dădeá dárea al aúş

GIVE A PIECE OF ADVICE *vb.* dau un anvéţ → ADVISE

GIVE A PIECE OF ONE'S MIND *vb.* (*to lesson*) ‖ ALR 1414: **Give him a piece of your mind!** S-lo aúrli!

GIVE AS GOOD AS ONE GETS *vb.* ‖ nu mi alás pri pádi, BASME 414

GIVE A SHRIEK *vb.* dau un zghic (ca şirpicát) → SHRIEK

GIVE A SOUND LICKING *vb.* úmflu sămárlu, ľ-u íntru; **Give him a sound licking!** Íntră-ľ-u! → BEAT, THRASH

GIVE A START *vb.* ľ-dau vímtu (*lit.* 'to give smb. a wind')

GIVE A SWEEP *vb.* ‖ trag cu mătura, BASME 161

GIVE AWAY *vb.* (*to divulge, to betray*) scot n páde; (*to present*) (a)hărzéscu

GIVE A YELL *vb.* dau un zghic

GIVE BIRTH *vb.* ▾amíntu, dizvóc, fac, ▾fét, nfáş, nfăşédz; **She does not make children** Nu amíntă fumeáľe; **When her time came to bring forth she gave birth to a girl** Cându ľ-víñe oára s-dizvoácă, feáţe nă feátă

GIVE EAR TO *vb.* ascúltu (di)

GIVE FREE REIN TO FUN *vb.* u fac uzungióva

GIVE IN *vb.* trag mâna (→ ABNEGATE), ▾alás, mi dau, părădhuséscu

GIVE IT TO SMB. STRONG AND HOT *vb.* (*to scold*) tălăéscu tu halé, lau cu ápa di sâmbătă, afúm nările, moľu tu ápă aráţe, moľu tu noauădzăţĭ noáuă di buéi

GIVE IT UP *vb.* li băgu mpáde

GIVEN (*as by God*) dat, hărzít

GIVEN NAME *s.* númă

GIVE NO CREDIT *vb.* apistiséscu

GIVE NOTICE *vb.* (*to let know*) dau glas, dau hăbáre, dau tu şteáre

GIVE OFF *vb.* (*to form and discharge*) (a)ndzămédz; **This stone is ~ing off water** Ndzămeádză ápă dit aéstă cheátră

GIVE ONE'S ATTENTION TO *vb.* ancúñu; **They do not give attention to him** Nu lu-ancúñe; (*in negative sentences*) l-dau di curáuă (*or* di mâneár)

GIVE ONESELF AIRS *vb.* ▾úmflu; *also:* ▾căbărdéscu, fac gilfédz, ▾făléscu, ▾frângu, ▾fuduléscu, ▾furduéscu, ▾mprustédz (*and* mbrustéz), mi ngroş, li ngroş lúcrili, li ngruşédz hăbările, li trag groáse, li trag mări, mi ţân a mári, trag măréţ múlte ‖ u scol cujáca; âl mut cáplu, DIARO 275

GIVE ONESELF AWAY *vb.* (*to betray oneself*) ‖ mi dau di páde, BASME 448

GIVE ONE'S KINDEST REGARDS TO *vb.* aduc (*or* dau, dzâc) múlti

GIVE ONE'S OPINION

ncľinăciúñ

GIVE ONE'S OPINION *vb.* ñ-dau nă mínte ‖ ñ-dau mínţăli, BASME 302

GIVE ONE'S WORD *vb.* dau zbor

GIVE OUT *vb.* (*to become used up*) ▾bitiséscu → FINISH

GIVER *s.* dătór; **the ~ of life** (*i.e., God*) dătórru a bániľĭ

GIVE RESPITE TO *vb.* dau oáră

GIVE SMTH. A REST *vb.* alás tu páde; u alás spindzurátă luyuría

GIVE SMB. BEANS *vb.* (*to trash*) afúm nările; tuchéscu di băteáre

GIVE SMB. LINE *vb.* ▾alás, dau bánă, alás tu síyă

GIVE SMB. NO PEACE *vb.* ‖ nu ľ-dau bánă, BASME 488

GIVE SMB. PLENTY OF ROPE *vb.* ľ-dau fáţă; **If you give children plenty of rope they do foolish things** ≈ Máca lă dai fáţă a fi-ciórilor, ti-ncálică pri gúşe

GIVE SMB. SHORT NOTICE *vb.* ľ-adún curăile, căpistruséscu

GIVE SMB. SOCKS *vb.* (*to beat*) tuchéscu di băteáre

GIVE SMB. THE AIR (*or* **THE BASKET, THE BIRD, THE CHUCK, THE MITTEN, THE SACK**) *vb.* dau ţărúhile, dau părtăľle → FIRE

GIVE SMB. A THICK EAR *vb.* ľ-astrág únă, ľ-surduéscu únă → SLAP SMB.'S FACE

GIVE SMB. THE RASPBERRY *vb.* ñ-arâd cu nâs

GIVE SMB. THE UP AND DOWN *vb.* mutréscu di la úngľi pân la cap

GIVE SMB. ONE'S WALKING PAPERS *vb.* ľ-dau ţărúhile → FIRE

GIVE SMB. THE GO-BY *vb.* (*to disregard*) nu lu bag tu (*or* tru) córnu ‖ (*to chase out*) ľ-aspún plătărle, BASME 226

GIVE SMB. THE RIGHT *vb.* dau driptáte

GIVE SMB. TO UNDERSTAND *vb.* dau si aducheáscă

GIVE THANKS TO SMB. *vb.* adúc birhuzúre → THANK

GIVE UP *vb.* ▾alás, li bag mpáde, ▾ncľín, para-dau, părădhu-séscu, ▾pridáu; trag mână (di) (→ ABNEGATE) ‖ BASME 411: ncľid ócľiľ; DIARO 223: fac cáli

GIVE UP ALL HOPE *vb.* ñ-ľau câştíga (di la); ñ-ľau curátile

GIVE UP AN OPINION *vb.* (*to abandon, to recede, to recant*) es di míntea a mea; **Ask everybody, but don't give up your opinion!** Tuţ s-ľi ntreghi ş di míntea a ta s-nu eşĭ!

GIVE UP DRINKING *vb.* mi cúrmu di beáre → THROW OFF

GIVE UP HOPING *vb.* (*to renounce, to forget about*) mi ľértu (di)

GIVE UP SMTH. FOR LOST *vb.* ľ-bag crúţea; *2 sg imper.* Băgă-ľ crúţea!

GIVE VENT TO vb. ▼discoápir

GIVE WAY TO TEARS vb. mi ľa (or mi mbáiră) lắcriñle; lăcrămédz, lăcrimédz

GIVING s. dăruíre, durusíre, pischisíre; ahărzíre; (as a treat) filipsíre

GIZZARD s. anat. ‖ ALR 364: (of birds) mámă

GLACIAL adj. arcurós, dzidzirós, virvirós; (of a wind) turinós

GLAD adj. hăriós (and hâ-), hărsít; hărăcóp, -oápă, -óchi, -oápe; yiós, -oásă, -óşǐ, -oáse; **to be ~** mi hăriséscu; **I am ~ that you are all right** Hărăsestu că hiţ ghini, HRISTU 65

GLADE s. misăreáuă, vuloágă ‖ *GSus:* bugeáchi, CL 39

GLADLY adv. hârós, hâriós

GLADNESS s. văsălíe → JOY

GLADSOME adj. → GLAD

GLAIVE s. apálă → SWARD

GLANCE s. bruítă, mutrítă; **at first ~** la videáre → LOOK

GLANCE vb. bruéscu, mutréscu

GLAND s. ǵíndură

GLANDERED adj. (affected with glanders, of a horse) bútur, săcăiárcu

GLANDERS s. vet. sacaí

GLARE s. (light) luñínă

GLARE vb. luñinédz

GLASS s. (material) yilíe, geáme; (container) scáfă, chélcă, chélce, chélcu, cúpă, putír or putíre; (small ~) (a)rucutír, (a)r-cutír; **to strike ~es** ▼cingărşéscu → CUPPING ~

GLASSES s. (spectacles) ócľi m pl; yilíi f pl; matuyeáľe f pl; **Put on your ~!** Bágă-ţ ócľiľ! ‖ *F:* matuyeáñ, SarD 114

GLASSWARE s. yilicádz m pl

GLASS WINDOWS s. geamlắche

GLAZED FROST s. arắchíş

GLAZIER s. geamgí, geamgíu

GLEAM s. lámpse, lícur, luţíre

GLEAM vb. licurédz, licuricéscu, licrăséscu; (as of hair) hrisuséscu

GLEAN vb. ▼adún

GLEANINGS s. adunătúră

GLEN s. glémur → RAVINE

GLIB

GLIB *adj.* **He has a ~ tongue** Ápă ĺ-ñárdze gúra

GLIDE *vb.* (a)lúnic, arúnic, alăchiúşur, şeárpic

GLIDE AWAY *vb.* (*as of days, weeks, remembrances*) ▾deápin

GLIMMER *vb.* → GLEAM

GLIMPSE *vb.* ▾mutréscu

GLITTER *s.* yílciu, anyílciu, yilcíre

GLITTER *vb.* (*as of amber*) ▾yilcéscu, (a)nyilcéscu → SPARKLE

GLITTERING *adj.* lumbărsít → BRILLIANT

GLITTERY *adj.* (*as of the moon*) (a)nyiliciós, ânyi-

GLOOM *s.* (*lowness of spirits*) ntuneáric, lăiáţă, milancolíe → DARKNESS

GLOOMILY *adv.* lângărós (*and* lângâ-), lângurós

GLOOMY *adj.* cérnu, ngérnu, jilós, lângărós, ntunicós, scur; **to become ~** ▾nigurédz; *3 sg* (*of the sky*) nigureádză, ngureádză

GLORIFICATION *s.* dhuxăsíre

GLORIFY *vb.* cântu, ▾álţu; (*to extol, as God*) dhuxăséscu, duxi-séscu, duxuséscu, dhoxologhiséscu

GLORIOUS *adj.* (*deserving or possessing glory*) mărít; **Glorious Lord!** Măríte Doámne! (*delightful*) ghiurghiulíu; (*excellent*) háscu, -ă (*no pl*); nişinlítcu ‖ MURNU 12: duxăsít

GLORY *s.* măríĺe, dhóxă (*and* dóxă), dhoxítă, camáră; **Lord, Your ~ is immense!** Máre ţ-u dhóxa, Doámne! **~ to you, Lord, that I have escaped!** Dhóxă-ţ, Doámne, că scăpái!

GLORY *vb.* (*to rejoice proudly*) arhundipséscu

GLOVE *s.* gántă, hirótă, mânúşe, pumânică; (*mitten*) brumáncă (*and* brumángă) ‖ **Pls, GSus:** mână, CL 256; **Prv:** hiĺórti, CL 253; **Cru:** mănícă, GOLAB 234

GLOW *s.* dugoáră, flóyă → BLAZE

GLOW *vb.* (*of a fire*) (a)ruşéscu, (a)ruşăscu; (*as of firewood*) njirédz, ▾duguréscu, guduréscu

GLOWING *s.* duguríre, luñináre

GLOWING *adj.* (*as of the sun in July*) dugurós, -oásă

GLOWWORM *s.* licuríciu, ĺuleác ‖ **SJos:** culuféxâ, *sg and pl*; **Prv:** culufuthéi [t-h], CL 43

GLUE *s.* tutcále, tupcálă; (*made of water and flour*) ciríş, ci-ríj

GLUE *vb.* ▾(a)lichéscu, alăchéscu, ▾aculséscu

GLUG-GLUG *ono.* gâl-gâl

GLUM *adj.* cérnu, mutrusít → SULKY

GLUT *vb.* ▾(a)ndés, ▾astúp → SATISFY

GLUTTED *adj.* sătúl, -úlă, -úľ, -úle; săturát

GLUTTING *s.* sătuleáţă → REPLETION

GLUTTON *s.* hap-húp ‖ ľúftă, BA 425

GLUTTONOUS *adj.* limós, oásă, óşĭ, -oáse → GREEDY

GLUTTONY *s.* límă, limăryíe, lixuríľe, lixuíre, lixurlíche, tă-măhchirlâche

GNASH ONE'S TEETH *vb.* zgroámic; scắrcic (*or* scâr-) dínţâľ, câr-ţânéscu, crâţânéscu, scârşnéscu

GNASHING *s.* (*of teeth*) scârcicáre, scârşníre, scărcăcáre

GNAT *s. ent.* musíţă, muşíţă, ciul

GNAW *vb* ▾(a)ród; (*of one's stomach*) si minteáşte; **I have a ~ing pain in my stomach** Ñ-si minteáşte ínima; *also:* Ñ-aúrlă luchi [luk'] tu pântică ≈ My stomach worm gnaws; ▾alúmtu; **Thoughts ~ at my heart** Mi alúmtă minduírĭli

GNAWED: **to be ~ by remorse** mi mâcă săráchea

GNAWING *s.* aroádire

GNOME *s.* ≈ giúgea, *pl* giúgeañ → DWARF

GO *vb.* ▾duc, *aor.* duş, *part.* dus; ñérgu, *aor.* ñérşu; ▾apórtu; **Where did he ~?** Cấtă iú dúsi? **~ after water!** Dú-te tr-ápă! **Let's ~!** S-nă ţém (*allegro from* duţém, *a var. of* dúţim); **Everybody went there** Toátă lúmea s-purtă acló; *2 sg* vai; **~ up to the hill** Vai m blai; **~ to grass!** (*Get lost!*) Adúnă-u di auá! → IT GOES WITHOUT SAYING

GO! *interj.* yízmadhe! yízmă-te!

GO A-BEGGING *vb.* yiftuéscu

GO AHEAD *vb.* dau năínte

GO AHEAD (AND...) ia; **Go ahead and ask him!** Ia lu-ntreábă!

GO AND WHISTLE FOR IT ≈ arămân ca găľína údă

GO AROUND *vb.* ▾şuţ

GO AWAY *vb.* (*to distance*) fug, ľau cior, trag ciciór, ▾dipár-tu, ▾dipărtédz; (*to ~ from home; to go abroad*) ▾xinitipséscu

GO BAIL FOR SMTH. *vb.* (*as to make a deposit for an engagement*) dau sémnul

GO BANKRUPT *vb.* mufluzipséscu

GO BEYOND *vb.* trec → SURPASS

GO BUGGY *vb.* → GO OUT OF ONE'S HEAD

GO DARK BEFORE ONE'S EYES *vb.* ‖ ñ-si ľa óćľiľ, BASME 53, 206, 281

GO DOWN *vb.* (*to descend*) ▾dipún; (*to ~ socially or economically*) cătăndiséscu (pri hála aéstă); (*of a swelling*) mi disúmflu (*or* disúflu)

GO DOWN IN ONE'S BOOTS *vb.* u aspár huzmétea; li yănuséscu (*or* hunuséscu) vásile di frícă; ▾păléscu; li úmplu (zmeánile) di frícă

GO FOR A WALK *vb.* ▾prímnu, priímnu, ghizipséscu

GO FOR BROKE *vb.* mi fac páde

GO GAPING ABOUT *vb.* şintéscu

GO HALF SHARES WITH *vb.* ngiumeátic, ▾ngiumitichédz

GO HALVES *vb.* ngiumeátic

GO HAYWIRE *vb.* u ľau giúngiula

GO INTO ONE'S TANTRUMS *vb.* ñ-yíne zurleáţa → GET INTO A TANTRUM

GO INTO THE WILD WORLD *vb.* (*as out of despair*) ñ-ľau míntea la cĭcioáre; ľau cálea a li púpăză; acăţ strématile; ñ-ľau pérlu ‖ BASME 403: ñ-ľau pérľi

GO IT! (*to urge to proceed*) ştu-cará

GO IT STRONG *vb.* ▾disíc năínte

GO MAD *vb.* mi apríndu, ▾zurléscu, ñ-ľa cáplu vímtu; (*of a dog, etc.*) túrbu, trub, turbédz, lisixéscu → MADDEN ‖ BASME 33: cher di mínte

GONE *adj.* dus ‖ CUVATA 6: **Marica was ~** Márica s-aveá dúsă

GO OFF *vb.* (*to follow a course*) ñeg, ñérgu

GO OFF THE HANDLE *vb.* ñ-arsáre scârpa → FLY INTO A TANTRUM

GO OFF ONE'S HEAD *vb.* ▾cicănéscu (di mínte *or* di cap); ▾°aspárgu di mínte

GO OFF THE HOOKS *vb.* → GO OFF ONE'S HEAD

GO ON *vb.* (*to happen*) cur; **in order to see what might be going on** s-veádă ca ţe va s-cúră

GO ON ALL FOURS *vb.* ▾abuşilédz, abuşulédz ‖ DIARO 161: ímnu abúşalui

GO ON AND ON *vb.* (*to let off hot air*) băndurédz, băbăléscu, zburăscu goále

GO ON A PILGRIMAGE *vb.* duc la hăgilâche, ñérgu n hăgilâche

GO ON A TRIP *vb.* fac sefér, mi duc tăxíe

GO ONE'S OWN GAIT *vb.* fac cúmu ñ-táľe cáplu → ACT

GO ONE'S WAY *vb.* (*to continue one's road*) ñ-trag calea; ñ-mu-tréscu di cále; (*to use one's own discretion*) fac cúmu ñ-táľe cá-plu (→ ACT)

GO ON FOOT *vb.* (*making large steps*) arúc jgľoáte

GO ON THE SPREE *vb.* (*to give free rein to fun*) u fac uzungióva

GO OUT *vb.* (*to exit*) es (*or* ies), aor. i(n)şíi *or* i(n)şái; *part.* işít (*or* inşít, inşát); (*to become extinguished*) ▼astíngu

GO OUT FOR A WALK *vb.* dau únă dévră, fac únă dévră

GO OUT OF ONE'S HEAD (*or* **MIND**) *vb.* ▼zurléscu, ▼aspárgu, ▼ciu-cănéscu di cáp (*or* di mínte); ñ-asboáră gáia; ▼cictiséscu, ▼cihtiséscu, ▼cicărdiséscu, ▼cildiséscu di mínte ‖ cher di mínte, BASME 496

GO OVER *vb.* (*to transgress*) scápit; (*to succeed*) u scot náparti

GO SHARES WITH SMB. *vb.* ▼cumăthiséscu

GO SHOPPING *vb.* psuniséscu, psunséscu

GO THE WRONG WAY UP *vb.* ñ-si dúțe tersiné

GO THE WHOLE HOG *vb.* u scot n cap, scot lucrulu n cap, ▼biti-séscu; **people decided to go the whole hog** oámiñ apufăsíț

GO THIRTEEN TO THE DOZEN *vb.* máțin pi virisíe

GO THROUGH *vb.* ▼spitrúndu; străbát

GO TO BED *vb.* ▼bag, ▼cúlcu, ľau viléndza dhípla; **He went to bed hungry** S-băgă ni-măcát; **Go to bed, my chick, go to bed!** Băgă-ñ-te, púľe, băgă-ñ-te!

GO TO CUFFS *vb.* ▼agiúngu la par, mi acáț di per (cu)

GO TO HELL! sictír! *Also:* na! **Go to hell! I don't care about your mind!** Na ş-tíne, ş-míntea-ț! Mâşcă-ț nările! Mâşcătureádză-te! Nclo, tu nec s-ñerdzi! S-ti ľa néclu! Túndi-ti! Dú-ti órca! ‖ DIARO 151: Dú-ti Brúsa! DIARO 305: s-ț-u da dzâpea (*or* dzâpita, dzâpitlu; BATSARIA 1: S-ti ľa dráclu! S-ț-u da cripátlu! *idem* 15: s-ti ľa hárlu! *idem* 73: s-ti ľa lăiáța; HRISTU 3: s-ti ia dracu

GO TO LAW WITH SMB. *vb.* lu scol.

GO TO THE DOGS *vb.* (*to go to the winds*) ‖ aor, 3 sg: li mâcă lúplu, BASME 364, *lit.* 'The wolf ate them'

GO TO THE LAND OF NOD *vb.* mi fúră sómnul

GO TO THE WINDS → GO TO THE DOGS

GO TOWARDS *vb.* (*to turn to*) ▼ľau

GO UNDER *vb.* (*to hide, as in a river*) ‖ mi dau de-a fúndu, BASME

410

GO UP *vb.* ▼alín; **Milk went up** (*became more expensive*) Láptile s-alină; ▼análţu **The smoke is going up** Si-análţă fúmlu nsus

GO WELL TOGETHER *vb.* ▼uidiséscu, iduséscu

GO WITH YOUNG *vb.* ▼acáţ ‖ armân sárţină, BASME 438

GO WRONG *vb.* (*to be in low water*) ñ-si dúţe tersiné; cacurizipséscu

GOAD *s.* (*pointed rod to urge on an animal*) acşále,; strimuráre, strâmburíre; *Tur:* strimburáre

GOAL *s.* scupó, lúcru tu-avináre; (*intention*) niéte

GOAT *s.* cápră, *dim.* căpríţă; (*young or small ~*) iádă; *coll.* căpráríu, căprâríu; **milking ~** muldzáră, muldzárcă; (*with a bell*) ciucánă; **wild ~** áyru-cápră

GOAT-DEALER *s.* ţăpár

GOAT HAIR *s.* căprínă

GOATHERD *s. G:* căprár, căprărár; (*female ~*) căpăráră

GOATSKIN *s.* (*container made of ~*) cheále → SATCHEL

GOB *s.* → LUMP

GOBBET *s.* → LUMP

GOBBLE *vb.* ▼apúc, ▼anciúp

GOBBLER *s.* cúrcu → TURKEY-COCK

GO-BETWEEN *s.* cudóş

GOBLET *s.* măstrăpă, tas, tásă

GOD *s.* Dumnidză, Dumnidzău, Aţél-di-Análtu; *voc.* Doámne! *or* Doámne-Dumnidzále! **God forgive them** ɖum-ľártă-ľ; **my God!** Hristé-mu! ‖ CUVATA 3: *voc.* Dumnidzálim!

GOD FORBID! (*don't!*) náca, nápa, năpă, nápu, núpu; vidém ‖ Lárgu di tíne! (*lit.* '[*May God keep it*] *far from you!*'), PARALLELE 128 *or* S-nu da Dumnidzău! PARALLELE 130

GOD REST HIS/ HER SOUL! Dum-leártă-ľ! ‖ HRISTU 103: ĭirtat s-ibă ('*May he be forgiven*')

GODCHILD *s.* hin, hiľín, hľin

GODDAUGHTER *s.* hínă, hiľínă, hľínă, cumbáră ‖ *Cru:* hăľínă, hľínă, GOLAB 219

GODFATHER *s.* cumbár; **~ fox** cumbáră vúlpe; nun

GODFATHERHOOD *s.* cumbărlíche, cumbărlíľe

GODLESS *adj.* m athéu f athéă, *m pl* athéi, *f pl* athée

GODMOTHER *s.* cumbáră, núnă ‖ *SJos:* cumbăríciă, CL 43

GODPARENT *s*. cumbár

GODSON *s*. hiľín → GODCHILD

GOGGLE AT *vb*. (a)zgârléscu ócľiľ (*or* dzíhľľi); **~ your eyes!** Azgârleá-ţ ócľiľ!

GOGGLE *adj*. (*of eyes*) zgârlós, zgârleáiu; cu ócľiľ hărvăľisíţ

GOGGLE-EYED *adj*. cu ócľiľ işíţ → GOGGLE

GOING *s*. imnătúră, dúcă, ducătúră

GOING DOWN *s*. dipuneáre, dipúnire

GOING OUT *s*. işíre, inşíre

GOING TO BED *s*. apuneáre, apúnire, culcáre

GOITER *s*. *anat*. mámă, gúşe; **He's got a ~** Alăsă mámă

GOITROUS *adj*. mămós, -oásă, -óşľ, -oáse

GOLD *s*. (a)málamă, amálumă

GOLDEN *adj*. di amálamă, di hrisáfe, di hrisózmă, di fluríe; glubudán, *m pl* -dáñ; **with his ~ sword** cu pála-ľ di fluríe; **~ coin** fluríe; **a girl with ~ hair** feátă cu pérlu fluríe ‖ (*having the color of gold*) malamatéñu, DIARO 97

GOLDEN WHITE *adj*. (*mainly of goats and sheep*) flor; beciu *m*, béce *f*

GOLDFINCH *s*. *orn*. ţínţur (*and* ţíndzur), ţuţundréu, ţuţundríu, maradóiu ‖ *SJos:* gíii, CL 46

GOLDSMITH *s*. fávru, hrísic, hríscu

GOLDSMITH'S CRAFT *s*. hrisiclíche

GOLD WIRE *s*. hrisáfe, hrisózmă, *pl*. hrisózmate

GONE *adj*. fugát, vgat; (*passed*) tricút; **~ to bed** apús; (*infatuated*) ayăchipsít; (*pregnant*) greáuă *f sg*, greále *f pl*; (*dead*) dus; (*ruined*) surpát; **They have been ~ since Monday** Súntu fugáţ di lúni; **Childhood is ~!** Tricútă-i ficiurímea! → BE ~

GONER *s*. chirút

GOOD *s*. ghíne, bun, ghineáţă; **Nobody runs away from ~** Di ghíne vâră nu fúdze; (*benefit*) ambăreáţă; **do ~ to smb.** fac bun, mi bunuéscu; (*of a remedy, of climate, of water*) mi acáţă

GOOD *adj*. bun, *f* búnă, *m pl* búñ, *f pl* búne; (*of a person*) bunác, bunşór; **Good day!** (*when greeting one person*) Búnă-ţ oára! (*when greeting two or more persons*) Búnă-vă oára! *or* Búnă-vă dzúua! **to be good at anything** ñ gioácă mâna la túte, ñ-ľa ócľul la túte

GOOD *adv*. ghíne, *F:* ghéni

GOOD FOR YOU!

GOOD FOR YOU! (*interjectionally*) áşculsun! ‖ BATSARIA 60: Calótih-vă!

GOOD LUCK *s*. báftă → LUCK ‖ *Cru:* ambăreáţă, GOLAB 197

GOOD MANNERS *s*. uminíľe

GOOD MILKER *s*. (*of a cow, a ewe or a goat*) lăptoásă *adj*.

GOOD NATURE *s*. (*of people's character*) imiráme, imireáţă

GOOD THINGS OF LIFE *s*. zéfchiă *or* zéfche, *pl.* zéfchi *or* zéfchiuri

GOOD TURN *s*. hăgilâche

GOOD-BYE! şedz cu sănătáte! Andámuse búnă! → BID ~ ‖ *F:* bună-videri, HRISTU 64 (cf. Alb. *mirupafshim*); **to bid ~ with one's hands** lă fac sănătati cu mănăli, HRISTU 65; oru sănătati, *ibid*.; STERGHIU 21: ñ-ľau adio

GOOD-FOR-NOTHING *s*. azvărnătúră; bandí *m*, bandoáñe *f*; calpuzán, călpudzán, capisâz, ceapcân, chimpazé, ciuhľán, cudár, dispuľát, *G:* dărmálă (*and* dâr-); mangusár, om di ciuchi, páľu-om, spindzu-rătúră, ţapaţúc, ţilipáie *m*, ţilipáiañ *pl*; ţârlós, vímtu-avínă, xipóltu, zgrumát (*of a woman*) gulubízdră, mángă, mangúfă ‖ BASME 702: stărchitúră, strărchitúră

GOOD-HEARTED *adj*. cu súflit; bun ca pânea ţea cáldă ‖ **He is ~** eásti ómlu alu Dumnidză, DIARO 430

GOOD-LOOKING *adj*. bírbu, *m pl* -rghi, *f pl* -rbe → HANDSOME

GOOD-NATURED *adj*. ímir, ímbru ‖ *GSus:* ári nidéii búnâ, CL 257

GOODLY *adj*. (*of pleasing appearance*) gustós; (*lárge*) *m/f sg* máre, *m/f pl* mări

GOODNESS *s*. bunáţă, buneáţă, bunătáte, bunăteáţă, ghinăteáţă; (*good deed*) sivápe

GOODS *pl*. (*merchandise*) prămătíe, părmătíe

GOODWILL *s*. bunăteáţă, ghinăteáţă; (*consent*) apodhixíre, căbíle

GOODY *s*. ghineáţă; muşitéţ, muşutéţ *pl*; **So many presents and goodies!** Ţe lai oáră şi ghinéţ! (*goodies brought for or sent to a young mother*) buguníţă, lănghídhă

GOOF *vb*. (*to blunder*) cálcu tu pítă

GOOFY *adj*. agudít → CRAZY, SILLY

GOOSE *s*. gâscă, hínă, pátă, pátcă; (*male*) gusác, gâscu; **wild ~** áyră gâscă → COOK SMB.'S ~

GORE *vb*. ▾spitrúndu, ▾spântic, ▾dispântic

GORGE *s*. (*narrow, usu. steep passage*) arăstoácă; *anat.* gărgălán, gărgălác → THROAT

GORGE ONESELF vb. (to glut) mi nfărmác

GORGEOUS adj. háscu, nişinlítcu, muşeát, bugdán, buydán; (of a woman or girl) piruşắnă, piruşeánă; (as of mountains) şcret, fanúmin

GORMANDIZE vb. (to eat ravenously) glăpuéscu → GULP DOWN

GOSHAWK s. orn. chirchinéc, **N:** ubíş

GOSLING s. ‖ **SJos:** hinóplu, CL 253; **Prv, Av:** pap, CL 257

GOSPEL s. vănghéľu (and vân-), vinghéľu; (the book of the four ~s) tetravánghel

GOSSIP vb. (to blab) máţin, discântu

GOT UP adj. (adorned) isusít, adărát, armătusít

GOURD s. (hard-rinded ~) curcubétă

GOURMAND s. ľúftă

GOVERNMENT s. chivérnise ‖ HRISTU 3: chivărisľi; gen. a li cheverisi, 27 (from Alb. qeverísi)

GOVERNMENT BOND s. (certificate of debt) caimée

GOVERNOR s. (of a province) valí; beiu or beu (voc. sg béo!); a ~'s wife biínă, bioáñe

GRAB vb. ▼apúc, ▼(a)nciúp, (a)ngiúp

GRACE n (clemency, pity) ñílă, isáfe, carémă, cherémi, cheremlâchi, doára-a Dómnului; (charm) gilfé, háre, harísmă; (beauty) muşuteáţă; (ease of movement) ľişureáţă

GRACEFUL adj. háriş; **a ~ mouth** gúră di cutíe

GRACIOUS adj. (kind) háriş; (merciful) ñilós

GRACKLE s. orn. chísă, gáie

GRADIENT s. giug → SLOPE

GRADUALISM s. părălâche

GRADUATED (one who studied) ≈ spudhăsít, spudhăxít

GRADUALLY adv. ‖ CUNIA 319: (cu) părălâche

GRAFT s. ambóľ, aşlamáie

GRAFT vb. ambuľiséscu, şurtéscu; fac aşlamáie

GRAFTED UPON adj. ambuľisít

GRAFT HORNS ON SMB. vb. (to deceive) ▼ampíhiur

GRAFTING s. ambuľisíre, şurtíre

GRAIN s. gărnúţ (**and** gâr-), găríţ, grănţu, grânúţ; dim. gărnuţíc; bob, pl boábe

GRAMMAR s. yramatichíe, yrămatichíe

GRANARY s. hambáre, ambáre

GRAND adj. m/f sg máre, m/f pl mărĭ

GRANDCHILD s. nipót

GRANDDAUGHTER s. nipoátă ‖ *Grăm, Hor, Kat, Plat:* nipótă, B-ARCH 474

GRANDE DAME s. chiráuă, madámă, bóje

GRANDEUR s. măríľe

GRANDFATHER s. tat, pl. táteañ; pap, pl: pachi, păpấñ, pápañ, pápeañ; ghiuş; táta mári

GRANDIOSE adj. évil, thiríu; ghigántu, ghigándu; div, m pl divĭ or diyĭ

GRANDMOTHER s. ómă, máuă, máie, bábă; (paternal ~) dádă ‖ *Cot, Kok:* mai [má•i]

GRAND-NEPHEW s. strănipót

GRAND-NIECE s. strănipoátă

GRANDOMANIA s. măríľe

GRANDSON s. nipót

GRANT vb. (a)hărzéscu

GRANT SMB. A RESPITE vb. dau oáră

GRAPE s. aúuă; (a variety with very large grapes) dábină; (sour unripe ~) ayurídhă; (wild ~) gríndză; (a)yrindzálă

GRAPE-GATHERING s. (a)yizmáre, (a)ghizmáre

GRAPE JUICE s. pitméze, picméze, pihméze

GRAPE VINE s. luzíncă

GRAPPLE s. băteáre; ncârligáre

GRAPPLE vb. ▾bat, ▾ncârlighédz

GRASP s. ncurpiľáre

GRASP vb. ▾apúc, ▾stríngu; *N* (rare): strấngu; (in or as in tongs) ncliştédz

GRASPING s. (a)nciupáre

GRASPING adj. zulumgí → RAPACIOUS

GRASS s. iárbă; bot. (Some nondescript plants and types of grass are:) brâzneáuă, burdulác, căşigíc, cípet, coáda-cálui, chinúş, lăpúş, oárdză, parádzină, preáznă, puh, sádină, scrádă, scrádză, séul găľínăľei, stiruvótan, sitrivótan, ţarţarác, vutánă → PUT SMB. OUT OF ~

GRASSY adj. irbós, -oásă, -óşĭ, -oáse

GRASSHOPPER s. ent. scarcaléc, carcaléc, scarcaléţ, carcaléţ, scarcalédz, carcalédz, ceatráfil

GRATE *vb.* (*to scratch, to abrade*) scălséscu; (*as of a door*) cârțânéscu, yrațânéscu ‖ CUNIA 230: (*to rub with smth. rough*) arin(ă)séscu, dau cu líma, dau cu arneála

GRATEFUL: to be ~ ľ-u am tu biricheávis → ACKNOWLEDGE

GRATE ONE'S TEETH *vb.* zgroámin → GNASH ONE'S TEETH

GRATER *s.* (*tool*) hístră

GRATIFY *vb.* ▾alín

GRATING *s.* (*framework of bars in a window*) parmác, părmác, părmáche, părmăclâche

GRATING *m.* (*sound*) cârțâníre, yrațânsíre

GRATIS *adj.*, *adv.* batiavá, bathavá [t-h], pi virisíe

GRATITUDE *s.* cunuşteáre, ahârzíre, ahâristisíre; **with much ~** cu máre ahâristisíre ‖ **Cru:** efharístise, GOLAB 214

GRATUITOUS *adj.* batiavá *invar.*

GRATUITY *s.* (a)rusféte, dáre

GRAVE *s.* groápă, murmíntu (*and* -míndu), mirmíntu, mârmíndu, **N:** mirmít; chiúngu, gúvă, túmbă ‖ (*usu. an old ~*) grúmur, CAPIDAN 151

GRAVE *adj.* (*threatening harm or danger*) gros, -oásă, -oşĭ, -oáse; greu, greáuă, grei, greále; laiu, *f* láie, *m/f pl* lăi

GRAVE-DIGGER *s.* grupár

GRAVEL *s.* chitríş

GRAVESTONE *s.* ploáce

GRAVEYARD *s.* murmínțâ (*and* -ndzâ), mărmínțâ *n pl* → CEMETERY

GRAVITATE *vb.* (*to move or tend to move toward smth.*) ‖ PC: trag tră, trag cătră

GRAY *adj.* săín; *also:* (a)múrgu, bágav, cănút; (*of goats: ~ with white head*) florucánat; găbúr (*and* gâ-), griv *or* yriv, yrivănúş; (*of beard or hairs*) yrivuít; (*as of mustaches*) măsinát; **G:** nalbástru; (*as of a horse*) psar, psăríc; siv, sumólcu

GRAYBEARD *s.* aúş → OLD MAN

GRAY-HEADED *adj.* (a)ncănuşít; (*somewhat ~*) cănutíc; şecherlíu

GRAYISH *adj.* şecherlíu

GRAZE *s.* sgârietúră, zgrâmătúră

GRAZE *vb.* (*to scratch*) ▾zgrâm, ▾sgâir

GRAZE *vb.* (*to feed on growing herbage*) páscu

GRAZING *s.* (*process*) páştire, păşteáre; (*pasture ground*) păşúne

GREASE *s.* grăsíme, umtúră

GREASE

GREASE *vb.* ▼(a)úngu

GREASE OF WOOL *s.* usâc, suc; (*containing such grease, adj.*) usâcós; (*the color obtained*) luláchiu

GREASING *s.* (a)úndzire

GREASY *adj.* (a)úmtu, -mtă, -mţâ, -mte; liydhós, -oásă

GREAT *adj.* (*solid, severe, as of a cold*) sănătós; (*very good, delicious*) scóntră *invar.*; (*deep, complete*) arắu *invar.*; ~ **desert** irñíe arắu; (*of people*) aţél máre *m*, aţeá máre *f*; **Tomorrow is Virgin Mary's Day** Mâni eáste Stă-Măría aţeá máre

GREAT BEAR *s. astr.* ursoáñe ‖ **Peş:** lătărpózle, CL 254; Cuscrí-ľa, DIARO 178

GREAT BOAST, SMALL ROAST ≈ Murí yífta ţe ti-alăvdá (*lit.* 'The Gypsy woman who used to praise you has died')

GREAT HAVENS! ≈ ba!

GREATHEARTED *adj.* (*brave*) inimárcu; (*magnanimous*) filótim, giumértu, sălghít

GREATNESS *s.* măríľe

GRECIZED AROMANIAN *s.* ‖ TULLIU 141: cărăgún

GREECE *s.* ‖ **Cru:** Eládhă, GOLAB 214

GREED *s.* límă, lexuríe, tămăhchirlâche

GREEDY *adj.* limós; *also:* hărbút, hărlăpút, hírtu, hârtu, lemáryu, líhud, lingársu, líxur; *3 sg pres.* nu ári sát (*or* nu ári sátur); tăhmăcheár, tămáh; (~ *of gain*) gulimán

GREEK *s.* and *adj.* élin; gắrcu, grec; *coll.* gricáme; *adj.* grâţéscu, grăţéscu, greţéscu ‖ (**I speak**) ~ (Zburắscu) gritseaşti, K-D 116

GREEN *adj.* (*color*) *m/f sg* veárde, *m/f pl* vérdzâ; (*dark-~*) carítcu; gángur, gálgur; (*immature; deficient in knowledge or training*) ghivréc (*lit.* 'cracker'), ni-agiúmtu, (a)rúd

GREEN CHESE *s.* (*fresh* ~) caş dúlţe, CAPIDAN 151

GREEN PEAS *s.* bizéľe, arucutéţ

GREEN PEPPER *s.* pipiryeáuă; *N:* ciúşcă, şúşcă

GREEN-EYED *adj.* ziľár → JEALOUS

GREENGROCER *s.* ‖ CUNIA 337: zărzăvăgí, zărzăvătcí, băhcivăngí

GREENHORN *s.* ageamí

GREENISH YELLOW *adj.* gángur

GREENNESS *s.* virdeáţă, nvirdzáme

GREENGROCER *s.* zârzâvăcí

GREENHORN s. (*inexperienced*) ni-fricát → IMMATURE

GREENS s. pl. zărzăváte (*and* zârzâ-)

GREET vb. ▾bunéscu, ▾ghinuéscu, călimirséscu; (*reciprocally*) ▾fac un yeásu-yeanásu, hiritiséscu, prişindéscu; (*to send greetings through*) dau hiritímate (di la) ‖ ALR 1312: **I ~ him** âľ dzâc bună-ţ oára; STERGHIU 14: mi ghiunuéscu (cu)

GREETING s. bunuíre, ghinuíre, ncľinăciúne *and* ncľinăciúnă; hiritisíre, hiritímate, apánghe

GREYHOUND s. hârtă, liyón, óşă

GREY LIFE OUT OF SMB. vb. ľ-mâc stuhicólu, ľ-scot geánlu

GRIDDLE s. távă, tâvă

GRIDIRON: **to be on the ~** şed ca pri schiñ

GRIEF s. cripáre; *also*: (a)ngúsă, bilé; caimó, camó, cărtíre (*and* câr-), căsăvéte, dor, găfă, gărămínă, ghiúcă, jále, lípe, *G*: măndălâche; máră, măráze, ñílă, nod la ínimă, nver, nverináre, nvernáre, virín ‖ BASME 490: plângu; STERGHIU 3: greáţă

GRIEVANCE s. nfărmăcáre, fărmăcáre, parápun

GRIEVE vb. ▾amărédz, crep, ▾jiléscu, lăiéscu (*and* lâ-), niurédz [ni•u•], ▾părăpuñiséscu;; **Calm down, my dear, do not ~!** Taţi, lai gióne, taţi, nu creápă! **Everybody ~ed** Tuţ niuráră [ni•u•]; (*to yearn*) ñ-alghéscu ócľiľ (tră); **It ~es me to the very heart** Ñ-si bágă ínima n páde ‖ BASME 403: Ñ-si diñícă ínima

GRIEVOUS adj. fărmăcát, fríptu, *m pl* -pţâ; cérnu *f* cérnă, *m pl* cérñi; ndzé(r)nu, ncimirát, nciumirát; cu límba scrumátă (*lit.* 'with scorched tongue')

GRIEVOUSLY adv. amár

GRILL s. (*cooking utensil*) scáră

GRILL vb. ▾pârjiléscu, pârjéscu

GRILLED STEAK s. burjólă, brujólă

GRILLING s. fridzeáre, frídzire

GRIM adj. (*cruel*) crud; (*savage*) áyru; (*fierce*) gúvru; (*harsh and forbidding in appearance*) fuvirós

GRIMACE s. strâmbătúră

GRIMACING WOMAN s. (*usu. a Gipsy*) cinghístră

GRIME s. (*soot, smut*) búştină, căpneáuă, furídzină

GRIME vb. ▾murdăripséscu → DIRTY

GRIND vb. chisédz; *S*: *also* csédz; (*to mill*) máţin, másnu; (*to sharpen, as a knife*) dau pi cheátră

GRINDING

GRINDING *s.* *(of teeth)* scărşníre, scărcăcáre, scărcicáre

GRINDSTONE *s.* mirácune

GRIP *s.* apucáre, apcáre, ţâneáre

GRIP *vb.* ▾apúc, ▾ţân

GRIPE *vb.* → GRIP; *(to distress)* ▾nver, ▾anvirédz, ▾mărín, ▾mărinédz

GRIPPE *s.* *med.* sirmíe → INFLUENZA

GRISLY *adj.* fuvirós, -oásă

GRIST *s.* gărnúţă *n pl* → BRING ~ TO ONE'S MILL

GRIST FOR ONE'S MILL *s.* ápă tu avláche → BRING GRIST TO ONE'S MILL

GRISTLE *s.* scârciu, scârcic

GRISTMILL *s.* moáră

GRIT ONE'S TEETH *vb.* zgroámic

GRITS *s.* ruiálă, uróv

GRIZZLY *adj.* sumólcu, *m pl* -mólţi, *f pl* -mólţe → GRAY

GROAN *s.* (a)ncăníre (*and* angă-), deápir, dzeámit, dzimeáre, plângut, plângu, pupuíre, schimuráre, şclim, şcĺímur, şcĺimuráre, şcĺimurát

GROAN *vb.* dzem, ▾nilséscu, nălséscu, şcĺímur, şcĺímbur, şcĺimurédz, şcĺumurédz, (a)ncănéscu (*and* angă-), âncănéscu

GROCER *s.* băcál, băcălă, *N:* băcălău *m*, -loáñe *f*; aryăstiryeár; *adj.* băcăléscu, -leáscă, -léşţâ, -léşti ‖ duchingí, DIARO 425

GROCERY *s.* aryăstír, băcălíche, dugáne, duyáne, măyăzíe

GROGGY *adj.* azmét; s(c)lab, *m pl* s(c)laghi, *f pl* s(c)lábe

GROIN *s.* *(of a horse)* slăbínţă, slăghínă, *N:* slăghină

GROOM *s.* *(bridegroom)* duduşeán, grambél, grambó; *(servant)* huzmicheár; *(one in charge of horses)* ipár

GROOM *vb.* *(to attend to the cleaning of an animal)* xistrisescu, histriséscu, sistriséscu; *(to make neat)* ▾cur, spăstréscu

GROOMSMAN *s.* *(sponsor of a wedding)* nun; *(friend of a groom at a wedding)* fărtát, furtát *m*, surátă *f*; căsăvyeár, sihădhyeár; *(boy involved in a wedding ceremonial)* călisár, călisitór

GROOVY adj. scóntră *invar.*

GROPE *vb.* huhuléscu

GROPING *vb.* pusputíre

GROPINGLY *adv.* cu ahulírea; *moves about* ~ ímnă cu ahulírea, ímnă cu tahmínea

GROSS *adj.* (*big*) *m/f* máre, *m/f pl* mări; (*bulky*) căbátcu; (*fat*) gras, strúmbul; (*rude*) păduríș; (**indecent**) dișuțât

GROTTO *s.* spílă → CAVE

GROUCH *s.* (*irritable person*) inagí

GROUND *s.* (*bottom of a body of water*) fúndu; (*soil*) páde, țáră; *to fall to the ~* (*to kill*) cúlcu n páde; **to the (very) ~** până mpáde → CUT THE ~ FROM UNDER SMB.'S FEET

GROUND *adj., part.* of GRIND (*reduced to small particles*) frâmtu; **~ chickpea** aróv frâmtu

GROUND *vb.* (*to base, to found*) thimiľuséscu

GROUND-IVY *s. bot.* poála a feátiľei

GROUNDRENT *s.* murtíe, murtíche

GROUNDS *s.* (*sediments of wine, etc.*) bărsíe → DREGS

GROUP *s.* bándă, bulúche, bluche, ceátă, táifă, tăráfe, tavabíe, tavambíe, tăbăbíe, tubăbíe, túbă

GROUSE *s.* ayru-cucót

GROUSER *s.* and *adj.* (a)ngrăñáric

GROVE *s.* tufáne, tufíș ‖ *Cru:* (*young ~*) pădúre, ɢᴏʟᴀʙ 241

GROVEL *vb.* (*to bow low*) fac taéte, fac timină

GROVELLING *adj.* azvărñár

GROW *vb.* (a)créscu; (*to appear*) arsár; (*as of fruits*) ▾fac

GROW ANGRY *vb.* ▾zbârléscu, zburléscu, ▾asplinséscu

GROW BIGGER *vb.* créscu, ▾ngráș

GROW CHEEKY *vb.* disgărdéscu → COCK ONE'S NOSE

GROW DARK *vb.* (*of the day*) *3 sg:* nsireádză, nupteádză, si ntúnică, ntuneárică

GROW GRAY *vb.* (*of hair*) alghéscu, cănuțéscu, ncănuțéscu, grivuéscu, yrivuéscu, mușcruéscu

GROW GREEN *vb.* nvirdzăscu, funduséscu

GROW HUNGRY *vb.* (*intensively*) ñ-si dúțe gúra la ureácľe

GROW HYPOCHONDRIAC *vb.* ▾ipuhundriséscu

GROW IMPATIENT *vb.* ▾sirhiséscu

GROW IN TUFTS *vb.* (*to become leafy again*) funduséscu

GROW KNOTTY *vb.* (*as of hands*) aruzuséscu, arizuéscu, ñ-si bat mâñle (di)

GROW LESS *vb.* ▾scad, ▾mpuțânédz, ▾ñicurédz, ▾ñicșurédz

GROW LIGHT *vb.* (*of a new day*) *3 sg impers:* algheáște, ápiră, creápă dzúua

GROW MILDER *vb. 3 sg impers. (as of weather)* moáľe

GROW MUDDY *vb.* (a)lăcéscu (*and* alâ-)

GROW OLD *vb.* auşéscu, ▼vicľéscu, (a)nvicľéscu, vicľédz, mbitârnéscu, mbătărnéscu, muşéscu, bătăľuséscu; ñ-arăţeáşte sândzile ‖ BASME 398: trec di vrâstă

GROW OVERCAST *vb.* vurcuséscu, vărcuséscu

GROW PALE *vb.* săhñiséscu

GROW POOR *vb.* ľau di híma, urfăn(ips)éscu

GROW PROUD OF *vb.* arhundipséscu

GROW RICH *vb.* bag zvércă, arhundipséscu

GROW ROUND *vb.* ▼ngurguľédz, ▼ngurlitédz

GROW SAD *vb.* ‖ STERE 29: mi prămpuséscu

GROW RUSTY *vb.* ▼zgurghiséscu

GROW SOFT-MINDED *vb. (to become weak or deficient mentally)* ñ-ľau míntea

GROW SOLITARY *vb.* irmuxéscu

GROW STRONG *vb.* ▼vârtuşéscu, ▼nvârtuşédz; *(as of a fire)* ▼săluéscu

GROW STUPID *vb.* glăréscu, hăzuséscu (di mínte), huţăscu, lişurédz

GROW SUSPICIOUS *vb.* íntru tu éryu ‖ BELIMACE 48: íntru tru şubéi

GROW TAME *vb.* ▼imirédz

GROW THICK *vb. (as of a river)* ▼alăcéscu, ▼cutúrbur

GROW THIN *vb.* ▼bitiséscu, ▼biţéscu, slăghéscu, sclăghéscu, ▼alăchéscu, atihéscu, mi fac hărăhástă; **Your face has grown thin** Ti bitisíşi la fáţă

GROW TIGHTER *vb.* mi apreadún, mi priadún

GROW TIRED *vb.* buhtiséscu → BE BORED

GROW TOO BIG FOR ONE'S BOOTS *vb.* mi ngroş → GIVE ONESELF AIRS

GROW TOO SMALL FOR *vb.* nu mi ncápe; **The whole palace grew too small for her** Pălátea ntreágă nu u ncăpeá

GROW UGLY *vb.* urăţéscu

GROW UP *vb.* créscu, ▼măréscu ‖ bag bóe, DIARO 311

GROW WARM *vb.* ▼ncăldurédz → WARM UP

GROW YELLOW *vb.* gălbinéscu, ngălbinéscu

GROWING *s.* creáştire, crişteáre

GROWING GREEN AGAIN *s. (of trees or fields)* nvirdzâre

GROWING THIN *s.* alăchíre, slăghíre

GROWL *vb.* ▾gărñéscu, ngărñéscu, ngrâñéscu; (*as of a bear*) mâ-râéscu ‖ TULLIU 58 (*of dogs*) angrăñéscu

GROWLING *s.* ngrâñíre (di câne)

GROWN *adj.* criscút

GROWN UP *adj.* *m/f* máre, *m/f pl* mări; mărít

GROWTH *s.* creáştire, crişteáre

GRUB *s.* (*a slovenly person*) áţala-máţala

GRUB *vb.* asgurñéscu → RUMMAGE

GRUBBY *adj.* alăsătóñu; pálaz, *m pl* -lajĭ; áţala-máţala *invar.*

GRUDGE *s.* dol, pícă; **to bear smb. a ~** ĺ-ţân pícă → ROD

GRUDGE *vb.* cărşilătiséscu, fac âncheáre, acáţ âncheáre

GRUEL *s.* dzámă

GRUESOME *adj.* fuvirós, -oásă, -óşĭ, -oáse

GRUFF *adj.* ni-ciuplít

GRUMBLE *s.* mumulíre

GRUMBLE *vb.* mi angrăñéscu; mi duc; **He keeps ~ing** S-dúţe zâr-zâr; (*to complain*) ▾buĭséscu, mumuléscu

GRUMBLER *s.* angrăñáric

GRUMPY *adj.* nizeárcu, *m pl* -rţi, *f pl* -rţe; ursúz, *m pl* -újĭ

GRUNT *s.* (*of a hog*) gruñáre

GRUNT *vb.* gruñédz, gurñédz, ▾gărñéscu, ▾ngărñéscu, ▾gurñéscu, ▾ngurñéscu

GUARANTEE *s.* → GUARANTOR

GUARANTOR *s.* chifíĺu, chifiĺót; **money lent with ~s** parádz daţ cu chifiĺóţ

GUARD *s.* apăráre, păzíre; *also:* afirítă, afiríre, avigĺáre, cărăulsíre ‖ (*a soldier attached to the person of the king, in Greece*) évzon, TULLIU 94

GUARD *vb.* ▾ápăr, ▾avégĺu, cărăulséscu, păzéscu

GUARDIAN *s.* (a)vigĺitór, *N:* avlighitór; cărăúle, cărăúlă, cărăulgí; (*at night*) cărătór, cráhtu, culúche, păzván, păzvándu, (*soldier*) nubicí; (~ *of a stud*) ipár, válmă (*and* vâl-); (~ *of the fields*) puleác (*and* puĺác), dăryát, pândár; strájă; (*trustee*) epítrop; (*protector*) apărătór ‖ *GSus:* simén, CL 260; cafás, gaváz, DIARO 189

GUARDIANSHIP *s.* epitrupíe

GUERDON *s.* muştináre

GUERILLA DETACHMENT s. ceátă ‖ *Cru:* cétă, GOLAB 210

GUESS s. angucíre

GUESS *vb.* gucéscu, cucéscu, (a)ngucéscu, anglicéscu, (a)n-gľíciu, ▾aduchéscu; ~, **if you can!** Aducheá, cari poţ! ‖ *Cru:* ăngucéscu *and* ăngucédz, GOLAB 205; (*to predict, as of a magician*) arúc tu steáli, DIARO 255

GUESS WORK s. angucíre

GUESSING s. aduchíre, aducheáre, angucíre; cu aduchírea (a *game*)

GUEST s. oáspe *m*, oáspită *f*; musafír; (*at a wedding party*) nuntár, numtár, lumtár; *coll.* (*guests brought by the godmother and godfather*) nunáme ‖ oáspit, CAPIDAN 153

GUFFAW s. păhăíre

GUFFAW *vb.* ▾păhăéscu → LAUGH

GUIDE s. călăyúz, călúz, culayúz ‖ *Gop, Mul:* cluz *m*, clúză *f*

GUIDING s. (*viewed as a profession*) călăuzlíche, culăzlíche, culayuzlíche

GUILD s. isnáfe

GUILDSMAN s. isnafcí

GUILE s. cătăryăríľe, dhol (*and* dol), punirlíche; ti vínde ş ti-acúmpără

GUILEFULNESS s. pispeáţă → GUILE, SLYNESS

GUILLOTINE s. caramanghiólă, cărămăñólă

GUILT s. măhănă

GUILTY *adj.* stipsít, ftixít, cu stípsu; **should you find me ~** cari s mi-aflăţ cu stípsu; **to be ~** am căbáte, éscu căbáte; fti-séscu, ftixéscu, stipséscu; **as if the whole world was ~** cánda ľ-stipseá duñáua

GUITAR s. chitháră (*and* chitáră)

GUITAR-PLAYER s. tamburagí

GULCH s. arâpă → RAVINE

GULL s. *orn.* (*with white brest*) ‖ *Prv, SJos:* psarufái, CL 259

GULL *adj.* (*dupe*) háhă, *pl m* háhañ → STUPID

GULL *vb.* ľ-bag cuváta, mi arâd → DECEIVE

GULLET s. *anat.* glâcă; (~ *of a jar*) gurgúľ

GULP: to take a ~ ľau nă gúră

GULP *vb.* arúc tu glâcă, glâcâéscu, ▾spăstréscu, ▾deápin, u adún tu fulínă, hăpuéscu, glăpuéscu (*and* glâ-), ylupuéscu, ciupléscu,

▼mâc ca nă lámñe, fac húmba; (to drink) ţucuéscu

GULPING DOWN s. hăpuíre, glăpuíre, ciuplíre

GUM s. anat. dzindzíe; (gelatinous substance on the edge of eyelids) ţálpă, pl ţălchĭ; sálcă ‖ **Prv:** ţímblă di la uócĭ, CL 263

GUM BOOT s. lástic, lástih

GUN-CARRIAGE s. cánă

GUNLOCK s. ceárcu

GUNNER s. tupcí

GUNPOWDER s. agzóte, avzóte, bărúte; vúlbură, búlvură

GUNSHOT s. plăscăníre, tufcheáuă, tufchileáuă

GURGLE s. gúrgur

GURGLE vb. (to drink with a liquid noise) ţucuéscu; (to flow gurgling) 3 sg: s-dúţe hor-hor

GUSH vb. (as of a spring) ▼(a)zvóm, azvurăscu, ▼vérsu

GUST s. (of wind) ‖ BASME 700: spíthă

GUT s.anat. maţ, pl máţă; (guts, courage) curáuă; (stamina) vârtúte, vârtuşáme

GUTSY adj. putút, vârtós

GUY s. (individual, fellow) om, soţ, ínsu, citămán

GUZZLE vb. beau, arucutéscu, arúc tu fulínă → TIPPLE

GYMNASTICS s. yimnástică

GYP vb. ancálţu → CHEAT, DECEIVE

GYPSY s. yíftu, ghéghiftu, cinghiné, curbét; (a black ~) carasóyiptu; (a ~ child) ghiftíciu; coll. yiftáme, ghiftáme, ghifturáme; derog. gáie, lit. 'crow'; adj. yiftéscu, ghighiftéscu; **She is a ~** Eáste di sóia a Hristólui (lit. 'She is Christ's relative')

GYRATE vb. ▼anvărtéscu

GYVE s. heáre n pl → MANACLES

H

HABIT s. (custom, addiction) adéte, (a)nvéţ, (a)réu, cúmpite f pl, (h)úche, idhíumă, idhiómă, mor, siníthise, sístimă; (bad ~)

HABITUATE

tabiéte, húie, *pl* hui; húche aráo; slábă

HABITUATE *vb.* ▾(a)nvéţ, ▾veţ, ▾mălăxéscu

HABITUATION *s.* (a)nvéţ, pleáme

HABITUDE *s.* pleáme, mălăxíre

HACK *s.* (*sorry horse*) cârcâm, *pl* cârcâmeañ

HACK *vb.* (*to chop*) toc

HACKLE *s.* tépcă

HACKLED WOOL *s.* (a)pálă

HACKNEY-COACH *s.* talíngă → CARRIAGE

HAEMORRHOIDS *s. med.* **Bl:** trănci

HAFT *s.* mânár

HAG *s.* muşurécă, muşarécă

HAGGARD *adj.* chirdút; s(c)lab, *m pl* s(c)laghi, *f pl* s(c)lábe

HAGGLE *vb.* yiftuséscu, ▾păzăripséscu

HAGGLING *s.* yiftusíre

HAIL *s.* grăndine (*and* grân-), gríndine, gríndină; (*process*) grindináre; (*rampage, of hail*) 3 sg impers. grândineádză ‖ **Gra, Rod, Perd, Ses:** gréndină, B-ARCH 19

HAIL *vb.* (*to salute, to greet*) ▾bunuéscu, ghinuéscu

HAIR *s.* per *m*, peri *pl*; *dim.* pirúş; (*a single ~*) şíľet; (*the ~ on the head*) chícă; *adv.* (*detailedly*) **to a ~** pân tu per ‖ (*goat hair*) căprínă, CAPIDAN 147 ‖ (*detailedly*) BELIMACE 44: hir cu per

HAIR ORNAMENT *s.* (*usu. of silver*) pirpindác

HAIRCUTTING *s.* bărbirisíre, bărbirsíre

HAIRPIN *s.* amúră, ciupráche; (*~ with an ornament*) pheástru ‖ DIARO 6: cârfíţâ

HAIR-RAISING *adj.* fuvirós, -oásă, -óşĭ, -oáse

HAIRY *adj.* pirós, -oásă, -óşĭ, -oáse

HALE *adj.* sănătós, putút; ntreg, *f* ntreágă, *m/f pl* ntredzĭ

HALE *vb.* ▾trag azvárna

HALF *s.* and *adj.* giumitáte, jumitáte, dis; **We ate ~ of the kid** Mâcăm díslu di ed; **We set free ~ of them** A díşilor lă deádim cále; **one and a ~ kilos** un ucă ş-dis; **It is ~ past one** Oára eáste únă ş-dísă; (*as of wine*) miţíu, giumétă; (*~ of a litre or so, unit of alcoholic drinks*) sutácă; **~ a meter** dis di métru; **~ a score** táľe → CUT BY ~

HALF MAN *s.* om di ciuchi → GOOD-FOR-NOTHING

HALF-BAKED *adj.* (*not thoroughly baked*) ni-agiúmtu, ni-cóptu;

(lacking intelligence or common sense) ni-tút

HALFHEARTED *adj.* hámin

HALF-TRUTH *s.* ≈ minciúnă → LIE

HALL *s.* *(large room)* sálă; *(entrance)* **G:** ghizintíe

HALLOW *vb.* ▾săntiséscu *(and* sân-*)*, sănţăséscu, ayiséscu, ayiu-séscu

HALLUCINATE *vb.* aĺurédz

HALLUCINATION *s.* aĺuráre

HALLWAY *s.* culghiós, **G:** ghizintíe

HALT *s.* cunáche; *(overnight ~ of a flock)* numíe → MAKE A ~

HALT *adj.* şcĺop, şcĺochi, şcĺoápă, -pe → LAME

HALT *vb.* (a)cundiséscu, (a)cudiséscu; *(to bring to an end)* ▾as-tămăţéscu, chindruséscu, chinduréscu; *(to sleep overnight)* lu-jéscu; *(to rest, as during a jurney)* pupuséscu → STOP

HALTER *s.* căpéstru, căpréstu

HALTING PLACE *s.* cunáche

HALTINGLY *adv.* várai-vára

HALVAH *s.* hâlvă

HALVAH DEALER *s.* hâlvangí

HALVE *vb.* ‖ ▾ngiumeátic, ngiumitichédz

HAMLET *s.* cătún ‖ *cătún is unknown by Arom. in ALB, who say* hoáră ñícă *(lit. 'small village'),* Brâncuş 555

HAMMER *s.* cioc, ciucán, daimác; *(small ~)* căngíc

HAMMER *vb.* bat cu ciócu

HAMPER *s.* coş → BASKET

HAMPER *vb.* ▾(a)ncheádic → SHACKLE

HAND *s. anat.* **S:** mână, **N:** mănă; *dim.* mâşíţă *(and* mă-*)*; mâşótă *(and* mă-*)*, mânşótă, mâjótă, mâşáţă, ciótă, mânuciótă, *(rare)* mă-nuşótă; **N:** mănúşcă; **at hand** *adj.* and *adv.* próir; **to be an old ~** hiu fricát → BE A GOOD ~ AT DOING THINGS, BE AN OLD ~ AT SMTH, BE ON THE GROWING ~, FROM ~ TO ~ ‖ ALIA 166: ménă *(13 cases)* and mánă *(3 cases)*

HAND *s. (of a clock)* ‖ **Peş:** căliúz, CL 41

HAND *vb.* ▾dau; *(to pass)* pára-dau

HAND AND GLOVE *(very good friends)* → BE ~ WITH SMB.

HANDCUFFS *s.* brángă → MANACLES ‖ ALR: heáră *n pl*; beligíţ

HAND DOWN *vb.* alás

HANDFUL *s.* mânátă *(and* mă-*)*, mnátă, púlmu; **a ~ of golden coins**

HANDGUN

un púlmu di fluríi; húftă

HANDGUN s. altípatlar, arăvóle, (a)ruvóle, ruvéle ‖ *SJos:* arivorvér, *pl* arivolvére (*sic*), CL 37

HANDICRAFTSMAN s. zanahcí, zănatcíu

HANDKERCHIEF s. (*pocket ~*) şimíe, şamíe; (*headgear*) cimbér → SHAWL ‖ *Amc:* tihíţă, SCHL 117

HANDLE s. (*of a pot, of abasket, of an axe, etc.*) coádă; mă-núşe (*and* mâ-); mânár; (*of a pot, of an earring*) turtoáre

HANDLE OVER vb. (*to transfer goods or custody*) fac tislíme

HAND-MILL s. moáră di café, moáră di pipér

HANDSEL s. (*lucky start*) sefté, sifté, xifté

HANDSEL vb. (*to inaugurate with a tocken of luck*) fac sefté

HANDSOME adj. aléptu, bírbu, bugdán, buydán, daiľán, daleán, scriát, *G:* platón; (*~ and strong*) livéndu ‖ BASME 12: chicát dit steále

HANDWRITING s. cundíľ

HANDYMAN s. theámin

HANG vb. ▼(a)spíndzur, ▼ascálin, ▼ascálnu, ▼acáţ; **~ up one's axe** (*to chock it up*) trag mână di (→ ABNEGATE)

HANG ABOUT SMB. vb. mi ţân scaľu (*lit. 'to stick to like a thistle'*)

HANG DOWN vb. discálnu, dispíndzur

HANG IN vb. (*to insist*) ľ-cad pri zvércă, para-ngréc, u ţân fúne

HANG IN THE WIND vb. (*to be reluctant*) strâmbu nárea → HESITATE

HANG ONE'S HEAD vb. ‖ HRISTU 41: apun capu

HANG UP ONE'S AX(E) vb. (*to renounce*) trag mână (di) → ABNE-GATE

HANGDOG s. capsâz, dărmálă, puşteán → GOOD-FOR-NOTHING; (*guilty*) stipsít

HANGER s. (*as a loop hanger of a coat*) ureácľe

HANGER ON s. (*parasite, of people*) hărămgí

HANGING s. (a)spindzuráre, acăţáre

HANGMAN s. gilát

HANGOVER s. (*after consumption of alcohol*) mahmurlâche, muhmur-lâche

HANK s. tex. cărúnă, jireágľe, jurébe, *Gop:* gârchínă

HANK WINDER s. dipinătór

HANKER *vb.* (*to long*) mi ľa dórlu (di), (*to yearn*) ñ-alghéscu ócľiľ (tră); (*to weary for/after*) ñ-si alăcheáşte ínima (di)

HANKY-PANKY *s.* tirtípe, a-plán, aplănisíre

HAP *s.* ugoádă, ugudíre

HAPHAZARD *s.* tíhe

HAPHAZARDLY *adv.* tu tíhe ‖ BASME 459: pri căsméte

HAPLESS *adj.* atíh; órbu, *f* oárbă, *m pl* órghi, *f pl* oárbe

HAPPEN *vb.* ▾tihiséscu, ▾ugudéscu, agudéscu, trăxéscu;; (*to come, esp. by way of injury or harm*) ▾pat, ▾păţăscu; **It ~ed that he had good eyes** S-tihisí că aveá ócľi buñ; **I ~ed to be there** Mi-agudíi acló; **in order to see what ~s** s-veádă ţe trăxeáşte; **What ~ed to you that you didn't come?** Ţe păţíşi di nu viníşi? **What has ~ed to you?** Ţe ti păţíşi? **It will ~ to him what has never ~ed to anyone** Vai pátă nipăţâta; (*what if*) náca, nácă **What if it happens that thieves come to rob us?** Náca fúrľi yin s-ni fúră?

HAPPEN WHAT MAY ţi s va las s híbă

HAPPENING *s.* ugoádă, ugudíre; **ill-fated ~** oáră láie; (*hazard*) tihisíre

HAPPINESS *s.* ambăreáţă, ghíne, ghineáţă, iftihíe

HAPPY *adj.* hărós, hăriós; hărăcóp, -oápă, -óchi, -oápe; calótih, calóhit, calurízic (*ant.* cacurízic); **to be ~** alghéscu; ñ-râde búdza (*lit.* 'my lip is laughing'), nu mi ţâne lóclu di ha-ráuă; **A ~ New Year!** Tră mulţ añ! ‖ álbu; **He did not have a single ~ day** Dzúuă álbă nu vidzú, CAPIDAN 150

HAPPY-GO-LUCKY *adj.* (*care-free*) fâră gailéi, cu căciúla scoásă

HARASS *vb.* scăñiséscu, nu dau bánă, acáţ limăreáua; **to ~ life out of smb.** aród dit hicáte, mâc hicátlu, uftichédz, uhtichédz; (*as of lovers*) mâc iñoára → PESTER

HARBINGER *s.* pródhrom

HARD *adj.* and *adv.* (*as of bread*) vârtós, scliró *invar*; (*heavy, painful*) greu, greáuă, grei, greále; dhíscul, hămăléscu;; **It is ~ for me** ñ-eáste greu; *adv.* hămăleáşte ‖ BASME 22: cu zóre

HARD CASH *s.* dismână, *adv.*

HARD OF HEARING *adj.* fudúl di ureácľi

HARD-BOILED *adj.* (*experienced*) păţât, trecút prit ţir ş-prit sítă → VERSED

HARDEN *vb.* (*as of the skin*) ▾ascurédz, vurtuşédz, ânvârtuşédz, vârtuşéscu

HARDENING

HARDENING *s.* nvârtuşáre; (*of steel*) călíre

HARDHEADED *adj.* aruşuţắt; (*willful*) uchealíu ‖ (*unfeeling*) no-ári uminitáte, PARALLELE 146

HARDHEARTED *adj.* ni-ñilós

HARDIHOOD *s.* găiréte, ínimă → COURAGE; (*vigor*) puteáre

HARDLY *adv.* cât, cât; **A cloud was ~ moving on** Un niór cât, cât s-miná ‖ **Cru:** cu-di-ayíia, GOLAB 196

HARDNESS *s.* vârtuşáme

HARDNESS *s.* ascuráme

HARDSHIP *s.* bréndă, zóre; **You don't know what ~ is** Tíne nu ştii ţe-i zórea; *cf. also* Nu şidzúşi cu cúrlu tu neáuă, *fig.* (*lit.* 'you have not sat bare assed on snow')

HARDWORKING *adj.* → INDUSTRIOUS

HARDY *adj.* (*robust*) vârtós, zdúmban; (*brave*) inimárcu → COURAGEOUS

HARE *s.* ľépur, ľépure (*and* lé-), ľópur; *dim.* lipuríş, lipuríciu → RUN THE WRONG ~ ‖ **P:** iépur, SarD 116; **Pls:** (*she-hare*) lipurárcâ, CL 255

HARE-BRAINED *adj.* hai-húi *invar.*; lişuráşcu (≈ 'easygoing')

HAREM *s.* haréme, *pl* haréñ

HARK *vb.* ascúltu

HARKEN *vb.* → HARK

HARL *s.* fuľór, fuiór, píciur; (*~ of wool*) pitríche, pitrícă

HARLOT *s.* cúrvă; *also:* chiúrhană, dósă, putánă, ruspíe

HARM *s.* săcătlíche, săcătlâche, vlápsim

HARM *vb.* (*to cause damage*) ▾zărăriséscu; (*to hurt*) agudéscu; (*to wound*) arănéscu, pliguéscu

HARMFUL *adj.* s(c)lab, -lábă, -laghi, -lábe

HARMLESS *adj.* (*free from injury*) ni-vătămát

HARMONICA *s.* muzichíe, múzică; **He is playing the ~** Cântă cu múzica

HARMONIOUSLY *adv.* (*in a friendly manner*) baríş

HARMONY *s.* (*agreement*) armuníe, udiséţă, udiseáţă, uidisíre, úidizmă

HARNESS *s.* ‖ PC: hamúti *n pl*; fârnuri *n pl*

HARNESS-MAKER *s.* ‖ DIARO 334: curâgí

HARP *s.* hárfă; **to agree like ~ and harrow** ≈ *3 sg* and *pl*: s-mâcă ca câñľi (*lit.* 'they eat each other like dogs')

HARP ON *vb.* (*to insíst, to persist*) mi duc arídhǎ, u ţân fúne

HARROW *s.* zvárnǎ ‖ *Pls:* bránǎ, CL 39; ALB, *Pe:* grápǎ, lésǎ, leásǎ, Brâncuş 557

HARROW *vb.* (*to torment*) ▾frimíntu, ▾fǎrmíntu, ▾vǎlǎnduéscu → PLAGUE, PESTER

HARRY *vb.* → TORMENT

HARSH *adj.* ágru; (*as of a wind*) áscur

HARSHLY *adv.* cu ţupáta, cu proñ; **I earn my living ~** Scot pânea cu proñ

HARSHNESS *s.* ascuráme

HART *s.* ţérbu, ţirbóñu → STAG

HARVEST *vb.* (*of a vineyard*) (a)yízmu, silixéscu, lixéscu

HARVESTER *s.* (*with a sickle*) siţirǎtór

HARVESTING *s.* (*with a sickle*) siţiráre

HARVESTING TIME *s.* adunǎtúrǎ

HAS *vb.* → HAVE

HASH *s.* → MAKE A ~ OF SMTH.

HASH *vb.* toc

HASP *s.* (a)rizé

HASSLE *s.* acǎţáre, nţirtáre, ncârligáre

HASSLE *vb.* ▾acáţ, ▾nţértu, ▾ncârlighédz

HASTE *s.* ayiueálǎ, ayiusíre, ayuñíe, ayuñisíre, curundáre, pristinisíre; **~ spells loss in every respect** (i.e., *haste makes waste*) Pristinisírea tu íţido lúcru eáste zulúme → MAKE ~, HURRY

HASTEN *vb.* ▾ayiuséscu, agunéscu, curundédz, vǎryéscu (*and* vâr-); ▾viiséscu [vi•i•] → HURRY UP

HASTILY *adv.* cu avrápǎ ‖ ALR 1346: **to act ~, to rush** mi-a-yuñisíi (*aor.*)

HASTINESS *s.* sirtlǎche

HASTY *adj.* ayisít, cu avrápǎ

HAT *s.* (*winter ~*) cǎciúlǎ, cǎciúuǎ [•ŭǎ]; (*summer ~*) capélǎ; (*a somewhat grotesque ~*) cǎvúche → PUT THE ~ ON ONE'S MISERY

HAT-AND-COAT RACK *s.* sǎrceáne

HATCH *vb.* (*of chicken*) clucéscu, cluţéscu, cucéscu, *N:* culcéscu; (*to stop hathing*) disclóţ; (*to plot*) nţirnuéscu, cruéscu únǎ cǎpáne

HATCHET *s.* bárdǎ (*and* bárdhǎ), bâltǎ; *Bǎi:* ľátǎ → AX(E)

HATCHING *s.* clucíre, glucíre

HATE

HATE *s.* úră, aurâre, amáhe, căréze, límă, şéri, şéră ‖ DIARO 433: ihtriţâľi; gâirézi

HATE *vb.* ▼(a)urăscu, am căréze, mi duc şéri; **They ~ each other** Si duc şéri; mi duc zăte (cu), ţân pícă, ehtrevséscu, ehtripséscu, hăzmuséscu, ▼uryiséscu ‖ BASME 405: ľi am seáte (máre)

HATEFUL *adj.* blăstimát, cacurízic ‖ DIARO 433: duşmânós, ihtráric

HATRED *s.* úră → HATE

HAUGHTY *adj.* daítcu, -tcă, -tţi, -tţe → ARROGANT

HAUGHTILY *adv.* cu săltănáte, cu cáplu n dzeánă, daí

HAUL *s.* (*the distance over which a load is transported*) cále

HAUL *vb.* ▼trag

HAULAGE *s.* chiragilâche

HAUNCH *s.* anat. gof, cipóc; (*of a horse*) ceréia-a ciupóclui; (*a piece of flesh from an animal*) búte di cárne

HAUNT *s.* (*hiding place of criminals, etc.*) limére, cuib di furi

HAUNT *vb.* (*to pursue*) ▼avín **Revenge is ~ing me** Mi-avínă sândzile

HAUGHTY *adj.* pirifán

HAVE *s.* avút → RICH

HAVE *vb.* pres. am, ai, áre, avém (*or* aém), avéţ (*or* aéţ), au (*F*: ar); *fut.* va si am, va si ai, *etc. or* vai am, vai ai, *etc.*; *ipf.* aveám (*or* aeám), *etc.*; *aor.* avúi; *pf* am avútă; *plupf.* aveám avútă *or* avusésim; *subj.* si (să, s-) am, si ai, *etc.*; *subj. ipf.* s-am (*or* si-ám) avútă; *cond.* si-aveárim; *past cond.* si-avúrim *or* vrea aveám; *also* si-aveám; *imper.* si ai tíne! si áibă el/ea! si avéţ voi! si áibă eľ/eále! *part.* avútă

HAVE A BEE IN THE BONNET *vb.* am bubulíţi ân cap, ñ-asboáiră (PC from *Brz*: [ñaz•bŭá•i•râ], *not* [ñaz•boáĭ•râ])

HAVE A BIT OF A TUSSLE WITH SMB. *vb. 3 pl*: şi-mâcă sămárile

HAVE A COLD *vb.* hiu arcurát, hiu plivricít

HAVE A CYLINDER MISSING *vb. 3 sg, fig.* ≈ ľ-lipseáşte únă scândură

HAVE A DOWN AGAINST SMB. *vb.* ľ-ţân cáche → HATE

HAVE A FANCY FOR *vb.* ‖ ñ-si dişcľíde ínima tră, BASME 90

HAVE A FIT OF EPILEPSY *vb.* cad nafoáră

HAVE A FOREBODING *vb.* ñ-yíne nóimă slábă

HAVE A GLIB TONGUE *vb.* gúra ñ-ñárdze ápă → TALK NINETEEN TO THE

DOZEN

HAVE A GLIMPSE OF *vb.* ▾(a)ndzăréscu → CATCH SIGHT OF

HAVE A GNAWING PAIN IN THE STOMACH *vb.* mi múşcă ínima

HAVE A GOOD FACE *vb.* (*to look well*) am fáţă búnă

HAVE A GOOD HEAD FOR *vb.* (*in neg. sentences*) nu-ñ táľe míntea (= *I can't figure it out, lit. 'my mind can't cut it'*)

HAVE A GOOD TIME *vb.* (*gaping about*) ylindipséscu, ylindiséscu, siryinséscu; (*as at a reception*) ▾curdiséscu, ▾curduséscu; ▾şui- téscu

HAVE A GOOD TUCK IN *vb.* mi adár fuşéche

HAVE A GRUDGE AGAINST SMB. *vb.* ţân pícă → HATE

HAVE A GUILTY CONSCIENCE *vb.* nu li am curáte zmeánile

HAVE A HUNCH *vb.* ñ-yíne nóimă, ñ-yíne nă măndátă, ñ-yíne érgu

HAVE A KILLING TIME *vb.* mi tuchésc tu lúcru

HAVE A LARK *vb.* (*to give free rein to fun*) u fac uzungióva

HAVE A LAUGH ON SMB. *vb.* ñ-arâd (cu nâs, *etc.*) → HOLD SMB. IN DERISION

HAVE ALL THE CARDS IN ONE'S HAND *vb.* ≈ ñ-gioácă cálu (*lit. 'my horse is dancing'*)

HAVE A MISCARRIAGE *vb.* lu-arúc crud (*lit. 'to throw it out raw'*)

HAVE AN ACHING VOID *vb.* mi múşcă ínima, ñ-si minteáşte ínima, mi múşcă buríclu

HAVE AN APOPLECTIC FIT *vb.* mi agudeáşte píca

HAVE AN ERUPTION *vb.* (*usu. on the lips*) ▾aruvérsu, ▾arăbudzâ- nédz

HAVE A NOTION TO DO SMTH. *vb.* ‖ ñ-bag tu mínte, BASME 14

HAVE A PRESENTIMENT *vb.* ▾aduchéscu, ñ-yíne nóimă

HAVE A SHIVERING FIT *vb.* ▾lăhtărséscu, mi trec furnídzi-fur- nídzi ‖ prit trup ñ-si duc híri-híri, BASME 35

HAVE A SLAP AT SMB. *vb.* ľ-astrág únă, ľ-alichéscu únă

HAVE A SNOOZE *vb.* ľ-coc un ócľu di sómnu

HAVE A SPREE *vb.* (*to give free rein to fun*) u-fác uzungióva

HAVE A STEAMING COLD *vb.* ñ-trag nărĭle → RUNNY NOSE

HAVE A STROKE *vb.* mi agudeáşte píca, mi áflă chícuta, nchicu- tédz, chicutédz, ñ-cáde chícută máre, mi-aseáşte chícuta, dăm- bluséscu

HAVE AT HAND *vb.* am próhir (*or* próhiră, próhire)

HAVE A TIFF WITH SMB.

HAVE A TIFF WITH SMB. *vb. 3 pl*: și-mâcă sămárile (cu)

HAVE A TILE LOOSE *vb.* u-am asbuirátă (PC: [az•bu•i•] → CRAZY

HAVE A TOOTH AGAINST SMB. *vb.* ñ-duc zắte → HATE

HAVE BATS IN THE BELFRY *vb.* am bubulíţi ân cap; ñ-asboáiră (míntea)

HAVE BEEN PUT THROUGH THE MILL *vb.* âñ tricú rúglu prit náre; hiu fricát

HAVE BETTER *vb.* (*it would be a good idea to*) nu cârteáşte să

HAVE BREAKFAST *vb.* (a)ngústu; **Come to ~ together!** yínu si-ngus-tăm!

HAVE CHILDREN *vb.* nfumiľédz; **They could not ~** Nu nfumiľá; **He had children with her** Cu dísa fumiľé

HAVE DIARRHEA *vb.* mi úrdină

HAVE DONE A BAD STROKE OF BUSINESS *vb. aor.* u adrái căcăteásca

HAVE DONE WITH SMB. *vb.* (*to break with smb.*) u-arúp cioára (cu)

HAVE ENOUGH TO KEEP THE WOLF FROM THE DOOR / AT BAY *vb.* puripséscu, prăpséscu

HAVE FRIENDS AT COURT *vb. am* plătắri

HAVE FUN *vb.* ▾ñir

HAVE HAD MORE THAN ENOUGH OF IT *vb.* ñ-si lăiáşte (*and* lâ-)

HAVE IN ABUNDANCE *vb.* ‖ CUVATA 19: para-am

HAVE IT ALL ONE'S OWN WAY *vb.* fac cum âñ táľe cáplu (*lit. 'I do as my head cuts it'*)

HAVE IT IN FOR SMB. *vb.* ţân pícă → HATE

HAVE LICE *vb.* ▾piducľédz, ▾piducľéscu

HAVE MERCY ON *vb.* → MERCY

HAVE NO CHOICE BUT *vb.* ≈ nu am ţe s-fac

HAVE NO IDEA *vb.* ‖ nu am hăbáre, BASME 486

HAVE NO NEWS OF *vb.* ľ-cher úrma

HAVE NO REFERENCE TO *vb. 3 sg*: nu áre crémase cu; **What you are saying has no reference to what he said** Ţe dzáţi tu nu-áre crémase cu ţe dzâse el

HAVE NOT ONE'S EQUAL *vb.* nu-ñ am uidía

HAVE ONE'S CAKE BAKED *vb.* ñ-si dúţe ambár, u trag chióşea dum-neáşte

HAVE ONE'S DAY *vb.* (*my day will come*) ľau tómbul tu mână (*lit. 'to take the whip in one's hand'*)

HAVE ONE'S HEART IN ONE'S MOUTH/THROAT *vb.* (*to get very scared*)

li úmplu (zmeánile), li yănuséscu (cicioárĭle, zmeánile), seámin aróv di frícă, cúrlu-ñ seámină aróv, li dau ármatile ‖ ñ-si adúnă ínima cât un púric, BASME 74

HAVE ONE'S MIND UNHINGED *vb.* ▾scol di mínte

HAVE ONE'S WAY *vb.* fac cum âñ táľe cáplu → ACT

HAVE ONE'S WEATHER EYE OPEN *vb.* (*to mind one's eye*) ñ-fac ócľiľ pátru

HAVE PINS AND NEEDLES (IN ONE'S LIMBS) *vb.* ▾furníc

HAVE RESPECT FOR SMB. *vb.* fac htibáre (+ *dat.*)

HAVE A SHIVERING FIT *vb.* *pt, 3 sg impers:* mi tricú prit íne

HAVE RATS IN THE ATTIC *vb.* am bubulíţi ân cap, ñ-asboáĭră (PC *from* **Brz**: [ñaz•bŭá•i•ră])

HAVERSACK *s.* diságă, tiságă, biságă

HAVE SMB. IN ONE'S POCKET *vb.* níţi la dzidzitíc nu lu am

HAVE SMB. ON A STRING *vb.* ñ-arâd (cu nâs, *etc.*)

HAVE SMTH. AT HEART *vb.* ñ-u am ca núca n sănătór

HAVE SMTH./SMB. ON ONE'S CONSCIENCE *vb.* am pri súflit, am pri gúşe, am pri zvércă, ľau pri gúşe, trag pri gúşe, ľau pri zvércă; *3 sg:* nu li-áre curáte zmeánile, *lit.* '(*he*) *does not have* (*his*) *underwear clean*'

HAVE SMB. ON TOAST *vb.* (*to put pressure upon smb.*) bag súla n coáste

HAVE SMB.'S EAR *vb.* am plătări

HAVE SMB. BY THE THROAT *vb.* lu-ascálin (*or* ascálnu) di gúşe

HAVE SMB./SMTH. IN ONE'S CARE *vb.* l-am (*f u ám*) angătán

HAVE SOWN ONE'S WILD OATS *vb.* (*to settle, to become wise*) di-pún mínte

HAVE SPARE TIME *vb.* adhyiséscu

HAVE SUPPER *vb.* ţin; **We have had our supper** Him ţináţ

HAVE THE BLUES: He has the blues ≈ Cánda ľ-si nicáră cărăyile, cánda ľ-mâcáră ágrulu púľi ‖ **Av:** cánda-ľ fudzíră căpărle dit căpărleádză, BASME 503

HAVE THE BRASS *vb.* am nări (tră *or* să)

HAVE THE BREEZE UP *vb.* u aspár huzmétea → GO DOWN ONE'S BOOTS

HAVE THE COURAGE (THE GUTS) *vb.* ñ(-u) ţâne, ñ-ţâne bíslu (**or** stricătoárea, cúrlu, curdheáua); **I don't have the guts** Nu mi ţân curáile

HAVE THE TRUMP CARD *vb.* ñ-gioácă cálu (*lit.* '*my horse is*

HAVE TO

dancing')

HAVE TO *vb.* *3 sg*: lipseáşte (ca să), prínde (ca să); (*need to*) va; **You have to get wet in order to eat fish** Va s-ti udz ca s-máţi péşţâ; ñ-cáde (să)

   HAVE TO DO WITH *vb.* am dáre-loáre cu ‖ am s-fac (cu), BASME 425

   HAVEN *s.* (*a place of safety*) apánghiu

   HAVOC *s.* irmuxíre, pundíre, şcrituíre, vlâpsitúră → DEVASTA-TION

   HAVOC *vb.* bag stróflu (tu)

   HAWK *s.* *orn.* ghirăchínă → FALCON

   HAWKER *s.* sirghingí

   HAWK-NOSED *adj.* yearacumít

   HAY → MAKE ~ OF SMTH.

   HAYCOCK *s.* cópă, cupíţă, căpíţă → RICK

   HAYRICK *s.* → HAYCOCK

   HAYSTACK *s.* → HAYCOCK, RICK

   HAYWIRE *adj.* cicănít → CRAZY

   HAZARD *s.* (*danger*) piríclu; (*chance*) tíhe; **at ~** tu tíhe ‖ pri căsméte, BASME 459

   HAZARD *vb.* căidiséscu → DARE

   HAZE *s.* négură, cătăcníe, cătăhníe, iámă

   HAZELNUT *s.* alúnă, liftócară; *Lac:* lúnă

   HAZEL TREE/BUSH *s.* alún, liftócar

   HAZEL WOOD *s.* alunáme, alunét

   HAZY *adj.* nigurós

   HE *pron.* el, -l, -şi, năs (*and* nâs), dâs, dis, díslu, *F:* is; **~ will be the boss** Ma máre el va híbă-l; **Where is ~?** Iu eásti-l? **where ~ was** acló iu şi-irá; **~ had offended her** Díslu u-aveá năi-rítă.

   HE- (*male*): bărbát; **he-dragon** lámña-bărbát

   HEAD *s.* cap, *pl.* cápite; *dim.* căpíc; *derog.* bétă, căpiţână, cărăfétă, ciufutínă; ciútură, ciútră, cócă, cófă, curcubétă, *G:* cărţúnă → COME TO A ~

   HEAD HORSE *s.* mbrustár

   HEAD OFF *vb.* (*to bar the way*) l'-tal'u cálea

   HEAD OVER HEELS *adv.* arócută, culutúmbă ‖ **to roll ~** ALR 1434: mi dau ceamceácu, mi dau ceambarlác

   HEADACHE *s.* scútură, pârjálă; **~ I have a ~** Am pârjálă máre n cáp-ñi (*sic*); **My head begins to ache** Mi-acáţă cáplu

HEAD-DRESS *s.* (*various types*) ambrúnă, călpáche, *G:* chiluvétă, *F:* ciupáre *and* ghiubéc; stóle, stolídhă, tăpáre, tepé → HEADGEAR

HEADGEAR *s.* bálţu; *G, Lvz:* cărâm, crâm; (*stripe around one's head*) ceálmă, cimbér, *G:* cípă; testeméle, desteméle, lăhúră, peá-tică, *Pls:* pétic; pihíţă; (~ *for elderly women*) pischíre; (*silk hat*) póşe, şamíe, şimíe; (*turban*) săríche; (*beret*) sucáie

HEADLONG *adj.* (*reckless*) distórsu, -toársă, -tórşi, -toárse

HEADMAN *s. G:* căliúş

HEADREST *s. N:* căpitíñu, *S:* căpitâñu, căpitúñu

HEADS *s.* (*of a coin*) ghéză; ~ **or tails?** túră i ghéză?

HEADSTALL *s.* căpéstru → BRIDLE

HEADSTRONG *adj.* uchealíu, capsumán

HEADWATER *s.* izvór, ízvur

HEADWAY *s.* → MAKE ~

HEADWORK *s.* minduíre, luyareazmó, hisápe, isápe

HEADY *adj.* (*shrewd*) şirét, -reátă, -réţ, -reáte; (*willful*) uchealíu; (*hasty*) ayisít

HEAL *vb.* ▾víndic, trec, ▾yitripséscu ‖ ALiA II q. 206 3 sg. (z)víndică, (a)sână, sâneádză, asâñeádză, adáră ghíni, adáră bun

HEAL THE BREACH *vb.* (*to calm; to smooth away difficulties*) a-răsbún, arăzbân, ▾asbún

HEALING *s.* vindicáre, yitripsíre

HEALTH *s.* sănătáte (*and* sânâ-)

HEALTHY *adj.* sănătós (*and* sânâ-), -oásă, -óşǐ, -oáse; sân, -ă, sâñ, sâne; san, sánă, sañ, sáne

HEAP *s.* (*as of ashes*) trâmbă; (*as of food*) dârlíc

HEAP UP *vb.* ▾stivăséscu

HEAR *vb.* ▾ávdu, § 31, 32; (*to ~ well; to ~ too much*) pára-ávdu; *N:* dăguéscu

HEARING *s.* (*power of perceiving sounds*) avdzâre

HEARKEN *vb.* ▾ascúltu

HEARSAY → FROM HEARSAY

HEART *s.* ínimă; *dim.* inimúşe, iñoáră; (*center, as of a forest*) buríc; (*cards*) cúpă → BY HEART ‖ *Po:* ímnâ, yímnâ, NEIESCU 248; (*cards*) aróş ('red') *or* di ínimâ, DIARO 204

HEART DISEASE *s.* lângoáre di ínimă, ciócut

HEARTBROKEN *adj.* căñisít

HEARTBURN *s.* căúră

HEARTEN *vb.* (*to encourage*) inimuséscu, ľ-fac găiréte [gă•i•]

HEARTH *s.* vátră, *N:* veátră, *dim.* vătrícă; fucurínă, *G:* ficu-rínă; (~ *of a furnace*) cirichínă

HEARTH-CAKE *s.* (*flat thin cake*) pișnícă, pugáce, puyáce

HEARTLESS *adj.* ni-ñilós, -oásă, -óșĭ, -oáse; scliró *invar.*

HEARTTHROB *s.* ciócut

HEARTY *adj.* (*sincere*) dișcľís; (*cordial*) inimárcu; (*healthy and strong*): **as ~ as a buck** ≈ sănătós ca grij di dzádă

HEAT *s.* căldúră, căroáre, culoáre, *S:* căloáre; dugoáră, flóyă, nădúf, zădúh, zudúh, zăbúh, părjálă (*and* pâr-) ‖ DIARO 197: cáñínâ

HEAT *vb.* ▾ncăldzăscu; (*as of the sun in July*) ▾păléscu; (*to singe*) ▾pârléscu; (*to make hot, as a furnace*) ▾árdu; **The woman ~ed the furnace** Muľárea lu-árse cireáplu

HEATED *adj.* (*as of a furnace*) ársu

HEATH *s. bot.* zărzăríche

HEATHEN *adj.* păngănitéscu → PAGAN

HEAVE *vb.* (*to rise, to lift*) ▾alín, ▾álțu, ▾análțu, ▾mut; (*to vomit*) vom, ▾azvóm, ▾vérsu

HEAVEN *s.* țer, uranó

HEAVENLY *adj.* dumnidzăscu, -dzáscă, -dzășțâ, -dzăști

HEAVES *s. vet.* tecneféz *n*, ticniféz, ticnăfése

HEAVY-HANDED *adj.* angricós, -oásă; astângu, -ngă, -ndzi, -ndze

HEAVILY *adv.* greu

HEAVY *adj.* greu, greáuă, grei, greále; **to be ~ at heart** ñ-u ghiúce; to **be ~ with sleep** cad di sómnu, hiu nsumnát, nsumnédz, mi neácă sómnul ‖ (*of the tongue of a very drunk person*) Ľ-si adră límba culeáș, *lit.* 'His tongue became polenta', DIARO 276

HEAVYHEARTED *adj.* dipús

HECKLE *vb.* pihtuséscu, uhtichédz

HECTOR *vb.* (*to intimidate*) cănuséscu; (*to heckle*) pihtuséscu; (*to scold*) ľau zbárdhu, dau un zbárdhu

HEDGE *s.* ploc

HEDGEHOG *s.* aríciu; *augm.* arióñu *m*, aricioáñe *f*; *also:* eg, *pl* edzĭ; júnă

HEED *vb.* ascúltu ‖ **You are not heeding me** Míni câtrâ voi, ș-voi câtrâ drați, DIARO 247

HEEDFUL *adj.* câștigós, -oásă

HEEDLESS *adj.* astráptu, azvimturát, ni-minduít; fấrã nisáfe nu áre meľ tu ciúturã → FOOLHARDY

HEEDLESSLY *adv.* fấrã nisáfe

HEE-HAW *vb.* (*of a donkey*) angãrséscu, zgher

HEEL *s. anat.* cãlcấñu (*and* cấl-); (*~ of a shoe*) tãcúne, tupúc; (*a contemptible person*) spindzurát ‖ *dim.* cấlcấñíţ, DIARO 196

HEFTY *adj.* zdúmban; *m/f* máre, *m/f pl* mãrĭ; greu, greáuã, grei, greále

HE-GOAT *s.* ţap, pârciu, pórciu; (*fore-front he-goat*) gâciu

HEIFER *s.* yiţáuã, júncã

HEIGH *interj.* (*used to call attention*) ‖ **Cru:** (*only when addressing a man*) álai, GOLAB 196

HEIGHT *s.* nãlţấme; (*stature*) bóie; **As for ~, they are tall** Di bóie, eľ sun análţâ; (*the height of a condition*) tu mburítã a; tu vãhátea a; **in the ~ of the heat** tu mburíta a cãloáriľei, tu vãhátea a li cãloáre; alţáre; **~ makes you lose your head** Alţárea mindeáşte di cap; ayíe

HEIGHTEN *vb.* ▾álţu, ▾análţu; (*to augment*) créscu, ▾adávgu

HEINOUS *adj.* blãstimát, s(c)lab, -bã, s(c)laghi, s(c)lábe

HEIR *s.* miraşigí, clinuróm

HEIRESS *s.* miraşigioáñe, clirunoámã

HEIRLOOM *s.* clironumíľe, miráze

HELL *s.* chísã, cólase, ginéme, fricuşeát, nfricuşeát ‖ *Prv, SJos:* cãtráne (*and* -ñe), CL 41 → GO TO ~!

HELL-BENT *adj.* apufãsít, dâldãsít

HELLEBORE *s. bot.* ştirigoáñe, ştrigoáñe, spíngiu

HELLO (*greeting word*) yeásu!

HELP *s.* agiutór, aştór, aştáre, intáte (*and* indáte), ndátã, apãndoáhã ‖ LITURG 123: agiãtór

HELMSMAN *s.* ‖ dumengí, timonér, DIARO 216

HELP *vb.* ▾agiút, yin indáte (a), dau indáte; **May I ~ you?** Ţe urséşti di la noi? **I can't ~** (+ *-ing*) mi astrádze lóclu; nu-ñ arávdã ínima ‖ (*outcry*) Agiutaţ! Agiutaţ! HRISTU 33

HELP OFF THE TIME *vb.* ‖ ñ-trec oára, BASME 409

HELPER *s.* agiutór, dhyeavér, dhyeavéran; (*wife*) muľáre

HELPFUL *adj.* fursatlí, fursãtlí

HELPLESS → BECOME ~

HELTER-SKELTER *adv.* cãtrã naľúrea

HELVE

HELVE *s.* tupurấşte, tăpurấşte

HEM *s.* (*of a shirt, etc.*) ori *f pl*; aruficătúră, birbíľ

HEM *vb.* aroáfic, aruféc; **hemmed** *adj.* mărdzinát

HE-MAN *s.* bărbát

HEM IN *vb.* nţércľu, ţírcľu, ţircľédz, ▾anvărlíg, ▾anvărli-ghédz, ▾anvărighédz ‖ prufiľédzu, DIARO 386

HEMLOCK *s. bot.* cucútă

HEMORRHOIDS *s. pl. med.* **Bl:** trănci *pl*

HEMP *s.* cânipă, cănáve; **field with ~** cănichíşte

HEMP-SEED *s.* cânâvúre

HE-MULE *s.* (*white ~*) ríză

HEN *s.* găľínă (*and* gâ-); *dim.* găľinúşe; (*young ~*) puľíţă, pľíţă

HEN HAWK *s. orn.* chirchinéc

HENBANE *s. bot.* măseáuă; **When you have a toothache apply ~.** Cându ti dor măséľĭle, bágă-lă măseáuă

HENCE *adv.* (*from this point*) di-auá

HENCEFORTH *adv.* → HENCE

HEN-HOUSE *s.* bufár, căsístră, cócină, cumás, cumáse, cumáş, cuşér, cuteáţă ‖ *Av:* câthístră, *GSus:* cucuşcárnec, CL 42

HEPATITIS *s. med.* gălbináre

HER 1. *pers. pron. dat.* ľi, -ľ, ľ-; *acc.* -o, u, -u, u-, ea; **seeing ~ so strong** vidzândalui-o ahântă gioánă; **Did you see ~?** Vidzúşi-u? **Take ~ and cut ~!** Ľa-u ş táľ-u! **Do you want ~, or not?** U-vréi, i nu u-vréi? **I haven't see her** Nu o vidzúi; **They caught him, but they didn't see ~** El lu-acăţáră, ea nu o vidzúră; 2. *poss. pron.* a ľei, -ľ, -i, -sa(i), sui; **~ mother's** a mă-sa-i; **~ mother** mái-sa; **She said to ~ daughter-in-law** Dzâse ea a nóră-sai; **Where are ~ parents?** Iu-ľ súntu părínţľi?

HERALD *s.* (*messenger*) sihăryeát

HERB *s.* iárbă, *pl* iérghĭ

HERBAGE *s.* (*abundant grass*) iárbă, amălăyíe

HERD *s.* gârdéľ, văcăríe ‖ *Peş:* văcreáţă, CL 263

HERDSMAN *s.* văcár

HERE *adv.* auá, auáţe, auáia; **from here** di-auáţe; **~ and there** pri-auá ş-pri-acló; lócuri-lócuri; aţía-di-aţía; (*hither*) ncoáţe (*and* ngoáţe), ncoa (*and* ngoa), nculeá; **Look ~!** Mutreá ngoa! **Don't come ~!** Mi yiñ nculeá! → **~ AND THERE** ‖ *Str:* anáţea, GOLAB 198; **~ I am!** Eá-mi! BASME 591; *F:* **~ and there** bilocuri-bilocuri, HRISTU 36

HERE *interj.* (*Look! or Take!*) na! ţâne! ~ **is a scale of mine** Na un sóldzu di a meu; ~ **is the coin I owe you** Ţâne-ţ yróslu ţe ţi-l voi; ~ **is the horse, take it!** Na calu, ľa-l! ~ **he/it is!** (*of a m/n sg noun*) Na-l! *pl m*: Ia-ľ! *or* Na-ľ! (**Look!** *or* **Listen!**) Ia [ĭa]! ~ **is how things are!** Ia cum sta lúcrulu! ‖ LITURG 124: aóţi

HERE AND THRE *adv.* pri-auá ş-pri-acló

HEREAFTER *s.* lúmea alántă; *adv.* tu lúmea náltă (*sic*)

HEREAFTER *adv.* (*in some future time or state*) ma nclo; ma nâpói; (*from now on*) di-auá; di-auá ş năínte

HERETOFORE *adv.* ‖ PC: până amú, până tóra

HERITAGE *s.* miráze → INHERITANCE

HERMAPHRODITE *s.* and *adj.* (*womanish, effeminate*) fiteái, *pl* fiteáiáñ

HERMIT *s.* érmu, aschitíu; *adj.* aschitipsít; **to become a** ~ mi aschitipséscu, aschitifséscu

HERMITAGE *s.* (*habitation of a heremit*) tiché, téche, aschitlíche

HERNIA *s. med.* sălăghíre

HERO *s.* búră, *pl* búrañ; gióne, ľundár, xiftér, schifter, sífter

HEROIC *adj.* (*relating to heroes*) junéscu *and* giu-; *f* -neáscă, *m pl* -néşţâ, *f pl* -néşti

HEROIC DEED *s.* ‖ *Cru:* giunáme, GOLAB 261

HERPES *s. derm.* cur di găľínă

HERRING *s. ichth.* ţir, ţiróñu, scumbríe

HER'S *poss. pron.* a ľei → HER

HERSELF *pron.* síngură; si (s, să + *vb.*); **dressed** ~ să viscú; *F:* ea ísăşi

HESITANCE, HESITANCY *s.* şuvăíre, induíre

HESITANT *adj.* da n coáste, *vb., 3 sg*

HESITATE *vb.* şuvăéscu, ▼induéscu, ñ-u dau n coástă, stau andoáuălea; *S:* anămiréscu; ▼strâmbu nárea; (*to be reluctant to consent*) ▼frângu coáste, ▼ncľín

HESITATION *s.* şuvăíre, induíre

HEW *vb.* (*to cut with blows of a heavy cutting instrument*) ▼pilichiséscu, ▼pilixéscu

HEX *s.* (a)măghipsíre, ligáre

HEX *vb.* (a)măghipséscu → EXORCISE

HEY *interj.* ‖ *Cru:* moi *and* omói, GOLAB 236 *and* 240

HEYDAY *s.* ≈ tu mburíta a, tu ayía a

HICCUP *s.* zéghe, suglíț, suglițáre

HICCUP *vb.* suglíț

HIDDEN *adj.* (a)scúmtu, (a)scúmsu; (*as of a place*) ascumtós, căipusít ‖ CARAFOLI 60: apitrusít

HIDDEN TREASURE *s.* (*or hidden money, esp. by elderly people*) picúľ

HIDE *s.* mișíne; (*a calf's dressed skin*) vidélă, vudhélă; (*from cattle*) taleatínă (*and* taľa-), teleátină, pustăcheáuă

HIDE *vb.* ▾ascúndu (→ § 32); (*in fear or at play*) păpăruséscu, zăruséscu, zuruséscu; ▾bag; **The viper hid in the firn** Nipírtica s-băgă tu feárică; ▾acáț gúva (*or* ▾acáț gúvile); **They hid** Acățără gúvile; (*to ~ from sight or from knowledge*) ľ-bag căpáchea a ipó-thisiľei; ALiA II: *3 sg.* ascúnde *and* ascúndi

HIDEOUS *adj.* slut, urât, urút, (a)ynusós

HIDEOUSNESS *s.* slutíche

HIDEOUT *s.* ascumtáľ, ascumtátic, cripsánă, limére ‖ BATSARIA 71: loc afirít

HIDING *s.* ascundeáre, ascúndire

HIEROGLYPH *s.* (*illegible script*) zgrâmătúră, cicioáre di găíñ

HIGGLEDY-PIGGLEDY *adv.* (*disorderly*) alandála, cióra-bóra, cioá-ră-boáră, darmadán, mintineáje

HIGH *adj.* análtu

HIGH *adv.* n dzeánă; **You've climbed too ~** Ti-alináși múltu n dzeánă; **~er** ma nsus

HIGH AND LOW *adv.* (*everywhere*) toátă rádha

HIGH SCHOOL *s.* líchiu, sholarhíu ‖ PC: scularhíu

HIGH-BORN *adj.* ciciór di scámnu (*lit. 'a leg of the throne'*)

HIGHBROW *s.* (*erudite*) iľumáie *f*, iľumăi *pl*

HIGH-HAT *adj.* pirifán → ARROGANT

HIGHLANDER *s.* sușán

HIGH-METTLED *adj.* azgutós, -oásă → HOT

HIGHNESS *s.* (*lordship or other high position*) afindíľi

HIGH-SPIRITEDNESS *s.* chéfe, chéifă

HIGHWAY *s.* geadé *m*, geadéi *f*; *N:* drúmul máre

HIGHWAYMAN *s.* haramíu, hărămít, chisăgí, chișigí; GBg: furcudár

HIKE *s.* (*long walk, travel*) imnáre; (*rise*) sculáre

HIKE *vb.* (*to rise*) ▾scol; (*to travel*) alág, ímnu, cálcu

HILARITY *s.* arâdeáre, arâdire

HILL *s.* dzeánă; *dim.* dzinícă; *also*: aráhe, băíre; (*steep* ~) píryu → HILLOCK

HILLBILLY *s.* păduríş

HILLOCK *s.* arudínă, măgúră, măyúlă, mărúlă, óhtu, túmbă ‖ *Peş:* muntác, CL 256; (*isolated hillock*) *Peş:* ţăpătuľe

HILLSIDE *s.* coástă

HILLTOP *s.* creáştit → TOP

HILLY *adj.* dzinós, -oásă

HILT *s.* mânár *or* mânáre

HIM *pron.* 1. *dat.* a lui, lui, ľĭ; **I gave to him, I didn't give to her** A lui ľĭ ded, a ľei nu-ľ ded; 2. *acc.* el, lu, -lu, -l, l-, ul; **They caught** ~ El lu-acáţără; **Go ahead and ask** ~! Ia lu-ntreábă! **Killng** ~ **he saved himself** Vătămndalui-lu, ascápă; **The door-keeper sent him to the devil** Cafázul ul sictărsí

HIMSELF *pron.* síngur, síngur-şi, ínsu, ínsuş; si, s, să (+ *vb.*); tut; **God** ~ ínsuşă Dumnidzău; **It was the dragon** ~ Insu vur-culáclu eará; **without being aware that he was her husband himself** fără s-lu cunoáscă că eáste bărbát-su ínsu; **The silversmith dressed (himself)** Hrísicu să viscú; **Cola will go with nobody else but Chita himsélf** S-dúţe Cóla cu tut Chíta

HIND *s.* ţeárbă, ţirboáňe

HINDER *vb.* ▾ncheádic, ▾stăpuéscu, ▾stivăséscu, ▾(a)mbudhisescu, ▾ambuţéscu → SHACKLE ‖ (*to oppose*) mi bag amplátea, DIARO 336

HINDER PART *s.* (*of a person*) şidzút

HINDMOST *adj.* códus, -să, -şĭ, -se; cudár; *also* coáda *invar.*

HINDRANCE *s.* cheádică

HINGE *s.* ţânţână, (a)rizé, reză

HINT *s.* → DROP A ~

HINT *vb.* → ALLUDE

HIP *s. anat.* bóşă, cipóc, ciupóc, cârţioáră, coápsă, gof, íľe *f pl*; schéle, *N:* slághină

HIP *s.* (*pile*) cup

HIP *adj.* (*hep*) câştigós, -oásă

HIRE *s.* (*the act of hiring*) păitíre, puitíre, arugáre; (*rent*) lăsáre

HIRE *vb.* ▾păitéscu, puitéscu, puituéscu, păltéscu, plătéscu, ▾aróg, ▾arughédz, ▾arudzéscu, ▾ndreg, ayuyi(p)séscu, ▾zburăscu;

HIRE ONESELF OUT

They ~ Bulgarian workers Puitéscu aryáţ vúryări; **The next day he ~ed some masons** Dzúua alántă păltí nâscânţâ másturĭ; **He ~ed him to graze horses** Lu-arugă s-páscă cáĺi; **They were ~ed as shepherds** Si-ndreápsiră picurári; **Put a good word for me to get hired by this man!** S-mi zburăşti la aístu

HIRE ONESELF OUT *vb.* mi bag ca huzmicheár → HIRE

HIRED *adj.* ndréptu, ndreáptă, ndrépţâ, ndreápte; **They were ~ as servants** Eará ndrépţâ ca huzmicheári

HIRING FEE *s.* chiră → RENT

HIRSUTE *adj.* pirós, -oásă, -óşĭ, -oáse

HIS poss. pron. a lui, alúi, -ĺ, ĺ-, -su, -sui, -sa, -şi, -siu; **with all ~ people** cu-a lúi-ĺi tuţ; **~ sight began to return** Ocĺiĺ acăţáră să-ĺ yínă; **Where are ~ parents?** Iu ĺ-súntu părínţĺi? **~ son** híĺ-su; **~ son's** a híĺ-sui; **~ mother's** a mă-sa-i; **~ (or her) lambs** ñéĺi-şi; **~ (or her) shadow** úmbra-şi

HISS *s.* (*as of the wind*) ţíur

HISTORY *s.* isturíe

HIT *s.* (*blow*) goádă, agudíre, aguditúră; (*as by a horse*) clóţă, cluţátă → MAKE A ~

HIT *vb.* ▾agudéscu, ▾aúrlu, ahuléscu, ĺ-u dau cu, axéscu, ĺi am únă, ▾árdu, ▾úmflu; **The vulture ~ the lamb into the head with its bill** Órñul ĺ-deáde n cap a ñélui cu cióclu; **He ~ him with a hammer** Ĺĭ áre únă cu cióclu; **~ him!** Aúrlă-ĺ vâră! **~ him with the rod!** Ahuleá-l cu veárga! (*to ~ a target, etc.*) ĺau; **and he ~ him just into his poor heart** şi-l lo trâşi tu iñoáră; (*to ~ with an arrow*) sădzitédz; **~ the ceiling** (*to jump with anger, fear, etc.*) arsár ca chipinát di şárpe

HITCH *s.* (a)stămătíre → BAR

HITCH *vb.* (*to move, to remove*) ▾mut; (*to drag, to pull*) ▾trag; (*to attach, to connect*) ▾leg; (*to marry*) ▾ĺau

HITHER *adv.* ncoa (*and* ngoa), ncoáţe, dincoá, dincoáţe

HITHERTO *adv.* pân tru hópa aístă

HIVE *s.* stup, (a)crínă di alghíñ, cufínă, cuşór, cuşóre

HO *interj.* ‖ (*addressing a man*) **Cru:** álai, GOLAB 196

HOARD *s.* thisavró → TREASURE

HOARDER *s.* adunătór, máză

HOARFROST *s.* brúmă, gazónă, siñác, ţeáfe, úchid ‖ **GSus, Prv:** şiñác, CL 261

HOARSE *adj.* (*of the voice*) (a)vrăhñisít, vrăhnós; **to become ~** (a)vrăhñiséscu, vrăhăséscu ‖ *Cru:* avărnăsít, *BdD':* avărcănisít, *Gop:* (a)frângâsít, vrăhnisít, *Mul:* avrângăsít, *Tir:* s-acáţă grumázlu, *Cu:* se cáţe buáţea, NEIESCU 187

HOARY *adj.* cănút, cu pérlu cáir

HOAX *s.* ncălţáre, réngă, rénghe

HOAX *vb.* (a)ncálţu → DECEIVE

HOBBLE *vb.* (*to limp along; to hesitate*) şuvăéscu; (*to fetter*) ncheádic; **hobbling along** *adv.* ciúpătă-ciúpătă, ţúpătă-ţúpătă, rúfu-n-búfu [rú•fum•bú•fu], várai-várai

HOBGOBLIN *s.* (*evil spirit*) Ñércurea; Gióia

HOBO *s.* (*vagrant, without a fixed home*) ≈ cu cása pri ciumágă (*lit.* 'with one's house [= belongings] on the cudgel')

HOCK *s. anat.* vasiľé

HOKUM *s.* chiritúri *f pl* → NONSENSE

HODGEPODGE *s.* ameástică, amisticătúră, mintitúră

HOE *s.* sápă; *Cľis:* cupăceárcă; (*with a broad blade*) sapă látă ‖ *Peş:* mutícă, CL 256; nópăcă, CL 257

HOE *vb.* prăşéscu, sărcľédz, *G:* plivéscu

HOG *s.* pórcu; **to live high on the ~** *vb.* huzuripséscu

HOGWASH *s.* lătúră

HOLD *s.* (*stronghold*) tábye, tăbyíe; (*confinement*) ncľideáre, ncľídire; (*prison*) ncľisoáre: (*grip*) ţâneáre → GET ~ OF, TAKE ~ OF

HOLD *vb.* (*to keep, to sustain, t halt, to contain*) ▼ţân

HOLD ALL THE WINNING CARDS (*to be in a favorable situation*) ≈ ñ-gioácă cálu (*lit.* 'my horse is dancing')

HOLD BACK *vb.* (*as from sins*) ▼stăpuéscu

HOLD DALLIANCE *vb.* (*to kill time*) ▼şintéscu

HOLD IN HIGH ESTEEM *vb.* lu fac mále

HOLD IN TRUST *vb.* lu-ám angătán

HOLD ON *vb.* (*to ~ mulishly*) u ţân fúne

HOLD ONE'S BREATH *vb.* ñ-ţân adiľáticlu

HOLD ONE'S GAB / NOISE *vb.* (*ant. to divulge, to reveal*) tac; nu dau pri toácă → HOLD ONE'S TONGUE

HOLD ONE'S SIDES WITH LAUGHTER *vb.* → SHRIEK WITH LAUGHTER

HOLD ONE'S TONGUE *vb.* tac; nu dau pri toácă

HOLD OUT *vb.* (*to present, to represent*) ▼părăstăséscu, ▼pă-

HOLD RESPONSIBLE

răstiséscu

HOLD RESPONSIBLE *vb.* arúc măhănălu (pri)

HOLD SMB. IN DERISION *vb.* nu lu fac mále, ñ-arâd (cu nâs), nu-l dau di mâneár, ñ-bat péză (cu)

HOLD SMB. IN RESPECT *vb.* fac htibáre (+ *dat.*)

HOLD TO SMB. *vb.* (*to follow annoyingly*) mi ţân scaľ

HOLD UP *vb.* (*by means of a prop or stay*) ▾(a)ndoápăr, ▾andrupăséscu → SUPPORT; (*to mock*) lu buiséscu, moľu tu noauădzăţinoáuă buiéi (*lit. 'to dip smb. in ninety-nine paints'*) ‖ (*to disgrace*) scot ócľiľ, BASME 244

HOLE *s.* gúvă, *dim.* guvícă, guvíce, guvălíce, guvăleáce; gávră, hăndác, hăndáche, *Gop:* hórhor; (~ *in the ground*) lac; (*lateral ~ in a furnace*) víglă, víylă → MAKE A ~   .

HOLEY *adj.* cărtiľát; (*of a road*) disfundát; **on ~ roads** prit căľuri disfundáte

HOLIDAY *s.* sărbătoáre; (*name day*) yiurtíe; **important** ~ sărbătoáre greáuă; **less important** ~ sărbătoáre uşoáră ‖ **Arm, Plat, Vot:** aryíe; **Prv:** skóli, B-ARCH 484

HOLLAND *s. tex.* (*linen*) hasé, -séi; pricál, pricálă, pércală

HOLLOW *s.* crúbă, cúfal, cúfală, cufálă, súdhă, trap; *G: dim.* tărpălíc ‖ **GSus:** căciúb, CL 40

HOLLOW *adj.* (*of a terrain*) cuvutós; cu súrpuri; (*as of a tree*) gof, goáfă, gohľ, goáfe; (*cavernous or spoiled, as of a nut*) cúfchiu, *m pl* cúfchi, *f sg/pl* cúfche

HOLLY TREE *s.* găirúş, gréuş, părnáre (*and* pâr-), purnáre; ~ **forest** pârnáríu, purnăreáuă ‖ **F:** ghiirúş, HRISTU 2

HOLLYWOOD *s.* purnăreáuă

HOLY *adj.* sâmtu, ayiu

HOLY GHOST *s.* Áyiul duh

HOLY OIL *s.* ñir

HOLY WATER *s.* (a)yeazmó

HOLY WEEK *s.* Săptămâna máre

HOMAGE *s.* ncľinăciúnă, ncľinăciúne

HOME *adv.* (a)cásă; **from** ~ di acásă; **A brave man does not die at** ~ Giónile nu moáre acásă

HOMELESS *adj.* (*as of a child*) di pri căľuri ‖ MERCA 35: cásă pri ciumág prit căľuri

HOMESTEAD *s.* nicuchirátă, nicuchireáţă

HOMEWARD *adv.* acásă, tu lóc-nă

HOMICIDE *s.* surpáre, uţídire, vătămáre

HOMOSEXUAL *s.* and *adj.* (*of men*) culumbră

HONE *s.* truhó → WHETSTONE

HONEST *adj.* curát, driptátic, cu érgi; om di-a dzâuăľei, om a cáľiľei; (*immaculate*) **He is not ~** Nu-i úşe di băseárică (*lit. 'He/she is not a church door'*)

HONESTLY *adv.* → ABOVEBOARD

HONESTY *s.* érgi *f*

HONEY *s.* ñáre, *N:* ñére; (*addressing people*) yem; **Go now, ~** Dú-ti, yem; **Whose are you, ~?** A cui hiţ, yem? (*of or to a little girl*) tănúşe ‖ *Tir, Kar, Po, Ştep, Pls, Gop:* ñéri, NEIESCU 124

HONEYBEE *s.* alghínă

HONEYCOMB *s.* buştínă ‖ *Av, GSus, Pls, Prv:* gúvâ di pítâ, CL 259

HONOR *s.* (a)nămúze, numúze, ihtibáre, htibáre, tiñíe → MAKE IT A POINT OF ~

HONOR *vb.* ▾tiñíséscu, tighiuséscu; **Parents ought to be ~ed** Părínţâľ vor tiñisíre

HONORABLE *adj.* tiñisít, cu anămúze

HOOD *s.* (*for the head*) capişónă, căpúş, cucúlă, *F:* culáre

HOODLUM *s.* (*assassin*) catíle; (*ruffian*) áscur, áyru, dilbidér, nihít

HOODWINK *vb.* ľ-bag pirdé tu ócľi → DECEIVE

HOOEY *s.* chiritúri *f pl* → NONSENSE

HOOF *s.* úngľe, *N:* cupítă ‖ *Kat, Perd:* únghe, B-ARCH 318

HOOK *s.* cârlíg; (*as in a door or window*) cărtéľu (*and* câr-); (*fishing ~*) anghístru; (*fastener, clasp*) závă máscură; (*of an earring*) turtoáre; (*as for hanging meat in a butcher's shop*) cénghiu, cinghéľ, cánge, yánge, căngíc, cârligár ‖ HRISTU 8: cărrig; (*~ for fishing*) ALB: *Dren, Për:* grep, BRÂNCUŞ 557. *See also* BY ~ OR BY CROOK

HOOK *vb.* (*to steal*) ▾ciun

HOOKAH *s.* ciubúche, mărcúş, narghilé(e)

HOOKED *adj.* (*as of the shape of a nose*) turnát

HOOKER *s.* putánă → HARLOT

HOOK IT *vb.* (*to run away*) li scármin → BOLT

HOOKNOSED *adj.* yearacumít

HOOP *s.* vărăgúce → RING ‖ *Gop:* arucót, GOLAB 202

HOOPOE *s. orn.* púpăză, púpuză ‖ *Pls:* púpă; *GSus, Prv:* púpiză, *SJos:* púpză, *Av:* púpzâ

HOOT *s.* (*shout of discontent at smb.*) alái

HOOT *vb.* ľ-fac alái

HOP *s.* (*dance, jump*) (a)săltáre

HOP *vb.* sáltu, ansár; ~ **it!** Adúnă-u di auá! → GET LOST

HOP ALONG *vb.* mi ľau cicioárĭle dinanúmirea

HOP THE HUTCH/ THE TWIG / THE PERCH *vb.* li tíndu → DIE

HOPE *s.* apăndoáhă, nádă, nădíe, nădăíre, ilpídhă, şpésă, umúte; **Our ~ vanished** Nădía a noástră si asteáse; **Don't set your ~ on me!** S-nu hiţ cu umútea la míne!; **to repose one's ~(s) in smb.** hiu cu umútea la ‖ STERGHIU 4: **with the ~ that** cu elpida că → ANCHOR ONE'S ~S IN/ON, SET ONE'S ~ ON, LOSE ~

HOPE *vb.* nădăéscu, elipséscu, ▾apăndăxéscu, ▾apăndixéscu, núpu; **I ~ he doesn't have anything serious** S-núpu áibă ţivá

HOPELESS *adj.* deáspir, fắră nádă, fắr-di-nádă, fắr-di-nădíe, a-pilpisít

HOPING *s.* elipsíre → HOPE

HOPPING *s.* (*as of sparrows*) puşputáre

HOPSCOTCH *s.* (*a game*) ≈ tricóte, triciu

HORAH *s.* (*round dance*) huró, cor; **to lead the ~** trag hurólu

HORIZON *s.* záre (*and* dzáre), zeáre, ţeáre

HORN *s. anat.* córnu ‖ *F:* pl coarră, HRISTU 38 → DRAW IN ONE'S ~S

HORN *vb.* (*of cattle*) (a)mpár, ▾(a)mbáir, ambúir, (a)mbúţ

HORNBEAM *s.* cárpin; *also:* cărănti, crănti, gávru, *Gop:* gáber; *Liv:* nărăndzu; scódhă, şcódhă; *coll.* cărpiníş ‖ *SJos:* miringéu, CL 255; *Av:* nărăngéu *and* nerăngió, CL 257; HRISTU 1: carpun

HORNED *adj.* ‖ *Gard:* cornút, *NPrv, Smx:* curnút, *GSus:* cărnút, *Arγ:* curút; cu coárni; *Pros et passim:* cu coárni; *Mi, Pdz:* cu córe, *Hor:* cu córi, B-ARCH 325

HORNED SHEEP *s.* ‖ *K:* cărnútă, GOLAB 225

HORNET *s. ent.* (a)yeáspe

HORN IN *vb.* ▾bag, ▾aúrlu

HORNLESS *adj.* şut, ciut, cărşút

HORNY *adj.* (*having horns*) curnút; (*calous*) bătút; **His hands were ~** Ľ-si aveá bătútă mấnle; (*excited, lascivious*) adzisít, azgân

HORRENDOUS *adj.* → HORRIBLE

HORRIBLE *adj.* fuvirós, -oásă; fricós, -oásă

HORRID *adj.* aurât → DETESTABLE

HORRIFY *vb.* ▼cişéscu, ▼lăhtărséscu, ▼fricuéscu

HORROR *s.* lăhtár, lăhtáră, lăhtáre

HORS D'OEUVRE *s.* mizé, mizilâche

HORSE *s.* cal, *pl* caľ; *dim.* călíc; hat, at; **chestnut** ~ algé; **Arabian** ~ cal arăpéscu; **sorry** ~ cârcâm, *pl* cârcâmeañ ‖ ALR 282: cal psohiu 'jade' ‖ *F:* pl cai, HRISTU 25

HORSEBACK: on ~ călár (pri); (a)ncălár; (*when* "the horse" *is a person*) ngrâcica [ngrâc•ka], ngrâşca

HORSE BAG *s.* ‖ *GSus:* zúbñic, CL 264

HORSEBEAN *s.*‖ fávă, CAPIDAN 148

HORSE-BELL *s.* (*also for other animals*) trácă

HORSE-DEALER *s.* geambáş, geambáz

HORSE-DEALER'S TRADE *s.* geambăzlâche

HORSE DRIVER *s.* ‖ *Cru:* ayuiát, GOLAB 196

HORSEFLY *s. ent.* dávan, tăún

HORSEKEEPER *s.* ipár; vălămă, vălmă,; *dim.* vălmíc

HORSEMAN *s.* călăréţ, sufarí, suvarí, căvălár, cavalară

HORSEPLAY *s.* glăreáţă → JOKE

HORSERADISH *s.* hrean, *Tur:* ólmu

HORSESHOE *s.* pétală

HORSESHOE NAIL *s.* guvójdu

HORSESHOER *s.* (*farrier*) nalbán, pitălár

HOSE *s.* ciúpăr, lăpúdă

HOSPITABLE *adj.* (*of a house*) dişcľís

HOSPITAL *s.* spitál

HOSPITALITY *s.* uspéţ; **gave him** ~ **for nine days** l-ţânú uspéţ náo dzâle; **to give** ~ ţân uspéţ

HOST *s.* (*multitude*) tabór, tabóre, tabúre, miriádhă, miríu; **a** ~ **of princes** un miríu di prínţâ

HOST *s.* (*one who receives guests*) nicuchír, (*rare*) gázdu

HOST *s.* (*the eucharistic bread*) (a)náfură

HOSTAGE *s.* chifíle, chifaléte, sclav, rob ‖ DIARO 43: amanéti

HOSTELRY *s.* (*inn*) háne

HOSTESS *s.* nicuchíră

HOSTILE *adj.* duşmănéscu, -neáscă, -néşţâ, -néşti; duşmănós

HOSTILITY *s.* duşmăníľe, hăseanlíche, éhtră, ihtríľe, zăte

HOT *adj.* (*of people*) agzutós, arăchít, sárpit, sărpit, sârpid, sértu, sértic; (*as of the sun*) dugurós; **a ~ day** dzúuă duguroásă; **~ weather** căroári *f*; **It is ~** Fáţi căroári; **I am ~** Ñ-eáste căroáre; *Mul:* ñ-éste acuroáre; (*of a liquid*) upărít; (*pungent*) mbipirát (*and* mpi-); (*as of eyes, of tears, etc.*) aprímtu, aprés → CATCH IT ~, MAKE IT ~ FOR SMB., BLOWING ~ AND COLD

HOT COCKLES *s.* (*a game*) péce; **to play ~** agióc péce

HOT PEPPER *s.* paparícă, pipércă, pipiryeáuă, *N:* ciúşcă, şúşcă ‖ DIARO 69: pipirúşi *f*

HOT POTATO *s.* ndzémă, ndzímă

HOT-BLOODED *adj.* arceátcu, *m pl* -tţi, *f pl* -tţe → ILL-TEMPERED

HOTCHPOTCH *s.* → HODGEPODGE

HOT-HEADED *adj.* sárpit → IMPETUOUS

HOTSHOT *s.* chischín, mástur

HOUND *s.* hártă, liyón, óşă

HOUND *vb.* ▼avín

HOUR *s.* oáră, săhát, săháte, săáte, sáte; (*moment*) **in the ~ of death** tru săhátlu a moártiľi; **the last ~** (*death*) oára-a oárăľei; **an ~'s journey** nă sáte cále; **at an early ~** próur; dinoápte; di c-noápte

HOUSE *s.* cásă, *pl.* căsi, cáse *and* (*rare*) căsuri; *dim.* căsícă, căscioáră, *Smr:* căşoáră; **rectangular ~** divítcă

HOUSEBREAKING *s.* aspárdzire, aspărdzeáre

HOUSECLEAN *vb.* născărséscu, (a)năschirséscu

HOUSECLEANING *s.* născărsíre

HOUSE-CLOTH *s.* păciúră, păcivúră

HOUSEHOLD *s.* (*property*) nicuchirátă ‖ MERCA 3, 49: duzéne

HOUSEHOLD ARTS *s.* nicuchiripsíre

HOUSEKEEPER *s.* nicuchír, icunóm; *adj.* nicuchiréscu

HOUSETOP *s.* acupirămíndu → ROOF

HOUSEWIFE *s.* (*married woman in charge of a household*) nicuchíră; (*container for needles*) pisúză, viluníthră

HOVEL *s.* arăbătíe ‖ *Peş:* paľúşpiti, CL 257

HOVER *vb.* (*to play attendance, to move to and fro from a place*) ‖ CARAFOLI 40: dau dulăi

HOW *adv.* cum, cúmu, cu ţi trop, cum di, cât; (*why?*) ţe, ţe sóie; **I don't know ~ to tell you** Nu ştiu cúmu s-ţ spun; **~ did you escape?** Cum di ascăpát? **Do you know ~ tall she is?** Stii cât análtu eáste? **Oh, ~ on earth was I not here at that time!** Ah, ţe nu mi-avúi draclu auá tu aţeá oáră! **He was thinking of ~ to destroy them** S-minduíă cu ţi trop si-ľ buréască; (when shopping) ~ **much?** ~ **much does it cost?** Cúmu-l daţ? Cum u daţ? (lit. 'how do you give it [out]'?)

HOW ARE YOU? (greeting formula) ‖ BATSARIA 50: Cum ľ-u treţ?

HOW COME? ‖ cum aşí? BASME 427

HOW FAR adv. (until where, up to which place) trâşi iu

HOW MANY interrog. and rel. câţ m, câte f/n; ~ **of you came?** Câţ di voi viñíră? cânţâ m,; cânte f/n

HOW MUCH interrog. and rel. cât (and căt) m/n, câtă f, cântu m/n, cântă f; **F:** chet

HOWEVER cj. cum ţi s híbă

HOWL vb. ▼aúrlu, **F:** aúrru

HOWLING s. aurláre, aurlătúră, **F:** aurráre (with rr < rl)

HOWSOEVER adv. cum ţi s híbă

HOY interj. ó-lai, á-lai, a-léi, a-leá, a, aĭ; **N:** la; a-lá and á-la

HUBBUB s. lávă, lăvătúră → UPROAR

HUCKLEBERRY s. afíngă, afínghe; **as huckleberries** (abundantly) cu mnáta

HUDDLE s. (meeting) adunáre

HUDDLE vb. (as of cold or fear) ▼(a)ndés, andiséscu, ▼nguzmu-lédz; (to curl up, to snuggle) mi adún gľem

HUDDLED UP adj. (with cold) nstugát (di arcoáre)

HUE interj. du-dú! hu-du-dú! dú! dúa! Dúa, lúpe!

HUE AND CRY interj. yiúha! or iúha!

HUFF s. inătusíre

HUFFY adj. inagí, inătcí

HUG s. ambrăţáre, angaľisire, gugustíre, hiriţíre

HUG vb. ▼ambráţ, ▼mbrăţăşédz, ▼mbrăţuşédz, ▼mbrăţitédz, ▼ngă-ľiséscu, puştuéscu, ▼stringu la sin, ncurpiľédz, ncurpulédz, ▼hiriţéscu, ▼gugştédz, ▼guguştéscu

HUGE adj. balaváncu, évil, ghigántu, yiyándu, thiríu

HUGGER-MUGGER s. (secrecy) ciuciuráre; (confusion) alăcíre

HULL s. coáje, céflă, flúdhă

HULL vb. ▼xifludhyi(p)séscu, xispirséscu

HULLABALOO s. ghiurultíe → HUBBUB

HUM

HUM *s.* zvngâníre, zângâníre

HUM *vb.* (*as of a spinning top*) z(v)ângânéscu, gărăéscu

HUMAN *adj.* uminéscu, -eáscă, -éşţâ, -éşti

HUMANE *adj.* uminéscu → HUMA

HUMANITY *s.* uminătáte, uminitáte

HUMANLY *adv.* umineáşte

HUMBLE *adj.* ncľinát, ñirusít, ñilúş, plicát, cu nările aplicá-
te, cu cáplu spindzurát, tápin, tăpinós; (*as before God*) efsevís
("*bookish Grecizm,*" DDA 528) → EAT ~ PIE

HUMBLE *vb.* mi fac túrtă → HUMILIATE

HUMBLEBEE *s. ent.* heávră, dzângânár, zăngrănă

HUMBLY *adv.* plicát → HUMBLE

HUMBUG *s.* (*nonsense*) curcubétă

HUMDINGER *s.* ≈ máre lúcru (di)

HUMID *adj.* vlăngu, *m pl* -ndzi; vlângós; (*as of walls, of rooms*)
nuţât, nutiós, nutós, nutirós ‖ **Peş:** mucirós, CL 256

HUMIDITY *s.* vlágă, vlăngă (*and* vlângă), vlănzíme, nóti, nutíe,
událiu; (*of walls*) iyrasíe ‖ **Nev:** umiditáte, CAPIDAN 150

HUMILIATE *vb.* cătăfrăniséscu, frângu nările, ▾fac túrtă ‖ **Cru:**
trag azvárna, GOLAB 204

HUMILIATED *adj.* cu nările frâmte, cătădhixít → HUMBLE

HUMMING *s.* (*of bells, of an approaching cart*) văzúră → RUMBLE

HUMMING TOP *s.* fúrlă, sfúrlă

HUMMOCK *s.* óhtu

HUMOR s. (*mood*) chéfe, chéifă; (*smth. designed to be comical or
amusing*) caraghiuzlắche; **in a bad ~** ≈ cu cúrlu n sús → PUT SMB.
OUT OF ~

HUMOR *vb.* ▾zdrudéscu, ▾hăidhipséscu; (*to let smb. have his
head; also of a horse*) ▾sălăghéscu

HUMOROUS *adj.* caraghiós, -oásă, -óşǐ, -oáse

HUMP *s.* cambúră, cusór ‖ **SJos:** cumbúră, CL 43

HUNCH *s.* (*intuitive feeling concerning a future event or result*) nóimă

HUNCHBACKED *adj.* cucuş(e)át, nguguşeát → CROOKED

HUNDRED *num. and s.* sútă, táľe; **one ~ horses** únă sută di caľ;
He records the ~s on his staff Seámnă tăľle pri cârlíg; (*bank-
note or coin*) sutăreáuă ‖ **almost one ~ meters** aproapia unăsută di
metri, HRISTU 30

HUNGARIAN *adj.* măgiréscu, măgiăréscu ‖ *Cru:* ungár, GOLAB 256

HUNGARY *s.* ‖ *Cru:* Ungaríe, GOLAB 256

HUNGER *s.* foáme, agiunáre; **rabid** ~ ≈ foámea ĺ-u ca ndúrlă (*lit.* *'His hunger is rather crazy'*) ‖ *Kat, Ses:* fómi, B-ARCH 227a; BELIMACE 116: agiunátic → BE OVERCOME BY ~

HUNGRY *adj.* agiún, agiunát, (a)fumitós, ni-măcát, ni-sătúl; **very** ~ supt di cătúşi (*lit.* *'sucked by cats'*); canda l-súpsiră cătúşile; **to be** ~ agiún, agiunédz; mi am dúsă gúra la ureácľe; ñ-aúrlă luchi [luk'] tu pântică (*lit.* *'wolves are howling in my belly'*) ‖ BASME 46: ñ-u foáme; *Amc:* **I am not** ~ nu ñ-eáste foáme, RÉCATAS 36; HRISTU 45: foamos

HUNK *s.* (*large piece*) bucátă, cumátă; ~ **of bread** (*with crust*) cultúc, márdzine di pâne; *Brz:* mărdziníčľe

HUNT *s.* avinátic → HUNTING

HUNT *vb.* ▼avín; (*to pursue*) (a)fug, alág dúpă; ~ **for bargains** alág dúpă pleácică [pleáĉ•kă]

HUNT THE WRONG HARE *vb.* ≈ u-adár taratóre

HUNTER *s.* avinătór, avgí, chiniyitór, chiniyătór ‖ *Rod, Smx.*, *etc.* chiniyó, *LvO:* chiniyár; *Mul:* lavgí, B-ARCH 359

HUNTING *s.* avináre, avinátic, chiníye ‖ *Peş:* avi, CL 37; MERCA 30: lov

HURDLE *s.* cheádică; **as thin as** ~ ≈ slăghít ca hiľán

HURL *s.* arucáre, arcáre, arucătúră, arcătúră

HURL *vb.* ▼arúc → RUSH, THROW

HURLY-BURLY *s.* lávă, vreávă → UPROAR

HURRIEDLY *adv.* n yíe, cu ayiuseálă, cu avrápă

HURRY *s.* ayiuseálă; **in a** ~ ayíu, cu ayiuseálă, pi-arăchíte; **to be in a** ~ mi ayuñiséscu ‖ **What's the** ~? Dzâlile nu intrără tu sac! BASME 11 (*lit.* *'Days have not entered into the sack!'*)

HURRY UP *vb.* u dau alága, ayunéscu, ayuñiséscu, ▼ayiuséscu; curundédz, ▼viiséscu, ▼sărgľéscu (and sâr-), ▼sarghéscu; ~ **up after a doctor!** Aguníţ di un lai yeátru! Căţáua ţe s-ayiuseáşte scoáte căţăľi órghi (*lit.* *'The bitch which hurries too much delivers blind puppies'* ≈ Haste makes waste; (*of an action performed with one's hands*) **Hurry up!** Áide, gioácă-ţ mâñle! (*i.e., keep working!*)

HURRY-SCURRY *adj. and adv.* (*as of smb.'s clothes*) cătră naľúrea

HURT *vb.* ▾agudéscu, ▾vlăpséscu; **It hurts me!** Mi doáre! **It doesn't** ~ Nu vlăpseáşte; **a piece of news that** ~**s** nă hăbáre ţe ti doáre ‖ CUVATA 4: **it** ~ **her** (*she was shocked*) u dărú; BATSARIA 13: **It hurts me badly** N-deáde dórlu tu hicáte

HURTFUL *adj.* zñiseáric

HUSBAND *s.* bărbát (*and* bâr-); *dim.* bărbătíc, soţ, mărít, *Băi:* hurhóñu ‖ **her** ~ burbasu (*i.e.,* bărbát-*su, E.V.*), HRISTU 10

HUSBANDMAN *s.* uráciu, zivyít

HUSBANDRY *s.* → ANIMAL ~

HUSH *vb.* tac; (*to impose silence, as trying to calm down a barking dog*) vâryéscu; (*to* ~ *away*) ~ **them away from here!** Vâr-yeá-ľ di-auá!

HUSH *interj.* câh, cârc, crâc, cítus, mâh, mútus, mólcĭ

HUSH-HUSH *adj.,* *adv.* ascumtá

HUSK *s.* păstăľe, spătáľe, (*of beans*) livídhă, (*of peanuts*) céflă; (*residual particles of wheat*) plătíţă; **This wheat has much** ~ Gáru ári múltă plătíţă ‖ *GSus:* (*as of beans*) capíşcă, CL 40; *Pls:* pustáľă, SarD 50

HUSK *vb.* (*as beans or corn*) cur

HUSKY *adj.* (*burly, robust*) vârtós, -oásă, -óşĭ, -oáse → STRONG

HUT *s.* călívă → COTTAGE

HUTCH *s.* (*pen*) bufár, cumáş

HYACINTH *s.* zambílă, zămbílă

HYGIENE *s.* iyiénă

HYMN *s.* cundác, hirovicó

HYPOCHONDRIA *s.* ipuhundríe, ipuhundríľe

HYPOCHONDRIAC *adj.* ipuhóndru, -ndră, -ndzri, -ndre

HYPOCORISTIC NAME *s.* númă di dizñérdu

HYPOCRISY *s.* ipucrisíe ‖ TC: prifăţeáre

HYPOCRITE *s.* *ipucrít;* şirét, şărét, cărbúne (*or* tucíne) anvă-lít, cătúşe, ócľi apúşi şi cur aprés; gúra lilíce şi ínima cir-níce; n gúră ñáre ş tu ínimă heáre; **Oh, you** ~ **Judas!** Oh, şăréte Iúdha!

HYPOCRITICAL *adj.* acupirít; ascúmtu, -mtă, -mţâ, -mte; ipucrít; şirét, -eátă, -éţ, -eáte; *also* şărét; alávdă făsúľíle ş-mâcă cárne (*lit.* 'praises beens but eats meat'); făţ-făţ eáste

I

I *pers. pron. nom.* míne, io [ĭo], **N:** iou [ĭoŭ], méni; (*rare*) eu; *dat.* añía, âñ, ñi, ñ-; **This is what the prelate whispered to me** Añía aşí ñ-abură dispótĭ; *acc.* míne, me, mi, io; **Wait for me!** Aştiptáţ ş-míne! **Stick to me!** Ţâni-te di míne! **This snake knows only me** şeárpile aéstu maşi míne mi cunoáşte; **You did not listen to me** Tíni io nu mĭ-ascultáşi; **without me** fără di io

ICE *s.* gľáţă, *pl.* gľéţuri ‖ MURNU 8, 14, 54: gľeţ *pl*

ICE CREAM *s.* **N:** dundurmáie, **S:** dundurmă

ICICLE *s.* (*hanging* ~) ţeáră (di gľáţă) aspindzurátă ‖ **Prv:** lâmbádhă, CL 254; **Pls:** păyúr, CL 258

ICON *s.* icoánă

ICON DEALER *s.* icunár

ICONOSTAS(IS) *s.* icunustás, témplu

ICTERUS *s. med.* (*jaundice*) gălbináre

ICY *adj.* ngľiţát, arcurós

IDEA *s.* (*opinion*) idhéi; (*inspiration*) fótise búnă; (*knowledge*) cunoáştire, cunuşteáre ‖ BATSARIA 54: **I have no ~** (*I cannot figure it out*) nu-ñ afeátă

IDENTICAL *adj.* únă, únă luyíe, únă sóie, únă turlíe; aparálat-cu; soţ *m*, soáţă *f*

IDENTICALLY *adv.* tut acşí (ca) ‖ HRISTU 102: tutaşă

IDIOCY *s.* glăreáţă, huţáme

IDIOT *adj.* ľócă *invar.* → STUPID

IDIOTIC *adj.* huţăscu, -ţáscă, -ţăşţâ, -ţăşti

IDLE *adj.* ayálnic, apráctu, *m pl* -cţă; apráhtu, *m pl* -hţâ; ciumagáră, *pl.* -gárañ; durñít; (*unemployed, free, available*) ni-acăţát; ~ **talk** zboáre di cácă, vrúte şi ni-vrúte; hăbări *f pl*

IDLE ABOUT *vb.* (*to loiter*) hălăndăréscu, misúr steálile (*lit.* 'to measure the stars')

IDLENESS *s.* şideáre; (*care-free* ~) bihulíche

IDLER *s.* haramufái → LOITERER

IDOL *s.* ídhol, ídhul

IDOLATER *s.* idhololátru

IDOLATRY *s.* idhulatríe

IF

I.E. (*id est*) va dzâcă, deméc

IF *cj.* **1.** ama că; **If he comes, let me know** Áma că va yínă, grea-ñ; **2.** ca (s); **If you wish, trade with us** Ca s-vrei, alăxeá cu noi; **3.** cára (s); **If he has not died, he may still be alive** Cára s-nu murí, vahi băneádză níca; **4.** (*unless, exept, on the condition that*) cari (s); **They are still alive if they have not died** Băneádză şi az cari s-nu muríră; **5.** (*in case*) dise, disi, dis; **if they have someting to sell** dísi au ţivá tră vindeáre; **6.** (*whether*) fúre-că, fúr-că ‖ **He could not tell for sure if it was a man or a woman** Nu aleápse ghíne fúre că-i bărbát i fúre că-i muľáre, BASME 78 ‖ **7.** ma (s); **Catch them, if you are so brave!** Acáţă-ľ, ma s-hii gióne! **If he sees you with me, he will kill you** Ma va ti veádă tíne cu míne, va ti vátămă; **8.** mácă, si, s; **if I had the strength** s-aveám putére; **If you knew what a hypocrite he is!** Si şteai ţe cătúşe eáste el! → AS ~ ‖ s-eáste că, s-fúre că, CAPIDAN 409; **~ such is the situation** mácă-i acşíţe, BASME 81

IF YOU WILL (*concessively*) ‖ CUVATA 10: maca vrei

IF NOT → OTHERWISE

IFFY *adj.* ni-síyur

IGNOBLE *adj.* (*base*) idipsâz, etep-, *m pl* -âjĭ, *f pl* -âze; (*of low birth*) suisâz, *m pl* -âjĭ, *f pl* âze; xisóiastu, *m pl* -şţâ, *f pl* -ste

IGNOMINIOUS *adj.* ar(u)şinós, próstih, pânghiós [•ǵós]

IGNOMINY *s.* şăneáţă, lăiáţă, paranamíľe → INFAMY

IGNORANCE *s.* ni-şteáre, niştíre, ni-scíre

IGNORANT *adj.* ni-ştiút; órbu, oárbă, órghi, oárbe; dărvár; li ncărcă pi cucót yrámotile (*lit. 'has loaded [all] his/her knowledge] on the rooster'*)

IGNORE *vb.* (*to neglect*) nu ancúñu, nu dau di mâneár

ILK *s.* sóie → KIND

ILL *s.* → EVIL, MISFORTUNE, SICKNESS, TROUBLE

ILL *adj.* lândzid; **to be ~** hivréscu, hiuvréscu; ▼lândzidizăscu; **to be slightly ~** nţân → SICK, FALL ~, MAKE ~; (*bad*) (a)rău; (*harsh*) ni-ñilós ‖ bâgát 'ill,' DIARO 321

ILL-BRED *adj.* păduríş → RUDE

ILLEGAL *adj.* paranóm

ILLEGALITY *s.* paranomíľe

ILLEGIBLE *adj.* (*of smb.'s script*) cioáre di găľíñ (*lit. 'chick-*

en feet')

ILLEGITIMATE *adj.* báştu, *m pl* báştâ, *f pl* báşte → BASTARD

ILL-FATED MOMENT *s.* oáră slábă

ILL GOTTEN, ILL SPENT ≈ haráme víñe, haráme s dúse

ILL-HUMORED *adj.* căchiós, -oásă; inagí

ILLICIT *adj.* para-nóm

ILLITERACY *s.* ni-ştíre, ni-scíre, ni-şteáre

ILLITERATE *adj.* ni-nviţát, ayrámat; órbu, oárbă, órghi, oárbe; nu li şti lăile (*lit. 'does not know the black ones,' i.e. the letters*)

ILL-LUCK *s.* tirsilâche

ILL-MANNERED *adj.* păduríş

ILL-MATCHED *adj.* ‖ RÉCATAS 50: ca púşca cu áilu (*lit. 'as vinegar with garlic'*)

ILL-NATURED *adj.* → ILL-TEMPERED

ILL-NATUREDLY *adv.* aráulea

ILLNESS *s.* lângoáre, ni-puteáre, ni-pteáre, ni-puteáţă

ILL OMEN *s.* cóbă, cubíľe, cubăíre, cubilíche (aráuă), grama-ráuă

ILL-OMENED *adj.* (*ill-starred*) năhusét, scurpisít

ILL-STARRED *adj.* **I am ~** ≈ am steáuă aráuă → ILL-OMENED

I'LL TELL YOU WHAT ciuleá ncoa!

ILL-TEMPERED *adj.* arăchít, arceátcu, astăľát, căţáuă, ghiurul-tagí, guşturát, yeáspe, yispinát, yispinós, ciftilâ, ciftilíu, dzăndzós (*and* dzân-), dzăndzăvós; dzâfnós; fesfesé; funicád; ina-cí, inacíu, inagí, mutrusít, nvipirát, slab, sclab, turc, puş-cľós, uhinát, zăpălít → BECOME ~

ILLUMINATE *vb.* luñinédz, fixéscu

ILLUMINATION *s.* luñináre, aprindeáre, apríndire; (*inspiration*) fótise

ILLUSION *s.* (*dream, fantasy*) păreáre; puľ di vímtu (*lit. 'wind chicks'*)

ILL WILL *s.* arăiáţă, slăbínţă, zăte

IMAGE *s.* figúră, iapíe ‖ GULI 29: iñíze

IMAGINARY *adj.* (*not real, fancied*) făndăxít

IMAGINATION *s.* (*fantasy*) făndăsíe, făndăzíe, făndăxíre

IMAGINE *vb.* (*to think, to believe, to fancy*) ▾făndăxéscu ‖ **I cannot ~ you being such** Nu ñ-te-acáţă ócľul ti ahtáre, BASME 178

IMBECILE

IMBECILE adj. ĺócă, *invar.* → STUPID

IMBECILITY s. (*silliness*) glăreáţă

IMBROGLIO s. mintitúră, ndézmă, ndízmă

IMBRUE vb. (*to drench in or with smth. that stains*) ▼(a)ncárcu, ▼mâryéscu

IMBUE vb. (*to saturate or impregmate with moisture, color, etc.*) ▼moĺu

IMMACULATE adj. curát; (*as of a fairy*) fắră minghinádhă → IN-NOCENT

IMMATURE adj. (a)rúd, crud, cu míntea ni-coáptă, gĺiciu, ni-agiúmtu, ni-agiúnsu, ni-cóptu, ni-fricát; nínga cu múţĭĺi tu nári-ĭ; *also:* și-eáste cu cămeáșea di la núna ‖ (*inexperienced, too young*) 3 sg: nu-acáţă ninga cĺag, DIARO 233; câcâtós, DIARO 192

IMMATURENESS s. ‖ STERE 66: agimlắchi

IMMEASURABLY adv. → BEYOND ALL MEASURE

IMMEDIATE adj. (*made or done on the spot*) tu loc

IMMEDIATELY adv. dinăoáră → SUDDENLY

IMMENSE adj. balaváncu, m pl -ánţi, f pl -ắnţi → HUGE

IMMENSELY adv. ‖ fắră márdzine, CAPIDAN 175

IMMERSE vb. (*to dip, to soak*) ▼afúndu, ▼(a)funduséscu, ▼(a)vuţéscu, ▼hăuséscu

IMMERSION s. fundusíre, hăusire

IMMOBILE adj. (*motionless*) ni-minát

IMMOBILITY s. ni-mináre

IMMOBILIZE vb. (*to circle, to drive into a corner*) ▼(a)plucuséscu

IMMODEST adj. (*indecent, shameless*) ni-aruș(i)nós, -noásă

IMMORTAL adj. ni-mórtu, (*rare*) athánat

IMMOVABLE adj. ni-minát

IMMUNE adj. (*protected from desease*) purbulít

IMMUNIZE vb. ▼vắţinipsescu, ▼simnédz

IMMUNIZED adj. vắţinát, vắţinipsít, simnát

IMMURE vb. (*to build into a wall*) stizmuséscu

IMP s. drăcúș, sírsen → DEVIL

IMPAIR vb. (*to cause damage, to deteriorate*) ▼zărăriséscu

IMPART vb. (*as terror*) ▼arăspândéscu; (*to grant*) dau

IMPARTIAL adj. driptátic

IMPASSIBILITY s. adhyeafuríe

IMPASSIVE *adj.* adhyeáfur

IMPASSIVELY *adv.* (*indifferently, carelessly*) cu alăsáre

IMPATIENCE *s.* nĭ-arăvdáre, ni-răvdáre

IMPATIENTLY *adv.* cu nĭ-arăvdáre ‖ (*waiting ~*) cu gúra căscátă, BA 7

IMPEACH *vb.* (*to bring an accusation against*) fac sibépi

IMPECCABLE *adj.* ni-stipsít

IMPEDE *vb.* (*to obstruct, to hinder*) ▾ambuţéscu, ▾ambudhiséscu, ▾ambudhuséscu → SHACKLE

IMPEDIMENT *s.* cheádică

IMPEL *vb.* (*to force, to constrain to action*)) sălnăéscu

IMPERFECTION *s.* cabáte, scárţu

IMPERIAL *adj.* (*excellent*) (a)mi(ră)réscu, vasilchéscu

IMPERIL *vb.* (*to endanger*) chindinipséscu

IMPERIOUS *adj.* (*lordly, arrogant*)) pitrít, daí, daítcu

IMPERISHABLE *adj.* athánat

IMPERTINENCE *s.* (*insolence*) nadanlắche

IMPERTINENT *adj.* arsíz, *m pl* -síjĭ; disgărdít; dângă ‖ fáţă-láie, BASME 313

IMPERTURBABLE *adj.* (*indifferent, cool, impassive*) adhyeáfur

IMPETUOUS *adj.* sárpit, sắrpit (*and* sâr-), sârpid, sértu, sértic; (*as of the wind*) himós, thimós, -oásă

IMPETUOUSLY *adv.* cu furţáte, bóra

IMPETUS *s.* (*moving force*) fúzmă, vánţu, vrápă, zvórimă; (*as of a river*) bóră

IMPIETY *s.* (*an impious act*) fắră cále → INFAMY

IMPINGE *vb.* (*to strike, to dash*) ▾ciucutéscu

IMPISH *adj.* (*mischievous*) drăc(ur)ós, -oásă, -óşĭ, -oáse

IMPLEMENT *s.* (*instrument, tool, utensil*) hăláte

IMPLEMENT *vb.* (*to fulfill, to perform*) ▾adár, ▾buréscu, ▾fac

IMPLEMENTATION *s.* adráre, buríre, făţeáre, fáţire

IMPLICATE *vb.* (*to involve*) ▾ameástic, ▾bag, fac sibépe

IMPLICIT *adj.* (*implied*) achicăsít

IMPLORE *vb.* ▾(a)ngréc, pălăcărséscu, părlăcăséscu, pricád, para-cád, ▾sprigiúr, ▾spigiúr, (*rare*) ▾rog; **We ~ you to stop crying** Nă angricắm si nu ma plấndzi; (**They**) **~ed him to give up** Lu sprigiuráră s-trágă mắnă

IMPOLITE *adj.* disgrădít → RUDE

IMPOLITIC

IMPOLITIC *adj.* (*injudicious, not wise*) ni-uidisít, glăréscu

IMPORTANT *adj.* (*of a holiday*) greu, greáuă, grei, greále; **an ~ holiday** sărbătoáre greáuă; lipsít; **it is very important that** eáste múltu lipsítă să; (*of consequence, speaking of people*) nişanlâ ‖ CUNTA 258: nişanlítcu

IMPORTUNATE *adj.* ≈ paľu ntr-ócľi (*lit. 'a straw in the eye'*)

IMPORTUNE *vb.* ‖ âñ sta tu coástâ, DIARO 268 (*lit. 'it stays in my rib'*)

IMPORTUNITY *s.* havalé, pirăxíre

IMPOSE *vb.* ▾arúc, bag ciciórlu, ▾cálcu; **~ expenses upon smb.** arúc hărgi; **You have ~ed huge expenses upon me** Mări hărgi ñ-arucát; (*to deceive*) ▾ncálţu ‖ (*a tax*) CUNIA 134: bag dáre

IMPOSING *adj.* (*beautiful, majestic*) fanúmin, lărgóñu

IMPOSSIBLE *adj.* cu niputeáre; nu-i cearé, **N:** nu-i cearée; **it is / it was ~ to** iu să; **It would have been ~ for the enemies to reach me** Iu s-mi alăcheáscă duşmáñľi! nu-i (*or* nu eáste) cu puteáre, nu s-fáţe; (*a superstition:*) **It is ~ to be beardless and good** şi spân, şi bun, nu s-fáţe

IMPOSSIBLY *adv.* adhínaton ‖ cu niputeáre, BASME 142

IMPOST *s.* bidéľu → TAX

IMPOSTOR *s.* (*deciever, cheat*) farmzón, şarlatán

IMPOTENCE, IMPOTENCY *s. med.* pútă

IMPOVERISH *vb.* (*to pauperize*) urfăn(ips)éscu, atirséscu, ▾scad, ▾minutédz, minuţăscu, sgulughéscu, dau di páde, ftuhipséscu, yiftuséscu; **He had ~ed** Aveá suflátă dráclu tu púngă (*lit. 'the devil had blown in his purse'*) ‖ scad di aveáre, PARALLELE 137

IMPOVERISHED *adj.* ftuhipsít, scădzút, sec, sgulughít, urfănipsít, cătră soáre; **He felt that the man was completely ~ed** Lu-aduchí că eásti dip cătră soáre

IMPOVERISHMENT *s.* scădeáre, sgulughíre, ftuhipsíre, urfănipsíre, urfănisíre

IMPRECATE *vb.* (*to invoke evil upon smb.*) ▾blástim, ▾blástin

IMPRECATION *s.* blăstém, cătáră, *G:* mândză

IMPRESSION *s.* entípuse, fiyúră

IMPRESSIVE *adj.* fanúmin, fiyurát; mă-sa ľ-fu!

IMPRESS ON ONE'S MEMORY *vb.* ▾stămbuséscu tru mădúuă

IMPRISON *vb.* bag brénda → JAIL

IMPRISONED *adj.* ncľis, flucusít

IMPRISONMENT s. âncľideáre, âncľídire, flucusíre, hăpsâníre

IMPROPER adj. (unsuitable) ni-uidisít

IMPROVE vb. (to correct, to amend) ▾ndréptu, ▾ndriptédz; (increase) créscu; (to embellish) mușiţắscu; (to heal) ▾víndic

IMPUDENCE s. (effrontery, insolence) nĭ-arușináre, ni-arușnáre, yumărlâche

IMPUDENT adj. (insulting, rude, saucy) nĭ-aruș(i)nát, nĭ-aru-ș(i)nós → SHAMELESS

IMPUISSANCE s. slăbeáţă → WEAKNESS

IMPULSE s. anăngăsíre

IMPULSION s. → IMPULSE

IMPULSIVE adj. astráptu, -ptă, -pţâ, -pte; himusít

IMPUNITY s. ni-pidhipsíre

IMPURE adj. ni-curát; (morally ~) pângân(ips)ít

IN adv. (within) năúntru (and năúndru), núntru; **They walked ~** Intráră núntru

IN prep. **1.** tu; **Do you have grape vine ~ your yard?** Ai luzíncă tu ubór? **2.** prit, prítu; **He lost his way ~ the woods** S-chirdú prit pădúrĭ; **3.** tru, ntr(u); **~ November** tru Brumár; **~ these pla-ces** tru aíste lócuri; **the wound that I have ~ my heart** arána ţe am ntru ínimă; **4.** pi, pri; **~ the days when** pi dzâlile cându; **~ the sunlight** pi soáre; **~ the moonlight** pri lúnă or pi lúnă; **You torment yourself ~ endless crying** Ti deápirĭ pri un plângu; **One of theirs is ~ danger** Un di-a lor eáste pi chíndhin; **5.** (rare) n, **N:** ân

IN A BAD HUMOR adj. cu cúrlu n sus

IN A BAD STATE adj. cătră soáre

IN A BLUE FUNK adj. cu ínima strímtă

IN ABUNDANCE adv. cu mnáta

IN A CRACK adv. tu-úna → IMMEDIATELY

IN A HURRY adj. and adv. ayisít, ayiusít, ayíu, ayuñisít, cu ayĭuseálă, pi-arăchíte

IN A JIFFY adv. (in a very short time) tu-úna → IMMEDIATELY

IN A LITTLE WHILE adv. dúpă niscântă oáră

IN ALL POSSIBLE WAYS adv. a mórtului

IN A LOW VOICE adv. păgăñór (and pâgâ-)

IN A MOMENT adv. tu-úna → IMMEDIATELY

IN AN AWFUL PLIGHT adv. cătră soáre, trâ nivideáre

IN

IN A PROPER MANNER *adv.* ‖ DIARO 326: cum-lipseáşti *adj, adv*

IN A SHAKE *adv.* tu-únă → IMMEDIATELY

IN A SORRY PLIGHT *adv.* trâ ni-videáre

IN A SPLIT SECOND *adv.* tu-únă

IN A TIGHT SQUEEZE *adv.* ndisít → TROUBLE

IN A TRICE *adv.* tu-únă → IMMEDIATELY

IN A TWINKLING *adv.* tr-únă hópă

IN BED *adj.* and *adv.* (*ant.* **out of bed**) culcát

IN BROAD DAYLIGHT *adv.* ñádză-dzúuă

IN CHARGE *s.* tăpár, máru

IN CHILDBED *adj.* mitrícă, mă-

IN COMPANY *adv.* carşí

IN DEFIANCE OF trâ píca a

IN DETAIL *adv.* pân tu per, pân la şíle

IN EAGER RIVALRY *adv.* cari di cari ma (+ *adj.*); un spri un di (+ *adj.*); **it is/was hard to decide who was more brave** ≈ ireá un spri un di gioñ

IN FOR A PENNY, IN FOR A POUND ≈ ‖ gioácă préftu di biľé, BASME 406

IN FRONT *adv.* nínte (*and* nínde), năínte, dinăínte, dinínte

IN FRONT OF *prep.* dinăínte di, dinăíntea a

IN GOOD TIME adv. → TIME

IN GREAT NUMBER *adv.* (*of people*) ca tră Stâ-Măríe (*lit.* 'as on St. Mary's [Day],' i.e. crowded)

IN LOW SPIRITS *adj.* (*depressed*) cu cúrlu n sus (*lit.* 'with one's ass upwards')

IN NO WAY *adv.* ‖ pa-pa-pá; ba-ba-bá; cu vâră trop, BASME 489; iuvaşuvá (*sic*), BASME 59

IN ONE'S OWN PERSON singuríc, singurúş

IN OPEN DAYLIGHT *adv.* ñádză-dzúuă

IN ORDER TO *cj.* s, să, tra s-, tra si, ca să, ca s-; **You have to get wet ~ eat fish** Va s-ti udz ca s-mâţi péşţâ ‖ *Cru:* tasă *or* tas, 253

IN OTHER WORDS deméc, óste, vadzâcă ‖ vai dzâţi, BASME 8; va-ľ dzâţi, BASME 336

IN PERSON *adv.* singuríc, singuríş

IN REALITY *adv.* (*indeed, actually*) naévea

IN SHORT (*to make few words of it*) ţe ncoa, ţe nclo

IN SOME WAY OR ANOTHER ‖ cum ni-cúm, BASME 256

IN SPITE OF trâ píca a; ~ **that** cu túte aíste ‖ BASME 487: cu túte-aéste

IN STREAMS *adv.* zăntúnă; **blood flew** ~ sândzile fudzeá zăntúnă

IN TERMS OF: You could not see anyone better ~ **behavior and youthfulness** Nu s-vidzú ma bun di port ş di ñáte

IN THE BEGINNING *adv.* ma naínte

IN THE BLOWING OF A MATCH *adv.* tu-úna → IMMEDIATELY

IN THE DEAD OF THE HEAT tu (a)yía a căloáriľei

IN THE DIRECTION OF *prep.* câtră (*and* cătră) → TOWARD(S)

IN THE DUMPS *adj.* (*depressed, down in the mouth*) cu cúrlu n sus

IN THE DUSK *adv.* tu amurdzítă, tu murdzítă, tu múrgu, tru murdzíş, *G:* tu múrgiu; cătră la toácă

IN THE END *adv.* tu soñ, nai tu sóne, nai ăn coádă, până ma dinăpói

IN THE FIRST PLACE (*first of all*) únă

IN THE FLOW OF CONVERSATION (*by dint of talking*) di zbor zbor

IN THE FUTURE (*from now on*) de-auă ş-nínte

IN THE MIDDLE OF *prep.* (*as* ~ *a forest*) tu buríclu a, tu buríclu di ‖ HRISTU 2: namăsa di

IN THE TWILIGHT *adv.* tru murdzíş → IN THE DUSK

IN THE TWINKLE OF AN EYE *adv.* ti un stic → SUDDENLY

IN THE UPPER PART OF *prep.* strâ

IN TIMES OF YORE *adv.* ‖ nă oáră ş-tu nă étă, BASME 84; tu nă étă, BASME 42

IN TROUBLE *adj.* ndisít

IN TWO TICKS *adv.* tu-úna → SUDDENLY

IN VAIN *adv.* áhristu, bathavá [t-h], batiavá, boş, geába, mátea, nafilé, n-cot, tu cácu, vânăt, vănátu; **His effort was** ~ N-cot âľ fu zahmétea *or* Cilistisirea ľ-fu vânătă; **All has been** ~ Nafilé sunt toáte; **But** ~, **Lena (Helen) was not for him** Ma, boş, Lena nu erá trâ nâs ‖ ciurúchi, DIARO 259; **I fed them** ~ lâ ded mâcári cuturú, DIARO 29; cot, HRISTU 3

INACTIVITY *s.* stáre, stăteáre, şideáre, ni-lucráre, aryíe, ripás

INANE *adj.* (*empty, insubstantial*) gol; (*silly*) glăréscu

INANITION *s.* foáme, ni-mâncáre

INAPPROPRIATE *adj.* (*not proper or suitable*) ni-uidisít

INAPT

INAPT *adj.* anícan → INCAPABLE

INATTENTIVE *adj.* (*heedless, unmindful*) bóşcu, -şcă, -şţâ, -ste

INAUSPICIOUS *adj.* (*unfavorable*) năhusét

INCALCULABLE *adj.* ni-numirát, ni-ruminát, ni-misurát

INCANTATION *s.* discântic, discântáre, discântătúră

INCAPABLE *adj.* anáxiu, *m pl* -cşi, *f pl* -xe; *also* náxu; anésustu, *m pl* -suşţâ, *f pl* -suste; aneaprócup, anaprócup, anícan

INCAPACITATE *vb.* (*to maim*) ▼săcătipséscu

INCARCERATE *vb.* chic năúntru → JAIL

INCARNATE *vb.* (*to embody*) ▼ântrupuéscu, ▼ntrupuşắdz ‖ CUNIA 160: chiuluéscu

INCARNATION *s.* ntrupuşáre

INCENSE *s.* thimñámă, thimeámă ‖ *GSus:* vasíleac, CL 263

INCENSE *vb.* (*to anger*) ▼furchiséscu, ▼inătuséscu, ľ-mâc urécĭile

INCENSE *vb.* (*to perfume with incense*) dau cu thimñatólu, ▼thimñiţéscu ‖ *Peş:* thimñituséscu, CL 262

INCENTIVE *s.* (*incitement, stimulus, spur*) mucaéte, ştiúri [ştĭú•ri] *f sg*, ştiuri [ştĭurĭ] *pl* (*1 syll.*)

INCEPTION *s.* apărñítă → BEGINNING

INCESSANT *adj.* (*ceasseless, unceasing, never-ending*) ni-curmát

INCESSANTLY *adv.* índa → CONTINUOUSLY

INCERTITUDE *s.* (*uncertainty*) ni-siyurlíche

INCH *s.* **not an ~** ≈ ni pálmă

INCIDENT *s.* (*occurrence, event*) cuşaméte; (*ill-fated ~*) oáră láie

INCITE *vb.* (*to urge on, to stimulate*) ▼schin, ▼scol, anăngăsăéscu

INCITEMENT *s.* schnătúră

INCITING *adj.* cârtilivós, -oásă; cărtilós, -oásă

INCIVILITY *s.* huryeátă

INCLINATION *s.* (*bow, bent, predilection*) aplicáre, prutimisíre, prutimsíre; (*talent*) doáră

INCLINE *s.* aripidínă → SLOPE

INCLINE *vb.* (*to bow*) ▼apléc, ▼ncľin

INCLINED *adj.* (*as of a tree*) arăvuít; (*as of a road, valley*) aripidinós, -noásă; aripidinát

INCLINE ONE'S STEPS TO *vb.* ľ-u dau cătră → TURN ONE'S STEPS TO

INCLUDE *vb.* ncurpilédz → COMPREHEND

INCOGNITO *adv.* tiptíle; **He was dressed** ~ Erá fáptu tiptíle

INCOME *s.* (a)iráte → EARNINGS

INCOMPATIBLE *adj.* ni-uidisít

INCOMPETENT *adj.* ni-ştiút, ni-fricát, ageamí, ageamíu ‖ CUNIA 7, 206: agimít, niprucupsít, nipurcupsít

INCOMPLETE *adj.* ni-bitisít, ni-burít

INCONCEIVABLY *adv.* ≈ cum soţ nu áre → MATCHLESSLY

INCONGRUITY *s.* ni-uidisíre

INCONSIDERATE *adj.* ni-uidisít, astráptu, -ptă, -pţâ, -pte

INCONSIDERATELY *adv.* fâră nisáfe

INCONSTANT *s.* nu sta pri únă; (*flighty*) nu-ľ angreácă míntea

INCONTESTABLE *adj.* (*authentic, genuine, pure*) di sárică

INCONTINENT *adj.* aspártu, -rtă, -rţâ, -rte

INCONVENIENCE *vb.* ▾angulcéscu, nu dau ariháte

INCORPORATED *adj.* (*of an artisan*) isnafcí

INCORRECT *adj.* stipsít → ERRONEOUS

INCORRIGIBLE *adj.* (*depraved*) aspártu. -rtă, -rţâ, -rte

INCREASE *s.* creáştire, cristeáre, ngruşeáre, adăvgáre, adăvgătúră, adăvgámíntu, avgáţíre; (*as of prices*) alináre, artirsíre

INCREASE *vb.* créscu; (*as of boiling milk, of dough, of a boaster*) ▾căbărdiséscu, ▾adávgu; **We want to ~ our wealth** Vrem s-nă adăvgăm aveárea; (*of a tax*) ▾angréc; **He wanted to ~ their duty** Vru s-lă angreácă; alín, artiriséscu, artirséscu, ▾nmulţăscu

INCREDIBLE *adj.* → UNBELIEVABLE

INCREMENT *s.* (*addition, increase*) adăvgáre, adăvgămíntu, adăvgătúră, creáştire, cristeáre

INCRIMINATE *vb.* fac sibépi

INCUBATE *s.* cluţéscu → HATCH

INCUBUS *s.* móră → NIGHTMARE

INCULPABLE *adj.* ni-stipsít ‖ PC: ni-căbătlí

INCUMBENT *adj.* (*imposed as a duty, obligatory*) ipuhriuticó

INCURSION *s.* irúse, irúşe, năvál, năválă

INDEBTED *adj.* burgilipsít; *s.* burgilâ

INDECENCY *s.* ni-aruş(i)şnáre

INDECENT *adj.* ni-aruş(i)nát

INDECISION *s.* induíre, ni-siyurlíche

INDECOROUS *adj.* (*unseemly, not in good taste*) zdángan

INDEED

INDEED *adv.* di alihea, di alíthhea [a•líth•h°a], dialíhealui;
N: alíhira; aríhina, avér, di-avér, *Gop:* drâhea, ca drâhea; tamamaná *(sic)*, tuónti ‖ de-a ghínealui, BASME 95

INDELICATE *adj.* *(of people)* zdángan

INDESCRIBABLE *adj.* ‖ *Cru:* nu ăncápe zbor, 205

INDEX FINGER *s.* anat. *(fore finger)* ‖ ALR 1604: pilicár

INDIAN CORN *s.* → CORN

INDIAN FILE *adv.* *(in single file)* arádha

INDICATE *vb.* *(to indicate, to poibt out)* ▾aspún, ▾făniruséscu,
▾părăstăséscu, ▾părăstiséscu

INDICATION *s.* *(solution)* căráre; **could not give him any** ~ nu
puteá si-ľ da vâră căráre

INDICT *vb.* *(to charge with an offense)* ▾cătiyurséscu

INDICTER *s.* *(prosecutor)* dâvăgí

INDICTMENT *s.* cătiyursíre, dâvăgilâche

INDIFFERENCE *s.* adhyeafuríe

INDIFFERENT *adj.* adhyeáfur; *(unbiased)* driptátic

INDIGENOUS *adj.* di-a lóclui

INDIGENT *adj.* *(needy)*) ni-avút → POOR

INDIGNATION *s.* → ANGER

INDIGO *s.* *(ca blue dye from plants)* civitlíe

INDIRECTLY *adv.* pri-lárgu

INDISCREET *adj.* dişcľís

INDISPOSED *adj.* ni-p(u)tút → SICK

INDISTINCT *adj.* alăcít, ni-acăchisít

INDIVIDUAL *s.* ínsu, om. citămán

INDOLENCE *s.* ni-mucaéte

INDOLENT *adj.* dânglâră, *f* -roáñe, *m pl* -rádz, *f pl* -roáñe;
haramufái, *pl* haramufáiañ; armăsătór; tăvlâmbă, -bádz, -boáñe

INDOLENTLY *adv.* cu alăsáre

INDOORS *adv.* núntru, núndru

INDUCE *vb.* úmplu cáplu, bag di cále → PERSUADE

INDUCEMENT *s.* umpleáre, úmplire

INDULGE *vb.* yăryărédz; *3 sg impers.* mi yăryăreádză s; **I ~ in**
strolling Mi yăryăreádză s-mi priímnu

INDULGE IN LECHERY *vb.* curvăriséscu

INDURATE *vb.* *(to make hard)* vârtuşéscu → HARDEN

INDUSTRIOUS *adj.* *(diligent)* ni-şidzút ‖ ALR 1619: lucrătór;

HRISTU 11: lucărtor

INEBRIATE *s.* ambitătór

INEBRIATE *vb.* ▼adár stíngăle → GET DRUNK

INEPT *adj.* (*unfit*) ni-uidisít, astângu, zérvu; (*incompetent*) apló; (*lacking sense or reason*) glar

INERT *adj.* (*sluggish*) muláşcu, -şcă, -şţâ, -şte

INESTIMABLE *adj.* arúspu, -spă, -schi, -spe; ni-ahărzít

INEXPENSIVE *adj.* éftin

INEXPENSIVENESS *s.* (*of goods on the market*) eftiníe, eftinătáte, eftineáţă

INEXPERIENCED *adj.* ageamí, ageamíu, ageamít, agimít, (a)rúd, ni-imnát, ni-ştiút

INEXPRESSIBLE *adj.* ‖ *Cru:* nu ancápe zbor, 205

INFAMOUS *adj.* átim, fáţă láie, póndu, sémnu → ABJECT

INFAMY *s.* atimíe, băbislíche, edepsâzlâche, fără-cále, firaunlâche, muşiteáţă, muşuteáţă, paranomíľe, pizivinglâche

INFANT *s.* níphiu → BABY

INFANTRY *s.* pizúră; **Turkish ~** nizáme

INFANTRY MAN *s.* aschirlí, ascherlâ, imnár, nifér; nizám; stratiót, suldát

INFATUATED *adj.* ayăpisít

INFECT *vb.* (*to catch or transmit a virus*) ▼mulipséscu, ▼ascúchiu; **Flies have ~ed the food** Mâcárea u-ascucheáră múştile

INFECTED *adj.* (*as of meat in a place with flies*) ascucheát

INFECTION *s. med.* mulipsíre

INFER *vb.* ▼angucéscu → GUESS

INFERIOR *adj.* (*in social origin, quality or taste*) *adj.* ápcu, ghi(ghi)ftéscu, próstih, di cătră la cúscra; (*as of the lower layer of a pie*) di prighiós; (*prefix*) paľu-, *as:* **an ~ man** paľuom; (*of low quality*) **an ~ sheep** paľu-oáie

INFERTILE FIELD *s.* ţârţârác

INFEST *vb.* (*with pest*) puşcľédz, mpuşcľédz

INFESTED WITH VERMIN *adj.* piducľós, biducľós; **to become ~** ▼piducľédz, piducľéscu, biducľéscu

INFIDEL *adj.* ápistu, *m pl* ápişţâ, *f pl* ápiste; cáúr, dinsâz, gheaúr, imansâz, pabés, babés; (*of a Muslim*) puríndu

INFIDELITY *s.* băbislíche

INFILTRATION *s.* intráre, pitrúndire

INFIRM

INFIRM *adj*. azmét, s(c)lab, *f* -bă, *m pl* s(c)laghi; vlângu

INFIRMITY *s*. săcătlíche, -lâche; slăbeáţă, -bíľe, -bínţă

INFLAME *vb*. ▼apríndu

INFLAMED *adj*. aprés, -reásă, -réşĭ, -reáse; aprímsu, -msă, -mşi, -mse; aprímtu, -mtă, -mţâ, -mte; ncăldurát, ncuñát

INFLAMMATION *s*. *med*. (*as of a boil*) coáţire, cuţeáre; ~ **of the spleen** (*of sheep*) dalácă, dălácă, duloáge; *adj*. dălăcós, -oásă

INFLATED *adj*. umflát, căbărdisít

INFLATION *s*. (*difficult time for ordinary buyers*) scumpeáte, scumpeátic, scumpíe

INFLEXIBLE *adj*. (*of people*) ni-apuadús, nĭ-apudús

INFLUENTIAL *adj*. greu, amisticát; **an ~ man** om amisticát

INFLUENZA *s*. arémă, sináhe, sirmíe

INFORM *vb*. dau habáre, ▼plirufuriséscu, ▼plirufurséscu → LET KNOW

INFORMATION *s*. plirufuríe, plirufurisíre, plirufursíre

INFRACTION *s*. călcáre

INFREQUENT *adj*. (a)rár

INFRINGE *vb*. (*to transgress, to violate*) ▼cálcu

INFRINGEMENT *s*. călcáre

INFURIATE *adj*. aprés → ANGRY, INFURIATED

INFURIATE *vb*. ▼arcédz, ▼ngíndu, ▼nşárpic

INFURIATED *adj*. arciuít, aprés, gindós, inătusít, vârlu

INGENIOUS *adj*. feámin, theámin, heámin, seámin

INGENUITY *s*. mínte

INGRATE *adj*. aháristu

INHABIT *vb*. şed, bănédz

INHERIT *vb*. clirunumséscu, afúm ugeáclu; **He is leaving behind no son to ~ him** Nu alásă hilu s-ľ-afúmă ugeáclu

INHERITANCE *s*. clirunumsíre, clirunumíe, numíľe, miráze

INHERITED *adj*. clirunumsít

INHIBIT *vb*. (*to deter*) dau ibréte (la)

INHUMATION *s*. ngrupáre → BURIAL

INHUME *vb*. ▼ngrop → BURY

INIMICAL *adj*. duşmănós, -oásă; duşmănéscu, -eáscă

INITIATE *vb*. (*to begin*) (a)hiurhéscu; (*to lay the foundation*) bag par; (*to instruct*) ▼(a)nveţ, ▼veţ; (*to take origin*) nţep → ORIGINATE

INJUDICIOUS *adj.* ni-aduchít

INJURE *vb.* (*to wrong, to hurt*) ▼agudéscu, ▼vlăpséscu

INJURED *adj.* (*morally, juridically, etc.*) adhichipsít; (*also physically*) frâmtu, -mtă, -mţâ, -mte

INJURIOUS *adj.* (*hurtful, detrimental*) zñiseáric

INJURY *s.* vlápsim (DDA 1274: *pl ?*)

INJUSTICE *s.* strâmbătáte, strămbeátic, ni-driptáte, ni-drip-tátică, adhichíe, dhichipsíre

INK *s.* miláne, muláme

INK-WELL *s.* călămár

IN-LAWS *s. coll.* cuscráme, cuscríme; (*the relationship of ~*) cuscríľe

INMATE *s.* âncľís, flucusít, hăpsânít

INN *s.* tavérnă, háne, cărvăsără ‖ BELIMACE 99: utél *and* utéle

INNARDS *s.* ľánumă → ENTRAILS

INNKEEPER *s.* hangí, mehengí, miengíu [mi•en•]; hăngioáñe *f*

INNOCENT *adj.* curát, ni-amártipsít, ni-stipsít, fâră níţi un stépsu, ápă di lituryíe, úşe di băseárică; **He/she is not ~** Nu-i úşe di biseárică → BLAMELESS

INNUMERABLE *adj.* ni-misurát, ni-numirát

INOCULATE *vb. med.* ▼văţinipséscu, ▼simnédz

INOCULATION *s. med.* văţináre, văţinipsíre, simnáre

INOPPORTUNE *adj.* achéryiu, **m pl** -ryi, *f sg/pl* -rye

INOPPORTUNELY *adv.* áchira

INQUIETUDE *s.* (*uneasiness*) angúsă

INQUIRY *s.* istindáche, xităsíre, xităxíre → MAKE INQUIRIES

INQUIRY *vb.* ‖ BELIMACE 99: scărmináre

INROAD *s.* năvál, năválă, irúse, irúşe

INSANE *adj.* zúrlu; **to become ~** hăzuéscu di mínte → CRAZY, MAD

INSANITY *s.* zurleáţă, zurláme, zurlíľe, cicărdisíre

INSATIABLE *adj.* ni-săturát

INSATIABILITY *s.* ni-săturáre

INSATIABLE *adj.* ásot

INSATIATE *adj.* ásot

INSCRUTABLE *adj.* nipitrúmtu; **~ darkness** únă lăiáţă nipitrúmtă

INSECT *s.* bubulíc, bumbărác, rímă; (*winged ~*) burdufoártică

INSECURE: to be ~ şuvăéscu, mi clátin

INSENSATE *adj.* (*foolish*) zúrlu; (*brutal*) fuvirós, -oásă

INSENSIBLE

INSENSIBLE *adj.* nĭ-aduchít

INSENSITIVE *adj.* ni-aduchít

INSEPARABLE *adj.* ni-dispărţât

INSERT *vb.* ▾bag

INSET *vb.* ▾bag

INSIDE *adv.* núntru (*and* núndru), năúntru, năíntru; **from ~** dinăúntru, dinaúntru

INSIDE OUT *adv.* anápudha, tersené, napudhíalui

INSIDIOUS *adj.* şirét, -reátă, -reţ, -reáte → CUNNING

INSIGHT *s.* pireáţă

INSINCERE *adj.* ≈ alávdă făsúľíle ş-mâcă cárne (*lit.* 'praises beans but eats meat')

INSINCERITY *s.* tácmă

INSIPID *adj.* análut, sárbit

INSIST *vb.* mi angréc, mi arúc, mi bag (s), ľ-cad furtíe, ľ-cad pri zvércă, mi duc arídhă, mi duc furtíe, mi duc furtúnă, mi duc índa, ľ-u íntru, ľ-u stau arídhă, u-ţân fúne, para-ngréc; **He ~ed a lot** ľ-si arcă múltu ‖ bag cicior, ʜʀɪsᴛᴜ 49

INSISTENCE *s.* (a)ngricáre, pricădeáre

INSOLENCE *s.* nadanlâche

INSOLENT *s.* arsíz, dângă

INSOMNIA *s.* (*sleeplessness*) ni-durñíre, ni-nsumnáre, ni-sum- náre, ni-sómnu

INSOUCIANCE *s.* (*unconcern, lack of care*) adhyeafuríe

INSPECTION *s.* (*checkout, appraisal*) xităxíre

INSPECTOR *s.* (*controller*) meimúr

INSPIRATIONfault *s.* (*illumination*) fótise, fótise búnă

INSPIRE WITH CONFIDENCE *vb.* am bésă; **The month of March does not inspire one with confidence** (*because winter may return*) Márţul nu-áre bésă

INSPIRIT *vb.* (*to infuse spirit or life*) inimuséscu

INSTALL *vb.* bag, ▾stălăéscu, ▾(a)stăséscu, ▾(a)stiséscu

INSTALMENT *s.* alíl-hisáp, hâşte, *f sg/pl*

INSTANCE *s.* (*case*) ‖ PC: únă

INSTANT *s.* minútă, stic, stih, stiymíe, ténghe, ténghiu, uríţă

INSTANTANEOUSLY *adv.* tu loc, pri loc, pi loc

INSTANTLY *adv.* máni-máni ‖ *Cru:* ódma, 239

INSTEAD OF *prep.* tu loc di; **~ goats they found dogs** Tu loc di căpri deádiră di câñ; n lóclu di, andí; **to ofer you an ordinary fur ~ a beaver** s ţ apúnă trâ castóre nă mişíne

INSTIGATE *vb.* (*to incite, to urge*) ▼schin

INSTIGATIVE *adj.* cârtilivós, -oásă; cârtilós, -oásă

INSTITUTION *s.* (*religious ~*) văcúfe

INSTRUCT *vb.* ▼veţ, ▼nveţ, dau ócľi; **He ~ed his son to run away** ľ-deáde ócľi a híľ-su s-fúgă; dhidhăxéscu → ADVICE, TEACH

INSTRUCTION *s.* (*studying*) spudhíe; (*teaching, advising*) dhidhăxíre

INSTRUMENT *s.* hăláte; (*~ of torture*) hălăţ di pidhimádz *f pl*

INSUBORDINATION *s.* nĭ-ascultáre

INSUFFERABLE *adj.* (*unbearable*) ‖ CUNIA 207: ni-străxít

INSULT *s.* yumărsíre, prusvulisíre, prusvulíe, ngiurătúră, tăxíre

INSULT *vb.* ▼angiúr, ▼tăxéscu → ABUSE, OFFEND

INSUPERABLE *adj.* ni-ntricút

INSURANCE *s.* siyurlíche; siyuripsíre

INSURE *vb.* ▼asfălséscu, săylămséscu, ▼(a)siyuripséscu

INSURGENT *s., adj.* sculát

INSURRECTION *s.* sculáre, minditúră, mintireáţă, panástase

INTACT *adj.* ni-cărtít; sustá *invar.*; (*not plundered*) ni-călcát

INTEGRITY *s.* (*moral ~*) érye

INTELLIGENCE *s.* mínte, mintéză (*and* mindéză); *also:* dişteptăciúne, cóngulă, góngulă, góngală; sicáră n cap (*lit.* 'rye in one's head')

INTELLIGENT *adj.* aflát; **~, but unlucky** om aflát, ma fără căsméte; *also:* aduchitór, ascăpirát, *3 sg* ári cap ligát, cu sicáră n cap (→ INTELLIGENCE), (cap) cu ţércľu, disfáptu, dişcľís, diştéptu, dişţiptát, duchít, duchitór, ligát, mintimén, pir *or* píră, pirgác, şpírtu, ştiút, theámin ‖ drac di váli, BASME 89; drac di sum púnti, BASME 404; (om) cu drăñ, BASME 429 ‖ **He is very ~** easti focu (di dişteptu), (easti) pirâ, şpirtu, yearyiru; Ári mínti şi-la cur, DIARO 389

INTEND *vb.* am di pri mínte (si), ñ-u am tu mínte (si), am niéte, fac niéte ‖ PC: mi minduéscu (să)

INTENDEDLY → DELIBERATELY, INTENTIONAL

INTENSE *adj.* (*as of a fire*) sâluiós, -ioásă → POWERFUL

INTENSIFY *vb.* (*as of a fire*) ▼sâluéscu

INTENTION *s.* niéte, năiéte, mínte, proéresi, scupó, *G:* imúte

INTENTIONAL, **-LY** *adj.*, *adv.* castílea, castíli *invar.* maxús *invar.*; xaryú *invar.*

INTER *vb.* ▾acoápir → BURY

INTERCEPT *vb.* ▾acáţ, bag tu mấnă

INTERCOURSE *s.* → COPULATION

INTERDICT *vb.* zăptiséscu, zăptăséscu, nu dau vóľe

INTEREST *s.* intirés, ntirés, sinfér; (*of money*) toc, dhyeáfur, gheáfru; **The ~ lessens the principal** Tóclu mấcă cáplu; **to return with ~** dau paradz cu gheáfru ‖ *GSus:* giáfru, CL 46; DIARO 99: simfér; **Everybody cares about his own ~** Cáthi om veádi simférlu a lui

INTERESTED *adj.* ntirisát; **to be ~** 3 *sg:* ▾sinfiriseáşte; ▾ntirisédz

INTERFERE *vb.* mi bag, mi ameástic; **Do not ~!** Şedz pri oáuă-ţ! (*lit. 'Sit on your eggs!'*); (*to clash*) mi ciucutéscu

INTERLACE *vb.* (a)mplătéscu (*and* amblă-), amplitéscu

INTERMARRY *vb.* ▾ľau

INTERMEDDLE *vb.* mi bag, ▾ameástic

INTERMEDIATE *adj.* ñijlucán, ñilgiucán, ñiljucán, nojlucán, nolgicán

INTERMENT *s.* ngrupáre → BURIAL

INTERMINABLY *adv.* índa → CONTINUOUSLY

INTERMINGLE *vb.* ▾mintéscu, ▾ameástic

INTERMIX *vb.* ▾ameástic

INTERPOSE *vb.* ▾bag

INTERPRET *vb.* (*to translate*) ▾xiyiséscu; (*to understand*) achicăséscu, acăchiséscu

INTERPRETATION *vb.* (*explanation*) exíyise, xíyise

INTERPRETER *s.* (*one who translates orally*) dragumán ‖ DIARO 420: tergimén

INTERROGATE *vb.* ‖ BELIMACE 98: scármin → EXAMINE

INTERROGATION *s.* (*law*) discoásire, istindáche

INTERRUPT *vb.* pricúrmu

INTERSECT *vb.* (*to meet on a road*) ▾stăvruséscu, ncruţilédz

INTERSECTION *s.* astălitúră

INTERSTICE *s.* arălíche

INTERVAL *s.* (*gap*) arălíche, arălâche

INTESTINE *s. anat.* maţ → GUT

INTIMATE *adj.* (*marked by warm friendship*): **they became ~** ş-ľa dúhurĭle

INTIMATELY *adv.* aproápe, aproápea

INTIMIDATE *vb.* cănuséscu; **Do not ~ him** Si nu-l cănuséşti

INTIMIDATION *s.* cănusíre

INTO *prep.* tu, pi

INTOLERABLE *adj.* ‖ CUNIA 207: ni-străxít

INTOXICATE *vb.* ▾mbét → GET DRUNK

INTOXICATION *s.* (a)mbitáre, (a)mbitătúră, (a)mbităţâľe, âmbităţâe

INTREPID *adj.* nĭ-aspăreát, dâldâsít

INTREPIDITY *s.* ni-aspăreáre

INTRICACY *s.* (*perplexity*) mintitúră → CONFUSION

INTRACTABLE *adj.* (*as of a horse*) jindáric, uchealíu; (*of animals and people*) huilâ *m*, huiloáñe *f*; tabietlâ, viţeárcu

INTRICATE *adj.* cărşileát

INTRIGANT *s.* curcusír → INTRIGUER

INTRIGUE *s.* mâcătúră, munăficlíche, munuflíche, muzevirlâche, nţăpătúră, scandál, schinătúră, scándala-mándala ‖ (*mean machination*) DIARO 274: cuduşlâchi

INTRIGUER *s.* curcusúr, culcusúrĭ, munăfíc, muzavír, zizanigí ‖ cútrâ, DIARO 339

INTRODUCE *vb.* (*to insert, to thrust in*) ▾bag, ▾părăstăséscu, părăstiséscu; (*to bring in for the first time*) scot; **They ~ed him to the emperor** Lu scoásiră la amirălu; (*to lead, to bring into society*) dişcľíd tu lúme

INTRODUCTION *s.* (*presentation*) părăstisíre

INTROMIT *vb.* ▾bag

INTRUDE *vb.* ▾arúc (tu), ▾aúrlu

INTRUDER *s.* (*uninvited guest*) guldánec *m*, guldáncă *f*; G: (*of a woman who butts in*) mblustélă

INUNDATE *vb.* (*to flood*) ▾nec

INUTILITY *s.* (*uselessness*) hristíe

INVADE *vb.* anăpădéscu, ncurpilédz, ncurpulédz, ncrupilédz

INVALID *adj.* săcát, sicát → CRIPPLED

INVALIDITY *s.* săcătlíche, săcătlâche

INVECTIVE *s.* cărínte

INVEIGLE

INVEIGLE *vb.* (*to beguile, to entice*) plănăséscu, bag pri sómnu

INVEIGLEMENT *s.* băgáre pri sómnu

INVENT *vb.* scot, sufséscu; (*to ~ a lie*) uidiséscu nă minciúnă ‖ CUVATA 3: chiuluéscu

INVENTION *s.* sufíe

INVENTORY *s.* cătăyrăfíe ‖ **Grannie knew** (*or* **remembered**) **things as if by ~** (*i.e., completely*) Máea li ştia túti câtâyrâfíe, DIARO 186

INVERSE *adj.* anápudh, -dhă, -dz, -dhe; (*adverbially*) anápudha

INVERTED WRY → WRY

INVEST *vb.* ▼bag; **~ your money in a bank!** Parádzľi s-ľi badzi la báncă

INVESTIGATE *vb.* bag sítă, xităxéscu, xităséscu; discărfuséscu (*and* -câr-), discurfuséscu; (*to search thoroughly*) asgurñéscu

INVESTIGATION *s.* exétase, xétase, xităxíre, sităxíre

INVETERATE *adj.* aruzusít, bătăľusít

INVIDIOUS *adj.* nchismatáric → ENVIOUS

INVINCIBLE *adj.* nĭ-asvímtu, -mtă, -mţâ, -mte

INVIOLABLE *adj.* → SACRED

INVISIBLE *adj.* căípe *invar.*

INVITATION *s.* (a)cľimáre, călisíre, cupusíre

INVITE *vb.* (a)cľém, chem, urséscu, ▼(a)căliséscu (*and* -ľi-), cupăséscu, cupuséscu, (a)dhixéscu; **You are ~ed to the table** Hii ursít la meásă; **It is me who ~ed you to have dinner with us** Io ñ-ti-acľimái pri meásă (*stress on* Io)

INVITED *adj.* (a)cľimát, călisít, cupusít

INVITING *adj.* (*pleasant*) nóstim, *m pl* -tiñ

INVOLVE *vb.* (*incriminatorily*) fac sibépi → IMPLICATE

INWARD *adv.* păgór; **The land has sunk ~ again** Lóclu si-a-lăsă năpói păgór

INWARDLY *adv.* (*mentally*) ‖ BELIMACE 65: ăn vétea-a mea

IODINE *s.* iodh

IODOFORM *s.* iodhufórmă

IOTA *s.* yióta *invar.*

IRASCIBILITY *s.* heáre, hulíe, inagilăche

IRASCIBLE *adj.* căchiós, -oásă; guşturát, inagí → ILL-NATURED

IRK *vb.* → IRRITATE

IRKSOME *adj.* paľu ntr-ócľi (*lit.* 'a straw in the eye')

IRON *s.* her, *pl* heáre; (~ *for pressing shirts, etc.*) her; ~ **good(s)** ceácră; *adj.* di her

IRON *vb.* (*to ~ clothes*) dau cu hérlu, cálcu

IRON-FOUNDRY *s.* hirăríe, hirăríľe

IRONMASTER *s.* hirár, yíftu, hălché, fávru, fávur

IRON-STORE *s.* ceacră, hirăríľe, hirăríe

IRRECONCILABLE *adj.* ni-mbunát

IRREGULAR *adj.* ‖ TULLIU 58: (*as of a zone lacking evenness*) grimós

IRRELIGIOUS *adj.* ápistu, -stă, *m pl* -şţâ, *f pl* -ste; dinsâz, *m pl* -âjĭ, *f pl* -âze; imansâz; pabés, -ésă, -éşĭ, -ése

IRREPROACHABLE *adj.* ni-stipsít

IRRESOLUTE *adj.* andáulea [•daŭ•] ‖ PC: ≈ nu mi nămăşéscu

IRRESOLUTION *s.* induíre

IRRIGATOR *s.* (*enema pump*) clistír, ylistír

IRRITABLE *adj.* inagí → HOT, ILL-NATURED, PEEVISH

IRRITATE *vb.* (*to vex*) ▼guştirédz, ▼năr(ă)éscu, ▼căchiuséscu; (*to make sore*) ▼afurñiséscu, asplinséscu, furchiséscu; **This garbage ~s the skin** Aéste cupríi afurñiséscu cheálea; (*to ruffle*) mâc urécľile ‖ CUNIA 99: ▼săcăldiséscu

IRRITATED *adj.* asplinsít

IRRITATING *adj.* (*uncomfortable, provocative*) paľu ntr-ócľi (*lit. 'a straw in the eye'*)

IRRITATION *s.* sâcâlmáie, asplindíre, asplinsíre; *dermat.* (~ *of the face because of much sweating*) ruspeásă

IRRUPT *vb.* (*to rush in violently*) năvăléscu

IRRUPTION *s.* anăpădíre, năvál *or* năválă, irúse, irúşe

IS *vb.*, *3 sg. of BE* eáste, i, -i [⁻ⁱ], i- [ⁱ⁻], u; **Love ~ gone** I vreárea dúsă (*or* Vreárea-i dúsă); **My mind ~ confused** Ñ-u míntea arăítă; **Life abroad ~ very difficult** Xeána şi-u múltu láie

ISLAMIZATION *s.* nturchipsíre, turchisíre

ISLAMIZE *vb.* ▼(a)nturţéscu, ▼nturchipséscu, ▼turchiséscu

ISLAMIZED *adj.* turchipsít

ISLAMIZED ALBANIAN *s.* Túrcu, *pl* -rţi, *f* Túrxă, *pl* -xe

ISLAND *s.* nisíe

ISSUE *s.* (*going or coming out*) işíre, inşíre ‖ (*outcome, result*) PC: inşíre, inşítă

ISSUE *vb.* (*to come*) yin; (*to emanate, to come out*) cur, ies *or*

ISSUE

es

ISSUE A CHALLENGE *vb.* u-cáftu (ngăceárea) cu luminárea (*lit.* 'to be searching for it [i.e., for trouble] with a candlelight')

ISTAMBUL *s.* Pole

IT *pron.* dis *m*, dísă *f*; nâs *m*, nâsă *f*; ís *m*, ísă *f*; ~ **is worthless!** S-ti chiş pr-ísă! (*lit.* 'You may piss on it!')

IT GOES WITHOUT SAYING ‖ *Av:* nu va zbor, BASME 503

IT IS DOWNING *vb. impers.* da dzúuă

IT IS NOT LAUGHING MATTER *vb.* nu-i a gioc

ITALIAN *adj.* italinéscu

ITALY *s.* ‖ *Cru:* Italíe, 222

ITCH *s.* făyúră; *derm.* mâcătúră; (*scabies*) zgáibă

ITCH *vb.* (*to have an*) mi mâcă; **Her tongue ~es** U mâcă límba; **to be ~ing for a drubbing** mi mâcă sândzile ‖ **Why were you ~ing to say it?** Ti mâca záva? DIARO 264

ITINERANT DEALER *s.* (*peddler*) manáfi, *pl* manáfeañ

IT'S ALL OVER dúsi; **The food benefits you have enjoyed are all over** ≈ Dúsi curmána di an!

ITSELF: **by ~** *adv.* (*with no interference or support*) di síngure; **a spinning-wheel that span by ~** únă cicrícă țe turțeá di síngură

IVORY *n* fíldiş

IVY *s. bot.* iádiră

J

JAB *s.* aguditúră; únă (*lit.* 'one,' i.e. 'one blow, a blow')

JABBER *vb.* discântu, máțin (pi virisíe)

JABBERWOCKY *s.* băbălíre

JACINTH *s. bot.* zambílă, zămbílă

JACK *s.* (*mechanical device used to lifte a heavy body*) arutél, măcără; (*a playing card*) fándi *m*; (*a male donkey*) tăróñu

JACK *vb.* ▾alín → INCREASE

JACKAL *s.* ceacál *m*, cicále *f*

JACKANAPES s. (*impudent*) ni-aruş(i)nát; (*conceited*) fudúl

JACKASS s. zool. tăróñu; (*a stupid person*) glar

JACKDAW s. orn. chísă ‖ **Cru:** gáie, 216

JACKET s. (*for women*) ceachét, geachét, cichét, jachétă; (*for men*) ilécă, iléche; *also:* cundándir, cundúş, cupărán, cupurán, dulâmă, dulumă, dulmă; dulméciu, dulmíciu, libadé; **Smr:** pişlí; săcáche, sălístră, sărăcúce, sitrée

JACKLEG s. măsturíciu, mbalumatí, cârpáciu, mpiticătór, ni-fri-cát, ni-imnát

JACK-PLANE s. (a)rucáne

JADE s. or adj. (*of a horse*) cârcâm, *pl m* -câñ; sarvál; (*dis-reputable woman*) dósă ‖ ALR 282: (*of a horse*) cal psohiu

JADE vb. tălăéscu; ľi scot pétalile → EXHAUST

JADED adj. (*exhausted*) frâmtu, -mtă, -mţâ, -mte

JAG s. chípită

JAGGED adj. ‖ (*as of a rock or of smb.' face*) chiuşilitícu, DIARO 278

JAIL s. hápse, hăpsáne, **N:** hăpsănáu [•ná•u]; *also:* bădrúme, budrúme, pudrúme, cúlă, filăchíe, fălochíe, ncľisoáre, săndáne, zăndáne (*and* zân-), zundáne; *in* ~ núntru; **to be in** ~ stau tu ară-ţíme ‖ VELO 49: zăndaníf

JAIL vb. ▾ncľid, bag brénda; bag tu-a boilor, bag (*or* chic) năúntru, flucuséscu, hăpsânéscu

JAILBIRD s. hăpsănít

JAM s. (*a fruit food*) măgiún, măgiúne

JAM vb. ▾cálcu, ▾ndes, nturtédz, ▾strimuxéscu

JAMB s. (*as of a window*) pirváză, pirváze

JAMBOREE s. băiráme

JANGLE s. cârţâníre

JANGLE vb. cârţânéscu

JANISSARY s. ianíţar, yeaniţár

JANUARY s. yinár; **N:** culugéu, culujég

JAPE s. ardeáre → JEST

JAPE vb. ngľim, nglimédz

JAR s. (*container*) chiup, chiúpă, chiúpe; birbíľu; ghium (~ *for preserves*) chisále; (*large* ~, *usu. for water*) pitháre

JAR s. (*a harsh sound*) cârţâníre; (*jolt*) zgăţănáre; (*quarrel*)

ncăcitúră (*and* ngă-)

JAR *vb.* cârţănéscu

JASMINE *s.* iasmín, iasimín

JAUNDICE *s.* gălbináre

JAUNT *s.* ghizére, priimnáre, piripát, tifiríce

JAUNTY *adj.* (*sprightly*) sárpit; (*lively*) şpítru *invar.*; (*debonair*) evắscu; sârbu, -rbă, -rghi, -rbe

JAVELIN *s.* cămác, cămáche

JAW *s. anat.* fálcă

JAW *vb.* băndurédz

JAWBONE *s. anat.* cioľ

JEALOUS *adj.* ftuñárcu, ziľár, zuľár, zuľáric, zilip(i)seáric →
MAKE ~

JEALOUSY *s.* ziľ, zălíe, zilíe, zúle; **out of ~** tră zilíe ‖ érgu,
BASME 220, 376, 405

JEER *vb.* ▾buiséscu → MOCK

JEHOVAH *s.* dumnidzắ

JEJUNE *adj.* (*dull*) ánustu, *m pl* ánuşţâ; (*childish*) ficiuréscu

JELLY *s.* (*fruit ~*) pelté; (*meat ~*) păcé, pihtíe; **to beat smb.
into a ~** chisédz oásile

JELLY *vb.* pihtuséscu

JENNET *s.* (*female donkey*) tăroáñe

JEOPARDIZE *vb.* chindinipséscu, dăldăséscu, dăldiséscu

JEOPARDY *s.* pirícľu

JERK *s.* (*tw*) zmuldzeáre, zmúldzire; (*a foolish person*) glar →
STUPID

JERK *vb.* ▾zmúlgu

JERSEY *s. Bit:* chină

JEST *s.* ardeáre, măitápe, mbizuíre, péză

JEST *vb.* **to ~ with edge tools** ≈ ñ-bag cáplu tu tástru

JESTER *s.* suitár *m*, suităroáñe *f*

JESTING *s.* măitápe → JEST

JET *s.* azvoámire, azvumeáre

JET *vb.* (a)zvóm → SPOUT

JETSAM *s.* nicătúră

JEW *s.* uvréu; *also:* cifút, ciufút, mătúr

JEWEL *s.* giuvaír *m, or* giuvaíre *f*; givaricó, giuvaricó; (*a
valuable person or thing*) máre lúcru di; **a ~ of a girl!** máre

lúcru di feátă!

JEWELLER *s.* giuvairgí

JEWESS *s.* uvreáuă, uvrídhă

JEWISH *adj.* uvréscu, -vreáscă, -vréşţâ, -vréşti

JIB *vb.* (*to refuse to proceed further*) ▼stăpuéscu

JIBE *vb.* ≈ hiu pri únă cále cu, hiu pri un zbor cu → AGREE

JIFFY *s.* minút, minútă → MOMENT

JINGLE *s.* zângâníre

JINGLE *vb.* zângânéscu

JINN *s.* stihíe, zân (*and* dzân)

JINX *vb.* leg, (a)măghipséscu

JITTERS *s.* sârbisláche; **to have the** ~ ≈ şápti-óptu ñ-si dúţe

JITTERY *adj.* nevricó, *m pl* -cádz

JOB *s.* (*work*) lúcru; (*occupation, chore, task, matter*) *G:* istréte; **a woman's** ~ istréte muľireáscă ‖ (*employment*) pâne, BASME 119 → TAKE A ~

JOB'S CAT → CAT

JOIN *vb.* ▼alăchéscu; *N:* ▼alichéscu, mi bag; **I ~ed the hora** Mi băgái tu cor; **to ~ hands with smb.** ñ-ľau mâna cu; (*to put together*) fac únă

JOINER *s.* maríngu → CARPENTER

JOINING *s.* alichíre

JOINT *s.* *anat.* prinód, ncľitúră, clídhuse → PUT ONE'S ARM OUT OF ~

JOINT *adj.* (*knitted, as of brows in anger, etc.*) (a)misticát; ~ **brows** dzeáne amisticáte

JOIST *s.* (*as in a ceiling*) témblă

JOKE *s.* şică, şicáe, şacáe; *N:* gľímă, ngľímă; gifă, schérţă, háze

JOKE *vb.* ngľim, ngľimédz, ngľimuéscu, ngľiñéscu, fac şicáe *or* fac ngľíme; *N:* şuguéscu, şiguéscu

JOKER *s.* şicăgí

JOKING *s.* ngľimáre

JOKINGLY *adv.* angľímea, ngľímă; (cu) aházea

JOLLITY *s.* hărăcupíľe, hilăríe

JOLLY *adj.* hăriós, -oásă; hărăcóp, -oápă, -óchi, -oápe

JOLT *s.* (*sudden shock*) zdrucináre, zdruncináre; (*a quick blow or knock*) agudíre

JOLT

JOLT *vb.* ▼asdrúţin, zdrúnţin, zdrúcin

JOLTING *s.* zgăţănáre

JOSTLE *vb.* ▼ciucutéscu

JOT: **not a** ~ cât ghitríşca; níţi únă chícută; cât trâ yitríe →
AT ALL

JOUNCE *vb.* zdrúţin, zdrúnţin, zdrúcin, zdrúncin; ▼ascútur

JOURNEY *s.* dúcă, sefér, tăxídhe; **I am undertaking a** ~ mi duc
tăxídhe; **an hour's** ~ nă sáte cále; **I wish you a good** ~ Oáră búnă!
Cále ambár! *or* Oáră búnă ş-cále-ambár! **to make a** ~ fac sefér

JOURNEY *vb.* alág, tăxidhipséscu

JOURNEYMAN *s.* mástur

JOVIAL *adj.* hăriós, -oásă; hărăcóp, -oápă, -óchi, -oápe

JOWL *s. anat.* fálcă, cǐoľ; (*cheek*) fáţă

JOY *s.* haráuă, *N:* hráo; *Gop, Mul:* hroa; hărăsíre, bucuríľe,
văsălíe; **He was jumping for** ~ Di hroa săltá → BE BESIDE ONESELF
WITH ~

JOY *vb.* ▼hăriséscu, ▼mbúcur; *obs.* mi búcur

JOYANCE *s.* haráuă, hărăsíre

JOYFUL *adj.* hăriós, hărós, hărăcóp → JOVIAL

JOYFULLY *adv.* hăriós, hărós

JUDAS *s.* (*hypocrite*) Iúdha

JUDGE *s.* giúdic, giudicătór, catí, mustăndíc

JUDGE *vb.* (*at law*) ▼giúdic, ▼criséscu; **We will have a trial in
court** Va nă giudicăm la huchiumáte; (*to think*) ▼giúdic; **Think and
then speak!** Giúdică şi-apóia zburá!

JUDGEMENT *s.* giudéţ, giudicátă, críse, fitfáe; **last** ~ nfricu-
şeátlu di giudéţ, giudéţlu putút; (*verdict*) ileáme (*and* iľá-),
ileáne

JUDICIOUS *adj.* aduchít; cu sicáră n cap (*lit.* '*with rye in
one's head*') → INTELLIGENCE; ~ **people** cápite cu ţércľu

JUDICIOUSLY *adv.* sustá

JUG *s.* ghium

JUGFUL: **not by a** ~ ≈ Sănătáte! (*lit.* '*[I wish you] health*');
Mútă-u míntea! (*lit.* '*change your mind [about that]*')

JUGGLER *s.* pihliván, ghioz-boiagí

JUGGLE SMB. OUT OF HIS/HER MONEY *vb.* (a)ghismédz

JUICE *s.* (*of a fruit; also the liquid part of cooked foods*)
dzámă

JUICY *adj.* dzămós, -oásă; mustós, -oásă

JUICE *vb.* (*usu. of grapes*) mustuséscu

JUICE UP *vb.* inimuséscu

JUJUBE *s.* ţindzífă, dzindzófă

JUJUBE-TREE *s.* ţindziféu

JULEP *s.* (*a drink*) salép *or* sălépe

JULY *s.* alunár, curíc, cuptór, iúliu

JUMBLE *s.* mintitúră (*and* mindi-), mintireáje (*and* mindi-), ghilíşti [•líştⁱ] *f pl*; **in a ~** (*disorderly*) *adv.* darmadán

JUMBLED *adj.* birdhipsít, mbirdhuít

JUMBLE UP *vb.* ▾mintéscu, ▾birdhipsescu, ▾mbirdhuéscu, nbirdhuéscu, ▾ambărtuséscu; (*of the sea, of smb.'s mind*) (a)lăcéscu

JUMP *s.* sáltă, (a)săltáre, ansăritúră, antrisătúră

JUMP *vb.* (a)nsár, arsár, alsár, antrisár (*and* andri-), (a)sáltu, dau nă sáltă; *N:* astrisár; **He ~ed over it** Ansărí prísti nâs; **to ~ too high** *or* **too far** paransár

JUMP FOR JOY *vb.* sáltu di hroa; **to jump out of one's skin for joy** ≈ ñ-si fítă Hristólu n cásă; nu mi ncap stráñile ‖ gioc pri únlu cior, BASME, 430

JUMPING *s.* (a)nsăríre; (*as a fence*) andrisăríre, astrisăríre

JUMPY *adj.* nevricó, *m pl* -ádz; sârbéscu, -eáscă, -éştâ, -éşti

JUNCTION *s.* (*of two roads*) triyeáuă

JUNCTURE *s.* (*a critical time or state of affairs*) anánghe

JUNE *s.* cirişeár, cireşár, ţirişár, cherşár, heristí, thiristí ‖ *F:* chirăşár, SarD 38

JUNIPER SHRUB *s.* găbjéu (*and* gâb-), giuneápine

JUNK *s.* vicĺitúră ‖ ciurúchi, DIARO 259

JUST *adj.* (*of people*) ndréptu, driptátic, mbróstu; cu crúţea n cap; *3 sg:* ímnă cu zíya n brâu

JUST *adv.* (**~ when**, **~ like**, *etc.*) tam, tamám, tamamá, tamamaná; trâşi, tăşi (*and* tâşi), tişi; **~ then** tâşi atúmţea; anílea; **~ like a dancing bear** anílea ca úrsa cându gioácă; cât *or* cât-cât; **The night had ~ fallen** Cât aveá murdzítă; ayiú; **I have ~ escaped!** Ayiú ascăpái ş-io! jústa; **Just fancy!** Ba! Bre-bre-bre! **~ in case** trâ sinudhíe

JUSTICE *s.* driptáte, driptátic\ă, dhíche ‖ **to administer ~** fac driptáti PC

JUVENILE *adj.* ficiuréscu, -eáscă, -éştâ, -éşti

K

KAFFEECLATCH s. láfe, muabéte

KAPUT adj. (utterly defeated) azvímtu, -mtă, -mţâ, -mte; bătút, surpát; (made useless) nturtát, adrát bóză

KARAKUL s. (fur) ‖ strayáni, DIARO 88; carachiúli, DIARO 179

KEEN s. (lamentation for the dead) boáţit

KEEN adj. (mentally alert) pir, pirgác; şpírtu invar.; (sharp) nturyisít, (s)truxít; (as of eyes) bun, m pl buñ; (nuts) miraclí

KEEN vb. ▾buţéscu

KEENNESS s. pireáţă, sirtlâche

KEEP vb. ţân; (to guard from harm) stănipséscu; ~ **your breath to cool your porridge!** ≈ Nu-ţ lipséscu căstrăvéţ truşíe? ‖ **to ~ tight** ţân sânătós, BASME 432

KEEP A FIRM HAND OVER SMB. vb. (to keep an iron rod over smb.) nu-ľ dau dínte álbu (lit. 'I give him / her no white touth')

KEEP A STIFF UPPER LIP vb. ▾disíc năínte, ▾cálcu ciciórlu, eneryiséscu

KEEP A TIGHT REIN OVER SMB. vb. nu-ľ dau dínte álbu

KEEP FAST vb. (to fast) ▾ţân păreásiñ

KEEP HANDS IN POCKETS vb. (to give no help) stau cu mâñle n sin

KEEP IN ONE'S HEAD vb. (to retain, to remember, to take notice of) bag tu cufíţă

KEEP IN VIEW vb. ▾(a)duchéscu; ~ **in view to buy salt!** Aducheáte si cúmpări sáre!

KEEP MUM vb. tac mútus-cítus; nu fac níţi dza; níţi nu cărlédz ‖ néca adíľu, BASME 275

KEEP OFF vb. ▾amfiréscu

KEEP ONE'S EYES (WELL) PEELED vb. (to look out) am ócľilu; am peána

KEEP ONE'S MOUTH SHUT vb. tac mútus-cítus

KEEP ONE'S OWN COUNCIL vb. nu cârlédz níţi dzău, nu cârlédz níţi un zbor

KEEP ONE'S TEMPER vb. ▾stăpuéscu ‖ (to stay cool) niţi că ñ-si báte ócľul, BASME 210

KEEP ONE'S TONGUE vb. (ant. to reveal, to divulge) nu dau pri toácă ‖ **He does not keep his tongue** Eásti cur discupirít, DIARO

377 (*lit.* '*He/she is uncovered ass*')

KEEP ONE'S WORD *vb.* mi ţân di zbor ‖ CUVATA 10: şed pi zbor

KEEP SECRET *vb.* am ascumtíşalui; **They kept their brotherhood oath secret** Frăţâľa u aveá ascumtíşalui

KEEP SILENT *vb.* tac; nu fac níţi dza

KEEP TRACE OF *vb.* (*not to lose sight of*) nu-ñ mut căştíga

KEEP UNDER CONTROL *vb.* fac azápe

KEEP UNDER LOCK AND KEY *vb.* ţân sum cátină (*or* sum catínă)

KEEP VIGIL *vb.* şed strájă → SENTINEL

KEEP WATCH AND WARD *vb.* cărăulséscu [•ră•ul•] → SENTINEL

KEEPER *s.* epítrop; pândár → GUARDIAN

KEG *s.* varélă → BARREL, CASK

KERATITIS *s. med.* chirítă, ghirítă

KERNEL *s.* (*of a nut, of a seed*) ñedz

KEROSINE *s.* gáze ‖ *GSus:* videálă, CL 263

KEY *s.* cľái [kľá•i], *pl* cľei [kľei]; *dim.* cľiíţă *or* cľíţă; dişcľidzătoáre; *G:* discľidzătoáre; *F* (*nr. Ohrid*): cheáie ‖ cătínă, CAPIDAN 148

KEYED UP *adj.* (a)scumbusit; **to be ~ for smth.** ▾(a)scumbuséscu ‖ bag poálile m-brâu, BASME 682

KHAKI *adj.* cachí *invar.*

KIBOSH *vb.* âľ vin di indiháche (*or* âľ vin di induháche) → PUT THE ~ ON SMB.

KICK *s.* cloáţă, cluţátă, culţátă, scluţátă, sculţátă; *N:* asclóţă

KICK *vb.* arúc (*or* trag) cluţắţ, dau cu scloáţa, ľi am nă cluţátă, cluţuéscu; (*to hit*) ▾âmprăñéscu

KICK THE BUCKET *vb.* li tíndu → DIE

KICK UP A ROW *vb.* (*to make a scene*) fac ghiurultíe

KICK UP ONE'S HEELS *vb.* li tíndu → DIE

KICK UP A DUST *vb.* (*to put on airs*) li trag groáse

KID *s.* **1.** (*of a goat*) ied, ed; mľor, mbľor *m*; mbľoáră *f*, mľoáră ‖ *GSus, SJos, Av:* iat, *pl* iăţ, CL 253; **2.** (*little boy, child*) piciu, ficiurác, ficiuríc, ficiurúş; *coll* (*of children*) cuchiláme

KIDNAP *vb.* ▾aráp, ▾aráchiu, ▾aráchéscu, arichéscu, archéscu

KIDNAPPED *adj.* arăchít, arăpút

KIDNAPPING *s.* arăchíre, arăcheáre, arăchitúră, arăpíre

KIDNEY *s.* *anat.* arnícľu *m*, rinícľu *m*, buburéc *m*, níre ‖ *GSus:* buréc, CL 40

KILL *vb.* ▾(a)spárgu; *also:* arcutéscu, ▾cher, cúlcu mpáde, ▾dizmáţ, ▾dispântic, ▾disúflu, ischédz, mâc, ľ-aláxéscu Stă-Víñirea, ľ-astíngu bána, ľ-astíngu cándíla, ľ-astíngu ţeára, ľ-ľau dzúua, ľau pri gúşe, ncrupuľédz, ncurpilédz, ngrupiľédz, pipiléscu, ▾spăstréscu, ▾spântic, súrpu, ▾uţíd, ▾vátăm, *N*: vátăn; vérsu máţăle; **Have you ~ed him?** L-disuflát? **Kill them all!** Ischeáţ-ľi pri tuţ! **You wanted to ~ me, you pagan!** Vruşi s-mi mâţi, óre pângâne! (*to survive smb.*) ľ-mâc colíva; mor; **I'll ~ you!** Va ti mor! **Are you not afraid that they may ~ you?** Nu ţ-u frícă s nu ti ncurpiľádză? **The enemy ~ed him** Lu-ncrupuľé duş-mánlu; **in order to ~ him** ca s-lu áibă spăstrítă

KILL TIME *vb.* ▾şintéscu

KILLED *adj.* aspártu, vătămát, vătănát, murít; (~ *by a bullet*) curşumát; ncurpiľát, spăstrít

KILLING *s.* vătămáre, vătănáre, arucutíre → MASSACRE

KILOGRAM *s.* chilódhram

KILOMETER *s.* chilómetru

KIN *s.* fáră, dzinúcľu; di un sândze

KIND *s.* turlíe, luyíe, sóie, sórtă; **all ~ of beautiful things** muşitéţ turlíi-turlíi; **He understands what ~ of person she is** U veáde ţe luyíe eáste; **all ~ of birds** puľ di túte sóíle (*or* sóǐ di sóǐ di puľ); **all ~ of goods** părmătíi di toáte sórtile (*or* di toáte turlíǐle); **There are all ~ of people** Săntu sórte-sórte di oámiñ ‖ **with all ~ of forms** cu soi di soi di formă, HRISTU 23; (*creature*) plázmâ; **What ~ of man is he?** Ţi plázmâ di om eásti aéstu? DIARO 307 → ALL ~ OF

KIND *adj.* bun, *m pl* buñ; (*very ~*) oáie al-Dumnidză (*lit.* 'God's sheep') → MILD

KINDHEARTED *adj.* bun, *m pl* buñ; ñil(ă)ós, -oásă

KINDLED *adj.* ncălurát

KINDLY *adv.* cu búnlu; **Try ~, man!** ≈ Vedz cu búnlu, bre crăştíne!

KINDNESS *s.* uminíľe ‖ DIARO 43: adâmlâchi

KINDRED *s.* sóie → RELATIVE

KINFOLKS *s.* → RELATIVE

KING *s.* văsilé (*and* vâ-), *N*: băsilău; (*a playing card*) ríya *m*, ríyañ *pl* ‖ (a *playing card*) préftu, DIARO 278 (*lit.* 'priest')

KINGDOM *s.* vasíliu [•sí•liŭ], văsilíe; (*state*) đuvléte

KINGLET *s. orn.* amirărúş, aroátă, cucuşúră; tripusáchĭ [•sák']
m

KINGLY *adj.* amirăréscu, amiréscu, văsilchéscu; **a ~ feast** meásă
văsilcheáscă

KINGLY *adv.* văsilcheáşte

KING'S EVIL *s. vet.* glíndură, plăscáre, prăscáre, priscáre,
sirigé, şirigé, sărăgé, sărăgeáe

KINK *s.* (*twist*) aruşuţâre; *med.* cârciór

KINSHIP *s.* sóie, yiñáuă, cuscríľe

KINSMAN *s.* sóie, di un sându ‖ *Cru:* fărtát, 215

KINSWOMAN *s.* → KINSMAN

KIP *s.* cheále → HIDE

KIRSCH *s.* (*a drink*) vişinátă, vişinádhă

KISMET *s.* căsméte

KISS *s.* băşeáre, băşáre, hiritisíre; (*a ~ on the eye*) ócľu; (*a
~ sent on the tip of one's fingers*) mătúľ

KISS *vb.* ▾baş; (*to ~ a lot*) spribáş; ▾guguştédz, guguştéscu;
(*to ~ smb. furtively on the eye*) fur un ócľu; (*to ~ an icon*) hiritiséscu

KISSING *s.* băşeáre, băşáre, hiritisíre

KITCHEN *s.* mayiryió, mayiuryió; *G:* mutváche ‖ *Cru:* măyirió, 234

KITCHEN STOVE *s. N:* şporét

KITE *n* (*toy*) zmeu; *Bit, Cru:* litácică [•tâĉ•kă], pitáche;
(*hawk*) ghirăchínă → FALCON

KITTEN *s.* ‖ *GSus:* cătuşíţă; *Av, Prv, SJos:* cătuşóplu, CL 41;
ALIA 17: cătuşícu; *also:* cătuşóc, cătuşóp, măţúc, macióc, mai-
cióc, pisóc

KLATCH *s.* (*informal conversation*) láfe

KNACK *s.* (*aptitude, skill*) háre ‖ PC: (*secret, key*) sórtă, cusúre; **I found its ~!** Ľ-aflái cusúrea!

KNAPSACK *s.* tástru

KNAVE *s.* antártu, antíhristu, cătúnă, ceapcân, edepsâz, zgrumát

KNAVERY *s.* cătăryăríľe, ceapcânlắche, edepsăzlắche, ilée

KNEAD *vb.* (*usu. dough*) ▾fărmíntu, firmíntu, fărmít, firmít; (*to
massage, to torment*) ▾zdrúmin, zdroámin ‖ (*to ~ dough*) disfíngu,

CAPIDAN 151

KNEADING s. frimintáre, frimitáre, frimtáre, firmintáre, firmitáre

KNEADING-TROUGH s. cuvắtă, căpisteáre; (a small ~ with two
handles) rácică [rác•kă], pl ráciche; pidhupinác (and pidupinác)

KNEE s. dzinúcl̯u, pl dzinúcl̯e ‖ also: dzinúchiu, ALIA 172; **Amc,
Fal, Smx:** ginúcl̯u, **An:** dzănucl̯u, B-ARCH 172; HRISTU 81: dzănuchl̯ă

KNEE vb. ndzinucl̯édz, ndzinúcl̯u, cad pri dzinúcl̯e, paracád

KNEELING s. ndzinucl̯áre

KNICKKNACK s. minuţắl̯e, pl minuţắl̯

KNIFE s. cuţút, cắţút, dim. cắţutáş, cắţutíc, cuţutíciu; (large
~, as for meat) sătâre, curtélă

KNIFE vb. (to stab) plântu cuţútlu

KNIFE DEALER s. cuţâtár, cắţutár

KNIFE-HANDLE s. mânár, mâneáre

KNIT s. cărlíg, cinghilác, andreáuă, undreáuă

KNIT vb. (a)mplătéscu; **to ~ one's brows** dipún dzeánile

KNITTED adj. (of brows) misticát

KNITTING s. chindisíre, ncărdzil̯eáre, mplitíre

KNITTING NEEDLE s. andreáuă, cârlíg (and căr-) di mplătíre,
cinghilác, ţinghilác ‖ **Peş:** cinghilát, CL 43

KNOB s. (rounded hill) óhtu, túmbă

KNOCK s. aguditúră

KNOCK vb. ▾ciucutéscu; **to ~ smb. into a cocked hat** (to beat severely) ndărséscu di chiutécă ‖ STERGHIU 13: dau; **He knocked at
the door twice and the master of the house came out** Deáde dáuă
ori pi poártă ş-l̯i insí huzmicheárlu a cásil̯ei

KNOCK DOWN vb. ▾arăstórnu, cúlcu mpáde, dau di páde, dărm,
▾răzuéscu, ruzuéscu, ▾súrpu, zdupănéscu, zdupunéscu ‖ zdupuséscu,
DIARO 120

KNOCK OFF vb. (to stop doing smth.) ▾acúmtin; (of prices) eftinipséscu; (to kill) aspárgu; (to rob) dispól̯u ‖ (of price)
alás, PARALLELE 144

KNOCK OVER vb. arăstórnu → OVERTURN

KNOCK SMB. TO FITS vb. scot míntea

KNOCK SPOTS OFF SMB. vb. ansár, ▾úmflu

KNOCK THE END IN/OFF vb. (to mar, to spoil) l̯-u adár bóză ‖
CUNIA 247: cálcu tu pítă

KNOCK TO PIECES vb. fac bucătíce, fac mâşcătúri-mâşcătúri, adár bucắţ, fac búcắţ (di bucắţ), disíc cumátă di cumátă

KNOCKDOWN s. zdupăníre, zdupuníre

KNOCKED DOWN adj. zdupănít

KNOCKED UP adj. (with work) dişilát

KNOLL s. óhtu

KNOT s. (in a thread) nod, nudătúră, píscu; (in a board, on a branch) aróz; **Gop:** cluj, **Smr:** jóngu

KNOT vb. ▾(a)nód, nudédz, ▾leg; **Knot the end of the rope!** Noádă cáplu di fórtumă!

KNOTTED adj. (a)nudát

KNOTTING s. (a)nudáre

KNOTTY adj. nodurós, aruzós, aruzusít, aruzeárcu, amzárcu

KNOW vb. ▾ştiu, **N:** sciu [scĭŭ], ñ-acắţă míntea, ñ-acắţă mâna, ñ-ľa ócľul (la), ▾apúc; (to be acquainted with) cunóscu; **Who knows? Cári-şti? N:** Cái-şci? **I don't ~ N:** Ciú-ştu? **This is the way we have known it of old** Acşí apucắm di pap-străpáp; **I/we don't know (who did it)!** ≈ Dhispóti! (lit. 'the bishop!'); **I ~ nothing about that** Nu-ñ cunóscu di lúcrulu aéstu; (to ~ smth. very well) pára-cunóscu; **to ~ a thing ot two** (to have had a lot of experience) 1 sg pt: âñ tricú rúglu prit náre; **to ~ how to speak** (as a foreign language) li-arúmig, li-aroámig; **to ~ inside out** ştiu pri dzeádite ‖ ştiu ca ápa, BASME 404

KNOW SMB. INTIMATELY vb. ‖ sáre ş-pâne mâcắm deadún (lit. 'we eat together salt and bread'), PARALLELE 127

KNOW THE ROPES vb. hiu fricát; âñ tricú rúglu prit náre

KNOW-HOW s. (expertise, skill, knowledge) chicazmó

KNOWING adj. şciút, achicắsít, mắstur

KNOWLEDGE s. cunoáştire, cunuşteáre ‖ **medical ~** ghitrắştízmă, VELO 98

KNOWLEDGEABLE adj. achicắsít, sciút, cunuscutór, cazamíe; **He is very ~** Cazamíe şi-eáste ‖ **He is very ~** u-ari mintea patru suti (lit. 'his mind is four hundred'); ári mínti şi la cur (lit. 'he/she has mind even at his/her ass'), DIARO 389

KNOWN adj. ştiút, cunuscút

KNUCKLE BONE s. vâşcľé, vâsiľé; also: alumă, anumă, amádhă, a(r)şíc, işíc, cócan, cociu; **N:** cuñác; ip; **Ohr:** ípă; mişíc; **Smr:** năíp; níp; (p)sáltu, sáutu [sáŭ-]; **N:** vángă m (sic); zbángu m

KOPECK s. cắpíc m

KORAN *s.* curán
KRAUT *s.* vérdzu di moáre

L

LABEL *s.* (*ticket, tag*) vulutínă
LABOR *s.* (*effort*) ayoánă, ayónă, ayunsíre, pidhipsíre; (*hard ~*)
hămălâche, hămălíche; *phys.* **Cru:** ~ híuri *f pl*, híme *f pl*
LABOR *vb.* lucrédz, píngu oáhte → WORK
LABORED *adj.* angricós, -oásă
LABORER → DAY ~
LABORIOUSLY *adv.* cu ócľi cripáţ
LACE *s.* ceapráz, găitán, găitáne; (*of gold or silk*) măgór;
(*cord, string*) báir, lutráe, utráe, truşínă; (*for trimming
sleeves, etc.*) bénchi *f pl*
LACEMAKER *s.* găităngí
LACE SMB.'S COAT / JACKET *vb.* (*to thrash, to tan smb.'s hide*)
ľ-scútur yicălu
LACK *s.* (*need, deficiency*) héră, scárţu, xíche
LACK *vb.* nu am (*lit. 'I do not have'*); **They ~ food** Nu-áu ciu-
meálă; **What do you ~?** Ţe ţ-u héra?
LACK PEP *vb.* *3 sg:* nu-ári yústu; **Wrangle without beating lacks
pep** Ncăceáre fâră băteáre nu-ári yústu
LACONIC *adj.* scúrtu, şcúrtu, *m pl* -rţâ, *f pl* -rte
LACRIMATION *s.* (*weeping*) lăcrămáre, lăcărmáre
LAD *s.* firfărúş, junóp
LADDER *s.* scáră
LADDIE *s.* junóp
LADEN *adj.* (*loaded*) ncărcát

LADLE *s.* hleárǎ, ciubánǎ; (*large* ~) ciútǔrǎ, ciútrǎ

LADY *s.* doámnǎ, **F:** doámǎ (*with the specific mn > m*); nicuchírǎ; (*usu. well dressed*) madámǎ, chiráuǎ, chiréuǎ, afindoáñe ‖ (*a bey's wife and fig.*) biancâ [bi•], DIARO 122-23

LADY-BIRD *s. ent.* (*lady-bug*) pǎscǎlíţǎ ‖ **GSus:** fítur, CL 45

LADY-BUG *s.* → LADY-BIRD

LADY-DAY *s.* (*March 25*) Vanghilizmó, Vanghilizmóu

LADYLOVE *s.* vrútǎ

LAG *s.* coáda (*lit. 'the tail'*)

LAG *vb.* ‖ PC: ar(ǎ)mân tu coádǎ

LAG *s.* (*of a barrel*) doágǎ, *pl* doádze *and* dodzǐ

LAGGARD *s.* alǎsǎtúrǎ, amǎnǎtór

LAGGING *adj.* ayálnic, yeaváşcu, amǎnǎtór

LAIR *s.* culcúş, pitúľu; (*a bear's* ~) **N:** bulóc

LAKE *s.* lac, ghióle; **Alpine** ~ nduhúñe

LAM *vb.* (*to flee hastily*) fug di nu mi ved → BOLT; (*to thrash*) bat, ciuléscu di bǎteáre, cruéscu un sumár, parabát, pǎpuriséscu, trag unǎ cǎláe, tuchéscu di bǎteáre

LAMB *s.* ñel *m*, ñáuǎ *or* ñálǎ *f; dim.* ñilúş, ñilíc, miľúr, mbľor, mľor *m*, mbľoárǎ, mľoárǎ *f;* (*lamb attached to people*) mânár; (*viewed as food*) ñel; cárne di mľor

LAMBASTE *vb.* → BEAT

LAMBDA *s.* lávdǎ

LAMBENT *adj.* (*marked by lightness*) luñinós, noásǎ

LAMBSKIN *s.* cheále, arñeacó

LAME *adj.* ş(c)ľop, -ľoápǎ, -ľochi, -ľoápe; tupál → MAIM

LAMEBRAIN *s.* glár → STUPID

LAMENT *vb.* buţéscu; *also:* arǎbdǎséscu, arǎvdǎséscu, arǎdǎséscu, arǎbdiséscu, arǎdhǎpséscu, cântu, ▼deápir, ▼jiléscu, ▼lipiséscu; ▼nilséscu, nǎlséscu, ▼plângu, şcľumurédz, zghiléscu ‖ (*for someone*) miryiuluséscu, DIARO 137

LAMENTATION *s.* boáţit, deápir, plângu; *also:* ciunáre, ciuñáre, ciuñát, cântic di mórtu, yonghizmó, miryiulóy, miryiulóiu, miryiuluxíre

LAMIA *s.* lámñe

LAMMERGEIER *s. orn.* stavraít → VULTURE

LAMP *s.* videálǎ, lámbǎ (*and* lámpǎ), lumínǎ → OIL-BURNING ~

LAMP-LIGHTER *s.* lambagí

LAND

LAND s. loc, uscát → DRY ~; (~ *good for plowing*) agru ‖ **Peş:** avrác, CL 38

LAND vb. (*to catch, as fish*) acáţ

LAND SMB. A BLOW vb. plăscănéscu únă ‖ amín únă, BASME 103

LANDLORD s. cifleaccí, ciufleaccí ‖ **Cru:** găzdắ, 217

LANE s. călíce, călişoárắ

LANGOR s. alăsáre, slăbeáţắ, slăbíľe, slăbínţă; ni-mucaéte

LANGOROUS adj. → LANGUISHING

LANGUAGE s. límbă, graiu; **abusive** ~ angiuráre, zbor di péză

LANGUID adj. lángur, lângurós, -oásă; mulăşcu, m pl -şţâ

LANGUISH vb. (*to linger, to lead a passive existence*) putri-dzắscu

LANGUISHING adj. lángur, lăngurós (*and* lân-), lungurós

LANKY adj. ciurligán, -ánă, -áñ, -áne

LANTERN s. fănáre, finére, filinár ‖ STERE 23: găziníc

LAP s. poálă, pudhyeáo, puryeáo, puzgheáuă

LAP vb. (*to fold*) dhipluséscu, ndhipluséscu

LAPEL s. ceapchén, cipchén, cipchéne

LAPFUL s. poálă (di)

LAPIDATE vb. (*to stone*) ▾ambuliséscu

LAPPET s. LAPEL

LAPSE vb. cad, hămbluséscu

LARCENY s. ciunáre → THEFT

LARCH s. dzádă

LARD s. usắndză, usắndze, axúnghe, pastó ‖ **Gop:** lígdă, GOLAB 232; **SJos:** ploáce, CL 259 ‖ **GSus:** lardí, **Mul:** lărdí, **Pro:** lărdhíe; **Amc, An, Arγ, Fal, Kat, Lep, Mi, Na, Pur, Src, Vil:** seu, B-ARCH 362

LANDAU s. carétă, cucíe, dálingă, tálingă; paitóne, caleáşcă, că-

LANDLORD s. cifleaccí

LARDON s. pastó ‖ ALR 1126: cumátă di lárdu

LARDOON s. → LARDON

LARGE adj. máre, m pl mắri *and* mari → BIG, SET AT ~

LARGESS(E) s. cuvurdhălâche

LARK s. orn. ciuciuríle, ciuciurleáiu, ciuciulán, ciuciulán; **Clis:** ciurleáiu; ţurţuleán; (*crested* ~) picurár ‖ **Prv:** caciulér, CL 40

LASCIVIOUS *adj.* dişuţât, azdisít

LASH *vb.* (*to whip; to blow, as of a cold wind*) frâştuéscu, jir-tuéscu, jurtuéscu, păléscu cu zvícilu + tuléscu, zăpăléscu, zăpătéscu

LASH *vb.* (*to bind*) ▾leg

LASHINGS *s.* (*lots of*) múltu *m/n*, múltă *f*, múlţâ *m pl*, múlte *f/n pl*

LASS *s.* feátă, fărfăľúşe

LASSIE *s.* → LASS

LASSITUDE *s.* alăsáre, curmáre, anusţâre

LASSO *s.* pidichíe; (a)láţ

LAST *s.* (*boot-last*) călăpódhe, călupódhe, călăpe, călúpe

LAST *adj.* din coádă; **during the ~ few months** tu méşiľ din coá-dă; dit soni; (*worst*) cudár; **the ~** coáda *invar.*; **~ night** ástă noápte; **~ winter** ástă ĭárnă; **at ~** artâc ‖ CUVATA 23: (*finally*) neise → BE ON ONE'S ~ LEGS

LAST *vb.* (*to survive, to endure*) ţân, şed; (*to ~ for a long time*) fturséscu ‖ ALR 783: ţăn; (*to continue, to go on, as of rain*) ţâne *3 sg* (*lit. 'holds'*), PARALLELE 135

LAST *adv.* tu coádă, tu sóne

LAST NAME *s.* ‖ paranúmă, 240

LATCH *s.* (*as in a door or gate*) clápă

LATCH *vb.* acáţ

LATCHET *s.* báir, truşínă; (*sandal strap*) nujíţă

LATE *adj.* (*after the usual or proper time*) amânát, tárdu, -rdă, -rdzâ, -rde; ntărdát; târ(d)zâu, -âie, *m/f pl* -âi; (*of a dead person*) ľirtát, dum-ľirtát; **your ~ grandmother** dumlirtáta di mă-ta; **to be too ~ in the field** ≈ arămân ca găľína údă

LATE *adv.* târdzâu; *also:* amânát, ntárdu, pára-oáră, paráură, şintít; **He is ~** Nu lu áre *or* Nu-şi lu-áre; **She is ~** Nu u áre *or* Nu-şi u-áre; **to be ~** ▾amân, ntărdédz; **Why are you ~?** Ţe amânáşi? **I am ~ because they put me off** Ñ-amânái că ñ-mi-amânáră; **We will be back ~** Vai amnăm s-yiním → BE TOO ~ IN THE FIELD

LATECOMER *s.* amânătór

LATER *adv.* ma năpói, ma nclo

LATH *s.* şíndră, pitávră, pitrăye; (*thin board*) apélă; **as thin as a ~** (*of people*) slăghít ca hiľán

LATHE *s.* strug ‖ *Prv:* zmilárĭe, CL 264

LATHER

LATHER *s.* spúmă → FOAM; (*dither*) hórhut, hirbeáre, heárbire

LATIN *s.* (*language*) latineásca; *adj.* lătinéscu, -eáscă

LATISH IN THE DAY *adv.* di cătră seáră

LATRINE *s.* işitór; *also:* căcăstoáre, **Grb:** căcăríu; căcătór, chinéfe, chişitór, halé, hríe, muştiréche

LATTEN *s.* (*tinplate*) pafíl

LATTICE *s.* cánghil

LAUD *s.* (*praise*) alávdă

LAUD *vb.* (*to praise*) ▾alávdu, ▾álţu

LAUGH *s.* arâs → LAUGHTER

LAUGH *vb.* ▾(a)râd, aríd (→ § 32); **~ oneself to death** arâd di mi lişín → SHRIEK WITH LAUGHTER

LAUGH UP ONE'S BEARD / SLEEVE *vb.* arâd pri su mustăţ

LAUGHINGLY *adv* cu arădeáre

LAUGHING-STOCK *s.* rizíľe, başúrlu a hoárălei, şúpirlu a li étă, şúpirlu a lúmiľei, mâscâroáña a lúmiľei ‖ DIARO 111: arizí-li, chipazé ; *He/she.* *is everybody's* **~** eásti ti curóidhu

LAUGHTER *s.* arâs, arâsut, arădeáre; **burst of ~** cachín → SHRIEK WITH ~

LAUNCH *vb.* (*to start*) nchiséscu, purnéscu; **to ~ out into** u bag tu *or* u bag pri

LAUREL *s.* *bot.* lávru, dáfnu, dáfin; (*leaf*) dáf(i)nă, váie

LAUREL BRANCH *s.* váie

LAVENDER WATER *s.* livándă

LAVISH *adj.* (*abundant*) bólcu, -lţi, -lţe; chíhtră *invar.*; (*generous*) cuvurdhă; giumértu, -rtă, -rţâ, -rte ‖ (*bestowing profusely*) CUNIA 261: aspărgătór

LAVISHLY *adv.* bólcu, chíhtră

LAW *s.* nom, zacóñu, zayón; **Ohr:** *obs.* leádze → TAKE THE ~

LAWSUIT *s.* ayuyíe, críse, giudicátă ‖ **Cru:** dăvíe, GOLAB 211

LAWYER *s.* avucát, dhichiyór

LAX *adj.* (*slack, loose, as of a belt*) distrés; (*having loose bowels*) căcătós; cufurít, cufuyeár, cufiryiós, cufurós

LAXATIVE *s.* cathártic, chiníse, chinitcó

LAY *adj.* (*secular*) cuzmicán, -áñ; laicó, *m pl* -cádz

LAY *vb.* ▾apún; **I laid my head on the pillow** Ñ-apúş cáplu pri căpitâñu; (*as: to ~ the table; also of falling snow*) ▾astérnu; ▾tíndu; **She shows up wherever a table is laid** Iu-i meása teásă, na-u ş ñâsă! [naŭ şnâ•să]

LAY A BET *vb.* mi acáţ cu báste

LAY A PLOT *vb.* cruéscu uñă căpáñe, plitéscu mplititúră

LAY A SNARE *vb.* bag stăpínţă → SET A TRAP

LAY A WAGER *vb.* → LAY A BET

LAY BARE *vb.* ▾guléscu → STRIP

LAY BLAME ON SMB. *vb.* arúc biléia pri, arúc fáia pri

LAY BY *vb.* icunumiséscu

LAY DOWN ONE'S ARMS *vb.* dipún ármile ‖ (*command*) Bâgáţ ármili-n-pádi! DIARO 370

LAY DOWN EVERYTHING *vb.* (*to sacrifice*) ñ-víndu luñína

LAY DOWN ONE'S LIFE *vb.* mi fac curbáne, cad curbáne

LAY EGGS *vb.* fet oáuă; **Doves ~ many times a year** Porúnghiľ feátă múlte ori tru an

LAY HOLD OF *vb.* (*to seize*) ▾acáţ

LAY IN A STOCK FOR WINTER *vb.* (*of food*) bag arnátic

LAY ONE'S HANDS (UP)ON *vb.* (*to catch, to capture*) bag mână pi

LAY SMTH. AT SMB.'S DOOR *vb.* (*to attribute, to blame*) arúc biléia pri, arúc fáia pri

LAY THE FOUNDATION / CORNER-STONE OF *vb.* bag par, thimiľuséscu

LAY THE TABLE *vb.* bag meása, ▾ndreg meása

LAY TO HEART *vb.* ▾amărédz, bag mără → TAKE TO HEART

LAY WASTE *vb.* şcretuéscu → DEVASTATE

LAYER *s.* strat; (*as of wool*) dhíplă; (*~ in a pie*) pétur; (*~ of earth, of stones*) arádhă; (*~ of snow, of hackled wool*) (a)pálă; **Snow began to fall abundantly** Neáua loa s-cádă pále, pále; (*~ of snow*) plásă

LAYING *s.* (*of eggs*) uuáre [u•ŭá•ri], uáre [u•á•ri]

LAYMAN *s.* cuzmián, laicó

LAYOFF *s.* scărchíre, ni-lúcru

LAYOUT *s.* (*arrangement*) arádhă; (*order*) nizáme

LAZE *vb.* ñ-angreácă

LAZINESS *s.* leáne, timbilâche

LAZY *adj* linăvós (*and* linâ-); *also:* acămát, (a)durñít, adhú-liftu, ambuţós, angricós, ápract, áprahtu, armăsătór, blanés, cacavátră, cinúşi-bibiľár, cioáre tu cinúşe, ciumagáră, *pl* ciumăgárañ; ciúşe *m*, ciúşañ *pl*; cúmban, edéc, haileás, hăileán, haín, hâín, haramulái, *pl* haramuláiañ; linós, mulắşcu, ni-adu-

LAZYBONES

chít, prăhár, tăvlâmbă *m*, tăvlâmboáñe *f*; timbél, tíndu-yómar; (~ *woman*) vacareásă ‖ BASME 512: áyru-cúmban ‖ *Cru:* iavaşlí *m*, iavaşloáñe *f*, GOLAB 223; *G, P:* haileáz, SarD 27; *Mul:* dângău; *Gra, Grăm, Hor:* dimbél; *Fal:* linuvós, B-ARCH 251 ‖ STERGHIU 28: linós

LAZYBONES *s.* timbél → LAZY

LEAD *s.* (*metal*) mulív, mulíve, pĺúmbu ‖ ALIA 33 (*rare*) plúmbu; *Pur:* mulíf, *Grăm:* mulíd, B-ARCH 33

LEAD *vb.* (*to cover or treat with lead*) mulidhuséscu

LEAD *vb.* (*to take, to bring*) duc, ambáir; (*of a road*) ▾acáţ, ▾apúc, ĺau; (*to conduct, as a hora*) ▾(a)pórtu; (*to run in a specific direction*) ies, aor. i(n)şíi *or* i(n)şái; **This path ~s to the river** Cálea aéstă iáse la arâu; (*to be ahead, as in a contest or a game*) éscu tu câp ‖ (*to command, to teach, to care for*) am tu mână, DIARO 284; (*to lay one's will on smb.*) trag di náre, BATSARIA 25

LEAD A DISORDERLY LIFE *vb.* ▾distórcu, ▾dişúţ → BECOME DISSOLUTE

LEAD A HAND-TO-MOUTH EXISTENCE *vb.* bat tămbărălu

LEAD ASTRAY *vb.* (*to set at fault*) fac buzgúne

LEAD AWAY IN CHAINS *vb.* (*to take prisoner*) ĺau sclav

LEAD A WONDERFUL LIFE *vb.* trag nă bánă ca di amirádz

LEAD IN *vb.* ▾bag

LEAD SMB. A MERRY CHASE *vb.* gioc pi tăpsíe, ancálţu şi discálţu

LEAD SMB. BY THE NOSE *vb.* trag di nări

LEAD SMB. INTO A FIGHT *vb.* ĺ-gioc únă hunére

LEAD SMB. IN(TO) THE RIGHT WAY *vb.* adúc pri cále driptática

LEADER *s.* (*boss*) ma máre, cap; câp, *pl* câpi *and* câchi; seíz; **Who is your ~?** Voi cari avéţ cap? **The ~ should drink first** Prótlu bea câplu; (*in some games*) múmă; **This game implies a ~** Gióclu aéstu şi-áre múmă ‖ *Cru:* (~ *of a guerrilla detachment*) vuivodă, GOLAB 259

LEAF *s.* frúndză (*and* frúnză), frândză; (*dead, dry* ~) şúmcă → PUT ON LEAVES ‖ *Cĺis, Gra:* fréndză, B-ARCH 45

LEAF *vb.* (*as of trees*) nfrundzăscu

LEAFY *adj.* frândzós, -oásă

LEAK *s.* (*hole*) gúvă; (*crack*) cripitúră, firídhă

LEAK *vb.* cur, ascáp

LEAKAGE *s.* (*loss, waste*) fíră

LEAN *adj.* s(c)lab; (*of meat*) mácru, amágru → BECOME ~

LEAN *vb.* ▼arádzim, arădzâm, ▼(a)ndoápăr, ▼(a)ndoápir, ▼ândúper, ▼andúpur, ▼andrupăscu, ▼acumbuséscu, ▼acumséscu; **to ~ on one's elbow** mi ndoápăr pri únlu cod

LEAP *s.* (a)săltáre

LEAP *adj.* (~ *year*) viséct, *m pl* -ctâ

LEAP FOR JOY *vb.* (a)sáltu di hroa ‖ BASME 430: gioc pri únlu cior

LEAP OVER *vb.* antrisár (*and* andri-), astrisár

LEARN *vb.* (*to find out*) ▼áflu, ľau di hăbáre, veţ, (a)nvéţ; ~ **how to read and write** ▼nvéţ cárte

LEARNED *adj.* nviţát, ştiút; **the ~** *s.* iliumáie *f sg*, iliumăi *pl*

LEARNING *s.* (*knowledge, education*) nviţătúră, yrámote *f pl*; cunoáştire, cunuşteáre

LEASE *s.* báltu; (*of horses*) ayuyi(p)síree ‖ (*of land*) **Peş:** igiáre, CL 255

LEASE *vb.* (*of horses*) ayuyi(p)séscu

LEASH *s.* cureáuă, **N:** curáo

LEAST → AT LEAST

LEATHER *s.* mişíne, misíne, cheále

LEATHER BOTTLE *s.* útre → SATCHEL

LEAVE *s.* (*authorized absence*) pápse, *pl* păpsuri; **to take one's ~** alás sănătáte → TAKE ~

LEAVE *vb.* (*to depart*) ▼duc, fug, nchiséscu, mi trag, ñ-ľau óčiiľ (di-acló), litéscu, (*rare*) ▼plec; u adún (coáda), u frângu; (*to cause or allow to be or remain in a specified con-dition*) ▼(a)lás ‖ fac; **Which way did he ~?** Cătră iu feáţe? BASME 427; STERGHIU 4, CUVATA 4: ñ-ľau calea

LEAVE A LEGACY TO SMB. *vb.* (*to bequeath*) ľ-alás dhyeátă

LEAVE ALONE *vb.* dau bánă, (a)lás (tu síyă); **He did not leave me alone even for a second** Nu-ñ da bánă un minút; **~ me alone, mother!** Lásă-ñ-me, dádo! ‖ CUVATA 15: lu-alás arăháti

LEAVE A MESSAGE *vb.* ‖ BASME 6: ľ-alás zbor

LEAVE (FAR) BEHIND *vb.* ľau loc múltu

LEAVE IN PEACE *vb.* → LEAVE ALONE

LEAVE NO STONE UNTURNED *vb.* tórnu lóclu anápudha; (*to do all in one's power*) mi fac páde

LEAVE ON SMB.'S CARE / RESPONSIBILITY *vb.* (*of an upleasant task*) ţi lo-alás pri zvércă-ţi (*lit.* 'I am leaving him / it on

LEAVE

your nape'), PARALLELE 135

LEAVE SMB. PENNILESS *vb.* (*as at cards*) (a)fuléscu (di parádz)

LEAVEN *s.* (*yeast*) maiáuă, măiáuă [-ĭá-]

LEAVEN *vb.* (*to prepare dough*) apríND aluát; mpărlíg

LEAVE-TAKING *s.* dúcă → DEPARTURE; (*farewell*) cále-ambár

LEAVING BEHIND *s.* antreáţire, astreáţire

LEAVINGS *s.* armăsătúră

LECHER *s.* futeái, *pl* futeáiañ

LECHERY *s.* curvărisíre; **to indulge in ~** curvăriséscu

LECTURE *s.* (*reproof*) zăvráche, zbárdhu

LECTURE *vb.* (*to scold*) culimbiséscu

LEECH *s. zool.* avdhélă, arveáuă, arvélă; *G:* pihávíţă; piuvíţă, sulĭúcă, (*rare*) sulúche) ‖ TULLIU 55: arveálă; *GSus:* dvélă

LEEK *s. bot.* preaş, praş, preas; **head of a leek** bărbútă di praş → EAT THE ~

LEER *s.* mutrítă

LEERY *adj.* ‖ PC: cu pripús

LEES *s.* ţípură → DREGS

LEFT *adj.* (a)stângu, -ngă, -ndzi, -ndze; **to the ~** astânga, nastânga; **on the ~ hand side** la stânga, a stânga, di nastânga

LEFT (*part. of* LEAVE) armás; **~ in the basket** (*disappointed, loser*) (armás) ca găľína údă; (armás) ca Sultána cu ucălu

LEFT EYE *s.* astângul

LEFT HAND *s.* astânga

LEFT-HAND *adj.* → LEFT; **on the ~ side** la stânga, a stânga, di nastânga

LEFT-HANDED *adj.* astângu; stângáciu, stângár, váncu (*and* văncu, văngu); zérvu, -rvă, -ryi, -rve

LEFTOVER *s.* armăsătúră, (a)réstu

LEFTWARD(S) *adv.* nastânga, astânga

LEG *s.* cior, ciciór, ciuciór; *S, P:* chiciór; *dim.* ciuciurúş; ciun, ciúciul, *pl* ciúce *or* ciúciule; *derog.* chilúnghe; **I'll break your legs!** Va-ţ frângu chilúnghea! (*of a child or animal*) pátă; (*of trousers*) sfrágan, pudhunár → BE ON ONE'S LAST ~S ‖ (*of pants*) *Peş:* pădhănáre, CL 258

LEGENDARY MAN *s.* (*in folklore*) şóşe, *m pl* şóşeañ

LEGION *s.* (*multitude*); **their name is ~** ≈ ca sprúna ş-ca arína; (múlţâ *m pl,* múlte *f, n pl*) câte steále (*lit.* 'like stars'); ñiľ di ñiľ (*lit.* '*thousands of thousands*')

LEGITIMATELY *adv.* driptátic, driptáticǎ

LEGUME *s.* → VEGETABLE

LEISURE *s.* zaharéñ *f pl*

LEISURELY *adj., adv.* pri-agálea

LEMON *s.* limón, limóñe ‖ *Cru:* limoáñe, GOLAB 232

LEMON TREE *s.* chítru, limóñu, limuñéu

LEMONADE *s.* limunádhǎ

LEMONADE MAN *s.* limun(ǎ)gí

LEMON-COLORED *adj.* limuníş

LEND *vb.* ▼mprumút, ▼mprumutédz (and *mbru-*), mprǎmutédz

LEND WINGS TO *vb.* dau vímtu (*lit.* '*to give wind*')

LEND WITH INTEREST *vb.* tuchiséscu

LENDING WITH INTEREST *s.* tuchisíre

LENGTH *s.* lundzíme, lundzeáme

LENGTHEN *vb.* ▼lundzéscu, spirlundzéscu

LENGTHENING *s.* spirlundzíre, lundzíre

LENGTHWISE *adv.* di-a-lúngului

LENIENCY *s.* imireáţǎ, imiráme

LENIENT *adj.* ímir, yeaváşcu, ayálnic

LENT *s.* câşleágǎ, *pl* câslédzi *and* câşleádze; cǎrleágǎ (*or* câr-)

LENTIL *s. bot.* línte (*and* línde), fáo, fáuǎ

LENTISK *s.* (*mastic tree*) mǎstícǎ, mǎstíhe

LEPER *s. med.* léprǎ; (*of a person*) cǎsidhyeár

LEPROSY *s.* léprǎ

LEPROUS *adj* liprós, cǎsidhyeár

LESION *s.* (a)ránǎ

LESS *adv.* nghios

LESS *prep.* fǎrǎ, fârǎ, fǎr-di

-LESS fǎrǎ de, fǎr-de; **waterless valley** vále fǎrǎ di ápǎ

LESSEN *vb.* ▼ñicşurédz → DIMINISH

LESSENING *s.* mpuţânáre (*and* mbu-), psânáre, psâníre, discreáştire, hirisíre, ñicşuráre, ñicuráre, ñicuráme, scǎdeáre, şcurticáre, şcurtáre

LESSON *s.* (*at school*) máthimǎ, *pl* mathímate; (*harsh reprimand*) ibréte; **to get a (good)** ~ ▼nveţ mínte, dipún mínte

LEST *cj.* tra s-nu (+ *vb*), s-nu (+ *vb*); ~ **he remain ignorant** s-nu armânǎ órbu ‖ HRISTU 27: ta s-nu vǎrsǎm sǎndzi '*lest we shed*

LET

blood'
   LET *vb*. (*to allow; to leave*) alás; **~ my puppy alone!** Alásă-ñ cățălu tu síyă! (*to rent, to lease a house, etc.*) ▾acáț; **Have you ~ a house?** Acățát cásă? ‖ **Let him / her come!** Las-yínă! PARALLELE 144
   LET DOWN *vb*. (*to lower*) ▾dipún; (*as of a belt*) sălghéscu
   LET DROP *vb*. (*to throw off*) ▾aleápid
   LET GO *vb*. ▾sărglʹéscu; **The emperor let them go** Âlʹ sărglʹí amirălu
   LET IN *vb*. (*to give entrance*) (a)dhixéscu (*and* adi-)
   LET IT BE as, ási → ALL RIGHT *and* SO BE IT
   LET KNOW *vb*. dau hăbáre, pitréc hăbáre, dau tu şteáre, gréscu, plirufuriséscu, plirufurséscu; **Let them know** Dă-le hăbáre; **Let me know** Grea-ñ (*lit*. 'speak to me')
   LET LOOSE *vb*. lʹ-dau díra, sălghéscu
   LET OFF HOT AIR *vb*. zburăscu goále
   LET ON *vb*. (*to reveal, to admit*) ▾aspún; (*to pretend*) mi fac (că), mi prifác (că)
   LET OUT *vb*. (*to free*) dau cále; (*as of a coat*) ▾lărdzéscu
   LET'S să, s-, háide *or* áide (să, s + *vb*.); ai, lási si, las, ştu-cará; **Let's turn back!** Lási si ni turnăm! **Let's go!** şpóru! ‖ **Let's eat!** a z măncăm, RÉCATAS 36
   LET SLIP *vb*. (*as of one's long hair*) sălăghéscu, sălghéscu
   LET SMB. GO TO HELL *vb*. ‖ 2 sg imper. (*with reference to a third person*) Scoáte-lʹ óclʹilʹ! BASME 231
   LETTER *s*. (*sign*) yrámă; (*written message*) cárte, pistulíe, scriitoáre, scriitúră; (*any written text*) lăile *f pl def*
   LETTUCE *s. bot*. lăptúcă, yilătídhă, cuştavár, guştevár; (*a poisonous variety*) pilʹ
   LETUP *s*. (**respite**) aryíe, oáră, lişuráre
   LEV *s*. ‖ BELIMACE 116: lev; 100: *pl*. lévañ
   LEVANTINE *adj. and s*. anatolít, anadulíş
   LEVEE *s*. (*as for preventing flooding*) dhési *f*, próhumă
   LEVEL *adj*. (*flat, plain*) buimátcu, -tcă, -tţi, tţe; íschiu
   LEVEL *vb*. ▾ischédz; **We are ~ing the ground** Ischém lóclu
   LEVELHEADED *adj*. aştirnút; cu sicáră n cap (→ INTELLIGENCE)
   LEVELING *s*. ischeáre
   LEVER *s*. (*wooden*) yeádham *m*; (*in a loom*) zănóz, zunóz

LEVITY *s.* lişuráme, fuscălíthră

LEVY *vb.* (*to ~ a tax on smb.*) arúc dátul; (*to ~ a fine*) glubuéscu, glubéscu

LEVY A DISTRAINT *vb.* (*to seize and hold property*) fac sucréstu

LEVY A TITHE UPON SMB. *vb.* (a)ghismédz, (a)ghízmédz

LEVY WAR AGAINST/ON *vb.* ▼apulimséscu

LEWD *adj.* dişuţât, azdisít

LEWDNESS *s.* dişuţâre

LEXICON *s.* lexicó

LIAISON *s.* (*link*) ligătúră

LIAR *adj.* and *s.* minciunós; *also:* bişinós, ialangíu, yealangíu, pséftu, *m pl* -fţâ; psimateár

LIBEL *vb.* zburăscu, cacuzburăscu ‖ (*to set a rumor about*) scot cântic (*lit.* 'to launch a song'), PARALLELE 139

LIBERAL *adj.* (*large*) filótim; (*~ in giving*) sălghít → GENEROUS

LIBERATE *vb.* elefthiriséscu, dau díra, ▼apulséscu, ▼sălăghéscu ‖ CUNIA 99: dau cále

LIBERATION *s.* elefthirusíre, sălăghíre

LIBERTINE *s.* puşt(e)ánă *f.*

LIBERTINE *adj.* curvár

LIBERTINISM *s.* birbăntlâche, săláne

LIBERTY *s.* ilifthiríe, huriéte, *N:* slobodíe

LIBIDINOUS *adj.* azdisít, dişuţât

LIBRA *s. astr.* Látură (*DDA is hesitant about this term*)

LIBRARY *s.* vivliutíche

LICENTIOUS *adj.* → LEWD

LICENTIOUSNESS *s.* dişuţâre

LICK *vb.* ▼(a)língu (→ § 32); **to ~ smb.'s coat** (*to give a beating*) âľ cruéscu un sumár, ľi úmflu sămárlu, ľ-u íntru; *imper. 2 sg:* Íntră-ľ-u! → BEAT; (*to defeat*) azvíngu; (*to run*) → AS HARD AS ONE CAN ~

LICKETY-SPLIT *adv.* ca curşúmlu

LICKING *s.* (a)lindzeáre, (a)líndzire

LID *s.* (*as on a pot*) căpáche, sústă, tápă; CARAFOLI 82, 106: (*baking ~*, Rom. ţest) gástru, yástru, gástur; ciriché

LIE *s.* (*untruth*) minciúnă, psémă, *pl* psémate; ialáne, yealáne, bişíñ di cuc; *coll.* mingiunáme ‖ **big ~** minciúnă groásă; minciúnă di la háni (*lit.* 'a lie from the inn'), BASME 100; minciúñ cu

LIE

coádi *pl* (*lit. 'lies with tails'*), DIARO 267

LIE *vb.* (*to tell lies*) (a)minciunédz;, mâc chétri (*lit. 'to eat stones'*), u-mpeátic (minciúna) (*lit. 'to patch it, to patch a lie'*, cruéscu nă minciúnă; **I didn't ~ to him** Nu lu am minciunátă ‖ trag nă minciúnă, BASME 79; **Cĺis, Els, LvO, Vil,** *etc.* (3 *sg*): dzâţi minciúñ; **An, Na:** dzâc psémata (*passim:* psémate, psémati); **Kat:** (3 *sg*) arídi; **Rod:** minciuneáşti (3 *sg*), B-ARCH 247; **He tells big ~s** Táĺe groáse (*lit. 'He cuts big ones'*), PARALLELE 150

LIE *vb.* (*to be or stay at rest, to remain*) dzac (*and* zac); hiu amplátea; **All the dead ~ in the black earth** Tuţ astéşĭĺi dzac tu láia ţáră; (*to ~ heavy*) ▼(a)ngréc

LIE DOWN *vb.* ▼apún, ▼bag, ▼cúlcu, ĺau vilénza dípla; **The bride had just lain down** Nveásta cât-cât si-apúse ‖ **Cru:** mi bag, GOLAB 207

LIE FLAT ON ONE'S BELLY *vb.* mi tíndu pri dínţâ, mi tíndu mpáde ‖ mi bag pi dínţâ, DIARO 321

LIE HEAVY ON THE STOMACH *vb.* (*as of unbaked bread*) ñ-cáde greu tu stumáhe, ñ-cáde pluvúc tu stumáhe

LIE IN AMBUSH *vb.* limiryiséscu, limirséscu, păndixéscu

LIE IN STORE FOR ONE *vb. impers.* 3 *sg:* mi adástă

LIE IN WAIT FOR *vb.* → LIE IN AMBUSH

LIFE *s.* bánă; yeáţă *or* gheáţă; trec *or* treácă; zuíe; (*way of living*) bănátă; (*difficult ~ abroad*) curbiţâĺe → COME TO ~; ESCAPE WITH ~ AND LIMB

LIFELESS *adj.* → DEAD

LIFE-RESTORING WATER *s.* (*in tales*) ápă di bánă, ápă yíe, ápă yíe fără moárte, apă yíe athanátă

LIFETIME *s.* ‖ MERCA 14: bănátic

LIFT *s.* mutáre

LIFT *vb.* ▼mut nsus, ▼scol, ▼análţu

LIFTED *adj.* mutát, mtat

LIFTING *s.* mutáre, mtáre, anălţáre, sculáre

LIGATE *vb.* (*to tie, to bind*) ▼leg

LIGHT *s.* (*illumination*) lumínă *or* luñínă; videálă, **S:** féxă; **The lamp was giving a lot of ~** Lámpa dideá nă máre videálă ‖ **F:** fosă, HRISTU 37, 151 → BRING TO ~, COME TO ~

LIGHT *adj.* (*not heavy*) ĺişór, nişór, ñişór, ñicşór

LIGHT *vb.* ▼apríndu, árdu; **The tapers are lit** Lumbărdzâle árdu;

(*to shed light*) luñinédz; **to light** (*to start*) **a fire** ancúñu (*and* angúñu); **They lit a cigarette** Anguñáră câte únă ţiyáră

 LIGHT OUT *vb.* li tíndu → BOLT

 LIGHTEN *vb.* (*to relieve of a burden, to become lighter*) lişu-rédz, ▾ñişurédz

 LIGHTEN *vb.* (*to give off flashes of lightning*) 3 *sg*: (si) ascápiră, (si) fúldziră, sfúldziră, sfúlgură, ‖ ALIA 15: astrăp-seáşte

 LIGHTENING *s.* (*alleviation*) lişuráre (*and* ľi-), lişuráme (*and* ľi-), ñişuráme

 LIGHTHEARTED *adj.* hărăcóp, -oápă, -óchi, -oápe; hăriós

 LIGHTHEARTEDNESS *s.* zburdălipsíre

 LIGHTHOUSE *s.* far

 LIGHTING UP *s.* (*illumination*) luñináre

 LIGHTLY *adv.* lişór, licşór

 LIGHT-MINDED *adj.* ľ-asboáiră míntea

 LIGHTNESS *s.* lişureáţă, lişuráme → LIGHTENING

 LIGHTNING *s.* sfúldzir, sfúlgu, sfúlgur, sfúlgure, fuldziráre, sfuldziráre; *also:* chícută, găríţ, găríş, ghiríţ, rufé, rufeáuă; (a)rufée, rófche, strápíe, vol ‖ ALIA 13: ascăpiráre, astrăpí, scápiră, strapóval, strapovál; *Prv:* străpoválă, CL 261

 LIGHTNING *adj.* (*extremely fast*) ca curşúmlu *adj. and adv.*

 LIGHTNING BUG *s.* licuríciu → FIREFLY

 LIGHTS *s.* anat. plămúnă → LUNG

 LIGHTSOME *adj.* (*nimble*) sárpit; (*cheerful*) hărăcóp, -oápă, -óchi, -oápe

 LIKE *adj.* → ALIKE

 LIKE *vb.* ▾arăséscu (*and* arâ-), ▾ariséscu, ñ-íntră tu ócľu; *obs.* ñ-pláţi; **He does not ~ anything** Ţivá nu-şĭ ariseáşte; **Let her marry the fellow she ~s** Pri carĭ gióne şi-arâseáşte, pri aţél nâsă si-şi lu ľa ‖ (*of food*) ñ-si mácă; **The old man ~ed the pie very much** Aúşlui âľ si mácá múltu píta, BASME 29 ‖ ALR 1641: **We don't like this wine** Noi nu-l vrem yínlu; ALR 1649: **They like roast beef** Alór lă e búnă fríptă cárne

 LIKE *prep.* ca; **He speaks ~ a prophet** Zburáşte ca prófit; **~ everybody else** (*i.e., normal*) ca tútă éta; **~ master ~ man** Ahtáre stână, ahtáre caş; Ahtáre picurár, ahtărĭ câñ; Spróti cap şi că-ciúlă ‖ DIARO 285: dúpâ om ş-mulárea

LIKE

LIKE *cj.* ca, cum; căt ‖ HRISTU 1: **a boulder ~ a house** nă şcămbă căt ună casă

LIKE MASTER, LIKE MAN → LIKE *prep.*

LIKENESS *s.* uidíe, uidisíre, úidizmă

LIKING *s.* (*preference*) prutímise; (*pleasure*) arâsíre, arisíre

LILAC *s. bot.* lilá, ghiurghiuván, argaván, argăván, arguván

LILIPUTIAN *adj.* (*tiny*) ñícăz, ñicăzán, ñicăzíc

LILY *s. bot.* crin, zâmbác, zambác, zămbácă

LIMB *s.* hăláte, *pl* hălăţ; mădulár, mudulár → ESCAPE WITH LIFE AND ~

LIMBECK *s.* lâmbíc

LIMBER *adj.* jílav, -vă, -yĭ, -ve

LIME *s.* (*mineral*) (a)zvéste, călchére, hălchére; **slaked ~** azvéste asteásă; **quicklime** azvéste ni-asteásă ‖ *Peş:* azvéstre, CL 38

LIME *vb.* (*to paint walls with lime*) azvistuéscu

LIME-BURNER *s.* azvistár

LIME-DEALER *s.* ‖ zvistár, CL 269

LIME KILN *s.* azvistăreáuă

LIMITATION *s.* piriorizmó [pi•ri•u•riz•mó], piriurisíre [•ri•u]; aprea-adunătúră

LIMIT *s.* (*boundary*) sémte, márdzină, márdzine, *Grb:* márne ‖ (*city limit*) *Cru:* sinúr, GOLAB 248

LIMIT *vb.* ▾piriurséscu [•ri•ur•], ▾apreadún

LIMITED *adj.* (*narrow-minded*) şcret, *f* şcrétă (*sic*) → STUPID

LIMP *s.* şcľupicáre

LIMP *adj.* (*weary*) curmát; (*weak, infirm*) vlângu, s(c)lab

LIMP *vb.* şcľoápic

LIMPID *adj.* lánghir, lăváră *invar*; lăyărós, límpide, límbit, límbid → CLEAR

LIMPIDITY *s.* dizlăcitúră

LIMPING *s.* şcľupáre, şcľupicáre

LIMPING *adj.* tupál

LIMPING ALONG *adv.* ţúpătă-ţúpătă → HOBBLING ALONG

LIMPINGLY *adv.* várai-vára; şľupicânda, şcľupicânda

LINDEN FLOWER *s.* filureáuă

LINDEN FLOWER INFUSION *s.* filureáuă

LINDEN-TREE *s.* tiľu, lípă; **~ grove** or **forest** filureáuă

LINE *s.* (*device for catching fish*) anghístru, grip, yrip, úñiţă, vlac; (*a rank of people*) sireáuă

LINE *s.* (*verse*) stih

LINE *vb.* (*a garment, etc.*) astăruséscu, căplădiséscu ‖ ALR 528: bag astáre; DIARO 202: dhipluséscu

LINEAGE *s.* (*descent*): **of princely ~** ciciór di scámnu (*lit. 'leg of chair, leg of throne'*)

LINED *adj.* (*as of a garment*) astărusít, căplădisít

LINEN *s.* pândză; **a piece of ~** pândzătúră; (*~ for jackets*) cundoándir ‖ (*sheet*) **Gop:** ciarşáfe, GOLAB 210

LINEN DEALER *s.* pândzár, trâmbâgí

LINGER *vb.* şed, hălăndăréscu, ntărdédz, putridzăscu; **All day long he ~ed indoors** N cásă putridză dzúua tútă

LINING *s.* căplădisíre, astărusíre; (*part of a garment*) astáre

LINK *s.* (*in a chain*) cinghéľu ‖ **Peş:** alcă, *pl* alcáţ, CL 36

LINT *s.* scámă

LION *s.* aslán, arslán; ľunár, ľundár ‖ **Peş:** arăslán, CL 37

LIONESS *s.* aslánă ‖ **Peş:** arăslánă, CL 37

LIP *s.* búdză, *N:* búză ‖ ALIA 157: budzínă → BITE ONE'S ~S; CURL ONE'S ~S

LIONHEARTED *adj.* inimárcu, -rcă, -rţi, -rţe; *3 sg impers:* ñ-ţâ-ne ‖ CUNIA 72: curajlí

LIQUID FOOD *s.* (*soup, tea, etc.*) muľitúră

LIQUOR *s.* (a)răchíe → BRANDY

LIRA *s.* (*former gold Turkish coin*) líră, rílă

LISP *vb.* bândurédz, gugurédz, gonghiuséscu

LISTEN *vb.* ▾ascúltu, ñ-bag urécľa, ▾acúmpăr; ▾ávdu; **Do not speak; just ~!** Tíne nu zbură, acúmpără!; ľau di uréacľe (*or di* urécľi) **Listen!** Si loáţă di urécľi! (*before anouncing pleasant news*) Sihăríche! **~ to me, woman!** Ávdză-mi, muľáre! ‖ HRISTU 29: **Girls should ~ more and talk less** fetili lipseşti mamult s-avdă şi puţănu s greastă ‖ BELIMACE 68: **listen to me!** ascúltă míne!

LISTENING *s.* ascultáre

LISTLESS *adj.* (*spiritless*) mólav, -vă, -vĭ (*sic!*), -ve

LISTLESSNESS *s.* anusţâre, curmáre

LITANY *s.* lităníe

LITERACY *s.* ştíre

LITERATE *s.* and *adj.* nvíţát, ştiút, loyiortát

LITHE

LITHE *adj.* ascuturát → SLENDER

LITHESOME *adj.* sárpit

LITIGATION *s.* daravérã

LITTER *vb.* (*to give birth to puppies, etc.*) ▼fet; (*to strew with litter*) aştérnu; (*to scatter about*) ▼aruvérsu, ▼arãspândéscu

LITTLE *adj.* and *adv.* niscântu (*and* niscându), nãscântu; **after a ~ while** dúpã niscântã oárã; **We boiled a ~ wheat** Heársim niscântu grân; niheámãtã, niheámãzã; **Do you want a ~ water?** Vrei nãheámãtã ápã? nãtheámã, nifeámã; **Give me a ~ help!** Agiútã-ñ nãfeámã! *dim.* himãzíc; **Please look at us a ~!** Ia mutríţ niheám la noi!; **very ~** cât trâ yitríe, cât ghitrúşca, cât chípita di ac; **in a ~ while** dúpã niheámãzã; nãnghídhã, un hir, puţân, pţân, psân, nichícuşe; **~ by ~** câte puţân, pãrãláche; **too ~** nichícãzã ‖ **~ by ~** anárga, pe-anárga, BASME 68, 214, 343; ALR 1488: chícutã di chícutã

LITTLE BEAR *s. astr.* ‖ Úrsa aţeá Ñícâ, Gâľinúşa, Clócea cu şã-siľi puľ DIARO 176

LITTLE FINGER *s.* (*pinkie*) dziditíc, dzidzitíc

LITTLENESS *s.* psânáme

LITTORAL *s.* (*shore*) mal, mázdã, márdzinã di amáre

LIVE *adj.* (*vivid, vigurous, quick*) aghíu, ayíu

LIVE *vb.* bãnédz (*and* bâ-), ľ-u trec, adíľu; **How do you ~?** Cum ľ-u treţi? **What a life we've ~ed!** Ţe bánã avém tricútã! (*to dwell*) stau, şed, cãtichiséscu; **Where do you ~?** Iu şidéţ?

LIVE AT SMB.'S EXPENSE *vb.* ▼mârşuséscu

LIVE COALS *s.* sprúnã, *N:* spúr(n)ã; *coll.* sprunáme

LIVE IN CLOVER *vb.* huzuripséscu, trec béica, trec biiáşte, bã-nédz ca dzúua ţea álbã, bãnédz tu bihulíche, u duc cu cãciúla scoásã, u trag chióşea dumneáşte ‖ trec ca dzúua ţea álbã, BASME 177

LIVE IN POVERTY *vb.* cacurizipséscu

LIVE TO SEE *vb.* ñ-u apúc; *imprec.* **May you not live to see to-morrow!** S nu-ţ apúţi!

LIVELINESS *s.* sirtláche, sârbisláche, sârpisláche, sârpiţâľe, spírtu, şpírtu

LIVELY *adj.* şpírtu *invar.* → SPIRITED, INTELLIGENT

LIVER *s.* hicát *n*, *pl* hicáte; ihcát *m*, ihcáţ *pl*; ipát ‖ *Also:* hicát laiu, ithcát, ALIA 181

LIVESTOCK *s.* (*seen as wealth*) tutíputã

LIVESTOCK RAISING s. (of sheep) picurărlíche, picurăríľe, picurărátă, picurlíche

LIVID adj. púhav, prú-, brú-; (livid and swollen) bútcav, m pl -cayĭ, f pl -cave; (as by bruising) vínit, víñit; siñicát; (ashen) măsinát; (enraged) inătusít ‖ **Peş**: bútcaf, CL 40

LIVING s. (being alive) bănáre; (way of ~) bănátă

LIVING adj. yiu, ghiu; **still alive** (of a person at death's door but able to speak) cu gúră (lit. 'with mouth')

LIZARD s. gúştir, gúştur, guşturíţă, ciupilár, ciupulár

LOAD s. furtíe, ncărcătúră, sárţină, sálţină; (half a load on a horse) sárţă, déngă, pl dénghi; dénghie, pl dénghiuri

LOAD vb. ▼ncárcu; **to ~ on one's back** ncarc pri plătări; úmplu; ▼furtuséscu; (to overwhelm, as with gifts) ▼ngľeg; **They ~ed her with goodies** U-ngľigáră di muşutéţ; (of a gun) cárcu

LOADED adj. ncărcát, ancărcát, âncărcát, mplin; (of a gun) um-plút

LOADING s. ncărcáre

LOAF s. (of bread) cărveáľe; **G:** bâzdrâmă; círecă, dérlic, sămúnă, sămúne, somúnă, sumúnă; (~ of white bread) frangiólă

LOAF vb. (to be idle) hălăndăréscu, misúr steálile

LOAFER s. birdhúş, capisâz, gulimán, haihúĭ, haihúm, pl haihú-meañ; hulandár, vagabóndu

LOAFING s. haileslíche → LAZINESS

LOAN s. mprumút, mbrumút; (making a loan) mprumutáre

LOAN SHARK s. zăráf, săráf

LOANSHARKING s. zărăflâche

LOATHE vb. (a)urăscu ‖ CUNIA: am tu hásmă

LOATHSOME adj. blăstimát → DETESTABLE

LOBBY s. (of a house) ghizintíe, hăiátă

LOBE s. (of ear) lăpúşe, ţúrţur

LOBSTER s. (fresh-water ~) cávur, cávru; (salt-water ~) astacó, astahó

LOCATED: **to be ~** vb. cad; **Where is your village ~?** Cătră iu cá-de hoára a voástră?

LOCATION s. (site, place, area) sémte

LOCK s. cătinár, cľáie; (built-in ~) brávă; (of hair) aráuă, avoálă, cilíe, ciulíe; cârcme, crácme f pl; ţălúfră, ţărúflă; zu-lúfe, pl zulúhi

LOCK

LOCK *vb.* bag tu cľái [kľá•i]; ▾ncľiédz

LOCKED *adj.* ncľiát, âncľiát

LOCKING *s.* ncľiáre

LOCKSMITH *s.* câtnă

LOCUST *s. ent.* lăcústă; *also:* acrídhă, gălăgústă, ɡulucústă, ɡulugústă, carcaléc, scarcaléc, scarcaléţ, carculéţ, scarculéţ, *Gop:* scuculéţ ‖ ALIA 125: bacác, bacacáchǐ, cărcăléci, scărcălíţă, cărcăléc, cicoáre, cicoáră, sicoáre, dzâcoáre

LODGE *s.* (*inn*) háne

LODGE *vb.* (*shelter*) ▾apreadún, ▾(a)próchiu, ▾aştéptu, ▾cúlcu; (*to thrust in*) ▾bag, plântu, nhig; **She implored the old man to ~ her** ăľ pricădzú a aúşlui s-u apreadúnă n cásă; **Please, ~ me tonight!** Aprucheáţ-mi aístă seáră! *or* Aştiptáţ-mi aéstă noápte!

LODGE A COMPLAINT *vb.* dau plângu (la), ▾plângu (la), arúc rgiuhále

LODGER *s.* → TENANT

LODGING EXPENSES *s.* hãñátic

LOFT *s.* (*kind of attic*) pótan, pótană

LOFTY *adj.* (*arrogant*) daítcu; (*noble*) chibár; (*high, tall*) análtu

LOFTINESS *s.* (*self-esteem, dignity*) cheaféte

LOG *s.* bucíne *m*, crăciún *m*

LOGGER *s.* (*lumberman*) chiristigí

LOGGERHEAD: *at* ~*s* pri cuţút *or* pri cemăúnă ‖ pri(tu) cuţúte, PARALLELE 147 → COME TO ~S

LOIN *s. anat.* cârţioáră, scârţioáră; curţórǐ *f pl*; şále *f pl*

LOITER *vb.* ▾misúr steálile (*lit.* 'to measure the stars')

LOITERER *s.* adúnă-vímtu (*lit.* 'wind-gatherer'); *G:* başinghél; ciumagáră *m*, ciumagárañ *pl*; haramufái, hărămgí, hásca, hascanífur

LOLL *vb.* ▾(a)rádzim, ▾acubuséscu, ▾acumséscu

LOLL ABOUT *vb.* hălăndăréscu, misúr steálile

LONELY *adj.* irñíu, irñít

LONENESS *s.* singuráme, singureáţă, singuritáte

LONESOME *adj.* ‖ síngur ca cúclu, BASME 409 (*lit.* 'as lonesome as the cuckoo')

LONG *adj.* lúngu; (*as of face*) spirlungós, sprilúngu, spirlúngu; (*as of smb.'s beard or hair*) bran; (*as of a road*) dipărtós ‖

(*longer than normal*) **Peş:** lungăvéţ, CL 255; **Av: as ~ as** *cj* únă ţe, BASME 502

LONG *vb.* (*to yearn*) ñ-u dor *and* ñi-i dor (tră, di, să)

LONG MAY YOU LIVE! ‖ La mulţi añ! L-añ múlţâ! Tră mulţi añ! Tr-añ múlţâ! PARALLELE 141

LONG SINCE *adv.* di múltu doáre, mi ľa dórlu, ñi-alghéscu ócľiľ (trâ), ñ-si alăcheáşte ínima (di), plângu di dor, ľ-trag dórlu; **We ~ for you very much** Múltu nă-i dor tră voi; **I have a mother who is ~ing for me** Ñ-m nă múmă ţe-ñ mi doáre → PINE

LONG *adv.* (*for a long time*) prilúngu

LONG LIVE! ‖ ALR 1315: z-băneádză!

LONG-EARED *adj.* dângľát, dângľinát, uricľát

LONGER *adv.* (*temporal*) cáma; **Will you wait for him any ~?** Va lu-aştépţâ cáma?

LONG-HAIRED *s.* (*as of a winter coat*) flucát, flucós

LONGING *s.* dor; **to feel a ~** mi ľa dórlu; (*solitary painful ~*) siclétă, săclétă

LONG-LEGGED *adj.* ciurligán; **G:** sprágăn

LONG-LIVED *adj.* lundzín

LOOK *s.* mu(n)trítă, m(u)tríre, ruítă; **He cast a ~ at the young man** şi-arcă mutríta pi gióne ‖ STERGHIU 3: mutrít *n*

LOOK *vb.* (*to gaze at, to watch*) mutréscu, mtréscu, muntréscu, mundréscu (→ § 32); **~ here!** Mutreá ncoa! **~ ahead!** Mutrea ghíne! (*to ~ at oneself*) ▾yilcéscu; **~ in the mirror!** yilcíţ-vă tu yilíe! ▾bruéscu, ▾bréscu; **It ~s like rain** Ţérlu angreácă ca ti ploáie; (*to seem*) par, ampár ‖ CUVATA 2: **she looked at me** mi mătrí → LOOK WELL

LOOK AFTER *vb.* (*to take care of*) cilistiséscu, cealăhtiséscu, cătăndiséscu, câştighédz, frundiséscu, frundixéscu, trag; **We used to look after large flocks of sheep** Trădzeám uiríu múltu

LOOK AROUND ONE *vb.* páscu di páturle părţâ, ñ-páscu ócľiľ di-varlíga

LOOK BLANK *vb.* l-háscu (*d/o m sg*), u háscu (*d/o f sg*)

LOOK DARKLY AT SMB. *vb.* mutréscu (mult) narău, mutréscu n aráulea

LOOK DOWN IN THE MOUTH *vb.* spíndzur nările; (*of smb.*) cánda ľ-si nicáră cărăyĭle (*or* ghimíĭle)

LOOK DOWN ON/UPON *vb.* cătăfroniséscu ‖ CUNIA 90: atimuséscu

LOOK

LOOK FONDLY AT SMB. *vb.* sórbu, ĺ-fac ócĺiĺ băcâre (dúpă)

LOOK FOOLISH *vb.* armân ti arâs (şi pizuírĭ); arămân ca găĺína údă

LOOK FOR *vb.* (*to check, to seek*) ▾ved; **Look for it in your pocket!** Védzâ-te n gépe!

LOOK FOR IT *vb.* (*to be cruising for a bruising*) u cáftu cu luminárea (*lit. 'to search it with a candlelight'*)

LOOK GLUM *vb.* ▾nigurédz (la fáţă)

LOOK LIKE *vb.* ▾undzéscu, ñ-u adúc pri → RESEMBLE

LOOK OUT *vb.* am ócĺilu, am peána; *Look out!* Ái-ţâ míntea! Ái-ţâ ócĺilu! Ái-ţâ peána! Sacân! Angătán! Várda!

LOOK SAVAGELY *vb.* ▾ayru-mutréscu

LOOK SMB. UP AND DOWN *vb.* mutréscu di la úngĺi pân la cap

LOOK WELL *vb.* am fáţă búnă; **He does not ~** Nu áre fáţă búnă ‖ DIARO 68: ĺau múltâ hári

LOOK WITH EAGER LONGING *vb.* ‖ fac ântr-ócĺi, BASME 309

LOOKING AFTER *s.* (*care*) câştigáre

LOOKING GLASS *s.* lăyíe → MIRROR

LOOKOUT *s.* vigĺáre, cumăndărsíre → BE ON THE ~ FOR

LOOM *s.* arăzbóiu, vălmént

LOONY *adj.* chirút → CRAZY

LOOP *s.* (*of hair*) ‖ DIARO 271: cúţcu

LOOSE *adj.* (*as of a belt*) distrés, distrímtu, lárgu, sălăghít, hábin; **to be ~ in the saddle** *vb.* (*to be insecure*) şuvăéscu

LOOSEN *vb.* (*as a belt*) disţíngu; (*a muscle, a bolt*) alás, ▾distríngu, lişurédz, sălghéscu

LOOSENING *s.* distríndzire, sălăghíre; (*of a belt*) disţíndzire

LOOT *s.* alimúră, yeáymă, iámă, prádă, spóĺe

LOOT *vb.* fac ghénga, *N:* mprad → PLUNDER

LOP *vb.* (*to cut off branches*) scriştéscu → TRIM

LOP *vb.* (*of branches*) vlăstăruséscu

LOPPING *s.* călărsíre, clădhipsíre, scrâştíre (a lumăchilor), vlăstărusíre

LOPSIDED *adj.* strâmbu, *m pl* -ânghi, *f pl* -âmbe

LOQUACIOUS *adj.* zburyeárcu → TALKATIVE

LORD *s.* (*God*) Dómnu; (*of the manor*) celepíu, cilibí, (*British nobleman*) lórdhu

LORD IT OVER SMB. *vb.* mi úmflu → GIVE ONESELF AIRS

LORDLY *adj*. (*proud*) pitrít; cu cáplu n dzeáná; (*haughty*) daítcu; (*proper and dignified*) prímtu; (*rich, aristocratic, as of a
wedding party*) cilnichéscu, dumnéscu, arhund(ich)éscu ‖ **Cru**: nicuchiréscu, GOLAB 238; afindéscu, CARAFOLI 25

LORDLY *adv*. dumneáşte, cu sáltănáte, cu cáplu n dzeáná

LOQUACIOUS *adj*. zburyeáric, -rcă, -rţi, -rţe → TALKATIVE

LOSE *vb*. ▾scherdu, chérdu, ▾cher, mărít; **to be losing** (*esp. of
money*) adár yróslu zloátă; **~ courage** ▾apilipséscu, chiutipséscu,
ñ-cherdu curáilu, ñ-arăţeáşte bişína; **~ hope** ▾apilipséscu

LOSE ONE'S BALANCE *vb*. (*to lose one's self-possession*) ▾pă-
léscu

LOSE ONE'S HEAD *vb*. ▾schérdu, ▾chérdu míntea, u-cher pusúla,
▾cilduséscu, cildiséscu, cictiséscu, cihtiséscu, ▾zurluséscu

LOSE ONE'S TEMPER *vb*. ñ-arsáre dzáfna → FLY INTO A TANTRUM

LOSE ONE'S WAY *vb*. ▾chérdu, ▾schérdu, ▾cher (*or* schérdu) cálea,
▾dzăgădéscu ‖ mi cher, BASME 35

LOSE SIGHT OF *vb*. cher ditr-ócľi; **not to lose sight of** nu-ñ mut
căştíga

LOSE SMB.'S TRAIL *vb*. ľ-cher tórlu, ľ-cher úrma

LOSE TRACK OF *vb*. ▾zăgădéscu; **In the house we don't lose track
of anything** Ân cásă nu nă si zăgădeáşte ţivá

LOSE WEIGHT *vb*. slăghéscu; (*to become very thin*) mi adár iáscă

LOSER *s., adj*. zimñusít, zñisít

LOSS *s*. cheárdire, chirdăciúne, schirdeáre, dâmă, gazépe, hătáie, zñíe; (*waste*) fíră; (*in some games: lost point*) bis, bij, sumár, zdârtă

LOST *adj*. (*no longer owned or known*) schirdút; (*unable to find
one's way*) dzăgădít; **~ in thought** minduít

LOT *s*. (*destiny*) soárte; (*on deciding by chance*) lahnó, **G**: lâh-
mă, lot, lótă, lotăríe, scúrtă, şcúrtă, şcurtíţă; **to cast ~s** arúc
şcurtíţa; **The ~ fell upon her** Ľĭ cădzú şcurtíţa a ľei ‖ CUVATA 4:
such was her ~ ahătă-ľ fu angrăsită → CAST ~S

LOT *s*. (*quantity, usu. large*) nă crímă di; **lots of** sumăreáuă →
A LOT OF

LOTTERY *s*. lahnó → LOT

LOUD *adj*. (*as of the voice*) vârtós, -oásă, silnăvós, -oásă ‖
HRISTU 52: aurrari analtă ('a ~ shout')

LOUDLY *adv*. cu boáţe; **The woman yelled ~** Muľárea zgľí cu

LOUDMOUTHED

boáṭe; pravatós, privatós, prâvatós, provatós ‖ sănătós, BASME
427; HRISTU 43: cu boaṭi mari

LOUDMOUTHED adj. ghiurultagí, m pl -geádz

LOUNGE vb. ▾şintéscu; (to gad about) alág sucắchile [su•kăk'-
•li]

LOUNGER s. durñít → LAZY

LOUNGING s. haileslíche → LAZINESS

LOUSE s. pidúcľu, bidúcľu, minciúşe, minciúş (and mingiúş);
G: yeátru; coll. biducľáme, minciuşáme ‖ **Peş: chicken** ~ şvélchi
di gắľínă, CL 261

LOUSY adj. **1.** (poor) ápcu, m pl ápṭi, f pl ápṭe; próstih, páľu-
(as in páľu-gắľátă 'a lousy pail') ‖ aclirát; **a ~ year** an aclirát, CL 36; ant. an berichitlâcu, CL 38 ‖ **2.** (infected with
lice) piducľós, biducľós, biducľát, mbiducľát, lindinós, mingiu-
şát ‖ **Amc:** mblínu di pidúcľi, SCHL 114

LOUT adj. cap di ghégan, muteái

LOVE s. vreáre; also: alughíre, ayápe, hicáte pl; sivdáe, siv-
dă, vilisíre; **The boy had a ~ for study** Ficiórlu aveá sivdắlu a
yrámatĭlor; **~ has no limits** Sivdáĭa nu áre márdzine; **Where is
their passionate ~?** Iu sunt a lor hicáte? **They are in ~** S-vor →
MAKE ~ TO SMB., BE IN ~ WITH

LOVE vb. voi, aor. vrui, part. vrut; am arán; **Tell me who you ~**
Spúne-ñ cai âñ ṭ-ai arán; ▾ayắp(i)séscu, ▾ayắchipséscu, ▾alu-
ghéscu, alăghéscu; iron. L-voi ca neáua n sin (lit. 'I love him
like snow in my bosom'); (to ~ intensely) pára-voi; dor; **if you
don't ~ him** di nu-l dori ‖ CUVATA 9: **Grandfather ~ed me very much
and I ~ed him** Páplu míni múltu mi vrea. Ş-míni-l vream

LOVE AS THE APPLE OF ONE'S EYE vb. l-voi ca luñína din cap;
l-voi ca gean ‖ BASME 191: voi ca ócľiľ din cap; HRISTU 46: ti vra
ca luñína a ochĭllu

LOVEMAKING s. (copulation) ambăiráre

LOVER s. (male) arán, iarán, yearán; (female) aránă, iaránă,
yearánă, moróză, muróză, farfúlă, fărfúlă, ayắpitoáñe ‖ **Cru:** ero-
mén, GOLAB 214; (fond of smth.) tiryeacľíu, tiriachíu, tiryeaclâ

LOVING adj. sivdalíu, sivdắlâ, sivdắlós; (affectionate) doľu, f
dóľe, m pl doľ, f pl dóľe ‖ (as of God) ‖ LITURG 126: dărútu

LOVINGLY adv. vrut

LOW adj. (of voice: quiet) dipús; in a ~ **voice** păgắñór (and pâgă-); cu boátea dipúsă; (*of prices: ridiculously* ~) bathavá, geába; (*as of a very modest house*) apús, CAPIDAN 151

LOW *vb.* (*of cattle*) mug, mudzéscu

LOWBRED *adj.* ni-adărát → RUDE

LOWBROW *s.* (*unintellectual*) apló

LOW-DOWN *adj.* (*contemptible*) cătăryár, idipsâz, *m pl* -âjĭ, *f pl* -âze; (*deeply emotional*) chirút

LOW-DOWN TRICKS/WAYS *s.* yumărlâche

LOWER (*comparative of LOW*) *adv.* nhímă

LOWER *vb.* ñicşurédz, scad; (*of prices*) eftinipséscu; (*as of a belt around one's waist*) sălghéscu (*and* sâl-)

LOWERING *s.* dipuneáre, dipúnire

LOWER ONESELF *vb.* mi scad

LOWING *s.* (*of cattle*) mudzíre

LOWLANDER *s.* câmpár; (*in a village*) ghioşán (*ant.* suşán)

LOWLY *adj.* tápin → HUMBLE

LOYAL *adj.* pistó, *m pl* pistádz → FAITHFUL

LOYALTY *s.* bésă

LUBBER *adj.* ócan, zdángan → STUPID

LUBRICATE *vb.* ▼(a)úngu

LUBRICATION *s.* (a)úndzire, (a)undzeáre

LUCERN *s.* (*alfalfa*) trifóľ, trifíľ, trăfíľ

LUCK *s.* (a)mbăreátă, báftă, calótihă, căsméte, tíhe, urbáre; **as ill ~ would have it** ca ti lăiátă; **to be down on one's ~** ñ-si dúte strâmbu, ñ-si dúte tersiné ‖ cánda dau ca di pri cheátră, BASME 99 ‖ *Greeting formula:* Cu ambăreátă te lucrát! '*Good luck in your endeavor!*'

LUCKY *adj.* hairlâtcu; tihiró; (*prosperous*) cu hăíre; **to be ~,** am (máre) tíhe, am steáuă búnă; **You have been so ~!** Calótiha di tíne! (*of good augure*) ugurlíu, agurlíu, ayurlíu; (*fortunate*) hará di; **~ is the mother who has such a son!** Hará di mă-sa ti ş-lu áre! ‖ **to be ~** ñ-ímnă tíhea, BASME 66; ugurlítcu, DIARO 96

LUGUBRIOUS *adj.* (*gloomy*) lăhtărós, -oásă

LUKEWARM *adj.* → TEPID

LULL *vb.* agălicéscu

LULLABY *s.* cânticáre

LULLABY *vb.* cântic

LULLABY *interj.* (*used to lull a child*) náni-náni; (*only in*

LUMBAR

songs) tărnă

LUMBAR REGION *s. anat* şále *f pl*

LUMBERMAN *s.* (*logger*) chiristigí, limnár

LUMINOUS *adj.* luñinós, -oásă

LUMMOX *adj.* (*clumsy*) angricós, -oásă

LUMP *s.* grúndă; **Cav:** (*as of cheese*) grúnghe; gumóĺ, gumúĺ, suráţ *m pl* (*sg.* suró); toc, top; (*~ of earth*) zvoĺ, zvólar, zvulár; (*a ~ in the throat*) nod; **He got a ~ in his throat** Boáţea ĺ-si nudă → BY THE ~; FEEL A ~ IN ONE'S THROAT

LUMP IT DOWN *vb.* (*when defeated in expectation or hope*) mâc călúpea

LUMP LARGE IN SMB.'S EYES *vb.* (*to have influence or credit*) am htibáre

LUMP TOGETHER *vb.* (*of sheep, 3 pl*) si-adúnă stúpă

LUMPISH *adj.* (*dull, sluggish*) (a)ngricós, -oásă

LUNACY *s.* zurleáţă, zurlíĺe

LUNATIC *adj.* zúrlu → CRAZY

LUNCH *s.* prândzu, prândzáre; **It's about time for ~** Eáste oára trâ prândzáre; **They came after ~** Viñíră prândzáţ; **~ time** a prândzalui

LUNCH *vb.* prândzắscu, prắndu (*and* prându), prắndzu (*and* prắn-)

LUNG *s. anat.* pulmúnă, plămúnă, pălmúnă, plimúnă, plămínă, plumóne, purmúnă, pârmúnă; plimún *m*, pilmún *m*; ‖ *Also:* plămóni, plimóni, pălămúne, albi-hicátu, ALIA 178

LURE *s.* băgáre pri sómnu, plănăsíre, culăchíe, culăchipsíre

LURE *vb.* bag pri sómnu, plănăséscu → BEGUILE

LURING *s.* → LURE

LURK *vb.* (*to lie concealed*) limiryiséscu, limirséscu; (*to sneak*) ▾stricór

LURKING PLACE *s.* cartére

LUSH *s.* (*slang:* '*drink*') biutúră; (*drunkard*) bicríu

LUST *s.* purníĺe, azdisíre, zilipsíre

LUST AFTER *vb.* zilipséscu

LUSTFUL *adj.* aspártu, azdisít, dişuţât, tileác, pânghiós

LUSTY *adj.* putút, livéndu, -ndă, -ndzâ, -nde; zdúmban

LUTE *s.* buzúche, lăútă

LUXATE *vb.* (*to dislocate, to displace a bone*) cluzunéscu, ▾strănguléscu

LUXATION *s. med.* cluzuníre, strǎngulsíre

LUXE *s.* lus, chibǎreáțǎ

LUXURIOUS *adj.* chibárcu ‖ BELIMACE 57: țivá éxtra di tut

LUXURIOUSLY *adv.* chibáre

LUXURY *s.* chibǎreáțǎ, lus *or* lúse, lúxu

LYE *s.* (a)lisívǎ, (a)lísvǎ, dzámǎ aráuǎ

LYING *s.* (*telling untruths*) minciunáre (*and* mingiunáre)

LYING *adj.* (*telling untruths*) minciunós, -oásǎ (*and* mingiunós)

LYING *adj.* (*stretched out*) tes, teásǎ, teşǐ, teáse; tímtu; **He found his wife ~ dead** şi-aflǎ nveásta teásǎ, moártǎ

LYING DOWN *adj.* (*resting, gone to bed*) apús → RECUMBENT

LYNX *s. zool.* arâs ‖ **Cru:** ciacál, GOLAB 210

LYRE *s.* (*musical instrument*) lírǎ, dzǎngǎrrǎ (*sic*)

M

MACABRE *adj*. fuvirós, -oásă → FRIGHTFUL

MACARONI *s*. macaróne *sg/pl*

MACE *s*. buzdugán, buzdugánă, buzdugáne

MACHINATION *s*. cruitúră, munăfíc, munăficlíche, mplititúră

MACHINE *s*. máchină

MACKEREL *s*. bilbíţă, harénghe

MAD *adj*. acăţát di hále, acâţát di nafoáră, ncuñát, turbát, trubát; vârlu, vúrlu; (*as of a dog*) lisixít; liseárcu, -rcă, -rţi, -rţe; **to be ~, to become ~** trub, túrbu, lisixéscu → DRIVE ~

MADCAP *s*. and *adj*. ciurtuít, şarafúra, dabóľa, tabóľa, tul; om fără hisápe; (*reckless*) distórsu

MADE *adj*. (*built, created, dressed, painted, shaped*) adrát, cruít, cuirít, ncľigát, plăsát ‖ HRISTU 4: ndrapt

MADDEN *vb*. ▾ayrédz, şuşuéscu, şuşéscu, túrbu, nglăréscu, glăréscu, ▾zurluséscu; (*to provoke, to anger*) ▾pizmuséscu

MADDENING *s*. şuşắre, şuşuíre, pizmusíre

MADDER *s*. *bot*. (a)rizáre, rúibu (*used in dyeing*)

MADDING *adj*. glărít, hăzusít

MADMAN *s*. zúrlu → MAD

MADNESS *s*. şuşuíre, turbáre, trubáre, zurleáţă

MAGICIAN *s*. may *m*, máyisă *f*; ghioz-boiagí

MAGNET *s*. magnéte, maynéti

MAGNETISM *s*. maynetizmó

MAGNIFICENCE *s*. măríľe

MAGNIFICENT *adj*. mărít

MAGPIE *s*. caracáxă, háşcă, *hâşcă*; hărăhástă, hăehástă, hărăháxă, hărácuľe, húľe ‖ *GSus:* cacaráscă, CL 40

MAID *s*. feátă ‖ BASME 315: dúlă

MAID OF HONOR *s*. surátă

MAIDEN *s*. feátă; *coll*. fitáme, fitiryió

MAIDENLY *adj*. (*as of a voice*) viryinéscu

MAIDSERVANT *s*. huzmicheáră

MAIL *s*. pósta, póştă; **by ~** pósta *or* cu pósta; **He wanted to send her a letter by ~ or by telegraph** Pósta i pri teľu vrea-ľ pitriţá nă cárte

MAIM *adj.* ólug → CRIPPLED, LAME

MAIM *vb.* ▾săcătipséscu, uludzéscu

MAIN: **with might and ~** *adv.* a mórtului

MAINSTAY *s.* ‖ SJos: dhiplár *m*, CL 44

MAINTAIN *vb.* (*to assert, to support, to provide for*) ▾ţân

MAINTENANCE *s.* ţâneáre, păstráre

MAIZE *s.* mísur → CORN

MAJOR *s.* (*in the Turkish army*) bimbắşé, bímbaşi

MAJOR *adj.* *m/f sg* máre, *m/f pl* mărĭ

MAKE *s.* adărătúră

MAKE *vb.* ▾fac, ▾adár; *also:* (*as of dough*) acáţ; (*to invent, to compose, as a song*) scol *or* scot; **Milk ~s skim** Láptile scoálă peáţă; (*to build, as a furnace*) ▾curduséscu; (*to prepare, to set in order*) ▾arădhăpséscu

MAKE A BAD BEGINNING *vb.* calc cu zévul

MAKE A DECISION *vb.* ‖ mi fac mucaéti (si) DIARO 364 → DECIDE

MAKE BAD BLOOD BETWEEN *vb.* bag zizáñe → BREED DISCORD

MAKE A BAD BREAK *vb.* u-adár dhálă → PUT ONE'S FOOT IN IT

MAKE A BLUNDER *vb.* u-adár taratóre

MAKE A BET *vb.* mi acáţ; mi acáţ cu báste

MAKE A BUNGLE OF SMTH. *vb.* (*to mix things up*) u-adár bóză, u adár taratóre

MAKE A DECISION *vb.* taľu píta; **A decision must be made!** Va tă-ľáre píta! *Also:* mi fac di căíle; **How did you make that decision?** Cum ti féţiş di căíle? → DECIDE ‖ BASME 682: ñ-bag poálile m-brâu

MAKE A BOW *vb.* mi ncľin

MAKE A DEPOSIT *vb.* (*for a contract or in view of engagement with a woman*) dau sémnul, dau seámne

MAKE A FOOL OF ONESELF *vb.* mi fac (tut) arizíle (*and* -zíľe) → MAKE ONESELF RIDICULOUS

MAKE A FOOL OF SMB. *vb.* ▾arâd, (a)ncálţu → DECEIVE

MAKE A FORTUNE *vb.* ▾acáţ maiáuă (*lit.* 'to catch yeast')

MAKE A FRIEND *vb.* acáţ un oáspe (nou)

MAKE A GIFT *vb.* → DONATE, PRESENT

MAKE A GOOD BARGAIN *vb.* adár căşáre (cu)

MAKE A HALT *vb.* ▾chinduréscu, ▾cundiséscu, ▾cundupséscu, lu-

MAKE

jéscu, nuptédz, pupuséscu; **He made a halt in another village**
Chindurí tu nă áltă hoáră → STOP

MAKE A HASH OF SMTH. *vb.* ľ-u adár bóză

MAKE A HIT *vb.* (*of thieves, etc.*) anăpădéscu

MAKE A HOLE *vb.* azvundzéscu, azundzéscu → BORE

MAKE A JOURNEY *vb.* fac sefér

MAKE A LAUGHING-STOCK OF ONESELF *vb.* mi nvăpséscu la tuţ bu-iangiádzľi

MAKE A LONG NOSE AT SMB. *vb.* ľ-dau mằndzăle (*or* múndzăle)

MAKE A LUCKY FIND *vb.* áflu mándră nicălcátă

MAKE A MESS OF SMTH. *vb.* u-adár culeáş → PUT ONE'S FOOT IN IT

MAKE A MISTAKE *vb.* (a)lăthipséscu, lăthăséscu, ftiséscu, fti-xéscu; fac aláth (*or* fac aláthos); para-cálcu, ▾para-ľau

MAKE A MOUNTAIN OUT OF A MOLEHILL *vb.* adár hírlu fúne, u-fac di per fúne (*lit. 'to make a rope out of a hair'*)

MAKE A NEAT JOB OF IT *vb.* u scot di nisáfe

MAKE AN EFFORT *vb.* ▾stríngu

MAKE AN END OF SMTH. *vb.* ▾bitiséscu → FINISH

MAKE A (NICE) MESS OF IT *vb.* u fac heártă (*lit. 'to make it boiled'*) → PUT ONE'S FOOT IN IT

MAKE A NOISE *vb.* (*as of a working device*) lăvăséscu

MAKE APPROPRIATE *vb.* 3 sg/pl ▾acáţă; **The white costumes suit you** Álbile vă-acáţă

MAKE A PRESENT *vb.* adúc nă pischési → PRESENT

MAKE A REGULAR THING OF SMTH. *vb.* li-ám tu pleáme

MAKE A RESOLVE TO DO SMTH. *vb.* → PLUCK UP ONE'S COURAGE ‖ ncľid ócľiľ (*i.e., to close one's eyes [and to do it, no matter how difficult the next step is or appears to be]*), BASME 206

MAKE A RETRIAL *vb.* prigiúdic

MAKE A ROLL (*as of a fabric*) trumbuéscu

MAKE A ROW *vb.* (*to create a scandal*) fac ghiurultíe

MAKE A RUSH *vb.* (*to scamper off*) li scármin → BOLT

MAKE A SACRIFICE (FOR) *vb.* fac dărmáne (tă)

MAKE A SHOW OF ONESELF *vb.* mi nvăpséscu la tuţ buiangiádzľi

MAKE A SIGN TO SMB. *vb.* fac sémnu

MAKE A SNOOK AT SMB. *vb.* ľ-dau mằndzăle (*or* múndzăle)

MAKE A SONG ABOUT SMTH. *vb.* (*to blame*) mi ncucutédz

MAKE A SPEECH *vb.* bag zbor

MAKE A STAND AGAINST *vb.* (*to resist*) dânâséscu, dândâséscu

MAKE A SWEET BUSINESS OF IT *vb.* u-adár căcăteásca → PUT ONE'S FOOT IN IT

MAKE A TO-DO *vb.* fac mútre, ▼strâmbu nárea

MAKE A TRIP *vb.* (*as of a carrier of goods*) arúc nă cále

MAKE A VOW *vb.* ▼leg

MAKE AWARE *vb.* ‖ *Cru:* bag pi mínte, GOLAB 207

MAKE A WOMAN PREGNANT *vb.* u-armân greáuă (*lit.* 'to leave her heavy')

MAKE BLIND *vb.* urghéscu

MAKE BLUE *vb.* albăstruéscu, murnéscu, nviñiţăscu

MAKE (BOTH) ENDS MEET *vb.* prăpséscu, puripséscu

MAKE CLEAR *vb.* (*of a liquid*) limbiséscu, limbidzăscu

MAKE DISAPPEAR *vb.* fac stifă or fac stífă; **He made everything disappear** Li feáţe stifă túte lúcrurile

MAKE DIZZY *vb.* ▼cirtăséscu → DIZZY

MAKE DRUNK *vb.* ▼mbet, ▼adár ciúrla, ▼adár stíngăle, ▼fac hrup

MAKE EASY *vb.* lişurédz, ▼ifculipséscu

MAKE EFFORTS *vb.* (*in attempting to defecate, etc.*) ▼sprem

MAKE EVEN *vb.* (*to level*) ▼ischédz

MAKE FEEL SICK *vb.* (*as of fatty fat food*) ▼angusédz

MAKE FIRM *vb.* ▼stiriuséscu; (*with nails*) ▼sfinuséscu

MAKE FOR *vb.* (*to go towards*) ▼ľau, ▼astáľu, ▼mbróstu or ▼mbrustédz

MAKE FRIENDS WITH SMB. *vb.* mi fac soţ; li apríndu aluáturile; *3 pl:* şi-ľa dúhurile; ▼ncuscrédz; **They made friends** Ncuscrárā ‖ *3 pl:* le-acáţă ghíne aloáturile, BASME 94

MAKE FRIENDS AGAIN *vb.* ▼disvér → RECONCILE

MAKE FUN OF *vb.* ▼arâd, ▼mâscâripséscu, ñ-bat péză (di) → RIDICULE ‖ strâmbu búdzâli, BASME 98

MAKE HASTE *vb.* agunéscu, ayiusescu, dau nă pálă, u dau alága

MAKE HAY OF SMTH. *vb.* fac cioáră ‖ DIARO 191: u cac huzmétea (*or* luguría); u (*or* li) li câcârusíi dípu

MAKE HEADWAY *vb.* (*to progress*) prudhipséscu

MAKE ILL *vb.* şúplic

MAKE INQUIRIES *vb.* xităxéscu, xităséscu

MAKE INTO PIECES *vb.* (*as of small pieces of bread put in one's*

MAKE

soup) ▼diñíc → DUNK

MAKE IT A POINT OF HONOR *vb.* ▼filutiniséscu, ▼filutinséscu

MAKE IT HOT FOR SMB. *vb.* itizăéscu

MAKE IT UP WITH SMB. *vb.* fac bărşíe

MAKE JEALOUS *vb.* bag tru zilíe

MAKE LESS SWOLLEN *vb.* ▼disúmflu, ▼disúflu

MAKE LOVE TO SMB. *vb.* mi zdrudéscu (cu) ‖ (*to a woman*) li-gioc meárile cu nâsă, BASME 255; *aor. 1 sg:* li băgái ghíne (cu), BASME 315

MAKE MERRY *vb.* ‖ ľ-dişcľíd iñoára, BASME 149

MAKE MERRY OVER SMB./SMTH. *vb.* strâmbu búdzâli → RIDICULE

MAKE MINCEMEAT OF SMB. *vb.* ‖ stifuséscu, BASME 171; lu spúlbir, BASME 700

MAKE MISCHIEF BETWEEN *vb.* bag zizáñe → BREED DISCORD

MAKE OFF *vb.* → TAKE ONESELF OFF

MAKE ONE'S EXIT *vb.* ies

MAKE ONESELF RIDICULOUS *vb.* mi fac (tut) arizíle (*and* -zíľe); agiúngu părămíth, mi nvăpséscu la tuţ buiangiádzľi

MAKE ONESELF SCARCE *vb.* li scármin → SCAMPER AWAY

MAKE ONESELF SMART *vb.* mi adár ca yambró

MAKE ONE'S ESCAPE *vb.* → ESCAPE

MAKE ONE'S PILE *vb.* adár căşeáre, ▼acáţ maiáuă → PROSPER

MAKE ONE'S WAY ALONG/TOWARDS *vb.* u ľau, mi ľau → TURN TO

MAKE OUT *vb.* (*to find or grasp the meaning of*) ▼achicăséscu; ▼alég

MAKE OUT ONE'S CASE *vb.* adúc tră mărtiríe

MAKE OVER *vb.* (*to remake, to remodel*) prifác, priadár

MAKE OVERABUNDANT *vb.* pára-agiúngu, paragiúngu

MAKE PEACE WITH SMB. *vb.* fac bāríşe

MAKE PROGRESS *vb. 3 impers.* ñ-cústă (lúcrulu); **Let's see who is not making enough progress in his/her work** S-vidém a cui nu-ľ cústă lúcrul; **I am not making any progress** Nu-ñ cústă lúcurlu → THRIVE

MAKE PROUD *vb.* ▼măréscu

MAKE QUIPS *vb.* → QUIP

MAKE REASONABLE *vb.* nsar

MAKE RICH *vb.* avuţăscu, ▼mbugăţăscu; **Commerce makes one rich** Tugearlâchea avuţăşte

MAKE RUDDY *vb.* ▾ruminéscu

MAKE SAD WORK OF IT *vb.* u scot di nisáfe → PUT ONE'S FOOT IN IT

MAKE SENSE *vb.* (*to be appropriate*) *3 sg impers*: acáţă

MAKE SHIFT TO LIVE *vb.* (*to resort to makeshifts*) bat tămbărălu

MAKE SMB. BEHAVE *vb.* (*threateningly*) lu-nvéţ eu panachída!

MAKE SMB. BESIDE HIMSELF *vb.* ľ-mâc urécľile → ENRAGE

MAKE SMB. DESERVE SMTH. *vb.* cataxiuséscu, cataxipséscu

MAKE SMB. QUAKE IN HIS SHOES *vb.* (*to come down hard upon smb.*) arát

MAKE SMB.'S ACQUAINTANCE *vb.* fac cunuşmáie cu, ▾cunóscu cu

MAKE SMB.'S HEAD REEL *vb.* scol di mínte, scot mădúua; **Quiet! You're making my head reel!** Tătéţ că-ñ scoásit mădúua! (*to ~ with excessive noise*) mâc urécľile ‖ *aor.* (*as a reproach*) ñi-l feáţişi cáplu drâşteálâ, DIARO 355

MAKE SMB. SIGH *vb.* suschír, súschir; **He made all the girls sigh** Túti feátile li suschirá

MAKE SOBER AGAIN *vb.* ▾disbét

MAKE SPORT OF SMB. *vb.* (*to make fun of smb.*) ñ-arâd (cu)

MAKE STIFF *vb.* ▾ncărfuséscu, ncrăfuséscu

MAKE SUITABLE *vb.* tiryiséscu

MAKE SWEET BUSINESS OF IT *vb.* u scot di nisáfe

MAKE THE BED *vb.* aştérnu trâ culcáre

MAKE THINNER *vb.* (*as of a thread*) ▾minutédz, minuţăscu

MAKE TRACKS *vb.* li scármin → SCAMPER AWAY

MAKE UGLY *vb.* urâţéscu

MAKE UNHAPPY *vb.* ▾curbisescu, ▾dhistihipséscu, ▾pisuséscu

MAKE UNSAVORY *vb.* ▾anusţăscu

MAKE-UP *s.* (*cosmetics*) buiáuă, măzeáuă, mâzíe; (*white make-up*) albeáţă → ROUGE

MAKE UP *vb.* (*to apply cosmetics*) ñ-adár fáţa cu bóie, ñ-dau cu buiáuă

MAKE UP ONE'S MIND *vb.* (*to make a decision*) taľu píta

MAKE WAR AGAINST/ON *vb.* ▾ampuliséscu → FIGHT

MAKE WARM *vb.* ▾apríndu; **Walking had made her feel warm** Imnânda u-aveá apreásă căldúra

MAKE WAY *vb.* părămirséscu

MAKE WHITE *vb.* (*as cloth*) biléscu → WHITEN

MAKE WORTHWHILE *vb.* ▾axĭuséscu [a•xi•u•], axéscu

MAKER

MAKER s. făcătór; fambricántu

MAKESHIFT: to resort to ~ bat tămbărălu

MAKING s. (*creation; putting together*) fáţire, făţeáre; adăráre, adráre; (*shaping*) turnipsíre; (*of dough*) frimintáre, frimitáre, firmitáre

MALADAPTED *adj.* ni-uidisít

MALADROIT *adj.* (a)stângu, -ngă, -ndzi, -ndze; zérvu, *m pl* zéryi

MALADY s. lângoáre → DISEASE

MALAPERT *adj.* (*impudently bold*) abrắşcu, ni-aruş(i)nát

MALARIA s. heávră, heávră lúngă, tétă; **fit of ~** hivríre; **sick
with ~** hivrít, hivrós ‖ **to have a fit of ~** mi hivreáşte, CAPIDAN
149

MALCONTENT *adj.* cripát, cărtít

MALE s. máscur, bărbát; **he-dragon** lámñea-bărbát

MALE *adj.* máscur (*ant.* theámin, feá-); bărbătéscu; (*part of an
Orthodox church reserved for men*) bărbăteásca

MALEDICTION s. anáthimă, anăthimáre, blăstém, blăstimáre, că-
tárǎ, cătăryisíre, culidzáre, hulidzáre; vlasfimíe

MALEFACTOR s. batác, cacurízic, catíle, *invar.*

MALEVOLENCE s. slăbeáţă → MALICE

MALEVOLENT *adj.* (a)rău, -ráuă, -răi, -rále; s(c)lab, urât

MALICE s. arăiáţă, slăbínţă, cáche, ináte, pícă, zăte; **to bear
~ against smb.** ñ-duc zăte; ĺ-ţân pícă, ĺ-ţân cáche

MALICIOUS *adj.* uhinát, vampír, vómbir, vurculác; **the ~ hags**
vurculáţile di moáşe ‖ arnăút *m*, -ă *f*, DIARO 75

MALICIOUSLY *adv.* aráulea

MALIGN *vb.* (*to speak ill of*) zburăscu, cacuzburăscu

MALIGNANT *adj.* ócĺu buín; **~ fate** tíhe neárcă, scriátă nfărmăcoásă

MALIGNITY s. ceapcânlắche

MALLET s. maĺ

MALLOW s. *bot.* nálbă; *also:* măláyă, muloáhă, ruyíţă

MALNOURISHED *adj.* (*undernourished*) ni-măcát

MALNUTRITION s. ni-măcáre

MALODOROUS *adj.* ambuţós, -oásă

MALODOROUSNESS s. → STENCH

MALTREAT *vb.* → ABUSE ‖ BASME 184: ĺ-scot ócĺul

MAMA s. → MOTHER

MAN *s.* om, *pl* oámiñ; (*male, husband*) bărbát; *coll.* bărbătáme; (*individual*) citămán ‖ HRISTU 5: burbat

MAN! *interj.* bre! (a)vre! re!

MAN-ABOUT-TOWN *s.* (om) amisticát

MANACLES *s. pl.* heáre *n pl*; prángă, *pl* prăndzi; *also* brăndzi

MANAGE *vb.* (*to succeed in doing; to reach or do in time*) pruf-tuséscu; **He did not ~ to hide** Nu pruftusí si s-ascúndă; (*to conduct business*) trag; **to ~ a sheep farm** trag cilnicátă; ▾chivir-niséscu, chivărniséscu, cumăndărséscu, ▾nicuchiripséscu

MANAGED *adj.* chivirnisít, cumăndărsít; (*well ~*) nicuchiripsít

MANAGEMENT *s.* chivernisíre, nicuchiripsíre, cilnicátă, cumăn-dărsíre, cumándă

MANAGER *s.* éfur, icunóm, -noámă, -nómĭ (*sic!*), -noáme; nicu-chír; *coll.* nicuchiráme; *adj.* nicuchiréscu, -reáscă, -réştâ, -réşti; **board of ~s** efuríe, efurlíche

MANDATE *s.* (*charge*) ncărcătúră

MANDATORY *s.* (*one given a mandate*) vichíľ

MANDATORY *adj.* ipuhriuticó (*no pl*)

MANDOLIN *s.* mandulín, mandulínă

MANDRAKE *s. bot.* mătrăgúnă

MANE *s.* coámă, grívă, hiote ‖ pérce, BASME 377

MANEUVER *s.* (*a calculated procedure*) tirtípe

MANFUL *adj.* căidigí, inimárcu, -rţi, -rţe; inimós, -oásă

MANGER *s.* (*as in a stable*) păhníe

MANGLE *vb.* chisédz, stúlţin, zdroámin

MANGY *adj.* (*with scabs*) arâñós, -oásă; arâñít, căsidheár, căsi-dhós, -oásă; psuryeár

MANHOOD *s.* bărbăteáţă, bărbăţâľe ‖ DIARO 116: andrâgâthíe

MANIPULATE *vb.* (*people*) ancálţu şi discálţu, gioc pi tăpsíe, víndu cu malámă şi acúmpăr cu górţă

MANIPULATIVE *adj.* → TRICKY

MANLY *adj.* bărbătéscu, -eáscă, -éştâ, -éşti

MANNA *s.* (*miraculous food*) mánă

MANNER *s.* aréu, trop, cúmpite *f pl*; háre; **bad manners** hări uráte; (*manners*) aducătúră → IN A PROPER ~

MANSERVANT *s.* huzmicheár

MANSION *s.* acaréte

MANSLAUGHTER *s.* → MASSACRE

MANTLE s. (*for women*) şcúrtă, şcúrtu, *pl* şcúrţâ

MANUFACTURE s. mălifătúră

MANUFACTURED adj. plăsát → MADE

MANUFACTURER s. fambricántu

MANURE s. cupríe, curpáie

MANURE vb. ▾cupriséscu

MANURING s. cuprisíre

MANY adj. múlţâ m, múlte f; ahânţi m, ahânte f; crímă di, jar di, plod di; ca tă Stâ-Máríe; ca aróiu di alghínă; (~ *people*) suflitáme; nă crímă di lúme; ~ **children** (*large family to take care of*) un jar di fumeáľe *or* nă crímă di ñaţi; ~ **times** mal di ori; ~ **years** málă di añ; **and ~ more** ahâte şi-ahâte; **Too ~ cooks** *spoil the broth* → COOK

MANY-COLORED adj. şáren, şirít

MAP s. hártă

MAPLE TREE s. giugástru, jugástru

MAR vb. (*as a chance*) ľ-u adár bóză; ~ **smb.'s mood** ľ-u aspárgu *or* ľ-aspárgu chéifa ‖ BELIMACE 8: ľ-frângu hătărea; *idem* 9: ľ-aspárgu hătărea

MARAUD vb. dau tărcoále

MARBLE s. mármură, mármar *or* mármară; mirmér; *adj.* mármar

MARCH s. márţu

MARCH! *interj.* *mil.* arş!

MARE s. iápă, *pl.* iápe

MARIGOLD s. *bot.* balţótă

MARINER s. cărăvyiót

MARJORAM *bot.* → WILD ~

MARK s. sémnu → SIGN

MARK vb. (*to set apart by a mark*) sémnu, (n)simnédz; simiuséscu [•mi•u•]

MARK DOWN vb. eftinipséscu

MARK UP vb. scunchéscu, scunghéscu

MARKDOWN s. eftinipsíre

MARKET s. păzáre, cirşíe, codur ‖ *Peş:* ciărsíi, ciărşíe, CL 43

MARKET PLACE s. códru, códur, for, misuhóre

MARKET-GARDENER s. bustangí, zârzâvăcí

MARKING s. simnáre

MARKUP s. scunchíre, scunghíre

MARMALADE *s.* măgiún, măgiúne, mângiún, anăcríme

MARRED *adj.* (*spoiled*) aspártu, -rtă, -rţâ, -rte

MARRIAGE *s.* loáre, ncrunáre; (*of women*) mărít, măritíş, măritáre, mártáre; (*of men*) nsuráre; **to negotiate a ~** pruxinséscu ‖ *F:* surari → ASK FOR SMB. IN ~

MARRIAGEABLE *adj.* tră măr(i)táre, ti mărít; mărtătoáre; di n călár

MARRIED *adj.* (*of a man*) nsurát, căstór; (*of a woman*) măritátă, mărtátă; (~ *by a priest*) ncrunát *m*, ncrunátă *f*; *pl.* loaţ ‖ *F:* surát, BASME 699

MARROW *s.* mădúuă, midúuă

MARRY *vb.* mi ľau (cu), ñ-leg cáplu, ▾curún, âncurún, ncrun, bag curúna, bag curúnile pe cap, bag surţeálile (n cap); (*of a man*) ▾nsor, *N:* mi sor, mi ngiug; (*of a woman*) ▾mărít (pi); **She married a very rich man** S-mărită pi un om dip avút ‖ ñ-bag lăile (cu), BASME 282 ‖ ALR 1265: **He married her** U lo ti mľáre

MARRY OFF *vb.* dau (pi)

MARSH *s.* azmác, váltu, varcó, vultúc

MARSHAL *s.* muşúr

MARSHY *adj.* băltós, -oásă, văltós, -oásă

MART *s.* păzáre

MARTEN *s.* zool. cunáve, nifíţă, nivistúľe, nvistaľán ‖ ALIA 101: (*rare*) ciciútă

MARTYR *s.* ispáti

MARTYR *vb.* (*to torture*) ▾munduéscu, ▾văsănipséscu, culăséscu

MARTYRDOM *s.* martíryiu, vásan, munduíre, schíngiu

MARVEL *s.* ciúdă, thámă, sámă, nişáne, sémnu; **She's an absolute ~ !** ≈ Ia mutreá ţe sémnu di feátă!

MARVEL *vb.* ▾(a)ñír, ▾apuriséscu, ▾ciudiséscu, ▾ciuduséscu, ▾ciuduéscu, ▾ncruţéscu, ▾thămăséscu, ▾thăvmuséscu, ▾uiñiséscu, ▾uñiséscu

MARVELLOUS *adj.* di próta, scóntră, spañiu

MASCULINE *adj.* máscur (*ant.* theámin)

MASHED POTATOES *s.* *Băi:* ciúmă di cârcăngi

MASK *s.* muţúnă, suráte, prusupídhă

MASKER *s.* aruguceár, babugheár, bubaír, *pl.* bubaíreañ; babugheár, ischinár; (*on the New Year*) liyuceár, ruguceár

MASON *s.* máistur, mástur

MASS[1] *s.* (*large body of people*) chíndră → CROWD; (*large amount, as of food*) dârlíc

MASS[2] *s.* (*as in a church*) aculuthíe, lutruyíe; **the holy ~** áyea lutruyíe; **~ for the dead** dáre

MASSACRE *s.* cărmoálă, cârdilíu, cârléşi [•léşi], cârligíe, cuţút, fănicó, lipídhă, machéľ, măchipsíre, spăstíre; **The Turks will begin the ~** Túrţiľ va bágă cuţút; **They began the ~** Băgáră lipídhă ‖ TULLIU 120: cârdălíe

MASSACRE *vb.* adár cârdilíu, bag coárdă, bag cuţút, ▾gilitipséscu, ▾măchilipséscu

MASSAGE *vb.* ‖ frec, DIARO 321

MAST *s.* (*nuts, as acorns, on the forest floor*) fágă, jir

MAST *s.* catárgu, *pl.* catárdzi; catártu, *pl.* catárte

MASTER *s.* (*owner*) aféndu, afindicó, dáşar, dómnu, nicuchír; (*skilled person*) ustă; **Like ~, like man** ≈ şi-află sáclu peáticlu

MASTIC *s.* măstícă, măstíhă

MASTICATE *vb.* mástic → CHEW

MASTURBATION *s.* malachíe

MAT *s.* aruguzínă ‖ *F:* lésă, HRISTU 2

MAT *vb.* (a)mplătéscu (*and* amblă-), mplitéscu

MATCH *s.* (*for fire*) chibrít, chibríte, chibrítă, şpírtu → STRIKE A ~

MATCH *s.* (*pair*) éşă, soáţă, uidíe; **He had no ~** Nu aveá soáţă *or* Nu aveá uidíe; **You should always search for your ~** Cáftă-ţ éşa tótna; **to meet one's ~** ñ-áflu căpáchea

MATCH *vb.* ▾uidéscu, ▾uidiséscu, ▾iduséscu, ▾tiryiséscu. dau plătárea (cu), sămâruséscu (un cu alántu); **We can't ~ him** Nu nă dăm plătárea cu nâs; **Idle words don't ~ you** Zboáre ánuste nu-ţi undzéscu

MATCH-BOX *s.* şpírtu, şpirtáră

MATCHLESS *adj.* făr-di-sóţ, fără uidíe, fâră preácľe

MATCHLESSLY *adv.* cum soţ nu áre

MATCHMAKER *s.* pruxinít

MATE *s.* soţ

MATE *vb.* (*of sheep or goats*) ▾mârléscu

MATING *s.* (*of sheep or goats*) mârlíre, mârlitúră

MATINS *s.* uóthură [ŭo•]

MATRIMONY *s.* loáre → MARRIAGE

MATRON *s.* nicuchírǎ

MATTED *adj.* (*as of a basket*) mblǎtít

MATTER *s.* (*object, question*) luyuríe, ipóthise; (*task, job, chore, work, thing*) istréte; **a ~ for women** istréte muľireáscǎ

MATTER *vb. med.* pruñédz; *also, 3 sg:* adúnǎ, coáţe

MATTER *vb.* (*to be of importance*) ‖ BATSARIA 48: **It dosen't ~ what his name is** Ţe-are s-fácǎ cum si-acľámǎ?

MATTINS *s.* → MATINS

MATTRESS *s.* duşéc, şiltée

MATURATE *vb.* ▼coc

MATURATION *s.* coáţire, cuţeáre

MATURE *adj.* agiúmtu, -mtǎ, -mţâ, -mte; cóptu, coáptǎ, cópţâ, coápte; *fig.* cu míntea coáptǎ

MAUDLIN *adj.* (*fuddled*) cǎlít

MAUL *s.* maľ

MAUL *vb.* ▼bat → BEAT

MAUNDER *vb.* (*to wander slowly and idly*) hǎlǎndǎréscu; (*to speak indistinctly or disconnectedly*) bǎbǎléscu, bâlbǎéscu, dǎrdǎréscu

MAW *s.* (*a bird's crop*) mámǎ, mámcǎ

MAWKISH *adj.* (*sickly or puerilely sentimental*) adiľós, -oásǎ; suschirós, -oásǎ; lǎcrimós, -oásǎ (*and* lǎcrǎ-); lǎcrǎmát

MAY *s.* (*the fifth month*) maiu

MAY *vb.* (*to be permitted*) am izíne; (*in wishes and imprecations*) mórvǎ, mórve, múrva; **~ you be accursed!** Anánghea s-ţu da! **Lord, ~ he not live to see tomorrow!** Mórve, Doámne, s-nu-şi apúcǎ! → BE WHAT ~, COME WHAT ~

MAYBE *adv.* poáte, poáte cǎ, bélchi, vahi; **~ it would have been good for me to die** Poáte cǎ erá ghíne s-mor; **~ he is asleep** Doárme vahi

MAY-BUG *s. ent.* bumbunár, zǎngǎnár; (*green variety*) júnǎ

MAYHEM *s.* sǎcǎtipsíre

MAYOR *s.* dhímarhu, gugeabáşi ‖ *Av, Prv, SJos:* muhtár, CL 256

MEADOW *s.* vǎloágǎ, vuloágǎ, pádinǎ *and* pǎdínǎ; gulivrágǎ; (*along a river*) ciíre, lúncǎ ‖ *SJos:* ceír, CL 43

MEADOW SAFFRON *s. bot. G:* lilínghe

MEAGER *adj.* s(c)lab, *m pl* s(c)laghi, *f pl* s(cl)ábe; iáscǎ *invar.* (*lit. 'tinder'*); loat la fáţǎ, slǎghít ca hiľán

MEAL *s.* (a)ngustáre; (*at about 4:00 - 5:00 PM*) mirínde, mirindáre; *adv.* **at ~s** la meásă → OBITUARY ~

MEALY *adj.* fărinós, -oásă

MEAN *adj.* babés, pabés, pânghiós [•ǵós], próstih ‖ DIARO 170: calpuzán

MEAN *vb.* (*to have in mind as a purpose*) numắţéscu

MEAN ILL *vb.* nu am mínte búnă

MEANDER *s.* (*as of a road*) şuţâtúră

MEANING *s.* (*sense*) nóimă

MEANINGFUL *adj.* (*and* **-~LY** *adv.*) cu mădúuă (*lit.* 'with brain')

MEANNESS *s.* băbislíche, cacurizilíche

MEANS *s.* (*smth. helpful in achieving an end*) cearé *and* **N:** cearée; *trop* → BY ALL ~ *and* BY NO ~

MEASLES *s.* purcuyíţă, prucuyíţă, pruhughíţă; **to get ~** scot prucuyíţă

MEASLY *adj.* minút, ñic

MEASURE *s.* misúră, métru; (*moderation*) usúle; **beyond ~** *adv.* prísti misúră → TAKE SMB.'S ~

MEASURE *vb.* ▼misúr, númir; **in order to ~ how deep the sea was** s-númiră cât ahândoásă erá amárea; **~ one's strength against smb.** mi misór cu; **to ~ smb. with one's eyes** mutrésc di la úngľi pân la cap → BEYOND ALL ~

MEASUREDLY *adv.* cu usúle

MEASUREMENT *s.* misuráre

MEAT *s.* cárne; **F:** cáră *or* cárră; (*children's language*) ţíţi; (*dishes with ~ as opposed to canonically fast meals*) purinteáţă; **G:** zubeálă; **preserved ~** căvrămă → EAT ~

MEAT DAY *s.* mâcătoáre

MEATBALL *s.* chifté, chióftă

MEDDLE *vb.* ▼bag, ▼ameástic

MEDDLESOME *adj.* **G:** (*of a woman*) mblustélă

MEDICINE *s.* yitríe, ghitríşcă, panádhă, pămádhă (*and* pâ-); ileáce; *obs.* ileáge; (*as a profession or branch of science*) yeatrăţâľe, yitrăţâľe, yeatrusíne

MEDIOCRE *adj.* mistótriv, *m pl* -trivĭ; nólgic

MEDITATE *vb.* arúmig, aroámig, ▼minduéscu, stau pri minduíre; ▼săluşéscu, ▼siluyiséscu

MEDITATION *s.* arumigáre, minduíre, siluyisíre

MEDITATIVE *adj.* minduít

MEDIUM *adj.* (*intermediate, average*) nólgic

MEDLAR *s.* muşmoálă, muzmúlă; *Lvz:* măşmúlă; soárbă, măceáşe

MEDLAR TREE *s.* muzmuléu (*and* muzmuľéu, muşmuléu), *Lvz:* brácean

MEDLEY *s.* ameástică, amisticătúră, mintitúră

MEED *s.* (*reward*) muştináre

MEEK *adj.* (*modest*) tápin → HUMBLE; (*deficient in spirit or courage*) andirsít

MEET *adj.* (*fit*) undzít

MEET *vb.* ▾astáľu (cu), mi aflu pri cále (cu), ▾tihiséscu, ▾mpichiu; *G:* ▾astăhiséscu; dau ócľi cu, ▾andămuséscu, anăpădéscu; ▾cunuştuséscu; **He did not ~ with us** Nu deáde ócľi cu noi; **We met him on the road** Lu-anăpădím pri cále; **and when he met them** şă di cára si cunuştusí cu năşi

MEET ONE'S MASTER *vb.* ñ-áflu másturlu ‖ *Prv:* ñ-áflu bárba, CL 38

MEET TROUBLE HALF-WAY *vb.* u cáftu ngăceárea cu luminárea

MEET WITH DIFFICULTIES *vb.* (*to be in trouble*) ved zóre; **He is meeting with great difficulties** Veáde zóre máre

MEETING *s.* adunáre, anáre, adunătúră, adămusíre, sobór

MEGLENO-ROMANIAN *s.* ‖ STERE 58: tucán

MELANCHOLY *s.* milancolíe

MELEE *s.* mintireáje (*and* mindi-), ambărtuíre

MELILOT *s. bot.* (*sweet clover*) sulfínă, sulhínă, sulchínă, surfínă, surhínă, struhínă; tindilínă

MELODIOUS *adj.* armătusít

MELODY *s.* miludhíe, ih

MELON *s.* gălbóñu *m*, peápine *m*, pipóñu *m*, pupóñu

MELON-BED *s.* şirchinăríe

MELT *vb.* ▾tuchéscu; (*as of snow*) ▾ihtiséscu; (*as of firewood*) hunipséscu; **The firewood ~ed away in the fire** Leámnile hunipsíră tu foc; curundédz; (*of a sick person*) **to ~ like wax** ▾tuchéscu di mpróstu

MELTED *adj.* (*of butter, etc.*) tuchít

MELTING *s.* tucheáre, tuchíre

MEMBRANE *s.* (*as the outmost layer of a plum*) coáje, peáje; (*a lamb's membrane*) típă → PEEL

MEMORY *s.* (*the power or procss of remembering*) ‖ PC: tâneáre di mínte

MEMBRUM

MEMBRUM VIRILE *s.* púlă (*vulg.*); *also:* ciulícă (*lit. 'tipcat'*), físe (*lit. 'nature'*), hăláte (*lit. 'tool'*), mándal (*lit. 'bolt'*), nánciu (*lit. 'rump'*), noáce (*lit. 'parson's nose'*), noádă (*lit. 'rump'*); púţă; sóche (*lit. 'bung'*); **a man with a big ~** pulără

MENACE *s.* fuvértă → THREAT

MENACE *vb.* (*to threaten*) ▾angréc; (*to be under threat*) mi páşte piríclʼul

MENACING *adj.* fuvirós, -roásă

MEND *vb.* ndréptu, mirimiţéscu, mirimitiséscu, măsturipséscu, mpeátic (*clothes, etc.*)

MENDACIOUS *adj.* plan

MENDER *s.* (*of clothes, stockings, etc.*) cârpáciu

MENDICANCY *s.* dicúñe, yiftilíche, yiftaryió, yifţălʼe

MENDICANT *s.* ţiritóñu → BEGGAR

MENDING *s.* miriméte; ~ *clothes* mpiticáre

MENFOLK *s.* oámiñ *m pl*

MENIAL *adj.* (*humble*) nclʼinát

MENINGITIS *s.* mininghítă

MENSES *s. pl.* mes, lunárile *f pl def;* arádhă ‖ PC: săhăţ *f pl;* cúscri

MENSTRUATION *s.* mes; **She's got her ~** lʼ-víñe méslu → MENSES

MENTALLY *adv.* (*to myself*) ‖ BELIMACE 65: ăn vétea-a mea

MENTION *s.* (*with reverence and devotion*) ‖ LITURG 123: acuitíră; acuitíra *f sg def*

MENTION *vb.* ▾anăfirséscu, fac ti măsláte; **He almost did not ~ her** Nu pára u fáţe ti măsláte; ▾adúc amínte (trâ); **He ~ed you** Pri tíne-amínte ti-aduţeá; **Why are you ~ing death?** Ţe adúţi amínte moárte? ‖ LITURG 23: acuitím *1 pl;*

MEOW *vb.* ñáur, ñiurédz

MEPHITIC *adj.* ambuţós, -oásă

MERCANTILE *adj.* tugiréscu, -eáscă, -éşţâ, -éşti

MERCER *s.* pândzár

MERCHANT *s.* émbur, tugeár, măyăzár, măyăjár, prămătár, părmătár, prămătéftu, părmătéfcu

MERCHANDISE *s.* prămătíe, părmătíe; (*livestock*) tutípută, málă; (*animals sold for meat*) săváte, suváte

MERCIFUL *adj.* ñil(ă)ós, -oásă; ímir

MERCILESS *adj.* ni-ñilós; (*speaking of fate*) tíhe neárcă; scriátă nfărmăcoásă

MERCURIAL adj. (changeable) 3 sg: nu sta pri únă

MERCURY s. gheárghir, yeáryir

MERCY s. ñílă; **at the ~ of** dúpă vola a, dúpă ñíla a; **to have ~ on** ñi-i ñílă di; **Have ~ on my house!** Di cása-ñ híbă-ţ ñílă! **it is a ~ that** calái-că → CLEMENCY

MERCY! interj. amán!

MERE s. báltă, blátă

MERGE vb. ▼fac únă

MERIT s. axíe, axítă

MERRIMENT s. (gaiety) hărăcupíľe, haréi, hilăríe; (good time) ziaféte, féstă

MERRY adj. hăriós, -oásă; hărăcóp, -oápă, -óchi, -oápe

MERRY-GO-ROUND s. drâmbálă, lişór, vârticóniţă, vărticoániţă

MESENTERY s. anat. bidzáre (and bizáre), bâdzáre

MESS s. căcătúră → FAILURE; MAKE A ~ OF SMTH.

MESS vb. (to dirty) ▼murdăripséscu; (to defecate, as of an infant) ▼fac

MESSAGE s. idhíse; (as from an authority) timbíhe, timbíe ‖ **to leave a ~** alás zbor, BASME 6

MESSENGER s. (as in a townhall) sihăryeát, sihăvyeár, purtóyir ‖ DIARO 335: psihudhróm

MESSY adj. căcătéscu, -eáscă, -éşţâ, -éşti

METAL s. métal

METER s. métru n; **two ~s** doáuă métri

METHOD s. mithoádă

METHODICALLY adv. cu husúle or cu usúle

METHODICALNESS s. usúle

METICULOUSNESS s. garaméte

METTLE s. físe → SHOW ONE'S ~

MEW vb. ñáur, ñiurédz [ñi•u•], fac meau ‖ ALIA 98, 3 sg: ñĭurseáşte, neuriseáşte, neaurisái, ceáună, cióne, ciuneádză, aúrlă, gărnéşte, plândze, zghileáşte

MEW! interj. meau, ñeau

MEW (UP) vb. (to confine) âncľíd tu căfése

MEWS s. ahúre → STABLE

MICA s. fáţa-a-lóclui

MICKEY-MOUSE ‖ ≈ **Cru:** ciaciúl-mangiúl, GOLAB 210

MIDAFTERNOON

MIDAFTERNOON s. chindíe

MIDDAY s. ñíză-dzâuă; *adj*. di ñiză-dzâuă; ~ **heat** căldúră di ñíză-dzâuă

MIDDEN s. cupríe

MIDDLE s. ñídză (*and* nídză, níză) ñádză, mése, nólgic, ñílgioc, ñólgiuc, ínimă, chéntru; **in the ~ (of)** tu mése (di), tu mésea di, (a)námisa (di), nídză (di), (tu) nóljuca (di), nólgiuca (di), nólgica (di); tu buríclu a *or* tu buríclu di; **in the ~ of the yard** nólgica di ubór; **in the ~ of the forest** tu buríclu a pădúrilei; **in the ~ of the summer** ñádză-veáră; **in the ~ of the winter** ñádză-iárnă

MIDDLE *adj*. ñijlucán, ñilgiucán, nulgicán; di meáse *or* dit meáse; aţél di mése

MIDDLE-AGED *adj*. misóchir

MIDDLE-CLASS s. arhundilâche, ciorbagilâche

MIDDLING *adj*. nólgic; (*mediocre*) misótriv, m pl -ótrivĭ (*sic*)

MIDGE s. *ent*. cunúpe, muşíţă, muşcóiu, ţânţár

MIDGET s. (*usu. as a nickname*) ficiu

MIDMOST *adj*. tu mése

MIDNIGHT s. ñadză-noápte; **at ~** ñadză-nópţâ; tu dísa di noápte; **until ~** până ñádză-nópţâ

MIDPOINT s. mése, chéntru

MIDST s. mése

MIDSUMMER s. ‖ CUVATA 11: ñadzăveáră

MIDSUMMER DAY s. Yianiú

MIDWIFE s. bábă, mămíe (*and* mâ-)

MIDWINTER s. ‖ BATSARIA 45: ñádză-iárnă

MIEN s. purtátic, fáţă, ópse

MIFF *vb*. ľ-u aspárgu

MIGHT: with ~ and main *adv*. a mórtului → FORCE, ENERGY

MIGHT *vb*. (*conjecturally*) va híbă

MIGHTY *adj*. (*as of God*) nvârtuşát

MIGRATION s. ‖ (*usu. of shepherds*) părcali, HRISTU 52

MIGRATORY *adj*. (*as of birds*) călătór, -oáre, -órĭ, -oáre

MILD *adj*. bunác; *m/f sg* moále, *m/f pl* moľ; muláşcu ‖ DIARO 159: bunáşcu

MILDEW s. mánă

MILDNESS s. (*of smb.'s character*) imiráme, imireáţă

MILFOIL s. bot. şuricínă, şurichínă, **G:** şiriuchínă; coádă şu-richínă

MILITARY CAREER s. armătulíche

MILITARY SERVICE s. aschirlắche

MILITIAMAN s. (of armed Greeks against the Ottoman rule) armatulắ; coll. armatuláme

MILK s. lápte, pl lắpturi n; **large quantity of** ~ lăptáriu; **sheep curled** ~ **G:** cutmáciu; **sour** ~ lápte vinít, lápte strivuít; **skim** ~ **Src:** beleníţă

MILK vb. múlgu (→ § 32) and múrgu; lăptuéscu

MILK CAKE s. lăptúcă

MILK PAIL s. ‖ **Cru:** găleátă, GOLAB 217

MILK TOOTH s. dínte di lápte

MILKER s. (worker) mulgătór, muldzár; (sheep) (a)plicătoáre ‖ (of sheep) **Peş:** pirét, CL 258

MILKING s. muldzeáre, murdzeáre, múldzire, lăptuíre

MILKMAN s. lăptár

MILKSOP s. muláşcu

MILKY WAY s. Cálea a láptilui, Cálea a páľilor (lit. 'The Way of Straws'), Cálea máre (lit. 'The Great Way') ‖ **SJos:** Brânu ura-nólui (lit. 'The Sky's Belt'); **Av:** Litrupódh, CL 254

MILL s. moáră → BRING GRIST TO ONE'S ~

MILL WHEEL s. vurvúra a moáráľei

MILL vb. ▾máţin, máţir, másnu; Iu ascúche únă hoáră máţină únă moáră ≈ **In unity there is strength** (lit. 'Where an entire village spits one can run a water mill')

MILL-DUST s. păspálă, pâspáľ

MILLER s. murár m, muráră f ‖ **Perd:** mulắr, **Plat:** măluná, **Kat:** mălonă, **Pro:** miluná, B-ARCH 352

MILLET s. meľ

MILLION s. miliúnă, miliúne [•li•ú•] ‖ **Cru:** ecatomírie, GOLAB 214

MILLIONAIRE s. miliunístru

MILLSTONE s. cheátră di moáră

MILLRACE s. ţăfúne (di moáră)

MINARET s. minarée

MINATORY adj. fuvirós, -oásă

MINCE vb. toc; chisédz; also **S:** csedz; **She ~ed the meat** U chisă

MINCEMEAT

cárnea

MINCEMEAT → MAKE ~ OF SMB.

MIND *s.* mínte (*and* mínde); (*reason*) fichíre, fichiúre; **to be in two ~s** stau andoáulea [an•dŭáŭ•lᵉa]; (*intelligence*) mădúuă ‖ (*opinion*) ʜʀɪsᴛu 29: **I am of a ~ with Viti** Mini estu pi mintia a li Viti → CHANGE ONE'S ~; BE OUT OF ONE'S ~; GIVE A PIECE OF ONE'S ~

MIND *vb.* ľau di ureácľe, ▾ciuléscu, saidiséscu, săldiséscu; am ménga la; **~ your lamb!** Ái-ţâ ménga la mânár! **mind one's eye** ñ-fac ócľiľ pátru ‖ ʙᴀsᴍᴇ 448: bag tu córnu; ʜʀɪsᴛu 58, *2 pl imper*: fiţeţi-i ochĭă patru!

MIND ONE'S OWN BUSINESS *vb.* ñ-trag cálea; **My friend, mind your own business!** Trádzi-ţ cálea, oáspe! *or* şedz pri oáuă-ţ! (*lit.* *'Sit on your (own) eggs!'*); *Also:* Nu-ţ lipséscu căstrăvéţ truşíe? (*lit.* *'Don't you need pickled cucumbers?'*) ‖ ʙᴀsᴍᴇ 82: Mutreá-ţ lú-crulu! (*lit.* *'Look (at) your (own) business!'*)

MIND (THE ...!) várda!

MINDFUL *adj.* câştigós, -oásă; mucaitlâ, *f* -loáñe, *m pl* -ládz

MINDFULNESS *s.* (*attention, consideration*) usúle, mucaitláche

MINDLESS *adj.* ni-minduít, astráptu, azvimturát; fâră nisáfe

MINE *poss. pron.* a mel *or* amél *m*; a mea *or* ameá *f*; a meľ (*or* améľ) *m pl*; a meále (*or* ameále) *f pl*; *g/d sg m* a milúi; *g/d pl m* and *f* a milór; **My people weren't happy** A milór nu lă părú ghíne ‖ ʟɪᴛuʀɢ 124: añéu *m*, amé *f*, añéi *pl m*

MINE *s.* (*source of supply*) madéme, madéne

MINERAL WATER *s.* ‖ **Cru:** ápă ácră, ɢoʟᴀʙ 196

MINER'S PICK *s.* dhicléle

MINGLE *vb.* ▾(a)meástic, ▾mintéscu

MINGLING *s.* (a)misticătúră

MINIMIZE *vb.* (*to belittle, to disparage*) fac mânică di tămbáre; nu-l dau di curáuă

MINT *s.* (*plant, pill, drink*) méntă (*and* méndă); (a)yeázmă, (a)yeázmu, yízmă

MINT *s.* (*establishment where coins are made*) tărăp(h)înă

MINUS *s.* (*lack, deficiency*) scárţu

MINUS *prep.* fâră (*and* fără)

MINUTE *s.* (*record of a meeting*) mâzbâtă

MINUTE *adj.* (*used with affection*) ‖ şimşiríc, ᴅɪᴀʀo 246

MINUTELY *adv.* pân la şíľe

MINX *s.* bandílă

MIRACLE *s.* ciúdă, ciudíe; *also*: nişeáne, nişáne, thávmă, thámă, sámă, *pl* thámate *or* sáme; thămăturyíe; **What a ~!** Máre thámă! *or* Sámă máre! **How did this ~ occur?** Cum s-feáţe sáma aístă? **to work ~s** adár tháme, adár thămăturyíi

MIRE *s.* (*mud*) tínă, láspe; (*alluvial ~*) alúnizmă, cuciumór

MIRROR *s.* yilíe, lăyíe, luyíe ‖ **Prv:** cathréfti, CL 40 ‖ **Amc, An, Cľis, Gra, Kast, Kok:** γilí B-ARCH 236 ‖ HRISTU 23: cutie

MIRROR *vb.* ▾yilcéscu, ▾lăyicéscu

MIRTH *s.* arâdeáre, arâdire

MIRY *adj.* glăburós, -oásă → MUDDY

MISADVENTURE *s.* → MISFORTUNE

MISAPPROPRIATE *vb.* ľau, ncálic

MISBEGOTTEN *adj.* (*illegitimate*) báştu, *m pl* -ştâ → BASTARD

MISCARRIAGE *s.* (*of sheep*) băgătúră, vătămătúră

MISCARRIED *adj.* (*messy, unsuccessful*) căcát *m/n*, căcátă *f* (*lit. 'shitty'*); **a ~ question** căcátă luyuríe

MISCARRY *vb.* lu-arúc crud (*lit. 'to throw it out raw'*); astrăchéscu, asturchéscu

MISCHANCE *s.* tirsilâche, lăiáţă → MISFORTUNE

MISCHIEF *s.* (*base act*) muşiteáţă, muşuteáţă → MAKE ~ BETWEEN

MISCHIEVOUS *adj.* s(c)lab, *m pl* s(c)laghi, *f pl* s(c)lábe; şirét, -reátă; urât, urút, muşmoálă; **a ~ child** geanabét; **a ~ girl** bandílă

MISCHIEVOUSLY *adv.* aráulea [•ráu•]

MISCHIEVOUSNESS *s.* vumbirlâche

MISCREANT *s.* batác

MISCUE *s.* sfálmă → MISTAKE

MISDEED *s.* slăbeáţă, -bíľe, -bínţă

MISER *adj.* zăráf, *pl* -ráhĭ → STINGY

MISERABLE *adj.* ndzérnu; túmtu, *m pl* -mţâ; **the ~ mother-in-law** túmta di soácră; ca vai di míne, ca vai di tíne, *etc.*

MISERLINESS *s.* filaryiríe → STINGINESS

MISERLY *adj.* stres, streásă, streşĭ, streáse; **A ~ person knows how to take, but does not know how to give** Stréslu s-ľa şti, nu şi s-da → STINGY

MISERY *s.* nivóľe, *pl* nivóľ *and* nivóľuri; anánghe, lipsítă

MISFORTUNE

MISFORTUNE s. arăiáţă; *also*: aráuă, atihíe, atihíre, bileáuă, cacurizilíche, cătráţă, chiaméte [k'i•a•], chícută, ciupulíc laiu, ciupulíc veárde, cóbă, curbisíre, dérte, *pl* dérturi; distihíe, ghidére, hálă, hăndăcusíre, lăiáţă, oáră láie, pácus *or* pácuz, páthimă, păţâre, pusoágă, stuhináre, taxiráte, târsilâche, tirsilâche, ugoádă, ugudíre; **The moment of ~ has come** Víñe oára a oárăľei; **What ~ has stricken her?** Ţe taxiráte u-áre aflátă? **Let him die in ~!** S-moáră tu lăéţ! **He was stricken by great ~** ăľ cădzú chícută máre ‖ STERE 8: trămăndáni

MISGIVING s. măndátă

MISHAP s. oáră láie → MISFORTUNE

MISHMASH s. mintitúră

MISJUDGE vb. ▼(a)plănăséscu, (a)plăniséscu, ▼plănéscu; am urbárea a găľíiñlor (*lit.* '*to have chickens' blindness'*)

MISLAY vb. → MISPLACE

MISLEAD vb. ▼plănéscu; **Your word has misled us** Nă plăním pi zbórlu a tău

MISPLACE vb. ▼(s)chérdu

MISS s. (*failure in some children's games*) úchi *f*

MISS vb. (*to escape*) cher; (*to feel the absence of*) mi ľa pónlu (di, să)

MISS THE MARK vb. (fig.) ≈ u-adár taratóre

MISS THE OPPORTUNITY vb. ‖ cher oára, BASME 38

MISSING: **to be ~** hiu cusúre, lipséscu

MISSION s. (*task*) sárţină, sálţină, nsărţináre, ncărcătúră

MIST s. négură, cătăcníe, cătăhnníe, iámă

MISTAKE s. sfálmă; *also*: aláth, (a)láthos, alăthipsíre, ftisíre, ftixíre, hătáie, stépsu, stipsíre → MAKE A ~

MISTAKEN adj. ftisít

MISTER s. chir *invar*

MISTLETOE s. bot. vâscu, véscu, ovéscu; **Florlu, Brz**: uvéz (*and* uvédz)

MISTRESS s. (*owner*) nicuchíră; (*lover*) ayăpitcoáñe, moróză, muşavéră

MISTREAT vb. yumărséscu, tălăéscu (tu halé)

MISTREATMENT s. catáhrise

MISTRUST s. afirítă

MISTY adj. nigurós, -oásă

MISUNDERSTANDING *s.* síyise

MISUSE *s.* catáhrise

MISUSE *vb.* ‖ CUNIA 3: catahriséscu

MITE: **not a ~** cât trâ yitríe → JOT

MITER *s.* (*liturgical headdress*) mítră

MITIGATE *vb.* mi moľu

MITTEN *s.* brumáncă, -ngă; mitáne, pumânică → GLOVE

MIX *vb.* ▾(a)meástic; *also:* ▾anăcătuséscu, hurhuléscu, ▾mintéscu (*and* mindéscu), ▾frângu; **Singing, the shepherds are mixing their milk** Láptile și-l frângu cântândalui căşăriľi ‖ **to ~ the cards** ALR 1272: *3 sg:* minteáşte cắrţăle

MIXED *adj.* (*as of liquids*) mintít (*and* mindít) ‖ ALR 1624: (**some good and** *some bad*) j-búne şi slábe

MIXED-UP *adj.* cutruburát → CONFUSED

MIXTURE *s.* ameástică, amisticătúră, mintíre (*and* mindíre)

MOAN *s.* dzeámit → GROAN

MOAN *vb.* dzem → GROAN

MOB *s.* ciuplicheáuă → CROWD

MOB *vb.* ▾stivăséscu

MOBSTER *s.* haramíu

MOCK *s.* (*one that is the object of derision*) şúpir, şúpirlu a lúmiľei

MOCK *vb.* ▾buiséscu → RIDICULE

MOCKER *s.* pizuitór, pizuiáric, mbizuiáric, şupăráiu

MOCKERY *s.* arâdeáre; *also:* pizuíre, mbizuíre, mbizuitúră, péză, şupăráre, şúpir, şúpur ‖ VELO 70: măzăli *f*

MOCKING *adj.* pizuiárnic → SCOFFING

MOCKINGLY *adv.* tr-arâdeáre, tră şúpir ‖ ti curoidhu [ku•rói•dhu], DIARO 111

MODE *s.* trop, ceará, *N:* cearée, aréu, luyíe, sóie, turlíe

MODEL *s.* (*pattern*) călapódhe; (*as in embroidery*) xómbľu, iurnécă, urnéche

MODERATE *adj.* (*average*) nólgic; (*as in eating or drinking*) luyursít

MODERATE *vb.* hăminédz

MODERATELY *adv.* cu métru

MODERATION *s.* (*measure, restraint, temperance*) métru, usúle; **He speaks with ~** Zburáşte cu métru

MODEST *adj.* tápin; **Be more ~!** Dipúni-ţ nările! → HUMBLE

MODIFY *vb.* ▾prifác

MODISH *adj.* galántu, prăpsít, prividzút, pruvidzút

MODISTE *s.* mudhístră

MODULATION *s.* (*of a song*) frămtúră (*and* frâm-)

MOIETY *s.* (*half*) giumitáte

MOIL: with ~ and toil *adv.* rúfu-n-búfu [•fum•bú•]

MOIRE s. tex. ghizíe

MOIST *adj.* nuţít → HUMID

MOISTEN *vb.* ▾nuţéscu

MOISTURE *s.* vlágă → HUMIDITY

MOLAR TOOTH *s.* măseáuă ‖ ALIA 60: muşeá, măşeáu, cărínt, că-ríndi, frâmceáu, frunimíntu, dínte máre, suprădánţ; *NPrv:* grínde, *Vil:* gríndi, B-ARCH 160

MOLD *s.* (*fungus*) múhlă

MOLD FRAME *s.* (*circular frame for molding the cheese called căşcăvál*) stifáne

MOLD *vb.* (*to give shape*) umbliséscu; (*to become moldy*) muhli-dzăscu

MOLDER *vb.* (*to crumble*) fármu, ▾zmínut

MOLDINESS *s.* muhlidzáme

MOLDING *s.* (*giving shape*) umblisíre; (*becoming moldy*) muhli-dzâre

MOLDY *adj.* múhlid, muhlidzât, muciulít

MOLE *s.* muşmán, muşuróiu, şumiróiu, şumuróiu ‖ ALIA 102: muşu-rói, măşărói, şărămói, şirimói, şirumói, şimirói, himurói, şir-mói, şoáric órbu, pundíchi, tiflunádă

MOLE-CRICKET s. ent. ‖ *GSus:* cânle dumnedzălui, CL 41

MOLEHILL *s.* ‖ óhtu di şumuróñu → MAKE A MOUNTAIN OUT OF A ~

MOLLIFY *vb.* ▾amóĺu; (*to soften*) agăliséscu; (*to solace*) ▾az-bún

MOLLYCODDLE *s.* muláşcu

MOLT *vb.* ‖ PC: alăxéscu pérlu

MOMENT *s.* oáră, *pl* ori; *also* hópă, stic, stiymíe; **crucial ~** oára a oárăĺei; **He was waiting for her to come at any ~** U-aş-tiptá oáră di oáră; (*favorable time*) **He found the ~** Ĺ-află oara; (*on the spot, immediately*) tr-un stic, tr-un stic di oáră; **for the ~** → FOR THE TIME BEING; **Wait a ~!** Aşteáptă-mă ună ténghe di oáră! ‖ HRISTU 28, 67, 99: op (*cf.* hópă)

MONACHAL *adj.* (*monastic*) călugăréscu, -eáscă, -éşţâ, -éşti

MONASTERY *s.* mănăstír (*and* mâ-), mânistér; (*small ~*) aschitar-yió

MONASTIC *adj.* călugăréscu, -eáscă, -éşţâ, -éşti

MONDAY *s.* lunĭ; *on ~* lúnea; **on a ~ towards the evening** únă lúne de cătră seárâ ‖ *Mul, Pal, Plat, Pur:* lúnă, *Gard, Perd:* lun, *Kat, Vil:* luñ, *Els:* lúne, B-ARCH 533

MONEY *s.* parádz, pradz *pl*, pară *sg* ('coi'); *also* pără (*and* pâ-ră); (*savings*) picúĭ; *N:* angărmárĭ, agărmári *and* gărmárĭ *pl*; **He does not have ~** Nu áre angărmárĭ; álghi *m pl* (*lit.* 'white [gadgets]'); (*~ solicited during a mass, etc.*) zítimă

MONEY BAG *s.* púngă, chésă

MONEY ORDER *s.* dimându di parádz

MONEY TALKS AND BULLSHIT WALKS ≈ Zboáre múlte, ftóhe máre (*lit.* 'many words [spell] big poverty')

MONEYBOX *s.* (*coin bank*) cumbără

MONEYCHANGER *s.* (*person*) zăráf, săráf

MONEYED *adj.* avút

MONITOR *vb.* (*to observe, to check*) privégľu

MONK *s.* călúgăr, călúgur, călúgru, calóir; *dim.* călugăráş

MONKEY *s.* maimúţă, maimúuă, maimún, măimún, múuă, jabéc, jubéc, şubéc

MONKEY TRICK *s.* maimunlíche

MONKEY WITH A BUZZ SAW *vb.* ≈ ñ-bag cáplu tu tástru

MONKISH *adj.* călug(ă)réscu, -eáscă, -éşţâ, -éşti

MONOGRAM *s.* (*a sultan's monogram on coins, etc.*) túră, dúră

MONOPOLY *s.* (*lease*) báltu

MONSTER *s.* móstru, ni-óm, săcătínă → DRAGON

MONSTROSITY *s.* ur(â)teáţă, ur(â)ţáme

MONTENEGRIN *s.* ‖ BELIMACE 19: caradác, *pl def* caradádzli, *ibid*

MONTENEGRO *s.* Cărădă ‖ BELIMACE 19: Múnte Lai, *def* Múntili Lai

MONTH *s.* mes *m, pl* meşĭ; (*rare*) lúnă; **one ~** únă lúnă *or* ună lúnă di dzăle; **about two ~s** ca doi meşi di dzâľe

MONUMENT *s.* ‖ *Cru:* spomeníc, GOLAB 250

MOO *vb.* mudzéscu

MOO *interj.* (*of cattle*) mu *or* muú

MOOCH ABOUT *vb.* hălăndăréscu, misúr steálile

MOOD

MOOD s. ori pl; **to be in a good** ~ hiu cu chéife, hiu tu ori, am búnile, am cuc; **in a bad** ~ cu cúrlu n sus; **to mar smb.'s** ~ → MAR ‖ **to be in no** ~ **(for)** nu-ñ árde (tră), BASME 469

MOODY adj. cu oáră, cu ori, cu órile

MOON s. lúnă; **full** ~ lúnă mplínă ‖ Cot: alúnă, B-ARCH 5

MOONLIGHT s. ‖ HRISTU 151: fosă di lună

MOONSTRUCK adj. (mentally unbalanced) aumbrát, agudít, (romantically sentimental) ayăchipsít

MOP THE FLOOR WITH SMB. vb. rizil(ips)éscu, tălăéscu tu halé

MOPE vb. (to become dejected) ▾cârtéscu

MOPPET s. (doll) păpúşe; (child) míncu

MOPPING s. aştirdzeáre, aşteárdzire

MORBID adj. (sickly) lângurós, -oásă

MORDANT adj. nţăpătós, -oásă, tăʎós, -oásă, tăʎitós, -oásă

MORE cáma; **Give me** ~ Dă-ñ cáma; ~ **than an hour** cáma di únă oáră; máta; **I will send** ~ Va máta pitréc; **once** ~ nícă únă oáră; ma and Smr: mai; **You've been to me** ~ **than a mother and** ~ **than a sister** Tíne-ñ fuşi ma di múmă ş-ma di sóră; (~ numerous) ma mulţ m, ma múlte f; ~ **lambs than rams** ma mulţ ñeli di birbéţi; **You want some** ~? Ma vrei? **and many** ~ ahâte şi-ahânte; tépăr; ~ **than** astáʎe di; ~ **and** ~: **Man's life shrinks** ~ **and** ~ Cioára a ómlui si-adúnă aţía-di-aţía; ~ **than** di prisúpră; ~ **than a week** nă siptămână ş-di prisúpră; di pri; **Good friends care of each other** ~ **than brothers** Búñʎi oáspiţ s-vor di pri fraţ → ANY ~ ‖ BASME 429: ma nsus di ‖ disúpră di; **I love my granny** ~ **than anyone else** disúpră di tuţ u voi máea, DIARO 357

MOREL s. bot. arţivúrţe f pl

MORELLO CHERRY-TREE s. víşin, víşan, yíşan; (the fruit) víşină, víşnă, víş ană

MORNING s. dimineáţă, tahináre, pl tahinări and tahinăi; tahináuă, tahínimă, tiheánă; **from** ~ **till night** di tahiná până seára, di dimineáţa păn(ă) cătră seáră, di dimineáţă pân tu ascápit; **once in the** ~ únă tahináuă; adv. tahiná [•hi•] or tainá [ta•i•]; HRISTU 27: dimiaţă

MORNING PRAYER s. uóthură

MORNING STAR s. luţeáfirlu di dimineáţă

MOROCCO LEATHER s. curdhuváne, saftiáñă, săhtiáne, săfheáne

MORON s. glar → STUPID

MOROSE *adj.* mutrusít; ursúz, *m pl* -újĭ, *f pl* -úze → SULKY

MOROSENESS *s.* schiviríe, ursuzlâche

MORROW *s.* a doáua-zĭ, dzúa alántă ‖ BASME 53: adoáua-z; BASME 54: adoá-ză

MORSEL *s.* (*a small piece*) bucătíce, cumătíce

MORTGAGE *m.* bifă

MORTAR *s.* dubéc, *pl* dubéţe; dubéche, *pl* dubéchi; ghiubéc, ghiubíc; **We grind coffee in a** ~ Cafélu l-chisăm tu dubéche; (*a bronze* ~) (h)ăváne

MORTICIAN *s.* (*undertaker*) muleaftă

MOSAIC *s.* (*small pieces of stone, etc.*) muzaíc

MOSQUE *s.* geamíe, jamíe; (~ *without a minaret*) micéte

MOSQUITO NET *s.* cunuphéră

MOSS *s.* múşcĺu, vlágă, zvoĺu *and* zvuĺu; **Rolling stone does not catch** ~ Cheátra arucutoásă vlágă nu acáţă

MOSSY *adj.* muşcĺós, -oásă

MOST *adv.* nai; **the** ~ **beautiful thing** nai cáma muşeátlu lúcru

MOTH *s. ent.* mólíţă; mulíţă (*and* -ĺí-), mólţă; saracufái, *pl* saracufáiañ → EMPEROR ~

MOTHER *s.* dádă; *also:* ímă, máică, mámă, mánă (Epir); mă, măníţă, múmă; (*old* ~) oámă; **my** ~ mú-mea, măníţa-ñ; **his** ~ mă-sa (*and* mâ-sa) ‖ *SJos:* băná, CL 38; **the** ~ **of the two children** măsa a doilu ñiţ, HRISTU 41

MOTHER-CHURCH *s.* mitrópule

MOTHER-IN-LAW *s.* soácră, soácără; **his/her** ~ soácăr-sa

MOTHER-OF-PEARLS *s.* sidéfe

MOTION: to set every spring in ~ mi fac páde

MOTIVE *s.* (*reason, cause*) furñíe

MOTTLED *adj.* şáren, şirít

MOTTLE WITH RED *vb.* plăvânédz; *adj.* (*of a sheep*) plăvântát

MOULD BOARD *s.* (*part of a plough*) pĺor

MOUND *vb.* → KNOLL

MOUNT *s.* (*an instance of mounting, as a horse*) (a)ncălicáre

MOUNT *vb.* (a)ncálic, angálic; ~ **on horseback** (*in children's speech*) mi bag décă (*or* déca); (*to give oneself airs*) **to** ~ **the high horse** mi ngroş; *tex.* ~ **the warp** năvădéscu

MOUNTAIN *s.* múnte, múnde *usu. m; occasionally f; adj.* (*a* ~ *horse, a* ~ *torrent*) muntíş, mundíş → MAKE A ~ OUT OF A MOLEHILL ‖

MOUNTAINOUS

Cru: múnte *f*, *as in* múntea tútă 'the whole mountain', GOLAB 236

MOUNTAINOUS *adj.* muntós, -oásă

MOUNTEBANK *s.* şarlatán

MOURN *vb.* zghiléscu → LAMENT

MOURNER *s.* and *adj.* jilít

MOURNING *s.* jále, jeále, jilíre, lípe, lut

MOURNING CLOTHES *s.* stráñe di písă; lăi *pl* ‖ **to put on ~** mi nvéscu tu lăi, BASME 460; tu lăi [lắ•i], DIARO 414

MOUSE *s.* şoáric, *dim.* şuricúş; (*female*) şuricoáñe; *coll.* şuricáme

MOUSE-TRAP *s.* bátcă, *pl* bắtţâ

MOUTH *s.* gúră, aróstru, aróstru; **He has many ~es to feed** Áre guri múlte; **graceful ~** gúră di cutíe; (**~ jar**) pífchiu, pífthhiu

MOUTH ORGAN *s.* ‖ fisarmónicâ, DIARO 75

MOUTHFUL *s.* búcă, gúră, mâşcătúră, *dim.* mâşcăturícă

MOVE *s.* ñişcáre, mânáre, mutáre, mtáre; (*maneuver*) tirtípe; (*grimace*) strâmbătúră; **You must be on the ~!** Dé-vă di auá!

MOVE *vb.* ▾mut, ▾min, mi bat dit loc, ▾strămút; **~ about** (*along or to and fro*) ▾úrdin ‖ gioc dit loc, CAPIDAN 176

MOVE AWAY *vb.* ▾dipărtédz ‖ STERGHIU 4: mi lărdzéscu (di); CUNIA 148: mi trag nanăpárti, ľau loc, ľau ciciór

MOVE HAVEN AND EARTH *vb.* (*as in search of smth.*) l-tórnu lóclu di-anántă párte, scol lóclu, mi fac páde, ▾apufác

MOVE HELL *vb.* (*to do all in one's power*) mi fac páde

MOVE OFF *vb.* (*to pack off*) ñ-ľau (*or* ñ-frângu) zvérca

MOVEMENT *s.* ñişcáre → MOVE

MUCH *adj.* múltu; *Smr:* mult; mală di, mal di; **He brought her ~ wool** ľ-adúse mal di lână; crímă di

MUCH *adv.* múltu; **no matter how ~** cătuchişdó (*and* câ-), cătuchişdó ţi s-híbă; **that ~** ahât ciómir di; **Why is it that you want so ~ water?** Ţe u vrei ahât ciómir di ápă? (*asking the price*) **How ~?** Cúmu-l daţ? (*m*); Cum u daţ? (*f*) Cum ľi daţ? *m pl*); Cum li daţ? (*f pl*); **as ~ as you can** cât ma múltu ‖ **Cru:** bághi, GOLAB 207; (*considerably, enough*) báea, DIARO 387; HRISTU 63: căt mult?

MUCK *vb.* (*to engage in aimless activity*) misúr steálile, hălăndăréscu

MUCOSITY *s.* mucoáre

MUD *s.* láspe, mâzgă, múzgă, tínă ‖ **Pro, Pros, Hal,** *etc.* lắschi;

Mul, Trn: gl̦ínă, B-ARCH 31

MUD *vb.* (*to make muddy*) ▼mintéscu, ▼túrbur

MUDDLE *s.* → TANGLE

MUDDLE *vb.* (*to act in a confused aimless way*) → MUCK; (*to make turbid, to grow thick*) (a)lăcéscu (*and* alâ-), ▼cutúlbur, ▼cutúrbur, *N:* ▼cutrúbur

MUDDLED *adj.* mindít → MUDDY

MUDDLEHEADED *adj.* chirút

MUDDY *adj.* (*of water, wine and fig., as of smb.'s mind*) túrbur *or* túrbure; cutúrbur, cutrúbur, cuturburát, cutulburát; alăcít; *also:* birdhipsít, mbirdhuít; glăburós, -oásă; mintít (*and* mindít), murdár, puvuiós, -oásă

MUFFLE *vb.* (a)nvăléscu

MULBERRY *s.* (a)múră, cirníce, dúdă, ţeríţă

MULBERRY TREE *s.* ciríciu, mureáuă

MULE[1] *s.* mul, múlă, muláre, mláre, mbláre; mulíciu *m*, mulíce *f*; múşcu; *dim.* mulăríţă ‖ *Cru:* muláre, *Gop:* mázgă, GOLAB 233

MULE[2] *s.* (*shoe*) méste, méstră, pătíche

MULE DRIVER *s.* ‖ *Cru:* ayuiát, GOLAB 196

MULETEER *s.* cărvănár → CARRIER

MULISH *adj.* (*recalcitrant*) viţeárcu, -rcă, -rţi, -rţe

MULL *vb.* ▼minduéscu → PONDER

MULLEIN *s. bot.* luminá́re; ţeára-al Dumnidzắu; coáda-a ñélui

MULLET *s. ichth.* chefál, sirtár

MULTIPLY *vb.* ▼(a)mulţắscu, ▼nmulţắscu

MULTITUDE *s.* multíme, mulţáme, multeáţă ‖ MERCA 8: **with a ~ of stars** cu mirminghiuslu di steáli → CROWD, LEGION

MUMBLE *vb.* băbăléscu

MUM'S THE WORD! ‖ nu fac níţi dza, BASME 73; níţi dzău, BASME 407

MUNCH *vb.* ▼ciumuléscu, arúmin

MUNIFICENT *adj.* (*princely*) pâşéscu, -eáscă; (*generous*) cuvurdhă

MURDER *s.* vătămáre, vătănáre

MURDER *vb.* ▼uţíd → KILL

MURDERER *s.* catíle

MURK *s.* ntuneáric

MURKY *adj.* ntunicós, -oásă

MURMUR *s.* múrmur, ciuciuráre, şuşuráre, şurşuráre, yonghizmó; (*of a river*) cúrsu

MURMUR

MURMUR *vb.* múrmur, murmurédz, şurşurédz, gârgâlédz, gârgârédz, gugurédz, gurgurédz, guguréscu; (*as of boiling water*) clucutéscu, yunghiséscu, gruhtéscu, hórhut, hurhuréscu

MURRAIN *s.* psof

MUSCLE *s.* anat. múşcĺu *m*

MUSHROOM *s.* bureáte *m.* buburéc, *N:* buréc; peciúrcă; *Cĺis:* ciupérnică, guguĺánă; (*a kind of flat ~*) túrtă ‖ ALIA 87: buréte, băréti, bureáche

MUSIC *s.* múzică

MUSIC TEXTBOOK *s.* muzichíe

MUSICAL INSTRUMENT *s.* latérnă (*DDA is not clear*)

MUSICIAN *s.* muzicándu, zângânár

MUSKY *adj.* (*as of soap*) mischíu, míşchiu

MUSKY SOAP *s.* muscusápnă, míschie săpúne

MUSLIM *adj.* (*of people*) ni-ñiruít

MUSS *s.* ni-arádhă; *G:* pálaz

MUSSEL *s.* zool. sulínă

MUSSILY *adv.* átacta, áţala-máţala

MUSSY *adj.* alócut → MUSSILY

MUST *s.* (*of grapes, etc.*) mústu, şíră

MUST *vb.* **3 sg impers.** prínde, lipseáşte ca s-, eáste múltu lipsítă s-; **You ~ be on the move!** Dé-vă di auá! ‖ *Alb:* va, CAPIDAN 176

MUSTACHE *s.* mustácă, *pl* mustăchi [•tăk']; mustáţă, *pl* mustắţ; *dim.* mustăcúşe, mustăcioáră → NOT YET

MUSTACHED *adj.* mustăcát

MUSTACHIOED *adj.* c-un tástru di mustắţ sun nări

MUSTARD *s.* sinápe

MUSTARD PLASTER *s.* sinapismó

MUSTER *vb.* (*to assemble, to accumulate, to congregate*) ▾adún; **to ~ up one's courage** ▾ncucutédz → PLUCK UP ONE'S COURAGE

MUSTINESS *s.* muhlidzáme

MUSTY *adj.* múhlid, muhlidzât, muciulít

MUST PRESERVES *s.* heámă

MUTABLE *adj.* *3 sg:* nu sta pri únă

MUTE *s.* and *adj.* mut; **as ~ as a fish** tac ca peáştile

MUTE *vb.* (*of birds*) ▾g(ă)ĺinédz

MUTENESS *s.* muţáme, (a)mutáĺ; (*becoming mute*) muţáre, muţâre

MUTILATE *vb.* ▾săcătipséscu

MUTILATION *s.* uludzíre; săcătipsíre, săcătlíche, săcătlâche

MUTINEER *s.* (*rebel*) scandzóhir

MUTING *s.* g(ă)ľináre

MUTINY *s.* (*revolt*) mintireáje

MUTINY *vb.* mut cap

MUTT *adj.* glar → STUPID

MUTTER *vb.* ▾angrăñéscu, ngrâñêscu, ngărñéscu (*and* ngâr-), discântu, cărlédz (*and* câr-), cărédz

MUTTERING *s.* căridzáre

MUZZLE *s.* muţ, múţă, múţcă

MUZZLE *vb.* (*to restrain from expression*) bag călúşlu n gúră → GAG

MY *poss. pron.* a meu, a ñeu, *and* a mel *m*; a mea, a meáo, a meáuă *f*; a ñei *m pl*; a meále *f pl*; *enclitic forms:* -mĭ, -m; **you, mother** lea dádo-m; ~ **heart** ínima-ñ ‖ *See also* § 24 *above*

MY BROTHER(S)! *interj.* cára; **It was blowing such a wind, ~, that** Cára trădzeá un vímtu

MY GOD! *interj.* oi-bobó! *or* o-bobó!

MYRIAD *s.* (*host, multitude*) miriádhă, miríu

MYRRH *s.* zmírnă

MYSELF *pron.* síngur-ñi (*sic*) ‖ BELIMACE 65: **to ~** (*mentally, inwardly*) ăn vétea-a mea

MYSTERY *s.* místiryiu

MYTHOLOGY *s.* mithuluyíe

N

NAB *vb.* acáţ, bag tu mână, príndu

NABOB *s.* pri-avút

NAG *s.* (*one who nags habitually*) (a)ngărñáric; (*decrepit horse; also: old person*) cârcâm, saravál

NAG *vb.* (*to reproach*) ľ-u scot análmă prit gúră (*or* prit nări); **to ~ the life out of smb.** lu aród dit hicáte (*lit.* 'to gnaw smb.'s liver'), ľ-mâc hicátlu (*lit.* 'to eat smb.'s liver')

NAIL

NAIL *s.* găvójdu, guvójdu, guvózdu, civíe, ţivíe, pénură, péndură, peróna; (*shoemaker's wooden nail*) prochiu, proácă; **to provide with a ~** ▼nguvujdédz; *anat.* úngľe, *dim.* ungľícă

NAIL *vb.* ▼sfinuséscu; (*to fasten with a nail*) pirunséscu; (*to crucify*) cărfuséscu, ncărfuséscu

NAILING *s.* sfinusíre, pirunsíre, ncărfusíre

NAIVE *adj.* ageamí, ageamíu, ageamít, agimít, apló, tivichél

NAKED *adj.* bilít; gol, goálă, goľ, goále; guliş(e)án; **stark ~** cuculíciu ‖ ALIA 177: (*over a large area*) gulăşán; *ibid.*: bilisírcu; zdipuít, zdu-, zipuít; chilibét, -vét; zárcu

NAKEDNESS *s.* gulăciúne

NAMBY-PAMBY *adj.* (*insipid*) sárbit; (*indecisive*) andóulea [doŭ•] *invar.*; (*weak, irresolute*) s(c)lab, zăíf, zăífcu

NAME *s.* númă; *also:* námă, náme, núme; **What's your ~?** Cúmu-ţ gréscu? Cum ti stríga? Cum ti-acľámă? **pet ~** númă di dizñérdu ‖ Cúmu-ţi dzâc? *or* Cúmu-ţi dzâc pri númă? (*lit.* 'How do they tell you? *or* 'How do they tell you by name?'), PARALLELE 151; *Cru:* **last ~** paranúmă, GOLAB 240; **What's your ~?** Cum oai (= u ai) numa? HRISTU 54

NAME *vb.* acľém

NAME DAY *s.* númă, yiurtíe

NAMELESS *adj.* ≈ ni-cunoscút

NAMELY *adv.* va dzâcă, deméc, dhiladhí

NANNY-GOAT *s.* → GOAT

NAP *s.* cĭúmă → FLOCK

NAP *s.* (*short sleep*) misimére ‖ un ócľu di sómnu (*lit.* 'an eye of sleep'), BASME 136

NAP *vb.* ‖ ľau un ócľu di sómnu (*lit.* 'to take an eye of sleep'; *the same in Albanian*, PARALLELE 121) → DOZE

NAPE *s. anat.* căşingíc, cheáfă, guryíţă, núcă, zvércă ‖ ALB: *Dren, Pe, Për:* zvércă; *Kërb:* dzvércă; *Pe, Sln:* zércă, Brâncuş 555

NAPHTHA *s.* néfte

NAPKIN *s.* şirvét, şirvéte, pischíre, piţétă; (*at a child's chin*) sáľar

NARCISSUS *s. bot. Amc:* gugúţă

NARGHILE *s.* (*Turkish pipe*) ciubúche, mărúş, narghilé, narghilée

NARIS *s. anat.* náre

NARRATE *vb.* ▼ambáir → TELL

NARROW *adj.* (a)ngústu, -stắ, -şti, -ste; strímtu, strâmtu

NARROW *vb.* ▼(a)ngustédz, ▼strimtédz, ▼minutédz, ▼supţârédz

NARROWING *s.* (a)ngustáre, angusteáţă, strimtáre, strimtúră, stringătúră

NARROW-MINDED *adj.* şcret, étă (*sic*), -eţ, -éte → STUPID

NARTHEX *s.* (*in a church*) ártică, nártică

NASAL CARTILAGE *s.* *anat.* cărţâle dit nări *f pl*

NASTINESS *s.* urâteáţă; *iron.* muşuteáţă, muşiteáţă

NASTY *adj.* (a)urât, (a)urút, slut; taxés, *m pl* -xéşĭ ‖ *Peş*: (*of weather*) cirúc; **The weather is ~** Eáste chirólu cirúc, CL 43

NATION *s.* miléte; (*race, tribe*) gínsă, ghímtă, yénos, laó, pópul, ráţă, zintúñe

NATIONALITY *s.* ruféte ‖ BELIMACE 109: plásă

NATIONALIZE *vb.* ľau trâ duvléte (*lit.* 'to take for the state')

NATIVE *adj.* di-a lóclui

NATIVE LAND *s.* pătrídhă (*and* pătrídă), vădăne (*and* vădăñe)

NATIVITY *s.* → CHRISTMAS

NATURAL *adj.* fisicó, *m pl* -ádz; **This is a ~ thing** Lúcru fisicó

NATURALLY *adv.* fisicá

NATURE *s.* pláse; (*the creative force of the univers*) físe; **~ has never created anyone lazier** Linăvós cum nu áre fáptă físea; (*character*) **Such is my ~** Acşí ñ-eáste fisicólu ‖ *GSus*: nidéĭi, CL 257

NAUGHT *s.* → ZERO

NAUGHTY *adj.* sirsém, *m pl* -séñ, *f pl* -séme; zevzéc

NAUSEA *s.* greáţă, *pl* greţ *and* gréţurĭ; (a)ngúsă

NAUSEATE *vb.* aynusédz, aynuséscu, ñ-i greáţă ‖ CUNIA 328: âñ víni s-vérsu

NAUSEATING *adj.* griţós, -oásă

NAVE *s.* (*in a church*) xóstră

NAVEL *s.* *anat.* buríc, bắríc, *N:* bric; mârdzeáuă (*lit.* 'bead')

NEAR *vb.* ▼apróchĭu → APPROACH

NEAR *adv.* aproápe, aproápea

NEAR *prep.* língă, níngă

NEAR AT HAND *adj.* próhir

NEARBY *adv.* → NEAR; (*close at hand*) próhir

NEARING *s.* aprucheáre

NEARLY *adv.* → ALMOST

NEAT *adj.* (*clean, tidy*) chischín, spástru; (*charming*) zâmbác; (*not mixed or diluted*) munát, curát ‖ CUNIA 201 *also:* manó

NEATHERD *s.* văcár

NEB *s.* → BEAK

NECESSARY *adj.* ananghiós, -oásă; lipsít, ofélim, *m pl* -liñ; *vb* 3 *sg impers.* prínde; **If ~, I can take an oath** S-lipseáre, ľau ş-giurát

NECESSARILY *adv.* ananghiós

NECK *s. anat.* gúşe, limăreáuă; (*~ of a bottle*) gúşe di bóţă ‖ ALIA 162: gurmádzu, gărmádzu; (*rare*) gât, gârdă

NECESSITOUS *adj.* (*needy*) nevóľin → NECESSARY

NECESSITY *s.* lipsítă → NEED

NECKERCHIEF *s.* limudhétă, limuvétă; (*for women*) buíme, buiúme

NECKLACE *s.* báir, báiur (di fluríi); fluríi *f pl*; (a)rădhăríche (di fluríi); culáne, ghirdáne, ghiurdáne, *dim.* ghiurdăníţă; *G:* (*~ made of artificial pearls*) măgúr, mógur; *G:* miruníc, muruníc; (*necklace-talisman*) mănóchir di gúşe, monóchir, munóchir, schicuríciu di fluríi

NECKTIE *s.* cravátă, pătlícă, pántlică, pánglică

NEED *s.* anánghe, *pl* anănghiuri; angusteáţă, héră, ihtizáe, ihtizắ, htizắ, lipsíre, lipsítă, nivóľe, strimtúră, zóre; **~ is the best teacher** Zórea ti-nveáţă; **A friend in ~ is a friend indeed** Oáspile si cunoáşte tru angusteáţă → BE IN ~

NEED *vb.* hărzăéscu, lipséscu, am anánghe (di), am ihtizáe (di); ('*is necessary*') va; **Thin cloth doesn't ~ a thick needle** La pândză minútă nu va ac gros; **I'd ~ a month to tell you the whole story** Va un mes s-ţă li mbáir [•ir]; **We may ~ this in a difficult moment** Poáte să lipseáscă t-únă oáră urâtă; **What do you ~?** Ţe anănghiuri ai? **We don't ~ you any longer** Ma múltu nu nă éşti lipsítă; **What a water mill needs is water, not big words** Moára va ápă, nu va groáse; *impers.* **you ~** ('*it is necessary, it takes*') prínde (să)

NEEDED *adj.* lipsít; ofélim, *m pl* -liñ; **it is ~** lipseáşte ‖ **Nothing else is ~** Ţivá nu lipseáşte, BASME 40

NEEDLE *s.* ac; **the eye of a ~** coáca a áclui, măgheáuă; **tip of a ~** chípită, súmig, súmigă; **large ~** sacuráfă, hundruvénal; *Tur:* chindríe ‖ *Els:* agu; *Gard:* vilónă, B-ARCH 432

NEEDLE *vb.* (*to prod, to incite*) yăryărédz

NEEDLE CASE *s.* pisúză. viluníthră

NEEDLESS *adj.* áhristu → USELESS

NEEDLESSLY *adv.* di-pistanéu; (*more than necessary*) di-prima-nsús

NEEDY *adj.* nevóľin, *m pl* -liñ

NEFARIOUS *adj.* pabés, -ésă (*sic*), -éşĭ, -ése → WICKED

NE'ER-DO-WELL *s.* om di ciuchi → GOOD-FOR-NOTHING

NEGATE *vb.* fac incheáre; nu u fac di căbúle

NEGATION *s.* incheáre, ncheáre

NEGATIVE *adj.* (*disapproving*) arniseáric

NEGATIVE vb. fac incheáre

NEGLECT *s.* ni-bruíre, ni-mutríre

NEGLECT *vb.* paralás, fac mânecă di tămbáre, nu-l dau di curáuă, nu-l dau di mâneár, nu lu-ancúñ

NEGLECTED *adj.* ni-bruít, ni-mutrít

NEGLECTFUL *adj.* → NEGLIGENT

NEGLIGENCE *s.* para-lăsáre

NEGLIGENT *adj.* (a)lăsát, alăsătóñu, -toáñe; dizbrânát, ni-mutrít

NEGOTIATE *vb.* (*as the price of smth.*) ▾păzăripséscu; (*to ~ a marriage*) pruxinséscu

NEGOTIATION *s.* păzáre, păzăripsíre, păzărlâche

NEGRO *s.* ‖ *Cru:* arápu, GOLAB 200

NEIGH *s.* (*of horses*) arujíre

NEIGH *vb.* arujéscu, azuréscu

NEIGHBOR *s.* viţín, yiţín; *coll.* viţináme. **All the ~s know of that** şti tútă viţinámea ‖ *Cru:* cumşoáñe *f*, GOLAB 228; *Rod:* văcín, *Kat, Plat, Pur:* yitón, *Gard:* yíţun, B-ARCH 493

NEIGHBOR *vb.* ▾viţinipséscu, ▾sinuripséscu

NEITHER... NOR... níţi... ni; ne...ne; ni...ni; úti... úti; **Neither does he come back nor does he write to me** Níţi s-toárnă, níţi ñ-scríe; **~ white ~ black** ne álbu, ne laiu; **~ I give, ~ he takes** ni io nu dau, ni el nu ľa; **~ you, ~ we** úti voi, úti noi; **~ fish ~ flesh** ni úda, ni uscáta ‖ HRISTU 46: **I ~ have ever seen, nor loved him** nică nu oam vădzută vărrăoară, nică oam vrută → EITHER... OR

NEIGHBORHOOD *s.* viţínă, viţinátă, viţinătáte, cumbuşóñe

NEMATODE *s.* (*intestinal worm*) limbríc, lâmbríc; **infected with**

nematodes adj. lâmbricós, -oásă

NEPHEW s. nipót ‖ *F, M:* năpót, SarD 38

NERVE s. névră

NERVE ONESELF UP TO DOING SMTH. vb. apufăséscu; âncl'íd ócl'il' şi (+ verb) → PLUCK UP ONE'S COURAGE

NERVOUS adj. nevricó, -coáñe, -cádz, -coáñe; sértu, sértic

NERVOUSNESS s. sârbislăche

NERVY adj. sârbéscu, -eáscă, -éşţâ, -éşti

NEST s. cuib, cuibár, cuibáir [•bá•ir], cuibáire, curbáiu [•báiŭ] ‖ *GSus:* cubáier [•bá•ier], CL 42

NEST EGG s. fol'u, *pl* fíl'e

NESTLE vb. *(to settle, to shelter)* fac cúibu, mi-adún ti cúibu, ▼apănghiséscu

NET s. plásă, leásă, poáhă, vurzóm, vurzón ‖ *(for catching fish)* **Av:** hrip, *GSus:* ahríp, CL 36; **Pls:** mréjdi, CL 256; **Prv:** pidhóval, CL 258 → BE CAUGHT IN THE ~

NET vb. *(to yield)* adúc, dau, fac

NETHERWORLD s. → UNDERWORLD

NETTLE s. *bot.* urtícă, urdzâcă; *coll.* urdzâcáme

NETTLE vb. ▼nţap, ▼urdzâc

NETTLE RASH s. *med.* hrúpă, blândă

NETTLESOME adj. nţăpătós, -oásă

NETTLING s. urdzâcáre

NEURALGIA s. nevralyíe

NEVER adv. vârnâoáră, vâroáră, puté; **I ~ eat olives** Eu vârnăoáră nu mâc másine; **You have ~ been married?** Nu ti nsuráşi vârnăoáră? *(not even once)* niţidânâoáră [•nâ•oá•]; *N:* barunoáră ‖ **Peş:** cănăoáră, CL 40; VELO 107: udepoté

NEVERTHELESS cj. cu túte aésti

NEVUS s. *derm.* dámcă

NEW adj. nou *m*, noáuă *f*, noi *pl*; *N:* nău *m*, náuă *f*, năi *m pl*, nále *f pl*

NEW MOON s. lúnă noáuă

NEW-ARRIVAL s. iabangíu

NEW-BORN s. fet, luţ, pup

NEWLY MARRIED s. yranghéi, yrangheádz *or* yrambádz *m pl*

NEWS s. hăbáre *(and* hâ-*)*, habáre; náo, *pl* nále; **He liked such ~** Lu arăseá ahtărĭ nále; şteáre, *pl* şteri; ştíre, *pl* ştiri; *(a ra-*

ther pleasant piece of ~) sihărícľe, sihăríche; (*rather unpleasant*) măndátă; **G:** burdúval; halát; **I am bringing you good** ~ V-a-
dúc hăbáre búnă; **What** ~ **do you have?** Ţe hâbări?

NEWSLETTER *s.* → NEWSPAPER

NEWSPAPER *s.* fimirídhă, thimirídhă, frândză, gazétă ‖ **Peş:** fe-
merídă, CL 45 ‖ **GBg:** vésnic, STERE 30

NEXT *adj.* alántu, -ntă, -nţâ, -nte; **the** ~ **day** dzúua alántă; **N:**
a doáz; ~ **summer** di veáră; **Come back** ~ **summer** S-ti tórñi di veáră; ~ **winter** tu iárnă; ~ **year** năínde; **We'll come back** ~ **year** Va
nă turnăm năínde ‖ (*the following*) PC: áltu; ~ **year** la ánlu, PA-
RALLELE 141; **the** ~ **day** alántă dzúă, CUVATA 8

NEXT *prep.* níngă, príngă, n viţinátă cu

NIBBLE *vb.* aród

NICE *adj.* bun, *m pl* buñ; muşát, *m pl* -áţ

NICELY *adv.* ‖ ghíne-muşát, BASME 420

NICETY *s.* micáme

NICK → COME IN THE ~ OF TIME

NICKER *vb.* → NEIGH

NICKNAME *s.* númă; *also*: parangóme, paranúmă, parasúmă; **G:** păr-
noáñe; **G:** prănoámă ‖ **Prv:** paraţúcle, CL 257

NICKNAME *vb.* bag númă, bag prănóñ, scot númă

NIECE *s.* nipoátă ‖ **F, M:** năpoátă, SarD 39

NIFTY *adj.* (*stylish*) galántu, *m pl* -nţâ, *f pl* -nte

NIGGARD *s.* stres → STINGY

NIGGARDLY *adj.* stres, streásă, streşĭ, streáse

NIGGARDLY *adv.* ‖ cu mână ncľísă (*lit. 'with close hand'*),
PARALLELE 136

NIGGARDLINESS *s.* schingiureáţă → STINGINESS

NIGGLING *adj.* garamitlíu, -tlíe, *m/f pl* -tlíĭ

NIGH *adj.* → CLOSE, NEAR

NIGH *adv.* (*near, almost*) aproápe, aproápea

NIGHT *s.* noápte, *pl* nópţâ; **at** ~ noáptea; oáră noápti; **good** ~!
búnă noápte; **Arabian** ~ halimáuă, *pl* halimăi; **fall of** ~ nsiráre →
BE CAUGHT BY THE ~ ‖ **the** ~ **before last Peş:** aprinduseáră, CL 37;
last night asar-noáptea, DIARO 84; *a wish to be OK next morning is*
Apirítă búnă! (*lit. 'Good dawn!'*), PARALLELE 159

NIGHT WATCH *s.* nihtéri *f*, nihtéryiu

NIGHTFALL *s.* (a)scăpitátă; *also*: (a)murdzíş, (a)murdzítă,

NIGHTINGALE

(a)murdzíre, murghízmă *and* murgheázmă, murgíş, múrgu, nsirátă, ntunicátă, nuptátă; **at ~** tu murdzítă

NIGHTINGALE *s.* aidhónă; *also:* bilbíĺ, birbíĺ, birbiĺóc, nibil-bíĺ, sirvíĺ, vigĺitoáre; *book.* filomélă

NIGHTMARE *s.* móră, pumoáră ‖ PC: yis urút

NIGRITUDE *s.* ntuneáric, chísă

NIL *s.* ţivá

NIMBLE *adj.* sárpit, sârbéscu, -eáscă, -éşţâ, -éşti; şaín; (~ *and brave*) siftér, xífter, schífter

NINE *num.* noáuă, *N:* náuă, náo; **at ~ o'clock** tu noáuăle [•uă•]; **the house of the ~ thieves** cása a noáurlor furi

NINETEEN *num.* noáuăsprădzaţe [•ŭă•], náusprădzaţe [náŭ•]; náuă-sprădzaţe; **His clack goes ~ to the dozen** ≈ ápă ĺ-ñárdze gúra (*lit.* 'his/her mouth goes like water,' *i.e. continuously, like a river*)

NINETY *num.* noauădzắţi, nauădzắţi; **~-nine** noáuădáţi-noáuă

NINNY *adj.* durñít → STUPID

NINTH *adj.* náurli *and* noáurlu

NIP *s.* (*sharp cold*) dzer, dzidzér, dzeádzir, ţingríme

NIP *s.* (*a small portion*) → BIT

NIP *vb.* ▾strângu, ▾zdrúmin, pliciutédz, plăsédz, *N:* astórcu; (*to steal*) ciun; (*to take tea or liquor in sips*) sórbu

NIPPERS *s.* ţimbídhă, ţimbístră → PLIERS

NIPPING *adj.* (*as of a thorn*) nţăpătós, -oásă

NIPPLE *s.* anat. gurgúĺu *m/n*, gurgúĺe and gurgúĺ *pl*; cap di ţâţă

NIPPY *adj.* (*sharp*) nţăpătós, -oásă; (*cold*) *m/f* aráţe, *pl* arăţĭ

NIT *s.* aminşuşíţă, líndină; *coll.* minţíme, minciuşáme ‖ *Amc:* coárdhă, SCHL 114

NITRIC ACID *s.* ghizáp, ghizápe

NITWIT *s.* lişurác

NIX *s.* ţivá

NO *adj.* (*not any, not a, hardly any*) can, dip, hici; **~ lamb did ever suck her** Ñel nu u súpse

NO *adv.* háca, áca, ba, mi, nu; *S:* ohi; *F:* no; **A thousand times ~!** Háşa ş háşa! - **Yes or ~?** (*i.e., You want it or not?*) - **No!** Vrei, i nu vrei? - Ba, ba, ba! *or* Ohi, nu u voi! **~, it burns me!** Áca, mi árde! *No, he said* Háca, dzâse

NO END GALORE *adv.* di-a sătúlui

NO MATTER (HOW, WHAT, WHO, *etc.***)** cât s-híbă (di); **An illiterate person, no matter how rich, is a servant of the learned** Ninviţátlu, cât avút s-híbă, eáste huzmicheár a nviţátlui

NO ONE → NOBODY

NO SOONER nu apucái tra s *(+ vb)*; nu bitisíi ghíne s *(+ vb)*; ~ **said than done** dzâca ş-fápta

NO SUCH THING ‖ aflấşi sắ... BASME 29

NOMAD *s.* ‖ HRISTU 1: nomadin

NOBILITY *s.* puristó

NOBLE *s.* celepíu, cilibí

NOBLE *adj.* chibár

NOBODY *pron.* vârnu, vâr, vâră, verún, vărrăúnu; ~ **runs away from good** Di ghíne vâră nu fúdze; cáinivá, canivá, cúnivá; **We harm ~** Arắu nu adúţim a cunivá; can *m*, cánă *f*; barún *m*, barúnă *f*; niţiún *m*, niţiúnă *f*; ţinivá; **but ~ will hear them** mea ţinivá nu va s-ĺi ávdă; **there is ~** nu-ári ţinivá; **absolutely ~** ţípit *or* cípit (di om); can; ~ **went there** Acló nu s-duţeá cípit di om; Can nu s-dúse; *(in negative sentences)* om; **You could see ~** Om nu z videá; **a little ~** om di ciuchi; pắrtál

NOCUOUS *adj.* zñiseáric

NOD ONE'S HEAD *vb.* ‖ tiñisescu cu capu, HRISTU 52

NODDLE *s.* ftínă

NODDY *s.* *(simpleton)* apló

NOEL *s.* cólindă, culíndă

NOGGIN *s.* **(a person's head)** curcubétă

NOISE *s.* ghiurultíe, yiurultíe; *also:* asunătúră, crot, lávă, lármă; *(hubub)* lăvătúră, lóngĭe, lóscut, sălăváte, scándal, şimắtă, vreávă, zbuc; *(of an explosion, of thunder)* vróndu, vrondusíre; *(as of trot)* (a)rupắţâre, tróput; *(of rain)* aróput di ploáie → MAKE A ~ ‖ *Str:* şómut, GOLAB 252

NOISEMAKER *s.* ghiurultagí

NOISILY *adv.* provatós → LOUDLY

NOISOME *adj.* *(harmful)* zñiseáric; *(disgusting)* aynusós, -oásă

NOISY *adj.* pravatós; *(as of a child)* sirsém, sirsén, asiyúriftu; *(stamping one's feet)* arupắţât; ~ **coming** viñítă arupăţâtă; *(boisterous)* dzardzára *m*, dzardzáră *f*, dzardzáreañ *m pl*

NOMAD *s.* cirigár

NOMADIC *adj.* cu cása pri ciumág, cu cása pri ciutáĺ

NONBAPTIZED *adj.* niñiruít; nu áre untulémnu pri nâs (≈ *unoiled*)

NONE *pron.* niţiún [•ţi•ún], *f* niţiúnă; *N* barún, *f* barúnă

NONETHELESS *cj.* NEVERTHELESS

NONPAREIL *adj.* făr-di-sóţ *invar.*

NONSENSE *n and interj.* bişíñ di cuc (*lit.* 'cuckoo's farts'), burlídz mbăiráte [•i•] *pl*; chiritúri *f pl*; cóľa-mbóľa *f pl*; curcubéte *f pl*; curcuféľ *f pl*; glăréţ *f pl*; guríţă *f pl*; lă-cărdíe, lăpărdíe; lişinătúri *f pl*; papurdhéle *f pl*; şahlamáră; zboáre tu cácă *n pl*

NONSENSICAL *adj.* (*silly*) şulúndu; **a ~ speech** zburâre şulúndă

NONESUCH *adj.* făr-di-sóţ *invar.*

NOODLES *s.* tămáciu, tumáciu, *no pl*

NOOK *s.* (*secluded place*) păt(i)ľáuă

NOON *s.* ñádză-dzúuă, prândzul máre; **from early morning until ~** din dzáre până n prândzul máre; **at ~** ñádză dzúuă, ñádză-prândzu

NOONTIME *s.* → NOON

NOOSE *s.* (a)láţ

NOR *cj.* níţi → NEITHER

NORM *s.* (*standard*) mucadéme

NORMAL *adj.* (*conforming to standards of propriety, good taste or morality*) ca tútă éta *invar.*

NORTH WIND *s.* turín, vimtu turinós, viríu, seávire; *Băi:* ţeáfir

NOSE *s.* náre, *dim.* năréce; nas → MAKE A LONG ~ AT SMB., PUT UP ONE'S ~

NOSE *vb.* (*to scent*) úlmic

NOSEGAY *s.* buchét, bubúche di flori

NOSTRIL *s.* náre

NOSY *adj.* períeryu, -yă, -yi, -ye

NOT nu

NOT A BIT → BIT, NOT AT ALL

NOT AT ALL cât trâ yitríe, cât ghitríşca; (*not half!*) am cum! (*no, no*) pa-pa-pá! ba-ba-bá! ‖ aflấşi să, BASME 29

NOT EVEN *adv.* níţi, néţi, níţe; un; **~ a colt is neighing** Un mândzu nu arujeáşte; **~ as little as** niţĭ cât

NOT HALF BAD ‖ príma, BASME 117

NOT IN THE LEAST *adv.* iuvá ş-iuvá → AT ALL

NOT MORE THAN *adv.* (*only*) dicât; (*He had*) *not more than three* (*golden*) *coins* maşi trei gálbine

NOT QUITE *adv.* nu pára-; **He does not see quite well** Nu pára-andzăreáşte; nu ca; **She is not quite in the mood** Nu ca áre chéfi

NOT UNFITTINGLY *adv.* driptátic, driptáticǎ

NOT WITHOUT GOOD REASON → NOT UNFITTINGLY

NOT YET *adv.* níngǎ; **Your mustache has shown up, but your mind has not yet~** Mustáţa ţ-inşí, míntea níngǎ

NOTABILITY *s.* nişalâ

NOTABLE *s.* gǎgán, ciurbagí *m*, ciurbagioáñe *f*; *coll.* prutáme

NOTCH *s.* (*gorge*) şilătúrǎ; (*mark in the ear of a sheep to be recognized*) coácǎ, cuceáfcǎ, cuceáftǎ, fúrcǎ; piľ *m pl* (*sic*); (~ *on a tally*) coácǎ pri (a)rǎbúş

NOTE *s.* (*written, usu. formal*) pusúlǎ

NOTE *vb.* (*to take note of*) bag tu mǎdúuǎ

NOTEBOOK *s.* tetrádhiu, filádhǎ ‖ DIARO 166: afládhâ

NOTED *adj.* (*notorious*) avdzât

NOTEWORTHY *adj.* nişanlâ ‖ CUNIA 258: nişanlítcu

NOTHING *pron.* ţivá; **I had ~** Eu nu aveám ţivá; **He wants to kill me for ~** Va s-mi cheárǎ trâ ţivá ici; **and ~ else** ş-tut; **That much money he had and ~ more** Ahâţ avea nâs tuţ parádz; cípit; **One could hear ~** Ne cípit nu s-avdzá; (*perfect silence*) tăţeáre máre, cípit; - **What's up? - Nothing** ‒ Ţe hâbǎrĭ? - Mâniţi di tâmbǎri! (*lit.* 'sleeeves of cloaks'); ~ **but** sadé; ~ **but pain and sorrow** sadé dureáre ş-tunusíre; ~ **loath** cu vreáre; ~ **to write home about** *3 sg aor.* ≈ adrǎ gúvǎ ntru ápǎ (*lit.* 'He/she made a hole in water'); ~ **truer** ≈ nu ânglĭmǎ (*lit.* 'no kidding') → COME TO ~ ‖ *Amc:* **nothing** canţiva, RÉCATAS 36

NOTICE *s.* hǎbáre

NOTICE *vb.* ▼pǎrǎtirséscu ‖ (*rare*) síntu, CAPIDAN 153; *Cru:* duchimiséscu, GOLAB 213; HRISTU 25: bag oárǎ (cǎ); DIARO 113: **I did not ~ what time it was** Nu bâgái oára cât eará oára

NOTIFY *vb.* pitréc hǎbáre → GIVE NOTICE

NOTION *s.* (*opinion*) mínte, hâvǎ, hǎvǎ; (*whim*) camómate *f pl*

NOTORIOUS *adj.* avdzât; cu númǎ (*lit.* 'with name')

NOTWITHSTANDING *prep.* cu tut, cu tútǎ, cu tuţ, cu túte

NOUGAT *s.* hásca

NOURISH *vb.* (*to feed*) ▼hrǎnéscu, hǎrnéscu, hǎréscu, ▼tǎyiséscu, tǎiséscu; (*to chew the food before it is given to an infant*) ▼ântríc, nitríc, ntric, mǎtríc; **They ~ each other like doves**

NOURISHMENT

Ntrícă ca porúnghi

NOURISHMENT s. hránă, năfăcă

NOVELTY s. náuă, noáuă; *G:* halát

NOVEMBER s. brumár, nuémbru; **It is** ~ I méslu al brumár

NOVICE s. múcio *invar;* adj. ageamít, agimít, ageamí, ageamíu, ni-fricát

NOW adj. di ádză, di tóra, di tórea

NOW adv. acúşi, amó, amú, amúşi, tóra; *Mul, Gop:* túra, tórea, túrea; **right** ~ úti tóra; ~... ~... ba (că)..., ba (că)...; ~ **you,** ~ **me** ba că tíne, ba că míne; ~ **a man,** ~ **an animal enter the vine-yard** Si arúcă tu ayíñe ba om, ba právdă, ba zlápe; ~ **and then** di oáră oáră; ~ **and then** arár → COME ~! ‖ ~ **is the decisive / crit-ical moment!** aoá-i aoá, DIARO 29

NOW THEN ştu-cará

NOWADAYS adv. adz, ádză (*and* áză), ásândzâ

NOWHERE adv. iuvá (*in neg. sentences*) **He is** ~ Nu lu-áre iuvá; **He was** ~ Nu lu-aveá iuvá

NOXIOUS adj. zñiseáric; (*poisonous*) → VENOMOUS

NUANCE s. ‖ (*of colors*) ton, HRISTU 1

NUBILE adj. mărtătoáre f, pl -tóri

NUDE adj. gol, goálă, goľ, goále → NAKED

NUDITY s. gulăciúne

NUISANCE s. biľé, ghiúcă ‖ *it came upon me as a* ~ âñ cădzú pri zvércă (*lit. 'it fell on my neck'*), PARALLELE 135 → GRIEF

NUMB adj. amurţât, amurtát

NUMBER s. númir, númire m or n; **in great** ~ (*of people*) ca tră Stâ-Măríe (*lit. 'like on Saint Mary's Day'*) ‖ **Cru:** broi, GOLAB 209; rúmir (*sic*), GOLAB 239

NUMBERLESS adj. ni-numirát, ni-ruminát; múltu, múltă, múlţâ, múlte → NUMEROUS

NUMBNESS s. amurţătúră, amurţáre, amurtáre; ~ **of the fingers** (*from cold*) dzidzirâtúră

NUMEROUS adj. flúmin di; ca aróiu di-alghínă → MANY, A LOT OF

NUMSKULL s. → STUPID

NUN s. călgăriţă, gălgăriţă, căluyríţă, căluguríţă, căluyreáuă

NUPTIAL(S) s. númtă, lúmtă

NUPTIAL adj. nuntár; **a** ~ **song** cântic nuntár

NUPTIAL PROCESSION s. (*at night, with torches*) muceáră

NURSE *s.* (*wet nurse*) para múmă, pára-mánă, mătrícă, mitrícă, mâtriţă; (*medical practitioner*) mâscă, mâţcă

NURSE *vb.* alăptédz, ţâţuéscu, apléc, áplic; (*to take care of*) frundiséscu, frundixéscu ‖ STERE 8: curipséscu

NURSE A GRUDGE AGAINST SMB. *vb.* ĺ-ţân pícă, ĺ-dúc zắte

NURSE ENMITY *vb.* ▼pizmuéscu

NURSLING *s.* ficiuríc → BABY

NURTURE *s.* → FOOD

NURTURE *vb.* ▼hrănéscu, ▼créscu

NUT *s.* cucoáşe, *dim.* cucuşícă, núcă; **be ~s about smb.** ñ-cáde tu vreáre máre → BE ~S ABOUT SMB.

NUTMEG *s.* moşcocáre

NUTRIENT *s.* → FOOD

NUTRITION *s.* hrăníre, hărníre

NUTRIMENT *s.* → FOOD

NUTS *adj. slang* (*enthusiastic, keen*) miraclí (*or* -clâ), *f* -cloáñe, *m pl* -cládz, *f pl* -cloáñe

NUTSHELL *s.* coáje di núcă

NYMPH *s.* (*minor divinity*) niráidhă, vílă

O

OAF *s.* glar → STUPID; (*countrified, unsofisticated*) păduríş

OAK *s.* árbur, árbure *m*; blădúh *m*, ceal**â**c *m*, chiminít *m*; cupáciu *m* or *n*; dúşcu *m*, ţer *m*; ~ *wood* arburét; cupăcínă, cupăcíñe, cupăcíñ ‖ **Alb:** dúşcu; **Dren, Kërb, Pe, Për, Sln:** cupáciu *and* (*rarely*) árbur, Brâncuş 554

OAR *s.* lupátă (di várcă)

OAT → OATS

OATH *s.* (a)giurát, jurát, giurátic, giuráre, órcu, urchisíre; *false* ~ yealán giurátic → TAKE AN ~, BREAK ONE'S ~

OATS *s.* uvédz (*and* uvéz), vróme

OBDURATE *adj.* scliró *invar.*

OBEDIENCE *s.* ascultáre

OBEDIENT *adj.* ascultătór, -oáre; tibié *invar.*

OBEISANCE *s.* ncľinăciúnă, ncľinăciúne

OBESE *adj.* ~ **and ugly** jibăcós, -oásă *and* jibicós; (*fat and clumsy*) stătút, BASME 422

OBEY *vb.* ascúltu, săidiséscu, săldiséscu, ▾ávdu (di); **This man does not ~ anyone** Aéstu om nu ávde di v**â**rnu ‖ âľ fac chéfea, BASME 8

OBITUARY MEAL: to offer an ~ *vb.* cum**â**ntu

OBJECT *s.* luyuríe

OBJECT *vb.* ‖ CUVATA 1: tórnu zbor

OBLATE *adj.* nturtát

OBLIGATION *s.* (*contract, promise*) ligămíntu, ipuhrisíre, a-puhréuse, ipuhréuse; (*duty*) dat; (*debt*) bórge, hreu, hréus, hréuse; (*bill payable to order*) emuluyíe, muluyíe, póliţă, sinéte; (*paper-money*) caimée; **to remain under an** ~ **to smb.** mi ndăturédz

OBLIGATORY *adj.* ipuhriuticó *no pl*

OBLIGE *vb.* ▾leg; **A gift ~s one** Dhoára ti leágă; ▾ipuhriuséscu, apuhriuséscu; (*to run into debt*) ▾burghilipséscu ‖ DIARO 93: ▾ngrec; **I do not want to ~ myself to anybody** Nu voi s-mi-ngrécu la áltu

OBLIGED *adj.* ipuhriusít

OBLIGING *adj.* próthim, *m pl* -thiñ; hătârgí, *m pl* -geádz

OBLIQUE *adj.* → ASLANT

OBLITERATE *vb.* ▾aştérgu

OBLITERATED *adj.* aştérsu, -eársă, -érşi, -eárse

OBLITERATION *s.* (a)şteárdzire, (a)ştirdzeáre

OBLIVION *s.* agărşáre, ultáre, xihăsíre → BURY IN ~

OBLONG *adj.* coárniş

OBNOXIOUS *adj.* salchíu, -íe, *m/f pl* -íĭ

OBOE *s.* ≈ zurnă

OBOIST *s.* zurnagí

OBSCENE *adj.* dişuţât, dişuţât; pânghiós [•ǵós], -oásă

OBSCENITY *s.* măscărlíche, mâscâríĭe, măscáră; (*lewdness*) di-şuţâre

OBSCURE *adj.* (*dark*) ntunicós, -oásă; scutidhós, -oásă; scuti-nós, -oásă

OBSCURE *vb.* ntúnic

OBSERVANCE *s.* (*of a holiday, etc.*) ţâneáre

OBSERVANT *adj.* căştigós, -oásă

OBSERVATION *s.* paratírise, paratírse, părătirisíre

OBSERVE *vb.* (*to keep track of, to, watch carefully*) ĭ-bag oára; ~ **him well!** Bágă-ĭ oára! (*to check, to monitor*) privégĭu; (*to honor or keep, as a holiday*) ţân; (*to see, to sense*) bag tu córnu

OBSOLESCENT *adj.* tricút, nvicĭát

OBSOLETE *adj.* nvicĭát; **to become** ~ ▾(a)nvicĭéscu, ▾(a)nvicĭédz, mbitărnéscu, bătăĭuséscu

OBSTACLE *s.* cheádică

OBSTINACY *s.* inagilâche, pruclitíe

OBSTINATE *adj.* nápran; (*as of a horse*) jindáric, viţeárcu

OBSTREPEROUS *adj.* ghiurultagí; provatós

OBSTRUCT *vb.* ▾astămăţéscu, ▾nchédic, ▾ambudhiséscu, ▾ambudhi-ţéscu, ▾mbudhuéscu, fac cărşilâche, cărşilătiséscu

OBSTRUCTION *s.* astămăţíre; (*blockage made with stones*) api-trusíre; (*opposition*) cărşilâche

OBTAIN *vb.* aflu, ▾agudéscu, ▾amíntu (*and* amíndu), scot

OBVIOUS *adj.* límpide, límbid

OCCASION *s.* apuhíe, ipuhíe, aráste, oáră; **You have found the ~** Ţ-afláşi apuhía; **We are waiting for the right ~** Aştiptăm arástea; **We may never again find such an ~** Áltă oáră nu-aflăm ahtáre oáră

OCCASIONAL *adj.* (*infrequent*) arár

OCCASIONALLY *adv.* arár

OCCIPUT *s.* mădulár

OCCUPATION *s.* (*work, business, job, matter*) *G:* istréte; **a woman's ~** istréte muľireáscă

  OCCUPY *vb.* (*to take or hold possession of*) ▾apúc, ľau, ▾ţân

  OCCUR *vb.* ▾fac, cur; **A misfortune ~s easily** Lăiáţa s-fáţe lișór; (*to come to mind*) ñ-cáde n córnu (*lit. 'it falls into my horn'*)

  OCCURRENCE *s.* (*chance*) ugoádă; (*unpleasant ~*) cușaméte

  OCEAN *s.* ucheán

  O'CLOCK: at three ~ A.M. tu tréile di noápte; **We'll be going tomorrow at eight ~** Mâne tu óptu oáră va s-ñárdzim; **at eleven ~** la úsprăs di săhắţă (*sic*)

  OCTOBER *s.* Samédru, Sămédru (*and* Sâ-), Sânmédru, Sânmădreán

  OCTOPUS *s. zool.* uhtapódhe, htapódhe ‖ HRISTU 26: octapodh

  ODALISQUE *s.* anâmă, hanúmsă, cadână

  ODD *adj.* (*unusual*) trónciu, *m pl* trónci, *f sg/pl* trónce; períeryu, -yă, -yi, -ye; curyiós, -oásă; (*disparate*) técă, techi

  ODDBALL *s.* (*one whose behavior is eccentric*) ciudós, paráxin

  ODDITY *s.* ciúdă

  ODDMENT *s.* aréstu, armăsătúră

  ODDNESS *s.* ciúdă

  ODDS AND ENDS *s.* vrúte și ni-vrúte

  ODIOUS *adj.* aurât → DETESTABLE

  ODIUM *s.* → HATRED

  ODOR *s.* ñurdíe, ñurízmă, mirudhyeáuă; (*offensive ~*) putoáre

  ODORIFEROUS *adj.* ñurizmós, -oásă; ñurzitór, -toáre → FRAGRANT

  OF *prep.* **1.** (*coming from, originating at/from*) di la, dit. **Can chickens come out ~ boiled eggs?** Dit oáuă heárte pot ca s-eásă puľ di trâși? **2.** (*caused by*) di; **It hurt him so badly that he was dying ~ pain** L-dureá că-l mureá di dor; **3.** (*so as to be separated from or relieved of*) di; **I got rid ~ them** Ascăpái di năși; **4.** (*composed or made of/from*) di; **sieve ~ silk** sítă di mătáse; *also without preposition:* **a bar ~ tin** nă veárgă yánumă; **5.** (*associated with or adhering to*) di; **all that tribe ~ shep-herds** tútă fără-aţeá di célniţi; **one ~ them** un di eľi; **6.** (*be-longing to or connected to/with*) **a ray ~ sun** múndă di soáre; **7.** (*possessing, having*) **the teeth ~ the wolves** dínţâļi a lúchilor;

8. (*containing or carrying*) di; **fifty pounds ~ cheese** ţindzắţi di ucádz di caş; 9. (*as if*) ca di; **The walls smelled ~ mold** Stízmile añurdzeá ca di múhlă; 10. (*a part of*) **He understood some ~ their language** Aducheá di límba a lor; 11. trâ; **remind smb. ~** ľ-adúc amínte (trâ)

OF COURSE *adv.* aiá, besbelé, bezbelé, curmátă, élbet, élbete, mútlac, nu va dzắcă, nu va vârnă dzắcă, sayláme, po, síyur, sígur, zắri ‖ ncápe zbor? BASME 492; fắră di álta, CAPIDAN 504-4; PC: cum mi vedz şi cum ti ved

OF GOOD FAMILY *adj.* di ugeáche; *ant.* (*of low birth*) cătrănár (*lit.* 'tar dealer')

OF OLD *adv.* → OLD

OF ONE'S OWN WILL *adv.* cu vreáre ‖ di la míni, DIARO 158

OF THE FIRST WATER (*first-rate*) mắ-sa-ľ fu!

OF YORE *adj., adv.* di zămáne, zămănéscu → OF OLD

OFF *vb.* → DEPART, GO, LEAVE

OFF *adv.* (*away*) alárgu, nafoárắ, la; **He went ~ in his carriage** Fudzí alárgu cu cărúţa a lui; **You drove ~ the road** Hii alárgu di cálea búnă; **~ with him!** Scutéţ-lu nafoárắ! **A wolf approached and stood ten paces ~** Un lup s-apruché j-dănăsí la dzáţi jghioáti

OFF *prep.* di la, di pi ‖ PC: **Florica cleared ~ the table** Fluríca li mutắ túti di pi siníi; **A button has come ~ your shirt** Chirúş un nástur di la cameáşe

OFF AND ON *adv.* (*intermittently*) cându să-l caţ *m*, cându s-u caţ *f*

OFF THE MAP *adv.* dúpă soáre

OFFAL *s.* minuţắľe, minţắľe, *pl* minuţắľ; *G:* yinómate *f pl*

OFFEND *vb.* prusvuliséscu, prusvulséscu

OFFENDED *adj.* hulisít (*and* -ľi-), hulusít, prusvulisít

OFFENSE *s.* (*insult, outrage*) prusvulíe, prusvulisíre

OFFENSE *vb.* prusvuliséscu, prusvulséscu

OFFENSIVE *adj.* (*of smells*) añurzít; **~ language** zbor di péză

OFFER *s.* dáre, durusíre; (*bid*) tăxíre

OFFER *vb.* ▾apún, dau, chirăséscu, ▾părăstăséscu, ▾părăstiséscu, méscu, tăxéscu; **the gifts he ~ed him** hắrile ţe ľ-apúse; **We were ~ed a glass of wine** Fum miscúţ cu câti un yín; **~ an obituary meal** cumântu (*and* cumându); **On Sunday we will ~ a meal for the dead** Dumânică va nă cumândắm mórţâľ a nóştri

OFFER

OFFER RESISTANCE *vb.* dân(d)âséscu, dăniséscu, cărşilătiséscu

OFFER THANKS TO SMB. *vb.* adúc birhuzúre → THANK

OFFER UP *vb.* (*to sacrifice*) afieruséscu; **to ~ one's life** cad curbáne, mi fac curbáne

OFFERING *s.* (*something offered*) afiérumă, curbáne

OFFICE FOR THE DEAD *s.* (*mass for the dead 40 days after burial*) sărindár

OFFICER *s.* (*one who holds an office of trust or authority*) zăpít, zăbít; (*Turkish soldier or officer*) agă, ayă

OFFICIANT *s.* ‖ LITURG 130: iusmetgí

OFFICIATE AN EUCHARIST *vb* lituryiséscu

OFFICIATING PRIEST *s.* lituryó

OFFSHOOT *s.* fidán → SUCKER

OFFSPRING *s.* → OFFSHOOT

OFTEN *adv.* des, dipriúnă, ndáse, nimal di ori, picná ‖ HRISTU 36: multiori

OGRE *s.* cap-di-câne, hap-húp; ≈ lámñe

OH *interj.* (*relief, sorrow, regret, etc.*) uf! uh! aí! vai! aú! uă! oi! léle! a-lelé! o(i)-lelé! (oi-)bobó! u-bubú! măricúie! alímunu! púpu! ~ **dear!** Vái-di-mini!

OIL *s.* untulémnu (*and* undu-); *also:* ladhi (*1 syll.*) *n*, ládhuri *pl*; ľóladh ‖ *G:* şirlán, şirligán, SarD 34; *F:* untulem, HRISTU 35; **flax ~** bizír, BELIMACE 10

OIL *vb.* ▾aúngu (→ § 32)

OIL ONE'S PALM *vb.* aúngu → BRIBE

OIL-BURNING LAMP *s.* căndílă (*and* cân-), finghít, fânghít

OILCLOTH *s.* muşamáe, muşămáe, muşimă, muşumă

OILING *s.* aúndzire, aundzeáre

OINK *s.* gurñíre, gurñáre

OINK *vb.* gurñédz, gurñéscu

OINTMENT *s.* alifíe, alfíe; *also:* agdă; (*made of wax and olium*) chiralfíe, chiréce, miyléme

OK *s.* (*approval, endorsment*) izíne, vóľe; (*consént*) astrăxíre, sinfonipsíre

OK *adj.* bun; *adv.* ghíne

OK *vb.* (*to consent, to allow*) dau izíne, dau vóľe; (*to agree to*) ▾astrăxéscu, căpséscu, sinfunipséscu

OLD *adj.* vécľu, vlechiu; **~ men and women** pachi ş-moáşe vécľi;

bitărnu, aúş; **You are very ~, uncle** Múltu aúş ésci, pap; máre;
You are ~er than he is Voi hiţ ma mări di el; tricút; **an ~ woman**
muľáre tricútă; di dimúltu; **~ tales** părămithe di dimúlt; di únă
étă; (*grown up*) máre; **How ~ is this horse?** Câţ guvójdzâ poártă
cálu aéstu? **of old** di pap-străpáp; di la aúşi-străaúşi, di zămáne, zămănéscu; **I am getting ~** yiramátile mi loáră ‖ (*older*) ma
máre; **my older brother** fráte-ñu aţél cama márle, PARALLELE 133;
How ~ are you? Di câţi añ hii? PARALLELE 141 → BECOME ~, MAKE ~,
GROW ~ ‖ *F:* vechi, HRISTU 2

   OLD AGE *s.* auşeátic, auşítă; *coll.* auşáme, alghitúră, vicľíme;
(*ant.* youth) yirámate *f pl*; **I am getting old** yirámatĭle mi loáră

   OLD-FASHIONED *adj.* auşéscu; *adv.* auşeáşte

   OLD MAID *s.* feátă armásă

   OLD MAN *s.* aúş, béhlu, bitârnu, burhóñu, geagiu, ghiuş, moş,
dim. muşíc; muşóñu, pap, pap-aúş, pleácă, prézvit, tot, *pl* tóteañ; (om) tricút; *coll.* auşáme, auşeáme

   OLDSTER *s.* aúş; *obs.* bitârnu

   OLD THING(S) *s.* vicľitúră

   OLD WOMAN *s.* bábă, băboáñe, bitârnă, máie, máuă, mămíe, moáşe,
dim. muşícă; *derog.* muşurécă, muşarécă; *coll.* măíme; *adj.* muşéscu
‖ *Cot, Kok:* mai [má•i], B-ARCH 212

   OLDTIMER *s.* → OLDSTER

   OLIO *s.* (*mixture*) ameástic, mintitúră, amisticătúră

   OLIVE *s.* másnă, máslă, másină; **green ~s** másne călugréşti

   OLIVE DRAB *adj.* măsinát

   OLIVE OIL *s.* untulémnu → OIL

   OLIVE TREE *s.* másin *m*; mâsnéu *m*; **wild ~** ayruleáuă

   OLIVE-GRAY *adj.* măsinát

   OLYMPUS *s.* Élimbul

   OMEN *s.* sémnu; (*ill ~*) tersiné, tersănă; *adj.* **of good ~** agurlíu, agurlíu, hairlâtic, hairlâtcu

   OMEN OF EVIL *vb.* ľ-u tórcu pri hírlu aţél laiu

   OMENTUM *s.* (*anat.*, *usually of lambs*) schépe

   OMINOUS *adj.* and **-LY** *adv.* fuvirós, lăhtărós

   OMNISCIENT *adj.* (*of people*) ‖ **He is ~** si-eáste câzâmíe, DIARO
190

   O MY! *interj.* vai di míni!

   ON *prep.* **1.** (*spatial*) stă; **A cuckoo is singing ~ Saint Mary's**

church Cântă un cuc sti Stă-Măríe; ~ **the table** pri meásă; stri; **They are the worst ~ earth** Sântu ațéĭ ma láiĭi stri loc; ~ **what shall I cut that?** Stri țe si-l taĭu? (*The preposition may be omitted, as in:* **They killed him ~ the seashore** L-vătămáră búdză di amáre); (*along*) pri; **He was walking ~ the seashore** S-priimná pri búdza di amári; 2. (*temporal*) tră, trâ; **You must be here ~ Saint Mary's Day** Trâ Stă-Măríe va hiț auá; ~ **Christmas Day** tră Crăciún; ti; ~ **the day of Epiphany** ti Boboátim; tu; ~ **departure** tu plicáre. (*The preposition may be absent, as in:* ~ **a Monday** únă Luni)

ON ALL FOURS *adj.* and *adv.* abușilát *adj*; t-abúșeala, t-abúșala *adv*.

ON BAD TERMS (WITH) *adj.* ncăceát (cu), tăcânsít (cu)

ON CONDITION THAT *cj.* (*provided that*) cu dimândárea să; cu căvúlea că; cu ligătúra s; cu simfunía si

ON CREDIT *adv.* pi virisíe

ON END *adj.* (*of smb.'s hair*) mbirșát

ON EARTH (*imprecatorily*) la daráți; to fleámă; (*from a tale*) **Where ~ is the dwarf?** Cătră iu, la daráți, si-áflă Bárbă-cot? **Where ~ have you been?** Iu tu fleámă ti dúsiși?

ON FIGHTING TERMS *adv.* pri ciamăúnă; **They were ~** Si-aflá pri ciamăúnă

ON FOOT *adv.* pri páde, pripáde, pedéstru, arcát; **I went ~ (and with no luggage)** Mi duș arcát

ON GOOD AUTHORITY ≈ (am) ápă di la múmă

ON HORSEBACK *adv.* ncălár; (*when "the horse" is a person, as in some children's games*) ngrâcica [ngrâč•ka], grâșca, ngrâșca

ON NO CONSIDERATION (*under no circumstances*) iuvá-ș-iuvá

ON PURPOSE *adv.* máxus, maxús → DELIBERATELY, INTENTIONALLY

ON ONE'S DEATH BED *adv.* (*last will*) cu límbă di moárte

ON STIPULATION THAT *cj.* → ON CONDITION THAT

ON THE CHANCE *adv.* tu tíhe

ON THE EVE OF *prep.* (a)piríndu; ~ **the wedding** apiríndu dzúuă di númtă

ON THE LEFT-HAND SIDE *adv.* di nastânga, la stânga, a stânga

ON THE QUIET *adv.* → QUIET

ON THE OFF CHANCE *adv.* cu tahmíne

ON THE ONE HAND ‖ pri di únă parte, BASME 2

ON THE OTHER HAND ‖ *PC:* pri di álta párte

ON THE OTHER SIDE *adv.* dincló, dingló; didínde, dínde; **We es-caped onto the other side (of the mountain)** Scăpăm didínde; ná-parte, na náparte ‖ *Cru:* anáparte, GOLAB 198; ~ **of** *prep.* náparte di; ~ **the Black sea** náparti di Láia-amáre; *S:* dincló di (*ant.* dincoá di, dincoáțe di, didingoá di)

ON THE SLY *adv.* tiptíle → STEALTHILY

ON THE SPOT *adv.* pi loc, pri lócu, tu loc, tu oáră, troáră, di-năoáră, dinăcále ‖ tru loc, BASME 17

ON THE WANE *adv.* tu ascápit; **Our life is** ~ Him tu ascápit

ON THIS SIDE OF *prep.* → ON THE OTHER SIDE OF

ON TOP *adv.* prisúpră ‖ *PC: prep.* prisúpră di

ONCE *adv.* úna oáră, nă-oáră; ~ **more** nínca úna oáră, nínca nă oáră; **only** ~ nă oáră; ~ **upon a time** una oáră ș-nă zămáne; ~ **in the morning** úna tahináuă; ~ **in a blue moon** tu-apreásă ș-tu chi-rítă; ~ **in a while** ori, ori → AT ~ ‖ ~ **a week,** *Av:* nă oáră tu siptămâna, BASME 502

ONCE *cj.* (*as soon as; at the moment when*) cára; ~ **you take the plunge** (*of getting married*) cára daț di vă nsuráț ‖ íțe, BASME 24

ONE *num.* un *m/n,* úna *f*

ONE *adj.* un *m;* úna *or* nă *f;* ~ **by** ~ di un un; un di un; un câte un; **They massacred them** ~ **by** ~ Łi tăłáră di un un; **It's** ~ **o'clock** Oára eáste úna; **He has** ~ **foot in the grave** Cu únlu cior lu ved tu groápă; ~ **after another** un dúpă alánt; un spri un; báir-báir

ONE NEVER KNOWS țí-șciu? țí-ști?

ONE-EYED *adj.* gav, -vă, gayĭ, gáve; chior, *f* chioáră; nciuricát

ONEROUS *adj.* ▾angricós, -oásă; căchiós, -oásă

ONESELF: by ~ di síngur

ONION *s.* țeápă, *dim.* țipícă; (*small* ~ *to be planted*) curcáre; *Prv:* curmídhă ‖ ALIA 79: ceápă (*in many places*); *Nij, Grăm:* țépă, *Ses:* cépă, B-ARCH 79

ONLOOKER *s.* mártir

ONLY *adj.* (*alone*) únu ș-tut; **He is an** ~ **child his parents have** Unu ș-tut i la părínță; (*dry, i.e. served or eaten without but-ter, jam, etc.*) gol; **dry bread** pâne goálă ‖ HRISTU 40: goálă așa 'only so'

ONLY *adv.* mași, mâși, ma; **She bore** ~ **girls** Mași feáte amintă; (*solely*) veci; ~ **God** Dumnidză veciu; mânghi; **He re-retted** ~ **one**

thing Mânghi di únă ĺĭ păreá arắu

ONLY *cj.* *(except that)* maşi că, ma

ONRUSH *s.* (a)urñíre

ONSET *s.* (a)urñíre

ONSLAUGHT *s.* irúse, irúşe, năvál, năválă

ONTO *prep.* pi, pristi, sti; **lest I direct the lightning ~ you** s-nu-amín chícuta sti tíne

ONWARD(S) *adv.* năínte, năínde

OODLES *s.* crímă, bunlúche, birichéte

OOZE *s.* láspe, tínă

OOZE *vb.* ▾sprilíngu, spilíngu

OOZE (AWAY) *vb.* stricór; **My strength is oozing from my body** ñ-si stricoáră putérĭle din trup

OOZE OUT *vb.* *(in drops)* ţipurédz

OOZING *s.* ndzămáre, sprilíndzire

OPEN *adj.* dişcĺís; **completely ~** *(as of a door or window)* urthánictu, -ctă, -cţâ, -cte; *(as if abandoned)* árvale *invar.*; **I am keeping my weather eye open** ñ-disfác óсĺiĺ pátru ‖ HRISTU 30: jdichis *(sic)*

OPEN *vb.* *(a door, a book)* ▾dişcĺíd; *(of a bottle, of one's ears)* ▾distúp; *(a letter)* dizvuluséscu *(one's eyes)* ▾disfác óсĺiĺ; *(a satchel with cheese, etc.)* disfóĺu; **to ~ one's eye's wide** (a)zgârléscu óсĺiĺ *(cătră)*; ñ-ansár dzíhile di căftáre; **with one's eyes ~ wide** cu óсĺiĺ hărvăĺisíţ; *(to look out)* ñ-disfác óсĺiĺ pátru ‖ HRISTU 17: jdichid; 43: **he ~ed his eyes** jdichisi ochiă **Amc, Mul, Prv, Smx:** *(3 sg, ~s a door)* disfáţe (úşa), B-ARCH 403; **Cru, BdD', Gop, Trn:** disfác; **Kĕr:** jdăcĺíd, NEIESCU 271; *(to inaugurate a school, a church, etc.)* disfác, BELIMACE 44

OPEN AN ACTION AGAINST SMB. *vb.* lu scol, l-dau tru judéţ

OPENHANDED *adj.* cuvárdă, giumértu, -mérţâ; filótim, -tiñ

OPENHANDEDLY *adv.* → GENEROUSLY

OPENHEARTED *adj.* *(frank)* cu priéplu dişcĺís

OPENHEARTEDLY *adv.* fără ticlífe

OPENING *s.* dişcĺideáre, dişcĺídire, dişcĺidzătură; *(hole)* gúvă, gávră

OPENLY *adv.* tu fáţă; **Say that to him ~!** Dzâ-ĺ-u tu fáţă! şichearé, aşichearée, fariná, fóra

OPEN-MINDED *adj.* dişcĺís

OPEN-MOUTHED *adj.* hásca *invar.* → STUPID, ASTONISHED

OPERATION *s.* *med.* ‖ CUNIA: inhírisi (*in a personal letter*)

OPIATE *s.* (*jam opium*) tiriácă, chirácă

OPINE *vb.* ñ-dau míntea ‖ ñ-dau mínţăľĭ, BASME 302

OPINION *s.* mónte, idhéi, arăsíre, hâvă; ticníre; **to be of the ~ that** hiu di mínte că → ADVANCE ONE'S ~, STICK TO ONE'S ~ ‖ **of a different ~** cu áltă mínte, BASME 418

OPINIONATED *adj.* naprán, *m pl* napráñ; cap di grij

OPIUM *s.* haşíş, aşíş, afhióne [af•hĭó•ni]

OPPORTUNE *adj.* uidisít

OPPORTUNITY *s.* (*a favorable juncture of circumstances*) oáră, apuhíe, aráste

OPPOSE *vb.* dândâséscu, dânâséscu, fac cărşilâche, cărşilăti-séscu, mi duc cóntră → DISAGREE

OPPOSED TO → BE ~

OPPOSITE *adj.* aynánghea; **looked at him from the ~ side** di aynánghea âl mutreá

OPPOSITE OF *prep.* ‖ *Gop:* cărşíi, GOLAB 226

OPPOSITION *s.* (*obstruction, hostility*) cărşilâche

OPPRESS *vb.* ▾cálcu, ▾ndes, ▾(a)ngrec; (*to persecute*) nduchéscu

OPPRESSION *s.* angricáre, (a)ngúsă, ndisáre; (*cruel or unjust exercise of authority or power*) zulúme

OPPRESSIVE *adj.* (*heavy, harsh*) ângusós, -oásă; **an ~ winter** únă iárnă ângusoásă

OPT *vb.* ▾alég, ▾ncľid (la); **Tell me what are you ~ing for** Spúne la ţe ncľidz

OPULENT *adj.* avút → RICH

OPULENCE *s.* → WEALTH

OR *cj.* ori, i, íli, ícă; **Should he kill him ~ not?** S-lu vátămă ori s-nu-l vátămă? **A boy ~ a girl?** Ficĭór, i feátă? **Are you a cousin ~ some kind of a relative?** Eştĭ cusurín íli vâră sóie? **~ else** íli, ílea; **~ else I'll chop off your head** íli cáplu va să-ţ ľau ‖ ma; BASME 236: **May I take it, ~ not?** Su-l ľau, ma nu? **OR NOT** i nu; **Will you make up your mind, ~?** Vă apufăsíţ, i nu? **OR SO** (*approximately*) váră, vâră; **She boiled them ten eggs ~** Lă heárse vâră dzáţe oáuă; **a month ~** ca váră lúnă

ORACH *s.* *bot.* (a)lóbodă; **~ pie** pítă di lóbodă

ORALLY *adv.* ‖ BELIMACE 45: cu gúra

ORANGE

ORANGE *s.* purtucálă, purdhucálă, purdhicáľe; (*a bitter variety*) niránge ‖ CUVATA 24: purdicáľ *f pl*

ORANGE *adj.* (*orange-colored*) purtucalíş; turungíu, -gíe, -gíĭ

ORBIT *s. anat.* cáfcală

ORCHARD *s.* livádhe (*and* liváde), pumét

ORDAIN *vb.* hirotuniséscu

ORDAINMENT *s.* hirotunisíre

ORDEAL *s.* páthimă

ORDER *s.* (*written ~ in Turkey*) firmáne, buiurdíe; (*command*) émri, endolíe; (*regular or harmonious arrangement*) órdu, úrdin, arádhă, nizáme, sără, táxe; *G:* udópsu; (*people united in a formal way*) táymă → PUT IN ~ ‖ *Cru:* dhiatayíe, GOLAB 214

ORDER *vb.* dau dimândáre, dimându; **The emperor ~ed to have him killed** Amirălu dimândă s-lo-aspárgă; ▾urséscu, părănghilséscu ‖ (*to give an ~ through smb.*) alás zbor, BASME 6

ORDERLY *adj.* (*neat*) chischín, *m pl* -chíñ; spástru, -ştri, -stre

ORDINANCE *s.* dhiatáymă

ORDINARY *adj.* paráspur, di-arádă; (*inferior*) ápcu, -că, -ţi, -ţe

ORDINATION *s.* (*of a priest*) hirotunisíre

ORDURE *s.* → EXCREMENT

OREGANO *s. bot.* (a)riyán

ORGAN *s.* (*musical instrument*) óryan

ORGANIZE *vb.* (*to arrange*) ▾arădhăpséscu

ORIFICE *s.* gúvă

ORIFLAMME *s.* (*church banner*) sígne

ORIGANUM *s. bot.* (a)ríyan

ORIGIN *s.* (*ancestry*) dămáră, vínă, bímă, sírtă, vitíl, răzgă, *G:* arâzgă; **He is of Gypsy ~** Eáste di dămáră yifteáscă; **She asked him what ~ he was** Lu-ntribă năsă d-iu ľĭ-eáste vína

ORIGINAL *adj.* (*witted, clever*) pirgác

ORIGINATE *vb.* (*to have an origin in/from*) azvurăscu, ▾vom; (*to initiate*) nţep; **Where does the river ~?** Di iu s-voáme aráulu?

ORNAMENT *s.* cârtónă

ORNAMENTAL *adj.* stulsít

ORNATE *vb.* ▾nvéscu

ORPHAN *n and adj.* oárfăn, ítin

ORTHODOX *adj.* orthódox

ORTHOPEDIST *s.* yeátru di cioáre

OSCILLATE *vb.* ▼induéscu; ñ-u dau n coástă

OSSUARY *s.* aştére

OSTENTATION *s.* alăvdătúră, piñisíre, sultănátă, săltănátă, fálă

OSTENTATIOUS *adj.* alăvdós, -oásă; fălós, -oásă

OSTENTATIOUSLY *adv.* chibáre, fóra

OTHER *pron.* ál(án)tu, váltu; **No ~ person would have done that** Cáre váltu va s-u fățeá? (*lit.* '*Who else would have done that?*')

OTHERWISE *adv.* al̦úmtrea, al̦úmtrealui, áltă lăghíe ‖ BASME 698: áltă sóie

OTHERWORLD *s.* (*afterworld*) éta alántă, lúmea alántă ‖ STERGHIU 9: to alantă etă

OTIOSE *adj.* (*idle*) adhúliftu, *m pl* -fțâ; blanés, -ésă, éşĭ, -ése; timbél; (*sterile*) stérpu, steárpă, stérchi, steárpe

OTTER *s. zool.* núrcă, vídră

OUGHT *vb. 3 sg impers*: va, prínde, âñ cáde; **you ~ not** nu-ț undzeáşte ‖ cádi, fáți *3 sg impers*: **we ~ to refrain from meat on Wednesdays** nu fáți s-máți cárni ñércurea, DIARO 194

OUR *adj.* nóstru *m*, noástră *f*, nóştri *or* nóşțrâ *m pl*, noástre *f pl*; (*short form poss dat.*) nă; **He broke ~ jar** Nă freádze pócilu [póc•lu]; **Let's go to ~ place** S-ñárdzim tu loc-nă, acásă; *F:* nost, *pl* noşti (**1 syll.**) *and* noci (**1 syll.**); *f* noástă, *f pl* noáste

OURSELVES *pron.* noi íşĭne *m*, noi ísăne *f*

OUST *vb.* avín din, scot din, *N:* azgunéscu

OUT *vb.* (*as of truth*) ies tu miydáne

OUT *adv.* nafoáră; **Out you go!** Adúnă-u di auá! → BE ~, PUT ONESELF ~

OUT OF *prep.* (*because of*) di, ti, trâ; (*from a tale*) **The crow did not talk to anyone ~ megalomania** Gáia nu zburá cu ținivá di măríl̦e; **~ pity for the children** ti ñíla a ficĭórilor; **out of revenge** trâ pícă

OUT OF BREATH *adv.* ‖ cu súfltlu la gúră (*lit.* '*with one's breath / soul in one's mouth,*' *i.e. precipitately*), PARALLELE 147

OUT-OF-DATE *adj.* arudzinát, di zămáne

OUT OF ORDER *adj.* aspártu, -rtă, -rțâ, -rte; părtătíd, săcát

OUT-OF-SORTS *adj.* **He is ~** Nu-i tu ori

OUT OF THE BLUE ‖ (*unexpectedly*) HRISTU 37: ca ună rufei tu

OUT

gălită

OUT OF THE SAME BATCH *adj., adv.* únă; **All were ~** Tuţ eará-ľ únă; di un lémnu (sun cruíţ) (*lit. 'made from the same (piece of) wood'*)

OUTBREAK *s.* arúpire, arupeáre

OUTBUILDING *s.* şăndrămáie, tream

OUTBURST *s.* arúpire, arupeáre; **unrestrained ~** ≈ u fac uzungióva

OUTCLASS *vb.* → SURPASS

OUTCOME *s.* (*result*) ‖ PC: işítă, inşítă

OUTCRY *s.* zghic, zghícut, istrigáre, strigáre

OUTFIT *vb.* (*a house, etc.*) ▼arădhi(p)séscu, arădhăpséscu

OUTDO *vb.* ▼antréc, *N:* ▼astrésc

OUTDOOR *adj.* di nafoáră

OUTDOORS *adv.* nafoáră

OUTERMOST *adj.* dítră márdzine ‖ BASME 442: **in the ~ room** tru óda di tru márdzine

OUTFIGHT *vb.* ▼azvíngu

OUTFIT *s.* (*equipage*) tăcâme

OUTFOX *vb.* ▼ncálţu

OUTGUESS *vb.* → OUTWIT

OUTHOUSE *s.* → TOILET

OUTLANDISH *adj.* strin; axén; (*bizarre*) paráxin, tránciu; trâ ciudíe ‖ STERE 29: (*of people*) badzară

OUTLAWED *adj.* ayunít, azgunít, xinumsít

OUTLET *s.* inşíre, işíre

OUTLINE *s.* (*as of smb.'s face*) măsídhă, misídhă, ñisídhă

OUTLIVE *vb.* ľ-u mâc colíva

OUTMODED *adj.* bătăľusít, nvicľát, vicľát

OUTNUMBER *vb.* ≈ ▼antréc (*lit. 'to surpass'*)

OUTPERFORM *vb.* ▼antréc, *N:* ▼astréc

OUTPLAY *vb.* → OUTPERFORM

OUTPULL *vb.* ▼trag, ▼(a)năpuéscu

OUTRAGE *s.* prusvulíe, prusvulisíre

OUTRAGE *vb.* ▼angiúr, yumărséscu → INSULT

OUTREACH *vb.* ≈ ▼antréc, *N:* ▼astréc

OUTRUN *vb.* ≈ ▼antréc, *N:* ▼astréc

OUTSET *s.* → BEGINNING, START

OUTSIDE *adv.* dinafoáră, nafoáră (*ant.* núntru); *prep.* nafoáră di

OUTSIDER s. ≈ ▾axén (*lit. 'stranger, foreigner'*)

OUTSKIRTS s. varóşe, văróşe

OUTSMART vb. (a)ncálţu → OUTWIT

OUTSPOKEN adv. aşichearí, fóra, cu gióne zbor

OUTSTANDING adj. nişanlâ *and* nişanlí, *f sg/pl* -loáñe, *m pl* -ládz ‖ CUNIA 258: nişanlítcu; mărít, PARALLELE 133

OUTSTRETCHED adj. spirlúngu, spri-, sprilungós; **his outstretched nose** nárea-ĺ sprilungoásă

OUTSTRETCHED ARMS s. (*viewed as an unit of length*) uryíe, urghíe (*about six feet*)

OUTSTRIP vb. ≈ ▾antréc, *N:* ▾astréc

OUTWEIGH vb. ≈ ▾antréc, *N:* ▾astréc

OUTWIT vb. (a)ncálţu; ▾arâd; **You can't ~ an Aromanian** Armânlu nu si ncálţă; **This time he couldn't ~ him** Nu putú s-lu ncálţă di aéstă oáră

OVEN s. → FURNACE ‖ **baking ~**, *K:* cireáp, GOLAB 210

OVER prep. **1.** (*more than, higher than*) ma nsus di, disúpră di, di prisúpră di, prísti, písti, nculó di, astáĺe di; **~ six hundred sheep and goats ~** oi, căpri, astáĺe di şeáse súte; **2.** (*excessively*) până di urécĺi; **3.** (*during*) **~ night** prísti noápti; **4.** (*in addition to*) stră; adv. (*of a change to the worse*) **It's all ~** Dúsi curmána di an! → ALL ~

OVER HERE adv. pir auáţi; **Come over here** S-yiñ pir auáţi

OVERABUNDANT → MAKE ~, BECOME ~

OVERALL adv. tu tot lóclu

OVERAWE vb. (*to subdue*) ▾apléc

OVERBAKE vb. pri-coc

OVERBEARING adj. pirifán, *m pl* -fáñ → ARROGANT

OVERBLOWN adj. (*pretentious*) căbărdisít

OVERBOIL vb. para-hérbu

OVERCAST adj. (*clouded over*) alăcít; cu ţérlu astupát; **to become ~** vb. vurcuséscu, vărcuséscu

OVERCOAT s. paltó, *N:* paltóne *and* páltu; *also:* căndúşe, cundúş; *N:* cupărán; górnă, gunélă, *or* guneálă; *Bl:* ĺáră; patatúc, şigúne, ţipúne; *S:* zăbúne

OVERCOME vb. (*to rush*) năvăléscu; **Longing for his mother ~s him** Dor di mámă 1-năvăleáşte; **to ~ a difficulty** lu ansár gárdul (*lit. 'to jump over the fence'*), lu ansár tráplu (*lit. 'to jump over*

the pit'); *(to defeat)* ▼azvíngu ‖ CUNIA 163: bag mpádi

OVERCONFIDENT *adj.* *(cocky)* saylámcu, -mcă, -mţi, -mţe

OVERDO *vb.* *(to exaggerate, to do to excess)* para-fác

OVERDONE *adj.* pri-cóptu, -coáptă, -cópţâ, -coápte

OVERDRINK *vb.* para-beáu

OVEREXERT ONESELF *vb.* ▼apu-fác

OVERFATIGUED *adj.* curmát

OVERFEED *vb.* ▼astúp, paramâc

OVERFILL *vb.* *(to satisfy to excess, to give in abundance)* artiriséscu, artirséscu; **May God ~ her with his blessings** Dumnidză s-u-artiriseáscă

OVERFLOW *vb.* *(as of a river)* ies, ▼dipún; ▼zgrum (di ápă múltă) **The river ~ed its banks** Dipúse *(or* dipună*)* arâulu

OVERFLOWING *adj.* *(as of a river)* dipús (túna), işít

OVERHEATED *adj.* *(as of a furnace)* ársu; *(tired)* asprímtu, -mţâ

OVERJOY *vb.* ▼hărăséscu

OVERJOYED → BE ~

OVERLOAD *s.* panuyóme

OVERLOAD *vb.* ▼parancárcu

OVERLOADED *adj.* (a)ncărcát, angricát; *(as with grief, bitterness)* dat (di fărmác)

OVERLOOK *vb.* *(to disregard)* cătăfroniséscu

OVERMATCH *vb.* *(to be more than a match of, as in a contest)* azvíngu

OVERNIGHT HALT OF A FLOCK *s.* numíe

OVERNIGHT STAY *s.* mas, numíe

OVERPASS *vb.* trec

OVERPLUS *s.* *(surplus)* báşă

OVERPOWER *vb.* ▼nec, ▼(a)pitruséscu, *N:* (a)putruséscu; *(as of thirst)* ▼cúrmu; **Sleep is ~ing me** Mi neácă sómnul; **A great thirst began to ~ him** Ahurhí să-l cúrmă ună máre seáte

OVERPROUD *adj.* căbărdisít

OVERRIPE *adj.* juľu *m,* júľe *f* ‖ PC: *m pl:* juľ, *f pl* júľi

OVERSCRUPULOUS *adj.* garamitlíu, -líe, *pl* -líĭ

OVERSEAS *adv.* tu axeáne

OVERSEER *s.* epistát

OVERSIGHT *s.* *(surveillance, care)* bruítă, mutríre, mutrítă; *(omission, error)* aláth, căbáte, fáie

OVERSLEEP *vb.* ‖ mi paradórmu; **Get up, my daughter, do not over-sleep!** Scoálă, feáta mea ş nu-ñ ţă paradórñi, Rec. 41

OVERSTATE *vb.* (*to exaggerate, to make a mountain out of a moll-hill*) fac di per fúne

OVERSTEP *vb.* (a)ntréc, *N:* ▾astréc

OVERTAKE *vb.* (*to reach*) ▾agiúngu, ▾apróchiu; (*to catch up to*) ▾acáţ, pruftuséscu; **Nobody could ~ me** Vârnu nu puteá s mi-aproáche; **I could not ~ him** Nu-l pruftusíi

OVERTAKEN → BE ~ BY THE NIGHT

OVERTHROW *vb.* ▾(a)răstórnu, (a)rustórnu → OVERTURN

OVERTHROWN *adj.* turculít, târ-; **He found him ~ on the ground** Lu-află turculít ân páde

OVERTOP *vb.* (*to surpass*) ▾antréc, *N:* ▾astréc

OVERTURN *s.* (a)răsturnáre

OVERTURN *vb.* ▾tórnu, ▾(a)răstórnu, aristórnu, alăstórnu, ▾am-báturlu; **This mule has the habit of ~ing the load** Múla toárnă; (*as of clouds or waves*) turculéscu → KNOCK DOWN

OVERWEENING *adj.* → ARROGANT

OVERWEIGHT *s.* fulínă

OVERWHELM *vb.* ▾nec, ▾(a)pitruséscu, *N:* aputruséscu; **A heavy sleep had ~ed them** Lí-aveá apitrusítă sómnu greu; (*as of dogs attacking a stranger*) ▾aplucuséscu; (*to seize, of fear, thirst, pity, etc.*) ▾cúrmu; **Despair ~s him** L-cúrmă jálea

OVERWHELMED → BE ~ BY LONGING

OVERWORK *vb.* ▾apu-fác, scot pétalile; **He used to ~ his mules** Lă scuteá pétalile a múlilor

OWE *vb.* voi, *aor.* vrui, *part.* vrut; hurséscu; am tră dáre; mi burgilipséscu; **Here is the piaster I ~ you!** Ţâne-ţ yróslu ţe ţâ-l voi! **How many liras were you ~ing him?** Câte líre ľi vreai? ‖ *Cru:* éscu bórge, GOLAB 208

OWE SMB. A GRUDGE *vb.* ţân pícă, ñ-duc zăte

OWED *adj.* (*as of money*) hursít; **money ~** parádz hursít

OWING TO *prep.* şúchiur al → THANKS TO

OWL *s. orn.* cucuveáuă, buf, búfă, búhă; **as stupid as an ~** (*i.e., very stupid*) cap-di-gáie

OWN *vb.* am, stăpuéscu ‖ CUNIA 239: ▾ţân

OWNER *s.* (*master, mistress*) nicuchír *m*, nicuchíră *f*; aféndu, dómnu ‖ *Cru:* (~ *of sheep*) chihăié, GOLAB 230

OX

OX *s.* bou, *pl* boi; **draft ox** giugătór ‖ *Mul:* giúncu curát, <small>B-ARCH</small> 314

OX-FLY *s. ent.* tăún, búmbar, bumbár, dávan, dávun, strécľe, strégľe

OXIDATION *ş.* (*esp. of copper*) băcríre, băcâryisíre; (*of iron*) arudzináre

OXIDIZE *vb.* (*of metals that produce verdigris*) băcréscu, ▼băcâryiséscu, mbăxéscu; (*to rust*) arudzinéscu

OYSTER *s.* burlídhă, sulínă

P

PACE *s.* → STEP

PACE *vb.* arúc jgľoáte, arúc úrme, fac paşi

PACIFICATION *s.* irini(p)síre

PACIFY *vb.* (*to calm*) ▼irini(p)séscu, ▼arihătipséscu; (*to appease*) aprea(a)dún

PACK *s.* (*of hounds, etc.*) licníe, ulmíe; (*load*) bal; (*package, set*) tisté; (*ballot*) *N:* bóhce *or* buhcé; hăráie; (*large bag, as with wool*) déngă; (*the content of a ~*) bohcealâche

PACK *vb.* (*to fill*) dânguséscu, durdurséscu, sursuséscu; (*to ~ smb. off, to dismiss, to fire*) ľ-dau ţărúhile, ľ-dau părtăľle; (*to ~ together, to cram*) ▼(a)ndés, (a)ndiséscu

PACK AWAY/OFF *vb.* li scármin → BOLT

PACK OFF *vb.* fug; mi frângu zvérca

PACK UP *vb.* **to ~ and be off** ñ-ľau păltărĭle, ñ-ľau cărăndíile; **to ~ bag and baggage** ñ-adún catrafúsili

PACKAGE *s.* (*as of cigarettes or tobacco*) tisté ‖ *GSus:* păchét, <small>CL</small> 258; *Pls:* bachét, *Prv:* băchétă, <small>CL</small> 38

PACKED TO CAPACITY *adj.* and *adv.* dénga di, dínga di; ndisát

PACKHORSE *s.* cal di mizíle

PACKSADDLE *s.* sămár, *dim.* sămáríciu → PUT THE ~

PACKSADDLE MAKER / DEALER *s.* sămârgí, sămâră (*and* sâ-), sumâră (*and* sumără); (*his profession*) sămârgilâche

PACKTHREAD *s.* cioáră

PACT *s.* (*agreement*) ligămíntu, ligătúră

PADDLE *s.* lupátă di várcă

PADDLE *vb.* avuzéscu

PADISHAH *s.* padişáh

PAEAN *s.* (*hymn*) hirovicó

PAGAN *adj.* pângân, -gáñ; *G:* păngâr; păngănitéscu, -teáscă, -téşti, -téşti; élin, *m pl* éliñ; (*of Turks*) puríndu, -ndzâ

PAGE *s.* (*messenger*) pisudhróm

PAID *adj.* plătít ‖ MERCA 9: păltíţ *m pl*

PAIL *s.* căldáre → BUCKET

PALLIATE *vb.* lişurédz

PAIN *s.* dor, caimó, duríme, dureáre, óndus, pon, *pl* pónuri; virvér; **He has a severe ~ in his bones** Áre dor máre tu oáse; **smart with ~** usturíme cu duríme; **She was caught by labor** U-acă-ţáră pónurile s-feátă; (*difficulty, effort*) múndă, munduíre, proñ, vásan, zahméte, ziétă; **with great ~s** *N:* cu zóre *or* cu zórte → ANGUISH, TORMENT

PAIN *vb.* (*to experience pain*) *3 sg:* ▾doáre, *3 pl:* ▾dor

PAINFUL *adj.* ≈ *vb 3 sg impers:* doáre ‖ DIARO 432: durirós, du-rurós

PAINFULLY *adv.* cu proñ, cu sândze ‖ cu óčľi cripáţi, BASME 388

PAINSTAKING *adj.* lucrătór, -toáre; ni-şidzút, cilistisít

PAINT *s.* (*for the face*) buiáuă, cânǎ

PAINT *vb.* dau buiáuă; dau cu bóiuri, dau réngă, dau cu (+ *color, as in*) **~ed with violet** dat cu civitlíe; ▾buiséscu, ▾chin-diséscu, ▾zugrăpséscu, ▾zugrăvséscu, ▾zigrăfséscu; **to ~ with yellow** gănguripséscu; **I have ~ed the house** Ded buiáuă a cásă-ľei; **to ~ one's face** (*to make up*) ñ-dau cu buiáuă; **to ~ the town red** (*to have fun*) u-fac uzungióva ‖ TULLIU 132: anvupséscu; *Cru:* amvăpséscu, GOLAB 209; *Gop:* şăréscu, GOLAB 282

PAINT-BRUSH *s.* cundíľ

PAINTED *adj.* văpsít, zugrăpsít, scriát

PAINTER *s.* zugráf

PAINTING *s.* zugrăfíe, zugrăfsíre

PAIR *s.* păreácľe, ciftée; **a ~ of boots** nă păreácľe di cíjme; (*a ~ of draft cattle*) giugíe, jugíe

PAL *s.* oáspe → FRIEND

PAL

PAL *vb.* (*to associate with*) mi fac soţ, li apríndu aluáturile, li-acáţ aluáturile

PALACE *s.* pălắte, palắte, sărái [•rá•i] *f*, sắrắi *f pl*

PALANQUIN *s.* tăhtăváne

PALATABLE *adj.* bun, *pl* buñ; nóstim, *pl* -tiñl gustós, -oásă; yu-

PALAVER *s.* láfe

PALAVER *vb.* băndurédz

PALE *s.* par *m*, **Gop**: pótpar *m*

PALE *adj.* sárbit, sálbit; mundó *invar.*; **to become ~** sãhñiséscu

PALISADE *s.* ngărditúră

PALL *vb.* ▾sátur, ▾năfătéscu

PALLID *adj.* gálbin, *m pl* -biñ *and* -ghiñ; sárbit, sálbit

PALLOR *s.* gălbineáţă, sáhnă

PALM *s. anat.* pálmă

PALM BRANCH *s.* váie

PALM SUNDAY *s.* Vaiú *m*

PALMY *adj.* (*prosperous*) tihiró, *m pl* -rádz, *f sg/pl* -roáñe; cu hãíre

PALPATE *vb.* pusputéscu

PALPATION *s.* pusputíre

PALPITATION *s.* ciócut, ciucutíre, zvăcníre

PALPITATE *vb.* (*as of the heart*) furfurédz → THROB

PALSY *adj.* i luát tot (*lit.* '(*He*) *is taken completely*')

PALTER *vb.* (*to equivocate*) li mintéscu

PALTRY *adj.* cácav, chirchinéc, pănghiós, andíhristu; **a ~ boy** un chirchinéc di ficiór

PAMPER *vb.* (*to baby, to spoil*) ▾cănăchipséscu, ▾dizñérdu, ▾gă-liniséscu, ▾hăidipséscu, pusputéscu, ▾zdrudéscu

PAMPERED *adj.* cănăcheárcu, -rţi; hadhyeárcu, -rţi

PAMPHLET *s.* (*booklet, brochure*) afládhă

PAN *s.* tigáne, tiyáne

PAN OUT *vb.* ñ-cústă → THRIVE, SUCCEED

PANCAKE *s.* lălănghítă

PANDEMIC *s.* mólimă → EPIDEMIC

PANDEMONIUM *s.* vreávă, ghiurultíe

PANDER *s.* cudóş → PIMP

PANE *s.* geam, geáme

PANEL *s.* (*of wood*) scândură; (*of stone*) ploáce

PANG *s. med.* giúngľu, stihíptu

PANHANDLE *vb.* ţer

PANHANDLER *s.* ţiritór

PANIC *s.* fríxe → FRIGHT

PANICKY *adj.* căcăciós, -oásă → COWARD

PANIC-STRICKEN *adj.* zurlusít

PANNIER *s.* coş → BASKET

PANORAMA *s.* (*sight*) aynánghiu ‖ vidzută, HRISTU 61

PANT *s.* (a)ngăníre ‖ **Peş:** ancăníre, CL 32

PANT *vb.* ancănéscu, angă-; ndăcanéscu

PANTALOONS *s.* (*Turkish baggy trousers*) şiliváre, şilváre, şuli-váre

PANTING *s.* → PANT

PANTING *adj.* ngănít; **~ing voice** boáţe ngăníta

PANTS *s.* pantalóne; (*large pants for men*) ceácşíri *f pl*; cidíc, cidíe; (*for women*) cinténe *f pl*; (*made of white wool*) **Bl:** gidíţĭ *f pl*; bécife [béĉ•fi] *and* béfce [béf•ĉi] *f pl*; bécică *f pl* (*sic*); (*large black ~*) brecúşe *f pl* ‖ **Gop:** (*slacks*) bécivi, GOLAB 208

PAPA *s.* → FATHER

PAPER *s.* (*material, document*) cárte, hărtíe; (*for cigarettes*) ţiyarohártă

PAPIST *n and adj.* papistán, *m pl* -stáñ

PAPRIKA *s.* chipér, ciúşcă, şúşcă, pipércă ‖ ALR 1107: chipér aróş

PAPULE *s.* → PIMPLE

PARABLE *s.* părăvulíe

PARADE *s.* (*ceremonial formation of a body of troops*) părátă; (*display, flaunt*) căbărdisíre

PARADE *vb.* ▾căbărdéscu → FLAUNT

PARADISE *s.* (a)ráiu, parádhis

PARAGRAPH *s.* paráyraf *m*

PARALLEL: with no ~ (*second to none*) cum soţ nu áre; fără-di-soţ

PARALYSIS *s.* acăţáre

PARALYTIC *n and adj.* chicutát, dămlusít, sicát

PARALYZE *vb. med.* dămluséscu; mi ľau (di mâñ, di cicioáre); **His legs became paralyzed** Si-acăţă di cioáre; (*to be paralyzed with fear*) ñ-beau sâdzile di frícă; (*to stun, to make powerless*)

PARALYZED

taĭu mâñle
   PARALYZED *adj. med.* loat (*lit. 'taken'*); loat di mâñ ş di ci-
cioáre
   PARANOIA *s.* zurleáţă, zurlíľe
   PARAPHERNALIA *s.* (*personal belongings*) catrafúse *f pl*; cărăndíe
   PARASITE *s.* (*profiteer*) hărămgí *m*, hărămgioáñe *f*
   PARCAE *s. pl.* ‖ Álbile *pl f def*, BASME 199
   PARCEL *s.* → PACKAGE
   PARCEL OUT *vb.* (*of dough*) disfíngu, *part.* disfímtu; (*as of a
property*) ▾cumăthiséscu
   PARCELLING OUT *s.* mâşcăturáre, disfíndzire
   PARCHED → BE ~ WITH THIRST
   PARDON *s.* ľirtáre; **ask/beg smb.'s** ~ ñ-ľau ľirtáre
   PARDON *vb.* ▾ľértu
   PARE *vb.* (*as skin or rind*) cur, ▾pilichiséscu
   PARE DOWN *vb.* (*to diminish*) ▾ñicşurédz, ▾scad, ▾şcurtédz
   PARENT *s.* pârínte ‖ HRISTU 24: prinţ *pl*
   PARENTAGE: of humble ~ suisâz, xisóiastu
   PARENTAL *adj.* părintéscu, -eáscă, -éşţâ, -éşti
   PARGET *s.* (*as for coating a wall*) curasáne
   PARGET *vb.* ▾lăspuséscu
   PARING *s.* (*peel*) peáje, *pl* peji
   PARING-KNIFE *s.* (*for trimming and cleaning the shoes of a
horse*) săndrácĪu
   PARIS *s.* ‖ *Cru:* Paríşľi, GOLAB 240
   PARISH *s.* inuríe, parohíe
   PARLOUS *adj.* → PERILOUS
   PARMESAN CHEESE *s.* ≈ caşére
   PAROCHIAL *adj.* văc(u)féscu, -eáscă, -éşţâ, -éşti
   PARROT *s.* papayál
   PARRY *s.* apăráre, afiríre
   PARRY *vb.* (*to ward off*) ▾ápăr; (*to evade*) ▾afiréscu
   PARSLEY *s. bot.* magdanós, macheadón, machiduníş
   PARSIMONY *s.* nichizlâhe → STINGINESS
   PARSON *s.* préftu; *coll.* priftáme → PRIEST
   PART¹ *s.* párte, méros; **from all** ~**s** di túte părţâle ‖ *K:* iséi *f*,
GOLAB 222
   PART² *s.* (*of hair*) ráuă

PART *vb.* ▼mpártu → PARCEL

PART COMPANY WITH SMB. *vb.* u-arúp cioára cu → FALL OUT WITH SMB.

PARTAKING COMMUNION *s.* cuminicáre

PARTICOLORED *adj.* ľar; (*a dog's name:* Ľárlu); péstru, -strắ, -ştri, -stre; şáren, şárcu; (*as of cattle*) chindisít

PARTICULAR *adj.* → BE VERY ~ ABOUT

PARTING *vb.* (*separation*) dispărţâre, disfắţeáre

PARTITE *adj.* mpărţât, dispárţât

PARTITION *s.* mpărţâre, âmpărtăciúne

PARTRIDGE *s.* piturnícľe, piturníche, pitruníche, pirdhíc *m*, pirdhícă *f*; thălăndză; **as plump as a ~** ≈ gras ca un peáşte

PARTITION *s.* mpărţâre, dispărţâre, dispărţâtúră

PARTNER *s.* soţ, urtác

PARTNERSHIP *s.* suţátă

PARTURITION *s.* (*childbirth*) amintáre (*and* amindáre), fáţire, fắţeáre: **to end the ~** *vb.* (*after forty days*) sărăndiséscu

PARTY[1] *s.* adunáre; (*entertainment*) muabéte, féstă, haréľ, ziaféte → EVENING ~ ‖ BASME 471: beáre máre

PARTY[2] *s.* (*usu. a political* ~) cómă, părtídhă; tăráfe; **What ~ do you belong to?** Di carľ cómă hii?

PARTY SPIRIT *s.* cărdăşlâche

PASCHAL EVENING WORSHIP *s.* ayripáie, ayrăpáie

PASHA *s.* paşă, păşé, pâşé, păşilă; **like a ~** *adv.* păşileáşte; **country governed by a ~** păşilâche

PASS *s.* buyáze → DEFILE

PASS *vb.* trec; **to ~ one's time** ñ-trec oára; (*to elapse, of time*) ▼axéscu; **A year has ~ed since he died** Axí un an di cându murí; **to ~ into a proverb** agiúng părămíth, mi fac părăvulíe

PASS ACROSS (*or* ~ **BEYOND**) *vb.* ▼astáľu; **The caravans ~ed beyond the mountain** Cârvắñle astắľáră la múnte

PASS ON *vb.* (*from one person to another*) ▼úrdin; (*to go one's way, to mind one's business*) ñ-trag cálea

PASS OUT *vb.* ▼lişín, ▼lişinédz, liyuséscu

PASS OVER *vb.* ▼leápid; **He mounted his horse and passed over the hill** Ancălícă cálu ş-lipídă dzeána

PASS THROUGH *vb.* ▼pitrúndu, spitrúndu; **This forest cannot be passed through** Pădúrea aéstă nu s-pitrúnde; (*to filter*) ▼stricór

PASS UP vb. (to decline, to reject) nu mi fac di căbúle, nu străxéscu (or strixéscu), dau cu ciórlu

PASSABLE adj., **-BLY** adv. (barely good) ceat-pat invar.

PASSERBY s. tricătór, dhyeavát

PASSING s. (coming to an end) treácă; ~ **by**, ~ **over**, etc. treá-ţire, triţeáre; (moving past another moving person) antriţeáre, astreáţire

PASSING DIMNESS OF SIGHT s. urbárea a gắľíñlor (lit. 'chickens' blindness')

PASSION s. (affection or rancor) path, páthus; (love) vreáre

PASSIONATE adj. sárpit, sărpit (and sâr-), sârpid, sértic; sértu, -rtă, -rţâ, -rţe

PASSPORT s. tischiré, tischirée, pasapórte ‖ BATSARIA 48 tischireáuă

PAST adj. tricút

PASTE vb. ▾alăchéscu, ▾alichéscu

PASTE SMB. ON THE FACE vb. (to slap) ľ-alichéscu únă, ľ-ancúñu únă

PASTEBOARD s. mucâvă

PASTIME s. (diversion) dhiaschédhase

PASTORAL adj. picu(ră)réscu, -eáscă, -éşţâ, -éşti

PASTORALLY adv. picurăreáşte

PASTRAMI s. păstrămă, păsturmă, pâstrâmă

PASTRY DEALER s. simicí, simigí(u)

PASTRY TART s. → FLAKY ~

PASTURE s. păşúne; also: (in a deforested area) arúncu, arúngu; ciré, ládzină, livádhe, liváde; miré, părleánţă, -leándză ‖ **GSus:** mireáuă, CL 255

PASTURE TAX s. utláche

PAT adj. (suited to the occasion) uidisít → ANSWER SMB. ~

PAT vb. (to tap lovingly) ▾zdrudéscu

PATCH s. ‖ PC: peátic

PATCH vb. mpeátic, măsturipséscu ‖ **Cru:** ămpeátic, GOLAB 204

PATCHWORK s. cărpitúră, călpitúră

PATCHY adj. (as of the garment of a poor) mpiticát

PATE s. (head) ftínă

PATENT s. (a document conferring a right) biráte

PATH s. căráre; (in the snow) năpărtécă; **to take the bad** ~ ľau cálea slábă

PATIENCE s. (a)răvdáre, (a)răvdăciúne, ipumuníe, sábre

PATIENT adj. arăvdătór, -oáre → BE ~

PATRIARCH s. patriárhu, patríc, patrícus, patríţ, patéran, patéra; (the ~'s office or residence) patriarhíe

PATRICIAN s. patríc, patrícus, patríţ

PATROL s. culúchel → GUARDIAN

PATRON s. → CLIENT

PATRON SAINT'S DAY s. pănăyír, păniyír; adj. pănăyiréscu, păni-

PATTER s. (a)róput

PATTER AWAY vb. dârdăréscu; 3 sg: dâr-dâr gúra ľ-si dúţe → BABBLE, PRATTLE

PATTERN s. (gauge) calapódhe; (as in embroidery) parádhíymă, xómbľu

PATTY s. chifté, chióftă

PAUNCH s. pântic → POTBELLY

PAUPER s. ni-avút, ftoh, oárfăn, fucără; adj. urfănéscu, -eáscă

PAUPERIZE vb. urfăn(ips)éscu

PAUSE s. acumtináre → STOP

PAUSE vb. ▼acúmtin

PAVE vb. fig. aştérnu cálea ‖ (~ a road with stone) aştérnu cu cheátrâ, DIARO 91

PAVED adj. (as of a road) ncălţát; (as of a yard) cu căldăr-mádz

PAVEMENT s. căldărâme, căldărmă, căndărmă, căndrămă

PAW s. (as a cat's ~) ‖ PC: putúnă

PAWN s. (security for a loan) amanéte

PAWN vb. (to deposit in pledge or as security) ‖ DIARO 7, CUNIA 10: bag amanéti

PAWN ONE'S WORD vb. dau zbor

PAY s. (a)rúgă, dhyeárā; (~ per day) gundulúche, undulâche → SALARY; (reward) muştináre

PAY vb. ▼plătéscu, păltéscu (and pâltéscu); ▼dau; **How much did you ~ for the cap?** Câţĭ câni deádişi pri căciúuă? **to ~ a visit** fac vizítă; vizitédz; **to ~ a drink** (to seal with a drink,of sellers and buyers, before or after a transaction) dau crâşmă

PAY ATTENTION vb. săidiséscu, săldiséscu, bindiséscu, ľ-bag

PAY

oárǎ; **What passes through the village and dogs don't even ~ to?**
(THE FOG) Țe treáțe prit hoárǎ ș-nu-ľ́ bágǎ câñľi oárǎ? (négura);
The evil spirits did not pay any attetion to him Dzânile nu-ľ́
bǎgárǎ oára; **She was not paying attention to me** Nu mi bin-diseá;
(to listen) ľau di ureácľe; **Let us ~ (to what they are saying)** S-
lom di ureácľe; (to pay little or no attention to) nu-l dau di
curáuǎ ‖ LITURG 125: 1 pl imper: as bǎgǎm urécľili (la); DIARO 93:
Pay attention to what you are doing! Bágâ-ț míntea ți fáți!

PAY A VISIT vb. fac vízitǎ, vizitédz; (to ~ when invited to attend a feast) mi duc uspéț

PAY BACK vb. (as a debt) ▾tórnu bórgea; *F:* tórru (with rr < rn)

PAY HEED TO SMB. vb. (to regard) lu fac mále

PAY NO HEED TO vb. (to feel no interest or concern) nu ñ-u mâc
ínima ‖ néca ñĭ si báte ureácľa, BASME 500

PAY SMART vb. (as a theat or curse) **You shall ~ for all that!**
Farmác va-ț iásǎ túte!

PAY THROUGH THE NOSE vb. ‖ plǎtéscu ca préftu (lit. 'to pay
like the priest'), BASME 104

PAY UP vb. (as a debt) plǎtésc borgea

PAYER s. pǎltǎtór

PAYMENT s. plátǎ, plǎtíre, pǎltíre, dáre

PEA s. mádzǎre; also: áfcu; **Tur:** arucutéț; bizéľe ‖ **GSus:** pǎ-
púdǎ, CL 258

PEACE s. ariháte; aríñe, iríne, isihíe, síyǎ; **to make ~** adár
iríne → MAKE ~ WITH SMB. ‖ **Cru:** dirmáne, GOLAB 212; LITURG 123:
aariaáti

PEACEABLE adj. (slow) minghét

PEACEFUL adj. arhǎtipsít, frónim, minghét

PEACH s. cheársicǎ, phéscǎ, pl phéști; **a ~ of a girl** un sémnu
di feátǎ; nǎ feátǎ, nǎ nișáne → APRICOT ‖ **Cru:** práscǎ, GOLAB 244;
P: virúchi, SarD 34

PEACH-TREE s. cheársic

PEACHY adj. (speaking of color or consistency)) ‖ caișitó [ka•
i•si•tó], DIARO 166

PEACOCK s. pǎún, paún, piunár, pionél ‖ **Prv:** frangócutâ, CL 45

PEAK s. creáștit or creáștid; also: aráhe, cacealíu, cǎcealíu,
chícerǎ, chípitǎ, chirchinédz, chíscu, cingǎrlíu, cípit, ciúcǎ,

ciucĭúlă, ciulubét, țulubét, ciúmă, *dim.* ciumulícă; ciungáne, cârcilíu, coácă, códru, creástă, **N:** creáștic, créstic; cucúľ, cúlmă, dzeánă, *pl* dzénuri; (~ *of a tree*) gucilíe, gugiulíe; giug, (~ *of a mountain*) huhútă; maiáuă, măyeáuă, míthcă, pic, pifilíc, sumíg *or* sumígă, tămpă, țipilíc, țuțuléu, țuțulíc

PEAK *vb.* (*to grow thin or sickly*) ñ-arățeáște bișína (*lit.* '*my fart is growing cooler*')

PEAL *s.* arăsunáre

PEAL *vb.* arăsún

PEANUT *s.* chéchiră, chíchir-míchir, țeáțire ‖ DIARO 42: chichi-ríchi

PEAR *s.* peáră, căicúșcă, *pl* căicúște; cheicúșă, gorță; **Nev:** gurníț; plisádhă; **bergamot** ~ górță apídhye; **flat** ~ curcúșe; **wild** ~ guríță, áyru-górță ‖ ALIA 59: dárdu, dángăt, górdzu, gorț

PEARL *s.* mărgăritár *or* mărgăritáre

PEAR-TREE *s.* per, górțu, dúșcu, căicúșcu, curcúș; (*wild*) agru-górțu

PEASANT *s.* → FARMER ‖ **Cru:** hurĭát, GOLAB 220

PEASANT *adj.* ‖ CUNIA 317: hurghitéscu; *cf.* DDA huryiteáște *adv.*

PEBBLE *s.* chitrițeále *f pl*; *sg* chitrițeáuă; **CÍis:** cutumág, *pl* cutumádze; (*white or whitish*) (a)bél, *pl* (a)beále; (*in children's games*) gurgúľ, gărgúľ

PEBBLY *adj.* stirnós, -oásă; ~ **area** hălíche

PECK *s.* chipitáre

PECK *vb.* (*as of chicken*) ▼chípit

PECKER *s.* (*vulg.*) → MEMBRUM VIRILE

PEDAGOGUE *s.* pidhayóy

PEDDLER *s.* manáfi [•náf^i], *pl* manáfeañ; (*esp. seller of fruit*) bașác *m*, bașachínă *f*

PEDIGREE *s.* (*ancestral line*): **of high** ~ ciciór di scámnu

PEDLAR *s.* → PEDDLER

PEEL[1] *s.* (*thin layer of organic material*) peáje, pijilínă; (*as on boiled milk*) peáță, peáză, coáje

PEEL[2] *s.* (*shovellike tool used by bakers*) pinacutó, pnacutó, placutó

PEEL *vb.* (*as potatoes*) cur, disbiléscu ‖ *derm.* **The skin on my face is ~ing** Ñ-si dispeátură cheálea di pi fáțâ, DIARO 381

PEEL OFF *vb.* (*a wall, a tree, etc.*) ▼dispeátur, dispiturédz;

PEELING

dizgóľu, disbiléscu

PEELING s. (as of a fruit) disbilíre

PEEP s. chiuráre [k'i•u•]

PEEP vb. chíur, chiurédz [k'i•u•] ‖ ALR 373 (as of very young chicken) ţíură 3 pl

PEEPHOLE s. (in a door) ‖ STERGHIU 16: ocľiu di uşi

PEER[1] s. soţ

PEER[2] s. → LOOK

PEERLESS adj. făr-di-soţ; cum soţ nu áre; fără uidíe

PEEVE vb. ▼sâcâldiséscu

PEEVISH adj. căvgăgí, dzăndz(ăv)ós, -oásă; mutrusít, ţifnusít, zăpălít

PEEVISHNESS s. dzándză, sirsimlấche

PEEWEE s. ñícăz, ñicşór

PEG s. (in a loom) virdzeáuă; (in children's games) pírle → TAKE DOWN A ~ OR TWO

PEG vb. ▼acáţ, pirunséscu, ▼ncărfuséscu

PEG TOP s. sfúrlă, fúrlă

PELAGE s. per m

PELLICLE s. (as a ~ of ice on a lake) ţípă → PEEL

PELISSE s. bidéne, búndă, gúnă, yúnă, şúbă

PELLET s. (ball) arómbu; ghilándru ‖ (as in polenta) vâvâlúşu

PELL-MELL s. darmadán invar → JUMBLE

PELL-MELL adv. alandála → DISORDERLY, HIGGLEDY-PIGGLEDY

PELLUCID adj. curát → CLEAR

PELT s. cheále, chiúrcu

PELT vb. (with stones, etc.) ▼ambuliséscu, N: amín

PELT DOWN vb. (of rain) veársă cu găleáta

PELTING RAIN s. stih di ploáie

PEN[1] s. (for writing, etc.) cundíľ, (a)peánă (lit. 'feather'); (made of reed) caléme

PEN[2] s. (for animals) coárdhă (and coárdă), cutár, cutăréţ, pătúľ, ţárcu, dim. ţărcóľu ‖ (for goats) căprăreáţă, căprăreádză, CAPIDAN 145; TULLIU 120: căpărleádză

PEN vb. (as sheep) bag tu coárdă

PENALIZE vb. culăséscu, girimiţéscu, girimitiséscu

PENALTY s. pidhipsíre, culăsíre, girimé(e)

PENCIL s. mulív

PENCILED EYES *s.* ‖ óclĭ scriáţĭ (*lit. 'written eyes'*), PA-RALLELE 153

PENETRATE *vb.* ▼(s)pitrúndu (→ § 32), spritúndu; trec prit

PENDULUM *s.* (*of a clock*) stúmbul di sǎháte

PENIS *s.* → MEMBRUM VIRILE

PENITENCE *s.* tǎñusíre → REPENTANCE

PENITENTIARY *s.* → JAIL

PENITENT *adj.* mitǎñusít; pişmán, mǎnipsít, tuñisít

PENKNIFE *s.* ceárche, custúrǎ, cȃstúrǎ, psifíe, psuthíe

PENNILESS *adj.* cacurizipsít, fǎrǎ prǎ, oárfǎn di parádz; tiniché *invar.*; **He is ~** Tiniché eáste; L̆-súflǎ vímtul tu púngǎ

PENNY *s.* **the penny drops / the penny's dropped** ≈ nu-ñ fátǎ; nu ñi si umplú ftína

PENNY ROYAL *s. bot.* cimburícǎ, ciburícǎ, ciumurícǎ, ţemurícǎ

PENNY WISE AND POUND FOOLISH ≈ ñilueáşte pétala ş-cheáre cálu (*lit. 'spares the horseshoe and kills the horse'*)

PENSIVE *adj.* minduít

PENNYWORTH *s.* chilipíre

PENT *adj.* nclĭis

PENTHOUSE *s.* şǎndrǎmáie

PENTECOST *s.* (A)rusálĭe

PENURIOUS *adj.* (*poor*) ftoh, ftoáhǎ; (*stingy*) stres, streásǎ, streşĭ, streáse; (*barren*) stérpu, -eárpǎ, -érchi, -eárpe

PEOPLE *s.* pláse *no pl*; duñáuǎ; **N:** diuñáie [d¹u•], duñáe; (a)lúme; ghíntǎ, ghíndǎ, ghímtǎ, gíntǎ, gímtǎ, gínsǎ; yénos; **Many ~ have come** Múltǎ pláse i-adunátǎ; **~ are dying of thirst** Moáre plasea di ápǎ; **Listen to ~'s opinion!** Ascúltǎ şi zboárile a duñáuǎlĭei! (*nation*) fárǎ, miléte, púpul; (*crowd*) flúmin, plod, suflitáme ‖ **Cru:** laó, GOLAB 231

PEP *vb.* (*to stimulate*) anǎngǎséscu, anǎngǎsǎscu, ▼ngǎsǎéscu → URGE

PEPPER *s.* chipér, pipér, şúşcǎ

PEPPER *vb.* mpipirédz (*and* mbi-), agudéscu tu pipér, bag pipér

PEPPER-BOX *s.* pipiríţǎ

PEPPERY *adj.* mbipirát (*and* mpi-)

PERCALE *s. tex.* pircálǎ, pricál

PERCEIVE *vb.* ▼aduchéscu

PERCH *s.* clárǎ, témblǎ, clémbǎ; lúrǎ, strop

PERCHANCE *adv.* vahi → MAYBE

PERCOLATE *vb.* ▼stricór

PERCUSSION-CAP *s.* (*of an explosive*) şpírtu

PER DIEM *s.* (*allowance*) undulâche

PERFECT *adj.* (*blameless*) făr di catmére

PERFECTLY *adv.* farsí, safí

PERFIDIOUS *adj.* afíşcu, -scă, -şţâ, -şţe; ápistu, *m pl* ápişţâ, *f pl* ápişte; firaón, -aún; punoróu, *m pl* -rádz; făţ-făţ eásti

PERFIDY *s.* apistíe, faraunlâche

PERFORATE *vb.* străpúngu → BORE

PERFORATION *s.* cărtiľáre

PERFORM *vb.* ▼adár, ▼fac, ▼buréscu, ▼mburéscu, ▼axéscu

PERFUME *s.* ghiúlsu; *rose* ~ ghiúlsu di trandáfle, livándu, mís-cu, míşchiu, móscu; **G:** târfóľ

PERFUME *vb.* bălsămuséscu, muscuvulséscu

PERFUMED *adj.* muscuvulsít

PERHAPS *adv.* poáte → MAYBE

PERICARDITIS *s. vet.* (*of lambs*) per

PERIL *s.* perícľu → DANGER

PERILOUS *adj.* s(c)lab, *m pl* s(c)laghi; pri perícul

PERIOD *s.* (*menstruation*) aráhă; lunárile *pl f def*

PERISH *vb.* ▼cher → DIE ‖ BASME 266 psuséscu, supséscu

PERJURER *s.* yealán-giurátic

PERJURY *s.* yealán-giurátic

PERK UP *vb.* ▼mprusţédz, ▼ncucutédz

PERKY *adj.* mprustát, ncucutát, ngu-

PERMISSIBLE *adj.* alăsát, dizligát; geaíze, *no pl*

PERMISSION *s.* alăsáre. dizligáre, geaíze, vóľe, vólă, adhíe, izíne; (*authorization*) trat → ASK FOR ~ ‖ **S:** ízili, SarD 95

PERMIT *vb.* ▼(a)lás → ALLOW

PERMITTED *adj.* geaíze; (*canonically* ~, *of food*) dizligát → BE ~

PERNICIOUS *adj.* s(c)lab, *m pl* s(c)laghi; (a)rău, (a)ráuă, (a)răi, (a)rále

PERPETRATE *vb.* ▼fac, ▼adár

PERPETUAL *adj.* di éta tutằ

PERPETUALLY *adv.* éta tútă, tru éta tútă; índa → CONTINUOUSLY

PERPLEX *vb.* ▼uñiséscu, ▼mintéscu, ▼cutúrbur, ▼cutúlbur

PERPLEXED *adj.* tulít, chirút → BEWILDERED *and* BE ~

PERPLEXITY *s.* birdhipsíre, mintitúră, síyise → CONFUSION

PERSECUTE *vb.* ▾avín, nduchéscu

PERSECUTION *s.* avináre

PERSEVERANCE *s.* eneryisíre

PERSEVERE *vb.* ▾disíc năínte; eneryiséscu → INSIST

PERSIFLAGE *s.* arâdeáre, măitápe, mbizuíre

PERSIST *vb.* ▾disíc năínte, eneryiséscu; (*to ~ stubbornly*) u ţân fúne → HANG IN

PERSON *s.* ínsu, citimán, ipuchímen, véte; *in ~* singuríc, singu-rúş

PERSONALITY *s.* (*a person of prominence*) o fáţă ânáltă

PERSONALLY *adv.* dizmână, síngur; singuríc, singurúş

PERSPICACIOUS *adj.* iáspir, tăľós, -ľoásă; tăľitós, struxít

PERSPICACITY *s.* pireáţă

PERSPICUOUS *adj.* → CLEAR

PERSPIRATION *s.* (a)sudoáre, asdáre, azdáre; **to break into ~** mi arúp sudóri ‖ HRISTU 28: sădoáră, 105: sădoră

PERSPIRE *vb.* (*in drops*) ţipurédz

PERSUADE *vb.* → CONVINCE

PERSUASION *s.* căndisíre, umpleáre, úmplire

PERT *adj.* abráşcu → IMPUDENT

PERTINACIOUS *adj.* → STUBBORN

PERTURB *vb.* (*to trouble*) andărlusescu, andrălăséscu, andrăli-séscu, ▾ndărséscu → UNSETTLE

PERTURBATION *s.* mintíre, cuturburáre, cutulburáre

PERVERSE *adj.* distórsu, -toársă, -tórşi, -toárse; năpudheáric, pónir, şuţât

PERVERSITY *s.* anăpudzâľe, distoárţire, distureáre

PERVERT *s.* aspártu, pânghiós [●ǵós] ‖ CUNIA 85: dizghirdát

PERVERT *vb.* ▾aspárgu

PESKY *adj.* căchiós, -oásă

PEST *s.* púşcľe → PLAGUE; **~iferous** *adj.* mpuşcľát

PESTER *vb.* ▾pidhipséscu, pihtusescu, ľ-cad furtíe ‖ BATSARIA 1: 2 *sg aor:* mi-aroásişi di hicáte; BASME 445: 3 *sg:* âñ sta n cap; DIARO 268: 3 *sg:* âñ sta tu coástâ; PARALLELE 127: mâc urécľile (*lit.* 'to eat smb.'s ears')

PESTERING *s.* pihtusíre

PESTHOUSE: to shun like the ~ ≈ fug ca uvréulu di cărăvádhă

PESTILENCE

PESTILENCE *s.* mólimă, pănúcľe

PESTLE *s.* stúmbu; *Cľis:* ciumarác

PET *vb.* ▾cănăchipséscu, ▾dizñérdu, ▾găliniséscu, ▾hăidhipsés-cu, pușputéscu, ▾zdrudéscu

PET NAME *s.* númă di dizñérdu

PETER OUT *vb.* ñicșurédz, ▾nicurédz, áscad

PETITE *adj.* ñicúṭ

PETITION *s.* (*formal request*) anafuráuă, arugiuhále, aruzuvále

PETITION *vb.* dau únă aruzuvále

PETRIFY *vb.* (*as of a smile on smb.'s lips*) ▾chitruséscu

PETTING *s.* disñirdáre

PETTISH *adj.* inagí, inací; mutrusít

PETULANCE *s.* → PEEVISHNESS

PETULANT *adj.* → PEEVISH

PEW *s.* (*in a church*) stálă, tisídhă

PHANTOM *s.* aúmbră, băbăľúr, fántasmă, fándazmă, fántase, scheástră, scheáhtru, stífă, stifă, stihíe, stihió, stihíu

PHARMACIST *s.* spiṭár, spiṭér

PHARMACOLOGY *s.* spiṭărlâche

PHARMACY *s.* spiṭăríe

PHEASANT *s.* *orn.* fașanó

PHIAL *s.* cunétă

PHILANTHROPIC *adj.* → PHILANTHROPIST

PHILANTHROPIST *s.* cuvurdhă, giuméru, slăghít, filanthróp

PHILANTHROPY *s.* filantrupíľe, filanthrupíe, sivápe

PHILOLOGIST *s.* filólog

PHILOLOGY *s.* filuluyíe

PHILOSOPHER *s.* filózof

PHILOSOPHY *s.* filuzufíe

PHLEGM *s.* hărboálă, hârpă

PHLEGMATIC *adj.* adhyeáfur

PHLYCTENA *s.* *derm.* arópun, rópan

PHONY, PHONEY *s.* șarlatán

PHOSPHOR *s.* fósfur

PHOTOGRAPH *s.* (*in books or magazines*) pap, pápean, pápan; **to take a ~** ▾futugrăfséscu ‖ *Cru:* fac pi cádru, GOLAB 214

PHOTOGRAPHER *s.* futuyráf

PHOTOGRAPH *vb.* ▾futugrăfséscu

PHTHISIS *s. med.* (*esp. pulmonary tuberculosis*) zúră

PHYSICIAN *s.* gheátru, ichím

PHYSICS *s.* fisichíe

PHYSIOGNOMY *s.* fisiunumíe

PIANO *s.* pheán

PIASTER *s.* câne *m*, aslán; **Give me a ~ to buy a loaf of bread** Dă-ñ un câne tra s-ľau pâne

PICK *vb.* (*to shell, to husk*) cur; (*to steal*) ▾agudéscu, ▾ahuléscu, ▾anvăléscu, ▾(a)nvărtéscu, ▾ciuléscu, ▾ciun; **to ~ a quarrel with smb.** trag tămbárea azvărna; u cáftu ngăceárea cu luminárea ‖ ALR 370: (*as of feeding chicken*) chípură 3 *sg/pl*

PICK AND CHOOSE *vb.* ▾strâmbu nárea

PICK HOLES IN SMB.'S COAT *vb.* ľ-áflu coáde, bag coáde, ľi áflu nă acăţătúră

PICK ON/UPON SMB. *vb.* (*to fix one's eyes on*) bag tu ócľu

PICK UP ONE'S WAY TOWARDS *vb.* (*to turn to*) ▾ľau

PICK UP SPEED *vb.* ľau vrápă

PICK UP *vb.* ▾adún → GATHER

PICKAXE *s.* chiuschíe, câzmă, dhichéle

PICKET *s.* pótpar *m*

PICKINGS *s.* sârme *f pl*

PICKLE *s.* (*cucumbers, etc.*) turşíe; **to be in a ~** li úmplu (di frícă)

PICKPOCKET *s.* lupudhít, pľaşcagí, zulumgí

PICKING *s.* alidzeáre, aleádzire

PICTURE *s.* cádhru, futugrăfíľe; (*in books or magazines, etc.*) pap, pápan, pápean; **The book is full with ~s** Cártea i mplínă di pápañ → PHOTOGRAPH ‖ *Cru:* cádru, cádhur, cádur GOLAB 223; **to have a ~ taken of oneself** mi fac cádru, GOLAB 214 ‖ ALR 1444: **(He is) the very ~ of his father** E tamán tát-su! E idhía ca tát-su!

PIE *s.* pítă, plăţíntă; **large ~** pităroáñe, pitu-, buyáce, căţăroáñe, lucumă; **cornmeal ~** badzáră ‖ *Ohr:* lucmáe, BASME 166

PIEBALD *adj.* ‖ *Cru:* álbastru, GOLAB 197

PIECE *s.* búcă, bucátă, *dim.* bucatíce; cumátă, *dim.* cumatíce, cumătúş; părceácľe; (*as of meat*) búte, filíe; (*as of cheese or sugar*) grúndă, grúndză; (*loaf of cheese*) dánă; *S:* grândză; (*as of bread*) ţópă; **With a large ~ of bread a dog gets full** Cu ţópa di pâne si sátură un câne; córnu; **a ~ of thread** un córnu di hir; (*a

PIECE

thing considered as a unit) *N:* grăţ; **five eggs** ţínţi grăţi di
oáuă; (*of wood*) blánă ‖ **large ~** cumâtoáñi, DIARO 153) → BREAK
INTO ~S, CUT INTO ~S, MAKE INTO ~S

PIECE *vb.* (*to repair*) (a)ndrég, măsturipséscu

PIECEMEAL *adv.* părălâche ‖ CUNIA 319: (cu) părălâche; PC: câti
psân, câti psân

PIECEWORK *s.* ‖ PC: lúcru cu cumáta

PIED *adj.* (*as of cattle*) chindisít

PIERCE *vb.* spitrúndu, pitrúndu → BORE

PIERCED *adj.* pitrúmtu, pitrúmsu; spitrundát, pitrumdát; **We are
~ with sorrow** di jále him pitrúmţ

PIERCING *s.* spitrundere, spitrundáre, pitrundeáre, pitrundáre,
pitrúndire, sfridináre, cărtiľáre

PIERCING OBJECT *s.* zahuráhe

PIETY *s.* ivlávie

PIFFLE *s.* bănduráre, láfe; zboáre tu cacu

PIFFLE *vb.* **He ~s** zburáşte goále

PIG *s.* pórcu, arâmătór; (*as an insult*) déri

PIGEON *s.* părúmbu → DOVE

PIGGISH *adj.* → GREEDY, STUBBORN

PIGGY BANK *s.* cumbără

PIGLET *s.* purţél *m*, -ţeáuă *f*; *dim.* purţilúş *m* ‖ *Grăm, Mul:* pur-
ţéu; *Arm, Cern, Pals:* purchícu, *An, Grbţ:* purchíclu, *LvO:* purcí-
clu; *Pros:* purţícu, B-ARCH 286

PIGMY → PYGMY

PIGPEN *s.* purcăreáţă, purcăreádză, purcaryió, cócina, cuteáţă,
cutumás

PIGSTY *s.* → PIGPEN

PIKE[1] *s. ichth.* túrnă

PIKE[2] *s.* (*tool or weapon*) gilít, cămác, cămáche, mastrác, măzdrác

PILAF *s.* pileáfe, pilafe, pileáf, piláf

PILASTER *s.* (*support*) arádzim, numíe

PILE[1] *s.* culéu, cup, grămádă; (*as of earth, of stones*) grúmbă,
grúmur, grúmbur; (*as of stones*) gumarádhă; (*as of coins*) stoc;
(*as of firewood*) stog, stívă, sumăreáuă, suríe, suró; (*of fabric, of flying birds, of clouds*) trâmbă → MAKE ONE'S ~ ‖ STERE
76: (*as of sunflower seeds*) cuculíci

PILE[2] *s.* (*support*) andoápir, fúrcă, pótpar

PILE UP *vb.* ▾stivăséscu

PILES *s. med.* suhădz, suhăţ *f pl;* **Bl:** trănci *n pl*

PILFER *vb.* ▾ciun → FILCH, PICK, STEAL)

PILFERING *s.* ciunáre → THEFT

PILGRIM *s.* (~ *to Jerusalem*) hagí *m,* hagioáñe *f*

PILGRIMAGE *s.* hăgilắche

PILING *s.* adunáre

PILL *s.* hap, hápe; (~ *of quinine*) scónă; (*poison*) scónă, fólă; **They poisoned him with a ~** L-fărmăcắră cu únă fólă

PILLAGE *s.* alimúră, yeá(y)mă, iámă, prádă, pridăciúne, spóľe

PILLAGE *vb.* fac ghénga → PLUNDER

PILLAGER *s.* haldúp, *pl* haldúpeañ; zulumgí, zulumcheár

PILLAR *s.* andoápăr, duréc, **N:** diiréc; stil, stur, ştiúlă → POST

PILLOW *s.* **S:** căpitâiu, **N:** căpitíñiu; pruschéfal

PILLOW-CASE *s.* călắfe, călúfe, culúfe ‖ **Peş:** pir, CL 258

PIMP *s.* arufcheán, cudóş, púştan, puşteán

PIMPLE *s.* gărnúţ (*and* gâr-), găríţă, *dim.* gârnuţíc; ciúmă; arápun, cucúdhă (*and* cucúdă); **with ~s** *adj.* gărnuţós, grâ-; gărnuţát ‖ **Pls:** puníe, CL 259

PIN *s.* cărfíţă ‖ **Peş:** ALR 523: ac cu ciófcă

PIN *vb.* (*to hold fast*) ▾ţân; (*to fasten with or as with a pin*) ncărfuséscu; (*to ~ one's hope on*) hiu cu umútea la; (*to assign the blame for*) arúc măhănălu pri; *to ~ smb. by the throat* lu-ascálin (*or* ascálnu) di gúşe

PINCER *s.* cleáşte *f* → PLIERS

PINCERS *s.* ţimbídhă, ţimbístră

PINCH *s.* (*an act of pinching*) chipinătúră; (*bit*) dhráme; (*arrest*) acăţáre; (*of snuff*) préză

PINCH *vb.* (*as of shoes*) stríngu; (*to compress painfully with one's thumb and index finger*) chíşcu, cepcuéscu, ▾chípur, ▾chípin; **Her little son ~ed her** Ficiórlu-a ľei u chipinắ; (*to steal*) sufruséscu

PINE *vb.* (*to yearn*) mi ľa dórlu (di), plâng di dor, ñ-alghéscu ócľiľ (tră); **Smr:** apórt dor; **She ~s after him** Trâ nâs apoártă dor; (*to weary for/after*) ñ-si-alăcheáşte ínima (di); (*to lose vigor, health or flesh*) ñ-arăţeáşte bişínă; **to ~ away** ▾usâc, usúc, ▾víntin → FADE, LONG

PINECONE

PINECONE s. aroábă, aroábulă, buşulíe; **G:** cucúciu, gugúciu (di chiñ); cuculíciu, mărúlă

PINE-FOREST s. chinét

PINE-TAR s. cătráne

PINE-TREE s. chin, *dim.* chinşór; (*mountain creeping ~*) **GBg:** slap, *pl* slachi [slɐk']; bor ‖ **Prv:** nuníclʹu, CL 257

PINK s. *bot.* (*dianthus*) garoáflă, garafílă

PINK *adj.* trandafilíu, trandafilʹát

PINKIE s. dzidzitíc, dziditíc

PINNACLE s. (*of a house*) papafíngu

PINPRICK s. nguvujdáre

PINWORM s. limbríc, lâmbríc

PIOUS *adj.* ivlaviós, -ioásă; thríscu, -scă, *pl.* thrískiĭ ‖ VELO 104: evlaghisít

PIP s. *bot.* sâmbur, sâmbure *m*, sâmbură *f*, súmbur *m*; **Src:** súmbru; os *n*; **Băi:** oásă *f*; (*as of plums*) cócală; (*as of melons*) puponʹu *m*; (*on the tongue of a bird*) ţífnă, ţíflă, dzífnă, dzână, dzífcă; **affected by ~** *adj.* (*of chickens*) dzifnusít; **to be sick with ~** ţifnuséscu ‖ **Peş:** pífcă, CL 258

PIPE s. (*for smoking*) lulé → PUT IT IN YOUR ~ AND SMOKE IT; (*with long stem*) cibúche, ciubúche, cʹubúcă; (*tube*) sulinár, píscală; (*flue*) chilúnge, chilúnghe, chiúncu, chiúngu, ciúnghe; (*long flute with five holes*) cavál

PIPE DOWN *vb.* tac, amuţắscu, **N:** amút

PIPE DREAM s. ‖ CUNIA 133: puʹ tu vímtu (*lit.* 'birds in the wind')

PIPE MAKER / DEALER s. ciubuccí

PIPER s. gaidagí

PIPE TO SMB.'S TUNE *vb. fig.* gioc cúmu-ñ cântă

PIPING HOT *adj.* clucutát, clucutít, culcutít

PIPKIN s. ulícă ‖ **Peş:** misúr, CL 256

PIPSQUEAK s. ţapaţúc, ţili-páie

PIQUANT *adj.* (*pungent*) pipirát; (*savory*) nóstim

PIQUE s. pícă, nţăpáre, nţăpătúră

PIQUE *vb.* (*to offend, to goad*) ▾nţap (*and* ndzap)

PIRATE s. cursár

PIROUETTE s. chíclă, fúrlă

PISS s. chişát *m*, cşat

PISTACHIO NUT *s.* făstácă, fistíche

PISTOL *s.* arăvóle, aruvóle, cumbúră, *N:* cumbúre, cubúre; piştoálă, piştólă, *dim.* piştulícă; ruvéle, tapánce; *derog.* bişinătoáre ‖ *Prv:* peristúf, CL 258

PIT[1] *s.* groápă, lac, yurníţă, trap; *G: dim.* tărpălíc; endéc, hindéche

PIT[2] *s.* (*seed*) → PIP

PITTANCE *s.* ≈ psân *adv.* → LITTLE

PIT-A-PAT *s.* (*as of a horse*) ▾aróput; (*of a clock, of the puls, etc.*) tic-tic; tâc-tâc

PITCH *s.* cătráne, pécură, písă, smólă ‖ BELIMACE 46: ~ **darkness** chísă zăndáne

PITCH A TENT *vb.* adár purávă

PITCH IN *vb.* ▾agiút, ▾bag

PITCHER *s.* urciór, stámnă; *also:* birbíľ, bot, buján, bujánă, căráfă, cătrúvă, cávan *m*, cănátă, cíngu; (*large ~, usu. for water*) dud, ghium, ghiúme, mâtâră, pifchiu, pociu, pucíc; *Tur:* putéţ, zvánă ‖ BA, 438: ghiumáce

PITCHFORK *s.* (*as for hay*) fúrcă, vílă, yílă; *G:* gârbu

PITEOUS *adj.* mărát

PITFALL *s.* → TRAP

PITH *s. bot.* mámă

PITIABLE *adj.* mărát, şulúndu

PITIFUL *adj.* mărát

PITIABLE *adj.* mărát

PITILESS *adj.* ni-ñilós, -oásă

PITILESSLY *adv.* fără di isáfe

PIT ONESELF AGAINST SMB. *vb.* mi acáţ cu, mi misór cu

PITTANCE *s.* tăíme → RATION

PITTER-PATTER *s.* ▾aróput

PITY *s.* isáfe, ñílă, ñiluíre; **it is a ~ that you** ... yeazác di voi că ...; **Take ~ on my house!** Di cásă-ñ híbă-ţ ñílă! ‖ MURNU: **Have ~ on us!** Ñiluiá-ñă! → CLEMENCY

PITY *vb.* ▾jăléscu, ñ-i ñílă, ▾ñiluéscu (di), ñi si fáţe ñílă (di), ñ-fac ínimă (di) ‖ BA, 80: ñ-fac di ínimă

PIVOT *s.* (*in the middle of a threshing area*) steájer

PLACATE *vb.* APPEASE

PLACE *s.* loc; **in ~s** *adv.* pri-auá ş-pri-acló; (*the ~ where one*

PLACE

lives) vădắne (*and* vădắñe); (*country*) pătrídhă (*and* pătrídă); (*plaza*) piáţă; (*an indefinite ~ far from human habitations*) meal ‖ biloc 'place,' HRISTU 26; a safe ~ un biloc asfilisit, *idem* 35 → PUT SMB. IN HIS/HER ~

PLACE *vb.* ▾pun, ▾bag, ▾análţu; (*to set, to install*) curdiséscu

PLACENTA *s. anat.* soárte

PLACID *adj.* arihătipsít

PLAGUE *s.* pănúcľe, púşcľe; **to contaminate or to be contaminated with ~** puşcľédz; *imprec.* **The ~ upon all!** Xíche si s-fácă túte! *or* Défi si s-fácă! **The ~ on you!** Défi s-ti faţi! Buiáua s-vă bátă! S-ti faţi răsădínă! Mori vătămát!

PLAGUE SMB. TO DEATH *vb.* (*to bother the life out of smb.*) ľi scot súflitlu; lu aród dit hicáte; ľ-mác hicátlu

PLAGUE-STRICKEN *adj.* puşcľát, puşcľós, -oásă

PLAIN *s.* câmpu, páde; (*small ~*) pádină, pădínă; (*rich ~*) mulălíche; (*~ surrounded by hills or mountains*) bátă, *pl* băţ; (*characteristic of a ~*) *adj.* câmpíş (*ant.* muntíş); **goods from the ~**O tutupútă câmpíşe

PLAIN *adj.* (*flat, smooth, level*) íschiu; **The place is level ~** Lóclu eáste íschiu

PLAINLY *adv.* (*categorically*) stres

PLAINSPOKEN *adj.* fanirá *invar.*

PLAINTIFF *s.* dâvăgí

PLAINTIVE *adj.* plângáciu, plângurós, plângărós, plâmtu; *also:* flivirós, lăcrimát, parapuñárcu, părăpuñós, suschirát, suschirós, şcľifurát, şcľifurós

PLAINTIVELY *vb.* plângurós, suschirós; cu graiu suschirát

PLAIT *s.* cusíţă, păltăníţă, pultăníţă

PLAIT *vb.* mplitéscu, (a)mplătéscu

PLAN *s.* (*contrivance, scheme*) cruitúră, daravéră

PLAN *vb.* cruéscu, **N:** curéscu; **They acted as they had ~ed** Feáţiră cum u cruíră ‖ **Cru:** cuiréscu, GOLAB 228

PLANE *s.* (*a tool for smoothing wood*) (a)rindé, rénde, réndză, rindeáuă, strug, (a)rucáne ‖ **GSus:** mazníi, CL 255

PLANE *vb.* arindiséscu, arândiséscu, arundiséscu, arucănséscu, aruncăséscu, struguéscu, ▾ischédz

PLANED *adj.* (*shaped with or as with a plane*) arundisít

PLANE-TREE *s.* páltin, plátăn, plátan, *dim.* plătăníc; plătănéu, *coll.* plătănáme; rápun, sfindán *m or* sfidáne *f*

PLANING *s.* arundisíre, pilixitúră, struguíre

PLANING KNIFE *s.* ‖ *GSus:* zmálă, CL 263; *Prv:* aréspâ *or* aréşpi, CL 37; *SJos:* scuáră, scáră, CL 260

PLANT *s. bot.* plántă (*DDA* 993 *mentions: bookish word*)

PLANT *vb.* (*a tree, a pole, a knife*) plântu, fitipséscu; (*forcefully*) ▼nhig; (*to ~ seeds*) seámin; (*as a trap*) ▼bag, ▼curdiséscu **Let's ~ some traps** S-băgăm băţ; **to ~ a standard** u scol pandéra

PLANT HORNS ON SMB. *vb.* ▼ampíhiur

PLANTAIN *s. bot.* pindánă, pindáne, pindănícă, pindánică, pindălícă, păndălícă

PLANTING *s.* (*of trees, etc.*) fitipsíre

PLASTER *s.* yeachíe, yeachíuă, ípsu, plástur, blástru, ţirót

PLASTER *vb.* ‖ (*to coat with clay*) dau cu loc, HRISTU 4

PLAT *s.* loc

PLATE *s.* căţân (*and* câ-), căţón (*and* câ-), căţână; *also:* blid, cíngu; (*of copper*) linghér; misúr, misúră, pheát, *dim.* pheatác; piát; san, săhán *or* săháne; tálir, tánir, tániră, tăľúr, tănír; tas *or* táse ‖ GBg: ciníi, STERE 50

PLATE *vb.* (*to cover*) vérsu, *part.* virsát; **a sword ~ed with gold** apálă tu amalámă virsátă ‖ ALR 1046: phiat

PLATEAU *s.* códru ‖ (*tableland*) CUVATA 5: plóştină

PLAY *s.* (a)gióc, joc

PLAY *vb.* (*to frolic*) ▼agióc; **They used to ~ together** Si-agiucá deadún; (*to ~ a musical instrument*) ▼bat; cântu cu, ľ-u dzâc; agudéscu; (*to ~ sadly*) blândurédz; **Shepherds are ~ing the flute** Picurári bat fluéri *or* cântă cu fluiára; **Do you know how to ~ the flute?** ştii si-agudéşti fluiără? **to ~ cards** ▼(a)gióc cărţâ ‖ BA, 430: gioc cu cărţáli ‖ **He is ~ing the flute** ľ-u dzâţe cu flueára (*lit. '[he /she] is telling it to it [sic!]'*), PARALLELE 151

PLAY A PRACTICAL JOKE ON SMB. *vb.* ľ-gioc, ľ-gioc pri tăpsíe, ľ-gioc nă fheácă, ľ-u gioc hunérea ‖ BA, 79: ľ-u adár; trag nă călúpe, PARALLELE 140

PLAY A SHABBY TRICK *vb.* ľi scot ócľiľ di cu tótalui, ľ-fac rénghe, u adár muşiteásca ‖ BATSARIA 10: ľ-u fac

PLAY DUCKS AND DRAKES WITH MONEY *vb.* (*to be prodigal*) tuchéscu

PLAY HAVOC *vb.* bag stróflu (tu) ‖ BASME 164: (*as of a turbulent child in a tidy room*) alúmtu cása

PLAY

PLAY THE BOTTLE *vb.* ĺ-arúc múltu tu cărcheáuă → DRINK

PLAY UPSTAGE *vb.* ▾ngroş → PUT ON SIDES, GIVE ONESELF AIRS

PLAY WITH FIRE *vb.* ≈ mut ciórlu ş-cáftu găvójdu; ñ-bag cáplu tu tástru

PLAY WITH SMB.'S NOSE *vb.* ñ-arâd (cu nâs)

PLAYER *s.* (a)giucătór → GAMBLER

PLAYFUL *adj.* fliturác, lişurác, zdurdít, zdrudít ‖ ândálic, DIARO 364 → FROLICSOME

PLAYFULNESS *s.* zburdălipsíre

PLAYING CARD *s.* cárte, hărtáche, pánto ‖ **Peş:** pánti *pl*, CL 257

PLAYMATE *s.* soţ

PLAYTHING *s.* (a)giucăreáuă, *pl* agiucăreále; agiucăríe

PLAZA *s.* piáţa, códru, códur

PLEAD *vb.* (*to appeal earnestly*) fac rigé, fac rigeáie, pălăcărséscu

PLEADER *s.* rigeagí

PLEASANT *adj.* arâsít; nóstim, *m pl* -tiñ; nustimác; cu hári

PLEASE *vb.* (*to ask, to beg*) (a)ór; ~ **tell me** Vă or s-ñi spúneţ; ▾ariséscu, urséscu, cupăséscu; ~ **come in!** Cupăseá năúntru (*or* Cupăseá n cásă!) *sg*; Ia ursíţ (*or* cupăsíţ) ân cásă *pl*; ~, **dinner is ready!** La mása scupăséşti! ‖ **Gop: it ~s me** mi bindisésci, GOLAB 208

PLEASE! *interj.* órse, urseá, oríste, buiúrun, buiúrum

PLEASED → BE ~

PLEASING *adj.* nóstim, *pl* -tiñ; pălít

PLEASURE *s.* plăţeáre; *also:* arisíre, arrâsíre, cănáche, chéfe, chéifă, gústu, hăidipsíre, háze, hăráuă, lizéte; (*caused by a trip, by an artistic performance, etc.*) siryeáne; **it is a ~** ti ĺa hăráua; (*sweet things, fig.*) zaharéñ *f pl.* (*sensual ~*) dizñirdăciúne ‖ BA, 501: **at one's ~** cât s-cáfţâ

PLEASURABLE *adj.* arâsít, nóstim, *m pl* -tiñ

PLEAT *s.* dhíplă; **a dress with many ~s** fustáne cu dhíple múlte

PLEDGE *s.* chifíle, chifaléte, chifiliméi, arăvoánă, căpărusíre, tăxíre; **to take a ~** → PLEDGE, SWEAR

PLEDGE *vb.* ▾leg, ▾căpăruséscu, ▾tăxéscu, ▾arăvuñiséscu; íntru chifíle; ~ **one's word** dau zbor ‖ leg zbor, CAPIDAN 176

PLEIADES *pl.* *astr.* Clóşca cu puĺ; Găĺinúşe; Púĺe ‖ **Peş:** Găĺinúşa, CL 254

PLENTIFUL *adj*. giumértu, *m pl* -rţâ → BOUNTIFUL, GALORE

PLENTY *adj*. bólcu, -lcă, lţi, lţe; **They want to have ~ of time** Vor si-áibă oáră bólcă → ABUNDANT

PLENTY *adv*. cu mnáta, birichéte ‖ MERCA 3: plíhtu

PLEURISY *s*. plivrít, plirít, pliyít, póndă, púndzire; **Ohr:** ân-dulţít (*sic*)

PLIABLE *adj*. **Cl'is:** jílav (DDA: *"flexible comme une verge"*)

PLIERS *s*. cleáşte (*and* cl'áş-), cleaciu (**1 syll.**), ţimbídhă, ţimístră

PLIGHT *s*. (*bad condition*) hálă, *pl* hăl'uri; **in a bad ~** trâ ni-videáre → QUANDARY

PLIGHT *vb*. (*to put or give in pledge*) ≈ íntru chifíle

PLOP *vb*. ‖ PC: ▾arucutéscu, ▾arcutéscu

PLOT *s*. loc; (*as for vegetables*) úrdin; (*scheme, machination*) cruitúră [kru•i•], mplititúră; **the ~ is thickening** (*things are becoming serious*) si-ngroáşe şicălu .

PLOT *vb*. cruéscu, ▾tórcu, ▾ţas, nţirnuséscu; **What is he ~ing?** Ţe lă toárţe? **We don't know what is being plotted** Ţe s-ţási nu ştim

PLOT AND SCHEME *vb*. bag fitíl'e, bag nţăpătúri, bag zizáñe

PLOTTER *s*. muzavír

PLOUGH *s*. arát; **Grbţ:** arátru; alétră; dămăl'úg, paramándă, paraméndă

PLOUGH *vb*. fac ágru; (*rare*) ar

PLOUGH WHEELS *s*. ‖ **SJos:** truhălíci, CL 262

PLOUGHED LAND *s*. **Zag:** arătúră

PLOUGHING *s*. aráre, airáre, avruguíre, nvrăgáre

PLOUGHMAN *s*. aráciu, uráciu, arătór, zivyít ‖ **F:** zăvyără; **P:** zivyâră, SarD 39; **An, Els, Prv, Rod, Ses, Vil:** zivyár, **Kok, Mal:** zivyăr; **GSus:** cifliccí [ĉi•flik•ĉí], B-ARCH 256

PLOUGHSHARE *s*. iníe, meş, vómiră

PLOWER *s*. → PLOUGHMAN

PLOWING *s*. → PLOUGHING

PLOY *s*. aplán, tirtípe

PLUCK *s*. (*of hair or feathers*) dipiráre

PLUCK *vb*. ▾trag, ▾deápir, zmúlgu, **N:** azmúlgu; (*to pick up, as flowers or berries*) adún → GATHER

PLUCK SMB.'S EYES OUT *vb*. scot burlídzle; (*as a threat*) **I'll**

PLUCK

pluck out your eyes! Va ţâ scot burlídzle!

PLUCK UP ONE'S COURAGE *vb.* bag per di lup; ñ-bag ciulíche la iñoárǎ; ľau ínimǎ; ▼ncucutédz

PLUCKY *adj.* bǎrbát, *f* -tǎ; cǎidigí, inimárcu, inimós, -oásǎ

PLUG *s.* (*poor or worn-out horse*) cârcâm, sarával ‖ CUNIA 191: gargásiu

PLUG *vb.* (*as a bottle*) ▼astúp; (*to hit with a bullet*) agudéscu

PLUM *s.* (*yellow ~*) prúnǎ, púrnǎ; (*bluish ~*) prúnǎ di Bósna; dhamaschínǎ ‖ *Fal:* ţápurnǎ, B-ARCH 60

PLUMAGE *s.* peáne *f pl*

PLUME *s.* peánǎ

PLUME *vb.* (*to indulge in pride*) ▼mǎréscu → BRAG

PLUMP *adj.* dúrdu, -rdǎ, -rdzâ, -rde; grozdavén, iľát, strúmbul, şut; **as ~ as a partridge** ≈ *Arom.* gras ca un peáşte

PLUME-TREE *s.* prun, púrnu, dhamaschín; *coll.* prunáme

PLUNDER *s.* alimúrǎ, yeáymǎ, yeámǎ, iámǎ, furlíche, géngǎ, pleácicǎ [pleáci•kǎ], prádǎ, spóľe

PLUNDER *vb.* ▼cálcu, ▼dispóľu, fac ghénga, ▼guléscu, ▼gulişinédz, guluşnédz, prad, *N:* mprad; prǎdédz; **These villages cannot be ~ed** Hórǐle-aéste nu si cálcǎ; **They began to ~** Ahiurhírǎ ghénga s-fácǎ

PLUNDERER *s.* haldúp, pleaşcagí (*and* pľáş-), zulumcheár, zulumgí

PLUNGE *s.* → TAKE THE ~

PLUNGE *vb.* ▼afúndu, ▼afundédz, ▼afunduséscu, ▼vuţéscu, ▼bag tu ápǎ, ▼bag pri ápǎ

PLUNGE INTO DESPAIR *vb.* ▼apilipséscu

PLUNGE INTO DIFFICULTIES *vb.* (*to get into trouble*) dau di a-rále

PLUVIAL *adj.* (*characterized by abundant rain*) pluiós, -ioásǎ; pluirós [plu•i•], -iroásǎ

PLY *vb.* ▼andúplic; *to ~ the distaff* ▼tórcu; *to ~ the bottle* beau, ciucutéscu; *to ~ smb. with food* ▼pristǎnscu, pristǎniséscu

PNEUMONIA *s.* póndǎ

POCKET *s.* gépe, geápe,, giópe; buzunár; (*inward pocket*) sâpáne, supáne; **to be out of ~** (*to be at a loss*) lu adár yróslu zlótǎ ‖ *dim.* gipícâ, DIARO 163

POCKET *vb.* (*to steal*) ciun

POCKET AN INSULT *vb.* mâc cǎlúpea ‖ *Cru:* ǎngĺít noáde, GOLAB 238

POCKETKNIFE *s.* ceárche ‖ CUNIA 33: pisufíe

POCKMARKED *adj.* chipitós, -oásǎ; muliţát (*and* muĺi-), mulţát, mǎlţidzát, mulţidzós, mǎl-; **to become ~** ▾chípit ‖ DIARO 258 chipurát, mâlţidzát

POD *s.* (*as of pea*) flúdhǎ ‖ *GSus:* capíşcǎ, CL 40; *SJos:* levídhǎ, CL, 254 → HUSK, HULL, RIND, SHELL

PODGY *adj.* → PUDGY

POINT *s.* (*as of a needle*) chípitǎ, chirchinédz, sumíg, sumígǎ, simígǎ, ţuţuléu, ţuţulíc → TIP, PEAK; BE ON THE ~ OF; TURNING ~; MAKE IT A ~ OF HONOR

POINT AT SMB. *vb.* aspún cu dzeáditlu

POINTED *adj.* chipitós, -oásǎ; simigós, sumi-, *f* -oásǎ; ânţepǎlicós, ânţepuliciós; **~ peaks** chíscuri chipitoáse; **~ object** zahuráhe, *pl* -rǎhi ‖ TULLIU 89: asuligós; CUVATA 7: suligós; BELIMACE 107: (*of a mosque*) nţuţulátǎ *f*

POINTER *s.* (*stick*) díhtur

POISON *s.* afrát, áxif, cémir, ncémir, ciómir, fǎrmác; mǎyilíc, virín; **rat ~** şuricoáñe

POISON *vb.* ▾fǎrmǎcuséscu, nfǎrmǎcuséscu, nfǎrmáciu, ▾fármǎc, ▾nciómir, ncioámir, ncimirédz, nciumirédz

POISON HEMLOC *s. bot.* fǎrmác

POISON IVY *s.* (*used as pesticide*) psiruvótan

POISONING *s.* fǎrmǎcáre, nfǎrmǎcáre

POISONOUS *adj.* toápsic, fârmâcós, -oásǎ; fǎrmǎchirós, -oásǎ

POKE¹ *s.* (*bag*) sac; (*small bag*) sǎcúĺ

POKE² *s.* aguditúrǎ, ampǎráre

POKE *vb.* (a)zgurñéscu, guzgunipséscu; (*of ember*) dijirédz; **He ~ed the fire with the fire-rake** Dijirǎ fóclu cu giugárlu

POKE AROUND *vb.* (*as if looking for smth.*) gurñédz, azgurñédz, gurñéscu, gruñéscu

POKER *s.* (*metallic rod*) cǎţíe, giugár, jóglu, lupátǎ, máşe

POLE¹ *s.* strop, ustúr, vig, vígǎ

POLE² *s.* (*person of Polish origin*) lǎhiót

POLEAXE *s.* ţupátǎ, *G:* bâltǎ

POLECAT *s.* tǎrtóciu ‖ *GSus:* por, CL 259; *SJos:* patcán laiu, CL 257

POLENTA *s.* (*made of cornmeal*) bǎcǎrdán, bǎrcǎdán, bǎrgǎdán, cǎ-

POLICE

cimác, cãciumác (*and* câ-), mãmulíc, mãmulíg, murmulíc, mãcãldárã
(*and* mâcâl-), mãclãdárã (*and* mâclâ-), tarapáş

POLICE *s*. (*authority*) pulíţã, *pl* puliţáñ; zabitlãcã; (*police-
men in search of thieves, rebels, etc. in the past*) pãyánã, *pl*
pãyãñ; potérã ‖ *Cru:* chivérnise, GOLAB 30

POLICEMAN *s*. pulíţ, *pl* puliţáñ; strãjeár; zãptié, zaptié, *pl*
zãptiédz *and* zãptíi

POLISH *s*. virníche

POLISH *vb*. daú másnã / máslã; lustruéscu; (*to chisel*) ▾pilichi-
séscu; ~ed *adj*. pilichisít ‖ *Also fig, Cru:* GOLAB 243

POLISHING *s*. fricãtúrã, pirdáfe, pirdáhe

POLITENESS *s*. pulíticã, pulitichíe

POLITICS *s*. pulíticã

POLKA *s*. (*a dance*) pólcã

POLL *vb*. ▾taľu; (*of hair or wool*) ▾túndu; (*to shorten, to trim*)
▾şcurtédz, ▾şcurtichédz

POLL TAX *s*. (*in the Ottoman Empire, taxation on non-Moslem
inhabitants*) haráce, hãráce

POLLEN *s*. búdrã di lilíce

POLLUTE *vb*. ▾murdãripséscu → DIRTY

POLLUTED *adj*. pângân(ips)ít

POLLUTION *s*. lãvãşíre, lirusíre, murdãripsíre

POLTROON *s*. pantalunár → COWARD

POLYP *s. zool*. uhtapódhe, htapóde

POMADE *s*. alifíe → OINTMENT

POMEGRANATE *s*. (a)ródhã ‖ *Cru:* aróidã, GOLAB 201

POMEGRANATE-TREE *s*. arudhéu

POMMEL *s*. (*of a saddle*) ublâncu, ublângu

POMP *s*. (*ceremonial*) sãltãnátã, táxe, ţirimóñe

POMPOUS *adj*. cu táxe

POND *s*. báltã, *G:* blátã; bárã, ghióle; *G:* hábinã; lac ‖ ALIA
24-25: abárã, bárnã, bárnisã, muceále. In ALB *báltã* is not known;
Kërb: burím, *Për:* pélgu, pelg, plégu, Brâncuş 552

PONDER *vb*. ▾arúmig, ▾aroámig, ▾criséscu, minduéscu, stau pri
minduíre, ▾sãluşéscu, ▾siluyiséscu, ▾ziyãséscu, ziyiséscu, zixéscu

PONDERING *s*. arumigáre, crisíre, minduíre, siluyisíre, ziyãsíre

PONDEROUS *adj*. angricós, -oásã

PONIARD s. şiş, (a)cámă → DAGGER

POOH interj. tu, ptiu, ptiu

POOH-POOH vb. cătăfroniséscu, ▾culédz, mpizuéscu (and mbi-), şúpir, şupirédz

POOL s. báltă → POND

POOR s. (the ~, coll.) urfănáme, urfănătáte, fucăráme ‖ discúlţañ pl, discúlţu sg., DIARO 377

POOR adj. (destitute, pauper) nĭ-avút, oárfăn, ftoh, fucâră, discúlţ, coáti-goáli; ~ **woman** invar cioáhă; ~ **as Job's cat** oárfăn alăchít, oárfăn ca chícuta, gol-golişán, oárfăn căpăít; nu áre cinúşe tu vátră, nu ári cu ţe si-şi súflă nările, nu ári níţi ascucheát ân gúră, nu ári níţi un cap di aľ, nu ári zmeánă la cur; tiflupéndar; şi-eáste ţínţirli-lipídhă ‖ **Smr:** ştoh, CL 261; cu métura s-trădzeái nu dădeái di ţivá, BASME 161; (assessing a year's harvest) **Peş:** aclirát (ant. birichitós), CL 36 ‖ (deserving compassion) marát, mărátlu-şi m, măráta-şi f; lăítlu or lăítlu-şi m, lăíta-şi f; córbu; fucărálu-şi; cápsu invar; mórva f; sărmáie f; múrlai or murlái; boiu m, bóie f; **our ~ horses** bóĭ caľ a nóştri; **The ~ mother wept**; Plâmse boiu múma; buiáuă invar; **Alas, the ~ boy died** U, buiáuă di ficiór murí; bógru, mbógru, gal; **Where are you going, ~ thing?** Iu ñérdzi, lai gále? (of or to a dear person) **Zag:** lai galé; **Oh, ~ us!** O, ca vai, ca vai di noi!

POPCORN s. cârcále n pl; păpădhúlă, púfcă, pl púfche

POPCORN DEALER s. pufcagí

POPE s. Pápa m

POP-EYED adj. hărvăľisít, zgârlít; zgârlós, -oásă

POPLAR s. plup, pľop, léfcă

POP OFF vb. (to depart unexpectedly or in a hurry) mi frângu zvérca

POP OUT vb. (to show up) ies, es; ▾zvom

POPPY s. bot. bălţotă, mac, păpărúnă, pirpirúnă ‖ DIARO 273: cucuţăl

PORCELAIN s. fărfăríu, fărfuríu

PORCH s. balcóne, tăráţă ‖ CUNIA 305: cirdáchi, ciurdáchi

PORE vb. PONDER

PORK s. (a pig's flesh) purţínă; (~ fried in a pan) tiyăñáuă

POROUS adj. guvunós, -oásă; (worn-out) găgăñós, -oásă

PORRIDGE s. dzámă

PORRINGER *s.* cuvátă, guvátă → BOWL

PORT *s.* (*for ships*) limáne, schéle, pórtu

PORTAL *s.* poártă

PORTEND *vb.* dau di şteáre, dau di hăbáre, fac hăbáre, adúc di hăbáre, pitréc hăbáre, dau zbor, dau glas; **to ~ evil** (*usu. of an owl's call*) cubăéscu

PORTENT *s.* (*smth. amazing or marvellous*) ciúdă, thámă; (*omen*) sémnu; (*of good portent*) ugúre *invar*

PORTENTOUS *adj.* (*amazing*) ciudós, -oásă; (*self-consciously weighty*) cămărusít, pirifán

PORTER *s.* hămál

PORTION *s.* (*ration*) curamánă, nárte, gărăvánă, tăíme, tăíne

PORTION *vb.* ▾mpártu

PORTLY *adj.* binalític ‖ CUNIA 65: builític; DIARO 298: binalítcu

PORTRAIT *s.* cádhru; (*people in books, magazines, etc.*) pap *or* pápean, pápan

PORTRAY *vb.* (*to describe, to depict*) ▾zugrăpséscu, zugrăvséscu, zugrăfséscu

POSE *vb.* (*to put or set in place*) ▾apún, ▾bag

POSITION *s.* (*the place or area occupied by smth.*) loc; (*office, post, job*) thése, *pl* thesi

POSITIVE *adj.* (*incontestable*) síyur → SURE, BE SURE

POSITIVELY *adv.* (*undoubtedly*) síyur, fắră di áltă

POSSESSED *adj.* aumbrós, -oásă; furchisít; loat di vímtu → MAD

POSSESSION *s.* (*property, estate, domain*) numíe

POSSIBLE *adj.* avóleto *invar.*; **It is not ~** Nu eáste cu puteáre; **This is never ~** Puté avóleto nu éste → BE ~

POST *s.* (*pillar, stake*) par *m*, *dim.* păríc, pălúc; *also:* andoápăr, duréc, **N:** diréc, drec; parpálangu, stil, stur, ştiúlă

POST SERVICE *s.* (*operated with horses*) mizíle *invar* ‖ MURNU 17, 18: póstă

POST-BOY *s.* (*as a messinger in a town-hall*) purtóyir; pisudhróm

POSTERIOR s. anat. şidzút → BUTTOCKS

POST-HORSE *s.* cal di mizíle

POSTMAN *s.* pustagí

POSTPONE *vb.* ▾amân, ▾şintéscu

POSTPONED *adj.* amânát

POSTPONEMENT *s.* amânáre, şintíre

POSY *s.* buchét, bubúche di flori

POT *s.* oálă, *dim.* ulícă; *also:* crup, hrup, ftínă; (*for milking*) mǎldzǎrúşe; (*with no handle*) sut, şútă; (*broken ~*) ciuváñiu ‖ CUVATA 2: cipceác → CHAMBER ~, COFFEE ~, EARTHEN ~

POTASSIUM *s.* nítru

POTATION *s.* (*drink*) biutúră; (*the act of drinking*) beáre

POTATO *s.* cartófe; *Băi:* cârcánge; *L:* bóţĭ *f pl*; *Brz:* bârboále; *Tur:* curcáce; cumpíre, nedz, ñédzlu a lóclui, pătátă, pǎpáte ‖ *Băi:* cǎlcánci *f sg*, CL 41; *GSus:* cúmbăr, CL 43; *Amc:* dǎrdúfǎ *and* budumeáre, CPad 129

POT-BELLIED *adj.* báfǎ *invar.*; bică; bǎzácǎ, bǎzǎcós, -oásǎ; zǎbácǎ; zǎbǎcós, -oásǎ; *also* jǎbǎ-, jibi-

POTBELLY *s.* pântică, pântiţe, tâmpâníciu, schimbé

POTENTATE *s.* cap, mǎimár, prot

POT-HANGER *s.* *P:* cârlápǎ

POTHER *s.* yiurultíe, lávǎ, vreávǎ

POT-HERBS *s.* zǎrzǎváte (*and* zârzâ-), mirizmádhǎ

POTHOOK *s.* cârlíg

POTION *s.* → DRINK; (*~ made by or as by a sorceress*) tatulát

POTSHERD *s.* ciuváñu, hrup

POTTER *s.* ulár, misurár; *G:* puceár; stǎmnár

POTTER ABOUT *vb.* misúr steálile, hǎlǎndǎréscu

POTTERY *s.* puceáme

POT-TREE *s.* → POT-HANGER

POTTY *adj.* (*slightly crazy*) şcret, -étǎ (*sic*), -éţ, -éte

POUCH *s.* ceántǎ

POULTICE *s.* (*made with seeds of flax*) lápǎ

POULTICE *vb.* plicuséscu; **They ~d Hristu with onion** Hrístul âl plicusírǎ cu ţeápe

POUNCE *vb.* (*upon or towards smb.*) ▼himuséscu, hiumuséscu; mi aleápid

POUND *vb.* (*to hit, to strike*) ▼agudéscu, dau, ▼pǎléscu; (*as sugar*) stumbuséscu, chisédz, *S:* csedz, *aor.* csai, *part.* csat; **to ~ to pieces** *vb* adár bucǎţ, adár muşcǎtúri, disíc cumátǎ di cumátǎ, fac bucatíce, fac bucǎţ di bucǎţ, fac mǎşcǎtúri-mǎşcǎtúri

POUND FOOLISH → PENNY

POUNDING *s.* cicǎtíre, ciucutíre (*as in a mortar*) stumbusíre

POUR

POUR *vb.* ▼vérsu; (*of rain*) 3 *sg*: veársă; veársă cu găleáta **It was pouring down** Ploáia virsá

POUR COLD WATER ON SMB. *vb.* (*to discourage, to dampen smb.'s appetite, etc.*) taľu tăcátea

POURING *s.* virsáre

POUT ONE'S LIPS *vb.* ▼mbudzinédz, ▼mbufunédz ‖ spíndzur búdzile or dipún búdzâle, PARALLELE 146

POUTING *s.* mbudzináre, cáche; ~ **is a major sin** Máre rrău (*sic*) éste cáchea

POVERTY *s.* urfáñe, urfăneáță, urfăníľe, nĭ-aveáre, ftóhe, fucăríme, fucârlíche; **to live in** ~ cacurizipséscu, bat tămbărălu

POWDER *s.* (*propelling charge*) bărúte, búlvură, vúlbură

POWDERED SUGAR *s.* tóze

POWER *s.* (*physical or moral capability*) → FORCE, STRENGTH; (*authority*) exusíe → DO ALL IN ONE'S ~

POWERFUL *adj.* nvârtuşát; siln(ăv)ós, silniós, silnăós, *f* -oásă

PRACTICABLE *adj.* (*usable, travelled, as of road*) urdinát

PRACTICAL JOKE *s.* téhne

PRACTICE *s.* píră, practichíe, práxe

PRACTICED, PRACTISED *adj.* (*experienced*) fricát

PRACTITIONER *s.* mâscă, mâtcă

PRAISE *s.* lávdă, (a)lăvdáre, (a)lăvdăciúne, épin

PRAISE *vb.* ▼alávdu, ▼álțu, ▼priñiséscu, mut di coádă

PRANK *s.* féstă, hunéră, hunére

PRATE *vb.* → CHATTER, PRATTLE

PRATER *s.* curcubitár, fărfár, fărfără, lafăzán, limbár, políloy, zburyeárcu

PRATTLE *s.* bănduráre, guguráre, láfe, poliloyíe

PRATTLE *vb.* (*to talk idly*) băndurédz, cicăléscu, discâtu, máțin, máțin pi virisíe

PRAY *s.* acățáre, ncăceáre, ncârligáre

PRAY *vb.* (*as to God*) ▼ncľin, cľin, (a)ór, urédz, fac duváe; *Băi:* ▼ruguéscu; **Let us ~!** S-nă cľinăm! **The anxious mothers are ~ing God** Durútile di máme la Dumnidzắu oáră; **And let us ~ like the blind man did** Să şi aurrắmu ca cum aură órbul; **He used to put them to ~** ăľ băgá duváe s-fácă ‖ mi rigiăescu, HRISTU 21

PRAYER *s.* duváe, ncľináre, ifchíe, ifhíe, ifcheáuă, pricădeáre; (*to God*) prusufhíe; (*to the Virgin*) paráclise; **morning ~** uóthură; (*one who prays*) âncl'inătór ‖ ~ **for the dead** trisáyiu, DIARO 6

PRAYER BOOK *s.* sínapse

PRAYERFUL *adj.* ivlaviós, -oásă

PREACH *vb.* chirixéscu; **to ~ to deaf ears** zburăsc pri víntu ‖ BASME 192: cánda li dzâc la chétri

PRECARIOUS *adj.* lai, *f* láie, *m/f pl* lăi; ni-síyur, s(c)lab

PRECAUTION *s.* pruvideáre

PRECENTOR *s.* (p)sáltu, anaynósţi [a•na•ynósti]

PRECEPT *s.* dhóymă, *pl* dhóymate

PRECIOUS *adj.* scúmpu, *m pl* scúnchi (*and* scúmbu, -nghi)

PRECIPICE *s.* (a)râpă, arúp, creac, chirítă, grem, hău, háuă; hímă, súrpu, surpătúră ‖ *Tur:* grimínâ, CL 45; *Cru:* anífur, GOLAB 199

PRECIPITATION *s.* (*haste*) → RUSH

PRECIPITOUS *adj.* súrpu; scârpós; **a ~ area** loc múltu súrpu

PRECISELY *adv.* sustá, tamám, tamamá; **He speaks ~** Zburáşte sustá

PRECURSOR *s.* pródhrom

PREDACIOUS *adj.* órñu → RAPACIOUS

PREDESTINATION *s.* (*ritual gathering in a family with a newborn*) trimeáre

PREDICAMENT *s.* → QUANDARY

PREDICATION *s.* (*sermon*) dhidhahíe

PREDICT *vb.* prufitipséscu → FORECAST

PREDICTION *s.* prufitíe, prufitipsíre

PREDILECTION *s.* prutimisíre, prutimsíre

PREEMINENT *adj.* → OUTSTANDING

PREEN *vb.* → BOAST

PREEMPT *vb.* → ARROGATE

PREFACE *s.* ‖ protozbór (*recent coinage*)

PREFECT *s.* (*~ of a district, in former Turkey*) mutesaríf ‖ *Av:* numárĭ, *Prv:* numárlu, CL 257

PREFER *vb.* ▼pruthimiséscu (*and* pruti-)

PREFERABLY *adv.* cál'a; mabúle

PREFERENCE *s.* (*option*) prutímise, prutimisíre, prutimsíre; (*a card game*) préfă

PREGNANT *adj.* greáuă, ncărcátă, cu pântica la gúră; **to become ~** armân greáuă, nchiséscu greáuă, armân sárţină, ▼nsárţin, ▼nsărţi-

PREJUDICE

nédz; *iron.* 3 aor. furắ curcubéta (*lit. '[She] has stolen the pumpkin'*); **All three were ~** Tréile erá sárţină → MAKE A WOMAN ~

PREJUDICE *s.* (*harm*) zñisíre

PREJUDICE *vb.* (*to harm*) apucupséscu, ▾zimñuséscu, ▾zñi(i)séscu

PREMATURE *adj.* (*born or arrived earlier than expected, as of a lamb, of spring or fall*) timpuríu; (*inopportune*) achéryiu

PREMATURELY *adv.* áchira

PREMEDITATED *adj.* xaryú

PREMISES *s. pl.* acaréte, *pl* acaréţ

PREOCCUPATION *s.* (*agitation*) prédhă (*and* prédă)

PREOCCUPIED *adj.* minduít

PREPARATION *s.* andreádzire, etimusíre, atimăsíe

PREPARE *vb.* ▾(a)ndreg (→ § 32), ândrég, ndirég; ▾etimăséscu; **The cook ~ed the dinner** Máyirlu ndreápse meása; (*to get ready*) ▾scumbuséscu; **~ for death!** Andreádzi-te tră moárte! → BRACE

PREPONDERATE *vb.* ntrec

PREPOSTEROUS *adj.* ni-minduít

PRESAGE *s.* sémnu

PRESAGE *vb.* ▾pruvéd; (*to portend smth. bad*) ĺ-u tórcu pri hírlu aţél laiu (*lit. 'to spin it on the black thread'*)

PRESAGE EVIL *vb.* (*to omen*) ĺ-u tórcu pri hírlu aţél laiu

PRESAGEFUL OF GOOD *adj.* agurlíu, ayu-; hairlâtcu, -lâtic

PRESENT *s.* (*gift*) dhoáră → MAKE A ~

PRESENT *vb.* (*to make a gift*) adúc nă pischési, (a)hărzéscu (*and* ahâr-), dau tră háre, dăruéscu, dhurséscu, fac háre, pischiséscu; **God ~ed them with a little boy** Dumnidză lă ahărzí un ficiuríc; (*to introduce smb.*) părăstăséscu (*and* părăsti-)

PRESENTATION *s.* părăstisíre

PRESENTIMENT *s.* nóimă

PRESENTLY *adv.* curúndu, crúndu

PRESERVATION *s.* păstráre

PRESERVE *s.* dúlţe, ylicó

PRESERVE *vb.* (*to keep for later use*) păstrédz

PRESIDENT *s.* proestó

PRESS *vb.* ▾ndes, ▾stríngu, *N:* (*rare*) strângu; (*to ~ one's hands*) ▾zdrúmin, zdroámin, ▾strimuxéscu; (*to mass, to cram, to crowd closely*) ▾(a)pitruséscu, *N:* (a)pu-; (*to hug*) stríngu la sin; (*in or as in tongs*) ncliştédz; **to ~ down** afiriséscu; **to ~ a**

point mi bag di-a mútra s (+ *vb.*); **to ~ each other close** priadún, ▾apreadún; (*to constrain*) bag súla n coáste

PRESSED *adj.* (*as wool in a bag*) ndisát; (*as of one's jaws*) ncliştát; ~ **by bodily necessities** ≈ ps., 3 pl. impers. mi loárã pri cioáre;

PRESSING *s.* ndisáre, stringãtúrã, strimuxíre

PRESSINGLY *adv.* ayóñea

PRESSURE *s.* (*burden*) angricáre → BLOOD ~; PUT ~ UPON SMB.

PRESSURE *vb.* (*to coerce*) bag súla n coáste

PRESTIGE *s.* ihtibáe, nãmúze, tiñíe

PRESUMPTION *s.* (*fantasy*) fãndãxíe

PRESUMPTUOUS *adj.* fãndãxít → BOASTFUL ‖ *Gop:* mãrés, GOLAB 234

PRESUPPOSITION *s.* pripúnire, pripuneáre

PRETENCE *s.* (*pretext*) furñíe

PRETEND *vb.* mi fac (cã), ▾prifác (cã); ~ **that you are sick!** Fã-te cã hii niptút! táha *adv*; **He ~s that he was trying to do a good deed to them** Táha mutrí s-lã fácã un ghíne

PRETENTIOUS *adj.* cãpriţusít ‖ PC: curuslític

PRETEXT *s.* acãţãtúrã, ascãlnãtúrã, furñíe; **He was seeking for a ~ to kill him** Cãftá vãrã furñíe tra si-l vátãmã

PRETTY *adj.* pãlít, daľán; (*of a face*) aumbrít, cu úmbrã; (*as of a flower*) nóstim, zdrob, zdrod, zâmbác; **to become ~** muşuţãscu → BEAUTIFUL

PRETZEL *s.* ghivréc, ghiuvréc, clúrã; (*for carol singers*) cólindu

PREVAIL ON SMB. TO *vb.* ▾andúplic → PERSUADE ‖ ľ-u tórnu mín-tea, BASME 120

PREVENT *vb.* (*to hinder, to stop, to hold back*) ▾stãpuéscu, bu-dhuéscu; **We should ~ them from doing bad things!** S-ľi stãpuím di rále lúcre! → HINDER

PREVISION *s.* (*foresight*) pruvideáre

PREY *s.* alimúrã, pleáşcã, pleácicã, prádã, spóľe

PREY *vb.* prad → PLUNDER

PRICE *s.* axíe, pãhã, pãzáre, tiñíe; **He offered him a low ~** Ľ-deáde unã pãdzáre ñícã; **fixed price(s)** nárche; **at a lower ~** eftinipsít; (*at a ridiculously low ~*) bathavá [bat•ha•] *adv.* ‖ **to set the ~** taľu pãzárea (*lit.* 'to cut the market'), PARALLELE 153

PRICELESS *adj.* scúmpu, *pl m* scúnchi (*and* scúmbu, *pl m* scúnghi)

PRICK

PRICK s. (*mark*) sémnu; (*an instance of pricking or a sensation of being pricked*) nţăpătúră, púndzire

PRICK vb. ▾(a)nţap (*and* andzáp), ▾schin; (*to repent, to be gnawed by remorse*) mi mâcă săráchea

PRICK UP THE EARS vb. (*of horses*) ▾ciuléscu urécľile

PRICKING s. nţăpătúră (*and* ndză-), nţăpáre; *fig.* munăficlíche

PRICKLE s. (*thorn*) schin m, ciupór n; **Tur:** chindríe; **a goad with ~** strămburáre cu chindríe

PRICKLE vb. → PRICK

PRICKLING s. schináre

PRICKLING adj. nţăpătós, -oásă; a ~ **object** zahuráhe

PRIDE s. cămáră (*and* câ-), cămărusíre, cheaféte, dăilíche, dăilâche, fálă, fidănlâche, fudulíche, fudulâche, fudulíe, fufuleáţă, ihtibáre, magurlăchi, măreáţă, pirifáñe, pirifăñíľe ‖ **Cru:** măríľe, GOLAB 234; *He is in the ~ of years* Eáste to-áñ → PRIME

PRIDE vb. (*to indulge in ~*) ▾măréscu → BRAG

PRIEST s. préftu; *also:* aféndu; paróh, părínte, pâpă *and* pópă; **officiating ~** lituryó; *derog.* ciúrlu-păpă; *coll.* priftáme; (*in a mosque*) hóge *or* hugé

PRIESTESS s. prifteásă

PRIESTHOOD s. (*the priests*) priftáme; (*character, vocation or office of a priest*) prifţâľe, ĭerosínă

PRIGGISH adj. mutrusít, căpriţusít; *as a vb.,* strâmbu nárea

PRIMAL adj. antâñu, -ñe, -ñ, -ñe; biringí, -gioáñe; prot, -tă

PRIMARY adj. → PRIMAL

PRIME: **in the ~ of youth** tu lilícea a áñlor → PRIDE

PRIMER s. (*for teaching to read*) alfavitáre

PRIMER s. (*in a cartridge*) şpírtu

PRIMP vb. ▾adár, ▾muşuţéscu

PRIMULA s. *bot.* ligoáce ‖ **Prv:** iárba vácăľei, CL 253

PRINCE s. vasilóplu, prínţu, vuivudă; **N:** cñeaz, *pl* cñeji; (*prime successor*) dhiádhoh

PRINCELY adj. amiréscu, -eáscă; pâş(i)léscu, -eáscă; văsilichéscu, -eáscă

PRINCIPAL s. (*money*) cap → INTEREST

PRINCIPAL adj. (*most important*) antâñu

PRINT s. (*cloth with a pattern*) chitabí *or* chitabíe; (*of books,* etc.) tip

PRINT *vb.* ▾stămbăséscu, stămbuséscu, ▾tipuséscu

PRINTED *adj.* stămbusít, tipusít

PRINTER *s.* (*compositor, typographer*) tipuyráf

PRINTING *s.* stămbusíre, tipusíre

PRINTING OFFICE *s.* tip, stámbă, tipuyrafíľe, tipuyrafíe

PRIOR *s.* iyúmin

PRIOR TO *prep.* năínte di

PRISON *s.* cúlă → JAIL, PUT IN ~

PRISONER *s.* sclav, rob; **to take** ~ ľau sclav

PRIVATION *s.* (*hardship*) zóre

PRIVILEGE *s.* (~ *granted to a monastery*) pronómiu

PRIZE *vb.* → VALUE

PROBE *vb.* (*as by thieves*) născărséscu; **They found the house ~ed from top to bottom** Aflără cása tútă născărsítă

PROBITY *s.* érgi, tiñíe

PROCEDURE *s.* mithoádhă, mithódhă

PROCEED AGAINST SMB. *vb.* lu scol

PROCEED TOWARDS *vb.* ľ-u dau cătră

PROCESS *s.* (*lawsuit*) críse, giudéţ, giudicátă; **to take out a ~ against smb.** lu scol

PROCLIVITY *s.* aplicáre

PROCRASTINATE *vb.* → POSTPONE

PROCRASTINATOR *s.* lăsát, om alăsát, alăsătóñu, alăsătúră

PROCREATE *vb.* (*to beget offsprings*) nfumiľédz

PROCREATOR *s.* (*father*) simnitór

PROCURATOR *s.* vichíľ, vichíle *m*

PROCUREMENT *s.* cuduşláche

PROCURER *s.* arufcheán, cudóş

PROCURESS *s.* cudoáşe

PROCURING *s.* (*making available for promiscuous purposes*) cuduşláche

PROD *vb.* ▾píngu, gărgărédz

PRODIGAL *adj.* sac arúptu; **to be ~** tuchéscu → PROFLIGATE

PRODIGALLY *adv.* cu sácul

PRODUCE *vb.* (*derog., as of lies, gossip, etc.*) vom ‖ (*to ~, as of land; to make in order to sell, as of a factory*) scot; **This land ~s tobacco** Lóclu aéstu scoáte tutúne, PARALLELE 138; **to ~ a**

PRODUCE

new machine scot nă noáuă mihăníe, PARALLELE 139

PRODUCE PROOFS *vb.* (*to prove*) adúc semn

PRODUCTS FROM SHEEP *s.* (*milk, cheese and wool*) prósfaľ; măxúle *no pl*

PROFESSION *s.* lúcru, téhne, zănáte; **What's your ~, my friend?** Ţi lúcru ai, oáspe?

PROFICIENT *adj.* → SKILFUL

PROFIT *s.* ayeáfur, amintátic, hăíre *or* hăríe; ânchédhu, nchédhu, prucuchíe, scoátire, scuteáre, ufélie; **Does it bring any ~?** Ári scuteári?

PROFIT *vb.* (*to gain, to take advantage*) ufiliséscu, filiséscu, hăiruséscu; **What will it ~ you?** (*i.e., It will be useless*) Va scoţ córnul?

PROFITABLE *adj.* cu hăíre; *3 sg:* **It is ~** Ari scuteáre

PROFITABLY *adv.* cu hăíre, cu prucuchíe

PROFITEER *s.* chilipirgí, chilipurgí, hâpsângí, haramgí *m*, haramgioáñe *f*

PROFLIGACY *s.* dişuţâre

PROFLIGATE *adj.* dizmălărát; *also:* aspártu, *m pl* -rţâ; dişuţât; púrnu, *m pl* -rñi; sac arúptu ‖ arâspândít, DIARO 235

PROFOUND *adj.* adâncós, -oásă (*and* adun-) → DEEP; (*of people*) mintimén (*and* mindi-), *f* -ménă, *m pl* -méñ; mindiós, mindu-

PROFOUNDLY *adv.* afúndu, adâncós, ahândós, afunducós

PROFUSE *adj.* giumértu, *m pl* -rţâ, *f pl* -rte; sălghít

PROFUSELY *adv.* di-primansús, di pri ma nsus (*sic*)

PROFUSION *s.* (*abundance*) artírizmă

PROGENY *s.* fumeáľe; *N:* fuméľ

PROGRAM *s.* próyramă

PROGRESS *s.* pródh, prucuchíe → MAKE ~

PROGRESS *vb.* prudhipséscu, ▼mprustédz → MAKE PROGRESS

PROHIBITED *adj.* yeasáche *invar.*

PROHIBITION *s.* astămăţíre, curmáre

PROJECT *s.* cruitúră

PROJECTILE *s. S:* ghiulé, *N:* ghiulée

PROLONG *vb.* ▼lundzéscu, spirlundzéscu

PROMENADE *s.* (*leisurely walk*) priimnáre, ghizére, ghizirsíre, tifiríce

PROMENADE *vb.* ▼priímnu, ▼prímnu, ghiz_iréscu

PROMINENT *adj.* nişanlâ, cu númă ‖ CUNIA 258: nişanlâtcu

PROMISCUITY *s.* săláne

PROMISE *s.* ipóshise, ipushisíre, ligământu, tăxíre, zbor

PROMISE *vb.* ▾tăxéscu, dau zbor, ipushiséscu

PROMOTION *s.* alţáre

PROMPT *adj.* (*ready to serve*) próthim, *m pl* -thiñ

PROMPT *vb.* (*to incite*) → URGE

PROOF *s.* sémnu; próvă; apódhixe; (*testimony*) ispáte

PROP *s.* andoápir → SUPPORT

PROP UP *vb.* ▾arádzim, arádzâm

PROPAGANDA *s.* propayánda

PROPEL *vb.* ▾púngu → PUSH

PROPENSITY *s.* híche, íche, húie

PROPER *adj.* (*suitable*) undzít; (*~ and dignified*) prímtu

PROPERLY *adv.* cum prínde

PROPERTY *s.* aveáre, cătúnă, cătúndă, cătundíe, căşeáre, fármă, nicuchirátă, nicuchireáţă

PROPHECY *s.* prufitíe, prifitipsíre

PROPHESY *vb.* profitipséscu → FORETELL

PROPHET *s.* prufít

PROPINQUITY *s.* aprucheáre, éşă, udiseáţă, uidisíre, viţinátă, viţinătáte

PROPITIOUS *adj.* fursatlí, *m pl* -tládz

PROPORTION *s.* análuy *no pl*

PROPOSAL *s.* (*~ of marriage*) pruxiníľe *f pl*

PROPOSE *vb.* (*to make an offer of marriage*) u cáftu nveástă

PROPRIETRESS *s.* nicuchíră

PROPRIETOR *s.* nicuchír

PROPRIETY *s.* (*decorum*) prep

PROSECUTE *vb.* giúdic

PROSECUTOR *s.* dâvăgí

PROSPER *vb.* ñ-si dúţi príma → THRIVE

PROSPERITY *s.* prucupsíre, ghineáţă ‖ **Cru:** yineáţă, GOLAB 221

PROSPEROUS *adj.* prucupsít, pur-, cu hăíre, amintát, tihiró

PROSTITUTE *s.* → HARLOT

PROSTITUTE *vb.* curvăriséscu

PROSTITUTION *s.* curvăríľe, curvaríe

PROSTRATE ONESELF *vb.* fac taéte, fac timínă

PROSTRATION

PROSTRATION *s.* taéte, timină, timinée

PROTECT *vb.* ▼afiréscu, amfiréscu; ▼ápăr, ▼păzéscu; am tru mână; **He ~s you with one hand and plucks out your hair with the other one** C-únă mână ti-ápără ş cu-alántă ti deápiră; **Lord, ~ him!** S-lu ai tru mână, Dumnidzále! ‖ amviléscu; LITURG 124: **protect us** *imper* amvilé-nă → WING

PROTECTED *adj.* (*shielded, covered, sheltered*) a(m)firít, (*watched over*) păzít, pi-

PROTECTION *s.* áripă; **under our ~** sun áripa a noástră; aúmbră; **Under whose ~ will we go to the wintering place?** Cu a cui aúmbră ñárdzim noi tru arníu? ‖ **to be under smb.'s ~** (*to be favored*) am plătări (*lit.* 'to have back, to have shoulders'), PARALLELE 154; **to of-fer one's ~** dau plătări; LITURG 124: (*shield, defense*) avi-limíntlu *sg def*

PROTECTOR *s.* apărătór

PRO TEMPORE *adv.* próschir

PROTEST *n* prutéstu

PROTOCOL *s.* (*record, minute*) mâzbâtă

PROTRACT *vb.* (*to extend*) ▼lundzéscu, ▼spirlundzéscu

PROTUBERANCE *s. med.* umflătúră

PROUD *adj.* sirbés, -ésă (*sic*), -éşĭ, -ése → ARROGANT

PROVE *vb.* adúc sémnu, ▼apudhixéscu

PROVE TO BE *vb.* ▼aspún; **They ~ very brave** Si-aspúsiră asláñ; ies, es; **She ~ed to be a virgin** Inşí feátă

PROVENANCE *s.* sírtă → ORIGIN

PROVERB *s.* părămíe, părimíe

PROVIDE FOR *vb.* (*to satisfy the needs of*) apudidéscu

PROVIDED *cj.* → PROVIDING

PROVIDENT *adj.* (*prudent*) luyeáric, lugheáric

PROVIDING *cj.* cu căvúlea că, cu ligătúra s, cu simfunía si; **~ he gives him his daughter** cu simfunía si ľ-u da híľ-sa → CONDITION

PROVISIONS *s.* (*food*) apsún *or* psúne; (a)rizáche, cumáşe *f pl*; **winter ~** arnátic, arnátcu

PROVOCATIVE *adj.* (*irritating, uncomfortable*) paľu ntr-ócľi (*lit.* 'a straw in the eye')

PROVOKE *vb.* (*to set on edge*) mâc urécľile (*lit.* 'to eat smb.'s ears'); ▼furchiséscu

PROWL *vb.* ▼(a)nvărtéscu, ▼şintéscu, şuntéscu; **Why are you ~ing here** Ţe ti-anvărtéşti pi-auáţi?

PROWLER *s.* capisâz, dilingí

PROWLING *s.* şuntíre

PROWESS *s.* giuneáţă → BRAVERY

PROXY *s.* (*document*) vichiliméie; (*administrator of an estate or mansion*) vichíle *m*, vichíľu *m*

PRUDE: to act the prude ▼strâmbu nárea

PRUDENT *adj.* câştigós, -oásă; lugháric, luyeáric; cu sicáră n cap (*lit.* 'with rye in one's head'); ári meľ tru ciútură (*lit.* 'he/she has millet in his/her bucket,' *i.e.* has mind in his/her head) ‖ HRISTU 37: mătăsit, cu căştigă

PRUNELLA *s.* (*the fruit of the blackthorn*) ţápurnă

PRUNING KNIFE *s.* clădhiftír

PRURITUS *s. derm.* făyúră

PRY *vb.* (*to look, to gaze*) ▼mutréscu

PSALM *s.* psalmó

PSALM-BOOK *s.* (p)săltíre, (p)săltichíe

PSALTER *s.* → PSALM-BOOK

PUB *s.* (*esp. for beer*) birăríe ‖ **SJos:** băcălíe, CL 38

PUCKER *s.* → WRINKLE

PUCKER *vb.* ▼zbârcéscu → WRINKLE

PUDDLE *s.* báră, băltác, bâltoácă, bâltóc, muceálă, muceáră, muciór

PUDENDUM *s.* → VULVA

PUDGY *adj.* şíşcu, -şcă, -şţâ, -şte

PUFF *s.* ávră, adiľáre, suflăre

PUFF OUT *vb.* (*to belch out smoke*) afúm

PUFF UP *vb.* (*of smb.'s face*) ▼buburédz, ▼zbuldzinédz, buldzinédz, ▼pârhâvuséscu; (*to give oneself airs*) ▼căbărdéscu

PUFFBALL *s. bot.* bişínă di vúlpe; pópurdhă

PUFFED UP *adj.* (*as of smb.'s face*) buburós, -oásă; pâhrâvós, -oásă; (*conceited, boastful*) ândârlu, -rlă, -rľi, -rle → BE ~

PUFFING UP *s.* (*as of smb.'s face*) pâhrâvusíre

PUFF-PASTRY TART *s.* pítă di péture; (*large ~*) pităroáñe, pitiroáñe, pituroáñe, pitroáñe

PUGNACIOUS *adj.* căvyă(n)gí, ghiurultagí

PUISSANCE *s.* → POWER, STRENGTH

PUKE

PUKE *vb.* → VOMIT

PULCHRITUDE *s.* muşiteáţă, muşuteáţă

PULL *vb.* ▼trag (→ § 32)

PULL DOWN *vb.* (*to do away with, to demolish*) dărâm, aspárgu, răzuéscu

PULL IN ONE'S BELT *vb.* (*to live in poverty*) bat tămbărălu

PULL OFF *vb.* (*to accomplish smth. successfully*) scot, u scot náparte, căturthuséscu ‖ CUNIA 259: u scot ân cále; acáţ péşti

PULL OFF SHOES AND SOCKS *vb.* ▼discálţu

PULL ONESELF TOGETHER *vb.* ñ-yin tu orĭ, ñ-yin n cále; *3 sg pt:* víne ânt-ésu (*lit. 'he is coming into himself'*); **After his father's death he pulled himself together** Dúpă moártea a tátă-sui víne ânt-ésu

PULL OUT *vb.* (*to extract, to stick out, to draw out, to remove*) scot; (*to uproot*) ▼(a)zmúlgu, ▼dizgrăbún

PULL OUT ONE'S TONGUE (AT SMB.) *vb.* lĭ scot límba nafoáră

PULL SMB.'S LEG *vb.* ñ-arâd (cu nâs) → HOLD SMB. IN DERISION

PULL THE WRONG BOW *vb.* ▼arădhăpséscu, taĭu pălăvri → TITTLE-TATTLE

PULL THROUGH *vb.* purbuléscu ‖ u scot ân cap (cu), BASME 461

PULL TO PIECES *vb.* adár bucăţ, adár muşcătúri, disíc cumátă di cumátă, fac bucatíce, fac bucăţ di bucăţ, fac păspăltáre, frângu chilúnghea

PULLBACK *s.* năpuíre → PULLOUT, RETREAT

PULLED TO PIECES *adj.* (*as of a goat caught by a bear*) aspártu; aspártu părceácĭe

PULLET *s.* (*of chicken*) púĭcă, púĭe, pulíţă

PULLEY *s.* (a)răteáuă, arutél; măcără (*and* mâcâ-), prísne; (*in a loom*) căirúş, călărúş

PULLING OUT *s.* (*as of nails*) discărfusíre, discurfusíre, scoátire, scuteáre

PULLOUT *s.* opistuhórise, pistuhórise

PULP *s.* (*of a fruit*) ñedz, ínimă

PULSATE *vb.* (*as of the heart*) ▼bat, furfurédz

PULVERIZE *vb.* → ANNIHILATE

PUMICE-STONE *s.* ghigór

PUMMEL *vb.* (*to pound, to beat*) agudéscu, ansár, ▼úmflu

PUMP *s.* (*device for absorbtion*) tulúmbă

PUMP *vb.* (*to question persistently*) ▾discúlţu → SOUND

PUMPKIN *s.* curcubétă; (*wild ~*) cítură; *~ pie* pítă di curcubétă; *G:* şúplă

PUNCH *s.* (*beverage*) pónci *f*; (*strike*) aguditúră, goádă

PUNCH *vb.* (*to hit*) agudéscu

PUNGENT *adj.* nţăpătós, -oásă; mpipirát, mbi-; (*as of hot pepper*) foc *invar.* (*lit. 'fire'*)

PUNISH *vb.* muştinédz, măştinédz ‖ **Cru:** căznuéscu, GOLAB 226; (*to ~ severely*) ĺ-chisédz pipér ân cap, BASME 624

PUNISHMENT *s.* muştináre, pidhipsíre; (*scourge*) pusoágă

PUNK *s.* (*dry spongy substance for starting a fire*) iáscă; (*young inexperienced person*) ni-fricát; (*a usu. petty gangster*) delbidér, nihít

PUNY *adj.* azmét, chirchinéc, piliciós, -oásă; pruzúme, *m pl* -zúñ; s(c)lab, *m pl* s(c)laghi; zăbún, *m pl* -búñ

PUP *s.* → PUPPY

PUPIL *s. anat.* mărdzeáuă, mărdzeáua a óćului (*lit. 'the bead of the eye'*) ‖ **Amc:** lâeáţă, SCHL 116; **Pls:** bébă, béba uóćui, CL 38

PUPPY *s.* căţăl; căţălác, -lúc, -líc, -lúş; **He follows me like a ~** yíni dúpă míni ca căţălúş ‖ **Nij:** căţéu, **Vel:** cânícu B-ARCH 92

PURBLIND *adj.* → BLIND, ONE-EYED; (*obtuse*) budălác → STUPID

PURCHASE *s.* (a)cumpăráre, **N:** ancumpráre; ancumprátă; **When you make a ~ open your eyes!** La acumpráre dişcĺídi-ţ óćiĺ!

PURCHASE *vb.* → BUY

PURCHASER *s.* muştirí

PURE *adj.* curát; (*innocent*) ápă di lituryíe (*lit. 'holy water'*); (*as of the sound of a bell*) trăgănós, -yănós, *f* -oásă

PUREBLOOD *adj.* di sóie *invar.*

PUREBRED *adj.* di sóie *invar.*

PURGATIVE *s.* cathártic, chinitcó

PURGE *vb.* cur

PURIFY *vb.* căthărăséscu → CLEAN

PURL *s.* ciúciur, múrmur, murmuráre

PURL *vb.* ciúciur, múrmur, murmurédz

PURLOIN *vb.* ▾ciun → STEAL

PURPLE *s.* (*stuff*) gariváldu, galiváldu

PURPLE *adj.* (*color*) álic, álcu, argăvanlíu, mórcu, móric

PURPOSE

PURPOSE s. máxus or maxús; niéte, scupó; on ~ castílea, xaryú;
He did this on ~ U feáţe xaryú; **as if on ~** cánda castílea ‖ CUVATA
7: ca ti ináti

PURPOSE vb. pripún, ñ-pripún să, am niéte [ni•é•] să , fac
niéte să; (to destine, to designate) număţéscu; to no ~ trâ oáuă
aróşă; **I don't think he is coming to no ~** Nu yíne trâ oáuă aróşă

PURPOSEFULLY adv. máxus or maxús → INTENTIONALLY

PURPOSELESSLY adv. **He is not coming ~** Nu yíne trâ oáuă aróşă

PURSE s. cheále, chésă, cărnéciu (and câr-), pirtufóle, portu-
fél, priftáciu; (~ made of a bladder) pungă, pungár; tăvărceác,
vúryă; **Amc:** zbârníc

PURSE ONE'S LIPS vb. ▼strâmbu búdzâle

PURSUE vb. (to chase) fug, **N:** afúg; (to haunt) ▼avín; (to follow) ľau n cicioáre

PURSUIT s. (of game, of a thief, etc.) ayunítă, avináre

PURULENCE s. pruñáre

PURULENT adj. pruñár, -ñát, -ñós; to be ~ pruñédz

PUS s. cuptúră, proñ

PUSH s. pindzeáre, píndzire, píndzur, píngu

PUSH vb. ▼ndes; ▼píngu (→ § 32), dau píndzur, dau un píngu; (to
urge) párachiniséscu; **As if the devil ~ed him** Cánda-l pímse
dráclu

PUSH ALONG / THROUGH vb. mi bag

PUSH IN vb. plântu, ▼nhig, hig

PUSILLANIMOUS adj. → FEARFUL

PUSS s. → CAT

PUSTULE s. med. (on the tongue or on the socket of a tooth)
tâmbúnă; (on the skin) cucúdă, făltácă, fultácă, zgáibă ‖ **Peş:**
fágusă, CL 45

PUSTULATE adj. derm. bubuchiós, -oásă; zgăibós, -oásă

PUT adj. (fixed, stationary) ni-minát

PUT vb. bag, mi arúc, ▼chic; (rare) ▼pun; ~ **the cake on the
table!** Bágă píta pri meásă! **He used to ~ them to pray** ăľ băgá
duváe s-fácă; **You may ~ it wherever you want to** Iu vrei âl puñ

PUT ABOARD vb. (to cause to go on board a boat) ▼vărcărséscu

PUT CLOSE TOGETHER vb. (to fill) ▼strimuxéscu

PUT DOWN vb. (to subdue) ▼căpistruéscu → BRIDLE; (to kill)
▼arucutéscu, arcutéscu

PUT FEAR IN SMB.'S HEART *vb.* dau ibréte (la), bag ceáşlu (tu)

PUT FORTH *vb.* (*of plants*) fitruséscu; náscu; **to ~ sprouts** mpu-
ĺédz

PUT IN *vb.* ▾bag

PUT IN A CHEST *vb.* sinduchiséscu

PUT IN A CLAIM *vb.* (*to lodge a complaint*) ‖ dau plângu, BASME
40; mi plângu (la), BASME 18

PUT IN CHAINS *vb.* ‖ arúc tu brángă, BASME 461

PUT IN ORDER *vb.* (*a room, a yard, etc.*) ▾ndreg, anăschirséscu,
anischirséscu, născărséscu, ▾arădhăpséscu, arădhyipséscu, ară-
dhiséscu ‖ *Cru:* ardăpséscu, GOLAB 201

PUT IN PRISON *vb.* chic năúntru → JAIL

PUT IT ACROSS SMB. *vb.* (*to get the better of smb.*) ĺ-u pot

PUT IT INTO ONE'S HEAD *vb.* ‖ BELIMACE 11: ñ-u bag tru mínte

PUT IT IN YOUR PIPE AND SMOKE IT! ≈ Țe s-ĺi faţĭ a étiĺei?

PUT IT ON *vb.* (*to give oneself airs*) mi ngroş

PUT OFF *vb.* (*to adjourn*) ▾amân, alás pri mâne; **I am late because they put me off** Ñ-amânái că ñ-mi-amânără; (*to flee*) li
scármin; **to put smb. off doing smth.** ĺ-taĺu tăcátea (*or* nările) ‖
(*to discontinue a bad habit*) **I put off drinking** O-a-lăsái arăchía
(*lit. 'I abandoned the liquor'*), PARALLELE 144

PUT ON *vb.* (*of clothes*) ▾véscu, nvéscu, ñ-pun, ▾alăxéscu (*and*
alâ-), ñ-trec; **If things look good, I'll ~ white clothes** Di-i tră
bun, álbe să-ñ pun; **They have not put on their shirts** Nu şi-au
tricútă cămeşile; ▾bag; (*of footwear*) ▾ancálţu (*and* angál-) ~
your glasses! Bágă-ţ óclĭiĺ! (*of a shawl*) ▾mbálţu; (*of a pair of
beads, of a hat, etc.*) chic; **She put them on around her neck** şi-
li chică di gúşe

PUT ON AIRS *vb.* ▾căbărdéscu → GIVE ONESELF AIRS

PUT ONESELF OUT *vb.* (*to try one's hardest*) cilistiséscu → CRACK
ON ALL HANDS

PUT ONESELF TO RIGHTS *vb.* ▾dreg, ndreg, andrég, ndirég

PUT ONE'S FOOT IN IT *vb.* u adár căcăteásca, u adár culeáş, u
adár dhálă, u adár dip hărdálă, u adár ghésă, u adár taratóre, u
fac ghésă, u fac heártă, ▾cálcu tu pítă

PUT ONESELF OUT *vb.* (*to do all in one's power*) mi fac páde

PUT ONE'S ARM OUT OF JOINT *vb.* ñ-scot mâna

PUT ONE'S SIGNATURE TO SMTH. *vb.* bag múndza → SIGN

PUT

PUT ON FLESH *vb.* *bag cárne;* (*as of sheep*) bag bóia, ▼iľédz, bag cárne tu urécľi, mi astúp cárne, mi adár şut

PUT ON LEAVES *vb.* (*as of a forest in spring*) funduséscu, nvirdzăscu, nvérdu

PUT ON THE RING *vb.* (*of a bear; fig. of people*) ľ-trec cărchéľlu di náre

PUT ON WEIGHT *vb.* mi adár şut → PUT ON FLESH

PUT OUT *vb.* (*a fire, a lamp*) ▼astíngu (→ § 32); (*to kill*) astíngu ţeára

PUT OUT SMB.'S EYE(S) *vb.* găvuséscu

PUT OUT ONE'S TONGUE AT SMB. *vb.* scot límba

PUT PRESSURE UPON SMB. *vb.* bag súla n coáste

PUT SMB. AWAY *vb.* bag năúndru → JAIL

PUT SMB. IN HIS/HER PLACE *vb.* ľ-u apléc nárea, ľi pliciutédz nările [nări•le]

PUT SMB. INTO PRISON *vb.* 1-chic núntru → JAIL

PUT SMB. OFF DOING SMTH. *vb.* ľ-taľu tăcátea (*or* nărĭle)

PUT SMB. OUT OF HUMOR *vb.* ľ-aspárgu chéfea, ľ-aspárgu gústul

PUT SMB. OUT TO GRASS *vb.* (*to put the skids under smb., to make leave*) ľ-dau purdheácica [•dheáĉ•ka]

PUT SMTH. TO FIRE AND SWORD *vb.* trec prit dínte

PUT SMB. TO HIS/HER WIT'S END *vb.* ľ-disíc cáplu

PUT SMB. TO THE SWORD *vb.* trec prit dínte, trec prit lipídhă

PUT SMB. TO THE TROUBLE *vb.* ľ-gioc únă hunére

PUT SMTH. INTO ONE'S HEAD *vb.* (*to intend to do*) ñ-u am tu mínte (să) ‖ âñ bag tu mínte (să), PARALLELE 156

PUT SMTH. THROUGH *vb.* (*to bring to an end*) u scot n cap, scot lúcrulu n cap

PUT THE HAT ON ONE'S MISERY *vb.* ≈ aéstu eáste bilélu a biľádzlor

PUT THE KIBOSH ON SMB. *vb.* *N:* ľ-vin idiháche

PUT THE PACK-SADDLE *vb.* ▼sămâruséscu; **Put the pack-saddle on the horses!** Sămărusíţ cáľi!

PUT THE SKIDS UNDER SMB. *vb.* (*to make leave*) ľ-dau părtáľile, ľ-dau ţărúhile → FIRE

PUT THE WIND UP SMB. *vb.* (*to intimidate, to scare*) bag ceáşlu (tu)

PUT TO BED *vb.* ▼cúlcu, ▼(a)pún

PUT TO RIGHTS *adj.* arădhyipsít, ardhyisít

PUT TO SHAME *vb.* aruşinédz, fac ciciór di ľepure, fac ciciór di câne, fac birbáte; **But watch out! Don't put us to shame!** Ma mutreá! Te-am vidzútă! → DISGRACE ‖ bag cu cáplu n loc, BASME 106

PUT TO SLEEP *vb.* bag pri sómnu; (*of little children*) bag to náni

PUT UP *vb.* (*at an inn, etc.*) ▾cundiséscu → MAKE A HALT

PUT UP A YARN *vb.* (*to tell, to narrate*) ▾ambáir; **This old woman will put up the whole story to you** Moáşea aéstă va ţâ li ambáiră túte

PUT UP ONE'S NOSE *vb.* am nările mutáte

PUT UP RESISTANCE *vb.* dândâséscu, dânâséscu

PUT UP WITH *vb.* (*to tolerate*) ‖ u-ári prâstúra lárgâ, DIARO 161

PUTREFACTION *s.* purtidzâre

PUTRESCENCE *s.* putridzâre

PUTRID *adj.* şúpliv, -vă, -yĭ, -ve → ROTTEN

PUTTING IN ORDER *s.* arădhyipsíre, arădhisíre

PUTTING TO SLEEP *s.* băgáre pri sómnu

PUZZLED *adj.* chirút; **I am ~** u-ám cumbúră

PUZZLE ONE'S HEAD ABOUT (AT, OVER smth.) *vb.* ni-disíc cáplu; ñ-frângu béta

PYGMY *adj. derog.* jabéc, jubéc; (*as of a goat*) júdav

Q

QUACK *s.* şarlatán → RASCAL

QUADRANGLE *s.* săndráciu

QUADRANT *s.* (*quarter*) cártu, ciuréc

QUAFF *vb.* sórbu, arufséscu

QUAIL *s. orn.* pripilíţă; *also:* şcurtéză, triyónă ‖ *SJos:* perdhícă, CL 258

QUAIL *vb.* (*to lose courage*) ▾lăhtărséscu; acáţ si seámin aróv (*lit. 'to begin to sow cickpea,' i.e. to break winds*); ñ-arăţeáşte bişína (*lit. 'my farts are growing cooler'*) ‖ PC: dau năpói (*lit. 'to give back'*)

QUAINT *adj.* (*odd*) trónciu → OUTLANDISH; (*pleasing*) nóstim

QUAKE *s.* cutrémur, trunduíre → EARTHQUAKE

QUAKE *vb.* (*with cold or fear*) treámur, treámbur, ▼cruţéscu, curţéscu, ▼trunduéscu, afiriséscu guvójdi; **to ~ in one's shoes** şápte-óptu ñ-si dúţe (*lit. 'I am breaking winds by seven-eight'*)

QUALIFIED *adj.* irbáp, *m pl* -báchi → ABLE

QUALITY: **of good ~** di háre; **of low ~** di cátră la cúscra

QUALMS: **to have ~** ‖ mi mâcâ, mi aroádi, mi mâcâ sáráchea, DIARO 289

QUANDRY *s.* birdhipsíre, mintitúră, síyise, sínyise

QUANTITY: **in ~s** cu mnáta

QUARREL *s.* ncăceáre; *also:* câvgă, căvyătúră, daravéră, filuníche, guşturáre, măcătúră, nguvujdáre, nţirtáre, scándal, strigáre, tăcânsíre, tăvătúră, dăvătúră ‖ HRISTU 39: şeri (*from Alb. sherr*)

QUARREL *vb.* ▼(a)ncáciu, angáciu; *also:* filunichiséscu, ▼ngrâñéscu, ▼nţértu, ▼tăcânséscu ‖ BELIMACE 10: mi áflu pri ngrăñe cu

QUARRELSOME *adj.* ghiurultagí; focurúsă *f*; **~ fellow** căvgă(n)gí → ILL-NATURED

QUARTAN FEVER *s. med.* tétă; arăspeáse, aru-

QUARTER *s.* (*a fourth part*) ciréc, ciuréc, **N:** ciréche; cártu; **a ~ of an hour** un ciréc di oáră, un cártu di oáră; **a ~ of a litre** (*unit for alcoholic beverages*) ţindzác *or* ţindzácă; (*division of a town or village*) măhălă ‖ **a ~ of an hour** un cirec di sati, HRISTU 172

QUART-POT *s.* lítră, mârâtác, mârtác

QUARTZ *s.* zealópetră, yealopétră

QUASH *vb.* ▼cúrmu, ▼astíngu

QUAVER *vb.* → SHIVER, TREMBLE

QUAY *s.* mol, scálumă

QUEASY *adj.* (*as of food*) aynusós, -oásă

QUEEN *s.* (*also ent.*) vasílsă, văsiloáñe; (*a playing card*) cucoánă (*lit. 'lady'*)

QUEER *adj.* trónciu → ODD

QUEER *vb.* (*to disrupt*) ▼aspárgu

QUELL *vb.* ▼urséscu; (*to put out, to quiet*) ▼cúrmu → CALM

QUESTION *s.* (*interrogation*) ntribáre, zítimă; (*matter*) ipóthise, luyuríe, **N**: luguríe ‖ **without** ~ nu va dzâcă, BASME 590

QUESTION *vb*. (a)ntréb, ântréb, discós → EXAMINE, SOUND

QUESTIONABLE *adj*. andoáulea [•dŭáŭ•] → DOUBTFUL

QUICK → BE ~ IN THE UPTAKE

QUICKLIME *s*. azvéste ni-asteásă

QUICK-COOKING *adj*. (*as of beans*) hirburíu

QUICKLY *adv*. ayóñea → FAST

QUICKSILVER *s*. yeáryir, gheárghir; *adj*. yearyearín, yearyearíu

QUICK-TEMPERED *adj*. arceátcu → ILL-NATURED

QUICK-WITTED *adj*. pirgác → INTELLIGENT ‖ şpirtuít, DIARO 238; dipirát, DIARO 369

QUIESCENT *adj*. agălisít, ísih, ímir

QUIET *s*. tățeáre → SILENCE ‖ STERGHIU 22: **on the** ~ (*secretively*) peascumtáti

QUIET *adj*. tăcút, ísih; (*in a low voice*) dipús; (*slow*) minghét; **to become** ~ amút, (a)muțáscu → BE SILENT

QUIET (DOWN) *vb*. (a)muțăscu, **N**: amút; (*to become calm, to make calm*) ▼apún, ▼irini(p)séscu ‖ STERE 29: pugădăséscu

QUIETLY *adv*. ariháte; (pri) ómñea

QUIETUDE *s*. arăpás ‖ STERE 23: pugádusi

QUILT *s*. yiuryáne, páplumă

QUILT MAKER *s*. yiuryangí [yⁱur•]

QUINCE *s*. gutúñe; *dim*. gutuñíță

QUINCE-TREE *s*. gutúñu, gâtúñu

QUININE *s*. sulfát, zulfát

QUINSY *s*. *med*. plăscáre, prăscáre, priscáre; gǐíndură

QUIP: to make ~**s** *vb*. gioc hunérea, gioc ună hunére

QUIRK *s*. tirtípe

QUIRKY *adj*. tirtipcí

QUIT *vb*. (*to abandon*) ▼(a)lás; (*to behave*) ▼apórtu

QUITE *adv*. (*to the greatest extent*) pri; **They are fresh and** ~ **warm** Sântu proáspite ş pri cálde

QUITS (*equal, even*) fit; **We are** ~ Him fit; Him ísea

QUIVER *vb*. (*with pain or fear*) ▼virvirédz; **to** ~ **like an aspen leaf** ≈ şápte-óptu ñ-si dúțe → SHIVER

QUIVERING *s*. (*thrill with fear, etc.*) nhiuráre, hiuráre

QUIZ *s*. (*eccentric person, joker*) trónciu; (*practical joke*) réngă, rénghe

QUIZZICAL *adj.* *(marked by bantering or teasing)* şicăgí
QUOIT *s.* asmádhă, chirséne, furcutáş
QUOTA *s.* *(share)* (a)rifiné

R

RABBET *s.* tăl'itúră
RABBIT *s.* l'épur(e)
RABBLE *s.* *(pile)* grămádă
RABID *adj.* *(as of a dog)* turbát, trubát; liseárcu
RABIES *s.* *med.* turbáre, trubáre; lisixíre
RACE *s.* *(current)* curáre
RACE *s.* ghíntă → PEOPLE
RACE *vb.* cur, fug; **to race along** mi u angán, fug di mi frângu,
fug di nu mi ved
RACK *s.* → DESTRUCTION
RACK *vb.* → TORMENT; ~ *one's brains about/over smth.* ▾frimíntu,
▾ciucutéscu cáplu *(or* míntea), ñ-disíc cáplu, ñ-vátăm míntea,
ñ-frângu béta, ▾văsănipséscu
RACKET *s.* *(confused chattering)* tăvătúră → HUBBUB, UPROAR
RADDLE *vb.* mplătéscu, mblătéscu
RADIANT *adj.* *(happy)* hăriós [•ri•ós], hărós, *(bright)* luñinós
RADISH *s.* répă, répură, (a)ripáne; mer dit loc *(lit. 'apple
from the earth')*
RAFT *s.* crímă di → LOT ‖ *Peş:* sále, *GSus:* ´sáli, CL 260

RAFTER *s.* *(one who maneuvers logs into position and binds them into rafts for conveyancce by water)* ‖ *Av:* varcadhór, CL 263

RAFTER *s.* *(as in a roof)* cálar, cálăr, călár, căvălár, căpri-ór, căprúľe, căprúľ, cărpúľu ‖ *SJos:* papafíngu, CL 257; *Av:* pă-pădhíţâ, CL 258

RAG *s.* cârpă, peátic, peática; *also:* *Smr:* cărcăşină, cioľu, léţcă, părtálă, părţáľe, şugánă; *(tatter)* récichiu [réĉ•k'u]

RAGAMUFFIN *s.* coáti-goáli *(lit. 'nacked elbows')*

RAGE *m.* yináte; **to boil over with ~** hérbu (pi) → ANGER

RAGE *vb.* bat; **hatred that ~s in the world today** líma ţe u báte lúmea di az; *(as of a blizzard)* 3 sg ntúrină, nturineádză; *(to ~ noisily, as of a storm)* huhutéscu

RAGGED *adj.* ţârţărós; **~ person** arúptu, dispuľitúră, partál, părtál, părtálcu, părtădít, recicamán [reĉ•ka•], ţârţărós; *(of a woman)* ca martíra ‖ HRISTU 49: arecĭcă f

RAGING *adj.* ncuñát, turbát → MAD

RAGOUT *s.* *(stew)* yeahné, iahníe, ahníe

RAID *s.* anăpădíre

RAID *vb.* anăpădéscu

RAIL *vb.* *(to complain angrily)* fac şimătă; *(to vituperate)* → SCOLD

RAILING *s.* părmác

RAILLERY *s.* arâdeáre, arâdire, măitápe, mbizuíre, mbizuitúră, péză

RAILROAD STATION *s.* staşióne, staşónă, staţióne, stathmó

RAIN *s.* ploáie, *Cľis:* dârce, *F:* zdârcă; **torrential ~** zof; **pelting ~** stih di ploáie; **drizzling ~** pluínă

RAIN *vb.* da ploáie; *also:* mpluiádză, pluireádză; *(to drizzle)* chícă ‖ *Kat, Perd, Plat:* da ploi, *Kar, Pur:* da ploai, B-ARCH 10; ALIA 10: arúcă ploáie, cáde ploáie; **it is ~ing cats and dogs** veársă cu găleáta

RAINBOW *s.* curcubéu ‖ *F:* cucubéu, SarD 105; beu, bélu, ALIA 17

RAINCOAT *s.* yeamburlúche, muşimă

RAINMAKER *s.* pirpiríţă, pirpirúnă

RAINSPOUT *s.* chilúnghe, chiulúnghe

RAINY *adj.* pluiós, pluirós

RAISE *s.* sculáre

RAISE *vb.* ▾álţu, ▾(a)scól; **I am ~ing the flag** U ascól pandéra;

RAISE

▾âmpróstu (*and* âmbróstu), ▾mpróstu, ▾mprustédz (*and* mbrustédz); ▾mut nsus, ▾nduréscu; (*to ~ from the dead*) nghiédz [nǵi•édz], an-ghédz, anyédz

RAISE A WHOOP *vb.* dau un zghic

RAISE PRICES *vb.* ▾scunchéscu → RIG

RAISE SUSPICION *vb.* ‖ dau şubée, BASME 446

RAISIN *s.* stăfídhă (*and* stafídă), stăhídhă

RAISING *s.* (a)nălţáre, sculáre, sculátă

RAKE *s.* (*a tool with prongs*) gráţă; **as thin as a ~** ≈ slăghít ca hiľán ‖ *SJos:* bunélă, CL 40

RAKE (*of people*) aspártu; *also:* birbántu, curvár, dişuţât, diz-mălărát, *G:* fatigéi invar; muľiráşcu, muľirúşu, muľirúşcu, púş-cľu, puşcľán, pústu, puştán, puşteán

RAKE *vb.* (*to gather with or as with a rake*) ▾adún

RAKISH *adj.* aspártu

RALLY *vb.* (*to arouse for action*) ▾scol; (*to join in a common cause*) ▾adún

RAM *s.* birbéc, birbeáţe; *dim.* birbicúş; areáte, arăiáte; (*in-completely castrated*) asmán ‖ *Mul, Ses:* bărbéc, *Amc, An, Arγ, Fal, Gard, Kat, Lep, Plat, Src, Ver:* bârbéc, B-ARCH 320; *SJos:* dumuzlúchi, CL 44; (*two-year old ~*) *Av:* stif, CL 261; *K:* (*the flock-leader, speaking of a ram*) gâciu, GOLAB 217

RAM *vb.* ▾agudéscu, ▾ndes, stimuxéscu, stúlţin, stúlcin

RAMADAN *s.* rămăzáne, armăzáne

RAMBLE *vb.* hălăndăréscu, misúr steálile

RAMBLE ON *vb.* (*to talk desultorily*) zburăscu goále

RAMBUNCTIOUS *adj.* ghiurultagí, pravatós

RAM-LAMB *s.* mľor, mbľor

RAMPAGE *s.* apríndire, aprindeáre, ariciuíre, inătusíre

RAMPAGE *vb.* (**to rush wildly about**) ▾apríndu, ▾arcédz, ▾ariciu-éscu, inătuséscu → GET ANGRY

RAMPAGEOUS *adj.* aprés, -eásă, -éşǐ, -eáse; inătusít

RAMPART *s.* mitiríze

RAMROD *s.* arbíe, hărbíe, hárbă, căsíe, veárgă

RAMSHACKLE *adj.* hárval

RANCID *adj.* aludzât; (*as of cheese*) *m/n* nţes, *f* nţeásă

RANCOR *s.* (*bitterness*) câníľe, heáre; **He is full of ~** Eáste maşi heáre

RANDOM: **at ~** cu tahmínea

RANGE *s.* ceárcu; **The wolf came within/into ~ of the gun** Lúplu cădzú tu ceárcu

RANGE *vb.* ▾ambáir, arădhăpséscu

RANGER *s.* (*warden*) păzván, păzvándu

RANK *s.* (*social class*) mânică, sóie, thése; **of high ~** di câpíe máre; **people of their ~** oámiñ di mânica a lor

RANK *adj.* (*offensive in odor or taste*) añurzít, ndâhânít, ndâhnít, xizumsít; (*of meat*) băiátcu → STALE

RANK *vb.* ▾arădhăpséscu

RANKLE *vb.* (*to cause anger*) ▾inătuséscu, ▾amărăscu, ▾amărédz; *med. 3 sg* (*as of a boil*): adúnă, adúnă proñ; coáţe

RANSACK *vb.* fac ghénga → PLUNDER

RANSACK ONE'S HEAD ABOUT/WITH SMTH. *vb.* (*to search thoroughly*) ñ-disíc cáplu, ñ-frângu béta ‖ âñ bat cáplu PARALLELE 143

RANSOM *s.* discumpăráre, xayuráuă, ayuráuă, ascăpáre

RANSOM *vb.* discúmpăr, ascáp

RANT *vb.* (*to talk loudly and wildly*) lăvăséscu; (*to scold*) vărghéscu, nţértu

RAP: (*a minimum amount or degree of*) **I don't care a ~** ≈ hăbáre nu am

RAP *s.* (*blow*) goádă, aguditúră, cloáţă, cluţátă

RAP *vb.* (*to strike*) agudéscu

RAPACIOUS *adj.* arăchitór; *also:* arpáy, baľúca *invar*; yearacumít, haldúp, *pl* haldúpeañ; órñu, zulumgí, zulumcheár; (*~ and vindicative*) şárcu; **How ~ you are!** Ţe baľúca hii!

RAPE *s. bot.* → COLZA ‖ *Prv:* bambacóla, CL 38

RAPE *s.* (*kidnaping*) arăchíre

RAPE *vb.* (*to seize, to ravish*) (a)ráp, (a)răchéscu

RAPIDITY *s.* curundeáţă

RAPIDLY *adv.* alága, cu-alága, agónea, agúnea, crúndu

RAPIDS *s.* ghirdápe

RARE *adj.* (a)rár, arítcu; réhav, *m pl* réhayĭ, *f pl* réhave

RAREFIED *adj.* arărít

RAREFACTION *s.* arăíre

RAREFYING *s.* arăíre → SCATTERING

RARELY *adv.* (a)rár, *N:* arétcu, arítcu

RASCAL *s.* pezevénghiu; *also:* chirătă, murláiu, nihít, păstúră,

RASCALITY

plăstúră, prăstúră, púşcľu, puşteán, puştán, spindzurát, şarlatán, zgrumát; **You devilish ~!** Plăstúra a dráclui! ‖ BATSARIA 67:
you, ~! bre nihíte!

RASCALITY s. muşuteáţă, edepsâzlắche

RASH s. *derm.* arópun, arupunáre, rópan, bişicáre, fultăcáre; **to
have a ~ on the lips** ▼arăbudzânédz arupunáre; (*on the lips*) arăbudzináre, arupunáre, aruvirsáre, aruvirsătúră, curi di găľínă,
piţíndzină; **to have a ~ on the face** mi arupunédz tu fáţă, scot
curi di găľínă

RASH adj. (*of people*) nu áre meľu tu ciútură pl → FOOLHARDY

RASP s. (*tool*) hístră, sístră

RASP vb. arinséscu ‖ CUNIA 230: dau cu líma, dau cu arneála

RASPBERRY s. (a)zñúră, gľúră

RASPBERRY-BUSH s. arúg, pilivúre

RASPINGS s. arăsătúră

RAT s. ‖ ALIA 104: pilécu, piléchiu, şóric, şóricu máre

RAT POISON s. şuricoáñe

RAT ON vb. (*to betray*) ▼prudhuséscu

RATE vb. → VALUE

RATION s. tăíme, tăíne; *also:* curamánă, gărăvánă, nárte

RATIONAL adj. (*sane*) aştirnút, duchít, duchitór; cu sicáră n
cap (*lit. 'with rye in one's head'*) → INTELLIGENT

RATTLE s. (*infant's toy*) vârvúră, zămbúnă

RATTLE vb. (*to confuse, to upset*) ▼mintéscu, ▼cirtuséscu, cirtuéscu

RATTLING adj. (*frolicsome*) astráptu

RAUCOUS adj. (*rough-sounding*) áscur, vrăhnós

RAVAGE s. chiaméte [k'i•a•], irmuxíre, pundíre, şcrituíre

RAVAGE vb. pustuéscu; **to ~ with fire and sword** trec prit dínte,
trec prit lipídhă → DEVASTATE

RAVE vb. bat n-aľúrea, xinu-zburắscu

RAVEL vb. → UNRAVEL

RAVELLING s. (*as of a woolen mitten*) strămáre, distrămáre, dis-
băiráre, disbăirătúră, dismăiláre, dizmăláre

RAVEL OUT vb. ▼distrămédz, strămédz, distrám, ▼dizbáir; (*rare*)
▼dizmál

RAVEN s. córbu; *also:* **N:** córac, curác; gávran, găvrán, gărván;
(*with white brest*) buducuşár, buducâşár

RAVEN *adj.* (*black*) laiu, láie, *m/f pl* lăi

RAVENING *adj.* hârtu, lémuryu → GREEDY, RAPACIOUS

RAVINE *s.* arâpă; *also:* grem, grémur, greb, gréblu, grímură, griméľ, milúră, súrpu, surpătúră

RAVISH *vb.* ▾aráp, ▾arăchéscu, archéscu

RAW *adj.* (*uncooked, unbaked, as of bread*) crud, yiu; (*unprocessed*) ni-lucrát; (*untrained*) agimí, agimíu, agimít, ageamít, ni-fricát; (*coarse*) ástur

RAWBONED *adj.* azmét, custăníc, *N:* costenlív; gúndu, piliciós, pruzúme

RAY *s.* → BEAM

RAZE *vb.* → DESTROY

RAZOR *s.* cusuráfe, xuráfe, suráfe

RAZZ *vb.* (*to deride*) ▾schin, rizil(ips)éscu

RE- *prefix* (*again, anew*) ≈ xana-; **Don't come out again!** S-nu xanaişíţ!

REACH *s.* (*power to comprehend*) aduchíre, (*rare*) aducheáre

REACH *vb.* ▾agiúngu (→ § 32); ▾alăchéscu; **Not even the devil could ~ us!** Dráclu nu nă alăcheá! (*to touch*) ▾aséscu, axéscu; **The dogs ~ed him** Cânľi lu-asíră; (*of age*) ▾úmplu; **He has ~ed 21 years** Umplú únsprăyinghiţ di añ

READ *vb.* ▾alég; (*~ aloud*) cântu; **to ~ smb.'s palm** arúc tíhea; arúc tu steáuă; **to ~ the sky** arúc tu steále ‖ **to know how to ~ and write** ştiu carte (*lit. 'to know book' or 'to know letter'*), PARALLELE 124; **I cannot ~ this letter, it is written badly** Nu pot si-u alég cártea, eásti scrísâ arău, DIARO 254; **to ~ aloud for smb.** dzâc; **My daughter-in-law read the letter for me** ñ-u dzâsi cártea nór-mea, DIARO 255

READER *s.* (*person*) yiuvăsitór

READINESS *s.* (*as ~ to serve smb.*) prothimíe; **to be in ~ for action** mi áflu sti cior → BE IN ~ FOR ACTION

READING *s.* ghiuvăsíre, yiuvăsíre

READY *adj. and adv.* (*finished, made, done*) adrát, étim, étmu, hazâre, hăzâre, hăzârcu, hârlu; (*prepared*) lésta, pri ciciór; (*dressed and waiting*) ndréptu; (*of money*) náhte, pişín; (*~ to serve, obliging*) poróthim, próthmu; **~ at hand** próhir ‖ ALB, **Për:** nu escu etum 'I am not ~,' Brâncuş 556

READY! *interj.* (It's the end of it! *a formula and an outcry in*

REAL

some children's games) táľa!

REAL *adj.* *(not imaginary)* yiu, ghiu; **a ~ vampire** vârcolác yiu ‖
Cru: dealíhea, GOLAB 211

REAL ESTATE *s.* edéc, múlche; *(small ~)* báşnă → ESTATE

REALISTIC *adj.* aştirnút → SERIOUS

REALITY: **in ~** *(indeed, actually)* naévea ‖ di d-arihina; **He
seemed to her older than he was in ~** ĭi apăru cama auş diţi ira
di d-arihina, HRISTU 68

REALIZE *vb.* (a)chicăséscu, (a)căchiséscu, ▾acúmpăr, ▾(a)duchés-
cu, *F:* bag tu cornu; **The priest ~ed how much the man was worth**
Préftlu lu-acumpără cât parádz fáţe; **He ~ed [much] too late what
the world was** Amânát duchí lúmea ţe eáste ‖ *(to understand)* ñ-vin
tu aéri, TULLIU 111

REALLY *adv.* alíhea, alíthhea [a•líth•h°a], alíhira, alíhiura ‖
Cru: dealíhea, GOLAB 211 ‖ ba; **~? I did't know that!** ba? nu u
ştiám şi-aéstu, DIARO 101

REALLY? *(Is it so?)* Ţe spuñ, aháră?

REALM *s.* văsilíe, vasíľ

REAP *vb.* *(to cut with a sickle)* seáţir, silixéscu, lixéscu; *(to
cut with a scythe)* cus(u)éscu

REAPER *s.* siţirătór, cosagí

REAPING *s.* siţiráre, cusuíre ‖ CUVATA 11: ţeáţir

REAR *adj.* códus, cudár; coáda *invar.* *(lit. 'the tail')*

REARWARD(S) *adv.* năpói, dinăpói

REASON *s.* mădé, mădée; **For what ~ are you killing the bastards?**
Tră ţe mădée lúţăľi âľ vătănáţă? *(justification, ground)* driptátic, driptática; gúră; **He has no ~ to speak** Nu-ári gúră s-greás-
că; *(motive)* cicuteálă, luyaryeazmó, isápe; **She may have her ~s**
Áre şi nâsă isápea a ľei; *(cause, blame)* itíe, fichíre, fichiúre
‖ *(rational ground or motive)* **I do not have any ~** to No-am zbor
si *(lit. 'I do not have word to')*, PARALLELE 151 → CAUSE; COME TO
~

REASON *vb.* ▾săluşéscu, ▾siliyiséscu

REASONABLE *adj.* *(possessing sound judgment)* duchít, duchitór →
MAKE ~

REBEL *s.* rébel, rebilipsít; *also:* *(Greek ~)* andárcu, andártu;
(Turkish ~) cumít, cumitagí; epanastát; scandzóhir; zurbă; *adj.*
andartichéscu

REBEL *vb.* ñ-mut cápu, u scol pandéra, rebilipséscu

REBELLION *s.* sculáre; *also*: andărsíe; *G*: cumitíe; panástase, rebilipsíre, ribiľó

REBELLIOUS *adj.* → RECALCITRANT

REBUKE *s.* pirdáfe, zăvráche, zbárdhu; (*abusive language*) rizilíre; *vb.* trag únă zăvráche → SCOLD

RECALCITRANT *adj.* năpudheáric, sirsém, sirsén, viţeárcu

RECALL *vb.* (*to bring to mind*) ▾anăfirséscu, tăcnéscu, ticnéscu, ticăéscu

RECANT *vb.* arniséscu, es di míntea a mea

RECEDE *vb.* (*to move back*) mi trag, mi trag năpói; **The river has ~ed** Ápa s-trápse; (*of rivers, lakes*) ▾scad; (*~ from an opinion*) es di míntea a mea

RECEIPT *s.* apódhixe

RECEIVE *vb.* ▾(a)próchiu, ľau; **~ this fellow well!** Aístu ficiór s-lu aprucheáţ ghíne! **N has received (gotten) a sad letter** Lo N nă cárte láie; (*to ~ a decoration*) ľau nişáne; (a)dhixéscu; **I heard that you have ~ed a piece of good news** Avdzâi că dixíşi hăbáre búnă; (*to be at home to visitors*) ▾aştéptu; **~ them as well as you can!** Aştiptáţ-ľi cât ma ghíne! **Is the emperor ~ing?** Aşteáptă amirălu? (*to ~ blows*) li-adún (*lit. 'to collect them'*)

RECEIVE COMMUNION *vb.* ľau cumnicătúră, ▾cumânic, cumínic

RECENT *adj.* nou, *m pl* noi, *f sg/pl* noáuă; fréşcu, proáspit, tazé, *f* -zée, *m pl* -zédz, *f pl* -zéi; din coádă

RECENTLY *adv.* adineávra, deaneávra, daneávra

RECEPTION *s.* (*as of money*) loáre; (*social gathering*) filipsíre; (*an instance of receiving*) dhixíre; (*welcome*) aştiptáre

RECESS *s.* (*hidden, secret or secluded place*) ascumtíş, ascumtáľ, ascumtátic, crispánă, dhóhe (*and* dóhe), doáhă, loc tr-ascundeári, pătiľáuă, pătľáuă

RECESS *vb.* ▾arăpás, ▾arăpăsédz

RECESSION *s.* trádzire, trădzeáre, opistuhórise, pistuhórise; (*reduced economic activity*) chisáte

RECKLESS *adj.* azvimturát, distórsu, -toársă, -tórşi, -toárse; cuturgí, ni-minduít, pristinisít; om fâră hisápe *s*

RECKON *vb.* fac isápe, ▾luyurséscu, ▾luyuryiséscu

RECKONING *s.* cicuteálă, dáre-loáre, hisápe, isápe, numiráre, misuráre; **Even ~ makes long friends** ≈ Oáspe, oáspe, ma dárealoárea curátă s-u-avém! *or* Fráte, fráte, ma cáşlu-i cu parádz!

RECLINE *vb.* ▾arăpăsédz → REST

RECLINED *adj.* andupirát, -rât, adupurát, ndupărát, -rât, antru-pát, arădzimát

RECLINING *adj.* culcát; tes, teásă, teşĭ, teáse

RECLUSE *adj.* căluyreáuă *f*; **my ~ life** bána-ñ căluyreáuă

RECOGNIZE *vb.* ▾cunóscu; **A madman does not have horns to be ~ed by!** Zúrlu nu áre coárne si-l cunóşti!

RECOIL *vb.* (*to shrink back in fear*) → QUAIL ‖ CUNIA 259: (*to retreat*) mi trag năpói dau năpói, mi frângu năpói, mi năpuéscu

RECOLLECT *vb.* ţân amínte → REMEMBER

RECOLLECTION *s.* ticníre, thimisíre, thimsíre → REMEMBRANCE

RECOMMENCE *vb.* pri-adár

RECOMMEND *vb.* părănghilséscu (*and* pârân-) ▾sistiséscu; (*as for getting a job*) ▾zburăscu; **~ me to him!** S-mi zburăşti la aístu

RECOMMENDATION *s.* sístase, sistisíre, părănghilíe, timbíe

RECOMPENSE *s.* muştináre, plátă

RECOMPENSE *vb.* (*to repay*) ▾plătéscu

RECONCILE *vb.* ▾(a)mbunédz, ▾mbun; **Let's ~!** S-nă mbunăm! ▾(a)z-bún, arăzbún, ▾disvér, fac băríşe; **Granny was trying to ~ them** Máia muntreá s-ĭi arăzbúnă → SOLACE

RECONCILED → BE ~

RECONCILIATION *s.* ambunáre → CONCILIATION

RECONDITE *adj.* (*abstruse*) **a ~ person** tártar

RECORD *s.* ‖ (*with recorded music or voice*) ‖ DIARO 405: ploáci *f*

RECORD *vb.* sémnu, nsimnédz → MARK

RECOVER *vb.* (*of health*) ▾nsănătuşéscu, sănătuşéscu, sănătuşédz; *also:* ĭau pri míne, ▾ncucutédz, ngiulnédz; nsânédz, sânédz, nturtărédz, ▾scol; (*to pull oneself together*) ñ-stríngu adiĭátlu, ñ-adún míntea cu míne, ñ-yin tu orĭ, ñ-yin pri mínte, ñ-yin pi véte; (*after childbirth*) sărăndiséscu; **to ~ one's breath** ñ-víñe sulúchea; (*as of a horse*) ĭau anásă; (*to ~ one's sere-nity*) ▾găléscu, ▾nsirín, nsirinédz; ‖ **to ~ one's sight** ñ-yin ócĭiĭ; **He began to recover his sight** Ócĭiĭ acăţără să-ĭ yínă, BASME 223; STERGHIU 22: ñ-vin la loc

RECOVERED *adj.* (*healthy again*) mprustát

RECOVERY *s.* ndriptáre, ngiulnáre, nsănătuşáre, nsânáre, sculáre; (*healing*) vindicáre

RECRUIT *s.* ridíf
RECRUIT ONE'S SPIRITS *vb.* ľau ínimă
RECRUITMENT *s.* (*in the army*) murmín
RECTANGLE *s.* sǎndráciu
RECTIFICATION *s.* ndriptáre
RECTIFY *vb.* ▾ndriptédz, ▾ndreg
RECUMBENT *adj.* (*lying down*) apús, culcát; tes, *f* teásǎ, *m pl* teşĭ, *f pl* teáse
RECUR *vb. med.* tórnu; **His disease has ~ed** Ál turnă lângoárea
RECURRENT MALARIAL FEVER *s. med.* tétǎ; arǎspeáse, arus- *f pl*
RED *s.* (*pigment or dye*) crépǎ
RED *adj.* (a)róş, *f* (a)róşe (DDA 209: "*not aroáşe*"), *m pl* (a)róşĭ, *f pl* aróşe; *m/f sg* cúche, *m pl* cuchi, *f pl* cúche; (*bright ~*) carpéz; (*dark ~*) ghivéz, ghiuvéze
RED BALL *s.* (*at billiards*) carambólǎ
REDDEN *vb.* aruşéscu
REDDENING *s.* aruşíre
REDDISH *adj.* (*of people*) (a)rús, (a)ruşcuván; (*of sheep*) cochi-róşil; (*~ mules*) váşe, *pl* váşi; (*of sheep, goats, mules*) ghes, *f* ghésǎ (*sic*), gheşĭ, ghése; (*reddish-brown*) cul, -lǎ, cuľ, cúle; (*as of clouds*) misu-aróş; *Gop:* (*of apples*) acărsát
REDEEM *vb.* ▾discúmpǎr (*and* discúmbǎr), discúmpru, discúmpur; a-scáp, ľişurédz, ▾ľértu
REDEMPTION *s.* discumpǎráre (*and* -cumbǎ-)
REDHAIRED *adj.* arús → REDDISH ‖ *Peş:* cǎstǎñác, CL 41
RED-HANDED *adj.* **He was caught ~** ≈ Lu-acǎţǎră tu-ayíñe (*lit. 'they caught him in the vineyard'*)
REDHEADED *adj.* (*as of sheep*) ròşuchéfal
REDNESS *s.* aruşitúrǎ
REDOLENT *adj.* ñurzitór, -oáre; ñurzimós, -oásǎ
REDOUBT *s. mil.* (*fortification*) tábye, tǎbyíe
REDOUBTABLE *adj.* fuvirós, -oásǎ; lǎhtǎrós, -oásǎ
REDRESS *s.* (*compensation, reparation*) plátǎ
REDRESS *vb.* ▾ndreg, ▾ndriptédz; (*of health*) ▾víndic → RECOVER; (*to pay back*) ▾tórnu, plǎtéscu
REDRESSING *s.* ndriptáre
REDUCE *vb.* ▾şcurtédz; **to ~ by half** ▾ngiumitichédz
REDUCED TO *adj.* cǎtǎndisít

REDUCTION *s.* ñicşuráre → LESSENING

REED *s.* (a)rugóz, arâgóz, răgóz, arugóş, căláme, şuvár, stuf, tréscă, trâscă

REED-MACE *s. bot.* (*cattail*) vuľár

REEK *s.* putoáre, (a)mbutoáre, voáhă, vrómă

REEK *vb.* ▼(a)mpút (*and* ambút), ampuţắscu

REEKY *adj.* ambuţós, -oásă

REEL *s.* (*for winding*) caléme → SKEIN-WINDER; MAKE SMB.'S BRAIN ~

REEL *vb.* (*to behave in a violent disorderly manner, usu. of animals*) vârléscu

REELING *s.* (*dizziness*) andrălăsíre

REELING OFF *s.* dipănáre, dipinătúră

REFINED *adj.* (*as of a fabric*) minút, supţáre, fin

REFINEMENT *s.* micáme

REFLECT *vb.* (*as of a mirror*) ▼yilicéscu, ▼nyilicéscu; (*to think*) → PONDER

REFLECTION *s.* (*meditation*) arumigáre

REFRACTORY *adj.* (*of people*) → RECALCITRANT

REFRAIN *vb.* ▼căpistruéscu, ▼căpistruséscu, ▼stăpuéscu, ▼ţân; **Let us ~ from sins** S-nă stăpuím di amărtii ‖ CUNIA 285: mi azăptăséscu

REFRESH *vb.* ▼avrédz, avréscu, ▼ncucutédz; **The wind ~ed them** Vímtul li ncucutắ

REFRESHED *adj.* avrát

REFRESHING *s.* avráre

REFRESHING *adj.* avrós, -oásă

REFUGE *s.* apánghiu → SHELTER, TAKE ~

REFUND *vb.* tórnu, plătéscu, păltéscu

REFUSAL *s.* incheáre

REFUSE *s.* (*from ravelling*) strămătúră

REFUSE *vb.* fac incheáre → DECLINE

REGAIN ONE'S SELF-CONTROL *vb.* ñ-yin tu orĭ → RECOVER

REGALE *vb.* (*to treat*) ▼filipséscu, uspitédz; (*to give a feast for smb.*) ľ-astérnu tavérnă

REGARD *s.* (*consideration*) hătâre; (*greetings*) **Give him** (*her, them*) **my ~s!** múltă sileáme la...; (múlti) ncľinăciúñ la...

REGARD *vb.* ▼(a)númir; (*to consider*) am ca; (*to take into con-*

sideration) fac mále; (*to set down as*) ľau ti

REGIMEN *s. med.* (*diet*) dhiétă, piríze

REGION *s.* loc; **in our ~** tu ļoclu a nóstru; náie; (*district, in former Turkey*) vilaéte, viléte

REGISTER *s.* cárte; **They recorded all of us in the ~** Pri tuţ nă tricúră tu cárte; catáloy, catástih, chitápe, chiutúc, chiutche, cóndică, tiftére, dhiftére

REGISTER *vb.* trec tu cárte

REGISTRAR *s.* (*clerk in a court*) chitíb

REGISTRATION *s.* cătăyrăfíe

REGRESS *vb.* ▾scad

REGRET *s.* caimó, ghiúce, miráche

REGRET *vb.* ñ-páre arău; (*to ~ bitterly or angrily*) ñ-múşcu mâñle (*lit.* 'to bite one's hands') → BE SORRY

REGULARLY *adv.* tahticá

REGULATE *vb.* (*to put in good order*) ▾arădhyipséscu, ▾arădhăp-séscu; (*to adjust*) ţivicuséscu

REIGN *s.* dumñíľe

REIGN *vb.* amirăripséscu, dumnéscu, văsilipséscu

REIMBURSE *vb.* ▾tórnu, ▾plătéscu, ▾păltéscu

REINFORCE *vb.* ▾nvârtuşédz → STRENGTHEN

REINS *s.* ‖ dizghíni, GOLAB 212

REJECT *vb.* (*with disdain*) ▾arúc; dau cu ciórlu

REJOICE *vb.* (*rare*) ▾mbúcur; *also:* ▾arăzbún, arăzbunédz, ▾hă-riséscu, hărséscu; ñ-páre ghíne; nu mi ţâne lóclu di haráuă ‖ créscu nă pálmă di haráuă, BASME 88; mi úmplu di haráo, BASME 75; ñ-yíne ca ghíne, BASME 100; DIARO 154: nu lu-ncáp stráñili di ha-ráuâ; 155: ľi-arâdi ínima di haráuâ

REJOICING *s.* hărisíre, hărsíre, hărăcupíľe

REJUVENATE *vb.* ntiniréscu, ntinirédz, scot peáne

REJUVENATION *s.* ntiniráre

RELATE *vb.* ambáir → TELL

RELATED *adj.* (*by blood or affinity*) sóie, (ú)nă sóie

RELATIONS *s.* (*relationship*) cioáră; **to break ~ with** u-arúp cioára (cu), u-táľu cioára (cu) ‖ (*good ~ with*) caliméra *invar.*

RELATIONSHIP *s.* shési, *pl* shesi; cioáră; (*contact*) (a)misticáre

RELATIVE *s.* (*by blood*) di un sândze; físe, plázmă, sóie, *G:* cârdu ‖ **close ~** sóe di cama-aproápea, BASME 432

RELAX

RELAX *vb.* ▾arăpás, arăpăsédz, arăpăséscu, aripás; *also:* apăn-ghiséscu, dispustuséscu; (*as of a muscle*) ▾distríngu → REST

RELAXATION *s.* dispustusíre, disvursíre, răpás

RELAXED *adj.* (*soft, mild*) mólav, *m pl* mólavĭ (*sic*); prăhár; (*loosened*) hábin; (*as after a good sleep*) arăpăsát, arăpăsít, dispustusít, disvursít ‖ CUVATA 2 (*quiet, not worried*) sărăsít

RELAXING *adj.* (*as of a place*) arihătós, -oásă

RELAY *s.* curcuşór

RELY *vb.* mi ncred, am ambithár

RELEASE *s.* elefthirusíre, sălăghíre, scăpáre; (*relief, discharge*) lişuráre; aurláre, *F:* aurráre

RELEASE *vb.* (*to set free, to let go*) ▾apulséscu, ▾elefthiriséscu; dau cále; ▾sărgléscu, sâlghéscu; **He used to ~ us at nightfall** Nă dădeá cále tu ntunicátă; (*to ~ a belt*) ▾distíngu

RELEASED *adj.* (*free, as of horses*) sălăghít

RELEGATE *vb.* ▾suryiunipséscu

RELEGATION *s.* (*exile*) suryiúne

RELENT *vb.* cătăprăéscu → SLACKEN, SLOW DOWN

RELENTLESS *adj.* únă-únă; zâr-zâr

RELIABLE *adj.* besalâ, saylám, saylámcu, sáicu, síyur, siyuripsít; **~ person** amanecí ‖ CUNIA 147: om di sănădíi

RELIANCE *s.* mbithár

RELICS *s.* (*of a saint*) moáşte *f pl*

RELIEF *s.* agălisíre, ifculipsíre, lişuráre, işuráme, oáră; **I am not giving him ~** Nu-ĺ dau oáră

RELIEVE *vb.* ▾discárcu, lişurédz; **to ~ smb.'s wants** (*to assist, to help*) yin indáte, yin agiutór

RELIEVED *adj.* avrát ‖ **they felt ~** lă viníră ípatli, CUVATA 8

RELIGION *s.* thrischíe → FAITH

RELIGIOUS *adj.* ivlaviós, -oásă

RELINQUISH *vb.* pára-dau, trag mână di → GIVE UP, RENOUNCE

RELOCATE *vb.* ▾mut

RELUCTANCE → AFFECT ~

RELUCTANTLY *adv.* di pristanéu ‖ fără ínimă → AGAINST

RELY ON FOR SUPPORT *vb.* ▾acúmtin, ▾apún, arádzim, arádzâm

REMAIN *vb.* (a)rămân, armân (→ § *32*); **to ~ agápe** lu háscu, u háscu; **to ~ all alone** rămân ca cucuveáua; **to ~ somewhere until dawn** ápir; **to ~ under an obligation to smb.** ▾ndăturédz ‖ **to ~**

agápe armân cu gúra căscátă, BASME 93

REMAINDER *s.* (*remnants*) (a)réstu, armăsătúră

REMAINS *s.* (*of the dead*) oáse *pl*; (*of a saint*) lipsán, lipsáná; moáşte *f pl*

REMAKE *vb.* pri-adár

REMARK *vb.* (*to notice, to make a remark*) ▼părătirséscu; (*to set one's heart on smth. /smb.*) bag tu ócľu

REMARKABLE *adj.* nişanlâ ‖ CUNIA 258: nişanlítcu

REMARRIED: (*a woman whose former husband has remarried*) símbră; (*a man whose former wife has remarried*) símbru

REMARRY *vb.* ñ-bag lắĭle adoáră

REMEDY *s.* cearé, **N**: cearée; dirmáne, ileáce, treácăt, vindicáre

REMEMBER *vb.* ñ-adúc amínte; *also*: (a)cuitéscu, ▼cuituéscu, ▼aduchéscu, ▼anăfirséscu, ▼thimiséscu, simiséscu; **God ~ed and did not forget me** şi-cuituí Dumnidză şi nu mi lăsắ; **~ to buy salt!** Aducheá-te si acúmpări sáre! **to ~ smb. to smb.** (*to greet*) dau hiritímate, dzâc (múlte) ncľinăciúñ la, hiritiséscu ‖ LITURG 123: acuitím *1 pl*

REMEMBERED *adj.* (*unforgotten*) ni-agărşít, thim(i)sít

REMEMBERING *s.* aburáre

REMEMBRANCE *s.* adúţire amínte, aduţeáre amínte, suviníre, thimisíre, simisíre, ticăíre

REMIND *vb.* adúc amínte, ▼aburédz; **~ him what I've told you!** Abureádză-ľ ţe ţâ dzâş; ▼thimiséscu, thimséscu, simiséscu

REMISS *adj.* alăsát → NEGLIGENT

REMISSION OF SINS *s.* (*forgiveness*) ľirtáre

REMIT *vb.* (*to pardon*) ľértu; (*to give or gain relief*) ľişurédz; (*to send*) pitréc

REMNANTS *s.* (a)réstu, armăsătúră

REMODEL *vb.* prifác, priadár [pri•a•]

REMORSE *s.* săráche, scrop, tunusíre; **to be gnawed by ~** mi mácă siráchea → REPENT

REMOTE *adj.* dipărtát, dipărtós

REMOTENESS *s.* dipărtáre (*and* dipâr-)

REMOVAL *s.* mutáre, mtáre

REMOVE *s.* dipărtáre, dipărtátic

REMOVE *vb.* ▼mut, scot; (*as a nail from a board, a board from a*

REMUNERATE

fence, etc.) ▾discărfuséscu, discărfi-, scărfuséscu; (*to cross out, to eliminate, as from a list*) fac arisíte

REMUNERATE *vb.* ▾plătéscu, ▾păltéscu

REMUNERATION *s.* plátă

RENCOUNTER *s.* (*casual meeting*) astăl̆áre, astăl̆itúră

REND *vb.* ▾disíc, ▾dizgl̆ín, dijgl̆ín; **to ~ one's hair** (*to tear out*) ñ-deápir péril̆i din cap

RENDER *vb.* ▾dau, ▾fac; **to ~ a blow** zdângânéscu úna; (*to melt down, as fat, hooves*) ▾tuchéscu; (*to translate*) ▾xiyiséscu

RENDER JUSTICE *vb.* dau driptáte

RENEGADE *s.* prudhót

RENEW *vb.* ▾znuéscu

RENNET *s.* (*part of an animal's stomach used in curdling milk*) arândză, cl̆ag, piteáuă, *G:* zaciu

RENNET *s. bot.* (*galium mollugo*) sărgúce, sârguríce, sândzeáná

RENOUNCE *vb.* ▾aleápid; trag mână (di) → ABNEGATE, GIVE UP

RENOUNCEMENT *s.* ‖ trádzire di mână, CAPIDAN 175

RENOWN *s.* (a)námă, anáme, númă, fáná, măríl̆e

RENOWNED *adj.* cu númă → FAMOUS

RENT *s.* (*split*) dizgl̆ináre, dij-, arupeáre, arúpire

RENT *s.* (*let*) niche, chéră, chiră; (*~ of a horse-drawn vehicle*) ayóye, lăsáre

RENT *vb.* (*as to ~ horses*) ayuyipséscu

REPAIR *vb.* ▾ndreg → MEND

REPAIRED *adj.* nd(i)réptu, *f* nd(i)reáptă, *m pl* nd(i)réptâ, *f pl* nd(i)reápte; ndres, *f* ndreásă, *m pl* ndreșĭ, *f pl* ndreáse; mirimi- tisít; (*of clothes*) mpiticát

REPARATION *s.* ndreádzire, ndridzeáre, mириméte, -mitisíre; (*of clothes*) mpiticáre; (*compensation*) plátă

REPAST *s.* (*meal*) mcáre, ngáre, ngustáre

REPAY *vb.* ▾plătéscu, ▾păltéscu; **to ~ in full** (*of a debt*) mi l̆au di bórge; **to ~ a kindness** ▾discúmpăr buneáţa

REPEAT *vb.* (*to do once more*) dhifturséscu

REPEL *vb.* agunéscu, *N:* azgunéscu

REPENT *vb.* ▾mâşcu, fac pişmáne, ▾mităñuséscu, ▾pişmănipséscu, ▾ăñuséscu, tuniséscu (*and* tuñi-, tunu-); (*to feel remorse*) mi mâcă săráchea → QUALMS, REMORSE

REPENTANCE *s.* tunusíre, tuñi-, tăñi-, mităñusíre, pişmănipsíre, canóne, canónă

REPENTANT *adj.* pişmănipsít → PENITENT

REPINE *vb.* *(to lament, to mourn)* ▾buţéscu, miryĭuluxéscu, ▾plấngu, ▾părăpuñiséscu

REPLETE *adj.* bólcu, -lcă, -lţi, -lţe; (m)plin, *m pl* -ñ

REPLETION *s.* *(usu. of food)* sat, sátru, săturáre, suturáre, sătuleáţă; *(affluence)* birichéte

REPLY *s.* apándise → ANSWER

REPLY *vb.* ĺ-u tórnu; *F:* torru ‖ BATSARIA 102: tórnu zbórlu

REPORT *s.* *(account)* tăcráre, tăcríre; *(of a gun)* plăscăníre, plâscănáme, tuficheáuă, tufichileáuă

REPORT *vb.* *(to present oneself)* cupăséscu; **in order to ~ to the palace** s-cupăseáscă pấnă la pălăte; *(to make a charge of misconduct against)* ▾plấngu; *(to make known)* dau tu şteáre

REPOSE *s.* arăpás → REST, SILENCE

REPREHENSIVE *adj.* ftixít

REPRESENT *vb.* ▾părăstăséscu, părăstiséscu

REPRESENTATIVE *s.* *(agent)* vichíle *m*, vichíĺu *m*

REPRESS *vb.* *(anger, a cough, a smile)* ▾cúrmu, ▾ţân; fac azápe

REPRESSION *s.* curmáre, (a)zápe

REPRIEVE *vb.* *(to give temporary relief to)* dau oáră

REPRIMAND *s.* zăvráche → SCOLDING

REPRIMAND *vb.* trag únă zăvráche, dau un zbárdhu; *(to chide)* ▾anăcréscu, ▾yumărséscu, ▾para-ĺau ‖ DIARO 231: giúdic; bag dinăpói

REPROACH *s.* ‖ *F:* romuză, HRISTU 69 (cf. Alb. *romúz* 'pointes, allusion, insinuation, sous-entendu,' COCONA 447)

REPROACH *vb.* ▾cătiyurséscu, ▾ncucutédz

REPROBATE *s.* cătúnă

REPRODUCTION *s.* *(of animals)* dămăzlấche, dumu-

REPROOF *s.* zăvráche → SCOLDING

REPROVE *vb.* → REPROACH

REPUDIATE *vb.* arniséscu → DENY

REPUGNANCE *s.* lăíĺe

REPUGNANT *adj.* ODIOUS

REPULSION *s.* yunós → DISGUST

REPULSIVE *adj* cătráne *invar.* **This is ~** *to me* Cătráne ñ-si páre

REPURCHASE *s.* căpităníĺe, xayuráuă, ayuráuă

REPUTABLE *adj*. cu anămúze

REPUTE *s*. ihtibáre, númă

REPUTATION *s*. númă

REPUTED *adj*. cu anúmă, alvdát, avdzât

REQUEST *s*. dimândáre, dimândátă, dimândăciúne; **at ~** pi dimân-dát; *also*: arigé, căftáre, pălăcáríe, părăcălíe, pricădeáre, tim-bíhe, timbíe, țireáre, țeárire, zítimă

REQUEST *vb*. ▾cáftu, dimândédz ‖ *Codex Dim. only*: țer, CAPIDAN 153

REQUIEM *s*. (*after 40 days*) sărindár, sărăndáre

REQUIRE *vb*. ▾cáftu; **Fried chestnuts ~ wine** Căstâñle frípte cáftă yin (*i.e., they are good with wine*)

REQUISITION *s*. angăríe

RESCUE *s*. (a)scăpáre

RESCUE *vb*. (a)scáp

RESEMBLANCE *s*. adúcă → SIMILARITY

RESEMBLE *vb*. ▾(a)undzéscu, ▾uidiséscu, adúc pri, ñ-u adúc pri; **He ~ed a bear more than a man** Ma múltu pri úrsă și-u aduțeá ca di pri om ‖ **He ~ed his father** L-aundzeá a tátă-sui, BASME 488

RESENT *vb*. ñi-ngreácă, ľ-țân cáche

RESENTMENT *s*. cărtíre, cărteáre

RESERVATION *s*. (*out of shame, fear, suspicion*) ticlífe

RESERVE *s*. *mil*. (*not full-time soldier*) ridífe

RESERVE *vb*. urséscu; *also*: numățéscu, prăxéscu; **He ~s me the worse fate** Ñ-prăxeáște cáma láia

RESERVED *adj*. (*of people*) ascúmtu, *m pl* -mță, *f pl* -mte; tăcút

RESERVOIR *s*. (*for water*) ‖ stérnă, BASME 414

RESIDE *vb*. armân, șed, bănédz

RESIDENCE *s*. (*domicile*) ≈ cásă

RESIDUE *s*. săbúră, săvúră; armăsătúră, réstu; (*~ of melted butter*) dráică

RESIGNATION *s*. (*deliberate renouncement*) parétise

RESIGN ALL HOPES *vb*. ñ-ľau curátile; *2 sg imper*. S-ță ľai curátile! *or* Ľa-ț curátile! → GIVE UP HOPING

RESIGNED *adj*. (*one who has given up*) arăvdătór, toáre

RESIN *s*. rițínă, arușínă, *G*: arucínă

RESIST *vb*. (*to stand, to endure*) ▾arávdu; (*to oppose, to obstruct*) fac cărșiláche, cărșilătiséscu; (*to make a stand*

against) dân(d)âséscu

RESISTANCE *s.* (*opposition, unwillingness*) cărşilâche; stricătoáre → PUT UP ~

RESOLUTE *adj.* apufăsít, dâldâsít, ligát → FIRM

RESOLVE *s.* → MAKE A ~ TO DO SMTH.

RESOLVED *adj.* → RESOLUTE

RESONANCE *s.* arăsunáre, arusunáre, avdzâtă

RESORT TO SLYNESS *vb.* (*to use psychology on smb.*) bag pi plan, ľau cu aplánlu

RESOUND *vb.* arăsún, arusún, ▾huhutéscu; **the valleys and the hills are ~ing** văľuri, pláiuri huhutéscu; (*of a rifle*) plăscănéscu; (*of bells*) ▾bat

RESOUNDING *adj.* asunătór, -oáre; (*a kiss, a slap, a pie with crust, etc.*) cârţănós, -oásă; **a ~ slap** nă báţă cârţănoásă

RESOURCEFUL *adj.* **The boy is ~** (*has an inventive mind*) âľ ľa caplu a ficiórlui, DIARO 174

RESPECT *s.* (*esteem*) htibáre, treácă; **to be held in ~** am htibáre

RESPECT *vb.* ▾tiñiséscu ‖ DIARO 390: câtândiséscu; **I have a good** (*respectful*) **daughter-in-law**: Am nórâ búnâ, nu-ñ dzâţi fă-ti mancló, DIARO 247

RESPECTABLE *adj.* tiñisít

RESPECTED *adj.* tiñisít; ca núnlu la númtă (*lit.* 'like the best man at a wedding')

RESPIRATION *s.* (*breathing*) anásă, sulúche

RESPITE *s.* aryíe, oáră, ripás, lişuráre

RESPLENDENT *adj.* (*as of a beautiful woman*) grindinát

RESPOND *vb.* → ANSWER

RESPONSE *s.* → ANSWER

RESPONSIBILITY: → TAKE ALL ~

RESPONSIBLE *adj.* (*reliable*) di bésă; aştirnút

REST *s.* (a)răpás, (a)răpăsáre, ripás, rupás, (a)riháte, arihătipsíre, discurmáre, dispustusíre; (*of sheep resting on hot afternoons*) amirizáre ‖ HRISTU 30: zdicurmari (*sic*)

REST *vb.* ▾arăpás, aripás, arupás, (a)răpăsédz, (a)răpăséscu, rupusédz, mi discúrmu, ▾dispustuséscu, ▾disvurséscu, dizvurséscu, ▾apănghiséscu; (*to calm down*) ▾arihătipséscu, arăhătipscu; (*to stop, to halt*) mi stăpuéscu; **The ark ~ed upon the mountain of Ararat** Cáticlu si stăpuí tru lóclu ţi s-cľámă Ararát; (*to rely* *for support*) ▼acúmtin, ▼apún, ▼arádzim, arádzâm; (*of people, after lunch*) prândzắscu; (*of sheep*) amirídz, añirídz ‖ HRISTU 19: mi zdicurmu

RESTED *adj.* (*ant.* TIRED) şidzút

REST ROOM *s.* hríe → TOILET

RESTING PLACE *s.* mas; (*of sheep*) (a)mirídz

RESTIVE *adj.* naprán, *G:* ciórnic

RESTLESS *adj.* (*fidgety*) ni-mpáde, pirídhrum

RESTORE *vb.* (*to return*) dau nắpói; (*of health*) nturturédz → RECOVER; (*to rejuvenate*) scot peáne ‖ PC: (*to put back into use*) bag nắpói

RESTORED *adj. med. and fig.* (*recovered*) mprustát, ngiulnát, turnát

RESTRAIN *vb.* ▼ţân; **to ~ one's astonishment** ñ-ţân apuría; cắpistruéscu; **to ~ oneself** ▼apreadún, apreaddún; **~ yourself!** Apreadúnắ-te! → BRIDLE

RESTRAINED *adj.* aştirnút, stắpuít

RESTRAINT *s.* (*moderation*) usúle, stắpuíre

RESTRICTION *s.* apreaadunáre, aptraadunắtúrắ, piriorizmó → LIMITATION

RESULT *s.* catórthose ‖ MERCA 19: (*beneficial effect, fruit*) siliméti *f*; PC: i(n)şítă

RESULT *vb.* ies, es, *aor.* i(n)şíi *or* i(n)şái, *part.* i(n)şít *or* i(n)şát

RESUME *vb.* (*as a conversation*) anắfirséscu

RESURGE *vb.* ▼scol

RESURGENCE *s.* sculáre

RESURRECT *vb.* (a)nắstắséscu, nyiédz, anyédz, anghédz; âmbắnédz (DDA: 688, bookish word)

RESURRECTED *adj.* (a)nắstắsít, anyeát, angheát

RESURRECTION *s.* anástase, nắstắsíre, angheáre, anyeáre, anyiáre; **They went to the ~ mass** S-dúsiră la Anástasi

RETAIL *vb.* (*to sell*) víndu

RETAIN *vb.* (*to keep, to hold*) ţân; (*to hire*) ľau; (*to keep in mind*) bag tu cufíţă

RETALIATE *vb.* → REVENGE

RETALIATION *s.* plátă, turnắtúră

RETARD *vb.* (*to delay, to slow*) ▼şintéscu, ▼ţân, ▼stắpuéscu

RETARDATION *s.* şintíre

RETARDED *adj.* ≈ nitót, *f* -toátă, *m pl* -tóţ, *f pl* -toáte

RETCH *vb.* (*to try to vomit*) bruzgăéscu

RETICENT *adj.* tăcút; ascúmtu, -mtă, -mţi, -mte

RETINUE *s.* táifă, tăcâme, tava(m)bíe ‖ CUNIA 294: ciumbuléche

RETIRE *vb.* ▾apún

RETIRING *adj.* → SHY, HUMBLE

RETRACT *vb.* (*take back, as a promise*) ñ-ľau zbórlu

RETREAT *s.* năpuíre, opistohórise, pistuhórise

RETREAT *vb.* mi frângu năpói, mi trag năpói, ▾năpuéscu; (*to ~ into one's den, hole, of animals*) ▾nguvédz → BACK UP

RETRENCH *vb.* ▾şcurtédz → SHORTEN

RETRENCHMENT *s. mil.* tábye

RETRIAL *s.* prigiudicátă → MAKE A ~

RETRIBUTION *s.* plátă

RETURN *s.* turnáre, turnátă, turnătúră, năpuíre

RETURN *vb.* ▾tórnu, ▾năpuéscu, yin năpói ‖ CUVATA 4: **I returned home** Mi turnái acásă

REVAMP *vb.* priadár [pri•a•], mirimiţéscu, mirimitiséscu

REVEAL *vb.* ▾discoápir, ▾dizvăléscu; (*to divulge*) dau pri toácă

REVEL *s.* (*wild party, celebration*) băiráme

REVEL *vb.* u-fác uzungióva

REVELER *s.* ‖ STERE 30: giumbuşlí

REVENGE *s.* áhte, arăzgán, arăzgănáre; sândze (*lit. 'blood'*); **out of ~** trâ pícă

REVENGE *vb.* → AVENGE; (*to be followed by the idea of taking revenge*) mi avínă sândzile

REVENGEFUL *adj.* irişárcu, -rcă, -rţi, -rţe

REVENUE *s.* (a)iráte

REVENUE OFFICE *s.* muhtărlíche

REVERE *vb.* tiñiséscu

REVERSAL *s.* disfáre, disfáţire

REVERSE *vb.* ▾tórnu, ▾arăstórnu, alăstórnu, arustórnu

REVERSED *adj.* (*upside-down, topsy-turvy*) darmadán

REVILE *vb.* (*to vituperate*) → ABUSE

REVIVE *vb.* (*to become flourishing again*) scot peána; (*to come back to life*) ▾ncucutédz

REVOLT *s.* mintireáje

REVOLUTION *s.* panástase

REVOLUTIONER *s.* cumitagí

REVOLVE *vb.* (*to spin*) ▾anvǎrtéscu

REVOLVER *s.* altípatlar → HANDGUN

REWARD *s.* mândílǎ, mujdé, mujdée, muştináre; (*repurchase, re-demtion*) (a)xayuráuǎ; (*benefit, satisfaction*) scuteáre

REWARD *vb.* mǎştinédz, muştinédz, discúmpǎr

REWARDING *adj.* **Is this ~?** Ári scuteáre? (*lit. 'Does it have profit?'*)

RHEUMY-EYED *adj.* ţǎlpós, -oásǎ

RHUBARB *s. bot.* rǎvénti

RIB *s.* coástǎ, *dim.* custícǎ

RIB *vb.* (*to tease, to make fun of*) → RIDICULE

RIBALD *adj.* dişuţât

RIBBON *s.* curdheáuǎ, curdhélǎ, *dim.* curdheláche; ciupáre; **Amc:** (*a ~ used to adorn the fez of the bride and groom*) lipiscánǎ

RICE *s.* uríz, aríz

RICH *adj.* avút; *also:* árhundu, *m pl* -ndzâ; arhundǎ, (m)bugát, bucát, cáldu, *m pl* -ldzâ, *f pl* -lde; greu, *f* greáuǎ, *m pl* grei, *f pl* greále; nicuchír, prucupsít, ţinghín, zinghín; **very ~** pri-a-vút, avút arúptu; greu nicuchír (*lit. 'heavy master'*); u-ári gǎ-ľína aţeá láia sǎnǎtoásǎ (*lit. 'his black hen is healthy,' i.e. his purse is full*); **He is ~** Ári cľag (*lit. 'He has yeast'*), Ari seu (*lit. 'He has fat'*), Ari midúuǎ (*lit. 'He has brains'*); U-ári coáda groásǎ (*lit. 'His tail is thick'*) → BECOME ~, MAKE ~ ‖ **Cru:** ambugát, GOLAB 198; **Kok, Smx, Vil,** *etc.* plusiu, B-ARCH 395

RICHES *s.* aveáre, máltǎ

RICK *s.* (*as of hay*) cópǎ, cǎpíţǎ, cupíţǎ ‖ **GSus:** cuculíş, CL 42; **Prv:** cúpâ, CL 44

RICKETY *adj.* (*shaky, unsound*) hárval → RAMSHACKLE

RID *vb.* ascáp (di), ▾discárcu (di)

RIDDLE *s.* angucitoáre, angľicitoáre, cucitoáre, ţiñitúrǎ; **Guess my ~** Angucíţ angucitoárea a meá ‖ **Gra, Pros,** *etc.* éniyma, B-ARCH 481

RIDDLE *s.* (*coarse sieve*) ţir, dirmóñiu

RIDE *vb.* trec, mi duc (pri *or* cu), ímnu (pri *or* cu), ▾priímnu (pri *or* cu); **to ~ one's high horse** ímnu daí, li ngroş hǎbǎrile, ▾ncucutédz, trag bózǎ máre

RIDER *s.* cavalará, sufarí, suvarí

RIDGE *s.* (*mountain*) areáhǎ, réhǎ, crástǎ, schinǎrát di múnte

RIDICULE *s.* mǎscǎlídhǎ, mâscârǎ, pézǎ, rizíle, şúpir; (*a laughing-stock*) mâscâroáñea a lúmiľei

RIDICULE *vb.* ▾arâd di, ▾buiséscu, ▾pizuéscu, mpizuéscu (*and* mbi-), ▾mâscâripséscu; moľu tu noauǎdzǎţi noáuǎ di buéi (*lit.* 'to dip smb. into ninety-nine paints'), rizil(ips)éscu, schin, şúpǎr, şupǎrédz, şúpir, şupirédz, şupurédz; **They began to ~ him** Acǎţǎrǎ s lu şúpǎrǎ; **to be a target/subject of ~** hiu tu şúpur ‖ ñ-bat pézǎ (di), BASME 73; ALR 1634: fac háze (di)

RIDICULED *adj.* pizuít, mbizuít

RIDICULOUS *adj.* → MAKE ONESELF ~

RIDING *s.* ampǎturáre, âmpǎturáre, âmpǎtuláre

RIDING *adj.* (*of horses and mules*) binéche, *pl* binéechi

RIDING WHIP *s.* vúrdhal

RIFLE *s.* tuféche, tféche; *also:* carabínǎ, carofílǎ, carupílǎ, dugrǎ, grǎ, martínǎ, sináuer, şişáne; *iron.* leánga; (*metaphorically*) daiľánǎ (*lit.* 'gorgeous') ‖ HRISTU 64: dufechi

RIFLE *vb.* (*to ransack and steal*) guzgunipséscu

RIFT *s.* crǎpǎtúrǎ, cripǎtúrǎ

RIG *vb.* (*of prices*) ▾scunchéscu, scunghéscu, artiriséscu, artirséscu, atǎrdiséscu; **They ~ed the price of grain** yípturile li-artirsírǎ

RIGGED (OUT) *adj.* (*equipped, decked out*) tǎcmǎlát

RIGHT *s. Str:* ndréptu → PUT ONESELF TO ~S

RIGHT *adj.* ndréptu ‖ BATSARIA 57: **You are ~** Ndréptu greáşti

RIGHT *adv.* (*exactly, precisely*) análtu; **~ now** úti tóra; méti, mídhi; únǎşunǎ; **~ after** únǎşunǎ dúpǎ; **to the ~** (a)ndreápta, nandreápta, nǎndreápta (*ant.* astânga, nastânga); **~ away** cât cáma tr-oárǎ; *N:* ayiú; ta-úna; ni únǎ ni áltǎ; **~ round** varlíga di varlíga → ALL ~, BE ~, DEEM IT ~ TO

RIGHT-HAND *s.* andreápta; **on the ~ side** *adv.* andreápta

RIGHT-HANDED *s., adj.* dripţáciu, ndripţáciu (*ant.* stângáciu)

RIGHTEOUS *adj. 3 sg:* ímnǎ cu zíya n brân (*lit.* 'walks with a scale at his belt,' *i.e. is always ready to impart justice*)

RIGHTEOUSNESS *s.* driptáte, driptáticǎ

RIGHTFUL *adj.* andréptu, *f* -eáptǎ, *m pl* -épţâ, *f pl* -eápte

RIGHTLY *adv.* andréptu

RIGHTWARDS *adv.* → RIGHT

RIGID *adj.* (*harsh, stern*) ni-apuadús, ni-apudús; (*stiff, as of a frozen body or limb*) cóţâ, córcan

RIGOR *s.* ascuráme

RIGOROUS *adj.* sértic; streṣ, -eásă, streṣĭ, -eáse

RILE *vb.* ▾guṣtirédz → VEX

RILL *s.* víe, avláchiu

RIM *s.* márdzină, márdzine; (*as the hem of a skirt*) yirlándă

RIME *s.* brúmă → HOARFROST

RIND *s.* coáje, coáră, flúdhă → HUSK, HULL, SHELL

RING *s.* (a)nél; **engagement** ~ arăvóne, arvoánă; (*at the end of a chain or rope*) cârcheálă, cârcheáuă, cârchéľu; vărăgúce, vărăgúciu, vărăgúţ; (*circle*) ţércľu ‖ HRISTU 9: **a golden** ~ un nel di flurii → PUT ON THE RING

RING *vb.* (a)sún; (*of bells*) ▾bat; **to~ the peal** dau cămbána; **to ~ the bells** cămbănédz

RING-BOLT *s.* (*of a steelyard*) sérghe

RINGDOVE *s.* gugúce → STOCK-DOVE

RINGING *s.* (*as of the bells of a church*) băteáre

RINGLEADER *s.* cap, căpíe, tăpár

RINGLET *s.* nel, *dim.* nilúṣ

RINSE *vb.* cļătéscu, clucutéscu (tu ápă), culcutéscu, trec tu ápă, ▾nyiurédz

RIOT *s.* sculáre

RIOT *vb.* ▾(a)scól

RIP *vb.* ▾disíc, crep

RIP OFF *vb.* ▾ancálţu, árdu, biléscu

RIP UP *vb.* arúp → TEAR

RIPE *adj.* cóptu, coáptă, cópţâ, coápte; agiúmtu *or* agiúmsu; asít, mătúr; (*overripe, as of pears*) juľu, para-agiúmtu

RIPEN *vb.* ▾coc, ▾agúngu, ▾aséscu, ▾fac ‖ ALIA 39: *3 sg:* s-coáţi, s-fáţi, s-adáră, scoáti, agiúndze, adzúndze, căréṣte, adúnă, z mătură

RIPENING *s.* coáţire, cuţeáre, agiúndzire, agiundzeáre

RIPPING OFF *s.* (*as a crust of bread*) dizguľáre, disguľíre; (*of skin and fig.*) biľíre

RIP-OFF *s.* (*robbery*) biľíre

RISE *s.* (*as of the sun*) apreásă, preásă; arsăríre, ansăríre;

(*the act of rising; ascent*) sculáre, sculátă; (*of prices*) scun-chíre

RISE *vb.* (*of stars*) arsár, dau, ies, ▼zvom; (*as of prices, of boiling milk, etc.*) ▼alín; (*to get up*) ▼mbróstu, ▼scol; **to ~ with the lark** (*to get up early*) ▼scol cu noáptea n cap; (*to take up arms*) ▼scol cap; (*of seeds and buds*) arăsár, arsár, alsár, ansár; (*to originate, as of rivers*) ▼vom; **to ~ up and flow forth** azvu-răscu; (*to ~ from the dead*) anghédz, ghiéz; **Christ has risen!** Hristólu anyé! **to ~ in rebellion** ▼scol panástase, u scol pandéra ‖ CUVATA 29: (*to stand up*) mi mut ămpróstu; DIARO 311: **the dough has risen** aloátlu viní (*or* criscú)

RISING *s.* sculáre

RISK *s.* cíndhin, perícľu, perícul; **at a ~** tu tíhe

RISK *vb.* dăldăséscu, dăldiséscu, dăvrănséscu; **I'll ~ it!** ≈ To tíhe!

RISKY *adj.* (*a job, a disease*) greu, greáuă, grei, greále

RITE *s.* (*division of Christian church*) thrischíe

RIVAL *vb.* ▼sinirséscu

RIVALRY: in eager ~ ≈ cari di cari; ntriţeáre

RIVER *s.* arău → RIVULET ‖ ALIA 23: rău, rreu, reu máre, ru, arú, arúu, arúuă, aréchi [a•rék'], vále

RIVERBANK *s.* mal, mázdă

RIVERBED *s.* ‖ *Prv, SJos:* putămíe, CL 260

RIVERSIDE *s.* mal

RIVET *vb.* ▼ncărfuséscu; **to ~ one's eyes on** mi si alăchéscu ócľiľ (di)

RIVETED *adj.* (*of eyes*) pirunsít

RIVULET *s.* (*small stream*) víe, avláchiu, puvóñu ‖ *Cot, Fal, Kok, Paleoh:* vále; *Cľis, Mal:* váli, *Cot:* valícă; *Cern, Flam:* váli ñícă; *Grăm, Nij, Rod, Trn:* rău; *Src:* râu; *Grbţ, Prv:* arău; *Gra:* reu; *Căl:* ñícă aréchi; *Ses:* trap, *Vot:* trap$_u$, *Pur:* trápu; *Lep:* ápă, B-ARCH 22

ROACH *s. ichth.* plătícă; **as sound as a ~** sănătos ca grij di dzádă ‖ sânătós hier, BASME 420

ROAD *s.* cále, *pl* căľuri, *F:* căľ; *N:* drum; **the large ~** cálea máre; **the small ~** cálea ñícă ‖ VELO 41: drum

ROAM (ABOUT, AROUND) *vb.* dau tărcoále, ímnu, hălăndăréscu; **You are ~ing about like a madcap** ímñi ca un dabóľa

ROAMER

ROAMER s. gulimán

ROAR s. (as of a river) (a)urláre, lávă

ROAR vb. ▾(a)úrlu; **to ~ with laughter** ▾căhtéscu, ▾păhăéscu

ROAST MEAT s. friptúră, friptáľ, chibápe, psitó, suylimă, *G:* civrimé

ROB vb. ayízmu, ▾aráp, biléscu, ▾dispóľu, ▾guléscu, gulişi-nédz, mut, zmúlgu; **Thieves ~ed us** Nă bilíră fúrľi

ROB ONE'S BELLY vb. ‖ CUVATA 2: ñ-lu cúrmu di gúră

ROBBED adj. ayizmát

ROBBER s. haramíu, *G:* furcudár

ROBUST adj. vârtós, -oásă → STRONG

ROCK s. şcămbă ‖ TULLIU 58: bígă; *Cru:* bărţíre, GOLAB 207; bizbí-ľe, GOLAB 208; *Gop:* cárpă, GOLAB 224; *Alb:* şómbură, BASME 708 → STONE

ROCK vb. ▾leágăn, mi dau cúñea, mi dau pi lişór, ▾drâmbălséscu

ROCKER: to be off one's ~ vb. ▾zurluséscu

ROCKY adj. chitrós, -oásă; **~ area** hălíţă

ROCKING s. drâmbălsíre

ROD s. veárgă; *also:* míşchi, prácică, purteácă, purtécă, şu-părteácă, şupurtécă, şulévcă, şúfră, víţă; (in a loom) virdzeá-uă; **to have a.~ in pickle for smb.** (to bear smb. a grudge) ľ-duc zăte, ľ-u coc, âľ pórtu múltă seáte, ľi pórtu un crínte, ľ-ţân cáche, ľ-ţân pícă

ROE s. (fish eggs stirred and salted) târâmă

ROE DEER s. căprioáră, şútă, zărcádhă, zărcângé, zârcângé ‖ *Av:* dhărcádâ, CL 44

ROEBUCK s. căpriór

ROGATION WEEK s. (before Ascension Day) siptămâna álbă

ROGUE s. bătăhcí, zgrumát

ROGUERY s. ceapcânlăche → KNAVERY

ROIL vb. cutúrbur, cutrúbur; (to vex) ▾guştirédz

ROLL s. (as of paper, or fabric) top, trâmbă, viláre; (small loaf of bread) simítă, simíte; (of coins) grup → MAKE A ~

ROLL vb. (to wallow) ▾anduchiléscu, ▾antăvăléscu, ntăvăléscu, cutăvăléscu, cutuvuléscu, cutuvléscu; turculéscu; **They found him rolling on the ground** Lu-afláră turculít ân páde; (to form into a ~) trumbuéscu; (to spin, to ~ down) ▾arucutéscu, arcutéscu; **to ~ over** ▾chilindéscu, ghilindéscu; (as of the warp on the cylinder of a loom) nvólbu, mvulbédz; **to ~ in** (to have in abundance or in excess) anót; **He was ~ing in sweat** Anutá tu sudóri; **~ head over heels** ▾turculéscu; **to ~ into a ball** or **to ~ oneself up** ▾fac culác; **to ~ out pasta** tíndu péturi; **to ~ the dough** mpétur ‖ (as a ball of paper) *Peş:* adár găgiumól, găgiumuléscu, CL 45

ROLL UP vb. (of one's sleeves) ▾(a)scumbuséscu, născumbuséscu

ROLLED adj. (as ~ in flour, in sugar, etc.) antăvălít

ROLLER s. (used with a rolling board) ‖ ALR 1054: şţálă

ROLLICK vb. (to move or behave in a carefree joyous manner) ▾zburdălipséscu

ROLLING s. anduchilíre, antăvălíre, arucutíre, ghilindíre, trumbuíre, turculíre

ROLLING BOARD s. cărpitór (and câr-), călpitór, cripitór, cârpitoáre, crâpitoáre

ROLLING DOWN s. arócut, arucutáre, arcutáre

ROLLING IN WEALTH adj. avút arúptu; priavút → RICH

ROLLING PIN s. şuţálă, şţálă

ROLY-POLY adj. (being short and pudgy) dúrdu, grăsíc, grozdavén

ROMAN CATHOLIC adj. (usu. of Albanians) Látin, m pl Látiñ

ROMANIA s. ‖ *Cru:* Rumăníe, GOLAB 246; Armănia, CUVATA 21

ROMANIAN s., adj. vlăhút, vlăhutéscu; (the ~ language) límba a vlăhúţilor, límba vlăhutéscă, vluhutéscă ‖ (Dacoromanian) iron. culeáşu ('polenta'), CarA 276

ROMP vb. (to frisk about) trub → FROLIC

ROOF s. acupirâmíndu, citíe, *Nev:* cupiríş; **to lift the ~** (to make a row) fac ghiurultíe ‖ *Prv:* ţitíe, *An:* stéĭi, *Gard, Lep, Src:* schipíe, B-ARCH 407; (protective cover) aplicâtoári, DIARO 62

ROOF s. anat. **~ of the mouth** ‖ *Peş:* cafcălea, CL 40

ROOF vb. ▾anvăléscu, amvăléscu

ROOFTOP s. → ROOF

ROOK s. orn. gáie, cioáră

ROOK vb. plănéscu → CHEAT, TRICK

ROOKIE s. (recruit) ridíf

ROOM s. (place) loc; (chamber) udă, *N:* ódă, udáie; dim. udíc, udíce, udíciu, udăíţă; also: ambínă, cámară; (winter ~, usu. with stove or fireplace) mândzát ‖ (the warm ~, the ~ with a stove) sóbâ, DIARO 417

ROOMY adj. lărguríu; ncăpătór, -oáre; vlíhur

ROOST

ROOST *vb.* (*of birds*) ▾apún

ROOSTER *s.* cucót, cócut; *dim.* cucuţăl; *also*: bindiríc, bindér-cu; *Băi*: cântâtoráş; cândăturáş, cântândăráş ‖ *GSus*: căcót, *Pls*: căcót, CL 40

ROOT *s.* (a)rădăţínă (*and* arădhă-), ariditţínă; *G*: zărăţínă; arăzgănă → TAKE ROOT ‖ *Cru*: arădăcínă, GOLAB 201; *G*: dârâţínă, dârţínă; zârţínă; *F*: rădzătínă; *P*: dhârâţínă, dhârţínă, *etc.*, SarD 85

ROOT *vb.* ▾răm, (a)râm; **Hard soil cannot be ~ed easily** LOC sănătós nu si-arâmă; **to ~ out** ▾zmúlgu; **to ~ up** scot dit rădăţínă

ROOTED *adj.* (*deep-rooted*) aruzusít

ROPE *s.* fúne; *also*: cúrmu, fórtumă, pălămár, sigíme, şigíme, truşínă

ROPE-DANCER *s.* pihliván

ROSARY *s.* (*string of beads*) ori *f pl*; cumbulóye, cumbulóie

ROSE *s.* trandáfilă, trandáflă, trandafiľáuă, rújă

ROSEATE *adj.* trandafilíu → ROSY

ROSE-BUSH *s.* trandafír, trandafiléu *m*

ROSEMARY *s.* *bot.* rosmarín, rismărínă

ROSE-WATER *s.* ghiuleápe, ghiúlsu

ROSIN *s.* măstíhe

ROSTER *s.* (*register*) băzmâtă

ROSY *adj.* giuleabíu; pembé *invar.*, trandafilíu, -fiľát, - flíş; (*blooming, as of a healthy girl*) arúmin, -nă, -ñ, -ne

ROT *s.* putrigâñu, putridzâñu, putridzâe; *also*: ciurúche, ciuru-cláche, trâhlă, smac

ROT *vb.* putridzăscu, ciurutipséscu; (*of eggs, etc.*) cluvyisés-cu ‖ CUNIA 150: prutidzăscu

ROTATE *vb.* ▾anvărtéscu, ▾arucutéscu

ROTTEN *adj.* pútrid, prútid, prúdit, putridzât, pâtârdzât; (*of food*) aludzât; (*of a nut*) şúpliv, *m pl* -pliyĭ, *f pl* -plive; şuplivós; (*of eggs*) clúvyiu; ~ **stuff** (*of wood, leaves*) trâhlă

ROTUND *adj.* → PLUMP

ROUÉ *s.* → RAKE

ROUGE *s.* (*cosmetic*) buiáuă, aruşeáţă, fcheasídhe, ucnă

ROUGED *adj.* ruşátă *f*

ROUGH *adj.* (*of ground*) frămtu; (*of the sea*) turburát; (*of leather, etc.*) áscur, ascurát; ~ **ground** *s.* rivéne ‖ *Cru*: (*wild*)

áyru, GOLAB 196

ROUGHCAST s. (for coating a wall) măltáre, párget

ROUGHCAST vb. ▾lăspuséscu

ROUGHCASTING s. lăspusíre

ROUGH-HEW vb. ▾pilichiséscu, pilichixéscu

ROUGH-HEWING s. pilichisíre, pilichixíre

ROUGHHOUSE s. ceamaúnă, câvgă, scandál, şimătă

ROUGHHOUSE vb. fac şimătă

ROUND adj. (as of smb.'s face or eyes) arucutós, nvărgós, nvrăgós, nvărligós; **with a ~ face** nvărgós tu fáţă; (as of eyes) mărdzilát; (as of a coin) gurguľitós, gurguľutós, strónghil; **to become ~** ▾gurgulitédz, ▾ngurgulédz

ROUND ABOUT adv. di-avărlíga, ţércľu di-avărlíga, varlíga di varlíga

ROUND UP vb. (as of sheep) ‖ **Cru:** adún, GOLAB 195

ROUNDING s. ngurguľáre

ROUNDISH adj. gurguľát, ngurguľát, gurguľutós, -toásă → ROUND

ROUNDLY adv. (bluntly) cu ţupáta

ROUSE vb. (to wake) ▾diştéptu; (to incite) azmúţ

ROUT s. (mob) suríe; (disturbance) mintíre, mintitúră, mintireáţă

ROUT vb. ▾aúrlu, ▾avín, agunéscu, ayunéscu ‖ PC: scot nafoáră

ROVE vb. ímnu, hălăndăréscu

ROW s. (quarrel, disturbance) ghiurultíe, tăvătúră → MAKE A ~ ‖ **to have a ~ with smb.** mi adár mâľáuâ, DIARO 230

ROW s. (line) arádhă, báir, chindinár; **the ~ of tall poplars** arădhăríchea a plúchilor análţâ; (a ~ of flowers, etc. in a garden) pat ‖ sărauă, HRISTU 100: **three weeks in a ~** trei stămăñ sărau

ROW vb. → QUARREL, WRANGLE

ROWDY adj. (d)zardzára, m pl (d)zar(d)záreañ → BOISTEROUS

ROYAL adj. (a)mi(ră)réscu, -eáscă; văsilchéscu, -eáscă

ROYALLY adv. văsilcheáşte

RUB vb. ▾frec; **to ~ out** ▾aştérgu; **to ~ one's skin off** ▾juléscu, ▾zgrâm

RUBBER BOOT s. lástic, lástică, lástih

RUBBING s. fricáre, fricătúră

RUBBISH s. vicľitúră ‖ ciurúchi, DIARO 259

RUBLE

RUBLE *s.* rúblă

RUBY *s.* rubín, rubíne

RUCKUS *s.* mintireáţă → ROW

RUDDER *s.* dumée, duméne, timóne

RUDDY *adj.* (*of cheeks, of apples, of a chicken in an oven*) ruminít; **to become ~** ▾ruminéscu

RUDE *adj.* ni-ciuplít; *also:* áscur, dângă, ni-adărát, ni-adurát, ni-duchít, ni-prăxít, ni-pulitipsít, păduríş; schizáre, zdángan; *3 sg:* u áre groásă cheálea (*lit.* 'his/her skin is thick'); (~ *language*) jupânéscu; (*insolent*) fíţă *f* ‖ **Peş**: distórsu, CL 44

RUDENESS *s.* huryeátă, nadanlâche; (*rude words*) zboáră di nadanlâche

RUE THE DAY *vb.* (*to regret*) mi tuñiséscu, mi tunu-

RUFFIAN *adj.* áyru, áscur

RUFFLE *vb.* (*to irritate smb.*) ĺ-mâc urécĺile (*lit.* 'to eat smb.'s ears')

RUFFLED *adj.* (*of smb.'s hair*) cearpér, geamálă, zbârlít

RUG *s.* chilím, chilíme, chilúme, *dim.* chilimícă; *also:* béliţă, bíliţă, cérgă, óplă, pârcoávă, sázmă, sigiadé, sigiadée ‖ (*long narrow rugs, usu. to cover benches, coll.*) mindirlâchi; (*small ~*) chilimúci [k'i•li•mú•ĉi], DIARO 303

RUGGED *adj.* (*rough, uneven, as of nuts*) cúncav, *m pl* -cayĭ, *f pl* -cave; costenlív (DDA 406); (*turbulent*) ghiurultagí; (*robust, sturdy*) trupós, zdúmban

RUGOSITY *s.* zgáibă

RUIN *s.* aspárdire, aspárdzeáre, dirín, hărápă, murísce, úrvală; (*loss, destruction, death*) chiríre, chireáre, chirdăciúne; *fig.* tíhtă; **A bad mother-in-law is her daughter-in-law's ~** Soácra aráuă eáste tíhta a nórăĺei

RUIN *vb.* ▾aspárgu, dărâm, ▾disvóc, lupuséscu, sutrupséscu **to ~ oneself** mi ihtiséscu; (*to start going wrong*) ĺau di híma (*lit.* 'to take it downward')

RUINATION *s.* arăvuíre, nilsíre, ruzuíre

RUINED *adj.* fríptu, -ptă, -pţâ, -pte; nilsít, părtădít; (*as at cards*) afulít → BE ~ FINANCIALLY

RULE *s.* (*the usual way of doing things*) aréu, arádhă, dat, dátă

RULE *vb.* dumnéscu, ▾urséscu; **Who is ruling this place?** Cari l-urseáşte lóclu aéstu? → REIGN

RULER *s.* (*as for guiding a pen in drawing lines*) hárac, hără-che, ríglă

RUMBLE *s.* văzúră, vróndu; (*as of approaching horses*) (a)róput; (*as of one's bowels*) gurgulidzáre, gurlidzáre

RUMBLE *vb.* aúrlu; (*as of a mill*) văzéscu, văxéscu (*as of a river*) gúrgur, gurgurédz, gurlédz; **my bowels ~** ñ-gurleádză mă-ţăle (di foáme); ñ-aúrlă luchi tu pântică (*lit. 'wolves are hawling in my belly'*; (*of canons*) bumbunédz

RUMBLING *s.* aurláre, gúrgur, gurgulíre, gurgulidzáre, văzíre

RUMINATE *vb.* (*to chew the cud*) ▾(a)roámig → CHEW

RUMMAGE *s.* căftáre, cirşíre, (a)sgurñíre, (a)zgurñíre, guzgunipsíre

RUMMAGE *vb.* gurñédz, gruñédz, gruñéscu, zgurñédz, (a)zgurñéscu, guzgunipséscu, născăréscu; **They ~ in other people's pockets and purses** Născăréscu géchile şi púndzile-a alăntór

RUMMAGED: ~ from top to bottom (*as by thieves*) născărsít

RUMMAGER *s.* zgurñáric, (a)sgruñáric

RUMOR *s.* zbor, glas; **it is rumored that** inşí zbórlu (că) ‖ DIARO 252: cúrâ un zbor (táha)

RUMP *s.* anat. *N:* noáce; (*~ of a horse; fig. of a mountain*) că-púľe *f*, căpúľu *n*

RUMPLE *vb.* (*of clothes, etc.*) ▾ciumuléscu → WRINKLE

RUMPUS *s.* nţirtáre → QUARREL

RUN *s.* alágă, alăgáre, fudzíre, fugáre, vdzíre, fúzmă, vánţu; (*brook*) víe; (*series*) báir, arádhă; (*the usual kind of*) turlíe; (*the regular course or route*) cále; (*enclosure for animals*) ţárcu → BREAK INTO A ~, TAKE A ~ ‖ *Cru:* alăgáre, GOLAB 197

RUN *vb.* ▾(a)fug, alág, adălág, dau alága;; **Let's ~ away!** S-fu-dzím! *or* S-nă fudzím! **I gave you legs to ~** Míne vă ded cicioáre tra si adălăgáţ; (*as a mill*) trag; (*exhortations:*) Spet! Spirtu-íţ-le! Plătările! Daţ fúga! **~ as hard as one can lick** fug di nu mi ved, fug di mi frângu, fug ca tórnic *or* fug ca (a)ndórnic ‖ fug di mâc lóclu (*lit. 'to run as if eating the earth'*), BASME 462; fug a niórihta, BASME 374

RUN ABOUT *vb.* (*to gad about, to travel*) cutríyir

RUN AWAY *vb.* ▾fug → BOLT ‖ (*to ~ for good*) ñ-ľau pérlu de-acló, BASME 4

RUN DOWN *vb.* (*to disparage*) săhunéscu; (*to overtake*) agiúngu;

▾apróchiu

RUN DRY *vb.* sec, (a)stråchéscu, stårchéscu; **The river had ~**
Arâulu aveá stårchítă

RUN FOR IT *vb.* (*to sling one's hook*) ľau cicioárile dinaúmi-
rea

RUN INTO DEBT *vb.* ▾hriuséscu [hri•u•], hurséscu, ▾burgilipséscu

RUN OFF *vb.* firiséscu, ▾scad → DIMINISH

RUN SHORT OF SMTH. *vb.* ñ-eáste lipsítă (di)

RUN THE WRONG HARE *vb.* u-adár taratóre

RUN THROUGH *vb.* (*as with a sword*) stråpúngu

RUN THROUGH *vb.* (*as of one's wealth*) tuchéscu

RUN UP A FLAG *vb.* (*to stand up against, to rise*) u scol pandéra

RUN UP AND DOWN *vb.* ▾cálcu, cutríyir

RUN WILD *vb.* mi ayrédz, ľau vímtu → FLY INTO A TANTRUM

RUNAROUND *s.* amânáre, amnáre, şintíre

RUNAWAY *s.* fúgă

RUN-DOWN *adj.* (*tired*) curmát, frâmtu, -mtă, -mţâ, -mte; (*in
poor repair*) → DILAPIDATED

RUNG *s.* (*of a ladder*) scalupátimă

RUN-IN *s.* → QUARREL

RUNLET *s.* víe, avláchiu

RUNNEL *s.* → RUNLET

RUNNING AWAY *s.* (*flight*) alágă, căpsălsíre, şpirtuíre

RUNNING KNOT *s.* thilíche, thileáuă

RUNNING START *s.* paramázmă → FLIGHT

RUNNY NOSE *s.* (a)rémă, bútur, ceáră, guhtíe, rúfă, simáhe,
sirmíe; *vb.* ñ-trag nărĭle

RUN-OF-THE-MILL *adj.* (*ordinary, common*) paráspur

RUNT *s.* (*an animal unusually small of its kind; a person of
small stature*) anghiúdhă, ñic(u)zót, şcurtabác, chirchinéc

RUPTURE *s.* arupeáre, arúpire; *med.* (*hernia*) sălăghíre

RUPTURE *vb.* ▾arúp

RUPTURED *adj.* (*with hernia*) sălăghít

RUSE *s.* (*imposture, trick*) arâdeáre

RUSH *s.* anăpădíre, fúzmă, sărghíre; **He is a ~** şi-eáste hai-hui
‖ **What's the ~?** ≈ Dzâlile nu intráră tu sac! BASME 11

RUSH *s.* *bot.* cánă, cucuvíţă ‖ *GSus:* şávăr, CL 261

RUSH *adj.* arăchít, arichít, aguñisít, ayu-, aghiusít

RUSH *vb.* albănséscu, ▼aľápid, ▼anăpădéscu, (a)pitruséscu, (a)putruséscu, (a)plucuséscu, ▼arăvuéscu, răvăéscu, ▼arúc pri, ▼astrág, (a)urñéscu (pri), ▼cităséscu, curundédz, dau iurúse (*or* irúse, irúşe), dau năválă, (ľ-u) fac fóra, fac yiurúse, fac năvál, ▼himuséscu, ▼ľuftéscu, ľuftuéscu, ▼nâburuéscu, ▼sălăghéscu (pri), ▼sărgľéscu, sărghéscu, ▼vérsu

RUSHLIGHT *s.* finghíd, finghídh

RUSSET *adj.* (*as of goats: reddish-brown or yellowish-brown*) cul

RUSSIA *s.* ‖ **Cru:** Russíe, GOLAB 246; **Russian tea:** ceáe di-Arusíe, DIARO 221

RUSSIAN *s.* Arús

RUST *s.* (a)rudzínă, (a)zguríe, zgúră

RUST *vb.* (a)rudzinéscu, (a)rudzinédz, ▼zgurghiséscu

RUSTIC *adj.* (*country*) ‖ PC: huryitéscu

RUSTICALLY *adv.* huryiteáşte

RUSTING *s.* (a)rudzináre, zgurghisíre

RUSTLE *s.* (*as of leaves*) hórhut, múrmur, şurşuráre

RUSTLE *vb.* (*as of leaves*) firfirédz, hurhutéscu, juñéscu → MURMUR

RUSTLING *s.* firfiridzáre, hurhutíre

RUSTY *adj.* (a)rudzinít, -nát, -nós; zgurghisít

RUTHLESS *adj.* (*merciless*) ni-ñilós, -oásă

RYE *n* sicáră; ~ **bread** sicăreáţă; ~ **field** sicáră *or* sicăríñe ‖ ALIA 69: vríză; **Lep, NPrv, Src:** sicáli, B-ARCH 69

S

'S *vb.* (*is, has*) → BE and HAVE

'S *poss.* a, al, a li; (*the wife of*) ţal; **Nica's wife** ţal Níca

SABER *s.* apálă → SWORD

SABLE *s.* zool. sămúră, sămúre, samúre; (*black color*) laiu

SACERDOTAL *adj.* priftéscu; ~ **clothes** priftéştile *f pl def.*

SACK *s.* sac

SACK *vb.* (*to plunder*) fac alimúră; (*to dismiss*) → FIRE

SACRED *adj.* ayisít; **their ~ hands** ayisítile-a lor mâñ

SACRIFICE s. (offering, smth. offered) afiérumă, curbáne, proscomidhíe, tiléfe; **I am ready to ~ my life for her** Tiléfe bána ñ-dau tră ea

SACRIFICE vb. (to offer up) afieruséscu; (to renounce for an ideal, belief or end) mi fac tiléfi (ti), DIARO 333 → MAKE A ~ FOR

SACRIFICER s. (Jewish ~) hahám

SACRILEGE s. lăiáţă, fără-cále, fără-di-zăcoáne (lit. 'awless')

SACRISTAN s. candilanáftu ‖ *SJos:* cliseátur, CL 42; *GSus:* him-ñitór, CL 253

SACROSANCT adj. → SACRED

SAD adj. cripát; also: acăţát, afumát, amărât, (a)nvirinát, anvirinós, búdză cripátă, căñisít, cărtít, dipús, fărmăcát, jilós; *Gop:* (â)nfuştát; lăcrimós, lăít, lipirós, mărămnát, mărănghisít, mărinát, ndzérnu, niurát [ni•u•], nci(u)mirát, ntunicát, pălít, părăpuñisít, plâmtu, póndu, văpsít, cu graiu plâmtu, cu ínima cărbúne, cu límba scrumátă, cu nările spindzuráte, cu sufrinţeáua dipúsă → BE ~, MAKE ~ WORK OF IT ‖ cu ínima frâmtă, BASME 193

SADDEN vb. ▼amărăscu, ▼nver, virinédz, (a)nvirinédz, căñiséscu, ▼cârtéscu, ▼fármăc, ñ-frângu ínima, ▼mărín or mărinédz, ▼nfuştédz ‖ STERE 29: mi prămpuséscu

SADDENED adj. dipús → SAD

SADDENING s. amărâre, nfărmăcáre

SADDLE s. şeáuă, şáo, sélă → BE LOOSE IN THE ~

SADDLE vb. ▼nşiédz [•nşi•édz], ▼nşiuédz [nşi•u•édz]

SADDLE ONESELF WITH vb. ncarc pri plătări

SADDLE-BOW s. ublăncu → POMMEL

SADDLE-GIRTH s. ghíncală, yínclă, yínglă

SADDLE-HORSE s. binéc (di caválă), cal di căválă, căválă, timbilíche → HORSE

SADNESS s. caimó, căñínă, jále, măráze, nvirináre, părăpuñisíre

SAFE adj. (freed from injury or risk) ascăpát, cutursít; (affording safety, secure from danger) apărát, síyur; (reliable) saylám, saylámcu ‖ CUVATA 30: **there was no ~ well to drink from** nu-aveá vără salámi fântănă

SAFEGUARD s. (precaution) afiríre, apăráre, apărătúră, pruvideáre, siyuripsíre

SAFEGUARD *vb.* ▾siyuripséscu → DEFEND, PROTECT

SAFEKEEPING *s.* afirítă, căştígă

SAFETY *s.* (*salvation, escape*) ascăpáre, siyuripsíre, sileaméte

SAFETY PIN *s.* paramánă

SAFFRON *s. bot.* croc, safrán, şafrán, şăfráne

SAG *vb.* hămbluséscu, ▾sălghéscu, ▾dipún

SAGACIOUS *adj.* duchít; duchitór, -oáre; cu sicáră n cap (*lit. 'with rye in one's head'*) → INTELLIGENT

SAGACITY *s.* chischimeáţă, chischineáţă

SAGE[1] *s. bot.* rusfăcheuă

SAGE[2] *s.* (*wise man*) mintimén (*and* mindi-), ştiút

SAGE *adj.* → WISE

SAID *part. of* SAY ; **so ~ so done** dzâca ş fápta

SAILOR *s.* cărăvyiót, cărăvyeár, cărăvúchil, náftu; *adj.* năftéscu ‖ *Peş:* cărvăchíre, CL 41

SAINT *s. and adj.* sâmtu (*and* sămtu), símtu, sântu, síntu; ayiu, ayiusít; ~ **Demeter** Su-Médru *or* Sân-Médru; ~ **Friday** Stă-Víniri; ~ **Elijah** Sâm-Ilíe; ~ **George** Sâm-Giórgiul; ~ **Mary** Stă-Măría; ~ **Peter** Sâm-Chétru, Sum-Chétru ‖ LITURG 123: a áyilor *gen pl*

SAKE: **for N's ~** ti hátra al N

SAL AMMONIAC *s.* (*ammonium cloride, used as expectorant*) muşidâre, nişidâre

SALACIOUS *adj.* (*obscene*) azdisít, dişuţât, pânghiós [•ǵós]

SALAD *s.* (*of vegetables*) cumbóst(r)ă, sălátă

SALAMANDER *s.* salaméndra ‖ *GSus:* siliméndră; *SJos:* soloméndră, *Prv:* suliméndră, CL 260

SALAMI *s.* (*from sheep or goat entrails*) bumbár, lumbár

SALARY *s.* (a)rúgă, dhyeáră, lufé, mistó, págă; (*~ for one day of work*) gundulúche, undulâche; **He cut off his ~** Ľ-u stărchí dhyeára

SALE *s.* víndire, vindeáre, alişveríşe, surdisíre; **for ~** di-a vínde *or* ti săváte; ~ **bargains** pătălămă, bâtâlâmă ‖ BATSARIA 76: **for ~** tri vindeáre

SALINITY *s.* (a)nsărătúră, sărătúră

SALIVA *s.* (a)scuchiát; bálă, *used mainly in pl:* bále ‖ ALIA 161, **Ary:** şcuchiát

SALLOW *adj.* sálbit, săhñisít

SALLY *s.* fúzmă, vánţu, zvórimă

SALMON

SALMON *s. ichth.* dhelfín

SALON *s. (elegant living room)* udắlu aţél búnlu

SALONIKA *s. (city in northeastern Greece)* Sărúnă

SALT *s.* sáre; *(the place where sheep get salt to lick periodically)* săríñe

SALT *vb.* ansár, ansărédz, bag sáre; *(season)* agudéscu tu sáre, păstoséscu

SALT-BOX *s.* pipiríţă, pipiḻíţă, sărătór

SALTING *s.* (an)sărătúră, (a)nsăráre; **The cheese needs to be salted** cáşlu va ansăráre

SALTLICK *s. (as for sheep)* săríñe

SALTNESS *s.* → SALINITY

SALTPETER *s.* nítru

SALTY *adj.* (a)nsărát; *(excessively ~)* bádrâ *invar.*; lísă *invar.*

SALUBRIOUS *adj.* sân, -nă, -ñ, -ne; sănătós, -oásă

SALUTARY *adj.* sănătós, -toásă; cu hăíre *(lit. 'with benefit')*

SALUTATION *s.* → GREETING

SALUTE *s. (of artillery)* pătăreáuă; **the rumble of the ~** văzúra a pătăréilor

SALUTE *vb. (to greet)* ▾ghinuéscu

SALVATION *s.* (a)scăpáre, nchiuluíre, sileaméte

SALVE *vb. (to assuage)* ▾asbún, ▾azbún

SALVIA *s. bot.* rusfăcheáuă

SAME *adj.* únă sóie, únă luyíe, únă; *adv.* tut acşí; *(that very)* ídhyiu, ídhyiu; **They worked, but not all the ~** Nâşi lucrá, ma nu toţ únă luyíe; **They were all the ~** Tuţ erá-ĺ únă; **It is all the ~ to me** Únă-ñ fáţe; **the ~ day** *(that very day)* ídhyea dzúuă; **the ~ thing** ídhyiu lúcru ‖ DIARO 8: tut aţélu *m*, tut aţeá *f*, tut aţéĺ *m pl*, tut aţeáli *f/n pl*

SAMPLE *s.* cişíte, dhuchimăsíre, móstră, próvă, sémnu

SAMPLE *vb.* dhuchimăséscu

SANCTIFICATION *s.* ayisíre, ayiusíre

SANCTIFY *vb.* ▾săntiséscu, ayiuséscu, ayiséscu ‖ LITURG 123: ayiusésti *2 sg* → HALLOW

SANCTIMONIOUS *adj.* ipucrít; prifáptu → HYPOCRITICAL

SAND *s.* arínă

SANDAL *s.* ţărúhe; **wooden ~** *Cĺis:* cléndză

SANDAL-MAKER *s.* ţăruhár

SANDAL-STRAP *s.* nujíţă, nuzíţă, truşínă

SANDSTONE *s.* greáse, greásă → WHETSTONE

SANDY *adj.* *(containing sand)* arinós; *(color)* arús, aróş

SANE *adj.* *(rationale, wise)* duchít; *(with normal mind)* ntreg *(lit. 'whole')*, *f* ntreágă, *m/f pl* ntredzĭ

SANGFROID *s.* ţâneáre

SANGUINARY *adj.* sândzinós, -oásă

SANGUINE *adj.* *(ruddy)* aruşcuván; *(cheerful)* hărăcóp, -oápă, -óchi, -oápe

SANICLE *s. bot.* şteáie

SAP *s.* *(as of a tree)* ‖ *SJos:* juľi, CL 254

SAP *vb.* *(to weaken)* adhinăţéscu

SAPLING *s.* pumíc

SAPPHIRE *s.* safír(e)

SARDINE *s.* sardhélă

SASH *s.* priváză, pirváză

SASHAY OFF *vb.* li aspél *(lit. 'to wash them')* → BOLT

SATAN *s.* Eusfór → DEVIL

SATANIC *adj.* drăcuréscu, -eáscă, -éşţâ, -éşti

SATCHEL *s.* cheále, foále, fulínă, *dim.* fulíc; útre, útur, vătăláh, vúryă → WALLET ‖ *Amc:* zbărnic, CPad 80 *and* 152

SATE *vb.* ▾sátur → SATISFY

SATIATE *vb.* → SATE

SATIATED *adj.* sătúl, *m pl* -túľ, *f pl* -túle → SATISFIED

SATIETY *s.* angusáre, sat → REPLETION

SATIN *s. tex.* atláze, tăláze, pélă

SATISFACTION *s.* *(contentment)* ambăreáţă, efharístise, uşnurlăcă

SATISFIED *adj.* *(esp. with food or drink)* sătúl, *m pl* -túľ; săturát, năfătít, fănătít; *(content)* efharistisít → BE ~

SATISFY *vb.* ▾sátur; *also:* ▾acáţ, ▾(a)năfătéscu, fănătéscu, fănitéscu, ▾tipuréscu; *(to content)* apudiséscu, efharistéscu, ifharistéscu; **He worked hard to ~ his family** S-tucheá di lúcru ca si-şi apudideáscă fumeáľa; **How could a crumb ~ him?** Nă lai sârmă ţe s-ľ-acáţă? **to ~ one's desire for smth.** ñ-fac chéfea ‖ *Cru:* sútur, GOLAB 251

SATURDAY *s.* sâmbătă ‖ *Amc, Mul:* sámbătă, *Gra, Kat, Perd:* sémbătă, B-ARCH 538

SAUCE *s.* dzámă, sálţă

SAUCEPAN *s.* tingére, tingíre, téngire, tingiré

SAUCER *s.* pheatác; *G:* taiŭ; zárfă *or* zárfu

SAUCINESS *s.* nadanlăche

SAUCY *adj.* abráşcu, -şcă, -şţi, -şte; ni-aruş(i)nát

SAUERKRAUT *s.* vérdzu di moáre

SAUNTER *vb.* ▾ghirizéscu, ▾priímnu → STROLL

SAUNTERER *s.* capisâz

SAUNTERING *s.* (*aimless stroll*) haileslíche [haĭ•lis•lí•ki]

SAUSAGE *s.* culéu, culucáncu; (*pork*) dorméñ *m pl*; lucáncu, lucá-nic, róman, sugiúc, şugiúc, şugiúche

SAVAGE *s.* ayru-óm

SAVAGE *adj.* (*untamed*) áyru; (*rude*) păduriş; (*furious*) gúvru, vârlu → MAD; *to* **become** ~ ayrăpséscu, ayripséscu → CUT UP ~

SAVE *vb.* (*to put aside, to spend stingily*) icunumiséscu, ▾stríngu; (*to keep for later use*) ▾(a)scól; **They ~ed the re-mainder of the cake for supper** Píta ţe armáse u sculáră ti seáră; (*to rescue*) (a)scáp, asuséscu; (*to get rid of*) cuturséscu; **to ~ one's life** ▾ascáp cu yeáţă

SAVE ONE'S FACE *vb.* ‖ ies cu fáţa álbă, BASME 142; ies cu fáţa curátă, BASME 162

SAVED *adj.* ascăpát, cutursít; n călár (*lit.* 'on horseback'); *We are* ~! Hímu n călár!

SAVING *s.* icunumíe, icunumisíre

SAVIOR *s.* (a)scăpătór, (a)scăpitór

SAVOR *s.* (*smth. of good taste*) nustimádhă, nustimeáţă

SAVORY *adj.* nóstim, *m pl* -tiñ, *f pl* -time → TASTY

SAVVY *vb.* → UNDERSTAND

SAW *s.* prióne, şáră; ‖ *GSus:* ciárcu, CL 43; trióne [tri•ó•], CL 262

SAW *vb.* şiruéscu

SAWDUST *s.* arucánizmă ‖ *Av, Grăm, Prv:* hram

SAWHORSE *s.* ‖ *Prv:* dhiyálâ, CL 44

SAW-WORT *s. bot.* gălbináre

SAWYER *s.* priună [pri•u•]

SAY *vb.* ▾aspún, dzăc, *N:* dzắc (→ § 32); cântu; fac (→ § 32); **What was the firman ~ing?** Ţe cântá firmánea? *impers.* **they** ~ cúră zbórlu (că); si zburáşte (că); táha; **They ~ he had descended from the heaven** Din ţer táha s-dipúse; **It cannot be said in any lan-**

guage Nu-áre tu vâr graiu spuneáre; **He died without ~ing a word**
Murí fâr-di spuneáre; **to ~ it to smb.'s face** ľ-u dzâc tu fáţă ‖
ALR 1469: **they say that (it is said that)** z-dzâţe că

SAY A PRAYER *vb.* ▾ncľín nă ncľinăciúne

SAY GOOD-BYE *vb.* alás cu sănătáte

SAY HELLO *vb.* călimirséscu → GREET

SAYING *s.* spuneáre, spúnire; **as the ~ goes** cúră nă cuvéndă

SCAB *s. derm.* coaje; (*of domestic animals*) aráña a óilor

SCABBARD *s.* teácă

SCABROUS *adj.* (*difficult*) greu, *f* greáuă, *m pl* grei, *f pl*
greále; (*rough to the touch*) áscur; (*squalid*) átim

SCABBY *adj.* aráñós, -oásă; **to become ~** aráñéscu → MANGY

SCABIES *s. derm.* (a)ráñe, căsídhă, psóră, zgáibă; **to get ~** aráñéscu

SCAD: **in ~s** *adv.* birichéte

SCALAWAG *s.* pezevénghiu

SCALD *vb.* ▾up(ă)réscu

SCALE *s.* sóldzu; *also:* áspru, flúdhă, ľúşpă, părdzíc

SCALES *s.* cândáre; **~ operator** cândârgí

SCALP → BE OUT FOR ~S

SCAMP *s.* zgrumát → RASCAL

SCAMPER AWAY/OFF *vb.* ñ-u arúp; **He took the book and ~ed away
with it** Lo cártea şi-u arúpse cu nâsă ‖ BATSARIA 41: **Let's ~,
brother!** Ai, fărtáte, s-li spilăm! → BOLT

SCANT *adj.* oárfăn, ni-avút

SCANTY OF WORDS *adj.* ≈ zboárile li-áre acumpăráte (*lit.* 'His /
her words are bought')

SCAPEGRACE *s.* → SCAMP

SCAR *s.* ‖ **Peş:** várză, CL 263

SCARAB *s. ent.* cărăbúş, zângânár

SCARCE: nişáne; **Water is very ~ here** Auá-i nişáne di ápă → MAKE
ONESELF ~

SCARCITY *s.* lipsítă → STRINGENCY

SCARE *s.* aspárizmă, aspárimă, fríxe

SCARE (AWAY) *vb.* aspár di-acló; (*of birds*) azboá(i)r; fuvirés-
cu; **The girl ~ed it [the bird] away** Lu-azbuiră feáta, lu-aspáré
di-acló; (*to intimidate*) ľ-aspún múnţâ (*lit.* 'to show smb. the
mountains') ‖ CUNIA 11: spun băstúnea (*lit.* 'tk show the stick')

SCARECROW

SCARECROW *s.* bóşe → BUGBEAR

SCARED *adj.* aspăreát, aspărít, bubuít, cănusít, nfricuşát → BE ~ ‖ cu ínima ngľiţátă (*lit.* 'with frozen heart'), BASME 177

SCARF *s.* limudhétă, limuvétă ‖ **Cru:** şchépe, **Gop:** şimíi, GOLAB 252

SCARF-PIN *s.* cărfíţă

SCARIFY *vb.* ▾hărăxéscu

SCARING *s.* aspăr(e)áre

SCARLET *s.* cârméze, criméze

SCARLET FEVER *s.* cochiníţă

SCARPED *adj.* (a)rápós, -oásă; scărpós, -oásă

SCATHE: **One does the ~ and another has the harm** ≈ Áltu fáţe şi-áltu bóra

SCATTER *vb.* (*as of snow driven by wind*) víntur (*and* víndur), (a)zvíntur, (a)zvântur, zvinturédz (*and* zvindu-), ▾spúlbir; (*to disperse, as a flock of sheep*) prâstuéscu, sârmu; **The shepherds are ~ing the sheep** Picurárĭľi sârmă óile; (*as of a piece of cloth*) arăschirédz → SPREAD

SCATTERBRAIN *s.* zevzéc → FLIBBERTIGIBBERT

SCATTERBRAINED *adj.* azvimturát; cap-di-gáie (*lit.* 'crow's head')

SCATTERED *adj.* (z)vinturát, spulbirát, prâstuít; (*as of sheep*) sârmát, arăschirát, arăşhirát

SCATTERING *s.* arăíre, (a)răschiráre, prâstuíre, scurp(i)síre, sârmáre

SCENE: **to make a ~** fac ghiurultíe

SCENT *s.* → ODOR

SCENT *vb.* ▾aduchéscu → SMELL; (*to get a ~ of*) ľau di hăbáre; (*to use the nose in seeking or tracking*) úlmic; **to ~ out** dau di úrmă; (*to perfume*) bălsămiséscu, muscuvulséscu

SCEPTER *or* **SCEPTRE** *s.* schíptru

SCHEME *s.* (*crafty action or plan*) dhóhe, mplititúră, tirtípe, daravéră

SCHEME *vb.* ▾ţas → PLOT

SCHEMER *s.* culcusúr, curcusúr, munăfíc; (*intriguer*) muzavír

SCHEMING *s.* munăficlíche, muzavirlắche

SCHISM *s.* schízmă

SCHOLAR *s.* ştiút, loyiotát

SCHOOL *s.* sculíe, sculó, mectepé; **secondary** ~ yimnáziu → DROP OUT OF ~ ‖ *Cru:* (*eight-year primary* ~) osmolétcă, GOLAB 240 (*word unknown in Albania and Greece*); MERCA 24: *pl* şcoľ; *pl def:* şcóili (*rhyming with* cu óili) 7, 8, 10, 15, 17, 22, *and* 23

SCHOOL BOARD *s.* muaríf [mu•a•]

SCHOOL-SATCHEL *s.* ceándă ti cărţâ, ghiuzdáne, sănătór, sărătór

SCHOOLTEACHER *s.* ânvăţătór, dháscal

SCHOOLMARM *s.* dhascálă

SCINTILLATE *vb.* (*as of smb.'s hair*) hrisuséscu

SCINTILLATION *s.* ascăpirătúră, ascăpăráre, scântiľáre

SCION *s.* ambóľu *n*, ambóľuri *pl*; fidáne, fidánă

SCISSORS *s.* foártică, foárfică

SCOFF *vb.* ▾buiséscu → RIDICULE

SCOFFING *adj.* mbizuitór, -oáre, pizuitór, -oáre; pizuiárnic

SCOLD *vb.* culédz, culimbiséscu; dau un zbúrdhu, giúdic, huléscu, ncáciu, ▾nţértu, trag un pirdáfe, trag únă zăvráche, văryéscu; **She used to ~ me all day long** Mi giudicá tútă dzúua; **Don't ~ me!** Nu mi vâryeá! ‖ *Cru:* ăncáciu, GOLAB 205

SCOLDING *s.* băzmátă, bâzmă, buzmă, culidzáre, culimbisíre, giudicáre, pirdáfe, rizilíre, văryíre (*and* vâr-), vurghíre, zăvráche, zbárdhu ‖ DIARO 414: bâsmátă

SCOOT *vb.* (*to sling one's hook*) ▾ľau cicioárile dinanúmirea

SCORCH *vb.* árdu; (*to overfry, of food*) ▾pârj(il)éscu, ▾ţicnuséscu

SCORCHED *adj.* (*as by the sun*) pârj(il)ít; *the soil is* ~ *by the heat of the summer* pârjilít di váră-i lóclu

SCORN *s.* arâdeáre, cătăfróñe, cătăfróñise, măitápe, mbizuíre, péză *f and* pez *n*, rizíle

SCORN *vb.* cătăfroniséscu, ▾pizuéscu, ▾mbizuéscu, şúpăr; (**you**) **who ~ the words of the prophet** ţi pizuíţă nómlu a profítlui

SCORNFUL *adj.* di péză; ~ **words** zbor di péză

SCORNFULLY *adv.* ti péză, tră şúper

SCORPION *s. zool.* scorpioánă, scorpiónă, scorpíu, scrap, şcrac

SCOT-FREE *adj.* ascăpát, ľirtát, ni-pidhipsít, ni-sudít

SCOUNDREL *s.* cătúnă ‖ CARAFOLI 117: sémnu

SCOUR *vb.* (*to clean in order to eliminate odours*) dispút

SCOUR AWAY/OFF *vb.* (*to take to the fields*) acáţ strématile

SCOURGE *s.* pácus, pusoágă → CALAMITY; (*lash*) cămíche → WHIP

SCOURING

SCOURING *s.* căthărsíre, născărsíre, spăstríre

SCOUT *vb.* buiséscu → RIDICULE

SCOWL *s.* mutrusíre

SCOWL *vb.* mutruséscu

SCRABBLE *vb.* (*as wool*) scármin

SCRAM *vb.* ▼căpsălséscu → GET LOST

SCRAP¹ *s.* (*as a ~ for repairing a shoe*) pór(n)ic; **not a ~** cât trâ yitríe → JOT

SCRAP² *s.* → FIGHT

SCRAP *vb.* → QUARREL, FIGHT

SCRAPE *vb.* ▼arád, ▼mintéscu, ▼scárchin; ▼zgrâm, ▼(a)râm (*to save wisely, little by little*) cilistiséscu, cilăstiséscu

SCRAPE ALONG TOGETHER *vb.* adún ayunséscu ‖ mi ndreg cu, BASME 84

SCRAPER *s.* (a)réndă, aréndză

SCRAPING *s.* (*slow accumulation of earnings*) cilistisíre

SCRAPPY *adj.* → QUARRELSOME

SCRATCH *s.* (*slight wound*) sgârietúră, zgrâmătúră, zgáibă, sgáibă, disbilitúră; **up to the ~** (*in good shape*) pri trup

SCRATCH *vb.* arâm, ▼zgrâm, ▼scárchin; (*with one's claws or paws, as in search of food*) scăléscu; (*to wound slightly*) ▼hărăxéscu

SCRATCHING *s.* scărchináre, scărchiráre, zgrâmáre

SCRAWNY *adj.* → SKINNY

SCREAM *s.* (i)strigáre, zghic

SCREAM *vb.* ▼aúrlu, strig; **to ~ with laughter** ▼căhtéscu, ▼păhăéscu

SCREW *s.* şurúb, şurúp, vídhă

SCREW *vb.* ▼vidhuéscu

SCREW UP ONE'S NOSE *vb.* (*to be or become conceited*) am nările mutáte

SCREWED *adj.* (*fastened*) vidhuít, vidhusít

SCREWING *s.* vidhuíre

SCREW-RING *s.* sérghe → EYE-BOLT

SCRIMPY *adj.* → STINGY

SCRIMP *vb.* (*to economize greatly*) dau cu ghiumáca, mâc cu ghiumáca, hărgiuéscu cu ghiumáca; mi stríngu, mi fac sclínciu

SCRIPTURE *s.* scriiáre, scriptúră; **the Holy ~** Áyea yrámă

SCROFULA *s. med.* (*esp. of horses*) sărăgé (→ KING'S EVIL); (*of people*) *G:* bábcă, broáscă, făľór

SCRUB *vb.* ▼frec

SCRUFF *s.* → NAPE

SCRUFFY *adj.* andíhristu, pânghiós [-ǵós] → SHABBY; **his mouth will never utter ~ words** din gúra a lui nu inşeá vârnăoară gráire pânghiose

SCRUMPTIOUS *adj.* mă-sa-ľ fú; **I took a ~ nap!** Ľi trápşu un sómnu, mă-sa-ľ fú!

SCRUPLE *s.* ≈ induiálă (*lit.* 'doubt')

SCRUTINIZE *vb.* ndzérnu, bag sítă, trec prit sítă (*lit.* 'to put through a sieve')

SCRUTINY *s.* xităxíre

SCUD *vb.* fug

SCUFF *vb.* trag azvárna

SCUFFLE *s.* alúmtă, alumtáre, băscâñe, ncârligáre

SCUFFLE *vb.* ñ-u dau cu; **The Greek began to ~ with the Turk** Élinlu şĭ-u da cu Túrcu; *3 pl*: şĭ-mâcă sămárile

SCULL-CAP *s.* sărpoáşe

SCUM *s.* spúmă, spumătúră, brúzgă, bărsíe; (*of people*) spindzurătúră → GOOD-FOR-NOTHING

SCUM *vb.* (*to remove the ~*) xispumédz

SCURF *s. derm.* flúdhă, mătreáţă, mătráţă

SCURRILOUS *adj.* zdángan, jupânéscu, ni-aruşnós

SCURRY *vb.* → BOLT

SCURVY *adj.* pânghiós [•ǵós] → CONTEMPTIBLE

SCUTTLE AWAY/OFF *vb.* → BOLT

SCUTTLEBUTT *s.* (*gossip*) zburâre

SCYTHE *s.* coásă, cósă; *Src:* căsáre

SEA *s.* (a)máre, pélay, thálasă; **the Black ~** Márea-láie → BE ALL AT ~ **SEAFARER** *s.* → SEAMAN ‖ *Trn:* móre, B-ARCH 26

SEA GULL *s. orn.* ‖ *GSus:* puľu pescár, CL 259

SEAL *s.* (*for stamping or marking*) dámcă, muhúre, mihúre, túră, dúră, vúlă; **wooden ~** svărhídă; (*~ for marking the consecrated bread with a cross*) simnătór, simnitór → BREAK THE ~

SEAL MAN *s.* (*dignity in the past*) miurgí [mi•ur•]

SEAL *vb.* bag dámca, dămcuséscu; **to ~ up** ▼vuluséscu, miuhiurlidiséscu); **to ~ one's lips** mistiryipséscu

SEALING *s.* dămcusíre

SEAM *s.* cusutúră

SEAMAN

SEAMAN *s.* cărăvyiót, náftu

SEAMSTRESS *s.* arăfteásă, arăftoáñe

SEAMY *adj.* urât

SEAR *s.* (*of a gunlock*) ceárcu

SEAR *vb.* (*to dry up*) ▾usâc, usúc

SEARCH *s.* căftáre → RUMMAGE

SEARCH *vb.* ▾cáftu; *also*: alág, ▾mutréscu, ▾ved, sătăxéscu, si-tăxéscu, xităséscu, xităxéscu; **He found what he was ~ing for** Ţe alăgá află; **~ in your pocket!** Védzâ-te n gépe! (*to interrogate thoroughly, to sift*) ndzérnu; (*to ~ earnestly*) l-tórnu lóclu di análtă párte; (*to sound*) discúltu

SEASHORE *s.* mal, márdzine di amáre, acruyeaľáuă; búdză di amáre (*lit.* 'lip of the sea')

SEA-SICKNESS: **to suffer from ~** mi-acáţă amárea (*lit.* 'the sea is catching me')

SEASIDE *s.* → SEASHORE

SEASON *s.* vârstă; **the ~ when ewes deliver** vârsta a fitáriľei

SEASON *vb.* (*as with salt*) agudéscu tu sáre, artiséscu

SEAT *s.* loc

SEAT *vb.* ▾apún, ▾curduséscu

SEATED *adj.* ncúrşi *invar.* → BE ~

SECEDE *vb.* ▾dispártu, mi trag năpói

SECLUDE ONESELF *vb.* ▾nguvédz, bănédz nguvát

SECLUDED *adj.* (*isolated*) nguvát; **~ place** pătiľáuă, pătľáuă ‖ MURNU 39: ascumtós

SECLUSION *s.* nguváre

SECOND *s.* (*instant*) uríţă, stic; **in a ~** tu uríţă; **in a split ~** tu-úna → IMMEDIATELY

SECOND *ord.* dóilu, a dóilui *m*, a doáua *f*; **the ~ time** a doára, a doáura [doáŭ•], d(e)adoára, dhéftira oáră, a dáo-oáră; **on the ~ of the month** tu doáule (*or* tu dáule) di mes; **~ to none** făr-di-soţ; cum soţ nu áre; **That girl was stupid ~ to none** Feáta ístă şi-irá gláră cum soţ nu-aveá ‖ DIARO 413: di-a-ndóilea *m*, di-a-ndoáulea *f*. K-D 71: dheftirlu, dheftirla → § 28.2 ‖ CUVATA 2: **for the ~ time** (*again*) *adv.* déftur

SECOND *vb.* (**to encourage**) inimuséscu; (*to assist*) agiút

SECOND LIEUTENANT *s.* melazâm, muľazím, miuľazím

SECONDHAND MERCHANDISE *s.* mărdáie; **He sells ~** Vínde mărdăi

SECOND-RATE *adj.* ápcu, *f* ápcă, *m pl* ápţi, *f pl* ápţe; próstih

SECRET *s.* acrifó, doáhă, dhoáhe, mistíryiu; **in ~** *adv.* pi ascúmtalui

SECRETARY *s.* (*cleark*) iazagí, yramaticó, yrămătíc; **~ of State** ipuryó

SECRETE PUS *vb.* pruñédz

SECRETIVE *adj.* ascumtós, -oásă; ascúmtu, -mtă, -mţi, -mte

SECRETLY adv. pi ascúmtalui, ascumtíşalui → STEALTHILY

SECULAR *adj.* cuzmicán, laicó

SECURE *vb.* asfăliséscu → ASSURE, INSURE

SECURITY *s.* (*bail, deposit, pledge of payment*) bifă, chifiliméi

SEDATE *adj.* (*serious*) aştirnút

SEDATELY *adj.* cu métru

SEDGE *s. bot.* tréscă → REED

SEDIMENT *s.* bărsíe, brúzgă, cómină

SEDUCE *vb.* plănéscu, (a)plănăséscu, plănipséscu; **~ a woman** li gioc meárile (cu nâsă)

SEDUCER *s.* ‖ farmazón, BASME 83 *and* 188

SEDULOUS *adj.* lucrătór, -oáre; cilistisít

SEE *vb.* ▾ved; ñ-si veáde; **to ~ how the land lies** discúltu; (*to perceive in the distance*) ▾andzăréscu ‖ *3 sg:* veáde, veádi; *Grăm, Kat, Mi, Plat, Perd:* védi, B-ARCH 188

SEE SMTH. OUT *vb.* (*to bring to a satisfactory conclusion*) u scot n cap; scot lúcrulu n cap

SEE YOU LATER! ≈ şedz cu sănătáte! (*lit. 'Stay with health!'*)

SEED *s.* simínţă, spor; *G:* (*tobacco ~*) artisáte; (*~ of a fruit*) → PIP ‖ *F:* sămíţă, SarD 101

SEEDY *adj.* (*inferior*) ápcu, ápcă, ápţi, ápţe; próstih; di cătră la cúscra; (*debilitated, as of a horse*) sarával

SEEK *vb.* cáftu; **to ~ a quarrel** u cáftu (ngăceárea) cu luminárea; **to ~ employment** ▾păitéscu; **to ~ trouble** ñ-bag cáplu tu tástru ‖ **to ~ smb.'s advice** ľ-cáftu míntea, BASME 10

SEEM *vb.* ñ-páre, (a)pár, ampár (*and* ambár), ▾(a)undzéscu; **It ~ed to him that nobody was prettier** Ľ-ampărú că nu-i vâră ma muşeátă; **This does not ~ to be a good sign** Nu undzeáşte s-híbă lúcru bun; **He does not ~ to me a rich man** Nu-ñ lu ľa ócľul tră avút

SEEMING s. (semblance) prep → APPEARANCE

SEEMLINESS s. undzítă, prindeáre, príndire

SEEMLY adj. undzít, umdzít

SEEP vb. (to percolate) ▼stricór

SEER s. PROPHET

SEETHE vb. hérbu

SEGMENT s. ≈ párte (lit. 'part [of]')

SEGREGATE vb. ▼dispártu, ▼alég

SEIGNEUR s. dómnu

SEIGNEURIAL adj. dumnéscu, -eáscă, -éşţâ, -éşti → LORDLY

SEISM s. → EARTHQUAKE

SEIZE vb. ľau, ▼apúc, ▼(a)nciúp (and angiúp); ▼mut; (to steal) úmflu; **The gray dog ~ed him by the nape** Cănútlu lu-nciupă di núcă; **They were seized and put in prison** Fúră mutáţ şi ncľíşi → TAKE

SEIZURE s. loáre

SELDOM adv. arár, areá, arétcu, arítcu; **~ seen, soon forgotten** ≈ Ócľi ţe nu s-ved curúndu sî-agărşéscu ‖ din Paşti-Paşti or di Paşti-n Cărciún (lit. 'from Easter to Easter' or 'from Easter to Christmas'), PARALLELE 150; CUNIA 252: tu apreásă ş-tu chirítă

SELECT adj. un şi un → CHOICE

SELECTION s. alidzeáre; aleádzire

SELF pron. síne; **in their own ~** tră sínea a lor

SELF-ASSURANCE s. embistosíne, mbithár

SELF-CONCEITED adj. făndăxít (and fândâ-) → BOASTFUL

SELFISH adj. arău, f aráuă, m pl arăi, f pl arále; cacurízic

SELF-EFFACING adj. → SHY

SELFLESS adj. → UNSELFISH

SELF-LIMITATION s. aprea-adunătúră → LIMITATION

SELF-POSSESSED adj. stăpuít → COLLECTED

SELF-RESPECT s. filutimíe, filutiñíe, (i)htibáre

SELF-RESTRAINT s. ţâneáre

SELF-SATISFIED adj. făndăxít

SELF-SUFFICIENCY s. dăilíche, dăilâche → ARROGANCE

SELFWILL s. pruclitíe, inagilâche

SELL vb. ▼víndu; **to ~ off** surdiséscu, dau sti zvércă, ▼xifac; (deceivingly) ▼chic, (a)ncălţu; **with the intention of ~ing to someone the load of dung as silk** cu míntea s-u chícă a vârnui furtía di bălidzi trâ sírmă; **to ~ a gold brick** ▾arâd → DECEIVE

SELL OUT *vb.* (*to betray*) prudhuséscu

SELLING *s.* víndire → SALE

SELVAGE *s.* úie, úvye

SEMBLANCE *s.* adúcă, prep → APPEARANCE

SEMESTER *s.* xámin

SEMOLINA *s.* simiydhále

SEMPSTRESS *s.* → SEAMSTRESS

SEND *vb.* amín, pitréc; **to ~ away from home** ▾xinitipséscu; **to ~ a wire** bat teľ; **to ~ forth** (*to utter*) cârlédz; **to ~ out roots** aruzuséscu, arizuéscu; **to ~ smb. away with a flea in his ear** ľ-bag cáplu tu loc; **~ smb. off** ľ-dau țărúhile (→ FIRE); **to ~ smb. out to grass** ľ-dau purdheácica; **to ~ word to smb.** pitrec hăbáre (→ LET KNOW); **to ~ to the devil** ľ-bag cuváta, ľ-bag láia, ngărmiséscu, ▾pătăxéscu, sictărséscu; **Send ~ him to the devil!** ≈ Các-lu n cap! ‖ *F:* **I have sent you** (*dat.*) ți pătărcui, HRISTU 63

SENDING *s.* pitreáțire, pitrițeáre

SENESCENCE *s.* (*the state of being old*) auș(e)átic; (*the process of becoming old*) aușíre

SENILE *adj.* → OLD

SENNA *s. bot.* (*Cassia acutifolia, used as purgative*) simănichíe

SENSATION *s.* sântíre, sintíre

SENSE *s.* (*meaning*) nóimă → MAKE ~; (*equilibrium*) → DRIVE SMB. OUT OF HIS ~S, COME TO ONE'S ~S

SENSE *vb.* (*to realize*) ciuléscu

SENSIBLE *adj.* aștirnút; cu (țivá) sicáră n cap (*lit.* 'with [some] rye in one's head'), cu țércľu; **~ people** cápite cu țércľu (*lit.* 'heads with circles')

SENSIBLY *adj.* (*rationally*) cu cále (*lit.* 'with way')

SENSITIVE *adj.* (*feeling*) adiľós, -oásă

SENSUAL *adj.* (*lascivious*) azgân, -ână, *m pl* -âñ, *f pl* -âne; cahpée *f sg*

SENSUALITY *s.* azgânláche, dizñirdăciúne

SENSUALIZE *vb.* azdiséscu, azgânipséscu

SENTENCED *adj.* giudicát, judicát

SENTIENT *adj.* aduchít

SENTIMENT *s.* → FEELING

SENTINEL *s.* cărăúle, cărăúlă → GUARDIAN

SENTINEL *vb.* cărăulséscu, şed cărăúle, şed strájă

SENTRY *s.* nubicí, strájă → GUARDIAN, SENTINEL

SEPARATE *vb.* ▼dispártu (di); *also:* ▼cúrmu (di), ▼disfác (di), ▼dizlăchéscu (di), ▼herăséscu (di), ▼mpártu (di)

SEPARATED *adj.* curmát, dispărţât, dizlăchít; **We are ~ from each other like lambs from sheep** Him curmáţ ca ñeľ di oi

SEPARATELY *adv.* ahór(y)ea, aľúrea, anámera (di)

SEPARATION *s.* dispărţâre, dispărţâtúră, dizlăchíre, disfăţeáre

SEPTEMBER *s.* (y)izmăciúñ, yismăciúne, sihteámvre, sihtémvre, septémvriŭ, stavrú; **in ~** tu méslu al ghizmăciúne ‖ HRISTU 48: părţari

SEPULCHRAL STILlNESS *s.* ţâpit → SILENCE

SEPULTURE *s.* ngrupáre → BURIAL

SEQUESTER *vb.* (*to seize*) fac sucréstu; (*to segregate*) ▼dispártu, ▼alég

SEQUESTRATION *s.* catáshise, sucréstu

SERAGLIO *s.* haréme

SERAPH *s.* ánghil, arhánghil

SERBIAN *adj.* sărbéscu, -eáscă, -éşţâ, -eáşti

SERENE *adj.* arihătipsít → STILL

SERF *s.* (*farmer ~*) cifcí → BONDMAN

SERGE *s.* adhímtu, dhímit

SERGEANT *s.* ceaúş, ónbaşi [•baş^i]; *adj.* ceauşéscu [ĉa•u•]

SERIOUS *adj.* (*of people*) aştirnút; (*devoted*) mbistimén; (*grave, dangerous*) laiu; (*as of a desease*) greu **Things are becoming ~** ≈ Si ngroáşe şicălu (*lit. 'The joke is getting thicker'*)

SERIOUSLY: → TAKE ~

SERMON *s.* dhidhăhíe; (*~ book*) cazamíe, căzâmíe

SERPENT *s.* → SNAKE

SERPOLET *s. bot.* (*wild thyme*) ţemurícă → PENNYROYAL

SERRATION *s.* (*as in a serrate margin of a dress*) zâmbă

SERRIED *adj.* strímtu, -mtă, -mţi, -mte

SERVANT *s.* huzmicheár, iuzmicheár, dhul, purtóiur, smichér, şcľau; (*for sheep*) peregé; **to be a ~** huzmitipséscu ‖ **Peş:** lăcrătór *m.*, lăcrătoáră *f*, CL 254; dúlă *f*, BASME 315 ‖ (*officiant*) iusmetgí, LITURG 130

SERVE *vb.* (*to work as a servant*) huzmitipséscu; (*to be of use*)

filiséscu; **to ~ smb. a bad trick** ľ-gioc nă féstă *or* nă hunére

SERVICE *s.* (*help, use, benefit*) huzméte, usméte, agiutór; **to be of ~** ufiliséscu ‖ (*job*) LITURG 130: iusméti

SERVICEABLE *adj.* (*obliging*) próthim, *m pl* -thiñ; próthmu, -mă

SERVICE-TREE *s.* cruş, sórbu, súrvu

SERVILE *adj.* tápin, *m pl* -piñ; tapinós, -oásă; tibié *invar.*

SERVITOR *s.* → SERVANT

SERVITORSHIP *s.* huzmichirlắche

SERVITUDE *s.* (*process*) arubuíre, sclăvuíre; (*state*) sclăvíľe, scl̦ăvíe, → BRING INTO ~

SESAME *s.* (a)susáme, sisáme

SESAME OIL *s.* şirlán

SET *s.* (*the fit of smth.*) tăcâme; (*group of persons associated by common interest*) suţátă, táymă, táifă

SET *vb.* (*to place*) bag, (a)pún; **He sat her on his lap** Pri dzinúcľe u púse; (*to appoint*) **They sat me as a servant** Purtóiur mi púsiră; (*of the sun*) 3 *sg*: apúne, (a)scápită, surupseáşte; **The sun was ~ing** Soárile erá trâ ascăpitáre ‖ ALIA 3: si ascúndi, fúdze; treáţi, văsilipseáşti ‖ (*to lay the table*) ▼tíndu; (*to establish, to schedule*) urséscu, ▼taľu, cruéscu; **The day set by the emperor arrived** Agiúmse dzúua ursítă di amiră; **God has set things this way** Dumnidzău acşí cruí; (*to form, as of fruit*) leg; **The trees have set** Póñľi ligáră poáme

SET A MARK OF DISGRACE UPON SMB. *vb.* ľ-u bag dámca, ľ-u bag vúla

SET A RUMOR ABOUT *vb.* → LIBEL

SET APART *vb.* ▼alég

SET AT LARGE *vb.* dau cále; *also:* ▼apulséscu, ▼elefthiriséscu, ▼sărgľéscu

SET A TRAP *vb.* bag aláţ, bag bátă, bag stăpânţă, bag príncă, ▼curdiséscu scăndilíe

SET AT VARIANCE *vb.* → BREED DISCORD

SET A WATCH *vb.* bag s priveágľe

SET BACK *vb.* ▼tórnu, ▼arăstórnu, ▼şúţ, ▼dau năpói

SET DOWN *vb.* (*to consider, to regard*) ľau ti ‖ **You are setting me down as a fool** Mi ľai ti om fără mínte, BASME 419

SET EVERY SPRING IN MOTION *vb.* mi fac páde (*lit.* 'I make myself flat')

SET

SET EYES ON *vb.* dau cu ócĺiĺ di → CATCH SIGHT OF

SET FIRE TO *vb.* ▼árdu ‖ HRISTU 36: bag foc

SET FORTH *vb.* ĺau cálea, litéscu, chin(i)séscu, nchiséscu, purnéscu

SET FREE *vb.* dau cale → RELEASE, SET AT LARGE

SET OFF *vb.* → SET FORTH

SET OFF RUNNING *vb.* li ascármin → SCAMPER AWAY/OFF

SET OF GARMENTS *s.* armátă di stráñe, adrămíntu di stráñe

SET ON EDGE *vb.* (*of teeth*) ñ-amúrtă (*or* ñ-amurţắscu) dínţăĺ

SET ONE'S CAP AT/FOR SMB. *vb.* (*to fix one's eyes on*) am ócĺu ‖ bag tu ócĺu, BASME 117; **He took hold of the vineyard on which he had set his eyes** Zăptăsí ayíña ţe lĺaveá ócĺu

SET ONESELF TO DO SMTH. *vb.* ▼acáţ; **Either do a job as it should be done, or don't set yourself to do it** I lu-adári un lúcru ca lúmea, i nu ti-acáţă

SET ONE'S HEART ON *vb.* ñ-armâne ípatlu la; bag tu ócĺu

SET ONE'S HOPE(S) ON *vb.* hiu cu umútea la

SET ONE'S SEAL TO *vb.* ĺ-bag dámca

SET ON FIRE *vb.* apríndu; **I'll set your hut on fire!** Va vă a-príndu călíva!

SET OUT *vb.* u adún (trâ, la), u angắn căţắua, u litéscu, mi min, nchiséscu, chiniséscu, chinséscu

SET PEOPLE BY THE EARS *vb.* bag zizáñe → BREED DISCORD

SET SMB. A TASK *vb.* ▼nsárţin, ▼nsărţinédz, nsărţănédz

SET SMB. AT ODDS *vb.* → BREED DISCORD

SET SMB. AT SOMEONE *vb.* (*a person or a dog*) azmúţ

SET SMB. ON FIRE *vb.* (*make jealous*) bag tru zilíe

SET SMB. ON HIS/HER LEGS AGAIN *vb.* nturturédz

SET THE FIRE *vb.* apríndu fóclu

SET THE TABLE *vb.* ▼ndreg meása

SET TO RIGHTS *vb.* (*to put in order a room, a yard, etc.*) ▼ndreg, anăschirséscu, anischirséscu, chirséscu, născărséscu

SET TO WORK *vb.* mi aştérnu tu (*or* pri) lúcru

SET UP *adj.* (*of people: eager to impart justice, exaggeratedly righteous*) ≈ ímnă cu zíya n brân

SET UP *vb.* (*to establish*) ▼taĺu; **A pay will be ~ for him** Va să-ĺ si táĺe unắ arúgă; (*to make, to build, to instale, to erect*) análţ, ▼(a)stăséscu, (a)stiséscu, ▼astălăéscu; **They set up swing**

under the veranda Astăsíră sun cirdáche únă drâmbálă; (*as a tent*) ▼mprustédz (*and* mbrus-); **to ~ a shout** dau un zghic

SET UPON A TASK *vb.* ▼acáţ

SET UP ONE'S COMB *vb.* (*to give oneself airs*) ▼ngroş

SETTING *s.* (*of the sun*) (a)scăpitáre, chirítă; (*~ in order*) (a)ndreádzire, ndridzeáre; (*~ on edge*) furchisíre; (*~ out*) purñíre → DEPARTURE

SETTLE *vb.* ▼aştérnu; **Fogs are ~ing on the mountains** Si-aşteárnă písti múnţâ néguri; (*of a liquid*) ▼dizlăcéscu, limbiséscu, limbizăscu, ▼lăyărséscu; (*to become quiet or orderly*) dipún mínte; (*to ~ the price*) ▼cúrmu păzárea ‖ MERCA 4: bag par

SETTLE DOWN *vb.* şed; **They ~ed down to dinner** şidzúră pri meásă; (*to take up a stable and honest life*) ▼aştérnu, ▼ncurduséscu, ncurdiséscu, curdhuséscu (*and* curduséscu); **You ~ed down to drink** Vă curdusít la beáre; **We ~ed down at his place** nă curdhusím la nâs acásă

SETTLE UP WITH SMB. *vb.* mi (a)láu (di); **I've ~ed up the debt** Mi lai di bórge

SEVEN *num.* şeápte, şápte; **Which of the ~ emperors?** Cai di şeáptiľi amirádz?

SEVENTEEN *num.* şeáptesprădzaţe

SEVENTH *ord.* ‖ şáptile, BASME 462; evdhómen, GOLAB 214 → § 28.2

SEVENTY *num.* şeaptedzắţi, şaptedzắţi

SEVER *vb.* ▼dispártu; **to ~ smb.'s head** ľ-ľau cáplu

SEVERAL *adj.* niscântu, nă- (*and* născându), *m pl* -nţâ *or* -ndzâ, *f pl* -nte *or* -nde; (â)ndói, *f* (â)ndoáuă *or* ndoáo; **Thus ~ years passed** Tricúră aşíţe ndoi añ

SEVERE *adj.* (*as of winter*) ásur; greu, -eáuă, grei, -eále; (*rough*) scliró *invar.*; sértic, -că, -ţĭ, -ţe; sértu, *m pl* -rţâ

SEVERITY *s.* ascuráme

SEVILLE ORANGE TREE *s.* nirángiu, miringéu

SEW *vb.* ▼cos; (*to ~ solidly*) arúc áţe múlte ‖ ânţapu

SEWING *s.* cuseáre, cseáre ‖ (*profession*) **GSus, SJos, Prv, Av:** araftţilâche, CL 37

SEWN *adj.* cusút, csut

SEXTON *s.* ‖ **SJos:** cliseátur, CL 42 → SACRISTAN

SHABBY *adj.* (*as of old clothes*) arós, -oásă; măcát, tuchít, fucăréscu, urfănéscu, cacurízic; (*ugly*) urât; (*dirty*) murdár;

SHABINNES

(*scruffy*) pânghiós, -oásă; (*threadbare*) părtálcu; (*mean*) ápcu

SHABBINESS *s.* cacurizilíche

SHACK *s.* călívă → COTTAGE

SHACKLE *s.* cheádică, chédică, ambódhyiu, purdhucľáuă

SHACKLE *vb.* ▾ancheádic, ▾ambudhiséscu, ambudhiţéscu, mbudhuéscu, zâgâdéscu; ~ **the horses!** Ncľidicáţ cáľi! (*to fasten*) ▾stiriuséscu

SHADE *s.* (a)umbrátă ‖ (*~ of color, nuance*) ton, HRISTU 1

SHADOW *s.* (a)úmbră; (*place in the shade for the sheep to rest at noon*) amirídz → CAST ~

SHADY *adj.* (a)umbrós, -oásă; (a)umbrát; ~ **area** cheáre

SHAFT *s.* ‖ PC: (*as a ~ of a hoe*) coádă

SHAGGY *adj.* (*as of smb.'s hair*) zbârlít; (*with much hair, as of a shepherd's winter coat*) pirós, -oásă; ñiţós, -oásă

SHAH *s.* şah

SHAKE *vb.* ▾ascútur, ▾azdrú(n)ţin, azdrúncin, ▾clátin, clătín, *N*: cleátin; ▾cutreám(b)ur, ▾trub, túrbu, ▾trunduéscu, ▾zgăţân; **to ~ in every limb** ▾cruţéscu (→ FEEL DITHERY); **to ~ off** (*as pears from a pear-tree*) ▾súrpu; **to ~ with laughter** ▾căhtéscu, ▾păhăéscu; **to ~ one's sides with laughter** nu-ñ ţân íľile di arâs; ~ **with fright** şápte-óptu ñ-si dúţe (→ QUAKE); ▾cutrumurédz; **to ~ the head** ▾mân cáplu ‖ ALR 1318: (*tilts, as of a table*) z-da

SHAKE DOWN *vb.* (*to become accustomed*) mi nveţ; (*to settle down*) mi aştérnu, mi curdhuséscu; (*to test*) cătăpăţéscu; (*to bring about a reduction of*) scad, ñicşurédz

SHAKE HANDS *vb.* ‖ BELIMACE 57: (*the king*) **shook hands with us** ş-lo mâna cu noi

SHAKING *s.* (a)scuturáre, asdrunţináre, clătináre, cruţíre, cutrem(b)uráre, trunduíre, virviridzáre, (*rare*) virviráre, zgăţănáre; (*~ of the head*) mânáre a cáplui

SHAKY *adj.* (*unsound, rickety*) hárval; ni-síyur; nu sta pri únă

SHALLOW *adj.* (*frivolous*) ľişór, -oáră; ľu-; lişurác, lişuráşcu

SHAM *s.* ≈ *adj.* cálpu, -lpă, -lchi, -lpe

SHAM *vb.* (*to pretend*) mi fac → FEIGN

SHAMBLE *vb.* ‖ PC: ímnu rúfu-m-búfu, mi trag azvárna

SHAME *s.* (a)rşíne, ruşíne, iazâche, yeazâc *or* yeazâcă; *N*: aípe; ~ **on you!** Túndi-te! *or* Iazâche s-ţâ híbă! ~ **on them!** Haráme s-lă híbă! → BURN WITH ~, DIE WITH ~, CRY ~ UPON, PUT TO ~

SHAME *vb.* ar(u)şinédz, aruşnédz

SHAMEFUL *adj.* trâ ascucheáre (*lit. 'such as to spit on'*)

SHAMEFACED *adj.* ar(u)şinát

SHAMELESS *adj.* abráş, abráşcu, arsâz, *m pl* -âjĭ; ni-aruşinát, ni-aruşinós, -oásă *or* ni-ruşinós, -oásă ‖ fáţă-láie, BASME 313

SHAMELESSNESS *s.* ni-aruş(i)náre

SHAMPOO *vb.* ▼(a)láu; *pres:* lau, lai, la, lăm, laţ, la; *ipf:* lam, lai, la, lam, laţ, la; *pt:* lai, laşi, lă, lăm, lat, láră; ~ **your hair!** Lă-ti n cap!

SHANTY *s.* călívă → COTTAGE ‖ paľióspitâ [pa•ľós•pi•tâ], DIARO 271

SHAPE *s.* slúpi *f* → CUT UP ~S, SHOW ~S

SHAPELESS *adj.* bicimsâz, -âză, -âjĭ, -âze

SHAPING *s.* turnipsíre

SHARD *s.* párte, bucătíce

SHARE *s.* párte; (*portion of food*) gărăvánă; (*~ due to or contributed by*) (a)rifiné

SHARECROPPING *s.* undălícă

SHARING *s.* mpărţáre, âmpărtăciúne

SHARK ON SMB. *vb.* aghismédz, aghizmédz

SHARP *adj.* tăľós, -oásă, tăľitós, -oásă; *also:* iáspir, ntruxít, nturhisít, struxít, turyisít; (*of a voice*) ânţăpulicós, -oásă; (*clear, evident*) ayimlíu ‖ (*~, as of a pole*) spirlúngu, BASME 700

SHARPEN *vb.* struxéscu, ntruxéscu, struhiséscu, sturhiséscu, truhiséscu, nturyiséscu, dau pi cheátră ‖ *Peş:* cucutéscu, CL 42; *Peş:* (*as of a scythe*) anturyiséscu, CL 37

SHARPENING *s.* struxíre

SHARPENING TOOL *s.* hrăblă

SHARPER *s.* călupcí, pişichér

SHARPY *or* **SHARPIE** *adj.* şpírtu *invar.* → SHARPER

SHARPNESS *s.* (*sourness*) acritúră

SHARPSHOOTER *s.* nişanlí, nuşanlíu, nişangí

SHATTER *vb.* ▼aspárgu, ▼disvóc → DAMAGE, RUIN

SHAVE *vb.* ▼arád, ▼bărbiriséscu, ▼xurséscu, surséscu, cusurséscu

SHAVING *s.* arádire, xursíre; (*additional, very close* ~) pirdáfe

SHAWL *s.* şal *or* şále; *also:* bálţu, bruboádă, cimbér, ciumbére, cióndă; *F:* ciupáre, *O:* ţipáre; ciuvré, civrée, cumáşe, dármă, dărmă, drámnă, dártmă, drápnă, dárpnă, tistiméle, distiméle,

SHE

dulbén, fachióle; *G:* lăhúră *or* lăhúre; mântílă (*and* mândílă), pétic, pética, peática, póşe, şamíe, şimíe, tarpoáşe; *G:* vláşcă → SHROUD ‖ *Prv:* búfcâ, CL 39

SHE *pron.* ea; dâsă, dísă, năsă; *dat. sg* âĭ, iĭ; -şĭ; **stupid as ~ was** ca chirútă ţe şĭ-erá; -u; **Where is ~?** Iu eásti-u? ‖ *F:* ĭa, BASME 591, 616; **Do you love her?** Tini u vrei ia? HRISTU 63

SHEAF *s.* mănúcĭu (*and* mâ-), mănúncĭu, mâldár, snop, făndáche, văndáche, dhimáte

SHEAR *vb.* (*to trim. to clip, usu. sheep*) **1.** (*under the belly*) suiĭédz; **2.** (*on the head and around the tail*) cápit, căpitédz

SHEARING *s.* suiĭát [su•i•], suiĭáre

SHEATH *s.* (*for a knife or sword*) teácă ‖ *Peş:* mirahúni, CL 255

SHEBANG *s.* (*affair, business, contrivance*) daravéră

SHE-BEAR *s.* úrsă, *N:* aúrsă

SHED *s.* (*usu. for people*) parángă, barángă; (*usu. for animals*) cumás(e), pĭánţă (*and* pĭándză)

SHED *adj.* (*of wine, milk, blood, etc.*) virsát

SHED *vb.* (*to pour down*) vérsu; (*to discard, as hair*) ▼pârjéscu; **to ~ bitter salt** (*to cry*) scârlédz

SHEDDING *s.* (*of hair*) pârjíre; (*of tears*) lăcrâmáre, lăcârmáre

SHE-DEVIL *s.* dráxă, drăcoáñe

SHEEN *s.* yilíciu, scântiĭáre

SHEEP *s.* oáie, *pl* oi; *dim.* uíţă; *coll.* uíme; *milking ~* (a)plicătoáre, muldzár(c)ă; **~ that has had lambs twice** oáie strífă; **two-year old ~** miĭór, ñiĭór, miĭúr, mbĭor, ñiór [ñi•ór] *m*; ñioáră [ñi•], miĭúră, strămĭoáră, ştrăpóri *f*; **horned ~** curnútă; **~ with a bell** ciucánă; *adj.* uín; **~ milk** lápte uín; **~ wool** lână uínă; **flock of ~** uínă; (*~ and goats*) nămáĭu, nimáĭu, numáĭu, *pl* -ĭe; *adj.* uiréscu [u•i•], -eáscă; **a shepherd's donkey** yumár uiréscu ‖ *Mul, Perd, Rod:* óie, *Kat,Plat:* oi, B-ARCH 322 → WET-NURSE ~

SHEEP BIRTHING SEASON (*or* **PLACE**) *s.* fitáĭ

SHEEP DOG *s.* câne picurăréscu

SHEEP FARMING *s.* picurăríĭe, picur(ă)líche; cilnicátă

SHEEP TICK *s. ent.* ‖ *SJos:* bubúşcă, bubúşche, CL 39

SHEEP-BELL *s.* ciocán di oi; *dim.* ciucăníc, ciucăníciu, cluputíc, cluputíciu

SHEEPFOLD *s.* căş(e)áre, căş(e)ár; *also:* cumáş, cuşér, cutár, mándră, stáne, stână, strúngă, tărúşte, turáşte, târáşte, turúşte; (*the place of a* ~) gărtu

SHEEP-OWNER *s.* célnic, cilnică, chihăié *m*, chihăoáñe *f*; scu-
tél; *coll.* cilnicáme

SHEEP-POX *s.* gălbádză, găḷbeáţă, mitíl; **contaminated with ~**
ngălbăgeát, gălbăgiós; **to get contaminated with ~** ngăbăgédz ‖
ALB, *Sln:* mulţădză, Brâncuş 555

SHEER *adj.* (*authentic, absolute*) curát

SHEET *s.* (*of paper*) (a)coálă, fílă; (*of a book*) frândză ‖ **linen**
~, *Gop:* ciarşáfi, GOLAB 210

SHEET-IRON *s.* lamarínă

SHELF *s.* aráfă, (a)ráfe, aráftu, ráfte; *also:* (*in a cheese-*
farm) curutmă, pat, pulíţă ‖ (~ *for cheese in a shepherd's shack*)
K: apát, GOLAB 200; curútmâ, DIARO 279

SHELL *s.* (*of a mussel*) burlídhă, sulínă ‖ *Peş:* zburlídhă, CL
263 ‖ (*of a snail or turtle*) sămár; (*of an egg*) cufcúlă, găuáľe,
guuáľe, găuáce, coáje; (*as of a nut*) coáje, căjoáľe, coáră, flúdhă (→ HUSK); (*of a canon*) ghiulé(e), tópă, vol

SHELL *vb.* (*as beans, nuts, peas, ears of Indian corn*) cur, ▼xi-
fludhyipséscu, xispirséscu

SHELL OUT *vb.* → PAY

SHELTER *s.* apărătúră, apánghiu, húncă; (*for animals*) puiátă,
buiátă; (*shadowy place where sheep rest at noon*) amirídz ‖ DIARO
14: **to take ~** mi apânghiséscu

SHELTER *vb.* ▼acúmtin; (*to lodge*) ▼apreadún, ▼aştéptu; **Please ~**
me tonight! Aştiptáţ-mi aéstă noápte! (*to offer ~*) dau apărătúră;
(*of sheep seeking for a shadowy place*) amirídz ‖ **Will you ~ me**
tonight? Me-apróchi astăseáră?

SHE-MULE *s.* túcă

SHENANIGAN *s.* tirtípe ‖ CUNIA 305: tărtíp; 299: duculeáchi

SHEPHERD *s.* picurár; *dim.* picurărúş; *coll.* picurărátă; (~ *of*
sheep) uiár; (~ *of rams*) birbicár; (~ *of bare ewes*) stirpár; (~
of young ewes) vituľár; (~ *of one-year old sheep*) nutinár; (~ *of*
milkïng sheep) mătricár, muldzár; (~ *of goats*) căprár; (*cheese-*
maker ~) căşeár; (*main* ~) baciu, (*rare*) bagiu; (*servant* ~ *in a*
sheepfold) peregé ‖ *Na:* giobán, B-ARCH 335; *K:* găvărár, GOLAB 217;
părvotár GOLAB 242; (*chief* ~) *Cru:* chihăié, GOLAB 23. In ALB: **Dren,**
Kërb, Për: căşáru, keşár, kişáru; *Sil:* cilinícu, Brâncuş 551.
"The term *baciu* is not known," *ibid.*

SHEPHERD *adj.* picurăréscu, -eáscă, -éşţâ, -éşti; di la oi; **a ~'s dog** câne picurăréscu *or* câne di la oi

SHEPHERD'S CROOK *s.* cârlíg; cľoágă (*and* gľoágă)

SHERBET *s.* şirbét, şirbéte

SHERIFF *s.* zăpít, zăpită, zăbít; cumisár

SHE-WOLF *s.* lupoáñe, lúpsă

SHIELD *s.* (*protection*) ‖ LITURG 124: avilimíntlu *sg def*

SHIELD *vb.* ▾ápăr → DEFEND, PROTECT

SHIEVER *s.* hiór, hir arắţe; *pl*: híre arắţi pi tu păltări

SHIFT *s.* (*dodge*) tirtípe

SHIFT ABOUT *vb.* ▾úrdin

SHIFT AWAY *vb.* li scármin → BOLT

SHIFTLESS *adj.* → LAZY

SHIFTY *adj.* → TRICKY

SHILLELAGH *s.* → CUDGEL

SHILLING *s.* silín

SHILLY-SHALLY *vb.* (*to put off acting*) ñ-u dau n coástă, ▾induéscu

SHIM *s.* scârpă

SHIMMER *vb.* → GLIMMER, SPARKLE

SHIMMERY *adj.* lumbărsít → BRILLIANT

SHIN *vb.* ▾angărlím (*and* angâr-) → CLIMB

SHINBONE *s. anat.* flúir → TIBIA

SHINE *s.* (*brightness*) yil(i)círe; (*liking, fancy*): **to take a ~ to** ñ-cáde tu ínimă

SHINE *vb.* lămbiséscu → SPARKLE

SHINE OUT *vb.* ▾luñinédz

SHINGLE *s.* (*made of wood*) şíndră

SHINING *adj.* scântiľós, -oásă → BRILLIANT

SHINY *adj.* scântiľós, -oásă

SHIP *s.* căráve, ghimíe, náie, pampóre

SHIPMENT *s.* pitreáţire, pitriţeáre

SHIPPING *s.* → SHIPMENT

SHIRT *s.* cameáşe, *dim.* cămişíţă, cămăşótă; *G:* ríză; **short-sleeved ~** camisólă ‖ *dim. also* câmişícâ, DIARO 199

SHIRTING *s.* pândză

SHIT *s.* căcát, *dim.* căcătíciu; mérdu, pângânătáte, păgâneáţă

SHIT *vb.* mi cac, ñ-scot ócľiľ; (*of infants*) ▾fac; (*soft con-*

sistency) ▼cufuréscu

SHIVER *s.* (*fragment*) hrup; ţívale *pl* ‖ ţistálâ, DIARO 248

SHIVER *s.* trimúră, hir aráţe, mpiruşáre, mbirşáre ‖ CUVATA 2: frắşti *f;* **a ~ passed over us** nă tricú ună frắşti tu pănticắ, Cuvata 9

SHIVER *vb.* ▼trémur, trámur, treám(b)ur; **Amc:** trímbur; ▼cutrém, cutrémur, cutreámbur, cutrémbur, cutrámur, ▼trunduéscu; (*to ~ with pain, cold, or fear*) ▼virvirédz

SHKODRA *s.* (*a town in Albania*): *adj.* şcodrănéscu, -eáscă

SHOCK *s.* (*shake*) trunduíre

SHOCK *s.* (*heap, pile*) cópă; (*a thick bushy mass, as of hair*) mănúcľu

SHOD *adj.* (*as of a horse*) ncălţát (*ant.* ni-ncălţát)

SHODDY *adj.* arós, -oásă; mâcát

SHOE *s.* curdhéľe, cundúră; *G:* gămáşe; yeméñe, pandóflă, păpúţă, pupúţă, scárpiñe; **a pair of ~** únă păreácľe di curdhéľe; (*children's talk*) pópă → MAKE SMB. CREAK IN HIS ~S

SHOE *vb.* (*of horses*) ▼ncálţu

SHOE-HORN *s.* os di curdhéľi

SHOEING *s.* (*of horses*) ncălţáre

SHOEING SMITH *s.* (a)nalbán, pitălár

SHOEMAKER *s.* curdhilár, curdhilắ; *also:* cundurgí, păpugí, pupugí, păpuţár, ţăruhár, ţuruhár, ţângár, ţârhắ ‖ *Mul:* cundrăgí; *almost everywhere:* ţăngár, B-ARCH 386; MERCA 30: cundrugí

SHOEMAKER'S KNIFE *s.* fălcétă

SHOEMAKER'S SHOP *s.* cunduragilâche

SHOE-MAKING *s.* cunduragilâche

SHOOT *s.* cľeciu, climbúciu → BRANCH ‖ *Av:* almăcúşâ, CL 36; *SJos:* clunáre, CL 42

SHOOT ONE'S GRANDMOTHER *vb.* (*i.e., to make a blunder*) u adár taratóre [*taratór* is a dish made of cold sour milk, cucumber and other ingredients]

SHOOT OUT ONE'S LIPS *vb.* ▼strâmbu búdzâle

SHOOT OUT ONE'S TONGUE AT SMB. *vb.* ľ-scot límba (nafoáră)

SHOOT THE BOLT(S) *vb.* trag sírtul

SHOOT *vb.* ▼arúc; **They shot and wounded me** Arcáră ş-mi pliguíră; *N:* amín; ▼trag; trag cu curşúñi; (*of a young plant*) fitruséscu; **~ at a target** amín, dau tu sémnu, trag tu nişáne

SHOOTING *s.* amináre

SHOP *s.* ducheánă, dugáne, duyáne; aryăstír, măgăză, măyăzíe

SHOP *vb.* fac păzáre, ▼nvistéscu → NEGOTIATE, BUY

SHOPKEEPER *s.* băcălă *m*, băcăloáñe *f*; măyăzár, măyăzătór

SHOPPING *s.* păzáre, psunsíre

SHORE *s.* mal, méjdă, mézdă; ~ **of the sea** acruyeaľáuă; márdzină di amáre

SHORE *vb.* (*to prop up*) ▼arádzim → LEAN

SHORING *s.* → SUPPORT

SHORN *adj.* cu pérlu tăľát

SHORT *adj.* scúrtu, *m pl* -rţâ *and* scúndu, *m pl* -ndzâ; apús; **in ~** cu un zbor; ~ **accounts make good friends** → ACCOUNT; **to be a button ~** ≈ ľ-lipséscu drăñ (*lit.* 'has missing boards'); ~ **of cash** cacurizipsít → PENNILESS)

SHORTCOMING *s.* catmére, cusúre, măhănă(u), mărdáie, smârdhă

SHORTCUT: to make a ~ astáľu cálea

SHORTEN *vb.* ▼scurtédz, şcurtédz; (*to decapitate*) **Cut off his head!** şcurteádză-l! ▼adún, apreadún; **With the passing of years the thread of life ~s** Cu áñľi cioára a ómului si-adúnă; (*to make a shortcut*) astáľu cálea

SHORT-EARED *adj.* (*of horses, sheep, or goats*) cip, *m pl* cipľ (*sic*)

SHORTENING *s.* şcurt(ic)áre

SHORT-HORNED *adj.* (*of cattle*) ciulác, şbut (PC: [źbut])

SHORT-LIVED *adj.* ntreáţit

SHORTLY *adv.* → SOON

SHORTNESS *s.* şcurtáme

SHORT-TEMPERED *adj.* căchiós, -oásă → ILL-TEMPERED

SHORT-WEIGHT *adj.*, *adv.* ixíche

SHOT *s.* (*lead or steel pellots; the charge of a shotgun*) aşíşe, bălătâñ *pl*; ciuciumág; **to make a bad ~** *fig.* u adár taratóre → TO SHOOT ONE'S GRANDMOTHER ‖ ALR 724: bălătín

SHOULD *vb.* 1. *3 sg*: va *or* vrea; *3 pl*: vor; **A debt ~ be paid** Bórgea va plătíre; **The thieves ~ be killed** Fúrľi vor vătămáre; 2. prínde; **You ~ comb** Prínde s-ti cheápţâñ; 3. fúri-că, fúreşi că; **should he really not have a father** fúri-că nu ári tátă; ~ **I be able to** fúreşi că va s-pot; 4. ai că fúre; ~ **it be a boy or a girl** ai că ficiór, ai că feátă fúre; 5. (*in case that*) ca să; ~ **I**

die ca si-ñ mor; ~ **he come, I'll give it to him** Ca s-yínă va
ľ-u dau; **6.** (*cond.*) ~ **it be necessary** (*i.e., if it were necessary*), **I shall take an oath** S-lipseáre, ľau ş giurát; **7.** fáţe; **He**
~ **not leave** Nu fáţe s-fúgă; **8.** cara s nu *or* cari s nu; **We would**
have died to a man ~ **we not have had you** Va s-chireám pân di un
cára s-nu erái tíne; ~ **he not be able to steal them** cari
s-nu poátă să-ľ ciúnă

SHOULDER *s.* (a)númir, úmir, plătáre, spálă, spátă; (*in a*
children's game: lásă-spátă); **on the** ~ *adv.* anúmirea, di-anúmi-
rea, dinanúmirea ‖ ALIA 163: pultáre, númur; *F:* **with a bag of**
clothing over his ~ cu un sac di strañă d-arumănă, HRISTU 60

SHOULDER BLADE *s. anat.* ármu, plătáre, spálă

SHOULDER STRAP *s.* (*of a rifle*) măgór

SHOUT *s.* aurláre, boáţe, huhútă, strigáre, zghic

SHOUT *vb.* aúrlu, (a)zghér, bag zghic, huéscu, ▾huhutéscu,
strig, zghiléscu ‖ bag boáţea, PARALLELE 156

SHOUT ONESELF HOARSE *vb.* ‖ *Don't shout yourself hoarse* (*i.e.,*
don't waste your breath) Nu-ţi aspárdzi gúra! (*lit. 'Don't break*
your mouth'!), PARALLELE 147

SHOUTING *s.* gríre

SHOVE *vb.* ▾bag

SHOVEL *s.* lupátă, *pl* -păţ

SHOW *s.* → CUT A ~, MAKE A ~ OF ONESELF

SHOW *vb.* ▾aspún (→ § 32), ▾făniruséscu, ▾părăstăséscu *and*
-sti-; (*rare*) arát; **If you want renown, you have to** ~ **that you**
are brave Ca si-ai anáme, prinde s ti-aspúñ gióne; **If you love**
your son, ~ **him the cudgel** S-eáste că-l vrei híľlu, spúne-ľ giu-
máclu; **to** ~ **one's mettle** scot; **Well,** ~ **your mettle now, son!** E,
scoáte tóra, híľi! **to** ~ **fight** nu-ñ mâcă coásta ţáră; **to** ~ **leg**
(*slang:* **to sling one's hook**) mi ľau cicioárile dinanúmirea; **to** ~
shapes l-gioc *or* l-gioc pri tăpsíe; **to** ~ **hospitality** l-ţân uspéţ;
to ~ **smb. much attention** ancúñu, dau di curáuă / di măneár

SHOW A CLEAN PAIR OF HEELS *vb.* li scármin → BOLT

SHOW FIGHT *vb.* (*to show hostility*) ‖ DIARO 173: **began to** ~ acáţă
şi-şi spúnâ cârínţâľi

SHOW IN *vb.* urséscu năúntru, cupăséscu năúntru, cupuséscu →
INVITE

SHOW ONESELF *vb.* ‖ MERCA 12: fac parón (*when the roll is called*)

SHOW UP *vb.* dau cap; *also:* ápir; ▼(a)spún; *(as of mustaches)* asúd, dau, arsár, alsár, (i)es; *(as of the moon)* ▼ñíşcu; *3 sg* lu-áre *m*, u-áre *f*; **My Lord, why isn't he showing up?** Doámne, ţe nu lu-áre?

SHOWING *s.* aspúnire, aspuneáre, arătáre

SHRED *s.* bucătíce

SHRED *vb.* ▼cumăthiséscu, ▼mâşcăturédz

SHREW *s.* *(of a woman)* dráxă, drăcoáñe, stríglă

SHREWISH *adj.* → ILL-TEMPERED

SHREWD *adj.* *(clever, sharp)* ayrăsít, iáspir, struxít, tăľós, tăľitós → SAGACIOUS; *(tricky)* ti vínde ş ti-acúmpără *(lit. 'he buys you and sells you off [easily]')* ‖ BASME 404: şirét; drac di sum púnte *(lit. 'devil from under the footbridge')*

SHRIEK *s.* zghic → SHOUT

SHRIEK *vb.* **to ~ at the top of one's voice** → LAUGHTER ‖ zghi-léscu cât mi ncápe gúra, *(lit. to shout as loudly as one's mouth allows it')* BASME 119

SHRILL *adj.* *(as of a whistle)* supţâre

SHRIMP *s.* *derog.* *(of people)* jabéc, jubéc; *(as of a feeble goat)* júdav ‖ *(of people, derog.)* căcătíciu, DIARO 192

SHRIMPY *adj.* chirchinéc; **a ~ child** un chirchinéc di ficiór; **a ~ person** căcărdác

SHRINK *vb.* ▼adún, ▼angustédz, ▼strâmtédz; *(of a fabric)* 3 *sg:* íntră (*and* índră); *(as of fear)* păpăruséscu, zăruséscu

SHRINKAGE *s.* → SHRINKING

SHRINKING *s.* adunáre, stríndzire, strindzeáre, scădeáre

SHRIVEL *vb.* ▼usúc, ▼usâc, ▼păléscu, ▼mărănédz, ▼arăhniséscu

SHRIVELLED *adj.* uscát, jabéc, preácăn, preángu, ţihărídă

SHROUD *s.* sávan, sávun, săvón, zăvón, zvon; *also:* (a)schépe, calimchéră, calimchére, căftáne, cípă, ţípă; *(bride's ~)* cimlér, ciumbér, sindhónă; şimíe, tarpóşe; *(mourner's ~)* **G:** turpáne; vláşcă → SHAWL

SHRUNKEN *adj.* găvunós, -oásă; jábec

SHUCK *s.* *(green pricking ~ of a chestnut)* júnă

SHUCK OFF *vb.* *(as nuts, Indian corn, etc.)* ▼xiludhipséscu, xi-ludhiséscu

SHUDDER *s.* hiór → SHIVER

SHUDDER *vb.* trémur, treámbur → SHAKE, SHIVER

SHUFFLE *vb.* ▾ambărtuéscu, ▾birdhipséscu, ▾mbirdhuéscu, hurhu-léscu

SHUFFLE THE CARDS vb. ‖ ALR 1272: *3 sg:* minteáşte cărţăle

SHUN *vb.* (*to ~ like the plague*) ≈ fug (di nâs) ca di per di lup

SHUT *s.* (*the act of shutting*) tufixíre, tufichisíre

SHUT *vb.* ▾ncľid (→ CLOSE); **to ~ one's yap** (*to keep a secret*) nu dau pri toácă; **~ up!** Máľaclu! Máľacura! Mâşcă-ţ límba! (*lit. 'Bite your tongue'!*) ‖ DIARO 51: (*~ up!*) taţi, anúti! 269: coási-u gúra! **to ~ smb.'s mouth** ľ-acáţ gúra, BASME 433

SHUT OFF *vb.* taľu

SHUT UP! → SHUT ‖ **~, you are talking garbage!** Uh, nu ti badzi amóľu, DIARO 50

SHUT UP SHOP *vb.* (*to hang up one's axe*) trag mânâ (di) → ABNE-GATE

SHUTDOWN *s.* (*layoff*) scărchíre

SHUTTER *s.* (*movable cover*) chipéne, chipénghe, chipinécă, cănát, glăvăníe

SHUTTLE: weaver's ~ suválţă, suvá(l)niţă; sválţă, zválţă; svu-líndză

SHY *adj.* ar(u)şinós, -oásă; aruşnós, -oásă; aruşdisít

SHY *vb.* (*to recoil*) aruş(u)téscu, aruşdiséscu, ▾aruşunédz

SHY DIRT AT SMB. *vb.* aúngu di la cap pânâ la cioáre; rizil(ips)éscu, tălăéscu tu halé

SHYNESS *s.* antírise (*and* andí-), ndílise, aruşdíe, aruşdisíre, ticlífe

SIBLING *s.* puľu

SIC *vb.* ‖ *Cru:* hiumuséscu, *BdD':* sâlâéscu, *Po:* ndârséscu, Ne-iescu 173; *Trn:* ~'em! să să să! NEIESCU 335

SICK *adj.* lânţid (*and* lândzid), lândzidzât, nip(u)tút, dzăcút, zaíf, zăífcu, zăbún(e) → ILL ‖ STERE 10: chifsăz; (*desgusted*) sătúl, săturát, ngustát → BE ~, BECOME ~, MAKE ~

SICK AND TIRED: I am ~ Ñ-se-acrí (*lit. 'It has turned sour to me'*), PARALLELE 151

SICKEN *vb.* hiuvréscu; (*to make sick*) şúplic

SICKLE *s.* seáţire, -ră; cusór, dhirpáne ‖ *GSus:* cusér, CL 43

SICKLY *adj.* lângurós, -oásă, lun-; *also:* cufurít, mărăjár, mârâjár, mârâjós, -oásă → AILING

SICKNESS *s.* (*ill health*) lângoáre, nipteáre; (*nausea*) greáţă,

SIDE

angúsă

SIDE *s.* párte; *(attitude, part)* ileácă; **on this ~** dincoá, dincoáţe; **on the other ~** dincló, dingló; didínde, *N:* dínde; *adj.* *(situated on the other ~)* anáparte; di didínde; **He went to the room situated on the other ~ of the house** Tricú tu óda di didínde; **on one ~** *(reclining)* pri câlcu → TAKE ~S, BE LIKE A THORN IN ONE'S ~, PUT ON SIDE

SIDE *vb.* *(with smb.)* ľ-ľau párte

SIDEBURNS *s.* aráuă

SIDEKICK *s.* soţ, urtác

SIDELONG *adv.* pládea, amplátea, ambládea

SIDEWALK *s.* căldărâme ‖ DIARO 168: gâdrâmă

SIEGE *s.* anvărligáre; **We fell into a heavy ~** Cădzú anvărligáre greáuă pri noi

SIEVE *s.* *(usu. for flour)* sítă ‖ **Cru:** *(for grain)* ţir, GOLAB 210

SIEVE-LIKE *adj.* *(as of an old cloth)* ndipirát

SIFT *vb.* ▾ţérnu, ▾ndzérnu

SIFTING *s.* ţirneáre, nţirneáre

SIGH *s.* uftáre, uhtáre, uhtát; *also:* scălizáre, scălizát, scălţádză, scălţáre, suschír, súschir, suschirát, suschiráre, suschináre

SIGH *vb.* uftédz, uhtédz; *also:* ñ-adún súflitlu, ▾nilséscu, nălséscu, nuchéscu, scăltíz, scălţédz, suschír, súschir → MAKE SMB. ~

SIGHT *s.* videáre, veádire; *also:* luñínă; ócľi *pl*; videálă; **His ~ began to return** Ócľiľ acăţáră să-ľ yínă; **at ~** la videáre; **at first ~** la videáre; *(panorama)* aynánghiu → CATCH ~ OF

SIGHTLY *adj.* muşát, nóstim, *m pl* -tiñ; nustimác, *m pl* -máţĭ

SIGN *s.* sémnu, *dim.* simníc; *also:* dhóymă, nişáne, simáde; *(start line in children's games)* apúchiu; **to put a ~** bag nişáne; *(mark cut on the ear of a sheep to show ownership)* coácă → MAKE A ~ TO SMB.

SIGN *vb.* *(to subscribe)* ▾ipuyrăpséscu, ñ-bag mândzăle, bag mândzále; bag dzeáditlu *(lit. 'to put one's finger')* ‖ MERCA 9: pugrăpséscu

SIGN UP *vb.* scriu

SIGNAL *vb.* *(with one's eyes)* ‖ ľ-dau ócľi, BASME 189

SIGNALIZE ONESELF *vb.* *(to distinguish oneself; to vote smb.*

into) ▾alég

SIGNATURE *s*. ipuyrắfíe, mândză, múndză, cundíľ, cundiľáuă; **This is not his ~!** Nu-i cundíľlu-a lui! → PUT ONE'S ~ TO SMTH.

SIGNING *s*. ipuyrăpsíre

SILENCE *s*. tăţeáre; **perfect ~** stámă, şteámă, ştámă, ţâpit; **~ please!** sst!

SILENCE *vb*. (*as to ~ a bell with one's hand*) ▾astúp; (*to talk smb. down*) ▾astúp gúra; ľ-bag lingureáua; **~ him!** Astupáţ-ľi gúra!

SILENT *adj*. tăcút → BE ~ ▾amút

SILKWORM *s*. budín

SILEX *s*. crémine, sturnáre

SILK *s*. sírmă; *also:* mătáse, mătáfe, mitáse, mitáxe; (*raw ~*) burungícă, (i)brisíme, (i)brişíme, (i)brăşíme; **fabrics of ~:** cumáşe, **G:** cumáş; curazé, **N:** curazée; geamfése, gron, gróndu, hachír, santacrútă, silimíe, silíncă, zófe ‖ (*~ of Indian corn*) **Peş:** bárbă, CL 38

SILLINESS *s*. curcubéte (di Chirásova) *f pl* → TRIFLE

SILLY *adj*. dabólea *invar*. şulúndu, -ndă, -ndzâ, -nde → STUPID; **~ talk** zburáre şulúndă

SILT *s*. alúnizmă, cuciumór

SILUROID *s*. *ichth*. (*catfish*) guľanó, soámă

SILVER *s*. asíme; (*articles of ~*) asim(i)có, asimicătúră

SILVER *adj*. (*color*) argheándu, *m pl* -ndzâ

SILVER *vb*. asimuséscu ‖ ALR 572: fumédz cu asíme

SILVERED OVER *adj*. asimusít

SILVERING *s*. asimusíre

SILVERSMITH *s*. fávru, hrísic, hríscu

SILVERWARE *s*. ‖ TULLIU 83: asimicó

SILVERSMITH'S CRAFT *s*. hrisiclíche

SIMILAR *adj*. aparálactu, *m pl* -cţâ; ómñu, *m pl* ómñi, *f sg/pl* ómñe ‖ **very ~ to** → AS LIKE AS TWO PEAS; *see also* BE ~ TO

SIMILARITY *s*. adúcă, uidíe, úidizmă

SIMILARLY *adv*. → IDENTICALLY

SIMPLE *adj*. (*pure, not mixed*) munát, schet; sadé(u) (*free from elaboration*) *m/f sg* apló, *m pl* apládz, *f pl* ? (DDA 175)

SIMPLE-MINDED *adj*. apló → STUPID

SIMPLETON *s*. *m/f* apló, *m pl* apládz (*f pl* ? DDA 175) → STUPID

SIMPLY *adv.* (*without ambiguity*) şi álta nu (*lit. 'and not other'*); ~ **and solely** ayní; **This soup is ~ and solely water** Dzáma eáste ayní ápă

SIMULATE *vb.* ▾fac → FEIGN

SIN *s.* picát, (a)mărtíe (*and* amâr-), crímă, fáie; **besetting ~** amărtíe greáuă

SIN *vb.* fac păcát, amărti(p)séscu, íntru tu amărtíe, ľau pri zvércă

SINAPISM *s.* (*mustard plaster*) sinapismó

SINCE *adv.* (*temporal*) di-ánda, dánda; di atúmţea; di cându; ~ **Adam** di únă étă ‖ ~ **then** → THEN

SINCE *cj.* (*in view of the fact that*) di oáră ţe, uná oáră ţe; .cari, **N:** di cari, **S:** dicára; cálai-că, délme, dírmi; ~ **discord appeared among them, they split** Cari lă intră ngrâña, si-mpărţă-ră; ~ **you have come, you will stay!** Dírmi viñíşi, va stai! ‖ *Cru:* ma; ~ **you have asked me, I will answer you** Ma m-intribáşi, va ţă spun, GOLAB 233

SINCERE *adj.* curát, dişcľís; **He is not ~** ≈ Nu li áre curáte zmeánile (*lit. 'His underwear is not clean'*) → HONEST

SINCERELY *adv.* curát; ndréptu ş curát

SINEW *s.* (*physical strength*) → STRENGTH

SINFUL *adj.* amărtiós, -oásă → WICKED

SING *vb.* ▾cắntu, ľ-u dzâc (*and* dzắc); (*of birds*) ▾bat; **That is the way the bird was singing** Acşí băteá púľlu; (*at church*) psăl(ti)séscu, psultiséscu, săltiséscu; **to ~ another tune** (*to change one's tune*) u şuţắscu frândza; (*said to someone who sings his/her own praise:*) Murí yífta ţi ti-alăvdá! **to ~ small** arăñés-cu; li dipún urécľile ‖ (*3 sg*) **Amc, Mul:** cántă, **An, Fal, Na, Vot, Ver:** cândă, **Perd:** chéntă B-ARCH 486; **Sing a song!** dzâ-ľ un cântic! (*lit. 'Tell him/it a song'*), PARALLELE 151

SING SMALL *vb.* → SING

SINGE *vb.* ▾pârléscu, ▾căpsălséscu, ▾ghimtuéscu; **You've ~ed your hair!** T-căpsălsíşi pérlu!

SINGER *s.* cântătór; **G:** dişcântă

SINGING *adj.* cântătór, -oáre

SINGLE *adj.* síngur, şúngru; (*not married*) ni-fumiľát; (*of a man*) ni-nsurát; (*of a woman*) ni-mărtátă; (*bachelor*) bicheár; (*odd*) techi [tek']

SINGLE FILE *adv.* arádha

SINISTER *adj.* lăhtărós, -oásă

SINK *s.* niruhíte; uz; **G:** vúdnic → DRAIN ‖ DIARO 243: niruhídhâ

SINK *vb.* (*to fall in*) ▼afunduséscu, ahunduséscu, ▼hăndăcusés-
cu; (*to enter deeply, as in a forest*) ▼huhutéscu; (*of smb.'s
eyes*) ▼hăuséscu; (*to fail in health or strength, as of the
heart*): **His heart sank** Inima ĺ-si ñicşură, ĺ-si feáţe ca pun-
gárlu; **to ~ in** ▼alás păgór; **to ~ into the earth for shame** mi
ngroápă lóclu (*or* lu-ngróp lóclu) di-arşíne; **to ~ into thoughts**
mi acáţă minduírea, ▼minduéscu ‖ ALR 859 (*of a ship*) 3 sg: s-a-
hunducuseáşte

SINKING *s.* fundusíre

SINLESS *adj.* ni-amărtipsít

SINNER *s.* amărtiós

SIP *s.* surghíre

SIP UP *vb.* sórbu; (*a little or little by little*) cuţubeau; (*as
of coffee*) arufséscu

SIR *s.* (*addressing a man*) eféndim ‖ **Av:** chiríu, CL 254

SISTER *s.* sóră, *pl* surări, sor; **Go to my elder ~** Si ti duţi la
márea-ñ sor; **He said to his ~ again** Ĺ-aspúse diznóu a sór-sai;
my ~ sór-mea; **your ~** sór-ta; **his/her ~** sór-sa; *dim.* surícă; surără-
rícă; **elder ~** dódă

SISTER-IN-LAW *s.* cumnátă, băginácă ‖ (*brother's wife*) nórâ di
fráti, DIARO 325

SIT: *to* **be on the anxious ~** şed ca pri schiñ

SIT *vb.* şed; stau (→ § 32); **to ~ down** ▼apún *or* şed ăn cur;
Raise so I can ~ down Scoálă tíne ca s-şed míne; **They sat down to
table** şidzúră pri meásă (*pres.* mi aşternu la meásă); **They sat
around me** Di-varlíga ñ-si-apúsiră; **~ down!** şedz pri cúr-ţâ! **to ~
cross-legged** şed a ncruţíşalui; **to ~ out** (*to stay away*) **S:** ană-
mirséscu; *to* **~ tight** ▼disíc năínte; nu cad ma nghios; **to ~ up** şed
pi şidzút; (*to watch*) privégĺu; **to ~ up on pins** şed ca pri schiñ;
(*of a dog*) stau sústa → BE SITTED

SIT ON THE FENCE *vb.* ñ-u dau n coástă → HESITATE

SIT PRETTY WARM *vb.* (*to prosper*) adár căşeáre

SIT TIGHT *vb.* → SIT

SIT UP *vb.* → SIT

SIT! (*to a dog*) sústa!

SITE *s.* sémte → LOCATION

SITTING UP TO WORK IN COMPANY *s.* ţícna-préfte

SITUATION *s.* catástasi; (*usu. bad ~*) hálă *or* hále; hăľúră; catándise; **I know your difficult ~** Vă ştiu hála; (*a complex and tricky ~*) lúcri cu fúndi (*lit.* 'things with bows of ribbon')

SIX *num.* şeáse, şáse; **sixes and sevens** (*of smb.'s clothes*) cătră naľúrea; ~ **hundred** şeáse súte

SIXTEEN *num.* şeásprădzaţe, şáspră

SIXTH *ord.* şásira; **at the ~ stair** la şásira scáră ‖ *Cru:* écatu, GOLAB 214; şásile, BASME 461 → § 28.2 *above*

SIXTY *num.* şaidzăţi

SIZABLE *adj.* mărişór, -oáră

SIZE *s.* (*as of shoes, shirts, etc.*) mizúră

SKEDADDLE *vb.* li scármin → BOLT

SKEIN *s.* cámată, crúnă, tiriplíche

SKEIN-WINDER *s.* (a)răşcľitór; *also:* caléme, dişcľitór, lăşchitór, lişcător; mutuvílă

SKID *s.* → PUT THE ~S UNDER SMB.

SKILFUL *adj.* chischín, -chinéţ, mástur; **to be very ~** ñ-acáţă mâna ‖ BA, 249: ñ-ľa ócľul la túti (*lit.* 'my eye catches all')

SKILL *s.* (*capacity*) tăcáte; (*artfulness*) micáme, muraféte

SKILLED *adj.* (*versed*) pir; ~ **worker** tihnít, usţă, zanahcí, zănătcíu

SKILLET *s.* tiyáñe

SKILLFUL *adj.* → SKILFUL

SKILLFULNESS *s.* chischineáţă, chischimeáţă, măsturíe, măsturlíche, murafitlâche

SKIM *s.* (*on boiling or boiled milk*) peáţă

SKIM MILK *s.* *Src:* beleníţă

SKIMP *vb.* ‖ PC: dau cu părălâche

SKIN *s.* cheále, *dim.* chilícă; **the ~ of the head** chifălăreáuă; **dressed ~** mişíne; **lamb ~** arñeacó ‖ ALIA 144: *also* chéli *and* fólă; ~ **and bone** cheáli ş-oási, BASME 46 ‖ ~ **of grapes after the last pressing** príştină di aúuă; ţípur, ţípură (→ DREGS)

SKIN *vb.* biléscu di cheále, ▾guléscu, ▾zmúlgu

SKINNY *adj.* alăchít (*and* alâ-, ali-); ca súptu di vómbiri (*lit.* 'as if sucked up by vampires'); iáscă *invar.*; slăghít ca hiľán (*lit.* 'like a toothpick')

SKIP *s.* sáltă, (a)săltáre

SKIP *vb.* → JUMP

SKIP OFF *vb.* li scármin → BOLT

SKIRMISH *s.* lúmtă, acăţáre, ncârligáre

SKIRT *s.* fústă, fútă, futắ; *G:* băcă

SKITTER *vb.* → SLIP

SKITTISH *adj.* (*capricious*) burdál, căpriceárcu, nizeárcu, zburdălipsít; (*easily frightened*) aspărós, -oásă

SKULKER *s.* (*poltroon*) pantalunár (*and* panda-)

SKULL *s.* căpiţắnă; *also:* cáfcală, cáfcă, cărápă, căr(ă)fétă ‖ *Pls:* tas di cap, CL 262; *SJos:* crăpăcínă; *Av:* crâpâţắnâ, CL 2; *Amc:* os di cap, SCHL 113

SKY *s.* ţer, uranó ‖ *Peş:* dumnidzá (*sic*), *Prv:* dumnedzắu, CL 44; **as blue as the ~** nalbástru ca dumnidzá

SKY-LARK *s.* ciuciurlíe → LARK

SLAB *s.* ploáce

SLACK *adj.* alăsát → NEGLIGENT

SLACKEN *vb.* ▾scad, cătăprăéscu; **Brigandage has ~ed** Furlíchile cătăprăíră; (*to ease, as a too tight belt*) ▾distríngu

SLACKENING *s.* distríndzire

SLAG *s.* zgúră, zgureáuă; *adj.* zgurós, -oásă; zgúrav, *m pl* -rayĭ

SLAKE *vb.* ▾cúrmu, ▾ayăliséscu

SLAKED LIME *s.* azvéste asteásă

SLAM *vb.* (*as a door*) zdupunéscu

SLANDER *s.* biuftáne, cacuzburáre, efteríe, muhtáne, săhúñ *f pl*

SLANDER *vb.* arúc efteríe (pri), arúc muhtáne (pri), zburắscu, cacuzburắscu, săhunéscu ‖ mâc chétri, BASME 346; acáţ ân gúrâ; ñ-strâmbu gúra, DIARO 121

SLANDERER *s.* ‖ DIARO 121: lafazán

SLANDEROUS *adj.* → SLANDERER

SLANT *vb.* ▾apléc, ▾nclʼin

SLAP *s.* báţă; **He had a ~ at him** Ľ-trápse únă báţă; *also:* (*~ in the nape of the neck*) ghiúştă, ghiuştăreáuă; fláscută, flíscută, flâscută, flúscută, plíscută, şúbă, şupleácă; únă (*lit.* 'one [blow]'); vâră; (*~ in the nape*) zvârcăreáuă ‖ **at a ~** *adv.* până s-ţă freţi óclʼiľ, BASME 10 (*lit.* 'before you rub your eyes') *or* până si-ascúchi, DDA 223

SLAP *vb.* ▾avrédz; ľ-trag (*or* ľ-súflu, ľ-şúir) únă báţă; *also*

SLASH

ľ-alichéscu únă, ľi am nă şupľácă, ľ-ancúñu únă, ľi-árdu vâră, ľ-
aséscu únă, ľi astrág únă, ľ-cârţânéscu una fľíscută, ľ-şurdués-
cu únă; **Have a ~ at him!** Alăcheá-ľ únă! Aseá-ľ únă! Avreádză-l!
şúiră-ľ una báţă!

SLASH vb. ▾taľu, ▾scad

SLASHING s. zâpâlíre

SLATE s. (for writing on) panachídă, pínac, pínacă; (also for
roofing) ploáce ‖ **GSus, Pls:** plácă, CL 259

SLATING s. (as of water) săturáre → REPLETION

SLAUGHTER s. mbizuíre, cârdilíu, cârléşi f, cârligíe, gili-
tipsíre, măchéľ, măchilipsíre

SLAUGHTER vb. ▾gilitipséscu, ▾măchilipséscu (and mâ-); (to
begin to ~) bag cuţút

SLAUGHTER HOUSE s. zalhané, zalhanée, zarhaná

SLAVE s. rob, **G:** rop; sclav ‖ LITURG 133: smichéru

SLAVER s. bále f pl, bálă sg

SLAVERY s. sclăvíľe, sclăvíe → SERVITUDE, THRALDOM

SLAVERY adj. (as of milk; also of people) bălós, -oásă

SLY vb. → KILL

SLEAZY adj. arós, -oásă; mâcát

SLED s. sáñe

SLEDGE s. sáñe

SLEEK adj. (of hair) ‖ **SJos:** hiľiciós, -oásă; **with ~ hair** cu
pérľi hi-ľiciós

SLEEVELESS FURRED COAT s. chiptár

SLEEP s. sómnu, dim. somnúş; to be heavy with ~ cad di sómnu,
mi neácă sómnul, nsumnédz; **heavy with ~** adj. nsumnát → BE OVER-
COME BY ~, DROP WITH ~, PUT TO ~ ‖ **F:** som, HRISTU 2 and somn 11

SLEEP vb. dórmu; l-ľau di ureácľe; **We lay down in order to ~** Nă
teásim si-l lom di ureácľe; (of little children) fac náni; **to ~
as fast as a church** dorm ca di ţáră di mórtu; **to ~ the sleep of**
death apudórmu; **As if he were expecting to ~ the sleep of death!**
Cánda aşteáptă si-apudoármă! ‖ **Sleep well!** Sómnu lişór! (lit.
'[Have a] light sleep'), PARALLELE 145

SLEEP IT OFF vb. ▾disbét

SLEEPER s. adurñít

SLEEPINESS s. agărşíre, apugărşíre

SLEEPING s. durñíre; **~ place, corner, shelter** guneáuă, STERE 24

SLEEPING BEAUTY s. ≈ Muşeáta-a-Lóclui (*lit. 'The Beauty of the Earth'*), Fáţa-a-Lóclui (*lit. 'The Face of the Earth'*)

SLEEPY *adj.* sumn(ur)ós, -oásă; **to be dead ~** cad di sómnu; **tired, upset, and ~** curmát, cripát şi nusumnát

SLEET s. jigărdhíţă, juyurdhíţă, lápă, lápuviţă, vlátură, *N:* vlăţúră, zăgărdíciu, zloátă

SLEEVE s. mânică; (*a ~ rolled up*) *G:* mănicoáce

SLEIGH s. → SLEDGE

SLEIGHT s. tirtípe → TRICK

SLENDER *adj.* (*handsomely ~*) (a)scuturát (ca brádul *or* ca fáglu); fidán, spăthát, supţârác; zvéltu; (*sickly ~*) umbărnát

SLENDERIZE *vb.* (*to make slender*) ▾supţârédz

SLEPT: durñít, sumnát; **I have not ~ for two days** Nu hiu durñít di doáuă dzále; **I have not slept at all for hours** Un somn nu hiu sumnát → SLEEP

SLICE s. filíe; (*as of pastrami*) şiníţă, şuníţă; (*big ~, as of bread*) cucutíciu di pâne; xifáre; *Clis:* bóje ‖ ALR 1068 (*~ of bread*) clin di pâne

SLICE *vb.* schizédz

SLICK *adj.* (*slippery*) arunicós, -oásă; (*intelligent*) → CLEVER

SLICKER s. calpuzán → SWINDLER

SLIDE s. arăchíş, arăchiúşur, arunicătúră, răgóciu

SLIDE *vb.* alúnic (→ SLIP) (*to move smoothly and winding*) şeárpic ‖ *Cru:* mi arăghiuséscu, GOLAB 201) ‖ **to ~ down** (*as of a bird of prey*) ▾aripidín; **to ~ off** (*to bolt*) li scármin

SLIDING s. arunicáre, alunicáre

SLIGHT s. cătăfronisíre, sictărsíre

SLIGHT *vb.* cătăfroniséscu, paralás, sictărséscu; nu ancúñu, nu dau di mâneár

SLIGHTLY *adv.* p(u)ţân, psân → SOMEWHAT

SLIM *adj.* → SLENDER

SLIM *vb.* supţârédz

SLIME s. (*sticky mud*) múzgă

SLING s. praşte, proáşte, téngală ‖ *G:* pleáşti; *G and P:* frăşti, SarD 69

SLING *vb.* → THROW

SLING ONE'S HOOK *vb.* ñ-lau cicioárile dinanúmirea → BOLT

SLINK *vb.* mi fur

SLIP

SLIP *vb.* alúnic, arúnic, arúdic, **Prv:** arúdhic; aylístu, (a)răgóciu, rugóciu, alăchiúşur, arăchiúşur, aruchiúşur, aruchiuşurédz; **Tears began to ~ down** Lăcriñle acăţără s alăchiúşură; (*to make a mistake*) (a)lăthipséscu, lăthăpséscu, ftixéscu, ftiséscu, para-cálcu; (*to creep into, to creep out, to creep away*) ▼şeárpic

SLIP AWAY (*or* **OUT**) *vb.* asuséscu, ▼ciun, ▼fur, (a)scáp

SLIP BY *vb.* (*of time*) mi deápir; **days slept by** Dzâlile s dipinără

SLIP OF A : *a slip of a girl* un nástur di feátă (*lit.* '*a button of a girl, a girl like a button'*)

SLIP OFF THE HANDLE *vb.* mi acáţă órile → FLY INTO A TANTRUM

SLIP OUT OF SIGHT *vb.* → DISAPPEAR

SLIP-KNOT *s.* thilíche

SLIPPER *s.* tărlíche (*and* târ-)

SLIPPERY *adj.* aruchiuşurós, -oásă; arunicós, -oásă; răguciós, oásă; **~ terrain** arăchíş, arăchiúşur, arunicătúră, răgóciu

SLIPPING *s.* aylisturáre, alunicáre, aruchişuráre, arăchiuşuráre, aru-

SLIPUP *s.* → MISTAKE

SLIT *s.* cripătúră; *also:* arălíche, arălâche, dişcľidzătúră, firádhă, ţânţână

SLITHER *vb.* mi fur

SLIVER *s.* → SPLINTER

SLOB *s.* pálaz

SLOBBER *s.* bále *f pl*

SLOBBER *vb.* ñ-cúrgu bálile

SLOE-TREE *s.* ţăpúrnu, ţăpurnéu

SLOPE *s.* (a)nífur, aplicátă, arădzâm, arâdzâm, arâpă, (a)ripidínă, arâpidínă, arâpâdzínă, arăpit, areápid, areápit, arúp, catífur, creac; **the ~ of the mountain** giúglu a múntilui; plaiu

SLOPE *vb.* ▼apléc, ▼ncľin; **to ~ downword** (*also fig.*) ľau catífurlu

SLOPING *adj.* (*as of a terrain*) aripidinát → INCLINED

SLOPPY *adj.* (*muddy*) mâzgós, -oásă; (*slovenly*) pálaz, *m pl* -ajĭ

SLOTH *s.* leáne, timbilâche

SLOTHFUL *adj.* linăvós, -oásă → LAZY

SLOUGH *s.* → LAZYBONES

SLOUCHED *adj.* (*as of a loaf of bread*) ncudurát

SLOUGH *s.* (*as from melting snow*) glắburi *f pl*; (*swamp*) lústră

SLOVENLY *adj.* alócut; átala-mátala *invar.*; **G:** pálaz, *m pl* -ajĭ

SLOW *adj.* (*as of smb.'s way of speaking*) (a)răshirát, minghét ‖
~ **of apprehension** cap di strúmciu, DIARO 150 → BE ~ IN THE UPTAKE

SLOW DOWN *vb.* ▾(a)cúmtin, agăliséscu, ▾dipún; **The rain had ~ed
down** Ploáia avea acumtinátă; **Please, ~ your drum!** Ia-l dipúne
tâmbârălu! (*to slacken*) cătăprăéscu → DEESCALATE

SLOWLY *adv.* (a)gále, (a)gálea, (a)yálea, priayále, ayalít, aya-
lía, payálea, (a)nárga, anárya, anárgalui, cătilín, **F:** câtelín,
câteañór ‖ **Cru:** preyále, peryále, GOLAB 245; **Pls:** peryále, **Av,
Prv:** păyálˈa, **GSus:** aprăyále, **SJos:** puyálea, CL 258

SLOW-WITTED *adj.* ta-o-tó *invar.* → STUPID

SLUG *vb.* (*to strike*) ▾agudéscu

SLUGGARD *s.* (a)mbutoáre, ciumagár, haramufái, prăhár

SLUGGISH *adj.* muláşcu, -şcă, -şchi, -şche (*sic*) → LAZY

SLUMBER *vb.* (*to fall asleep*) apugărşéscu → DOZE, SLEEP

SLUMBEROUS *adj.* (*sleepy*) sumn(ur)ós, -oásă; (*peaceful*) arhătip-
sít; frónim, *m pl* -niñ

SLUMP *s.* chisátă

SLUMP *vb.* cad, ▾aruvuéscu

SLUSH *s.* (*watery snow*) lápă, lápuviţă, **Bit:** lăpăíţă; (*soft mud*)
múzgă

SLUT *s.* ncălicătúră → HARLOT

SLY *adj.* şirét, -eátă; şă-; **the ~ fox** şireáta di vúlpe; *also:*
cumalíndru, hítru; mástorsă *f sg*, *as* mástorsa di vúlpe 'the ~
fox'; mălăyár; muşmoálă *m/f*; píspu, *m pl* píschi; pónir, tirtipcí;
vúlpe (*lit.* 'fox'), vulpóñu *m*, -poáñe *f*; **to become ~** puniripséscu

SLYLY *adv.* cu vulpíˈe

SLYNESS *s.* (a)plán, pispeáţă, şiretlắche; vulpíˈe (*lit.* 'foxiness')

SMACK *s.* (*flavor*) aroámă, arúmă, (a)ñurízmă; (*slight trace*)
úrmă

SMALL *adj.* ñic, -cşór, -cút, -cuz, -căzán, -căzíc, -cuzáncu,
-c(u)zót; ñícăz; ciuflíc ‖ CUVATA 2: *dim. m sg* ñicăzancu, *f*
-zancă, *m pl* -zánţă, *f pl* -zănchi

SMALL SHOT *s.* (*of metal*) bălătáñ *f pl*; ciuciumág, şuşumág ‖
Peş: bălătíñ, CL 38

SMALL

SMALL TALK *s.* hăbări *f pl*; vrúte şi nivrúte *f pl* (*lit.* 'wanted and unwanted')

SMALLPOX *s.* luţítă, mălteádză, mulţeádză, mălţeádză, mălteádza aţeá láia; **to be sick with ~** ▾muľiţédz, ▾chípit, ▾chipitédz, ▾nchipitédz

SMART *s.* (*smarting pain*) arduríe, ústur, usturáre, usturíme

SMART *adj.* (*neat, trim*) → MAKE ONESELF ~; (*clever, intelligent*) şciút, achicăsít, mástur ‖ **You are ~, but I am smarter!** cându ti duţeái tíni, míni yineám, DIARO 119 → QUICK-WITTED

SMASH *vb.* aspárgu, dărâm; **to ~ smb. to a pulp** ansár, úmflu → PULL TO PIECES

SMEAR *s.* líydhă → SPOT

SMEAR *vb.* ▾(a)úngu

SMEARING *s.* (a)undzeáre, (a)úndzire

SMELL *s.* (*the power of ~*) añurdzíre; (*odor*) (a)ñúrizmă, ñurdíe; **offensive ~** putoáre; **heavy ~** añurzíre greáuă; **~ of burning** (*as in the ken*) ţícnă

SMELL *vb.* ▾(a)ñurzéscu, (a)ñuzéscu; (*to feel, to perceive*) ▾aduchéscu; **They ~ed him** Lu-añurzíră; **The dogs ~ed him** Lu-aduchíră cânľi; **That ~s like gunpowder** Añurdzeáşte bărúte; **to ~ stale** ▾dâhnéscu, ndâhnéscu ‖ DIARO 1: **It ~s like fish** Añurdzeáşti a péscu

SMELL A RAT *vb.* ‖ DIARO 118: eásti lúcru bişít *3 sg*

SMELLY *adj.* (*malodorous*) ambuţós, -oásă → STINKING

SMIDGEN *s.* → BIT

SMILE *s.* hamu-arâdeáre, hamu-arâs

SMILE *vb.* hamu-arâd, sumarâd ‖ HRISTU 81: bag budza pi arăsu

SMIRCH *vb.* (*to dirty*) ▾murdăripséscu, ▾pângân(ips)éscu; (*to bring disgrace*) fac di arşíne

SMITE *vb.* (*to strike*) ▾agudéscu → KILL

SMITH *s.* hirár → IRONMASTER

SMITHEREENS *s.* sârmă; **The ship was broken into ~** U feáţe pampórea sârme → BREAK TO ~

SMITTEN *adj.* (*enamoured*) erotipsít

SMOKE *s.* fum; **a lot of ~** fumăríe → EMIT ~, END IN ~

SMOKE *vb.* ▾afúm; **I used to ~ the entire room with incense** Toátă óda ñ-afumám cu fúmlu di thimñámă; (*to burn with ~*) (a)núñu; (*of a smoker*) beau ţiyáră (*lit.* 'to drink a cigarette'), trag ţiyáră

(*lit. 'to draw a cigarette'*)

SMOKING *s.* (*treat with smoke*) afumáre

SMOOTH *adj.* buimátcu, -tcă, -tţi, -tţe; dúze *invar.* ‖ **Cru:** ănyiliceát, GOLAB 205; CUNIA 207: máznu

SMOTHER *vb.* ‖ CUNIA 293: ▾zăbunuséscu, ▾zmúrtic

SMUDGE *s.* liché → SPOT

SMUDGE *vb.* ▾lichiséscu, ▾dămcuséscu, ▾chic

SMUG *adj.* făndăxít

SMUGGLING *s.* cacearmáie

SMUT *s.* (*a wheat fungus*) tăciúne

SMUTCH *s.* → SMUDGE

SNACK *s.* (a)mbucáre

SNAIL *s.* cărnáş, zmélciu

SNAKE *s.* năpărtică, şárpe, şeárpe, şirpoáñe; **large** ~ buľár; **jumping** ~ strit; **large harmless** ~ ófchiu; (*a certain venomous* ~) săpít ‖ ALB: **Dren, Kërb, Pe, Për, Sen:** bulár(u) 'red snake,' 'blind snake'; *This blind and fatty snake is believed to open his eyes and see only on April 23, i.e. on St. George's day* (**Për**). *Other terms:* **Kërb:** sulvál 'a long snake'; **Pe:** şughétu máre, Brân-cuş 551

SNAP *s.* anciupáre, acăţáre

SNAP *vb.* (*to throw*) (a)rúc, arúncu; (*to land a blow*) zdângânés-cu únă; (*to grasp with or as with the teeth*) ▾anciúp, angiúp; (*of a firearm*) plâscănéscu; **to** ~ **a pistol** (*at smb.*) arúc cu cumbúra (pri)

SNAPPING *adj.* (*resounding*) zvângânós, -oásă

SNAPPISH *adj.* arăchít

SNARE *s.* (*also fig.*) laţ → TRAP, BE CAUGHT IN THE ~, DEVISE A ~

SNARL[1] *s.* (*tangled situation*) cărşiľáre, ncărşiľáre

SNARL[2] *s.* (*a surly angry growl*) ngrâñe, ngrâñíre

SNARL₁ *vb.* (*to tangle*) ▾cărşiľédz, ▾ncărşiľédz

SNARL[2] (*to express with a snarl*) ▾ngrâñéscu, ▾ngârñéscu

SNATCH *vb.* ▾apúc, ▾anciúp, ▾aráp, ▾zmúlgu

SNEAK *vb.* (*to lurk*) mi stricór, mi fúr; **to** ~ **away / off** mi fac căípe

SNEAKINGLY *adv.* acrifá, ascumtá, bizgúlea, tiptíle

SNEER *s.* múndză

SNEER *vb.* ▾mundzuéscu, ▾mundzuséscu → MOCK

SNEEZE

SNEEZE *s.* stărnutáre, stirnutáre

SNEEZE *vb.* strănút, stărnút, (a)ştirnutédz, **F:** sturrutédz ‖
Peş: frumuxéscu, CL 45

SNEEZING *s.* strănutáre, ştirnutáre

SNIDE *adj.* pânghiós, -oásă

SNIFF *vb.* añurdzăscu; (*to detect*) áflu

SNIFFLE *s. med.* ▾aréme, bútur, ceáră, rúfă

SNIP *vb.* ▾taľu, túndu

SNIPPERSNAPPER *s.* om di ciuchi, mâscâră

SNIVEL *s.* plángut

SNIVEL *vb.* şcľimurédz

SNOOK *s.* múndză, măndză → COCK A ~, CUT A ~, MAKE A ~

SNOOZE *s.* → DROP INTO A ~

SNOOZE *vb.* ľ-coc un sómnu (*lit. 'I bake [it!] a sleep'*), ľ-coc
un ócľu di sómnu (*lit. 'I bake [it!] an eye of sleeping'*) → DROP
INTO A ~ ‖ **F:** fac un ochi di som, HRISTU 2

SNORE *s.* hărbulíre, hărchíre

SNORE *vb.* bútur, fac hor-hor, hărbulédz, hăr(ă)chéscu; hérbu
făsúľe (*lit. 'to cook beans'*) ‖ (*of horses*) fărnuxéscu, STERE 3

SNORTING *s.* (*of horses*) buturáre

SNOT *s.* muc, múcă, mir, ñir, míxă; **a grain of dried ~** căcăstór; *vet.*(*a horse disease*) sacaí

SNOTTY *adj.* mucós, -oásă; muţós, -oásă; mixós, -oásă; **a ~ child**
un cópan di ficiór; (*of horses*) bútur, săcăiárcu; (*annoyingly or
spitefully unpleasant*) abráşcu, -şcă, -şţi, -şte

SNOUT *s.* biciu, múţă, zurnă ‖ DIARO 144: múţcâ

SNOW *s.* (a)neáuă, neáo, ródă; **~ drift** năváľu, năváiu, niváiu,
nimusórizmă ‖ **Amc, Kok, LvO, Mal, Mi, Prv, Suf, Vot:** neau; **Plat,
Kat, Pur:** ñau; **Ses, Trn:** ñeu, B-ARCH 20

SNOW *vb.* 3 *sg:* da neáuă

SNOWBALL *s.* tópă di neáuă

SNOWBANK *s.* năváľu, nimusórizmă

SNOWDRIFT *s.* → SNOWBANK

SNOWDROP *s.* culeastrándu, culeástrandu

SNOWFALL *s.* neáuă (*lit. 'snow'*)

SNOWSTORM *s.* azvimturáre, năváiu, turín, ntúrin, nturináre,
sindilíe di neáuă, tufáne, vinturáre (*and* vindu-)

SNOW-WHITE *adj.* ≈ alb ca scămánghea (*lit. 'as white as cotton'*)

SNOWY *adj.* (*with* ~) cu neáuǎ; (*comparison*) ca neáua

SNUB *vb.* (*to slight*) cătăfroniséscu

SNUB-NOSED *adj.* cârnu, *m pl* -rñi; *also:* cíple *invar.*, cuciumít, ânciuvăñát, năréciu, *m pl* -réci, *f sg/pl* -réce; şpârtu, *m pl* -rţâ

SNUFF *s.* (*tobacco*) bărnúte, tabác; ~ **dealer** bărnuticí

SNUFF OUT *vb.* li tíndu → DIE

SNUFF PURSE *s.* cărnéciu, cărníciu di bărnúte

SNUFFBOX *s.* tăbăchérǎ

SNUG *adj.* (*comfortable*) nóstim, *m pl* -tiñ, *f pl* -time

SNUGGLE *vb.* mi adún, mi adún ģľem, mi adún guzmóľ

SNUGGLED *adj.* adunát, adunát ģľem (*or* adunát guzmóľ)

SO *adv.* (*in this/that manner*) aşí, aşâ, aşíţi; (*to this/that extent*) ahântu, ahtât; **Why are you ~ cruel?** Ţi ñ-éşti ahtânt niñiloásǎ? (*then*) de; ~, **what did you say to me?** Ţi-ñ dzâseşi, de?

SO *cj* (*with the result that, in order that*) ‖ culái DIARO 241

SO BE IT (*concessively: all right*) as, ási

SO FAR *adv.* pân tu hópa aístǎ

SO GOT, SO GONE ≈ haráme víñe, haráme s-dúse (*lit.* '*[as or since] it came unlawfully, it went unlawfully*')

SO LET IT BE néise [néĭ•si]

SO LONG! şedz cu sănătáte!

SO LONG AS *cj.* (*since*) ‖ **Av:** únǎ ţe, BASME 502

SO MANY MEN, SO MANY MINDS ≈ câte miléţ, ahâţ dumnidzádz (*lit.* '*so many races, so many gods*'); cáthiun cu hâvǎlu-ľ (*lit.* '*everyone with his tune*') ; cáthe puľu ş-bateárea-ľ (*lit.* '*each bird with its [specific] call*')

SO SAID SO DONE ≈ dzâca ş fápta

SO SO *adv.* (*not too good, but not too bad either*) ceat-pat

SO THAT *cj.* di, tra s; **The mule lowers so that I mount it** Múla si-apleácǎ di-ncálic; **I have created the sea so that you can feed from it** Míne u feciu amárea tra s-vǎ hǎríţǎ di nâsǎ

SO WHAT? ‖ ţi cára? em ş-ţi cára? DIARO 344

SOAK *vb.* ▾muculéscu, ▾nghihurédz, ud, ▾ud muceále, ▾(a)móľu; **to ~ to the skin** mi fac pupúľu (di ploáie, di asudórĭ); mi fac sara-gárǎ; *Cľis:* mi fac mucľíşte

SOAKED TO THE SKIN *adj.* bľóndǎ *invar*; ud (a)móľ, ud mucilít, ud muceále, ud pupúľ; (*by rain*) mpluát, muľát lércǎ

SOAP

SOAP *s.* săpúne; **cake of** ~ călúpe di săpúne; **the rope and the ~!** fúnea şi săpúnea!

SOAP *vb.* ▾săpunéscu, ▾săpunédz ‖ ALR 1224: dau cu săpúne

SOAP-BOILER *s.* (*soap-maker*) călupcí, săpungí, săpunár

SOAPING *s.* săpunáre, săpunsíre

SOAPWORT *s. bot.* sărpúñe, *G:* şărpúne ‖ *Prv:* sulufát, CL 261

SOAR *s.* fúzmă → IMPETUS

SOAR *vb.* (*as of prices*) ľau vánţu; **to ~ forward** ▾azvímtur

SOARING → BE ~

SOB *s.* scâlţáre → SIGH

SOB *vb.* scâlţédz

SOBER *adj.* (*not intoxicated*) ni-biút [ni•bi•út] → MAKE SMB. ~ AGAIN

SOBER DOWN *vb.* ▾disbét

SOBERING *s.* disbitáre, disbătătúră

SOBRIQUET *s.* → NICKNAME

SOCIETY *s.* (*association*) itaríe, sinastrufíe, suţátă

SOCK *s.* părpóde, pripódhă, pripóde; călciún, călciúne, călcâñe, ciúpăr, lăpúdă, pătúnă, scufúne ‖ DIARO 251: pârpudúşcâ *dim*

SOCK *vb.* ▾agudéscu → BEAT

SOCKET *s.* → EYE ~

SOD *s.* zvólar, zvulár

SODA WATER *s.* sodhă

SODDEN *adj.* (*heavy or doughy*) crud; ni-cóptu, -coáptă, -cópţâ, -coápte

SOEVER *adv.* (*in any degree or manner*) di-acutótalui; (*at all*) hici, ici, dip

SOFA *s.* canapé *m*, **N:** canapéi *f*; mindér, mindére, mindíre, sufă, sufáte, sufălắche

SOFIA *s.* (*city in Bulgaria*) ‖ BELIMACE 100: **we left the famous capital city** ~ alăsăm scámnul alăvdátlu a Sufiiľei

SOFT *adj.* (*soothing, gentle*) dúlţe; (*as of wool*) *m/f sg* moále, *m/f pl* moľ; (a)rúd; **as ~ as cotton** bumbăcós, bâm-; (*of a person's character*) evăşcu, ímir; *the~ part of a loaf of bread, of a fruit, etc.* ñed ‖ HRISTU 7: zdrod; **with ~ voice** cu boţe zdrodă

SOFTEN *vb.* ▾(a)ndulţéscu; (*to make more bearable*) ▾(a)móľu, ▾fruminéscu; *med.* (*esp. of old men*) mi vérsu n púndzi

SOFTENING *s.* muľáre; (*spoilage*) aludzâre

SOFTLY *adv.* moále, dúlţe

SOFTNESS *s.* (*~ of character*) imireáţă, imiráme

SOFTY *s.* and *adj.* (*of people*) aluát

SOGGY *adj.* ud, údă, udz, úde

SOIL *s.* (*earth*) ţáră; **barren ~** hărhálă

SOIL *vb.* ▾murdăripséscu, ▾pângân(ips)éscu, ▾smaryéscu, ▾úmplu (di) ‖ *Gop:* mărghéscu, GOLAB 234 (*to disgrace*) fac di arşíne

SOILED *adj.* smâryít, mâryít, putusít, lichisít, lirusít

SOILING *s.* pângân(ips)íre → BESMIRCHMENT

SOJOURN *vb.* → RESIDE

SOLACE *s.* arăzbunáre, azbunáre, sămănáre, păriyuríe

SOLACE *vb.* asbún, azbún, ▾păriyuriséscu, părăyuriséscu, păryuriséscu → COMFORT, RECONCILE

SOLDIER *s.* suldát; **Greek ~** stratiót; **Turkish ~** ayă, agă, aschirlí, ciulé (*and* -ľé), emşerí; (*Turkish ~ with large pants*) dudúm; (*nickname for a Turkish ~*) banabác; **Turkish ~** *derog.* jabéc ‖ *Cru:* vuiníc, GOLAB 259

SOLD OUT *adj.* vindút

SOLE *s. anat.* pátă; pătúna a ciórlui; (*of boots, shoes, etc.*) bálă, ghion, ghiónă, ghióne, péţumă, şóľe; (*~ for sandals*) poáhă; **half-~** mingiuşóle, mişuşóle

SOLE *adj.* → SINGLE

SOLE *vb.* piţuséscu, trec mingiuşóle

SOLELY *adv.* maşi, veciu ‖ *Cru:* sámo, GOLAB 247

SOLEMN *adj.* písim, *m pl* -siñ

SOLICIT *vb.* → ASK, BEG, TEMPT

SOLICITOUS *adj.* (*worried*) sicliţít

SOLICITUDE *s.* căştígă, frundídhă, săráche

SOLID *adj.* (*compact*) mplin, vârtós, -oásă; scliró *invar.*; (*reliable*) sănătós, -oásă ‖ (*as good as it should be*) nu e şică, BASME 500 (*lit. 'it is not a joke'*)

SOLING *s.* piţusíre

SOLITARY *adj.* axólit, irñít, irñíu, nguvát → ALONE

SOLITUDE *s.* singuráme → ALONENESS

SOLUTION *s.* cearé, *N:* cearée

SOLVE *vb.* (*a riddle, a problem*) ▾dizlég; ľi áflu căpáchea (*lit. 'I can find its lid'*), ľi áflu cearélu (*lit. 'I can find its remedy'*); ľ-dau di fúndu (*lit. 'I am getting down to its bottom'*)

SOMBER, SOMBRE adj. nigurát; also: cérnu, m pl -rñi; âmpumurát; mundó invar.

SOME țivá, văr m, vără f; várnu (and vârnu)) m, várnă f; ~ hair(s) of wool văr per di lână; (~ kind of) should you have ~ kind of ... di si-ai tínc vârnu (or vârnă); He was chasing after ~ pray Alăgá tră vâră prádă; while ~ ..., ~ other ... áltu ..., áltu...; álțâ..., álțâ...; níște, nâște; (some, a certain amount of) He un-derstood ~ of their language Aducheá di límba a lor

SOME- (in compounds, as something, etc.) -vá (enclitic only)

SOMEBODY càrevá, càinivá, ținivá, vâr, vârnu, nușcáre; Apparently ~ is ringing at the gate Asúnă cánda vârnu la poártă; ~ else's adj. xen, xeánă, xeñ, xeáne ‖ DIARO 180: carivá: Call ~ to help you! Cľámâ carivá s-ti-agiútâ; This is ~'s house, he does not want to tell his name Cása-i a curivá ți nu va și-și spúnâ núma

SOMEBODY ELSE ‖ DIARO 40: áltuvârnu

SOMEHOW adv. (with difficulty) rufu-n-búfu [rú•fum•bú•fu]; (by all means) cum di cum

SOMEONE → SOMEBODY

SOMERSAULT s. drâclă, túmbă, culutúmbă ‖ Peș: ceambarlác, ceamceác, CL 43

SOMERSAULT vb. fac túmba, fac nă culutúmbă, fac culutúmbe ‖ Peș: 3 sg pt: z deáde ceamceácu, z deáde ceambarlác, CL 43

SOMETHING níște, nâște, țivá, țíșciu, N: ciúșciu; He needs to tell him ~ Ciúșciu áre s-ľi spúnă

SOMETIME adv. áltăoară

SOMETIMES adv. niscânte ori ‖ Cru: căti várnoáră, GOLAB 226; CUNIA 322: cátivăroáră

SOMEWHAT adv. (to some degree) ca, theámă; This seems to me ~ heavy Ca greu ắñ páre

SOMEWHERE adv. iuvá, tr-un loc; ~ else aľúrea; We are from ~ else Noi him di aľúrea ‖ t-un loc, BASME 19; ~ else áltuiuva [al•tu•iu•vá], DIARO 41

SOMNAMBULIST s. loat, loát di lúnă, lunátic

SOMNOLENT adj. → SLEEPY

SON s. ficiór, hiľu, dim. hiľór

SON OF A BITCH s. ‖ BELIMACE 83 and 84: puľu di cáni

SONG s. cắntic (and cântic, cândic), cântáre; N: hấvă, hăváie;

Sing us a ~! Cântă-nă un hâvă! → MAKE A ~ ABOUT SMTH.

SONGSTER *s.* cântătór

SONGSTRESS *s.* cântătoáre

SON-IN-LAW *s.* dzínire, dzinirác ‖ *Cru:* grambóu, GOLAB 217; *Cern, Flam, Prv, Vot:* grambóu, B-ARCH 469

SONOROUS *adj.* asunătór, -toáre

SOON *adv.* ayóñea, anghíu, c(u)rúndu; **Seldom seen, ~ forgotten** ≈ Óčΐi țe nu s-ved curúndu si agărșéscu; **as ~ as possible** cât cama tr-oáră; **He wrote us to flee as ~ as possible** Nă scriá si-angănăm cât ma tr-oáră cățáua; **As ~ as he returns, call me** Áma că va yínă, yrea-ñ; (*after a little while*) dúpă niscântă oáră; tră puțăn chiró

SOONER *adv.* cáma tr-oáră

SOOT *s.* furídzină, fulídzină, búștină, căpñáuă, fum

SOOTH *s.* → TRUTH

SOOTHE *vb.* azbún → COMFORT

SOOTHING *adj. m/f sg* dúlțe, *m pl* dúlți, *f pl* dúlțe (DDA 506 *sic*)

SOOTHSAYER *s.* mándu, prufét,

SOOTHSAYING *s.* măndíe, măndipsíre, prufitipsíre

SOP *s.* → BRIBE, GRATUITY

SOP *vb.* moΐu, aúngu

SORB *s.* sórbu, súrvu; (*fruit*) súrvă

SORB-APPLE *s.* crúșe

SORCERER *s.* măyístru, palongheár

SORCERESS *s.* mándisă, măyístră, palongheáră, stríg(l)ă

SORCERY *s.* (a)máye, (a)máie

SORDID *adj.* (a)zvărñár, urât; cacavátră *invar.* → DIRTY

SORDIDLY *adv.* troc

SORE *s.* afurñisíre

SORE *adj.* ≈ 3 *sg:* ▾doáre (*lit.* '[it] hurts')

SORREL *s. bot.* bumbunárică, brumánică, burbunácă, nánă, nénă

SORROW *s.* angúsă, cripáre → GRIEF

SORROWFUL *adj.* jilós, -oásă; șcΐimurós, -oásă

SORRY *adj.* → BE SORRY ‖ *Cru:* **I feel ~** Ñ-yíne arău, GOLAB 201; **~ plight** luyuríe streásă, BASME 10 *and* 52

SORT *s.* sóie, turlíe; **all sorts of beauties** mușitéț turlíi-turlíi

SORT *vb.* ▾alég, ▾arădhăpséscu

SORTING *s.* (*selection*) alidzeáre, aleádzire

SOT *s.* → DRUNKARD

SOUGH *s.* (*sigh*) uhtáre

SOUGH *vb.* (*as of wind or water*) văzéscu (*and* vâ-), vuzuéscu; (*to sigh*) uhtédz

SOUL *s.* súflit ‖ LITURG 134: súfitu; **save our ~s!** scápă-nă su-fitlu PC from ALB: súlfit

SOUND *s.* asunătură

SOUND *adj.* (*free from injury*) ni-vătămát; (*strong, healthy*) sayláme; **as ~ as a bell** sănătós ca grij di dzádă ‖ *also:* sânătós her (*lit.* '*as healthy / strong as iron*') BASME 420

SOUND *vb.* (*to explore, to investigate*) ▾discós, ▾discúlţu, dis-cúltu, ▾scărfiséscu, ▾discărfuséscu (*and* -câr-, -cur-), xităses-cu; **Take him aside and ~ him well!** Loaţ-lu di unâ párte şi dis-culţáţ-lu ghíne! ‖ **Why are you ~ing me so thoroughly?** Ţí-ñ-lu cáfţâ zbórlu ahât? DIARO 208

SOUND *vb.* (*to ~ loudly, as of a rifle*) plăscănéscu, plâscâ-)

SOUNDLY *adv.* (*tightly, solidly*) pravatós

SOUP *s.* hirtúră, ciórbă, dzámă; (*made of bread*) dzămătúră, prosfáyiu; (*brine ~*) armózmu, dzámă di moáre; (*~ with dough ras-pings*) tărhănă (*and* târhâ-), trâhănă; **to be in the ~** (*scared*) ≈ li úmplu (di frícă) (*lit.* '*to fill it up,*' *where* **it** *stands for one's underweare*')

SOUPÇON *s.* (*trace, a little bit*) úrmă

SOUP-TUREEN *s.* suphéră [sup•hé•ră]

SOUPY *adj.* (*densely foggy or cloudy*) nigurát, nigurós

SOUR *adj.* ácru; **~ milk** lápte ácru; (*of a person*) acreárcu

SOUR CREAM *s.* álică, áică, álcă, prăzgu, teáră

SOUR MILK *s.* lápte ácru, lápte bătút, lápte vinít

SOUR *vb.* ▾acréscu, acrédz, ▾aludzăscu, ▾puscuéscu; (*to embit-ter*) ▾nfărmác

SOURCE *s.* (*spring*) fântână (*and* fândână), *N:* funtână; ízvur; (*point of origin of a river*) cap-di-arâu; vitíl; múmă (*lit.* '*mo-ther*')

SOURING *s.* (*as of wine*) acríre, puscuíre

SOURISH *adj.* acrişór, -oáră; maióşcu, -óşcă (*sic*); (*also of people*) acreárcu, -rcă, -rţi, -rţe

SOURNESS *s.* acríş, acrătúră, anăcríme, anăcríciu, puscăitúră

SOUSE *s.* → BRINE

SOUSE *vb.* (*to make drunk*) ▾ambétu

SOUTH *s.* ñadzădzâuă; (*Epir, Thessalia*) misiméră

SOUTH WIND *s.* iug, not

SOUTHERN-WOOD *s. bot.* pilóñu-di-Muzichíe

SOW *s.* poárcă ‖ *Am, Mal:* scrófă, B-ARCH 285

SOW *vb.* seámin; ~ **dicord** bag zizáñe, bag anghídz

SOWING *s.* siminére

SOWN FIELD *s.* siminătúră

SPACE *s.* (*room, distance*) loc

SPACIOUS *adj.* lărguríu, vlíhur

SPADE *s.* câzmă, dhichéle ‖ *Prv, SJos:* lizgáre, CL 254; DIARO 202: spathí (spathí 'clubs' *in the* DDA 1104 *is an error*)

SPAHI *s.* spahíu

SPAN *s.* (*distance from the end of the thumb to the end of the little finger*) făltác, făşcátă, fuşcátă

SPANGLE *s.* părdzíc, pitalúryă

SPANK *vb.* dau ună plíscută

SPAR *vb.* (*verbally*) trag un cărínte

SPARE *vb.* ▾ñiluéscu; (*to lay by, to save*) cumăndărséscu, icunumiséscu, purbuléscu; ~ **the rod and spoil the child** ≈ Pârjína-i dátă di Dumnidzău (*lit.* 'the rod has been given by God')

SPARE CLOTHES *s.* alăxămíntu

SPARED *adj.* cumăndărsít, icunomisít

SPARING *adj.* icunumisáric; máză *invar.*

SPARK *s.* scânteáľe, scânteáľu, spíthă, scăndălóthră, scărdzălóthră

SPARK *vb.* (*to produce sparks*) (a)scápir, scrăpuéscu

SPARKLE *vb.* ▾nyil(i)céscu, anyilíciu; *also:* hrisuséscu, lăyicéscu, liyicéscu, licrăséscu, lămbiséscu, limbiséscu, lămbruséscu, lămburséscu, lumbrăséscu, lumbărséscu, lumbriséscu, luñinédz, luţéscu, scântéľu, scântiľédz, sfúldzir, şcrăpuéscu; **His sword is sparkling** Pála-ľ sfúldziră

SPARKLING *s.* ascăpiráre → SPARKLE

SPARKLING *adj.* lumbărsít → BRILLIANT

SPARROW *s.* anghídhă, ciónă, cioñiu, harabél, harabéu, harabéľu, ţărnăpúľu, vrápciu ‖ ALIA 115: cinginé, pui *and* puľu, puľíţă; (*rare*): dzundzán, gealgeán; *GSus:* púică, CL 259; *SJos:*

SPARROW

spruít, CL 261

SPARROW HAWK s. sfrântéľu, sfrâmtéľu, sfrindzél; pizóvlu

SPARSE adj. arăít

SPASM s. spazmó

SPAT s. and vb. → QUARREL

SPATTER vb. ▼(n)ciumulscu, ▼pruscuchéscu

SPAWN s. (mixed salted fish eggs) târâmă

SPEAK vb. zburăscu, acuvântédz, cuvintédz, dzâc, gréscu; **They do not ~ to each other** Nu-şi gréscu (cu gúra); **to ~ continuously** ñ-ñárdze gúra; **to ~ ill of smb.** zburăscu, trec n gúra; **Don't ~ ill of me!** Nu mi treáţe n gúra! **to ~ in vain** zburăsc pi víntu; **to ~ the truth** spun ndrept; **to ~ up** zburăscu ndisát ‖ *Mul, Smr:* 3 sg zbráşte , B-Arh 477

SPEAR s. cundár, gilít, mastrác, măzdrác

SPEAKING s. gríre, grítă

SPEARMINT s. méntă (and méndă), yízmă, ayeázmă

SPECIAL adj. (made upon demand, as of a hat) maxutárcu, -rcă, -árţi, -árţe or -ărţi ‖ (distinguished, superior) ayóryea; **N. is ~ N.** u-ári caliméra ayór-yea, DIARO 368

SPECIES s. (sort, kind, model) iurnécă

SPECIMEN s. (individual) derog. clir

SPECIOUS adj. cálpu, -lpă, -lchi, -lpe; cálpic; ehlé invar.

SPECK s. (stain) liché: (particle) dhráme; **not a ~** cât trâ yitríe → JOT

SPECKLE vb. ▼pluscutéscu → SPLASH

SPECTACLES s. yilíi f pl → GLASSES

SPECTER s. fandázmă → PHANTOM

SPEECH s. zbor, zburáre, zburâre, graiu, greiu, griu; (dialect, way of speaking) cuvéndă → MAKE A ~

SPEECHLESS adj. tăcút ‖ **to be / to remain ~** armân fără gúra (lit. 'to remain without mouth') PARALLELE 147

SPEED s. (a)vrápă, curundeáţă ‖ **to run at breakneck ~** fug di mâc lóclu (lit. 'to run [as if] eating the earth'), BASME 500

SPELL[1] s. amáie, măyíe, măghíe; **evil ~** văscăníe → BE UNDER A ~, CAST A ~ UPON

SPELL[2] s. (at work or duty) schímbu; (a period of rest) (a)răpás → REST

SPELL vb. (to relieve, to take the place of) ▼schímbu

SPELLBOUND *adj.* mărmurisít, di fáptu; **as if ~** ca di fáptu

SPEND *vb.* (*usu. of money*) (a)spárgu, fac jir, hărgéscu, hărgiuéscu, hărjéscu, scap, spătăľuséscu, xudh(y)ipséscu; **He has
spent all his money** Scăpă parádzľi; **to ~ the summer** nvirédz; **We
will ~ the summer in the lowland** Va nvirăm tu câmpu → SQUANDER ‖
(*to ~ wastefully*) adár ghíne, fac ghíne, BASME 607; (*to ~ time*)
fac; **He spent three years abroad** Feáțe trei añ tu xeáne, BASME 98;
(*to help off the time*) ñ-trec oára, BASME 409

SPENDING OF SUMMER *s.* niviráre

SPENDTHRIFT *adj.* aspártu, -rtă, -rţâ, -tre; hărgiuitór, mână
aspártă, sac arúptu; spátal, *m pl* -taľ, *f pl* -tale

SPERM *s.* spérmă

SPEW *vb.* → VOMIT

SPICY *adj.* nóstim, *m pl* -tiñ, *f pl* -time

SPICK-AND-SPAN *adj.* prividzút; ca scos dit ou (*lit. 'as if
taken out from an egg'*)

SPIDER *s.* páingu, páiangu, pángu, maramágă, maramángă, meramá-
gă, mirimágă, mirimángă, mirumágă

SPIDER'S WEB *s.* pândză di pángu, pândzină di páiangu

SPIGOT *s.* cep, sóche → FAUCET

SPICK-AND-SPAN *adj.* nou, nău; (*spotlessly clean*) spástru, curát

SPIKE *s. bot.* schic; (*nail*) pénură

SPIKE *vb.* (*to fasten with nails*) ▾ncărfuséscu

SPILL *vb.* ▾vérsu

SPIN *vb.* ▾tórcu (→ § 32); **to ~ a yarn;** (*to tell a story*)
▾ambáir

SPINACH *s.* spanác, spănáche

SPINDLE *s.* fus, drug; **the disk of the ~** prísne, rătél

SPINDLE MAKER *s.* fusár

SPINNING *s.* (*the process*) turţeáre, toárţire; **Begin your ~!**
Acăţáţ-vă di turţeáre!

SPINNING TOP *s.* sfúrlă

SPINNING WHEEL *s.* cicrícă, cicríche, cicărícă; *also:* andéme,
arudheáuă, dipinătór, rudáne, vărténiţă (*and vâr-*), vărteániţă,
vărteánţă ‖ *Peş:* arhotar, CL 37

SPIRIT *s.* duh, pnévmă; (*~ believed to protect a house or a
village*) stihíe; **the Holy ~** Áyiul duh; **in low spirits** cu cúrlu n
sus; (*beverage*) şpírtu, inóplimă ‖ CUVATA 11: **he was not in good**

SPIRIT

~s nu eará pi chéfi ‖ LITURG 32: súfitlu *sg def*

SPIRIT AWAY *or* **SPIRIT OFF** *vb.* ▼ahuléscu

SPIRITED *adj.* aflát, căidagí, inimárcu, inimós, pirgác, sárpit, sărpit (*and* sâr-), sârpid; (*courageous*) → PLUCKY

SPIRITUOUS *adj.* (*of liquors*) șpirtós

SPIT¹ *s.* (*thin rod for holding meet on fire*) súlă

SPIT² *s.* (*saliva*) (a)scucheát; (*an act or instance of spitting*) (a)scucheáre, (a)scuchitúră

SPIT *vb.* (*to eject saliva*) ▼ascúchiu, *Gop:* ▼stichéscu (*sic*)

SPITE *s.* ináte, ceapcânlâche, chíme; **in ~ of that** țécă!
in ~ of cu tut (*f* cu tútă, *m pl* cu tuț, *f/n pl* cu túte)

SPITEFUL *adj.* dușmănós, nguvujdát, nipârticát, nșirpicát, nvipirát, pușcľós, s(c)lab, uhtinát, urât, urút; **~ fate** tíhe neárcă *or* scriátă nfărmăcoásă ‖ pângân, BASME 680

SPITEFULLY *adv.* aráulea

SPITEFULNESS *s.* háre → WICKEDNESS

SPITTED LAMB (*or any other edible animal*) curbán

SPITTLE *s.* (a)scucheát

SPLASH *vb.* ▼pluscutéscu, pluscuchéscu, pruscuchéscu, prăscutéscu, pruscutéscu, ▼muciuléscu; **to ~ one's money about** hiu mână aspártă

SPLASHING *s.* pluscutíre, pluscuchíre, muciulíre

SPLATTER *vb.* → SPATTER

SPLAY *adj.* → CLUMSY

SPLEEN *s.* anat. splínă; **He has a problem with his ~** Áre splínă

SPLENDID *adj.* háscu, -scă, *no pl*; nișinlítcu, -tcă, -tți, -tțe

SPLENDOR *s.* nișáne; **What a horse, what a ~!** Țe cal, țe nișáne! (*glitter; attractiveness*) lumbărsíre

SPLENETIC *adj.* gușturát → ILL-NATURED, SPITEFUL

SPLINTER *s.* (*of wood*) áscľe, cľin, scârpă, scârpoáce, *G:* licătúră; luschídhă, luțeáthră; (*~ of glass*) aspărgătúră

SPLIT *s.* dijgľináre, curmáre, arupeáre, arúpire

SPLIT *vb.* ▼cúrmu, disfác, ▼disíc, ▼dispártu, ▼mpártu; **to ~ one's sides with laughter** arâd di mi lișín (→ SHRIEK WITH LAUGHTER); **to ~ smb.'s ears** ľau urécľile; **to ~ with smb.** u-arúp cioára (cu) ‖ HRISTU 19 (*of a road*) mi zdifac (*sic*)

SPLOTCH *s.* → SPOT, STAIN

SPLUTTER *vb.* → SPUTTER

SPOIL *s.* alimúră, yeáymă, yeámă, iámă, prádă, spóľe

SPOIL *vb.* ▾stric, ▾aludzắscu; **~ed meat** cárne aludzâtă; (*of teeth, of nuts, etc.*) cufchiséscu; (*of milk, of soup, etc.*) ▾astáľu; (*to ~ a child*) ľ-dau fáţă; (*to ~ a plan, an opportunity*) cacurizipséscu, u adár bóză; **to ~ the fun** aspárg chéifa; **to ~ for a fight** trag tâmbárea azvắrna, trag brâmlu azvárna; u cáftu ngăceárea cu luminárea; **Too many cooks ~ the broth** ≈ Iu-s mămíi múlti lu scot ficiórlu órbu (*lit. 'Where there are too many midwives the child comes out blind'*)

SPOILAGE *s.* stricáre; *also:* aludzâme, aludzâre, astăľáre, cufchisíre

SPOILED *adj.* ciurúc, -úcă, -úţi, -úţe; stricát; (*empty, with holes, as of teeth or of nuts*) cúfchiu; (*usu. of food*) aludzât, astăľát; (*as of cheese or flour*) aprés, nţes; (*morally ~*) aspártu, -rtă, -rţâ, -rte; **~ supplies** viştínă

SPOILER *s.* aspărgătór

SPOILING *s.* → SPOILAGE

SPOKE *s.* (*rung of a ladder*) scalupátimă ‖ (*~ of a wheel*) **Prv:** pălmáche, CL 258

SPOKEN *adj.* zburât

SPOLIATION *s.* bilíre, dispuľáre

SPONGE *s.* sfúnghe, sfúngu, sfănghíe, sfungáre

SPONGE ON SMB. *vb.* (a)ghismédz, (a)ghizmédz; **~ on them as much as you can!** Aghizmáţ-ľi cât ma múltu!

SPONGE OUT *vb.* ▾agắrşéscu; Apă şi sáre! (*lit. 'water and salt,' i.e. Let's sponge out the past!*)

SPONSORSHIP *s.* (*of a wedding*) nuníľe

SPOOF *s.* ncălţáre

SPOOF *vb.* (a)ncálţu, trag únă căláie → DECEIVE

SPOOK *s.* → GHOST

SPOOK *vb.* ▾aspár

SPOOL *s.* măsúr, ţáye, ţáie, cótcă, cărúľu

SPOOL FORK *s.* (*Y-shaped*) ftínă; furcáce, furcáce de cicríche

SPOON *s.* língură, língră, *dim.* linguríce; (*large ~*) hľáră; (*a shepherd's ~*) ciubánă

SPOON MAKER *s.* (*of wooden spoons*) lingurár

SPOONY → BE ~ ON SMB.

SPOOR *s.* úrmă

SPORADIC

SPORADIC *adj.*, **SPORADICALLY** *adv.* arár

SPORT *s.* → FUN, MAKE ~ OF SMB.

SPOT *s.* liché → STAIN

SPOT *vb.* → STAIN; (*to recognize, to identify*) cunóscu

SPOTLESS *adj.* curát, fără lichédz, fâră minghinádhă → CLEAN

SPOTTED *adj.* smâryít

SPOUSE *s.* (*husband*) **Băi:** hurhóñu

SPOUT *vb.* (*to eject a liquid*) ▾(a)zvóm, azvurăscu; (*to show up, of a fluid or semifluid*) andzămédz

SPRAIN *s.* cluzuníre, străngulsíre

SPRAIN *vb.* cluzunéscu, ▾străngulséscu ‖ I ~ed my hand Ñ-scoşu mâna (*lit. 'I pulled out my hand'*), PARALLELE 138

SPRAWL *vb.* ▾tíndu

SPRAY *s.* (*aigrette*) sărgúce

SPREAD *adj.* aştirnút; tímsu, -mşi, -mse; tímtu, -mţâ, -mte

SPREAD *vb.* ▾(a)răspândzu, arăspândéscu, ▾arăéscu, aruéscu, ▾prâstuéscu; (*to scatter*) ▾scropiséscu, scrupséscu, scurpiséscu, ▾xiruíndu; (*of a gossip*) iáse zbor (că); (*as of a piece of news*) feráre, *invar.*; **May your word be ~ everywhere!** Zbórlu-a tău s s-fácă feráre! ‖ MERCA 4: mi aspărăndéscu

SPREAD OUT *vb.* ▾aştérnu

SPREADING *s.* arăspândíre, arăíre, prâstuíre, scrupsíre; (~ out) aştirneáre xirutíndire

SPREE → BE ON THE ~

SPRIGHTLINESS *s.* sirtlâche

SPRIGHTLY *adj.* aflát → INTELLIGENT, SPIRITED

SPRING *s.* (*source*) ízvur, *dim.* izvuríc; fântână, *dim.* fântâní-că, fântâneáuă, fântâñoáră; (*season*) primveáră, primuveáră; **at the beginning of the ~** tu cáplu a primuveárăľei; (*elastic body in a mechanism*) zumbăréche, zimbireche

SPRING *adj.* primuviréscu; **~ cheese** cáş primuviréscu

SPRING *vb.* (*to originate*) azvurăscu; **to ~ at smb.** ▾nhimuséscu; **to ~ up** (*as of a plant*) fitruséscu

SPRINKLE *vb.* (*with salt, pepper, flour, etc.*) pispiléscu; (*with water, as flowers in a garden*) ▾ud, ▾aruvín, aruvinédz, arăvi-nédz, ▾pruscuséscu, pruscuhéscu, pruscutéscu, nţilistrédz; (*to ~ holy water*) (a)yizmuéscu, (a)yizmuséscu, ▾fuţéscu

SPRINKLING *s.* (*as of sugar*) pispilíre; (*of a liquid, usu. wa-*

ter) aruvináre, pruscutíre, pruscuchíre, udătúră; (*of holy water*) (a)yizmuíre, (a)yizmusíre

SPRINT *s*. fúgă

SPRINT *vb*. fug di mi frângu → RUN

SPRITE *s*. → GHOST

SPROUT *s*. cľeciu, climbúciu; (*rudiment of a plant*) fítru; *to put forth sprouts* *vb*. mpuľédz

SPROUTING *s*. (*germination*) fitrusíre

SPRUCE *s*. arób, róbul, mănícľu, mănúcľu; *G:* mulíftu

SPRUCE *adj*. mutrít, prăpsít, pruvidzút, prividzút

SPRUCE UP *vb*. ▾andrég, ▾adár, ▾adár ca yambró

SPRY *adj*. → NIMBLE

SPUME *s*. → FOAM

SPUNK *s*. → COURAGE

SPUNK *vb*. ▾apríndu

SPUN TREAD *s*. drúgă, tórtu, tul

SPUR *s*. (*at a rider's heels*) măhmúze (*and* mâh-), muhmúze, *pl* măhmúzi

SPUR *vb*. anăngăsăéscu, bag măhmúzea (a cálui)

SPURIOUS *adj*. minciunós, -oásă; pséftu, -ftă, -fţâ, -fte

SPURT *s*. fúzmă, vánţu, zvórimă

SPURT *vb*. (*to gush*) ▾azvóm, azvurăscu; **to ~ out** ▾zvom → ORIGINATE

SPY *s*. spiún, şpiún, spión; *also:* cişít, seíd, sâíz

SPY *vb*. páscu; **I have been ~ing on him for an hour** L-páscu di únă oáră di chiró

SPYING *s*. culayuzlâche, călăyuzlâche, spiunlâche [•i•un•]; **~ will cost you your head** Culayuzlâchea va-ţ mâcă cáplu ‖ CARAFOLI 41: spiuniľi

SQUABBLE *vb*. ▾ncaciu, ▾nţértu

SQUABBLER *s*. căvgăgí

SQUAD *s*. táifă

SQUADRON *s*. (*naval unit*) stol

SQUALID *adj*. átim, *m pl* -tiñ; murdár, ni-bruít, ni-mutrít

SQUALL *s*. (a)zvinturáre (di neáuă)

SQUALOR *s*. ni-mutríre

SQUANDER *vb*. (*as one's money*) ▾spătăľuséscu, tuchéscu, dau stâ zvércă; **to ~ one's time** (*in vain*) ñ-cher săpúnea → SPEND

SQUANDERER *s.* hărgiuitór, -toáre; ásot; aspártu, -rtă, -rţâ, -rte; spátal, *m pl* -taĭ, *f pl* -tale ‖ DIARO 235: arâspândít, aspârgâtór

SQUANDERING *s.* spătăĭusíre

SQUARE *s.* (*four equal sides*) săndráciu → BE ~ WITH SMB.

SQUASH *vb.* (*as of grapes taken on a rough trip*) ▾zdrúmin, zdroámin, strúcin, stúrcin, strucinédz, ▾zmoátic; (*to press, to crush*) ▾(a)pitruséscu, (a)putruséscu

SQUAT *adj.* şíşcu, -şcă, -şţâ, -şte; muşmoálă, -múlă

SQUAT *vb.* păpăruséscu; zăruséscu, zuruséscu

SQUEAK *vb.* (*of mice*) ‖ cârţâtéscu, DIARO 243

SQUEAK-SQUEAK *ono.* (*of mice*) ‖ cârţ-cârţ, DIARO 243

SQUEAL *vb.* ‖ ALR 332: (*of a pig*) gurleádză; (*of a piglet*) ţíură

SQUEEZE *vb.* ▾stríngu (→ § 32); (*as of a wet shirt*) ▾stricór; (*to crush with one's hands, as of grapes*) ▾zdrúmic, ▾zdroámin; **to ~ out** (*of oneself*) ▾spreámit; **to ~ to one's heart** ▾stríngu la sin

SQUEEZING *s.* stríndzire, strindzeáre, sticuráre, zdrumináre

SQUINT-EYED *adj.* ceacâr, strióclĭu, strâ- ‖ *Av:* ciacârcu, zăvumát, CL 43

SQUIRM *vb.* mi şuţ, mi turculéscu, mi târculéscu → FIDGET ‖ nu mi-acáţă lóclu, BASME 61

SQUIRREL *s.* virviríţă ‖ ALIA 100: vervéră, virvéră; *also:* chétur, cunáve, ayrupísă

SQUIRT *s.* (*toy*) păşpácă (*and* pâş-), plíscă, sălístră, silístră, ţilístră ‖ *GSus:* ţârţânítă, CL 63

STAB *vb.* plântu cuţútlu

STABLE *s.* ahúre, patós, pleámţă, pleánţă, plénţă, stáulă; *F:* dámă

STABLE *adj.* ni-minát, sănătós, -oásă; (*mentally well-balanced*) aştirnút

STABLE-BAG *s.* (*for horses*) liyutástru

STACK *s.* (*usu. of hay*) cópă → RICK

STAFF *s.* (*as of a flag*) purtécă, purteácă; (*stick*) puleán → CUDGEL

STAG *s.* ţérbu, ţirbóñu, *dim.* ţirbóplu; *also:* buyắ, elén, ndrél, plătún

STAG-BEETLE *s.* ent. ‖ *SJos:* zarcádhă, CL 263

STAGGER *vb.* ▾trunduéscu → SHIVER

STAGGERS: marked by ~ adj. (of animals) vârlu, vârlít

STAGNANT adj. (of a body of water) stătút

STAGNATION s. (low economic activity) chisáte

STAIN s. liché; also: bátă, dámcă, lăvíle, léră, minghinádhă ‖ **Peş:** vúlă, CL 263; **Cru:** mănghinádhă, GOLAB 234; **Na:** léche, **Grăm:** lichéu, B-ARCH 438

STAIN vb. ▾chic; **You have ~ed your shirt** Ti chicaşi pri cămeá-şe; also: ▾lichiséscu, ▾dămcuséscu, ▾lăvăşéscu; (usu. with blood) ▾mârşuéscu, ▾mustuéscu → DIRTY ‖ ALR 1369: ▾ncárcu: **I ~ed myself with blood** Mi ancărcái di sândze

STAINED adj. (as of the walls of a room) chicát; (~ with blood) ncărcát di sândze, sândzinát, sândzirát

STAKE s. (as a burning log in the middle of a fire) rug; (post) par; (smth. that is staked for gain or loss) apáie

STAKED adj. **~ beans** făsúle di análtu (ant. făsúle di páde)

STALACTITE s. ‖ CUVATA 27: ghígor

STALE adj. stătút, şidzút; also: (as of bread) băiáte; (of water) ndâhânít, ndâhnít; (of flour) xizumsít; **~ supplies** viştínă ‖ (as of cheese or fruit) nţes, CAPIDAN 149

STALK s. **slender ~** şíľe

STALK vb. ▾avín ‖ CUNIA 324: mi ţân dúpă, ľau ân cicioáre, ľau ân tor

STALL s. (for animals) cumás; (in a church) stálă, stisídhă, tisídhă, (a)stăsídhă

STALL HOLDER s. sirghingí

STALLION s. areáte, arăiáte; hat, at ‖ **GSus:** diót, CL 44; **Cru:** aigăr, GOLAB 196; **Mul:** iágăr; **Amc, LvO:** cálu bârbát, **Kast:** cal más-cul; **CĽis, Pro, Pros:** mândzu; passim: cal, B-ARCH 305

STALWART adj. (robust) zdúmban, m pl -bañ, f pl -bane

STAMINA s. vârtúte, vârtuş → VIGOR

STAMMER vb. bâlbăéscu, băbăléscu, dărdăréscu, ngulişédz; **Their tongues are ~ing** Lă si ngulişeádză límba

STAMMERER s. peltéc; also: chec, gângu, **Bl:** gângăvéţ

STAMMERING s. băbălíre, bănduráre, dărdăríre

STAMP s. (device for stamping) vúlă (→ SEAL); (postal ~) puľu

STAMP vb. (to pound, to crush with or as with a pestle) stúlţin, zdroámin; (to ~ one's feet) (a)rupăţéscu, rupuţéscu; **to ~ off** (as snow) ▾(a)scútur; **Please ~ off the snow!** Ascuturáţ-vă di

STAMPEDE

neáuă! **to ~ on the mind** ▼stămbuséscu (tu mădúuă)

STAMPEDE *vb.* (*of domestic animals*) vârléscu → GIDDY, REEL

STAMPING ONE'S FEET *s.* arupăţâre

STAND *s.* → MAKE A ~ AGAINST

STAND *vb.* (*to endure*) ▼arávdu, ▼apufirséscu, (a)stărxéscu (*and* astâr-); (*to withstand, to held*) stănipséscu, dăinséscu, dindiséscu, dănăséscu, dăniséscu, dănséscu, hunipséscu; **He could not ~ it any longer** Nu putú z-dăniseáscă cáma múltu; **Skin does not ~ cold** Cheálea nu dindiseáşte tu arcoáre; *impers.* s-trádze; **One cannot ~ this heat** Nu s-trádzi căldúra aístă; (*of smb. or smth. repulsive*) nu luám tu stumáhe; (*to be in an upright position*) şed mpróstu; **to ~ aghast** l-háscu *or* l-háscu n gúră; **to ~ gaping about** ylindipséscu, siryinséscu; **to ~ aside** părămirséscu; **to ~ by smb.** (*to side smb.*) ĺ-ĺau párte; **to ~ in smb.'s way**, *3 sg*: ñ-şeáde ntr-óčĺi; **to ~ on end** (*to stick up, of one's hair*) ñ-si mútă pérlu făltác; **to ~ out** (*to keep a stiff upper lip*) ▼cálcu ciciólu; **to ~ sentinel over** cărăulséscu (→ SENTINEL); **to ~ a treat, a drink** dau únă mişteáre; **to ~ still** (*as of children*) ĺ-ţân lóclu; **Children cannot ~ still** Ficiórĺi nu ştiu si-ĺ ţână lóclu; **to ~ up** ▼mbrustédz; **to ~ up against** (*to defy*) ĺi stau cucót, ▼ţân cheptu; **to ~ upon ceremony** → CEREMONY

STAND TRANSFIXED *vb.* ‖ *Amc:* armân lóclui, RÉCATAS 37

STANDARD *s.* (*accepted pattern*) mucadéme → FLAG

STANDARD-BEARER *s.* bairahtár

STANDING *s.* (*rank*) arádhă

STANDING *adj., adv.* mpróstu (*and* mbros-), di proáste

STANDING ARMY *s.* sifére

STAR *s.* steáuă, steáo

STAR OF BETHLEHEM *s. bot.* (a)ngulíce, gulíce, guláce, lilícea a Hristólui, lúşcă

STARCH *s.* cólă, acoálă, nizisté

STARCH *vb.* culărséscu, culurséscu

STARCHED *adj.* (*of collars, etc.*) culărsít

STARCHING *s.* culărsíre

STARE *vb.* hărvăĺiséscu, (a)zgârléscu óčiĺ (cătră); **to ~ smb. up and down** mutréscu di la úngĺi pân la cap

STARER *s.* zgârĺáiu

STARK *adj.* (*strong*) vârtós, -oásă; (*rigid*) scliró *invar.*;

(*strict*) áscur; (*desolate*) érmu, *m pl* érñi

STARLING *s.* zgârlíre

STARLING *s. orn.* cărăvéľu, gărăvéľu

START *s.* (*run, soar*) fúzmă → IMPETUS; (*sudden bodily movement*) astrisăríre

START *vb.* (*to give an involuntary tw or jerk*) astrisár, antrisár (*and* andri-); (*to move forward, to rush upon*) urñéscu; (*to cause to leave, as a hare*) sârmu; **to ~ violently** (*as of a storm*) ▾arúp; (*to commence*) → BEGIN

STARTING LINE *s.* (*line traced on the ground, in some games*) apúchiu

STARTLE *vb.* ▾anăbăréscu

STARTLED → BE ~

STARVATION *s.* foáme, foámită; *also:* agiuneáţă, agiunátic, agiunáre, agiunáme, ni-mâncáre

STARVE *vb.* agiún, agiunédz, bag ploci pri pântică, bat tămbărălu, ñ-gurleádză máţăle di foáme

STARVING *adj.* líhud, -hudă, -hudz, -hude

STATE *s.* (*political organization*) duvléte, vasíľu ‖ CUNIA: crat (*private letter*); HRISTU 1: stat; *Gop:* dărjávă, GOLAB 211 ‖ (*condition*) rádă, nizáme; **in a bad ~** (*in a sorry plight*) cătră soáre

STATE *vb.* dzâc ‖ (*to ~ one's point of view*) ñ-dau mínţăli, BASME 302

STATELY *adj.* bugdán, buy-; mărít; pirifán, *m pl* -fáñ

STATEMENT *s.* (*account*) tăcráre, tăcríre; (*oral ~*) dzâcă

STATION *s.* (*stopping place on a transportation route*) staţióne, staşióne, staşiónă

STATIONARY *adj.* ni-minát

STATUE *s.* áyalmă, ágalmă

STATURE *s.* stătút; **of the same ~ and color** aţél stătút, aţeá buiáuă

STATUS *s.* (*condition of a person*) arádhă; (*state of affairs*) luyuríe

STAUNCH *adj.* (*fixed*) ni-minát; (*determined*) dâldâsít, apufăsít

STAVE *s.* (*as in a barrel or bucket*) doágă ‖ CUNIA 91: ceambér *and* doágă

STAVE IN *vb.* (*of a cask*) disfúndu

STAVE OFF *vb.* (*to stop one's stomach*) ñ-apúc gúra

STAVING

STAVING IN *s.* (*as of a cask*) disfundáre

STAY *vb.* (*to stop, to dwell, to live*) armấn; (*to prop up*)
▼arádzim → LEAN

STAY ONE'S HUNGER *vb.* ▼năfătéscu foámea

STAY OVERNIGHT *vb.* ▼cundiséscu, nuptédz → MAKE A HALT

STAY-AT-HOME *s., adj.* dumuşár, dumuşárcu; *derog.* cacavátră

STEADFAST *adj.* (*determined*) apufăsít, dâldâsít; (*constant,
fixed*) ni-minát

STEADILY *adv.* cu métru

STEADY *adj.* (*firm, reliable*) sănătós ‖ (*of smb.'s mind*) cu
míntea tu loc, BASME 347

STEAK *s.* (*grilled ~*) burjólă, brujólă

STEAL *s.* (*the act of stealing*) furáre; (*bargain*) chilipúre ‖
STERGHIU 30: furátic

STEAL *vb.* ▼(a)fúr; *also:* afúm (*lit. 'to smoke'*), ▼agudéscu,
ñ-agudeáşte mâna, ▼anvăléscu, amvăléscu, ▼ahuléscu, ▼apúc, bag tu
mânică di tămáre, bag tu tástru, ▼căléscu, ▼ciun, ▼ciupléscu,
▼nciuléscu, ciuléscu, ▼căpsălséscu, ▼mut, sec, ñ-seácă mâna,
▼spăstréscu (*lit. 'to clean'*), sufruséscu, úmflu, úmflu ngrâşca ‖
TULLIU 135: aruşúţ

STEAL AWAY *vb.* u căléscu, li scármin → BOLT

STEALING *s.* ciunáre; **He is an expert at ~** Eáste gióne tu ciunáre → STEAL

STEALTH → STEAL; *by ~* pri afuríşalui → STEALTHILY

STEALTHILY *adv.* acrifá, (a)furíşalui, pri (a)furíşalui, ascúmtalui, pri ascúmtalui, bisgúlea, furíş, pri niaduchíte, tiptíle

STEAM *s.* ábur ‖ HRISTU 44: duh

STEAM *vb.* ▼aburédz, hérbu ahnó

STEAM ENGINE *s.* ‖ **Peş:** cap di paóre, CL 40

STEAMER *s.* paór, paóre

STEAMING *adj., adv.* ahnó *invar.*

STEAMSHIP *s.* pampór, pampóre

STEAMY *adj.* aburós, -oásă

STEED *s.* → HORSE

STEEL *s.* (*piece of ~ for sharpening knives, etc.*) arbínă, cilí-
che, ciulí-, ciulé-; măsát(e) ‖ GULI 43: ciléche; (*~ for strike-
a-light*) amnáre, amneár, cicmác ‖ **GSus:** mănár, CL 255; **SJos:**

muñár, CL 256

STEEL *vb.* (*to make strong, to strngthen*) cilicuséscu

STEELYARD *s.* zíyă

STEEP *adj.* (a)râpós, -oásă; n hímă *invar.*; scârpós, -oásă

STEEP *vb.* (*to soak*) ▾(a)móľu, ▾ud

STEEPLE *s.* → BELL TOWER

STEEPLY UPHILL *adv.* ‖ *Cru:* anífur, GOLAB 199

STEER *s.* (*young ox*) giúncu, mândzát

STEER *vb.* (*to guide, to inspire*) âñ şúiră ‖ **how God will ~ him** cum va-ľ şúiră Dumnidzău, BASME 149

STEERSMAN *s.* → HELMSMAN

STEIN *s.* bucál → MUG

STEM *s.* bot. (*~ of a gourd*) cúrpin, cúrpan, *Scruf:* scrúpen; climătăryeáuă; (*~ of a narghile*) mărcúş ‖ (*~ of a tree*) *Amc,* *AMer, Els, Fal, Gra, Lvz, LvO, Mul, Na, Prv, Rod, Smx, Suf:* trup

STENCH *s.* putoáre, ambutoáre, ndâhâníre, ndâhníre, voáhă, vrómă

STEP *s.* ceálpă, ceálpu, ceápă, giglátă, jgľoátă, zgľoátă; *Gop:* jgľot; **at each ~** la cáthi şgľot; ciciór, drăşcľáuă, úrmă; **to take a false ~** cálcu strâmbu, pára-cálcu; **He made a couple of steps forward** Arcă trei-pátru úrme; **to bend one's ~s to/toward** ľ-u dau cătră, ▾ľau cătră; (*~ of a stair-case*) scáră, scalupá-timă; **~ by ~** scară di scáră

STEP ASIDE *vb.* părămirséscu ‖ ▾trag năpói, BASME 615; ALR 1376: mi dau na nă párte

STEP BACK *vb.* (*to retreat*) ▾trag năpói; **~, you shrimps!** Trádziţ-vă, jabéţ, năpói!

STEP OFF *vb.* (*to die*) li tíndu

STEPCHILD *s.* proyón *m* ‖ DIARO 294: pruyoánâ *f*

STEPDAUGHTER *s.* hiľástră

STEPFATHER *s.* tátă nércu

STEPMOTHER *s.* năeárcă, nueárcă, neárcă

STEPSON *s.* hiľástru

STERILE *adj.* (*of women, of sheep*) stérpu, steárpă, stérchi, steárpe; (*of sheep and goats*) mărmáră ‖ **~ ewe** biroáñe, GOLAB 208; (*of a field*) hărhálă, ţâţârác → BECOME ~

STERILIZATION *s.* (*usu. of a sheep*) stirpuíre

STERILIZE *vb.* (*usu. of sheep*) stirpuéscu, stirpéscu

STERN *adj.* (*austere*) áscur; (*sturdy*) vârtós, -oásă

STEW

STEW s. yeahníe, iahníe, căpămă; **stewed beans** făsúle yeahné; ~ **fruit** cuşáfe, huşáfe, uşáfe

STEWARD s. icunóm, cumandărgí

STEWPAN s. tengíre → SAUCEPAN

STICK s. (*for stirring boiling milk*) mintătór, spăteádză; (*rod*) ciumág, giumác, puleán; **little ~** (a)fínge, (a)fínje; **to be at ~ and lift** bat tămbărălu; **to beat smb. all to sticks** ansár, stul-cinédz di chiutécă → CUT ONE'S ~

STICK vb. ▾alichéscu (di), alăchéscu; ▾ţân (di); **~ to me!** Ţâni-te di míne! **to ~ like a burr** mi ţân scaľu (di), ľ-acáţ yéaca; **to ~ it on/up** (*to give oneself airs*) mi ngroş; **to ~ in the mire** vărcuséscu, vultuséscu; **to ~ in one's throat** ñ-si acáţă; *imprec.* **May it ~ in his throat!** Si-ľ si-acáţă! **to ~ one's spoon in the wall** (*to die*) li tíndu; **to ~ to business** mi aştérnu pri (*or* tu) lúcru; **to ~ to one's opinion** u ţân fúne, u leg că (→ HOLD ON; STUBBORNLY); **to ~ to one's word** mi ţân di zbor

STICK OUT vb. scot; **to ~ one's tongue at smb.** ľ-scot límba nafoáră

STICK UP vb. (*of a plant*) fitruséscu; (*of one's hair when in terror*) ñ-si mútă pérlu din cap făltác

STICKING OUT: with ~ ears adj. plahúrcu, pľa-, f -rcă, m pl -rţi, f pl -rţe; maltécicu, -că, -cichi [čki], -ciche

STICKY adj. mâzgós, -oásă ‖ (*of unbaked bread*) gľiciós, DIARO 272 **STIFF** adj. (*as of joints*) ncărfusít, nturusít, ndirusít, ncu-cinát, ngu-; (*as with cold*) ngárdu, ngľiţát → MAKE ~

STIFF-DEAD adj. scândurát

STIFFEN vb. ancúñu, limnuséscu; **His body has ~ed** Trúplu ľ-an-cuñí; (*as with cold*) ▾ncărfuséscu, ncrăfuséscu, ▾ndiruséscu, ▾nturuséscu, ▾ncucinédz, ngu-; ngurdéscu; (*with terror*) ngľeţ di frícă ‖ (~ *with cold*) ngu28ncinéscu, BATSARIA 46

STIFFENING s. ncărfusíre; (*of cold*) ncucináre, ngu-; ngurdíre

STIFF-NECKED adj. → HAUGHTY, STUBBORN

STIFFNESS s. ngurdíre, limnusíre

STIFLE vb. zdrúmin di gúşe, ▾zgrum; (*to block with stones, as a snake*) ▾(a)pitruséscu, **N:** (a)putruséscu

STIFLING s. (*suffocation*) ndăhníre, zădúh

STIFLING adj. (*of voice*) ndăcănít, ndăhănít

STILL adj. (*quiet*) tăcút; (*calm*) arihătipsít, frónim, ísih,

sirín; (*without motion*) ni-minát **to be as ~ as a mouse** ≈ nu fac
níţi dza → STAND ~

STILL adv. (*continuance of an action or condition*) tut, nícă,
níca, níngă; (*in spite of*) cu tútă aístă; **He is ~ a chick** Níca
éste puľu

STILLNESS s. arăpás; **sepulchral ~** ţâpit → SILENCE

STILTED adj. (*pompous*) cu táxe

STILT OF PLOUGH s. mânǎ di dămăľúg ‖ *GSus, Pls:* coádă

STILTS s. călingóci f pl; călingoáce sg; nalǎne f pl ‖ *Peş:*
năgáltă, pl năgălţâ, CL 257

STIMULATE vb. ▼schin, anăngăséscu, ngăsăéscu → PEP

STIMULATION s. anăngăsíre

STIMULUS s. mucaéte

STING s. (*an act of stinging or the result of it*) nţăpătúră;
(*the pointed organ of a bee*) ac

STING vb. nţap (*and* ndzap), mâc; **Are the flies stinging you?**
Músca ti mâcă?

STINGINESS s. filaryiríe, icunumíe, nichizlâche, sclingiureáţă, schingiureáţă, sclinceáme, şclinceáme, titizlâche

STINGING s. (*by or as by a wasp*) nyispáre, yispináre

STINGING adj. nţăpătós, -oásă

STINGY adj. stres, streásă, streşĭ, streáse; ţânút; *also:* cim-
brós, cľáia a dráclui (*lit. 'devil's key'*), filáryir, nichéz, săráf, şcľínciu, şcľinciuít, titíz; 3 sg: ş-di púric va s scoátă
seu (*lit. 'willing to squeeze fat even out of a flea'*) ‖ *Av:*
ciúngu, CL 43; *Pls:* schifupát, CL 261; *Amc, An, Arγ, Cľis, Lvz,
Na, Pdz, Pur, Ses, Vil:* ţingún; *Els:* spañu; *Grăm:* schifrumén; *Am:*
sclângítu, *Kast:* sclindzítu, B-ARCH 241

STINK vb. ▼(a)mpút (*and* ambút), ampuţăscu

STINKARD s. (*male or female*)‖ CARAFOLI 54: amputoári

STINKING adj. (a)mpuţât (*and* ambuţât), ambuţós, vrumñár

STINT vb. (*to restrict to a scant allowance*) ▼scad, ▼hiriséscu;
(*to be sparing*) ▼chivirnăséscu

STINT ONESELF vb. (*to restrain, to press, to limit*) ▼apreadún,
priadún

STIR s. lávă, mintitúră, vreávă

STIR vb. (*as the ember in a stove*) ▼mintuéscu; (*of beaters*)
▼aúrlu; **to ~ heaven and earth** (*i.e., to do one's damned best*)

STIR

▼apufác

STIR UP vb. anăngăséscu, ▼avín; (to incite) azmúţ, ▼sălăghés-cu, ▼scol; **The dogs were stirred up** Cân̄ľi eará sălăghíţ; (of fire) ascrúm, ▼aschín (fóclu)

STIRRUP s. (of metal) zănghíe; (of rope) scárǎ, dim. scărícă ‖ **Peş:** zinghíe, CL 263

STIRRUP LEATHER s. stríngľe

STITCH s. (as in knitting) ócľu; to drop a ~ n̄-ascápǎ un ócľu; (a)láţ; **stitches in a stocking** láţuri di lăpúdǎ

STITCH vb. ‖ ALR 525: cos lárgu

STITCH s. med. amurţât, giúngľu, giungľáre, mâşcáre, púndzire; **Cľis:** stihíptu; **to have a ~** mi giungľádzǎ

ST. JOHN'S WORT s. bot. căntăríe

STOCK s. (block of wood) búcium; (handle) coádǎ; (farm animals) tutíputǎ; (not distributed cards) scártu; (a stupid person) glar

STOCKDOVE s. dudíe, dhicuhtúrǎ (lit. 'eighteen'); fásǎ, gugúce, gugúfcǎ, gugúfce → DOVE

STOCKY adj. şíşcu, -şcǎ, -şţâ, -şte → THICKSET

STODGY adj. angricós, -oásǎ

STOKE vb. (to stir up, as a fire) mintéscu

STOLE s. (ecclesiastical vestment) pătrăhíľe, pitrăhíľe

STOLEN adj. (a)furát, afumát, loat di furi

STOLID adj. (phlegmatic, apathetic) adhyeáfur

STOMACH s. stumáh, stumáhe, mámǎ, ínimǎ, arândzǎ; **He filled up his ~** şi-umplú máma; (→ RENNET); (a ruminant's ~) amúrǎ; **~ discomfort** plácumǎ

STOMACH vb. (to stand) hunipséscu; **I cannot ~ him** Lu-ám şíľe ntr-ócľi

STOMACH ACHE: I have a ~ Mi mâşcǎ ínima cólicǎ; Mi mâşcǎ buríclu

STONE s. cheátrǎ; (small ~) şómbur, şómburǎ; (~ of grape) sâmbure; (of cherry) os; (of a peach) ciucurdécǎ → PIP

STONE vb. (to lapidate) ▼ambuliséscu

STONE-CUTTER s. chitrár

STONED adj. → DRUNK

STONING s. ambulisíre

STONY adj. stirnós, -oásǎ; **~ area** scârcǎ, hălíche

STOOL: to have a ~ ies afoárǎ, mi scoáte (nafoárǎ); **I've had**

one ~ Mi scoáse nă mấnă; **I had three ~s** Mi scoáse trei mấñ; **How
many ~s did you have yesterday?** Cấte ori inşít afoárã aéri?

STOOP *vb.* (*to condescend*) cătădhixéscu; (*to lower oneself
morally*) ▼scad

STOP *s.* acumtináre, astămăţíre, păfsíre, puşíre; (*halt*) chin-
druíre, cunáche, lujíre

STOP *vb.* stau (→ § *32*); ▼ţấn, ▼adún, cúrmu; **Only the cricket
was not stopping its singing** Maşi chirchinéclu nu-şi adună gúra;
(*to bar, to stop running*) (a)stămăţéscu, ▼(a)cúmtin, acumtinéscu,
N: ▼ascúmtin; **He ~ed going** Si acumtină din cále; **the tears she
could not ~** lăcriñle ţe nu puteá si li-ascúmtină; **to ~ talking**
tac; (*as a request*) **Stop talking!** Moári-u láfea! (*to make a
halt*) chindurséscu, chinduréscu, lujéscu, pupuséscu, zăptăséscu,
zăptiséscu; *G:* **Stop it!** Fă sábine! (*to interrupt, to discontinue*)
pricúrmu; (*to hinder, to prevent*) mbudhuéscu; **to ~ favoring smb.**
ĺ-ĺau hárea; **to ~ one's stomach** ñ-apúc gúra; **Eat something to
stop your stomach!** Mấcă s ţ apúţi gúra! ‖ STERGHIU 29: (*don't!
stop it! wait a minute!*) dinăseá!

STOPPER *s.* (a)stupătoáre, stúpumă, stuputór, şiróf ‖ *SJos:* tápă, *Prv, Smr:* tápâ, CL 261

STORE *s.* ducheánă *and* ducheáne; aryăstír, dugáne

STORE *vb.* (*to lay away*) păstrédz; **to be** (*or* **to lay**) **in ~ for
one** *impers.* mi adástă

STOREHOUSE *s.* hămbáre, ambáre

STOREKEEPER: **army ~** zapită ‖ (*one that operates a retail
store*) duchingí, DIARO 425

STOREROOM *s.* ţilár, cămáră → CELLAR

STORK *s.* lélic, liléc, luléc; *N:* ululéc, ulaléc, uĺuléc; pilicán, ştấrcu, ştrăc ‖ ALB, *Dren, Kërb, Pe, Për, Sln:* luléc, liléc, Brâncuş 552

STORM *s.* furtúnă; *also:* bóră; (*terrible ~*) chiaméte; *CĺIS:*
dârce, sindilíe de ploáie (*or* di neáuă); vímtu ‖ *Av:* zof, BASME
743

STORM *vb.* (*as in a battle*) ▼fac fóra; (*to rage, of weather*)
bat, huhutéscu

STORMY *adj.* furtunós, -oásă

STORY *s.* (*account, anecdote*) părăvulíe ‖ (*circumstances*) **the
whole ~** ţi ş-cum, BASME 418

STORY *s.* pat → FLOOR; *also:* BE WRONG IN THE UPPER ~

STOUT *adj.* zdúmban, *m pl* -bañ, *f pl* -bane → THICK-SET

STOVE *s.* sóbă; (*small portable* ~) mângáne ‖ STERE 70: chiumbé

STOVEMAKER *s.* sobagí

STOW AWAY *vb.* ▾stríngu, ▾ascúndu

STRADDLE *vb.* (*of legs*) ▾discácăr

STRADDLING *s.* discăcăráre, discăcărătúră

STRAGGLE *vb.* (*to rove*) mi abát, mi dipărtédz; (*to stray*) hă-lăndăréscu

STRAIGHT *adj.* (*free from curves*) d(i)réptu, -eáptă, -épţâ, -eápte; (*even, adequate*) íschiu, *m pl* íschi, *f sg/pl* ísche; dúze *invar.*

STRAIGHT *adv.* (a)ndréptu, ísea, íşea; (*ant.*, *iron.*: ndrept ca fúnea tu tástru) ‖ ~ **ahead** cálea ndréptu, BASME 486

STRAIGHT-BUILT *adj.* subţârác

STRAIGHTEN *vb.* ▾mbróstu, ▾ischédz; **to ~ things out** ▾li andrég lúcrurile

STRAIGHTFORWARD *adj.* (*candid, honest*) nămuzlí, -zloáñe, -zládz

STRAIGHTFORWARDLY *adv.* ndréptu; fắră ticlífe

STRAIGHTFORWARD *adv.* fanirá → OPENLY

STRAIGHT-HAIRED *adj.* (*as of a puppy*) pârjít

STRAIN *s.* (*stretch*) tindeáre, tíndire; *phys.* spreámită → TE-NESMUS; (*compression, grip, embrace*) strândzire, strândzeáre

STRAIN *vb.* (**to stretch**) ▾tíndu; (*to squeeze or clasp tightly*) ▾stríngu; *phys.* ▾sprem; (*to cause to pass through a strainer*) ▾stricór **to ~ one's eyes** (*as in search of smth. important*) ñ-an-sár dzíhile (di căftáre); **to ~ to one's heart** (*to press, to hug*) ▾stringu la sin; **to ~ one's back** mi tuchéscu tu lúcru ‖ (*to pass through a strainer*) F: sticór, SarD 1o5; (*to strain oneself, as to defecate*) PC: mi (a)stríngu; CUNIA 272: âñ scot gúşa

STRAINER *s.* (*metallic*) ghirghír; (*of cloth*) sticătoáre, sti-cătoáre ‖ F: stăcători, HRISTU 50

STRAINING *s.* (*through or as through a strainer*) stricuráre

STRAIT *s.* strimtúră

STRAIT *adj.* stres, streásă, streşǐ, streáse

STRANGE *adj.* ciudós, -oásă; paráxin, *m pl* -xiñ; toáfe *invar.*

STRANGELY *adv.* toáfe

STRANGER *s.* aúmbră, (a)xinitór; **Who is the ~?** Aúmbra cári eáste?

STRANGLE *vb.* ▼zgrum, zgrumuéscu, zdrúmin di gúşe

STRANGLED *adj.* zgrumát

STRANGLING *s.* zgrumáre, zgrumătúră

STRANGULATION *s.* → STRANGLING

STRAP *s.* fáşe; (*belt*) ghíncală, yínglă

STRAP *vb.* (*to bind*) ▼leg (*as a saddle on a horse*) yingluséscu

STRAW *s.* paľu, *pl* páľe, *dim.* păľúş ‖ (*pl tantum*) **Mul, Perd:** páie, (*sg*) **Kat, Mal:** paiu, **Flam, Mi:** pai, B-ARCH 275

STRAW BOSS *s.* cap, măimár

STRAW MAT *s.* aruguzínă, psá(n)thă

STRATUM *s.* arádhă, dhíplă, pétur

STRAWBERRY *s.* căpşúnă, căpşeánă; *also:* (a)frángă, căpúşe, cărăşínă, fránţă, frándzu, gľúră, liliştrúfă, lulustúfă

STRAY *vb.* mi abát, hălăndăréscu

STRAYING *s.* urbáre; *also:* schirdeáre, zăgădíre

STREAK *s.* yir, yiur [yⁱur], yiúră; (*trace*) úrmă

STREAK OF LUCK *s.* urbáre; **He had a ~** Ľ-víñe urbárea

STREAKED *adj.* ľar; péstru, -stră, -ştri, -stre

STREAM *s.* (*brook*) víe, şuruínă, zănătúnă; **My blood was flowing in ~s** Sândzile cúra di míne şuruíñ; **in ~s** *adv.* zănătúnă; **Blood flew in ~s** Sândzile fudzeá zănătúnă → TORRENT ‖ **Cru:** (*flow, drip*) şóput, GOLAB 252

STREAMLET *s.* → RIVULET

STREET *s.* sucáche, úliţă; **town streets** sucáchi di pulitíe

STREETWALKER *s.* → HARLOT

STRENGTH *s.* puteáre, pteáre → FORCE; BEYOND SMB.'S ~

STRENGTHEN *vb.* ▼nvârtuşédz, ▼stiriuséscu, ▼vârtuşéscu

STRENUOUS *adj.* (*strong*) sărchirós, -oásă; (*requiring effort or stamina*) garamitlíu; greu, greáuă, grei, greále

STRETCH *vb.* ▼tíndu (→ § 32); (*to expand, to spread out, to lie or lay down*) ▼trag; **as far as the sea ~es** cât trádze amárea; **He lay near his wife** Níngă nveásta-a lui si tímse; **to ~ out** ▼lărdzéscu; **to ~ one's eyes** zgârléscu ócľiľ

STRETCHED *adj.* tes, teásă, teşľ, teáse; tímtu, *m pl* -mţâ; ântíntu; **~ flat** (*on the ground, on the floor*) tes, tes pri pântică, tes pri dínţâ; **~ out on the grass** ântíntu pi virdeáţă

STRETCHER: **to carry on or as on a ~** adúc patalóne

STREW

STREW *vb.* (*to disperse*) spúlbir, ▾arắéscu, ▾aruvérsu, ▾scrup-éscu, ▾pristuéscu; **The wind is ~ing (the dust, the snow)** Vímtul spúlbiră

STREWING *s.* spulbiráre

STRICKEN *adj.* (*hit*) agudít; (*wounded*) pliguít; (*by or as by a lightning*) sfuldzirát, sfulguít, sfulgurát, sfulgusít; (*crazy*) agudít

STRICT *adj.* sértic ‖ PC: arós

STRICTURE *s.* (*critical remark*) cătiyuríľe, cătiyuríe; (*narrowing*) angustáre

STRIDE *s.* drăşcľáuă máre

STRIDE *vb.* (*to walk with long steps*) arúc drăşcľéi mări

STRIFE *s.* ncăceáre → FIGHT, QUARREL

STRIKE *s.* agudíre, ciucutíre, cruíre, pălíre

STRIKE *vb.* (*to go*) ▾đuc, ▾trag, ▾trag pri cále; (*to turn one's steps to*) u ľau cálea (di cătră la), ľ-u dau; (*to come upon*) ▾agiúngu; (*to hit*) ▾agudéscu, ▾aúrlu, ▾luvéscu, trag, cruéscu únă, ľ-u dau, ľ-u asún, zăpăléscu únă; **to ~ a blow whith the hoof** trag únă cluţátă; **~ him!** Aúrlă-ľ vấră! (*to ~ with a whip*) jirtuéscu, jurtuéscu; **The swine struck to the forest** Poárca lo pădú-rea; **The thieves struck to the village of Sâmtu** Fúrľi loáră cá-lea di cătră la Sâmtu; **They struck across villages** Ľ-u deádiră prit hoáre; ‖ acáţ; **Where should he ~ to?** Cấtră iu s-acáţă? BASME 57 ‖ **to ~ across** apúc plainá; **to ~ a knife into smb.** ▾hig (*or* nhig) cuţútlu; plấntu cuţútlu; **to ~ a light** (a)scápir; **to ~ a match** şpirtuéscu; **to ~ an average** (*as bargaining over price*) u fac cumătúră; **to ~ dumb** ľau gúra; **to ~ off smb.'s head** ľau cáplu; **~to oil** (*i.e., to make a lucky find*) ≈ áflu mándră ni-călcátă; **to ~ roots** aruzuséscu, arizuséscu; **to ~ smb. down** arúc áde; **to ~ off** (*to eliminate, to remove*) 1-fac (a)risíte; **~ them** (*i.e., their names*) **off!** Fă-ľ arisíte! **to ~ terror into smb.'s breast** bag ceáşlu (tu), dau ibréte (la); (*to come to mind*) ñ-cá-de n córnu; **to ~ upon an idea** ñ-íntră; fotiséscu; **What could have stricken them to separate?** Ţe lă intră să si mpártă? **to ~ up friendship with smb.** li apríndu aluáturile (cu); **to ~ up to smb.** ľi stau cucót; (*of apoplexy*) chicutédz, nchicutédz; (*to clink glasses*) ▾cingărşéscu; (*to ~ red eggs on Easter*) ▾cingărşéscu; (*of clocks*) dau; **The clock struck five** Săhátea deáde ţínţi; (*of* *lightning*) *3 sg:* sfúldziră; *imprec.* **May God's lightning ~ you!** Dumnidzău s ti sfúldziră!

STRIKE UP *vb.* → BEGIN

STRIKING *s.* agudíre, agudeáre; (*of bells*) asunáre

STRING *s.* măgór, truşínă; (*as of a violin*) coárdhă; (*as for fastening a load*) fórtumă; (*group of objects in or as in line*) trâmbă → CORD, ROPE ‖ *Cru:* **~ of beads** báir, GOLAB 207; şigíme, GOLAB 252

STRING *vb.* (*as beads*) ▾(a)mbáir, ambúir, âmbár, mbar; **Let us ~ out one after the other** Un di un si mbăirăm

STRINGENCY *s.* (*scarcity*) lipsítă; (*trouble, difficulty*) anánghe, ihtiză, ihtizáe

STRIP *s.* (*band of fabric, leather, etc.*) lurídhă

STRIP *vb.* ▾dispóľu, ▾guléscu, ▾gulişnédz, gulişnédz; **to ~ smb. of money** (*as at cards*) afuléscu ‖ DIARO 393: ▾dizgóľu

STRIPE *s.* (*as on a wall*) răcáie (*and* râ-), răncáie; (*~ of different color in a fabric*) căráre; (*~ showing the rank of an officer*) galón, yalóne; (*kind, sort*) turlíe ‖ DIARO 430: yiúrâ

STRIPED *adj.* bétic ‖ *Av:* pârdhălós, CL 259

STRIPLING *s.* ficiurác, hilándru, giunél; *derog.* mucós, muxós

STRIPPING OFF *s.* dispuľáre, gulişináre, gulişnáre

STRIVE *vb.* (*to apply oneself to, to lay oneself out to*) cilistiséscu, cealăhtiséscu

STROKE *s. med.* agudĭtúră, apuplixíe, chícută, nchicutáre, dămláie, dumláie, dâmbľă, loáre di lúnă, pícă

STROKE *vb.* (*to caress*) adíľu, puspútéscu, puşpútéscu

STROLL *s.* ghizére, ghizirsíre, priimnáre, piripát, sulát, suláţă, tifiríce,; **to take a short ~** dau sulăţ; **We went for a ~** Ñársim tifiríce, vóltă; **There was no ~ing in the plaza** Nu aveá vólte prit piáţă

STROLL *vb.* dau sulăţ, ▾ghiziréscu, ▾priímnu

STRONG *adj.* putút, ptut; *also:* babáşcu, babáşcan, bărbătín, cadăr, cădăr, cădâr, cadăre, cudumán, gióne, greu, ndrúmin, puţâră, sărcós, sărchirós, sfârciu, silnăvós, silnós, vârtós, zdúmban, zófnic; ári zvércă sănătoásă; (*of a ~ woman*) oámă; ca birbeácă; **He is of the ~ ones** Éaste di gréiľi; **~ in health** sănătós ca grij di dzádă; (*durable*) nu ári moárte (*lit.* 'It does not have death') ‖ ALIA 143: sân, sănătós, sinitós

STRONGHOLD

STRONGHOLD *s.* tábye, tabyíe

STRONGLY *adv.* vârtós

STRUCK *adj.* ~ **by lightning** sfuldzirát → STRICKEN; **to be ~ with horror** ñ-acáţ limăreáua, ▼cruţéscu, curţéscu

STRUGGLE *vb.* (*as for existence, for a better life*) ‖ mi dau, mi ciucutéscu, DIARO 249

STRUMPET *s.* cúrvă → HARLOT

STRUT *vb.* ▼fuduléscu, ▼făléscu

STUB *s.* (*of a tree*) cúciub, cuciúbă → STUMP; (*the end part of smth.*) cápit, coádă, armăsătúră

STUBBLE FIELD *s.* călămñáuă ‖ *Pls, GSus:* agríşti, *Peş:* agrâşte, CL 36; *SJos:* călămeáuă, CL 6

STUBBORN *adj.* anăpudzât, aruşuţât, capsumán, cap di grij; *G:* ciórnic, ntórnic, inatcí, naprán, pruc'ĺét; (*to have a fit of stubbornness*) u leg ca yumárlu pri púnte; **to become ~** anăpudzăscu

STUBBORNLY *adv.* ‖ ca yumárlu pri púnte (*lit. 'like the donkey [in a certain Balkan anecdote] on the footbridge'*), BASME 488; únă ş-búnă (*i.e., he / she has a fixed idea; the same expression in Mod. Greek and Alb.*), PARALLELE 134 → STICK

STUBBORNNESS *s.* anăpudzâre, anapudzâĺe, inagilâche, pruclitíe

STUCK-UP *adj.* (*conceited*) făndăxít

STUCK UP *vb.* (*of one's hair*) ñ-si mútă pérlu (di frícă)

STUD *s.* areáte → STALLION; (*group of horses*) irghilé, irghilíe; *adj.* irghilíş ‖ *F:* arghilă, SarD 35 ‖ (*stable*) ahúre → TAKE THE STUDS

STUDENT *s.* (*college ~*) sóftă; (*elementary school ~*) mathití ‖ *Cru:* (*old generation talk*) mathití; (*young generation talk*) uceníc, GOLAB 256

STUDHORSE *s.* → STALLION

STUDIED *adj.* (*intentional*) castílea *or* -li, maxús, xaryú

STUDY *vb.* (*to examine carefully*) sap, spudhăxéscu; (*to be enrolled in a school*) ▼nveţ cárti

STUDYING *s.* spudhăxíre

STUFF *vb.* (*with food*) ▼pristănéscu, prâstânéscu, ▼nfĺămác → CRAM

STUFFY *adj.* (*oppressive, close*) ânclĺís, astupát; (*stodgy*) angricós, -oásă

STULTIFICATION *s.* nglăríre, glăríre, hăzusíre, şuşăre

STULTIFY *vb.* buiséscu, glăréscu, hăzuséscu, şuşéscu

STUMBLE *s.* anchidicáre, scundipsíre

STUMBLE *vb.* ▾cheádic, (a)ncheádic, scundipséscu

STUMP *s.* trup; *also:* bábnic, băndíc, brándu, búcium, ciúbă, chiutúc, cúciub, -bă, câciub, cuciubéu, cuciubeáuă, cúfal, cúţur, crăciún, grij ‖ ALIA 41: căciúmbă, chiciúmbă, cuţ, cur di pom

STUN *vb.* ▾cirtuséscu, cirtăséscu, ▾ciurtuéscu, ▾mintéscu (*and* mindéscu); (*to make lose one's head*) tuléscu, vârléscu, zăléscu; **You have ~ed me** Mi vârlíşi di cap; **It is very cold; it stuns one** Arcoáre mare, ti tuleáşte; (*as of drinking too much wine*) ñ-u da n cap; **The wine ~ed him** yínlu ľ-u deáde n cap ‖ DIARO 48: ânvârléscu

STUN GUN *s.* (*usu. of elder*) → SQUIRT ‖ **GSus:** ţârţânítă, CL 263

STUNNED *adj.* (*astonished*) ndărsít → DIZZY

STUNTED *adj.* astrăchít, azmét, chirchinéc, jibicós, jibă-, zăbă-; pilicós, zvumút; p(r)uzúme; străchitúră *invar.*, vumutúră *invar.*

STUPEFACTION *s.* mărmurisíre

STUPEFIED *adj.* mărmurisít → ASTONISHED

STUPID *adj.* glar, *dim.* glărúşcu, -şcă, -şţâ, -şte; hut, *m pl* huţ, *f pl* húte; *also:* agudít (*or* agudít la cap), ahmác, anóit; *m/f sg* apló, *m pl* apládz, *f pl* ? (DDA 175); argheándalu (di), **G:** başinghél, *m pl* -ghéľ, *f pl* -ghéle; budălác, -lácă, -láţĭ, -láţe; budâlă, *m pl* -ládz, *f sg/pl* -loáñe; buf, *m pl* buhĭ; cap clúvyiu, cap di curcubétă, cap di crínă, cap di gáie, cap di grij, cap di muláre, cap di şiníc, cap di tayáre, cápu mplin di páie, cap vuryăréscu, cărăfétă groásă, chirút, chiutúc, crau *invar.*, cu ciútra goálă, cşúra, *f* cşúră, *m pl* cşúrañ, *f pl* cşúre; cu cămeáşa di la núna, cu trei scânduri (*lit.* 'with three boards' [*instead of four*]), cúţur, dabóľa, ta- *invar.*, datu n cap, di doáuă oáuă (*lit.* '[valuing] two eggs'), **G:** dúmba *invár.*; fâră mădúuă (*lit.* 'brainless'), háhă, *pl m* háhañ; haihúi *invar.*, haihúm, *m pl* -húmeañ; hásca *invar.*, hascanífur, hazó, -záuă, -zádz, -zále; hazúscu, -zúşcă, -zúşţâ, -zúşte; *m/f sg* hľára, *m pl* hľárañ; leángă *invar. and* leángu, -ngă, -ndzi, -ndze; ľ-si vărsă mădúua; ľócă *invar.*; **Smr:** manglár; *m/f sg* măscălídhă, *m pl* -lídz; **G:** mbógru; mbróstu, -roástă, -róşţâ, -roásre; mbrustişór, -óără *and* mbrustu-; mighétă, *m pl* -ghéteañ; mínte di dintánă gálbină, mu-

STUPIDITY

teái, *m pl* -teáiañ; mutuleá(n)gă, *m pl* -leá(n)gañ; ncľis di
mínte, netót, -toátă, -tóţ, -toáte; *G:* nitút *or* nitút la mínte;
nibún, ndârlu *and* ndúr-, ntréşcu, -réşcă, -réşţi, -réşte; nu ári
mădúuă tu cócă, nu ári meľ tru ciútră, ócan, -nă, -ñ, -ne; právdă
al Dumnidzău, schizáre (DDA 1099: *"morceau de bois"*); şábşa, şápşa
invar.; şápşal, şahúlcu, -lcă, -lţi, -lţe; şamandúr, -ră, -ri,
-re;, şcret, -étă -eţ, -éte; şeápti-găľíñ (*lit. 'seven hens'*),
şop, *m pl* şópañ; şóşe, *m pl* şóşañ (*in* DDA 1155 *with* ?); şulúndu, *m
pl* -ndzâ, *f pl* -nde; tabóľa *invar.*, ta-o-tó *invar.*; témblă; tu
lişoára eáste; túmsu, -msă, -mşi, -mse *and* túmtu, -mtă, -mtâ,
-mte; túrlu, -rlă, -rľi, -rle; uzún, -nă, -ñ, -ne; vácă (*lit.
'cow'*), zdángăn, zgurghisít ‖ lişór di mínte, BASME 42; lişurác,
ibid.; şcúrtu di mínte, BASME 54; ľi áre tră dáre al Miháli [-
háľ]; **Don't you know how ~ he is**? Nu lu ştii cât ľi áre tră dáre
al Miháli? BASME 231; DIARO 145: bou *m*, boáuâ *f* (sic!); DIARO 188:
câtráne di Breáza

STUPIDITY *s.* glăríľe, glăríme, glăreáţă, glarumáră; *also:* ah-
măclíche (*and* -cľí-), ahmăclâche, anoisíe, chiritúră, hazu-máră,
huţáme, huţâľe; (*passing ~*) urbáre ‖ lişureáţă, BASME 63

STURDY *s.* vet. vârlíre

STURDY *adj.* (*resolute*) apufăsít; (*robust*) trupós, zdúmban

STUTTER *vb.* ngulişédz → STAMMER

STUTTERER *s.* peltéc

STUTTERING *s.* dărdăríre

STY *s.* (*pen for swine*) căsístră, cócină, cutumás

STY *or* **STYE** *s.* med. arciór, ulciór, uliciór, grânişór

STYLISH *adj.* frâncu, galántu, hu, prăpsít; **There is something ~
about him** Áre hu

SUAVE *adj.* muşát; nóstim, *m pl* -tiñ, *f pl* -time

SUBDUE *vb.* ▾apléc, ▾căpistruéscu, ▾căpistruséscu

SUBDUING *s.* (a)zápe, căpistruíre, căpistrusíre, zăptăsíre

SUBJECT *s.* (*theme*) thémă

SUBJUGATE *vb.* (a)rubuéscu, ▾sclăvuéscu, ▾sclăvuséscu

SUBMERGE *vb.* ▾afúndu, (a)funduséscu, ▾(a)vuţéscu ‖ *Peş:* ahundu-
cuséscu, CL 36

SUBMERSE *vb.* → SUBMERGE

SUBMISSION *s.* (*compliance*) pára-ascultáre, parascultáre

SUBMISSIVE *adj.* ascultătór, tápir, tibié

SUBMIT *vb.* (*to comply, to obey*) pára-ascúltu, parascúltu; (*to
put forward an opinion*) ñ-dau míntea, ñ-dau nă mínte

SUBPREFECTURE *s.* căimăcănlíche

SUBSCRIBE *vb.* (*to sign*) ▾ipuyrăpséscu

SUBSIDE *vb.* (*as of a river*) ▾scad, ▾trag

SUBSIDE INTO SILENCE *vb.* ‖ CUVATA 13: nu scot ni ah ni léle din gúră (*to suffer in silence*)

SUBSIST *vb.* puripséscu

SUBSTANCE *s.* usíe

SUBSTITUTE: *as a ~ for* tu loc di

SUBTERFUGE *s.* tirtípe

SUBTLE *adj.* (*thin, refined*) supţâre, minút; (*shrewd*) → SLY

SUBTRACT *vb.* ▾scad

SUBURB *s.* varóşe, văróşe

SUBVERT *vb.* (*to overturn or overthrow, as in search of smth.*) ▾ambáturlu; (*to corrupt*) aspárgu

SUCCEED *vb.* (*esp. economically*) adár căşáre, ▾prucupséscu, pricupséscu; (*to get trough*) u scot náparti; (*to bring off*) căturthuséscu; **to ~ each other** ▾urdín ‖ (*to attend a desired end*) HRISTU 38: ies naparti

SUCCESS *s.* ‖ BELIMACE 4: (*accomplishment*) azvíndză *pl*

SUCCESSFUL *adj.* prucupsít, purcupsít; *to be ~* ñ-cústă, ñ-si dúţe príma → THRIVE

SUCCESSION *s.* (*inheritance*) miráze

SUCCESSIVELY *adv.* azvárna, azvárnalui, arţivúrţe

SUCCINCT *adj.* scúrtu, şcúrtu

SUCCOR *s.* agiutór, lişuráre

SUCCOR *vb.* ▾agiút, lişurédz

SUCCUMB *vb.* (*to give up*) ▾andúplic; (*to die*) mor

SUCH *adj.* a(h)táre, *N:* aftáre; táre; dhína *invar*; fileán *invar*; tádhe *invar*; **Why should we live ~ a life?** Te aftáre bánă; **in ~ a village** tu aţáre hoáră; (*so much, so many*) ahántu; **~ and ~** atáre

SUCK *vb.* sug (→ § 32); **No lamb has ever ~ed her** Ñel nu u súpse; (*as a pipe for smoking*) muţ; **to ~ in** sórbu; (*to ~ noisily*) arufséscu

SUCKER *s.* bot. cľeciu, climbúciu, fidán, prácică [prač•kă]; vlăstár, vlăstáre, lăstár, lăstáre; **to throw out ~s** mpuľédz (*also of animals*)

SUCKING *s.* sudzeáre, súdzire; **~ in** soárbire, surghíre, surbeáre, arufsíre

SUCKLE *vb.* alăptédz, ţáţuéscu

SUCKLING *s.* (*unweaned baby*) nat, ñic di chéptu; (*lamb or kid*) sugár, *dim.* sugáríc, sugárúş

SUCTION *s.* súdzire, sudzeáre

SUDDEN *adj.* éxafnu, -fnă, -fñi, -fne; **had a ~ death** murí troáră; **~ flush** (*passing sensation of heat*) mpiruşáre, mbiruşáre

SUDDENLY *adv.* diunăoáră [di•u•nă•oá•ră], dinăoáră, dioáră [di•oa•], di-unặ-cále [di•u•], dinăcále, ni únă ni áltă, tr-únă

hópă, tru-oáră, tuoáră [tu•oá•], tu uríţă, tr-un stic, tr-un stic
di oáră, ta úna, tu úna, tu un súflit, únă şi-únă, úti tóra; *G:*
párafta ‖ *Cru:* di năpăndícă, GOLAB 237; ca dit loc, BASME 44

SUE *vb.* (*in court*) scol, dau tru judéţ ‖ scol la giudéţ (*lit.*
'*to raise smb. to court*'), PARALLELE 121

SUET *s.* usândză (*and* -săn-)

SUFFER *vb.* ▾arávdu, ▾pat, ▾trag; **I have ~ed so much bitterness!**
Câte fărmáţe nu-ám tráptă! **He ~s from epilepsy** Páte di nafoáră;
(*to torment*) dor, ▾apufirséscu, ▾părăpuñiséscu; **His heart ~s because of you** Ínima-ľ doáre trâ tíne ‖ CARAFOLI 22, 69: vălăndu-
séscu

SUFFER THE CONSEQUENCES *vb.* ‖ **I suffered the consequences** Ñ-işí
prit nări (*lit.* '*it came out through my nose*') PARALLELE 148

SUFFERING *s.* câñíľe, dértă, dureáre, múndă, parápun, părăpuñisíre, trádzire, trădzeáre, vásan ‖ HRISTU 26: *pl* stărdzer mări;
34: pădhimo; *Cru:* (*constant ~*) path, GOLAB 241; CUVATA 22: patimati
pl

SUFFERANCE *s.* vásan → SUFFERING

SUFFICE *vb.* agiúngu; (*to have enough*) ñ-aseáşte

SUFFICIENT *adj.* distúr; *Mul:* distúl; di nimál → ENOUGH

SUFFICIENTLY *adv.* distúr

SUFFOCATE *vb.* ▾asfixédz; (*with food*) ▾zgrum

SUFFOCATION *s.* zădúh, ndăhníre, ndăcăníre

SUFFRAGE *s.* (*vote*) psif

SUFFUSE *vb.* ▾arăspândzăscu, arăspândzu, ▾arăspândéscu

SUGAR *s.* záhare, şichér ‖ **We do not have ~ to make coffee** nu
avém di-álba, s-făţém únu laiu (*lit.* '*We do not have the white
(stuff) to make the black (stuff)*', DIARO 33

SUGAR *vb.* zăhăruséscu, zăhăriséscu

SUGAR-CANDY *s.* cándyiu, pitruzáhare

SUGARED *adj.* zăhărusít, zăhări-

SUGAR-LOAF *s.* căpiţână, top

SUGARY *adj.* zăhărusít, zăhări-

SUIT *s.* (*of garments*) adrămínt di stráñe, armátă di stráñe; (*in
a courtroom*) ayuyíe

SUIT *vb.* (*to be or to make appropriate*) ▾acáţă, ▾prínde, ñ-da
di mână, undzéscu, umdzéscu, ▾uidiséscu, iduséscu; **If so, it ~s
me** Ñ-da di mână ma i-aşíţe; **to ~ smb. down to the ground** âñ ghíne
pi gáidă → FIT, MATCH

SUITABILITY *s.* uidisíre, undzíre

SUITABLE *adj.* uidisít, undzít, umdzít → BE ~, MAKE ~

SUITCASE *s.* baúlă, sipéte, valíţă

SUITED *adj.* (*pat*) uidisít

SUITOR *s.* pruxinít

SULK *vb.* ▼mărinédz, niurédz [ni•u•]

SULKY *adj.* cacuríscu, ncérnu, ngér-, mutrusít, pahóm, *f* -hómă, *m pl* pahóñ, *pl f* -hóme; ursúz, *m pl* -sújĭ, *f pl* -súză; ursúscu, văpsít → GLOOMY

SULLEN *adj.* mutrusít → SULKY

SULLENNESS *s.* ursuzlâche, schiviríe

SULPHUR *s.* schífură, scl̆ífur, sclífură, şclífur, teáfe

SULTAN *s.* sultán

SUM *s.* súmă

SUMMARY *adj.* scúrtu, şcúrtu

SUMMER *s.* veáră; *adj.* viréscu; ~ **is coming** nvireádză

SUMMIT *s.* (*of a hill, etc.*) ţipilíc → PEAK

SUMMON *vb.* (*to convoke*) acl̆ém

SUMMONS *s.* clíse, iczáre ‖ cárti, DIARO 254

SUMMON UP COURAGE *vb.* l̆au ínimă, ▼ncucutédz → PLUCK UP ONE'S COURAGE

SUN *s.* soáre, *dim.* suráţel, suránţel, suríc ‖ *Lvz, Trn, Ses, Gra, Plat, Perd:* sóri, B-ARCH 1

SUNBURNT *adj.* caramúz, -ză, -jĭ, -ze → BLACKISH

SUNDAY *s.* dumânică, *N:* dumínică‖ *Mul, Rod:* dumánică, *Gra:* dumé-nică, *Arγ, Plat, Pur:* dumǎnică, B-ARCH 539

SUNFLOWER *s.* ócl̆ul-al-soáre ‖ *GSus:* sânciuglét, CL 261

SUNRISE *s.* (a)preásă; **at** ~ tu tahínimă; di (a)ndzáre

SUNSET *s.* (a)scăpit, (a)scăpită, (a)scăpitát, ascăpitătă, (a)scăpităre, surúp ‖ chiar, CAPIDAN 176

SUNSHADE *s.* aumbrátă

SUN-SPONGE *s.* *bot.* aréu

SUNUP *s.* → RISE

SUP *s.* (*mouthful*) gúră

SUP *vb.* (*to eat the evening meal*) ţin

SUPER *adj.*, *adv.* príma

SUPERANNUATED *adj.* (*antiquated*) arudzinát

SUPERB *adj.* háscu, -că, *no pl*

SUPERCILIOUS *adj.* pirifán, -ánă, -áñ, -áne → ARROGANT

SUPERFICIAL *adj.* (*of people*) lişurác, lişuráşcu

SUPERFICIALLY *adv.* prisúpră

SUPERFLUOUS *adj.* di-pri-súpră, di pristanéu, parapaníş

SUPERFLUOUSLY *adv.* di-pristanéu, di-pistanéu, di primansús, di-prisúpră

SUPERINTENDENT *s.* epistát

SUPERIOR *s.* and *adj.* (~ *in rank or office*) ma máre, ma-márlu, máru, tăpár; (*upper*) di prisúpra

SUPERNATURAL *adj.* (*as of a horse or snake in tales*) achică-şóñu, api- *m pl* -şóñ, *f sg/pl* -şoáñe

SUPERPOSING *s.* băgáre

SUPERVISE *vb.* vigľédz, cumndărséscu

SUPERVISOR *s.* epistát → BOSS

SUPPER *s.* ţínă, ţináre; ~ **is ready!** La meásă s cupuséşti! ‖ Cľis: mâcári di seáră, LvO: iévma di seáră; **AMer, Mal, Vil,** *etc.* seáră, **Ses:** séră, B-ARCH 220

SUPPER *vb.* ţin ‖ miríndu, CAPIDAN 153

SUPPLE *adj.* Cľis: jílav

SUPPLEMENT *s.* adăvgămíntu, adăvgătúră

SUPPLEMENT *vb.* ▾adávgu, avdág

SUPPLIANT *adj.* rigeagí

SUPPLICATE *vb.* ▾cáftu, ţer

SUPPLICATION *s.* angricáre; (*towards God*) lităníe

SUPPLIES *s.* cumáñe *f pl;* **stale ~** viştínă → PROVISIONS

SUPPLY ONESELF *vb.* psuniséscu

SUPPORT *s.* acúmtil, acúmtin, (a)ndoápir, andrupătúră, apăndoáhă, arádzim, arádzâm, reádzâm, dăiáche, ndupăciúne, ndupărăciúne, numíe, stur ‖ MERCA 3: andróhe

SUPPORT *vb.* ▾acumbuséscu, ▾acumséscu, ▾(a)ndoápăr, (a)ndoápir, ndúper, ▾andrupăséscu, andrupăscu, ▾arádzim, ▾arádzâm; (*to feed*) ▾ţân; (*to undergo successfully*) diriséscu

SUPPORTED *adj.* (*held*) ândupărát, ndupărát, ândupărít, ndupărít, andrupát

SUPPOSE *vb.* (*to believe, to think*) ▾cred, ñ-u am că; (*to expect*), ▾aştéptu, apăndăxéscu

SUPPOSED *adj.* pripús

SUPPOSEDLY *adv.* (*as if*) táha

SUPPRESS *vb.* (*to bring under control*) ▾căpistruéscu → BRIDLE

SUPPRESSION *s.* (*quieting*) (a)zápe

SUPPURATE *vb.* (a)ndzămédz; *med.* pruñédz

SUPREME COURT *s.* urfié, rufié

SURCEASE *s.* curmáre

SURCINGLE *s.* ghíncală, yínglă

SURE *adj.* (*confident*) ulút, síyur, sígur; **Are you ~?** Hiţ ulúţ? → BE ~

SURELY *adv.* (*yes*) po; (*undoubtebly*) cum mi vedz ş-cum ti ved; (*there is no doubt that*) aiá

SURFACE: at the ~ la videálă

SURFEIT *s.* (a)ngusáre → EAT TO A ~

SURFEIT *vb.* (*to make feel sick*) ▾angusédz; (*to cloy*) ▾adár pântica ţáie, mi fac ţáe, ▾anăfătéscu, fănătéscu, fănitéscu,

▼apudiséscu, u adár (pântica) ciufulícă (or ciuféică, ciuflécă), ▼pristănéscu, pristinéscu, prâstănéscu

SURFEITED *adj.* săturát, sătúl

SURGE *s.* chímă, tăláze, úndă

SURGE *vb.* ▼álţu

SURGEON *s.* giráh, hirúryu

SURLY *adj.* mutrusít → SULKY

SURLINESS *s.* schiviríe, sirsimlâche, ursuzlâche

SURMISE *vb.* ▼angucéscu, ▼făndăxéscu

SURMOUNT *vb.* (*to defeat*) nvíngu; ~ *a difficulty* u scot náparti, lu ansár tráplu

SURPASS *vb.* ▼(a)ntréc, *N:* ▼astréc; (*to ~ in jumping*) *N:* lu astrisár; **to ~ smb. with no difficulty** ≈ níţi la dzidzitíc nu lu am (*i.e., 'He is weaker than my little finger'*) ‖ astálu, DIARO 370

SURPASSED *adj.* (a)ntricút, astricút

SURPLUS *s.* báşă

SURPLUS *adj.* parpaníş, primansús

SURPRISE: by ~ *adv.* pri ni-aştiptáte, aniórihta [a•ni•ó•]

SURPRISE *vb.* ľau pri ni-aştiptáte

SURRENDER *s.* pridáre

SURRENDER *vb.* ▼pridáu, li bágu áde; mi paradáu → GIVE UP ‖ (*as of a criminal*) ▼ncľin, BASME 653; *3 sg pt:* să paradedi, HRISTU 76

SURREPTITIOUSLY *adv.* tiptíle → STEALTHIDLY

SURROUND *vb.* ▼(a)nvărlíg, ▼anvărlighédz, nţércľu, nţircľédz, ţircľédz, anăpădéscu, ▼leg, ▼anvârtéscu, amvârtéscu, ncurpilédz, ncurpuľédz, ncrupíľu; **The army ~ed the forest** Aschérea ligă pădúrea; **to ~ with walls** stizmuséscu

SURROUNDED *adj.* (a)nvărligát, nverigát, ncircľát, nţircľát

SURROUNDING *s.* (a)nvărligáre

SURVEILLANCE *s.* vigľáre, bruítă, mutrítă, mutríre → WATCH

SUSPECT *adj.* ípaptu, ípuptu, şubiilâ, şubeilâtic

SUSPECT *vb.* (*to conjecture*) pripún

SUSPEND *vb.* (*to debar temporarily, to fire*) cúrmu; (*to postpone*) ▼amân; (*to hang*) ▼(a)spíndzur

SUSPENDED *adj.* (*fired*) aryó invar.

SUSPENDERS *s.* (*to support trousers*) tarăndzâ *f pl*

SUSPENSION *s.* curmáre

SUSPICION *s.* pripús, éryu, ipupsíe; şubié, şubée → RAISE ~, GROW SUSPICIOUS

SUSTAIN *vb.* ▼ţân, dinăséscu → SUPPORT)

SUSTENANCE *s.* (*food*) măcáre (*and* mâ-); (*support*) andoápir

SUSURRATION *s.* şuşuráre → MURMUR

SUTURE *s.* cusutúră

SVELTE

SVELTE *adj.* *(slender)* ascuturát

SWADDLE *vb.* *(usu. an infant)* nfaş, nfăşédz; *(to wrap up)* ▾amvăléscu ‖ BELIMACE 15: *(to toilet a very sick person)* culupănséscu

SWADDLING BAND or CLOTHES *s.* fáşe, culupán, culpán, nfăşimându, scútic, spárgan, spárgăn, speáse; *coll.* spărgăn ‖ **Peş:** imbulíce, CL 254

SWAG *s.* *(spoils)* prádă

SWAGGER *vb.* ▾făléscu → BOAST

SWAGGERER *s.* tartabés → BOASTFUL

SWAGGERING *s.* fălíre, cămáră *(and* câ-*)* → BRAGGING

SWAIN *s.* picurár → SHEPHERD; *(suitor)* pruxinít

SWALLOW *s.* *orn.* (a)rândură, (a)rândurícă, (a)ládură *(and* ală-*)*, lândurúşe, lăndureáuă, hilidhónă; nod, *pl* noáde ‖ **SJos:** hilidhón, CL 253

SWALLOW *s.* *(an act of swallowing)* (a)ngľitáre ‖

SWALLOW *vb.* (a)ngľít; *also:* ascápit, bucuséscu; **~ it and keep quiet!** Ngľíte ş-taţi! **to ~ down** *(to eat greedily or in haste)* ▾deápin; **to ~ a shame** ascápit nódlu, ngľit aruşínea, mâc călúpea; **He ~ed his bread in tears** Pânea ţe u mâcá fărmác şi nódurĭ ľ-si duţeá

SWALLOWWORT *s.* *bot.* alânduríşe → CELANDINE

SWAMP *s.* váltu, varcó ‖ **Cru:** bătáche, GOLAB 207

SWAMP *vb.* ▾nec; **The river has ~ed our garden** Arâulu nă u nică grădína

SWAMPLAND *s.* → SWAMP

SWANKY *adj.* *(showily smart)* fanfarón, -oánă; pripsít

SWAY *adj.* băltós, -oásă *and* văltós, -oásă

SWAN *s.* *(fig., as of a gracious bride)* yerăchínă

SWAP *s.* trámpă, dare-loáre, daravéră

SWAP *vb.* fac trámpă

SWARM *s.* (a)róiu; *(~ of people)* crímă di lúme ‖ alghínă, CAPIDAN 151

SWARM *vb.* *(to form a swarm, to comport oneself like a swarm)* ruiéscu; *(of a static crowd)* ▾furníc, hérbu; *(of an advancing crowd)* yin ca roiu di-alghíne

SWARTHY *adj.* búşcu, gáie → DARK-COMPLEXIONED

SWAT *vb.* ▾agudéscu

SWATHE *vb.* nfăş, nfăşédz

SWAY *s.* ligănáre

SWAY *vb.* ▾leágăn, ▾dau cúñea

SWEAR *vb.* *(to attest, to promise)* ▾(a)giúr, ▾urchiséscu; *(formula)* pri pâne! *(lit. 'upon [my daily] bread!')* or (▾giur) pri

ócľiľ a mei! (lit. '(I ~ upon (my) eyes!'); to ~ false agiúr strâmbu ‖ ▼giur şi sprigiúr, BASME 8; (to curse) ▼angiúr, dzâc să-rindár;
STERE 12: (to attest, to promise) bag besă

SWEAT s. (a)sudoáre → PERSPIRATION ‖ **by the ~ of one's brow** cu
ócľi cripáţi, BASME 388

SWEAT vb. asúd; (because of heat) ncălduRédz, ngăl-; (in drops)
ţipurédz; **to ~ one's guts out** (to overwork) mi tuchéscu tu lúcru

SWEATING s. asudáre, azdáre

SWEATING adj. asudát

SWEEP s. arníre, arneálă, mituráre

SWEEP vb. arnéscu, métur; to ~ the oven păñiséscu

SWEEP AWAY/OFF vb. zvíntur, zvinturédz

SWEEPING s. (a)născărsíre, anăschirsíre, născăríe, arnitúră,
căthărsíre, spástră → SWEEP

SWEEPINGS s. curpăi f pl

SWEET s. arusticó ‖ dulţeánă, BASME 426

SWEET adj. m/f sg dúlţe, m pl dúlţi, f pl dúlţe (sic in DDA 506)
(charming) zâmbác; ~ **damn all!** (penniless) tiniché ‖ (charming)
nustimáşcu, DIARO 421 → MAKE ~ BUSINESS OF IT

SWEET CLOVER s. bot. sulfínă

SWEET MARJORAM s. bot. mandzuránă

SWEET PEPPER s. pipiryeáuă, **N:** ciúşcă, şúşcă

SWEETBRIER s. bot. arúg, zíyră → EGLANTINE

SWEETEN vb. (a)ndulţéscu, (â)ndulţéscu

SWEETHEART s. vrut m, vrútă f; also: yearán, iarán, arán, dáşur,
durút; dudía-a-meá, gugúce, guguleánă, gutuníţă

SWEETLY adv. dúlţe

SWEETMEATS s. zaharéñ f pl

SWEETNESS s. dulţeáţă, dulţáme

SWEET-SMELLING adj. ñurzitór, -oáre; ñurizimós, -oásă

SWELL adj. (stylish) pripsít; (excellent) aléptu, spáñu

SWELL vb. ▼úmflu, ▼căbărdéscu; (to puff up one's cheeks)
▼mbulbuchédz

SWELLED HEAD s., adj. fudúl, făndăxít

SWELLING s. umflătúră; also: ciúmă, cocoşúră, cucúľu, nigoádă,
şútă, şúşcă; **G:** (at the neck) trágăn, úimă

SWIFT-FOOTED: He is ~ ľ-gioácă ciciórlu

SWIFTLY adv. ayóñea, anyíe, n yíe, c(u)rúndu, prápa, n prápă

SWIG vb. arúc tu fulínă

SWIM s. (act or period of swimming) not

SWIM vb. (a)nót; (to float) (a)mplătéscu (and amblă-), avuzéscu;
to ~ across trec

SWIMMING s. not, nutáre

SWIMMING

SWIMMING IN THE HEAD *s.* andrălăsíre, ndărsíre, scútură

SWINDLE *vb.* (a)ncálţu → DECEIVE

SWINDLER *s.* bătăhcí (*and* bâtâh-) *m*, bătăhcioáñe *f*; făgă, muşmúlă, muşmoálă, pleaşcagí (*and* pľáş-), zulumgí

SWINDLING *s.* bătăhcilâche → DECEIT

SWINEHERD *s.* purcár

SWING *s.* cúñe; (*rotative ~*) drâmbálă, vârticóniţă, vărticoáñiţă

SWING *vb.* ▾leágăn, ▾dau cúñea; **to ~ one's hips** ñ-fac căţămǎchi

SWINGING *s.* (*~ of the body as if to give oneself airs*) căţămáche

SWIPE *vb.* (*as of a strong wind*) ▾bat, ▾agudéscu; (*to steal*) ciun

SWIRL AWAY *vb.* (*speaking of the wind*) 3 *sg*: spúlbiră

SWISHING: to get a ~ → GET A SOAKING

SWITCH *s.* dărmă, drămă (*and* drâmă), lúră, şuvélcă, vig, vígă, víţă → ROD; (*a blow with a switch*) jirtuíre

SWITCH *vb.* (*to punish or urge with or as with a switch*) jirtuéscu

SWOLLEN *adj.* umflát; (*~ and pale*) búhav, bútcav, prúhav → BECOME LESS ~, MAKE LESS ~

SWOON *s.* lişín, lişinătúră, cǎhtíre

SWOON *vb.* lişín → FAINT

SWORD *s.* apálă, ceálme, coárdhă (*and* coárdă), hoárdhă, lipídhă, spáthă (*and* spátă) → PUT SMB. TO THE ~

SWORD-BAYONET *s.* cǎlâce ‖ *GSus:* ştic, CL 261

SYCOPHANCY *s.* guduráre, guduríre

SYCOPHANT *adj.* cólac, marghiól, maryiól

SYLLABICATION *s.* (*syllabling*) silavisíre

SYLLABIZE *vb.* silaviséscu

SYLLABLE *s.* silávă, silavíe

SYMPATHETIC *adj.* (*given to compassion*) ñil(ă)ós; (*appropriate, kind, pleasant, not discordant*) háreş, nóstim, pălít; cu hári

SYMPATHIZE *vb.* ▾jǎléscu

SYMPATHY *s.* (*favor, compassion*) simbatíe; (*an expression of sorrow for another's grief*) păriyuríe

SYMPTOM *s.* sémnu; dhóymă, *pl* dhóymate

SYNAGOGUE *s.* hávră

SYNOD *s.* sinúdh, sinódhă

SYPHILIS *s.* malufrándză, mălăfrándză, mulufrándză

SYPHILITIC *adj.* mălăfrăndzós, -dzoásă

T

TABLE *s.* meásă, *dim.* misícă; sófră, sufră, súfăr, *dim.* sufríc; trápez *or* -peză; (*small ~ in a shepherd's hut*) tijáche; **Clean the ~!** Mutáţ meása! **around the ~** pri meásă → SET THE ~ ‖ *Cru:* másă, *Gop:* meásă, GOLAB 233; *Prv:* bángu, CL 38; *Mul:* másă, B-ARCH 414; *plurals: Cru, Trn:* măsur¹,. *BdD':* máse; *Cu, Mul, Pls:* mási, NEIESCU 145

TABLECLOTH *s.* misále

TACITURN *s.* tăcút, abóristu, pahóm, ursúz, ursúscu; zboárile liáre acumpăráte; (*~ person*) muleaftă ‖ *Pls:* mâtúf, CL 256

TACK *vb.* (*to affix with tacks*) ‖ *Av:* tipuséscu, *Pls:* tuẹpuséscu (*sic*), CL 262

TACKY *adj.* (*sticky*) mâzgós, -oásă; (*of poor quality*) → INFERIOR

TACTFULLY *adv.* cu usúle

TADPOLE *s. zool.* călúyriţă, jághină

TAFFETA *s. tex.* táftă

TAG *s.* (*libel, ticket*) vulutínă

TAG *vb.* (*to follow closely*) mi ţân di / dúpă; ľau n cicioáre

TAIL *s.* coádă, *dim.* cudíţă

TAIL *vb.* (*to follow*) → TAG

TAILLESS *adj.* cóluv, -vă, -yĭ, -ve

TAILOR *s.* (a)ráftu *m*, arăfteásă *f*; cusór; **modern ~** frángu-aráftu

TAILS *s.* (*of a coin*) túră, turáuă; (*ant.* yeáză 'heads')

TAINT *s.* cusúre, ciurúche

TAINT *adj.* (*as of meat*) stătút

TAINT *vb.* ▾aspárgu

TAINT WITH RED *vb.* plăvântédz; *adj.* (*of sheep*) plăvântát

TAKE *vb.* ľau (→ § 32); **to ~ by force** ľau cu stañólu; **The devil ~ him!** ≈ Scoáti-ľ ócľiľ! *or* Văpseá-l! (*to lead, of a road*) apúc; 2 *sg. imper.* Na! 'Take!'; 2 *pl:* Ná-vă! ‖ (*to apprehend, to seize*) *Amc:* **~ him!** luázlu, RÉCATAS 37

TAKE ACCOUNT OF *vb.* nu-ñ cáde mpáde; **He takes account of his word (of his advice)** Zbórlu-a lui nu-ľ cáde mpáde

TAKE ACTION AGAINST *vb.* → SUE

TAKE A DECISION *vb.* taľu → DECIDE

TAKE ADVANTAGE *vb.* ufiliséscu, filiséscu, hăiruséscu

TAKE A FALSE STEP *vb.* cálcu strâmbu, pára-cálcu → MAKE A MISTAKE

TAKE A FANCY TO SMB. *vb.* ñ-cáde cu vreáre máre ‖ ñ-ľa ócľul, BASME 418

TAKE A GOOD LESSON *vb.* dipún mínte, ▾nvéţ mínte

TAKE A GULP *vb.* ľau nă gúră

TAKE A HAND IN THE WORK *vb.* bag mâna pi lúcru

TAKE AIM

TAKE AIM *vb.* (a)nchiléscu, nişinipséscu ‖ ľau la óčľu, BASME 488

TAKE A JOB *vb.* íntru tu pâne

TAKE A JOURNEY *vb.* fac sefér

TAKE ALARM *vb.* ▼aspár

TAKE ALL RESPONSIBILITY *vb.* ñ-u ľau prisúpră-ñ; ľau pri míne

TAKE A MOUTHFUL *vb.* ľau nă gúră

TAKE AN AIRING *vb.* ‖ ľau vímtu, BASME 2

TAKE A NAP *vb.* ľ-coc un sómnu, ľ-coc un óčľu di sómnu, ľ-trag un sómnu ‖ ľau un óčľu di sómnu, BASME 49

TAKE AN OATH *vb.* ľau giurát

TAKE A PHOTO *vb.* → PHOTO

TAKE A PLEDGE *vb.* mi giur şi mi sprigiúr → SWEAR

TAKE A REST *vb.* → TAKE A NAP ‖ (*usu. in bed*) âñ ľau dhípla, DIARO 321; (*to draw breath, to fetch one's breath*) dizvruséscu, RÉCATAS 47

TAKE ARMS *vb.* ▼armătuséscu

TAKE A RUN *vb.* (*as before jumping*) ľau vímtu

TAKE AS HARD AS ONE CAN LICK *vb.* (*to run*) fug ca tórnic, fug ca (a)ndórnic

TAKE A SHINE TO *vb.* ñ-cáde tu ínimă

TAKE A SIGHT AT *vb.* ñ-arâd (cu nâs, *etc.*) ‖ strâmbu búdzăli, BASME 98

TAKE A STROLL *vb.* dau sulăţ

TAKE A TRIP *vb.* mi duc tăxídhe

TAKE A TURN *vb.* fac únă dévră, dau únă dévră

TAKE A WALK *vb.* fac únă dévră, dau únă dévră

TAKE AWAY CAPTIVE *vb.* acáţ sclav, ľau sclav

TAKE AWAY/OFF *vb.* scot

TAKE BACK ONE'S WORD *vb.* (*to retract*) ñ-ľau zbórlu

TAKE BREATH *vb.* ľau ánasă; (*to recover one's strength*) âñ yíne ípatlu

TAKE CARE *vb.* ▼caftu, ▼mutréscu; *also:* lu am angătán, am ménga (la), am óčľul, am peána, ñ-bag oára, cătăndiséscu, cilihtiséscu, cealăhtiséscu, câştighédz, cumăndărséscu, frundiséscu, frundi-xéscu, ▼preaadún, preadún,; trag căştíga, ▼ved; **~ of them** (*of your goats*)**! Ái-li angătán! ~ of your lamb! Ái-ţâ ménga la mânár! There is nobody to ~ of us today** Nu-i vârnu s-nă trágă az câştíga; **They thought how on earth to take better care of their children** Mutríră cum di cum si câştigheádză cama múltu trâ fumeáľe; **~ of this lamb!** Nélu aéstu preaadunáţ-lu! **I was sick and you did not ~of me** Fui lândzit mea nu mi vidzút; **Take care!** (*Watch out!*) Angătán! *or* Bá-gă-ţ oára!

TAKE CARE! Mutreá! → WATCH OUT!

TAKE COURAGE *vb.* ľau ínimă, ▼mbărbătédz, ▼ncucutédz; *3 sg/pl aor.*
cápra u mută coáda n sus → PLUCK UP ONE'S COURAGE

TAKE DISGUST *vb.* ▼aynuséscu, aynusédz, ▼dizvăléscu

TAKE DOWN *vb.* (*as from a hook or a peg*) dispíndzur

TAKE DOWN A PEG OR TWO *vb.* ľĭ pliciutédz nările

TAKE EFFECT *vb.* (*as of a medicine*) surdiséscu; **The medicine took
effect well** Mi surdisí múltu yitría

TAKE FIRE *vb.* ▼apríndu, ľau foc

TAKE FRIGHT *vb.* ▼aspár, âñ fúdze buríclu di frícă, âñ beau
sândzile di frícă, ľau păvríe → BE FRIGHTENED

TAKE HOLD OF *vb.* (*of a feeling*) ▼năvăleáşte; **Longing for his
mother is taking hold of him** Dor di mámă l-năvăleáşte; (*to get hold
of*) bag tu mână; **If only I could ~ of you!** S-ti băgárim tu mână!
arúc cătuhíe (pri); (*to usurp*) zăptiséscu

TAKE HOLIDAY *vb.* ľau páfse

TAKE-IN *s.* ncălţáre

TAKE IN *vb.* (*to deceive*) ▼(a)ncálţu, ▼arâd; (*to absorb*) beau; **The
earth took in the rain** Ploáia u biú lóclu

TAKE IN(TO) *vb.* ▼bag

TAKE IN CUSTODY *vb.* ‖ DIARO 7o: (*to arrest*) ľau, scol, mut

TAKE INTO ACCOUNT *vb.* (*as of a piece of advice*) bag tu mădúuâ;
(*to intend*) mutréscu, ñ-u am tu mínte (să), saidiséscu (*sic*), săldiséscu; (*to esteem, to regard*) lu fac mále ‖ muntréscu, BASME 418;
bag tu córnu, BASME 488; CUNIA 212: bag oáră că; (*to take into consideration*) baģu tu isápi; CARAFOLI 43, 48, 76: ľau di vij; DIARO 94:
dau di mánár; dau simásie

TAKE IT ON THE CHIN *vb.* ▼mâc păpáră, ▼mâc pri zvércă (múlte)

TAKE IT ON THE LAM *vb.* → LAM

TAKE IT TO HEART *vb.* (*to go into the wide world, as of dispair*)
âñ ľau míntea la cioáre

TAKE IT TO THE FIELDS *vb.* ľ-u dau năpói nclo

TAKE LEAVE *vb.* ľau páfse

TAKE OFF *vb.* (*to remove, as one's hat*) scot ‖ **~ your hat!** Scoáte-
ţi capéla! PARALLELE 138

TAKE ON *vb.* ‖ (*to take the responsibility*) ľau pri ģúşe (*lit. 'to
take on one's nape'*), PARALLELE 135

TAKE IT SERIOUSLY *vb.* → BELIEVE ‖ ľau tră búne, BASME 399

TAKE NOTICE OF *vb.* bag tu córnu, bag tu ócľu; (*to get the wind
of*) ľau di vij, ľau di viş; **without taking notice of us** fâră ca
s nă ľa di vij

TAKE OFF/OUT *vb.* ▼(a)rúp, scot, afiriséscu; **Don't ~ a cent of it!**
Un pară s nu-ñ arupéţ! (*to undress*) ▼dizlăxéscu (di); **~ your new
clothes!** Dizlăxíţ-vă di stráñile aţeálea noáule! (*to ~ one's hat*)

TAKE OFFENSE

▼discufuséscu; (to ~ one's shoes or socks) ▼discúlţu; (to depart very early in the morning) tăhinipséscu, tuhinipséscu → TAKE ONE-SELF OFF

TAKE OFFENSE vb. mi ayrédz, ▼filutimiséscu, ▼filutiñiséscu, ľau vímtu → FLY INTO A TEMPER

TAKE ON vb. (to lay to heart) bag márã; **Don't ~!** Nu bágã márã!

TAKE ONESELF OFF vb. li aspél → BOLT

TAKE ONE'S LEAVE vb. alás sănătáte

TAKE ONE'S OWN COURSE vb. ‖ fac cum mi táľe cáplu, BASME 411

TAKE ONE'S REVENGE vb. (to be followed by the idea of taking revange) mi avínã sândzile

TAKE ONE'S VALE vb. (as from a moribund) mi ľértu (di)

TAKE ON ONE'S BACK vb. ľau ncrâşca (and ngrâşca)

TAKE OUT vb. scot (→ § 32); **to ~ a process against smb.** lu scol; **to ~ walking** (to go for a walk) ▼priímnu

TAKE OVER vb. (liabilities) ľau pri míne; **He took over all the liabilities** Túte éxudhile şi-li lo pri nâs

TAKE PITY ON SMB. vb. → PITY

TAKE PLACE vb. cur

TAKE REFUGE vb. ▼acúmtin; **cells for the monks to ~ in** chilíi tra si s acúmtinã călúgăríľi

TAKE REVENGE vb. → AVENGE

TAKE ROOT vb. aruzuséscu, aruziséscu

TAKE RUN vb. ľau fúzmã, ľau paramázmã, ľau vánţu, ľau vímtu, ľau zvórimã

TAKE SIDES vb. ľau párte

TAKE IN vb. (to invite) cupăséscu năúntru, cupuséscu or urséscu năúntru; (to dupe) ľ-bag samárlu

TAKE INTO ONE'S CONFIDENCE vb. ▼ximistiripséscu → CONFESS

TAKE SMB.'S DUST vb. → DUST

TAKE SMB. UNDER ONE'S WING vb. ‖ LITURG 130: ľeu sumsórã; **take us under your wing** ľé-nã sumsórã

TAKE SERIOUSLY vb. lu dau di mânár, hăbărséscu; **They do not take him seriously at all** Nu-l hăbărséscu ti ţivá

TAKE SMB.'S ADVICE vb. ‖ DIARO 286: ľ-ľau mâna; **I am not going to take his advice** Nu va ľ-ľau mâna a lui

TAKE SMB.'S BREATH AWAY vb. → BREATH

TAKE SMB.'S HEART OUT vb. (to exasperate) scot súflitlu

TAKE SMB.'S MEASURES vb. (to eye carefully) mutréscu di la ún-gľi pân la cap

TAKE SMB.'S TRACE vb. (to start to pursue) ľau n cicioáre; **He took her trace** U lo n-cicioáre

TAKE SMB. TO BE vb. ‖ ñi lu ľa ócľul trã; **He looked at him from**

head to foot and took him to be a good man L-mutrí di la cap la cioári şi-ľ lu lo ócľul tră om bun, BASME 428

TAKE TO HEART vb. ▼amărédz → EMBITTER

TAKE THE AIR vb. ľau vímtu

TAKE THE BAD PATH vb. ľau cálea slábă

TAKE THE BITE vb. cad tu stăpíţă → FALL INTO THE TRAP

TAKE THE CHILL OFF vb. ▼dizgľéţ

TAKE THE HUFF vb. dipún búdzâle, dipún dzeánile, dipún mútrile; spândzur nările → HUFF

TAKE THE LAW ON SMB. vb. lu scol

TAKE THE PLUNGE vb. (to make a decision) taľu píta

TAKE THE ROAD vb. apărñéscu, purñéscu (and purnéscu), fug, ñ-ľau cálea di gúşe (şi ímnu); ▼nchiséscu, trag cále; (as out of despair) acáţ strématile → LEAVE, SET OUT

TAKE THE STUDS vb. (to be stubborn) u leg tu greáua (or tu greáuă)

TAKE THE WIND OUT OF SMB.'S SAILS vb. ľ-taľu mâñle

TAKE THE WRONG SOW BY THE EAR vb. u adár taratóre

TAKE TO HEART vb. ▼nvirín, (a)nvirinédz, bag márà ‖ ñ-mâc ínima, BASME 461

TAKE TO ONE'S HEELS vb. ñ-ľau cicioárĭle dinanúmirea → SLING ONE'S HOOK

TAKE TO THE HILLS vb. li-aspél → BOLT

TAKE TO THE WOODS vb. (as of outlaws) li ţíngu (ármatĭli)

TAKE TO THE ROAD vb. acáţ strématile

TAKE UMBRAGE AT vb. ▼ariciu(s)éscu, ▼zbârléscu, zbur-

TAKE UP vb. (a trade, a profession) ľau; **He took up the mili-tary profession** Lo armătulíchea

TAKE UPON ONESELF vb. âñ ľau prisúpră-ñ

TAKE UP ONE'S COURAGE vb. ľau ínimă → PLUCK UP ONE'S COURAGE

TAKE UP WITH vb. (to pal, to associate with) li apríndu aluáturile (cu)

TAKEN adj. (as by sleep) apucát

TAKEN CARE OF adj. mutrít → TAKE CARE

TAKING adj. (attractive, captivating) nóstim, m pl -tiñ

TALE s. (account) părămíth, părmíth, părămís, pirmíth, pirimís; (falsehood) tácmă; (gossip) zbór, zburáre

TALENT s. (a notable capacity or gift) doáră ‖ PC: doáră di la Dumnidză

TALER s. (silver coin) tálir

TALK s. zbor, zburáre, zburâre; **to become the ~ of the town** agiúngu părămíth ‖ **Let's have a ~** Hai s-fâţém unâ cuvéndâ, DIARO 292 → EMPTY ~

TALK

TALK *vb.* zburắscu; **to ~ a lot of punk** zburắscu goále; **to ~ bunkum** ▼arădhăpséscu; **to ~ claptrap** cântu; **I've got a headache from your talking claptrap** Mi doáre cáplu di cấte ñ-cântáşĭ; **to ~ idly** máţin (pi virisíe); discântu, fârfáréscu, parazburắscu; **to ~ nonsense** arucutéscu bizbíľe; ▼bat naľúrea, xinuzburắscu; **Stop talking rot!** Ia nu bătéţ naľúrea! **to ~ nineteen to the dozen** gúra ñ-ñárdze á pă; límbi-límbi ñi si dúţe gúra; gúra ñ-si dúţe vârvura; ñ-si dúţe gúra ca túrtura; ca ļimădhúra ñ-si dúţe gúra ‖ BELIMACE 104: zbrắéscu; **to ~ incoherently, irationally,** *3 sg* dzấţi álti-ti-álti, DIARO 32

TALK DOWN *vb.* (*to silence*) ‖ ľ-acáţ gúra, BASME 433

TALKATIVE *adj.* limbuţéscu *m*, -ţéşcă *f* (*sic*); ni-tăcút, políloy, zburyeárcu, -eáric ‖ **Cru:** zburutór, GOLAB 260

TALKING *s.* zboáre, *n pl*; **by dint of ~** di zbor zbor *or* di cuvéndă cuvéndă

TALKING-TO *s.* zăvráche → SCOLDING

TALL *adj.* (a)náltu, lúngu ‖ **Amc, An, Els, Na:** anáłtu, **Mul:** anáu-tu, B-ARCH 140 ‖ **F:** lung, HRISTU 75

TALLOW *s.* seu

TALLY *s.* (a)răbúş, arăbój

TALON *s.* zgrắñe, sgrâie

TAMBOURA *s.* tâmpără (*and* tắmpără, tắmbără), dumbârắ, támbură

TAMBOUR FRAME *s.* ghirghéfe

TAMBOURINE *s.* dairé, dắiré

TAME *adj.* ímbru, ímir, imiripsít, imirisít

TAME *vb.* ▼imirédz, imiri(p)séscu, ▼fruminéscu, piculéscu; **to ~ down** (*as of one's hungar*) apún

TAMER: bear ~ ursár

TAMING *s.* imiri(p)síre

TAMP *vb.* ▼astúp

TAMPER *vb.* (*to bribe*) ▼aúngu, ▼acúmpăr; (*to alter*) ▼şuţ, ▼aspárgu

TAN *vb.* (*to expose oneself to sun*) ▼lăiéscu (la soáre); ▼pâr-jiléscu *or* pârjéscu (la soáre); (*to convert hide into leather*) ▼aryăséscu; **to ~ smb.'s hide** (*to beat the tar out of smb.*) tuchéscu di băteáre

TANGLE *s.* mintitúră, síyise

TANGLE *vb.* (*to engage in conflict*) ▼ambărtuéscu, ▼birdhipséscu, mbirdhuéscu; (*to make or become entangled*) ▼cărşiľédz; (*as of the hair*) ▼ciufuléscu; **Your hair has ~ed** Ţi si ciufulí pérlu

TANK *s.* (*container*) buduvái, stérnă

TANNED *adj.* lăít di soáre; (*converted into lather by tanning*) aryăsít

TANNERY *s.* tabacaryió

TANNER *s.* tăbác, tăbán ‖ **Prv:** tăbắcă; **Av, SJos:** tăbăcărgí, CL 262

TANNING s. (of hides) aryăsíre

TANTALIZE vb. ▾amân

TAN-YARD s. tabacaryió

TANTRUM s. **to fly into a ~** → FLY INTO A PASSION

TAP s. (spigot) sóche

TAPER s. lumináre, ţeáră, ţéră; (large white ~) lumbárdhă; **wax ~** lumbárdhă di ţeáră

TAPER vb. → DIMINISH

TAPERING adj. (as of a pear) surlutós, -oásă

TAPEWORM s. strúnă, téñe

TAR s. cătráne, smólă; **to beat the ~ out of smb.** ĺ-scútur yi-călu (lit. 'to shake smb.'s collar')

TAR DEALER / MANUFACTURER s. cătrănár

TAR vb. ▾cătrănéscu, ▾cătrănăséscu, cătărnăséscu

TARADIDDLE s. minciúnă → LIE

TARDINESS s. amânáre, şintíre, alăsătúră

TARDY adj. amănătór, -oáre; (derog., of people) alăsătúră invar.

TARE s. (speaking of weight) tár, dáră

TARE vb. firiséscu

TARGET s. (a mark to shoot at) ‖ sémnu, BASME 487

TARIFF s. tarífă, cústu, păhă

TARNISH vb. ▾chicuséscu, ▾(a)úngu, ▾lăvăşéscu, ▾murdăripséscu; (to ~ with or as with mud) ▾mâzgăléscu

TARNISHED adj. (as of a flower) bubuchisít

TARNISHING s. (as of a consumptive person) umbărnáre

TARRY vb. şed, ▾amân, putridzăscu

TARSUS s. anat. cărcinár; **They hang sheep by the ~** Numáĺlu di cărcinár si-aspíndzură

TART s. pítă; (large ~) pităroáñe, pituroáñe; **puff-pastry ~** pítă di péture; (prostitute) → HARLOT

TART adj. acrişór, -oáră; maióşcu, -óşcă (sic), -şţi, -şte

TASK s. sárţină, sálţiñă, nsărţináre, mândátă, lúcru; **to set a ~** ▾nsárţin, ▾nsărţinédz

TASSEL s. ciléngă

TASTE s. gústu, yústu; (preference, inclination) chéfe

TASTE vb. gústu, ▾purindédz ‖ ngústu, BASME 657

TASTELESS adj. blánav, f -vă, m pl -yĭ, f pl -ve; sárbit ‖ HRISTU 46: bizdisit (cf. Alb. bezdísshĕm 'ennuyeux,' Ko, s.v.

TASTY adj. gustós, -oásă and yu-; nóstim, m pl -tiñ ‖ **very ~** s-ţi-alíndzi dzeáditle, BASME 416, 429 (lit. 'you lick your fingers')

TATTER s. cârpă, récichiu → RAG

TATTERDEMALION s., adj. ţârţârós, -oásă

TATTERED adj. arúptu, părtălós, recicamán; (of a woman) ca mar-

tíră; **She does not know how to dress and goes** ~ Nu şti si si
nveáscă, ímnă ca martíra; **He was dressed in** ~ **clothes** Erá viscút
recicamán

 TATTLE *vb.* băndurédz, băbăléscu, dărdăréscu

 TATTLER *s.* pălăvrăgí

 TAUNT *s.* → INSULT

 TAUNT *vb.* ▾buiséscu → MOCK

 TAUT *adj.* (*tightly drawn*) tes, teásă, teşĭ, teáse; (*extremely*
nervous) sértic, -tu; nevricó, *m pl* -cádz; (*tidy*) mutrít, (m)brit

 TAVERN *s.* lucántă, mihenă, mihéne, miéne, mianée, tavérnă

 TAVERN KEEPER *s.* ambirigí, lucantagí

 TAWDRY *adj.* jupănéscu, -eáscă, -éşţâ, -éşti

 TAX *s.* dáre; *also:* bidéĭu, dat, dátlu cătră amirăríĭe, for, hárge
di chivérnise; (*taxation on sheep*), bidéĭu uiréscu, gilép,
spăhidlâche, viryíe ‖ GSus: bírnic, CL 39; CUNIA 134 *also:* décat

 TAX *vb.* **to** ~ **one's ingenuity** ▾frimíntu

 TAX COLLECTOR *s.* băjdár, imbruccí, yimbruccí, muhtár, miuftár,
taxildár, taxidár

 TEA *s.* ceai

 TEACH *vb.* ▾véţ, nveţ, dhidhăxéscu, părădhuséscu; **He taught him**
how to speak Lu nviţă cum si zburáscă; **He will** ~ **you!** Va s-ti veá-
ţă! ‖ (**to scold**) ALR 1414: aúrlu

 TEACHER *s.* nviţătór, dháscal *m*, dháscală *f*; (*iron.*) purdháscal ‖
dim., *iron.* dhâscălíciu, DIARO 353; *In GR* **nviţătór** *is an obsolete*
word today, EV.

 TEACHING *s.* dhăscălíe, dhăscălíche, -láche; (*education*) părădhusíre

 TEAM *s.* ≈ soţ *m pl*; suţátă, bándă

 TEAM *vb.* mi adún (cu), mi fac urtác (cu) ‖ CUNIA 18: fac suţátă
(cu), mi fac únă (cu)

 TEAR *s.* lácrămă, lácrimă, lăcrimeáuă; **to give way to tears** mi-
mbáiră lăcriñle ‖ HRISTU 11: lăcărñ *pl*

 TEAR *vb.* ▾(a)rúp (→ § 32); **to** ~ **one's hair** ñ-deápir pérĭĭi din
cap; **to** ~ **away** ▾zmúlgu, ▾dizgrăbún; **to** ~ **to pieces** (a)rúp făşi-
făşi, beau, ▾diñíc, disíc, dizvóc; **The dogs were about to** ~ **me to**
pieces Vrea mi bea cáñĭi; **to** ~ **one's skin off** ▾zgrâm, ▾sgâir

 TEAR ALONG *vb.* mi u angán → BOLT

 TEAR AWAY (*or* **OUT, UP**) *vb.* scot

 TEAR OUT ONE'S HAIR *vb.* ñ-deápir pérĭĭi din cap

 TEARFUL *adj.* lăcrimát; plâmtu, -mtă, -mţâ, -mte; asplímtu

 TEARING *s.* arupeáre, arucheáre, arúpire

 TEASE *vb.* ▾schin, pirăxéscu, scăñiséscu (*and* scă-), căscăndiséscu; **They began to** ~ **him** Acăţără s-lu schínă ‖ mâc, BASME 68

TEASER *s.* (*worker who disentangles wool*) lânár

TEASING *s.* scăñisíre, schináre, pirăxíre

TEASING *adj.* schinătór, -oáre

TEAT *s. anat.* gurgúľu *n or m*; (*artificial nipple*) lástic, lástică, lástih

TEDIOUS *adj.* ánustu, -stă, -şţâ, -ste

TEDIUM *s.* aurâre → BOREDOM

TEEM *s.* → SWARM

TEEM *vb.* (*to abound with*) hérbu; **This place ~s with thieves** Lóclu aéstu heárbe di furi

TEENAGER *s.* firfărúş *m*, firfiríţă *f*, fărfăľúşe f, hilándru *m*, hilándră *f*

TEENY *adj.* ñicúţ

TEETER *vb.* ▾clátin, *N:* ▾cleátin

TEETH *s.* (*as in a lace*) zâmbe *f pl*

TELEGRAM *s.* tel, teľu, tiléyraf

TELEGRAPH: by ~ pri sírmă, pri teľu; **~ wire** sírmă

TELEGRAPH *vb.* tiliyrăfséscu

TELEGRAPHIST *s.* telegrafcí

TELEPHONE WIRE *s.* sírmă

TELESCOPE *s.* chéle, ɖulbíe

TELL *vb.* dzâc, ▾(a)spún; (*as a story*) ▾ambáir, ▾deápir, cântu, discântu; **to ~ cock-and-bull stories** taľu papardhéle; **to ~ the truth** (a)spún drept, aspún a cálealui; **Either you ~ me the truth, or you have no escape from me!** Ori ñ-aspúñ a cálealui, i nu ai ascăpáre di míne! **to ~ lies** (a)minciunédz; **to ~ fortune with a shell** arúc tu mărdzeáuă; **to ~ smb. so in his/her face** ľ-u dzâc tu fáţă; **to ~ tall tales** taľu palăvri

TELL SMB. OFF *vb.* ľ-pliciutédz năříle

TEMERITY *s.* cutidzáre, fidănlâche

TEMPER *vb.* (*to dilute, to soften, to calm down*) hăminédz, apún, moľu (*to harden, of steel and fig.*) ▾cilicuséscu, ▾căléscu; **to fly into a ~** → FLY INTO A PASSION

TEMPERAMENT *s.* físe → CHARACTER

TEMPERANCE *s.* misúră, usúle

TEMPERATE *adj.* (*as in eating or drinking*) luyursít

TEMPERATURE *s.* căldúră, heávră, cápse ‖ *Cru:* foc, GOLAB 215

TEMPERED *adj.* (*of steel*) cilicusít, călít

TEMPERING *s.* (*of steel*) călíre

TEMPEST *s.* furtúnă, vímtu

TEMPESTUOUS *adj.* furtunós, -oásă

TEMPLATE *s.* călăpódhe

TEMPLE *s. anat.* tâmplă

TEMPLE

TEMPLE *s.* (*edifice*) náo
TEMPORARY *adj.* próschir
TEMPORARILY *adv.* próschir
TEMPT *vb.* ▼ngăsăiéscu, ▼plăniséscu
TEMPTATION *s.* pirazmó, plănipsíre, plănăpsíre; **Fasting keeps away ~s** Păreásiñle azñéscu pirazmázľi ‖ LITURG 125: **and do not lead us into ~** şă nu nă băgă tru fármucu
TEMPTED → BE ~
TEMPTING *adj.* (*attractive, pleasant*) nóstim, *m pl* -tiñ
TEN *num.* dzáţe; táľe, *pl* tăľ; **I was a little boy of ~ plus** Erám ciulimán di únă táľe ş-cáma di añ
TENACIOUS *adj.* apufăsít
TENACITY *s.* apufăsíre, eneryisíre
TENANT *s.* ‖ DIARO 242: nichiyó [ni•ki•yó]
TENCH *s.* *ichth.* gľinár
TEND *vb.* mutréscu, ved, vigľédz
TENDER *s.* (*steward*) cumandărgí
TENDER *adj.* (*affectionate*) adiľós, -oásă; durút; (*as of choice meat*) trifirúşcu; (*fresh, delicate*) **Gop, Mul:** créfcu, créftu, créhtu → ~ POINT
TENDER POINT *s.* mărdáie; *fig.* sfínă; **I alone know his ~** Maşľ io ľi ştiu sfína
TENDER THANKS *vb.* adúc birhuzúre → THANK
TENDERHEARTED *adj.* ñil(ă)ós, -oásă
TENDERLOIN: pork ~ ‖ cárni di la psaronévri, CL 245
TENDERLY *adv.* durút, vrut; **She kept shouting ~** Durút ea tut strigá
TENEBROUS *adj.* ntunicós, -oásă; scutinós, scutidhós
TENESMUS *s.* sprimeáre, sprimáre, splimáre; (*effort, strain*) spreámiţă
TENET *s.* dhóymă
TENSE *adj.* tes, teásă, teşľ, teáse
TENSE *vb.* ▼tíndu
TENT *s.* cidâre, ceádră, purávă, téntă (*and* téndă)
TENTH: on the ~ of the month tu dzáţile di mes
TENUOUS *adj.* (*as of smoke, of a cloth*) arétcu, arítcu, aréhav
TEPID *adj.* căldişór, -oáră; hámin, hábin, *m pl* -biñ
TERM: to be on bad ~s with hiu ngrâñít cu, hiu cârtít cu; **in ~s of** di; **You could not see anyone better in terms of behavior and youthfulness**
s-vidzú ma bun di port ş di ñáte → COME TO ~S WITH
TERMINAL ILLNESS *s.* léle
TERMINATE *vb.* → FINISH

TERMINATION *s.* bitisítă → END

TERRACE *s.* (*along the outdoor walls of a rural house*) pidzúľu; *G:* preáspă; (*verande, porch*) cirdháche (*and* cirdáche)

TERRAIN *s.* loc

TERRIBLE *adj.* (*fearful*) (a)rău, (a)ráuă, (a)rắi, (a)ríle; fuvirós; (*extreme*) máre, *pl* mắri

TERRIBLY *adv.* (*very, awfully*) múltu (*followed by an adj. or adv.*)

TERRIFIC *adj.* and *interj.* vârtós, -oásă

TERRIFY *vb.* bag ceáşlu (tu); dau ibréte

TERROR *s.* lăhtár → FRIGHT

TERROR-STRICKEN *adj.* cişuít, ciuşuít, cişiít, cutrimburát

TERRORIZE *vb.* → TERRIFY

TERSE *adj.* şcúrtu

TEST *s.* (*trial*) dhuchimíe, dhichimăsíre, prová; (*verification*) cătăpăţíre

TEST *vb.* cătăpăţéscu, ▾dhuchimăséscu; **He taught him to ~ her** Lu nviţă s-u cătăpăţeáscă;

TESTED *adj.* (*verified, checked*) cătăpăţít

TESTICLE *s. anat.* coľ, *pl* coáľe; *also:* arómbu, boáşă, *pl* boáşe; hărhăndéľu, *pl* hărhăndeáľe; tópă, *pl* toápe

TESTIFY *vb.* ▾martiriséscu, mărtiriséscu

TESTIMONY *s.* mărturíľe, -tiríe, -tirisíre, ispáte; (*receipt*) apódhixe

TESTING *s.* cătăpăţíre, dhuchimăsíre

TESTY *adj.* (*irascible*) căchiós, -oásă; inací(u), inagí(u)

TETHER *s.* (*rope*) cúrmu; *vb.* leg

THAN *cj.* di, dicât, di per, di pércă, pércă, péryea, dípi, prícă; (*rare*) ca; **better green ~ black** ma ghíne veárde dicât laiu; **It is better to live just one minute at home ~ a whole life abroad** Di per tu xeáne bánă..., tu lóclu-a meu ma ghíne nă síngură minútă; **It is better to be a rooster for just one day ~ a hen for one year** Ma ghíne s-hii únă dzúuă cucót prícă un an găľínă; **rather a coward ~ a bold man** ma múltu fricós percă om cu ínimă; **There is no one more handsome ~ you** Cáma muşát ca tíne nu eáste níţi un ‖ **It would be better if God cut off my life ~ to let me live** ma ghíne s-mi táľe Dumnidzắu di percă z-bănédz, BASME 165; **He seemed to her older than he was in reality** ĭi apăru cama auş di ţi ira d-arihina, HRISTU 68

THANK *vb.* ifhăristiséscu, adúc birhuzúre; **~ God (that)** cála, cála-i ţe, cálai că; **~ God that you've come!** Cála-i ţi viñíşi! alácherím! biricheát virsân; **Thank you!** Efharistó! şúchir! ‖ LITURG 128: **Let us thank God** as fáţim şiuchiúr; *Cru:* **~ you very much** Múltu haristó, GOLAB 219; **~ God** Vru Dumnidzău, BASME 588 ‖ **~ you very much!** Vi tiñisestu dit inimă, HRISTU 51

THANK GOD! ‖ BATSARIA 77: Dóxă-ţ, Doámne!

THANKFUL *adj.* → BE ~

THANKING *s.* efharistíe, birhuzúre, şúchir, şuchiur

THANKS TO *prep.* şúchiur al, spuláite; birhuzúre; ~ **to God** şúchiur al Dumnudzău ‖ *K:* bircheávis, GOLAB 208; di (+ *dat.*), hár(i)tâ (+ *dat.*), DIARO 350

THAT *dem. pron.* aţél, aţăl; *Smr:* aţéu *m*, aţeá(ua) *f*, aţéľ *m pl*, aţeále *f pl*; *Smr:* ţeu, ţea, ţeľ. ţeále; *O:* (a)ţelacló *m*, (a)ţea-acló *f*; (*all that, all those who*) cât, câţ, câtă, câte; **From those who left only one has returned** Di câte fudzíră maşi únă s-turnă ‖ DIARO 8: **that one** aéstâ-acló *sg*, aésti-acló *pl*; *also* aţeá aoá *sg*, aţeáli-aoá *pl*, *and* aţeá-acló *sg*, aţeáli-acló *pl*

THAT *rel. pron.* ţe; **during the eight days ~ I stayed there** óptuli dzâle ţe şidzúi acló ‖ *See also* § 25 *above*

THAT *adv.* ahât, ahântu (*and* ahându), ahtât; ~ **few, that much, that little, that many** ahântu, ahântă, ahânţâ, ahânte

THAT *cj.* că, câ, ţi, tră; **They told me ~ you had died** Ñ-spúsiră că tíne muríşĭ; **She was so lazy ~ she would not even touch work** Irá linăvoásă ţi nu băgá mâna pi lúcru; **People knew ~ he was very poor** Lúmea lu ştea tră tiflupéndar

THAT BEATS THE DEVIL! ≈ (Aéstu eáste) bilélu a bileádzlor!

THATCHED HUT *s.* cătúnă → COTTAGE

THAT IS TO SAY va dzâcă, s-cľámă, deméc, dhiladhí, óste ‖ HRISTU 41: vra s-dzăcă

THAT'S ALL, THAT WAS ALL! ai! **A week and that was all - he kicked the bucket!** Nă stămână şi-ái, li teáse!

THAT'S RICH! *interj.* bá!

THAT WAY *adv.* (*manner*) aşí, acşíţe, ahtáre; (*direction*) ncloáţe; nclo, nculeá

THAUMATURGIST *s.* (*wonder-worker*) thavmaturgó, thavmaturgóu

THAW *s.* dizgľiţáre; (*damp weather*) múină, muládhă, udáľu

THAW *vb.* ▾dizgľéţ

THEATER *s.* théatru

THEFT *s.* fúrtu, (a)furáre, furlíche; (*petty* ~) ciunáre ‖ *Cru:* furíľe, GOLAB 216

THEIR *poss. pron.* a lor (*long form*), lă (*short form*); **Such is ~ chirping** Băteárea lă eáste acşí; **helped by ~ destiny** di míră-lă agiutáţ; ~ **own** -şi; **They see ~ village in ~ dreams** Hoára-şi ved tu yíse; ~ **name was legion** ≈ ñiľ di ñiľ (*lit.* 'thousands of thousands')

THEM *pers. pron. dat.* a lor (*long form*), lă *or* lâ (*short form*) - **Send ~ a letter! - I won't!** - Pitreáţi-lă cárte! - Nu lă pitréc! *acc.* (*long forms*) eľ *m*, eále *f*; (*short forms*) ľi, -ľ, ľ- *m*; li *f*; **He did not find them** (*3 pl f*) Eále nu li-află; **Why should you** (*2 sg*) **kill them** (*3 pl m*)? Cắţé si-ľ váţâñ?

THEME *s.* thémă, *pl* thémate

THEMSELVES: sínguri *m pl*, síngure *f pl*; si, să, s; **The bells began to ring by ~** Cămbăñle nchsíră s-asúnă di síngure; **They dressed ~** Să viscúră

THEN *adv.* (*soon after that*) apói(a), deapóia, dapóia, daporpóia, di priapóia, napói, năpói; (*at that time*) tu aţeá óără; atúnţi, (a)túmţea, (a)túmţealui, (a)túnţealui; **just ~** tiși atúmţea; (*in that case*) cára, daporpóia; **Good-bye ~, take care!** Oáră búnă cára, dú-te! (*shows a necessary consequence*) am; **Gardani, of course! If not him, ~ who else?** Gardani, am cari? ‖ **since ~** di astumsăne, HRISTU 12 → EVERY NOW AND ~

THEOLOGIAN *s.* theólog

THEOLOGY *s.* theoloyíe

THEORY *s.* theoríe

THERE *adv.* aculó, acló, aclóţe, aţía, anculeá, aculeá, acó, clo; *F:* arcó; (*to that place*) cătră acló ‖ *F:* acó, BASME 243 → BE NOT QUITE ALL ~; EVERY ~ AND ~

THERE! *interj.* iácă; ba; **~, the priest is coming!** Ia că víne ș-préftlu! **~ you go! ~ he goes!** ba! ‖ *Cru:* **~ he is!** Ia-ţ-ul! Ia-s-lu! GOLAB 222

THERE IS / THERE ARE: *pres.* si áflă; áre, *ipf.* aveá; **Do you know that there are ghosts over here?** știţ că áre stihíi auáţe? **A stupid man believes that ~ no one brighter than himself** Chirútlu și-u áre că áltu ca nâs nu áre; **There aren't many sheep in the mountains this year** Est-an nu áre oi múlte tu múnţâ; **There were no signs that he was about to finish** Nu aveá seámne s-bitiseáscă; **There is a lot of wool at home** Lână acásă si-áflă crímă ‖ **there is still more** (*to do, to see, etc.*) ning-avém, BASME 11

THERMOMETER *s.* thermométru

THEY *pers. pron.* nâși, năși, dâși *m*; năse, dâse, díse *f*; *also*: eľ, -ľi *m*; -le *f*; **~ were like masters in their house** Ca domñi eará-ľ pri cásă-lă; **~ were all the same!** Tuţ eará-ľ únă! **Were are the magpies?** Hăscile iú-le súntu? **Where are those chicken?** Púľi aţéľ iu súntu-ľ?

THEREFORE *cj.* tr-aţeá *or* di tr-aţeá ‖ *Av:* de-aéstă, BASME 504; *Cru:* teaţeá, GOLAB 253

THICK *adj.* gros, -oásă, groșĭ, -oáse; (*as a forest, a sieve, a comb*) des, deásă, deșĭ, deáse; picnós, -oásă; spes, -eásă, speșĭ, -eáse; (*of fog*) ndisát; (*a tree, a forest, smb.'s hair*) (s)tuf(ut)ós; (*of a forest*) greu; (*obtuse*) glar → STUPID; **~ and short** zófnic ‖ ALIA 141 (*thickset*) gros, gărós, cros; (*of hair*) *Tir:* ndes,

THICKET

ndăsát, *BdD'*: ntufós, *Gop*: ntăfós, NEIESCU 148

THICKET *s.* dégă, deágă, **drâzgă**, tufáne, tufíş, iánură, jánură (DDA 695), ľanúră, yeánură

THICKEN *vb.* ▾ngroş, ▾ngruşédz ‖ **The plot is ~ing!** Si-ngroáşe şicălu! BASME 8; Si-ngroáşe luyuría! BASME 510

THICKENING *s.* ngruşeáre

THICK-HEADED *adj.* cap di grij ‖ HRISTU 46: dudum → STUPID

THICK-LIPPED *adj.* budzós, mbudzát

THICKSET *adj.* gros, bătálcu, căbátcu, şíşcu, şişmán, zdúmban

THIEF *s.* (a)fúr *m*, fúră *f*; haramíu; lupudhít; *GBg*: furcudár; **petty ~** furác, găľinár; **Turkish ~** chisangí, chisăgí, chişigí; **expert ~** fur cu bandéră, fur cu cízme, fur cu dhíplumă; *coll.* furáme; **~ head of thieves** arhilisťín; (**~** *in a candle*) muc

THIEVERY *s.* afuráre, ciulíre

THIEVISH *adj.* furéscu, -eáscă; **~LY** *adv.* fureáşte

THIGH *s.* (*of venison*) ármu; (*haunch*) búte (di cárne) *m*; (*anat., of a horse*) cârâdzéľu ‖ ALIA 173: búcă di chiciór, but, búti, gof, coápsă

THIMBLE *s.* didzitár, diftilídhe, dhihtălíthră, dăhtilíthră

THIN *adj.* (*lean*) s(c)lab, slăbúşcu; **as ~ as a lath** slăghít ca hiľán; (*subtle, as of skin*) minút; supţáre; **~ person** azmét, psănác, piliciós, -oásă, ţărós, -ásă; *derog.* chirchinéc, pruzúme → THINNER

THIN *vb.* supţârédz

THING *s.* lúcru, lúcur; **Here is how ~s are** Ia cum sta lúcrulu; luguríe, lugríe, luyuríe, luyríe; **~s are becoming serious!** Si ngroáşe şicălu! ‖ HRISTU 28: luc (*spelled* lluc)

THINK *vb.* giúdic, ▾mintuéscu (*and* minduéscu); **Think and then speak!** Giúdică şi-apóia zburá! **When you are prosperous, ~ a little of tomorrow!** Cându ai, minduiá ş-tră mâne! (*to remember*) (a)cuitéscu, cuituéscu; **God thought of me and did not abandon me** Si cuituí Dumnidză ş-nu mi lăsă; ▾luyurséscu, ▾siluyiséscu, ▾ziyăséscu, ziyiséscu, zixéscu; (*to believe, to have the feeling that*) ñ-u am că; (*to be menentally with*) ñ-u míntea la; **I was thinking of you** La tíne ñ-erá míntea; (*to assess things correctly*) criséscu; **a man who does not ~** om ţe nu crisáşte; **to ~ better of it** ▾mut míntea; **Son, think better of it!** Ficiór, mútă-u míntea! **to ~ it proper to** u áflu cu cále să, áflu mundăsípe; **~ no small beer of oneself** li trag groáse *or* li trag mări; (*to ~ up, to plot, to cook smth. up*) sufséscu; (*to believe, to hope*) pistipséscu ‖ **~ well!** Mintuia-ti ghini! HRISTU 86

THINK TOO MUCH OF ONESELF *vb.* ‖ mi trag mári, DIARO 307

THINNER *adj.* → BECOME ~, MAKE ~

THINNING *s.* minuţáre, minuţâre
THIN-SKINNED *adj.* căchiós, -oásă
THIRD *ord.* tréilu, trélu *m*, a tréia, a trea *f*; **on the ~ day** a treáz, treádzâ ‖ K-D 71: tritlu, trita; **the ~ time** a treuară, K-D 72; **the ~ night** a ntreilea noapti, HRISTU 43 → § 28.2
THIRST *n* seáte; **to be parched with ~** crep di seáte ‖ **to be seized by ~** mi ľa seátea, BASME 35
THIRSTY *adj.* sitós, -oásă; sátru; ni-biút; **very ~** ársu di seáte; **I am thirsty for conversation** Nu am sátru (*or* sat) di cuvéndă
THIRTEEN *num.* trésprădzaţi; **His clack goes ~ to the dozen** Ápă ľ-ñárdze gúra (≈ *his/her mouth runs like water*)
THIRTY *num.* treidzắţi, tridzắţi, triadzắţi; **~-one** treidzắţi únă; **~-nine houses** tridzăţinoáuă di căsi ‖ 31 treidzaţse unu, K-D
THIS *dem. pron.* aíst(u), aést(u), íst(u), aţístu, aţéstu *m*; aístă, aéstă, ístă, aţístă, aţéstă *f*; **~ time** di aéstă cále *or* di cálea aéstă; **~ way** aşí, acşíţe ‖ *F:* **the landlady of these houses** doámna iştór cási, BASME 478; *see also* § 25 **above**; DIARO 8: **this one** aéstâ-aoá *sg*, aésti-aoá *pl*
THISTLE *s. bot.* scaľ
THITHER *adv.* (*to that place*) nclo, âncló, nculó, ânculeá
THORN *s.* schin *m*; *also:* cârnicóciu, curnucóciu, guvujdél, -vuzdél, -vuzdéľ *m* → BE LIKE A ~ IN ONE'S SIDE
THORNBUSH *s.* schin, păľúr
THORNY *adj.* schinós, -oásă
THORNY AREA *s.* schináme, păľurét, păľuríu
THOROUGH *adj.* bitivíu, arắu, aráuă, arắi, arále; **~ emptiness** irñíe arắu
THOROUGHBRED *adj.* di sóie, suilâtcu, di dămáră, dămărlâtcu
THOROUGHGOING *adj.* apufăsít
THOROUGHLY *adv.* ghíne, arắu, bitivíu ‖ cum lipseáşte, BASME 407 (*lit. 'as it should be'*); de-a ghínealui, BASME 95 ‖ (*exhaustively, as of a deposition before a court*) pânâ tu per, DIARO 281
THOUGH *cj.* cánai că, că ţi că, cu túti că → AS IF ‖ *as ~* táha, GOLAB 253
THOUGHT *s.* minduíre, méngă; **I see that your ~s are elsewhere** ≈ Ved că-ţ asboáră
THOUGHTFUL *adj.* arumigát, minduít
THOUGHTLESS *adj.* astráptu, fâră socoteálă, ni-minduít; (oámiñ) cari nu au meľ tu ciútură (*lit. 'people with no millet in their bucket,' i.e. with no brain in their head*)
THOUSAND *s. or num.* ñíľe; (*a bill of one ~*) hiľárcă
THRALL *s.* rob, sclav
THRALDOM *s.* sclăvíľe, sclăvíe, arubuíre

THRASH

THRASH *vb.* → BEAT; (*as a walnut tree*) (a)scútur

THRASHING *s.* avráre → BEATING

THREAD *s.* áţă, cioáră, coárđhă (*and* coárdă), hoárdhă, hir, *dim.* hiríc, hirúş, sfoáră, spángu; (*spun* ~) cheádin, tórtu, tul; **a piece of ~** un córnu di hir; **the ~ of life** cioára a ómlui

THREAD *vb.* (*to ~ a needle*) (a)mpíhiur (hírlu tu ac), mpihiór

THREADBARE *adj.* părtálcu, -lcă, -lţi, -lţe; arós, tuchít

THREAT *s.* fuvértă, fuvéră, fuvirsíre, cănusíre

THREATEN *vb.* ▼angréc, fuvirséscu, ▼cănuséscu ‖ CUNIA 11: ascútur dzeáditlu, spun băstúnea

THREATENED → BE ~

THREATENING *adj.* fuvirós, -oásă

THREE *num.* trei *or* treĭ; **all ~** amintréili *m*, amintréile *f*; şámintreiľi, ámiştreiľi, antréiľi *m*, antréile *f*; **the ~ of us** tréľi-nă (DDA 852); **~ times** trei orĭ; **I'll ask the ~ of you a riddle** Vă bag a tréilor cấte nă angucitoáre ‖ *Amc*: **there are ~ young men and the ~ of them are hanged** sấntu trei lai gioñ şamen treľi spindzurấţ(â), RÉCATAS 41

THRESH *vb.* alunséscu, tríyir, tríir ‖ *3 sg*, *Amc, An, Els, Na*: aluniseáşte, B-ARCH 272

THRESHING *s.* alunsíre, triiráre

THRESHING FLOOR *s.* alóne, árye, árghie; *obs.* árie

THRESHOLD *s.* prag, preág; prágură (di úşe) → CROSS THE ~

THRIFT *s.* cumándă, icunumíe

THRIFTLESS *adj.* hărgiuitór, -oáre; spátal, *m pl* -taľ

THRIFTY *adj.* adunătór; (*sparing*) icunumisáric; máză, *invar.*

THRILL *s.* hiór → SHIVER

THRILL *vb.* (*as of the water of a spring*) trăsár; (*to feel a thrill*) tríhir, trihirédz; ▼nhiurédz [nhi•u•]

THRIVE *vb.* amíntu, acáţ maiáuă, adár cásă, adár căşáre, adár cătúnă, am cľág, fac aveáre, ñ-cústă, ñ-gioácă cálu (DIARO 167: cállu), ñi si dúţi príma, ñ-ñárdzi príma, ▼pricupéscu, prucupséscu, purcupséscu, prudhipséscu; **I am not ~ing in my work** Nu-ñ cústă lúcrulu → TO GET ON WELL

THRIVING *s.* prudhipsíre **THRIVING** → BE ~

THROAT *s. anat.* gărgălác, gărgălán, gărgăľán, gârgal, gârcinár, grumádz, gurmáz; *to pin smb. by the* ~ lu-ascálin di gúşe

THROAT-WASH *s.* yăryáră

THROB *s.* ciócut ‖ **His heart gave a ~** Ľi si bătú ínima, BASME 42

THROB *vb.* (*usu. of the heart*) âñ báte, âñ cicăneáşte, âñ ciucuteáşte, âñ furfureádză, âñ zvâcneáşte; (*as of an eye*) âñ flítură; mi zbat

THROBBING *s.* cicăníre, zvâcníre, flituráre

THRONE *s.* scámnu, thron
THRONG *s.* multíme, suríe → CROWD, FLOCK
THROTTLE *vb.* zdrúmin di gúşe, ▼zgrum, zgrumuéscu
THROUGH *adj.* (*direct*) ndréptu; (*finished*) bitisít
THROUGH *prep.* pit, prit, pitu, pitru; **Various thoughts were flashing ~ his mind** Minduíri âľ triţeá prit mínte; (*via*) pri → PUT SMTH. ~
THROW *s.* arucătúră
THROW *vb.* ▼(a)rúc, arúncu, **N:** arrúcu; aríc; **N:** amín; ▼aúrlu; azvârlu, azvârléscu; (*as stones*) ▼astrág, bumbunédz; (*as into a cell*) huhutéscu, plăscănéscu; (*to cause to fell*) tălcéscu; **He threw the apple and hit him in the head** Amină mérlu ş-lu-agudí n cap; **He threw the fish from the basket** Arcă peáşţăľi dit cuşóre; **They threw him inside** L-huhutíră naúntru; **to ~ against the ground** dau di páde, zdupănéscu (di páde), zdâpânéscu, zdupunéscu; **to ~ down** arúc mpáde; **to ~ dirt at smb.** rizil(ips)éscu; **to ~ off one's shyness** ľau ínimă, ▼ncucutédz; **to ~ smb. off his/her guard** (*to deceive, to lure*) ▼acáţ óčľi; **to ~ smb. into a fever** ľ-frig máţăle; **to ~ into confusion** (*of people*) ▼scol di mínte; (*as of a neat room*) fac cioáră; **to ~ oneself from side to side** (*to toss*) mi zbat
THROW APART *vb.* (*of one's legs*) ▼discácăr
THROW DOWN *vb.* ▼súrpu, ▼răzuéscu, ruzuéscu, (a)răstórn → OVERTURN
THROW OFF *vb.* (*as a bad habit*) mi cúrmu (di), mi aleápid (di); **~ your drinking!** Cúrmă-ti di beáre!
THROW ONESELF UPON *vb.* ▼arúc pri → RUSH
THROW OUT *vb.* arúc nafoáră
THROW UP *vb.* *phys.* vom; (*to build*) análţu, adár, fac
THROWING *s.* aruncáre, arcáre, amináre, astrádzire, astrădzeáre, aurláre, azvârlíre; **~ down** (a)răsturnáre, ▼arusturnáre
THRUSH[1] *s.* *orn.* stúrdz, strudz, **Cľis:** stúrgiu; chirchirínă
THRUSH[2] *s.* *med.* părzătúră
THRUST *s.* (*as with the horns*) ambuiráre, ambuţâre, mbuţ, ampăráre; (*as with a knife, with a sharp pole, etc.*) hidzeáre, hídzire, plântáre, băgáre
THRUST *vb.* (*with or as with the horns*) ▼(a)mbúir, ▼(a)mbúţ, **G:** mbut; ampár; (*to force in*) hig, nhig, plântu, ▼bag; (*a door, an adversary, etc.*) zdupănéscu, zdupunéscu ‖ DIARO 147: dau un píngu
THRUST AWAY ONE'S HUNGER *vb.* (*to stop one's stomach*) ñ-apúc gúra
THRUST DOWNWARD *vb.* ▼ndes
THRUST IN *vb.* ▼bag
THRUST OUT ONE'S TONGUE AT SMB. *vb.* ľi scot límba nafoáră
THUMB *s.* pălicár, pulicár ‖ **Peş:** pilicár, CL 258
THUMB ONE'S NOSE AT SMB. *vb.* ľ-dau măndzăle (*or* múndzle);

THUMBNAIL

▼mundzuséscu, ▼mundzuéscu, țifnuséscu

THUMBNAIL *adj.* (*brief, concise*) şcúrtu, -rtă, -rţâ, -rte

THUMP *s.* aguditúră

THUMP *vb.* → POUND

THUNDER *s.* (a)rófche, (a)rufée, rufeáuă, rufé; astrăpíe, bumbu-nidzáre, gărníş, *G:* ghiríţ; sfúlgu, tun ‖ *GSus:* chirút, CL 254; *Prv:* străpoválă, CL 261

THUNDER *vb.* 3 *sg:* bumbuneádză, bubuneádză, túnă, toánă, *Src:* detúnă, vrunduseáşte ‖ ALIA 16: asúnă, atúnă, bumbăneádză, bu-bunídză, cârţăneáşte

THUNDERBOLT *s.* chícută

THUNDERSTORM *s.* ≈ furtúnă

THUNDERSTRUCK *adj.* limnusít → DUMBFOUNDED

THURSDAY *s.* gioi; **All ~s should be observed because ~ is very vicious** Túte gióile vor ţâneáre, că gióia i múltu aráuă ‖ *Kok:* dzoi, *Mul:* jóă, *Pal, Pur:* gióiă, B-ARCH 336; *Gop:* joi, NEIESCU 131

THUS *adv.* acşiá, aşiá, aşá, aşíţe, aşâţe, aşâ, aşí, aşé; *N:* acşé; *F:* aşă; dicára

THUS FAR *adv.* pân tru hópa aístă

THUS *cj.* ileachím, lipón

THWACK *s.* aguditúră

THWACK *vb.* ▼agudéscu

THWART *vb.* (*to obstruct, to balk*) cărşilătiséscu; (*to outwit*) ncálţu

THWART *adv.* → ATHWART

THYME: **wild ~** ţemurícă → PENNYROYAL

TIBIA *s. anat.* arídă (*and* arídhă), chilúnghe, fler

TICK *s. ent.* căpúşe, *N:* căpúş; căpúţ, căcimór, cârléj

TICK *vb.* **to ~ smb. off** (*to bring smb. to his bearings*) ľi pliciutéscu nările

TICKET *s.* (*label, tag*) vulutínă ‖ (*permit*) pusúlâ, DIARO 161

TICKLE *vb.* ▼gâdil (*and* gă-), ▼gădălíc, gădilíc, *N:* gâdic ‖ Ba-tsaria 62: gădic → BE ~ED TO DEATH

TICKLING *s.* gâdiláre, gădălicáre, gădilicáre, gâdicáre, yăryări-dzáre

TIDE ON *vb.* (*to progress, to advance*) prudhipséscu

TIDE OVER *vb.* (*to stave off hunger*) ñ-apúc gúra

TIDY *adj.* (*neat*) → chischín; (*large, substantial*) máre, *pl* mări

TIDY *vb.* ▼arădhăpséscu

TIE *s.* pánglică, pătlícă, cravátă ‖ ligâtúrâ, DIARO 304

TIE *vb.* ▼leg, ▼(a)nód; **to ~ smb. down** ľ-taľu mâñle

TIED *adj.* anudát

TIE-IN *s.* ligătúră

TIER *s.* (*layer*) dhíplă, arádhă, pétură

TIFF *s.* → QUARREL, HAVE A ~ WITH SMB.

TIFF *vb.* *3 pl:* și-mâcă sămárile → QUARREL

TIGER *s.* tíyru ‖ HRISTU 8: tigur

TIGHT *adj.* (*as of a knot*) stres, -eásă, -eșĭ, -eáse; (*serried, as of lips*) strímtu, -mtă, -mțâ, -mte

TIGHTENING *s.* strândzeáre, strândzire

TIGHTEN *vb.* ▾stríngu

TIGHTLY *adv.* stres, pravatós, pri-, prâ-, pro- ‖ sânătós, BASME 432

TILE *s.* ploáce, *dim.* plucícă; chirimídhă ‖ túlă, CAPIDAN 150

TILE-MAKER *s.* chirimidhár

TILL *prep.* pântu; ~ **one's dying day** pân-la ploáce → UNTIL

TILL *vb.* ‖ fac ágru, BASME 512

TILLAGE *s.* (*agriculture*) zivyărlíche

TILLER *s.* aráciu, uráciu, zivyít

TILT: at full ~ an pátrulea, ambátrulea

TILT *vb.* ▾apléc; ~ **over** ▾arăstórnu; ~ **against** ▾himuséscu (pri); (*as of shaking table, 3 sg*) z-da → SHAKE

TILTH *s.* zivyărlíche

TIMBER *s.* chiristé(e)

TIME *s.* chiró, étă, ipuhíe, oáră, văcâte, zămáne; **A long ~ has past since then** Tricú di atúmțea zămáne múltă; **What ~ is it?** Țe oáră-avém? **The ~ came for him to die** Ĺ-víñe oára tra si-șĭ moáră; **Let's run away until there is ~!** S-fudzím pân-avém oáră! **this ~** di oára iástă; **the first ~** próta oáră *or* ântâñea oáră; **the second ~** di-adoára; **three ~s** trei ori; **three-four ~s** trei-pátru ori; **one ~** (*in the past*) nă oáră; **many ~s a year** múlte ori tru an; **a long ~ ago** di-oáră; **for the ~ being** tră oáră; **this ~** ástă-oáră *or* di aéstă cále; **in a short ~** (*soon*) tră puțână oáră *or* tră puțân chiró; **long ~** málă di oáră *or* mal di chiró; **at ~s** ori ori; **At ~s he wants it, at ~s he does not** Ori ori va, ori ori nu; **It did not rain all the ~** Nu déde ploáie tru éta tútă; **at one ~** tu únă étă; **to the end of ~** păn tu éta a étiĺei; **~ out of mind** di éta a li éte; **at their ~** tu ipuhía a lor; **in good ~** di timpuríu ‖ CARAFOLI 43: *the watchman could not observe in good time what was going on* cărăúĺa nu putú s-ĺa di vij di timpuríu → TIMES

TIME-KEEPER *s.* (*inspector*) meimúr

TIME-OUT *s.* aryíe

TIMES *prep.* ori → A *prep.*

TIMEWORN *adj.* ros, vicĺát, nvicĺát

TIMID *adj.* fricós, -oásă; *3 sg:* áre ínimă di ĺépure → FEARFUL

TIMON *s.* (*of a carriage*) ‖ *GSus:* coádă, CL 42

TIN

TIN *s.* tiniché(e), călái, căláie, yánumă, gánumă, pafíl ‖ *Cern,*
Mi, Src: calái, B-ARCH 34

    TIN *vb.* yănuséscu, yu-, gu-

    TINDER *s.* iáscă

    TINGE *vb.* (*of colors*) ▾buiséscu → DYE

    TINGLE *vb.* jujuéscu

    TINKER *s.* → TINMAN

    TINKLE *vb.* asún

    TINKLING *s.* văzúră; **the ~ of the church bell** văzúra a cămbánă-ľei

    TINMAN *s.* (*tinsmith*) tinichigí(u), yanóş, yunusár, gu-, gănustár,
yălăngí; (*bungler*) mbalumatí; *adj.* gunusăréscu

    TINNER *s.* → TINMAN

    TINNING *s.* yănusíre, gu-

    TINPLATE *s.* lamanínă, lămărínă, pafíl, tiniché

    TINSEL *s.* teľu, hrisáfe

    TINSMITH *s.* → TINMAN

    TINT *vb.* ▾buiséscu

    TINY *adj.* ciuflíc, ciufléc, ñicúţ, şámcure → SMALL

    TIP¹ *s.* (*as of a needle*) simígă, sumígă, míthcă ‖ *Peş:* (*~ of a*
finger, of a scythe, etc.) ţăpătuľe, ţípătuľe

    TIP² *s.* (*gratuity*) dáre, băhcíşe, meáştire; (*gratuity given to*
one's friends when leaving the village) pinitádhă

    TIP *vb.* (*to present*) méscu; (*to impart a piece of information*)
▾aspún, dau hăbáre; (*to overturn*) ▾arăstórnu; **He ~ed me with a**
golden coin Mi miscú un arúspu

    TIPCAT *s.* báche, ciulícă, cilécă, ciuléngă, stíngăle, tíngăle,
şcľéndză, şcľándză

    TIPPLE *vb.* ▾sórbu, mi afúm; (*by habit or to excess, 3 sg.*)
ľ-arúcă múltu tu cărcheáuă → DRINK, GET TIPSY

    TIPSY *adj.* adărát → DRUNK

    TIPTOE *vb.* ñérgu pri úngľile di cioáre

    TIP-TOP *adj.* (*excellent*) nişanlí(u); príma *invar.*; spániu, -nie,
m/f pl -niĭ; safí *invar.*

    TIRE *vb.* ▾cúrmu, apustuséscu, avurséscu, avruséscu; (*to overwork*)
▾dişilédz, scot pétalile; mi tuchéscu (tu lúcru), ▾zgrum (tu lúcru); **when I ~ed myself out** cari mi curmái

    TIRED *adj.* curmát; *also:* apustusít, avursít, stătút, vătămát; **ve-**
ry ~ arúptu ‖ cu límba scoásă di curmáre, BASME 27; **~ to death (from**
work) dijgľinát di lúcru, DIARO 363

    TIRELESS *adj.* ni-curmát

    TIRESOME *adj.* ánustu, -stă, -şţâ, -ste

    TISSUE *s.* ţesătúră

    TIT¹ *s. orn.* ‖ *GSus:* puľu chindisítu, CL 259; *Smr, Băi:* yrămătíc, CL 46

TIT² s. anat. → TEAT

TIT³ s. **not the least** ~ cât ghitrúşca

TITANIC adj. évil, -lă, -ľ, -le

TITHE s. dhécat, for, ghísmă; **not a** ~ cât trâ yitríe

TITHE vb. (a)ghizmédz, ayízmu

TITILLATE ONESELF vb. ‖ **Cru:** mi duzduséscu, GOLAB 213

TITIVATE vb. ▾adár, ▾andrég

TITLE¹ s. (*proof of ownership*) tăpíe; (~ *of a book*) títlu; (*dignity*) sémnu; **He took the** ~ **of pasha** şi-lo sémnul di păşé

TITTLE²: **not a** ~ cât trâ yitríe → JOT

TITTLE-TATTLE vb. ▾arădhăpséscu, másin curnuţeále, máţin măslăţ, taľu crúde ş-coápte, taľu pălăvri, zburăscu chiritúrĭ; (*braggingly*) taľu groáse

TIZZY s. şişirmáie, şiştamără, şiştimără

TO prep. (*direction*) tră, ntre trâ, trâşi, tăşi; **We went** ~ **Salonika** Nă dúsim trâşi Sărúnă; **The per is going** ~ **the well** S-dúţe pócilu [póĉ•lu] ntre ápă; (*in view of*) pri; **He kept them** ~ **supper** Ľ-ţânú pri ţínă; (*towards*) câtră; (*for*) ti; **She is poison** ~ **us** Ea-i fărmác ti noi; ~ **and fro** F: pi-aroá pi-arcó → TOWARD(S)

TO verb connective (*in order to*) di, tea s, tra si, trea si, tra să; **I went** ~ **see him** Mi duş di-l vidzúi; **When fear began** ~ **take hold of us** ... Cari víñe fríca di nă lo ...; **I did not want** ~ **kill** Eu nu vream tea s-vátăm; **I am not able** ~ **count them** Nu pot si-ľ númir; **She couldn't stand it any longer** Nu ma putú tra s-arávdă

TO A HAIR adv. (*everything*) pân tu ac ‖ pănă tu per, BASME 446

TO A MAN adv. (*everybody*) di un; pân di un

TO AND FRO adv. ‖ DIARO 433: ţâsâ-n vâsâ; sírta-férta

TO ONE'S HEART'S CONTENT adv. di-a-sătúlui

TO ONE'S LAST BREATH adv. pân tu amín → TO THE BITTER END

TO PUT IT BLUNTLY ≈ ţe ncoa, ţe nclo (*lit.* 'why [should we go] to and fro?')

TO THE BITTER END adv. pân tu amín, pân la ploáce

TO THE LAST FARTHING adv. (*everything*) pân tu ac

TO THE LAST GASP adv. → TO THE BITTER END

TO THE UTMOST EXTENT adv. a mórtului; di-a mútra

TO WIT adv. → NAMELY

TOAD s. jábă

TOADY adj. (*sycophant*) cólac, -că, -ţĭ, -ţe; marghiól, -oálă

TOADY vb. ▾gúdur, guduréscuu ‖ dau coáda (pri nângă), BASME 2

TOAST vb. ▾ghinuéscu, chinu-; ▾chirăséscu, méscu; **The two in-laws drank toasts** S-ghinuíră cúscri; (*to brown by heat*) ▾pârjiléscu

TOASTED adj. (*as of a slice of bread*) pârjilít

TOBACCO

TOBACCO *s.* tutúne, tutúme, tătúme, tăbác (*and* tâbác), tubác, duyeán; (*snuff*) bărnúte; (~ *for narghile*) tumbíche

TOBACCONIST *s.* tutungí

TOCK-TOCK *ono.* tâc-tâc; **His heart was going** ~ Tâc-tâc âľ fățeá ínima

TODAY *adv.* adz, ádză (*and* ádzâ), az, áză; ástăndzâ (*and* ástândzâ), ásăndzâ, ástăz, ástăză, ánză ‖ ándzâ, BASME 348

TODDLE ONE'S WAY ALONG *vb.* ñ-trag cálea, ñ-mutréscu cálea năínte

TO-DO *s.* (*fuss, uproar*) **G:** giufă → MAKE A ~

TOGETHER *adv.* deadún, dadún, âmpriúnă, mpriúnă, dipriúnă, bárabára, soáță; **They are** ~ **day and night** Dzúua ş-noáptea súntu bárabára → COME ~, PUT CLOSE ~

TOGGERY *s.* stráñe *n pl*, strañu *sg*

TOG OUT *vb.* ▾anvéscu, ▾andrég

TOGS *s.* → TOGGERY

TOIL AND MOIL *vb.* (*to work hard*) lucrédz discufút, ▾píngu oáhte ‖ DIARO 272: mi-ndúplic di lúcru

TOILET *s.* halé, halée; *also:* **Grbț:** căcăríu; căcătór, căcăstoáre, chinéfe, chişitór, hríe, işitór, muştiréche ‖ **Cru:** hăríe, GOLAB 219

TOIL *s.* lúcru, múndă, pidhimó ‖ CARAFOLI 53: agónă; 91: agoánă

TOILS *s.* (*noose*) (a)láț → BE TAKEN IN THE ~

TOIL UP A HILL *vb.* ľau dzeána

TOILWORN *adj.* curmát

TOLERABLE *adj.* misótriv, *m pl* -vĭ (*sic*); ceat-pat *invar.*

TOLERANCE *s.* (*endurance*) văstăxíre → PATIENCE

TOLERATE *vb.* ▾arávdu → ENDURE, PUT UP WITH, STAND

TOLL *s.* (*as of bells*) asunáre

TOLL *vb.* asún

TOMAHAWK *s.* bâltă → AX(E)

TOMATO *s.* dumátă; **Brz:** frangómină ‖ ALIA 78: dhumátă, tomátă, pătărgeánă, pătlâgeánă ‖ STERE 52: fréncă

TOMB *s.* túmbă → GRAVE

TOMBSTONE *s.* ploáce

TOMCAT *s.* cătúş, macióc, măcióc, macearóc, mărói ‖ ALIA 94: maróñu, maț, măcióc, pis

TOME *s.* tom

TOMFOOLERY *s.* (*nonsense*) chiritúră; (*trick*) féstă, tirtípe

TOMORROW *adv.* mâne; **the day after** ~ păimâne (*and* pâi-), alántă mâne

TONGS *s.* țimbídhă, țimbístră; (*for ember*) mâşé, **N:** máşe; (*in a shoemaker's shop*) dânáľe, tănále ‖ VELO 109: máşe

TONGUE *s.* límbă, *dim.* limbúşe → BRIDLE ONE'S ~, PUT OUT ONE'S ~ AT SMB.

TONGUE-LASH *vb.* → SCOLD

TONIGHT *adv.* astáră, ástă seáră, aístă seáră, noáptea aéstă

TONING DOWN *s.* (a)zápe

TONSIL *s.* glíndură

TONSILLITIS *s. med.* paradhángală, plăscáre

TONSURE *s.* túndire, tundeáre

TOO *adv.* (*exceedingly*) múltu, pri; **~ much** cu sáclu; fâră nisáfe; **~ few** múltu puţâñ; **~ late** pri amânát

TOOL *s.* hăláte, ípiryu, iryălíe; **the ~s for ploughing** hălăţle di aráre ‖ *Gop:* aláti, GOLAB 197

TOOTH *s.* dínte; **milk teeth** dínţâ di lápte ‖ ALIA 154: díndi

TOOTHLESS *adj.* jímbu, -mbă, -nghi, -mbe; *also* jú-; strábal, -lă, -ĺ, -le

TOOTHPICK *s.* hiĺán

TOOTHSOME *adj.* → nóstim, -timă, -tiñ, -time → TASTY

TOOTHY *adj.* cărinţós, -oásă ‖ dinţâlós, DIARO 405

TOP *s.* (*~ of a mountain or hill*) ţăpălíc (→ PEAK); (*~ of the head*) creáştit, cârcilíulu cáplui; (*~ of the nose*) chípita di náre; (*~ of a tree*) angheáuă; **on ~** *adv.* pisúpră ‖ (*~ of a scythe, of fingers*) *Peş:* ţípătuĺe, ţăpătuĺe, CL 262

TOP *vb.* → COVER, SURPASS

TOPE *vb.* ▾ambét

TOPER *s.* → DRUNKARD

TOPFLIGHT *s.* → TIP-TOP

TOPIC *s.* thémă, *pl* thémate

TOPKNOT *s.* (*of hair*) túfă

TOP-NOTCH *adj.* → TIP-TOP

TOPPLED *adj.* turculít, târ-

TOPPLE DOWN *vb.* ▾súrpu, zdupunéscu di páde

TOPPLE OVER *vb.* ▾arăstórnu

TOPS *adj.* → TIP-TOP

TOPSOIL *s.* ≈ loc

TOPSY-TURVY *adj., adv.* cióra-bóra, darmadán; **make ~** ▾fac cioáră

TOQUE *s.* (*a woman's brimless hat*) ghiubéc

TORCH *s.* (*of larch*) dzádă, zádă

TORMENT *s.* dirín, dirináre, dirnáre; *also:* múndă, munduíre, mursicáre, pidhimó, pidhipsíre, tiráñu, vălăndúră, zahméte ‖ DIARO 173: canónâ

TORMENT *vb.* ▾alúmtu, ▾deápir; ▾frimí(n)tu, fărmí(n)tu, firmí(n)tu; ▾munduéscu, ▾pat, ▾pidipséscu, pidhi-, ▾vălănduséscu, ▾văsănipséscu; **~ smb.** ĺ-fac tiráñu; **What devil is ~ing me today?** Ţe drac mi páte ádză? **Long-ing was ~ing him** Un dor âl firmitá (*or* âl dipirá) ‖ MERCA 9: mi tirinséscu

TORMENTED

TORMENTED *adj.* *(after consumption of alcohol the previous day)* mahmúr, mahmurlíu, muhmarlí; bărliv, *m pl* -liyĭ

TORN *adj.* *(tattered)* arúptu; *(as of a goat torn apart by a bear)* aspártu

TORPID *adj.* adurñít, agărşít, minghét

TORPOR *s.* slăbeáţă, adurñíre, nsumnáre, leánc

TORRENT *s.* proiu, puvóñu, şuruínă, vále; **What a big ~ is coming down!** Ţi vále máre yíne! → STREAM

TORRID *adj.* căldurós, -oásă; aprés, -eásă, -éşĭ, -eáse; aprímtu, -mtă, -mţâ, -mte; **~ weather** curoáre

TORRIDNESS *s.* váhte

TORSION *s.* strâmbáre

TORTUOSITY *s.* strâmbătúră

TORTUOUS *adj.* *(twisted)* strâmbu, -mbă, -nghi, -mbe; birdhipsít; *(devious)* plan, *m pl* -ñ

TORTURE *s.* schíngiu; *(punishment)* culăsíre, văsinipsíre → TORMENT

TORTURE *vb.* ▼munduéscu, culăséscu, văsănipséscu → PUNISH, TORMENT

TOSS *vb.* ▼zbat; *also:* ▼ciucutéscu, ▼dirín, ▼turculéscu, târcu-

TOTAL *adj.* ntreg, -eágă, -edzĭ; *also* ndreg; bitivíu, -íe, -íĭ

TOTALLY *adv.* dicutót, di-a-cutótalui, dibină, dip, fáre

TOTTER *vb.* ▼cl(e)átin, clătín; ▼trunduéscu; ▼ñíşcu

TOUCH *s.* *(a light ~)* arăcíre; *(a light stroke)* cimşíre, cârtitúră

TOUCH *vb.* *(to reach)* ▼acúndin, arăcéscu, aricéscu, cimşéscu, cimcéscu, bag mâna (pi), dau di, mâc; **No one should ~ the house** Ţivá s-nu da di cásă; **The ball ~ed the ground** Tópa mâcă ţára; *(to feel)* ▼ahuléscu; **They saw and ~ed each other** S-videá, s-ahuleá; *(admonitorily, as to a child)* **Don't ~ it!** Tea! tea! *(to examine by the feel)* pusputéscu, păspătéscu, pusputipséscu, ▼cârtéscu (di); **He even would not ~ her** Nâs níţi nu s cârteá di ea; **Don't ~ my belongings!** S nu ti cârtéşti di lúcrile a meále! ‖ DIARO 94: dau; **Don't ~ me, I don't love tou!** Nu dă di míni, câ nu ti voi! *Don't ~ the wall because it has been painted recently* Nu ti dă di stízmâ câ-i aúmtâ; cârtéscu: **Let me in peace, don't ~ me, I'm upset!** Alásâ-mi, nu mi cârteá, câ hiu cripátâ, *ibid.* → ~ UPON, ~ WOOD!

TOUCH UPON *vb.* *(to remind, to make a hint)* adúc di amínte (trâ) ‖ *Av:* adúc zbórlu di, BASME 503

TOUCH WOOD! ≈ S nu-ţ di óclĭu! *(i.e., may the evil eye avoid you)*

TOUGH *adj.* *(marked by absence of softness)* ascúr, ascurát

TOUGHNESS *s.* ascuráme

TOUCHY *adj.* *(ill-natured)* căchiós, guştirát, inagí

TOUGH *adj.* *(strong, firm)* putút, vârtós, -oásă; *(severe)* áscur; *(difficult)* greu, greáuă, grei, greále; *(determined)* apufăsít;

(*stubborn*) anăpudzât; (*enduring*) arăvdătór, -toáre

TOUGHNESS *s.* vârtuşáme

TOUSLE *vb.* (*to disarrange*) ▾stric, cârtéscu (*and* căr-), tălăéscu; (*to dishevel*) ▾ciumuléscu

TOUSLED *adj.* (*dishevelled*) ciumulít

TOUT *vb.* (*to ballyhoo*) ▾alávdu

TOW *s.* fuľór; (*of flax*) stúpă, stupíe, ciup, *pl* ciuchi *m*

TOW *vb.* ▾azvărnuéscu, ▾trag azvárna

TOWARD(S) *prep.* cátră, câtră, cátă, câtă, spri, sti, trât; ~ **evening** cátră di seáră *or* di cátră seáră; **Three people were coming ~ me** Spri míne viñá trei oámeñ; **lest I direct the lighting ~ you (onto you)** s-nu-amín chícuta sti tíne; **He is tending ~ the hereafter** Trádzi trât lúmea alántă ‖ ~ **the sea** câtră a máre, BASME 441

TOWEL *s.* pischíre, pişchíre, prusópe, pişteamál, piştamál, pişteamálă; (*to be given to the bridegroom*) ilícă ‖ *GSus, Peş:* distiméľ, CL 44; *Pls:* păştămál, CL 258

TOWER *s.* cúlă, agúlă, píryu, turón, turró

TOWER ABOVE SMB. *vb.* (*to be far better than smb.*) níţi la dzidzitíc nu lu am

TOWHEAD *s., adj.* albér, arús

TOWN *s.* căsăbă; *also:* apulitíe, păzáre

TOWN LIMIT *s.* ‖ *Cru:* sinúr, GOLAB 248

TOWN COUNCIL *s.* dhimuyerundíe

TOWN COUNCILLOR *s.* dhimuyerúndu

TOWN-CRIER *s.* tălál → CRIER

TOWN HALL *s.* bilidé *or* bilidíe

TOWNSMAN *s.* câsâbúñu, pulít

TOY *s.* agiucăríe, agiucăreáuă

TOY *vb.* ▾agióc

TRACE *s.* úrmă, úlmă, dâră, trágă; (*as of a fox*) tor, *G:* toáră; **not a ~** níţi úrmă; (*at all*) cât trâ yitríe; cípit → TAKE SMB.'S ~

TRACE *vb.* dau di úrmă; **to ~ smb. over** âľ ľau dâra *or* âľ ľau tórlu

TRACK *s.* (*visible mark or sign*) úrmă; (*of game*) dâră → TRACE; **to be hot on the ~ of** ▾avín → MAKE ~S

TRACK *vb.* dau di úrmă, ľi áflu úrma, dau di trágă; **They couldn't ~ them** Di úrma a lor nu putúră s-da; (*to ~ with or as with one's sense of smell*) úlmic

TRACKING *s.* (*using one's sense of smell*) ulmicáre

TRACTABLE *adj.* ascultătór, -oáre

TRACTION *s.* trádzire, trdzeáre

TRADE *s.* (*profession, skill*) măsturíľe, téhne, zănáte; (*commerce*) tigearéte

TRADE *vb.* ▾alăxéscu, emburipséscu, fac tigearéte, fac trámbă

TRADE-GUILD

TRADE-GUILD s. câlfălâche, suţátă

TRADE-NAME s. fírmă

TRADER s. tugeár

TRADITION s. arádhă, adéte

TRADUCE vb. (to slander) zburăscu

TRAGEDY s. (misfortune) ‖ **Cru:** fănicó, GOLAB 215

TRAIL s. → TRACE

TRAIL vb. (to drag along) trag azvárna, ▾azvărnuéscu; (to follow the trail) ▾avín, ľau n cicioáre, ľau tórlu

TRAIN s. tren, máchină, sidhiródhrum ‖ **Peş:** paóre, CL 257

TRAIN vb. (to form by instruction, to drill) ▾nveţ, dhăscălipséscu, ▾fac hăzâre

TRAINEE s. (apprentice) cálfă, câlfă; mathití

TRAINING s. nviţáre

TRAIT s. (as of smb.'s face) măsídhă, misídhă, ñisídhă

TRAITOR s. prudhót

TRAMMEL s. cheádică, purdhucľáuă

TRAMMEL vb. ▾(a)ncheádic → SHACKLE

TRAMP s. (succession of sounds made by the beating of feet on a road) tróput ‖ (a begging or thieving vagrant) ceapatórean, DIARO 222

TRAMP vb. ímnu, hălăndăréscu

TRAMPLE vb. (as of grapes) ▾zdrúmin, ▾zdroámin, ▾stúlcin, ▾stulţin

TRAMPLED ON adj. (as of grass) târât

TRANQUIL adj. arihătipsít → STILL

TRANQUILLITY s. arihătlâche

TRANSACT vb. ▾păzăripséscu

TRANSACTION s. alişveríşe, arişveríşe, dare-loáre, daravéră, ipáthise, păzăripsíre

TRANSFER s. (conveyance) pitreáţire, pitriţeáre

TRANSFER vb. (to convey) pitréc; (to deliver, to hand over) fac tislíme

TRANSFORM vb. (to alter, to turn into) ▾prifác, priadár

TRANSGRESS vb. ▾astáľu, ascápit, ▾cálcu, trec; **The others have just ~ed the hill** Cât ascăpitáră alánţâ dúpă dzeánă

TRANSGRESSION s. (as of a law) călcáre

TRANSITORY adj. ntreáţit

TRANSLATE vb. ▾xiyiséscu

TRANSLATED adj. xiyisít

TRANSLATION s. turnătúră, xiyisíre

TRANSLATOR s. dragumán ‖ DIARO 420: tergiménu

TRANSMIT vb. (to deliver) ▾dau, pitréc, fac tislíme

TRANSPIERCE *vb.* ▾străpúngu

TRANSPIRE *vb.* ţipurédz

TRANSFIXED *adj.* (*as with surprise*) limnusít → DUMBFOUNDED ‖ **to stand ~** *Amc:* armân nlóclui, RÉCATAS 37

TRANSFORMATION *s.* prifáţire, prifăţeáre

TRANSMISSION *s.* pitreáţire, pitrieáre

TRANSPORT *s.* ‖ CUVATA 11: (*as of the harvast from the field*) vuzeári

TRANSPORT *vb.* ▾pórtu; (*to make a trip with or as with a cargo*) fac únă cále, arúc únă cále

TRAP *s.* aláţ, avróhe, bátă, căpáne, clápă, yrip, păyídhă, prín-că (*and* príngă), stăpíţă, scăndilíe, scundilíe → BE CAUGHT IN THE ~, SET A ~

TRAP *vb.* ▾acáţ, bag tu mână; apitruséscu; **It's just here that we trapped the snake** Auá apitrusím nipârtica

TRAPDOOR *s.* glăvăníe

TRAPS *s.* catrafúse *f pl*, cărăndíi *f pl*

TRASH *s.* armăsătúri *f pl*; curpăi *f pl*; viclitúrĭ *f pl* ‖ (*junk, rubbish*) ciurúchi, DIARO 259

TRAVAIL *s., vb.* → TOIL, TORMENT

TRAVEL *s.* tăxídhe → JOURNEY

TRAVEL *vb.* alág, tăxidhipséscu

TRAVELLED *adj.* (*of roads*) bătút, imnát ‖ (*experienced, well travelled*) alăgát, BASME 45

TRAVELLER *s.* călătór, călitór

TRAVELLING BAG *s.* sipéte → SUITCASE

TRAVERSE *vb.* (*as a mountain*) trec; ▾pitrúndu, spitrúndu

TRAY *s.* dhíscu, dâblă, távă, tâvă, táblă, távlă, tăvlíe; (*of copper*) (a)pládhă

TRAY *vb.* ▾dizmál, ▾distrám, ▾arúp

TREACHEROUS *adj.* pónir, plan

TREACHERY *s.* tácmă

TREAD *vb.* (*to walk on*) ▾cálcu; **to ~ in the step of** ▾cálcu pi úrma a ‖ (*of birds*) cálcu, DIARO 196

TREAD DOWN *vb.* (*as of a house*) ▾(a)pitruséscu, *N:* (a)putruséscu; ▾aplucuséscu; (*to ~ under one's feet*) ▾zdrúmin, zdroámin, stulcin, stúlţin, cluţéscu

TREADING *s.* călcáre, călcătúră

TREADLE *s.* (*in a loom*) pătíche, pudhuríţă, pudhăríţă; *G:* pârdă-ríţă ‖ *GSus:* pătăríţă, CL 258

TREASON *s.* pridáre, prudáre, prudhusíe, prudhusíre

TREASURE *s.* hăznă (*and* hâz-), (a)yisteáre, chisavró, thisavró, málă

TREASURE

TREASURE *vb.* ‖ **to ~ as the apple of one's eye** voi ca ócĭiĭ din cap, BASME 191

TREASURER *s.* hăznătár

TREASURY *s.* → TREASURE

TREAT *s.* (*wine, coffee, etc.*) mişteáre

TREAT *vb.* (*to offer*) chiräséscu ‖ STERE 39: chirniséscu; (*to regale*) ▼filipséscu, uspitédz; **to ~ smb. as mud** rizil(ips)éscu

TREE *s.* árbur, ábure, oárbări *m*, *dim.* arburíc; *also:* cupáciu, pom; **young ~** fidán, fidánă; **dried ~** xérac ‖ *F:* oárbure, SarD 28; ALIA 40: órbăre, órbire, cupát, cupáţ, ľémnu ‖ DIARO 69: *dim.* arburíciu

TREE-FROG *s.* zool. báfă, broátic, *dim.* bruticúş, *coll.* bruticáme

TREFOIL *s.* trifóľu, tărfóľu ‖ ALIA 84: detelínă, tărăfóľu, ugé

TREMBLE *vb.* trémur, treámbur → SHAKE, SHIVER; **to ~ all over** şeápte-óptu ñi si dúţe → FEEL DITHERY; **to ~ with cold** adár guvójdi, afiriséscu guvójdi, fac guvójdi, taľu guvójdi ‖ HRISTU 32: ntramur

TREMBLING *s.* trémur, trimur, trímură, trimuráre, trimburáre, treámbur

TREMOR *s.* trimuráre → TREMBLING

TREMULOUS *adj.* → TIMID

TRENCH *s.* (a)vláchiu

TRENCHERMAN *s.* ľuftă, mâncătór

TREPIDATION *s.* → TREMBLING

TRESPASS *s.* (*violation*) amărtíe, călcáre

TRESPASS *vb.* (*to sin*) fac păcát; (*to intrude, to encroach*) cálcu

TRIAL *s.* (*test, verification*) cătăpăţíre, dhuchimíe, dhuchimăsíre, próvă; (*in court*) giudicátă, giudéţ, judéţ, dâvă, dăvíe, dăváie; **to bring to ~** scol; (*suffering*) dértă ‖ *Prv:* (*~ in court*) clíşi, CL 42 ‖ *Gop:* judicátâ, judicári, NEIESCU 240

TRIBE *s.* fáră; (*~ of Aromanian shepherds*) fălcáre; (*rare*) pălcáre; (*race, nation*) zintúñe

TRIBULATION *s.* arăiáţă, pusoágă, taxiráte

TRIBUNAL *s.* giudéţ, judéţ, huchimáte, huchiumáte, iuchiuméte, istináfe

TRIBUTARY *s.* (*non-Muslim subject in former Turkey*) arâié, arié

TRIBUTE *s.* (*annual ~ for non-Muslim residents*) haráce, hăráce, haráţumă

TRICE *s.* minút, minútă; *in a ~* tr-únă hópă, tr-un stih di oáră → INSTANT, MOMENT

TRICK *s.* dubăráie, féstă, fheácă, ilée, muraféte, ncălţáre, réngă *or* rénghe, téhne, tirtípe; **monkey ~** măimulắche

TRICK *vb.* ncálţu; ľ-bag cuváta, ľ-bag şáua ‖ PARALLELE 140: trag nă călúpe; BATSARIA 41: **Don't ~ me!** Nu mi-ancálţă!

TRICKERY s. alingíe, avucătlíche, zăvúle, zăvyíe, zăvlíe → TRICK

TRICKLE vb. (to dribble) chic, chícur, chicurédz; (to ~ down in a thin stream, as of a tear) ▾prilíngu

TRICKSTER s. apatión, călupcí, călpuzán, pişichér

TRICKY adj. ariditór, -oáre; calpuzán, -áñ; G: ehlé; mălăyár, minciunós (and mingiunós), plan; (manipulative) ti vínde ş ti-acúmpără; (of a woman) mastórsă; **the ~ vixen** mastórsa di vúlpe

TRICTRAC s. táblă

TRIED adj. (experienced) fricát; **A ~ man knows a lot** Omlu fricát şti múlte

TRIFLE s. bărcudíi f pl; bişíñ di cuc f pl; búfche (lit. 'chicken guts') f pl; burlídzi mbăiráte (lit. 'shells on a string') f pl; căcát; chiritúri f pl; curcubéte or curcubéte di Chirásova f pl; curcuféľi or curcuféxale f pl; lilíce di ureácľe; lişinătúri f pl; mándzale or grándzale-mándzale f pl; mániţi di tâmbări f pl; papardhéle f pl; púfchi f pl; zácate f pl; zăcătúră f sg ‖ **It is no ~** nu giucăreálă, BASME 500; CARAFOLI 24: lúcri di canţivá pl

TRIFLE vb. (to act heedlessly) ▾avín guşturíţăle; **to ~ away one's time, effort, etc.** ñ-cher săpúnea (lit. 'to waste one's soap') ‖ cher milăñle tu cácu, BASME 489

TRIG adj. (stylish) prăpsít; (tidy) chischín, m pl -ñ

TRILL s. frămtúră (and frâm-)

TRIM s. (as of a horse): **in good ~** pri trup

TRIM adj. (neat) chischín, m pl -ñ, f pl -ne

TRIM OFF vb. (to lop) călărséscu, clărséscu, ▾ciuléscu, clădhip-séscu, scrâştéscu, scriştéscu

TRIMESTER s. triminíe

TRIMMED adj. (lopped) scrăştít; (of a vineyard) clărsít; (pared, adorned) adărát, armătusít, isusít

TRINITY s. Triádhă; **The Holy ~** Áyia Triádhă

TRINKET s. minuţáľe → BANGLE

TRIP[1] s. (journey) tăxídhe; (a síngle round or tour on a business errand) cále → MAKE A ~

TRIP[2] s. (a maneuver causing someone to stumble or fall) cheádică, nchidicătúră, purdhucľáuă, pirdhucľáuă, birducľáuă

TRIP vb. ▾ncheádic, bag cheádică, scundipséscu

TRIPLET s. (born at the same date) tirñác

TRIPOD s. (a three-legged metalic stand as for a caldron) pirus-tíe, pirustríe

TRIUMPHANT adj. asvingătór, -oáre; also az-

TRIVET s. pirustríe, pirustíe

TROLLOP s. → HARLOT

TROMP vb. (to beat) ▾bat; (to defeat) (a)mpót; (to tramp, to *march*) ▾cálcu

TROOP *s.* (*collection of people*) urtáuă; tabór, tabóre, tabúre

TROOP THE COLORS *vb.* u scol pandéra

TROOPER *s. coll.* căvălăríe

TROT *s.* (*the sound of a ~*) tróput, aróput, tópur; **at a round ~** *adv.* (*very fast*) tu apáľi, tu únă apálă ‖ *adv.* alága-alága, BASME 54

TROT AWAY *vb.* u adún; **You ~!** Adúnă-u di auá! → GET LOST

TROTH *s.* (*fidelity*) bésă

TROUBLE *s.* biľé, **N:** biľáuă *or* biľáie; *also;* chidére, ghidére, dirín, dirináre, dirnáre, hále; mărăţíñ *m pl* (*lit.* 'thorns'); ndízmă, nivóľe, strimtúră; (*distress*) nvirín; (*effort*) cópus; **Here is my ~** Ia ţe ñ-eáste hálea. **I have more and more ~s** Ghidérile a meále créscu; **in ~** *adj.* ndisít; **We are in ~** Hímu ndisíţ; **to put smb. to the ~** ľ-gioc únă hunére; **This is the greatest ~!** Eásti biľélu a biľeádzlor! ‖ **When they realized that they were in ~** ... Cari u vidzúră streásă ..., BASME 48; pon; ALR 1691: **Let me tell you all my ~** S-ţ-aspún tot pónlu ţe-am; DIARO 154: buclúchi; **They got into big ~** Deadirâ di mari bucluchi

TROUBLE *vb.* ▾mintéscu, ▾stinuhursescu; **to ~ one's mind about smth.** ñ-disíc cáplu

TROUBLED *adj.* (*insane*) cărtít, cărtít di mínte

TROUBLEMAKER *s.* căvyăgí, scandaľár

TROUBLESOME *adj.* căchiós, -oásă

TROUBLESOMELY *adv.* ‖ cu ócľi cripáţ, BASME 388

TROUGH *s.* cópan, cupánă, cupáñe

TROUNCE *vb.* (*to thrash*) ▾bat → BEAT

TROUSER STRAP *s.* stáflă

TROUSERS *s.* pănăvrắchi *f pl;* (*Turkish baggy ~*) şiliváre, *dim.* şilvărúşe; (*short ~*) pături, púturi, putúri *f pl*

TROUT *s. ichth.* péstruv, péstrav, péstruvă, păstrávă, létnă; **N:** córan ‖ **Pls:** cupán, CL 43

TROWEL *s.* mistríe

TRUCE *s.* (*armistice*) paidós; (*relief*) aryíe

TRUCK *s.* → SWAP

TRUCK *vb.* fac trámpă

TRUCKLE *vb.* ▾alás, ▾ncľin, (a)ndúplic ‖ CUNIA 47: hăbinédz

TRUCULENT *adj.* áscur, crud, -dă, -dz, -de; fuvirós, -oásă

TRUDGE ALONG *vb.* ímnu, ñeg, ñérgu, ▾cálcu; arúc jgľoáte (*lit.* 'to throw steps')

TRUE *adj.* (*genuine, authentic*) tamamá, tamaná, alíthhea [th-h], alihiós, alithinós; sayláme *invar.;* **All this is ~** Túte aéste súntu alíthhea; (*of pure origin, speaking of Aromanians*) di sárică; **He is a ~ Aromanian** Eáste di sárică; (*real*) mplin; **Madam, are the words**

you are saying ~? Gréşti mplíne, muľáre? → COME ~

TRUE *vb.* ţivicuséscu

TRUE-BLUE *adj.* pistó, *m pl* -stádz → FAITHFUL, RELIABLE

TRUEHEARTED *adj.* → FAITHFUL

TRULY *adv.* avér, di-avér, alíhea, *N:* alíhira, alíhiura; a cálea-lui; **Either you tell me everything ~, or you won't get rid of me** Ori ñ-aspúñ a cálealui, i nu ai ascăpáre di míne ‖ *Gop:* cadilíhea, GOLAB 223

TRUMPET *s.* buríe, burazáne, trumpétă (*and* trumbétă), turumbétă, rumbétă; **the sound of a ~** turu-tutú → BLOW ONE'S ~

TRUMPETER *s.* trumbicí

TRUNCATE *vb.* ▼şuntédz, ▼taľu

TRUNDLE *vb.* ▼anvărtéscu, ▼arucutéscu

TRUNK *s.* (*of a tree*) trup (→ STUMP); (*chase*) săndúche

TRUSS *s.* ligătúră, stiriusíre

TRUSS *vb.* ▼leg, stiriuséscu, ▼ncărfuséscu → BIND

TRUSS UP BAG AND BAGGAGE *vb.* ñ-adún catrafúsili

TRUST *s.* virisé, virisíe, thărusíre; **on ~** pi virisíe

TRUST *vb.* ▼ncred, ñ-u ľau pri míne, thărăséscu, thăruséscu; (*to believe smb., to trust*) pistipséscu, pristupséscu; **Don't ~ before seing!** Nividzútă s-nu pistupséşti! → BELIEVE, RELY

TRUSTEE *s.* epítrop, **G:** apicúndu

TRUSTEESHIP *s.* epitrupíe

TRUSTWORTHY *adj.* besalâ, *m pl* -ládz; saylámcu; sáicu, -că, -ţi, -ţe; síyur, siyuripsít; **~ man** amanecí

TRUSTY *adj.* (*reliable*) saylám, -ámă, -áñ, -áme

TRUTH *s.* driptáte, ndriptáte, alíthhea [a•líth•hea], talíhea, dhíche, háche; **~ will out** Alíhea éásă tu páde ‖ **~ to say** şi; (*Commentary after the death of an old couple:*) **~ to say, they were very old** Era ş-áúşi múltu, BASME 400; ALR 1396: **Tell me the ~!** Aspú ni-ñ dealíhea!

TRUTHFUL *adj.* cu érgi → HONEST

TRY *vb.* (*to attempt*) ▼bat să, cătăpăţéscu, dau să, ▼dhuchimăsés-cu, mutréscu să; **They tried to calm him down with nice words** Cu graie dúlţi dădeá s lu-apúnă; **He was ~ing to find a piece of wood** Băteá s-áflă vâră lémnu; (*to taste foods or drinks*) gústu, (a)ngús-tu; **to ~ hard** cilihtiséscu, ▼stríngu, ▼sprem; **to ~ one's hardest** mi fac páde; **~ one's strength against smb.** mi misór cu

TRY CONCLUSIONS WITH SMB. *vb.* ‖ ñ-u bag míntea cu; **Why are you trying conclusions with a child?** ti ţi ţ-u badz míntea cu un fi-ciuríc? DIARO 113

TRYING-ON *s.* (*as in a tailor's shop*) dhuchimăsíre, próvă

TRYING *adj.* (*difficult*) greu, greáuă, grei, greále

T-SHIRT *s.* ≈ tricó

TUBERCULAR *s.* ufticós, uhticós

TUBERCULOSIS *s.* óftică, óhtică, ftíse, tíhtă; **touched by** ~ cărtít; **to have** ~ ▾umbărnédz

TUCK *s.* bástă

TUCK *vb.* ▾bag, ▾andúplic ‖ PC: fac nă bástă

TUCK UP *vb.* (*of sleeves*) ▾(a)scumbuséscu, născumbuséscu → ROLL UP

TUCKER OUT *vb.* (*to exhaust*) ▾cúrmu

TUESDAY *s.* márţă ‖ *Amc, Căl, Fu, Hor, Kat, Lep, NPrv, Pdz, Ses:* marţ, B-ARCH 234

TUFT *s.* giugiúfcă, ciuciúlă, fúndă; (*as on the top of a cap*) ciúmă; (~ *of feathers*) búfcă; (*on a bird's head*) cucúľu; **to become** ~**ed** (*as of the tail of an animal*) tufuséscu; (*of forests in spring*) funduséscu; nvirdzăscu

TUFTED *adj.* tufós, -oásă, -óşĭ, -oáse; fundutós, stuf(u)tós; (*of some birds*) cucuľát; cu búfcă → BECOME ~

TUFTY *adj.* (*of hair*) ‖ *GSus:* stăpós, CL 261

TUG *s.* trádzire, trădzeáre

TUG *vb.* ▾trag

TULIP *s.* laléi *f*; spăteádză

TUMBLE *vb.* cad; **to** ~ **down** súrpu, dau di páde; **to** ~ **in** ▾apún, ▾cúlcu, aúrlu núntru; **to** ~ **on smb./smth.** ▾áflu; **to** ~ **out** cad, aúrlu nafoáră; **to** ~ **over** ▾arucutéscu, ▾târculéscu, turculéscu; **to** ~ **to** achicăséscu; **to** ~ **upon smb./smth.** astáľu; **to** ~ **smb. down** *or* **over** arúc áde

TUMBLE: in a ~ *adv.* darmadán

TUMBLEDOWN *adj.* (*dilapidated*) hárval, -lă, -ľ, -le

TUMBLER *s.* (*of a firearm*) ceárcu

TUMID *adj.* umflát, căbărdisít

TUMMY *s.* → BELLY

TUMOR *s.* ciúmbă, giúmbă, giúmcă, júmbă, şúmbă; (*in the leg of a horse*) cărăcúş → SWELLING

TUMULT *s.* vreávă → NOISE

TUMULTUOUS *adj.* alăcít, mintít, túlbur

TUNA FISH *s.* (*salted*) lăchérdhă

TUNE *s.* blândur, ih; (*for violin*) nubéte; (*Turkish* ~) manéi, *pl* manéi

TUNE *vb.* (*a violin, etc.*) curdhuséscu ‖ DIARO 11: curdiséscu

TUNIC: a priest's ~ stiháre

TUNISIAN *adj.* di Tunúză

TUNNEL *s.* gălúme, gălâme, glâme, lăyúme, luyúme

TUQUE *s.* bărbărúsă

TURBAN *s.* cărâm, crâm; (*a* ~-*cloth around one's hat*) pap, şirvét, şirvéte

TURBID *adj.* túrbure → MUDDY

TURBULENT *adj.* dzardzára, *pl* -dzáreañ; minditór, -toáre; năpu-dheáric; sirsém, -émă, -éñ, -éme; sirsén; zevzéc, -écă, -éţĭ, -éţe

TUREEN *s.* cinác, cinácă, cináche → BOWL

TURGID *adj.* umflát, căbărdisít

TURK *s.* túrcu *m*; turxă *or* turcálă *f*; dómnu; *coll.* turcáme, tur-căríe, dumnáme; (*nickname given by Christians*) báfă; **the ~s** Lăiľi ‖ TULLIU 88: carbaerean

TURKEY *s.* Turchíe, Turţeásca; *in ~* tu Turţeásca

TURKEY-COCK *s.* cúrcu, hórhan, misírcu, misiróc, míscu, pilicán

TURKEY-HEN *s.* curcoáñe, hórhană, misírcă, míscă ‖ *GSus:* mísă, CL 256

TURKISH *s.* (*language*) Turţeásca; **He speaks ~ fluently** Turţeásca u zburáşte farsí

TURKISH *adj.* (n)turţéscu, dumnéscu; **to become ~** ▾turchipséscu; **This is a ~ neighborhood** Măhălălu aéstu eáste dumnéscu; **~ army** Turcăríe; *adv.* a-la-Túrca (*ant.* a-la-Fránga)

TURKISH COFFEE *s.* laiu, Scr: négru; **Give me a cup of ~** Dă-ñ un négru; **We've come over to get a cup of ~** Viñím la tíni s-bem un laiu

TURKISH DELIGHT *s.* lucúme

TURMOIL *s.* alăcíre

TURN *s.* arucutíre, turnătúră, şuţâtúră, frâmtúră; (*tric*) hunéră, hunére; **My turn will come** ≈ Va yínă chízda tu cinúşe → TAKE A ~, DO A BAD ~

TURN *vb.* (*to rotate*) ▾nvărtéscu, arucutéscu; (*to twist*) ▾şuţ *or* şuţăscu; (*to wrench*) cluzunéscu; (*to twist, to luxate*) ▾străngul-séscu; (*to reverse, to move around*) ▾tórnu, *F:* tórru; (*to upset, to disorder, to disarrange*) ▾mintéscu; (*to disperse*) arăiéscu; (*to become, to transform*) ▾adár, ▾fac, ▾prifác; (*of a road*) acáţ, apúc; (*of time, age*) ▾úmplu, ▾ncľid, ▾cálcu tu (*followed by a numeral*); **He just was ~ing tewnty-one** Ncľideá tamán únsprăyinghiţľi di añ; **Next spring the boy will ~ nineteen** Prumuveára ficiórlu va călcă tu yínghiţ ‖ HRISTU 28: u turră capu cătă munţ 'turned his head toward the mountains'

TURN ABOUT: to ~ smth. in one's mind *vb.* ▾frimíntu

TURN ALL THE COLORS OF THE RAINBOW → CHANGE COLOR

TURN ASIDE *vb.* ▾abát, părămirséscu

TURN BLUE / BLUISH *vb.* murnéscu, nviniţăscu (*and* nviñi-)

TURN DOWN *vb.* nu căpséscu, nu străxéscu, nu simfunipséscu

TURN GREEN *vb.* nvirdzăscu, nvérdu

TURN IN *vb.* (*to deliver up, to hand over*) fac tislíme

TURN

TURN OFF *vb.* (*to deviate*) ▼abát; (*as a lamp*) astíngu; (*cut off*) cúrmu

TURN ON *vb.* (*of light*) fac luñínă; (*of water*) ▼sălghéscu

TURN ONE'S HANDS TO SMB. *vb.* ▼acáț

TURN OUT *vb.* (*to expel, to evict*) scot, scot nafoáră; (*to renverse*) tórnu anáschila; (*to end*) ▼bitiséscu; (*to become in maturity*) agiúngu, cătăndiséscu (*to become obvious, to prove to be in the result or end*)) ies; es tu páde; **It ~ed out that she was a virgin** Işí feátă

TURN ONE'S STEPS TO *vb.* ľ-u dau cătră

TURN OVER *vb.* (*as meat on a grill*) ▼şuț

TURN PALE *vb.* săhñiséscu

TURN RIGHT / LEFT *vb.* u-ľau andreápta / astânga; ▼frângu andreápta / astânga

TURN ROUND *vb.* ▼şuț

TURN SICK *vb.* (*disgusted*) ñ-víne greáță

TURN SMB.'S HEAD *vb.* ľ-u tórnu míntea

TURN SMB. INTO RIDICULE *vb.* fac ciciór di ľépure

TURN SMB. ROUND ONE'S (LITTLE) FINGER *vb.* ncálțu şi discálțu; gioc pi tăpsíe

TURN SOUR *vb.* ▼acrédz, acréscu

TURN THE CONVERSATION (UP)ON *vb.* adúc di-amínte (trâ); **By dint of talking we turned the conversation on the engagement** Di cuvéndă cuvéndă adúsim di-amínte şi trâ isusíre

TURN TO *vb.* (*to address, to make for*) mi ndréptu cătră

TURN TO/INTO *vb.* ▼fác, prifác; *to ~* **ashes** fac scrum

TURN TOPSY-TURVY *vb.* fac cioáră

TURN UP *vb.* (*to come to light*) ies tu páde; **~ one's mustache** ▼şuț mustățile; **to ~ one's nose** (*as of a pretentious person*) fac năji, ▼strâmbu nárea; **to ~ one's sleeves** ▼(a)scumbuséscu, născumbuséscu; **to ~ one's toes/heels** (*i.e., to die*) li tíndu

TURN UPSIDE DOWN *vb.* arăstórnu → OVERTURN

TURN YELLOW *vb.* gălbinéscu, ngălbinéscu

TURNABOUT *s.* turnătúră

TURNER *s.* strugár

TURNING *s.* (*bend*) curmătúră

TURNING BLUE / BLUISH *s.* vinițâre, nvinițâre (*and* nviñi-), murníre

TURNING POINT *s.* oára a oárăľei

TURPENTINE *s.* trimindínă

TURPITUDE *s.* cătăryăríľe, edepsâzláche

TURTLE *s.* broáscă, cáthă, *N:* cắthă ‖ *GSus:* broáscă cu cásă; *SJos:* broáscă cu sămár; *Av, Prv:* broáscă cu os, CL 39

TURTLE-DOVE *s.* túrtură, turtúră, turtureáuă ‖ *GSus:* túrteză *f;* túrtiuz *m,* CL 262

TUSSLE *vb.* ñ-mâc sămárlu cu; ñ-u dau cu → SCUFFLE

TUTOR *s. G:* apicúndu

TWADDLE *s.* (*silly idle talk*) chiritúri *f pl;* căcát

TWAIN *s.* păreácľe → PAIR

TWEAK *s.* chipináre → PINCH

TWEAK *vb.* ▾chípin

TWELVE *num.* dósprădzaţe, dausprădzaţe, dióspraţi, diósprăs; **I can tell that you are one of those** ~ Ved că hii di dósprăľ

TWENTY *num.* yínghiţ, yíyinţ; **~-one** únsprăyimghiţ (di), únăsprăyinghiţ (di) *and Smr:* yínyiţ únă; **~-two** dósprăyinghiţ *m,* doáuăsprăyinghiţ *f;* **~-three** trésprăyinyiţ, trésprăyiyiţ *or* tresprăyiyit; **a ~-cent coin** *s.* icusár *m* ‖ *M:* yíñiţ, SarD 96; yiyinţ, yiyindzâ, K-D 70 ‖ MERCA 17: **twenty-five** ţisprăyínghiţ; STERGHIU 4: **26 years** şasprăyinghiţ di-añ

TWICE *adv.* doáu-ori ‖ di dáo ori, BASME 37; ndau ori, HRISTU, 43

TWIDDLE *vb.* (*to play negligently with*) mi agióc (cu), şuţ; **to ~ one's mustache** şuţ mustăţile → TWIRL

TWIG *s.* vreáză, vreáje, *pl:* vréşturi *or* vreáşturi; **rot ~** trâhlă; **slender ~** liyăreáuă; **dry ~** gâñe ‖ STERE 14: (*fuel*) *pl.* părpătúri

TWILIGHT *s.* ‖ *Cru:* murgíş, GOLAB 236

TWIN *s.* and *adj.* dzeámin; *also:* bisnát, bliznác, didimárcu **two ~s** doi fraţ dzeámiñ; **a ~ chestnut** căstâñe dzeámină ‖ *LvO, Pdz, Prv, Gard:* diplăţ, *Paleoh, Src:* dhídhimi, B-ARCH 462

TWINE *vb.* → TWIST

TWINGE *s.* dor → PAIN

TWINKLE *vb.* (*of light*) 3 *sg/pl:* bubureádză

TWIRL ONE'S MUSTACHE *vb.* ▾şuţ mustăţile; ▾aruşúţ *or* aruşuţăscu mustáţa

TWIST *s.* aruşuţâre; (*unexpected development*) turnătúră

TWIST *vb.* şuţ; ▾aruşúţ, aruşuţăscu

TWIST ABOUT *vb.* ▾turculéscu, târculéscu

TWISTED *adj.* şuţât, (a)ncârligát, anvârligát, strâmbu; (**of leggs**) ciurigát; *iron.* adréptu ca fúnea tu tástru (*lit.* 'as straight as a piece of rope in a bag') ‖ TULLIU 55: cănghiľát

TWISTING *s.* şuţâre, aruşuţâre, strâmbáre; (*of the body*) târculíre

TWIT *vb.* ▾arâd (di), ▾nţap (*and* ndzp), ▾schin

TW *s.* zmuldzeáre, zmúldzire; *vb.* ▾zmúlgu → THROB

TWITTER *s.* ţíţir-víţir, ţíur

TWO *s.* (*a playing card*) duiár *or* dúe, *art.* dúea, DIARO 413

TWO *num.* doi *m;* dáuă *or* doáuă *f;* ~ **by** ~ doi câti doi; **between the**

TWO-FACED

~ of us ntră noi doĭi; **the ~ rosy apples** dáule meáre giuleabíi;
They returned at ~ o'clock S-turnáră tu doáuăle

  TWO-FACED *adj.* → HYPOCRITE
  TWO-PENCE *s.* ≈ duiár; dhyeáră, *pl* dhyeri
  TWO-TIME *vb.* ▾ampíhiur, bag cuváta
  TYPE *s.* turlíe → KIND, SORT
  TYPHUS *s. med.* buíţă, ñáţă, tif
  TYPOGRAPHER *s.* tipuyráf
  TYPOGRAPHY *s.* tip
  TYRANNICALLY *adv.* ca vâră bulubáş
  TYRANNIZE *vb.* ▾tirănséscu
  TYRANNY *s.* tirăníe
  TYRANT *s.* ghilát, ghiľát, sufarí, suvarí, tirán
  TYRO *s.* múcio *invar.*

U

  UDDER *s.* údzăre, **G:** údzir, **Cru:** údzur; **K:** údzăr, GOLAB 257
  UGLIFICATION *s.* uruţâre, urţâre
  UGLIFIED *adj.* ur(u)ţât, -ţâtă, -ţâţ, -ţâte
  UGLIFY *vb.* uruţéscu, urâ-
  UGLINESS *s.* uruteáţă, urâţáme, slutíche
  UGLY *adj.* urút, urât; taxés, -xésă, -xéşĭ, -xése; (*formless*) bi-cimsâz, *m pl* -sâjĭ, *f pl* -sâze; **very ~** si-l beai tu hrup; **as ~ as sin** urút ca lóclu, urút ca fáţa lóclui
  ULCER *s.* pleágă, yiră, (a)ránă
  ULEMA *s.* (*Moslem priest*) imám
  ULTIMATE *adj.* (*last*) coáda *invar.* (*lit. 'the tail'*)
  UMBILICUS *s.* buríc, băríc, **N:** bric
  UMBRAGE *s.* úmbră → TAKE ~
  UMBRELLA *s.* umbrélă
  UNABLE *adj.* ni-ácşu, náxu; anésustu, -suşţâ, -suşte; anícan
  UNACCEPTABLE *adj.* ‖ DIARO 7: ti loári tu ureácľi
  UNACCUSTOMED *adj.* ni-nviţát
  UNAFRAID *adj.* ni-aspăreát, ni-fricuít
  UNAMBIGUOUSLY *adv.* cum mi vez şi cum ti ved
  UNASHAMED *adj.* ni-aruş(i)nát
  UNASSUMING *adj.* (*modest*) tápin, tapinós, -oásă ‖ DIARO 134: (*soft, low-keyed; ant.* **strenuous**) plahúrcu (*rare*)

UNATTENDED *adj.* síngur

UNATTRACTIVE *adj.* slut → UGLY

UNAVAILING *adj.* áhristu, -stă, -şţâ, -ste

UNAWARES *adv.* (*unexpectedly*) aróndu, aniórihta, apándica, pri ni-aştiptáte

UNBAKED *adj.* crud, -dă, -dz, -de; gľiciu, *f sg/pl* -ce, *m pl* glici; yľiciu; ~ **bread** plivúc, pluvúc; *Gop:* gliţimácă

UNBALANCED *adj.* (*mentally disordered*) ni-aştirnát, ni-aştirnút

UNBAPTIZED *adj.* ni-pătidzát

UNBEARABLE *adj.* ni-arăvdát; **This heat is** ~ Nu s-trádzi căldúra aéstă; ~ **person** schínu ntr-ócľi (*lit.* 'a thorn in the eye')

UNBEATEN *adj.* ni-bătút

UNBECOMING *adj.* ni-uidisít, ni-aştirnát, zdángăn

UNBELIEVABLE *adj.* (*extraordinary, hard to express*) ‖ CUVATA 8: ţi nu să spúni

UNBIASED *adj.* driptátic

UNBIND *vb.* ▾dizlég, ▾disfác

UNBLEMISHED *adj.* curát

UNBLENDED *adj.* (*simple, pure*) munát, sadéu; schet, *f* schétă

UNBLUSHING *adj.* → SHAMELESS

UNBOILED *adj.* (*not boiled or insufficiently boiled*) ni-hértu

UNBOLT *vb.* trag sírtul

UNBORN *adj.* ni-fáptu, -ptă, -pţâ, -pte

UNBOSOM *vb.* → REVEAL

UNBOUND *adj.* (*not tethered, as of a dog*) dizligát

UNBOUNDEDLY *adv.* făr di nisáfe

UNBRAID *vb.* (*of hair*) ▾displătéscu ‖ *Cru:* dispăltéscu, GOLAB 212

UNBUCKLE *vb.* ▾disţíngu

UNBUCKLED *adj.* disţímtu, -mtă, -mţâ, -mte

UNBUCKLING *s.* (*of a belt*) disţíndzire

UNBURDEN *vb.* ▾ñişurédz, lişurédz, ▾efculipséscu; (~ *one's heart*) ▾discárcu ‖ alúmbu, DIARO 384

UNCANNY *adj.* (*as in tales, usu. of a horse*) căntát (*lit.* 'en-chanted')

UNCAUGHT *adj.* ni-acăţát

UNCEASINGLY *adv.* nicurmát; *also:* ápă, dipriúnă, dzúua ş noáptea, fâră acúmtin, fâră acumtináre, fâră (a)răpás, fâră (a)ripás, fâră (a)rupás, índa, ni-păpsít, ni-păxít, picná, únă, únă-únă, zâr-zâr tútă dzúa, BASME 38 (*lit.* **'zâr-zâr all day long'**)

UNCERTAIN *adj.* ni-síyur → DOUBTFUL

UNCERTAINTY *s.* ni-siyurlíche

UNCHANGEABLE *adj.* ni-minát

UNCHANGED *adj.* ni-minát

UNCHANGING

UNCHANGING *adj.* ni-minát

UNCHASTE *adj.* dămusít, lichisít

UNCIVIL *adj.* disgrădít → RUDE

UNCIVILIZED *adj.* pădurís → RUDE, WILD

UNCLAD *adj.* dispuľát, dizlăxít

UNCLE *s.* lálă, *pl* lălăñ; (*brother of one's father or father-in-law*), pára-cúscru; (*senior male*) pap, prezvít; (*term of consideration for a male*) bíro, *voc.* o bíro, vre bíro, *or* vre biro-m; *iron.* áide, bíro curcubétă!

UNCLEAN *adj.* ni-curát

UNCLEANED *adj.* ni-curát

UNCLEAR *adj.* alăcít

UNCLOSED *adj.* ni-ncľís

UNCLOTHE *vb.* ▼dizvéscu, ▼guléscu

UNCLOTHED *adj.* dizviscút, dizlăxít

UNCLOUDED *adj.* curát

UNCOMBED *adj.* ‖ dischiptinát, DIARO 384

UNCOMELINESS *s.* slutíche

UNCOMFORTA0BLE *adj.* (*irritating*) paľu ntr-ócľi (*lit.* 'a straw in the eye')

UNCOMFORTED *adj.* ni-păriyursít

UNCOMMUNICATIVE *adj.* ursúz, -úză, -újĭ, -úze

UNCONCEALED *adj.* disсľís, tu fáţă

UNCONCERN *s.* alăsáre, adhyeafuríe

UNCONCERNED *adj.* adhyeáfur

UNCONCERNEDLY *adv.* cu căciúla scoásă, BASME 405

UNCONSOLED *adj.* ni-păriyursít

UNCOOKED *adj.* crud, -údă, -udz, -úde

UNCORK *vb.* ▼distúp

UNCORKING *s.* distupáre

UNCOUNTABLE *adj.* ni-numirát

UNCOUTH *adj.* (*awkward*) zérvu, -rvă, -ryi, -rve; astângu; (*rude*) ni-ciuplít

UNCOUTHLY *adv.* huryiteáşte

UNCOVER *vb.* ▼dicoápir, ▼dizvăléscu

UNCOVERED *adj.* dizvălít, ni-acupirít ‖ HRISTU 43: zdivilit (*sic*)

UNCOVERING *s.* discupiríre

UNCTION *s.* (*in religion rituals*) efhéle, efchéľu, hrísmă; **extreme ~** dhyeávase

UNDAMAGED *adj.* ni-cârtít

UNDAUNTED *adj.* ni-aspăreát

UNDECIDED **adj.** induít, andáulea

UNDECIDEDLY *adv.* ‖ (*of oral requests, answers or statements*) cu giumitát di gúră (*lit.* *'with half mouth'*), PARALLELE 135

UNDEFEATED *adj.* ni-frâmtu, ni-azvímtu, ni-bătút

UNDER prep. sum, sun, su, pri sun (DDA: 1148), pri su, pi; **~ the stars** pi steále ‖ ALR 1352: **~ my very eyes** diníntea mea

UNDER NO CIRCUMSTANCES pa-pa-pa; ba-ba-ba ‖ dip-di-dip, DIARO 241

UNDERBAKED BREAD *s.* cľiciu, gľici, yľiciu; pâne crúdă

UNDERDONE *adj.* ni-cóptu, ni-hértu

UNDEREDUCATED *adj.* ni-nviţát

UNDERESTIMATE *vb.* arúc náparti

UNDERESTIMATION *s.* arcári náparti

UNDERGO *vb.* (*to experience, to go through*) trec prit

UNDERGROUND CANAL *s.* ghiríz *or* ghiríze

UNDERHAND *adj.* paranóm (*f sg/ pl, m pl absent in the* DDA) ascúmtalui, afuríşalui

UNDERHANDEDLY *adv.* ascumtá, (pi-)ascúmtalui; furíş, acrifá

UNDERMINE *vb.* ‖ BELIMACE 60: lu sap timéľu a

UNDERNEATH *adj. and adv.* din ghios, dighiós, di prighiós

UNDERNOURISHED *adj.* ni-măcát ‖ BATSARIA 76: nihărnít

UNDERRATE *vb.* arúc náparti

UNDER-SHERIFF *s.* subáşi

UNDERSHIRT *s.* tricó

UNDERSTAND *vb.* achicăséscu, acăchi-, apucupséscu, ▼(a)duchéscu, acúmpăr, **F:** bag tu córnu, ľau, ľau di urécľi, ñ-afeátă cáplu, ñ-afeátă míntea, ñ-acáţă míntea, ñ-táľe, ñ-táľe cáplu; **to ~ a foreign language** li-aroámig, li-arúmig, (*rare*) ▼nţâlég; ▼príndu; **You have not understood us well** Nu nă prínseşi ghíne; **to ~ quickly** ľau n yíe; **I do not ~** Nu-ñ ľa cáplu; Nu-ñ táľe cófa; Nu li bag tu cófă ‖ **N:** alég, CAPIDAN 151; **Have you understood?** Loaş di hăbari? HRISTU 32

UNDERSTANDING *s.* (*comprehension*) achicăsíre, acăchi-, chicazmó; (*harmonious relationship*) búnă treácă

UNDERSTATE ONE'S AGE *vb.* (*trying or as if trying to look younger*) mi túndu cu noátiñľi

UNDERTAKE *vb.* mi leg (să); **to ~ the risks and dangers** dăvrănséscu

UNDERTAKER *s.* (*at burials*) muleáftă

UNDERTAKING *s.* (*promise, pledge*) ligămíntu, tăxíre

UNDERWEAR *s.* alăxămíntu; (*for Turkish women*) firigé, firigée

UNDERWEIGHT *s.* ixíche, xíche

UNDERWEIGHT *adj.* firisít

UNDERWORLD *s.* lúmea nántă, éta di nsus; (*adverbially*) tu éta-alántă, tu alántă étă lúmea lántă, BASME 5; lúmea ţealántă, BASME 476; lúmea di ghios, BASME 158, éta di dighiós, BASME 265

UNDERWRITE *vb.* ▼ipuyrăpséscu

UNDESERVING

UNDESERVING *adj.* ni-ácşu

UNDESERVEDLY *adv.* haráme; **I eat bread ~** Haru mâc pânea

UNDISTURBED *adj.* ni-cărtít, ni-pirăxít

UNDO *vb.* ▾disfác

UNDO ONE'S BELT *vb.* ▾dizbrânédz

UNDOING *s.* disfáre, disſáţire, disfăţeáre

UNDOUBTEDLY *adv.* bezbilé; fără-di-áltă; cum mi vedz ş-cum ti ved

UNDRESS *vb.* ▾dizvéscu, ▾dizlăxéscu ‖ *Cru:* ▾dispóľu, GOLAB 212

UNDRESSED *adj.* ni-ndréptu, ni-nviscút, dizviscút, dizlăxít, gol, goálă, goľ, goále; ALIA 177: dispuľát

UNDRESSING *s.* dizvişteáre, dizveáştire, dizlăxíre

UNDULATION *s.* undáre

UNEARTH *vb.* dizgróp

UNEASINESS *s.* (*regret, distress*) (a)ngúsă, ghiúce, sicléte, săcléte; (*difficulty*) strimturáre; (*timidity*) andirisíre; (*pain*) nivóľe

UNEASY *adj.* antirsít (*and* andirsít); **to become ~** mi păleáşte peána

UNEMPLOYED *adj.* aryó *invar.*; ni-acáţát, rébil; cu sfârlícilu dinanúmirea (*lit. '[to go] with the churn paddle on one's shoulder,' initially said of unemployed shepherds*)

UNEMPLOYMENT *s.* ni-lúcru

UNENDURABLE *adj.* ni-arăvdát

UNENLIGHTENED *adj.* ni-nviţát

UNEQUALLED *adj.* cum soţ nu áre → MATCHLESS

UNEXPECTED *adj.* ni-aştiptát, éxafnu, ni-apăndixít

UNEXPECTEDLY *adv.* pri niaştiptáte; ni únă, ni áltă; a(ni)pándiha, dinapándiha, áxafna → SUDDENLY

UNEXPERIENCED *adj.* ni-fricát → IMMATURE

UNEXPLORED *adj.* ni-călcát, nizgruñít

UNFAIR *adj.* ni-dréptu, -eáptă, -pţâ, -eápte → UNJUST

UNFAIRLY *adv.* ádhica (*and* ádica), haráme

UNFAITHFUL *adj.* ápistu, -stă, -şţâ, -ste; dinsâz, *m pl* -âjĭ, *f pl* -âze; pabés, -ésă (*sic*), -éşĭ, -ése; prudhót, -ótă (*sic*), -óţ, -óte

UNFASTEN *vb.* (*to set free*) ▾sălghéscu

UNFAVORABLE *adj.* anápudh; (*as of a wind*) laiu, térsu

UNFEELING *adj.* ni-durút

UNFEIGNED *adj.* dişcľís, curát

UNFINISHED *adj.* ni-bitisít, ni-burít

UNFITTING *adj.* (*unsuitable*) ni-uidisít

UNFOLD *vb.* (*as of a fabric*) arăschirédz

UNFOLDING *s.* arăschiráre

UNFORSEEN *adj.* éxafnu

UNFORTUNATE *adj.* jilít → WRETCHED

UNFRIENDLY *adj.* dușmănós, -oásă; dușmănéscu, -neáscă

UNFRIENDLINESS *s.* hăseanlíche → HOSTILITY

UNGLUE *vb.* ▼dizlăchéscu

UNGODLY *adj.* pângân, **G:** păngâr

UNGOVERNABLE *adj.* → UNRULY

UNGRATEFUL *adj.* aháristu, *m pl* -rișțâ, *f pl* -riste

UNGUENT *s.* (*smear*) grăsíme; *med.* alifíe, alfíe, chiralfíe

UNHANDY *adj.* (*lacking in skill or dexterity*) angricós, -oásă; astângu, -ngă, -ndzi, -ndze; zérvu, -rvă, -ryi, -rve

UNHAPPY *adj.* buisít, cacurízic, curbisít, déspir, di cătráne, di chísă, lăít, nvápsu, -psă, -pși, -pse; ânvupsít, ni-arâs, oárfăn, stuhinát → WRETCHED, MAKE ~

UNHARMED *adj.* ni-cârtít, ni-pliguít

UNHEALTHY *adj.* zăbún → SICK

UNHEARD-OF *adj.* ni-avdzât, făr-di-sóț, ni-vidzút ‖ ți nu s-áre spúsă, BASME 173

UNHINGE *vb.* (*to confuse*) ▼glăréscu, ▼nglăréscu

UNH *vb.* ▼sălăghéscu

UNHOBBLE *vb.* (*to unfetter, as of horses*) discheádic

UNHOBBLING *s.* dischidicáre

UNHOOK *vb.* discálnu, dispíndzur

UNHOOKING *s.* dispindzuráre

UNHORSE *vb.* (*to dislodge from or as if from a horse*) súrpu di pi cal

UNHURRIED *adj.* (*serious, considerate*) aștirnát

UNHURT *adj.* ni-cârtít

UNIFY *vb.* ▼fac únă

UNIMPORTANT *adj.* (*as of a holiday*) lișór, -oáră

UNINHABITED *adj.* érmu, -rmă, -rñi, -rne

UNINJURED *adj.* ni-cârtít, ni-pliguít, sustá

UNITE *vb.* (*as by marriage*) ▼ndzeámin, ▼ndzimănédz

UNINTELLIGENT *adj.* glar → STUPID

UNINTERRUPTED *adj.* (*as of a noise*) nităcút

UNINTERRUPTED *adj.* ni-curmát

UNINTERRUPTEDLY *adv.* → UNCEASINGLY

UNINTERRUPTEDNESS *s.* ni-curmáre, ni-cuntiníre, ni-păpsíre

UNINVITED *adj.* ni-acľimát

UNION *s.* (*association*) suțátă, sinastrufíe

UNITE *vb.* (*to coalesce into one*) ▼mi fac únă

UNIVERSE *s.* cózmu → WORLD

UNIVERSAL *adj.* catholichíe

UNJUST *adj.*, **-LY** *adv.* ni-dréptu, strâmbu, *m pl* -nghi; ádhic

UNJUSTNESS

UNJUSTNESS *s.* strâmbătáte

UNKEMPT *adj.* discăceát, ni-chiptinát

UNKEPT *adj.* ni-ţânút

UNKIND *adj.* ágru, áscur; scliró *invar.*

UNKNOWN *adj.* ni-cunuscút, ni-ştiút ‖ HRISTU 7: ni cănăscut

UNLACE *vb.* ▾dizlég

UNLADE *vb.* ▾discárcu

UNLATCH *vb.* trag sírtul

UNLAWFUL *adj.* para-nóm

UNLEARNED *adj.* ni-nviţát, ni-fricát

UNLEASH *vb.* ▾dizlég

UNLEAVENED *adj.* (*of dough*) ni-viñít; (*of bread*) ftazmítcu, lip-sunévat

UNLEAVENED BREAD *s.* ádzâmă, ázimă, afreáţă, túrtă

UNLETTERED *adj.* ni-ştiút → IGNORANT

UNLIKE *adj.* (*different, differently*) aľúmtrea(lui), áltă sóie, áltă turlíe, áltă lăghíe → BE ~

UNLIMBER *vb.* (*to prepare for action*) ▾ndreg

UNLOAD *vb.* ▾discárcu; (*of a gun*) amín ‖ HRISTU 6: zdicarcu (*sic*), 1 pl zdăcărcăm, HRISTU 57

UNLOADED *adj.* discărcát; (*of a gun*) aminát

UNLOADING *s.* discărcáre, discătúră; (*of a gun*) amináre

UNLOCK *vb.* dişcľiédz

UNLOCKING *s.* dişcľiiáre

UNLOOSE *vb.* ▾sălăghéscu, ▾ dizlég

UNLOVED *adj.* ni-vrút, ni-durút

UNLUCKY *adj.* órbu, oárbă, órghi, oárbe; átih, cu tíhe láie, cu tíhe oárbă; 3 *sg:* áre tíhe aráuă ‖ buclucgí *m*, -gioáñi *f*, DIARO 154

UNMAKING *s.* disfáţire, disfăţeáre

UNMANLY *adj.* fricós, -oásă, -óşi, -oáse; bişinós, căcătós

UNMANNERLINESS *s.* huryeátă

UNMANNERLY *adj.* păduríş → RUDE

UNMARRIED *adj.* (*of a man*) ni-nsurát; (*of a woman*) ni-măritátă, ni-mărtátă ‖ nincurunát, BASME 205; **Amc:** xóltu, PADIOTU 152

UNMASK *vb.* ▾scot tu páde

UNMATCHED *adj.* 1. (*odd*) făr-di-soţ ‖ BATSARIA 60: nu-ám preácľe; (*inappropriate*) ni-uidisít ‖ RÉCATAS 50: (*inappropriate*) ca púşca cu-áilu (*lit. 'as vinegar with garlic'*)

UNMERCIFUL *adj.* ni-ñilós

UNMINDFUL *adj.* bóşcu

UNMIXED *adj.* curát, munát, sadéu, schet

UNMOVED *adj.* → FIRM, RESOLUTE

UNNAIL *vb.* (*to remove smth. nailed*) ▾scărfiséscu ‖ CUNIA 69: discărfuséscu, discărfiséscu

UNNATURAL *adj.* (*rare*) afísic

UNNECESSARY *adj.* áhristu, -stă, -şţâ, -ste → USELESS

UNNOTICED *adj.* ni-părătirsít

UNNUMBERED *adj.* ni-numirát

UNOBSERVED *adj.* ni-părătirsít

UNOCCUPIED *adj.* ni-acăţát

UNPACK *vb.* ▾disfác

UNPAID *adj.* ni-plătít, ni-păltít

UNPARALLELED *adj.* făr-di-soţ

UNPASTE *vb.* dizlăchéscu, dizlichéscu

UNPERCEIVED *adj.* ni-părătirsít

UNPITYING *adj.* ni-ñilós, -oásă, -oşĭ, -oáse

UNPLAIT *vb.* ▾displ̦ătéscu, dispăltéscu, ▾displéc

UNPLAITING *s.* displătíre; displicáre

UNPLEASANT *adj.* salchíu; (*as of an ugly dream*) văpsít

UNPOLISHED *adj.* păduríş → RUDE

UNPOLLUTED *adj.* curát

UNPRECEDENTED *adj.* ni-vidzút, ni-avdzât ‖ ţi nu s-áre spúsă, BASME 173

UNPREDICTABLE *adj.* (*as of the market*) térsu, -rsă, -rşi, -rse

UNPREPARED *adj.* ni-ndréptu

UNPRETENTIOUS *adj.* tápin → HUMBLE

UNPRINCIPLED: ~ **person** nu ţâne păreásiñ ('He/she does not observe fast days')

UNPROCESSED *adj.* ni-adrát

UNPROFITABLE *adj.* nu áre scuteáre

UNPROTECTED *adj.* ni-apărát

UNPUNISHED *adj.* ni-pidhipsít

UNPURPOSEFULLY *adv.* ‖ tră oáuă aróşă, BASME 165 (*lit.* 'for the sake of red eggs')

UNQUESTIONABLY *adv.* fără di áltă, sígur, síyur, sáicu

UNQUIET *adj.* (*restless*) asiyúriftu, pirídhrum, ni-mpáde (*and* ni-mbáde)

UNRAVEL *vb.* ▾disfác, ▾dişúţ, ▾strămédz; (*to disentangle, to elucidate*) ĺ-dau di fúndu ‖ (*as a fabric*) dizmál, CAPIDAN 146; disprufiĺédzu, DIARO 386

UNREASONABLE *adj.* ni-minduít, glăréscu, huţăscu

UNRELIABLE *s.* (*of people*) nu adári strúngă cu nâs (*lit.* 'You cannot run a sheep farm with him'); nu-áre bésă; ni-síyur

UNREMITTING *adj.* ni-acumtinát

UNREMITTINGLY *adv.* únă-únă, índa, tótna

UNREQUESTED *adj.* ni-ntribát; **to speak** ~ zburăscu ni-ntribát,

UNRESPONSIVE

zburắscu pri niântribátă
UNRESPONSIVE *adj.* tăcút, nguvát
UNREST *s.* alăcíre
UNRIGHTEOUS *adj.* ni-dréptu, -eáptă, -épţâ, -eápte; strâmbu, -bă, -nghi, -mbe
UNRIGHTEOUSNESS *s.* strămbeátic
UNRIPE *adj.* (*fig.*, *of children or young people*) ghivréc → IMMATURE ‖ ALR 112: (*of Indian corn*) yiu
UNRIPPING *s.* disfăţeáre, disfáţire
UNRUFFLED *adj.* (*poised and serene*) sirín, stăpuít
UNRULY *adj.* (*turbulent*) năpudheáric, sirsém, sirsén; (*as of a horse*) uchealíu → INTRACTABLE
UNSAFE *adj.* ni-síyur
UNSALTED *adj.* ni-sărát, ni-nsărát, blánav, blániv
UNSAVORY *adj.* blánav, -avă, -ayĭ, -ave → MAKE ~
UNSCATHED *adj.* ni-cârtít
UNSCHOOLED *adj.* ni-nviţát; órbu, oárbă, órghi, oárbe
UNSCREW *vb.* ‖ dizvidhuséscu, DIARO 390
UNSEAL *vb.* (*as an envelope*) dizvuluséscu, dizvuliséscu
UNSEASONABLY *adj.* achéryiu, *m pl* -ryi, *f sg/pl* -rye
UNSEEMLY *adj.* abráșcu, -șcă, -ști, -ște; pânghiós [•ǵós], -oásă; ni-uidisít [ni•uĭ•]; zdángan
UNSEEN *adj.* ni-vidzút, áfan, áfandu; cáĭpe *invar.*
UNSELFISH *adj.* giumértu, -rtă, -rţâ, -rte → GENEROUS
UNSETTLE *vb.* (*to disturb, to upset, as things in a room*) ▾alúmtu, ▾fac cioáră
UNSETTLED *adj.* ni-aștirnát, ni-aștirnút, alăcít, cutulburát; andáulea *invar.*; (*as of a debt*) ni-plătít; (*not occupied by settlers*) ni-acăţát
UNSEW *vb.* (*to undo sewn*) ▾discós
UNSEWING *s.* discusătúră, discuseáre
UNSEWN *adj.* discusút
UNSHACKLED *adj.* sălăghít, dizligát
UNSHOD *adj.* discúlţu, -lţă, -lţâ, -lţe; xípoltu, -ltă, -lţâ, -lte
UNSHOE *vb.* (*a horse*) ▾discálţu
UNSHOEING *s.* discălţáre
UNSIGHTLY *adj.* urât, urút
UNSIGHTLINESS *s.* slutíche → UGLINESS
UNSKILLED *adj.* ageamí(u), ageamít, ni-fricát, ni-nviţát
UNSKILLFUL *adj.* cu téhnea aráuă
UNSOCIABLE *adj.* asbóristu, -stă, -șţâ, -ste; ursúz, -úză, -újĭ, -úze; ursúscu, -scă, -șţâ, -ște; pahóm, pahómen, munólcu, *G:* manóleac

UNSOILED *adj.* curát, ni-stipsít

UNSOPHISTICATED *adj.* (*of people*) apló, ageamít

UNSOUND *adj.* (*shak*) hárval; (*depraved, rotten*) geadíu

UNSPARING *adj.* (*ruthless*) ni-ñilós; (*profuse*) giumértu

UNSPEAKABLE *adj.* (*detestable*) cacurízic

UNSPOILED *adj.* curát, ni-stipsít

UNSPOTTED *adj.* curát, ni-stipsít

UNSTABLE *adj.* (*shaky*) hárval; nu sta pri úná

UNSTAINED *adj.* → UNSPOTTED

UNSTICK *vb.* ‖ dizlichéscu, dizlâchéscu, DIARO 395

UNSTRING *vb.* ▾disbáir

UNSTRINGING *s.* disbãiráre

UNSUBMISSIVENESS *s.* ni-ascultáre

UNSUCCESSFUL *adj.* (*of people*) fâră cătúná; (*of a project, of an attempt*) căcát

UNSUITABILITY *s.* ni-uidisíre

UNSUITABLE *adj.* ni-uidisít

UNSUITED *adj.* ni-uidisít

UNSURE *adj.* ni-síyur

UNSURPASSED *adj.* ni-ntricút; (*of a horse*) ni-astăľát

UNSWATHE *vb.* ▾disfáş

UNSWATHING *s.* (*as of an infant*) disfăşeáre

UNSWEPT *adj.* ni-arnít

UNTANGLE *vb.* ▾discáciu, ▾dizlég

UNTAUGHT *adj.* ni-nviţát

UNTHANKFUL *adj.* aháristu

UNTHINKABLE *adj.* ni-avdzât, adhínaton

UNTHREAD *vb.* ▾disbáir

UNTHREADING *s.* disbãiráre

UNTIDILY *adv.* áţala-máţala, átacta

UNTIDINESS *s.* ambăturláre, ambătruláre

UNTIDY *adj.* áţala-máţala *invar.;* alócut, *G:* pálaz

UNTIE *vb.* ▾dizlég, ▾disfác

UNTIL *prep.* pănă la, pân la, pân tu, pân di, pănă cându, trâşi; ~ **now** pănă tru hópa aístă; **Let's run away ~ it is too late** S-fudzím pân-avém oáră; **We waited for you ~ last evening** Trâşi aseáră ti aştiptăm; (*as far as*) ~ **the end of the world** pănă tu ascápitlu a lóclui; **Wait ~ fall** şceáptă pân di toámnă

UNTIMELY *adj.* áchira, achéryiu; (*premature*) timpuríu

UNTOLD *adj.* (*numberless*) ni-numirát; (*vast*) tímtu; (*unheard-of*) ni-avdzât

UNTOUCHED *adj.* (*unharmed*) sustá; (*not plundered*) ni-călcát; ni-pirăxít

UNTRAINED *adj*. ni-nviţát, ni-ştiút, ni-fricát

UNTRAVELLED *adj*. (*of people*) ni-imnát; (*of roads or areas*) ni-călcát

UNTRIED *adj*. (*not tested*) ni-dhuchimăsít

UNTROD *adj*. ni-călcát

UNTROUBLED *adj*. siríń → STILL

UNTRUE *adj*. ápistu, -stă, -şţâ, -ste; imansâz, -sâjĭ, -sâze

UNTRUTH *s*. tácmă

UNTRUTHFUL *adj*. cálpu, -lpă, -lchi, -lpe; cálpic; plan

UNTRUSTWORTHY *adj*. ápistu, -stă, -şţâ, -ste → UNFAITHFUL

UNTWIST *vb*. ▼dişúţ, ▼distórcu

UNTWISTING *s*. dişuţâre

UNUSED *adj*. ni-nviţát ‖ CUNIA 206: ni-aryăsít

UNUSUAL *adj*. (a)rár

UNVEIL *vb*. ▼dizvăléscu; (*reveal oneself*) ▼aspún

UNVEILED *adj*. dizvălít

UNWASHED *adj*. ni-lat; **He is ~** Lu-alímsiră cătúşile (*lit*. 'Cats have licked him')

UNWEARIED *adj*. ni-curmát

UNWELL *adj*. lânţid; **to feel ~** atihiséscu; mi-arúc a arắului → SICK

UNWEPT *adj*. ‖ PC: ni-plâmtu

UNWHOLESOME *adj*. zñiseáric

UNWIELDY *adj*. angricós, -oásă

UNWILLINGLY *adv*. di pristanéu

UNWISE *adj*. glăréscu, -eáscă, -éşţâ, -éşti

UNWORTHY *adj*. ni-ácşu

UNWOUNDED *adj*. ni-pliguít

UNWRAP *vb*. ▼disfác

UNWRINKLE *vb*. ▼disufruţéscu

UNYOKE *vb*. dizgiúg

UNYOKING *s*. dizgiugáre

UP *adj*. (*out of bed*) sculát

UP *adv*. nsus, nsus; **~ and down** ≈ *F*: pi-aroá, pi-arcó ‖ DIARO 334: **What's up?** Ţi cúrâ? → BE ~ TO

UP *interj*. (*in a traditional Aromanian game*) ţícna

UP STREAM *adv*. di(n)ghiós, dipri(n)ghiós

UP TO *prep*. pân di; **so that I fly ~ the clouds** ca si-azbór pân-di niór; **The water was ~ the neck** Ápa eará pân di gúşe; **~ the chin** ≈ până di uréčʹi → BE ~

UP TO NOW / PRESENT *adv*. până tóra, pân tru hópa aístă

UP TO THE SCRATCH *adj*., *adv*. (*in good shape, as of a horse*) pri trup

UPBRAID *vb.* → SCOLD

UPBRINGING *s.* (a)creáştire, prăxíre, tirbié, tirbiéte

UPCHUCK *vb.* → VOMIT

UPEND *vb.* ▾alín

UPGRADE *vb.* ▾créscu, ▾análţu

UPGROWTH *s.* creáştire, crişteáre

UPHEAVAL *s.* arăsturnáre, buzgúne, mintitúră

UPHILL *adv.* nsus; (*on a road*) stră cále (*ant.* sum cále) ‖ Epirus: mblai, CAPIDAN 501; **Cru:** anífurlu, GOLAB 199

UPHOLD *vb.* (*as against an opponent*) ▾ţân, ▾ndoápir

UPLAND ≈ sus; sus tu múnţâ

UPLANDER *s.* suşán (*ant.* giosán)

UPLIFT *s.* sculáre

UPLIFT *vb.* ▾ascól → RISE

UPON *prep.* pri; ~ *God!* Pri Dumnidzắu! mi giur! ‖ BATSARIA 49, 57, 74: pri păni! (*lit. 'upon bread'*); ~ **my word!** ţă dau zbórlu, BATSARIA 1

UPON DEMAND → DEMAND

UPPER *adj.* di prisúpră; ~ **leather** (*in a shoe*) căpútă

UPPISH *adj.* → ARROGANT

UPRIGHT *adj.* (*perpendicular, vertical, standing*) mbróstu, -oástă, -óşţâ, -oáste; (*morally ~*) nămuzlí; ímnă cu zíya n brâu (*i.e., goes with a yardstick under his belt, as if ready to measure in order to be impartial*)

UPRIGHTNESS *s.* (*moral rectitude*) tiñíe

UPRISE *vb.* ▾ascól → RISE

UPRISING *s.* panástase, ribiľó ‖ CUNIA 254: sculáre; **Cru:** vustaníie, GOLAB 259

UPROAR *s.* lává, lăvătúră; *also:* dăndănă,; făsăríe, ghiurultíe, *G:* giufă; giurgiúnă, lóscut, păltúră, sălăváte, şimătă, tăvătúră, vreávă; (*of the roar of a river*) cúrsu

UPROOT *vb.* ▾zmúlgu; scot dit rădăţínă

UPROOTED *adj.* zmúlsu, -lşă, -lşi, -lse; zmúltu, -ltă, -lţâ, -lte; arúptu, -ptă, -pţâ, -pte

UPRIGHT *adj.* (*morally ~*) Imnă cu zíya n brâu (*i.e., goes with the yardstick under his belt, as if ready to measure in order to be impartial*) ‖ (*on one's feet, vertical / vertically*) ân cicioáre; pri cicioáre, PARALLELE 129

UPSET *s.* răsturnáre, arusturnáre

UPSET *vb.* (*to overturn*) ▾arăstórnu; (*to disarrange, to throw into disorder*) alúmtu, aspárgu, ▾ambáturlu; (*to disturb, to afflict*) ▾părăpuñiéscu; **to ~ smb.'s plan** ľ-aspárgu plánlu; (*to be distressed*) nu-ñ yíne ghíne; **He was somewhat ~** Ca nu-ľ víñe ghíne

UPSETTING

UPSETTING *s.* (a)răsturnáre, (a)rusturnáre; (*disillusion*) nfărmăcáre

UPSHOT *s.* catórthose

UPSIDE-DOWN *adj.* (a)răsturnát, (a)rusturnát, alusturnát

UPSIDE-DOWN *adv.* darmadán ‖ **Cru:** anápudha, GOLAB 198

UPSTAIRS *adv.* sus, nsus

UPSTANDING *adj.* (*erect*) mprustát; (*honest*) nămuzlí

UPSTART *vb.* ▾ansár, ▾arsár, ▾alsár

UPSURGE *s.* creáştire, crişteáre

UPTAKE *s.* achicăsíre → BE QUICK ON THE ~

UPTIGHT *adj.* (*in difficulty*) tru angusteáţă; (*tense, nervous, uneasy*) sicliţít; (**indignant**) yinătós → ANGRY

UPWARDLY *adv.* nsus, cătră nsus ‖ HRISTU 36: cátă sus

URBANITE *s.* câsâbúñu, pulít

URCHIN *s.* (a *mischievous youngster*) geanabét

URGE *s.* (*exhortation*) parachínise; ştiúri [şti•ú•ri] *f*; zóre

URGE *vb.* anăngăséscu, angăsăiéscu, parachin(i)séscu; **to ~ on** (*as horses*) văryéscu

URGENT *adj.* ananghiós, -oásă, -óşĭ, -oáse

URGENTLY *adv.* ayóña

URINATE *vb.* ▾chiş, ñ-fac ápa, ñ-fac ápa minútă; (*children's talk*) fac pişi, fac ciuş

URINATION *s.* chişáre, cşáre

URINE *s.* chişát, cşát, ud; ápă minútă (*lit. 'small water'*), ápa aţeá minútă

US *pers. pron.* nă, nâ

` **USE** *s.* ufélie

USE *vb.* ufiliséscu; **~ one's own discretion** fac cúmu ñ-táľe cáplu; **to ~ up** fac ghíne (→ SPEND); **to ~ one's strength** xizumséscu

USE UP *vb.* ▾bitiséscu

USED UP *adj.* făcút ghíne, mâcát, xizumsít → WORN-OUT

USEFUL *adj.* lipsít, ofélim

USEFULNESS *s.* ufélie

USELESS *adj.* ni-lipsít, di-prisúpră, adhyeafórit, adhyeafurisít; (*vain*) áhristu; **a ~ thing** lúcru di-prisúpră

USELESSNESS *s.* hristíe

USUAL *adj.* mălăxít → ORDINARY

USURER *s.* ‖ ALR 1005: kehăié

USURP *vb.* ▾zăptiséscu

USURPATION *s.* zăptisíre

USURY *s.* gheáfru (→ INTEREST); zărăflíche, zărăflâche

UTENSIL *s.* hăláte → TOOL

UTILIZATION *s.* ufilisíre, nchirdhăsíre

UTILIZE *vb.* (*to make use of*) ufiliséscu; (*to turn to profitable use*) nchirdhăséscu

UTILITY *s.* (*usefulness*) ufélie

UTTER *vb.* şcrăpuéscu, cârlédz; **He couldn't ~ anything in Latin** Nu şcrăpuiá can Lătineásca; **Don't ~ a word!** Nu cârleádză! (*in negative statements*) nu scot cípit; (*as of lies*) vom

UTTERANCE *s.* dzâcă

UVULA *s. anat.* stăfilít, stăflít; límba aţeá ñícă ‖ om ñic (*lit. 'little man'; same pattern in D-Rom., Alb., and Bulg.*), PARALLELE 146

V

VACANCY *s.* (*vacant site*) viráne

VACANT *adj.* (*empty*) gol, goálă, goĭ, goále; ni-acăţát; (*stupid, foolish*) glar; glăréscu, -eáscă, -éşţâ, -éşti

VACANT SITE *s.* măidáne, miydáne, viráne

VACATE *vb.* ▾guléscu ‖ PC: alás gol

VACATION *s.* (*period of rest from work*) páfse, pápse

VACCINATE *vb.* ▾văţinédz, ▾văţinipséscu, ▾simnédz; **The girl was ~ed on her right arm** Feata i simnátă la mâna ndreáptă

VACCINATION *s.* văţináre, văţinipsíre, simnáre

VACILLATE *vb.* ñ-u dau n coástă, ▾induéscu

VACUITY *s.* (*something which is vacuous or insane*) gulăciúne

VACUOUS *adj.* (*empty*) gol, goálă, goĭ, goále; (*stupid*) glar

VAGABOND *s. and adj.* birdhúş, ciuhľán, ciumagáră, *pl* ciumagárañ; dilingíu, hulandár, vagabóndu; (*of a child*) ficiór di prit căľuri ‖ DIARO 222: ceapatoreán

VAGARIOUS *adj.* (*capricious, whimsical*) căpriceárcu, -rcă, -rţi, -rţe; nizeárcu, -rcă, -rţi, -rţe; cu oára

VAGARY *s.* → WHIM

VAGRANT *s.* dilingíu → VAGABOND

VAIL *vb.* ▾ncľin

VAIN: in ~ in vímtu → VAINLY

VAINGLORY *s.* ▾alăvdătúră, fălíre, fudulíre, piñisíre

VAINGLORIOUS *adj.* fudúl, -úlă, -úľ, -úle → ARROGANT

VAINLY *adv.* boş, geába, mátea, ncot (*and* ngot), ti éră ş-ti séră, tângăr-mângăr, tu cácu

VALE *s.* → VALLEY

VALE: to take one's ~ (*to depart from a moribund*) mi ľértu (di)

VALET *s.* dhul, huzmicheár

VALIANT *adj.* gióne, -oánă, -oñ, -oáne → BRAVE

VALIANTLY

VALIANTLY *adv.* giuneáşte

VALISE *s.* baúlă → SUITCASE

VALLEY *s.* vále, *pl* văľuri, *dim.* vălícă, văľúră; clíncă; **small hollow** ~ trăpíc

VALOR *s.* sărpiţâľe → BRAVERY

VALOROUS *adj.* ghirăchín → BRAVE

VALUABLE *s.* (*thing of value*) háre **valuables** lúcre ahărzíte, BASME 289

VALUABLE *adj.* ahărzít, aléptu, -eáptă, -pţâ, -pte; arúspu, -spă, -schi, -spe; scúmpu, -mpă, scúnchi, -mpe (*and* scúmbu)

VALUE *s.* axíe, tiñíe, pâhă; **This idea is of no ~ at all** Idéia nu áre níţi un pâhă; **to set in high** ~ fac htibáre

VALUE *vb.* (*to appraise, to evaluate, to prize, to rate*) ahărzéscu ‖ muntréscu, BASME 418

VAMPIRE *s.* vampír, vómbir, vârcólac, vurcólac, vurculác, vărculác; **~s suck blood** Vurculáţľi sug sândzi

VANISH *vb.* mi fac căípe, mi ahunduseáşte lóclu; **He seemed to have ~ed into the air** Cánda lu-aveá ahundusítă lóclu **to ~ from sight** ñcheáre ditr-ócľi, BASME 61 → DISAPPEAR

VANISHING *s.* spulbiráre

VANITY *s.* (*senselessness*) vânătáte; (*empty pride*) fudulíre, făndăxíre

VANQUISH *vb.* → DEFEAT; (*to gain mastery over*) ▼stăpuéscu, ▼ţân

VAPID *adj.* análut, ánustu

VAPOR *s.* ábur *m*

VAPOR *vb.* ‖ PC: scot áburi

VARIABLE *adj.* nu sta pri únă

VARIANCE *s.* ceamăúră, ni-achicăsíre → QUARREL, SET AT ~

VARICELLA *s. med.* mălteádză a pădúriľei

VARICOLORED *adj.* ľar, péstru

VARIEGATED *adj.* ľar, péstru

VARIOLA *s. med.* mălteádza aţeá láia → SMALLPOX

VARLET *s.* (*attendant, servant*) huzmicheár; (*scoundrel, knave*) cătúnă

VARNISH *s.* (*of leather*) iurgáne; lustríñe, virníche; (*luster*) máslă, másnă

VARNISHED LEATHER *s.* (a)ruyáne, iurgáne

VASE *s.* (*container*) vas; (*expensive* ~) vaz

VAST *adj.* tes, teásă, teşĭ, teáse; tímtu; *sg* máre, *pl* mări

VAT *s.* (*as for the fermentation of fruit*) cârblă, crâblă, cârbă, crâbă, gărbă, gârbă, cádză → CASK

VAULT[1] *s.* (*storage*) bímţă, pímniţă, pleámniţă, catóye, cămáră, ízbă, ţălár, ţăláre, *G:* zímnic; (*as decoration on the top of a*

building) thol; (*cupola*) **S:** cubé, gubé, **N:** cubée; ~ **of vine** pérgură, pirguríe

VAULT² *s.* (*leap*) sáltu, sáltă, vóltă

VAULTED *adj.* → ARCHED

VAUNT *vb.* ▼fuduléscu → BOAST

VEER *vb.* ▼abát, părămirséscu ‖ CUNIA 76: mi trag di nă párte

VEGETABLE *s.* zărzăváte (*and* zârzâ-), veárdză; **early** ~ turfandá, báclă

VEGETABLE GARDEN *s.* băhcé, buhcé, bustáne, grădínă (*and* grâ-); *dim.* grădiníciu, grădinúşe

VEHEMENCE *s.* stañó

VEHEMENT *adj.* sértu, -rtă, -rţâ, -rte; silnă(v)ós, -oásă

VEIL *s.* vel *or* vélă; *also:* (a)şchépe, bálţ, bărbúľu, mândílă, sávan, sávun, tuvlétă, duvléte, **G:** duvalé; ţípă, ţiţiroáñe, zvon, zăvón

VEIN *s. anat.* vínă, stríngľe, flévă ‖ MERCA 13: (*stock, descendant*) jílă

VEINED *adj.* vinós, -oásă

VEINY *adj.* vinós, -oásă

VELVET *s.* catifé, **N:** catifée; pilúş ‖ **Peş:** bilúş, CL 39; **stripet** ~ şaitan-bizír, DIARO 188

VENAL *adj.* aspártu, -rtă, -rţâ, -rte

VEND *vb.* ▼víndu

VENDEE *s.* (*buyer*) muştirí, muştiră

VENERABLE *adj.* ayímtu, tiñisít; **the** ~ **priests** ayímţâľi aféndzâ

VENERATE *vb.* tiñiséscu

VENETIAN *adj.* vinétic

VENGEANCE *s.* → REVENGE, CRY FOR ~

VENGEFUL *adj.*‖ PC: mplin di áhte

VENOM *s.* fărmác, áxif, ciómir, émir, ceámerru (*sic*); hulíe; (*from hellebore*) ştrigoáñe

VENOMOUS *adj.* fârmâcós, -oásă; toápsec, -ecă, -eţĭ, -eţe

VENOUS *adj.* (*full of veins*) vinós, -oásă

VENT *s. anat.* → ANUS; (*outlet*) işíre, inşíre

VENT PEG *s.* (*of a barrel*) sóche

VENTURE *s.* dăldăsíre → RISK

VENTURE *vb.* (*to undertake a risk*) căidăséscu, dăvrănséscu, am iárbă di ţâneáre → DARE

VENTURESOME *adj.* cuturgí; cu érghi

VENTUROUS *adj.* → VENTURESOME

VERACIOUS *adj.* cu érghi → HONEST

VERANDA *s.* tăráţă → PORCH

VERBALLY *adv.* ‖ BELIMACE 45: cu gúra

VERBOTTEN

VERBOTEN *adj.* yeasáche *invar.*

VERDICT *s.* ileáme, ileáne, sigilíe

VERDURE *s.* nvirdzáme, virdeáţă, virdzătúră, prisinádhă

VERGE *s.* márdzină, márdzine → EDGE

VERGE *vb.* (*to border*) ▾viţinipséscu; (*to incline toward the horizon*) ▾dipún

VERGER *s.* (*sacristan, sexton*) candilanáftu

VERIFICATION *s.* cătăpăţíre; (*of a scale*) airáre

VERIFIED *adj.* (*checked, tested*) cătăpăţít

VERITABLE *adj.* curát, yñisíu

VERITY *s.* driptáte → TRUTH

VERJUICE *s.* acríme

VERMICELLI *s.* **S**: fidé *m,* **N**: fidéi [•dé•i] *f*

VERMIN *s.* (*lice*) *coll.* biducľáme, minţíme, minciuşáme

VERMINOUS *adj.* biducľós, -oásă; biducľát

VERSE *s.* (*a single line of poetry*) stih, vérşă

VERSED *adj.* (*of a thief*) cu bandéră, cu cízme, cu dhíplumă, cu scórne

VERSET *s.* vérşă

VERSUS *prep.* (*face to face with*) tru; **Dona alone ~ seven girls** Dona un tru şeápte feáte

VERTEBRAL COLUMN *s. anat.* schinărát

VERTEX *s. anat.* creáştit

VERTICAL *adj.* mbróstu, -oástă, -óşţâ, -oáste

VERTIGO *s.* scútură → DIZZINESS

VERVAIN *s. bot.* yirghínă

VERY *adv.* múltu; *also*: aráu, câtu s-dzâţi, dip, foc, píră, vârtós; (*of a good student*) **He is doing ~ well** Píră nveáţă; **~ intelligent** diştiptát foc ‖ **~ much so!** Am cum? (*lit. 'How [could it be] otherwise?'*) BASME 31

VESPERS *s.* (*a service of evening worship*) ayripníe → EASTER ~

VESSEL *s.* (*container, bowl*) vas; (*for milk*) meáră; (*ship*) caráve; **G**: cărádhi; ghimíe, náie

VEST *s.* (*for men*) ilécă, iléche, saltamárca; (*for women*) ceachét, geachét, ţichétă, şcurtác, şcurtácă; (*of wool*) peş; sărăcúce

VESTIBULE *s.* hăiáte

VESTIGE *s.* úrmă → TRACE

VETCH *s. bot.* mădzirícľe, mărdzinícľe, vic ‖ **GSus**: fii, CL 45

VETERAN *s.* (*a person of long experience in an occupation or skill*) fricát *adj.*

VEX *vb.* aród dit hicáte, ▾căchiuséscu, ▾guştirédz, mâc hicátlu, ▾nărăéscu, ▾nţap, scot peri álghi

VEXATION *s.* căchiusíre, cărtíre, cârtitúră, hulusíre, ngúsă

VEXATIOUS *adj.* căchiós, -oásă; mintitór, -oáre; năpudeáric, sirsém, *m pl* -séñ; zarzára, *f* -ră, *m pl* -reañ, -re

VEXED *adj.* cărtít, mbudzinát, mbufnát → BE ~ WITH SMB.

VIA *prep.* pri, prít, prin

VIAL *s.* cunétă

VICAR-GENERAL *s.* prutusínghil

VICE *s.* slábă, tăbiéte

VICE *prep.* tu lóclu a

VICE VERSA *adv.* anáschile

VICIATE *vb.* aspárgu, murdăripséscu

VICINAGE *s.* (*a neighboring or surrounding area*) viţinátă, viţinătáte

VICINITY *s.* → VICINAGE

VICIOUS *adj.* aspártu, -rţă, -rţâ, -rte; chiutandál; (*spiteful*) nvipirát; şirpát, şirpóñu, Turc, vampír, vómbir, vurculác; **a ~ man** om di arăiľi; **What a ~ son she has!** Ţe vómbir ficiór áre!

VICISSITUDE *s.* alăxíre

VICISSITUDINOUS **adj.** (*unsteady, shaky*) nu sta pri únă *3 sg.*

VICTIM *s.* zimñusít

VICTIMIZATION *s.* zimñusíre

VICTIMIZE *vb.* ▼zimñuséscu

VICTORIOUS *adj.* azvingătór, -oáre

VICTORY *s.* azvindzeáre, anixíre, nichisíe

VICTUALS *s.* (a)psún, psúne, zairé, zăirée

VIE *vb.* (*to contend*) mi sinirséscu (cu)

VIENNA *s.* (*Wien*) Béşľi, Béşiľi [béşĭ•ľi]

VIEW *s.* (*the act of seeing*) videáre; (*inspection*) mutríre; (*aspect*) vidzútă; (*panorama, sight*) aynánghiu; (*objet, purpose*) isápe

VIEW *vb.* mutréscu

VIGIL *s.* privigľáre, strájă

VIGILANCE *s.* căştígă (*and* câş-), méngă

VIGILANT *adj.* câştigós, -oásă; *3 sg*: áre méngă

VIGOR *s.* vârtúte, virtúte, vârtuş→ FORCE

VIGOROUS *adj.* sărchirós, -oásă

VIGOROUSLY *adv.* vârtós

VILE *adj.* (*despicable*) idipsâz, *m pl* -âjĭ; pânghiós, -oásă; zgrumát; (*of little worth*) mízav, *m pl* -ayĭ; (*repulsive*) aynusós; ~ **person** azvărnătúră; ~ **language** grăíre pânghioásă ‖ laiu, BASME 283

VILENESS *s.* lăiáţă

VILIFY *vb.* zburăscu, cacuzburăscu

VILLAGE *s.* hoáră, *dim.* hurícă; **Aromanian ~** vlahuhoáră; **king's ~** vasiluhóre; **independent ~** chifaluhoáră ‖ LITURG 129: hóră

VILLAGER *s.* huryeát

VILLAIN

VILLAIN *s.* cătúnă

VILLAINY *s.* şăneáţă, edepsâzlâche

VIM *s.* → VITALITY

VINDICATE *vb.* ▾ascúmpăr → REVENGE

VINDICATIVE *adj.* irişárcu, -rcă, -rţi, -rţe

VINE *n.* (*stem of* ~) ghítă, ayítă, ayíñc; (*young* ~) fitheáuă ‖ *Prv:* călimáte, CL 41

VINE BRANCH *s.* ayítă, sărméţ; (*with grapes on it*) bígă; (*dried out* ~) climăţídhă

VINE TRELLIS *s.* clivătăreáuă, climătăreáuă

VINEGAR *s.* púscă; **Get some ~, it will calm you down!** Bea púscă s-ţâ treácă!

VINEGAR DEALER *s.* puscár

VINEGARY *adj.* ácru

VINE-STOCK *s.* ayítă, clímă, *pl* clímate

VINEYARD *s.* (a)yíñe; (*young* ~) sad

VINTAGE *s.* (a)yizmăciúne, ayizmáre

VIOLACEOUS *adj.* (*color*) yioáră *invar.*

VIOLATE *vb.* ▾cálcu; **to ~ an oath, a promise** ▾cálcu giurátlu, ▾cálcu zbórlu

VIOLATION *s.* călcáre

VIOLENCE *s.* stañó, zurbălâche

VIOLENT *adj.* sâlniós, -uiós, -năvós, -năós; pléşcav; **He is ~** Ca ianiţár fáţe (*lit.* 'behaves like a janisary')

VIOLENTLY *adv.* cu furţáte

VIOLET *s. bot.* ghioáră [ǵi•oá•], yioáră [yi•], manuşáche, musáhe ‖ *Amc:* ayioáră, PADIOTU 119

VIOLET *adj.* yioáră [yi•oá•], luláchiu

VIOLIN *s.* zângână → FIDDLE

VIPER *s.* năpârtică, nipârtică, uheáuă ‖ *Prv:* aştrít, CL 37

VIRAGO *s.* dráxă, drăcoáñe, căţáuă, căţáo

VIRGIN *s., adj.* feátă, vírghină, vírghiră, (feátă) vérgură, (feátă) viryinádhă; ghirgheánă; **the Virgin Mary** Parádhisa ‖ ~ **forest** păduri ni cărtită di mâna a omu, HRISTU 86

VIRGINAL *adj.* (*as of a voice*) viryinéscu

VIRGINITY *s.* virghireáţă, virghirătáte

VIRILE *adj.* bărbătín; bărbătéscu, -eáscă, -éşţâ, -éşti

VIRTUE *s.* érye, aretíe

VIRULENT *adj.* (*noxious*) (a)rắu, (a)ráuă, (a)rắi, (a)rále; (*venomous*) fârmâcós, oásă; toápsec, *m pl* -pseţĭ

VISA *s.* (*on a passport*) cáide; *vb.* ñ-fac cáide pasapórtea

VISAED *adj.* (*of a passport*) cáide *invar*

VISAGE *s.* fáţă; (*physiognomy*) iapíi

VISCERA *s.* ľánumă; minuţáľe *f pl*; (*broiled lamb*) arumáne; cu-curéciu

VISCOUS *adj.* mâzgós, -oásă

VISE *s.* minghiné

VISION *s.* (*sight*) videáre ‖ (*as in a dream or trance*) PC: as-puneáre

VISIT *s.* vízită

VISIT *vb.* fac vizită, vizitédz → PAY A VISIT

VITALITY *s.* tăcáte, puteáre

VITIATE *vb.* cacurizipséscu

VITTLES *s.* → VICTUALS

VITUPERATE *vb.* trag un cărínte → SCOLD

VITUPERATION *s.* cărínte

VIVA *interj.* víva

VIVACIOUS *adj.* aflát; pirgác

VIVACITY *s.* sirtlâche

VIVID *adj.* fréşcu, -şcă, -şţâ, -şti

VIVIDNESS *s.* sirtlâche

VIXEN *s.* vúlpe; (*shrew*) dráxă, drăcoáñe

VIZI(E)R *s.* vizír, satrazám, zadrazám

VOCABLE *s.* zbor

VOCIFERATE *s.* → SHOUT

VOCIFERATION *s.* strigáre

VOGUE *s.* (*fashion*) módhă

VOICE *s.* boáţe; **with low ~** cu boáţea dipúsă; **in a low ~** păgăñór (*and* pâgâ-)

VOID *adj.* gol, goálă, goľ, goále; ni-acăţát

VOID *vb.* ▾guléscu

VOLATILE *adj.* ni-síyur; nu sta pri únă

VOLE *s. zool.* şoáric

VOLLEY ABUSE AT SMB. *vb.* rizil(ips)éscu

VOLUBLE *adj.* → TALKATIVE

VOLUMINOUS *adj. m/f* máre, *m/f pl* mărĭ; căbátcu, -tcă, -tţi, -tţe

VOLUNTEER *s.* thilundí, filundí

VOLUPTUARY *adj.* aspártu; *G:* fatigéi *s. or adj. invar.*

VOLUPTUOUS *adj.* cârţănít; (*of a woman*) cahpée

VOLUPTUOUSNESS *s.* dizñirdăciúne; azgânlâche

VOMIT *s.* (*disgorged matter*) vumutúră, bruzgăitúră, gălbinitúră; **to ~ smoke** (*to belch out smoke*) afúm

VOMIT *vb.* ▾vérsu, vom, ▾(a)zvóm

VOMITING *s.* virsătúră, voámire, voámită, (z)vumeáre

VORACIOUS *adj.* limós, -oásă

VORTEX *s.* viró, zuryió

VOTE

VOTE *s.* psif

VOTE *vb.* ▾alég, psifiséscu; **We will ~ him into the leader** Va lu-alidzém ma-máre

VOUCH *vb.* (*to give personal assurance*) íntru chifíle, mi fac chi-féľ

VOUCHER *s.* (*a person*) chifí, chifiľót, chifíľu, chifaléte; (*a document*) izmáe

VOW *s.* → MAKE A ~

VOYAGE *s.* sefér; **to go on a ~** fac sefér → JOURNEY

VULGAR *adj.* jupânéscu, -eáscă, -éşţâ, -éşti; ni-adărát, ni-ciuplít, păduríş; (*obscene*) dişuţât

VULTURE *s.* vúltur, vultúr (*and* vâl-, văl-) → FALCON

VULVA *s.* chízdă (*vulg.*); *also:* heárhiră, hérhică (*lit.* 'peach'); hícă (*lit.* 'fig'); píce

W

WAD *s.* (*fibrous material used to clean firearms*) paciúră, păci-vúră ‖ (*a small mass, bundle or tuft*) găgiumól, găgiămól, CL 45

WADDING *s.* bumbác; scămánghe; vátă

WADDLE *s.* furduíre

WADDLE *vb.* ▾furduéscu

WADE *vb.* trec, străbát, stribát

WADING *s.* treáţire, triţeáre

WAFT *s.* (*breeze*) ávră → PUFF

WAFT *vb.* ▾min, ▾duc

WAG *s.* (*joker*) şicăgí

WAG *vb.* şuvăéscu

WAG ONE'S CHIN *vb.* (*to puff oneself up*) ▾căbărdéscu

WAGE *s.* (a)rúgă → SALARY

WAGE WAR *vb.* ▾a(m)puliséscu

WAGER *s.* acăţătúră, báste, iádiş, iádeţ acăţáre, BASME 508

WAGGERY *s.* (*practical joke*) féstă

WAGGISH *adj.* *m/f* muşmoálă; sirsém, *m pl* -séñ; şicăgí; zevzéc

WAGON *s.* car, cárră, cărúţă, caróţă, chéră; (*large ~*) arâbă ‖ *Cru:* (*cart*) amáxe, GOLAB 198

WAGON DRIVER *s.* căruţár, căruţér

WAGTAIL *s.* *orn.* bátură; coádăbátură, cudubátură, cutrubátă ba-jáncă, culusúsă

WAIF *s.* (*of people or animals*) birdhús, capisâz; ciuhleán; ciulandár

WAIL *s.* şcľimurát

WAIL *vb.* ▼şcľimurédz → LAMENT

WAILFUL *adj.* şcľimurós, -oásă

WAIN *s.* carúţă; (*rare*) car

WAIST *s.* mése, nólgic; *N:* bârnu

WAISTBAND *s.* zónă, zúnă; brăn, *N:* bârnu

WAIT *vb.* (a)ştéptu; *Cru, M:* astéptu, şcéptu; ▼adástu, agăléscu; **to ~ on smb.** (*as on a guest*) bag nătheám di meásă; **to ~ on smb. hand and foot** ţân pri pálme, ţân ca pri pălñi

WAITER *s.* ‖ *Cru:* garsón, GOLAB 216

WAITING *s.* aştiptáre, păndixíre

WAIVE *vb.* (*to give up claim to*) trag mâna (→ ABNEGATE); ▼alás; (*to postpone*) amân

WAKE[1] *s.* (*track left behind*) úrmă

WAKE[2] *s.* (*watch over the body of a dead person*) cărăulsíre, nihtéri

WAKE *vb.* (*to awake*) ▼diştéptu

WAKEFUL *adj.* diştiptát, ni-durñít; câştigós, -oásă

WAKING *s.* diştiptáre, diştiptátă

WALE *s.* (*a streak or ridge made on the skin*) yir, yiur ‖ CUNIA 96: vărdză, băirúş

WALK *s.* imnáre; (*for or as if for pleasure*) ghizére, ghizirsíre, priimnáre, primnáre, piripát, suláţă, suláţ, tifiríce; (*as in search of smth.*) âmpăturáre; **to take a ~** dau únă dévră; (*to take a turn*) dau únă duláie

WALK *vb.* ímnu; ñérgu (*and* nérgu → § 32), *G:* ñeg; trag cále, trag di-a lúngului; (*to ~ very fast*) li tíndu ciúnile; **to ~ back and forth** mi ţas, mi úrdin; **to ~ in single file** ľau ciórlu-ciórlu; **to ~ one's legs off** (*to do all in one's power*) mi fac páde; **to ~ on tiptoe** ñérgu pri úngľile di cioáre; **to ~ over** trec; **to ~ round smb./smth.** adúc vârlíga ‖ CARAFOLI 64: dau nă vóltă

WALK ASIDE *vb.* ‖ ALR 1376: mi dau na nă párte

WALKING *s.* imnáre, imnátă, imnátic, imnătúră, ñárzire, ñirdzeáre

WALKING STICK *s.* băstún, băstúne; (**in icebound areas**) budéc ‖ *Str:* ciumúc, GOLAB 207

WALL *s.* stízmă; *also:* greb, mur, tih ‖ *Cru:* (*inner ~ from straw and clay*) bulmée, GOLAB 201

WALLET *s.* priftáciu, purtufóle; (*pilgrim's ~, shepherd's ~*) tástru, tărástru, tráştu, tráştir, tăyărcícă, tărgăcícă, trăyăcícă, tăvărceác, târváciu, târváş → SATCHEL

WALLOP *s.* (*collision*) agudíre

WALLOP

WALLOP *vb.* (*to thrash soundly*) tuchéscu (di băteáre) → BEAT

WALLOW *vb.* ▼anduchiléscu, ▼tăvăléscu, antăvăléscu (*and* andă-), cutăvăléscu, cutuvăléscu

WALLOWING *s.* andăvălitúră, anduchilitúră

WALNUT TREE *s.* nuc, cucóş

WAN *adj.* s(c)lab, -bă, s(c)laghi, -be; lângurós, umbărnát

WAND *s.* veárgă

WANDER *vb.* (*to become delirious*) aľurédz; **to ~ about** alág lócu di lócu, misúr steálile, hălăndăréscu

WANDERING *adj.* dilingí, dilingíu, cu cása pri ciumág (*or* pri ciutáľ)

WANE *s.* scădeáre, mpuţânáre

WANE *vb.* discréscu, ▼mpuţânédz; **when the moon ~s** tu mângáta a lúnăľei (*lit.* '*at the eating of the moon*')

WANGLE *vb.* plănéscu, (a)plănăséscu, (a)plănipséscu, lu-árdu, trag călúpea

WANT *s.* **to be in ~ of smth.** ñ-eáste lipsítă (di)

WANT *vb.* *pres.* voi, vrei, va, vrem, vreţ, vor; *ipf:* vream; *aor.* vrui; *also:* alág, caftu, ñ-si urixeáşte; **Does he ~ it or not?** Va i nu va? **Whether I ~ it or not, I'll go** Voi, nu voi, va mi duc; **He found what he ~ed** Ţe alăgá află; **What do you ~ from me?** Di la míne ţe căftáţ? **She ~ed apples** Ľ-si urixí meáre; **He ~s two-pence in the shilling** ≈ Ľ-lipseáşte únă scândură (*lit.* '*He is missing one board,*' *cf. Engl.* *He is missing some marbles*) ‖ HRISTU 67: vroi; **I ~ to talk to you** Vroi să zburăstu cu tini

WANTING *prep.* ('*lacking*') fâră

WANTON *s.* (*merry*) hăriós; (*frolicsome*) burdal, zdurdít; (*lewd*) → LUSTFUL; (*merciless*) ni-ñilós

WAR *s.* pólim; **to begin a ~** mut pólim ‖ *GSus:* póľum, CL 259 → MAKE ~ AGAINST / ON

WARBLING *s.* (*of birds*) ţíur

WARD *s.* pândár → GUARDIAN

WARDEN *s.* păzván, păzvándu

WARE *s.* prămătíe, părmătíe → EARTHEN ~

WAREHOUSE *s.* dipózit

WARLOCK *s.* → SORCERER

WARM *adj.* cáldu, -ldă, -ldzâ, -lde; *dim.* căldişór, -oáră; căldurós, -oásă; (*as of water*) hámin, hábin; hľo *invar.*, *dim.* hľúşcu, -că, *no pl*; diháñu, *f* -ñe (*pl ?* DDA 470) → MAKE ~

WARM *vb.* ▼ncăldzăscu, ncăldurédz (*and* ngăl-), ncălurédz; (*with one's own breath, usu. of hands*) ▼ahuléscu; ▼apríndu

WARMING UP *s.* ncăldzâre, ncăluráre, ncălduráre

WARMTH *s.* căloáre, căroáre, căldúră

WARN *vb.* cănuséscu ‖ CUNIA 11: ascútur dzeádzitlu

WARP *s.* (*in a loom*) urdzătúră, usúră

WARP *vb.* (*to mount the warp*) (a)năvădescu, urdzăscu

WARP UP *vb.* (*to twist*) ▾şuţ, ▾strâmbu; (*to pervert*) aspárgu

WARP-BEAM *s.* bărbătór, vălvătór

WARPING *s.* (*of trees, of wood*) dispituráre; *tex.* năvădíre, nvul-báre, urdzâre

WARRANT *vb.* ‖ ALR 1010: me-acáţ chifilíi

WARRANTOR *s.* ‖ ALR 1009: chifíľu

WARRANTY *s.* chifaléte → VOUCHER

WART *s. derm.* lúzmă, aríciu, bărgăvíţă, băzdrăvíţă

WART-CRESS *s. bot.* pândălícă → PLANTAIN

WART-WEED *s. bot.* aréu

WARY *adj.* câştigós, -oásă → BE ~ OF

WAS *vb.* → BE

WASH *vb.* ▾(a)láu, ▾(a)spél, ▾şpuľuéscu, ▾spriláu, ▾yăryăláu; **to ~ out** es, *aor.* i(n)şíi, i(n)şái; **(This dirt) does not ~ out** Nu eáse; **Beating and shame do not ~ out** (*i.e., they are not forgotten*) şcóplu şi arşínea nu es, *lit.* 'they do not come out') ‖ (*~ thoroughly as to eliminate unpleasant odors; to deodorize*) ▾dispútu

WASH BASIN *s.* → WASHBOWL

WASHED *adj.* spilát, (a)lát, yăryălát; **~ and bleached** grândinát

WASHED-OUT *adj.* (*exhausted*) curmát

WASHING *s.* (a)láre, (a)spiláre, spilătúră; (*usu. of white cloth in order to make it whiter*) bilíre

WASHBOWL *s.* liyén, liyéne, liéne, iléne

WASHY *adj.* s(c)lab, -bă, s(c)laghi, -be; sálbit, sárbit

WASP *s. ent.* (a)yeáspe

WASP NEST *s.* yispár

WASPISH *adj.* arceátcu, inací, inacíu, inagí, inătcí, sértic; sértu, -rtă, -rţâ, -rte

WASTAGE *s.* aroádire, cheárdire, chirdeáre

WASTE *s.* (*desert*) irñíu, urñíe, pundíe, pustilíe; (*leakage*) firă; (*dissipation*) spătăľusíre; (*~ of time*) hasuméri; **in mere ~** *adv.* dipri-súpră

WASTE *adj.* (*barren, desolate, empty*) gol, goálă, goľ, goále

WASTE *vb.* ▾cher, ngărmiséscu, tuchéscu; (*to ~ time*) hăsumirséscu; (*~ one's time in vain*) ñ-chérdu săpúnea (*lit.* 'to ~ one's soap'); (*to ruin, as one's best years*) stuhinédz; (*to emaciate*) mi adár iáscă, slăghéscu ca cártea; **to ~ words** zburăsc pi víntu

WASTE AWAY *vb.* ▾pustuéscu, ▾pustixéscu, ▾irmuxéscu

WASTE GROUND *s.* puľánă, viráne

WASTE ONE'S TIME *vb.* cher săpúnea, cher milăñle tu cácu ‖ cher

WASTE

oára, BASME 424; chérdu oára, BASME 99; cher chiró, BASME 50; ALR 775:
He is wasting time doing nothing Cheáre chirólu ţivá

WASTE PRODUCT *s.* armăsătúră

WASTED *adj.* (*thin, enfeebled*) loat la fáţă; (*careworn*) sicliţít

WASTEFUL *adj.* dismălărát, hărgiuitór, spátal; **a ~ person** mână spártă, sac arúptu → PROFLIGATE

WASTELAND *s.* irñíu, irñíe, chirítă

WATCH¹ *s.* săháte, sááte, oáră

WATCH² *s.* (*surveillance*) vigľáre, păzíre, sinudhíe, nubéte; (*night ~*) nihtéri, nihtéryiu → SET A ~

WATCH *vb.* vigľédz, (a)végľu, privégľu, ▾hărnéscu, ▾pitéscu; **~ out!** Aveágľi-te! Sacân! Mutreá! Ắi-ţâ míntea! Bágă-ţ míntea ghíne! (A)ngătán! ‖ BATSARIA 74: *2 pl imper* Mutríţ! HRISTU 86: (*think well*) *2 sg imper* mintuia-ti ghini!

WATCH HOLE *s.* (*as in a fortress*) víglă, víylă

WATCH OUT *vb.* → WATCH

WATCH PLACE *s.* cartére, pusíe, sémte

WATCH TOWER *s.* pindurníţă, pândruníţă

WATCHED OVER *adj.* păzít, pizít

WATCHER *s.* vigľitór → GUARDIAN

WATCHFUL *adj.* câştigós, -oásă

WATCHFULNESS *s.* afiríre, afirítă

WATCHMAKER *s.* săhătcí, uruluyă

WATCHMAN *s.* vigľitór → GUARDIAN

WATER *s.* ápă, *dim.* apşoáră; **holy ~** ayeazmó; **~ of youth** ápă di bánă; ápă yíe fără moárte; apă yíe athanátă → BE IN LOW ~

WATER *vb.* (*to wet, to get soaked*) ▾ud; (*to give water to people, animals or plants*) ▾adáp; (*to anticipate spontaneously smth. tasty, usu. of food*) ñ-fug bále ‖ CUNIA 289: (*to sprinkle*) (a)sprucuchéscu; (*of smth. tasty*) BASME 239: límba ápă-ñ lásă n gúră

WATER GLASS *s.* yilíe, lăyíe, putír(e)

WATER PIPE *s.* şóput

WATER WAGON *s.* stérnă

WATER RESERVOIR *s.* avúz, hăvúze

WATER-BOTTLE *s.* mâtâră

WATERCRAFT *s.* ghimíe

WATERED *adj.* (*of animals, of a garden*) adăpát, biút

WATERER *s.* (*one who supplies water to gardens*) arădhár

WATERFALL *s.* ghirdápe

WATERING *s.* udătúră, adăpáre, adăpatură

WATERING CAN *s.* ştrac

WATERLOGGED *adj.* ud moľu

WATERMELON *s.* himuníc, hiumuníc, carpúz, şirchín; (*unripe ~*) cu-

cumbíciu ‖ CUVATA 1: hiumăníc

WATER-PLANTAIN *s. bot.* mâna a li Stă-Măríe

WATERPROOF *s.* muşímă (*a fabric*)

WATERSIDE *s.* méjdă, mézdă

WATERSPOUT *s.* şitrăváne

WATERY *adj.* após, -oásă; apătós, -oásă

WATTLE¹ *s.* (*as a turkey's ~*) hărháľe, hărháľu

WATTLE² *s.* ‖ (*sticks interwoven with twigs*) *GSus:* cóşniţă, CL 42

WAVE *s.* úndă; *also:* chímă, *pl* chímate; dálgă, taláză; (*multitude*) flúmin; **~s of young men** flúmin di ficióri

WAVE *vb.* (*as a handkerchief*) ▼min; (*of a flag, etc.*) arăschiredz; (*of a river*) undédz

WAVER *vb.* ▼âncľín → HESITATE

WAX *s.* ţeáră

WAX RESIDUE *s.* ‖ *GSus:* fóştină, CL 45

WAX *vb.* chiruséscu

WAX-CANDLE *s.* spirmaţétă, axunguchére

WAX LIGHT *s.* (*taper*) ţeáră

WAY *s.* (*manner*) ciré, cearé, *N:* cearée; trop; **There is only one ~** Maşi ún cearé eáste; **There was no ~ for me to escape** Nu erá trop si-ascáp; **In what ~?** Cu ţi trop? **in no ~!** pa-pa-pá! ba-ba-bá! **that ~** pri-acló; **the ~ you are putting it** aşí cum dzáţi; **the wrong ~** *adv.* anápudha, térse, tirsiné; **He put on the cloak the wrong ~** Nviscú sárica anápudha; **out of the ~** (*mistaken*) ni-uidisít; alăthipsít (*situation, circumstances*) **I am in a bad ~** Ñ-si dúţe strâmbu, BASME 280 ‖ *F:* (*direction*) **that ~** cătă aco, HRISTU 22 → MAKE ~, MAKE ONE'S ~ ALONG / TOWARDS

WAY OUT *s.* (*exit, escape*) inşíre, işíre, culáiu; **We'll find a ~** Va-i aflăm vâr culái si-ascăpăm

WAYLAID: to be ~ cad tu yrip → FALL INTO THE TRAP

WAYLAY *vb.* păndixéscu, ▼stăvruséscu, astáľu cálea, stau tu cartére

WE *pers. pron. 2 pl* noi; *dat.* (*long form*) (a) noáuă, (a) náo; (*short form*) nă; *acc.* (*long form*) noi; (*short form*) nă; **Say a kind word to us!** Dzâ-nă şi-anoáuă un zbor bun! **Did you see us?** Nă vidzút noi?

WEAK *adj.* (*frail*) vlângu, -ngă; nu áre arândză; (*as of starvation*) s(c)lab, -bă, s(c)laghi, -be; súptu, -ptă, -pţâ, -pte; (*sluggish, poor, as of sales*) átih, adhínat ‖ *Bil:* (*ant. of 'fat'*) uscát; *Gop:* ('frail') trom, NEIESCU 122

WEAKEN *vb.* slăghéscu, adhinăţéscu

WEAKENING *s.* slăghíre, adhinăţíre

WEAKLY *adj.* s(c)lab, ţârós, zaífcu, zaíf ‖ *Peş:* mărăjgľós, CL 255

WEAKNESS *s.* sclăbeáţă, sclăbeáţă, sclăbíľe, sclăbíľe, slăbínţă, sclăbínţă, adhinămíe

WEAL *s.* ghineáţă

WEALTH *s.* aveáre; *G:* aburíe; arhundíľe, arhundilíche, avuţâľe, avuţáme, bugătlăcă, căşeáre, cătándă, cătăndíe, cătúnă, periusíe, seu; **He has ~** Are seu; (*livestock viewed as ~*) tutípută picúľu, picúñu, CAPIDAN 144

WEAN *vb.* nţárcu, nţércu; apucupséscu, cúrmu

WEANING *s.* nţărcáre, curmáre, apucupsíre

WEAPONS *s.* **pl.** ármate

WEAR *vb.* (*as of clothing*) apórtu; **to ~ a chip on one's shoulder** trag tămbárea azvărna; **to ~ mourning for smb.** ţân jálea, hiu di har, hiu di jále

WEAR OUT *vb.* ▼zmúrtic; *also:* apustuséscu, ▼băildéscu, ▼căpăéscu (di), mi deápir, liyuséscu, ▼aród, ▼mâc, tălăéscu, ▼tuchéscu; vicľédz *or* vicľéscu **The boat was worn out by storms** Cărávea u vicľíră furtúñle

WEARINESS *s.* apustusíre, avursíre, buhtíre, curmáre, lăvrusíre

WEARISOME *adj.* ánustu, -stă, -şţâ, -ste

WEARY *adj.* (*tired*) curmát

WEARY *vb.* (*to overwork*) lăvruséscu, scot pétalile; **to ~ out** alúmtu; **Heavy rains ~ them out** Ľ-alúmtă plóíle; **to ~ smb.'s life out** (*to harass the life out of smb.*) mâc iñoára, mâc hicátlu, aród dit hicáte

WEARY FOR / AFTER *vb.* (*to pine*) ñ-si-alăcheáşte ínima di

WEASEL *s.* *zool.* nvistaľán → MARTEN; CATCH A ~ ASLEEP

WEATHER *s.* chiró, chiróu, chiról, oáră; **bad ~** chiró urút, uruteáţă; **fine ~** bunáţă ‖ ALIA 6 (*bad ~*) urutéţă, eáră, furtúnă, slábă dzúuă; *also various adjectives preceding the noun* **chiró**: scláb, sălábu, nebún, acăţát, paľu, paľó; *Na:* cacocherí (*ant.* calocherí), B-ARCH 6 *and* 7 → TORRID

WEATHER *vb.* (*to bear up against successfully*) trec

WEATHERBEATEN *adj.* **I am ~** ≈ âñ tricú rúglu prit náre

WEAVE *vb.* ▼ţas; (*to interlace*) (a)mplătéscu (*and* amblă-), mblitéscu

WEAVER *s.* ţăsătór

WEAVING *s.* ţăseáre, ţăsătúră

WEAVING LOOM *s.* arăzbóiu

WEB *s.* ţăsătúră

WEB *vb.* ▼ţas

WEE *adj.* ñicúţ

WEENY *adj.* → WEE

WED *vb.* ‖ *Cru:* ăncurún, GOLAB 206;

WEDDING s. númtă, núntă, haráuă, haréi; **at your** ~ la haráua-ţ;
Happy ~! Stifăñ búne! ‖ *Cru:* ăncurunáre, GOLAB 206; *also* PARALLELE
143; *LvO, Rod, Smx:* númptă, B-ARCH 448
    WEDGE s. (*for cleaving wood*) scârpă, sfínă
    WEDGE vb. (*to fasten*) ▾sfinuséscu
    WEDLOCK s. (*of women*) mărít
    WEDNESDAY s. ñércuri ‖ *Ses:* ñércur, *Na:* ñércură, B-ARCH 535
    WEED s. *N:* jumeáră ‖ ALR 40: iárbă
    WEED vb. plivéscu, prăşéscu, sărcĺédz, scălséscu
    WEEK s. siptămână, stămână; **Holy** ~ Siptămâna máre; **Rogation** ~
Siptămâna álbă
    WEEKDAY s. (dzúuă) lălătoáre ‖ *Amc, Src, Tur:* lăvrătoáre
    WEEP vb. arăvdăséscu, arăbdăséscu; **to ~ bitter tears** scârlédz;
plângu cu sugĺíţuri → LAMENT
    WEEPER s. (*female* ~) váie
    WEEPING s. plândzeáre, plândzire, asplândzire
    WEEPING adj. plâmtu, -mtă, -mţâ, -mte; lăcrămós, -oásă *and*
lăcrimós; lăcrimát
    WEEPY adj. lăcrimát, şcĺimurós, -oásă; *also* şcĺiu-
    WEEVIL s. ent. ‖ *Prv:* mumúdhâ CL 256
    WEFT s. trámă
    WEIGH vb. trag tu zíyă; ▾yixéscu, *N:* yiséscu; ▾ziyăséscu,
ziyiséscu; **to ~ heavy** (*as of smb.'s words*) 3 sg cádi greu, 3 pl
trag greu *or* trag greu tu cândáre; (*to press down with or as with
a heavy weight*) ▾(a)ndés; ▾ngrec ‖ DIARO 93: **Iron ~s a lot, wool does
not** Hérlu ângreácâ múltu, lâna nu-ngreácâ
    WEIGH DOWN vb. ▾(a)ngréc, dipún, ▾useléscu; (*as of an old house*)
hămbluséscu, hlâmbuséscu; (*to overwhelm, as diseases or concerns*)
pulcuséscu
    WEIGH HEAVILY UPON vb. ñi-ngreácă → OPPRESS
    WEIGHING s. ziyisíre, zixíre
    WEIGHT s. angricáre → PUT ON ~
    WEIGHTLESS adj. lişór, -oáră
    WEIGHTY adj. greu, greáuă, grei, greále; angricós, -oásă
    WELCOME vb. ‖ BATSARIA 35: **Welcome him in!** Dzâ-ĺ si urseáscă!
    WELCOME! ‖ DIARO 131: sg. Ghíni viníş! *or* S-hii ghíni vinít! pl.
Ghíni vinítu! *or* S-hiţ ghíni viniţ! (*The usual answer is* Ghini ti
aflái! (*sg*) *or* Ghini vi aflái! (*pl*)
    WELKIN s. (*the vault of the sky*) ţer, uranó
    WELL s. fântână (*and* fândână); *N:* funtână; *dim.* fântâneáuă, fân-
tâñoáră, fântâníce; puţ, ízvur, bunár, piyádhe; **artesian** ~ şitrăváne ‖ ALR 850: (~ **with wheel**) apúţ cu cicrícă
    WELL vb. (*to run*) ▾(a)zvóm, ndzămédz

WELL

WELL *adv.* ghíne, muşeát, de-a muşátlui, príma → BE DOING ~

WELL *cj.* méţi; ~, **so be it!** Méţi, şi-aşá! (*expostulation*) amí

WELL ON IN THE NIGHT *adv.* noáptea pára-oáră; paráură

WELL SET UP *adj.* ímnă cu zíya m brâu

WELL-ADVISED *adj.* achicăsít, câştigós, -oásă ‖ cu míntea tu loc, BASME 347

WELL-BALANCED *adj.* aştirnút

WELL-BEING *s.* ghineáţă

WELL-BELOVED *adj.* vrut, zdrod, *f* zdródă (*sic*); ñícă *f*

WELLBORN *adj.* celepíu, cilibí, di lăgámă

WELL-BRED *adj.* pilichisít, prăxít; tirbietlâ, *f* -tloáñe, *m pl* -tládz, *f pl* -tloáñe

WELL-CONDITIONED *adj.* sănătós, -oásă; zófnic

WELL-CONSIDERED *adj.* (*as of statements*) minduít

WELL-DISPOSED: I am ~ Am búnile; Am cuc (*lit. 'to have cuckoo'*)

WELL-DRAWN *adj.* (*well designed, as of smb.'s nose, brows, etc.*) cundiľát, cundiľisít, yrăpsít, scriát

WELL-FED *adj.* (*of a horse*) urdzát

WELL-FIXED *adj.* amintát; arhúndu, -ndă, -ndzâ, -nde; avút

WELL-FOUNDEDLY *adv.* cu usíe

WELL-GROOMED *adj.* mutrít ‖ anviscút ca dit ou, BASME 421 (*lit. 'dressed as if from an egg'*)

WELL-GROUNDED *adj.* (*as of an opinion*) thimiľós, -oásă

WELL-HEELED *adj.* → WELL-FIXED

WELL-KNIT *adj.* (*of people*) plătărós, -oásă; *also* pultărós

WELL-MANNERED *adj.* pilichisít, pripsít, prăpsít

WELL-OFF *adj.* nicuchír → BE ~; RICH

WELL-SET *adj.* (*strongly built*) ‖ fáptu ghíne, adărát ghíne, PA-RALLELE 134

WELL-TIMED: (*opportune*) ~ **moment** apuhíe, aráste

WELL-TO-DO *adj.* amintát → PROSPEROUS

WELL-TRAVELLED *adj.* alăgát, tăxidhipsít; **A ~ person knows many things** Alăgátlu múlte şti

WELL-TURNED *adj.* (*of the shape of a nose*) cu nările trápte

WELT *s.* (*blow or bump from a blow*) şúşcă

WELT *vb.* → HIT, STRIKE

WELTER *s.* alăcíre

WELTER *vb.* (*to become deeply sunk or involved*) ▼afúndu, ▼afundédz

WENCH *s.* (*girl*) feátă; (*female servant*) huzmicheáră

WEND *vb.* trag cálea; ~ **one's way** ľ-u dau cătră

WERE *vb.* 2-6 *past tense* of BE →

WEST *s.* (a)scăpitátă a soárilui; chirítă

WESTWARD *adv.* cătră tu ascăpitáta a soárilui

WET *adj.* ud, udát, muľát; (~ *with dew*) aruvinát ‖ HRISTU 44: aud
WET NURSE *s.* (*of a person*) pára-mánă; (*of sheep*) (a)plicătoáre
WET *vb.* ▼ud; **Wet the flowers!** Udáţ lilícile! (*to pay for a drink on the occasion of a personal success, etc.*) **This should be wetted!** Va udáre!
WETLAND *s.* → MARSH
WETTING *s.* udáre udătură
WHACK (*condition, proper working order*): **out of** ~ aspártu
WHACK *vb.* (*to strike*) agudéscu, agudéscu únă
WHALE *vb.* (*to thrash*) → BEAT
WHARF *s.* mol
WHAT *rel. and interrog. pron.* ţe, *N:* ţi; ţe? *N:* ţi? ~ **a** ... ţe lai ...; ~ **a kingly wedding party!** Ţe lai númtă amirăreáscă! (*disparagingly*) ~ **a comical idea!** Ţe s-ti ñirĭ! ~ **wind blows you here?** Ţe pân-auá? (*with omitted subject and verb*)
WHAT ABOUT *cj.* am; ~ **the other two?** Am alánte doáuă?
WHATEVER *pron.* íţe, íţi, íţişi, íitipása; *N:* císci, cíşci, ciúşciu
WHATNOT *s.* (*for keeping spoons*) *Băi:* lingurár
WHATSOEVER *pron.* hici, ici, can, dip; **I am not scared** ~ Dip nu mi aspár
WHEAL *s. derm.* cucúdă (*and* cucúdhă)
WHEAT *s.* gârnu (*and* gărnu), grân, găr; **best sort of** ~ arusíe, aruseáuă, fluríţă; **white** ~ cutruľáuă; **spring** ~ trimíľu, trimíñu
WHEEDLE *vb.* culăchipséscu, hăidhipséscu, bag pri sómnu
WHEEL *s.* (a)roátă, (a)rócut, *G:* arucoátă; ghirghíl, furcutáş; **mill** ~ arócut di moáră ‖ *Prv:* aroátă, aródhă, CL 37; *Pls:* răcătóciu, CL 260; *SJos:* techerliéc, CL 262; *GSus:* arăcóthor, CL 37; *Peş:* arăcóthar, *ibid.*
WHEELBARROW *s.* ‖ *GSus:* măxícă, CL 255; *SJos:* căruţícă, CL 41; DIARO 204: câruţáchi
WHEELWRIGHT *s.* ‖ *Av, SJos:* arăbăgí, CL 37; *Prv:* caropió, CL 40; *Peş:* măxár, CL 255
WHEEZE *s.* (*a sound of wheezing*) ndăcăníre; (*gag*) → JOKE
WHEEZE *vb.* ndăcănéscu
WHELP *s.* (*the process and the place*) fitáľu; (a)fitáre
WHELP *vb.* ▼fet, *N:* afét
WHEN *adv.* cându, *N:* cănd; cari, car, cára, cárea, dicára, ánda, nda, íţe, íţi, íţişi, ţe, stícă, únă ţe; ~ **he saw that death was approaching** ... Iţi vidzú că hárlu si-apruché ...; **the day** ~ **he was born** dzúua ţe s-află; ~ **fear began to seize us** ... cari víñe fríca di nă lo ...; ~ **you come, let me know** Ánda s-yiñ, si-ñ dai hăbáre; ~ **you leave, call me** Cánda va s-fudzi, grea-ñ; ~ **they saw that,**

WHEN

they stopped talking Cára vidzúră aşí, tăcúră ‖ CUNIA: iu; **I squan-
dered a couple of days when I didn't work at all** chirúi ăndáuă
dzăli iu nu lucrai dip (*in a private letter*)

WHEN HELL FREEZES OVER ≈ când va angheádză mórtul (*lit. 'when the
dead resurrects'*); cându va s-ţâ scoátă límba peri (*lit. 'when your
tongue will have hair'*); cându va si s-fácă márea liváde (*lit.
'when the sea becomes an orchard'*); va s-creáscă meáre n pluchi; pi
coádă di cripitór; noápte búnă (*lit. 'good night!'*) ; va yínă ca di
cheátra ‖ PARALLELE 126: cându va-ñ ved cótlu (*lit. 'when I see my
elbow'*); DIARO 91: stăi si-adúnâ méľlu!

WHENCE *adv.*, *cj.* di iu

WHENEVER *adv.* cănţi, cánţido, cănţidó; *N:* cănchişdó ‖ CUNIA 217:
cănţi s-híbă

WHENSOEVER *adv.* → WHENEVER

WHERE *adv.* iu, cătă iu, clo iu, ţe; **Hi, ~ are you going?** Iu, oáră
búnă; **He went to the mountain ~ there were few houses** S-dúse la
múnte ţi erá psâne căsi

WHEREIN *adv.* iu

WHEREVER *adv.* iudó, iuchişdó, iúţi, iuţidó, iúţi s-híbă

WHEREWITHAL *s.* parádz *m pl*

WHET *vb.* ▼truhiséscu → SHARPEN

WHETHER *cj.* fúri-că, fúreşi că, ai că fúre

WHETSTONE *s.* greáse; *also:* acóne, mirácune, truhó ‖ *GSus:* murá-
coni, CL 256; *G:* minácuri, *F:* mureáhănă, SarD 27; ALB: *Kёrb*, *Pe:*
gríă, gríe; *Pe:* măreáhnă; *Sln:* măréră, mâréră; *Pёr:* meráhănă, *Dren:*
măráhănă, Brâncuş 558

WHEY *s.* dzăr, şar

WHICH *pron.* ţe, cáre, cari, *N:* cai, cáie; *g/d* a curór; **Not a single day passed on ~ they did not intrude into his vineyard** Nu triţeá dzúuă ţe s-nu-ľ si-arúcă tu-ayíñe; **~ shepherds did you meet on
your way?** Cari picurári astăľáşi n cále?

WHICHEVER *pron.* iţidó, ítipása (*sic*)

WHICKER *vb.* → NEIGH

WHIFF *s.* (*puff*) sufláre

WHIFF SMOKE *vb.* (*to belch out smoke*) afúm

WHILE *s.* chiró, oáră; **after a ~** dúpă oáră; **a little ~** niheámă,
niheámătă, niheámăză; **after a little ~** dúpă niheámăză

WHILE *cj.* cum; **~ they were at play** cum si-agiucá; **~ some of them
..., some others ...** áltu ..., áltu ...

WHILE AWAY *vb.* ▼şintéscu **to ~ the time** ñ-trec oára, BASME 409

WHILOM *adv.* (*formerly*) năoáră, unăoáră, unoáră

WHIM *s.* chéfe, chéifă, fărfúdă; camómate *f pl*; **They satisfied her
every ~** Túte chéhĭle ľi li făţeá (*sic*) → CAPRICE

WHIMPER *s.* schimuráre

WHIMPER *vb.* nciñédz, nciuñédz, nciurédz, schímur, şcľímur, şcľimurédz, şcľumurédz

WHIMPERER *adj.* ngrâñárcu, -rcă, -rţi, -rţe

WHIMPERING *adj.* (*as of a child*) ngrâñárcu, -rcă, rţi, -rţe; (*of a river*) şcľimurós, -oásă; *also* şcľimurát

WHIMSICAL *adj.* cu órile → CAPRICIOUS

WINCE *vb.* mi trag năpói; ▾şuţ, ▾aruşúţ

WHINE *s.* ancăníre → GROAN

WHINE *vb.* ciunédz, schímur ‖ scľímur, şcľímur, CAPIDAN 150

WHINNY *s.* arujíre

WHINNY *vb.* → NEIGH

WHIP *s.* cămíche, cărbáţă, gărbáce, gărbáciu, sficiu, zviciu, vúrdhal; (*in children's games*) tómbu, tómbul ‖ **Pls:** hângíc, CL 253; **Peş:** cămişíc, cămâşíc CL 41

WHIP *vb.* jirtuéscu, frâştuéscu, păléscu, zăpăléscu, árdu vâră; **Get lost before they ~ you!** Fudzi că va-ţ árdă únă! (*to bite, of frost*) 3 *sg*: ñ-ciuleáşte urécľile

WHIP AWAY *vb.* mi fac căípe → DISAPPEAR

WHIPPED *adj.* jirtuít, frâştuít

WHIPPERSNAPPER *s.* măscără, mâscără; om di ciuchi

WHIPPING *s.* jirtuíre, frâştuíre

WHIR(R) *s.* văzúră → RUMBLE

WHIRL *s.* vâltoáre

WHIRLING *adj.* ‖ (*as of smoke*) **a white ~ smoke** un fum albu cair-cair, HRISTU 33; (*of a river*) burdulác, BELIMACE 102

WHIRL ALONG *vb.* mi u angán → BOLT

WHIRLPOOL *s.* vâltoáre, viró, zuryió

WHIRLWIND *s.* (*evil genius of the wind*) vinturíţă

WHISK AWAY *vb.* mi fac căípe → DISAPPEAR

WHISKER *s.* mustácă, mustáţă

WHISPER *s.* şupturáre, şuptiráre, şuputíre, şúrşur, şurşuráre, şuşuráre, ciuciuráre puşpuráre, puşpuríre, pâşpuráre, puşpur ‖ 3 *sg pt:* murmurí, HRISTU 63

WHISPER *vb.* şúptur, şupturédz, şupirédz, şurşurédz, şuşurédz, ciúciur, ciuciurédz, pâşpurédz, pişpurédz, puşpurédz

WHISPERING *s.* şurşuráre, şuşuráre → WHISPER

WHISTLE *s.* flúir, fluér, fluiáră, fiľoáră, píscă, pízgă, piscálă, pilipíscă, pilipísche, şuiáră; (*made of clay*) bilbíiu

WHISTLE *vb.* şúir, şíur; (*speaking of the wind*) ţíur; **You may ~ for it!** ≈ Ľa-ľ ciulíca (carĭ poţ)! Ľa-ñ coáda, lúpe! (*lit. 'Wolf, take my tail!'*); Va-ñ mâţĭ coáľile! (*lit. 'You'll eat my balls!'*); Va-ñ ľai cúrlu! (*lit. 'You'll take my ass!'*) ‖ ş-áltu ţe? BASME 26

(lit. 'And what else?')

WHISTLE DOWN THE WIND vb. (i.e., in vain) zburắscu pi víntu

WHISTLE OFF vb. (to take oneself off) li aspél

WHISTLING s. şuiráre, şuirát, şuirătúră

WHIT: **not a ~** cât trâ yitríe; cât yitrúşca → AT ALL

WHITE s. (the ~ of the eye) albeáţa a ócĺului; (~ from an egg) albúş, albeáţă

WHITE adj. álbu, álbă, álghi, álbe; (of an old person) cu pérlu cáir; **G**: (of horses) cil; (of a mule) bárdz → MAKE ~ ‖ HRISTU 1: cu albi 'wearing ~ clothing'

WHITE FROST s. (hoarfrost) brúmă

WHITE SHEEP WITH BLACK HEAD / LEGS s. oácărnu, ócren

WHITE-FACED adj. sálbit, săhñisít

WHITEHEAD s. derm. arópun → PIMPLE

WHITE-LEGGED adj. (of sheep and goats) pudhrúşcu

WHITEN vb. (usu. cloth) alghéscu, biléscu; **This cloth does not ~ well** Pândza aéstă nu s-bileáşte ghíne

WHITENESS s. albeáţă

WHITENING s. alghíre

WHITE-REDDISH adj. (usu. of sheep) ghesucánat, -cánut

WHITEWASH vb. azvistuéscu

WHITEWASHING s. azvistuíre

WHITHER adv. iu

WHITHERSOEVER adv. iuţidó, iúţi s-híbă, iuchişdó

WITHIN prep. ‖ TULLIU 81: **Real life was to begin ~ three months** di-anculeá trei meş eară bána

WHITISH adj. (usu. of sheep and goats) asprucánat, bărdhúş

WHIT-SUNDAY s. ‖ **Cru**: arsáĺe, GOLAB 201

WHITTLE vb. ▾pilichiséscu ‖ **Cru**: arád, GOLAB 200

WHIZ(Z) s. şuiráre, şiuráre, vângâníre, zvângâníre

WHIZ(Z) vb. şúir, şíur, vângânéscu, zvângânéscu

WHIZZING s. şuiráre, şuirát, şuirătúră

WHO interrog. and rel. pron. cári, cari, **N**: acári, ácari; cai, cáie, ţe, ţi; (rare) ţíne; **~ knows how circumstances brought her here** Cári-şte cum u-adúse oára; **I, ~ have killed the dragon?** Míne, ţe vătămái lámñea? **Who are you going to leave me with?** Míne cu cáie va mi aláşi? ‖ STERGHIU 4: (to a stranger) Cari hiţ voi? 'Who are you'; BELIMACE 55: **~ are you, sir?** Dómnul cáre eáste? **~ knows how much / many** cá-şti-cátu, cá-şti-câtâ, cá-şti-câţ, cá-şti-câti, DIARO 219; **who knows who** ţí-şti cári; **who knows what** ţí-şti ţi, DIARO 220

WHOEVER pron. ichişdó, iţindó, iţidó, careţidó, cárechişdó, cáriţindó, cáiţidó, cáriţi, ítipása, íţi om va híbă, ţiuşticáre, ţenuşcáre, ţéştucáre; **to whomever** a cuichişdó, a cuinivá; **Give it to**

whomever you want Dă-ľ a cuiţidó s-híbă; ~ **saw him called him** Cai âl videá âľ strigá

WHOLE *adj.* ntreg (*and* ndreg), -eágă, *m/f pl* ntredzĭ; (*total*) bitivíŭ ‖ **a ~ year** → YEAR

   WHOLEHEARTED *adj.* curát, dişcľís; hăriós [•ri•ós]

   WHOLEHEARTEDLY *adv.* dintr-ínimă cu doáule mâñ, BASME 498

   WHOLFSALE *adv.* tuptáne

   WHOLESALER *s.* tuptangí(u)

   WHOLESOME *adj.* sân, -nă, -ñ, -ne; sănătós, -oásă; cu hăíre

   WHOM *pron.* ţe, ţi → WHO

   WHOOP *s.* aurláre, strigáre, huhutíre

   WHOOP *vb.* ▾aúrlu, strig, *N:* astríg; huéscu, huhutéscu

   WHOOPING COUGH *s.* túse aráuă; crep, cripát; dzâpit, dzâpită

   WHOPPING LIE *s.* minciúnă di la háne (*lit.* 'a lie from the inn')

   WHORE *s.* dósă → PROSTITUTE

   WHORTLEBERRY *s.* afíngă, afínghe ‖ *Av:* ţápurnă, CL 262

   WHOSE *poss. pron.* a cui, ţe, ţi ‖ ALR 1684: **~ is this horse?** A curi om eáste cálu aéstu?

   WHY *cj.* ţe, tră ţe, că ţe; **Rush out and see ~ the dogs are barking** Aleápidă-te s-vedz ţe bat câñľi; **Liar, ~ did you deceive me?** Bre pséfte, ţe mi-arăsişi? **~ are you not saying anything?** Că ţe nu gréşti? ‖ BELIMACE 47: ti ţi itíe

   WICK *s.* fitíľe, fitíľu; **~ support** (*in an oil lamp*) şamandúră

   WICKED *adj.* afíşcu, cătrăceárcu, chiutandál, ni-ñiruít, pabés, ba-; puşcľós, -oásă; s(c)lab, -bă, s(c)laghi, -be; Turc, turcanácat; vómbir

   WICKED MAN *s.* bubuşár

   WICKEDNESS *s.* arăiáţă, câníľe, heáre, hulíe, vumbirlâche

   WICKER *s.* ‖ PC: lumáche di rắchítă

   WICKET *s.* (**small gate**) purtíţă, părníşcă

   WIDE *adj.* lárgu, -rgă, -rdzi, -rdze; lat, -tă, laţ, -te; vlíhur

   WIDE-AWAKE *adj.* aştirnút, diştéptu, lugheáric

   WIDE-EYED *adj.* → AMAZED; (*naive*) apló *invar.*; tivichél

   WIDEN *vb.* ▾lărdzéscu, lărguéscu

   WIDENING *s.* (*as of a shirt*) lărdzíre

   WIDESPREAD *adj.* arăspândít

   WIDOW *s.* véduuă

   WIDOW *vb.* (*to survive as a ~ or widower*) nviduéscu, viduéscu

   WIDOWED *adj.* nviduít, viduít

   WIDOWER *s.* véduu; *dim.* (*or young ~*) vidúşcu

   WIDOW(ER)HOOD *s.* viduíre

   WIDTH *s.* lărdzíme, viryeáne

   WIFE *s.* muľáre, mgľáre, mgheáre; niveástă, nveástă, *dim.* nivistícă, curcoáñe; *Băi:* hurhoáñe; (*one of the wives of an Albanian*) şémbară, şămbară; **a priest's** ~ prifteásă; **a shepherd's** ~ picuroáñe, picurăroáñe; **a fisher's** ~ piscăroáñe; **a miller's** ~ murárä; **a lumberman's** ~ limnăroáñe ‖ *Mul:* muiére, B-ARCH 452; **young** ~ nivistúľe, PARALLELE 141

WIG *s.* pirúcľe

WIGGLE *vb.* ▾clátin, ▾clătín, ▾ñíşcu, ▾mut

WILD *adj.* áyru, păduríş; (*turbulent*) zevzéc; ~ **animal** príce ‖ *Cru:* (~ *animal*) ayríme, GOLAB 196 → BE ~ WITH DELIGHT, RUN ~

WILD APPLE *s.* ayrómbal, ayrómin, *G:* grómin

WILD BOAR *s.* ‖ HRISTU 36: porc ayăr

WILD GRAPE *s.* ayrandzaľáuă

WILD MARJORAM *s. bot.* (a)ríyan

WILDFIRE *s.* foc, yeangâne

WILD-GOOSE CHASE *s.* puľ tu vímtu

WILD-LOOKING *adj.* chirdút

WILDLY *adv.* áyru

WILE *s.* → TRICK

WILE *vb.* → ENTICE, LURE

WILL *s.* vreáre; dhyeátă, dheátă, thélimă; **at smb.'s** ~ dúpă vóla a; **God's** ~ **be done!** Al Dumnidzău si s-fácă! (*'will' is omitted*); **by last will** (*before death*) *adv.* cu límbă di moárte → AT ONE'S OWN SWEET ~, OF ONE'S OWN WILL

WILL (*aux. for the fut.*) va, vai; *sporadically, as in Gop, Mul:* a; **I** ~ **leave** Va mi dúc; **We** ~ **leave** Va nă dúţim; **They** ~ **drown** Va si s neácă; **They** ~ **not hear his flute** Nu a s-ávdă-a lui fluiáră; **He** ~ **be either sleeping, or singing** I vai doármă, i vai cântă

WILLFUL *adj.* (*as of a horse*) ucheaļíu → INTRACTABLE

WILLFULNESS *s.* inagilâche

WILLIES *s.* ori *f pl*; nevricádz *m pl*, nevricó *sg*

WILLING OR NOT *adv.* (*willy-nilly*) cu vreáre, cu nivreáre; di vreáre, di nivreáre

WILLOW *s.* răchítă, sálţe, *dim.* sălţioáră ‖ *Cru:* sálcu, *pl* sálţă, GOLAB 247

WILLY-NILLY → WILLING OR NOT

WILT *vb.* (*to fade*) păléscu; (*to loose courage or spirit; to lower the spirit or force of*) ▾apilipséscu

WILY *adj.* plan, -nă, -ñ, -ne → TRICKY

WIMBLE *s.* sfrédin → DRILL

WIN *vb.* amíntu (*and* amíndu); (*to finish before the other players, esp. at cards*) ies, *aor.* i(n)şíi *or* i(n)şái

WIN OVER *vb.* (*as a town*) ľau

WINCE: to ~ **as if whipped** arsár ca chipinát di şárpe ‖ (*as of*

fear or pain): arsár năpói; mi trag năpói, mi astrág năpói

WIND *s.* víntu, vimtu; **strong** ~ sindilíe, şindéľu, spídhă (*and* spídă) ‖ ALIA 11: víndu, vímptu, aiéră; **Arm, Pals, Pdz**: avímptu, B-ARCH 11; **the ~ is blowing**: *Mul*: báte víntu, *Amc, Na, Vil*: súflă; *An*: trádzi aéras, B-ARCH 12; STERGHIU 24: *voc.* vímte! → PUT THE ~ UP SMB., NORTH ~, SOUTH ~

WIND *vb.* (*to* ~ *a clock*) ▾cruţéscu, ▾curdiséscu, ▾curdhuséscu (*and* curduséscu); ~ **up my clock!** Curdiseá-ñ oára *or* Cruţeá-ñ oára! (*to manipulate*) ~ **smb. round one's little finger** (a)ncálţu şi discálţu; (*to have a curving course*) ▾stricór; (*to encircle with smth. pliable*) ▾ncurpilédz (*and* ngur-), ▾şuţ, ▾aruşúţ

WIND GAP *s.* coácă, şilătúră

WIND OFF / UP *vb.* (*of thread*) ▾deápin

WINDBAG *s.* (*an very talkative person*) lafăzán, năpudheáric, políloy, zburyeáric, zburyeárcu

WINDER *s.* vârteániţă, vârteánţă, cicrícă, cicríche

WINDER MAKER *s.* (*a manufacturer of winders*) cicriccí [ĉi•krik•ĉí]

WINDFALL *s.* báftă → LUCK

WINDING *s.* (*of thread*) dipănáre; (*of a road*) şuţâtúră, turnătúră; (*grimace*) strâmbătúră

WINDING DEVICE *s.* aruidheáuă, cicrícă, dipinătór, rudáne, vărteániţă, vârteánţă, vârténiţă

WINDING UP *s.* (*as a clock*) cruţíre, curţíre

WINDING-SHEET *s.* (*shroud*) sáván, sávún

WINDOW *s.* fireástă, fireástră, cripitúră, firídhă (*and* firídă), geáme, pălăthíre, pingére; **small** ~ mâzgálă ‖ **Amc, An, Na**: parádhir, **Els**: pirdhíri, **Kat, Perd**: firídhă, B-ARCH 401; VELO 11: frídă

WINDOW FRAME *s.* pirváze, márgură

WINDOW GLASS *s.* geam *n or* geáme *f, pl* geñ

WINDOW SASH *s.* ciurciuvé, circivé, ciurcĭuvée

WINDOW-CATCH *s.* cărcheáuă

WINDOW-SHUTTER *s.* cănát, cănáte ‖ **Peş**: căpáche, CL 41

WINDSTORM *s.* ‖ PC: vímtu

WINDY *adj.* vintós, -oásă; *also* vimtós

WINE *s.* yin; **thin** ~ lánghir; **red** ~ aruşitúră; ~ *brought to church on one's birthday or name day* anámă

WINE CELLAR *s.* bímţă

WINE DEALER *s.* yinár

WINE SHOP *s.* tavérnă → TAVERN

WINEGROWER *s.* ‖ **GSus**: simén, CL 260

WING *s.* áripă, árpă, áripită, árpită, áriptă ‖ ALIA 108: peáne, péne, pupíţă; VELO 10: árpă → TAKE SMB. UNDER ONE'S ~

WINGDING *s.* (*party*) băiráme, muabéte [mu•a•], ziaféte [zi•a•]

WINGED

WINGED *adj.* azbuirătór, -toáre ~ **creature** pitúmin

WINK AT SMB. *vb.* fac cu ócľul, ñ-fac ntr-ócľu, cálcu cu ócľul, dau cu nóima; ~ **with one's left eye** fac sémnu cu-astângul

WINNER *s.* azvingătór

WINNING *adj.* (*as at cards*) câştigós, -oásă

WINNOW **vb.** (*to remove chaff, etc. by a current of air*) víntur, azvíntur, azvímtur

WINTER *s.* iárnă, iárănă, *N:* iáră; **last ~** *adv.* ástă-iárnă ‖ *rn* > *n in* **Gra, Grăm, Hor, Kar, Kat, Mi, Pdz, Plat, Rod,** B-ARCH 454

WINTER *adj.* ~ **supplies** arnátic, arnátcu; ~ **pears** górţă arnareáte; ~ **coat** (*from sheep skin*) cujúc, cojóc

WINTER *vb.* (*to pass the winter*) irnédz, iernédz, airnédz, arnédz ‖ **passed the winter** *3 sg/pl* irra, HRISTU 3

WINTER SEASON *s.* iárnă, irnáre, arnáre, irnát

WINTERING QUARTERS *s.* (*for shepherds and their flocks*) irnát, arnát, aríu, arníu, aríe; câşlă; **In winter time this place is good quarters for sheep** Auá iárna eásti câşlă bun trâ oi; **I am going to the ~** Mi duc arníe

WINTERTIME *s.* → WINTER

WINTRY *adj.* (*cold*) *m/f sg* aráţe, *m/f pl* arăţi

WIPE *s.* (*cleaning*) sfungărsíre

WIPE *vb.* ▼(a)ştérgu (→ § 32); (*with a sponge*) sfungărséscu; *fig.* ~ **the floor with smb.** rizilipséscu → REPRIMAND

WIPED OUT *vb.* aştérsu

WIPING *s.* (a)şteárdzire; (a)născărsíre, ▼anăschirsíre, spăstríre

WIPING OUT *s.* (a)şteárdzire

WIRE *s.* sírmă

WIRE *vb.* (*to send word by telegraph*) bat teľu

WIRE-PULLER *s.* tirtipcí

WISDOM *s.* mínte, mintéză (*and* mindéză), mintiminíľe

WISDOM TOOTH *s.* măseáua di mínte; streápită

WISE *adj.* mintiós, -oásă (*and* mindiós, minduós), mintimén (*and* mindi-); diştiptát, ştiút; cu sicáră n cap (*lit. 'with rye in one's head'*) → INTELLIGENCE); *pl:* cápite cu ţercľu; **with ~ words** cu zboáre ştiúte; prónim; **to become ~** bag mínte búnă

WISEACRE *s.* calpuzán

WISELY *adv.* auşeáşte; cu cále

WISH *s.* dimândáre, vólă, vreáre; (*invocation*) uráre, urát; ursíre; **You have fulfilled your ~** Tíne ursírea ţ-u fiţéşi ‖ **last ~** (*before death*) dórlu dit sóne, BASME 430

WISH *vb.* (*to dream*) dor; (*to whim, to fancy*) *3 sg impers.* ñ-si urixeáşte; **He ~ed to have a child** Dureá s-áibă un ficiór; **She ~ed a rose** Ľ-si urixí nă trandáfilă; (*to desire*) **His mother ~ed to**

kiss him Mă-sa dureá să-l báşe; **We will give you as much as you ~** Va-ţ dăm cât va u-ái tu vreáre; (*to die to, to desire desperately*) crep, plăscănéscu; (*to long*) ñ-víñe dórlu, mi ľa dórlu; (*to bid*) (a)ór, urédz, dau urăciúnea să; **He ~ed them all the best** Lă ură câti búni sun pri loc

WISHING FOR THE MOON ≈ ‖ fum di hióle! (*to indulge in illusions*), RÉCATAS 50

WISHY-WASHY *adj.* ánustu, -stă, -şţâ, -ste

WISP *s.* (*bunch*) mânátă, mnátă

WISTFUL *adj.* lângărós, -oásă

WIT *s.* mínte; *to* **be at one's ~'s end** nu-ñ táľe puscárlu → TO PUT SMB. TO HIS/HER ~'S END

WIZARD *s.* măyístru *m*, măyístră *f*; mándisă *f*; Máia-Gáia; palang-heár

WITCH *vb.* măyipséscu → BEWITCH

WITCHCRAFT *s.* amáie, (a)máye, măndíe

WITCHERY *s.* → WITCHCRAFT

WITCHING *s.* măyipsíre, nămătisíre

WITH *prep.* cu; **to cut ~ a knife** taľu cu cuţútlu; di; **He keeps the house ~ trifling sums** di şíle, di páľe ţâne cásă; **~ all one's forces** cât pot; a mórtului; **~ bag and baggage** cu síndu, cu pándu; **~ bent head** cu cáplu spindzurát (*or* plicát); **~ good reason** drip-tátic *or* driptática; **~ moil and toil** rúfu-n-búfu; **~ many small children** (*of a family*) minút, *as in*: Are fumeáľe minútă ('He has a family ~ many small children'); **~ folded arms** cu mâñle ncruţíte (*or* ncruţiľáte); **~ might and main** *adv.* a mórtului

WITHDRAW *vb.* ▾trag năpói; trag mână (→ ABNEGATE);, ▾cúrmu; **The river has withdrawn** Ápa s-trápse; **We withdrew the boy from the sheep** Ficiórlu l-curmăm di la oi

WITHDRAWAL *s.* ‖ (*renouncement*) trádzire di mână, CAPIDAN 174

WITHDRAWN *adj.* (*isolated, secluded*) nguvát, axólit, pahóm

WITHE *s.* liyăreáuă, lúră, veárgă

WITHER *vb.* ▾(a)spárgu → FADE

WITHHOLD *vb.* ▾ţân, ▾căpistruséscu, ▾acumtinéscu

WITHIN *prep.* tu; **~ rifle shot** to tuféche; **~ a short time** dúpă niscântă oáră

WITHOUT *prep.* and *cj.* fără, făr-di, fără să; **~ saying a word** fără să scoátă zbor din gúră; **~ doubt** fără di áltă ‖ **~ much ado** níţi únă, níţi doáuă, BASME 500; níţi únă, níţi áltă, BASME 60; **~ question** nu va (vârnă) dzâcă, BASME 590

WITHSTAND *vb.* ▾ţân, ▾ţân chéptu, dă(i)năséscu, dăniséscu, stă-nipséscu, văstăxéscu; (*to abide*) ▾arávdu → STAND

WITNESS *s.* mártur, mártir, şaít; **to bear ~** ▾mărtiriséscu, ▾măr-

WITTED

tirséscu

WITTED *adj.* pirgác

WITTY *adj.* theámin → CLEVER

WIZARD *s.* măyístru → W

WIZARDRY *s.* (*magic skill*) (a)máye, amáie; (*great skill*) măsturíľe, măsturíe

WIZENED *adj.* (*dried up*) uscát

WOBBLE *vb.* ▼trunduéscu → SHIVER

WOE *s.* → SUFFERING

WOE *interj.* mar (di); cavái; ~ **me!** Mar di míne!

WOEBEGONE *adj.* cripát → SAD

WOEFUL *adj.* (*afflicted*) amărât; (*paltry*) pânghiós [•ǵós], -oásă

WOLD *s.* (*upland area*) plaiu

WOLF *s.* lup; (*in fairy tales*) Mástur Nicóla

WOMAN *s.* muľáre, mbľáre, mgľáre, mgheáre; *coll.* muľiráme; **strong** ~ muľiroáñe, bărbătoáñe ‖ ALIA 139: mľáre, mľére, bleáre; *Vil:* miáre, *GSus:* m'áre; *Mul:* muiére, B-ARCH 139; *Cru:* nveástă, mveástă, GOLAB 239

WOMAN IN CHILDBED *s.* lihoánă; *adj.* lihuñéscu

WOMANISH *adj.* muľiréscu, -eáscă, -éşţâ, -éşti

WOMB *s. anat.* mítră

WONDER *s.* ciúdă → MIRACLE

WONDER *vb.* ▼(a)ñír, ▼apuriséscu, ▼ciudiséscu, ▼ciuidiséscu, ciudéscu, ciuduéscu, ñ-frec ócľiľ, ▼limnuséscu, ▼ncruţéscu; ▼thămăséscu, ▼uiñiséscu, ▼uñiséscu

WONDERFUL *adj.* nişinlítcu, -tcă, -tţi, -tţe; scóntră *invar.*

WONT *s.* tabiéte, nveţ

WONTED *adj.* (*accustomed*) nviţát

WOOD *s.* (*forest*) pădúre; (~ *full with thickets*) drâzgă; (*material*) lémnu; (*much* ~) limníu; (*colored* ~) aváijivă; (*yellow* ~) ţermandél ‖ *F:* lémmu, SarD 98; lem, HRISTU 1; ('forest') *Els:* múnte, *Cern, Flam, Kast, LvO, Mal:* múndi

WOOD EMBERS *s. coll.* spúză, sprunáme, *N:* spúr(n)ă

WOOD PECKER *s. orn.* ciplitoáre, ciucutoáre, chétru ‖ *Smr:* ciclitoári, CL 43; *Prv:* ciupătoáre, CL 44; *SJos:* tripocsán, CL 262; *GSus:* puľu cu ciópcă, CL 259

WOODBORER *s. ent.* → BORER

WOODCOCK *s. orn.* bicáţă

WOODCRAFT *s.* ≈ măsturíe, măsturíe, măsturlíche

WOODCUTTER *s.* limnár, cupăceár, dărvár; (*his wife*) limnăroáñe

WOODED *adj.* pădurós, -oásă; sâlniós, -oásă *G:* sânluós, -oásă

WOODEN *adj.* limnós, -oásă; di lemnu; ~ **houses** căsi limnoáse

WOOD-FRETTER MOTH *s. ent.* saracufái

WOODLAND *s.* → FOREST

WOODLOT *s.* pădurícă, păduríce

WOOD-PIGEON *s. orn.* gugúce → STOCK-DOVE

WOODY *adj.* (*abounding in woods*) pădurós, -oásă; (*made or consisting of wood*) limnós, -oásă

WOOL *s.* lână; (*rough ~*) súmă; (*best ~*) cărmínă; (*inferior ~*) chéndic, chióndic; (*~ from around the tail*) códină, suélu; (*~ from the head*) cápit; (*mixed ~*) similână; (*hackled ~*) (a)pálă; (*the whole ~ from one sheep*) báscă; fălcáre di lână; (*lamb ~*) arnăpáche; (*a heap of ~ carded by hand*) clăndzu, **Smr:** clíndzu; (*a flock of ~*) ñiţ *or* ñíţă; ~ **waste** ştim, tălaciu, tălmáciu; **Much cry and little ~** ≈ Cari táţe fáţe → CRY ‖ ALR 435: **best ~** arúdă; **worst ~** áscură; ALB: **Dren, Kërb, Pe, Për, Sln:** báscă 'the whole ~ from one sheep,' Brâncuş 553

WOOL-COMBER *s.* chiptinár, hălăciu

WOOLEN FABRIC *s.* málină

WOOLEN GOODS *s.* (i)spápe

WOOLY *adj.* lânós, -oásă

WOOZINESS *s.* andrălăsíre

WOOZY *adj.* (*befuddled*) călít → DRUNK; (*dizzy, weak*) andrălăsít

WORD *s.* zbor, cuvéndă, dzácă, gráir, graiu, greiu, *pl* gréire; **N:** greaiu, *pl* greáire; **empty ~s** goále; **big ~** groáse; **Fine ~s butter no parsnips** ≈ Zboáre múlte - ftóhe máre (*lit.* 'many words [spell] great poverty') → IN OTHER ~S ‖ **Cru:** **~s cannot express** nu ăncápe zbor, GOLAB 205 → BREAK ONE'S ~; DEPART FROM ONE'S ~; MAKE ~S

WORDLYWISE *adj.* fricát, amisticát

WORK *s.* lúcru, **N:** lúcur; lucráre; **G:** (*occupation*) istréte; (*exhausting or villain ~*) hămălâche, pidhipsíre; (*accomplishment*) adărămíntu

WORK *vb.* lucrédz; **to ~ too much** pára-lucrédz; **to ~ grimly** lucrédz discufút, ▾pidhipséscu, ▾píngu oáhte; **~ oneself to death** mi tuchéscu tu lúcru; mi misucupséscu; (*to ~ with good results*) *3 sg impers:* ñ-cústă; (*to ~ well, to take effect*) surdiséscu; **~ miracles** *vb.* fac thámă

WORK HAVOC UPON SMTH. *vb.* trec prit dínte, trec prit lipídhă, bag stróflu (tu)

WORK IN *vb.* ▾bag

WORK OUT *vb.* cătăpăţéscu

WORKADAY *adj.* (*ordinary*) di-arádhă

WORKER *s.* lucrătór, lucrătóñu *m*, lucrătoáñe *f*; aryát; lăcrătór ‖ **F:** lăcătór, SarD 105; **Cru:** lucărtór, GOLAB 232; **An, Arm, Căl, Cern, Clis, Cot, Els, Gra, Kok, Lvz, Mi, Na, Pals, Pdz, Pro, Pros, Ses, Vil:** eryát, B-ARCH 250

WORKINGMAN

WORKINGMAN *s.* lucrătór
WORKMAN *s.* mástur
WORKMANSHIP *s.* (*craftsmanship*) micáme
WORKOUT *s.* (*test*) cătăpățíre
WORKSHOP *s.* aryăstír
WORLD *s.* a) lúme; (*the earth*) loc; (*people*) duñáuă; (*the uni-verse*) cózmu, duñáuă; (*a state of existence*) bánă ‖ **Cru:** duñáie, GOLAB 213
WORM *s.* yérmu; (*on goats*) vúngu ‖ ALIA 137: ghérmu, iérmu, iérru
WORM *vb.* (*to obtain by artful or insidious pleading*) scot
WORM-EATEN *adj.* yirmít
WORMWOOD *s. bot.* pilóñu
WORMY *adj.* yirm(in)ít; yirminós, -oásă; **to be ~, to become ~** yirm(in)éscu; **This cheese is ~ing** Cășcăválu aéstu yirmineáște
WORN *adj.* (*as of the heels of a boot*) mâcát; (*as of a blanket*) cingăñós, -oásă; găgăñós, -oásă; tráptu, -ptă, -pță, -pte; tuchít; **~ out** (*exhausted*) tălăít
WORN-OUT *adj.* arós, -oásă; mâcát, tuchít
WORRIED *adj.* sicliít, sinhisít, tu gailéi, tu pihtíe ‖ STERE 10: găilipsít
WORRISOME *adj.* (*inclined to worry or fret*) siclițít
WORRY *s.* cripáre, vălăndúră ‖ (*agitation*) murzueri, HRISTU 37; miracu, HRISTU 78 → CONCERN
WORRY *vb.* ▾ciurtuéscu, ▾minduéscu, ▾sinhiséscu, ▾sicliţéscu, am frundídz, am (máre) angătán, am zóre, mi mâcă sárachea, mi mâcă únă sárache, ñ-dă cripáre (*or* crăpări), trag cripárea a, ñ-u mâc ínima; **Don't ~!** Nu ti minduiá! Nu-ái zóre! Bágă-u (fésea) strâmbă! **Don't ~ me!** Nu-ñ dă cripări! ‖ **Don't ~!** Nu-i țivá! BASME 420; S-nu-ț ímnă míntea! BASME 237; mi murzuescu, HRISTU 22; **Don't ~, father!** Nu ai miracu, tate! HRISTU 78
WORRY ONE'S BRAINS WITH *vb.* ñ-vátăm míntea, ▾văsănipséscu
WORRY THE LIFE OUT OF SMB. *vb.* scot súflitlu, scot peri álghi, aród hicátlu, aród dit hicáte
WORRYWART *adj.* sicliţít, ciurtuít
WORSE *adj.* and *adv.* bitér. bitíre, cáma rău → BECOME WORSE
WORSEN *vb.* (*as of a wound*) cacurizipséscu ‖ (*only in Codex Dimonie*) ▾măriţăscu, CAPIDAN 149
WORSHIP *vb.* tiñiséscu, alávdu
WORST *adj.* cudár, dip ma răulu *m*, dip ma ráua *f*; nai ma răulu *m*, nai ma ráua *f*
WORSTED *s.* (*woolen cloth*) ‖ CARAFOLI 25: adímtu
WORTH (*deserving of*): **Is it ~?** Ari scuteári? **to become ~** ▾axéscu, ▾axiuséscu → BE ~, MAKE ~
WORTHLESS *adj.* mízav *and* mizáv; ni-ácșu, náxu; *3 sg* nu áre níți

un pâhă → BE ~

WORTHWHILENESS *s.* scuteáre, scoátire

WORTHY *adj.* ≈ *3 sg:* axizeáşte ('it is ~')

WOULD *auxiliary of the conditional:* vrea, vreai; va; **He ~ sell it** Vrea si-l víndă; **He ~ die** (*or* **He ~ have died**) vreai moáră; **I ~ have seen** vrea ved; **we ~ have seen** vrea vidém; **you ~ have seen** (*2 sg*) va videái; (*2 pl*) va videáţ; **he ~ have seen** va vidzú; **they ~ have seen** va vidzúră

WOUND *s.* (a)ránă, disbelitúră, yir; pleágă; (*by a bullet*) lăvuitúră

WOUND *vb.* ▾aránéscu, ▾agudéscu; (*to ~ with an arrow*) sădzitédz; ▾lăvu(s)éscu, pliyuséscu, pliguéscu; **I was ~ed at Yanina** Iánina mi pliyuíră

WOUNDED *adj.* (a)rănít; (*by a bullet*) curşumát, pliguít, -yu-

WOUNDING *s.* lăvusíre, lăvuíre, pliguíre, -yu-

WOW! *interj.* oá! úa! hui! ui! húhe! i! ih! (*amazement*) vii! o-popó!

WRACK *s.* nilsíre

WRACK ONE'S BRAINS OVER *vb.* ñ-disíc cáplu; ▾frimíntu

WRAITH *s.* stihíe → PHANTOM

WRANGLE *s.* nţirtáre, filunichíe → DISCORD

WRANGLE *vb.* ▾nţértu → QUARREL; (*to compete*) ▾sinirséscu

WRANGLER *adj.* (*brawler*) ghiurultagí

WRANGLING *s.* ngârta-mârta, ngrắñe

WRAP *s.* anvălitoáre

WRAP *vb.* (*to cover by winding*) ▾anvăléscu, ▾anviléscu, ▾nvârtéscu, anvârtéscu; **Death is wrapping me up** Moártea-ñ mi-anvăleáşte ‖

WRAPPED *adj.* nvârtít, anvărtít

WRAPPER *s.* bog, *pl* bodzi; (*article of clothing*) antiríu; căpót, capótă, giup, sâié; **dressed in ~s** nviscúţ tu sâiádz

WRAPPING *s.* (a)nvălíre, (a)nvălitúră, (a)nvârtíre

WRATH *s.* (*rage*) amăníe; (*divive chastisement*) uryíe

WREAK *vb.* culăséscu; mi discárcu

WRECK *s.* aspărgăciúne, aspărgătúră

WRECK *vb.* aspárgu, dărâm

WRECKAGE *s.* → RUIN

WRENCH *s.* şuţáre

WRENCH *vb.* ▾anvârtéscu, amvârtéscu; (*to distort, to twist*) ▾şuţ, ▾aruşúţ; (*to cause to suffer anguish*) ▾munduéscu → TORMENT, TORTURE; **Why are you ~ing our conversation this way?** Te u-anvârtéşti cuvénda acşí?

WRENCH OUT *vb.* stricór, *N:* astórcu

WREST *s.* astoárţire

WREST

WREST *vb.* astórcu → WRENCH
WRESTLE *s.* alúmtă, alumtáre
WRESTLE *vb.* ▾alúmtu, ▾azvíngu
WRETCH *s.* zgrumát
WRETCHED: **the ~** urfănámea
WRETCHED *adj.* antíhristu di (*and* andi-), aspindzurátlu di, (a)stímtu di, buisítlu di, bumbunidzát di Dumnidzău, cacómir, caimén, capsumán, cătrán, di cătráne, cacurídz, chisusítlu di (*and* pisusítlu di), córbu, curbisítlu di, dhaľu, dispuľátlu di, dhuľát (*and* duľát), dhístih, érmu, gramén, yramén, funipsít, furtunát, jilít, láie ş-tihiláie, lai córbe-curbişáne! lăítlu di, lipisít, mbógrulu di (*or* bógru di), miláne, mórvu, mpuşcľát, ncérnu, ngérnu ş-corbu; (*of destiny*) tíhe neárcă; ni-apucát, ni-arâs, nihít, óhru di, órbu, părsítlu di, piscătrán, póndu di, pundătúrlu di, pústu di, scurpisít, seclu di, stuhinátlu di, şcrétlu di, şcrituít, tihiláiu, túmsu, túmtu, uryisít, vápsu (*or* nvápsu), văpsítlu di, vătămát; (*unhappy*) **that ~ mother** túmsa-aţeá di múmă; aístă ni-arásă mámă; (*ugly*) **a ~ dream** un văpsít di yis; **the ~ old man** stihinátlu di aúş (*of destiny*) nfărmăcós, BASME 126 ‖ CUVATA 4: (*miserable*) ca bătut di grăndínă; DIARO 25: (*contemptible, despicable*) hândâcusít, handacúmen
  WRIGGLE *vb.* (*as of clouds or waves*) ▾şuţ, ▾târculéscu (*and* tăr-), turculéscu; (*to fling about, to toss*) mi dirín
  WRING *vb.* **~ one's hands** ñ-frágu mâñle; **to ~ linen dry** (a)stórcu
  WRINKLE *s.* súfră ‖ **Peş**: (*on the forehead*) avlăchiuri *f pl*, CL 38
  WRINKLE *vb.* ▾sufruséscu, ▾zbârcéscu, ▾stăfidhuséscu; (*of a dress*) ▾ciumuléscu, jubărjéscu ‖ CUNIA 148: **to ~ one's brows** adún sufrânţeálili; alăxéscu ópsea
  WRINKLED *adj.* sufrusít, zbârcít, jubărjít
  WRINKLING *s.* sufrusíre, zbârcíre, jubărjíre
  WRIST *s. anat.* ALIA 170: anódu, bilingiúcă, bilindzúcă, bilingécă, bilingíticu; cľái [kľá•i] di mână, clíduse (*and* cľíduse, cľídhuse), clídere, gúşă di mână
  WRITE *vb.* (n)yrăpséscu, grăpséscu; ascríu, scriu (→ § *32*), scriír, scriéscu ‖ adár: **He wrote a letter** Adră nă cárti, BASME 47
  WRITE OFF *vb.* (*to cancel*) ▾aştérgu
  WRITHE *vb.* (*as ~ in pain*) mi turculéscu, târculéscu; mi dirín; (**to ~ of shame**) mi ngroápă lóclu di arşíne
  WRITING *s.* (n)yrăpsíre, scriiáre, scriitúră *adj.* scriát, yrăpsít
  WRITTEN *adj.* scriát, yrăpsít; (*as with a nail or a knife*) ‖ GULI 5: zgrămát
  WRONG *s.* strâmbătáte, adhichipsíre
  WRONG *adj.* strâmbu; **~ in the upper story** nu lu-ári súbaşi la lóc; **the ~ side out** tersené; **What's ~ with her**? (*What's happened to*

her?) Ţe taxiráte u-áre aflátă? ‖ **You are far ~** Te-arâde míntea, BASME 355 → MISTAKEN, BARK UP THE ~ TREE, RUN THE ~ HARE, BE ~ IN THE UP-PER STORY, BE FAR ~

WRONG *vb.* (*to injure, to hurt*) ▾vlăpséscu, ▾adhichipséscu, ▾adhichiséscu, (a)ncálic → OPPRESS

WRONGLY *adv.* (*the ~ way*) ádhica (*and* ádică), térse, tersiné

WRONGDOER *s.* batác, bătác

WRONGHEADEDLY *adv.* anápuda

WROTH *adj.* → ANGRY

WROUGHT *adj.* turnipsít

WRY *adj.* strâmbát

WURST *s.* → SAUSAGE

X

XMAS *s.* → CHRISTMAS

Y

YAHOO *s.* gaľamán

YANK *s.* dizgrăbunáre, zmúldzire, zmuldzeáre

YANK *vb.* ▾dizgrăbún, ▾zmúlgu

YAP: keep one's ~ shut ≈ nu dau pri toácă (*as a secret*)

YAP *vb.* (*as of dogs*) ▾alátru

YARD *s.* (*closure*) cúrte; *also:* avlíe, trúsă, ubór, ugrádă

YARN *s.* (*woolen ~*) cheádin, chédin

YARROW *s. bot.* şuricínă

YATAGHAN *s.* yităgáne, yiutăgáne

YAWN *vb.* cáscu, háscu

YAWN(ING) *s.* căscáre, hăscáre

YEAR *s.* an *m*; **last ~** an; **the ~ before last** anţărţu (*and* adzărţu); **this ~** éstan; **next ~** alántu an; di vârnă oáră; **the ~ after next** andó năínte; **A happy new ~!** Tră mulţ añ! **three ~s** trei añ di dzále (*lit.* 'three ~s of days') ‖ **the ~ before last** adzărtsu, K-D 116; **next ~** la ánlu, PARALLELE 141; **a whole ~** un an cu ánlu, *ibid.*

YEARLING *s.* (*of sheep*) noátin, vitúľu

YEARN

YEARN *vb.* (*to long for, after*) ñ-alghéscu óčĭiĭ, mi ĭa dórlu (di)
→ PINE

YEARNING *s.* dor; *adj.* lângărós, -oásă

YEAST *s.* ‖ *Prv:* fatazmítcâ, CL 45

YEAST *vb.* ‖ (*to ferment, of dough*) asfíngu, CAPIDAN 148

YESTERYEAR *s., adv.* an

YEASTY *adj.* (*frivolous*) lişurác; (*unsettled*) ni-aştirnát, ni-aştirnút

YELL *s.* zghic, zghícut, zghilíre, ceáună, ciuñát, huhutíre, strigáre

YELL *vb.* dau un zghic, zghiléscu, zgĭéscu, strig; **~ with laughter** ▾cãhtéscu, ▾păhăéscu

YELLING *s.* huhutíre → YELL

YELLOW adj. gálbin, limuníş; **light-~** hímil

YELLOWISH *adj.* gălbinós, -oásă; gălbinúş, gălbiñór, -ñoáră; (*pale*) gălbúñu, -ñe, -ñ; gâlbâgiós, -oásă; **~ brown** (*of goats*) cul

YELP *vb.* (*usu. of dogs or children*) ▾nciuñédz (*and* ngiu-); (*rare*) cioñu

YES ahá, ahă; *also:* hoa, málista; *N:* po; péchi ‖ (*indicating polite interest or attentiveness*) ursea! HRISTU 6; (*yes, I've heard you*) e, avdzâi, DIARO 343

YESTERDAY *adv.* (a)iéri; **~ evening** aseáră, asáră; **the day before ~** auáltari, aláltari, láltari, auártari, auáltadz (*and* -taẓ) culoáltădz ‖ *Cru:* aualtădz, GOLAB 199; ALIA 525: aér, aiéri, aseáră, aséră

YET *adv.* (*up to now*) nínga, până tóra, pân tu hópa aístă; (*eventually*) ună-oáră

YET *cj.* ş-năpói; **Beasts are wild and ~ they do not abandon their offspring** Ayríñle, ţi săntu ayríñ, ş-năpói fumeáĭa nu şĭ-u alásă; (*nevertheless*) cu túte aésti

YEW-TREE *s.* tísă

YIELD *vb.* (*to give off/out; to produce*) dau; fac; (*to ~ lies, gossip*) vom; (*to renounce, to truckle*) ▾alás; trag mână di (→ ABNEGATE); **to ~ to temptation** dau coáda (*lit.* 'to give one's tail')

YIELDING adj. (*submissive*) ascultătór, -oáre; tápir; tibié *invar.*

YOGURT s. mârcát, yeaúrte [y°a•úr•ti]

YOGURT SELLER s. mârcâtgí, iargí [ĭar•]

YOKE s. giug [ĝug]

YOKE vb. (*of draft animals*) ▾ngiug, ▾giuguéscu

YOKING s. ngiugáre

YOLK s. gălbinúş, gălbineáţă, croc

YORE: **of ~** adj. di zămáne, zămănéscu ‖ **in days of ~** tu nă étă, BASME 42; nă oáră ş-tu nă étă, BASME 84

YOU pers. pron. *2 sg*: tíne *and* (*almost extinct*) tu; *dat.* (*long form*) a ţâia; (*short forms*) ţâ, ţ, âţ; **It seems to ~** A ţâia ţâ si páre; **I told ~** Ţâ dzâş; **What do you want me to tell ~?** Ţe vrei s-ţâ dzâc? *acc.* (*long form*) tíne; (*short form*) ti; **All of them jumped on ~** Tuţ si-arcárã pri tíne; **Did I hurt ~?** Eu ti-agudíi? **The advice I am giving ~ will get ~ out of trouble** Cálea ţe-ţ dau io va ti scoáte năpárti; *2 pl*: voi; **You are not the way we are** Voi nu hiţ ca noi; *dat.* (*long form*) a voáuă; (*short form*) vă, vâ, -vă; **It seems easy to ~** A voáuă vă si páre lişór; (*addressing more than one person*) **Good day to ~!** Búnă-vă dzúua! *acc.* (*long form*) voi; (*short form*) vă; **They saw ~ last night** Vă vidzúrã aseárã; Hey, ~! (*interj.*) ghídi! bre, vre, re *or* aré (*only when addressing men*); lai; **~ witch!** Ghídi stríglă! **~ head of an ass!** Ghídi cap di muľáre! **Why did you shout, ~ stupid man!** Ţe greai, vre gláre! **~ my sons!** Vre hiľ! **Is it ~?** Tíni hii, aré? **Why are ~ hitting me this way?** Aré, ţe dai acşí? **~ wretched man, I am sorry for ~!** Ñ-eáste ñílă di tíne, lai lipsíte! ‖ (*reverent or ironical 'you'*) afindíľa-ţi (*Germ. Herrlichkeit*) PARALLELE 139

YOUNG adj. ñic, ñic di añ, tínir, tínir di añ; **~ people** *coll.* tiniráme; **two younger sisters** doáuă surắrĭ ma ñiţĭ; **We are not ~** Nu him tu ñáte; (*characteristic of young people*) tiniréscu

YOUNG MAN s. gióne, schitíu; *coll.* giunáme, ficiuráme, cuchiláme

YOUNGISH adj. tinirúşcu, -şcă, -şţă, -şti

YOUNGSTER s. ficiór, ficiurác, ficiurángu; *also:* cântătoráş (*and* cândă-), cătândoráş, schitíu, talabáciu; (*handsome and brave*) fidán

YOURS

YOUR(S) *poss. adj. or pron.* **1.** *(one possessor)* *(of a m sg or n sg object)* a tău, atău; a tăl; *(of a f sg object)* a ta, atá, a tále; *N:* a táo; *(of m pl objects)* a tăĭ, a tăi; *(of f or n objects)* a tále; **~s** *(m ± f)* **have arrived** A tăĭ viñíră; **~ fields** ágrâle a tále *(n pl)*; *(Short dat. sg. forms of the pers. pron. may also be used)*: **~ knife** cuţútlu-ţ; **You will have me on ~ conscience** Va mi-ái pri súflit-ţâ; **~ tongue** límba-ţ; **All ~ young men are leaving** Gĭóñĭi tuţ âţ fug; **~ ears** *(f pl)* urécĭile-ţ; **~ brother with ~ mother** fráti-tu cu mâ-ta; **2.** *(two or more possessors)* a vóstru *(the object is m sg or n sg)*; a voástră, *f sg*; a vóştri *or* a vóşţrâ, *m pl*; a voástre, *f or n pl*; *(The short dat. pl. form may also be used)*; **Go to ~ home(s)!** Ñirdzéţ acású-vă!

YOURSELF *pron.* ínsuţ; síngur-ţâ; **Go ~!** Dú-te síngur-ţâ!

YOUTH *s.* *(young male)* ficiór, firfirúş ; *(the time and state when one is young)* giunátic, tinireáţă, ñátă **my ~** ñátile meále ‖ *F:* ti-niraţă, HRISTU 1

YOUTHFULNESS *s.* ñátă

YULE *s.* → CHRISTMAS

YUMMY *adj.* bun, búnă, búñ, búne; nóstim, *m pl* -tiñ, *f pl* -me; scóntră *invar.*

Z

ZANY *adj.* astráptu, -ptă, -pţâ, -pte → CRAZY

ZAP *vb.* aspárgu, súrpu → DESTROY, KILL

ZEAL *s.* zési *f*

ZEALOUS *adj.* aprés, -eásă, -éşĭ, -eáse

ZEPHYR *s.* *(light wind)* ávră; *tex.* zafíre, zefiráche

ZERO *s.* sâfâr, sâfâre, núlă

ZEST *s.* nustimádhă, nustimeáţă

ZESTFUL *adj.* nóstim, -timă, -tiñ, -time

ZIBELINE *s.* *zool.* iulmáe

ZIGZAG *s.* frimtúră

ZIGZAG *vb.* (*to turn to the right and to the left*) ▼strâmbu ‖ CUNIA 66: frângu cálea

ZIGZAGGEDLY *adv.* strâmbândalui

ZINC *s.* țíngu, cíngu

ZONKED *adj.* (*being under the influence of alcohol*) mbitát ‖ CUNIA 49: călít → DRUNK